LICENSING
INTELLECTUAL PROPERTY

ASPEN CASEBOOK SERIES

Licensing Intellectual Property

Law and Application

Fourth Edition

Robert W. Gomulkiewicz
UW Law Foundation Professor of Law
Director, Intellectual Property Law & Policy Graduate Program
University of Washington School of Law – Seattle

Xuan-Thao Nguyen
Gerald L. Bepko Chair in Law
Director, Center for Intellectual Property and Innovation
IU Robert H. McKinney School of Law – Indianapolis

Danielle M. Conway
Dean and Professor of Law
University of Maine School of Law

Published by Wolters Kluwer in New York.

Wolters Kluwer Legal & Regulatory U.S. serves customers worldwide with CCH, Aspen Publishers, and Kluwer Law International products. (www.WKLegaledu.com)

To contact Customer Service, e-mail customer.service@wolterskluwer.com, call 1-800-234-1660, fax 1-800-901-9075, or mail correspondence to:

Wolters Kluwer
Attn: Order Department
PO Box 990
Frederick, MD 21705

Printed in the United States of America.

1 2 3 4 5 6 7 8 9 0

ISBN 978-1-4548-9269-4

Library of Congress Cataloging-in-Publication Data

Names: Gomulkiewicz, Robert W. author. | Nguyen, Xuan-Thao N., author. | Conway, Danielle M. author.
Title: Licensing intellectual property : law and application / Robert W. Gomulkiewicz, UW Law Foundation Professor of Law, Faculty Director of the Law, Technology & Arts Group University of Washington School of Law, Seattle; Xuan-Thao Nguyen, Gerald L. Bepko Chair in Law, Director, Center for Intellectual Property and Innovation IU Robert H. McKinney School of Law, Indianapolis; Danielle M. Conway, Dean and Professor of Law University of Maine School of Law.
Description: Fourth edition. | New York : Wolters Kluwer, [2018] | Series: Aspen casebook series | Includes index.
Identifiers: LCCN 2017056957 | ISBN 9781454892694
Subjects: LCSH: License agreements — United States. | Patent licenses — United States. | Copyright licenses — United States. | Intellectual property — United States. | LCGFT: Casebooks
Classification: LCC KF3145 .G66 2018 | DDC 346.7304/8 — dc23
LC record available at https://lccn.loc.gov/2017056957

About Wolters Kluwer Legal & Regulatory U.S.

Wolters Kluwer Legal & Regulatory U.S. delivers expert content and solutions in the areas of law, corporate compliance, health compliance, reimbursement, and legal education. Its practical solutions help customers successfully navigate the demands of a changing environment to drive their daily activities, enhance decision quality and inspire confident outcomes.

Serving customers worldwide, its legal and regulatory portfolio includes products under the Aspen Publishers, CCH Incorporated, Kluwer Law International, ftwilliam.com and MediRegs names. They are regarded as exceptional and trusted resources for general legal and practice-specific knowledge, compliance and risk management, dynamic workflow solutions, and expert commentary.

· SUMMARY OF CONTENTS ·

· CONTENTS ·

TWO
INTELLECTUAL PROPERTY LICENSING

THREE
LICENSING IN BUSINESS AND INDUSTRY

· PREFACE ·

A WORD ABOUT USING THIS BOOK

This book will seem different than other casebooks that you have used. Most casebooks integrate excerpts from cases, articles, and statutes into the text of the chapter. This book begins each chapter with an Overview that gives the reader an overall picture of licensing in a particular context (say, for example, licensing in the software industry). Think of this Overview section as an extended nutshell or an abbreviated hornbook. The Overview cites cases, statutes, and articles but does not contain excerpts from them.

The excerpts come after the Overview in a section called Materials. The Materials are there to be used as primary source material to explore the multitude of issues that arise in licensing. They are there to serve as the platform and catalyst for discussion of issues about legal doctrine, public policy, business strategy, litigation tactics, and contract drafting.

The chapters also include Problems and Drafting Exercises. These you will find after the Materials. They provide different settings in which to apply the information from the Overview and the Materials, and introduce new issues and perspectives.

We think this format will allow the discussion of licensing law to be freer, deeper, and richer than if we suggested the importance of the materials by their placement in each chapter's text. We also think it allows you to experience the materials as you will in law practice. In law practice, materials do not come neatly packaged in a context suggesting their usefulness. Instead, it is up to the reader to glean their significance.

You might be interested to know that this format is both cutting edge and old school. It is cutting edge in the sense that it is largely new to modern readers. It is old school in the sense that the original casebooks were largely a compilation of unedited cases. Whether our format represents new or old or both, we hope it provides a useful way to learn about licensing.

A final word about format: Part One of the book contains a general introduction to licensing transactions and law. It also contains a chapter discussing the common provisions that are found in a license agreement and a chapter that addresses the craft of drafting a license agreement. Part One sets up the rest of the book. Part Two contains chapters on the licensing of all the major types of intellectual property. Part Three contains chapters on licensing in certain contexts, such as the software industry and university technology transfers, as well as chapters on how various commercial laws bear on licensing.

Robert W. Gomulkiewicz
Xuan-Thao Nguyen
Danielle M. Conway

January 2018

· ACKNOWLEDGMENTS ·

We are grateful to many people who helped us take this project from the idea stage to a casebook with Aspen's signature red cover.

For excellent research assistance and comments from a student perspective, we give thanks to Kent Diamond and Bill Snyder from the University of Washington School of Law; Adrianne Speas, Julianna Mott, Amy Mendez, Joe Lenard, Elizabeth Polk, Peggy Ho, Michelle Tran, and Shruti Krishnan from SMU Dedman School of Law; Robert Sherman and Georgette Yaindl from the University of Hawai'i, William S. Richardson School of Law; and Kelly Leong from the George Washington University Law School. We are also grateful to the law firm, Pierce Atwood, LLP, specifically its Portland-based partner, Peter Guffin, who also serves the University of Maine School of Law as Visiting Professor of Practice, for his contributions related to information privacy. We are especially grateful to Ewa Davison, Tristan Kenyon-Schultz, and Jim Sfekas who "beta tested" a draft of the book in a classroom setting. Signe Brunstad, Jeff Maine, and Sean O'Connor provided helpful comments on early drafts.

Rachel Allison, Josephine Ah Ching, Nancy Eagan, and Jennifer Snider provided invaluable administrative support.

Finally, thanks are due the staff of the Marian Gould Gallagher Law Library, especially Nancy McMurrer, Cheryl Nyberg, and Mary Whisner.

LICENSING
INTELLECTUAL PROPERTY

PART ONE

FOUNDATIONS OF LICENSING

1

LICENSING TRANSACTIONS AND LAW

I. OVERVIEW OF LICENSING TRANSACTIONS AND LAW

A. From Sales of Goods to Licenses of Information

Sales of goods dominated the economy in the industrial age. Now, we live in the so-called "information economy." This means that production has shifted from the manufacture of hard goods to the creation of ideas and information. The products of the information economy are intangibles and hybrids of goods and services. Licensing is the predominant transaction model in the information economy, although licensing is as old as intellectual property itself.[1] Modern licensing arises in a wide variety of contexts: mass market consumer transactions, business to business product development deals, university technology transfers, government contracts, business financing, and corporate mergers and acquisitions.

Licenses come with many labels. Depending upon the setting, they may be called covenants not to sue, permissions, releases, waivers, clearances, assignments, or sales. Not only do licenses come with many labels, they come in a variety of styles. Licenses with the federal government are very formal; indeed, the substantive terms are in the Code of Federal Regulations. The software industry tends to use written licenses, negotiated and standard form, in paper and electronic formats. The movie industry often operates informally with oral permissions.

The use of licenses underlies two important aspects of the information economy. First, it enables creators of information, technology, and intellectual property to do the sharing and collaboration that lead to the creation of new information products, from

---

1. Licensing is specifically mentioned in the Venetian Patent Act, which dates from the fifteenth century. *See* Venetian Senate's 1474 Act: "It being forbidden to every other person in any of our territories and towns to make any further device conforming with and similar to said one, without the consent and license of the author, for the term of 10 years."

the production of an epic motion picture to the development of complex software. In other words, licensing underlies creativity and technological innovation. Second, licensing enables parties of all sizes and from all sectors to bring information products to market in a multitude of ways. In other words, licensing also underlies business model innovation. The role that licenses play in creativity and innovation of all types is illustrated throughout this book.

B. The Nature of a License

A "license" is a grant of permission. In everyday life people encounter many types of licenses. The permission to drive a car is known as a driver's license. Lawyers and engineers must be licensed by a professional organization to practice in their respective fields. Airlines give passengers the right to occupy a seat on an airplane at a certain hour on a certain day bound for a certain destination. A concert ticket gets a patron into the concert hall to hear a symphony, and a baseball ticket gets a fan into the ballpark to watch a game.

A license grants permission, but why is such permission needed for intellectual property, software, or information? There are several reasons that permission may be necessary.

Intellectual property laws grant exclusive rights. Later, this chapter describes intellectual property rights in detail. Without permission, no one (subject to certain exceptions, such as "fair use") has authority to exercise those rights. Without permission, copying a song or modifying software may be a copyright infringement; fabricating a microprocessor using a certain process may be a patent infringement; using a logo on a T-shirt may be a trademark infringement; taking a formula to a new employer may be a trade secret misappropriation.

Intellectual property laws do not protect all products of the information economy. Uncopyrightable data provides a good example. For these products, physical control creates the need for permission. Sometimes physical control is simply a lock and key, or a security guard at the door. For information stored on computer systems, it comes in the form of passwords or other software-related security measures.

The physical protection is often bolstered by legal protection. Even if someone manages to pick a lock and evade the security guards, the person still may be subject to civil or criminal liability. In the digital world, the Digital Millennium Copyright Act,[2] for instance, contains provisions which make it illegal to circumvent copy protection devices. The Computer Fraud and Abuse Act[3] and Economic Espionage Act[4] make it illegal to break into computer systems without permission. Courts

---

2. 17 U.S.C. §§1201 *et seq.*
3. 18 U.S.C. §§1030 *et seq.*
4. 18 U.S.C. §§1831 *et seq.*

sometimes transport the concept of trespass from the physical world into the electronic world to add legal force to physical control. *See* eBay, Inc. v. Bidder's Edge, Inc., 100 F. Supp. 2d 1058 (N.D. Cal. 2000); *but see* Ticketmaster Corp. v. Tickets.com, Inc., 54 U.S.P.Q. 2d 1344 (C.D. Cal. 2000) (no trespass claim where there was an open system).

C. Introduction to the Sources of Licensing Law

Contract law for sales of goods played an important role in facilitating transactions in the industrial age. Indeed, contract law and practice evolved alongside changes in product development and distribution. As the need for speedy and efficient product development and distribution came to the fore, contract law evolved to uphold flexible contracting practices, address the proliferation of standard forms, offer implied and gap filler terms, and incorporate terms from industry custom into the contract. Article 2 of the Uniform Commercial Code (UCC 2) embodies many of these contract law innovations.

Licensing law has also grown up in tandem with the information economy. There is a large and diverse collection of laws that bear on and shape licenses. We call this body of law "licensing law" although it is a looser and less formalized body of law (at least at this point in history) than many bodies of law such as real property law, secured transactions, or even traditional contract law for the sale of goods.

Contract law is one of the most important ingredients in licensing law. Most licenses are contracts, so licensing law fundamentally involves contract law. That principle is simple to state but the reality is complex. Licensing contract law comes from a wide variety of different sources, including the common law and UCC 2.

Besides contract law, intellectual property law is an important component of licensing law. Intellectual property law influences licenses in a variety of ways. In some instances, intellectual property law provides contract rules, such as a statute of frauds for exclusive copyright licenses. In other cases it provides the backdrop for licenses, and so influences the content and interpretation of licenses. In still other cases, the fact that intellectual property is the subject of the contract places boundaries around freedom of contract. These boundaries, expressed in terms of antitrust, misuse, and preemption, are an important aspect of licensing law.

1. Contract Law

a. State Common Law of Contracts

The traditional source of contract law in the United States is judge-made state common law. Each of the 50 states and each U.S. territory has its own body of contract law that can be ascertained by studying the relevant case law. The American Law Institute (ALI) in its *Restatement of Contracts* has attempted to draw together common principles from the states (the common common law, so to speak) as have scholars such as Williston,[5] Corbin,[6] and Farnsworth[7] in their contract treatises,[8] but it is the judges' precedents in each state and territory that have the force of law.[9]

The common law of contracts governs many licenses. It provides the contracting principles for most patent, copyright, trademark, and trade secret licenses. It also serves as the contract law for many software and information licenses, although, as explained below, UCC 2 and the Uniform Computer Information Transaction Act (UCITA) may also come into play.

b. Uniform Commercial Code Article 2

Uniform Commercial Code Article 2 on its face applies to transactions in goods, not licenses of intangibles. Its drafters tailored UCC 2's provisions to typical goods-related sales. However, courts have applied it to licenses in some cases, either directly (by interpreting the terms "transactions" and "goods" broadly) or by analogy.[10] There are several reasons for this.

The first reason is convenience. A state's common law may be diffuse and incomplete in its coverage of contract law, so UCC 2 provides a comprehensive, systematic, readily ascertainable set of contract rules. The second reason is that UCC 2 contains many general principles of contract law that apply nicely to many contractual contexts. The third reason is that some transactions involve both an intangible and a good, such as the purchase of a smartphone or a computer gaming device. These transactions have the "feel" of a sale of goods, so courts treat them that way in the contract law they employ.

c. Uniform Computer Information Transactions Act

In the 1990s, some people began to see the need for a cohesive body of contract law for licensing software and information. The organization that created UCC 2,

---

5. Richard A. Lord, WILLISTON ON CONTRACTS (4th ed. 2003). Professor Williston was the Reporter for the original *Restatement of Contracts* and the Uniform Sales Act.

6. Joseph M. Perillo, CORBIN ON CONTRACTS (rev. ed. 1993). Professor Corbin served as Special Advisor for the original *Restatement of Contracts* and the Reporter for the chapter on remedies.

7. E.A. Farnsworth, FARNSWORTH ON CONTRACTS (3d ed. 2003). Professor Farnsworth was the Reporter for the *Restatement (Second) of Contracts*.

8. The earliest treatises on sales of goods date from the mid-1800s. *See, e.g.,* Colin Blackburn, A TREATISE ON THE EFFECT OF THE CONTRACT OF SALE ON THE LEGAL RIGHTS OF PROPERTY AND POSSESSION IN GOODS, WARES, AND MERCHANDIZE (1847); William W. Story, A TREATISE ON THE LAW OF SALES OF PERSONAL PROPERTY (1847).

9. In creating common law, judges draw contract principles for licensing law from a variety of sources including the general common law of contracts, the Uniform Commercial Code Article 2 (UCC 2), and sometimes the Uniform Computer Information Transactions Act (UCITA). The ALI's *Principles of Software Contracts* also proposes principles of licensing law. The Federal Circuit has been influential in creating the common law of licensing. *See* Robert W. Gomulkiewicz, *The Federal Circuit's Licensing Law Jurisprudence: Its Nature and Influence*, 84 WASH. L. REV. 199 (2009).

10. Not all courts or commentators think UCC 2 works well for licenses. *See, e.g.,* Raymond T. Nimmer, *An Essay on Article 2's Irrelevance to Licensing Agreements*, 40 LOY. L.A. L. REV. 235 (2006); Lorin Brennan, *Why Article 2 Cannot Apply to Software Transactions*, 38 DUQ. L. REV. 459 (2000); iLAN Systems, Inc. v. Netscout Serv. Level Corp., 183 F. Supp. 2d 328, 332 (D. Mass. 2002) ("Article 2 technically does not, and certainly will not in the future, govern software licenses, but for the time being, the Court will assume it does.").

the Uniform Law Commission (ULC),[11] looked at this picture and decided to create a separate article of the UCC to deal specifically with licenses. This statute was known as UCC Article 2B (UCC Article 2 for sales, 2A for leases, and 2B for licenses).

The Article 2B project created intense debate, especially about the contract law/intellectual property law interplay,[12] enforceability of mass market licenses,[13] and use of electronic self-help.[14] ULC's partner in the UCC projects, the American Law Institute, eventually withdrew its support. Nonetheless, ULC decided to move forward and renamed the project the Uniform Computer Information Transactions Act (UCITA). ULC approved UCITA in 1999, and Maryland and Virginia enacted it shortly thereafter. *See* MD. CODE ANN. COM. LAW §§22-101 *et seq.*; VA. CODE ANN. §§59.1-501.1 *et seq.* Since that time no other state has enacted UCITA and several states have passed legislation purporting to preclude any contractual choice of law choosing UCITA.[15] However, some courts have looked to UCITA for guidance in deciding cases involving licensing law issues.[16]

---

11. At the time of the UCITA project the ULC called itself the National Conference of Commissioners on Uniform State Laws (NCCUSL).

12. *See* David McGowan, *Free Contracting, Fair Competition, and Article 2B: Some Reflections on Federal Competition Policy, Information Transactions, and Aggressive Neutrality,* 13 BERKELEY TECH. L.J. 1173 (1998); Raymond T. Nimmer, *Breaking Barriers: The Relation Between Contract and Intellectual Property Law,* 13 BERKELEY TECH. L.J. 827 (1998); UCITA §105 (Relation to Federal Law). In response to criticisms about the intellectual property/contract law interplay, the 2002 Amendments to UCITA limit a licensor's ability to prohibit "reverse engineering" by contract. UCITA §118 (Terms Relating to Interoperability and Reverse Engineering); *see* Jonathan Band, *Closing the Interoperability Gap: NCCUSL's Adoption of a Reverse Engineering Exception in UCITA,* 19 COMPUTER & INTERNET LAW 1 (2002). Compare this approach to the Federal Circuit's ruling in Bowers v. Baystate Techs., 320 F.3d 1317 (Fed. Cir. 2003), permitting contractual prohibitions on reverse engineering.

13. *See* Mark A. Lemley, *Beyond Preemption: The Law and Policy of Intellectual Property Licensing,* 87 CAL. L. REV. 113 (1999); Robert W. Gomulkiewicz, *The License Is the Product: Comments on the Promise of Article 2B for Software and Information Licensing,* 13 BERKELEY TECH. L.J. 891 (1998); UCITA §112 (Manifesting Assent; Opportunity to Review) and §209 (Mass-Market License).

14. *See* Julie E. Cohen, *Copyright and the Jurisprudence of Self-Help,* 13 BERKELEY TECH. L.J. 1089 (1998); David Freidman, *In Defense of Private Orderings: Comments on Julie Cohen's* "Copyright and the Jurisprudence of Self-Help," 13 BERKELEY TECH. L.J. 1151 (1998); UCITA §815 (Right to Possession and Prevent Use) and §816 (Limitations on Electronic Self-Help). ULC's 2002 Amendments to UCITA ban the use of electronic self-help, even if the parties agree to it.

15. Iowa, North Carolina, Vermont, and West Virginia have passed such legislation in various forms. *See* IOWA CODE 554D.104; N.C. GEN. STAT. 66-329; 9 VT. STAT. 2463a; W. VA. CODE 55-8-15. Legislation to prevent the application of UCITA has come to be known as "bomb shelter" legislation. ULC responded to some of the criticisms of UCITA by passing a series of amendments in 2002, but no additional states have adopted UCITA. Note that Maryland and Virginia adopted UCITA prior to the 2002 Amendments.

16. *See, e.g.,* Specht v. Netscape Communications Corp., 306 F.3d 17 (2d Cir. 2002) (looking to UCITA for guidance on formation of contract issue); Rhone Poulenc Agro, S.A. v. DeKalb Genetics Corp., 284 F.3d 1323 (Fed. Cir. 2002) (looking to UCITA for guidance on bona fide purchaser rule in patent licensing case); AGT Int'l, Inc. v. Level 3 Communications, 2002 WL 31409879 (S.D. Ohio 2002) (looking to UCITA for guidance on duration of object code license where copy of software is delivered for fixed fee). *See also* 12A OKLA. ST. ANN. §2-105(1) Official Comment ("A reasoned and studied articulation of the differences between Article 2 and concepts governing information is available from the Uniform Computer Information Transactions Act. Even though it has not been enacted in the jurisdiction, a court might well look to it for guidance . . .").

d. The Significance of the Source of Contract Law

Uncertainty about the source of contract law that applies to licenses is more than just an inconvenience; it can impact the substantive terms of the license. Let us look, for example, at the impact on warranties. The common law of contracts leaves warranties up to the parties to decide. If the parties do not agree on any warranties, then the license does not contain any. UCC 2 represents a different paradigm.

UCC 2 contains both implied and gap filler warranties. If the parties do not consider any warranties, then UCC 2 interjects its gap filler warranties into the contract by operation of law. In addition, a collection of implied warranties (e.g., merchantability) come into the contract automatically unless the parties disclaim them in a certain manner.

The source of contract law has an impact on other provisions of a license as well: for example, the duration of the license, the rules for rejecting deliverables, choice of law, risk allocation, and remedies. Chapter 2 examines the impact of the source of contract law in more detail in the context of its discussion of common license provisions.

2. Intellectual Property Law in Licensing

Contract law forms the base of licensing law but it is shaped and molded by intellectual property law. This section describes intellectual property law and its role in licensing law.

a. Copyrights

The U.S. Constitution gives Congress the power to "promote the Progress of Science and the useful Arts" by granting to authors and inventors exclusive rights in their works for a limited time. U.S. CONST. art. I, Sec. 8, cl. 8. Using that power, Congress passed the Copyright Act. Copyright protection applies to "original works of authorship fixed in any tangible medium of expression." 17 U.S.C. §§101 *et seq.* Works of authorship include: literary works; musical works; dramatic works; pantomimes and choreographic works; pictoral, graphic, and sculptural works; motion pictures and other audiovisual works; sound recordings; and architectural works. Certain things do not qualify for copyright protection: ideas; processes; systems; methods of operation; concepts; principles; or discoveries "regardless of the form in which it is described, explained, illustrated, or embodied" in a work. To put it another way, copyright applies to the expression of an idea but never to the idea itself. Mazer v. Stein, 347 U.S. 201, 217-18 (1954); Data East USA, Inc. v. Epyx, Inc., 862 F.2d 204, 207 (9th Cir. 1988).

For each copyrighted work, the author receives a set of exclusive rights, namely: the right to reproduce, create derivative works, distribute copies, and publicly perform or display the work. 17 U.S.C. §106. The author's exclusivity lasts for a discrete, limited period of time. During the period of exclusivity no one may exercise the author's exclusive rights without the author's permission.[17] The copyright holder does not have to license his or her exclusive rights all together. The rights are infinitely divisible. It is often said that a copyright holder's exclusive rights can be thought of as a bundle of sticks. *See* New York Times Co. v. Tasini, 533 U.S. 483 (2001). A license agreement allocates the sticks. This is a powerful and useful image, but it only begins to describe the richness of licensing copyrights. The bundle of sticks image implies that once a stick is given, the bundle is reduced. However, the nature of copyright is that the stick can be given without taking it out of the bundle. It is given yet it remains to be given again. Economists say this makes copyrights "nonrivalrous." *See generally* Posner & Landes, THE ECONOMIC STRUCTURE OF INTELLECTUAL PROPERTY (2003).

Chapter 8 explores copyright licenses in greater detail.

b. Patents

The same authority in the U.S. Constitution that gives Congress the power to enact copyright protection also gives Congress the authority to enact patent protection. U.S. CONST. art. I, Sec. 8, cl. 8. Using that power, Congress passed the Patent Act. *See* 35 U.S.C. §§1 *et seq.*

Patents can be granted by the United States Patent and Trademark Office (PTO) and foreign governments for new, non-obvious, useful inventions. There are various types of patents: utility, process, plant, and design. Like a copyright, a patent gives the holder exclusive rights for a certain limited period of time. The patent holder has the right to exclude others from making, using, selling, offering to sell, distributing, or importing things that practice the patented invention. The license allocates the exclusive rights of the patent or serves as a covenant not to sue for exercising these rights.

Unlike copyrights, patents are not infinitely divisible. A patent holder may not assign only partial claims of the patent or some claims to one party and other claims to another. It may, however, grant different parties each of its exclusive rights — for example, one party the right to make products based on its patent and another party the right to sell products. And for each right it may grant the right for different fields, such as a grant to one party to sell in one territory and to another party for a different territory.

Chapter 6 explores patent licenses in greater detail.

c. Trademarks, Service Marks, Trade Dress

A trademark is a name, symbol, or other device used to identify the source of a good. A service mark is a mark used to identify services. Trade dress protects product

---

17. However, anyone may make a "fair use" of a copyrighted work. A potential fair use is measured by a non-exhaustive list of factors: (1) the purpose and character of the use, including whether such use is of a commercial nature or is for nonprofit educational purposes; (2) the nature of the copyrighted work; (3) the amount and substantiality of the portion used in relation to the copyrighted work as a whole; and (4) the effect of the use upon the potential market for or value of the copyrighted work. 17 U.S.C. §107. *See* Campbell v. Acuff-Rose Music, Inc., 510 U.S. 569 (1994).

packaging and configurations.[18] Upon use in commerce, a trademark, service mark, or trade dress is protected under state common law; federal protection (national in scope) may be acquired by registering with the United States Patent and Trademark Office. *See* 15 U.S.C. §§1051 *et seq.* (the federal trademark statute is known as the Lanham Act). Unlike copyrights and patents, trademarks, service marks, and trade dress do not give the owner a bundle of exclusive rights. They give the holder the right to exclude others from using confusingly similar marks and the right to control usage of the mark in conjunction with goods or services. Consequently, the license grant in a trademark or service mark license speaks in terms of the use of the mark with goods or services.

Chapter 4 explores trademark, service mark, and trade dress licenses in greater detail.

d. Trade Secrets

A trade secret is information that holds independent economic value because it is held in secrecy. Trade secret law protects the trade secret holder from unlawful misappropriation of the information. Trade secrets are protected by state and federal law. Most states have adopted a version of the Uniform Trade Secrets Act. *See, e.g.,* RCW §§19.108 *et seq.* (Washington State's version of the UTSA). Those states that have not passed the UTSA tend to apply principles set out in the *Restatement (First) of Torts* §757. In addition, federal law provides protection through the Defend Trade Secrets Act and the Economic Espionage Act. *See* 18 U.S.C. §§1831-1839. The license grant in a trade secret license describes the use that the licensee may make of the information, helps maintain the secrecy of the information, and can affect the duration of the trade secret.

Chapter 7 explores trade secret licenses in greater detail.

e. Data and Information

Intellectual property does not protect all intellectual creations. Data, pure ideas, and information are seldom protected under U.S. law, unless they are held as trade secrets. Copyright law protects a unique arrangement of information but never the information itself. *See* Feist Publ'ns, Inc. v. Rural Tel. Serv. Co., 499 U.S. 340 (1991).

Nonetheless, courts have provided some protection for information that qualifies as "hot news." *See* International News Service v. Associated Press, 248 U.S. 215 (1918) (holding that the news originally collected by Associated Press was not copyrightable, but copying of AP's compiled news violated unfair competition law); National Basketball Ass'n v. Motorola, 105 F.3d 841 (2d Cir. 1997) (recognizing and affirming "hot news" misappropriation as a valid claim). Federal legislation can protect information in certain contexts. The Computer Fraud and Abuse Act (CFAA) §1030(g) provides for both criminal and civil actions for breaking into information systems to steal information. In certain cases state law claims of trespass to chattels have been used

---

18. *See generally* Wal-Mart Stores, Inc. v. Samara Bros., Inc., 529 U.S. 205 (2000).

to prevent the taking of information when it causes injury to the information processing systems. *See* eBay, Inc. v. Bidder's Edge, Inc., 100 F. Supp. 2d 1058 (N.D. Cal. 2000) (court relies on trespass to chattels doctrine to prevent the defendant's computer bots from crawling eBay's auction Web site for the purpose of using eBay's data along with data from other auction Web sites to yield a larger aggregate auction Web site); *but see* Intel Corp. v. Hamidi, 30 Cal. 4th 1342, 71 P.3d 296, 1 Cal. Rptr. 3d 32 (2003) (denying Intel's request for an injunction premised upon a trespass to chattels theory).

In contrast to the limited protection provided under U.S. law, the European Union protects databases and collections of information in its Database Directive. *See* Directive 96/9/EC of the European Parliament and of the Council of 11 March 1996 on the Legal Protection of Databases, OJ L 77, 27.3.1996, 20-28. The Directive provides: (1) a harmonized level of protection of "original" databases under copyright for the structure of a database — but not its contents — by reason of its arrangement and selection; and (2) the introduction of a new *sui generis* right to protect investments in databases, specifically, protecting against unauthorized extraction of all or a substantial part, considered quantitatively or qualitatively, of the contents of any database produced through substantial investment.

The license grant for data, ideas, and information describes as accurately as possible the uses to which it may be put in a given context. Chapter 10 explores data and information licenses in greater detail.

f. Software

Software is protected in the United States under a variety of intellectual property laws. Copyright law protects the source code, object code, and visual displays of software. *See* Apple Computer, Inc. v. Franklin Computer Corp., 714 F.2d 1240 (3d Cir. 1983) (source and object code); Apple Computer, Inc. v. Microsoft Corp., 35 F.3d 1435 (9th Cir. 1994) (visual displays). Patent law protects a variety of software-related inventions, although patent protection for software has proven to be a hot topic. *See In re Allapat*, 33 F.3d 1526 (Fed. Cir. 1994); Bilski v. Kappos, 130 S. Ct. 3218 (2010); Alice Corp. v. CLS Bank, Int'l, 134 S. Ct. 2347 (2014). Trade secret law also protects software when the software developer decides to hold source code or other aspects of software as a trade secret. Software licenses must account for this wide variety of applicable intellectual property rights.

Chapter 9 explores software licenses in greater detail.

g. Publicity Rights

The right of publicity gives a person a proprietary interest in his or her image or persona. It may apply to a name, voice, and other identifiable personal traits and includes a person's likeness as depicted in a photo, portrait, or other medium. The license grant for a publicity right describes the trait and the manner and context in which the trait may be exploited.

Chapter 5 explores publicity rights licenses in greater detail.

h. Intellectual Property Law Rules and Overlays for Licenses

Sometimes intellectual property law contributes to licensing law by providing a specific rule. For example, the Copyright Act states that an exclusive license or an assignment of rights must be made in a signed writing. 17 U.S.C. §204. It also states that for a work by an independent contractor to qualify as a "work made for hire" the work must be of a certain type and the parties must so agree in a signed, written agreement which uses the words "work for hire." 17 U.S.C. §§101, 201. If the parties fail to follow these contracting rules, the erstwhile (as the case may be) exclusive license, assignment, or work for hire agreement becomes (at most) a non-exclusive license. *See* Community for Creative Non-Violence v. Reid, 490 U.S. 730 (1989); Effects Associates v. Cohen, 908 F.2d 555 (9th Cir. 1990).

Federal intellectual property law influences the transferability of licenses. For example, a non-exclusive patent license is not transferable without the consent of the licensor as a matter of federal policy. *See* Everex Sys. v. Cadtrak Corp., 89 F.3d 673 (9th Cir. 1996), which is contained in the Materials section of this chapter. *See also* Harris v. Emus Records Corp., 734 F.2d 1329, 1333 (9th Cir. 1984); Unarco Indus., Inc. v. Kelley Co., 465 F.2d 1303, 1335 (7th Cir. 1972). Under the Computer Software Rental Amendments Act the right to transfer software by rental, lease, or lending is subject to the authorization of the copyright holder. 17 U.S.C. §109(b). In the context of trademarks, a licensee in bankruptcy may not be permitted to assume the licensed trademark because trademarks are personal and thus cannot be assigned without the consent of the licensor. *See* Marketing Group Inc. v. Blanks, 337 B.R. 230 (D. Nev. 2005).

Sometimes intellectual property law influences the wording of the license. The license grant section of a patent or copyright license typically uses the nomenclature of the exclusive rights granted under copyright or patent. For example, if a licensor wants to allow someone to modify a copyrighted work, he or she talks in terms of "derivative works." If the licensor wants to let someone manufacture a product under his or her patent, the license grants the right to "make" products under the patent.

Intellectual property law influences the content of licenses in other ways as well. A trademark license must contain provisions allowing the licensor to retain quality control over goods displaying the mark. A trade secret license must describe the measures that will be used to protect the secrecy of the licensed information. If a license contains warranties, disclaimers of warranty, or limitations of liability, these provisions should all speak in terms of the intellectual property that is the subject of the license: For instance, if patents are being licensed, the license should either take on or refuse to take on liability for patent infringement.

Intellectual property law also bears on the interpretation of the license. State contract law usually provides that ambiguous contract language should be construed against the drafter. *See* RESTATEMENT (SECOND) OF CONTRACTS 206 (1981); 1 E.A. Farnsworth, FARNSWORTH ON CONTRACTS 4.24 (1990). Some courts have altered that equation for licenses, saying that the wording of license grants should be construed with a favorable eye toward the owner of the intellectual property rights being licensed (the licensor). *See* S.O.S., Inc. v. Payday, Inc., 886 F.2d 1081 (9th Cir. 1995), which is contained in the Materials section of this chapter; *but see* Bourne v. Walt Disney Co., 68 F.3d 621 (2d Cir. 1995) (applying traditional principles of contract interpretation).

Intellectual property law's overlay on a license determines whether a litigation claim is for breach of contract or copyright infringement. If someone exploits a copyrighted work beyond the scope of license, then that person may be a copyright infringer. It is usually worse to be deemed a copyright infringer than a contract breacher. Copyright infringers may be liable for statutory damages, enhanced damages, and attorneys' fees, as well as subject to injunctive relief, which may top normal measures of damages for breach of contract. *See* Jacobsen v. Katzer, 535 F.3d 1373 (Fed. Cir. 2008), which is contained in the Materials section of Chapter 9, and MDY Industries v. Blizzard Entertainment, 629 F.3d 928 (9th Cir. 2011), which is contained in the Materials section of this chapter.

3. Boundaries

Not all license provisions or practices are fair game. Freedom of contract remains the touchstone of contract law in the United States, but several laws constrain licenses. These boundaries are particularly important in licenses because licenses often involve intellectual property, which provides limited monopolies to rights holders. Courts are keen to maintain the limits on these monopolies and the power they confer. Below is a brief introduction to some boundaries on licenses; later chapters provide a more detailed discussion.

a. Antitrust

Antitrust law is one of the most important bodies of law placing a boundary around the use of licenses. Prior to the 1980s, the U.S. government used antitrust policy to restrict many licensing practices. *See* Roger B. Andewelt, *Department of Justice Antitrust Policy*, 1 DOMESTIC AND FOREIGN TECHNOLOGY LICENSING LAW 401 (1982). Subsequently, the U.S. government concluded that most licensing practices were procompetitive, and that attitude prevails today. *See* U.S. DEPT. OF JUSTICE AND FED. TRADE COMMISSION, ANTITRUST GUIDELINES FOR THE LICENSING OF INTELLECTUAL PROPERTY (2017). The U.S. Supreme Court has upheld licensing practices in many cases, including the use of collective rights organizations for licensing public performance rights in music. *See* Broadcast Music v. C.B.S., 441 U.S. 1 (1979), which is contained in the Materials section of this chapter.

However, antitrust law still provides an important boundary for licenses. In *United States v. Microsoft Corp.*, the court took Microsoft to task for a number of its licensing practices. The court ruled that these practices were used by Microsoft to illegally maintain its Windows operating system monopoly. 253 F.3d 34 (D.C. Cir. 2001) (en banc). The *Microsoft* case is contained in the Materials section of Chapter 9.

b. Misuse

The doctrine of "misuse" can be employed by courts to police against using licenses to unfairly extend intellectual property monopolies. The patent misuse concept, grounded in equity theory, arose out of the Supreme Court's decision in Morton Salt Co. v. GS Suppiger Co., 314 U.S. 488 (1942), though its reach was later modified by Congress to apply only if the "patent owner has market power in the relevant market for the patent or patented product on which the license or sale is conditioned." 35 U.S.C. §271(d)(5) (1994).

The misuse doctrine has been extended to limit copyright licenses too. *See* Video Pipeline, Inc. v. Buena Vista Home Enter., Inc., 342 F.3d 191 (3d Cir. 2003), which is contained in the Materials section of this chapter, and Lasercomb America, Inc. v. Reynolds, 911 F.2d 970 (4th Cir. 1990), which is contained in the Materials section of Chapter 9. The "misuse" in *Lasercomb* arose from use of a standard form license purporting to restrict licensees from developing competing products for a period of 99 years. Misuse does not invalidate the copyright, but it does prevent the copyright holder from enforcing it until the misuse has been purged.

c. Preemption

Federal law preemption provides another possible source of limits on licenses. *See* Vault Corp. v. Quaid Software Ltd., 847 F.2d 255 (5th Cir. 1988) (finding state law dictated contract terms conflicted with Section 117 of the Copyright Act). Federal preemption disallows state laws or regulations that conflict with federal laws. In copyright, preemption could arise under either Section 301 of the Copyright Act or the Supremacy Clause of the U.S. Constitution. 17 U.S.C. §301(a); U.S. CONST. art. VI, cl. 2. A successful challenge to the license on this basis would allow a party to avoid abiding by a term of a license, such as a condition on a license grant or a prohibition on reverse engineering the software, or limit the causes of action or remedies in a lawsuit.

Courts have concluded in many cases that contract law and copyright law do not involve the same rights, and have refused to preempt licenses. *See, e.g.,* ProCD, Inc. v. Zeidenberg, 86 F.3d 1447 (7th Cir. 1996); National Car Rental Sys., Inc. v. Computer Assocs. Int'l, Inc., 991 F.2d 426 (8th Cir. 1993). As a general matter, license-related breach of contract claims are not preempted. Also, challenges to certain software license provisions have been rejected by the courts, such as challenges to limitations on an end user's scope of use or ability to reverse engineer software. *See* Blizzard Entertainment, Inc. v. Jung, 422 F.3d 630 (8th Cir. 2005) and Bowers v. Baystate Tech., 320 F.3d 1317 (Fed. Cir. 2003), which are contained in the Materials section of this chapter. However, some courts have upheld copyright preemption challenges, particularly when a litigant attempts to recover damages under both intellectual property laws and state laws such as conversion and misappropriation. *See* Kabehie v. Zoland, 102 Cal. App. 4th 513, 124 Cal. Rptr. 2d 721 (2002) (discussing a variety of preemption cases). Copyright law also preempts publicity rights claims in certain cases. *See* Baltimore Orioles, Inc. v. Major League Baseball Players Ass'n, 805 F.2d 663 (7th Cir. 1986), *cert. denied,* 480 U.S. 941 (1987); *but see* Waits v. Frito-Lay, 978 F.2d 1093 (9th Cir. 1992) (voice sound-alike claim not preempted).

Preemption can arise in other contexts as well. Courts have struck down state laws that provide patent-like protection, such as a Florida boat hull protection statute in

Bonito Boats, Inc. v. Thunder Craft Boats, Inc. 489 U.S. 141 (1989); *but see* Kewanee Oil Co. v. Bicron Corp., 416 U.S. 470 (1974) (state trade secret law not preempted).

d. Fair Use

Under the Copyright Act certain uses of copyrighted works, though technically infringing, are socially beneficial and thus constitute "fair uses." 17 U.S.C. §107. A party asserts its right to a "fair use" as a defense to a suit for copyright infringement. For example, in the context of software, a fair use defense is often raised by defendants who have reverse engineered software to discover unprotectable ideas to create a compatible or competing product. Courts have consistently held that such reverse engineering to discover unprotectable ideas is a fair use. *See, e.g.*, Sony Computer Entertainment, Inc. v. Connectix Corp., 203 F.3d 596 (9th Cir. 2000). If a license prohibits reverse engineering, however, most cases have upheld this limitation. *See, e.g.*, Blizzard Entertainment, Inc. v. Jung, 422 F.3d 630 (8th Cir. 2005), which is found in the Materials section of this chapter, and Bowers v. Baystate Tech., 320 F.3d 1317 (Fed. Cir. 2003), which is located in the Materials section of Chapter 9.[19]

Fair use concepts also exist outside of copyright law. Trademark law permits third parties to use a mark when necessary to refer to a product marked with the mark or to use the mark in parody — this is known as referential or nominative use. *See, e.g.*, Mattel, Inc. v. MCA Records, 296 F.3d 894 (9th Cir. 2002) (song using "Barbie" mark in parody). Free speech concepts also limit publicity rights by allowing news reporting of celebrities and public discussion of them, including in parody. *See, e.g.*, Hoffman v. Capital Cities/ABC, 255 F.3d 1180 (9th Cir. 2001); Cardtoons, L.C. v. Major League Baseball Players' Association, 95 F.3d 959 (10th Cir. 1996).

e. Unconscionability and Fundamental Public Policy

Courts can strike down license terms that are "unconscionable." This allows courts to guard against abusive contract terms (substantive unconscionability) and contracting practices (procedural unconscionability). The basic test is whether, in light of the commercial circumstances, the clauses involved are so one-sided as to be unconscionable under the circumstances existing at the time of making the terms. UCC 2-302. For example, courts have stricken down certain binding arbitration and exclusive venue provisions in consumer transactions. *See, e.g.*, Comb v. PayPal, Inc., 218 F. Supp. 2d 1165 (N.D. Cal. 2002) (binding arbitration); America Online, Inc. v. Superior Court, 90 Cal. App. 4th 1, 108 Cal. Rptr. 2d 699 (2001) (exclusive forum).

---

19. In 1991, the European Union passed a directive on legal protection for computer software (Software Directive). COUNCIL DIRECTIVE 91/250/EEC ON THE LEGAL PROTECTION OF SOFTWARE PROGRAMS (May 14, 1991). One part of the Software Directive addresses the issue of "reverse engineering." The Software Directive provides that if a software developer needs to discover information about another software program to interoperate with it and the information is not otherwise available, the programmer may reverse engineer the software to learn how to interoperate with it even if a contract prohibits this act. This Directive is addressed again in Chapter 9.

Apart from challenges based on unconscionability, there may be instances where a fundamental public policy outweighs the parties' private contractual terms. The *Restatement (Second) of Contracts* §178 summarizes this principle as follows: "A promise or other term of an agreement is unenforceable on grounds of public policy if legislation provides that it is unenforceable or the interest in its enforcement is clearly outweighed in the circumstances by a public policy against enforcement of such terms." The Uniform Computer Information Transactions Act contains a similar provision. *See* UCITA §105.

f. Policy-Based Objections to Licensing and Licensing Practices

Although the use of licenses is pervasive in the information economy, their use has stirred controversy. The forums for expressing concerns about licensing have been diverse but they include the law review literature (especially in reaction to the Seventh Circuit's *ProCD* decision,[20] which you will find in the Materials section of this chapter), and during the UCITA drafting process.

Licensing raises several important policy-related issues. First, and most fundamentally, licensing represents an intersection between two venerable legal doctrines: contract law's principle of freedom of contract and intellectual property law's grant of limited exclusive rights. Some scholars express concern that the use of licenses will disrupt the delicate balance in the intellectual property laws between exclusive rights and public access. *See, e.g.*, Mark A. Lemley, *Beyond Preemption: The Law and Policy of Intellectual Property Licensing*, 87 CAL. L. REV. 113 (1999); Robert P. Merges, *Intellectual Property and the Costs of Commercial Exchange: A Review Essay*, 93 MICH. L. REV. 1570 (1995); *but see* Raymond T. Nimmer, *Breaking Barriers: The Relation Between Contract and Intellectual Property Law*, 13 BERKELEY TECH. L.J. 827 (1998) (arguing that intellectual property and contract work in "comfortable tandem"). The primary concern is that private ordering, represented by licensing, will be used to expand the exclusive rights granted to the rights holder or pare back the rights reserved for the public under intellectual property laws.

For example, some commentators argue that copyright holders should not be able to alter the rights of the purchaser of a copy described in Copyright Act's "first sale" provision, 17 U.S.C. §109. *See* John A. Rothschild, *The Incredible Shrinking First Sale Rule: Are Software Resale Limits Lawful?*, 57 RUTGERS L. REV. 1 (2004). (This "first sale" provision is explained below in section D and is contained in the Materials section of this chapter.) In other words, commentators argue that copyright holders should not be permitted to use a contract to control the use of a copy of a work, as permitted by the court in the *ProCD* case, or prevent redistribution. There is also a concern that using a contract to control access to non-copyrightable data disrupts the balance in copyright law by, in essence, encumbering information from the public

---

20. *E.g.,* Michael J. Madison, *Legal Ware: Contract and Copyright in the Digital Age*, 67 FORDHAM L. REV. 1025 (1998) (criticizing the *ProCD* decision on contract law grounds); Maureen A. O'Rourke, *Copyright Preemption After the* ProCD *Case: A Market-Based Approach*, 12 BERKELEY TECH. L.J. 53 (1997) (agreeing with *ProCD* on contract grounds but offering criticism on preemption grounds).

domain—again, the *ProCD* case raises this issue. *See* David Nimmer et al., *The Metamorphosis of Contract into Expand*, 87 CAL. L. REV. 17 (1999); *but see* Joel Rothstein Wolfson, *Contracts and Copyright Are Not at War: A Reply to "The Metamorphosis of Contract into Expand*," 87 CAL. L. REV. 79 (1999). These issues often arise in the context of software end user licenses, software distributor licenses, and Web site terms of use, so they will be explored in more detail in Chapters 9 and 10.

A second concern relates to use of take-it-or-leave-it standard form licenses in the mass market. In this context, many scholars express concern that the contract formation process is flawed, particularly the practice of "pay first, terms later," which some call "layered" or "rolling" contracts[21] and others deride as "sneak wrap"[22] contracts. There is also concern that this mode of licensing too easily permits licensors to press one-sided or unfair terms on end users, particularly consumers. *See generally* Robert A. Hillman & Jeffery R. Rachlinski, *Standard Form Contracting in the Electronic Age*, 77 N.Y.U. L. REV. 429 (2002). Moreover, scholars express concern that the practice of presenting terms in standard forms can result in something akin to private legislation, which, echoing the concern expressed in the prior paragraph, disrupts the balance in the intellectual property laws to the advantage of rights holders. *See, e.g.*, David A. Rice, *Public Goods, Private Contract and Public Policy: Federal Preemption of Software License Prohibitions Against Reverse Engineering*, 53 U. PITT. L. REV. 543 (1992); *but see* Tom W. Bell, *Fair Use vs. Fared Use: The Impact of Automated Rights Management on Copyright's Fair Use Doctrine*, 76 N.C. L. REV. 557 (1998) (criticizing the "private legislation" metaphor).

This section is intended to alert you to some of the policy-related concerns that have been raised about licensing; it is not intended to provide a deep or comprehensive treatment. These concerns will resonate in various forms in the Materials sections and in the Problems throughout the rest of this book. There, you will see them arise as they present themselves in various settings.

D. Transaction Models Other Than Licenses

Licensing has emerged as the predominant transaction model for software, information, and intellectual property. However, it is not the only model, and sometimes a license is not the best fit. It is wise to consider all potential transaction options. This section explores some of the other candidates.

---

21. *See* Robert A. Hillman, *Rolling Contracts*, 71 FORDHAM L. REV. 743 (2002).

22. *See* Jean Braucher, *Amended Article 2 and the Decision to Trust the Courts: The Case Against Enforcing Delayed Mass-Market Terms, Especially for Software*, 2004 WIS. L. REV. 752 (2004) (objecting to the terms rolling and layered contracts, and proposing the term "sneak wrap").

1. Copyright Act First Sales

Under the Copyright Act, an author may choose to sell copies of his or her work. Sales of copies are known as "first sales." *See* 17 U.S.C. §109(a); Kirtsaeng v. John Wiley & Sons, 133 S. Ct. 1351 (2013). In a first sale transaction, the purchaser of the copy acquires the right to freely use and transfer the copy. For software, the purchaser also gets the right to make an archival copy and any copies (usually copies in RAM) or modifications that are essential steps in running the software. *See* 17 U.S.C. §117. In some settings this is an excellent transaction model: It provides the perfect set of rights without the fuss of a written contract. That is why newspapers, books, and magazines are sold that way.

It is important to understand that a first sale provides only a discrete, rather limited set of rights to do things with the one copy. It is not a sale of the copyright itself. The purchaser of a copy cannot make additional copies or create derivative works. In substance, a first sale is really akin to a limited license. The *Vernor v. Autodesk* case in the Materials section of this chapter and the *UMG v. Augusto* case in the Materials section of Chapter 8 explore the distinction between a first sale and a license.

In many modern settings, a first sale transaction model is inadequate. Several common examples from the software industry illustrate this. If a software publisher wants to allow a business user to make an extra copy of the software for home use, a first sale is not up to the task. If a software publisher wants its users to be able to make and distribute derivative works of clip art, a first sale would not grant these rights. If a software developer wants to put his or her code on the Internet so that anyone can reproduce and fix bugs, a first sale cannot accomplish that objective.

2. Patent Exhaustion

In patent law the first sale doctrine is known as "patent exhaustion." United States v. Univis Lens Co., 316 U.S. 241, 250 (1943). Under the patent exhaustion doctrine, if a customer purchases a patented product from either the patent holder or its licensee, the customer may freely use or resell the product. *See* Impression Products, Inc. v. Lexmark Int'l, Inc., 137 S. Ct. 1523 (2017), which is contained in the Materials section of Chapter 6.

Like a Copyright Act first sale, patent exhaustion allows the purchaser to use a product and dispose of it as he or she desires.[23] Also like a Copyright Act first sale, these are the only rights the purchaser acquires — the purchaser does not acquire other patent rights such as the right to manufacture a second product from the first one. *See* Bowman v. Monsanto, Co., 569 U.S. 278 (2013), which is contained in the Materials section of this chapter. In substance, patent exhaustion provides a limited right to use and resell a particular item rather than a broad license to the patent itself.

---

23. Like copyright and patent law, trademark law has a doctrine of exhaustion. *See* Sebastian Int'l, Inc. v. Longs Drug Stores Corp., 53 F.2d 1073 (9th Cir. 1995). Trademark licensing is explored in Chapter 4.

Just like copyright holders, patent holders may choose the transaction model that suits them best, including a conditional sale of a patented product. However, if a patent holder makes a conditional sale of an item, then the patent holder will only be able to enforce the condition using contract remedies. An unconditional sale of an item is often an excellent transaction model because it can be done with minimal terms and conditions; however, in other cases a license is better. *See, e.g.,* Monsanto Co. v. Scruggs, 459 F.3d 1328 (Fed. Cir. 2006).

3. Assignment of Rights

A complete, absolute transfer of title to an intellectual property right is usually called an "assignment." If an owner of intellectual property rights wants to sell a copyright, patent, or trademark, he or she assigns it to someone else. An assignment conveys all right, title, and interest in the intellectual property.

The completeness and finality of this transaction model means that it is only useful in certain circumstances. Normally an author, inventor, or the creator of a trademark intends to exploit its intellectual property on an ongoing basis. However, when the goal is to create, obtain value (monetary or otherwise), and then move on to something else, an assignment works nicely.

4. Dedicating a Work to the Public Domain

Dedicating a work to the public domain is another way to completely give up the title to it. Some works automatically fall into the public domain because the statutory term of exclusivity has run or, prior to the United States' acceptance of the Berne Copyright Treaty in 1989, if certain copyright marking formalities were not observed.[24] A trademark may fall into the public domain if the trademark holder has not been a good steward of its use or abandons it.[25]

Some copyright holders *choose* to place their works in the public domain. Some do so for altruistic reasons: They have a desire to give works away for others to use freely. Their reward is simply seeing others use and appreciate their work. Others do it because it makes business sense. For example, an artist might place some of her early works in the public domain to get widespread distribution, hoping that people will become familiar with her name, like the works, and be willing to pay for future works.

---

24. Prior to 1989, U.S. copyright law followed the Universal Copyright Convention. Universal Copyright Convention, 25 UST 1341. This Convention allowed signatories to require certain formalities to obtain copyright protection, such as marking a work with © or the word "copyright." The Berne Convention does not permit formalities: "enjoyment of [the] rights [of authorship] shall not be subject to any formalities." Berne Convention, Article 5(2).

25. Chapter 4 discusses this in more detail.

5. Leasing and Renting

A lease grants permission to use and possess real or personal property. A rental agreement does essentially the same thing as a lease but "rental" has become the preferred nomenclature in certain contexts (e.g., rental cars, apartments). The "rental" terminology also carries the connotation that the right is granted for a relatively short term. Rental as a transaction model is used for home viewing of movies and sometimes to acquire copies of scripts and musical scores for performing plays (e.g., to perform *The Sound of Music*).

Leasing and renting seem a lot like licensing: All of these transaction models grant permission but do not transfer title. What is the distinction? The primary distinction is that leases involve the transfer of something tangible. A lease confers exclusive possession of physical property to the lessee.

Licenses, by contrast, often grant permission to use an intangible such as an intellectual property right or some information. A license to practice a patent or to use a trademarked name often does not involve the delivery of anything tangible. That is not to say, however, that a tangible item is never part of the equation. A software developer may deliver code on a diskette or loaded on a computer hard drive as part of a copyright and patent license; a motion picture producer may deliver a motion picture on celluloid film as part of a copyright license; a franchisor may deliver camera-ready artwork of a logo design in conjunction with a trademark license; a biotech company might deliver biological material in tubes as part of a patent license; a database producer might deliver the data on a CD-ROM to enable an information license. However, the tangible medium does not represent the predominant value in the transaction; the intangible intellectual property or information does, along with the contract to use it.

E. Reasons That Licensing Is Often Chosen as a Transaction Model

Among the transaction models available, licensing has emerged as a dominant transaction model in the information economy. Licensing enables holders of intellectual property or information to do multiple things with it. Later chapters explore many examples, but here are some brief examples to begin the discussion:

- A copyright license allows the copyright to be applied to a variety of products and form the basis of new works: *Superman* comic strips lead to comic books, TV shows, movies, figurines, and pajamas;
- Licensing enables the creators of a John Madden football computer game to use Mr. Madden's name and likeness;
- A trade secret license allows a sports drink beverage to be mixed and bottled by third parties around the world;
- A trademark license allows the Starbucks Coffee Company to open distinctive coffee bars around the world;

- A patent license allows Intel Corporation to have its microprocessors fabricated by other companies;
- Patent cross licensing and licenses from a patent pool allow music to be distributed in the MPEG format;
- A patent license allows an entrepreneur to commercialize a new medicine discovered by a university professor;
- An information access license allows consumers to get information online from Consumer Reports to choose a new car;
- A software end user license enables a software publisher to license word processing software to business users for one price, home users for a lower price, students for a lower price still, and charitable organizations for free.

"Free" and "open source" software (FOSS) is one of the best current illustrations of the powerful use of licenses in product development. Briefly, a FOSS development project gets started when a programmer creates a software program and posts it on the Internet with a license granting others the right to freely use, copy, modify, and distribute the code. The developer chooses to grant these broad permissions because this encourages other developers to fix bugs and improve the code. As open source developer Eric Raymond likes to put it: "Given enough eyeballs, all bugs are shallow." The notion of open source licensing has begun to expand beyond the realm of software to biotech, music, and other works and technologies. The Materials section of this chapter contains an open source license created by an organization called Creative Commons for use with copyrighted works. Chapter 9 examines FOSS licensing in greater detail.

It is often said that licensing gives the licensor the ability to control intellectual property or information. This characterization, though true as far as it goes, sheds insufficient light on the rationale for licensing. Intellectual property rights or physical possession already provides the means to control. The better understanding of licensing is that it is a tool for doing a wide variety of productive things. More often than not, licensing enables flexibility, diversity, and choice: multiple products, a variety of price points, creative distribution models, innovative collaboration, and new works and inventions.

II. MATERIALS

These Materials contain items that will enable you to learn more about license transactions and the laws that make up the body of law that we call licensing law. Of course, it is best to begin by examining an actual license. Thus, the Materials contain a license known as the Creative Commons Attribution 4.0 International Public License. It was created by an organization called Creative Commons, whose mission is to assure that there will always be a rich body of publicly available creative works. *See http://www.creativecommons.org/* for further information about Creative Commons. This Creative Commons license is designed for authors to use who wish to allow others to freely copy, distribute, and make derivatives of their works so long as the author receives attribution. Creative Commons provides a "human-readable" summary of the license called a License Deed as well as a detailed license contract.

Next, you will find two provisions from the United States Copyright Act. The first provision, 17 U.S.C. §109, contains the so-called "first sale" doctrine and exceptions to it. The accompanying Historical and Statutory Notes provide some important elaborations that help put licensing transactions in context. The second provision, 17 U.S.C. §201(d), also provides a backdrop for licensing because it describes a copyright holder's right to transfer a copyright. The Materials also include a provision from the Uniform Computer Information Transactions Act, Section 103, to illustrate how difficult it can be to distinguish between transactions that are licenses of information and transactions that are sales of goods.

Following these statutory provisions, you will find cases that discuss the general legal basis for licensing. One case, ProCD, Inc. v. Zeidenberg, 86 F.3d 1447 (7th Cir. 1996), discusses copyright and data licenses; and another case, Bowman v. Monsanto, Co., 569 U.S. 278 (2013), discusses patent licenses. Cases in later chapters discuss copyright, data, and patent licensing in more detail, but these two cases provide a foundation for those later chapters. Following the *ProCD* and *Bowman* cases, Vernor v. Autodesk, 621 F.3d 1102 (9th Cir. 2010), explores the distinction between licenses and copyright first sales.

To illustrate the influence of intellectual property law on license contracts, the Materials contain excerpts from three cases. First, Everex Systems, Inc. v. Cadtrak Corp., 89 F.3d 673 (9th Cir. 1996), shows how patent law influences whether a license is freely transferable. Second, S.O.S., Inc. v. Payday, Inc., 886 F.2d 1081 (9th Cir. 1989), shows that the breach of a license can lead to a copyright infringement as well as a breach of contract. Third, MDY Industries LLC v. Blizzard Entertainment, Inc., 629 F.3d 928 (9th Cir. 2010), discusses which license agreement provisions are merely contractual covenants (the breach of which leads to a breach of contract claim) and which are conditions on intellectual property license grants (the breach of which leads to a copyright infringement claim).

Finally come three cases that introduce the idea that laws place boundaries on licenses. Blizzard Entertainment, Inc. v. Jung, 422 F.3d 630 (8th Cir. 2005), examines whether enforcement of a contractual prohibition on reverse engineering in a mass market license is preempted by federal intellectual property law. Broadcast Music, Inc. v. Columbia Broadcasting System, Inc., 441 U.S. 1 (1979), looks at one of the important boundaries of licenses: Antitrust law. In this case, the Supreme Court ruled on whether the use of licenses in a collective rights organization violates U.S. antitrust laws. Finally, Video Pipeline, Inc. v. Buena Vista Home Enter., 342 F.3d 191 (3d Cir. 2003), deals with the defense of copyright misuse and determines whether the defense can overcome a contractual provision that limits the licensee's free speech and fair use rights. Cases in later chapters explore these boundaries further, but the latter three will serve as an introduction.

* * *

Section 1 — Definitions.

a. **Adapted Material** means material subject to Copyright and Similar Rights that is derived from or based upon the Licensed Material and in which the Licensed Material is translated, altered, arranged, transformed, or otherwise modified in a manner requiring permission under the Copyright and Similar Rights held by the Licensor. For purposes of this Public License, where the Licensed Material is a musical work, performance, or sound recording, Adapted Material is always produced where the Licensed Material is synched in timed relation with a moving image.

b. **Adapter's License** means the license You apply to Your Copyright and Similar Rights in Your contributions to Adapted Material in accordance with the terms and conditions of this Public License.

c. **Copyright and Similar Rights** means copyright and/or similar rights closely related to copyright including, without limitation, performance, broadcast, sound recording, and Sui Generis Database Rights, without regard to how the rights are labeled or categorized. For purposes of this Public License, the rights specified in Section 2(b)(1)-(2) are not Copyright and Similar Rights.

d. **Effective Technological Measures** means those measures that, in the absence of proper authority, may not be circumvented under laws fulfilling obligations under Article 11 of the WIPO Copyright Treaty adopted on December 20, 1996, and/or similar international agreements.

e. **Exceptions and Limitations** means fair use, fair dealing, and/or any other exception or limitation to Copyright and Similar Rights that applies to Your use of the Licensed Material.

f. **Licensed Material** means the artistic or literary work, database, or other material to which the Licensor applied this Public License.

g. **Licensed Rights** means the rights granted to You subject to the terms and conditions of this Public License, which are limited to all Copyright and Similar Rights that apply to Your use of the Licensed Material and that the Licensor has authority to license.

h. **Licensor** means the individual(s) or entity(ies) granting rights under this Public License.

i. **Share** means to provide material to the public by any means or process that requires permission under the Licensed Rights, such as reproduction, public display, public performance, distribution, dissemination, communication, or importation, and to make material available to the public including in ways that members of the public may access the material from a place and at a time individually chosen by them.

j. **Sui Generis Database Rights** means rights other than copyright resulting from Directive 96/9/EC of the European Parliament and of the Council of 11 March 1996 on the legal protection of databases, as amended and/or succeeded, as well as other essentially equivalent rights anywhere in the world.

k. **You** means the individual or entity exercising the Licensed Rights under this Public License. **Your** has a corresponding meaning.

Section 2 — Scope.

a. **License grant**.
   1. Subject to the terms and conditions of this Public License, the Licensor hereby grants You a worldwide, royalty-free, non-sublicensable, non-exclusive, irrevocable license to exercise the Licensed Rights in the Licensed Material to:
       A. reproduce and Share the Licensed Material, in whole or in part; and
       B. produce, reproduce, and Share Adapted Material.
   2. Exceptions and Limitations. For the avoidance of doubt, where Exceptions and Limitations apply to Your use, this Public License does not apply, and You do not need to comply with its terms and conditions.
   3. Term. The term of this Public License is specified in Section 6(a).
   4. Media and formats; technical modifications allowed. The Licensor authorizes You to exercise the Licensed Rights in all media and formats whether now known or hereafter created, and to make technical modifications necessary to do so. The Licensor waives and/or agrees not to assert any right or authority to forbid You from making technical modifications necessary to exercise the Licensed Rights, including technical modifications necessary to circumvent Effective Technological Measures. For purposes of this Public License, simply making modifications authorized by this Section 2(a)(4) never produces Adapted Material.
   5. Downstream recipients.
       A. Offer from the Licensor — Licensed Material. Every recipient of the Licensed Material automatically receives an offer from the Licensor to exercise the Licensed Rights under the terms and conditions of this Public License.
       B. No downstream restrictions. You may not offer or impose any additional or different terms or conditions on, or apply any Effective Technological Measures to, the Licensed Material if doing so restricts exercise of the Licensed Rights by any recipient of the Licensed Material.
   6. No endorsement. Nothing in this Public License constitutes or may be construed as permission to assert or imply that You are, or that Your use of the Licensed Material is, connected with, or sponsored, endorsed, or granted official status by, the Licensor or others designated to receive attribution as provided in Section 3(a)(1)(A)(i).

b. **Other rights.**
   1. Moral rights, such as the right of integrity, are not licensed under this Public License, nor are publicity, privacy, and/or other similar personality rights; however, to the extent possible, the Licensor waives and/or agrees not to assert any such rights held by the Licensor to the limited extent necessary to allow You to exercise the Licensed Rights, but not otherwise.

2. Patent and trademark rights are not licensed under this Public License.
3. To the extent possible, the Licensor waives any right to collect royalties from You for the exercise of the Licensed Rights, whether directly or through a collecting society under any voluntary or waivable statutory or compulsory licensing scheme. In all other cases the Licensor expressly reserves any right to collect such royalties.

Section 3 – License Conditions.

Your exercise of the Licensed Rights is expressly made subject to the following conditions.

a. **Attribution.**
   1. If You Share the Licensed Material (including in modified form), You must:
      A. retain the following if it is supplied by the Licensor with the Licensed Material:
         i. identification of the creator(s) of the Licensed Material and any others designated to receive attribution, in any reasonable manner requested by the Licensor (including by pseudonym if designated);
         ii. a copyright notice;
         iii. a notice that refers to this Public License;
         iv. a notice that refers to the disclaimer of warranties;
         v. a URI or hyperlink to the Licensed Material to the extent reasonably practicable;
      B. indicate if You modified the Licensed Material and retain an indication of any previous modifications; and
      C. indicate the Licensed Material is licensed under this Public License, and include the text of, or the URI or hyperlink to, this Public License.
   2. You may satisfy the conditions in Section 3(a)(1) in any reasonable manner based on the medium, means, and context in which You Share the Licensed Material. For example, it may be reasonable to satisfy the conditions by providing a URL or hyperlink to a resource that includes the required information.
   3. If requested by the Licensor, You must remove any of the information required by Section 3(a)(1)(A) to the extent reasonably practicable.
   4. If You Share Adapted Material You produce, the Adapter's License You apply must not prevent recipients of the Adapted Material from complying with this Public License.

Section 4 – Sui Generis Database Rights.

Where the Licensed Rights include Sui Generis Database Rights that apply to Your use of the Licensed Material:

a. for the avoidance of doubt, Section 2(a)(1) grants You the right to extract, reuse, reproduce, and Share all or a substantial portion of the contents of the database;

b. if You include all or a substantial portion of the database contents in a database in which You have Sui Generis Database Rights, then the database in which You have Sui Generis Database Rights (but not its individual contents) is Adapted Material; and

c. You must comply with the conditions in Section 3(a) if You Share all or a substantial portion of the contents of the database.

For the avoidance of doubt, this Section 4 supplements and does not replace Your obligations under this Public License where the Licensed Rights include other Copyright and Similar Rights.

Section 5 — Disclaimer of Warranties and Limitation of Liability.

a. Unless otherwise separately undertaken by the Licensor, to the extent possible, the Licensor offers the Licensed Material as-is and as-available, and makes no representations or warranties of any kind concerning the Licensed Material, whether express, implied, statutory, or other. This includes, without limitation, warranties of title, merchantability, fitness for a particular purpose, non-infringement, absence of latent or other defects, accuracy, or the presence or absence of errors, whether or not known or discoverable. Where disclaimers of warranties are not allowed in full or in part, this disclaimer may not apply to You.

b. To the extent possible, in no event will the Licensor be liable to You on any legal theory (including, without limitation, negligence) or otherwise for any direct, special, indirect, incidental, consequential, punitive, exemplary, or other losses, costs, expenses, or damages arising out of this Public License or use of the Licensed Material, even if the Licensor has been advised of the possibility of such losses, costs, expenses, or damages. Where a limitation of liability is not allowed in full or in part, this limitation may not apply to You.

c. The disclaimer of warranties and limitation of liability provided above shall be interpreted in a manner that, to the extent possible, most closely approximates an absolute disclaimer and waiver of all liability.

Section 6 — Term and Termination.

a. This Public License applies for the term of the Copyright and Similar Rights licensed here. However, if You fail to comply with this Public License, then Your rights under this Public License terminate automatically.

b. Where Your right to use the Licensed Material has terminated under Section 6(a), it reinstates:
   1. automatically as of the date the violation is cured, provided it is cured within 30 days of Your discovery of the violation; or
   2. upon express reinstatement by the Licensor.

For the avoidance of doubt, this Section 6(b) does not affect any right the Licensor may have to seek remedies for Your violations of this Public License.

c. For the avoidance of doubt, the Licensor may also offer the Licensed Material under separate terms or conditions or stop distributing the Licensed Material at any time; however, doing so will not terminate this Public License.

d. Sections 1, 5, 6, 7, and 8 survive termination of this Public License.

Section 7 — Other Terms and Conditions.

a. The Licensor shall not be bound by any additional or different terms or conditions communicated by You unless expressly agreed.

b. Any arrangements, understandings, or agreements regarding the Licensed Material not stated herein are separate from and independent of the terms and conditions of this Public License.

Section 8 — Interpretation.

a. For the avoidance of doubt, this Public License does not, and shall not be interpreted to, reduce, limit, restrict, or impose conditions on any use of the Licensed Material that could lawfully be made without permission under this Public License.

b. To the extent possible, if any provision of this Public License is deemed unenforceable, it shall be automatically reformed to the minimum extent necessary to make it enforceable. If the provision cannot be reformed, it shall be severed from this Public License without affecting the enforceability of the remaining terms and conditions.

c. No term or condition of this Public License will be waived and no failure to comply consented to unless expressly agreed to by the Licensor.

d. Nothing in this Public License constitutes or may be interpreted as a limitation upon, or waiver of, any privileges and immunities that apply to the Licensor or You, including from the legal processes of any jurisdiction or authority.

UNITED STATES CODE ANNOTATED: TITLE 17. COPYRIGHTS

§109. Limitations on exclusive rights: Effect of transfer of particular copy or phonorecord

(a) Notwithstanding the [exclusive right "to distribute copies or phonorecords . . . to the public by sale or other transfer of ownership, or by rental, lease, or lending"] of section 106(3), the owner of a particular copy or phonorecord lawfully made under this title, or any person authorized by such owner, is entitled, without the authority of the copyright owner, to sell or otherwise dispose of the possession of that copy or phonorecord.

(b)(1)(A) Notwithstanding the provisions of subsection (a), unless authorized by the owners of copyright in the sound recording or the owner of copyright in a computer program (including any tape, disk, or other medium embodying such program), and in the case of a sound recording in the musical works embodied therein, neither the owner of a particular phonorecord nor any person in possession of a particular copy of a computer program (including any tape, disk, or other medium embodying such program), may, for the purposes of direct or indirect commercial advantage, dispose of, or authorize the disposal of, the possession of that phonorecord or computer program (including any tape, disk, or other medium embodying such program) by rental, lease, or lending, or by any other act or practice in the nature of rental, lease, or lending. Nothing in the preceding sentence shall apply to the rental, lease, or lending of a phonorecord for nonprofit purposes by a nonprofit library or nonprofit educational institution. The transfer of possession of a lawfully made copy of a computer program by a nonprofit educational institution to another nonprofit educational institution or to faculty, staff, and students does not constitute rental, lease, or lending for direct or indirect commercial purposes under this subsection.

(B) This subsection does not apply to —

(i) a computer program which is embodied in a machine or product and which cannot be copied during the ordinary operation or use of the machine or product; or

(ii) a computer program embodied in or used in conjunction with a limited purpose computer that is designed for playing video games and may be designed for other purposes.

(c) Notwithstanding the provisions of section 106(5), the owner of a particular copy lawfully made under this title, or any person authorized by such owner, is entitled, without the authority of the copyright owner, to display that copy publicly, either directly or by the projection of no more than one image at a time, to viewers present at the place where the copy is located.

(d) The privileges prescribed by subsections (a) and (c) do not, unless authorized by the copyright owner, extend to any person who has acquired possession of the copy or phonorecord from the copyright owner, by rental, lease, loan, or otherwise, without acquiring ownership of it.

(e) Notwithstanding the provisions of sections 106(4) and 106(5), in the case of an electronic audiovisual game intended for use in coin-operated equipment, the owner of a particular copy of such a game lawfully made under this title, is entitled, without the authority of the copyright owner of the game, to publicly perform or display that game in coin-operated equipment, except that this subsection shall not apply to any work of authorship embodied in the audiovisual game if the copyright owner of the electronic audiovisual game is not also the copyright owner of the work of authorship.

REVISION NOTES AND LEGISLATIVE REPORTS: 1976 ACTS

Notes of Committee on the Judiciary, House Report No. 94-1476

Effect on Further Disposition of Copy or Phonorecord. Subsection(a) of section 109 restates and confirms the principle that, where the copyright owner has transferred ownership of a particular copy or phonorecord of a work, the person to whom the copy or phonorecord is transferred is entitled to dispose of it by sale, rental, or any other means. Under this principle, which has been established by the court decisions and section 27 of the present law [former section 27 of this title], the copyright owner's exclusive right of public distribution would have no effect upon anyone who owns "a particular copy or phonorecord lawfully made under this title" and who wishes to transfer it to someone else or to destroy it.

Thus, for example, the outright sale of an authorized copy of a book frees it from any copyright control over its resale price or other conditions of its future disposition. A library that has acquired ownership of a copy is entitled to lend it under any conditions it chooses to impose. This does not mean that conditions on future disposition of copies or phonorecords, imposed by a contract between their buyer and seller, would be unenforceable between the parties as a breach of contract, but it does mean that they could not be enforced by an action for infringement of copyright. Under section 202 [section 202 of this title] however, the owner of the physical copy or phonorecord cannot reproduce or perform the copyrighted work publicly without the copyright owner's consent.

Effect of mere possession of copy or phonorecord. Subsection [d] of section 109 qualifies the privileges specified in subsections (a) and (b) by making clear that they do not apply to someone who merely possesses a copy or phonorecord without having acquired ownership of it. Acquisition of an object embodying a copyrighted work by rental, lease, loan, or bailment carries with it no privilege to dispose of the copy under section 109(a) or to display It publicly under section 109(b). To cite a familiar example, a person who has rented a print of a motion picture from the copyright owner would have no right to rent it to someone else without the owner's permission.

§201. Ownership of copyright

(d) Transfer of Ownership—

(1) The ownership of a copyright may be transferred in whole or in part by any means of conveyance or by operation of law, and may be bequeathed by will or pass as personal property by the application of the intestate succession.

(2) Any of the exclusive rights comprised in a copyright, including any subdivision of any of the rights specified by 106, may be transferred as provided by clause (1) and owned separately. The owner of any particular exclusive right is entitled, to the extent of that right, to all of the protection and remedies accorded to the copyright owner by this title.

UNIFORM COMPUTER INFORMATION TRANSACTIONS ACT

Section 103. Scope; Exclusions

(a) [**Scope in general.**] This [Act] applies to computer information transactions.

(b) [**Mixed transactions.**] Except for subject matter excluded in subsection (d), if a computer information transaction includes subject matter other than computer information or subject matter excluded under subsection (d), the following rules apply:

(1) [**Computer information and goods.**] If a transaction includes computer information and goods, this [Act] applies to the part of the transaction involving computer information, informational rights in it, and creation or modification of it. However, if a copy of a computer program is contained in and sold or leased as part of goods, this [Act] applies to the copy and the computer program only if:

(2) [**Computer information and motion pictures.**] Subject to subsection (d)(3)(A), if a transaction includes an agreement for creating, or for obtaining rights to create, computer information and a motion picture, this [Act] does not apply to the agreement if the dominant character of the agreement is to create or obtain rights to create a motion picture. In all other such agreements, this [Act] does not apply to the part of the agreement that involves a motion picture excluded under subsection (d)(3), but does apply to the computer information.

(3) [**All other cases.**] In all other cases, this [Act] applies to the entire transaction if the computer information and informational rights, or access to them, is the primary subject matter, but otherwise applies only to the part of the transaction involving computer information, informational rights in it, and creation or modification of it.

(c) [**Article 9 governs.**] To the extent of a conflict between this [Act] and [Article 9 of the Uniform Commercial Code], [Article 9] governs.

(d) [**Exclusions.**] This [Act] does not apply to:

(1) a financial services transaction;

(2) an insurance services transaction;

(3) an agreement to create, perform or perform in, include information in, acquire, use, distribute, modify, reproduce, have access to, adapt, make available, transmit, license, or display;

(4) a compulsory license;

(5) a contract of employment of an individual, other than an individual hired as an independent contractor to create or modify computer information, unless the independent contractor is a freelancer in the news reporting industry as that term is commonly understood in that industry;

(6) a contract that does not require that information be furnished as computer information or a contract in which, under the agreement, the form of the information as computer information is otherwise insignificant with respect to the primary subject matter of the part of the transaction pertaining to the information;

(7) unless otherwise agreed between the parties in a record;

(8) subject matter within the scope of [Article 3, 4, 4A, 5, [6,] 7, or 8 of the Uniform Commercial Code].

(e) [**Definitions.**] In this section:

(1) "Audio or visual programming" means audio or visual programming that is provided by broadcast, satellite, or cable, as defined or used in the Communications Act of 1934 and related regulations as they existed on July 1, 1999, or by similar methods of delivery.

(2) "Enhanced sound recording" means a separately identifiable product or service the dominant character of which consists of recorded sounds, but which includes (i) statements or instructions whose purpose is to allow or control the perception, reproduction, or communication of those sounds or (ii) other information, as long as recorded sounds constitute the dominant character of the product or service.

(3) "Motion picture" means:

(A) "motion picture" as defined in Title 17 of the United States Code as of July 1, 1999; or

(B) a separately identifiable product or service the dominant character of which consists of a linear motion picture, but which includes (i) statements or instructions whose purpose is to allow or control the perception, reproduction, or communication of the motion picture or (ii) other information, as long as the motion picture constitutes the dominant character of the product or service.

* * *

PROCD, INC. v. ZEIDENBERG
86 F.3d 1447 (7th Cir. 1996)

EASTERBROOK, Circuit Judge.

ProCD, the plaintiff, has compiled information from more than 3,000 telephone directories into a computer database. We may assume that this database cannot be copyrighted, although it is more complex, contains more information (nine-digit zip codes and census industrial codes), is organized differently, and therefore is more original than the single alphabetical directory at issue in Feist Publications, Inc. v. Rural Telephone Service Co., 499 U.S. 340 (1991). ProCD sells a version of the database, called SelectPhone on CD-ROM discs. (CD-ROM means "compact disc — read only memory." The "shrinkwrap license" gets its name from the fact that retail software packages are covered in plastic or cellophane "shrinkwrap," and some vendors, though not ProCD, have written licenses that become effective as soon as the customer tears the wrapping from the package. Vendors prefer "end user license," but we use the more common term.) A proprietary method of compressing the data serves as effective encryption too. Customers decrypt and use the data with the aid of an application program that ProCD has written. This program, which is copyrighted, searches the database in response to users' criteria (such as "find all people named Tatum in Tennessee, plus all firms with 'Door Systems' in the corporate name"). The resulting lists (or, as ProCD prefers, "listings") can be read and manipulated by other software, such as word processing programs.

The database in SelectPhone cost more than $10 million to compile and is expensive to keep current. It is much more valuable to some users than to others. The combination of names, addresses, and SIC codes enables manufacturers to compile lists of potential customers. Manufacturers and retailers pay high prices to specialized information intermediaries for such mailing lists; ProCD offers a potentially cheaper alternative. People with nothing to sell could use the database as a substitute for calling long distance information, or as a way to look up old friends who have moved to unknown towns, or just as an electronic substitute for the local phone book. ProCD decided to engage in price discrimination, selling its database to the general public for personal use at a low price (approximately $150 for the set of five discs) while selling information to the trade for a higher price. It has adopted some intermediate strategies too: access to the SelectPhone database is available via the America Online service for the price America Online charges to its clients (approximately $3 per hour), but this service has been tailored to be useful only to the general public.

If ProCD had to recover all of its costs and make a profit by charging a single price — that is, if it could not charge more to commercial users than to the general public — it would have to raise the price substantially over $150. The ensuing reduction in sales would harm consumers who value the information at, say, $200. They get consumer surplus of $50 under the current arrangement but would cease to buy if the price rose substantially. If because of high elasticity of demand in the consumer segment of the market the only way to make a profit turned out to be a price attractive to commercial users alone, then all consumers would lose out — and so would the commercial clients, who would have to pay more for the listings because ProCD could not obtain any contribution toward costs from the consumer market.

To make price discrimination work, however, the seller must be able to control arbitrage. An air carrier sells tickets for less to vacationers than to business travelers, using advance purchase and Saturday-night-stay requirements to distinguish the categories. A producer of movies segments the market by time, releasing first to theaters, then to pay-per-view services, next to the videotape and laserdisc market, and finally to cable and commercial TV. Vendors of computer software have a harder task. Anyone can walk into a retail store and buy a box. Customers do not wear tags saying "commercial user" or "consumer user." Anyway, even a commercial-user-detector at the door would not work, because a consumer could buy the software and resell to a commercial user. That arbitrage would break down the price discrimination and drive up the minimum price at which ProCD would sell to anyone.

Instead of tinkering with the product and letting users sort themselves — for example, furnishing current data at a high price that would be attractive only to commercial customers, and two-year-old data at a low price — ProCD turned to the institution of contract. Every box containing its consumer product declares that the software comes with restrictions stated in an enclosed license. This license, which is encoded on the CD-ROM disks as well as printed in the manual, and which appears on a user's screen every time the software runs, limits use of the application program and listings to non-commercial purposes.

Matthew Zeidenberg bought a consumer package of SelectPhone in 1994 from a retail outlet in Madison, Wisconsin, but decided to ignore the license. He formed Silken Mountain Web Services, Inc., to resell the information in the SelectPhone database. The corporation makes the database available on the Internet to anyone willing to pay its price — which, needless to say, is less than ProCD charges its commercial customers.

In the end, the terms of the license are conceptually identical to the contents of the package. Just as no court would dream of saying that SelectPhone must contain 3,100 phone books rather than 3,000, or must have data no more than 30 days old, or must sell for $100 rather than $150 — although any of these changes would be welcomed by the customer, if all other things were held constant — so, we believe, Wisconsin would not let the buyer pick and choose among terms. Terms of use are no less a part of "the product" than are the size of the database and the speed with which the software compiles listings. Competition among vendors, not judicial revision of a package's contents, is how consumers are protected in a market economy. Digital Equipment Corp. v. Unig Digital Technologies, Inc., 73 F.3d 756 (7th Cir. 1996). ProCD has rivals, which may elect to compete by offering superior software, monthly updates, improved terms of use, lower price, or a better compromise among these elements. As we stressed above, adjusting terms in buyers' favor might help Matthew Zeidenberg today (he already has the software) but would lead to a response, such as a higher price, that might make consumers as a whole worse off.

BOWMAN v. MONSANTO, CO.

569 U.S. 278 (2013)

Justice **KAGAN** delivered the opinion of the Court:

Under the doctrine of patent exhaustion, the authorized sale of a patented article gives the purchaser, or any subsequent owner, a right to use or resell that article. Such a sale, however, does not allow the purchaser to make new copies of the patented invention. The question in this case is whether a farmer who buys patented seeds may reproduce them through planting and harvesting without the patent holder's permission. We hold that he may not.

I

Respondent Monsanto invented a genetic modification that enables soybean plants to survive exposure to glyphosate, the active ingredient in many herbicides (including Monsanto's own Roundup). Monsanto markets soybean seed containing this altered genetic material as Roundup Ready seed. Farmers planting that seed can use a glyphosate-based herbicide to kill weeds without damaging their crops. Two patents issued to Monsanto cover various aspects of its Roundup Ready technology, including a seed incorporating the genetic alteration. *See* Supp. App. SA1-21 (U.S. Patent Nos. 5,352,605 and *RE39,247E*); *see also* 657 F.3d 1341, 1343-1344 (CA Fed. 2011).

Monsanto sells, and allows other companies to sell, Roundup Ready soybean seeds to growers who assent to a special licensing agreement. That agreement permits a grower to plant the purchased seeds in one (and only one) season. He can then consume the resulting crop or sell it as a commodity, usually to a grain elevator or agricultural processor. But under the agreement, the farmer may not save any of the harvested soybeans for replanting, nor may he supply them to anyone else for that purpose. These restrictions reflect the ease of producing new generations of Roundup Ready seed. Because glyphosate resistance comes from the seed's genetic material, that trait is passed on from the planted seed to the harvested soybeans: Indeed, a single Roundup Ready seed can grow a plant containing dozens of genetically identical beans, each of which, if replanted, can grow another such plant — and so on and so on. The agreement's terms prevent the farmer from co-opting that process to produce his own Roundup Ready seeds, forcing him instead to buy from Monsanto each season.

Petitioner Vernon Bowman is a farmer in Indiana who, it is fair to say, appreciates Roundup Ready soybean seed. He purchased Roundup Ready each year, from a company affiliated with Monsanto, for his first crop of the season. In accord with the agreement just described, he used all of that seed for planting, and sold his entire crop to a grain elevator (which typically would resell it to an agricultural processor for human or animal consumption).

Bowman, however, devised a less orthodox approach for his second crop of each season. Because he thought such late-season planting "risky," he did not want to pay the premium price that Monsanto charges for Roundup Ready seed. He therefore went to a grain elevator; purchased "commodity soybeans" intended for human or animal consumption; and planted them in his fields. Those soybeans came from prior harvests of other local farmers. And because most of those farmers also used Roundup Ready seed, Bowman could anticipate that many of the purchased soybeans would contain Monsanto's patented technology. When he applied a glyphosate-based herbicide to his fields, he confirmed that this was so; a significant proportion of the new plants survived the treatment, and produced in their turn a new crop of soybeans with the Roundup Ready trait. Bowman saved seed from that crop to use in his late-season planting the next year — and then the next, and the next, until he had harvested eight crops in that way. Each year, that is, he planted saved seed from the year before (sometimes adding more soybeans bought from the grain elevator), sprayed his fields with glyphosate to kill weeds (and any non-resistant plants), and produced a new crop of glyphosate-resistant — *i.e.*, Roundup Ready — soybeans.

After discovering this practice, Monsanto sued Bowman for infringing its patents on Roundup Ready seed. Bowman raised patent exhaustion as a defense, arguing that Monsanto could not control his use of the soybeans because they were the subject of a prior authorized sale (from local farmers to the grain elevator). The District Court rejected that argument, and awarded damages to Monsanto of $84,456. The Federal Circuit affirmed. It reasoned that patent exhaustion did not protect Bowman because he had "created a newly infringing article." 657 F.3d, at 1348. The "right to use" a patented article following an authorized sale, the court explained, "does not include the right to construct an essentially new article on the template of the original, for the right to make the article remains with the patentee." *Ibid*. Accordingly, Bowman could not "replicate Monsanto's patented technology by planting it in the ground to create newly infringing genetic material, seeds, and plants." *Ibid*. We granted certiorari to consider the important question of patent law raised in this case, and now affirm.

II

The doctrine of patent exhaustion limits a patentee's right to control what others can do with an article embodying or containing an invention. Under the doctrine, "the initial authorized sale of a patented item terminates all patent rights to that item." *Quanta Computer, Inc. v. LG Electronics, Inc.*, 553 U.S. 617, 625 (2008). And by "exhaust[ing] the [patentee's] monopoly" in that item, the sale confers on the purchaser, or any subsequent owner, "the right to use [or] sell" the thing as he sees fit. *United States v. Univis Lens Co.*, 316 U.S. 241, 249-250 (1942). We have explained the basis for the doctrine as follows: "[T]he purpose of the patent law is fulfilled with respect to any particular article when the patentee has received his reward . . . by the sale of the article"; once that "purpose is realized the patent law affords no basis for restraining the use and enjoyment of the thing sold." *Id.* at 251.

Consistent with that rationale, the doctrine restricts a patentee's rights only as to the "particular article" sold, *ibid.*; it leaves untouched the patentee's ability to prevent a buyer from making new copies of the patented item. "[T]he purchaser of the [patented] machine . . . does not acquire any right to construct another machine either for his own use or to be vended to another." *Mitchell v. Hawley*, 16 Wall. 544, 548 (1873); *see Wilbur-Ellis Co. v. Kuther*, 377 U.S. 422, 424 (1964) (holding that a purchaser's "reconstruction" of a patented machine "would impinge on the patentee's right '*to exclude others from making*' . . . the article" (quoting 35 U.S.C. §154 (1964 ed.))). Rather, "a second creation" of the patented item "call[s] the monopoly, conferred by the patent grant, into play for a second time." *Aro Mfg. Co. v. Convertible Top Replacement Co.*, 365 U.S. 336, 346 (1961). That is because the patent holder has "received his reward" only for the actual article sold, and not for subsequent recreations of it. *Univis*, 316 U.S., at 251. If the purchaser of that article could make and sell endless copies, the patent would effectively protect the invention for just a single sale. Bowman himself disputes none of this analysis as a general matter: He forthrightly acknowledges the "well settled" principle "that the exhaustion doctrine does not extend to the right to 'make' a new product." Brief for Petitioner 37 (citing *Aro*, 365 U.S., at 346).

Unfortunately for Bowman, that principle decides this case against him. Under the patent exhaustion doctrine, Bowman could resell the patented soybeans he purchased from the grain elevator; so too he could consume the beans himself or feed them to his animals. Monsanto, although the patent holder, would have no business interfering in those uses of Roundup Ready beans. But the exhaustion doctrine does not enable Bowman to make *additional* patented soybeans without Monsanto's permission (either express or implied). And that is precisely what Bowman did. He took the soybeans he purchased home; planted them in his fields at the time he thought best; applied glyphosate to kill weeds (as well as any soy plants lacking the Roundup Ready trait); and finally harvested more (many more) beans than he started with. That is how "to 'make' a new product," to use Bowman's words, when the original product is a seed. Brief for Petitioner 37; *see* Webster's Third New International Dictionary 1363 (1961) ("make" means "cause to exist, occur, or appear," or more specifically, "plant and raise (a crop)"). Because Bowman thus reproduced Monsanto's patented invention, the exhaustion doctrine does not protect him.

Were the matter otherwise, Monsanto's patent would provide scant benefit. After inventing the Roundup Ready trait, Monsanto would, to be sure, "receiv[e] [its] reward" for the first seeds it sells. *Univis*, 316 U.S., at 251. But in short order, other seed companies could reproduce the product and market it to growers, thus depriving Monsanto of its monopoly. And farmers themselves need only buy the seed once, whether from Monsanto, a competitor, or (as here) a grain elevator. The grower could multiply his initial purchase, and then multiply that new creation, *ad infinitum* — each time profiting from the patented seed without compensating its inventor. Bowman's late-season plantings offer a prime illustration. After buying beans for a single harvest, Bowman saved enough seed each year to reduce or eliminate the need for additional purchases. Monsanto still held its patent, but received no gain from Bowman's annual production and sale of Roundup Ready soybeans. The exhaustion doctrine is limited to the "particular item" sold to avoid just such a mismatch between invention and reward.

Our holding today also follows from *J. E. M. Ag Supply, Inc.* v. *Pioneer Hi-Bred Int'l, Inc.*, 534 U.S. 124 (2001). We considered there whether an inventor could get a patent on a seed or plant, or only a certificate issued under the Plant Variety Protection Act (PVPA), 7 U.S.C. §2321 *et seq.* We decided a patent was available, rejecting the claim that the PVPA implicitly repealed the Patent Act's coverage of seeds and plants. On our view, the two statutes established different, but not conflicting schemes: The requirements for getting a patent "are more stringent than those for obtaining a PVP certificate, and the protections afforded" by a patent are correspondingly greater. *J. E. M.*, 534 U.S., at 142. Most notable here, we explained that only a patent holder (not a certificate holder) could prohibit "[a] farmer who legally purchases and plants" a protected seed from saving harvested seed "for replanting." *Id.*, at 140; *see id.*, at 143 (noting that the Patent Act, unlike the PVPA, contains "no exemptio[n]" for "saving seed"). That statement is inconsistent with applying exhaustion to protect conduct like Bowman's. If a sale cut off the right to control a patented seed's progeny, then (contrary to *J.E.M.*) the patentee could *not* prevent the buyer from saving harvested seed. Indeed, the patentee could not stop the buyer from *selling* such seed, which even a PVP certificate owner (who, recall, is supposed to have fewer rights) can usually accomplish. *See* 7 U.S.C. §§2541, 2543. Those limitations would turn upside-down the statutory scheme *J. E. M.* described.

Bowman principally argues that exhaustion should apply here because seeds are meant to be planted. The exhaustion doctrine, he reminds us, typically prevents a patentee from controlling the use of a patented product following an authorized sale. And in planting Roundup Ready seeds, Bowman continues, he is merely using them in the normal way farmers do. Bowman thus concludes that allowing Monsanto to interfere with that use would "creat[e] an impermissible exception to the exhaustion doctrine" for patented seeds and other "self-replicating technologies." Brief for Petitioner 16.

But it is really Bowman who is asking for an unprecedented exception—to what he concedes is the "well settled" rule that "the exhaustion doctrine does not extend to the right to 'make' a new product." *See supra*, at 5. Reproducing a patented article no doubt "uses" it after a fashion. But as already explained, we have always drawn the boundaries of the exhaustion doctrine to exclude that activity, so that the patentee retains an undiminished right to prohibit others from making the thing his patent protects. *See, e.g., Cotton-Tie Co.* v. *Simmons*, 106 U.S. 89, 93-94 (1882) (holding that a purchaser could not "use" the buckle from a patented cotton-bale tie to "make" a new tie). That is because, once again, if simple copying were a protected use, a patent would plummet in value after the first sale of the first item containing the invention. The undiluted patent monopoly, it might be said, would extend not for 20 years (as the Patent Act promises), but for only one transaction. And that would result in less incentive for innovation than Congress wanted. Hence our repeated insistence that exhaustion applies only to the particular item sold, and not to reproductions.

Nor do we think that rule will prevent farmers from making appropriate use of the Roundup Ready seed they buy. Bowman himself stands in a peculiarly poor position to assert such a claim. As noted earlier, the commodity soybeans he purchased were intended not for planting, but for consumption. *See supra*, at 2-3. Indeed, Bowman conceded in deposition testimony that he knew of no other farmer who employed beans bought from a grain elevator to grow a new crop. *See* App. 84a. So a non-replicating use of the commodity beans at issue here was not just available, but standard fare. And in the more ordinary case, when a farmer purchases Roundup Ready seed *qua* seed—that is, seed intended to grow a crop—he will be able to plant it. Monsanto, to be sure, conditions the farmer's ability to reproduce Roundup Ready; but it does not—could not realistically—preclude all planting. No sane farmer, after all, would buy the product without some ability to grow soybeans from it. And so Monsanto, predictably enough, sells Roundup Ready seed to farmers with a license to use it to make a crop. *See supra*, at 2, 6, n. 3. Applying our usual rule in this context therefore will allow farmers to benefit from Roundup Ready, even as it rewards Monsanto for its innovation.

Still, Bowman has another seeds-are-special argument: that soybeans naturally "self-replicate or 'sprout' unless stored in a controlled manner," and thus "it was the planted soybean, not Bowman" himself, that made replicas of Monsanto's patented invention. Brief for Petitioner 42; *see* Tr. of Oral Arg. 14 ("[F]armers, when they plant seeds, they don't exercise any control . . . over their crop" or "over the creative process"). But we think that blame-the-bean defense tough to credit. Bowman was not a passive observer of his soybeans' multiplication; or put another way, the seeds he purchased (miraculous though they might be in other respects) did not spontaneously create eight successive soybean crops. As we have explained, *supra* at 2-3, Bowman devised and executed a novel way to harvest crops from Roundup Ready seeds without paying the usual premium. He purchased beans from a grain elevator anticipating that many would be Roundup Ready; applied a glyphosate-based herbicide in a way that culled any plants without the patented trait; and saved beans from the rest for the next season. He then planted those Roundup Ready beans at a chosen time; tended and treated them, including by exploiting their patented glyphosate-resistance; and harvested many more seeds, which he either marketed or saved to begin the next cycle. In all this, the bean surely figured. But it was Bowman, and not the bean, who controlled the reproduction (unto the eighth generation) of Monsanto's patented invention.

Our holding today is limited — addressing the situation before us, rather than every one involving a self-replicating product. We recognize that such inventions are becoming ever more prevalent, complex, and diverse. In another case, the article's self-replication might occur outside the purchaser's control. Or it might be a necessary but incidental step in using the item for another purpose. Cf. 17 U.S.C. §117(a)(1) ("[I]t is not [a copyright] infringement for the owner of a copy of a computer program to make . . . another copy or adaptation of that computer program provide[d] that such a new copy or adaptation is created as an essential step in the utilization of the computer program"). We need not address here whether or how the doctrine of patent exhaustion would apply in such circumstances. In the case at hand, Bowman planted Monsanto's patented soybeans solely to make and market replicas of them, thus depriving the company of the reward patent law provides for the sale of each article. Patent exhaustion provides no haven for that conduct. We accordingly affirm the judgment of the Court of Appeals for the Federal Circuit.

VERNOR v. AUTODESK, INC.
621 F.3d 1102 (9th Cir. 2010)

CALLAHAN, Circuit Judge.

Timothy Vernor purchased several used copies of Autodesk, Inc.'s AutoCAD Release 14 software ("Release 14") from one of Autodesk's direct customers, and he resold the Release 14 copies on eBay. Vernor brought this declaratory judgment action against Autodesk to establish that these resales did not infringe Autodesk's copyright. The district court issued the requested declaratory judgment, holding that Vernor's sales were lawful because of two of the Copyright Act's affirmative defenses that apply to owners of copies of copyrighted works, the first sale doctrine and the essential step defense.

Autodesk distributes Release 14 pursuant to a limited license agreement in which it reserves title to the software copies and imposes significant use and transfer restrictions on its customers. We determine that Autodesk's direct customers are licensees of their copies of the software rather than owners, which has two ramifications. Because Vernor did not purchase the Release 14 copies from an owner, he may not invoke the first sale doctrine, and he also may not assert an essential step defense on behalf of his customers. For these reasons, we vacate the district court's grant of summary judgment to Vernor and remand for further proceedings.

I.

A. Autodesk's Release 14 Software and Licensing Practices

The material facts are not in dispute. Autodesk makes computer-aided design software used by architects, engineers, and manufacturers. It has more than nine million customers. It first released its AutoCAD software in 1982. It holds registered copyrights in all versions of the software including the discontinued Release 14 version, which is at issue in this case. It provided Release 14 to customers on CD-ROMs.

Since at least 1986, Autodesk has offered AutoCAD to customers pursuant to an accompanying software license agreement ("SLA"), which customers must accept before installing the software. A customer who does not accept the SLA can return the software for a full refund. Autodesk offers SLAs with different terms for commercial, educational institution, and student users. The commercial license, which is the most expensive, imposes the fewest restrictions on users and allows them software upgrades at discounted prices.

The SLA for Release 14 first recites that Autodesk retains title to all copies. Second, it states that the customer has a nonexclusive and nontransferable license to use Release 14. Third, it imposes transfer restrictions, prohibiting customers from renting, leasing, or transferring the software without Autodesk's prior consent and from electronically or physically transferring the software out of the Western Hemisphere. Fourth, it imposes significant use restrictions:

> YOU MAY NOT: (1) modify, translate, reverse-engineer, decompile, or disassemble the Software . . . ; (3) remove any proprietary notices, labels, or marks from the Software or Documentation; (4) use . . . the Software outside of the Western Hemisphere; (5) utilize any computer software or hardware designed to defeat any hardware copy-protection device, should the software you have licensed be equipped with such protection; or (6) use the Software for commercial or other revenue-generating purposes if the Software has been licensed or labeled for educational use only.

Fifth, the SLA provides for license termination if the user copies the software without authorization or does not comply with the SLA's restrictions. Finally, the SLA provides that if the software is an upgrade of a previous version:

> [Y]ou must destroy the software previously licensed to you, including any copies resident on your hard disk drive . . . within sixty (60) days of the purchase of the license to use the upgrade or update. . . . Autodesk reserves the right to require you to show satisfactory proof that previous copies of the software have been destroyed.

Autodesk takes measures to enforce these license requirements. It assigns a serial number to each copy of AutoCAD and tracks registered licensees. It requires customers to input "activation codes" within one month after installation to continue using the software.[26] The customer obtains the code by providing the product's serial number to Autodesk. Autodesk issues the activation code after confirming that the serial number is authentic, the copy is not registered to a different customer, and the product has not been upgraded. Once a customer

---

26. Prior to using activation codes, Autodesk required users to return one disc of an earlier version of the software to upgrade to a later version. Autodesk has abandoned this return policy, deeming it slow and unworkable.

has an activation code, he or she may use it to activate the software on additional computers without notifying Autodesk.

B. Autodesk's Provision of Release 14 Software to CTA

In March 1999, Autodesk reached a settlement agreement with its customer Cardwell/Thomas & Associates, Inc. ("CTA"), which Autodesk had accused of unauthorized use of its software. As part of the settlement, Autodesk licensed ten copies of Release 14 to CTA. CTA agreed to the SLA, which appeared (1) on each Release 14 package that Autodesk provided to CTA; (2) in the settlement agreement; and (3) on-screen, while the software is being installed.

CTA later upgraded to the newer, fifteenth version of the AutoCAD program, AutoCAD 2000. It paid $495 per upgrade license, compared to $3,750 for each new license. The SLA for AutoCAD 2000, like the SLA for Release 14, required destruction of copies of previous versions of the software, with proof to be furnished to Autodesk on request. However, rather than destroying its Release 14 copies, CTA sold them to Vernor at an office sale with the handwritten activation codes necessary to use the software.

C. Vernor's eBay Business and Sales of Release 14

Vernor has sold more than 10,000 items on eBay. In May 2005, he purchased an authentic used copy of Release 14 at a garage sale from an unspecified seller. He never agreed to the SLA's terms, opened a sealed software packet, or installed the Release 14 software. Though he was aware of the SLA's existence, he believed that he was not bound by its terms. He posted the software copy for sale on eBay. . . .

II.

In August 2007, Vernor brought a declaratory action against Autodesk to establish that his resales of used Release 14 software are protected by the first sale doctrine and do not infringe Autodesk's copyright. . . . In October 2009, the district court entered judgment for Vernor, and Autodesk timely appealed.

III.

Copyright is a federal law protection provided to the authors of "original works of authorship," including software programs. 17 U.S.C. §§101-103. The Copyright Act confers several exclusive rights on copyright owners, including the exclusive rights to reproduce their works and to distribute their works by sale or rental. *Id.* §106(1), (3). The exclusive distribution right is limited by the first sale doctrine, an affirmative defense to copyright infringement that allows owners of copies of copyrighted works to resell those copies. The exclusive reproduction right is limited within the software context by the essential step defense, another affirmative defense to copyright infringement that is discussed further infra. Both of these affirmative defenses are unavailable to those who are only licensed to use their copies of copyrighted works.

This case requires us to decide whether Autodesk sold Release 14 copies to its customers or licensed the copies to its customers. If CTA owned its copies of Release 14, then both its sales to Vernor and Vernor's subsequent sales were non-infringing under the first sale doctrine.[27] However, if Autodesk only licensed CTA to use copies of Release 14, then CTA's and Vernor's sales of those copies are not protected by the first sale doctrine and would therefore infringe Autodesk's exclusive distribution right.

A. The First Sale Doctrine

The Supreme Court articulated the first sale doctrine in 1908, holding that a copyright owner's exclusive distribution right is exhausted after the owner's first sale of a particular copy of the copyrighted work. *See* Bobbs-Merrill Co. v. Straus, 210 U.S. 339, 350-51, 28 S. Ct. 722, 52 L. Ed. 1086 (1908). In *Bobbs-Merrill,* the plaintiff-copyright owner sold its book with a printed notice announcing that any retailer who sold the book for less than one dollar was responsible for copyright infringement. *Id.* at 341, 28 S. Ct. 722. Plaintiff sought injunctive relief against defendants-booksellers who failed to comply with the price restriction. *Id.* at 341-42, 28 S. Ct. 722. The Supreme Court rejected the plaintiff's claim, holding that its exclusive distribution right applied only to first sales of copies of the work. *Id.* at 350-51, 28 S. Ct. 722. The distribution right did not permit plaintiff to dictate that subsequent sales of the work below a particular price were infringing. *Id.* The Court noted that its decision solely applied to the rights of a copyright owner that distributed its work without a license agreement. *Id.* at 350, 28 S. Ct. 722 ("There is no claim in this case of contract limitation, nor license agreement controlling the subsequent sales of the book.").

Congress codified the first sale doctrine the following year. *See* 17 U.S.C. §41 (1909). In its current form, it allows the "owner of a particular copy" of a copyrighted work to sell or dispose of his copy without the copyright owner's authorization. *Id.* §109(a) (enacted 1976). The first sale doctrine does not apply to a person who possesses a copy of the copyrighted work without owning it, such as a licensee. *See id.* §109(d); *cf.* Quality King Distribs., Inc. v. L'anza Research Int'l Inc., 523 U.S. 135, 146-47, 118 S. Ct. 1125, 140 L. Ed. 2d 254 (1998) ("[T]he first sale doctrine would not provide a defense to . . . any non-owner such as a bailee, a licensee, a consignee, or one whose possession of the copy was unlawful.").

B. Owners vs. Licensees

We turn to our precedents governing whether a transferee of a copy of a copyrighted work is an owner or licensee of that copy. We then apply those precedents to CTA's and Vernor's possession of Release 14 copies.

1. United States v. Wise, 550 F.2d 1180 (9th Cir. 1977)

In *Wise,* a criminal copyright infringement case, we considered whether copyright owners who transferred copies of their motion pictures pursuant to written distribution agreements

---

27. If Autodesk's transfer of Release 14 copies to CTA was a first sale, then CTA's resale of the software in violation of the SLA's terms would be a breach of contract, but would not result in copyright liability. *See* United States v. Wise, 550 F.2d 1180, 1187 (9th Cir. 1977) ("[T]he exclusive right to vend the transferred copy rests with the vendee, who is not restricted by statute from further transfers of that copy, even though in breach of an agreement restricting its sale.").

had executed first sales. *Id.* at 1187. The defendant was found guilty of copyright infringement based on his for-profit sales of motion picture prints. *See id.* at 1183. The copyright owners distributed their films to third parties pursuant to written agreements that restricted their use and transfer. *Id.* at 1183-84. On appeal, the defendant argued that the government failed to prove the absence of a first sale for each film. If the copyright owners' initial transfers of the films were first sales, then the defendant's resales were protected by the first sale doctrine and thus were not copyright infringement.

To determine whether a first sale occurred, we considered multiple factors pertaining to each film distribution agreement. Specifically, we considered whether the agreement (a) was labeled a license, (b) provided that the copyright owner retained title to the prints, (c) required the return or destruction of the prints, (d) forbade duplication of prints, or (e) required the transferee to maintain possession of the prints for the agreement's duration. *Id.* at 1190-92. Our use of these several considerations, none dispositive, may be seen in our treatment of each film print.

For example, we reversed the defendant's conviction with respect to Camelot. *Id.* at 1194. It was unclear whether the Camelot print sold by the defendant had been subject to a first sale. Copyright owner Warner Brothers distributed Camelot prints pursuant to multiple agreements, and the government did not prove the absence of a first sale with respect to each agreement. *Id.* at 1191-92, 1194. We noted that, in one agreement, Warner Brothers had retained title to the prints, required possessor National Broadcasting Company ("NBC") to return the prints if the parties could select a mutual agreeable price, and if not, required NBC's certification that the prints were destroyed. *Id.* at 1191. We held that these factors created a license rather than a first sale. *Id.*

We further noted, however, that Warner Brothers had also furnished another Camelot print to actress Vanessa Redgrave. *Id.* at 1192. The print was provided to Redgrave at cost, and her use of the print was subject to several restrictions. She had to retain possession of the print and was not allowed to sell, license, reproduce, or publicly exhibit the print. *Id.* She had no obligation to return the print to Warner Brothers. *Id.* We concluded, "While the provision for payment for the cost of the film, standing alone, does not establish a sale, when taken with the rest of the language of the agreement, it reveals a transaction strongly resembling a sale with restrictions on the use of the print." *Id.* There was no evidence of the print's whereabouts, and we held that "[i]n the absence of such proof," the government failed to prove the absence of a first sale with respect to this Redgrave print. *Id.* at 1191-92. Since it was unclear which copy the defendant had obtained and resold, his conviction for sale of Camelot had to be reversed. *Id.*

Thus, under *Wise*, where a transferee receives a particular copy of a copyrighted work pursuant to a written agreement, we consider all of the provisions of the agreement to determine whether the transferee became an owner of the copy or received a license. We may consider (1) whether the agreement was labeled a license and (2) whether the copyright owner retained title to the copy, required its return or destruction, forbade its duplication, or required the transferee to maintain possession of the copy for the agreement's duration. *Id.* at 1190-92. We did not find any one factor dispositive in *Wise*: we did not hold that the copyright owner's retention of title itself established the absence of a first sale or that a transferee's right to indefinite possession itself established a first sale.

2. The "MAI Trio" of Cases

Over fifteen years after *Wise*, we again considered the distinction between owners and licensees of copies of copyrighted works in three software copyright cases, the "*MAI* trio." *See* MAI Sys. Corp. v. Peak Computer, Inc., 991 F.2d 511 (9th Cir. 1993); Triad Sys. Corp. v. Se. Express Co., 64 F.3d 1330 (9th Cir. 1995); Wall Data, Inc. v. Los Angeles County Sheriff's Dep't, 447 F.3d 769 (9th Cir. 2006). In the *MAI* trio, we considered which software purchasers were owners of copies of copyrighted works for purposes of a second affirmative defense to infringement, the essential step defense.

The enforcement of copyright owners' exclusive right to reproduce their work under the Copyright Act, 17 U.S.C. §106(1), has posed special challenges in the software context. In order to use a software program, a user's computer will automatically copy the software into the computer's random access memory ("RAM"), which is a form of computer data storage. *See MAI*, 991 F.2d at 513. Congress enacted the essential step defense to codify that a software user who is the "owner of a copy" of a copyrighted software program does not infringe by making a copy of the computer program, if the new copy is "created as an essential step in the utilization of the computer program in conjunction with a machine and . . . is used in no other manner." 17 U.S.C. §117(a)(1).

The Copyright Act provides that an "owner of a copy" of copyrighted software may claim the essential step defense, and the "owner of a particular copy" of copyrighted software may claim the first sale doctrine. 17 U.S.C. §§109(a), 117(a)(1). The *MAI* trio construed the phrase "owner of a copy" for essential step defense purposes. Neither Vernor nor Autodesk contends that the first sale doctrine's inclusion of the word "particular" alters the phrase's meaning, and we "presume that words used more than once in the same statute have the same meaning throughout." Moldo v. Matsco, Inc. (In re Cybernetic Servs., Inc.), 252 F.3d 1039, 1051 (9th Cir. 2001). Accordingly, we consider the *MAI* trio's construction of "owner of a copy" controlling in our analysis of whether CTA and Vernor became "owner[s] of a particular copy" of Release 14 software.

In *MAI* and *Triad*, the defendants maintained computers that ran the plaintiffs' operating system software. *MAI*, 991 F.2d at 513; *Triad*, 64 F.3d at 1333. When the defendants ran the computers, the computers automatically loaded plaintiffs' software into RAM. *MAI*, 991 F.2d at 517-18; *Triad*, 64 F.3d at 1333, 1335-36. The plaintiffs in both cases sold their software pursuant to restrictive license agreements, and we held that their customers were licensees who were therefore not entitled to claim the essential step defense. We found that the defendants infringed plaintiffs' software copyrights by their unauthorized loading of copyrighted software into RAM. *MAI*, 991 F.2d at 517-18 & n. 5; *Triad*, 64 F.3d at 1333, 1335-36. In *Triad*, the plaintiff had earlier sold software outright to some customers. 64 F.3d at 1333 n. 2. We noted that these customers were owners who were entitled to the essential step defense, and the defendant did not infringe by making RAM copies in servicing their computers. *Id.*

In *Wall Data*, plaintiff sold 3,663 software licenses to the defendant. *Wall Data*, 447 F.3d at 773. The licenses (1) were non-exclusive; (2) permitted use of the software on a single computer; and (3) permitted transfer of the software once per month, if the software was removed from the original computer. *Id.* at 775 n. 5, 781. The defendant installed the software onto 6,007 computers via hard drive imaging, which saved it from installing the software manually on each computer. It made an unverified claim that only 3,663 users could simultaneously access the software. *Id.* at 776.

The plaintiff sued for copyright infringement, contending that the defendant violated the license by "over-installing" the software. *Id.* at 775. The defendant raised an essential step defense, contending that its hard drive imaging was a necessary step of installation. *Id.* at 776. On appeal, we held that the district court did not abuse its discretion in denying the defendant's request for a jury instruction on the essential step defense. *Id.* at 784. Citing *MAI*, we held that the essential step defense does not apply where the copyright owner grants the user a license and significantly restricts the user's ability to transfer the software. *Id.* at 784-85. Since the plaintiff's license imposed "significant restrictions" on the defendant's software rights, the defendant was a licensee and was not entitled to the essential step defense. *Id.* at 785.

In *Wall Data*, we acknowledged that *MAI* had been criticized in a Federal Circuit decision, but declined to revisit its holding, noting that the facts of *Wall Data* led to the conclusion that any error in the district court's failure to instruct was harmless. Even if the defendant owned its copies of the software, its installation of the software on a number of computers in excess of its license was not an essential step in the software's use. *Id.* at 786 n. 9 (citing NIMMER on Copyright §8.08[B][1][c] at 8-136; DSC Commc'ns Corp. v. Pulse Commc'ns, Inc., 170 F.3d 1354, 1360 (Fed. Cir. 1999) (criticizing *MAI*)).

We read *Wise* and the *MAI* trio to prescribe three considerations that we may use to determine whether a software user is a licensee, rather than an owner of a copy. First, we consider whether the copyright owner specifies that a user is granted a license. Second, we consider whether the copyright owner significantly restricts the user's ability to transfer the software. Finally, we consider whether the copyright owner imposes notable use restrictions.[28] Our holding reconciles the *MAI* trio and *Wise*, even though the *MAI* trio did not cite *Wise*. *See* Cisneros-Perez v. Gonzales, 451 F.3d 1053, 1058 (9th Cir. 2006) ("[W]e are required to reconcile prior precedents if we can do so.").

In response to *MAI*, Congress amended §117 to permit a computer owner to copy software for maintenance or repair purposes. *See* 17 U.S.C. §117(c); *see also* H.R. Rep. No. 105-551, pt. 1, at 27 (1998). However, Congress did not disturb *MAI*'s holding that licensees are not entitled to the essential step defense.

IV.

A. The District Court's Decision

[Omitted.]

B. Analysis

We hold today that a software user is a licensee rather than an owner of a copy where the copyright owner (1) specifies that the user is granted a license; (2) significantly restricts the user's ability to transfer the software; and (3) imposes notable use restrictions. Applying our holding to Autodesk's SLA, we conclude that CTA was a licensee rather than an owner of

---

28. Although use restrictions were not dispositive in the *MAI* trio, we considered them in each case. *See MAI*, 991 F.2d at 517 n. 3 (license limited user to making one working and one backup copy of the software, and forbade examination, disclosure, copying, modification, adaptation, and visual display of the software); *Triad*, 64 F.3d at 1333 (license prohibited software duplication and third-party use); *Wall Data*, 447 F.3d at 775 n. 5 (license permitted software use on single computer, prohibited multicomputer and multi-user arrangements, and permitted transfer to another computer no more than once every thirty days).

copies of Release 14 and thus was not entitled to invoke the first sale doctrine or the essential step defense.

Autodesk retained title to the software and imposed significant transfer restrictions: it stated that the license is nontransferable, the software could not be transferred or leased without Autodesk's written consent, and the software could not be transferred outside the Western Hemisphere. The SLA also imposed use restrictions against the use of the software outside the Western Hemisphere and against modifying, translating, or reverse-engineering the software, removing any proprietary marks from the software or documentation, or defeating any copy protection device. Furthermore, the SLA provided for termination of the license upon the licensee's unauthorized copying or failure to comply with other license restrictions. Thus, because Autodesk reserved title to Release 14 copies and imposed significant transfer and use restrictions, we conclude that its customers are licensees of their copies of Release 14 rather than owners.

CTA was a licensee rather than an "owner of a particular copy" of Release 14, and it was not entitled to resell its Release 14 copies to Vernor under the first sale doctrine. 17 U.S.C. §109(a). Therefore, Vernor did not receive title to the copies from CTA and accordingly could not pass ownership on to others. Both CTA's and Vernor's sales infringed Autodesk's exclusive right to distribute copies of its work. *Id.* §106(3).

Because Vernor was not an owner, his customers are also not owners of Release 14 copies. Therefore, when they install Release 14 on their computers, the copies of the software that they make during installation infringe Autodesk's exclusive reproduction right because they too are not entitled to the benefit of the essential step defense. 17 U.S.C. §§106(1), 117(a)(1).

Although unnecessary to our resolution of the case, we address the legislative history in order to address the arguments raised by the parties and amici. That legislative history supports our conclusion that licensees such as CTA are not entitled to claim the first sale doctrine. The House Report for §109 underscores Congress' view that the first sale doctrine is available only to a person who has acquired a copy via an "outright sale." H.R. Rep. No. 94-1476, at 79 (1976), *reprinted in* 1976 U.S.C.C.A.N. 5659, 5693. The report also asserts that the first sale doctrine does not "apply to someone who merely possesses a copy or phonorecord without having acquired ownership of it." *Id.*

Our conclusion that those who rightfully possess, but do not own, a copy of copyrighted software are not entitled to claim the essential step defense is also supported by the legislative history. Congress enacted §117 following a report from the National Commission on New Technological Uses of Copyrighted Works ("CONTU") proposing Copyright Act amendments. DSC Commc'ns Corp. v. Pulse Commc'ns, Inc., 170 F.3d 1354, 1360 (Fed. Cir. 1999) (citing Final Report of the National Commission on New Technological Uses of Copyrighted Works, U.S. Dept. of Commerce, PB-282141, at 30 (July 31, 1978)). CONTU's proposed version of §117 was identical to the version that Congress enacted with one exception. *Id.* CONTU's version provided, "[I]t is not an infringement for the rightful possessor of a copy of a computer program to make or authorize the making of another copy or adaptation of that program. . . ." *Id.* Without explanation, Congress substituted "owner" for "rightful possessor." *Id.* This modification suggests that more than rightful possession is required for §117 to apply — i.e., that Congress did not intend licensees subject to significant transfer and use restrictions to receive the benefit of the essential step defense.

C. Vernor's Four Counterarguments Are Not Persuasive

. . .

3. The Supreme Court's Holding in Bobbs-Merrill

Vernor contends that *Bobbs-Merrill* establishes his entitlement to a first sale defense. *See* Bobbs-Merrill Co. v. Straus, 210 U.S. 339, 28 S. Ct. 722, 52 L. Ed. 1086 (1908). However, *Bobbs-Merrill* stands only for the proposition that a copyright owner's exclusive distribution right does not allow it to control sales of copies of its work after the first sale. *Id.* at 350, 28 S. Ct. 722. Decided in 1908, *Bobbs-Merrill* did not and could not address the question of whether the right to use software is distinct from the ownership of copies of software. Moreover, the Supreme Court in *Bobbs-Merrill* made explicit that its decision did not address the use of restrictions to create a license. *Id.* ("There is no claim in this case of contract limitation, nor license agreement controlling the subsequent sales of the book.")

4. Economic Realities of the Transaction

Finally, Vernor contends that "economic realities" demonstrate that Autodesk makes "first sales" to its customers, because Autodesk allows its customers to possess their copies of the software indefinitely and does not require recurring license payments. We held *supra* that neither of these factors is dispositive. Vernor cites no first sale doctrine case in support of this proposition. Rather, he cites In re DAK Indus., 66 F.3d 1091, 1095 (9th Cir. 1995), a case in which we interpreted the Bankruptcy Code to decide whether a particular transaction should be considered a pre-petition sale. We commented that "[w]hen applying the bankruptcy code to this transaction, we must look through its form to the 'economic realities of the particular arrangement.'" *Id.* Nothing in *DAK* is contrary to our reconciliation of *Wise* and the *MAI* trio.

V.

Although our holding today is controlled by our precedent, we recognize the significant policy considerations raised by the parties and amici on both sides of this appeal.

Autodesk, the Software & Information Industry Association ("SIIA"), and the Motion Picture Association of America ("MPAA") have presented policy arguments that favor our result. For instance, Autodesk argues in favor of judicial enforcement of software license agreements that restrict transfers of copies of the work. Autodesk contends that this (1) allows for tiered pricing for different software markets, such as reduced pricing for students or educational institutions; (2) increases software companies' sales; (3) lowers prices for all consumers by spreading costs among a large number of purchasers; and (4) reduces the incidence of piracy by allowing copyright owners to bring infringement actions against unauthorized resellers. SIIA argues that a license can exist even where a customer (1) receives his copy of the work after making a single payment and (2) can indefinitely possess a software copy, because it is the software code and associated rights that are valuable rather than the inexpensive discs on which the code may be stored. Also, the MPAA argues that a customer's ability to possess a copyrighted work indefinitely should not compel a finding of a first sale, because there is often no practically feasible way for a consumer to return a copy to the copyright owner.

Vernor, eBay, and the American Library Association ("ALA") have presented policy arguments against our decision. Vernor contends that our decision (1) does not vindicate the law's aversion to restraints on alienation of personal property; (2) may force everyone purchasing copyrighted property to trace the chain of title to ensure that a first sale occurred; and (3) ignores the economic realities of the relevant transactions, in which the copyright owner permanently released software copies into the stream of commerce without expectation of return in exchange for upfront payment of the full software price. eBay contends that a broad view of the first sale doctrine is necessary to facilitate the creation of secondary markets for copyrighted works, which contributes to the public good by (1) giving consumers additional opportunities to purchase and sell copyrighted works, often at below-retail prices; (2) allowing consumers to obtain copies of works after a copyright owner has ceased distribution; and (3) allowing the proliferation of businesses.

The ALA contends that the first sale doctrine facilitates the availability of copyrighted works after their commercial lifespan, by inter alia enabling the existence of libraries, used bookstores, and hand-to-hand exchanges of copyrighted materials. The ALA further contends that judicial enforcement of software license agreements, which are often contracts of adhesion, could eliminate the software resale market, require used computer sellers to delete legitimate software prior to sale, and increase prices for consumers by reducing price competition for software vendors. It contends that Autodesk's position (1) undermines 17 U.S.C. §109(b)(2), which permits non-profit libraries to lend software for non-commercial purposes, and (2) would hamper efforts by non-profits to collect and preserve out-of-print software. The ALA fears that the software industry's licensing practices could be adopted by other copyright owners, including book publishers, record labels, and movie studios.

These are serious contentions on both sides, but they do not alter our conclusion that our precedent from *Wise* through the *MAI* trio requires the result we reach. Congress is free, of course, to modify the first sale doctrine and the essential step defense if it deems these or other policy considerations to require a different approach. . . .

VACATED AND REMANDED.

EVEREX SYSTEMS, INC. v. CADTRAK CORPORATION

89 F.3d 673 (9th Cir. 1996)

PREGERSON, Circuit Judge.

In a 1986 agreement, as modified by a 1989 supplemental agreement, Cadtrak, in return for a one-time $290,000 payment, granted CFLC, a personal computer company, a royalty-free, worldwide, nonexclusive license to use certain computer graphics technology for which Cadtrak holds a patent (the "Cadtrak license"). The license agreement specified, among other things, that the license was non-transferrable, that it extended to any company more than 50% of which was owned by CFLC, that it conferred on CFLC no right to sublicense, that it could be terminated by Cadtrak upon CFLC's bankruptcy, and that it was to be construed according to California law.

On January 4, 1993, CFLC began a Chapter 11 proceeding, in the course of which it sold certain divisions, foreign subsidiaries, and assets for nearly $20 million. It then sought and received approval to sell "substantially all" of its remaining assets to Everex. The sale closed on November 12, 1993; Everex paid approximately $4 million.

The sale agreement provided that the parties would seek the assumption and assignment by CFLC to Everex of certain designated executory contracts. Bankruptcy Judge Randall J. Newsome denied the motion as to the Cadtrak license.

The statutes governing patents are basically silent on the issue of licenses. The construction of a patent license is generally a matter of state contract law, Lear, Inc. v. Adkins, 395 U.S. 653, 661-62 (1969) ("[T]he California Supreme Court's construction of the 1955 licensing agreement is solely a matter of state law."), except where state law "would be inconsistent with the aims of federal patent policy," *id.* at 673. See also McCoy v. Mitsuboshi Cutlery, Inc., 67 F.3d 917, 920 (Fed. Cir. 1995) ("Whether express or implied, a license is a contract 'governed by ordinary principles of state contract law.'"); Power Lift, Inc. v. Weatherford Nipple-Up Systems, Inc., 871 F.2d 1082, 1085-86 (Fed. Cir. 1989) (holding that "license agreement is a contract governed by ordinary principles of state contract law" and examining whether state relief from forfeiture provision was preempted). Two circuits have found such an inconsistency and expressly held that "[q]uestions with respect to the assignability of a patent license are controlled by federal law." PPG Industries, Inc. v. Guardian Industries Corp., 597 F.2d 1090, 1093 (6th Cir.), cert. denied, 444 U.S. 930 (1979); Unarco Industries, Inc. v. Kelley Co., 465 F.2d 1303, 1306 (7th Cir. 1972), cert. denied, 410 U.S. 929 (1973) ("[T]he question of assignability of a patent license is a specific policy of federal patent law dealing with federal patent law. Therefore, we hold federal law applies to the question of the assignability of the patent license in question."). See also In re Alltech Plastics, Inc., 71 B.R. 686, 689 (W.D. Tenn. 1987) ("The right[] of the patent owner to license the use of his invention is a creature of federal common law as is the right of the licensee to have the license construed. . . . [I]t follows that questions regarding the assignability of patent licenses are controlled by federal law.").

Federal patent policy . . . does justify the application of federal law here. The fundamental policy of the patent system is to "encourag[e] the creation and disclosure of new, useful, and non-obvious advances in technology and design" by granting the inventor the reward of "the exclusive right to practice the invention for a period of years." Bonito Boats, Inc. v. Thunder Craft Boats, Inc., 489 U.S. 141 (1989). Allowing free assignability — or, more accurately, allowing states to allow free assignability — of nonexclusive patent licenses would undermine the reward that encourages invention because a party seeking to use the patented invention could either seek a license from the patent holder or seek an assignment of an existing patent license from a licensee. In essence, every licensee would become a potential competitor with the licensor-patent holder in the market for licenses under the patents. And while the patent holder could presumably control the absolute number of licenses in existence under a free-assignability regime, it would lose the very important ability to control the identity of its licensees. Thus, any license a patent holder granted — even to the smallest firm in the product market most remote from its own — would be fraught with the danger that the licensee would assign it to the patent holder's most serious competitor, a party whom the patent holder itself might be absolutely unwilling to license. As a practical matter, free assignability of patent licenses might spell the end to paid-up licenses such as the one involved in this case. Few patent holders would be willing to grant a license in return for a one-time lump-sum payment, rather than for per-use royalties, if the license could be assigned to a completely different company which might make far greater use of the patented invention than could the original licensee.

Thus, federal law governs the assignability of patent licenses because of the conflict between federal patent policy and state laws, such as California's, that would allow assignability.

Federal law holds a nonexclusive patent license to be personal and nonassignable and therefore would excuse Cadtrak from accepting performance from, or rendering it to, anyone other than CFLC. "It is well settled that a non-exclusive licensee of a patent has only a personal and not a property interest in the patent and that this personal right cannot be assigned unless the patent owner authorizes the assignment or the license itself permits assignment." Gilson v. Republic of Ireland, 787 F.2d 655, 658 (D.C. Cir. 1986) (Friedman, J.). See also Stenograph Corp. v. Fulkerson, 972 F.2d 726, 729 n.2 (7th Cir. 1992) ("Patent licenses are not assignable in the absence of express language."); PPG Industries, 597 F.2d at 1093 ("It has long been held by federal courts that agreements granting patent licenses are personal and not assignable unless expressly made so."); Unarco, 465 F.2d at 1306 ("The long standing federal rule of law with respect to the assignability of patent license agreement provides that these agreements are personal to the licensee and not assignable unless expressly made so in the agreement."); E.I. du Pont de Nemours & Co. v. Shell Oil Co., 498 A.2d 1108, 1114 (Del. 1985) (rights conveyed by nonexclusive patent license are personal to licensee and not susceptible to sublicensing unless specific permission given). The only decision cited to the contrary is Justice Traynor's opinion in Dopplmaier. While that opinion raises not insignificant questions about the actual holdings, relevance, and continued vitality of the nineteenth-century Supreme Court decisions which are cited for the origins of the federal rule, Troy Iron & Nail Factory v. Corning, 55 U.S. (14 How.) 193 (1852), those questions are not so significant as to compel departure from the uniform rule of modern federal decisions reading those precedents as defining nonexclusive patent licenses as personal and non-assignable.

Because federal law governs the assignability of nonexclusive patent licenses, and because federal law makes such licenses personal and assignable only with the consent of the licensor, the Cadtrak license is not assumable and assignable in bankruptcy under 11 U.S.C. §365(c). The decision of the district court is therefore AFFIRMED.

S.O.S., INC. v. PAYDAY, INC.
886 F.2d 1081 (9th Cir. 1989)

FLETCHER, Circuit Judge.

This appeal from grants of summary judgment turns on the interpretation of a computer software agreement and presents issues of copyright law as well as pendent state law claims arising under trade secret, contract, and tort law. We affirm in part, reverse in part, and remand.

S.O.S., Inc. specializes in furnishing computer hardware and software to companies that process payrolls, ledgers, and accounts receivable. Payday, Inc. is a company which provides payroll and financial services to the entertainment industry.

The district court granted Payday's motion for summary judgment on S.O.S.'s claim of copyright infringement. The district court concluded that because Payday had a license to use the payroll programs, it could not infringe S.O.S.'s copyright. It also held that California law required that the contract be construed against S.O.S., placing the burden on S.O.S. explicitly to restrict Payday from making modifications. Absent such a restriction in the contract, the district court held, Payday acquired the unrestricted right to adopt and utilize the program.

The district court erred in assuming that a license to use a copyrighted work necessarily precludes infringement. A licensee infringes the owner's copyright if its use exceeds the scope of its license. Gilliam v. American Broadcasting Cos., 538 F.2d 14, 20 (2d Cir. 1976). The critical question is not the existence but the scope of the license.

The license must be construed in accordance with the purposes underlying federal copyright law. Cohen v. Paramount Pictures Corp., 845 F.2d 851, 854 (9th Cir. 1988); *Harris*, 734 F.2d at 1334. Chief among these purposes is the protection of the author's rights. *Cohen*, 845 F.2d at 854. We rely on state law to provide the canons of contractual construction, but only to the extent such rules do not interfere with federal copyright law or policy. See Fantastic Fakes, Inc. v. Pickwick Int'l, Inc., 661 F.2d 479, 482-83 (5th Cir. 1981) (state law rules of contract construction not preempted by federal law; however, application of state law to supply implied terms in copyright license would raise preemption question).

The district court applied the California rule that the contract should be interpreted against the drafter, see Heston v. Farmers Ins. Group, 160 Cal. App. 3d 402, 415 (1984), thereby deeming S.O.S. to have granted to Payday any right which it did not expressly retain. This result is contrary to federal copyright policy: copyright licenses are assumed to prohibit any use not authorized. Cf. *Cohen*, 845 F.2d at 853 (license analyzed to determine what uses it affirmatively permits); 17 U.S.C. §204(a) (transfer of copyright ownership must be in writing).

The contract between S.O.S. and Payday states, "This series of programs is the property of SOS, and PAYDAY is acquiring the right of use, SOS retains all rights of ownership." This language is unambiguous. Payday acquired the right to use the software, but S.O.S. retained all ownership rights. In the context of the parties' entire agreement, it is clear that the "right of use" was not intended to refer to copyright use. The contract does not refer explicitly to copyright or to any of the copyright owner's exclusive rights.

S.O.S. concedes that Payday had a right to use the software on its own machines, but insists S.O.S. retained title to any copies. We agree. The literal language of the parties' contract provides that S.O.S. retains "all rights of ownership." This language plainly encompasses not only copyright ownership, but also ownership of any copies of the software. Payday has not demonstrated that it acquired any more than the right to possess a copy of the software for the purpose of producing "product" for its customers. We conclude that Payday exceeded the scope of its license when it copied and prepared a modified version of the programs without S.O.S.'s permission. Whether these acts, unshielded by any license, infringed S.O.S.'s copyright will be a matter for the district court to determine on remand.

MDY INDUSTRIES LLC v. BLIZZARD ENTERTAINMENT, INC.
629 F.3d 928 (9th Cir. 2011)

IKUDA, Circuit Judge.

Blizzard Entertainment, Inc. ("Blizzard") is the creator of World of Warcraft ("WoW"), a popular multiplayer online role-playing game in which players interact in a virtual world while advancing through the game's 70 levels. MDY Industries, LLC and its sole member Michael Donnelly ("Donnelly") (sometimes referred to collectively as "MDY") developed and sold Glider, a software program that automatically plays the early levels of WoW for players. MDY brought this action for a declaratory judgment to establish that its Glider sales do not infringe Blizzard's copyright or other rights, and Blizzard asserted counterclaims under the Digital Millennium Copyright Act ("DMCA"), 17 U.S.C. §1201 et seq., and for tortious interference with contract under Arizona law. The district court found MDY and Donnelly liable for secondary copyright infringement, violations of DMCA §§1201(a)(2) and (b)(1), and tortious interference with contract. We reverse the district court except as to MDY's liability for violation of DMCA §1201(a)(2) and remand for trial on Blizzard's claim for tortious interference with contract.

I.

A. World of Warcraft

In November 2004, Blizzard created WoW, a "massively multiplayer online role-playing game" in which players interact in a virtual world. WoW has ten million subscribers, of which two and a half million are in North America. The WoW software has two components: (1) the game client software that a player installs on the computer; and (2) the game server software, which the player accesses on a subscription basis by connecting to WoW's online servers. WoW does not have single-player or offline modes. WoW players role play different characters, such as humans, elves, and dwarves. A player's central objective is to advance the character through the game's 70 levels by participating in quests and engaging in battles with monsters. As a player advances, the character collects rewards such as in-game currency, weapons, and armor. WoW's virtual world has its own economy, in which characters use their virtual currency to buy and sell items directly from each other, through vendors, or using auction houses. Some players also utilize WoW's chat capabilities to interact with others.

B. Blizzard's Use Agreements

Each WoW player must read and accept Blizzard's End User License Agreement ("EULA") and Terms of Use ("ToU") on multiple occasions. The EULA pertains to the game client, so a player agrees to it both before installing the game client and upon first running it. The ToU pertains to the online service, so a player agrees to it both when creating an account and upon first connecting to the online service. Players who do not accept both the EULA and the ToU may return the game client for a refund.

C. Development of Glider and Warden

Donnelly is a WoW player and software programmer. In March 2005, he developed Glider, a software "bot" (short for robot) that automates play of WoW's early levels, for his personal use. A user need not be at the computer while Glider is running. As explained in the Frequently Asked Questions ("FAQ") on MDY's website for Glider: "Glider moves the mouse around and pushes keys on the keyboard. You tell it about your character, where you want to kill things, and when you want to kill. Then it kills for you, automatically. You can do something else, like eat dinner or go to a movie, and when you return, you'll have a lot more experience and loot." Glider does not alter or copy WoW's game client software, does not allow a player to avoid paying monthly subscription dues to Blizzard, and has no commercial use independent of WoW. Glider was not initially designed to avoid detection by Blizzard. The parties dispute Glider's impact on the WoW experience. Blizzard contends that Glider disrupts WoW's environment for non-Glider players by enabling Glider users to advance quickly and unfairly through the game and to amass additional game assets. MDY contends that Glider has a minimal effect on non-Glider players, enhances the WoW experience for Glider users, and facilitates disabled players' access to WoW by auto-playing the game for them. In summer 2005, Donnelly began selling Glider through MDY's website for fifteen to twenty-five dollars per license. Prior to marketing Glider, Donnelly reviewed Blizzard's EULA and client-server manipulation policy. He reached the conclusion that Blizzard had not prohibited bots in those documents. In September 2005, Blizzard launched Warden, a technology that it developed to prevent its players who use unauthorized third-party software, including bots, from connecting to WoW's servers. Warden was able to detect Glider, and Blizzard immediately used Warden to ban most Glider users. MDY responded by modifying Glider to avoid detection and promoting its new anti-detection features on its website's FAQ. It added a subscription service, Glider Elite, which offered "additional protection from game detection software" for five dollars a month. Thus, by late 2005, MDY was aware that Blizzard was prohibiting bots. MDY modified its website to indicate that using Glider violated Blizzard's ToU. In November 2005, Donnelly wrote in an email interview, "Avoiding detection is rather exciting, to be sure. Since Blizzard does not want bots running at all, it's a violation to use them." Following MDY's anti-detection modifications, Warden only occasionally detected Glider. As of September 2008, MDY had gross revenues of $3.5 million based on 120,000 Glider license sales.

D. Financial and Practical Impact of Glider

Blizzard claims that from December 2004 to March 2008, it received 465,000 complaints about WoW bots, several thousand of which named Glider. Blizzard spends $940,000 annually to respond to these complaints, and the parties have stipulated that Glider is the principal bot used by WoW players. Blizzard introduced evidence that it may have lost monthly subscription fees from Glider users, who were able to reach WoW's highest levels in fewer weeks than players playing manually. Donnelly acknowledged in a November 2005 email that MDY's business strategy was to make Blizzard's anti-bot detection attempts financially prohibitive: "The trick here is that Blizzard has a finite amount of development and test resources, so we want to make it bad business to spend that much time altering their detection code to find Glider, since Glider's negative effect on the game is debatable." . . . [W]e attack th[is] weakness and try to make it a bad idea or make their changes very risky, since they don't want to risk banning or crashing innocent customers. . . .

III.

. . .

To establish secondary infringement, Blizzard must first demonstrate direct infringement. See A & M Records, Inc. v. Napster, Inc., 239 F.3d 1004, 1019, 1022 (9th Cir. 2001). To establish direct infringement, Blizzard must demonstrate copyright ownership and violation of one of its exclusive rights by Glider users. *Id.* at 1013. MDY is liable for contributory infringement if it has "intentionally induc[ed] or encourag[ed] direct infringement" by Glider users. MGM Studios Inc. v. Grokster, Ltd., 545 U.S. 913, 930 (2005). MDY is liable for vicarious infringement if it (1) has the right and ability to control Glider users' putatively infringing activity and (2) derives a direct financial benefit from their activity. *Id.* If Glider users directly infringe, MDY does not dispute that it satisfies the other elements of contributory and vicarious infringement. As a copyright owner, Blizzard possesses the exclusive right to reproduce its work. 17 U.S.C. §106(1). The parties agree that when playing WoW, a player's computer creates a copy of the game's software in the computer's random access memory ("RAM"), a form of temporary memory used by computers to run software programs. This copy potentially infringes unless the player (1) is a licensee whose use of the software is within the scope of the license or (2) owns the copy of the software. See Sun Microsystems, Inc. v. Microsoft Corp., 188 F.3d 1115, 1121 (9th Cir. 1999) ("Sun I"); 17 U.S.C. §117(a). As to the scope of the license, ToU §4(B), "Limitations on Your Use of the Service," provides: "You agree that you will not . . . (ii) create or use cheats, bots, 'mods,' and/or hacks, or any other third-party software designed to modify the World of Warcraft experience; or (iii) use any third-party software that intercepts, 'mines,' or otherwise collects information from or through the Program or Service." By contrast, if the player owns the copy of the software, the "essential step" defense provides that the player does not infringe by making a copy of the computer program where the copy is created and used solely "as an essential step in the utilization of the computer program in conjunction with a machine." 17 U.S.C. §117(a)(1).

A. Essential Step Defense

We consider whether WoW players, including Glider users, are owners or licensees of their copies of WoW software. If WoW players own their copies, as MDY contends, then Glider users do not infringe by reproducing WoW software in RAM while playing, and MDY is not secondarily liable for copyright infringement. In Vernor v. Autodesk, Inc., we recently distinguished between "owners" and "licensees" of copies for purposes of the essential step defense. Vernor v. Autodesk, Inc., 621 F.3d 1102, 1108-09 (9th Cir. 2010); see also MAI Sys. Corp. v. Peak Computer, Inc., 991 F.2d 511, 519 n. 5 (9th Cir. 1993); Triad Sys. Corp. v. Se. Express Co., 64 F.3d 1330, 1333, 1335-36 (9th Cir. 1995); Wall Data, Inc. v. Los Angeles County Sheriff's Dep't, 447 F.3d 769, 784-85 (9th Cir. 2006). In *Vernor*, we held "that a software user is a licensee rather than an owner of a copy where the copyright owner (1) specifies that the user is granted a license; (2) significantly restricts the user's ability to transfer the software; and (3) imposes notable use" restrictions. 621 F.3d at 1111 (internal footnote omitted).

Applying *Vernor*, we hold that WoW players are licensees of WoW's game client software. Blizzard reserves title in the software and grants players a non-exclusive, limited license.

Blizzard also imposes transfer restrictions if a player seeks to transfer the license: the player must (1) transfer all original packaging and documentation; (2) permanently delete all of the copies and installation of the game client; and (3) transfer only to a recipient who accepts the EULA. A player may not sell or give away the account. Blizzard also imposes a variety of use restrictions. The game must be used only for non-commercial entertainment purposes and may not be used in cyber cafes and computer gaming centers without Blizzard's permission. Players may not concurrently use unauthorized third-party programs. Also, Blizzard may alter the game client itself remotely without a player's knowledge or permission, and may terminate the EULA and ToU if players violate their terms. Termination ends a player's license to access and play WoW. Following termination, players must immediately destroy their copies of the game and uninstall the game client from their computers, but need not return the software to Blizzard. Since WoW players, including Glider users, do not own their copies of the software, Glider users may not claim the essential step defense. 17 U.S.C. §117(a)(1). Thus, when their computers copy WoW software into RAM, the players may infringe unless their usage is within the scope of Blizzard's limited license.

B. Contractual Covenants vs. License Conditions

"A copyright owner who grants a nonexclusive, limited license ordinarily waives the right to sue licensees for copyright infringement, and it may sue only for breach of contract." *Sun I*, 188 F.3d at 1121 (internal quotations omitted). However, if the licensee acts outside the scope of the license, the licensor may sue for copyright infringement. *Id.* (citing S.O.S., Inc. v. Payday, Inc., 886 F.2d 1081, 1087 (9th Cir. 1989)). Enforcing a copyright license "raises issues that lie at the intersection of copyright and contract law." *Id.* at 1122. We refer to contractual terms that limit a license's scope as "conditions," the breach of which constitute copyright infringement. *Id.* at 1120. We refer to all other license terms as "covenants," the breach of which is actionable only under contract law. *Id.* We distinguish between conditions and covenants according to state contract law, to the extent consistent with federal copyright law and policy. Foad Consulting Group v. Musil Govan Azzalino, 270 F.3d 821, 827 (9th Cir. 2001). A Glider user commits copyright infringement by playing WoW while violating a ToU term that is a license condition. To establish copyright infringement, then, Blizzard must demonstrate that the violated term — ToU §4(B) — is a condition rather than a covenant. *Sun I*, 188 F.3d at 1122. Blizzard's EULAs and ToUs provide that they are to be interpreted according to Delaware law. Accordingly, we first construe them under Delaware law, and then evaluate whether that construction is consistent with federal copyright law and policy. A covenant is a contractual promise, i.e., a manifestation of intention to act or refrain from acting in a particular way, such that the promisee is justified in understanding that the promisor has made a commitment. See Travel Centers of Am. LLC v. Brog, No. 3751-CC, 2008 Del. Ch. LEXIS 183, *9 (Del. Ch. Dec. 5, 2008); see also Restatement (Second) of Contracts §2 (1981). A condition precedent is an act or event that must occur before a duty to perform a promise arises. AES P.R., L.P. v. Alstom Power, Inc., 429 F. Supp. 2d 713, 717 (D. Del. 2006) (citing Delaware state law); see also Restatement (Second) of Contracts §224. Conditions precedent are disfavored because they tend to work forfeitures. *AES*, 429 F. Supp. 2d at 717 (internal citations omitted). Wherever possible, equity construes ambiguous contract provisions as covenants rather than conditions. See Wilmington Tr. Co. v. Clark, 325 A.2d 383, 386 (Del. Ch. 1974). However, if the contract is unambiguous, the court construes it according to its terms. AES, 429 F. Supp. 2d at 717 (citing 17 Am. Jur. 2d Contracts §460 (2006)). Applying these principles, ToU §4(B)(ii) and (iii)'s prohibitions against bots and unauthorized third-party software are covenants rather than copyright-enforceable conditions. See Greenwood v. CompuCredit Corp., 615 F.3d 1204, 1212 (9th Cir. 2010) ("[H]eadings and titles are not meant to take the place of the detailed provisions of the text," and . . . "the heading of a section cannot limit the plain meaning of the text." (quoting Bhd. of R.R. Trainmen v. Balt. & Ohio R.R., 331 U.S. 519, 528-29 (1947))). Although ToU §4 is titled, "Limitations on Your Use of the Service," nothing in that section conditions Blizzard's grant of a limited license on players' compliance with ToU §4's restrictions. To the extent that the title introduces any ambiguity, under Delaware law, ToU §4(B) is not a condition, but is a contractual covenant. Cf. Sun Microsystems, Inc. v. Microsoft Corp., 81 F. Supp. 2d 1026, 1031-32 (N.D. Cal. 2000) ("Sun II") (where Sun licensed Microsoft to create only derivative works compatible with other Sun software, Microsoft's "compatibility obligations" were covenants because the license was not specifically conditioned on their fulfillment).

To recover for copyright infringement based on breach of a license agreement, (1) the copying must exceed the scope of the defendant's license and (2) the copyright owner's complaint must be grounded in an exclusive right of copyright (e.g., unlawful reproduction or distribution). See Storage Tech. Corp. v. Custom Hardware Eng'g & Consulting, Inc., 421 F.3d 1307, 1315-16 (Fed. Cir. 2005). Contractual rights, however, can be much broader: [C]onsider a license in which the copyright owner grants a person the right to make one and only one copy of a book with the caveat that the licensee may not read the last ten pages. Obviously, a licensee who made a hundred copies of the book would be liable for copyright infringement because the copying would violate the Copyright Act's prohibition on reproduction and would exceed the scope of the license. Alternatively, if the licensee made a single copy of the book, but read the last ten pages, the only cause of action would be for breach of contract, because reading a book does not violate any right protected by copyright law. Id. at 1316.

Consistent with this approach, we have held that the potential for infringement exists only where the licensee's action (1) exceeds the license's scope (2) in a manner that implicates one of the licensor's exclusive statutory rights. See, e.g., Sun I, 118 F.3d at 1121-22 (remanding for infringement determination where defendant allegedly violated a license term regulating the creation of derivative works). Here, ToU §4 contains certain restrictions that are grounded in Blizzard's exclusive rights of copyright and other restrictions that are not. For instance, ToU §4(D) forbids creation of derivative works based on WoW without Blizzard's consent. A player who violates this prohibition would exceed the scope of her license and violate one of Blizzard's exclusive rights under the Copyright Act. In contrast, ToU §4(C)(ii) prohibits a player's disruption of another player's game experience. Id. A player might violate this prohibition while playing the game by harassing another player with unsolicited instant messages. Although this conduct may violate the contractual covenants with Blizzard, it would not violate any of Blizzard's exclusive rights of copyright. The anti-bot provisions at issue in this case, ToU §4(B)(ii) and (iii), are similarly covenants rather than conditions. A Glider user violates the covenants with Blizzard, but does not thereby commit copyright infringement because Glider does not infringe any of Blizzard's exclusive rights. For instance, the use does not alter or copy WoW software. Were we to hold otherwise, Blizzard — or any software copyright holder — could designate any disfavored conduct during software use as copyright infringement, by purporting to condition the license on the player's abstention from the disfavored conduct. The rationale would be that because the conduct occurs while the player's computer is copying the software code into RAM in order for it to run, the violation is copyright infringement. This would allow software copyright owners far greater rights than Congress has generally conferred on copyright owners.[29]

We conclude that for a licensee's violation of a contract to constitute copyright infringement, there must be a nexus between the condition and the licensor's exclusive rights of copyright.[30] Here, WoW players do not commit copyright infringement by using Glider in violation of the ToU. MDY is thus not liable for secondary copyright infringement, which requires the existence of direct copyright infringement. We thus reverse the district court's grant of summary judgment to Blizzard on its secondary copyright infringement claims. Accordingly, we must also vacate the portion of the district court's permanent injunction that barred MDY and Donnelly from "infringing, or contributing to the infringement of, Blizzard's copyrights in WoW software."

BLIZZARD ENTERTAINMENT, INC. v. JUNG
422 F.3d 630 (8th Cir. 2005)

SMITH, Circuit Judge.

FACTUAL BACKGROUND

Blizzard, a California corporation and subsidiary of Vivendi, creates and sells software games for personal computers.

In January 1997, Blizzard officially launched "Battle.net," a 24-hour online-gaming service available exclusively to purchasers of its computer games. The Battle.net service has nearly 12 million active users who spend more than 2.1 million hours online per day. Blizzard holds valid copyright registrations covering Battle.net and each of its computer games at issue in this litigation. Battle.net is a free service that allows owners of Blizzard games to play each other on their personal computers via the Internet. Battle.net mode allows users to create and join

---

29. A copyright holder may wish to enforce violations of license agreements as copyright infringements for several reasons. First, breach of contract damages are generally limited to the value of the actual loss caused by the breach. See 24 Richard A. Lord, Williston on Contracts §65:1 (4th ed. 2007). In contrast, copyright damages include the copyright owner's actual damages and the infringer's actual profits, or statutory damages of up to $150,000 per work. 17 U.S.C. §504; see Frank Music Corp. v. MGM, Inc., 772 F.2d 505, 512 n. 5 (9th Cir. 1985). Second, copyright law offers injunctive relief, seizure of infringing articles, and awards of costs and attorneys' fees. 17 U.S.C. §§502-03, 505. Third, as amicus Software & Information Industry Association highlights, copyright law allows copyright owners a remedy against "downstream" infringers with whom they are not in privity of contract. See *ProCD, Inc.*, 86 F.3d at 1454.

30. A licensee arguably may commit copyright infringement by continuing to use the licensed work while failing to make required payments, even though a failure to make payments otherwise lacks a nexus to the licensor's exclusive statutory rights. We view payment as sui generis, however, because of the distinct nexus between payment and all commercial copyright licenses, not just those concerning software.

multi-player games that can be accessed across the Internet, to chat with other potential players, to record wins and losses and save advancements in an individual password-protected game account, and to participate with others in tournament play featuring elimination rounds. Players can set up private "chat channels" and private games on Battle.net to allow players to determine with whom they wish to interact online. These Battle.net mode features are only accessible from within the games.

Like most computer software, Blizzard's games can be easily copied and distributed over the Internet. Blizzard has taken steps to avoid piracy by designing Battle.net to restrict access and use of the Battle.net mode feature of the game. Each time a user logs onto Battle.net, a Battle.net server examines the user's version of the game software. If a Blizzard game does not have the latest software upgrades and fixes, the Battle.net service updates the customer's game before allowing the game to play in Battle.net mode.

With the exception of "Diablo," each authorized version of a Blizzard game comes with a "CD Key." A CD Key is a unique sequence of alphanumeric characters printed on a sticker attached to the case in which the CD-ROM was packaged. To log on to Battle.net and access Battle.net mode, the game initiates an authentication sequence or "secret handshake" between the game and the Battle.net server. In order to play the Blizzard game contained on a CD-ROM, a user must first install the game onto a computer and agree to the terms of the End User License Agreement ("EULA") and Terms of Use ("TOU"), both of which prohibit reverse engineering. At the end of both the EULA and TOU, Blizzard includes a button with the text, "I Agree" in it, which the user must select in order to proceed with the installation. Users are also required to enter a name and the CD Key during installation of Battle.net and Blizzard games.

The outside packaging of all Blizzard games, except for Diablo, contains a statement that use of the game is subject to the EULA and that use of Battle.net is subject to the terms of the TOU. The terms of neither the EULA nor the TOU appear on the outside packaging. If the user does not agree to these terms, the game may be returned for a full refund of the purchase price within thirty (30) days of the original purchase. Combs, Crittenden, and Jung installed Blizzard games and agreed to the terms of the EULA. Crittenden and Jung logged onto Battle.net and agreed to the TOU.

The users of Battle.net have occasionally experienced difficulties with the service. To address their frustrations with Battle.net, a group of non-profit volunteer game hobbyists, programmers, and other individuals formed a group called the "bnetd project." The bnetd project developed a program called the "bnetd.org server" that emulates the Battle.net service and permits users to play online without use of Battle.net. The bnetd project is a volunteer effort and the project has always offered the bnetd program for free to anyone. Combs, Crittenden, and Jung were lead developers for the bnetd project.

The bnetd project was organized and managed over the Internet through a website, www.bnetd.org, that was made available to the public through equipment provided by Internet Gateway. The bnetd.org emulator provides a server that allows gamers unable or unwilling to connect to Battle.net to experience the multi-player features of Blizzard's games. The bnetd.org emulator also provides matchmaking services for users of Blizzard games who want to play those games in a multi-player environment without using Battle.net. Bnetd.org attempted to mirror all of the user-visible features of Battle.net, including online discussion forums and information about the bnetd project, as well as access to the program's computer code for others to copy and modify.

To serve as a functional alternative to Battle.net, bnetd.org had to be compatible with Blizzard's software. In particular, compatibility required that bnetd.org speak the same protocol language that the Battle.net speaks. By speaking the same protocol language, the bnetd programs would be interoperable with Blizzard games. Once game play starts, a user perceives no difference between Battle.net and the bnetd.org.

By necessity, Appellants used reverse engineering to learn Blizzard's protocol language and to ensure that bnetd.org worked with Blizzard games. Combs used reverse engineering to develop the bnetd.org server, including a program called "tcpdump" to log communications between Blizzard games and the Battle.net server. Crittenden used reverse engineering to develop the bnetd.org server, including using a program called "Nextray." Crittenden also used a program called "ripper" to take Blizzard client files that were compiled together in one file and break them into their component parts. Crittenden used the ripper program to determine how Blizzard games displayed ad banners so that bnetd.org could display ad banners to users in the format that Blizzard uses on the Battle.net service. Combs tried to disassemble a Blizzard game to figure out how to implement a feature that allowed bnetd.org to protect the password that a user enters when creating an account in Battle.net mode. Crittenden made an unauthorized copy of a Blizzard game in order to test the interoperability of the bnetd.org server with multiple games.

PREEMPTION

The Copyright Act provides the exclusive source of protection for "all legal and equitable rights that are equivalent to any of the exclusive rights within the general scope of copyright as specified by . . . [§]106" of the Copyright Act. See 17 U.S.C. §301(a). The Copyright Act preempts state laws that attempt to protect rights exclusively protected by federal law. See Nat'l Car Rental Sys., Inc. v. Computer Assocs. Intern., Inc., 991 F.2d 426, 428 (8th Cir. 1993). Conversely, the Copyright Act does not preempt state law from enforcing non-equivalent legal or equitable rights. Id. A state cause of action is statutorily or expressly preempted if: (1) the work at issue is within the subject matter of copyright as defined in §§102 and 103 of the Copyright Act, and (2) the state-law-created right is equivalent to any of the exclusive rights within the general scope of copyright as specified in §106. Id. at 428-29 (citing Harper & Row Pub., Inc. v. Nation Enter., 723 F.2d 195, 200 (2d Cir. 1983)). Express preemption is no longer at issue in this case.

This case concerns conflict preemption. Conflict preemption applies when there is no express preemption but (1) it is impossible to comply with both the state and federal law or when (2) the state law stands as an obstacle to the accomplishment and execution of the full purposes and objectives of Congress. Pacific Gas & Elec. Co. v. Energy Res. Conservation and Dev. Comm'n, 461 U.S. 190, 204 (1983); Jones v. Rath Packing Co., 430 U.S. 519, 525 (1977). Appellants, relying upon Vault v. Quaid Software Ltd., 847 F.2d 255, 268-70 (5th Cir. 1988), argue that the federal Copyright Act preempts Blizzard's state law breach-of-contract claims. We disagree.

In Vault, plaintiffs challenged the Louisiana Software License Enforcement Act, which permitted a software producer to impose contractual terms upon software purchasers provided that the terms were set forth in a license agreement comporting with the statute. *Id.* at 268. "Enforceable terms [under the Louisiana statute] include the prohibition of: (1) any copying of the program for any purpose; and (2) modifying and/or adapting the program in any way, including adaptation by reverse engineering, decompilation or disassembly." *Id.* at 269 (citation omitted). The Louisiana statute defined reverse engineering, decompiling or disassembling as "any process by which computer software is converted from one form to another form which is more readily understandable to human beings, including without limitation any decoding or decrypting of any computer program which has been encoded or encrypted in any manner." *Id.* (citation omitted). The Fifth Circuit held that the Louisiana statute conflicted with the rights of computer program owners under the Copyright Act, specifically 17 U.S.C. §117, which permits a computer program owner to make an adaptation of a program provided that the adaption is either created as an essential step in the utilization of the computer program in conjunction with a machine or is for archival purpose only. *Id.* at 270.

Unlike in *Vault*, the state law at issue here neither conflicts with the interoperability exception under 17 U.S.C. §1201(f) nor restricts rights given under federal law. Appellants contractually accepted restrictions on their ability to reverse engineer by their agreement to the terms of the TOU and EULA. "[P]rivate parties are free to contractually forego the limited ability to reverse engineer a software product under the exemptions of the Copyright Act[,]" Bowers v. Baystate Techs, Inc., 320 F.3d 1317, 1325-26 (Fed. Cir. 2003), and "a state can permit parties to contract away a fair use defense or to agree not to engage in uses of copyrighted material that are permitted by the copyright law if the contract is freely negotiated." *Id.* at 1337 (Dyk, J., dissenting). See also *Nat'l Car Rental Sys., Inc.*, 991 F.2d at 434 (holding that the Copyright Act does not preempt a breach of contract action based on prohibited use of software contained in a license agreement). While *Bowers* and *Nat'l Car Rental* were express preemption cases rather than conflict preemption, their reasoning applies here with equal force. By signing the TOUs and EULAs, Appellants expressly relinquished their rights to reverse engineer.

Summary judgment on this issue was properly granted in favor of Blizzard and Vivendi.

BROADCAST MUSIC, INC. v. COLUMBIA BROADCASTING SYSTEM, INC.
441 U.S. 1 (1979)

Justice **WHITE** delivered the opinion of the court:

This case involves an action under the antitrust and copyright laws brought by respondent Columbia Broadcasting System, Inc. (CBS), against petitioners, American Society of Composers, Authors and Publishers (ASCAP) and Broadcast Music, Inc. (BMI), and their members and affiliates. The basic question presented is whether the issuance by ASCAP and BMI to CBS of blanket licenses to copyrighted musical compositions at fees negotiated by them is price fixing per se unlawful under the antitrust laws.

CBS operates one of three national commercial television networks, supplying programs to approximately 200 affiliated stations and telecasting approximately 7,500 network programs per year. Many, but not all, of these programs make use of copyrighted music recorded on the soundtrack. CBS also owns television and radio stations in various cities. It is " 'the giant of the world in the use of music rights,' " the " 'No. 1 outlet in the history of entertainment.' "

Since 1897, the copyright laws have vested in the owner of a copyrighted musical composition the exclusive right to perform the work publicly for profit, but the legal right is not self-enforcing. In 1914, Victor Herbert and a handful of other composers organized ASCAP because those who performed copyrighted music for profit were so numerous and wide-spread, and most performances so fleeting, that as a practical matter it was impossible for the many individual copyright owners to negotiate with and license the users and to detect unauthorized uses. "ASCAP was organized as a 'clearing-house' for copyright owners and users to solve these problems" associated with the licensing of music. 400 F. Supp. 737, 741 (S.D.N.Y. 1975). As ASCAP operates today, its 22,000 members grant it nonexclusive rights to license nondramatic performances of their works, and ASCAP issues licenses and distributes royalties to copyright owners in accordance with a schedule reflecting the nature and amount of the use of their music and other factors.

BMI, a nonprofit corporation owned by members of the broadcasting industry, was organized in 1939, is affiliated with or represents some 10,000 publishing companies and 20,000 authors and composers, and operates in much the same manner as ASCAP. Almost every domestic copyrighted composition is in the repertory either of ASCAP, with a total of three million compositions, or of BMI, with one million.

Both organizations operate primarily through blanket licenses, which give the licensees the right to perform any and all of the compositions owned by the members or affiliates as often as the licensees desire for a stated term. Fees for blanket licenses are ordinarily a percentage of total revenues or a flat dollar amount, and do not directly depend on the amount or type of music used. Radio and television broadcasters are the largest users of music, and almost all of them hold blanket licenses from both ASCAP and BMI. Until this litigation, CBS held blanket licenses from both organizations for its television network on a continuous basis since the late 1940's and had never attempted to secure any other form of license from either ASCAP or any of its members. Id., at 752-754.

Though agreeing with the District Court's fact finding and not disturbing its legal conclusions on the other antitrust theories of liability, the Court of Appeals held that the blanket license issued to television networks was a form of price fixing illegal per se under the Sherman Act. 562 F.2d 130, 140 (CA2 1977). This conclusion, without more, settled the issue of liability under the Sherman Act, established copyright misuse, and required reversal of the District Court's judgment, as well as a remand to consider the appropriate remedy.

In construing and applying the Sherman Act's ban against contracts, conspiracies, and combinations in restraint of trade, the Court has held that certain agreements or practices are so "plainly anticompetitive," National Society of Professional Engineers v. United States, 435 U.S. 679, 692 (1978); Continental T.V., Inc. v. GTE Sylvania, Inc., 433 U.S. 36, 50 (1977), and so often "lack . . . any redeeming virtue," Northern Pac. R. Co. v. United States, 356 U.S. 1, 5 (1958), that they are conclusively presumed illegal without further examination under the rule of reason generally applied in Sherman Act cases. This per se rule is a valid and useful tool of antitrust policy and enforcement. And agreements among competitors to fix prices on their individual goods or services are among those concerted activities that the Court has held to be within the per se category. But easy labels do not always supply ready answers.

The blanket license, as we see it, is not a "naked restrain[t] of trade with no purpose except stifling of competition," White Motor Co. v. United States, 372 U.S. 253, 263 (1963), but rather accompanies the integration of sales, monitoring, and enforcement against unauthorized copyright use. See L. Sullivan, Handbook of the Law of Antitrust §59, p. 154 (1977). As we have already indicated, ASCAP and the blanket license developed together out of the practical situation in the marketplace: thousands of users, thousands of copyright owners, and millions of compositions. Most users want unplanned, rapid, and indemnified access to any and all of the repertory of compositions, and the owners want a reliable method of collecting for the use of their copyrights. Individual sales transactions in this industry are quite expensive, as would be individual monitoring and enforcement, especially in light of the resources of single composers. Indeed, as both the Court of Appeals and CBS recognize, the costs are prohibitive for licenses with individual radio stations, nightclubs, and restaurants, 562 F.2d, at 140, n. 26, and it was in that milieu that the blanket license arose.

A middleman with a blanket license was an obvious necessity if the thousands of individual negotiations, a virtual impossibility, were to be avoided. Also, individual fees for the use of individual compositions would presuppose an intricate schedule of fees and uses, as well as a difficult and expensive reporting problem for the user and policing task for the copyright owner. Historically, the market for public-performance rights organized itself largely around the single-fee blanket license, which gave unlimited access to the repertory and reliable protection against infringement. When ASCAP's major and user-created competitor, BMI, came on the scene, it also turned to the blanket license.

With the advent of radio and television networks, market conditions changed, and the necessity for and advantages of a blanket license for those users may be far less obvious than is the case when the potential users are individual television or radio stations, or the thousands of other individuals and organizations performing copyrighted compositions in public. But even for television network licenses, ASCAP reduces costs absolutely by creating a blanket license that is sold only a few, instead of thousands, of times, and that obviates the need for closely monitoring the networks to see that they do not use more than they pay for. ASCAP also provides the necessary resources for blanket sales and enforcement, resources unavailable to the vast majority of composers and publishing houses. Moreover, a bulk license of some type is a necessary consequence of the integration necessary to achieve these efficiencies, and a necessary consequence of an aggregate license is that its price must be established.

This substantial lowering of costs, which is of course potentially beneficial to both sellers and buyers, differentiates the blanket license from individual use licenses. The blanket license is composed of the individual compositions plus the aggregating service. Here, the whole is truly greater than the sum of its parts; it is, to some extent, a different product. The blanket license has certain unique characteristics: It allows the licensee immediate use of covered compositions, without the delay of prior individual negotiations and great flexibility in the choice of musical material. Many consumers clearly prefer the characteristics and cost advantages of this marketable package, and even small-performing rights societies that have occasionally arisen to compete with ASCAP and BMI have offered blanket licenses. Thus, to the extent the blanket license is a different product, ASCAP is not really a joint sales agency offering the individual goods of many sellers, but is a separate seller offering its blanket license, of which the individual compositions are raw material. ASCAP, in short, made a market in which individual composers are inherently unable to compete fully effectively.

With this background in mind, which plainly enough indicates that over the years, and in the face of available alternatives, the blanket license has provided an acceptable mechanism for at least a large part of the market for the performing rights to copyrighted musical compositions, we cannot agree that it should automatically be declared illegal in all of its many manifestations. Rather, when attacked, it should be subjected to a more discriminating examination under the rule of reason. It may not ultimately survive that attack, but that is not the issue before us today.

We reverse [the Court of Appeals'] judgment . . . and remand for further proceedings to consider any unresolved issues that CBS may have properly brought to the Court of Appeals. Of course, this will include an assessment under the rule of reason of the blanket license as employed in the television industry, if that issue was preserved by CBS in the Court of Appeals.

Justice **STEVENS**, dissenting.

The Court holds that ASCAP's blanket license is not a species of price fixing categorically forbidden by the Sherman Act. I agree with that holding. The Court remands the cases to the Court of Appeals, leaving open the question whether the blanket license as employed by ASCAP and BMI is unlawful under a rule-of-reason inquiry. I think that question is properly before us now and should be answered affirmatively.

Antitrust policy requires that great aggregations of economic power be closely scrutinized. That duty is especially important when the aggregation is composed of statutory monopoly privileges. Our cases have repeatedly stressed the need to limit the privileges conferred by patent and copyright strictly to the scope of the statutory grant. The record in this case plainly discloses that the limits have been exceeded and that ASCAP and BMI exercise monopoly powers that far exceed the sum of the privileges of the individual copyright holders. Indeed, ASCAP itself argues that its blanket license constitutes a product that is significantly different from the sum of its component parts. I agree with that premise, but I conclude that the aggregate is a monopolistic restraint of trade proscribed by the Sherman Act.

VIDEO PIPELINE, INC. v. BUENA VISTA HOME ENTERTAINMENT, INC.

342 F.3d 191 (3d Cir. 2003)

AMBRO, Circuit Judge.

In this copyright case we review the District Court's entry of a preliminary injunction against Video Pipeline, Inc.'s online display of "clip previews." A "clip preview," as we use the term, is an approximately two-minute segment of a movie, copied without authorization from the film's copyright holder, and used in the same way as an authorized movie "trailer." We reserve the term "trailer" for previews created by the copyright holder of a particular movie (or under the copyright holder's authority).

BACKGROUND

Video Pipeline compiles movie trailers onto videotape for home video retailers to display in their stores. To obtain the right to distribute the trailers used in the compilations, Video Pipeline enters into agreements with various entertainment companies. It entered into such an agreement, the Master Clip License Agreement ("License Agreement"), with Disney in 1988, and Disney thereafter provided Video Pipeline with over 500 trailers for its movies.

In 1997, Video Pipeline took its business to the web, where it operates VideoPipeline.net and VideoDetective.com. The company maintains a database accessible from VideoPipeline .net, which contains movie trailers Video Pipeline has received throughout the years. Video Pipeline's internet clients — retail web sites selling home videos — use VideoPipeline.net to display trailers to site visitors. The site visitors access trailers by clicking on a button labeled "preview" for a particular motion picture. The requested trailer is then "streamed" for the visitor to view (because it is streamed the trailer cannot be downloaded to or stored on the visitor's computer). The operators of the web sites from which the trailers are accessed — Video Pipeline's internet clients — pay a fee to have the trailers streamed based on the number of megabytes shown to site visitors. Video Pipeline has agreements to stream trailers with approximately 25 online retailers, including Yahoo!, Amazon, and Best Buy.

As noted, Video Pipeline also operates VideoDetective.com. On this web site, visitors can search for movies by title, actor, scene, genre, etc. When a search is entered, the site returns a list of movies and information about them and allows the user to stream trailers from VideoPipeline.net. In addition to displaying trailers, VideoDetective.com includes a "Shop Now" button to link the user to a web site selling the requested video. Visitors to VideoDetective.com can also win prizes by playing "Can You Name that Movie?" after viewing a trailer on the site.

Video Pipeline stores the clip previews in its database and displays them on the internet in the same way it had displayed the Disney trailers. In content, however, the clip previews differ from the trailers. Each clip preview opens with a display of the Miramax or Disney trademark and the title of the movie, then shows one or two scenes from the first half of the movie, and closes with the title again. Disney's trailers, in contrast, are designed to entice sales from a target market by using techniques such as voice-over, narration, editing, and additional music. Video Pipeline's clip previews use none of these marketing techniques.

Fair Use

Congress's constitutional power to provide for copyright protection "is intended to motivate the creative activity of authors . . . by the provision of a special reward, and to allow the public access to the products of their genius after the limited period of exclusive control has expired." Sony Corp. of Am. v. Universal City Studios, Inc., 464 U.S. 417, 429 (1984). At times, however, "rigid application of the copyright statute . . . would stifle the very creativity which that law is designed to foster." Campbell v. Acuff-Rose Music, Inc., 510 U.S. 569, 577 (1994). When that is the case, the fair use doctrine may be implicated.

Congress codified the judicially created "fair use" defense at §107 of the 1976 Copyright Act, which permits a "fair use of a copyrighted work." 17 U.S.C. §107. A fair use, although not specifically defined by the statute, is one made "for purposes such as criticism, comment, news reporting, teaching . . . , scholarship, or research." *Id.* It is an affirmative defense for which the alleged infringer bears the burden of proof.

In judging the fairness of a particular use, courts must take into account the following non-exhaustive list of factors:

1. the purpose and character of the use, including whether such use is of a commercial nature or is for nonprofit educational purposes;
2. the nature of the copyrighted work;
3. the amount and substantiality of the portion used in relation to the copyrighted work as a whole; and
4. the effect of the use upon the potential market for or value of the copyrighted work.

Id. The four statutory factors "do not represent a score card that promises victory to the winner of the majority." Pierre N. Leval, *Toward a Fair Use Standard*, 103 HARV. L. REV. 1105, 1110 (1990). Rather, each factor is "to be explored, and the results weighed together, in light of the purposes of copyright." *Campbell*, 510 U.S. at 578 (citations omitted). Thus, as we apply copyright law, and the fair use doctrine in particular, we bear in mind its purpose to encourage "creative activity" for the public good. Sony Corp., 464 U.S. at 429.

1. Purpose and Character of the Use

Once again, the first factor requires that we consider "the purpose and character of the use, including whether such use is of a commercial nature or is for nonprofit educational purposes." §107(1).

If a new work is used commercially rather than for a nonprofit purpose, its use will less likely qualify as fair. *Campbell*, 510 U.S. at 585. As Video Pipeline charges a fee to stream the clip previews, its use of the copies is commercial (as the District Court found).

The commercial nature of the use does not by itself, however, determine whether the purpose and character of the use weigh for or against finding fair use. *Id.* at 583-84. We look as well to any differences in character and purpose between the new use and the original. We consider whether the copy is "transformative" of the work it copied because it "alter[ed] the first with new expression, meaning, or message," or instead "whether the new work merely supersedes the objects of the original creation." *Id.* at 579 (citations and alteration in original omitted).

Given the shared character and purpose of the clip previews and the trailers (so that the clips will likely serve as a substitute for the trailers) and the absence of creative ingenuity in the creation of the clips, the first factor strongly weighs against fair use in this case.

2. Nature of the Copyrighted Work

The second statutory fair use factor directs courts to consider "the nature of the copyrighted work." §107(2). "This factor calls for recognition that some works are closer to the core of intended copyright protection than others, with the consequence that fair use is more difficult to establish when the former works are copied." *Campbell*, 510 U.S. at 586. Fictional, creative works come closer to this core than do primarily factual works. Harper & Row Publishers, Inc. v. Nation Enters., 471 U.S. 539, 563 (1985). The Disney movies at issue — including, for example, *Beauty and the Beast, Fantasia, Pretty Woman*, and *Dead Poet's Society* — are paradigms of creative, non-factual expression. And Disney's trailers share imaginative aspects with the originals.

Disney's movies and trailers contain mainly creative expression, not factual material, [which] suggests that the use is not fair regardless of the published or unpublished status of the original. See e.g., *Campbell*, 510 U.S. at 586 (holding that the song *Pretty Woman* fit "within the core of the copyright's protective purposes" because of its creative expression, without considering that the original had already been made available to the public).

3. Amount and Substantiality of the Work Copied

The third factor requires an analysis of "the amount and substantiality of the portion used in relation to the copyrighted work as a whole." §107(3).

As Video Pipeline points out, its previews excerpt only about two minutes from movies that last one and a half to two hours. Quantitatively then, the portion taken is quite small. [A]s advertisements, the clip previews are meant to whet the customer's appetite, not to sate it; accordingly, they are not designed to reveal the "heart" of the movies. Simply put, we have no reason to believe that the two-minute clips manage in so brief a time, or even intend, to appropriate the "heart" of the movies. Compare *Harper & Row*, 471 U.S. at 564-55, 105 S. Ct. 2218 (weighing this factor against finding fair use because the alleged infringer "took what was essentially the heart of the book").

Because the clip previews copy a relatively small amount of the original full-length films and do not go to the "heart" of the movies, this factor . . . weighs in favor of finding fair Video Pipeline's display of its clips.

4. Effect on Potential Market or Value

Finally, courts should evaluate "the effect of the use upon the potential market for or value of the copyrighted work." §107(4).

As mentioned above, this final factor "must take [into] account not only . . . harm to the original but also . . . harm to the market for derivative works." *Campbell*, 510 U.S. at 590, 114 S. Ct. 1164.

In light of Video Pipeline's commercial use of the clip previews and Disney's use of its trailers as described by the record evidence, we easily conclude that there is a sufficient market for, or other value in, movie previews such that the use of an infringing work could have a harmful effect cognizable under the fourth factor.

We have already determined that the clip previews lack transformative quality and that, though the clips are copies taken directly from the original full-length films rather than from the trailers, display of the clip previews would substitute for the derivative works. As a result, the clips, if Video Pipeline continues to stream them over the internet, will "serve[ ] as a market replacement" for the trailers, "making it likely that cognizable market harm to the [derivatives] will occur." *Campbell*, 510 U.S. at 591. For instance, web sites wishing to show previews of Disney movies may choose to enter licensing agreements with Video Pipeline rather than Disney, as at least 25 have already done. And internet users searching for previews of Disney films may be drawn by the clip previews to web sites other than Disney's, depriving Disney of the opportunity to advertise and sell other products to those users.

Consequently, "'unrestricted and widespread conduct of the sort engaged in by [Video Pipeline] . . . would result in a substantially adverse impact on the potential market' for the [derivative works]." *Id.* at 590 (quoting 3 M. Nimmer & D. Nimmer, Nimmer on Copyright §13.05(A)(4) (1993)). We therefore hold that the District Court should have weighed this factor against recognizing the fair use defense in this case.

Three of the four statutory factors indicate that Video Pipeline's internet display of the clip previews will not qualify as a fair use. From our consideration of each of those factors, we cannot conclude that Video Pipeline's online display of its clip previews does anything but "infringe[ ] a work for personal profit." *Harper & Row*, 471 U.S. at 563. The District Court therefore correctly held that Video Pipeline has failed to show that it will likely prevail on its fair use defense.

Copyright Misuse

Video Pipeline further contends that Disney has misused its copyright and, as a result, should not receive the protection of copyright law. Video Pipeline points to certain licensing agreements that Disney has entered into with three companies and sought to enter into with a number of other companies operating web sites. Each of these licensing agreements provides that Disney, the licensor, will deliver trailers by way of hyperlinks for display on the licensee's web site. The Agreements further state:

> The Website in which the Trailers are used may not be derogatory to or critical of the entertainment industry or of [Disney] (and its officers, directors, agents, employees, affiliates, divisions and subsidiaries) or of any motion picture produced or distributed by [Disney] . . . [or] of the materials from which the Trailers were taken or of any person involved with the production of the Underlying Works. Any breach of this paragraph will render this license null and void and Licensee will be liable to all parties concerned for defamation and copyright infringement, as well as breach of contract. . . .

As Video Pipeline sees it, such licensing agreements seek to use copyright law to suppress criticism and, in so doing, misuse those laws, triggering the copyright misuse doctrine. The misuse doctrine extends from the equitable principle that courts "may appropriately withhold their aid where the plaintiff is using the right asserted contrary to the public interest." *Morton Salt*, 314 U.S. at 492. Misuse is not cause to invalidate the copyright or patent, but instead "precludes its enforcement during the period of misuse." Practice Management Info. Corp. v. American Med. Assoc., 121 F.3d 516, 520 n.9 (9th Cir. 1997) (citing Lasercomb America,

Inc. v. Reynolds, 911 F.2d 970, 979 n.22 (4th Cir. 1990)). To defend on misuse grounds, the alleged infringer need not be subject to the purported misuse. *Morton Salt*, 314 U.S. at 494, 62 S. Ct. 402 ("It is the adverse effect upon the public interest of a successful infringement suit in conjunction with the patentee's course of conduct which disqualifies him to maintain the suit, regardless of whether the particular defendant has suffered from the misuse of the patent."); *Lasercomb*, 911 F.2d at 979 ("[T]he fact that appellants here were not parties to one of Lasercomb's standard license agreements is inapposite to their copyright misuse defense. The question is whether Lasercomb is using its copyright in a manner contrary to public policy, which question we have answered in the affirmative.").

The "ultimate aim" of copyright law is "to stimulate artistic creativity for the general public good." *Sony Corp.*, 464 U.S. at 432; see also Eldred v. Ashcroft, 537 U.S. 186 (2003) ("[C]opyright's purpose is to promote the creation and publication of free expression."). Put simply, our Constitution emphasizes the purpose and value of copyrights and patents. Harm caused by their misuse undermines their usefulness.

Anti-competitive licensing agreements may conflict with the purpose behind a copyright's protection by depriving the public of the would-be competitor's creativity. The fair use doctrine and the refusal to copyright facts and ideas also address applications of copyright protection that would otherwise conflict with a copyright's constitutional goal. See *Eldred*, 123 S. Ct. at 789; *Campbell,* 510 U.S. at 575 & n.5. But it is possible that a copyright holder could leverage its copyright to restrain the creative expression of another without engaging in anti-competitive behavior or implicating the fair use and idea/expression doctrines.

The licensing agreements in this case do seek to restrict expression by licensing the Disney trailers for use on the internet only so long as the web sites on which the trailers will appear do not derogate Disney, the entertainment industry, etc. But we nonetheless cannot conclude on this record that the agreements are likely to interfere with creative expression to such a degree that they affect in any significant way the policy interest in increasing the public store of creative activity. The licensing agreements do not, for instance, interfere with the licensee's opportunity to express such criticism on other web sites or elsewhere. There is no evidence that the public will find it any more difficult to obtain criticism of Disney and its interests, or even that the public is considerably less likely to come across this criticism, if it is not displayed on the same site as the trailers. Moreover, if a critic wishes to comment on Disney's works, the fair use doctrine may be implicated regardless of the existence of the licensing agreements. Finally, copyright law, and the misuse doctrine in particular, should not be interpreted to require Disney, if it licenses its trailers for display on any web sites but its own, to do so willy-nilly regardless of the content displayed with its copyrighted works. Indeed such an application of the misuse doctrine would likely decrease the public's access to Disney's works because it might as a result refuse to license at all online display of its works.

Thus, while we extend the patent misuse doctrine to copyright, and recognize that it might operate beyond its traditional anti-competition context, we hold it inapplicable here. On this record Disney's licensing agreements do not interfere significantly with copyright policy (while holding to the contrary might, in fact, do so). The District Court therefore correctly held that Video Pipeline will not likely succeed on its copyright misuse defense.

III. PROBLEMS

1. Kate Gero created a software product called "EasyRiter" that makes it simple for kids to write stories, create cards and fliers, and put together slide shows. Gero wants to incorporate into EasyRiter some artwork created by her friend Gannon Hill.

   1.1 Advise Gero on the advantages and disadvantages of various transaction model(s) for acquiring the artwork from Hill. Which transaction model(s) would work best?

   1.2 How would you counsel Hill if you were advising him in the best model(s) for the transaction?

   1.3 Advise Gero on the best transaction model(s) for providing EasyRiter to end user customers. How will the transaction between Gero and Hill affect your advice?

   1.4 If Gero wants to provide free copies of EasyRiter to public schools and children's hospitals but charge for all other copies, what advice would you give Gero on the appropriate transaction model(s)?

2. Alexis Hernandez grows apples in Wenatchee, Washington. Through meticulous experimentation, Hernandez has developed and patented a variety of apple with a yellow skin that is crisper, firmer, sweeter, and more flavorful than the Golden Delicious apple. Hernandez calls this apple the GoldieGirl. Hernandez is willing to provide seeds for the GoldieGirl to Washington orchardists but to no one else.

   2.1 Advise Hernandez on the best transaction model(s) for commercializing her seeds.

   2.2 If Hernandez wants to allow Washington State University (which has a tree fruit research center in Wenatchee) to continue to improve the GoldieGirl variety, what transaction(s) would enable that?

   2.3 Assume Hernandez wants to get out of apple growing and into grape growing. What transaction models would allow her to provide her patent and trademark rights to WSU?

3. Rashmi Khaki has developed formulas for several perfumes for dogs. The perfumes are designed to combat unpleasant doggy odor. Khaki recently filed for a patent on several unique chemical compositions that allow the perfume to permeate a dog's oily coat. She has recorded the recipes in a journal, along with a description of and names for the scents and some doggerel, all to be used for marketing purposes. Khaki would like to license the recipe and accompanying names and poems to the leading French perfume manufacturer, Tres Tres Chic ("Chic").

   3.1 How would you advise Khaki if she wanted to include a lengthy non-compete provision in the license? What about a provision for royalty payments for 100 years?

   3.2 How would you analyze a request by Chic to sublicense any patent obtained by Khaki to a coalition of French perfume makers who operate a patent pool for perfume compositions?

    3.3 How would you advise Khaki on a request by Chic only to license the compositions and not the names and poems (assuming Khaki only wants to license the package)?

    3.4 Assume Khaki and Chic enter the license but Chic decides the doggerel are too goofy for its French customers so it creates more elegant poems based on the doggerel. Does Chic have the right to do this? Anticipating this issue, what could Khaki do in the license?

4. If you were a judge on the court of appeals receiving the case on remand from the U.S. Supreme Court in the *Broadcast Music* case, how would you rule on BMI's blanket license scheme under a "rule of reason" analysis?

5. Do you agree with the court's ruling in the *Video Pipeline* case that the use of the clips was not a fair use? Do you agree that the challenged provisions in Disney's license did not constitute a copyright misuse? Given the nature of copyrights when contrasted to patents, do you agree that just because a doctrine of patent misuse exists that a doctrine of copyright misuse makes sense? If the license provisions were not a copyright misuse, are there other grounds to challenge this provision?

6. Do you agree with the court in Blizzard Entertainment v. Jung that parties should be able to contract away their right to raise the fair use defense? Should it depend on the circumstances? Must a court always abide by a contractual provision purporting to eliminate fair use? Compare the treatment of fair use in Blizzard Entertainment v. Jung to the treatment in *Video Pipeline*.

7. If a licensee exceeds the scope of the license grant, can the licensor sue for breach of contract and infringement of intellectual property rights, or must the licensor choose between the causes of action? What are the pros and cons of each type of action? How do you distinguish between the breach of a pure contractual covenant and a condition on a license grant? For a discussion of the latter issue, including the role that license drafting can play in the distinction, *see* Robert W. Gomulkiewicz, *Conditions and Covenants in License Contracts: Tales from a Test of the Artistic License*, 17 TEX. INTELL. PROP. L.J. 335 (2009), and Robert W. Gomulkiewicz, *Enforcing Open Source Software Licenses: The MDY Trio's Inconvenient Complications*, 14 YALE J.L. & TECH. 106 (2011).

8. The court in the *Everex Systems* case ruled that federal patent policy bears strongly on the assignability of a patent license. Would federal patent policy bear just as strongly on all provisions of the license? Should federal copyright policy or trademark policy bear just as strongly on the assignability of copyright or trademark licenses, respectively? What if evidence showed that application of federal intellectual property law was contrary to the normal expectations of the parties — should that matter?

9. Many observers have declared that UCITA will not and should not be enacted by additional states. *See, e.g.*, David A. Szwak, *Uniform Computer Information Trans- actions Act: The Consumer's Perspective*, 63 LA. L. REV. 27 (2002); *but see* Raymond T. Nimmer, *UCITA and the Continuing Evolution of Digital Licensing Law*, 21 COMPUTER & INTERNET LAW 10 (2004). Nonetheless, some commentators have renewed the call for a new uniform licensing law — either an improved version of

UCITA or something entirely new. *See* Nim Razook, *The Politics and Promise of UCITA,* 36 CREIGHTON L. REV. 642 (2003); Maureen O' Rourke, *An Essay on the Challenges of Drafting a Uniform Law of Software Contracting,* 10 LEWIS & CLARK L. REV. 925 (2006) (describing the ALI project on software contracts). What are the advantages and disadvantages of creating a uniform licensing law statute? How would you describe transactions to which this statute should apply? As a point of reference, *see* UCITA §103 in the Materials section of this chapter. What would you think about applying the common law of contracts to all licenses? If the common law applies, where will judges look for guidance in deciding licensing cases? What would you think about applying UCC 2 to all licenses?

10. How does the current diversity of sources of contract law for licenses affect the way you advise clients? For example, think of how you would advise a client who wanted to give certain warranties but did not want to give any others?

11. As mentioned in the Overview, some commentators view Copyright Law's "first sale" provision as a "right." Other commentators view it as one potential transaction model for distributing copyrighted works. What is your analysis? What are the advantages and disadvantages of each position?

2

COMMON LICENSE PROVISIONS

I. OVERVIEW OF COMMON LICENSE PROVISIONS AND A MYTHICAL LICENSE AGREEMENT

When parties to a transaction decide to license intellectual property or information, they need to create a license agreement that reflects their particular objectives. Through years of usage in a variety of transactions, licenses have evolved to address common issues, such as the scope of the license grant or how the parties will allocate risk. In other words, licenses share common provisions even though the provisions may be crafted in a different manner in any given license arrangement.

The best way to learn about these common license provisions is to look at examples. Accordingly, this chapter contains the provisions of a mythical license agreement between a university called "Pine University" and a mythical company known as "Conway Racket Ltd." Pine University has invented new tennis racket frame technology that it plans to patent. Conway Racket wants to make tennis rackets in Texas based on that technology and distribute the rackets to the European market under Pine University's "FlexPower" trademark. Below is the complete license agreement, followed by a discussion of each of its provisions:

LICENSE AGREEMENT

This license agreement (hereafter "Agreement") is entered into this 25th day of June, 2010 (hereafter "Effective Date"), by and between Pine University, a land grant university of the State of Washington, with its principal place of business at One Saturn Way, Spokane, Washington, U.S.A. (hereafter "University"), and Conway Racket Ltd., a Delaware corporation, with its principal place of business at 500 Surf Road, Honolulu, Hawaii, U.S.A. (hereafter "Racket").

1. Recitals

Whereas University has developed new tennis racket frame technology;

Whereas University has applied for patent protection in the United States of America for this technology;

Whereas Racket desires to manufacture tennis rackets based on this technology at its facilities in Texas;

Whereas Racket desires to distribute tennis rackets based on this technology in the European market;

Now, therefore, the parties agree as follows:

2. Definitions

For purposes of this Agreement, the following terms have the following meanings whenever capitalized:

2.1. "Technology" shall mean University's tennis racket frame technology as described in Attachment 1.

2.2. "Patent" shall mean any United States patent that issues from U.S. Patent Application number XXX, including continuations and divisionals.

2.3. "Manual" shall mean University's manual titled *Procedures for Manufacturing Tennis Racket Frames* as that manual exists on the Effective Date, and any revisions to it.

2.4. "Know How" shall mean all of University's confidential know how relevant to manufacturing the tennis rackets based on the Technology, including information contained in the Manual.

2.5. "Manufacturing Facility" shall mean Racket's tennis racket manufacturing facility located in Dallas, Texas, at 500 Star Street.

2.6. "European Market" shall mean the countries which are members of the European Union as of the Effective Date and any countries that are admitted during the term of this Agreement.

2.7. "FlexPower Logo" shall mean University's *FlexPower* logo which is used in conjunction with the Technology.

2.8. "Quality Standards" shall mean the quality standards as described in Attachment 2.

2.9. "Net Sales" shall mean gross sales minus returns.

2.10. "Maximum Payment" shall mean U.S. $5,000,000.00.

3. License Grant

3.1. University hereby grants to Racket an exclusive license under the Patent to:

    (a) make and use tennis rackets based on the Technology at the Manufacturing Facility;

    (b) sell, offer to sell, import, and distribute tennis rackets based on the Technology in and to the European Market for amateur tennis players.

3.2. University hereby grants to Racket a non-exclusive license to use the Know How for the sole purpose of making tennis rackets based on the Technology at the Manufacturing Facility;

3.3. University hereby grants to Racket a non-exclusive license under University's copyrights to use and reproduce the Manual for the sole purpose of making the tennis rackets based on the Technology at the Manufacturing Facility.

3.4. University hereby grants to Racket an exclusive license to use the FlexPower Logo in conjunction with the rights granted in 3.1 above;

3.5. All rights other than those licensed in paragraphs 3.1, 3.2, 3.3, and 3.4 above are reserved by University.

4. Delivery of Manual and Logo Artwork

4.1. University shall deliver the Manual in hard copy and electronic forms to Racket at the Manufacturing Facility no later than ten (10) days after the Effective Date.

4.2. University shall deliver camera-ready artwork of the FlexPower Logo to Racket's headquarters in Honolulu, Hawaii, no later than ten (10) days after the Effective Date.

5. Delivery, Inspection, and Acceptance/Rejection of Rackets

5.1. Racket shall deliver to University twenty (20) tennis rackets based on the Technology manufactured by Racket at the Manufacturing Facility, no later than one (1) year after the Effective Date.

5.2. University shall evaluate the tennis rackets to determine whether they meet the Quality Standards. The Quality Standards shall be the sole measure to determine whether the rackets meet an acceptable level of quality. University shall notify Racket in writing of its acceptance or rejection of the level of quality within thirty (30) days of receipt from Racket. In the event University fails to notify Racket in writing within the thirty (30) day time period, the quality shall be deemed acceptable. If University rejects the quality, its notice of rejection shall include a detailed description of the reasons for its rejection.

5.3. In the event University timely notifies Racket of its rejection of the level of quality, then Racket shall have six (6) months to improve the quality of its manufacturing process and resubmit the tennis rackets for evaluation by University. The evaluation and acceptance/rejection process shall be as described in paragraph 5.2 above. In the event University rejects the level of quality, University shall have the right either to grant an additional period of time for Racket to improve quality or terminate the Agreement.

6. Payment

6.1. Racket shall pay to University the following payments according to the following schedule. All payments shall be made in U.S. dollars via wire transfer to account 12345 at Wells Fargo Bank.

   (a) $500,000.00 on the Effective Date;
   (b) $500,000.00 five (5) days following receipt of University's notice of acceptance of the quality of the tennis rackets;
   (c) 1% of Net Sales of the first 100,000 tennis rackets sold;
   (d) 2% of Net Sales of the next 250,000 tennis rackets sold;
   (e) 3% of Net sales for any additional tennis rackets sold.

6.2. In no case shall payments exceed the Maximum Payment. Upon payment of the Maximum Payment, the license grants in the Agreement shall be fully paid up.

7. Accounting; Audits

7.1. Racket shall keep such books and records as are reasonably necessary to account for the payments due under the Agreement.

7.2. University shall have the right on an annual basis to audit the records of Racket at Racket's headquarters in Honolulu, Hawaii, to ensure that Racket's payments to University are full and accurate. Such audit shall be conducted by certified public accountants on at least one week's prior written notice during Racket's normal business hours. Racket shall cooperate fully with University's auditors during the audit.

7.3. The audit described in paragraph 7.2 above shall be at University's sole expense unless the auditors discover an underpayment of at least 5% of the amount due and owing for that year, in which case the audit shall be paid for at Racket's expense.

8. Duration

8.1. Initial Term. The Agreement shall be in effect from the Effective Date until five (5) years from the Effective Date.

8.2. Renewal. The Agreement automatically renews for up to five (5) additional one (1) year terms unless one party gives the other party written notice of its intent not to renew prior to the start of a renewal term.

9. Cancellation and Survival of Obligations

9.1. Cancellation. Either party may cancel the Agreement if the other party is in material breach thereof by providing written notice of breach to the other party describing the nature of the breach. A party receiving notice of breach shall have thirty (30) days to cure the breach. If the party receiving notice of breach has not cured the breach within such thirty (30) day period, the Agreement shall automatically end.

9.2. Obligations upon Cancellation or Termination. Following cancellation or termination of the Agreement, Racket shall promptly return to University any copies of the Manual and any tennis rackets based on the Technology in Racket's possession or under its control.

9.3. Survival of Obligations. Following cancellation or termination of the Agreement, all confidentiality obligations, obligations to return materials, limits on liability, and dispute resolution provisions shall survive and continue in full force and effect.

10. Limitation of Liability

NEITHER PARTY SHALL BE LIABLE FOR ANY INCIDENTAL, CONSEQUENTIAL, SPECIAL, OR PUNITIVE DAMAGES THAT ARISE OUT OF OR RELATE TO THE AGREEMENT, EVEN IF A PARTY HAS BEEN ADVISED OF THE POSSIBILITY OF SUCH DAMAGES.

11. Warranties

11.1. University warrants that the Manual does not infringe the copyright of any third party.

11.2. University warrants that it owns all right, title, and interest in and to the Manual, free from any encumbrances as to title or ownership.

11.3. University warrants that application of the Know How to manufacture tennis rackets based on the Technology does not, to the best of University's actual knowledge, infringe the patent rights of any third party.

11.4. Racket warrants that tennis rackets based on the Technology meet the Quality Standards.

12. No Other Warranties and Disclaimers of Implied Warranties

THE WARRANTIES DESCRIBED IN SECTION 11 ARE THE ONLY WARRANTIES OF ANY KIND PROVIDED BY UNIVERSITY. UNIVERSITY DISCLAIMS ALL OTHER WARRANTIES, INCLUDING THE IMPLIED WARRANTIES OF MERCHANTABILITY AND FITNESS FOR A PARTICULAR PURPOSE.

13. Indemnification; Defense of Actions

University shall indemnify, hold harmless, and defend Racket from and against any claims, losses, liabilities, damages, costs, or expenses from any and all suits and causes of action incurred by Racket arising out of or related to breach of the warranties of non-infringement and title. University shall employ legal counsel to defend such suit or action at University's expense. Racket shall have the right to approve such counsel, but Racket may not unreasonably withhold its approval. Upon notice of any suit or action, Racket shall promptly notify University and Racket shall cooperate in University's defense. Racket shall have the right, at its sole expense, to employ separate legal counsel to participate in the defense.

14. Choice of Forum

Any cause of action arising out of the Agreement shall be brought exclusively in the state or federal courts sitting in Honolulu, Hawaii, U.S.A.

15. Choice of Law

Any cause of action arising out of the Agreement shall be governed by the laws of the State of Delaware, U.S.A.

16. Attorneys' Fees

In the event a party brings an action to enforce its rights under the Agreement, the prevailing party shall be entitled to receive its reasonable litigation costs, including reasonable attorneys' fees.

17. Restrictions on Exports

The Know How and the Manual are subject to export controls. The parties agree that they will comply with all domestic and international export laws and regulations, including restrictions on destinations, users, and uses.

18. Complete Agreement

The Agreement constitutes the complete agreement between the parties with respect to the subject matter described herein, merging and superseding any prior or contemporaneous agreements. The Agreement can only be amended by a written amendment signed by both parties.

19. Severability

If any provision of the Agreement becomes invalid, illegal, void, or unenforceable under any law that is applicable to the Agreement, each such provision shall be deemed amended to conform to applicable law or, if it cannot be amended without materially altering the terms of the Agreement, such provision shall be deleted.

20. Assignability

The Agreement may not be assigned by either party without the prior written consent of the other.

21. Notices and Requests

All notices and requests shall be sent via overnight courier as follows (or to such other address as is provided by one party to the other party from time to time):

To University:

Provost	cc: General Counsel
Pine University	Pine University
One Saturn Way	One Saturn Way
Spokane, Washington, U.S.A.	Spokane, Washington, U.S.A.

To Racket:

President	cc: General Counsel
Conway Racket Ltd.	Conway Racket Ltd.
500 Surf Road	500 Surf Road
Honolulu, Hawaii, U.S.A.	Honolulu, Hawaii, U.S.A.

Agreed to this 25th day of June, 2010. This Agreement may be signed in counterparts or via fax.

FOR UNIVERSITY: FOR RACKET:

_____   _____
Signature   Signature

_____   _____
Printed Name   Printed Name

_____   _____
Title   Title

_____   _____
Date Signed   Date Signed

II. DISCUSSION OF COMMON LICENSE PROVISIONS

Each subpart of this section explains the objectives and law behind each provision of the License Agreement. The explanation of the law will be abbreviated, just enough to acquaint you with the basic legal principles that underlie the provision (in some cases, entire treatises have been written on the legal topic). This chapter concludes with a set of Problems that relate to the provisions in the License Agreement; Drafting Exercises based on the License Agreement are contained in Chapter 3.

A. Parties and Effective Date

LICENSE AGREEMENT

This license agreement (hereafter "Agreement") is entered into this 25th day of June, 2010 (hereafter "Effective Date"), by and between Pine University, a land grant university of the State of Washington, with its principal place of business at One Saturn Way, Spokane, Washington, U.S.A. (hereafter "University"), and Conway Racket Ltd., a Delaware corporation, with its principal place of business at 500 Surf Road, Honolulu, Hawaii, U.S.A. (hereafter "Racket").

---

1. Parties

A license agreement usually begins by identifying the parties who are entering into the transaction. If a party is an individual person the license identifies him or her by name. Sometimes the individual will be a sole proprietor with a business name, so the license will name the person and the "doing business as" or "d/b/a" name as well. One or both parties to the license may be a corporation, partnership, or other type of legal entity, in which case the entity will be named as a party. Sometimes this becomes complicated as one entity is a division or subsidiary of another entity.

2. Effective Date

A license agreement needs a date that marks the beginning of each party's rights and duties. In some cases, determining that point in time is simple: It is the date both parties sign the license. In other cases, the matter is more complicated. For instance, the license may be signed after the parties have begun to perform or signed by one party and then sent to the other party for signature. Sometimes the parties do not sign and date the license at all because it has been entered into electronically, orally, or by conduct.

Knowing the effective date is more than just a matter of curiosity. Many terms of the license are triggered or affected by it. Here are some examples:

- Royalties. Royalty payments become due and owing X days from the effective date;
- Duration. The license agreement automatically terminates X years from the effective date;
- License Grant. The start of the license grant is tied to the effective date;
- Exclusivity. An exclusive license grant becomes a non-exclusive license grant X years from the effective date;
- Warranty. A warranty runs X months from the effective date;

- Delivery. A deliverable must be delivered within X days of the effective date;
- Return. A deliverable must be returned, if unacceptable, within X days of the effective date;
- Damages. Damages litigation over a license may be tied to the effective date.

B. Recitals

---

1. Recitals

Whereas University has developed new tennis racket frame technology;

Whereas University has applied for patent protection in the United States of America for this technology;

Whereas Racket desires to manufacture tennis rackets based on this technology at its facilities in Texas;

Whereas Racket desires to distribute tennis rackets based on this technology in the European market;

Every license agreement arises out of particular facts and circumstances, and it is conceived of and drafted by certain individuals. As time passes, individuals who did not draft or negotiate the license need to implement and interpret it. If a dispute arises about the license agreement, a mediator, arbitrator, judge, or government official may need to understand it. The Recitals can be helpful in determining the parties' intent. *See, e.g.*, Motorola, Inc. v. Analog Devices, Inc., 2004 U.S. Dist. LEXIS 15607 (E.D. Tex. 2004) (court uses recitals to interpret patent license grant); McGraw-Hill Companies, Inc. v. Vanguard Index Trust, 139 F. Supp. 2d 544 (S.D.N.Y. 2001) (court uses preamble to interpret trademark license grant). The Recitals are sometimes called the Preamble because they come before the binding promises as a prelude, or the "whereas clauses" because the sentences often begin with the word "whereas."

The primary legal issue raised about Recitals is whether they are binding. As a general rule, they are not. The parties normally do not intend for the Recitals to be treated as covenants, and courts do not treat them as such. However, there are two contexts in which the Recitals may be binding.

First, they are binding in the sense that they are an authoritative description of the context for the license. A party cannot later claim the setting for the license is different than described in the Recitals. This becomes important when the Recitals are used by a court as an aid to interpret the binding covenants in the license. For example, the Recitals may be considered in determining whether the license as a whole suffers from an ambiguity that would warrant the admission of extrinsic evidence.

Second, the parties may draft the Recitals in such a way as to make them part of a covenant. They do this by referring to the Recitals in the operative part of the license.

If a Recital is incorporated by reference, it becomes part of the binding agreement as if it were a covenant. A Recital may also become part of the binding agreement if the agreement says the Recital is to be treated in this manner.

C. Definitions

---

2. Definitions

For purposes of this Agreement, the following terms have the following meanings whenever capitalized:

2.1. "Technology" shall mean University's tennis racket frame technology as described in Attachment 1.

2.2. "Patent" shall mean any United States patent that issues from U.S. Patent Application number XXX, including continuations and divisionals.

2.3. "Manual" shall mean University's manual titled *Procedures for Manufacturing Tennis Racket Frames* as that manual exists on the Effective Date, and any revisions to it.

2.4. "Know How" shall mean all of University's confidential know how relevant to manufacturing the tennis rackets based on the Technology, including information contained in the Manual.

2.5. "Manufacturing Facility" shall mean Racket's tennis racket manufacturing facility located in Dallas, Texas, at 500 Star Street.

2.6. "European Market" shall mean the countries which are members of the European Union as of the Effective Date and any countries that are admitted during the term of this Agreement.

2.7. "FlexPower Logo" shall mean University's *FlexPower* logo which is used in conjunction with the Technology.

2.8. "Quality Standards" shall mean the quality standards as described in Attachment 2.

2.9. "Net Sales" shall mean gross sales minus returns.

2.10. "Maximum Payment" shall mean U.S. $5,000,000.00.

The Definitions section defines key terms that will be used throughout the license agreement. As such, it is one of the most important sections. It is a place where knowledge of the business deal and context are particularly important because the definitions describe the subject matter of the license such as an invention, data, a logo, a picture, or software.

What happens when the license agreement does not define a key term? Sometimes a court will consult a dictionary to determine the ordinary meaning. Use of dictionaries has its drawbacks. The dictionary may provide multiple definitions, with one party claiming one and the other party another. Also, in many license agreements the dictionary definition is not what either party has in mind because the license is using a technical term or term of art in a certain industry. This leads courts to consult specialized or technical dictionaries in certain cases.

Apart from dictionaries, courts may look to analogous terms used in intellectual property statutes. Other times courts will utilize various principles of contract law as an aid, such as course of dealing or course of performance. *See* Effects Assocs., Inc. v. Cohen, 908 F.2d 555, 558 (9th Cir. 1990) (using course of dealing to help establish implied license); UCC 1-205. Courts may look to a definition that others in the industry would consider standard. This is called industry custom or usage of trade. For example, if most software developers think that a certain type of defect is a "bug," that understanding would define the term "bug" in a license that obligates one of the parties to fix bugs. Usage of trade is established through technical dictionaries or other literature from the industry or by expert testimony. Needless to say, the parties can improve the clarity and certainty of their contract by defining key terms in their license agreement rather than leaving it to judicial interpretation at a later date.

D. License Grants

---

3. License Grant

3.1. University hereby grants to Racket an exclusive license under the Patent to:

    (a) make and use tennis rackets based on the Technology at the Manufacturing Facility;

    (b) sell, offer to sell, import, and distribute tennis rackets based on the Technology in and to the European Market for amateur tennis players.

3.2. University hereby grants to Racket a non-exclusive license to use the Know How for the sole purpose of making tennis rackets based on the Technology at the Manufacturing Facility;

3.3. University hereby grants to Racket a non-exclusive license under University's copyrights to use and reproduce the Manual for the sole purpose of making the tennis rackets based on the Technology at the Manufacturing Facility.

3.4. University hereby grants to Racket an exclusive license to use the PowerFlex Logo in conjunction with the rights granted in 3.1 above;

3.5. All rights other than those licensed in paragraphs 3.1, 3.2, 3.3, and 3.4 above are reserved by University.

The License Grant section is the heart of the license agreement. It is the place where the rights in intellectual property, information, or software are granted. The license grant gets formed as the licensor answers two questions: What is being licensed, and what are the contours of the permission?

1. What Is Being Licensed?

Often a license agreement grants rights in intellectual property. In creating the license grant, the potential licensor determines the types of intellectual property that might be licensed: copyrights, patents, trademarks, or trade secrets. Licenses may also grant permission to use information or publicity rights. If patent rights or copyrights are licensed, the licensor determines which of the exclusive rights will be granted: for copyrights, the right to reproduce, distribute, publicly perform or display, or make derivatives; for patents, the right to make, use, sell, offer to sell, and import products based on the patent.

2. What Are the Contours of the License Grant?

As explained above, the license grant clause spells out the types of intellectual property being licensed, and within each category of intellectual property, which of the exclusive rights. That answers the question of "what is being licensed." The rest of the license grant describes on what conditions and for what purposes things are being licensed. For example, a license may grant rights only for a certain number of geographical territories.

Licenses grant rights on either an exclusive or non-exclusive basis. Out of these two choices arise many possibilities. A non-exclusive license, as the words suggest, means the license is available to multiple comers. Licenses of this nature encourage widespread distribution and usage of the thing being licensed.

An exclusive license grant restricts the licensor. Within the grant of exclusive rights, the licensor may not license to another or itself exercise the rights being licensed. Some exclusive licenses are as limiting for the licensor and others as the name suggests. If a patent holder grants someone an exclusive license to use the patent in all fields of use under all circumstances, then the licensee truly has use of the patent to the exclusion of everyone else. Many exclusive licenses, however, do not grant such encompassing exclusivity. They, instead, grant exclusive rights for a given use or context. Consequently, they open up many licensing possibilities for the same intellectual property.

Some license grants state that the license is "personal." In other words, the rights are being granted to someone who is familiar to or specially chosen by the licensor. The licensor trusts that particular someone with a trade secret, trademark, copyrighted work, invention, data, or idea. The licensor may not trust others similarly. Several examples illustrate this point:

- A beverage company may be willing to license its root beer recipe to an independent bottler but not its direct competitor in the beverage business;

- A French designer of high-end, stylish shoes may be willing to license its trademark for use in conjunction with shoes crafted by one Italian cobbler but not another;
- A stock exchange may be willing to license its real-time data to brokerage houses but not rival stock exchanges;
- A novelist may be willing to grant derivative works rights to one playwright but not another;
- A famous sports figure may be willing to grant a publicity right to a tennis clothes designer but not a swimsuit designer.

Historically most licenses were personal in nature, so license grants were presumed to be personal. This is still the case in many areas. Intuitively we know that trademark and trade secret licenses are personal. As licensing has become a ubiquitous transaction model in the modern global economy, however, many licenses clearly are not personal. They are licenses literally offered to anyone in the world. The best example of this is the mass market licenses often used in software transactions. Consequently, the presumption about the personal nature of licenses may have changed — people now assume that many licenses are impersonal. This change in perspective makes it prudent for licenses that are personal to state that they are "personal" rather than rely on the historical understanding for context.

In addition to describing the grant of rights as exclusive or non-exclusive or personal, the license grant section may describe a variety of other contours. For example, the license grant may set out geographic parameters for distribution, grant rights for use of a work or invention with only a particular product, or grant rights for usage in only certain business fields of use. There are as many license grant possibilities as there are business opportunities.

3. Construing License Grants and Reservations of Rights

a. Construing Grants

It is the nature of human language that people will disagree over the meaning of words. State contract law deals with this reality by providing a rule of construction that ambiguous contract language should be construed against the drafter. Courts are divided over whether this rule should apply when construing license grants for intellectual property. Some cases hold that the traditional state contract law principle of construing ambiguous language against the drafter should apply. *See* Bourne v. Walt Disney Co., 68 F.3d 621 (2d Cir. 1995). Other cases hold that license grants should be viewed differently because they are grants of government-provided exclusive rights. As such, the intellectual property rights holder should only be deemed to be granting those exclusive rights which the holder explicitly gives away. *See* S.O.S., Inc. v. Payday, Inc., 886 F.2d 1081, 1088 (9th Cir. 1989).

b. Reservation of Rights Clauses

One response to the uncertainty about license grant construction is a "reservation of rights" clause. *See* Section 3.5 of the License Agreement. This provision clarifies that the licensor keeps any rights not explicitly granted in the license grant. To put it another way, in litigation the reservation of rights clause informs a court that the licensor means only to grant rights clearly granted and no others by implication.

E. Delivery and Inspection; Acceptance or Rejection

---

4. Delivery of Manual and Logo Artwork

4.1. University shall deliver the Manual in hard copy and electronic forms to Racket at the Manufacturing Facility no later than ten (10) days after the Effective Date.

4.2. University shall deliver camera ready artwork of the FlexPower Logo to Racket's headquarters in Honolulu, Hawaii, no later than ten (10) days after the Effective Date.

5. Delivery, Inspection and Acceptance/Rejection of Rackets

5.1. Racket shall deliver to University twenty (20) tennis rackets based on the Technology manufactured by Racket at the Manufacturing Facility, no later than one (1) year after the Effective Date.

5.2. University shall evaluate the tennis rackets to determine whether they meet the Quality Standards. The Quality Standards shall be the sole measure to determine whether the rackets meet an acceptable level of quality. University shall notify Racket in writing of its acceptance or rejection of the level of quality within thirty (30) days of receipt from Racket. In the event University fails to notify Racket in writing within the thirty (30) day time period, the quality shall be deemed acceptable. If University rejects the quality, its notice of rejection shall include a detailed description of the reasons for its rejection.

5.3. In the event University timely notifies Racket of its rejection of the level of quality, then Racket shall have six (6) months to improve the quality of its manufacturing process and resubmit the tennis rackets for evaluation by University. The evaluation and acceptance/rejection process shall be as described in paragraph 5.2 above. In the event University rejects the level of quality, University shall have the right either to grant an additional period of time for Racket to improve quality or terminate the Agreement.

---

1. Delivery

Some licenses grant a permission and do little more. These licenses are sometimes viewed simply as covenants not to sue or waivers of rights. In other cases, however, the parties will be delivering tangible things to one another in support of a license to use an intangible. The Delivery section of the license agreement (or a section with a similar, more aptly descriptive title for that particular transaction) contains these obligations. A few examples illustrate the situations that the Delivery section may cover:

- A Subway sandwich restaurant franchisee receives Subway logo artwork to use on store signage;
- A Two Pesos restaurant franchisee receives specifications for laying out and decorating the restaurant to emulate the total look and feel of Two Pesos' trade dress;
- The licensor of the Tommy Hilfiger brand receives samples of clothing marked by the brand from the licensee to monitor product quality;
- A movie theater receives a copy of the *Lord of the Rings* motion picture on celluloid film or disk;
- A famous murder mystery author delivers a book manuscript to his publisher;
- Red Hat software company delivers Linux source code on CD-ROMs to its customer who will use the code to fix critical bugs;
- Intel Corporation delivers microprocessors and motherboards to Dell Computer so it can make and sell personal computer systems under Intel's patents;
- Shell Oil Company receives the chemical ingredients from E.I. du Pont de Nemours & Co. necessary to make a certain chemical mixture under DuPont's patents;
- Charles Schwab brokerage receives an electronic feed of stock quotes from the NASDAQ stock exchange as part of a license for stock price data.

Describing what needs to be delivered can take many forms, from a simple description to an elaborate specification. Beyond describing what needs to be delivered and by whom, the Delivery section also describes when, how, and where things must be delivered.

What are the rules about delivery if the parties do not describe the rules in the license agreement? In transactions where UCC 2 applies, it provides for certain default rules. For example, delivery must be at a reasonable hour and needs to conform to any oral agreements between the parties. UCC 2-503; *see also* UCITA §606(a). If one party's performance is contingent on the other party's performance, the one party does not have to perform until the other party has performed. UCC 2-307; *see also* UCITA §607(a)(1).

2. Inspection

A counterpart to the Delivery section is the Inspection section. The Inspection section describes the process for evaluating a deliverable so that the recipient can ultimately accept or reject the deliverable. In many cases the parties do not spell out the inspection and acceptance/rejection process. What happens then?

In jurisdictions that apply UCC 2 to licenses, certain default rules can come into play. For example, if the agreement does not address inspection, UCC 2 allows a party receiving a deliverable to inspect the deliverable at a time, a place, and in a manner that is reasonable under the circumstances. *See* UCC 2-513. In jurisdictions that have adopted UCITA, the recipient of confidential information may be required to protect the confidentiality of the information in certain cases and, unless trade usage indicates otherwise, there is no right to inspect where giving the recipient the information equals the value of getting the information.[1] *See* UCITA §604.

3. Acceptance

When does a party "accept" a delivery? Often the license agreement will have a section that sets out the criteria and manner for accepting deliverables. Apart from acceptance as defined in a written license agreement, UCC 2 describes many types of actions and circumstances[2] of the receiving party that may qualify as acceptance in 2-606:

- Signifying acceptance or acting in a manner that indicates that the party is willing to accept the deliverable (even if it is not perfect);
- Failing to effectively refuse the deliverable;
- Doing any act inconsistent with the seller's ownership.

4. Rejection

Written license agreements often explain the process for rejecting a deliverable. If the license does not provide rules for rejection, however, then general rules of contract law come into play.

The *Restatement (Second) of Contracts* follows the "material breach" approach. RESTATEMENT (SECOND) OF CONTRACTS 241; *see also* UCITA §704(a) (non-mass market licenses). This approach favors holding contracts together whenever possible. Consequently, if a licensor delivers something that substantially conforms to the contract, the licensee cannot reject the deliverable but may only recover damages for breach of contract if the licensor does not correct the deliverable. A minor defect in a deliverable does not allow the receiving party to cancel the entire contract.

This rule works well for many licenses for two reasons. First, software and information often contain small errors, imperfections, or incompleteness so that complete, perfect performance is almost never the norm in commerce. Second, a license often involves ongoing activity and multiple aspects, so it is unfair for one party to be able to cancel the entire deal over an immaterial issue. The party who receives something with a small defect does have recourse in damages, offsets, or correction but not in canceling the entire contract.

---

1. For example, in a license to view a picture or see stock price quotes, the licensee receives the value of the license the very instant that the licensee sees the picture or prices quotes — in this situation, there is no right of inspection under UCITA.

2. In jurisdictions that have adopted UCITA, UCITA §609 also provides that a deliverable is accepted if it becomes inextricably commingled with the software or information of the receiving party or the receiving party receives substantial value or benefit from the deliverable.

UCC 2 provides for what is called "conforming tender," though some use the nomenclature "perfect tender." *See* UCC 2-601; *see also* UCITA §704(b) (following this approach for mass market licenses). Under the conforming or perfect tender rule, if the deliverable does not conform to the contract, the recipient may reject the deliverable. The implication is that the recipient can reject the deliverable for any non-conformance no matter how small. So, in theory, a recipient could reject for a minor non-conformity or, to put it another way, require "perfect" tender. However, Professors White and Summers note that they have found no case that "grants rejection on what could fairly be called an insubstantial non-conformity." J. White & R. Summers, Uniform Commercial Code (4th ed. 1995).

F. Consideration/Payment

---

6. Payment

6.1. Racket shall pay to University the following payments according to the following schedule. All payments shall be made in U.S. dollars via wire transfer to account 12345 at Wells Fargo Bank.

   (a) $500,000.00 on the Effective Date;
   (b) $500,000.00 five (5) days following receipt of University's notice of acceptance of the quality of the tennis rackets;
   (c) 1% of Net Sales of the first 100,000 tennis rackets sold;
   (d) 2% of Net Sales of the next 250,000 tennis rackets sold;
   (e) 3% of Net sales for any additional tennis rackets sold.

6.2. In no case shall payments exceed the Maximum Payment. Upon payment of the Maximum Payment, the license grants in the Agreement shall be fully paid up.

Every license involves an exchange of consideration, of course, but consideration takes many forms. *See* Robert A. Hillman & Maureen A. O'Rourke, *Rethinking Consideration in the Electronic Age*, 61 Hastings L.J. 311 (2009). Sometimes the consideration for one license is another license. On other occasions one party trades a license for services, such as editing, marketing, or distribution capabilities. Still other times a license is traded for some type of payment that may take the form of stock, notes, or cash.

When the consideration is the payment of money, these payments are often called royalties. There are endless ways to structure royalties. Tax considerations often play a role in the choice of royalty structure, as explained in the final chapter of this book. Antitrust law may influence how long royalties will be paid — payments beyond the exclusive term of an intellectual property right may be improper. Most importantly, however, the parties will choose a structure that creates the right incentives and rewards for their contributions.

The parties might choose an escalating royalty. This royalty structure allows the licensee to keep more proceeds at the beginning of the contract, and then pay increasingly more to the licensor as the contract progresses. This structure is used when: the licensee may be poorly capitalized and needs to retain significant proceeds at the beginning of the deal to fund the costs of ramping up production; the parties want to create a large incentive for the licensee to develop and market the product quickly; the licensor's contribution to the overall license arrangement (via support, marketing, etc.) will increase over time.

On the other hand, the parties may choose a de-escalating royalty. This structure is normally used when the licensor's contribution to the deal decreases over time or when the parties expect that the volume of royalties will increase over time so that, while the rate is lower, the total proceeds may actually be equal or greater as the contract progresses. It also creates an incentive for the licensee to become successful quickly so that it can ship sufficient volume to qualify for the lower rate.

The parties could choose a flat rate royalty. This structure provides predictability and certainty. This has advantages for planning, payment, and accounting for royalties.

At a certain point the parties may decide that the licensor has earned sufficient revenue for its contribution to the license agreement. When this happens, a cap is a useful contract drafting tool. Caps can apply to periodic royalty payments, such as payment of a variable royalty up to a cap of X dollars, or can be used to cap overall payments in the license agreement.

The royalty payments, regardless of the rate structure, could be triggered in various ways. One common trigger is the licensee's receipt of revenue. This allows the parties to share money as it comes in the door. It makes them partners in the financial success of the license agreement. Another way to structure royalties is by triggering various payments based on units of product shipped. This structure may be easier to track than royalties based on net sales while at the same time allowing each party to share in the success of the venture.

G. Audits and Accounting

---

7. Accounting/Audits

7.1. Racket shall keep such books and records as are reasonably necessary to account for the payments due under the Agreement.

7.2. University shall have the right on an annual basis to audit the records of Racket at Racket's headquarters in Honolulu, Hawaii, to ensure that Racket's payments to University are full and accurate. Such audit shall be conducted by certified public accountants on at least one week's prior written notice during Racket's normal business hours. Racket shall cooperate fully with University's auditors during the audit.

> 7.3. The audit described in paragraph 7.2 above shall be at University's sole expense unless the auditors discover an underpayment of at least 5% of the amount due and owing for that year, in which case the audit shall be paid for at Racket's expense.

What happens if the party bound to pay does not pay or there is a suspicion that the party is not paying the appropriate sum? One course of action is to sue for breach of contract. However, many licenses include an Audits section so that the parties can attempt to resolve payment-related issues short of litigation.

H. Duration

> **8. Duration**
>
> 8.1. Initial Term. The Agreement shall be in effect from the Effective Date until five (5) years from the Effective Date.
>
> 8.2. Renewal. The Agreement automatically renews for up to five (5) additional one (1) year terms unless one party gives the other party written notice of its intent not to renew prior to the start of a renewal term.

The parties often agree specifically on how long a contract will run. When they do not, contract law must fill in the duration. Under the common law of contracts, a contract for an unspecified duration may be terminable at will. If UCC 2 applies, the default term is "a reasonable time," which "may be terminated at any time by either party" upon "reasonable notification." UCC 2-309. In jurisdictions that have adopted UCITA, it follows the UCC 2 rule for most licenses but the duration is perpetual for transactions in which a software publisher delivers software in object code form and either makes a first sale or delivers a copy for a single fixed fee. UCITA §308(2)(A). UCITA also provides a perpetual duration as a default rule when the license grants rights to incorporate or use information from multiple sources in a combined work for public distribution or public performance. *Id.* §308(2)(B).

Intellectual property law also bears on duration. As discussed in Chapter 9, Section 203 of the Copyright Act gives licensors a window of time in which to terminate a license or assignment. In addition, obligations to pay royalties longer than the life of an intellectual property right may constitute a misuse or unfair competition issue. *See* Brulotte v. Thys, 379 U.S. 29 (1964); Kimble v. Marvel Entertainment, 135 S. Ct. 2401 (2015).

I. Termination, Cancellation, Obligations upon Termination or Cancellation

---

9. Cancelation and Survival of Obligations

9.1. Cancellation. Either party may cancel the Agreement if the other party is in material breach thereof by providing written notice of breach to the other party describing the nature of the breach. A party receiving notice of breach shall have thirty (30) days to cure the breach. If the party receiving notice of breach has not cured the breach within such thirty (30) day period, the Agreement shall automatically end.

9.2. Obligations upon Cancellation or Termination. Following cancellation or termination of the Agreement, Racket shall promptly return to University any copies of the Manual and any tennis rackets based on the Technology in Racket's possession or under its control.

9.3. Survival of Obligations. Following cancellation or termination of the Agreement, all confidentiality obligations, obligations to return materials, limits on liability, and dispute resolution provisions shall survive and continue in full force and effect.

When a license agreement ends according to its terms, this is called "termination." The parties may describe any number of reasons to terminate a license: a period of time passes, a project is completed, certain events transpire.

In terminable at will license agreements there is no particular event triggering the end of the contract — either party may simply end the license agreement at its discretion. If UCC 2 or UCITA apply, however, the party terminating the license agreement may be required to provide reasonable notice to the other party. UCC 2-309(c); UCITA §607(b).

In terms of the form of a notice, it may come as a written document, an e-mail, a fax, a telephone call, or simply an action that, in effect, ends the license for all practical purposes. In terms of timing, reasonableness may require notice prior to termination in some circumstances, but in other circumstances the notice may coincide with an act that ends the license for all practical purposes. In terms of the delivery mechanism, any method reasonably calculated to reach the other party should suffice — in this day and age, an e-mail or text message or call to a mobile phone may be faster and as reliable as a fax or letter sent via the mail.

Termination differs from cancellation — cancellation occurs when a party ends a contract for breach, often material breach.[3] *See* Kane v. Roxy Theaters Corp, 65 F.2d

---

3. Note, however, that practicing lawyers and courts sometimes use the terms cancel, terminate, and revoke interchangeably. *See, e.g.*, Welles v. Turner Entm't Co., 488 F.3d 1178 (9th Cir. 2007).

324, 326-27 (2d Cir. 1933); Valeo Intellectual Property, Inc. v. Data Depth Corp., 368 F. Supp. 2d 1121, 1126 (W.D. Wash. 2005) (failure to place agreed copyright tag on works was material breach, but failure to place copyright notice was not material breach); UCC 2-106(4); UCITA §102(8). Cancellation may be a remedy for breach of a license agreement. *See* UCC 2-703; UCITA §802(a). The party injured by the breach is not required to cancel the contract — canceling is optional. The injured party instead may opt to pursue a claim for damages, collect liquidated damages, or sue for specific performance.

Sometimes the parties require notice prior to cancellation but the parties may choose to dispense with notice. This is enforceable unless its operation would be unconscionable. *See* UCC 2-309(c); UCITA §617(c).

In general, the termination or cancellation of a license agreement means that the licensee loses the right to use licensed intellectual property rights, data, or information. Some license agreements provide that the agreement or a term in the agreement may not be cancelled. These license grants are "perpetual and irrevocable" even if a party is in breach. These agreements are enforceable unless, of course, they run afoul of antitrust law or create a patent or copyright misuse. They do not, however, limit an aggrieved party's right to sue for damages.

Whether cancellation has officially occurred (did the licensor send a notice of cancellation after the licensee was in breach?) can have an impact on the status of the license agreement and the licensor's rights if the licensee is in a bankruptcy proceeding. *See* Chapter 14 for a discussion of this.

When a license agreement ends, certain obligations may survive. These are either bargained-for rights or duties that the parties agreed should continue or obligations related to unwinding the contract. For example, the parties may agree that a license grant continues on, a limitation of liability stays in place, or a party must return or destroy copies of confidential information.

J. Limitation of Liability

---

10. Limitation of Liability

NEITHER PARTY SHALL BE LIABLE FOR ANY INCIDENTAL, CONSEQUENTIAL, SPECIAL, OR PUNITIVE DAMAGES THAT ARISE OUT OF OR RELATE TO THE AGREEMENT, EVEN IF A PARTY HAS BEEN ADVISED OF THE POSSIBILITY OF SUCH DAMAGES.

Many license agreements attempt to limit the liability of one or more of the parties. These contractual provisions beg an important question — what liability do the parties face for breach of contract? Contract law allows an injured party to recover various types of damages. A party may recover damages to compensate for unpaid fees or consideration received by the breaching party but never paid. These damages are known as "direct damages." "Incidental damages" are another measure of damages. These are the reasonable charges, expenses, or commissions incurred incident to a breach. *See* UCC 2-715(1).

An injured party may also recover "consequential" damages. *See* 2 E.A. Farnsworth, FARNSWORTH ON CONTRACTS 12.14 (2d ed. 1998); UCC 2-715(2). Consequential damages are any loss of anticipated benefits resulting from the inability to use the licensed material or intellectual property of which the breaching party, at the time of contracting, had reason to know and could not be reasonably prevented. This may include lost profits or royalties that could have been collected, as well as damage to reputation, loss of privacy, lost value of a trade secret from wrongful disclosure, and lost or damaged data.

Often the parties agree to limit the type or the amount of damages that may be recovered. Limitations of liability are common, but are they enforceable? Generally they are enforceable in commercial transactions. UCC 2, for example, says that "the agreement may provide for remedies in addition to or in substitution for those provided in this Article and may limit or alter the measure of damages recoverable under this Article. . . ." UCC 2-719(1)(a).

The policy for this is simple: Allocating risk is a fundamental part of freedom of contract. The parties know best how to formulate the remedies most appropriate to their transaction. They know what fits best and what else is being traded off in the contract (e.g., price) when remedies are limited, enhanced, or adjusted. Outside of the business to business context, however, the Uniform Commercial Code or consumer protection laws often place limits on the ability to disclaim or eliminate damages. The policy for this is also simple: Consumers need special protection because they may lack sophistication and bargaining power.

K. Warranties

---

11. Warranties

11.1. University warrants that the Manual does not infringe the copyright of any third party.

11.2. University warrants that it owns all right, title, and interest in and to the Manual, free from any encumbrances as to title or ownership.

11.3. University warrants that application of the Know How to manufacture tennis rackets based on the Technology does not, to the best of University's actual knowledge, infringe the patent rights of any third party.

11.4. Racket warrants that tennis rackets based on the Technology meet the Quality Standards.

The common law of contracts leaves warranties up to the parties to decide. If the parties do not agree to any warranties, then no warranties become part of the contract. *See, e.g.*, Cordis Corp. v. Medtronic, Inc., 780 F.2d 991, 996 (Fed. Cir. 1984), *cert. denied*, 476 U.S. 1115 (1986).

UCC 2 and UCITA take a different approach. These statutes use the concept of warranties in three ways: express, gap filler, and implied. Express warranties arise from express language in the license agreement or conduct of the parties. UCC 2-313(a). Gap filler warranties may come into a license agreement when the parties did not address the particular term in their negotiations. For instance, UCC 2 and UCITA have gap filler warranties on intellectual property infringement. Implied warranties are promises so fundamental to transactions that the promises should be assumed to exist in every contract unless the parties clearly express a contrary intent. Implied warranties include ones of merchantability and fitness for a particular purpose. *See* UCC 2-314, 2-315.

L. Disclaimers of Warranty

---

12. No Other Warranties and Disclaimers of Implied Warranties

THE WARRANTIES DESCRIBED IN SECTION 11 ARE THE ONLY WARRANTIES OF ANY KIND PROVIDED BY UNIVERSITY. UNIVERSITY DISCLAIMS ALL OTHER WARRANTIES, INCLUDING THE IMPLIED WARRANTIES OF MERCHANTABILITY AND FITNESS FOR A PARTICULAR PURPOSE.

If a license is governed by the common law, there is no need to disclaim implied warranties because the common law does not imply warranties into contracts. UCC 2 allows parties to disclaim implied or default-rule warranties in their agreement; however, certain rules may apply. For example, to make a valid exclusion or modification of the implied warranty of merchantability, the licensor must mention "merchantability," and if the disclaimer is in a written contract, it must be conspicuous. UCC 2-316(1); *see also* UCITA §405(b). Some states do not allow disclaimers of these implied warranties in consumer contracts. *See, e.g.*, Conn. Gen. Stat. 42a-2-316(5); Mass. Gen. Laws 106 2-316(A).

Warranties and disclaimers are also drafted in the shadow of the federal Magnuson-Moss Warranty Act (MagMoss). MagMoss, by its terms, applies to written warranties that accompany sales of tangible consumer products. 15 U.S.C. §§2301-2312. Though many licenses do not involve tangibles or consumer products,[4] many licenses are drafted as if MagMoss could apply.

---

4. In 2000, the Federal Trade Commission held a symposium on whether to expand the reach of Mag-Moss. *See* Symposium on Warranty Protection for High-Tech Products and Services at *http://www.ftc.gov/bcp/workshops/warranty/index.html*. To date, Congress has not revised MagMoss.

M. Indemnity

---

13. Indemnification; Defense and Actions

University shall indemnify, hold harmless, and defend Racket from and against any claims, losses, liabilities, damages, costs, or expenses from any and all suits and causes of action incurred by Racket arising out of or related to breach of the warranties of non-infringement and title. University shall employ legal counsel to defend such suit or action at University's expense. Racket shall have the right to approve such counsel, but Racket may not unreasonably withhold its approval. Upon notice of any suit or action, Racket shall promptly notify University and Racket shall cooperate in University's defense. Racket shall have the right, at its sole expense, to employ separate legal counsel to participate in the defense.

An indemnity provision provides another way for parties to allocate risk on top of provisions which, as previously discussed, allocate risk by giving and disclaiming warranties, by shaping and molding remedies, and by eliminating the right to recover certain types or amounts of damages. For example, it is common to allocate risk by requiring one party to indemnify the other party in the event the indemnifying party breaches a warranty. A contractual indemnity works like private insurance — if a party suffers a loss due to a breach of warranty, it submits a claim to the other party, who then reimburses the aggrieved party for losses suffered.

The indemnity provision may also include an obligation on a party to defend any litigation brought against the other party arising out of a breach of warranty. This is called a defense obligation. Again, this parallels what happens in a typical insurance contract — if an insured party is in an automobile accident, the insurance company provides a lawyer to defend the insured party. Not every indemnity obligation comes with a defense obligation — these are two separate obligations.

N. Choice of Forum

---

14. Choice of Forum

Any cause of action arising out of the Agreement shall be brought exclusively in the state or federal courts sitting in Honolulu, Hawaii, U.S.A.

The issues related to contractual choices of forum are complex, and the discussion in this chapter is brief. In evaluating the enforceability of a choice of forum, a threshold question must first be answered: Does the court have personal jurisdiction over the parties? This, of course, is a question ultimately for courts to decide based on "traditional notions of fair play and substantial justice." International Shoe Co. v. Washington, 326 U.S. 310, 316 (1945); *see* Hildebrand v. Steck Mfg. Co., 61 U.S.P.Q.2d 1696 (Fed. Cir. 2002) (sum of contacts in patent license context were not enough to establish minimum contacts for personal jurisdiction).

Assuming a court has personal jurisdiction, contractual choices of forum are presumptively valid. *See* Bremen v. Zapata Off-Shore Co., 407 U.S. 1 (1972); Carnival Cruise Lines, Inc. v. Shute, 499 U.S. 585 (1991). According to the Supreme Court, choice of forum clauses serve a significant commercial purpose by allowing parties to control uncertainty and the cost it creates. *Carnival Cruies Lines* at 585-86. This is particularly important in electronic commerce to lower the risk that a merchant, primarily a small one, must litigate disputes in any forum around the world. If the parties want a choice of forum to be exclusive, they must say so expressly in their license agreement. *See* Docksider Ltd. v. Sea Tech Ltd., 875 F.2d 762, 764 (9th Cir. 1989).

Despite the commercial benefits, however, there remains a serious concern that litigating in a contractually chosen forum may be a hardship for one of the parties, particularly a consumer in a standard form contract setting. While a disparate impact will not be enough to defeat a choice of forum, the choice is not enforceable if it is unreasonable or unjust. *Carnival Cruise Lines* at 585-86. For example, it may be unjust for a U.S. company to require a U.S. consumer to pay a $100 arbitration fee and arbitrate a dispute in London over a $50 product. *See* Brower v. Gateway 2000, Inc., 676 N.Y.S.2d 569 (A.D. 1998).

O. Choice of Law

---

15. Choice of Law

Any cause of action arising out of the Agreement shall be governed by the laws of the State of Delaware, U.S.A.

Like choice of forum, the jurisprudence of choice of law is complex, so this chapter will only provide a brief introduction to help provide the backdrop for a choice of law clause.[5] Unlike choice of forum, which is primarily concerned with whether it is fair for the parties to litigate in a particular place, choice of law is focused on whether it is sound for a court to apply the law of a jurisdiction chosen by the parties over the law of another jurisdiction that otherwise *could* apply to the transaction (absent the parties' contractual choice).

---

5. *See* Richman & Reynolds, UNDERSTANDING CONFLICT OF LAWS 241 (2d ed. 1992) (characterizing choice of law theory as "in considerable disarray" and "marked by eclecticism and even eccentricity"); Brilmayer, CONFLICT OF LAW: FOUNDATIONS AND FUTURE DIRECTIONS (1991).

Courts typically uphold the parties' choice of law in a license agreement. *See, e.g.,* Medtronic, Inc. v. Jans, 729 F.2d 1395 (11th Cir. 1984). However, contractual choices of law are not enforceable to the extent they are unconscionable or violate a fundamental public policy. Lambert v. Kysar, 983 F.2d 1110, 1118 (1st Cir. 1993). The Uniform Commercial Code also requires that the parties' choice of law have a "reasonable relationship" to the transaction. UCC 1-105.

What law applies if the parties do not expressly make a choice of law in their license? The *Restatement (Second) of Conflicts of Law* §188 provides that the law of the jurisdiction with the most significant relationship to the transaction should apply. Applying this test causes courts to weigh the following factors "according to their relative importance with respect to the particular issue":

- Place of contracting;
- Place of negotiation;
- Place of performance;
- Location of the subject matter of the contract;
- Domicile, residence, nationality, place of incorporation, and place of business of one or both parties.

Needless to say, this balancing approach has the advantage of flexibility but the disadvantage of uncertainty, which is why parties often elect to choose governing law in their license agreements.

P. Attorneys' Fees

---

16. Attorneys' Fees

In the event a party brings an action to enforce its rights under the Agreement, the prevailing party shall be entitled to receive its reasonable litigation costs, including reasonable attorneys' fees.

In the United States parties pay their own court costs, litigation expenses (expert witness fees, court reporter costs, etc.), and attorneys' fees, even if they prevail in the case. Given that backdrop, parties may agree in their license agreement that the prevailing party will be entitled to recover its litigation costs and attorneys' fees. In addition, attorneys' fees may be available under intellectual property statutes if the breach of a license agreement results in an infringement. *See* Fantasy v. Fogerty, 510 U.S. 517 (1994).

Attorneys' fees clauses have the salutary effect of discouraging frivolous litigation. If a party knows that it will have to pay its litigation expenses and the other side's litigation expenses if it loses, the party may take a more conservative approach to pursuing litigation. It will have an incentive to pursue non-litigation options first.

Q. Export Controls

---

17. Restrictions on Exports

The Know How and the Manual are subject to export controls. The parties agree that they will comply with all domestic and international export laws and regulations, including restrictions on destinations, users, and uses.

The Departments of Commerce and State of the U.S. government control exports from the United States. Most exports are not restricted in any way; they are exportable under a so-called "general license." If government regulations list your product as qualifying for a general license, you may export it.

The U.S. government does restrict the export of certain types of products and to certain countries. For example, the government restricts the export of products that could be used for military applications. There are also certain embargoed countries, such as Cuba and North Korea, to which the government restricts virtually all exports. Violation of export control laws could result in large fines or even loss of export privileges.

R. Complete Agreement/Merger/Amendments

---

18. Complete Agreement

The Agreement constitutes the complete agreement between the parties with respect to the subject matter described herein, merging and superseding any prior or contemporaneous agreements. The Agreement can only be amended by a written amendment signed by both parties.

The parties to a license agreement may agree that the written terms and conditions constitute the complete and final expression of their bargain. The clause in a license expressing this agreement is often called the "merger" clause because it merges all terms, including those from prior oral or written communications. The clause is also called the "complete" or "exclusive" agreement clause to emphasize that there are no other agreements outside the four corners of the written document.

The Complete Agreement provision must be understood in the context of what is known as the Parol or Extrinsic Evidence Rule. The Parol Evidence Rule arises when a party offers extrinsic evidence to explain, supplement, or contradict a provision of a contract. The law on the Parol Evidence Rule is complex; however, several generalizations help understand the context for the Complete Agreement provision.

First, when the parties have expressed, through a Complete Agreement clause, their intent that a written instrument contains their integrated and entire agreement, the terms in the written instrument may not be contradicted by evidence of a previous written or oral agreement. *See* RESTATEMENT (SECOND) OF CONTRACTS 209; UCC 2-202; Data General Corp. v. Grumman Support Corp., 36 F.3d 1147 (1st Cir. 1994). The basic policy behind the rule is that a record of the contract is the best and primary source for determining the terms of the agreement of the parties. Second, if the parties have not stated that the written record is the "complete and exclusive" statement of their terms, the court may look to evidence of consistent additional terms. Third, some courts will also admit extrinsic evidence to explain an ambiguous term, *see, e.g.*, Kepner-Tregoe, Inc. v. Vroom, 186 F.3d 283 (2d Cir. 1999), and explain or supplement terms by course of performance, course of dealing, or usage of trade, *see, e.g.*, Random House, Inc. v. Rosetta Books, LLC, 283 F.3d 490 (2d Cir. 2002).

S. Severability

---

19. Severability

If any provision of the Agreement becomes invalid, illegal, void, or unenforceable under any law that is applicable to this Agreement, each such provision shall be deemed amended to conform to applicable law or, if it cannot be amended without materially altering the terms of the Agreement, such provision shall be deleted.

As discussed in Chapter 1, a court may strike a provision of a license agreement because it is unconscionable, violates public policy, constitutes a misuse, or violates antitrust laws. In most cases, the parties would like the license agreement as a whole to survive such challenges to individual provisions. The Severability clause serves this purpose.

T. Assignability

---

20. Assignability

The Agreement may not be assigned by either party without the prior written consent of the other.

As discussed in Chapter 1, many licenses are considered personal, which means the parties only intend the license to be transferred to another trusted party whom they approve in advance. General principles of contract law favor free assignability of contracts, although, as discussed in Chapter 1, this may be overridden by principles of intellectual property law. Rather than leaving the matter to background rules, most parties use the license agreement to describe explicitly when and if the license may be assigned.

U. Notices

---

21. Notices and Requests

All notices and requests shall be sent via overnight courier as follows (or to such other address as is provided by one party to the other party from time to time):

To University:

Provost	cc: General Counsel
Pine University	Pine University
One Saturn Way	One Saturn Way
Spokane, Washington, U.S.A.	Spokane, Washington, U.S.A.

To Racket:

President	cc: General Counsel
Conway Racket Ltd.	Conway Racket Ltd.
500 Surf Road	500 Surf Road
Honolulu, Hawaii, U.S.A.	Honolulu, Hawaii, U.S.A.

Most written licenses have a section that sets out where notices are to be sent, to whom, and by what method. For example, the license agreement may say notices must be sent to the corporate CEO at the corporate headquarters via overnight courier with a courtesy copy to the General Counsel. The notice provision is important because certain provisions of the license agreement may require notice as a prerequisite to some action or consequence.

V. Manifesting Assent

Agreed to this 25th day of June, 2010. This Agreement may be signed in counterparts or via fax.

FOR UNIVERSITY: FOR RACKET:

_____   _____
Signature   Signature

_____   _____
Printed Name   Printed Name

_____   _____
Title   Title

_____   _____
Date Signed   Date Signed

Many written license agreements conclude with the signatures of the parties. This is the simplest, most straightforward way for the parties to manifest assent to the license agreement. A signature may be a handwritten signature or an electronic signature. *See* Electronic Signatures in a Global and National Commerce Act (E-Sign), 15 U.S.C. §§7001 *et seq.*; Uniform Electronic Transactions Act (UETA).[6] Signatures may be applied simultaneously or in counterpart copies, in person or by exchange of faxes.

Many license agreements do not contain signatures. In general, parties may form a license agreement in any manner sufficient to show agreement, including by conduct of the parties or the interaction of electronic agents. "The manifestation of assent may be made wholly or partly by written or spoken words or by other acts or failure to act." RESTATEMENT (SECOND) OF CONTRACTS §19(1).

Determining when assent is sufficient is no simple matter. Many commentators have weighed in on this issue, some applauding the flexibility of modern contracting practices[7] and others criticizing the drift away from meaningful agreement in contract law.[8] In this book, that debate is presented primarily in the context of software mass market licensing in Chapter 9.

---

6. E-Sign and UETA generally put electronic signatures on par with traditional handwritten signatures. Despite predictions that digital signatures would become commonplace, traditional signatures and non-signature manifestations of assent are most common in licensing transactions.

7. *E.g.*, Robert A. Hillman & Jeffrey J. Rachlinski, *Standard Form Contracting in the Electronic Age*, 77 N.Y.U. L. REV. 429 (2002).

8. *E.g.*, Margaret Jane Radin, *Boilerplate Today: The Rise of Modularity and the Waning of Consent*, 104 MICH. L. REV. 1223 (2006).

III. PROBLEMS

1. (Parties): The process of identifying the parties, though often unremarkable, can yield useful information or raise issues that need to be addressed in the license. What information can be gleaned in the following situations?

   1.1 XMart, a regional convenience store chain, considers licensing credit card processing software from a software publisher called Reliable Software Company. This software will be critical to XMart's business — if the software is not reliable it will cost XMart thousands of dollars in lost sales. In the draft license agreement provided by Reliable, XMart learns that Reliable is a d/b/a for a sole proprietorship operating out of an apartment in Vancouver, B.C.

   1.2 Katie O'Grady is a professor at Cascade Mountain College. She has developed a new type of automobile fuel from used cooking oil and has received several patents for her inventions. Discount rental car company Cars4Less, Inc. decides to license the patented inventions. In the draft license agreement provided by Professor O'Grady, Cars4Less notices that Professor O'Grady is named as a party to the license while Cascade Mountain College is not.

   1.3 GuzzleUp Sports Co. produces a popular thirst-quenching sports drink. The drink contains several secret ingredients that, when used in the right proportions, replace electrolytes far better than other sports drinks. GuzzleUp decides to increase distribution of its drink by licensing its formula to GoFoods, Inc., a restaurant company that has facilities at youth soccer fields around the world. The draft license provided by GoFoods describes the company as a division of a corporate conglomerate that distributes a competitive thirst-quenching beverage.

2. (Recitals): If a license agreement does not contain a Recitals section, how would a court learn about the background of the license?

3. (Definitions)

   3.1 In a patent license the definition of the licensed patent may discuss whether or not the license includes continuations or divisionals. Should the license include continuations or divisionals if the parties are silent on the matter? *See* Intel v. Negotiated Data Solutions, 703 F.3d 1360 (Fed. Cir. 2012).

   3.2 If a license grants rights to distribute a copyrighted work "in Europe" but does not define that term, how should the licensee interpret the term? How should a court interpret the term?

   3.3 If a software license obligates the licensor to fix "major bugs" but does not define that term, how would a court determine the meaning in case the parties disagree over the meaning?

4. (License Grant)

   4.1 Does an exclusive license grant mean that the licensee is the only one who has rights in the licensed intellectual property or information?

   4.2 If you were a legislator creating a contract statute for licenses, would your statute provide that ambiguous license grant language should be construed against the drafter or that the ambiguous grant language should be construed narrowly, or would you choose some other principle of construction?

4.3 In a license for a U.S. patent, if the parties do not mention any geographical limitation on distribution, should a court assume that distribution is for the United States or worldwide? What if the license was for a copyrighted work? A trademark?

4.4 The License Grant section provides a license for Know How. The definition of Know How indicates that it is confidential information. In light of that, what provisions should be added to the License Agreement?

5. (Delivery and Inspection)

5.1 If you were a legislator drafting a statutory default rule for electronic delivery of information, when and where would you say that "delivery" and "receipt" occurs?

5.2 If you were a legislator drafting a statutory default rule for inspection of information whose value is extinguished as soon as the licensee see it, what would that rule provide?

6. (Acceptance and Rejection): Should licensees have the right to reject information or software that has immaterial defects and end the entire license transaction? Why or why not? What approach does UCC 2 take? If the licensee cannot end the license, what recourse does the licensee have?

7. (Payment)

7.1 What incentives does an escalating royalty rate create? A declining royalty rate? A flat rate? In what business contexts might you use each of these approaches?

7.2 In what contexts might the parties agree to a cap on royalties?

7.3 Why might the parties agree on pre-paid royalties or some other form of advance payment?

8. (Accounting and Audits): Which party benefits from an audit right?

9. (Duration): If you were a legislator drafting a statutory default rule for duration of licenses, what rule would you choose? Terminable at will? A "reasonable" time? For the exclusive term of the intellectual property right? Something else?

10. (Survival of Obligations): If you were a legislator drafting a statutory default rule for survival of obligations, which license provisions should survive?

11. (Limitation of Liability)

11.1 If you were a legislator drafting a statutory default rule for whether parties could recover consequential damages for breach of license, what rule would you provide? If research showed that over 90 percent of licenses disclaimed consequential damages, would that affect the rule you created? What about survey data showing that over 90 percent of businesses believed that excessive consequential damage awards were detrimental?

11.2 Should parties be able to limit or exclude certain types of damages in a contract? Always? Sometimes? In some contexts and not others?

11.3 What contract doctrines inherently limit parties' ability to limit or exclude damages?

12. (Warranties and Disclaimers of Warranty)

 12.1 If you were a legislator drafting statutory implied warranties, would you create an implied warranty of merchantability? An implied warranty that the licensed work or invention does not infringe any third-party intellectual property right? What are the pros and cons of creating such implied warranties? What challenges would you face in drafting such warranties to apply to a wide range of license transactions?

 12.2 If you were a legislator, would you allow parties to disclaim implied warranties for license agreements? Would you allow disclaimers if your state's UCC 2 allowed for disclaimers for sales of goods?

13. (Indemnity): When might you ask the other party to indemnify you for breach of warranty? When might you ask the other party to defend a claim? When might you choose not to ask for an indemnity or an obligation to defend?

14. (Choice of Forum and Choice of Law)

 14.1 Should the parties be able to choose a forum to resolve disputes about their license? Why or why not? In all cases? What about the governing law? Why or why not? In all cases?

 14.2 When might the parties choose the forum but not the governing law? What about the governing law but not the forum? Would it ever be prudent for the parties to leave open the choice of law or forum?

 14.3 When might the parties choose arbitration? What are the pros and cons of arbitration in license transactions?

15. (Attorneys' Fees): Does an attorneys' fees provision favor licensors or licensees? Large or small parties?

16. (Export Controls): Why should a license contain an export control provision when the provision is merely restating the export laws?

17. (Complete Agreement): What are the terms and conditions of a license that does not contain a Complete Agreement clause?

18. (Notices): What happens if the addresses or names of the parties change from the ones listed in the Notices clause?

19. (Assent)

 19.1 Do you agree with the trend in modern contract law to permit assent in a variety of ways? What are the advantages and disadvantages of this flexibility? Does technology sharpen or dampen the disadvantages?

 19.2 If you were a legislator drafting a rule describing when a licensee should be bound by a standard form license, what would that rule say?

DRAFTING LICENSES

I. OVERVIEW OF DRAFTING LICENSES

Drafting license agreements is an essential part of licensing law practice. Well drafted licenses can help facilitate transactions by accurately documenting the deal points and serving as a roadmap for the parties to perform under the contract. Poorly drafted licenses, on the other hand, can cause friction in the business relationship or even lead to litigation. There is no reason why a law student cannot draft a license agreement. Drafting is both easier and harder than meets the eye: harder in the sense that it takes a lot of skill to become an excellent draftsperson; but easier in the sense that there are many ways to write the words and the drafter seldom needs to start from scratch.

This chapter introduces the craft of drafting license agreements. It begins with a discussion of the principles of good drafting and a practical drafting primer. The balance of the chapter is devoted to a series of drafting examples based on the License Agreement presented in Chapter 2. Subsequent chapters contain drafting exercises to practice drafting in various contexts.

II. THE CRAFT OF DRAFTING

Just as novelists and playwrights have their unique writing styles, so do drafters of license agreements. A variety of license drafting styles can work. Regardless of an author's style, following certain core principles will improve the quality of a license agreement.

Know the Business Context. Each licensing transaction operates in the broader context of the things that are going on in a particular industry—be aware of this broader context. If the parties are licensing a patent for a stem cell line, for instance, the drafter should be aware of developments in the scientific or political areas that could bear on the license. In a software license for browser software, the drafter should understand that there are both binary use and open source programs, some distributed stand-alone and others bundled with software or hardware.

Know the Business Deal.   License agreements get drafted because two parties see the value of a transaction. Each party has its reasons for wanting to enter into the deal. The license drafter needs to understand what each side is trying to accomplish in the transaction.

Make Your Client Your Partner.   Clients often think that creating a license agreement falls solely in the domain of lawyers. They think that because a license is a legal document, only lawyers need to understand it in any detail. Yet the client knows the business deal best. The author of a license should treat the client as a partner in the drafting process by having the client review iterations of the license to make sure it captures the business deal in its proper context.[1]

Know the Goal of Each Provision.   Each provision in a license agreement serves a particular purpose, as discussed in Chapter 2. The author of the license needs to know that purpose. The hardest part of drafting often lies in the thinking that goes into the choice of words, not the writing of them. This may be common sense but many superfluous or ill chosen words are added to license agreements because the author did not think carefully about the purpose of the words.

Know the Law Behind the Language.   The author needs to know the background law against which each license provision operates, as introduced in Chapter 2. What cases or statutes bear on the provision? If you draft no words at all, what would the law provide by default? For example, the warranty section requires knowledge about the types of implied and gap-filler warranties that could come into play, as well as any cases ruling on how to draft a conspicuous disclaimer.

Pay Attention to Interactions Between Provisions.   Various provisions of a license agreement tend to interact with one another. As each section of the license agreement is created and revised, the author should be aware of the impact on other parts of the agreement. A change in the definitions section might influence the breadth of the license grant; a change from a non-exclusive to an exclusive license might influence the commitments owed in the marketing section; a change in the geographic scope of the license grant might influence the warranties or indemnification offered; the addition of confidential information to the license grant might create the need to add an additional provision dealing with the protection of confidential information.

Think Litigation.   Always bear in mind that a license agreement could land in litigation. That is not to say that the author should add additional provisions to the agreement simply out of undue concern over litigation. In fact, sometimes deletions

---

1. *See* Robert W. Gomulkiewicz, *Getting Serious About User-Friendly Mass Market Licensing for Software,* 12 Geo. Mason L. Rev. 687, 692-94, 699-705 (2004) (describing the real world of license creation).

change to a definition may have implications for the license grant. Make sure your client also reviews revised or newly created provisions. Eventually, if the business deal holds together (not a given, by any means), then you will prepare the Final Version. Like all drafts, read and think through this Final Version once more with a skeptical eye. You may be weary but make sure that you and your client are satisfied.

The End of the Beginning.   To borrow from Winston Churchill, the Final Version is not necessarily the end but, perhaps, the end of the beginning. Most likely you will be called on to interpret the license for your client: does the license allow this or that; what happens if we do X or Y? Over time it is common for parties to decide that they need to amend their license. This reflects the changing business climate and actual experience of living with the terms of the license. What may have seemed sensible on the effective date of the Final Version may no longer make sense; terms that seemed clear then may seem ambiguous later. As a consequence, the license drafting process begins anew.

IV. DRAFTING EXAMPLES

The set of examples in this section are designed to give you a taste of what it is like to draft the provisions of a license. We hope to demystify the drafting process and encourage you to try the Drafting Exercises in the rest of the book.

A. Definitions

The Definitions section of a license agreement contains the glossary of terms that will be used throughout the license agreement. It often captures important business terms, such as the parameters of an exclusive market. From a drafting standpoint, definitions allow the license drafter to write more efficiently because a term does not need to be written in expanded form time after time.

The license agreement between Pine University and Conway Racket in Chapter 2 gives Conway Racket exclusive distribution rights in Europe. Anticipating that the license agreement will need to contain a license grant reflecting this deal point, the Definitions section contains a definition of the European market:

> "European Market" shall mean the countries that are members of the European Union as of the Effective Date and any countries that are admitted during the term of the Agreement.

How would this definition be redrafted if the parties agreed that Conway Racket would also have exclusive distribution rights in Russia (which is not, at present, a member of the European Union)? One approach is to add an additional sentence to the definition of European Market to expand the definition: *It shall also include the Russian Federation.* Another approach is to add Russia to the existing sentence: *"European Market" shall mean the Russian Federation, any countries that are members of the European Union, and any countries that are admitted to the European Union during the term of the Agreement.* Both approaches work equally well.

What changes would be needed if the parties agreed to add Brazil and Argentina to the exclusive market? The word "European" is no longer apt since the exclusive market now contains South American countries. By dropping the word "European" and listing the new countries, redrafting is relatively simple: *"Market" shall mean Brazil, Argentina, any countries that are members of the European Union, and any countries that are admitted to the European Union during the term of the Agreement.*

What if the parties decided that the exclusive market would include all of Europe and South America? This complicates the drafting. Which countries are considered part of Europe — what about Great Britain, Russia, Turkey, or Georgia? What if new countries emerge, such as the states that were formerly a part of the Soviet Union or Yugoslavia? One important question for the license drafter to ask is: do the parties intend an expansive view of "Europe" and "South America," a narrow view, or something in between? The answer to this question will guide the drafting.

If the parties intend an expansive view of Europe, the definition can reflect that intent by specifically including all countries that are in the gray areas: *"Market" shall mean any country in South America and any country in Europe or that is a member of the European Union, including Great Britain, Russia, Georgia, and Turkey.* If the parties intend a narrow view of Europe, the definition can reflect that intent by being very precise about the countries included: *"Market" shall mean any country in South America and any European country listed in Attachment 1 to this Agreement.*

Finally, how would the definition of "Market" change if the parties decided that Conway Racket would have exclusive distribution rights in South America but non-exclusive rights in Europe? The drafter needs to anticipate that the license agreement will have two distribution license grants: one exclusive and one non-exclusive grant. To facilitate the drafting of those grants, it would be useful to divide the definition of Market into two definitions, one that will be used in the exclusive grant and one in the non-exclusive grant:

> *"South American Market" shall mean any country in South America. "European Market" shall mean any countries that are members of the European Union, and any countries that are admitted to the European Union during the term of the Agreement.*

If the license agreement needs to refer to both the European and South American markets without regard for whether the distribution grant is exclusive or non-exclusive (e.g., in reference to Conway Racket's right to manufacture rackets for both Europe and South America), then a third definition could be created drawing on the prior two: *"Licensed Market" shall mean the South American Market and the European Market.*

Suppose, next, that the parties have decided to license Conway Racket a set of photographs of prototype rackets that were taken by Pine University. Conway Racket will use these photos in promotional materials only. The drafter must create a new definition. Before drafting the definition, the drafter needs to learn as much as possible about the photos: How many? What form? Where are they located? Who took them?

Are all the photos taken of the prototypes to be licensed? Will any new photos be included?

Based on the answers, the author will draft the new definition. It might say something like: *"Photos" shall mean University's entire collection of photographs of prototype tennis rackets based on the Technology created prior to the Effective Date, in digital, print, and negative forms.* Note that the definition does not include any mention of a copyright license or limit use to promotional purposes. That is because these issues should not be addressed in the Definitions section — the place to address them is in the License Grant section.

B. License Grants

Drafting the license grant requires the author to ask a series of questions:

- What types of intellectual property are in play?

Some license agreements grant permission to exploit one discrete thing, such as an invention or work of authorship, covered by one discrete type of intellectual property, such as a patent or copyright. In these cases, thinking through the type of intellectual property that might be licensed in the transaction is a simple exercise. However, many licensing transactions involve multiple types of objects covered by multiple types of intellectual property as well as associated know how, data, and other things not protectable under intellectual property laws. When this is the case, the author needs to think systematically through all the types of rights and other licensable items that *potentially could* be licensed in the particular transaction and then decide which ones *actually should* be licensed.

- Within each type of intellectual property, which rights should come into play?

Once the author determines which categories of intellectual property should be licensed, he or she must determine which rights within each category should be granted. For copyrights, the author must decide whether to grant the right to reproduce, distribute, create derivative works, or publicly perform or display, and for patents whether to grant the right to make, use, sell, offer to sell, or import under its patents.

- Are there any conditions or parameters that need to be placed around use of the rights being licensed?

The final task of the author is to describe any conditions on or parameters around the rights being granted under the intellectual property. These are what shape and form the license grant so that it fits the business deal. For example, in the license between Pine University and Conway Racket, the distribution license grant is limited to "amateur tennis players" and the right to manufacture the tennis rackets must be done "at the Manufacturing Facility."

1. Patent License

The license agreement between Pine University and Conway Racket contains the following license grant under University's patent:

University hereby grants to Racket an exclusive license under the Patent to:

(i) make and use tennis rackets based on the Technology at the Manufacturing Facility;

(ii) sell, offer to sell, import, and distribute tennis rackets based on the Technology in and to the European Market for amateur tennis players.

This license grants Conway Racket certain manufacturing and distribution rights on an exclusive basis. What if the parties decided that the rights should be granted on a *non*-exclusive basis? A straightforward revision could accomplish that result: change the word in the grant from "exclusive" to "non-exclusive."

What changes would be needed if the parties decided that Conway Racket could have exclusive rights for amateur and professional tennis players? One approach is to simply delete the words "for amateur tennis players." These words had the effect of narrowing the grant so deleting them broadens it. Another approach is to add the words "and professional" following the word "amateur." Yet another approach is to delete the word "amateur," leaving the words "tennis players."

Consider next the changes necessary if the parties agreed that the license grant for amateurs would be exclusive but the grant for professionals would be non-exclusive. To accomplish that, several approaches could work. One approach would be to add another grant for the non-exclusive license:

University hereby grants to Racket a non-exclusive license under the Patent to sell, offer to sell, import, and distribute tennis rackets based on the Technology in and to the European Market for professional tennis players.

Another approach is to delete the initial use of the word "exclusive" and then add in the word "non-exclusive" or "exclusive" as applicable to the existing grant:

University hereby grants to Racket the following rights under the Patent:

(i) *an exclusive license to make and use tennis rackets based on the Technology at the Manufacturing Facility;*

(ii) *an exclusive license to sell, offer to sell, import, and distribute tennis rackets based on the Technology in and to the European Market for amateur tennis players.*

(iii) *a non-exclusive license to sell, offer to sell, import, and distribute tennis rackets based on the Technology in and to the European Market for professional tennis players.*

Finally, assume that the parties agreed that all patent licenses would be non-exclusive. This, of course, is a major change from a substantive point of view.

The change to the license grant would be easy to make but this change should spur the drafter to re-examine other license provisions: Do the parties need to adjust the royalty rate or marketing obligations? Is a strong warranty or indemnification appropriate?

2. Copyright License

The license agreement between Pine University and Conway Racket contains a license under University's copyrights to use and copy a certain University technical manual:

> University hereby grants to Racket a non-exclusive license under University's copyrights to use and reproduce the Manual for the sole purpose of making the tennis rackets based on the Technology at the Manufacturing Facility.

What needs to be added to the license grant if the parties agree that Conway Racket should have the right to modify the Manual? University needs to give Conway Racket the right to create derivative works:

> *University hereby grants to Racket a non-exclusive license under University's copyrights to use, reproduce, and create derivative works of the Manual. . . .*

Now assume that the Manual is a published work, available for free download from University's Web site or in hard copy form from the University for a nominal per-copy fee. How should the license grant be changed? Under these circumstances, there may be no need for a copyright license at all. If Conway Racket wants hard copies, the license agreement could require University to deliver a certain number of copies to Conway Racket — this would be done in the Delivery section and Conway Racket's rights under copyright simply would be first sale rights.

Alternatively, assume that the parties want Conway Racket to have exclusive rights to control the use and evolution of the Manual. Several drafting approaches could be taken. First, the license agreement could assign Pine University's copyright in the Manual to Conway Racket:

> *University hereby assigns to Racket all right, title, and interest in and to University's copyrights in the Manual.*

Second, Pine University could grant Conway Racket an exclusive license under all of its copyrights:

> *University hereby grants to Racket an exclusive license under University's copyrights to use, reproduce, distribute, publicly perform or display, and create derivative works of the Manual.*

If the parties wanted to give Conway Racket this license indefinitely, even if the rest of the license agreement ends, then they would add the word "irrevocable" to the grant and, in the Survival provision, provide that this license grant survives termination or cancellation of the license agreement.

C. Warranties

Warranties in license agreements are promises about the quality of the products delivered or about whether use of the licensed intellectual property will lead the licensee into an infringement. The license agreement between Pine University and Conway Racket contains the following warranty:

> University warrants that the Manual does not infringe the copyright of any third party.

This is an unequivocal promise. Suppose, however, that the Manual contains factual information from several third-party sources. Pine University believes that the information is not copyrightable but it does not want to risk being in breach of the license agreement if it is wrong. Thus Pine University only wants to promise non-infringement of copyright to the best of its knowledge. To implement this change, the parties could revise the warranty as follows:

> *University warrants that, to the best of its knowledge, the Manual does not infringe the copyright of any third party.*

The license agreement between Pine University and Conway Racket also contains a warranty about patents:

> *University warrants that the application of the Know How to manufacture tennis rackets based on the Technology does not, to the best of University's actual knowledge, infringe the patent rights of any third party.*

Assume that Conway Racket wants a straight up warranty rather than one qualified by "best of University's actual knowledge." Making this revision simply entails deleting the latter words.

Assume, instead, that Pine University just discovered a patent that may tread on its Technology. There are several drafting approaches to this situation. One is to call out the patent as an exception to the warranty:

> *Except for patent number XXX, University warrants that the application of the Know How to manufacture tennis rackets based on the Technology does not, to the best of University's actual knowledge, infringe the patent rights of any third party.*

Another approach is to delete the warranty because Pine University can no longer make this promise. Still another approach is to get the advice of patent counsel and, if patent counsel gives an opinion of non-infringement or invalidity, then give the warranty knowing that there is some risk that a court may find patent infringement but not a high enough risk to take the warranty out of the license agreement.

D. Boilerplate

As illustrated above, modern license drafting often involves starting from existing language — a form or prior license — and revising from there. The provisions that require the most original drafting tend to be provisions such as the Definitions, the boundaries in the License Grants, Delivery and Marketing obligations, and sophisticated royalty schemes. Some provisions remain relatively constant from license to license. These provisions are often called "boilerplate." They include Complete Agreement (also known as Merger), Disclaimer of Warranty, and Choice of Law or Forum, and Attorneys' Fees.

In the boilerplate sections, the important job of the license drafter lies not in crafting new words but in thinking about whether a particular provision belongs in the license at all. Should the license agreement contain a Complete Agreement provision if important deal points were agreed to orally? Should the license agreement disclaim consequential damages when that type of damage may be the primary measure of damages that could be recoverable (e.g., in a software source code license)? Should a forum or choice of law be selected? Is an Attorneys' Fees provision in the best interest of the parties? These are the questions the skilled license drafter asks before including them in a draft agreement. The Exercises present some of these issues for you to work through.

E. Learning from Cautionary Tales and Pitfalls

The examples above try to teach through best practices; the ones below teach through cautionary tales and pitfalls.

1. Cautionary Tales

Definitions Example. Assume the License Agreement contains the following:

> "Manual" shall mean University's manual titled *Procedures for Manufacturing Tennis Racket Frames,* which is attached to the Agreement and which University agrees to update from time to time.

First, Definitions should not contain covenants or promises. Definitions provide the grist for covenants and promises but those should be drafted in other provisions. Second, it is common practice to attach an exhibit to a License Agreement, but it is probably unrealistic to attach a lengthy technical manual. If the manual does not get attached, then you have created an ambiguity in the license: What version of the manual is canonical?

There is another cautionary tale about attachments that is just as important. Often lawyers will reference an attachment that is prepared by a business client and, often, the lawyer will not review the attachment (thinking that it is not in his or her domain). However, the attachment's contents can have significant consequences (they may expand or contract definitions or license grants) or there may be extraneous language in the attachment that bears on or even contradicts provisions in the license.

License Grants Example.   Assume the License Agreement contains the following:

> University hereby grants to Racket a non-exclusive license under University's copyrights to use, reproduce, and distribute the Manual, provided that Racket does not develop any competing technology for making fiberglass rackets or the like for a period of 99 years from the Effective Date.

First, this provision points out a danger in the conventional wisdom often expressed that the license drafter should take as aggressive a position as possible in drafting a license agreement. In licensing, an overly aggressive position can create a copyright or patent misuse or run afoul of antitrust laws as explained in Chapter 2. Here, the 99-year non-compete proviso may well have that effect.

Second, the words "fiberglass rackets or the like" create ambiguities that could cause problems later. Is the term "fiberglass" defined well enough in the industry to avoid future confusion — does this include composite materials? Perhaps the words "or the like" broaden it sufficiently but what about rackets made with graphite, carbon, aluminum, or other natural metals? Use the Definitions or additional words in the license grant to reduce ambiguity. The chapters on Copyright and Multimedia Licensing explore ways to anticipate technological changes in licensing.

Warranty Disclaimer Example.   Many licenses purport to disclaim *"all warranties, express or implied."*

First, this provision raises an important question: Can you disclaim express warranties? To put it another way, can you give an express warranty in one place in the license agreement or orally and then take it back by disclaiming it? The answer is "no," you usually cannot. The law does not allow that (unless you do it very explicitly). In fact, in extreme situations, trying to disclaim an express warranty can be considered an unfair trade practice. Second, can you always disclaim implied warranties? Not all states or nations permit this. That is why many licenses contain the language "some jurisdictions do not allow disclaimers of warranty so these disclaimers may not apply to you." By omitting this language, your license agreement may lead to allegations of unfair trade practices (in addition to being unenforceable).

Limitation of Liability Example.   Some licenses purport to eliminate the ability to recover *"any and all damages of any kind, including direct, indirect, special, and consequential. . . ."*

Perhaps it is truly the intent of both parties in a negotiated license to eliminate the possibility of recovering any damages for breach of the license. However, the primary concern tends to be consequential damages because they can lead to immense sums of damages. Parties in a negotiated transaction seldom intend to eliminate the right to recover direct damages. On top of that, particularly in standard form licensing, disclaiming all damages may create a situation where the contract fails of its essential purpose. If a court finds that a contract has so failed, it may be willing to open the door to the recovery of all types of damages, even consequential damages, notwithstanding language to the contrary in the license. Make sure the license agreement contains some remedy, whether that be repair, replacement, refund, or leaving open the right to recover direct damages.

Cases.   There are many more lessons about drafting that you can learn from the cases in the Materials sections of this book. As you read the cases, be attuned to drawing lessons about license drafting as well as learning the legal rules and policies that are normally the focus of case reading.

2. Top Ten Pitfalls

Now that we have described the best approach to drafting, where do things tend to go wrong? The Cautionary Tales provide a few clues, but here's a list of the Top Ten License Drafting Pitfalls that can serve as a quick reference:

10. Putting binding terms in the Definitions section;
9. Failing to clearly specify the duration and scope of the license grant;
8. Assuming that all warranties and damages should be disclaimed;
7. Failing to review attachments or appendices to the license agreement;
6. Creating purposefully ambiguous language in hopes your client can exploit it later in ways the other side did not agree to;
5. Failing to anticipate that technology, distribution methods, and business models change;
4. Proposing or accepting a provision because "it's always been done that way";
3. Using legalese instead of plain language (except when necessary to present a legal term of art);
2. Sending a draft to the other side before your client reviews it;
1. Assuming that imperfect drafting is the end of the world — that's what amendments are for.

V. DRAFTING EXERCISES

Use the License Agreement in Chapter 2 as the baseline for these Drafting Exercises.

1. Add two additional recitals to the Recitals section.
2. In the Payments section:
   2.1 Re-draft the current provision so that the two initial payments are treated as down payments for the percentage royalties owed rather than as separate payments on top of the percentage royalties.
   2.2 Draft a provision that would permit Conway Racket to buy out all royalty payments for a fee of $3 million.
   2.3 Draft a provision for a flat rate royalty of 2 percent.
   2.4 Change the payment triggers from rackets shipped to total net sales of $1 million and then $2 million.

3. Assume that the rackets will be fitted with grips, strung, and covered at a facility in Australia. Re-draft the definition of Manufacturing Facility to account for this.

4. Draft a warranty stating that the *FlexPower* logo does not infringe any other trademarks.

5. Draft a mandatory arbitration provision.

6. Re-draft the Notices section to allow e-mail notices to qualify.

7. Revise the copyright warranty to reflect that a "best of knowledge" standard means actual knowledge.

8. Revise the Choice of Forum section so that any litigation must be brought in the home jurisdiction of the defendant.

9. Revise the Assignability section to permit assignment to subsidiaries and affiliates. Add a provision saying that consent to any other assignment will not be unreasonably withheld.

10. Make any changes needed to permit the parties to assent to the license using electronic signatures.

PART TWO

INTELLECTUAL PROPERTY
LICENSING

· CHAPTER ·

4

TRADEMARK LICENSING

I. OVERVIEW OF TRADEMARK LICENSING

A. Introduction

Trademarks are perhaps the oldest type of intellectual property. The use of markings in commerce has been around for thousands of years. With the increase of cross-border transactions and the movement of goods in global trade, many trademarks today enjoy a high degree of consumer recognition across national boundaries. Take a look at a laptop computer — the marks of companies from around the world can be found on it. Acer, Dell, Lenovo, Samsung, Intel Inside, and the Apple or Windows logo are just a few of the marks that you might find.

Trademarks are important corporate assets. Trademarks function as source identifiers to the consumer. Trademarks speak for the goodwill and reputation of the products and services and, in turn, the company. To expand the market for certain trademarked goods or services into new geographical territories, the trademark holder can either directly be involved or the holder can license the trademark to a third party who may have resources and expertise to achieve the expansion. For example, Calvin Klein clothes are neither designed nor manufactured by the designer. Warnaco Group, Inc. controls most of the tasks, and Calvin Klein, Inc. is a wholly owned subsidiary of Phillips-Van Heusen Corporation.

Trademark law is significantly different from other types of intellectual property laws. A trademark holder does not own a trademark outright as the patentee or a copyright holder does with respect to patents and copyrights. A trademark holder has the right to enjoin others from using its trademark when it is likely to cause consumer confusion. That is how trademark law protects the investment, the goodwill, and reputation that the trademark holder has invested in the trademark through years of use and marketing.

Consequently, trademark licensing is unique. A trademark holder can license a trademark for use in connection with goods and services in different fields of use and geographical markets, as long as the trademark is in use and under quality control by the trademark holder. There is no definite terminable life of a trademark that is in use. By contrast, a patentee cannot license its patent beyond the legal term of protection provided under the patent statute. Trademark licenses can last as long as the parties to the license agreement wish and as long as there is no abandonment of the trademark.

B. Assignment Versus License of Trademarks

1. Assignment

A trademark may be sold together with or without the ongoing business concern, as long as the transfer of trademark includes the associated goodwill. If the goodwill was not assigned together with the trademark, the trademark assignment is "in gross," which passes no rights to the assignee. It is not uncommon for the trademark owner, upon assignment, to receive a license-back to use the trademark on certain products from the assignee. Such assignment-and-license-back schemes are permissible and explored later in this chapter.

In an assignment, the trademark holder assigns all of its title, rights, and interest in the trademark, together with the goodwill, to the assignee. In some cases, however, the owner of a trademark may choose to transfer certain rights, but not all of the rights in the trademark. This is an assignment of partial rights, but not an assignment of the entire ownership in the trademark. Under tax law, such a transfer may not be deemed as a *sale* of the trademark. Whether a transfer is deemed a sale or a license is important to the seller and purchaser of the trademark with respect to the taxation of the transaction and in bankruptcy proceedings. *See* Chapters 14 and 15.

2. License

The holder of trademarks can exploit the commercial power of the trademarks by licensing them to others for use in connection with new products or in new markets. Trademark licensing enables trademark holders to capitalize on the comparative advantage of their partners, such as better knowledge of local markets, expertise in product design, manufacturing capacity, or access to a superior distribution network. In other words, trademark licensing enhances the trademark holder's reach and scale. To get a better grasp of trademark licensing in the real world consider the following transactions:

- National Football League Properties, Inc. (NFLP) is a California corporation jointly owned by the member clubs of the National Football League (member clubs) founded in 1963. Each member club grants an exclusive license to NFLP to act as licensing representative for the trademarks of the member clubs. NFLP then authorizes manufacturers to produce merchandise bearing the NFL member club's marks. An NFLP licensee is required to pay to NFLP a royalty fee of a certain percentage of all net sales of licensed products.

- Hershey Chocolate (predecessor of Hershey Foods) first began manufacturing and selling various food and milk products throughout the United States as HERSHEY'S in 1894. Hershey Creamery, founded by the Hershey brothers, began manufacturing and selling ice cream products, using the same HERSHEY'S trademark in 1910. Hershey Creamery filed suit in the Southern District of New York against Hershey Chocolate for trademark infringement in 1966 based on the fact that Hershey Creamery had learned that Hershey Chocolate was planning to make a foray into the ice cream business by licensing Consolidated Foods Corporation to use the HERSHEY'S trademark on ice cream bars coated with HERSHEY'S chocolate. The parties later settled the law suit. As part of the settlement agreement, Hershey Creamery agreed to drop its claims against Hershey Chocolate and to allow Hershey Chocolate to license its HERSHEY'S trademark for use in connection with ice cream bars coated with HERSHEY'S chocolate, subject to various restrictions on the manner in which the mark is displayed on the packaging.

- McDonald's Corporation is a Delaware corporation that franchises and operates fast food restaurants. McDonald's expands its business through the franchise system. By contract, all of the McDonald's franchisees must operate their restaurants in compliance with the "McDonald's System," a series of business practices and procedures employed, in part, to ensure uniform restaurant and food quality at all McDonald's locations. The franchise documents generally consist of a franchise letter agreement, a license agreement, and an operator's lease to the real property upon which the restaurant is located. The License Agreement allows the franchisee to adopt and use the McDonald's trade names, trademarks, and service marks on the condition that they comply with the obligations specified in the Agreement. The Materials section of this chapter contains an excerpt from a franchise agreement.[1]

- Hugo Boss USA is a group of U.S.-based, wholly owned subsidiaries of Hugo Boss Germany, which is a designer and manufacturer of expensive men's clothing and accessories. HB Germany exclusively licenses trademarks to Hugo Boss USA for use on Hugo Boss products. The Boss Manufacturing Company (BMC) is a manufacturer of industrial and outdoor clothing and accessories such as shoes, boots, garden gloves, and mittens. Both BMC and Hugo Boss sell items bearing the term "BOSS." BMC became concerned about possible infringement by Hugo Boss on certain products. As a result, in 1990, BMC and Hugo Boss entered into a Concurrent Use Agreement wherein Hugo Boss agreed not to sell or license others to sell gloves, mittens, or boots with a mark that incorporates the word "BOSS." BMC and Hugo Boss also agreed to cross-license

---

1. Franchise agreements are also regulated by both state and federal law. *See* Federal Trade Commission's FTC Franchise Rule, 16 C.F.R. 436; *see, e.g.,* RCW 19.100 *et seq.* and WAC 460-80 (Washington Franchise Investment Protection Act).

their trademarks for certain products at designated price points representing separate consumer markets. The purpose of the Agreement along with the cross-license was to establish guidelines that would prevent consumer confusion and would keep the parties from infringing each others' trademark rights.

- The powerhouse toy store chain Toys "R" Us owns numerous trademarks in the United States. Toys "R" Us formed the Geoffrey Company, a wholly owned subsidiary in Delaware, to hold all of its trademarks. "Geoffrey" is the name of the Toys "R" Us mascot, Geoffrey the Giraffe. Toys "R" Us assigned all of its trademarks to Geoffrey in exchange for 100 percent of Geoffrey's stock. Geoffrey then licenses the trademarks back to Toys "R" Us in exchange for periodic royalty payments. Toys "R" Us deducts the royalty payments as expenses. Geoffrey does not pay state income on the royalty income because Delaware does not tax passive holding companies.

3. Assignment and License-Back

In some transactions, on the one hand, the assignor wants to continue using the assigned trademark in connection with certain areas of the assignor's business, after the execution of the trademark assignment to the assignee. On the other hand, the assignee wants to be the sole owner of the assignor's right, title, and interest in and to the assigned trademarks. To fulfill the parties' wishes, the assignor and assignee would enter into an assignment and license-back arrangement where the assignor assigns the trademarks to the assignee and the assignee licenses the trademarks back to the assignor. Below are provisions from an assignment and license-back agreement.

A. Assignor owns the trademark "E-MACHINES" with respect to fully and partially completed or assembled computer equipment (including CPUs and monitors) and computer related products and parts (including spare parts) if any thereof, the marketing, advertising, selling, distribution, maintenance and servicing thereof, and all business and activities incidental thereto, together with United States Trademark Registration No. 1,758,158 (collectively, the "Trademark") and has the right to assign all right, title and interest in and to the Trademark;

B. Assignee desires to obtain all of Assignor's right, title and interest in and to the Trademark; and

NOW, THEREFORE, in consideration of the mutual covenants and agreements hereinafter contained and other good and valuable consideration, the receipt and adequacy of which are hereby acknowledged by each party hereto, it is understood and agreed between the parties herein as follows:

1. Promise to Assign. Assignor hereby agrees to assign to Assignee all right, title and interest worldwide in the Trademark by executing the form of assignment attached to this Agreement as Exhibit A (the "Assignment").

> 2. License-Back for Assignor. In partial consideration of the assignment of the Trademark, Assignee and Assignor agree to grant, after the Assignment, a perpetual exclusive royalty-free license in favor of Assignor, without warranties, to use the mark in the Republic of Korea, subject to advice of Korean counsel with respect to the timing and the form of a license, taking into account availability of the Trademark in the Republic of Korea and the need for a trademark application to be perfected for the license to be effective.

C. Exclusive and Non-Exclusive Trademark License

An exclusive trademark license often means that the licensor grants the licensee the right to use the trademark in connection with certain goods or services in a particular region and that no other licensees received similar rights to use the trademark on similar products in the same territory. Exclusive licensees of trademarked goods may have "the right by agreement with the owner of the trademark to exclude even him from selling in their territory." Quabaug Rubber Co. v. Fabiano Shoe Co., 567 F.2d 154, 159 (1st Cir. 1977).

Below is a sample provision of an exclusive trademark license.

SECTION 4

Trademark Rights

4.1 Trademark License; Use of Name. Assignor hereby grants Assignee an exclusive license to use the mark "Knowlton" solely on or with products for use in the Field, and Assignee agrees that all such products will use the "Knowlton" mark, except as may otherwise be required by law. Assignee shall secure trademark protection for the "Knowlton" marks related to the product arising from the Intellectual Property, such protection to include applying for registrations with the United States Patent and Trademark Office and, where appropriate, foreign trademark offices. Such applications shall be prosecuted at Assignee's expense and owned by Assignor. . . .

In the above exclusive trademark license provision, the owner of the trademark only grants the exclusive license to use the trademark within a particular field of use, as the term "Field" is defined in the Definition provision that often appears toward the beginning of a trademark license agreement. The owner of the trademark also imposes a number of requirements on the licensee. The licensee bears the financial responsibility to register the trademark domestically and internationally.

Non-exclusive license means that the licensee is not the only party using the trademark in connection with the goods or services or within a particular geography. By agreement the licensor sets forth the terms describing the parameters of the grant.

A non-exclusive license is generally non-transferable by the licensee to a third party without the express consent of the trademark holder.

Below are provisions in a non-exclusive trademark license agreement where Apple grants a non-exclusive, nontransferable, royalty-free license to use Apple's logo design (the "Works with iPhoto" graphic design). In this type of trademark license agreement, the licensee's use of the trademark will generate goodwill and the goodwill belongs to the licensor, the owner of the trademark. The owner of the trademark must exercise certain quality control of the licensee's use of the trademark in order to avoid trademark abandonment, as discussed below in section D, Quality Control.

> Upon acceptance of this Agreement, Apple grants Licensee a non-exclusive, nontransferable, royalty-free license to use Apple's "Works with iPhoto" graphic design ("Logo") on and in connection with the sale, promotion and advertising of Licensee products identified above ("Products"), subject to the following conditions. . . .
>
> . . . Nothing in this Agreement shall give Licensee any right, title or interest in and to the Logo. Licensee acknowledges and agrees that Apple is the exclusive owner of rights, title or interest in and to the Logo and the associated goodwill therein. Licensee's use of the Logo shall exclusively inure for the benefit of Apple. . . .

D. Quality Control

One of the prominent features in trademark licensing arrangements is quality control of the licensed trademark. Quality control parameters are necessary for the maintenance of trademark rights and protection. An unsupervised license, called a "naked license," can amount to an abandonment of the trademark and result in the loss of trademark rights. These parameters include the licensor's affirmative duty to take reasonable measures to detect and prevent misleading uses of its trademark by licensees. Otherwise, the licensor risks cancellation of its federal registration and abandonment of its trademark. The rationale for such a duty is that the consumer should be assured that the quality and nature of the licensed goods or services are the same as they were before the trademark was licensed.

Whether the licensor exercises adequate quality control is a case-by-case inquiry and what degree of control is necessary depends on the factual circumstances. Some courts require strict oversight by licensors of the licensed marks. Dawn Donut Co. v. Hart's Food Stores, Inc., 267 F.2d 358, 368 (2d Cir. 1959) (requiring actual control by the licensor, not just the right to control stated in the license agreement). Other courts, however, adopt the view taken by the *Restatement (Third) of Unfair Competition*, which advocates a flexible approach, allowing licensors to rely on the reputation and expertise of the licensees. *See* RESTATEMENT (THIRD) OF UNFAIR COMPETITION §33, cmt. c (1995).

The reason for the trend toward a flexible approach is the practical reality that a licensing arrangement may entail some loss of control over product quality. But as long as the licensor maintains reasonable control over product quality, consumers ultimately do rely upon the licensor's quality control. Consumers generally are oblivious to the corporate structure relating to trademark transfers or licenses. Therefore, as long as the licensor's quality standard has not significantly changed through the licensing arrangements, the licensor's rights in the trademark remain intact and no abandonment occurs. *See* TMT N. Am., Inc. v. Magic Touch GmbH, 124 F.3d 876, 885-86 (7th Cir. 1997) (accepting reasonable amount of control as sufficient). *Compare* Freecycle Sunnyvale v. Freecycle Network, 626 F.3d 509 (9th Cir. 2010) (holding licensor failed to establish that it had exercised actual quality control of trademark usage by member licensees and licensor failed to show that it had a close working relationship with its members wherein the licensor could rely on the members to exercise quality control measures).

Below is a sample provision from the "Knowlton" exclusive trademark license, but with quality control added in italics for emphasis.

SECTION 4

Trademark Rights

4.1 Trademark License; Use of Name. Assignor hereby grants Assignee an exclusive license to use the mark "Knowlton" solely on or with products for use in the Field, and Assignee agrees that all such products will use the "Knowlton" mark, except as may otherwise be required by law. Assignee shall secure trademark protection for the "Knowlton" marks related to the product arising from the Intellectual Property, such protection to include applying for registrations with the United States Patent and Trademark Office and, where appropriate, foreign trademark offices. Such applications shall be prosecuted at Assignee's expense and owned by Assignor. *Assignor shall have the right to review and approve any such use of the mark "Knowlton" prior to Assignee's use thereof, which approval shall not be unreasonably withheld. If Assignor and Assignee do not agree upon use of mark, then Assignor has the right to withdraw the use of the mark.*

E. Litigation Issues in Trademark Licensing

1. Standing and Jurisdiction

When the National Football League Properties Inc. (NFLP) enters into a license agreement with a manufacturer to produce merchandises such as jerseys, sportswear, caps, and accessories bearing the trademark of a particular National Football League team, NFLP (like any good licensor) would anticipate the creation and distribution of counterfeits and other infringing products, and parties to a trademark license should decide how those acts are to be resolved and by whom during the term of the license agreement. The NFLP would want to reserve the right to decide to initiate any infringement action against a third party. If the NFLP allows too many third-party infringing activities to occur, it runs the risk of weakening the strength of its mark and trademark abandonment. The licensee, on the other hand, would like to know whether it is obligated to serve as a co-plaintiff with the licensor in an infringement action against a third party, whether it has any input into the decision of initiating the litigation, and who would bear the litigation cost.

To specify the obligations of each party in litigation against a third party, trademark license agreements often include provisions relating to whether the licensee can unilaterally bring an infringement action against a third party. Some license agreements permit the licensee to initiate such an action if the licensee obtains express approval from the licensor. The provision may state that the licensor may in its discretion decide to join the suit. Some license agreements, however, may fail to include such a provision.

Depending on the terms of the license agreement, courts will permit or deny exclusive licensees the right to bring a trademark infringement action. *See* ICEE Distributors, Inc. v. J&J Snack Foods Corp., 325 F.3d 586 (5th Cir. 2003) (holding that the exclusive licensee did not have standing to bring a trademark dilution suit, although the licensee had the exclusive right to use the trademarks in its territory for the life of the trademarks, the right to sue for trademark infringement in its territory, and an unconditional right to transfer or assign its rights in the trademarks to another). *Compare* Bliss Clearing Niagara, Inc. v. Midwest Brake Bond Co., 339 F. Supp. 2d 944 (W.D. Mich. 2004) (holding that the clutch manufacturer had standing, as licensee of the trademark, to sue a competitor for alleged trademark infringement and dilution, given that the manufacturer had the exclusive and perpetual right and license to use the mark throughout the world and the right to pursue actions for infringement, and that the license lacked many features indicative of a license agreement, such as quality control provisions and geographical limitations, such that manufacturer had substantial rights in the mark, including the right to enforce its rights against third parties).

Parties to a trademark license agreement sometimes resort to litigation to resolve disputes between themselves. The disputes may cover topics such as failure to make royalty payments, trademark usage beyond the scope of the license grant, and licensor's breach by allowing another licensee to use the trademark in the exclusive licensed territory. *See* Eureka Water Co. v. Nestle Waters North America, Inc., 690 F.3d 1139 (10th Cir. 2012), which is included in the Materials section of this chapter.

Whether an action between the parties to a trademark license agreement is about breach of contract, trademark infringement, or both breach of contract and trademark infringement may dictate the proper forum to adjudicate the dispute. If it is purely a breach of contract case, the dispute will be in state court; if it involves primarily trademark infringement, the action is in federal court. The mere existence of a trademark in a case does not establish federal jurisdiction. If the action involves both breach of contract and trademark infringement, federal courts will have subject matter jurisdiction and supplemental jurisdiction to hear the entire action. Federal courts generally have dismissed actions that fundamentally assert contract claims and only incidentally involve trademarks. *See* International Legwear Group, Inc. v.

Americal Corp., 2010 WL 3603784 (E.D.N.C. Sept. 8, 2010) (finding that the licensee has no objective reason to remove the trademark license contract dispute action from state court to federal court and awarding reasonable costs and attorneys' fees incurred by the licensor as a result of the licensee's removal action).

2. Licensee Estoppel Defense

Unlike patent law, the trademark licensee is estopped from contesting the validity of its licensor's trademark based on facts that arose during the term of the license. By virtue of the license agreement, the licensee has recognized the licensor's trademark rights. Therefore, the licensee may be estopped from raising the abandonment defense in a case where the licensee asserted that the licensor did nothing to insure the quality of the trademark during the term of the license. *See, e.g.*, Creative Gifts, Inc. v. UFO, 235 F.3d 540 (10th Cir. 2000) (holding that the licensees were estopped from asserting that the trademark holders' failure to police or control their use of the trademark during the term of the license amounted to granting a naked license); Seven-Up Bottling Co. v. The Seven-Up Co., 561 F.2d 1275 (8th Cir. 1977) (affirming the district court's finding that the bottling company's admission as a licensee prevented it from making claims of invalid trademarks against the licensor). *Compare* Fair Isaac Corp. v. Experian Information Solutions, Inc., 650 F.3d 1139 (8th Cir. 2011) (allowing the non-licensee party whom the licensor failed to establish as the alter ego of the licensee to assert trademark invalidity against the licensor).

The licensee cannot use the licensor's action (or inaction) during the term of the license to prove abandonment. Only once the license is terminated can the licensee use the licensor's action subsequent to termination to prove abandonment. That means the former licensee is still estopped from challenging the validity of its former licensor's trademark based upon facts which arose during the course of the license. *See, e.g.*, John C. Flood of Va., Inc. v. John C. Flood, Inc., 642 F.3d 1105 (D.C. Cir. 2011); Henry v. Pro 10 Originals, LLC, 698 F. Supp. 2d 1279 (D. Wyo. 2010); Westco Group, Inc. v. K.B. & Associates, 128 F. Supp. 2d 1082 (N.D. Ohio 2001).

F. International Issues in Trademark Licensing

A foreign trademark holder and manufacturer of certain trademarked goods may want to export its goods to the U.S. market. Generally, the manufacturer will enter into a distribution agreement with a U.S. company in which the manufacturer grants the distributor the exclusive right to use the trademark in connection with the distribution and sales of the goods within the U.S. territory. For trademark registration purposes, the distributor will act as the authorized agent of the manufacturer. In international trademark licensing agreements, the parties often include provisions relating to choice of law and forum for solving disputes. *See* ASA v. Pictometry International Corp., 2010 WL 4922636 (W.D.N.Y. Dec. 2, 2010) (ICC arbitration clause included).

The availability of cheap labor overseas allows U.S. trademark holders or brand owners to engage foreign companies to manufacture various products for distribution worldwide. Once the products are manufactured they will be distributed in accordance with the trademark owner's plan. The trademark owner may enter into numerous distribution and license agreements with various distributors. Some products will be distributed in developing countries, others in the United States, Japan, or Europe. Depending on the trademark law in the country of the licensee, the U.S. trademark holder may encounter issues relating to registration of the licensed trademark, recordation of the license agreement with appropriate governmental agency, and distribution of "gray market" goods.

A brief walk along Canal Street in Manhattan will lead tourists to a street of both counterfeits and "gray market" goods. Most of the luxury goods with global brand names such as Gucci, Chanel, Calvin Klein, Nike, Puma, and the like are available at very low prices. Electronic products with recognized names are also available for purchase. The lure of inexpensive prices invites the tourists back to Canal Street year after year. The brand owners believe that both counterfeits and "gray market" goods destroy the prestige of the goodwill in the trademarks and cause post-sale consumer confusion.

Counterfeit trademarked goods are those bearing, without authorization, a trademark which is identical to a registered trademark for the same goods. The distributor or seller of counterfeits has no license agreement with the owner of the trademark. The counterfeits are made and sold without the trademark owner's permission. Counterfeits are often of inferior quality.

Unlike counterfeits, gray market goods are trademarked goods authorized by the trademark owner for sale in a particular country, but the goods are then diverted for sale to another country without the authorization of the trademark owner in the receiving country. Gray market goods are also referred to as parallel import goods. Here is an illustration. Nike enters into an agreement with a company in China to make a certain type of Nike walking shoes. The shoes are only to be distributed and sold in China and Southeast Asian countries. The shoes are then legitimately purchased in China and subsequently shipped to the United States for retail sales. The U.S. importer of the shoes has no license agreement with Nike to sell the shoes in the United States.

Gray market goods reveal several economic interests and concerns. For example, in the Nike-shoes hypothetical, because the shoes cost less to purchase in China, the U.S. importer will be able to sell the shoes at a lower price than those Nike shoes sold in U.S. stores with Nike's consent. From the consumer's perspective, some consumers are happy to purchase gray market goods because they are not counterfeits; they are, after all, shoes authorized by the trademark owner, Nike. From Nike's perspective, as a global brand owner, it wants to control the quality of its trademarked goods within different territories. Nike wants certain types of shoes of a certain quality to be sold within a designated territory. Nike does not want to see the same shoes finding their way to a different territory competing with Nike shoes of a different quality level or different price range. By controlling the territory for distribution and sale of trademarked products, Nike is in control of the price differentials and collects optimal pecuniary returns.

U.S. trademark owners often rely on the "genuine" goods doctrine under the Lanham Act for recourse against the importation of gray marked goods. *See* Societe Des Produits Nestle, S.A. v. Casa Helvetia, Inc., 982 F.2d 633, 635 (1st Cir. 1992), which is included in the Materials section of this chapter. *See also* Bose Corp. v. Ejaz, 732 F.3d 17 (1st Cir. 2013).

II. MATERIALS

The Materials below provide you an opportunity to learn about trademark licensing law from primary sources comprised of a trademark assignment, a trademark license agreement, a franchise agreement, and several cases. The initial documents provide you an opportunity to see the practice side of trademark licensing. The trademark license agreement has many provisions, some of which are necessary to prevent an "assignment in gross" such as the grant and the quality control provisions. The juxtaposition of these documents provides an opportunity to compare and contrast the trademark license agreement and the trademark assignment. The franchise agreement allows you to see trademark use in that context.

The Materials also include seven cases on various aspects of trademark licensing law. These cases illustrate the intersection between contract law and trademark law in a trademark licensing context. In the first case, Barcamerica International USA Trust v. Tyfield Importers, Inc., 289 F.3d 589 (9th Cir. 2002), the licensing of the trademark between the licensor and its licensees became an issue as the third-party defendant relied on the licensor's conduct as a defense. Specifically, the Court must decide whether the owner of a trademark had abandoned its trademark through its lack of quality control of the trademark licensed for use in connection with wine products.

The second case, NAACP v. NAACP Legal Defense and Education Fund, Inc., 753 F.2d 131 (D.C. Cir. 1985), is an illustration of a trademark license arrangement between two non-profit entities and explains how the license agreement was not a revocable contract. The case also highlights the laches defense raised by the defendant in hopes that it would have the right to continue to use the trademark outright.

The next case, Eureka Water Co. v. Nestle Waters North America, Inc., 690 F.3d 1139 (10th Cir. 2012), offers some valuable lessons on contract drafting. The case centers on whether the agreement between the contracting parties was a trademark license governed by contract law or a sale of goods governed by the Uniform Commercial Code. Some trademark owners only sell their products through authorized distributors. The trademark owners offer warranty and other services in connection with the purchase of the trademarked products from authorized distributors. In Beltronics USA, Inc. v. Midwest Inventory Distribution, LLC, 562 F.3d 1067 (10th Cir. 2009), the Court addressed the "first sale" doctrine defense raised by the reseller of the trademarked products while not offering warranty and other services for the products. Licensing relationship may go sour for various reasons. Benihana, Inc. v. Benihana of Tokyo, 784 F.3d 887 (2nd Cir. 2015) illustrates a contentious contract dispute over the scope of the trademark license and arbitration provision.

Known brands transcend borders. Many trademark license agreements today are concerned with global trademark usage in connection with products and services. The next two cases address problems arising in connection with international licensing of trademarks. TMT North America, Inc. v. Magic Touch GmbH, 124 F.3d 876 (7th

Cir. 1997), is about a rather common problem related to ownership of trademarks licensed in connection with an international distribution of trademarked goods. Societe Des Produits Nestle, S.A. v. Casa Helvetia, Inc., 982 F.2d 633, 635 (1st Cir. 1992), provides a comprehensive view of the international trademark licensing arrangements of Perugina chocolates and legal protection to the trademark owner facing the influx of "gray market" Perugina chocolates.

TRADEMARK ASSIGNMENT AGREEMENT

This TRADEMARK ASSIGNMENT AGREEMENT, dated as of _____, is by and between [Seller], a _____ ("Assignor"), and [Purchaser], a Delaware corporation ("Assignee").

Recitals

WHEREAS, pursuant to the Asset Transfer and Acquisition Agreement, dated as of _____, by and among _____, concurrently herewith, are selling, and Assignee is acquiring, the Business (such term and, except as otherwise defined herein, all other capitalized terms used herein, shall have the meanings set forth in the Acquisition Agreement) and certain related assets of Assignor as described in the Acquisition Agreement, including, without limitation, certain intellectual property of Assignor, upon the terms and subject to the conditions set forth in the Acquisition Agreement; and

WHEREAS, in consideration of the transactions contemplated by the Agreement, Assignor desires to sell, assign and transfer to Assignee all of Assignor's right, title and interest in and to the trademarks, service marks and trade names set forth on Schedule A attached hereto (collectively, the "Marks") and all goodwill symbolized by and associated with the business conducted under such Marks, which business is ongoing and existing, and Assignee desires to purchase, and accept the assignment and transfer of, all of Assignor's right, title and interest in and to such Marks and all goodwill symbolized by and associated with the business conducted under such Marks.

NOW, THEREFORE, by this document, and for good and valuable consideration, the receipt and sufficiency of which is hereby acknowledged, Assignor does hereby sell, assign and transfer to Assignee, and its successors and assigns, its entire right, title and interest in and to: (i) the Marks; (ii) any and all goodwill symbolized by and associated with the business conducted under the Marks; (iii) all registrations and applications (including intent-to-use applications) for the Marks together with the portion of the business of Assignor to which these Marks apply, which business is ongoing and existing; (iv) all income, royalties, damages and payments in respect of the Marks which become due or payable following the Closing; and (v) all causes of action (either in law or in equity) and the right to sue, counterclaim and recover for infringement of the Marks which occurs following the Closing; provided, however, that Assignor shall retain (a) all right, title and interest in and to any income, royalties, damages and payments in respect of the Marks due or payable prior to the Closing and (b) all causes of action (either in law or equity) and the right to sue, counterclaim and recover for any infringement of the Marks which occurred prior to the Closing. Assignor hereby agrees to execute all papers and to perform such other proper acts as Assignee or its successors or assigns may deem reasonably necessary to secure for Assignee or to its successors or assigns, or to evidence the rights, hereby transferred. WHEREFORE, Assignor has caused this Trademark Assignment Agreement to be duly executed below, on the date indicated.

[Date, Signature Block for the Seller/Assignor and Purchaser/Assignee, and Notary Public page are included].

Date: _____   [SELLER]

                                      By:_____

                                      Name:

                                      Title:

Agreed and Acknowledged:

[PURCHASER]

By: _____

Name:

Title:

* * *

TRADEMARK LICENSE AGREEMENT

THIS TRADEMARK LICENSE AGREEMENT ("Agreement") is made and entered into effective as of August 1, 2007 (the "Effective Date") by and between _____ Inc., a Delaware corporation ("Licensor"), and _____ Corporation, a Delaware corporation ("Licensee").

WHEREAS, Licensor has adopted, has registered with the United States Patent and Trademark Office and the trademark offices of various foreign countries, and is using the trademark _____ ("Trademark") throughout the world in connection with computer graphics hardware, software, and related services; and

WHEREAS, Licensee desires to use the Trademark, in both block letter and stylized form, in connection with Licensee's "Interactive Video" display (the "Video") to promote the fact that certain of Licensor's applications are compatible with Licensor's _____ (TM) Processor throughout the world ("Territory"); and

WHEREAS, Licensor, subject to the terms and conditions set forth in this Agreement, is willing to permit Licensee to use the Trademark in connection with the Video for the mutual benefit of Licensor and Licensee.

NOW, THEREFORE, in consideration of the above premises, the mutual covenants set forth below, and other good and valuable consideration, the receipt and sufficiency of which are hereby acknowledged, the parties hereto agree as follows:

Section 1

License

1.1 Scope of License. Subject to the terms and conditions set forth in this Agreement, Licensor grants to Licensee a non-exclusive, non-transferable, royalty-free license to use the Trademark in connection with the Video throughout the Territory. Licensee shall make no other use of the Trademark.

1.2 Non-Assignment. Licensee acknowledges and agrees that the rights granted to Licensee by and obtained by Licensee as a result of or in connection with this Agreement are license rights only, and nothing contained in this Agreement constitutes or shall be construed to be an assignment of any or all of Licensor's rights in the Trademark.

Section 2

Licensor's Control

In order to protect and preserve Licensor's rights in the Trademark, Licensee understands, acknowledges, and agrees that (i) prior to the first date of Licensee's use of the Trademark in connection with the Video, Licensee shall obtain Licensor's approval of all aspects of such use; and (ii) once Licensee's use of the Trademark in connection with the Video is initially approved by Licensor, any subsequent alteration, modification, or change in such use must be reviewed and approved by Licensor prior to implementation of such alteration, modification, or change.

Section 3

Use of the Trademark

3.1 Trademark Format. Licensor retains the right to specify, from time to time, the format in which Licensee shall use and display the Trademark, and Licensee shall only use or display the Trademark in a format approved by Licensor.

3.2 Proper Notice and Acknowledgment. Every use of the Trademark by Licensee shall incorporate in an appropriate manner an "R" enclosed by a circle or the phrase "Reg. U.S. Pat. & Tm Off."

3.3 Impairment of Licensor's Rights. Licensee shall not at any time, whether during or after the term of this Agreement, do or cause to be done any act or thing challenging, contesting, impairing, invalidating, or tending to impair or invalidate any of Licensor's rights in the Trademark or any registrations derived from such rights.

3.4 Licensor's Rights and Remedies. Licensee acknowledges and agrees that Licensor has, shall retain, and may exercise, both during the term of this Agreement and thereafter, all rights and remedies available to Licensor, whether derived from this Agreement, from statute, or otherwise, as a result of or in connection with Licensee's breach of this Agreement, misuse of the Trademark, or any other use of the Trademark by Licensee which is not expressly permitted by this Agreement.

Section 4

Term and Termination

4.1 Term. The term of this Agreement shall be for two (2) years from the Effective Date; provided, however, that either party may terminate this Agreement, with or without cause, by delivering written notice of termination to the other party, and, unless a later date is specified in such notice, termination shall be effective sixty (60) days after the date such notice is given.

4.2 Termination for Cause. Notwithstanding the provisions of Section 4.1 of this Agreement, this Agreement and all rights granted hereby, including but not limited to Licensee's right to use the Trademark, shall automatically terminate without notice from Licensor if (i) Licensee attempts to assign, sublicense, transfer or otherwise convey, without first obtaining Licensor's written consent, any of the rights granted to Licensee by or in connection with this Agreement; (ii) Licensee fails to obtain Licensor's approval of Licensee's use of the Trademark in accordance with Section 2 of this Agreement; (iii) Licensee uses the Trademark in a manner in violation of, or otherwise inconsistent with, the restrictions imposed by or in connection with Section 3 of this Agreement; or (iv) Licensee uses the Trademark in a manner not expressly permitted by this Agreement.

4.3 Effect of Termination. All rights granted by this Agreement, including, without limitation, Licensee's right to use the Trademark, shall expire upon termination of this Agreement, and upon termination Licensee shall immediately cease and desist from all further use of the Trademark.

Section 5

Miscellaneous

5.1 Assignment. Licensee shall not assign, sublicense, transfer, or otherwise convey Licensee's rights or obligations under this Agreement without Licensor's prior written consent. Licensee shall indemnify and hold harmless Licensor against all liability, costs, and expenses, including but not limited to a reasonable attorneys' fee, arising out of or in connection with claims relating to an attempted assignment, sublicense, transfer, or other conveyance of Licensee's rights and obligations.

5.2 Applicable Law. This Agreement shall be interpreted, construed, and enforced pursuant to, and in accordance with, the laws of the State of Alabama.

5.3 Entire Agreement. This Agreement supersedes all previous agreements, understandings, and arrangements between the parties, whether oral or written, and constitutes the entire agreement between the parties.

5.4 Amendments. This Agreement may not be modified, amended, altered, or supplemented except by an agreement in writing executed by the parties hereto.

5.5 Waivers. The waiver by either party of a breach or other violation of any provision of this Agreement shall not operate as, or be construed to be, a waiver of any subsequent breach of the same or other provision of this Agreement.

5.6 Notice. Unless otherwise provided herein, any notice, demand, or communication required, permitted, or desired to be given hereunder shall be in writing and shall be delivered by hand, by telex or telecopy, by facsimile, or by registered or prepaid certified mail through the United States postal service, return receipt requested, addressed as follows:

Attn: General Counsel   Attn: Legal Department
_____ Inc.   _____ Corporation
_____   _____
_____   _____

or to such other address, and to the attention of such other persons or officers as either party may designate by written notice. Any notice so addressed and mailed shall be deemed duly given three (3) days after deposit in the United States mail, and if delivered by hand, shall be deemed given when delivered, and if telecopied, telexed, or sent by facsimile, shall be deemed given on the first business day immediately following transmittal.

5.7 Counterparts. This Agreement may be executed in several counterparts, each of which shall be an original, but all of which together shall constitute one and the same Agreement.

5.8 Articles and Other Headings. The articles and other headings contained in this Agreement are for reference purposes only, and shall not affect in any way the meaning or interpretation of the terms of this Agreement.

IN WITNESS WHEREOF, the parties hereto have caused this Agreement to be executed by their duly authorized representatives as of the date first set forth above.

_____ INC.   _____ CORPORATION

*   *   *

SEATTLE'S BEST COFFEE FRANCHISE AGREEMENT

THIS AGREEMENT (the "Agreement") is made this _____ day of _____,
200_____, by and between CINNABON, INC., SUCCESSOR IN INTEREST TO
SEATTLE'S BEST COFFEE, LLC, a Washington corporation, with offices at Six Concourse
Parkway, Suite 1700, Atlanta, Georgia, 30328-5352 U.S.A. ("Franchisor" or
"SEATTLE'S BEST COFFEE") and _____, [jointly and severally where more than
one], ("Franchisee").

WITNESSETH:

WHEREAS, Seattle's Best Coffee, LLC has developed and owns a unique and
distinctive system for the development, establishment and operation of retail Cafes
("SBC Cafes") and Kiosks ("SBC Kiosks") (collectively, "SBC RETAIL UNITS")
specializing in the preparation and sale of specialty coffee beverages, proprietary
coffee products and other menu items developed and owned by Franchisor (the
"Seattle's Best Coffee System", "SBC System" or "System");

WHEREAS, the distinguishing characteristics of the SBC SYSTEM include, without
limitation, the name "SEATTLE'S BEST COFFEE"; distinctive interior and exterior design
and layouts, decor, color schemes, and furnishings; confidential food formulae and
recipes used in the preparation of food products, formulas and specifications for
preparing specialty coffee drinks and other coffee and non-coffee-based products;
specialized menus; standards and specifications for equipment, equipment layouts,
products, operating procedures, and management programs, all of which may be
changed, improved, and further developed by Franchisor from time to time;

WHEREAS, Franchisor identifies the SBC SYSTEM by means of certain trade names,
service marks, trademarks, logos, emblems, and other indicia of origin, including, but
not limited to, the marks "SEATTLE'S BEST COFFEE", "SBC" and such other trade
names, service marks, trademarks and trade dress as are now, or may hereafter, be
designated by Franchisor for use in connection with the SBC SYSTEM (collectively
referred to as the "Proprietary Marks");

WHEREAS, pursuant to a Master License Agreement and First Amendment thereto,
both dated July 13, 2003, by and between Cinnabon Inc., SBC and Seattle Coffee
Company, SBC granted a license to CBI for the use of the SBC System and proprietary
marks in performing its obligations under this Agreement;

WHEREAS, Franchisor continues to develop, use, and control the use of such
Proprietary Marks in order to identify for the public the source of services and products
marketed thereunder in the SBC SYSTEM and to represent the System's high
standards of quality, appearance, and service;

WHEREAS, Franchisee wishes to be assisted, trained, and licensed by Franchisor as an SBC franchisee and licensed to use, in connection therewith, the SBC SYSTEM and to continuously operate one SBC Retail Unit at the location specified in Section 1.01 herein (the "Franchised Location");

WHEREAS, Franchisee understands the importance of the SBC SYSTEM and SEATTLE'S BEST COFFEE'S high and uniform standards of quality, cleanliness, appearance, and service, and the necessity of opening and operating SBC RETAIL UNITS in conformity with the SBC SYSTEM;

NOW, THEREFORE, the parties hereto agree as follows:

I. Appointment

1.01. Franchisor grants to Franchisee a franchise to open and operate an SBC Unit (the "Franchised Unit," or "Franchised Business") at one location only, such location to be described as:

STORE NUMBER:

FRANCHISED
LOCATION:

UNIT FORMAT: [ ] SBC Cafe   [ ] SBC Kiosk
                     [ ] Traditional Venue   [ ] Captive Venue

upon the terms and conditions herein contained and subject to the terms and conditions contained in the development agreement between Franchisor and Franchisee, dated ___, (the "Development Agreement"), which is incorporated herein by reference; and a license to use in connection therewith Franchisor's Proprietary Marks and the SBC SYSTEM. Franchisee may not operate the Franchised Unit at any site other than the Franchised Location.

1.02. Except as otherwise set forth herein, (a) the franchise granted to Franchisee under this Agreement is non-exclusive, and grants to Franchisee the rights to establish and operate the Franchised Unit at only the specific location set forth hereinabove, (b) no exclusive, protected or other territorial rights in the contiguous area or market of such Franchised Unit or otherwise is hereby granted or to be inferred and (c) Franchisor and/or its affiliates have the right to operate and grant as many other franchises for the operation of SBC Retail Units, anywhere in the world, as they shall, in their sole discretion, elect. In addition to the foregoing, Franchisor may sell SBC brand coffee and related coffee products anywhere, including, but not limited to, sales on the Internet, by mail order, or through wholesale distribution channels, including, but not limited to independent coffee retailers, department stores, food marts, restaurants, cafes and grocery stores, during and after the term of this Agreement ("Wholesale Accounts"). Wholesale Accounts of Franchisor may, in return, sell SBC coffee and related products under the same or different trademarks.

1.03. Nothing herein shall be deemed to be a grant to Franchisee of any rights as a commercial agent or distributor of SBC Coffee and/or coffee products in any jurisdiction. Franchisor reserves the right, in its sole discretion, to grant such rights to any third party, during or after the term of this Agreement. Franchisee may not sell any SBC Coffee Products (as defined herein) and/or any other materials, supplies, or inventory bearing the Proprietary Marks anywhere except at the SBC Retail Unit, without SBC's prior written consent. Franchisee shall specifically be prohibited from selling any such items at wholesale, except as specifically agreed to, in writing, by Franchisor. The foregoing restriction shall not apply to catering events and/or the offer of samples of SBC coffee products at or directly in front of the Franchised Unit.

1.04. Franchisee acknowledges that, over time, Franchisor has entered, and will continue to enter, into franchise agreements with other franchisees that may contain provisions, conditions and obligations that differ from those contained in this Agreement, including, without limitation, franchise agreements for the operation of SBC Retail Units. The existence of different forms of agreement and the fact that Franchisor and other franchisees may have different rights and obligations does not affect the parties' duty to comply with the terms of this Agreement.

II. Term [...]

III. Fees

3.01. In consideration of the franchise granted to Franchisee herein, Franchisee shall pay to the Franchisor the following:

A. franchise fee of ___ THOUSAND DOLLARS ($___) payable upon execution of this Agreement by Franchisee. . . .

B. A recurring, non-refundable royalty fee of [. . .].

3.02. In addition to the payments provided for in Section 3.01. hereof, Franchisee, recognizing the value of advertising and the importance of the standardization of advertising and promotion to the goodwill and public image of the System, agrees to pay to the SEATTLE'S BEST COFFEE national marketing fund (the "NMF," f/k/a "NCP Fund") a recurring, non-refundable contribution ("NMF Contribution," f/k/a "NCP Fund Contribution") in an amount to be determined by Franchisor, in its sole discretion, up to [ ] PERCENT (1%) of the Gross Sales. . . .

IV. Accounting and Records [...]

V. Proprietary Marks

5.01. It is understood and agreed that the franchise granted herein to use Franchisor's Proprietary Marks applies only to use in connection with the operation of the Franchised Unit franchised in this Agreement at the location designated in Section I hereof, and includes only such Proprietary Marks as are now designated or which may hereafter be designated, in the Confidential Operating Standards Manual or otherwise in writing as a part of the SBC System (which might or might not be all of the Proprietary Marks pertaining to the System owned by the Franchisor), and does not include any other mark, name, or indicia of origin of Franchisor now existing or which may hereafter be adopted or acquired by Franchisor.

5.02. With respect to Franchisee's use of the Proprietary Marks pursuant to this Agreement, Franchisee acknowledges and agrees that:

A. Franchisee shall not use the Proprietary Marks as part of Franchisee's corporate or other business name;

B. Franchisee shall not hold out or otherwise use the Proprietary Marks to perform any activity or incur any obligation or indebtedness in such manner as might, in any way, make Franchisor liable therefor, without Franchisor's prior written consent;

C. Franchisee shall execute any documents and provide such other assistance deemed necessary by Franchisor or its counsel to obtain protection for the Proprietary Marks or to maintain the continued validity of such Proprietary Marks; and

D. Franchisor reserves the right to substitute different Proprietary Marks for use in identifying the System and the franchised businesses operating thereunder, and Franchisee agrees to immediately substitute Proprietary Marks upon receipt of written notice from Franchisor.

5.03. Franchisee expressly acknowledges Franchisor's exclusive right to use the marks "SEATTLE'S BEST COFFEE" and "SBC" for restaurant services, coffee products, and other related food and beverage products; the building configuration; and the other Proprietary Marks of the System. Franchisee agrees not to represent in any manner that it has any ownership in the Proprietary Marks or the right to use the Proprietary Marks except as provided in this Agreement. Franchisee further agrees that its use of the Proprietary Marks shall not create in its favor any right, title, or interest in or to the Proprietary Marks, and that all of such use shall inure to the benefit of Franchisor.

5.04. Franchisee acknowledges that the use of the Proprietary Marks outside the scope of this license, without Franchisor's prior written consent, is an infringement of Franchisor's exclusive right to use the Proprietary Marks, and during the term of this Agreement and after the expiration or termination hereof, Franchisee covenants not to, directly or indirectly, commit an act of infringement or contest or aid in contesting the validity or ownership of Franchisor's Proprietary Marks, or take any other action in derogation thereof.

5.05. Franchisee shall promptly notify Franchisor of any suspected infringement of, or challenge to, the validity of the ownership of, or Franchisor's right to use, the Proprietary Marks licensed hereunder. Franchisee acknowledges that Franchisor has the right to control any administrative proceeding or litigation involving the Proprietary

Marks. In the event Franchisor undertakes the defense or prosecution of any litigation relating to the Proprietary Marks, Franchisee agrees to execute any and all documents and to do such acts and things as may, in the opinion of counsel for Franchisor, be necessary to carry out such defense or prosecution. Except to the extent that such litigation is the result of Franchisee's use of the Proprietary Marks in a manner inconsistent with the terms of this Agreement, Franchisor agrees to reimburse Franchisee for its out-of-pocket costs in doing such acts and things, except that Franchisee shall bear the salary costs of its employees.

5.06. Franchisee understands and agrees that its license with respect to the Proprietary Marks is non-exclusive to the extent that Franchisor has and retains the right under this Agreement:

A. To grant other licenses for the Proprietary Marks, in addition to those licenses already granted to existing franchisees;

B. To develop and establish other franchise systems for the same, similar, or different products or services utilizing proprietary marks not now or hereafter designated as part of the System licensed by this Agreement, and to grant licenses thereto, without providing Franchisee any right therein; and

C. To develop and establish other systems for the sale, at wholesale or retail, of similar or different products utilizing the same or similar Proprietary Marks, without providing Franchisee any right therein.

5.07. Franchisee acknowledges and expressly agrees that any and all goodwill associated with the System and identified by the Proprietary Marks used in connection therewith shall inure directly and exclusively to the benefit of Franchisor and is the property of Franchisor, and that upon the expiration or termination of this Agreement or any other agreement, no monetary amount shall be assigned as attributable to any goodwill associated with any of Franchisee's activities in the operation of the Franchised Unit granted herein, or Franchisee's use of the Proprietary Marks.

5.08. Franchisee understands and acknowledges that each and every detail of the SBC SYSTEM is important to Franchisee, Franchisor, and other franchisees in order to develop and maintain high and uniform standards of quality and services, and hence to protect the reputation and goodwill of SBC RETAIL UNITS. Accordingly, Franchisee covenants:

A. To operate and advertise the Franchised Unit, at Franchisee's own expense, under the name "SEATTLE'S BEST COFFEE," without prefix or suffix;

B. To adopt and use the Proprietary Marks licensed hereunder solely in the manner prescribed by Franchisor;

C. To observe such reasonable requirements with respect to trademark registration notices as Franchisor may from time to time direct in the Confidential Operating Standards Manual or otherwise in writing.

5.09. In order to preserve the validity and integrity of the Proprietary Marks licensed herein and to assure that Franchisee is properly employing the same in the operation of the Franchised Unit, Franchisor or its agents shall at all reasonable times have the right to inspect Franchisee's operations, premises, and Franchised Unit and make periodic evaluations of the services provided and the products sold and used therein. Franchisee shall cooperate with Franchisor's representatives in such inspections and render such assistance to the representatives as may reasonably be requested.

5.10. Franchisee shall not hold out or otherwise employ the Proprietary Marks to perform any activity, or to incur any obligation or indebtedness in such a manner as might, in any way, make Franchisor liable therefor, without Franchisor's prior written consent.

VI. Obligations of Corporate or Partnership Franchisee [...]

VII. Confidential Operating Standards Manual

7.01. In order to protect the reputation and goodwill of Franchisor and the SBC SYSTEM and to maintain uniform standards of operation under Franchisor's Proprietary Marks, Franchisee shall conduct the Franchised Business in accordance with Franchisor's Confidential Operating Standards Manual (hereinafter, together with any other manuals created or approved for use in the operation of the Franchised Business granted herein, and all amendments and updates thereto, the "Manual").

7.02. Franchisee shall at all times treat the Manual, and the information contained therein, as confidential, and shall use all reasonable efforts to keep such information secret and confidential. Franchisee shall not, at any time, without Franchisor's prior written consent, copy, duplicate, record, or otherwise make the Manual available to any unauthorized person or entity.

7.03. The Manual shall at all times remain the sole property of Franchisor.

7.04. In order for Franchisee to benefit from new knowledge information, methods and technology adopted and used by Franchisor in the operation of the System, Franchisor may from time to time revise the Manual and Franchisee agrees to adhere to and abide by all such revisions.

7.05. Franchisee agrees at all times to keep its copy of the Manual current and up-to-date, and in the event of any dispute as to the contents of Franchisee's Manual, the terms of the master copy of the Manual maintained by Franchisor at Franchisor's home office, shall be controlling.

7.06. The Manual is intended to further the purposes of this Agreement, and is specifically incorporated, by reference, into this Agreement. Except as otherwise set forth in this Agreement, in the event of a conflict between the terms of this Agreement and the terms of the Manual, the terms of this Agreement shall control.

VIII. Training

8.01. Franchisee, a partner of Franchisee if Franchisee is a partnership, or a principal shareholder of Franchisee if Franchisee is a corporation (or a principal member of Franchisee if Franchisee is a limited liability company), must complete, to Franchisor's satisfaction, the SEATTLE'S BEST COFFEE New Franchisee Orientation Program ("NFOP") prior to opening the first franchised SBC RETAIL UNIT operated by Franchisee. NFOP shall consist of up to three (3) days of workshops and seminars conducted at a training facility and designated by Franchisor.

8.02. In addition to completing the NFOP, Franchisee (or a partner, principal shareholder, principal member of Franchisee, or an Operations Director/District Manager designated by Franchisee, and at least one designated management employee of Franchisee (and, in all instances, a senior management employee of Franchisee responsible for daily operations of the Franchised Unit), must attend and complete, to Franchisor's satisfaction, the SBC FRANCHISE ACADEMY PROGRAM ("FAP"), prior to opening the Franchised Unit. FAP consists of up to four (4) weeks of classroom and and operations training at an SBC Cafe designated by Franchisor (an "SBC Certified Training Cafe"). A management employee of Franchisee that successfully completes FAP, shall be certified by Franchisor as an "SBC Certified Manager."

8.03. Franchisee shall maintain the number of FAP Certified Managers designated by the Franchisor in the employ of the Franchised Unit throughout the term of this Agreement, which in no event shall be less than one (1). In the event that Franchisee or any SBC Certified Manager ceases active employment at the Franchised Unit, Franchisee must enroll a qualified replacement in FAP within thirty (30) days of cessation of such individual's employment. The replacement employee shall attend and complete the next regularly scheduled FAP to Franchisor's satisfaction.

8.04. The cost of conducting the initial NFOP and FAP (instruction and required materials) shall be borne by Franchisor. All other expenses during NFOP and FAP, including meals and lodging, wages and travel, shall be borne by Franchisee.

8.05. Franchisor reserves the right to test any and all SBC Certified Managers at any time, and may require such individuals to attend and complete additional training at a training facility designated by Franchisor, and at Franchisee's sole cost and expense, in the event they fail to achieve a satisfactory score on such test. Additionally, Franchisor may make available to Franchisee or Franchisee's employees, from time to time, such additional training programs as Franchisor, in its sole discretion, may choose to conduct. Attendance at said training programs may be mandatory. The cost of conducting such additional training programs (instruction and required materials) shall be borne by Franchisor. All other expenses during the training period, including meals and lodging, wages and travel, shall be borne by the Franchisee.

IX. Duties of the Franchisor

9.01. Franchisor will make available to Franchisee standard plans and specifications to be utilized only in the construction of the Franchised Unit. No modification to or deviations from the standard plans and specifications may be made without the written consent of Franchisor. Franchisee shall obtain, at its expense, further qualified architectural and engineering services to prepare surveys, site and foundation plans, and to adapt the standard plans and specifications to applicable local or state laws, regulations or ordinances. Franchisee shall bear the cost of preparing plans containing deviations or modifications from the standard plans.

9.02. Franchisor shall provide consultation and advice to Franchisee as Franchisor deems appropriate with regard to construction or renovation and operation of the Franchised Unit, building layout, furnishings, fixtures and equipment plans and specifications, employee selection and training, purchasing and inventory control and those other matters as Franchisor deems appropriate.

9.03. Franchisor will make available to Franchisee such continuing advisory assistance in the operation of the Franchised Business, in person or by electronic or written bulletins made available from time to time, as Franchisor may deem appropriate.

9.04. Franchisor, in its sole discretion, may provide opening assistance to Franchisee at the Franchised Unit.

9.05. Franchisor will loan one (1) copy of the Manual to Franchisee for the duration of this Agreement, which Manual contains the standards, specifications, procedures and techniques of the SBC System.

9.06. Franchisor will continue its efforts to maintain high and uniform standards of quality, cleanliness, appearance and service at all SBC Retail Units, to protect and enhance the reputation of the SBC System and the demand for the products and services of the System. Franchisor will establish uniform criteria for approving suppliers; make every reasonable effort to disseminate its standards and specifications to prospective suppliers of the Franchisee upon the written request of the Franchisee, provided that Franchisor may elect not to make available to prospective suppliers the standards and specifications for such food formulae or equipment designs deemed by Franchisor in its sole discretion to be confidential; and may conduct periodic inspections of the premises and evaluations of the products used and sold at the Franchised Unit and in all other SBC Retail Units.

9.07. Franchisor will provide training to Franchisee as set forth in Article VIII hereof.

X. Duties of the Franchisee

Franchisee understands and acknowledges that every detail of the System is important to Franchisor, Franchisee and other franchisees in order to develop and maintain high and uniform operating standards, to increase the demand for SEATTLE'S BEST COFFEE products and services, and to protect the reputation and goodwill of Franchisor. Accordingly, Franchisee agrees that:

10.01. Franchisee shall maintain, at all times during the term of this Agreement, at Franchisee's expense, the premises of the Franchised Unit and all fixtures, furnishings, signs, systems and equipment (hereinafter "improvements") thereon or therein, in conformity with Franchisor's high standards and public image and to make such additions, alterations, repairs, and replacements thereto (but no others, without Franchisor's prior written consent) as may be required by Franchisor, including but not limited to the following:

A. To keep the Franchised Unit in the highest degree of sanitation and repair, including, without limitation, such periodic repainting, repairs or replacement of impaired equipment, and replacement of obsolete signs, as Franchisor may reasonably direct;

B. To meet and maintain the highest governmental standards and ratings applicable to the operation of the Franchised Business;

C. At its sole cost and expense, to complete a full reimaging, renovation, refurbishment and modernization of the Franchised Unit, within the time frame required by Franchisor, including the building design, parking lot, landscaping, equipment, signs, interior and exterior decor items, fixtures, furnishings, trade dress, color scheme, presentation of trademarks and service marks, supplies and other products and materials, to meet Franchisor's then-current standards, specifications and design criteria for SBC Retail Units, including without limitation, such structural changes, remodeling and redecoration and such modifications to existing improvements as may be necessary to do so (hereinafter, a "Franchised Unit Renovation"). Franchisee shall not be required to perform a Franchised Unit Renovation if there are less than three (3) years remaining on the term of this Agreement, and/or the lease for the premises occupied by the Franchised Unit. Nothing herein shall be deemed to limit Franchisee's other obligations, during the term of this Agreement, to operate the Franchised Unit in accordance with Franchisor's standards and specifications for the SBC System, including, but not limited to, the obligations set forth in this Section X.

10.02. Franchisee shall operate the Franchised Unit in conformity with such uniform recipes, methods, standards, and specifications as Franchisor may from time to time prescribe in the Manual or otherwise in writing, to insure that the highest degree of quality, service and cleanliness is uniformly maintained and to refrain from any deviation therefrom and from otherwise operating in any manner which reflects adversely on Franchisor's name and goodwill or on the Proprietary Marks, and in connection therewith:

A. To maintain in sufficient supply, and use at all times, only such ingredients, products, materials, supplies, and paper goods as conform to Franchisor's standards and specifications, and to refrain from deviating therefrom by using non-conforming items, without Franchisor's prior written consent;

B. To sell or offer for sale only proprietary "Seattle's Best Coffee" brand coffee products and such other products and menu items that have been expressly approved for sale in writing by Franchisor, meet Franchisor's uniform standards of quality and quantity and as have been prepared in accordance with Franchisor's methods and techniques for product preparation; to sell or offer for sale the minimum menu items specified in the Manual or otherwise in writing; to refrain from any deviation from Franchisor's standards and specifications for serving or selling the menu items, without Franchisor's prior written consent; and to discontinue selling or offering for sale such items as Franchisor may, in its discretion, disapprove in writing at any time;

C. To use the premises of the Franchised Unit solely for the purpose of conducting the business franchised hereunder, and to conduct no other business or activity thereon, whether for profit or otherwise, without Franchisor's prior written consent;

D. To keep the Franchised Unit open and in normal operation during such business hours as Franchisor may prescribe in the Manual or otherwise in writing;

E. To permit Franchisor or its agents, at any time during ordinary business hours, to remove from the Franchised Unit samples of any ingredients, products, materials, supplies, and paper goods used in the operation of the Franchised Unit, without payment therefor, in amounts reasonably necessary for testing by Franchisor or an independent laboratory, to determine whether such samples meet Franchisor's then-current standards and specifications. In addition to any other remedies it may have under this Agreement, Franchisor may require Franchisee to bear the cost of such testing if any such ingredient, products, materials, supplier or paper goods have been obtained from a supplier not approved by Franchisor, or if the sample fails to conform to Franchisor's specifications;

F. To purchase, install and construct, at Franchisee's expense, all improvements furnishings, signs and equipment specified in the approved standard plans and specifications, and such other furnishings, signs or equipment as Franchisor may reasonably direct from time to time in the Manual or otherwise in writing; and to refrain from installing or permitting to be installed on or about the premises of the Franchised Unit, without Franchisor's written consent, any improvements, furnishings, signs or equipment not first approved in writing as meeting Franchisor's standards and specifications;

G. To comply with all applicable federal, state and local laws, regulations and ordinances pertaining to the operation of the Franchised Business; and

H. Franchisee shall grant Franchisor and its agents the right to enter upon the premises of the Franchised Unit at any time during ordinary business hours for the purpose of conducting inspections; cooperate with Franchisor's representatives in such inspections by rendering such assistance as they may reasonably request; and, upon notice from Franchisor or its agents, and without limiting Franchisor's other rights under this Agreement, take such steps as may be necessary immediately to correct the deficiencies detected during any such inspection, including, without limitation, immediately desisting from the further use of any equipment, promotional materials, products, or supplies that do not conform with Franchisor's then-current specifications, standards, or requirements.

10.03. To maintain the quality and distinct characteristics of fine specialty coffee flavors that customers associate with the SBC System and the Proprietary Marks, Franchisee shall offer and sell only SEATTLE'S BEST COFFEE brand coffee and coffee products at or from the Franchised Unit and must purchase all of its coffee and coffee products from Franchisor or its designee ("SBC Coffee Products"), and prepare all coffee products at the Franchised Unit using Franchisor's proprietary recipes and methods of operation. Franchisor will sell SBC Coffee Products to Franchisee on standard purchase terms that may vary from time to time, F.O.B. Franchisor's designated distribution center, with all freight, duties and shipping charges at Franchisee's sole cost and expense. Franchisor will give prior notice of any material changes in purchase terms.

10.04. Franchisee shall purchase all other ingredients, products, materials, supplies, and other items required in the operation of the Franchised Unit which are or incorporate trade-secrets of Franchisor, as designated by Franchisor ("Trade-Secret Products") only from Franchisor or suppliers designated by Franchisor.

10.05. Franchisee shall purchase all other ingredients, products, materials, supplies, paper goods, and other items required for the operation of the Franchised Business, except SBC Coffee Products and Trade-Secret Products, solely from suppliers who demonstrate, to the continuing reasonable satisfaction of Franchisor, the ability to meet Franchisor's reasonable standards and specifications for such items; who possess adequate quality controls and capacity to supply Franchisee's needs promptly and reliably; and who have been approved in writing by Franchisor and such approval has not thereafter been revoked. If Franchisee desires to purchase any such items from an unapproved supplier, Franchisee shall submit to Franchisor a written request for approval, or shall request the supplier itself to seek approval. Franchisor shall have the right to require, as a condition of its approval, that its representatives be permitted to inspect the supplier's facilities, and that samples from the supplier be delivered, at Franchisor's option, either to Franchisor or to an independent laboratory designated by Franchisor for testing prior to granting approval. A charge not to exceed Franchisor's reasonable cost of inspection and the actual cost of testing shall be paid by the supplier or Franchisee.

Franchisor reserves the right, at its option, to reinspect the facilities and products of any such approved supplier from time to time and to revoke its approval upon failure of such supplier to continue to meet any of the foregoing criteria.

10.06. Advertising Cooperative. Franchisor shall have the right, in its sole discretion, to designate any geographic area (which may consist of any portion of a country or jurisdiction and/or more than one country or jurisdiction) for the purposes of establishing an advertising cooperative ("Cooperative"). . . .

10.07. Franchisor disclaims all express or implied warranties concerning any approved products or services, including, without limitation, any warranties as to merchantability, fitness for a particular purpose, availability, quality, pricing or profitability. Franchisee acknowledges that Franchisor may, under appropriate circumstances, receive fees, commissions, field-of-use license royalties, or other consideration from approved suppliers based on sales to franchisees, and that Franchisor may charge non-approved suppliers reasonable testing or inspection fees.

10.08. All local advertising by Franchisee shall be in such media, and of such type and format as Franchisor may approve; shall be conducted in a dignified manner; and shall conform to such standards and requirements as Franchisor may specify. Franchisee shall not use any advertising or promotional plans or materials unless and until Franchisee has received written approval from Franchisor, pursuant to the procedures and terms set forth in Section 10.09 hereof.

10.09. All advertising and promotional plans proposed to be used by Franchisee or the Cooperative, where applicable, except such plans and materials that have been previously approved by Franchisor shall be submitted to Franchisor for Franchisor's written approval (except with respect to prices to be charged) prior to any use thereof. Franchisor shall use its best efforts to complete its review of Franchisee's proposed advertising and promotional plans within fifteen (15) days after Franchisor receives such plans. If written approval is not received by Franchisee or the Cooperative from Franchisor within fifteen (15) days after receipt by Franchisor of such plans, Franchisor shall be deemed to have disapproved such plans.

10.10. Franchisee shall, at Franchisor's request, require all of its supervisory employees, as a condition of their employment, to execute an agreement prohibiting them, during the term of their employment or thereafter, from communicating, divulging, or using for the benefit of any person, persons, partnership, association, corporation or other entity any confidential information, trade secrets, knowledge, or know-how concerning the SBC System or methods of operation of the Franchised Unit which may be acquired as a result of their employment with Franchisee or other franchisees. A duplicate original of each such agreement shall be provided by Franchisee to Franchisor immediately upon execution.

10.11. If Franchisee operates more than five (5) Franchised Units, Franchisee shall have a supervisor, which may be Franchisee, to supervise and coordinate the operation of the Franchised Units (hereinafter, a "Supervisor"). In addition to the foregoing, Franchisee shall employ an additional Supervisor upon the opening of Franchisee's sixth (6th) Franchised Unit and upon the opening of each successive fifth (5th) Franchised Unit thereafter. Each Supervisor shall attend and successfully complete the CMT program set forth in Section 8.02 hereof prior to assuming any supervisory responsibilities and shall meet such other standards as Franchisor may reasonably impose. No Supervisor may have supervisory responsibility for more than five (5) Franchised Units.

10.12. If at any time the Franchised Unit is proposed to be operated by an entity or individual other than the Franchisee, Franchisor reserves the right to review and approve the operating entity or individual and to require and approve an operating agreement prior to such party's assumption of operations. Franchisor may, in its sole discretion, reject either the operating entity, the individual operator or the operating agreement. If approved by Franchisor, the operating entity and/or individual shall agree in writing to comply with all of Franchisee's obligations under the Franchise Agreement as though such party were the franchisee designated therein, on such form as may be designated by Franchisor. The operation of the Franchised Unit by any party other than Franchisee, without Franchisor's prior written consent, shall be deemed a material default of this Agreement for which Franchisee may terminate this Agreement pursuant to the provisions of Section 15.02 hereof.

10.13. Franchisee shall become a member of any purchasing cooperative established by Franchisor for the SEATTLE'S BEST COFFEE System and shall remain a member in good standing thereof throughout the term of this Agreement and shall pay all reasonable membership fees assessed by such purchasing association.

10.14. Franchisee shall, within thirty (30) days from receipt of written notice from Franchisor, at its sole cost and expense, purchase and install at the Franchised Unit and/or at Franchisee's principal business office such computer hardware and software equipment, required dedicated telephone and power lines, modems, printers and other computer related accessory and peripheral equipment as Franchisor specifies in the Manual or otherwise in writing (the "Required Computer Equipment"). The Required Computer Equipment shall include telecommunications devices and may include a single software program or set of programs, all of which must be obtained in accordance with the Franchisor's standards and specifications. The Required Computer Equipment shall permit 24 hour per day electronic communications between Franchisor and Franchisee including access to the internet and Franchisor's current intranet, or any successor thereto. Franchisee shall only be required to purchase and install the Required Computer Equipment at one, central location, which shall satisfy the conditions of this Section 10.02 (or its equivalent) for all Franchised Units operated by Franchisee, provided information for all Franchise Units is maintained at such location.

10.15. Franchisee shall comply with all other requirements set forth in this Agreement.

XI. Insurance [...]

XII. Confidential Information

12.01. Franchisee shall not, during the term of this Agreement or thereafter, communicate, divulge, or use for the benefit of any other person, persons, partnership, association, corporation or other entity, any confidential information, knowledge or know-how concerning the construction and methods of operation of the Franchised Business which may be communicated to Franchisee, or of which Franchisee may be apprised, by virtue of Franchisee's operation under the terms of this Agreement. Franchisee shall divulge such confidential information only to such employees of Franchisee as must have access to it in order to exercise the franchise rights granted hereunder and to establish and operate the Franchised Unit pursuant hereto and as Franchisee may be required by law, provided Franchisee shall give Franchisor prior written notice of any such required disclosure immediately upon receipt of notice by Franchisee in order for Franchisor to have the opportunity to seek a protective order or take such other actions as it deems appropriate under the circumstances.

12.02. Any and all information, knowledge, and know-how, including, without limitation, drawings, materials, equipment, recipes, prepared mixtures or blends of spices or other food products, and other data, which Franchisor designates as confidential, and any information, knowledge, or know-how which may be derived by analysis thereof, shall be deemed confidential for purposes of this Agreement, except information which Franchisee can demonstrate came to Franchisee's attention prior to disclosure thereof by Franchisor; or which, at the time of disclosure thereof by Franchisor to Franchisee, had become a part of the public domain, through publication or communication by others; or which, after disclosure to Franchisee by Franchisor, becomes a part of the public domain, through publication or communication by others.

[Remainder of Franchise Agreement provisions have been deleted — Eds.]

IN WITNESS WHEREOF, the parties hereto, intending to be legally bound hereby, have duly executed, sealed, and delivered this Agreement in triplicate on the day and year first above written.

WITNESSES: CINNABON, INC., SUCCESSOR IN INTEREST TO
                    SEATTLE'S BEST COFFEE, LLC
_____   By:_____

_____   Title:_____

            DEVELOPER:
_____   By:_____

_____   Title:_____

BARCAMERICA INT'L USA TRUST v. TYFIELD IMPORTERS, INC.
289 F.3d 589 (9th Cir. 2002)

O'SCANNLAIN, Circuit Judge.

We must decide whether a company engaged in "naked licensing" of its trademark, thus resulting in abandonment of the mark and ultimately its cancellation. This case involves a dispute over who may use the "Leonardo Da Vinci" trademark for wines.

Barcamerica International USA Trust (Barcamerica) traces its rights in the Leonardo Da Vinci mark to a February 14, 1984 registration granted by the United States Patent and Trademark Office (PTO), on an application filed in 1982. On August 7, 1989, the PTO acknowledged the mark's "incontestability." See 15 U.S.C. §1115(b). Barcamerica asserts that it has used the mark continuously since the early 1980s. In the district court, it produced invoices evidencing two sales per year for the years 1980 through 1993: one to a former employee and the other to a barter exchange company. Barcamerica further produced invoices evidencing between three and seven sales per year for the years 1994 through 1998. These include sales to the same former employee, two barter exchange companies, and various sales for "cash." The sales volume reflected in the invoices for the years 1980 through 1988 range from 160 to 410 cases of wine per year. Barcamerica also produced sales summaries for the years 1980 through 1996 which reflect significantly higher sales volumes; these summaries do not indicate, however, to whom the wine was sold.

In 1988, Barcamerica entered into a licensing agreement with Renaissance Vineyards (Renaissance). Under the agreement, Barcamerica granted Renaissance the nonexclusive right to use the "Da Vinci" mark for five years or 4,000 cases, "whichever comes first," in exchange for $2,500. The agreement contained no quality control provision. In 1989, Barcamerica and Renaissance entered into a second agreement in place of the 1988 agreement. The 1989 agreement granted Renaissance an exclusive license to use the "Da Vinci" mark in the United States for wine products or alcoholic beverages. The 1989 agreement was drafted by Barcamerica's counsel and, like the 1988 agreement, it did not contain a quality control provision. In fact, the only evidence in the record of any efforts by Barcamerica to exercise "quality control" over Renaissance's wines comprised (1) Barcamerica principal George Gino Barca's testimony that he occasionally, informally tasted of the wine, and (2) Barca's testimony that he relied on the reputation of a "world-famous winemaker" employed by Renaissance at the time the agreements were signed.[2]

(That winemaker is now deceased, although the record does not indicate when he died.) Nonetheless, Barcamerica contends that Renaissance's use of the mark inures to Barcamerica's benefit. See 15 U.S.C. §1055.

Cantine Leonardo Da Vinci Soc. Coop. a.r.l. (Cantine), an entity of Italy, is a wine producer located in Vinci, Italy. Cantine has sold wine products bearing the "Leonardo Da Vinci" tradename since 1972; it selected this name and mark based on the name of its home city, Vinci.

---

2. After the commencement of this litigation, Barcamerica proposed a new agreement to Renaissance. The proposed agreement included a quality control provision, and the letter from Barcamerica's attorney proposing this new agreement acknowledged that the agreement "addresses requirements of trademark law that the licensor maintain some control over the licensed product." Renaissance never accepted Barcamerica's invitation to enter into this new agreement. In 1999, Barcamerica again acknowledged it had an obligation to perform quality control for the licensed product and requested that Renaissance execute a declaration stating, inter alia, that Barcamerica had been involved in the quality control of the licensed product. Renaissance refused to execute this declaration, because it was "neither truthful nor accurate." Indeed, in a letter to Barcamerica, Renaissance's counsel stated:

[N]ever at any time, to [Renaissance's] knowledge, has Mr. Barca ever had any involvement of any kind whatsoever regarding quality, quality control, the use of the Da Vinci label, or the marketing of the Da Vinci label wines, nor has he ever "examined" Renaissance's wine, "sampled" it, or had any involvement whatsoever regarding the quality of the wine and maintaining it at any level.

Cantine began selling its "Leonardo Da Vinci" wine to importers in the United States in 1979. Since 1996, however, Tyfield Importers, Inc. (Tyfield) has been the exclusive United States importer and distributor of Cantine wine products bearing the "Leonardo Da Vinci" mark. During the first eighteen months after Tyfield became Cantine's exclusive importer, Cantine sold approximately 55,000 cases of wine products bearing the "Leonardo Da Vinci" mark to Tyfield. During this same period, Tyfield spent between $250,000 and $300,000 advertising and promoting Cantine's products, advertising in *USA Today*, and such specialty magazines as *The Wine Spectator, Wine and Spirits*, and *Southern Beverage Journal*.

Cantine learned of Barcamerica's registration of the "Leonardo Da Vinci" mark in or about 1996, in the course of prosecuting its first trademark application in the United States. Cantine investigated Barcamerica's use of the mark and concluded that Barcamerica was no longer selling any wine products bearing the "Leonardo Da Vinci" mark and had long since abandoned the mark. As a result, in May 1997, Cantine commenced a proceeding in the PTO seeking cancellation of Barcamerica's registration for the mark based on abandonment. Barcamerica responded by filing the instant action on January 30, 1998, and thereafter moved to suspend the proceeding in the PTO. The PTO granted Barcamerica's motion and suspended the cancellation proceeding. Although Barca has been aware of Cantine's use of the "Leonardo Da Vinci" mark since approximately 1993, Barcamerica initiated the instant action only after Tyfield and Cantine commenced the proceeding in the PTO. A month after Barcamerica filed the instant action, it moved for a preliminary injunction enjoining Tyfield and Cantine from any further use of the mark. The district court denied the motion. Thereafter, Tyfield and Cantine moved for summary judgment on various grounds. The district court granted the motion, concluding that Barcamerica abandoned the mark through naked licensing. The court further found that, in any event, the suit was barred by laches because Barcamerica knew several years before filing suit that Tyfield and Cantine were using the mark in connection with the sale of wine. This timely appeal followed. . . .

III

We now turn to the merits of the appeal. Barcamerica first challenges the district court's conclusion that Barcamerica abandoned its trademark by engaging in naked licensing. It is well-established that "[a] trademark owner may grant a license and remain protected provided quality control of the goods and services sold under the trademark by the licensee is maintained." Moore Bus. Forms, Inc. v. Ryu, 960 F.2d 486, 489 (5th Cir. 1992). But "[u]ncontrolled or 'naked' licensing may result in the trademark ceasing to function as a symbol of quality and controlled source." McCarthy on Trademarks and Unfair Competition §18:48, at 18-79 (4th ed. 2001). Consequently, where the licensor fails to exercise adequate quality control over the licensee, "a court may find that the trademark owner has abandoned the trademark, in which case the owner would be estopped from asserting rights to the trademark." *Moore*, 960 F.2d at 489. Such abandonment "is purely an 'involuntary' forfeiture of trademark rights," for it need not be shown that the trademark owner had any subjective intent to abandon the mark. McCarthy §18:48, at 18-79. Accordingly, the proponent of a naked license theory "faces a stringent standard" of proof. *Moore*, 960 F.2d at 489.

Judge Damrell's analysis of this issue in his memorandum opinion and order is correct and well-stated, and we adopt it as our own. As that court explained, in 1988, [Barcamerica] entered into an agreement with Renaissance in which [Barcamerica] granted Renaissance the non-exclusive right to use the "Da Vinci" mark for five years or 4,000 cases, "whichever comes first." There is no quality control provision in that agreement. In 1989, [Barcamerica] and Renaissance entered into a second agreement in place of the 1988 agreement. The 1989 agreement grants Renaissance an exclusive license to use the "Da Vinci" mark in the United States for wine products or alcoholic beverages. The 1989 agreement was to "continue in effect in perpetuity," unless terminated in accordance with the provisions thereof. The 1989 agreement does not contain any controls or restrictions with respect to the quality of goods bearing the "Da Vinci" mark. Rather, the agreement provides that Renaissance is "solely responsible for any and all claims or causes of action for negligence, breach of contract, breach of warranty, or products liability arising from the sale or distribution of Products using the Licensed Mark" and that Renaissance shall defend and indemnify plaintiff against such claims.

The lack of an express contract right to inspect and supervise a licensee's operations is not conclusive evidence of lack of control. "[T]here need not be formal quality control where 'the particular circumstances of the licensing arrangement [indicate] that the public will not be deceived.'" *Moore Bus. Forms, Inc.*, 960 F.2d at 489. Indeed, "[c]ourts have upheld licensing agreements where the licensor is familiar with and relies upon the licensee's own efforts to control quality." Morgan Creek Prods., Inc. v. Capital Cities/ABC, Inc., 22 U.S.P.Q.2d 1881, 1884 (C.D. Cal. 1991).

Here, there is no evidence that [Barcamerica] is familiar with or relied upon Renaissance's efforts to control quality. Mr. Barca represents that Renaissance's use of the mark is "controlled by" plaintiff "with respect to the nature and quality of the wine sold under the license," and that "[t]he nature and quality of Renaissance wine sold under the trademark is good." [Barcamerica]'s sole evidence of any such control is Mr. Barca's own apparently random tastings and his reliance on Renaissance's reputation. According to Mr. Barca, the quality of Renaissance's wine is "good" and at the time plaintiff began licensing the mark to Renaissance, Renaissance's winemaker was Karl Werner, a "world famous" winemaker.

Mr. Barca's conclusory statements as to the existence of quality controls is insufficient to create a triable issue of fact on the issue of naked licensing. While Mr. Barca's tastings perhaps demonstrate a minimal effort to monitor quality, Mr. Barca fails to state when, how often, and under what circumstances he tastes the wine. Mr. Barca's reliance on the reputation of the winemaker is no longer justified as he is deceased. Mr. Barca has not provided any information concerning the successor winemaker(s). While Renaissance's attorney, Mr. Goldman, testified that Renaissance "strive[s] extremely hard to have the highest possible standards," he has no knowledge of the quality control procedures utilized by Renaissance with regard to testing wine. Moreover, according to Renaissance, Mr. Barca never "had any involvement whatsoever regarding the quality of the wine and maintaining it at any level." [Barcamerica] has failed to demonstrate any knowledge of or reliance on the actual quality controls used by Renaissance, nor has it demonstrated any ongoing effort to monitor quality.

[Barcamerica] and Renaissance did not and do not have the type of close working relationship required to establish adequate quality control in the absence of a formal agreement. See, e.g., *Taco Cabana Int'l, Inc.*, 932 F.2d at 1121 (licensor and licensee enjoyed close working relationship for eight years); *Transgo*, 768 F.2d at 1017-18 (licensor manufactured 90% of components sold by licensee, licensor informed licensee that if he chose to use his own parts "[licensee] wanted to know about it," licensor had ten-year association with licensee and was familiar with his ability and expertise); Taffy Original Designs, Inc. v. Taffy's Inc., 161 U.S.P.Q. 707, 713 (N.D. Ill. 1966) (licensor and licensee were sisters in business together for seventeen years, licensee's business was a continuation of the licensor's and licensee's prior business, licensor visited licensee's store from time to time and was satisfied with the quality of the merchandise offered); Arner v. Sharper Image Corp., 39 U.S.P.Q.2d 1282, 1995 WL 873730 (C.D. Cal. 1995) (licensor engaged in a close working relationship with licensee's employees and license agreement provided that license would terminate if certain employees ceased to be affiliated with licensee). No such familiarity or close working relationship ever existed between [Barcamerica] and Renaissance. Both the terms of the licensing agreements and the manner in which they were carried out show that [Barcamerica] engaged in naked licensing of the "Leonardo Da Vinci" mark. Accordingly, [Barcamerica] is estopped from asserting any rights in the mark.

On appeal, Barcamerica does not seriously contest any of the foregoing. Instead, it argues essentially that because Renaissance makes good wine, the public is not deceived by Renaissance's use of the "Da Vinci" mark, and thus, that the license was legally acceptable. This novel rationale, however, is faulty. Whether Renaissance's wine was objectively "good" or "bad" is simply irrelevant. What matters is that Barcamerica played no meaningful role in holding the wine to a standard of quality — good, bad, or otherwise. As McCarthy explains,

> It is important to keep in mind that "quality control" does not necessarily mean that the licensed goods or services must be of "high" quality, but merely of equal quality, whether that quality is high, low or middle. The point is that customers are entitled to assume that the nature and quality of goods and services sold under the mark at all licensed outlets will be consistent and predictable.

McCarthy §18:55, at 18-94. And "it is well established that where a trademark owner engages in naked licensing, without any control over the quality of goods produced by the licensee, such a practice is inherently deceptive and constitutes abandonment of any rights to the trademark by the licensor." First Interstate Bancorp v. Stenquist, 16 U.S.P.Q.2d 1704, 1706, 1990 WL 300321 (N.D. Cal. 1990).

Certainly, "[i]t is difficult, if not impossible to define in the abstract exactly how much control and inspection is needed to satisfy the requirement of quality control over trademark licensees." McCarthy, §18:55, at 18-94. And we recognize that "[t]he standard of quality control and the degree of necessary inspection and policing by the licensor will vary with the wide range of licensing situations in use in the modern marketplace." Id., at 18-95. But in this case we deal with a relatively simple product: wine. Wine, of course, is bottled by season. Thus, at the very least, one might have expected Barca to sample (or to have some designated wine connoisseur sample) on an annual basis, in some organized way, some adequate number of bottles of the Renaissance wines which were to bear Barcamerica's mark to ensure that they were of sufficient quality to be called "Da Vinci." But Barca did not make even this minimal effort.

We therefore agree with Judge Damrell, and hold that Barcamerica engaged in naked licensing of its "Leonardo Da Vinci" mark — and that by so doing, Barcamerica forfeited its rights in the mark. We also agree that cancellation of Barcamerica's registration of the mark was appropriate.

For the foregoing reasons, the decision of the district court is AFFIRMED.

NAACP v. NAACP LEGAL DEFENSE & EDUC. FUND, INC.
753 F.2d 131 (D.C. Cir. 1985)

BAZELON, Senior Circuit Judge.

Two civil rights organizations contend for the right to use the initials "NAACP" as their trademark. The National Association for the Advancement of Colored People (the Association) alleges that the continued use of the NAACP initials by the NAACP Legal Defense and Education Fund, Inc. (the LDF) constitutes a trademark infringement. The LDF replies that the Association irrevocably granted it the right to use the initials. The LDF also maintains, inter alia, that the Association's suit is barred by laches.

The material facts are undisputed. The Association, known as "the NAACP," was founded in 1909, and listed among its goals:

> to promote equality of rights and eradicate caste or race prejudice among the citizens of the United States; to advance the interests of colored citizens; to secure for them impartial suffrage; and to increase their opportunities for securing justice in the courts, education for their children, employment according to their ability, and complete equality before the law.

The Association has sought to achieve its goals through educational work, legislative activity, and litigation.

As early as 1936, the Association's Board of Directors voted to organize a national defense fund to raise money for its litigation program. Besides serving as a means to ensure on-going financing of civil rights litigation, the creation of the LDF provided an important tax advantage. The Bureau of Internal Revenue had ruled that contributions to the Association were not deductible for federal income tax purposes because of the Association's lobbying work. Hence, the creation of a separate organization to perform the Association's legal work allowed contributors wishing to support its nonpolitical activities to receive tax deductions.

The Association's Board of Directors was informed by the New York Secretary of State that a certificate of incorporation could be processed only if the new corporation obtained "consent" from the Association to the use of the NAACP initials. The Association's Board of Directors then passed the following resolution on October 9, 1939:

> BE IT RESOLVED, that the Board of Directors of the National Association for the Advancement of Colored People grant permission for the use of the initials, "N.A.A.C.P." by the "N.A.A.C.P. Legal Defense and Education Fund, Inc." and authorize the President and Secretary to execute whatever papers might be necessary to carry out this resolution.

In 1957, however, the LDF and the Association mutually agreed to the LDF's independence. A gradual shift in that direction had suddenly been accelerated by external forces. The U.S. Treasury Department and several Southern state officials challenged the LDF's tax-exempt status. The Southern state officials claimed that the LDF had too close a relationship with the Association, which was engaged in lobbying and political activities. The U.S. Treasury Department objected to the sharing of board members and the NAACP initials. In response, the Association and LDF decided that the LDF should retain its NAACP initials but should sever all direct connections with the Association. On May 16, 1957, the LDF's board adopted a resolution that "no person should be a Board member, officer or employee of this corporation who is also a Board member, officer or employee of the N.A.A.C.P." . . .

Because such scrupulous organizational separation precluded "direct and formal control of the Inc. Fund [LDF] by the NAACP Board," cooperation between the two parties relied upon personal ties and common policy interests. But by the 1960's, however, tensions between the two organizations became evident, despite the formation of several liaison committees established between 1960-62 and 1965-66. These strained relations resulted from a heightening of direct competition in fundraising. There was also a dispute over who should take public credit for successful civil rights litigation. Although both organizations publicly attempted to deemphasize any explicit competition, the tensions between them continued to heighten.

In July 1965, the Association's Board adopted a resolution:

> it was VOTED that the Inc. Fund [the LDF] be approached by the Chairman of the Board, the Executive Director, the Treasury, and the Chairman of the Special Contribution Fund for the purpose of requesting the Inc. Fund to voluntarily reincorporate under a name that does not include NAACP; or to bring the Inc. Fund back into Special Contribution Fund status; and, if they refuse to do so, the NAACP should go into court and enjoin them from use of the name NAACP.

The Association's Executive Director orally conveyed this request and threat of suit to the Director of the LDF, who rejected the demand. At the Association's September 12, 1965 meeting, the Association's Board formally withdrew the language of its resolution threatening suit.

On February 24, 1966, representatives of both sides met to discuss their relationship. It was suggested again that the LDF change its name but the LDF declined. During the next twelve years, from 1966 through 1978, the Association remained silent concerning the LDF's use of the NAACP initials. The Association did not give clear notice to the LDF about reserving its exclusive claim to the NAACP initials. There were no negotiations. Cooperative interchanges between the LDF and the Association's attorneys waned. The Association itself indicated that during this time, the LDF "pursued an independent course of action . . . without consultation with the NAACP as to either policy or program." At least since 1966, the LDF has included a disclaimer on its stationery disavowing any present relationship with the Association. During this period of no negotiations, the LDF continued to build up its goodwill — indeed, these were the salad days for the LDF's litigation practice. The LDF continued to spend time and millions of dollars in soliciting gifts and recruiting legal talent using the NAACP initials. Many public interest groups now use the term "legal defense fund" in emulation of the LDF's success.

Negotiations were initiated by a letter from the Association to the LDF on December 29, 1978. The correspondence indicated concern about confusion stemming from LDF's use of the NAACP initials. On June 28, 1979, the Association's board adopted a resolution that rescinded the resolution of October 9, 1939 and revoked permission to use the NAACP initials. The Association registered the NAACP initials with the Patent and Trademark Office on January 26, 1982. On May 25, 1982, the Association initiated this suit.

The Association alleged that its 1939 resolution granted only a revocable license for use of the NAACP initials, and that the LDF's continued use of the initials constituted a trademark infringement. In response the LDF maintained that the 1939 resolution was an irrevocable grant, and that estoppel, acquiescence, and laches prevent the Association from belatedly asserting its claim. After a period of discovery, the parties made cross-motions for summary judgment. . . .

II. THE LACHES DEFENSE

The doctrine of laches bars relief to those who delay the assertion of their claims for an unreasonable time. Laches is founded on the notion that equity aids the vigilant and not those who slumber on their rights. Several aims are served by requiring the reasonable diligence of plaintiffs in pursuing their legal rights. Plaintiffs are encouraged to file suits when courts are in the best position to resolve disputes. As claims become increasingly stale, pertinent evidence becomes lost; equitable boundaries blur as defendants invest capital and labor into their claimed property; and plaintiffs gain the unfair advantage of hindsight, while defendants suffer the disadvantage of an uncertain future outcome.

Here almost thirteen years passed from 1966 through 1978 during which this case was ripe for judgment. Laches may not have been applicable if the Association had pursued negotiations during this time rather than going directly to court. Understandably these two civil rights organizations were reluctant to air publicly a fight among brothers and sisters. But legal precedent requires that this well-meaning motive be objectively evidenced by ongoing negotiation to excuse a stale claim. The Association fails to offer reasons why negotiations were not possible.

A. The Doctrine

The essential elements of laches are well-defined by common law. There are three affirmative requirements: (1) a substantial delay by a plaintiff prior to filing suit; (2) a plaintiff's awareness that the disputed trademark was being infringed; and (3) a reliance interest resulting from the defendant's continued development of goodwill during this period of delay. Courts also look for factors that may negate the invocation of laches by excusing the delay: (1) ongoing negotiations; and (2) conscious fraud or bad faith by the defendant.

Laches may bar injunctive relief when the defendant has established a substantial reliance interest. The district court failed to recognize this principle. It is true that "mere delay" by itself does not bar injunctive relief if the defendant did not invest resources that contribute to a trademark's future value. But injunctive relief may be appropriately barred when the defendant invested substantial labor and capital that builds the trademark's goodwill. This future property interest, resulting from reliance during the plaintiff's negligent delay, therefore prevents the enjoining of the defendant's continued use of the trademark.

The district court erred in denying the defense of laches. Although considerable deference is given to the trial judge's discretion on the question of laches, here the material facts are not in dispute according to both the parties and the district court.

B. The Affirmative Requirements

The requirements of laches are satisfied by the facts of this case. First, the Association delayed for almost thirteen years before resuming negotiations over the LDF's use of the NAACP initials. This length of time is comparable to that in other cases in which the laches doctrine has been applied. While mere delay by itself does not bar injunctive relief, here there was substantial investment by the LDF during this considerable time lapse. Because the Association did not give clear notice of its exclusive claim to the NAACP initials during this hiatus, the Association failed to reserve its rights. Such delay invites reasonable reliance by strengthening the defendant's belief that its use of a trademark will not be challenged. The cases cited by the district court do not tolerate the length of the delay found here.

Second, it is undisputed that the Association had knowledge of the LDF's alleged infringement. These two organizations knew each other intimately. In 1957, it was a mutual decision to separate and to allow the LDF to retain its NAACP initials. In the 1960's, the Association was also aware of the direct competition that was developing between the parties. The Association had ample opportunity to resort to a suit. In fact, the Association did threaten litigation, but withdrew its threat.

Third, the Association's conduct gave the LDF reasonable justification to rely on the Association's inaction, and to invest resources based upon this reliance. We again emphasize that, while mere passage of time does not bar injunctive relief, here the defendant's use of the NAACP initials resulted from both the plaintiff's inaction and conduct that encouraged continued use of the trademark. The Association failed to reserve its rights during the twelve-year period. Indeed, it had previously agreed to the LDF's independence without asserting an exclusive claim to the NAACP initials. The prejudice resulting from the reliance interest building during the years of delay in this case was substantial. The LDF continued to develop "[t]he universal esteem in which the [NAACP] initials are held." The LDF invested substantial labor and millions of dollars in pressing important civil rights suits, soliciting gifts, and recruiting legal talent using the NAACP initials. Because many organizations have names virtually identical to the LDF's except for the NAACP initials, it is only these initials that distinguish the LDF from its emulators.

Courts have never imposed an affirmative obligation upon a defendant to clarify its right to use a disputed trademark during the plaintiff's delay. The undisputed facts of this case point to the reasonableness of the LDF's reliance upon the Association's delay in enforcing its claims. The passing of almost thirteen years without any clear reservation of rights by the Association creates a presumption of reasonable reliance. The Association's conduct included affirmative acts of encouragement. Besides having agreed to the LDF's independence, the Association continued as a client of the LDF and did not protest the LDF's use of the initials despite the LDF's independent dealings with other clients. Finally, the LDF was aware that the Association had threatened to sue but did not. The LDF's good-faith reliance was reasonably based upon both the Association's prolonged passivity and its affirmative acts.

C. The Absence of Negating Factors

The district court correctly indicated that courts tolerate delays if the parties are negotiating a settlement. But the undisputed facts show that from 1966 through 1978 there were no negotiations. In the total absence of negotiations, delay "stemming from an abhorrence of time-consuming and costly litigation" does not preclude laches. Nor was there any evidence presented that suggested bad faith or conscious fraud by the LDF. Indeed, both parties have cooperated in exchanging donations attributed to the wrong organization. The LDF's disclaimer on its stationery further indicates good faith efforts to reduce any possible public confusion over its use of the NAACP initials. In conclusion, there is an absence of factors that might counsel our hesitation in applying laches.

III. THE LACK OF LICENSING ARRANGEMENTS

The Association alleges that from 1966-78 the LDF possessed only a revocable license to use the NAACP initials. The Association bases this view upon a non-profit parent organization's right to revoke use of its name when an affiliate dissociates itself from the parent. Our review of the case law reveals no separate rule for non-profit organizations. The cases relied upon by the Association involve local chapters of national organizations whose right to use the parent's name was conditioned — in the organization's bylaws or charter — on the local's continued affiliation with the national organization. The agreements between the Association and the LDF contained no such condition. Even examined in the most favorable light, these cases do not establish that an affiliate's right to use the parent's name ceases anytime the parent chooses. Rather, they establish that the affiliate's right expires when the affiliation ceases. The parent organization therefore must assert its exclusive claim to the trademark when disaffiliation occurs. Here the affiliation between the Association and the LDF ceased in 1957. Nevertheless, there was mutual agreement to the LDF's continued use of the NAACP initials as an independent organization.

A revocable license cannot be contrived from the record. Such trademark licensing requires (1) explicit contractual arrangements indicating revocability; and (2) supervision and controls by the licensor over the licensee. Indeed, there was no contract between the parties which contained the words "revocable license," much less any exchange of consideration for this alleged license. The record before us is clear that there was no mutual agreement to a revocable licensing arrangement. There were no provisions which indicated (1) that this alleged license was revocable at will, or (2) under what conditions the license would be revoked. We can find no cases in which a revocable trademark license was imputed when there was a twelve-year delay while the defendant was developing a significant reliance interest during this time. In fact, in the absence of qualifying language upon a license, the right to use the license may be deemed perpetual. Although we need not decide whether the 1957 agreement constituted an irrevocable license, certainly the record does not support the finding that a revocable license was granted. The parties mutually agreed to the LDF's independence and continued use of the NAACP initials. The Association's right as a parent organization to deny an affiliate's use of its name was ripe for determination at that time. It does not seem reasonable to impute retroactively a revocable license during the twelve-year time span in which the LDF was expending resources in reliance upon the Association's inaction.

IV. CONCLUSION

The National Association for the Advancement of Colored People and the NAACP Legal Defense and Education Fund, Inc. share common ideals and a distinguished common heritage. History suggests that they were jointly responsible for the revolution in civil rights that led to and has been epitomized by the Supreme Court's decision in *Brown v. Board of Education*. The passage of time coupled with the reliance between the parties leads this court to conclude that laches bars the injunctive relief sought by the Association. These two great organizations, like brilliant but quarreling family members, must continue to share the NAACP initials with which they were born. The judgment is reversed. The case is remanded to the district court with directions that the suit be dismissed.

EUREKA WATER CO. v. NESTLE WATERS NORTH AMERICA, INC.

690 F.3d 1139 (10th Cir. 2012)

HARTZ, Circuit Judge.

I. BACKGROUND

A. Ozarka Spring Water and Ozarka Drinking Water

As early as 1907 Ozarka Water Company sold water that it obtained from a spring in Arkansas. It entered into franchise agreements to allow regional dealers to bottle Ozarka spring water and sell it in specified territories. Eureka was such a regional franchisee. Arrowhead Puritas Waters, Inc. purchased Ozarka in the late 1960s.

In 1971 Dave Raupe purchased Eureka, which sold only spring water. Shortly thereafter, Arrowhead concluded that Ozarka's supply of spring water was inadequate for further expansion and informed its franchisees that it was shutting down its springs. The franchisees could, however, start distributing facsimile drinking water, which was to be made from purified water by adding mineral concentrates for taste. Arrowhead ceased bottling spring water under the Ozarka label. Eureka and Arrowhead memorialized this arrangement in a 1972 franchise agreement, under which Eureka paid royalties on each gallon of drinking water that it sold.

A few years later Arrowhead and Eureka renegotiated their relationship. Their 1975 agreement (the 1975 Agreement) called for a one-time payment of $9,000 by Eureka in exchange for "a royalty-free, paid-up right and license to use the said OZARKA mark in connection with the processing, bottling, sale and distribution within [Eureka's territory] of purified water and/or drinking water made from OZARKA drinking water concentrates."

Arrowhead and Eureka independently began bottling spring water in 1983. In 1987 Arrowhead was acquired by Perrier Group of America, Inc. Two years later, Perrier began packaging Ozarka-branded water in single-serve plastic bottles (PET bottles).

Nestle purchased Perrier in 1992 and began selling Eureka its PET spring water at below-market prices for resale to Eureka wholesale customers. (For convenience, we will now refer to the Perrier/Nestle entity as Nestle, even if the described events predate Nestle's purchase of Perrier.) In 1997, however, Eureka discovered that Nestle had been directly shipping Ozarka PET spring water to Sam's Club and Wal-Mart stores within Eureka's territory. In response to Eureka's claim that these sales violated the 1975 Agreement, Nestle agreed to pay Eureka 50 cents a case on all PET spring-water products and 30 cents a case for all bulk products (1-gallon and 2.5-gallon packages) that Nestle sold in Eureka's territory. The parties refer to the payments as royalties or invasion fees. Nestle did not pay royalties to any other bottler in the country. From 1997 until October 15, 2007, Eureka received 67 royalty checks totaling about $2.5 million.

In late 2003 Nestle unilaterally reduced the royalty rates for both PET and bulk cases to 25 cents a case. Although Eureka continued to invoice Nestle for the difference, it was not paid.

In a May 2007 meeting, William Pearson, Vice President and chief financial officer of Nestle, told Steve Raupe, Eureka's CEO, that Nestle was losing money doing business with Eureka and that something had to change. Three months later Pearson wrote Raupe a letter stating that as of October 15, 2007, Nestle no longer would pay royalties or offer Eureka a lower price on Ozarka spring water than what Nestle charged comparable purchasers. This lawsuit followed.

The jury awarded Eureka $9.2 million on the contract claim and $5 million on the tortious-interference claim. After the jury returned its verdict, the district court entered a declaratory judgment that the 1975 Agreement applies to all Ozarka products, including Ozarka spring water.

II. DISCUSSION

On appeal Nestle argues that it is entitled to (1) JMOL on the contract claim because the unambiguous terms of the license agreement do not cover Ozarka spring water; (2) JMOL on the tortious-interference claim because its conduct was privileged and justified as a matter of law. . . . We begin with Nestle's first two issues.

A. Contract Claim

Nestle argues (1) that its agreement with Eureka was not a contract for the sale of goods and was therefore governed by Oklahoma common law rather than the UCC; (2) that under Oklahoma common law, extrinsic evidence is not admissible to create an ambiguity; and (3) that the 1975 Agreement unambiguously covers only purified water and drinking water, not spring water. We agree.

1. Applicability of UCC

In our view the UCC does not govern the 1975 Agreement. Article 2 of the Oklahoma UCC governs "transactions in goods." Okla. Stat. tit. 12A, §2-102. "'Goods' means all things (including specially manufactured goods) which are movable at the time of identification to the contract for sale. . . ." Okla. Stat. tit. 12A, §2-105(1). This circuit has held that when a contract involves the sale of both goods and non-goods, an Oklahoma court would apply the "predominant factor" test to determine whether the UCC governs. See Specialty Beverages, L.L.C. v. Pabst Brewing Co., 537 F.3d 1165, 1174 (10th Cir. 2008). To explain why the Agreement is not under the UCC, we first summarize the Agreement, which consists of the recitals and seven numbered sections.

The recitals name Arrowhead (Nestle's predecessor) as "SUPPLIER" and Eureka as "DISTRIBUTOR" and summarize the parties' 1972 franchise agreement, which licensed Eureka to use the Ozarka trademark in return for paying royalties on each gallon of purified water and drinking water sold. Next the recitals state:

> The parties now believe that it will be to their mutual advantage to terminate the continuing obligation of DISTRIBUTOR under said Franchise Agreement to pay said royalties in consideration of a lump sum payment for a paid-up license; and to discontinue all obligations of SUPPLIER under said Franchise Agreement except for the obligation to furnish OZARKA drinking water concentrates at SUPPLIER's cost, the

continued exercise of control over the quality of the drinking water sold by distributor under the OZARKA mark, and the maintenance of OZARKA registrations in the United States Patent Office for drinking water and for refrigerated and evaporative coolers for drinking water.

After stating that Eureka has paid Nestle $9,000, the Agreement sets forth the parties' rights and obligations.

Section 1 ("LICENSE TO DISTRIBUTE, BOTTLE, ADVERTISE, AND SELL OZARKA PRODUCTS") grants Eureka:

> a royalty-free, paid-up right and license to use the said OZARKA mark in connection with the processing, bottling, sale and distribution within [Eureka's territory] of purified water and/or drinking water made from OZARKA drinking water concentrates and in connection with coolers and dispensers therefor, subject to the terms and conditions hereinafter set forth.

The section requires that "[a]ll OZARKA [purified and] drinking water bottled or sold by DISTRIBUTOR" be labeled and produced in accordance with specified standards, *id.* at 9398, and gives Nestle the right to inspect Eureka's production facilities and to terminate the agreement if Eureka fails to correct any deficiencies in its production process. In addition, the section prohibits Nestle from granting any other party within Eureka's territory "a license to process, bottle or sell OZARKA drinking water."

Section 2 ("THE SUPPLY OF OZARKA DRINKING WATER CONCENTRATES TO DISTRIBUTOR") requires that Nestle "furnish to DISTRIBUTOR OZARKA drinking water concentrates in such quantities as may be required by DISTRIBUTOR for production of OZARKA drinking water, charging DISTRIBUTOR therefor at its own cost plus freight." *Id.* at 9402. It further provides, however, that "DISTRIBUTOR may obtain OZARKA drinking water concentrates from a party other than SUPPLIER." *Id.* Once Eureka identifies the third-party supplier and Nestle is satisfied that the third party can maintain quality standards, Nestle will provide the formulation for the concentrates to the third party. (Nestle stopped providing the concentrates to Eureka by 1987, and perhaps a number of years before that.)

Under Section 3 ("TERM AND TERMINATION") the 1975 Agreement "shall continue in full force and effect so long as DISTRIBUTOR shall continue the use of the OZARKA mark as licensed hereunder." *Id.* Section 4 ("INFRINGEMENT BY THIRD PARTY") requires each party "to notify the other of any infringements of the trademark OZARKA within [Eureka's] Territory." *Id.* at 9403 (internal quotation marks omitted). Section 5 ("NOTICES") states that all mailings to Nestle are considered delivered when sent by registered mail to the specified address. *Id.* And Section 6 ("ASSIGNMENT") prohibits Eureka from assigning its rights under the Agreement to anyone without Nestle's written consent, unless it is selling its entire business. *Id.* at 9404. Finally, under Section 7 ("PRODUCT LIABILITY") Eureka bears sole liability for any third-party product-liability claims based on injury from the OZARKA products or their containers.

Nestle argues that the 1975 Agreement is not a transaction in goods because it is a license for a trademark, which it claims is not a good under the UCC. We agree with Nestle that the Agreement includes a trademark license. Section 1 grants Eureka "a royalty-free, paid-up right and license to use the . . . OZARKA mark in connection with the processing, bottling, sale and distribution . . . of purified water and/or drinking water." We also agree with Nestle that a trademark license is not a "good" as that term is used in the UCC. Intellectual property is not a movable thing, see Okla. Stat. tit. 12A, §2-105 ("'Goods' means all things . . . which are movable at the time of identification to the contract for sale. . . ."); rather, it is a type of intangible property, see Penguin Group (USA) Inc. v. Am. Buddha, 609 F.3d 30, 36 n. 4 (2d Cir. 2010) ("a copyright [is] . . . an intangible thing"); 1 McCarthy on Trademarks and Unfair Competition §2:14 (4th ed. 2012) ("[I]n discussing 'ownership' of a trademark, we must recognize that we are dealing with intangible, intellectual property."). Although one can express the content of intellectual property in a movable medium (such as a trademark registration form), the intellectual property remains intangible. See United States v. Brown, 925 F.2d 1301, 1307 (10th Cir. 1991) ("Purely intellectual property . . . can be represented physically, such as through writing on a page, but the underlying, intellectual property itself, remains intangible."). Therefore, the grant of a trademark license is not a transaction in goods under the UCC. See Lamle v. Mattel, Inc., 394 F.3d 1355, 1359 n. 2 (Fed. Cir. 2005) ("[A] license for intellectual property . . . is not a sale of goods."); Emerson Radio Corp. v. Orion Sales, Inc., 253 F.3d 159, 161, 170 (3d Cir. 2001) (three-year exclusive license to use a trademark); Grappo v. Alitalia Linee Aeree Italiane, S.p.A., 56 F.3d 427, 432 (2d Cir. 1995) (nonexclusive license for copyrighted material); JRT, Inc. v. TCBY Sys., Inc., 52 F.3d 734, 739 (8th Cir. 1995) (contract for services and use of a trademark).

Admittedly, as Eureka points out, the 1975 Agreement also contemplates the sale of goods. Section 2 of the Agreement states that Nestle "shall furnish to [Eureka] OZARKA drinking water concentrates in such quantities as may be required by [Eureka] for production of OZARKA drinking water." Drinking water concentrates are goods. The question, then, is whether the license or the sale of goods is the predominant factor in the contract. See *Specialty Beverages*, 537 F.3d at 1174.

Here, there is little doubt that the license — not the right to purchase drinking-water concentrates — is what motivated the transaction. Eureka's right to purchase drinking-water concentrates was a matter of financial indifference to Nestle. The Agreement required Nestle to sell Eureka the concentrates at Nestle's cost plus freight. And from Eureka's point of view, although the concentrates enabled it to sell Ozarka drinking water, it could not engage in those sales without the license granted by the Agreement. See *Grappo*, 56 F.3d at 432 (training manuals would have been useless absent a copyright license to use them). Moreover, the Agreement could be fully consummated without any sales of concentrates from Nestle to Eureka; if Eureka found a suitable supplier, Nestle would provide the supplier with the intellectual property (the formulation for the concentrates) necessary to produce the concentrates for Eureka.

Eureka relies on Pepsi-Cola Bottling Co. of Pittsburg, Inc. v. PepsiCo, Inc., 431 F.3d 1241 (10th Cir. 2005), where we held that New York's version of the UCC governed a contract granting a bottling company an exclusive territory to bottle and distribute Pepsi-Cola. See *id.* at 1248, 1255-56 n. 7. But *Pepsi-Cola Bottling* is distinguishable. The contract in that case required the bottling company to purchase all its Pepsi-Cola concentrate from PepsiCo, see *id.* at 1248 ("[T]he Company will sell to the Bottler, and the Bottler will purchase, at the Company's then price or prices . . . at the time of each sale, the Bottler's requirements of

Pepsi-Cola concentrate or syrup for the bottling of Pepsi-Cola hereunder." (internal quotation marks omitted)), and PepsiCo was not required to sell the syrup at cost. Presumably, PepsiCo made its money by selling the syrup. Although the bottler did not purchase the concentrate directly from PepsiCo, it did so indirectly, as a member of a 27-bottler cooperative. See *id.* at 1248 n. 1. The financial core of the contract was the purchase and sale of syrup—a good.

To be sure, we observed in *Pepsi-Cola Bottling* that "an overwhelming majority of . . . jurisdictions have held that distributorship contracts are sales contracts and thus governed by the UCC." *Id.* at 1256 n. 7; see also *Specialty Beverages*, 537 F.3d at 1174-75 (Oklahoma Supreme Court would, in accordance with the majority rule, apply the UCC to a distribution agreement because the sale of goods is the predominant factor). And we recognize that the 1975 Agreement refers to the parties as "Supplier" and "Distributor." But it is the substance of the Agreement that controls, and the substance is not a distribution contract. "In the world of goods, a distribution contract is a commitment by a manufacturer to sell products to a distributor with the expectation that the distributor will resell them to others in the stream of commerce." Raymond T. Nimmer, Through the Looking Glass: What Courts and UCITA Say About the Scope of Contract Law in the Information Age, 38 Duq. L. Rev. 255, 294-95 (2000). Under the 1975 Agreement, unlike a distribution agreement, the sale of goods from "Supplier" to "Distributor" is only an incidental, and perhaps nonexistent (Nestle quit supplying the concentrates no later than 1987), component of the contractual relationship.

Accordingly, we hold that the UCC does not govern the 1975 Agreement; rather, Oklahoma common law governs.

2. Admissibility of Extrinsic Evidence Under Oklahoma Common Law

Eureka argues that under Oklahoma common law the circumstances surrounding execution of a contract are admissible to establish intent. But the most recent Oklahoma case authority that it cites is from 1980. Whatever the law may have been then, that is not Oklahoma law now. Under current Oklahoma common law, extrinsic evidence is not admissible to create an ambiguity in a contract that is unambiguous on its face. In Mercury Investment Co. v. F.W. Woolworth Company, 706 P.2d 523, 529 (Okla. 1985), the state supreme court wrote:

> [T]he practical construction of an agreement, as evidenced by the acts and conduct of the parties, is available only in the event of an ambiguity. But where a contract is complete in itself and, as viewed in its entirety, is unambiguous, its language is the only legitimate evidence of what the parties intended. The intention of the parties cannot be determined from the surrounding circumstances, but must be gathered from a four-corners' examination of the contractual instrument in question.

We therefore turn to the question whether the 1975 Agreement is ambiguous regarding whether it covers all Ozarka products, including spring water, or covers only purified water and drinking water. "Whether a contract is ambiguous and hence requires extrinsic evidence to clarify the doubt is a question of law for the courts." Pitco Prod. Co. v. Chaparral Energy, Inc., 63 P.3d 541, 545 (Okla. 2003); see King v. PA Consulting Group, Inc., 485 F.3d 577, 589 (10th Cir. 2007) ("Whether a contract is ambiguous is a question of law that we review de novo.").

i. Facial Ambiguity

"A contract is ambiguous if it is reasonably susceptible to at least two different constructions. To decide whether a contract is ambiguous we look to the language of the entire agreement. A contract must be considered as a whole so as to give effect to all its provisions." *Pitco*, 63 P.3d at 545-46 (footnotes omitted). In our view, the 1975 Agreement is not reasonably susceptible to two different constructions regarding the type of water that it concerns. Its plain language grants Eureka a right to use the Ozarka trademark only in connection with purified water and what it terms drinking water.

The language granting Eureka a license to use the Ozarka trademark is unequivocal:

The Franchise Agreement between the parties of [Arrowhead] and [Eureka] is hereby terminated and [Eureka] is granted a royalty-free, paid-up right and license to use the said OZARKA mark in connection with the processing, bottling, sale and distribution within [a specified region] of purified water and/or drinking water made from OZARKA drinking water concentrates. . . .

No reasonable reading of this paragraph could extend Eureka's right to use the Ozarka trademark to spring water. The provision lists only "purified water" and "drinking water" without referencing any other products.

At least three other parts of the Agreement further support this conclusion. First, §1 sets forth detailed standards that Eureka must follow in producing and labeling purified water and drinking water, with no reference to spring water or any other Ozarka products. The purified-water provision states that "[a]ll purified water sold under the OZARKA mark . . . shall be designated as purified water with the method of preparation specified" and that "[t]he mineral content of any such purified water sold . . . shall not at any time exceed ten (10) parts per million by weight." *Id.* at 9398. The drinking-water provision states that "[a]ll OZARKA drinking water sold by DISTRIBUTOR shall be produced from purified water plus OZARKA drinking water concentrates" and that "[a]ll OZARKA drinking water bottled or sold by DISTRIBUTOR shall be produced in accordance with the production and control specifications of drinking water . . . supplied to DISTRIBUTOR by SUPPLIER." *Id.* Later §1 states that "SUPPLIER . . . shall have access to the purification and drinking water production facilities of DISTRIBUTOR at all times during normal operations hours for the purpose of checking . . . the quality of the purified and/or drinking water produced by DISTRIBUTOR," *id.* at 9399; and that "[a]ll labels employed by DISTRIBUTOR for use on or in connection with OZARKA drinking water and/or OZARKA purified water shall first be approved in writing by SUPPLIER for trademark usage," *id.* at 9400. The language of §1 unequivocally establishes that neither purified water nor drinking water encompasses spring water.

All OZARKA drinking water bottled or sold by DISTRIBUTOR shall be produced in accordance with the production and control specifications of drinking water effective March 7, 1972 supplied to DISTRIBUTOR by SUPPLIER, and DISTRIBUTOR shall conform in all respects to the quality control provisions respecting concentration, sanitation, sampling, and other procedures set forth in said production and control specifications.

Likewise, §2 of the Agreement makes no mention of spring water. It provides terms for the supply of materials necessary for producing drinking water, saying that Nestle "shall furnish

DISTRIBUTOR OZARKA drinking water concentrates . . . for the production of OZARKA drinking water." *Id.* at 9402.

We also note that the recitals reference only purified water and drinking water. The summary of the 1972 franchise agreement states that under that agreement Eureka had "installed facilities for production of OZARKA 'scientifically prepared' drinking water produced by adding OZARKA drinking water concentrates to purified water" and "ha[d] been engaged in the sale of such OZARKA drinking water and OZARKA purified water in [Eureka's territory]." *Id.* at 9396. In short, nothing in the Agreement indicates that it covers spring water.

Eureka responds that the Agreement is ambiguous because on several occasions it uses the terms Ozarka products and Ozarka waters. But "[a] contract must be considered as a whole so as to give effect to all its provisions without narrowly concentrating upon some clause or language taken out of context." *Mercury Inv. Co.*, 706 P.2d at 529; see also Okla. Stat. tit. 15, §157 ("The whole of a contract is to be taken together, so as to give effect to every part, if reasonably practicable, each clause helping to interpret the others."). When viewed in light of the Agreement's focus on purified water and drinking water, the references to Ozarka products and waters cannot reasonably be read to expand the scope of the licensing provision beyond the only two specific products mentioned. Rather, the unmodified terms products and waters are clearly used only as shorthand for the products and waters specified elsewhere, just as we have often referred to the 1975 Agreement as "the Agreement." For example, Eureka points to the licensing provision's heading: "LICENSE TO DISTRIBUTE, BOTTLE, ADVERTISE, AND SELL OZARKA PRODUCTS." Aplt. App., Vol. 29 at 9397. But immediately following the heading is the statement that the license granted is "in connection with the . . . distribution . . . of purified water and/or drinking water." *Id.* The only licensed Ozarka "products" are purified water and drinking water. The heading cannot reasonably be interpreted as expanding the coverage of the provision. Similarly, the sole appearances of the term Ozarka water(s) in the Agreement are in subsections 1(d) and 1(f), which allow Nestle to inspect Eureka's purification and drinking-water production facilities and which require Eureka's compliance with production standards that are applicable only to purified water and drinking water—the only "waters" of interest.

Eureka also claims that the Agreement's reference to trademark registration number 836,026, which is a registration for Ozarka drinking water, creates an ambiguity because in 1967, when Ozarka (Arrowhead's predecessor) registered the trademark, it sold only Ozarka spring water. Eureka argues that "[i]t is reasonable to conclude that based on the reference to this trademark, Arrowhead and Eureka believed that spring water and drinking water are sufficiently alike that a trademark or license for one necessarily covers the other." Aplee. Br. at 25. Eureka's argument fails because it relies on extrinsic evidence—evidence that in 1967 Ozarka sold only spring water. But even if we could consider the evidence, and even if whoever filed the trademark thought that "drinking water" encompassed spring water, that does not tell us the meaning of "drinking water" in the 1975 Agreement eight years later. The Agreement specifies that the drinking water it covers must be produced by adding concentrates to purified water, and no one has suggested that spring water is so produced.

ii. Latent Ambiguity

Eureka seeks to escape the Oklahoma rule against the use of extrinsic evidence to interpret an unambiguous contract by invoking an exception to the general rule—the exception for latent ambiguities. "A 'latent ambiguity' is one not evident from the face of the instrument alone but becomes apparent when applying the instrument to the facts as they exist." Ryan v. Ryan, 78 P.3d 961, 964 (Okla. Civ. App. 2003). "It arises when language is clear and intelligible and suggests but a single meaning, but some extrinsic fact or some extraneous evidence creates a necessity for interpretation or a choice between two or more possible meanings." *Id.* at 965.

Here, Eureka has failed to identify any latent ambiguity in the 1975 Agreement. Perhaps the latent-ambiguity doctrine might allow Eureka to prove that the parties understood the term purified water or drinking water in the 1975 Agreement to mean something broader than the purified water or drinking water described in that Agreement, although one could doubt whether such proof would be possible in light of the precise language of the Agreement defining purified water and drinking water. In any event, all that is referred to in Eureka's brief on appeal to show a latent ambiguity is the following:

(1) Trademark No. 836,026 suggests that Arrowhead believed that drinking water and spring water were functionally interchangeable; (2) Nestle aggressively sought to buy from Eureka a right which it now claims Eureka did not possess under the 1975 Bottling Agreement and that it could regain by merely terminating a supplemental agreement with reasonable notice; (3) for nearly two decades, Nestle extended special pricing and paid invasion fees to Eureka for sales made into its territory, all applicable to Ozarka spring water; and (4) for nearly thirty years, Nestle and its predecessors-in-interest were aware of and acquiesced to Eureka's continued expansion of Ozarka products in Oklahoma.

We have previously concluded, however, that the trademark application does not indicate that the term drinking water as defined in the 1975 Agreement encompasses spring water. And items 2, 3, and 4 do not show how the parties defined the terms purified water or drinking water but are simply evidence of the parties' general intent in entering into the Agreement. This evidence was used at trial to prove that the agreement was meant to include more than the purified water and drinking water specified in the Agreement, not that the term purified water or drinking water actually encompassed spring water. Such evidence of general intent, not tied to the specific usage of a particular word or term, does not establish a latent ambiguity. If it did, the latent-ambiguity exception would swallow the general rule barring extrinsic evidence.

Thus, we hold that the 1975 Agreement applies only to purified water and drinking water. The declaratory judgment and the jury's verdict to the contrary (including the damages award) must be reversed. We remand to the district court for entry of judgment in favor of Nestle on the contract claim.

BELTRONICS USA, INC. v. MIDWEST INVENTORY DISTRIBUTION, LLC

562 F.3d 1067 (10th Cir. 2009)

TACHA, Circuit Judge.

Defendants-Appellants are a consumer electronics company, its owners, and its trade names (collectively, "Midwest"). Plaintiff-Appellee ("Beltronics") is a provider of aftermarket vehicle electronics, including radar detectors. Midwest appeals the district court's order preliminarily enjoining it from selling Beltronics equipment not bearing an original Beltronics serial number label. We have jurisdiction under 28 U.S.C. §1292(a)(1) and AFFIRM.

I. BACKGROUND

As early as 2003, Beltronics began selling electronics equipment under its Beltronics trademark. At all times relevant to this case, Beltronics sold its equipment to at least two authorized distributors who agreed to sell the products for a specified minimum price. Apparently in violation of their distribution agreements, those distributors sold Beltronics radar detectors to Midwest, which in turn resold them as "new" on the internet auction site eBay. To prevent Beltronics from discovering that Midwest's inventory had been supplied by the two distributors, the distributors either replaced each radar detector's original serial number label with a phony label or removed the original label altogether before shipping equipment to Midwest. On rare occasions, when the distributors supplied Midwest with a radar detector bearing an original serial number label, Midwest removed the label prior to resale.

It is Beltronics's policy that only those who purchase Beltronics radar detectors bearing an original serial number label are eligible to receive certain products and services, including software upgrades, rebates, product use information, service assistance, warranties, and recalls. Beltronics learned that its radar detectors were being sold without original serial labels when Midwest's purchasers contacted Beltronics with warranty requests for detectors that had phony serial numbers. A Beltronics customer service manager submitted an affidavit stating that those purchasers were confused, thinking that they were entitled to a warranty from Beltronics. The customer service manager further stated that the customers expressed their belief that they did not receive what they thought they had purchased and that Beltronics had deceived them. He explained that they became irate when they learned their radar detector was not covered by Beltronics's warranty and did not come with other services such as recalls and product upgrades, and that this is extremely harmful to Beltronics's reputation and goodwill.

In September 2007, Beltronics filed this action against Midwest. The complaint asserted (1) counterfeiting and federal trademark infringement under 15 U.S.C. §1114; (2) false designation or origin under 15 U.S.C. §1125; and (3) trademark infringement, unfair competition, and passing off in violation of state law. Beltronics also sought a preliminary injunction. . . .

B. Trademark Infringement Claim

Under §32 of the Lanham Act, "[t]he unauthorized use of any reproduction, counterfeit, copy, or colorable imitation of a registered mark in a way that is likely to cause confusion in the marketplace concerning the source of the different products constitutes trademark infringement." First Sav. Bank, F.S.B. v. First Bank System, Inc., 101 F.3d 645, 651 (10th Cir.1996). Thus, the central inquiry in a trademark infringement case is the likelihood of consumer confusion. Midwest argues that the district court erred both legally and factually in determining that Midwest's sale of Beltronics radar detectors is likely to cause confusion in the marketplace. First, Midwest claims that its sale of radar detectors under the Beltronics trademark is protected by the first sale doctrine and the district court committed an error of law in concluding otherwise. Alternatively, Midwest argues that even if the first sale doctrine does not apply, the district court's determination that its disclosure to consumers was insufficient to alleviate confusion involved errors of both law and fact. We evaluate each of these claims in turn.

1. First Sale Doctrine

Those who resell genuine trademarked products are generally not liable for trademark infringement. See Davidoff & CIE, S.A. v. PLD Int'l Corp., 263 F.3d 1297, 1301 (11th Cir.2001); NEC Elecs. v. CAL Circuit Abco, 810 F.2d 1506, 1509 (9th Cir.1987). "The reason is that trademark law is designed to prevent sellers from confusing or deceiving consumers about the origin or make of a product, which confusion ordinarily does not exist when a genuine article bearing a true mark is sold." NEC Elecs., 810 F.2d at 1509. Accordingly, under the "first sale" doctrine, "the right of a producer to control distribution of its trademarked product does not extend beyond the first sale of the product." Australian Gold, 436 F.3d at 1240-41 (10th Cir. 2006). In our circuit's only case evaluating this doctrine in connection with a Lanham Act claim, we observed that "the essence of the 'first sale' doctrine [is] that a purchaser who does no more than stock, display, and resell a producer's product under the producer's trademark violates no right conferred upon the producer by the Lanham Act." Id. at 1241.

It logically follows that the first sale doctrine is not applicable "when an alleged infringer sells trademarked goods that are materially different than those sold by the trademark owner." Davidoff, 263 F.3d at 1302. A materially different product is not genuine and may generate consumer confusion about the source and the quality of the trademarked product. See Gamut Trading Co. v. U.S. Int'l Trade Comm'n, 200 F.3d 775, 779 (Fed. Cir. 1999); Iberia Foods Corp. v. Romeo, 150 F.3d 298, 303 (3d Cir.1998). We hold, as other federal circuit courts have held, that the unauthorized resale of a materially different trademarked product can constitute trademark infringement.[3]

We emphasize that not all differences are material. Some differences between products "prove so minimal that consumers who purchase the alleged infringer's goods get precisely what they believed they were purchasing [and] consumers' perceptions of the trademarked goods are not likely to be affected by the alleged infringer's sales." Iberia Foods, 150 F.3d at 303. A guiding principle in evaluating whether a difference between two products bearing the same trademark is material is whether the difference "confuses consumers and impinges on the . . . trademark holder's goodwill." Nestle, 982 F.2d at 638. For this reason, the materiality analysis must be undertaken "on a case-by-case basis" and must include "an examination of the products and markets at issue." Brilliance Audio, 474 F.3d at 371. Although no mechanical process exists for determining the threshold for materiality, a difference is material if "consumers [would] consider [it] relevant to a decision about whether to purchase a product." Davidoff, 263 F.3d at 1302. Because many factors influence such considerations, the threshold "must be kept low to include even subtle differences between products." We review de

---

3. We recognize that these cases and others cited in this opinion involve the sale of "gray market" goods — goods that bear a United States trademark, are authorized for exclusive production and sale in a foreign country, and are subsequently imported and sold in the United States without the trademark owner's consent. The rationale in gray goods cases applies with equal force in this context. Thus, we agree with the Third and Eleventh Circuits that the rule "is not limited to gray goods cases." Iberia Foods, 150 F.3d at 302; Davidoff, 263 F.3d at 1302 n.5.

novo the question of whether differences between trademarked goods and goods sold by an alleged infringer are material.

In support of its argument that the first sale doctrine applies in this case, Midwest contends that material differences are limited to differences in physical quality or in control procedures designed to ensure a trademarked product's physical quality at the time of resale. It asserts that the absence of Beltronics's warranties and other services are "collateral" to the radar detectors' physical quality, and therefore no material differences distinguish Beltronics's radar detectors from those sold by Midwest. Accordingly, Midwest claims the first sale doctrine shields it from liability under the Lanham Act.

In evaluating this line of reasoning, we turn again to what we have called "the essence of the 'first sale' doctrine," which is that "a purchaser who does no more than stock, display, and resell a producer's product under the producer's trademark violates no right conferred upon the producer by the Lanham Act." *Australian Gold*, 436 F.3d at 1241. In this case, it is undisputed that something more than stocking, displaying, and reselling radar detectors is at issue. Additionally, although we have never had occasion to review whether differences in warranties or service commitments may constitute material differences, at least two federal circuit courts have held or observed that they may. The Federal Circuit has held that "physical material differences are not required to establish trademark infringement . . . because trademarked goods originating from the trademark owner may have nonphysical characteristics associated with them, including services, such that [the sale of] similar goods lacking those associated characteristics . . . may mislead the consumer and damage the owner's goodwill." SKF USA Inc. v. Int'l Trade Comm'n, 423 F.3d 1307, 1312 (Fed. Cir. 2005). Similarly, the First Circuit has observed that "the appropriate test [for materiality] should not be strictly limited to physical differences," but should include other differences such as "warranty protection or service commitments [that] may well render products non-identical in the relevant Lanham Trade-Mark Act sense." *Nestle*, 982 F.2d at 639 n.7. We are aware of no federal circuit court that has held or observed otherwise when considering the specific question of whether material differences may include warranties and service commitments. Accordingly, we conclude that the district court did not commit an error of law in concluding that material differences may include the warranties and services associated with Beltronics's radar detectors.

Midwest expresses concern about the policy implications for such a decision. It claims that this interpretation of the material difference exception to the first sale doctrine would permit any trademark owner to eliminate the resale of its goods, shut down its competitors, and ultimately fix the price of its product simply by limiting its warranty coverage and service commitments to those who buy from it directly. Because under this scenario those who purchase a trademarked product from a reseller would not receive the same warranty and services as those who purchase from the trademark owner, Midwest asserts the product would be materially different and all resellers would be unavoidably and invariably liable under the Lanham Act.

Were the first sale doctrine the only legal principle shielding resellers from liability in this scenario, Midwest's argument might avail. See *Davidoff*, 263 F.3d at 1301 (observing that the first sale doctrine "does not hold true . . . when an alleged infringer sells trademarked goods that are materially different than those sold by the trademark owner."). However, the fact that "the resale of a trademarked product that is materially different can constitute a trademark infringement," see *id.* at 1302, does not mean that it always does. The Lanham Act does not proscribe material differences per se; it proscribes sales and offers for sale that are "likely to cause confusion, or to cause mistake, or to deceive." 15 U.S.C. §1114(a)-(b). The purpose of the material difference test is to assist courts in determining whether allegedly infringing products are likely to cause confusion in the marketplace and undermine the goodwill the trademark owner has developed in its trademarked goods. So long as resellers of materially different products take the necessary steps to adequately alleviate this confusion and prevent injury to the trademark's goodwill—by, for example, sufficiently disclosing that the product differs from the originally sold product—those differences will be unlikely to trigger the liability Midwest envisions. See Matrix Essentials, Inc. v. Emporium Drug Mart, Inc., 988 F.2d 587, 591 (5th Cir. 1993) (explaining that in several cases where trademark infringement was associated with the resale of materially different goods, an essential element was that "a consumer would not necessarily be aware of the [differences] and would thereby be confused or deceived."). We therefore conclude that Midwest's policy argument is unavailing.

BENIHANA, INC. v. BENIHANA OF TOKYO
784 F.3d 887 (2d Cir. 2016)

LYNCH, Circuit Judge.

BACKGROUND

I. The License Agreement

This case arises from a dispute between the parties resulting from the 1994 corporate division of the well-known Benihana restaurant chain. Under the parties' Amended and Restated Agreement and Plan of Reorganization (the "ARA"), Benihana America received the right to operate Benihana restaurants and use Benihana trademarks in the United States, Latin America, and the Caribbean, while Benihana of Tokyo received those rights for all other territories. The one exception to this clean split was Hawaii: the ARA provided that Benihana America would grant Benihana of Tokyo a license to continue operating an existing Benihana restaurant in Honolulu.

Accordingly, on May 15, 1995 the parties entered into a License Agreement (the "Agreement"), governed by New York state law, granting Benihana of Tokyo a license and franchise to operate Benihana restaurants in Hawaii, subject to the terms of the Agreement. In the Agreement, Benihana of Tokyo acknowledged the "necessity of operating the [restaurant] in conformity with [Benihana America's] standards and specifications," many of which are spelled out in the Agreement. Most relevant here, the Agreement restricts Benihana of Tokyo's menu selection and use of Benihana trademarks. Article 6.3 requires Benihana of Tokyo to "sell or offer for sale only such products and services as have been expressly approved for sale in writing" by Benihana America, provided that "such approval shall not be unreasonably withheld." Similarly, under Article 8.1(c), Benihana of Tokyo agreed "[t]o advertise, sell or offer for sale only those items which are sold by [Benihana America] in its company-owned restaurants or such other products as are approved by [Benihana America] in writing, which shall not be unreasonably withheld, prior to offering the same for sale." Article 5.2 provides that "[a]ny and all advertising ... or other matter employing in any way whatsoever the words 'Benihana,'

'Benihana of Tokyo' or the [Benihana] 'flower' symbol shall be submitted to [Benihana America] for its approval prior to publication or use. [Benihana America] shall not unreasonably withhold approval for any such publication or use."

The Agreement also sets forth conditions and procedures governing termination. Under Article 12.1, Benihana America has good cause to terminate the Agreement in the event of either: (I) a violation of "any . . . substantial term or condition of th[e] Agreement [that Benihana of Tokyo] fails to cure . . . within thirty days after written notice from [Benihana America]"; or (II) "three notices [by Benihana America] of any default hereunder (and such defaults are thereafter cured), within any consecutive twelve-month period." The Agreement also provides that violation of certain articles — including Article 5.2 restricting Benihana of Tokyo's trademark use and Article 8.1(c) restricting the items Benihana of Tokyo may advertise or sell — "would result in irreparable injury to [Benihana America] for which no adequate remedy at law may be available" and for which Benihana America may obtain "an injunction against [such] violation . . . without the necessity of showing actual or threatened damage."

Finally, Article 13 contains two arbitration provisions:

> 13.1 If this Agreement shall be terminated by [Benihana America] and [Benihana of Tokyo] shall dispute [Benihana America's] right of termination, or the reasonableness thereof, the dispute shall be settled by arbitration at the main office of the American Arbitration Association in the City of New York in accordance with the rules of said association and judgment upon the award rendered by the arbitrators may be entered in any court having jurisdiction thereof. The arbitration panel shall consist of three (3) members, one (1) of whom shall be chosen by [Benihana America], and (1) by [Benihana of Tokyo] and the other by the two (2) so chosen.

> 13.2 In the event that any other dispute arises between the parties hereto in connection with the terms or provisions of this Agreement, either party by written notice to the other party may elect to submit the dispute to binding arbitration in accordance with the foregoing procedure. Such right shall not be exclusive of any other rights which a party may have to pursue a course of legal action in an appropriate forum. Enforcement of any arbitration award, decision or order may be sought in any court having competent jurisdiction.

II. The Licensing Disputes

Things proceeded amicably enough under the Agreement for over fifteen years. But in 2012 Benihana America was purchased by Angelo Gordon & Co., which proved to be a more hands-on licensor. In May 2013, Benihana America wrote to Benihana of Tokyo that it had recently learned that Benihana of Tokyo was selling hamburgers — called "BeniBurgers" — at its Honolulu location. Benihana America reminded Benihana of Tokyo that the Agreement required Benihana America's approval of new menu items, noted that hamburgers were not an authorized menu item, and demanded that the hamburgers be removed from the menu. When no remedial action was forthcoming, Benihana America sent a second letter on July 30, 2013 notifying Benihana of Tokyo that it was in breach of the Agreement and had thirty days to cure.

After receiving two extensions of the cure period from Benihana America, Benihana of Tokyo brought suit on September 24, 2013 in the New York State Supreme Court seeking an injunction to stay the running of the cure period pending arbitration of whether selling hamburgers violated the Agreement. Benihana America promptly removed the suit to federal court. At a hearing before the district court on October 1, 2013, Benihana of Tokyo did not dispute that the Agreement prohibited selling hamburgers but argued that Benihana America had waived its right to enforce that prohibition by failing to monitor the Honolulu restaurant for many years. The district court rejected the waiver argument as precluded by the plain language of the Agreement, found that each of the relevant factors weighed against staying the cure period, and accordingly denied the motion. The court also rejected Benihana of Tokyo's backup request at oral argument for "a very short stub period for the cure," explaining that it had "applied the standards and determined that they don't justify extending the cure period." Later that day, counsel for Benihana of Tokyo submitted to Benihana America certain financial documents required by the Agreement and represented that Benihana of Tokyo "will not be selling hamburgers in Hawaii." On December 13, 2013 Benihana America sent another notice of breach based on asserted deficiencies in the submitted financial documentation and violations of the Agreement's advertising restrictions.

On January 13, 2014, the day on which the latest cure period expired, Benihana of Tokyo filed an arbitration demand with the American Arbitration Association seeking "a declaratory judgment that the claimed defaults do not exist, but, if the panel finds that the claimed defaults do exist, then [Benihana of Tokyo] requests sufficient time to cure the alleged defaults.

Despite its assurances to the contrary, Benihana of Tokyo continued to sell hamburgers at its Honolulu location. An onsite inspection by Benihana America on January 21, 2014 allegedly revealed that, in place of the BeniBurger, Benihana of Tokyo was now serving a "Tokyo Burger," as well as a "Beni Panda" children's meal consisting of two mini-burgers served with rice and arranged to resemble a panda face. These menu offerings were advertised using the Benihana name and other trademarks in a manner allegedly not authorized by the Agreement.

That discovery prompted Benihana America on February 5, 2014 to send Benihana of Tokyo a notice of termination of the Agreement effective February 15, 2014. The notice asserted that good cause for termination existed under either prong of Article 12.1: (I) failure to cure within thirty days; and (II) three notices of default within twelve months. The notice also stated that Benihana of Tokyo's "attempt to relitigate [before an arbitral panel] the question of whether [Benihana of Tokyo] may wait to cure until after the arbitration 'panel finds that the claimed defaults do exist,' an argument rejected by [the district court] in October, suggests a level of contempt so extreme that termination of the License Agreement is [Benihana America's] only option." That same day, Benihana America filed a counterclaim in the arbitration seeking confirmation of its termination.

Two days later, Benihana America petitioned the district court for injunctive relief in aid of arbitration pursuant to Federal Rule of Civil Procedure 65 . . .

DISCUSSION

Where the parties have agreed to arbitrate a dispute, a district court has jurisdiction to issue a preliminary injunction to preserve the status quo pending arbitration. The standard for such an injunction is the same as for preliminary injunctions generally. We review the grant of a preliminary injunction for abuse of discretion, reversing only if the injunction is based on an error in law or a clearly erroneous assessment of the evidence, or if it cannot be located within the range of permissible decisions.

I. Injunction Against Unauthorized Menu Items and Use of Trademarks

The first two components of the district court's injunction do not require extensive discussion, and because Benihana of Tokyo's arguments as to them largely overlap, we consider them together. We conclude that the district court acted within its discretion in finding that each of the factors for a preliminary injunction favored Benihana America and accordingly in granting those portions of the injunction.

A. Likelihood of Success on the Merits

Benihana of Tokyo concedes what it describes as "technical violations of two ancillary provisions" of the licensing agreement — namely, the menu and advertising restrictions. But, it contends, when assessing likelihood of success on the merits, that the question is not simply whether it has breached the Agreement, but whether its breaches were grounds for termination. Assuming that this is indeed the correct question, the answer depends largely on the accuracy of Benihana of Tokyo's characterization of the violations as "technical" and the provisions as "ancillary." Benihana of Tokyo does not fare well on either front.

The district court properly found that, far from committing merely trivial violations, Benihana of Tokyo was "blatantly not complying with the license agreement," even after it "could not have been more clear at [an earlier] hearing in acknowledging that it was forbidden under the license agreement to sell burgers," and even after it represented that it would cease doing so. Instead, Benihana of Tokyo continued to flout the terms of the Agreement, relying on, as the district court aptly put it, "justification[s] utterly and unusually unconvincing," such as that burgers with rice and shaped as "panda ears" are not burgers. The menu item and advertising restrictions of the Agreement were clear, and Benihana of Tokyo was clearly violating them.

Nor do we agree with Benihana of Tokyo that the breached provisions are "ancillary." Control over menu and advertising is presumably a central concern for a licensor of a restaurant brand, and the Agreement reveals precisely such a concern in this case. The Agreement begins by explaining that Benihana America has "created and developed a unique system of high-quality restaurants" and that Benihana of Tokyo "understands and acknowledges . . . the necessity of operating the business franchised hereunder in conformity with [Benihana America's] standards and specifications." Moreover, the Agreement included the menu and advertising restrictions among the provisions for violation of which Benihana America could seek an injunction without showing irreparable harm.

As a fallback, Benihana of Tokyo contends that Benihana America is not likely to prevail in the arbitration because, under the Agreement, had it submitted the menu items and advertisements for approval, Benihana America could not have unreasonably withheld its consent. Thus, Benihana of Tokyo argues, its advertisements and "burger sales are impermissible only if [Benihana America] acts reasonably in prohibiting [the advertisements and] burger sales to begin with." We express no view on whether Benihana America's withholding such consent would have been reasonable, for that question is beside the point. The Agreement required Benihana of Tokyo to seek consent before taking these actions. Failure to do so put Benihana of Tokyo in breach; it also meant that Benihana America's obligation not to withhold its approval unreasonably was never triggered. We therefore reject Benihana of Tokyo's contention that Benihana America's conduct makes it unlikely to prevail in the arbitration.

B. Irreparable Harm

Nor did the district court abuse its discretion in finding that "the sale of these burgers under a Benihana name will irreparably harm [Benihana America] by undermining the distinct image it has worked so hard to create in the minds of consumers." . . .

C. Balance of Hardships and Public Interest

We also agree with the district court that it is no hardship for Benihana of Tokyo to refrain from menu offerings and trademark uses that are not permitted under the Agreement, whereas Benihana America faces harm to its brand from the Agreement's violation.

. . .

CONCLUSION

For the foregoing reasons, we AFFIRM the order of the district court insofar as it enjoins Benihana of Tokyo, pending resolution of the arbitration, from selling hamburgers or other unauthorized menu items or engaging in unapproved advertising at its Hawaii location. . . .

TMT NORTH AMERICA, INC. v. MAGIC TOUCH GMBH
124 F.3d 876 (7th Cir. 1997)

KANNE, Circuit Judge.

TMT GmbH is a German company that has developed a specially-coated paper for use in transferring images onto fabrics. Color photocopiers can transfer images onto the paper, and with the use of heat and pressure, the images can be transferred from the paper to the fabric. In 1990, TMT GmbH entered into an agreement with TMT-1, making TMT-1 the exclusive North American distributor of TMT GmbH's image transfer products. The distribution agreement stated that TMT-1 was "required to display the trademark and instructions supplied by TMT [GmbH] on all promotional materials, packaging and any other related materials produced by [TMT-1] in a manner agreed upon by both parties prior to production." TMT GmbH thereafter shipped the image transfer paper to TMT-1, which distributed the paper under the two trademarks at issue in this case, "The Magic Touch" and "The Magic Touch . . . my one and only." Initially, TMT GmbH shipped the paper in its final form to TMT-1 for distribution. By the beginning of 1992, however, TMT GmbH began to ship only rolls of the raw paper from its French manufacturer, and TMT-1 would then have the paper converted into individual sheets and packaged for sale.

Early on in this contractual relationship, TMT-1 filed an application to register "The Magic Touch . . . my one and only" with the U.S. Patent and Trademark Office. TMT-1's president and vice president both testified that they always understood TMT GmbH to own the trademarks, but TMT-1's chairman of the board, Martin Schwartz, filed a federal trademark application that listed TMT-1 as the owner. Schwartz had discussions with TMT GmbH's principal, Juergen Hagedorn, regarding the registration, but it is unclear whether Hagedorn knew the registration was in TMT-1's name rather than TMT GmbH's. Schwartz testified that Hagedorn knew TMT-1 was filing on its own behalf, but Hagedorn denied such knowledge.

Over approximately the next two years, TMT-1's business did not go well. When TMT-1 fell behind in its payments to TMT GmbH, three new investors were recruited to put money into either TMT-1 or its distribution arm, TMT Services, Inc. All three of these investors testified that they understood TMT-1 to own the trademarks and that Hagedorn, who was involved with recruiting the investors, never said anything to suggest otherwise. In late 1992, one of these investors, along with three new investors, formed TMT-2 which acquired the assets of TMT-1. In the Asset Purchase Agreement, TMT-1 explicitly represented that it owned and was transferring the trademarks. TMT GmbH was not a party to the Asset Purchase Agreement, but it did enter into a Memorandum of Agreement with the TMT-2 investors. The Memorandum called for the parties to sign a distributorship agreement and for the new company to pay TMT GmbH substantial consulting fees.

. . . TMT GmbH and TMT-2 were unable to negotiate a distributorship agreement. In February 1993, TMT GmbH sent TMT-2 a letter terminating the Memorandum of Agreement and a second letter stating that "no Intellectual Art, Patents and/or Trademarks and/or related rights have been traded, transferred, provided and/or assigned." Both parties, meanwhile, attempted to secure federal trademark registrations. In February 1993, TMT-1 filed a federal trademark application for "The Magic Touch" (which was granted in 1994), and in April 1993, TMT GmbH filed its own federal trademark application (which apparently was unsuccessful). Nonetheless, TMT GmbH and TMT-2 continued their distribution relationship without a written contract until June 1996 when TMT-2 terminated its distributorship and filed suit against TMT GmbH. TMT-2 now has its own source of the raw paper product and thus no longer needs TMT GmbH's paper.

TMT-2's complaint pleaded numerous counts against TMT GmbH, invoking §43(a) of the Lanham Act (15 U.S.C. §1125(a)), §35 of the Lanham Act (15 U.S.C. §1117), and the state common-law torts of unfair competition and interference with business relationships. TMT-2 specifically requested a declaratory judgment establishing its ownership of the trademarks, both preliminary and permanent injunctive relief preventing TMT GmbH from using the marks in any way, and damages. One of the ways that the law extends the benefits of trademarks and protects incentives to develop them is by allowing trademark owners to license the use of their marks to distributors and franchisees. Such licensing allows more information to be conveyed to more consumers without the licensor having to risk losing title to its mark. Indeed, trademarks would be of much less value to society if only vertically-integrated firms could safely take advantage of trademark law's protections. Similarly, trademark law creates a presumption that, in the absence of an assignment of trademark rights, a foreign manufacturer retains all rights to a trademark even after licensing the use of the trademark to an exclusive U.S. distributor. See Global Maschinen GmBH v. Global Banking Systems, Inc., 227 U.S.P.Q. 862, 866 (T.T.A.B. 1985). Such a distributor "does not acquire ownership of a foreign manufacturer's mark anymore than a wholesaler can acquire ownership of an American manufacturer's mark, merely through the sale and distribution of goods bearing the manufacturer's trademark." 4 McCarthy, supra, §29:8. Turning finally to the facts of the present case, the magistrate judge found that TMT GmbH originally owned the trademarks and that the initial distribution agreement "implicitly licensed TMT-1 for the duration of the agreement to use the marks then owned by TMT GmbH." Moreover, the magistrate judge concluded that TMT-1's registration of the marks (and even the notice given to Hagedorn of the registration) did not indicate transfer of ownership of the marks "in the context of the relationship between [TMT-1 and TMT GmbH] at the time." Based on our review of the record and the applicable case law, we agree with these conclusions. The parties certainly did not expressly agree to transfer the marks, and the evidence is speculative even with regard to any implied transfer. See Automated Prods., Inc. v. FMB Maschinenbaugesellschaft mbH & Co., 34 U.S.P.Q.2d 1505, 1515 (N.D. Ill. 1994) ("[T]here was no express transfer of any sort, and any argument of an implied transfer is crushed by the language of the exclusive agency agreement which reserves all rights to the foreign manufacturer."); cf. 1 Jerome Gilson, Trademark Protection and Practice §3.02[13] (1997) ("In light of the strong initial presumption of manufacturer trademark ownership and the rather strict requirements for express transfers, a finding of transfer to a distributor by implication would be quite rare.").

Of course, it is both possible and logical that a distributor might have a license to use the trademark only during the distributorship. It is also frequently the case that the licensee will attempt to "holdover" and retain the trademark even after the distributorship has ended.

On the one hand, the magistrate judge reasoned that Hagedorn's conduct was tantamount to an implied agreement to transfer ownership of the marks to TMT-2. Such an implicit agreement would make TMT-2 the exclusive owner and allow TMT-2 to enjoin all other uses of the marks. We do not think, however, that the magistrate judge's own findings of fact are sufficient to support a conclusion that this case involved such a complete transfer of rights. Assignments of trademark rights do not have to be in writing, but an "implied agreement to transfer" requires conduct manifesting agreement, not just conduct that might be characterized as being shady or otherwise inequitable. See 2 McCarthy, supra, §18:4. Indeed, one prominent trademark commentator suggests that without documentary evidence, an assignment "may be proven by the clear and uncontradicted oral testimony of a person in a position to have actual knowledge." *Id.*; see also Diebold, Inc. v. Multra-Guard, Inc., 189 U.S.P.Q. 119, 124 (T.T.A.B. 1975). Requiring strong evidence to establish an assignment is appropriate both to prevent parties from using self-serving testimony to gain ownership of trademarks and to give parties incentives to identify expressly the ownership of the marks they employ. Cf. 15 U.S.C. §1060 (requiring assignments of federal trademark registrations to be "by instruments in writing").

In this case, however, both the documentary evidence and oral testimony are ambiguous and contradictory. Hagedorn disputed all of the TMT-2 investors' allegations, and TMT-2 made no mention of trademark ownership in the Memorandum of Agreement with TMT GmbH, which was signed roughly at the same time TMT-2 was negotiating with TMT-1. And after the Memorandum of Agreement, TMT-2's own drafts of a distribution agreement suggest that TMT GmbH still owned the trademarks. . . . The evidence on the record now, however, is simply insufficient to show that the parties agreed to a wholesale transfer of trademark rights.[4]

---

4. In this case, the distribution agreement between TMT GmbH and TMT-1 explicitly provided that TMT-1 was "required to display the trademark and instructions supplied by TMT [GmbH]." With TMT GmbH's initial ownership of the marks established by the agreement, TMT GmbH could lose its rights by assignment or by abandonment, but not by some nebulous balancing test.

SOCIETE DES PRODUITS NESTLE, S.A. v. CASA HELVETIA, INC.

982 F.2d 633, 635 (1st Cir. 1992)

SELYA, Circuit Judge.

This bittersweet appeal requires us to address the protection that trademark law affords a registrant against the importation and sale of so-called "gray goods," that is, trademarked goods manufactured abroad under a valid license but brought into this country in derogation of arrangements lawfully made by the trademark holder to ensure territorial exclusivity.

I. BACKGROUND

PERUGINA chocolates originated in Italy and continue to be manufactured there. They are sold throughout the world and cater to a sophisticated consumer, a refined palate, and an indulgent budget. Societe Des Produits Nestle, S.A. (Nestle S.P.N.) owns the PERUGINA trademark.

For many years, defendant-appellee Casa Helvetia, Inc. was the authorized distributor of PERUGINA chocolates in Puerto Rico. On November 28, 1988, however, Nestle S.P.N. forsook Casa Helvetia and licensed its affiliate, Nestle Puerto Rico, Inc. (Nestle P.R.), as the exclusive Puerto Rican distributor.

At this point, the plot thickened. Nestle S.P.N. had previously licensed an independent company, Distribuidora Nacional de Alimentos La Universal S.A. (Alimentos), to manufacture and sell chocolates bearing the PERUGINA mark in Venezuela.[5] The Venezuelan sweets differ from the Italian sweets in presentation, variety, composition, and price. In March 1990, without obtaining Nestle S.P.N.'s consent, Casa Helvetia began to purchase the Venezuelan-made chocolates through a middleman, import them into Puerto Rico, and distribute them under the PERUGINA mark.

This maneuver drew a swift response. Charging that Casa Helvetia's marketing of the Venezuelan candies infringed both Nestle S.P.N.'s registered trademark and Nestle P.R.'s right of exclusive distributorship, Nestle S.P.N. and Nestle P.R. (hereinafter collectively "Nestle") sued under the Lanham Act. They claimed that Casa Helvetia's use of the PERUGINA label was "likely to confuse consumers into the mistaken belief that the Venezuelan chocolates are the same as the Italian chocolates and are authorized by Nestle for sale in Puerto Rico." And, they asserted that, because the PERUGINA name in Puerto Rico is associated with Italian-made chocolates, the importation of materially different Venezuelan chocolates threatened to erode "the integrity of the PERUGINA trademarks as symbols of consistent quality and goodwill in Puerto Rico." The district court held that the differences between the Italian-made and Venezuelan-made candies did not warrant injunctive relief in the absence of demonstrated consumer dissatisfaction, harm to plaintiffs' goodwill, or drop-off in product quality. This appeal followed.

---

5. Under the licensing agreement, Alimentos may not sell or distribute the Venezuelan product in the United States without written authorization from Nestle S.P.N. Moreover, the licensing agreement states that Alimentos "cannot export the products under the 'trademarks' to [countries outside Venezuela], either directly or indirectly," except via Nestle S.P.N. Insofar as the record reveals, the licensing agreement remains in effect.

II. THE LANHAM TRADE-MARK ACT CLAIMS

A. The Philosophy of the Lanham Act

Two amaranthine principles fuel the Lanham Act. One aims at protecting consumers. The other focuses on protecting registrants and their assignees. These interlocking principles, in turn, are linked to a concept of territorial exclusivity.

1. Animating Principles. Every product is composed of a bundle of special characteristics. The consumer who purchases what he believes is the same product expects to receive those special characteristics on every occasion. Congress enacted the Lanham Act to realize this expectation with regard to goods bearing a particular trademark. The Act's prophylaxis operates not only in the more obvious cases, involving the sale of inferior goods in derogation of the registrant's mark, but also in the less obvious cases, involving the sale of goods different from, although not necessarily inferior to, the goods that the customer expected to receive. By guaranteeing consistency, a trademark wards off both consumer confusion and possible deceit. The system also serves another, equally important, purpose by protecting the trademark owner's goodwill. See Keds Corp. v. Renee Int'l Trading Corp., 888 F.2d 215, 218 (1st Cir. 1989); see also S. Rep. No. 1333, supra, 1946 U.S. Code Cong. Serv. at 1274 ("where the owner of a trademark has spent energy, time, and money in presenting to the public the product, he is protected in his investment from its misappropriation by pirates and cheats"). Once again, this protection comprises more than merely stopping the sale of inferior goods. Even if an infringer creates a product that rivals or exceeds the quality of the registrant's product, the wrongful sale of the unauthorized product may still deprive the registrant of his ability to shape the contours of his reputation.

2. Territoriality. In general, trademark rights are congruent with the boundaries of the sovereign that registers (or recognizes) the mark. Such territoriality reinforces the basic goals of trademark law. Because products are often tailored to specific national conditions, a trademark's reputation (and, hence, its goodwill) often differs from nation to nation. Because that is so, the importation of goods properly trademarked abroad but not intended for sale locally may confuse consumers and may well threaten the local mark owner's goodwill. It is not surprising, then, that the United States Supreme Court long ago recognized the territoriality of trademark rights. See, e.g., A. Bourjois & Co. v. Aldridge, 263 U.S. 675 (1923) (per curiam); A. Bourjois & Co. v. Katzel, 260 U.S. 689 (1923). . . .

Of course, territoriality only goes so far. By and large, courts do not read Katzel and Aldridge to disallow the lawful importation of identical foreign goods carrying a valid foreign trademark. Be that as it may, territorial protection kicks in under the Lanham Act where two merchants sell physically different products in the same market and under the same name, see, e.g., Lever Bros., 877 F.2d at 107, for it is this prototype that impinges on a trademark holder's goodwill and threatens to deceive consumers. Indeed, without such territorial trademark protection, competitors purveying country-specific products could exploit consumer confusion and free ride on the goodwill of domestic trademarks with impunity. Such a scenario would frustrate the underlying goals of the Lanham Act, the "plain language and general sweep" of which "undeniably bespeak an intention to protect domestic trademark holders." Lever Bros., 877 F.2d at 105. Thus, where material differences exist between similarly marked goods, the Lanham Act honors the important linkage between trademark law and geography.

B. The Provisions at Issue Here

In this court, as below, the plaintiffs ground their trademark infringement and unfair competition claims in Lanham Act sections 32(1)(a), 42, and 43(a)(1), 15 U.S.C. §§1114(1)(a), 1124, 1125(a)(1) (1988). The district court considered and rejected each provision as a basis for relief. In so doing, the court misinterpreted the proper scope of the protection these three sections confer. . . .

C. Synthesis

In this case, all roads lead to Rome. Whether the fulcrum of plaintiffs' complaint is perceived as section 32(1)(a), section 42, or section 43(a), liability necessarily turns on the existence *vel non* of material differences between the products of a sort likely to create consumer confusion. Because the presence or absence of a material difference—a difference likely to cause consumer confusion—is the pivotal determinant of Lanham Act infringement in a gray goods case, the lower court's insistence on several other evidentiary showings was inappropriate. . . .

III. THE MATERIALITY THRESHOLD

When a trial court misperceives and misapplies the law, remand may or may not be essential. Here, a final judgment under the correct rule of law requires only the determination of whether reported differences between the Venezuelan and Italian products are material. It follows, then, that we must examine the legal standard for materiality before deciding whether to remand.

Under the Lanham Act, only those appropriations of a mark that are likely to cause confusion are prohibited. Ergo, when a product identical to a domestic product is imported into the United States under the same mark, no violation of the Lanham Act occurs. See, e.g., *Weil*, 878 F.2d at 668. In such a situation, consumers get exactly the bundle of characteristics that they associate with the mark and the domestic distributor can be said to enjoy in large measure his investment in goodwill. By the same token, using the same mark on two blatantly different products normally does not offend the Lanham Act, for such use is unlikely to cause confusion and is, therefore, unlikely to imperil the goodwill of either product.

The probability of confusion is great, however, when the same mark is displayed on goods that are not identical but that nonetheless bear strong similarities in appearance or function. Gray goods often fall within this category. Thus, when dealing with the importation of gray goods, a reviewing court must necessarily be concerned with subtle differences, for it is by subtle differences that consumers are most easily confused. For that reason, the threshold of materiality must be kept low enough to take account of potentially confusing differences—differences that are not blatant enough to make it obvious to the average consumer that the origin of the product differs from his or her expectations.

There is no mechanical way to determine the point at which a difference becomes "material." Separating wheat from chaff must be done on a case-by-case basis. Bearing in mind the policies and provisions of the Lanham Act as they apply to gray goods, we can confidently say that the threshold of materiality is always quite low in such cases. See *Lever Bros.*, 877 F.2d at 103, 108 (finding minor differences in ingredients and packaging between versions of deodorant soap to be material); *Ferrero*, 753 F. Supp. at 1241-49, 1247 (finding a one-half calorie difference in chemical composition of breath mints, coupled with slight differences in packaging and labeling, to be material); PepsiCo Inc. v. Nostalgia, 18 U.S.P.Q.2d at 1405 (finding "differences in labeling, packaging and marketing methods" to be material); PepsiCo v. Giraud, 7 U.S.P.Q.2d at 1373 (finding differences not readily apparent to the consumer — container volume, packaging, quality control, and advertising participation — to be material); *Dial Corp.*, 643 F. Supp. at 952 (finding differences in formulation and packaging of soap products to be material). We conclude that the existence of any difference between the registrant's product and the allegedly infringing gray good that consumers would likely consider to be relevant when purchasing a product creates a presumption of consumer confusion sufficient to support a Lanham Act claim. Any higher threshold would endanger a manufacturer's investment in product goodwill and unduly subject consumers to potential confusion by severing the tie between a manufacturers' protected mark and its associated bundle of traits.

IV. MATERIALITY IN THIS CASE

Having fashioned the standard of materiality and examined the record in light of that standard, we are drawn to the conclusion that remand is not required. Hence, we proceed to take the lower court's supportable findings of fact, couple them with other, uncontradicted facts, and, using the rule of law articulated above, determine for ourselves whether the admitted differences between the Venezuelan-made chocolates and the Italian-made chocolates are sufficiently material to warrant injunctive relief.

A. A Catalog of Differences

The district court identified numerous differences between the competing products. Because the record supports these findings and the parties do not contest their validity, we accept them. We add, however, other potentially significant distinctions made manifest by the record.

1. Quality Control. Although Nestle and Casa Helvetia each oversees the quality of the product it sells, the record reflects, and Casa Helvetia concedes, that their procedures differ radically. The Italian PERUGINA leaves Italy in refrigerated containers which arrive at Nestle's facility in Puerto Rico. Nestle verifies the temperature of the coolers, opens them, and immediately transports the chocolates to refrigerated rooms. The company records the product's date of manufacture, conducts laboratory tests, and destroys those candies that have expired. It then transports the salable chocolates to retailers in refrigerated trucks. Loading and unloading is performed only in the cool morning hours.

On the other hand, the Venezuelan product arrives in Puerto Rico via commercial air freight. During the afternoon hours, airline personnel remove the chocolates from the containers in which they were imported and place them in a central air cargo cooler. The next morning, employees of Casa Helvetia open random boxes at the airport to see if the chocolates have melted. The company then transports the candy in a refrigerated van to a warehouse. Casa Helvetia performs periodic inspections before delivering the goods to its customers in a refrigerated van. The record contains no evidence that Casa Helvetia knows or records the date the chocolates were manufactured.

2. Composition. The district court enumerated a number of differences in ingredients. The Italian BACI candies have five percent more milk fat than their Venezuelan counterparts, thus prolonging shelf life. Furthermore, the Italian BACI chocolates contain Ecuadorian and African cocoa beans, fresh hazelnuts, and cooked sugar syrup, whereas the corresponding Venezuelan candies are made with domestic beans, imported hazelnuts, and ordinary crystal sugar.

3. Configuration. The district court specifically noted that the Italian chocolates in the Maitre Confiseur and Assortment collections come in a greater variety of shapes than the Venezuelan pieces.

4. Packaging. The district court observed differences in the "boxes, wrappers and trays" between the Italian and Venezuelan versions of the various chocolate assortments. *Id.* For example, the packages from Italy possess a glossy finish and are either silver, brown, or gold in color. The Venezuelan boxes lack the shiny finish. They are either blue, red, or yellow in color. While the Italian sweets sit in gold or silver trays, their Venezuelan counterparts rest on white or transparent trays. The Italian boxes depict the chocolates inside and describe the product in English, French, and Italian. The Venezuelan packages describe the contents only in Spanish and English. Moreover, only the BACI box illustrates what is inside.

5. Price. The district court pointed out that while the Venezuelan and Italian BACI collections contain the same quantity of chocolate (8 oz.), the Italian BACI sells for $12.99 and the Venezuelan BACI costs $7.50. See *id.* at 163. The record also reflects that the Italian version of the Assortment collection (14.25 oz. for $26.99) weighs less and is more expensive than the Venezuelan version (15.6 oz. for $22.99).

B. Applying the Standard

Applying the legal standard discussed in Part III, supra, to the record at bar, it is readily apparent that material differences exist between the Italian and Venezuelan PERUGINA. These differences—which implicate quality, composition, packaging, and price—if not overwhelming, are certainly relevant. We run the gamut.

Differences in quality control methods, although not always obvious to the naked eye, are nonetheless important to the consumer. The precautions a company takes to preserve a food product's freshness are a prime example. Here, the parties' quality control procedures differ significantly. Even if Casa Helvetia's quality control measures are as effective as Nestle's—a dubious proposition on this record—the fact that Nestle is unable to oversee the quality of the goods for the entire period until they reach the consumer is significant in ascertaining whether a Lanham Act violation exists. Regardless of the offending goods' actual quality, courts have issued Lanham Trade-Mark Act injunctions solely because of the trademark owner's inability to control the quality of the goods bearing its name. Thus, the substantial variance in quality control here creates a presumption of customer confusion as a matter of law. See *id.* at 108. The differences in presentation of the candies are also material. Although the district court dismissed the differences in packaging as "subtle," *Societe Des Produits Nestle*, 777 F. Supp. at 166, subtle differences are, as we have said, precisely the type that heighten the presumption of customer confusion. Consumers are more likely to be confused as to the origin of different goods bearing the same name when both goods are substantially identical in appearance. Furthermore, the differences in presentation and chocolate shape strike us as more than subtle. Glossy veneers, gold and silver wraps, and delicate sculpting add to the consumer's perception of quality. In the market for premium chocolates, often purchased as gifts, an elegant-looking package is an important consideration. The cosmetic differences between the Italian-made and the Venezuelan-made PERUGINA, therefore, might well perplex consumers and harm Nestle's goodwill. We are also hesitant to dismiss as trivial the differences in ingredients. While the district court may be correct in suggesting that "the ultimate consumer is [not] concerned about the country of origin of cocoa beans and hazelnuts," *id.* at 166-67, the measure of milk fat in the chocolates is potentially significant. Certainly, consumers care about the expected shelf life of food products.

Price, without doubt, is also a variable with which purchasers are concerned. To the consumer (perhaps a gift buyer) who relishes a higher price for its connotation of quality and status, as well as to the chocolate aficionado who values his wallet more than his image, a difference of nearly five and a half dollars (or, put another way, 73 percent) on a half-pound box of chocolate is a relevant datum. Furthermore, the fact that consumers are willing to pay over five dollars more for the Italian-made chocolate than for its Venezuelan counterpart may suggest that consumers do care about the other differences between the two products. Afforded perfect information, consumers indifferent between the two would presumably not be willing to pay more for one than for the other.

We need go no further. Given the low threshold of materiality that applies in gray goods cases, we find the above dissimilarities material in the aggregate. The use of the same PERUGINA label on chocolates manifesting such differences is presumptively likely to cause confusion. Casa Helvetia could, of course, have offered evidence to rebut this presumption—but it has not done so. There is no proof that retailers explain to consumers the differences between the Italian and Venezuelan products. The record is likewise devoid of any evidence that consumers are indifferent about quality control procedures, packaging, ingredients, or price. Because the differences between the Italian and Venezuelan PERUGINA chocolates are material, the district court erred in denying plaintiffs' trademark infringement and unfair competition claims under Lanham Act sections 32(1)(a), 42, and 43(a)(1).

Reversed and remanded for the entry of appropriate injunctive relief and for further proceedings not inconsistent herewith. Costs to appellants.

III. PROBLEMS

1. There are different types of royalty payments. (1) Lump Sum Payment in Full is where the licensee pays a one-time fee in exchange for the use of the trademark and the payment is at the time the license agreement commences. (2) Running Royalty is where the licensee agrees to make periodic payments based on calculation of agreed percentage of sales, shipments, distributions, or manufacturing. (3) Minimum Royalty Payments is where the licensee pays a fixed amount regardless of the volume of sales, shipments, distributions, or manufacture of the licensed products or services. Under (2) and (3), the licensor sometimes insists that the licensee pay a lump sum payment first and then either the Running Royalty or Minimum Royalty payments for the duration of the license agreement. What are

some reasons a trademark holder would like to have a lump sum payment at the execution of the license agreement instead of periodic payments over a period of time? What method of payments would be preferred by the licensee?

2. Compare "first sale" goods and "gray market" goods. Discuss the "material difference" exception to the first sale doctrine.

3. With the increase in globalization and free movement of goods, should the United States change the law with respect to gray market goods? Explain your reasons. Can you think of reasons why some developed countries and developing countries permit gray market goods?

4. Consider the following Quality Control provision. Will the provision satisfy the requirement for quality control of trademark licensing?

QUALITY CONTROL:

(a) All work performed "shall be of reasonable quality and shall be performed by experienced personnel," materials shall be "particularly selected for the particular job" and shall be of reasonable quality, all complaints regarding repairs performed shall be investigated and shall be remedied to the satisfaction of the customer, unless the demands are unreasonable.

(b) The manner in which Licensee uses the trademarks, and the quality of the licensed products marketed by Licensee under the trademarks (and all related advertising, promotional business materials and packaging), will be commensurate with, and at least as high as, the quality, style, and manner in which Licensor has used the trademarks. In no event shall the licensed products be sold under any terms or circumstances that would injure the prestige or goodwill of Licensor or the trademarks.

(c) Licensor shall approve the design and quality of the licensed products (including the packaging and labeling) and the proper use of the trademarks. Prior to the commercial manufacture, promotion, distribution or sale of any new licensed product, Licensee shall submit to Licensor for its written approval, at Licensee's own expense, three (3) prototype samples of the new version of the licensed product bearing the trademarks.

(d) Licensee shall produce one or more samples of the licensed product. Licensor agrees to inspect and/or test the sample licensed product and to notify Licensee in writing of its approval within fifteen (15) business days of receipt of such sample, and, if not approved, to advise Licensee, in writing within fifteen (15) business days of receipt of such sample, of any and all corrections reasonably required by Licensor for the licensed product to be approved. The quality of the licensed product for sale by Licensee shall be identical to that of the approved licensed product if such product has been approved.

5. When is an agreement deemed a trademark license or a sale of goods? Explain fully.

6. Many trademark license agreements contain a Post-Termination provision relating the use of the trademark. Read the Post Termination provision below and explain the rationale for its inclusion.

> **POST TERMINATION:** In the event of termination of this Agreement in any manner, LICENSEE shall have the right to complete any and all contracts which it may be obligated to fulfill, paying the royalties thereon, but it shall not further use, either directly or indirectly, the trademarks or trade names, any trade secrets or valid, protected patented processes of LICENSOR, or use or employ any imitations of LICENSOR'S trade names, trademarks, or valid, protected patented processes, if acquired during the term of this Agreement; and these obligations shall continue after termination of this Agreement.

7. Consider the following scenario. The licensee has been granted the exclusive right to exploit the trademark and the right to bring infringement suit against a third party, but the licensor retains the ownership of the trademark. Does the licensee have standing to bring an infringement suit against a third party?

8. Section 10.02.F. of the SBC Franchise Agreement requires the Franchisee "To purchase, install, and construct, at Franchisee's expense, all . . . equipment . . . as Franchisor may reasonably direct from time to time in the Manual or otherwise in writing. . . ." Assume that the Franchisor sends a letter to the Franchisee directing the Franchisee to use a new type of espresso machine. After testing the new machine, the Franchisee firmly believes the new machine actually produces espresso that is more bitter than before—this seems to go against SBC's claim that its coffee is bold but smooth. Can the Franchisee refuse to install the new machine? What if the Franchisor had decided to use the new machine because Starbucks Coffee Co. had begun a new marketing campaign lauding its new and improved espresso machines? *See* La Quinta Corp. v. Heartland Properties LLC, 603 F.3d 327 (6th Cir. 2010), for a case considering a franchisee's obligation to install new equipment.

IV. DRAFTING EXERCISES

1. Digital Equipment Corporation (Digital) wants to grant a non-exclusive license to Alta Vista Inc. to use the DEC trademark either as a corporate name or as part of a URL for a website. Digital wants the assurance that Alta Vista will not use the DEC trademark in connection with any product or service offered by Alta Vista. In the event that Alta Vista is owned by another company, after the execution of the license agreement, Digital does not want the license to be transferred to the new company or any third party. Digital requests that you draft a license grant provision for the in-house counsel's review. Submit your draft. Is there additional

information that you would like to obtain from Digital for the purpose of drafting the grant provision?

2. Digital, your client in the previous problem, comes back to see you again. Digital wants to enter into an agreement with EKD for the distribution and sales of Digital's latest DMA software worldwide. EKD will be responsible for the advertisements and sales literature for the DMA software. EKD will sell the software worldwide. The term of the agreement is five years. EKD has agreed to pay Digital a one-time lump sum payment of $2 million. Digital is located in Boston, Massachusetts, and EKD in San Jose, California. Digital requests that you submit a short draft license agreement that contains Grant of Trademark License, Quality Control, Licensee's Obligations, Term (Duration), Royalty, and Choice of Law provisions. You may ignore the remainder provisions for now.

3. Shanghai Toys Inc. (STI) is a toy manufacturing company located in Shanghai, China. Geoffrey, Inc. is a wholly owned subsidiary of Toys "R" Us corporation. Geoffrey owns all the trademarks used in connection with the sales of toys and children's items in the United States. Geoffrey wants an exclusive arrangement with STI wherein Geoffrey will send various toy designs to STI for mass production. The toys will bear various trademarks owned by Geoffrey and be shipped to the United States for distribution by Geoffrey's sister companies across the United States. Geoffrey is concerned about gray market goods and would like you to draft an agreement with STI, specifically the grant provision relating to the use of the trademarks provided by Geoffrey to STI.

4. Redraft the grant provision on Eureka's behalf in the *Eureka v. Nestle* case. Explain how your new grant provision avoids the problems articulated by the Court in that case.

5. Consider the following forum selection clause in a trademark license agreement:

> The parties agree to submit all disputes arising hereunder to the courts situated in Miami, Florida, and not otherwise.

What does "and not otherwise" mean? Should you keep the phrase in the forum selection clause? Why or why not?

6. Draft a quality control provision for the trademark license in *Barcamerica v. Tyfield Importers* that would be sufficient to avoid a naked license.

· CHAPTER ·

5

LICENSING THE RIGHT OF PUBLICITY

I. OVERVIEW OF RIGHT OF PUBLICITY LICENSING

A. Introduction

Celebrities from the sports and entertainment industries are a major part of culture, both in the United States and abroad. Businesses, eager to capitalize, have signed up celebrities to endorse everything from sportswear to motor oil. We all know that a yellow football jersey with "Ronaldinho" or "Rothlesberger" is far more valuable than one without the name. Our choice of cars, clothing, or cuisine is often influenced by what an actress or singer drives, wears, or eats. The proliferation of sports, infotainment, and entertainment-related interactive multimedia products has created a new celebrity rights licensing landscape. Online advertising, Web sites, social media, and blogs have opened and expanded markets for exploiting the value of a celebrity's identity or persona for commercial gain.

But entertainment figures are not the only celebrities of interest to business ventures. A *Financial Times* article reported on the indecent feeding frenzy to cash in on the Nelson Mandela name. According to the article, Mandela is everywhere, from gold coins, to art projects, to Web sites. Apparently requests, often from companies completely unrelated to Mandela or his causes, are clogging the queue to use his name and likeness. Although South Africa relies on a common law approach to protect publicity rights, the Nelson Mandela Foundation struggles with how to deal with the issues surrounding the use of Mandela's name and likeness in the context of branding and merchandising. In addition to creating a code of conduct banning the commercialization of Mandela's name or image by his four official charities, the Foundation is looking at examples internationally of similar situations, most notably Princess Diana in the United Kingdom and Martin Luther King, Jr. and Albert Einstein in the United States, to discern how best to control the Mandela legacy. *See The Mandela Name*, 4/25/05 Bus. Day 8, 2005 WLNR 6436613.

B. Nature of the Right of Publicity

Despite judicial protection for the right of publicity and its treatment as intangible property, commentators and scholars continue to debate the nature of the right of publicity, routinely inquiring whether the right is better characterized as a personal right or privacy right. Judicial and state legislative approaches have generally treated the right of publicity as a property right, *see* Haelen Labs., Inc. v. Topps Chewing Gum Inc., 202 F.2d 866 (2d Cir. 1956) (stating that "a man has a right in the publicity value of his photograph, *i.e.*, the right to grant the exclusive privilege of publishing his picture, and that such a grant may validly be made 'in gross,' *i.e.*, without an accompanying transfer of a business or of anything else"), specifically rejecting claims for redress by celebrities based upon privacy interests. Scholars challenge the property rights theory dominant in right of publicity case law by, among other arguments, asserting the inalienability of certain tort-based personal or privacy aspects of the right of publicity that were at the claim's origin.

Inquiries about intellectual property rights analogues to the right of publicity are also expressed in judicial case law and academic literature. There is no question that the right of publicity is different in many ways from other intellectual property rights, most notably patent, copyright, trademark, and trade secret rights, which are fully alienable. Some commentators assert that the value of the right of publicity is in the control of identity or persona, an assignment of which would be conditional, such that a third party would not obtain unfettered or unrestricted use of the right. Instead, an assignment of the right of publicity would operate like a license, with the assignor retaining the right of control over the residual uses of the publicity right. Most jurisdictions, however, recognize the right of publicity as an intangible property right that is capable of being transferred for commercial purposes. *See* Factors, Etc., Inc. v. Creative Card Co., 444 F. Supp. 279, 284 (S.D.N.Y. 1977) (identifying that "recent decisions have clearly labeled the 'right of publicity' a species of 'property.'" [citations omitted]).

Courts and commentators have also addressed the unique aspects of the right of publicity by extolling that the persona of a celebrity has important expressive and communicative impacts on society and, therefore, the granting of publicity rights has the potential to create tensions between the right and the First Amendment. Consider the following excerpt:

> [B]ecause celebrities take on personal meanings to many individuals in the society, the creative appropriation of celebrity images can be an important avenue of individual expression. As one commentator has stated: "Entertainment and sports celebrities are the leading players in our Public Drama. We tell tales, both tall and cautionary, about them. We monitor their comings and goings, their missteps and heartbreaks. We copy their mannerisms, their styles, and their modes of conversation and of consumption. Whether or not celebrities are 'the chief agents of moral change in the

United States,' they certainly are widely used—far more than are our institutionally anchored elites—to symbolize individual aspirations, group identities and cultural values. Their images are thus important expressive and communicative resources: the peculiar, yet familiar idiom in which we conduct a fair portion of our cultural business and everyday conversation." *See* Comedy III Prods., Inc. v. Gary Saderup, Inc., 25 Cal. 4th 387, 397, 106 Cal. Rptr. 2d 126, 21 P.3d 797, 803 (2001).

This quote reflects the modern significance of the right of publicity to celebrities and to the general public. This significance is not diminished by claims that the right of publicity is less compelling than those that justify rights in trademarks or trade secrets or that the commercial value of a person's identity often results from success in endeavors such as entertainment or sports that offer their own substantial rewards. The reality is that lending a celebrity name or likeness to products and services in the global marketplace facilitates business transactions. Accordingly, these transactions will be supported by licensing as one of the most effective means of controlling the transfer of the right of publicity from the person holding the right to those interested in using the right.

C. *Protecting the Right of Publicity*

The right of publicity is a right granted by state common law or statute. *See* Stephano v. News Group Publications, Inc., 474 N.E.2d 580 (1984) (explaining that New York has not created a statutory right of publicity nor does it recognize a common law right of publicity; instead, the New York statutory right of privacy applies to any use of a person's picture or portrait for advertising or trade purposes whenever the defendant has not obtained the person's written consent to do so. Therefore, the right of publicity is already subsumed in the statutory right of privacy.). Despite the controversy regarding whether it is a personal or property right, generally the modern legal doctrine of the right of publicity grants proprietary rights to anyone, even noncelebrities. *See* Gridiron.com v. National Football League Players Ass'n, 106 F. Supp. 2d 1309, 1315 (S.D. Fla. 2000) (stating "[t]he right to publicity is a legally protected, transferable interest."). The right of publicity provides celebrities and non-celebrities alike the control over the commercial value of their persona or identity. The right of publicity is defined as the right of every person to prevent the unauthorized commercial use of his or her identity. The purpose of the right of publicity is to protect the proprietary interest that people, especially celebrities, have in their identities. Thus, people have a right to license or assign this right and, consistent with a valid transfer, an exclusive licensee of the right to exploit persona or identity has a proprietary interest assignable in gross to the extent permitted under a licensing agreement.

D. *Comparison to Trademarks*

Trademarks are only analogous, and not identical, to the right of publicity. As a general rule, a person's image or likeness cannot function as a trademark, unless one particular image is consistently used in advertising and sales to identify those goods or services such that the image or likeness functions as a mark. Thus, convergence of the right of publicity and trademarks occur, as the exception, when a person's identity is equivalent to a source identifier. *Cf.* Miller v. Glenn Miller Prods., Inc., 318 F. Supp. 2d 923, 938-39 (C.D. Cal. 2004) (stating that "in practice, many licenses convey both trademark rights and publicity rights. In such cases, the special rules of trademark licensing must be followed in order to preserve the trademark significance of the licensed identity or persona."). The *Miller* case is excerpted in the Materials section of this chapter.

Although the right of publicity has, over time, the ability to function as a trademark, these two protections are not the same. Trademark law protects the source identifying characteristics of marks, while the right of publicity protects the commercial value of one's human identity. Trademarks protect the goodwill bound up in the source identifying mark, while the right of publicity protects against the unauthorized commercial use of a person's actual identity. Trademark rights exist only upon prior adoption and use of a mark in a commercial context; the right of publicity, however, has inherent commercial value without regard to prior use. Trademark law requires a showing of likelihood of confusion as a condition precedent for an infringement action; infringement of the right of publicity, however, requires only a showing that the injured party is identifiable. Finally, trademark law prohibits assignments in gross and naked licenses; the right of publicity, however, is freely assignable in gross.

E. Comparison to Copyrights

Over time, the right of publicity can also morph into the copyright area. For example, a person may claim a right of publicity in a song, artwork, picture, or sound recording, the latter of which is also the subject matter of copyrights.

Copyright law protects original works of authorship fixed in tangible mediums of expression. To the extent that the right of publicity is connected to a character — for example, that is highly developed, delineated, or distinct — that character may be entitled to copyright protection. To a greater degree, characters are protected by copyright if they comprise both the character and a graphic component. Courts have long held that characters with graphic components such as cartoon or comic book characters are more readily protectable under copyright than purely literary characters because of their visual characteristics. In contrast, however, in Landham v. Lewis Galoob Toys, Inc., 227 F.3d 619, 625-26 (6th Cir. 2000), the Sixth Circuit held that Landham, a fringe actor who played supporting roles in several motion pictures, had failed to show a violation of his right of publicity when defendant marketed an action figure of a character he had played but which did not bear a personal resemblance to him. The Sixth Circuit found that Landham had failed to show that his persona had significant value or that the toy invoked his persona as distinct from that of the fictional character he played.

Accordingly, the subject matter of the right of publicity does not generally fall into the category of copyright subject matter. Thus, personal names, voice, and physical likeness are generally excluded from the subject matter of copyright. This subject matter is typically left unprotected under copyright because the subject matter is not sufficiently delineated as to rise to the level of expression.

F. Assignment Versus Licensing the Right of Publicity

The majority of states view the right of publicity as proprietary and, therefore, freely assignable. Both the right of publicity and licensing law are flexible tools of commercialization; both tools make it possible for people with otherwise limited property interests to exploit that which they will always retain — control or possession of an identity or persona, and the freedom to enter into agreements to commercialize and exploit that persona. While an outright sale of the right of publicity is possible, as a business matter, this type of transaction is probably undesirable because the value of identity typically derives from the very person from whom the identity springs. Accordingly, the commercial value of the identity traded will likely diminish if that identity is forever disassociated with the person responsible for the existence of that identity. As such, the most likely mechanism for capitalizing on the commercial value of identity or persona is a license.

With respect to the right of publicity, an assignment is distinguishable from a license. Licensing is often the most effective means of controlling the transfer of the right of publicity from the person holding the right to those interested in using the right. A license is a limited right to use the right of publicity. A license is a form of consent that establishes the terms under which the licensee may exploit the licensor's identity but does not purport to transfer ownership of the commercial value of the identity. The licensor is merely estopped from challenging the licensee's use of the property under a valid licensing agreement. Principally then, a license is temporary, provisional, or conditional. Questions to consider when drafting or analyzing publicity rights licenses include:

- Who owns the right of publicity?
- What is the scope of the right of publicity license — name, likeness, and/or image?
- Is celebrity content being licensed?
- In what territory will the right of publicity be used?
- In what media will the right of publicity be used?
- Who seeks the license of the right of publicity?
- What bundle of rights is available under common law/statutory law?
- When does the license commence?
- What is the duration of the license?
- Under what circumstances can the license be terminated?
- Will the right of publicity be sub-licensed?

- What payments will be received?
- How will payments be received?
- Are there fair uses of the persona or identity?
- When is a waiver or release used?
- What are the quality control requirements?

G. Standard Right of Publicity Release Agreements

In general, publicity rights release agreements are considered non-exclusive licenses of a personal nature. A release agreement is a form of consent that establishes the terms under which a licensee may exploit the licensor's identity, short of transferring outright ownership. *See* RESTATEMENT (THIRD) OF UNFAIR COMPETITION §46, cmt. g. Release agreements protect licensees from claims of infringement that the licensor could have brought but for the license. Release agreements can range from the formal to the informal. For example, a professional athlete may execute a release agreement as part of her employment contract, while a sports fan by purchasing a ticket automatically acquiesces to the release terms printed on the back of his ticket of entry.

A release agreement is a binding contract by which a person waives or gives up any rights to sue arising from certain activities engaged in by another. As courts generally construe release agreements consistent with general state law contract principles, the intent of the parties controls the scope of the release. Accordingly, the language of the release agreement is the first place to start in deciding what the parties to the release agreement intended. The general practice in drafting release agreements is to keep them short and uncomplicated. The rationale for brevity in drafting release agreements correlates directly with what is being granted. The standard release agreement merely extracts permission from a person (typically a noncelebrity) to make use of that person's identity or persona for limited purposes, durations, and in specific contexts.

H. Litigation Issues in the Licensing of the Right of Publicity

1. Standing

Because the tort of misappropriation is premised on a person's economic interest in publicity rights, the range of plaintiffs who have standing to make a misappropriation claim expands to the extent that such publicity rights are assignable. *See* MJ & Partners Rest. Ltd. v. Zadikoff, 10 F. Supp. 2d 922, 930 (N.D. Ill. 1998). Thus, an exclusive licensee of the right to exploit a celebrity's name, likeness, or personality has a right of publicity interest assignable in gross to the extent permitted under the original licensing agreement. *See* Haelan Labs., Inc. v. Topps Chewing Gum, Inc., 202 F.2d 866 (2d Cir. 1956). Accordingly, an exclusive licensee of a celebrity's name, likeness, or personality may state a cause of action for misappropriation of the right of publicity.

2. Defenses

The defenses to a claim of misappropriation of the right of publicity include consent by the holder of the right of publicity, constitutional privilege, the first sale/exhaustion doctrine, and preemption. Thus, where a licensee demonstrates that valid consent was given by the licensor to use the publicity right, there will be a cognizable defense to a claim of misappropriation. Figuring prominently in right of publicity misappropriation actions are defenses based upon constitutional privileges. When an individual's right of publicity is used for comment, news reporting, or noncommercial speech, then that expression is entitled to the protection of the First Amendment. These constitutional privileges are often codified by statute along with the protection for the right of publicity. In addition, the first sale/exhaustion doctrine is available as a defense to limit protection of the right of publicity. Finally, where right of publicity actions are equivalent to the rights protected by copyright, the preemption doctrine can be invoked as a defense to misappropriation.

3. Antitrust Litigation and the Right of Publicity: The Special Case of Student-Athletes, Athletic Conferences and Licensing Agencies, and Television Networks

The student–athlete arena has produced a spate of litigation around the recognition and protection of the right of publicity of college athletes on the one hand and the degree to which NCAA amateurism rules create restraints on these athletes and their attempts to leverage their names, images, and likenesses on the other hand. The tug of war between college athletes on one side and university-affiliated athletic conferences, licensing agencies, and broadcast networks on the other side has been on exhibition in federal district and circuit courts around the nation. As well, this exhibition has produced varied outcomes with respect to the breadth and scope of the right of publicity of these athletes as well as varied analytic approaches regarding the question of whether conference amateurism rules are anticompetitive with respect to recognizing actions by college athletes to protect their publicity rights, either individually or collectively.

In 2013, the United States Courts of Appeals for the Third and Ninth Circuits rejected First Amendment defenses raised by video game manufacturer Electronic Arts, the latter having been found to have used the likenesses and personas of two college quarterbacks in violation of these athletes' right of publicity. The decisions were based on determinations that defendant's uses in both cases were insufficiently transformative. *See* In re NCAA Student-Athlete Name & Likeness Licensing Litigation, 724 F.3d 1268, 1271, 1276 (9th Cir. 2013), and Hart v. Elec. Arts, Inc., 717 F.3d 141, 166-70 (3d Cir. 2013). Garnering speed and attention, the class action case of O'Bannon v. NCAA, 802 F.3d 1049 (9th Cir. 2015), opened yet another type of action — specifically antitrust — that provided a window of opportunity for student-athletes to allege violations for restraining trade in relation to players' names, images, and likenesses. With its favorable conclusion affirming the district court's findings that the plaintiff identified not one but two economic markets that were potentially affected by the challenged NCAA rules and the United States Supreme Court declining to review the opinion, current and future plaintiffs must look to the circuits for holdings relating to antitrust issues.

While some cases have recognized student-athlete right of publicity claims, subsequent cases in other jurisdictions have espoused narrow and clearly defined limits on the right of publicity for student-athletes. One of these limiting cases is Marshall v. ESPN Inc., 111 F. Supp. 3d 815 (M.D. Tenn. 2015). In rejecting plaintiffs' arguments — based on In re NCAA Student-Athlete Name & Likeness Litigation — that college athletes have rights of publicity associated with sports broadcasts, the court reiterated that whether athletes have such publicity rights is a matter of state law. Accordingly, where the *Marshall* plaintiffs' right of publicity claims are based exclusively on Tennessee law, that law "recognizes no right of publicity in sports broadcasts."

II. MATERIALS

The cases in this section were selected to illustrate the scope and protection of the right of publicity. Specifically, ETW v. Jireh Publ'g, Inc., 332 F.3d 915 (6th Cir. 2003), offers a thorough discussion of the right of publicity and how the right can be distinguished from rights granted by trademark law. In addition, this case introduces the concept of implied licenses supported by the First Amendment, which requires courts to balance state law rights of publicity against the public interest in freedom of expression. A more expansive, yet controversial, application of the First Amendment in the right of publicity licensing context is C.B.C. Distrib. & Mktg., Inc. v. Major League Baseball Advanced Media, L.P., 505 F.3d 818 (8th Cir. 2007). *See also* In re NCAA Student-Athlete Name & Likeness Licensing Litigation, 724 F.3d 1268 (9th Cir. 2013). Infringement of the right of publicity is analyzed in Ryan v. Volpone Stamp Co., 107 F. Supp. 2d 369 (S.D.N.Y. 2000), a case that offers an illustration of the boundaries of use of the right of publicity subsequent to the termination of an exclusive license agreement. An interesting case at the intersection of the right of publicity, false endorsement, copyright preemption, the First Amendment, and contractual releases is Facenda v. N.F.L. Films, Inc., 542 F.3d 1007 (3d Cir. 2008). This case illustrates the competing interests of intellectual property rights holders and how the courts are being forced to balance, weigh, and prioritize each party's legitimate interests in commercial markets for multimedia content. The Materials include Miller v. Glenn Miller Prods., Inc., 318 F. Supp. 2d 923 (C.D. Cal. 2004), which embraces the trademark principle that a licensor's express permission is required before a licensee may further license the use of the right of publicity to a sublicense. This case also provides an example of an ambiguous scope of grant license provision that fueled the litigation between the parties regarding the right to sub-license publicity rights to third parties and the failure to obtain consent for sub-licensing in breach of the relevant license agreement. Finally, the Materials include two cases O'Bannon v. NCAA, 802 F.3d 1049 (9th Cir. 2015), and Marshall v. ESPN Inc., 111 F. Supp. 3d 815 (M.D. Tenn.

2015) — both provided to demonstrate the interplay between federal antitrust injury based on the right of publicity and the requirement that state law actually recognize the right of publicity in order to further recognize and compensate for an antitrust violation.

ETW v. JIREH PUBL'G, INC.

332 F.3d 915 (6th Cir. 2003)

GRAHAM, District Judge sitting by designation.

Plaintiff-Appellant ETW Corporation ("ETW") is the licensing agent of Eldrick "Tiger" Woods ("Woods"), one of the world's most famous professional golfers. Woods, chairman of the board of ETW, has assigned to it the exclusive right to exploit his name, image, likeness, and signature, and all other publicity rights. ETW owns a United States trademark registration for the mark "TIGER WOODS" (Registration No. 2,194,381) for use in connection with "art prints, calendars, mounted photographs, notebooks, pencils, pens, posters, trading cards, and unmounted photographs."

Defendant-Appellee Jireh Publishing, Inc. ("Jireh") of Tuscaloosa, Alabama, is the publisher of artwork created by Rick Rush ("Rush"). Rush, who refers to himself as "America's sports artist," has created paintings of famous figures in sports and famous sports events. A few examples include Michael Jordan, Mark McGuire, Coach Paul "Bear" Bryant, the Pebble Beach Golf Tournament, and the America's Cup Yacht Race. Jireh has produced and successfully marketed limited edition art prints made from Rush's paintings.

In 1998, Rush created a painting entitled *The Masters of Augusta*, which commemorates Woods's victory at the Masters Tournament in Augusta, Georgia, in 1997. At that event, Woods became the youngest player ever to win the Masters Tournament, while setting a 72-hole record for the tournament and a record 12-stroke margin of victory. In the foreground of Rush's painting are three views of Woods in different poses. In the center, he is completing the swing of a golf club, and on each side he is crouching, lining up and/or observing the progress of a putt. To the left of Woods is his caddy, Mike "Fluff" Cowan, and to his right is his final round partner's caddy. Behind these figures is the Augusta National Clubhouse. In a blue background behind the clubhouse are likenesses of famous golfers of the past looking down on Woods. These include Arnold Palmer, Sam Snead, Ben Hogan, Walter Hagen, Bobby Jones, and Jack Nicklaus. Behind them is the Masters leader board.

The limited edition prints distributed by Jireh consist of an image of Rush's painting which includes Rush's signature at the bottom right hand corner. Beneath the image of the painting, in block letters, is its title, "The Masters of Augusta." Beneath the title, in block letters of equal height, is the artist's name, "Rick Rush," and beneath the artist's name, in smaller upper and lower case letters, is the legend "Painting America Through Sports."

As sold by Jireh, the limited edition prints are enclosed in a white envelope, accompanied with literature which includes a large photograph of Rush, a description of his art, and a narrative description of the subject painting. On the front of the envelope, Rush's name appears in block letters inside a rectangle, which includes the legend "Painting America Through Sports." Along the bottom is a large reproduction of Rush's signature two inches high and ten inches long. On the back of the envelope, under the flap, are the words "Masters of Augusta" in letters that are three-eighths of an inch high, and "Tiger Woods" in letters that are one-fourth of an inch high. Woods's name also appears in the narrative description of the painting where he is mentioned twice in twenty-eight lines of text. The text also includes references to the six other famous golfers depicted in the background of the painting as well as the two caddies. Jireh published and marketed two hundred and fifty 22½″ × 30″ serigraphs and five thousand 9″ × 11″ lithographs of *The Masters of Augusta* at an issuing price of $700 for the serigraphs and $100 for the lithographs.

ETW filed suit against Jireh on June 26, 1998, in the United States District Court for the Northern District of Ohio, alleging trademark infringement in violation of the Lanham Act, 15 U.S.C. §1114; dilution of the mark under the Lanham Act, 15 U.S.C. §1125(c); unfair competition and false advertising under the Lanham Act, 15 U.S.C. §1125(a); unfair competition and deceptive trade practices under Ohio Revised Code §4165.01; unfair competition and trademark infringement under Ohio common law; and violation of Woods's right of publicity under Ohio common law. Jireh counterclaimed, seeking a declaratory judgment that Rush's art prints are protected by the First Amendment and do not violate the Lanham Act. Both parties moved for summary judgment.

The district court granted Jireh's motion for summary judgment and dismissed the case. *See* ETW Corp. v. Jireh Pub., Inc., 99 F. Supp. 2d 829 (N.D. Ohio 2000). ETW timely perfected an appeal to this court. . . .

III. TRADEMARK CLAIMS UNDER 15 U.S.C. §1125(a) BASED ON THE UNAUTHORIZED USE OF THE LIKENESS OF TIGER WOODS

Section 43(a) of the Lanham Act, 15 U.S.C. §1125(a), provides "a right of action to persons engaged in interstate and foreign commerce, against deceptive and misleading use of words, names, symbols, or devices, or any combination thereof, which have been adopted by a . . . merchant to identify his goods and distinguish them from those manufactured by others[.]" Federal-Mogul-Bower Bearings, Inc. v. Azoff, 313 F.2d 405, 408 (6th Cir. 1963). . . .

ETW has registered Woods's name as a trademark, but it has not registered any image or likeness of Woods. Nevertheless, ETW claims to have trademark rights in Woods's image and likeness. Section 43(a) of the Lanham Act provides a federal cause of action for infringement of an unregistered trademark which affords such marks essentially the same protection as those that are registered. . . .

The Lanham Act defines a trademark as including "any word, name, symbol, or device, or any combination thereof" used by a person "to identify and distinguish his or her goods . . . from those manufactured or sold by others and to indicate the source of the goods, even if that source is unknown." 15 U.S.C. §1127. The essence of a trademark is a designation in the form of a distinguishing name, symbol or device which is used to identify a person's goods and distinguish them from the goods of another. . . . Not every word, name, symbol or device qualifies as a protectable mark; rather, it must be proven that it performs the job of identification, *i.e.*, to identify one source and to distinguish it from other sources. If it does not do this, then it is not protectable as a trademark. . . .

Here, ETW claims protection under the Lanham Act for any and all images of Tiger Woods. This is an untenable claim. ETW asks us, in effect, to constitute Woods himself as a walking, talking trademark. Images and likenesses of Woods are not protectable as a trademark because they do not perform the trademark function of designation. They do not distinguish and identify the source of goods. They cannot function as a trademark because there are undoubtedly thousands of images and likenesses of Woods taken by countless photographers, and drawn, sketched, or painted by numerous artists, which have been published in many forms of media, and sold and distributed throughout the world. No reasonable person could believe that merely because these photographs or paintings contain Woods's likeness or image, they all originated with Woods.

We hold that, as a general rule, a person's image or likeness cannot function as a trademark. Our conclusion is supported by the decisions of other courts which have addressed this issue. In Pirone v. MacMillan, Inc., 894 F.2d 579 (2d Cir. 1990), the Second Circuit rejected a trademark claim asserted by the daughters of baseball legend Babe Ruth. The plaintiffs objected to the use of Ruth's likeness in three photographs which appeared in a calendar published by the defendant. The court rejected their claim, holding that "a photograph of a human being, unlike a portrait of a fanciful cartoon character, is not inherently 'distinctive' in the trademark sense of tending to indicate origin." The court noted that Ruth "was one of the most photographed men of his generation, a larger than life hero to millions and an historical figure[.]" The Second Circuit Court concluded that a consumer could not reasonably believe that Ruth sponsored the calendar:

> [A]n ordinarily prudent purchaser would have no difficulty discerning that these photos are merely the subject matter of the calendar and do not in any way indicate sponsorship. No reasonable jury could find a likelihood of confusion.

Id. at 585. The court observed that "[u]nder some circumstances, a photograph of a person may be a valid trademark — if, for example, a particular photograph was consistently used on specific goods." The court rejected plaintiffs' assertion of trademark rights in every photograph of Ruth.

In Estate of Presley v. Russen, 513 F. Supp. 1339, 1363-1364 (D.N.J. 1981), the court rejected a claim by the estate of Elvis Presley that his image and likeness was a valid mark. The court did find, however, as suggested by the Second Circuit in Pirone, that one particular image of Presley had been consistently used in the advertising and sale of Elvis Presley entertainment services to identify those services and that the image could likely be found to function as a mark. . . .

Here, ETW does not claim that a particular photograph of Woods has been consistently used on specific goods. Instead, ETW's claim is identical to that of the plaintiffs in Pirone, a sweeping claim to trademark rights in every photograph and image of Woods. Woods, like Ruth, is one of the most photographed sports figures of his generation, but this alone does not suffice to create a trademark claim.

The district court properly granted summary judgment on ETW's claim of trademark rights in all images and likenesses of Tiger Woods.

IV. LANHAM ACT UNFAIR COMPETITION AND FALSE ENDORSEMENT CLAIMS, OHIO RIGHT TO PRIVACY CLAIMS, AND THE FIRST AMENDMENT DEFENSE

A. Introduction

ETW's claims under §43(a) of the Lanham Act, 15 U.S.C. §1125(a), include claims of unfair competition and false advertising in the nature of false endorsement. ETW has also asserted a claim for infringement of the right of publicity under Ohio law. The elements of a Lanham Act false endorsement claim are similar to the elements of a right of publicity claim under Ohio law. In fact, one legal scholar has said that a Lanham Act false endorsement claim is the federal equivalent of the right of publicity. *See* Bruce P. Keller, *The Right of Publicity: Past, Present, and Future*, 1207 PLI Corp. Law and Prac. Handbook, 159, 170 (October 2000). Therefore, cases which address both these types of claims should be instructive in determining whether Jireh is entitled to summary judgment on those claims.

In addition, Jireh has raised the First Amendment as a defense to all of ETW's claims, arguing that Rush's use of Woods's image in his painting is protected expression. Cases involving Lanham Act false endorsement claims and state law claims of the right of publicity have considered the impact of the First Amendment on those types of claims. We will begin with a discussion of the scope of First Amendment rights in the context of works of art, and will then proceed to examine how First Amendment rights have been balanced against intellectual property rights in cases involving the Lanham Act and state law rights of publicity. Finally, we will apply the relevant legal principles to the facts of this case.

B. First Amendment Defense

The protection of the First Amendment is not limited to written or spoken words, but includes other mediums of expression, including music, pictures, films, photographs, paintings, drawings, engravings, prints, and sculptures. *See* Hurley v. Irish-American Gay, Lesbian and Bisexual Group of Boston, 515 U.S. 557, 569 (1995) ("[T]he Constitution looks beyond written or spoken words as mediums of expression.") [Citations omitted.]

Speech is protected even though it is carried in a form that is sold for profit. *See* Smith v. California, 361 U.S. 147, 150 (1959) ("It is of course no matter that the dissemination [of books and other forms of the printed word] takes place under commercial auspices.") [Citations omitted.] The fact that expressive materials are sold does not diminish the degree of protection to which they are entitled under the First Amendment. City of Lakewood v. Plain Dealer Publ'g Co., 486 U.S. 750, 756 n.5 (1988).

Publishers disseminating the work of others who create expressive materials also come wholly within the protective shield of the First Amendment. *See, e.g.,* Simon & Schuster, Inc. v. Members of New York State Crime Victims Bd., 502 U.S. 105, 116 (1991) (both the author and the publishing house are "speakers" for purposes of the First Amendment) [citations omitted]. Even pure commercial speech is entitled to significant First Amendment protection. *See* City of Cincinnati v. Discovery Network, Inc., 507 U.S. 410, 423 (1993). Commercial speech is "speech which does 'no more than propose a commercial transaction[.]'" [Citation omitted.]

Rush's prints are not commercial speech. They do not propose a commercial transaction. Accordingly, they are entitled to the full protection of the First Amendment. Thus, we are called upon to decide whether Woods's intellectual property rights must yield to Rush's First Amendment rights. . . .

D. Right of Publicity Claim

ETW claims that Jireh's publication and marketing of prints of Rush's painting violates Woods's right of publicity. The right of publicity is an intellectual property right of recent origin which has been defined as the inherent right of every human being to control the commercial use of his or her identity. [Citation omitted.] The right of publicity is a creature of state law and its violation gives rise to a cause of action for the commercial tort of unfair competition.

The right of publicity is, somewhat paradoxically, an outgrowth of the right of privacy. [Citation omitted.] A cause of action for violation of the right was first recognized in Haelan Laboratories, Inc. v. Topps Chewing Gum, Inc., 202 F.2d 866 (2d Cir. 1953), where the Second Circuit held that New York's common law protected a baseball player's right in the publicity value of his photograph, and in the process coined the phrase "right of publicity" as the name of this right.

The Ohio Supreme Court recognized the right of publicity in 1976 in Zacchini v. Scripps-Howard Broadcasting Co., 351 N.E.2d 454 (1976). In *Zacchini*, which involved the videotaping and subsequent rebroadcast on a television news program of plaintiff's human cannonball act, the Ohio Supreme Court held that Zacchini's right of publicity was trumped by the First Amendment. On appeal, the Supreme Court of the United States reversed, holding that the First Amendment did not insulate defendant from liability for violating Zacchini's state law right of publicity where defendant published the plaintiff's entire act. *See* Zacchini v. Scripps-Howard Broadcasting Co., 433 U.S. 562 (1977). *Zacchini* is the only United States Supreme Court decision on the right of publicity. . . .

When the Ohio Supreme Court recognized the right of publicity, it relied heavily on the RESTATEMENT (SECOND) OF TORTS, §652. . . . The court quoted the entire text of §652(C) of the RESTATEMENT, as well as comments a., b., c. and d. . . .

In §47, comment c, the authors of the RESTATEMENT note, "The right of publicity as recognized by statute and common law is fundamentally constrained by the public and constitutional interest in freedom of expression." In the same comment, the authors state that "[t]he use of a person's identity primarily for the purpose of communicating information or expressing ideas is not generally actionable as a violation of the person's right of publicity." Various examples are given, including the use of the person's name or likeness in news reporting in newspapers and magazines. The RESTATEMENT recognizes that this limitation on the right is not confined to news reporting but extends to use in "entertainment and other creative works, including both fiction and non-fiction." The authors list examples of protected uses of a celebrity's identity, likeness or image, including unauthorized print or broadcast biographies and novels, plays or motion pictures. According to the RESTATEMENT, such uses are not protected, however, if the name or likeness is used solely to attract attention to a work that is not related to the identified person, and the privilege may be lost if the work contains substantial falsifications.

We believe the courts of Ohio would follow the principles of the RESTATEMENT in defining the limits of the right of publicity. The Ohio Supreme Court's decision in *Zacchini* suggests that Ohio is inclined to give substantial weight to the public interest in freedom of expression when balancing it against the personal and proprietary interests recognized by the right of publicity.

There is an inherent tension between the right of publicity and the right of freedom of expression under the First Amendment. This tension becomes particularly acute when the person seeking to enforce the right is a famous actor, athlete, politician, or otherwise famous person whose exploits, activities, accomplishments, and personal life are subject to constant scrutiny and comment in the public media. In *Memphis Development Foundation*, 616 F.2d at 959, this court discussed the problems of judicial line drawing that would arise if it should recognize the inheritability of publicity rights, including the question "[a]t what point does the right collide with the right of free expression guaranteed by the First Amendment?" In *Carson*, after noting that the First Amendment protects commercial speech, Judge Kennedy opined in her dissent that "public policy requires that the public's interest in free enterprise and free expression take precedence over any interest Johnny Carson may have in a phrase associated with his person." *Carson*, 698 F.2d at 841. In *Landham*, we noted "the careful balance that courts have gradually constructed between the right of publicity and the First Amendment [.]" 227 F.3d at 626.

In a series of recent cases, other circuits have been called upon to establish the boundaries between the right of publicity and the First Amendment. In *Rogers*, the Second Circuit affirmed the district court's grant of summary judgment on Rogers' right of publicity claim, noting that commentators have "advocated limits on the right of publicity to accommodate First Amendment concerns." That court also cited three cases in which state courts refused to extend the right of publicity to bar the use of a celebrity's name in the title and text of a fictional or semi-fictional book or movie.

In *White*, television celebrity Vanna White, brought suit against Samsung Electronics, alleging that its television advertisement which featured a female-shaped robot wearing a long gown, blonde wig, large jewelry, and turning letters in what appeared to be the "Wheel of Fortune" game show set, violated her California common law right of publicity and her rights under the Lanham Act. The Ninth Circuit, with Judge Alarcon dissenting in part, reversed the grant of summary judgment to defendant, holding that White had produced sufficient evidence that defendant's advertisement appropriated her identity in violation of her right of publicity, and that the issue of confusion about White's endorsement of defendant's product created a jury issue which precluded summary judgment on her Lanham Act claim. In so holding, the court rejected the defendant's parody defense which posited that the advertisement was a parody of White's television act and was protected speech.

A suggestion for rehearing *en banc* failed. Three judges dissented from the order rejecting the suggestion for a rehearing *en banc*. *See* White v. Samsung Electronics America, Inc., 989 F.2d 1512 (9th Cir. 1993). Judge Kozinski, writing the dissenting opinion, observed, "Something very dangerous is going on here. . . . Overprotecting intellectual property is as harmful as underprotecting it. Creativity is impossible without a rich public domain." Later, he commented:

> Intellectual property rights aren't free: They're imposed at the expense of future creators and of the public at large. . . . This is why intellectual property law is full of careful balances between what's set aside for the owner and what's left in the public domain for the rest of us[.]

Id. at 1516. In *Landham*, this court declined to follow the majority in *White* and, instead, cited Judge Kozinski's dissent with approval.

In Cardtoons, L.C. v. Major League Baseball Players Assoc., 95 F.3d 959 (10th Cir. 1996), the Tenth Circuit held that the plaintiff's First Amendment right to free expression outweighed the defendant's proprietary right of publicity. The plaintiff in *Cardtoons* contracted with a political cartoonist, a sports artist, and a sports author and journalist to design a set of trading cards which featured readily identifiable caricatures of major league baseball players with a humorous commentary about their careers on the back. The cards ridiculed the players using a variety of themes. The cards used similar names, recognizable caricatures, distinctive team colors and commentaries about individual players which left no doubt about their identity. The Tenth Circuit held that the defendant's use of the player's likenesses on its trading cards would violate their rights of publicity under an Oklahoma statute. Addressing the defendant's First Amendment claim, the court held:

> Cardtoons' parody trading cards receive full protection under the First Amendment. The cards provide social commentary on public figures, major league baseball players, who are involved in a significant commercial enterprise, major league baseball. While not core political speech . . . this type of commentary on an important social institution constitutes protected expression.

Cardtoons, 95 F.3d at 969. The Tenth Circuit rejected the reasoning of the panel majority in *White*, and expressed its agreement with the dissenting opinions of Judges Alarcon and Kozinski. . . . In striking the balance between the players' property rights and the defendant's First Amendment rights, the court in *Cardtoons* commented on the pervasive presence of celebrities in the media, sports and entertainment. The court noted that celebrities are an important part of our public vocabulary and have come to symbolize certain ideas and values:

> As one commentator explained, celebrities are "common points of reference for millions of individuals who may never interact with one another, but who share, by virtue of their participation in a mediated culture, a common experience and a collective memory." John B. Thompson, *Ideology and Modern Culture: Critical Social Theory in the Era of Mass Communication* 163 (1990). Through their pervasive presence in the media, sports and entertainment celebrities come to symbolize certain ideas and values. . . . Celebrities, then, are an important element of the shared communicative resources of our cultural domain.

Cardtoons, 95 F.3d at 972. . . .

In Comedy III Productions, Inc. v. Gary Saderup, Inc., 21 P.3d 797 (2001), the California Supreme Court adopted a transformative use test in determining whether the artistic use of a celebrity's image is protected by the First Amendment. Saderup, an artist with over twenty-five years experience in making charcoal drawings of celebrities, created a drawing of the famous comedy team, The Three Stooges. The drawings were used to create lithographic and silk screen masters, which were then used to produce lithographic prints and silk screen images on T-shirts. Comedy III, the owner of all rights to the former comedy act, brought suit against Saderup under a California statute, which grants the right of publicity to successors in interest of deceased celebrities.

The California Supreme Court found that Saderup's portraits were entitled to First Amendment protection because they were "expressive works and not an advertisement or endorsement of a product." *Id.* 21 P.3d at 802. . . .

We conclude that in deciding whether the sale of Rush's prints violate Woods's right of publicity, we will look to the Ohio case law and the RESTATEMENT (THIRD) OF UNFAIR COMPETITION. In deciding where the line should be drawn between Woods's intellectual property rights and the First Amendment, we find ourselves in agreement with the dissenting judges in *White*, the

Tenth Circuit's decision in *Cardtoons*, and the Ninth Circuit's decision in *Hoffman*, and we will follow them in determining whether Rush's work is protected by the First Amendment. Finally, we believe that the transformative elements test adopted by the Supreme Court of California in *Comedy III Productions*, will assist us in determining where the proper balance lies between the First Amendment and Woods's intellectual property rights. We turn now to a further examination of Rush's work and its subject.

E. Application of the Law to the Evidence in This Case

The evidence in the record reveals that Rush's work consists of much more than a mere literal likeness of Woods. It is a panorama of Woods's victory at the 1997 Masters Tournament, with all of the trappings of that tournament in full view, including the Augusta clubhouse, the leader board, images of Woods's caddy, and his final round partner's caddy. These elements in themselves are sufficient to bring Rush's work within the protection of the First Amendment. The Masters Tournament is probably the world's most famous golf tournament and Woods's victory in the 1997 tournament was a historic event in the world of sports. A piece of art that portrays a historic sporting event communicates and celebrates the value our culture attaches to such events. It would be ironic indeed if the presence of the image of the victorious athlete would deny the work First Amendment protection. Furthermore, Rush's work includes not only images of Woods and the two caddies, but also carefully crafted likenesses of six past winners of the Masters Tournament: Arnold Palmer, Sam Snead, Ben Hogan, Walter Hagen, Bobby Jones, and Jack Nicklaus, a veritable pantheon of golf's greats. Rush's work conveys the message that Woods himself will someday join that revered group.

Turning first to ETW's Lanham Act false endorsement claim, we agree with the courts that hold that the Lanham Act should be applied to artistic works only where the public interest in avoiding confusion outweighs the public interest in free expression. The *Rogers* test is helpful in striking that balance in the instant case. We find that the presence of Woods's image in Rush's painting *The Masters of Augusta* does have artistic relevance to the underlying work and that it does not explicitly mislead as to the source of the work. We believe that the principles followed in *Cardtoons, Hoffman* and *Comedy III* are also relevant in determining whether the Lanham Act applies to Rush's work, and we find that it does not.

We find, like the court in *Rogers*, that plaintiff's survey evidence, even if its validity is assumed, indicates at most that some members of the public would draw the incorrect inference that Woods had some connection with Rush's print. The risk of misunderstanding, not engendered by any explicit indication on the face of the print, is so outweighed by the interest in artistic expression as to preclude application of the Act. We disagree with the dissent's suggestion that a jury must decide where the balance should be struck and where the boundaries should be drawn between the rights conferred by the Lanham Act and the protections of the First Amendment.

We further find that Rush's work is expression which is entitled to the full protection of the First Amendment and not the more limited protection afforded to commercial speech. When we balance the magnitude of the speech restriction against the interest in protecting Woods's intellectual property right, we encounter precisely the same considerations weighed by the Tenth Circuit in *Cardtoons.* These include consideration of the fact that through their pervasive presence in the media, sports and entertainment celebrities have come to symbolize certain ideas and values in our society and have become a valuable means of expression in our culture. As the Tenth Circuit observed "[c]elebrities . . . are an important element of the shared communicative resources of our cultural domain." *Cardtoons*, 95 F.3d at 972. . . .

[A]pplying the transformative effects test adopted by the Supreme Court of California in *Comedy III*, we find that Rush's work does contain significant transformative elements which make it especially worthy of First Amendment protection and also less likely to interfere with the economic interest protected by Woods' right of publicity. Unlike the unadorned, nearly photographic reproduction of the faces of The Three Stooges in *Comedy III*, Rush's work does not capitalize solely on a literal depiction of Woods. Rather, Rush's work consists of a collage of images in addition to Woods's image which are combined to describe, in artistic form, a historic event in sports history and to convey a message about the significance of Woods's achievement in that event. Because Rush's work has substantial transformative elements, it is entitled to the full protection of the First Amendment. In this case, we find that Woods's right of publicity must yield to the First Amendment.

V. CONCLUSION

In accordance with the foregoing, the judgment of the District Court granting summary judgment to Jireh Publishing is affirmed.

C.B.C. DISTRIB. & MKTG., INC. v. MAJOR LEAGUE BASEBALL ADVANCED MEDIA L.P.

505 F.3d 818 (8th Cir. 2007)

ARNOLD, Circuit Judge.

C.B.C. Distribution and Marketing, Inc., brought this action for a declaratory judgment against Major League Baseball Advanced Media to establish its right to use, without license, the names of and information about Major League Baseball players in connection with its fantasy baseball products. Advanced Media counterclaimed, maintaining that CBC's fantasy baseball products violated rights of publicity belonging to the players and that the players, through their association, had licensed those rights to Advanced Media, the interactive media and Internet company of Major League Baseball. The Major League Baseball Players Association intervened in the suit, joining in Advanced Media's claims and further asserting a breach of contract claim against CBC. The district court granted summary judgment to CBC and Advanced Media and the Players Association appealed. We affirm.

I.

CBC sells fantasy sports products via its Internet website, e-mail, mail, and the telephone. Its fantasy baseball products incorporate the names along with performance and biographical data of actual Major League Baseball players. Before the commencement of the major league baseball season each spring, participants form their fantasy baseball teams by "drafting" players from various Major League Baseball teams. Participants compete against other fantasy baseball "owners" who have also drafted their own teams. A participant's success, and his or her team's success, depends on the actual performance of the fantasy team's players on their respective actual teams during the course of the Major League Baseball season. Participants in CBC's fantasy baseball games pay fees to play and additional fees to trade players during the course of the season.

From 1995 through the end of 2004, CBC licensed its use of the names of and information about Major League players from the Players Association pursuant to license agreements that it entered into with the association in 1995 and 2002. The 2002 agreement, which superseded in its entirety the 1995 agreement, licensed to CBC "the names, nicknames, likenesses, signatures, pictures, playing records, and/or biographical data of each player" (the "Rights") to be used in association with CBC's fantasy baseball products.

In 2005, after the 2002 agreement expired, the Players Association licensed to Advanced Media, with some exceptions, the exclusive right to use baseball players' names and performance information "for exploitation via all interactive media." Advanced Media began providing fantasy baseball games on its website, MLB.com, the official website of Major League Baseball. It offered CBC, in exchange for a commission, a license to promote the MLB.com fantasy baseball games on CBC's website but did not offer CBC a license to continue to offer its own fantasy baseball products. This conduct by Advanced Media prompted CBC to file the present suit, alleging that it had "a reasonable apprehension that it will be sued by Advanced Media if it continues to operate its fantasy baseball games."

The district court held that CBC was not infringing any state-law rights of publicity that belonged to Major League Baseball players. The court reasoned that CBC's fantasy baseball products did not use the names of Major League Baseball players as symbols of their identities and with an intent to obtain a commercial advantage, as required to establish an infringement of a publicity right under Missouri law. The district court further held that even if CBC were infringing the players' rights of publicity, the first amendment preempted those rights. Finally, the district court held that CBC was not in violation of the no-use and no-contest provisions of its 2002 agreement with the Players Association because "the strong federal policy favoring the full and free use of ideas in the public domain as manifested in the laws of intellectual property prevails over [those] contractual provisions." [Our review of the] district court's grant of summary judgment, our review is de novo. We also review de novo the district court's interpretation of state law, including its interpretation of Missouri law regarding the right of publicity.

II.

A.

An action based on the right of publicity is a state-law claim. In Missouri, "the elements of a right of publicity action include: (1) That defendant used plaintiff's name as a symbol of his identity (2) without consent (3) and with the intent to obtain a commercial advantage." The parties all agree that CBC's continued use of the players' names and playing information after the expiration of the 2002 agreement was without consent. The district court concluded, however, that the evidence was insufficient to make out the other two elements of the claim[s].

With respect to the symbol-of-identity element, the Missouri Supreme Court has observed that "'the name used by the defendant must be understood by the audience as referring to the plaintiff.'" The state court had further held that "[i]n resolving this issue, the fact-finder may consider evidence including 'the nature and extent of the identifying characteristics used by the defendant, the defendant's intent, the fame of the plaintiff, evidence of actual identification made by third persons, and surveys or other evidence indicating the perceptions of the audience.'"

Here, we entertain no doubt that those players' names that CBC used are understood by it and its fantasy baseball subscribers as referring to actual major league baseball players. CBC itself admits that: In responding to the appellants' argument that "this element is met by the mere confirmation that the name used, in fact, refers to the famous person asserting the violation," CBC stated in its brief that "if this is all the element requires, CBC agrees that it is met." We think that by reasoning that "identity," rather than "mere use of a name," "is a critical element of the right of publicity," the district court did not understand that when a name alone is sufficient to establish identity, the defendant's use of that name satisfies the plaintiff's burden to show that a name was used as a symbol of identity.

It is true that with respect to the "commercial advantage" element of a cause of action for violating publicity rights, CBC's use does not fit neatly into the more traditional categories of commercial advantage, namely, using individuals' names for advertising and merchandising purposes in a way that states or intimates that the individuals are endorsing a product. But the Restatement, which the Missouri Supreme Court has recognized as authority in this kind of case also says that a name is used for commercial advantage when it is used "in connection with services rendered by the user" and that the plaintiff need not show that "prospective purchasers are likely to believe" that he or she endorsed the product or service. We note, moreover, that in Missouri, "the commercial advantage element of the right of publicity focuses on the defendant's intent or purpose to obtain a commercial benefit from use of the plaintiff's identity." Because we think that it is clear that CBC uses baseball players' identities in its fantasy baseball products for purposes of profit, we believe that their identities are being used for commercial advantage and that the players therefore offered sufficient evidence to make out a cause of action for violation of their rights of publicity.

B.

CBC argues that the First Amendment nonetheless trumps the right-of-publicity action that Missouri law provides. The Supreme Court has directed that state law rights of publicity must be balanced against First Amendment considerations and here we conclude that the former must give way to the latter. First, the information used in CBC's fantasy baseball games is all readily available in the public domain, and it would be strange law that a person would not have a First Amendment right to use information that is available to everyone. It is true that CBC's use of the information is meant to provide entertainment, but "[s]peech that entertains, like speech that informs, is protected by the First Amendment because '[t]he line between the informing and the entertaining is too elusive for the protection of that basic right.'" We also find no merit in the argument that CBC's use of players' names and information in its fantasy baseball games is not speech at all. We have held that "the pictures, graphic design, concept art, sounds, music, stories, and narrative present in video games" is speech entitled to First Amendment protection. Similarly, here CBC uses the "names, nicknames, likenesses, signatures, pictures, playing records, and/or biographical data of each player" in an interactive form in connection with its fantasy baseball products.

Courts have also recognized the public value of information about the game of baseball and its players, referring to baseball as "the national pastime." A California court, in a case where Major League Baseball was itself defending its use of players' names, likenesses, and information against the players' asserted rights of publicity, observed, "Major League Baseball is followed by millions of people across this country on a daily basis. . . . The public has an enduring fascination in the records set by former players and in memorable moments from previous games. . . . The records and statistics remain of interest to the public because they provide context that allows fans to better appreciate (or deprecate) today's performances." Gionfriddo v. Major League Baseball, 94 Cal. App. 4th 400, 411, 114 Cal. Rptr. 2d 307 (2001). The Court in *Gionfriddo* concluded that the "recitation and discussion of factual data concerning the athletic performance of [players on Major League Baseball's website] command a substantial public interest and, therefore, is a form of expression due substantial constitutional protection."

In addition, the facts in this case barely, if at all, implicate the interests that states typically intend to vindicate by providing rights of publicity to individuals. Economic interests that states seek to promote include the right of an individual to reap the rewards of his or her endeavors and an individual's right to earn a living. Other motives for creating a publicity right are the desire to provide incentives to encourage a person's productive activities and to protect consumers from misleading advertising. But Major League Baseball players are rewarded, and handsomely, too, for their participation in games and can earn additional large sums from endorsements and sponsorship arrangements. Nor is there any danger here that consumers will be misled, because the fantasy baseball games depend on the inclusion of all players and thus cannot create a false impression that some particular player with "star power" is endorsing CBC's products.

Then there are so-called non-monetary interests that publicity rights are sometimes thought to advance. These include protecting natural rights, rewarding celebrity labors, and avoiding emotional harm. We do not see that any of these interests are especially relevant here, where baseball players are rewarded separately for their labors, and where any emotional harm would most likely be caused by a player's actual performance, in which case media coverage would cause the same harm. We also note that some courts have indicated that the right of publicity is intended to promote only economic interests and that noneconomic interests are more directly served by so-called rights of privacy. "Publicity rights . . . are meant to protect against the loss of financial gain, not mental anguish." [W]e hold that CBC's First Amendment rights in offering its fantasy baseball products supersede the players' rights of publicity. . . .

III.

We come finally to the breach of contract issue. The 2002 contract between the Players Association and CBC specifically provided: "It is understood and agreed that [the Players Association] is the sole and exclusive holder of all right, title and interest in and to the Rights." CBC undertook not to "dispute or attack the title or any rights of Players' Association in and to the Rights and/or the Trademarks or the validity of the license granted," either during or after the expiration of the agreement (the no-challenge provision). CBC also agreed that, upon expiration or termination of the contract, it would "refrain from further use of the Rights and/or the Trademarks or any further reference to them, either directly or indirectly" (the no-use provision). The Players Association maintains that the no-challenge and no-use provisions of the 2002 agreement are fatal to CBC's claim. We disagree.

Although the parties did not cite to it in their briefs, the agreement does contain what we believe is a warranty of title . . . in §8(a). The agreement provides that its interpretation will be governed by New York law. In New York, a contractual warranty is defined as "'an assurance by one party to a contract of the existence of a fact upon which the other party may rely.'" Section 8(a) of the agreement provides that the Players Association "is the sole and exclusive holder of all right, title and interest" in and to the names and playing statistics of virtually all major league baseball players. This is quite obviously a representation or warranty that the Players Association did in fact own the state law publicity rights at issue here. For the reasons given above, the Players Association did not have exclusive "right, title and interest" in the use of such information, and it therefore breached a material obligation that it undertook in the contract. CBC is thus relieved of the obligations that it undertook, and the Players Association cannot enforce the contract's no-use and no-challenge provisions against CBC. For the foregoing reasons, the district court's grant of summary judgment to CBC is affirmed.

COLLOTON, Circuit Judge, dissenting.

I agree with the court's discussion of the right of publicity in Missouri and the application of the First Amendment in this context. I would resolve the contractual issues differently, however, and I therefore respectfully dissent.

Advanced Media and the Major League Baseball Players Association ("MLBPA") contend that CBC has violated two provisions of the applicable License Agreement as set forth in the majority opinion—the "no-challenge" provision and the "no-use" provision. CBC does not really dispute that it violated the restrictions, but it contends that the contractual provisions are unenforceable. I disagree with the court's conclusion, *sua sponte*, that the provisions are unenforceable because MLBPA breached a warranty set forth in section 8(a) of the agreement.

Section 8(a) appears under a heading "Ownership of Rights." It provides as follows: "It is understood and agreed that MLBPA is the sole and exclusive holder of all right, title and interest in and to the Rights and/or Trademarks for the duration of this Agreement." Given the court's resolution of issues concerning the right of publicity and the First Amendment, section 8(a) wins the day for CBC only if it is a warranty by MLBPA that CBC does not have rights under the First Amendment to use the players' names and statistics in its fantasy baseball games.

Assuming that section 8(a) does address CBC's constitutional rights (as opposed merely to the players' state-law rights of publicity, which are accurately represented), and assuming that one party's prediction about the constitutional rights of another party is the sort of "fact" that can be warranted under New York law, section 8(a) does not purport to make such a warranty. The provision states that the parties "agree" that MLPBA is the sole and exclusive holder of all right, title and interest in and to the Rights. CBC surely can "agree," as a matter of good business judgment, to bargain away any uncertain First Amendment rights that it may have in exchange for the certainty of what it considers to be an advantageous contractual arrangement. That CBC later decided it did not need a license, and that it preferred instead to litigate the point, does not relieve the company of its contractual obligation. For these reasons, I would reverse the district court's grant of summary judgment in favor of CBC.

RYAN v. VOLPONE STAMP CO.

107 F. Supp. 2d 369 (S.D.N.Y. 2000)

HAIGHT, Senior District Judge.

This action arises out of a dispute between a licensor and ex-licensee over the use of former Major League Baseball pitcher Nolan Ryan's name, likeness and signature in association with the sale of several products including stamps, coins, teddy bears, model trains and autographed items. Plaintiff Nolan Ryan brought this action under §43(a) of the Lanham Act, 15 U.S.C. §1125(a), New York Civil Rights Law §§50-51, and applicable common law alleging, *inter alia*, trademark infringement and breach of contract. Plaintiff moves for a preliminary injunction enjoining and restraining Defendant from manufacturing, causing to be manufactured, selling, causing to be sold, licensing or otherwise exploiting any products bearing Nolan Ryan's image. Defendant cross-moves to dismiss the action in deference to the pending New York State Court action between the parties, or in the alternative pursuant to Rules 12(c) and 19(b) of the Federal Rules of Civil Procedure.

I. BACKGROUND

Plaintiff Nolan Ryan, a former Major League Baseball player, pitched seven no-hitters during his career and continues to hold the record for most strikeouts. He was inducted into the Baseball Hall of Fame and voted by fans onto Baseball's All-Century Team. In light of his accomplishments and illustrious career, Ryan currently derives substantial revenue from endorsements, commercials, and the licensing of his name and image. Ryan is represented with respect to these matters by his agent Mattgo Enterprises, Inc. ("Mattgo"), a New York corporation. Matt Merola is the president of Mattgo. Neither Mattgo nor Merola are currently parties to this action.

Defendant Volpone Stamp Company, Inc. d/b/a Sport Stamps Collectors Association ("Volpone") is in the business of selling sports-related merchandise. Bernie Neumark is the president of Volpone.

In 1998 Ryan through Mattgo entered into a licensing agreement with Volpone (the "Master Agreement"). The Master Agreement was dated March 2, 1998 and was signed by Neumark for Volpone, Merola for Mattgo, and Ryan himself. The Master Agreement granted Volpone exclusive rights to manufacture, sell, and sub-license numerous Nolan Ryan products, including, stamps, coins and medals, cards and all products with facsimile Nolan Ryan signatures. It also granted Volpone non-exclusive rights with respect to two styles of watches as well as plates and figurines. The Master Agreement was for a term of two years with an effective starting date of January 1998. In return Volpone promised to pay royalties equal to ten percent of its wholesale price and guaranteed minimum royalties of $150,000 the first year and $175,000 the second year to be paid according to a schedule outlined in the Master Agreement. The Master Agreement also provided that Ryan would personally sign an unlimited quantity of baseballs at $25 per item, and an unlimited quantity of cards, flats and stamps at $20 per item. Finally, in case of nonpayment of the minimum royalties, Volpone would have sixty days to cure any default, after which the Master Agreement would terminate and all licensing rights would revert to Mattgo.

On November 23, 1998, the third and final agreement between the parties was executed granting Volpone the license to manufacture, sell and sub-license Nolan Ryan Plush Teddy Bears (the "Teddy Bear Agreement"). This contract required royalty payments amounting to ten percent of wholesale sales and guaranteed a minimum payment of $5,000 due on June 30, 1999. The Teddy Bear Agreement also expired on December 31, 1999.

The instant action arises out of a dispute that began in the summer of 1999. In accordance with the Master Agreement and the Teddy Bear Agreement, Volpone delivered checks covering its minimum guarantee payments in late June 1999. Specifically, he tendered two checks payable to Mattgo in the amounts of $43,750 (the second quarterly minimum guarantee payment for 1999 under the Master Agreement) and $5,000 (the minimum guarantee payment due under the Teddy Bear Agreement). Although the payments were due no later than June 30, 1999, both checks were post-dated July 31, 1999. According to Merola, Mattgo accepted the post-dated checks as an accommodation to Neumark. Merola deposited the post-dated checks on August 2, 1999. The checks were returned for insufficient funds. Volpone claims that payment was deliberately stopped.

Sometime in July 1999, Ryan autographed numerous items, including baseballs and photos, for Volpone in accordance with the Master Agreement. Volpone then tendered two additional checks compensating Ryan according to the rates agreed upon. One of the two checks was made payable to Nolan Ryan in the amount of $38,035. The other check was made payable to the Nolan Ryan Foundation in the amount of $2,117; this check represented a nominal fee for the Foundation's services in facilitating the signing of the objects and delivery of the items to Volpone. Thereafter payment was stopped on both checks.

Volpone justifies its actions based on the belief that Plaintiff had breached the Master Agreement which granted Volpone exclusive rights to Ryan's name, image and facsimile signature with respect to several products. As early as April 15, 1999, Neumark sent a letter to Merola expressing concern that the Master Agreement had been breached or that other companies were selling unauthorized merchandise.

Neumark sent another letter to Merola dated July 28, 1999 demanding a list of all licensing agreements Mattgo had made for Nolan Ryan products. He also requested that Merola not deposit the outstanding checks until the matter was resolved. Merola did not heed his plea and deposited the checks on August 2, 1999. Nevertheless, as previously stated, Volpone never made good on any of the four checks tendered in June and July 1999. On August 9, 1999, Neumark informed Merola by letter that he had stopped payment on the checks made payable to Nolan Ryan and the Nolan Ryan Foundation because Merola disregarded his request not to deposit the checks made out to Mattgo. He also reiterated his request for the list of licensing agreements Mattgo has made for Nolan Ryan products.

On August 10, 1999 counsel for Ryan wrote a letter to Volpone stating that its allegations concerning violations of the Master Agreement did not justify its failure to make the minimum guarantee payments. Such failure to pay, the letter continued, constituted a breach of the licensing agreements, and, therefore, the letter was to serve as notice that the licensing agreements were terminated. The letter stated in no uncertain terms that Volpone was no longer authorized to "manufacture, cause to be manufactured, sell, market or otherwise distribute or promote any products bearing Nolan Ryan's name, photograph, signature, image, etc."

Plaintiff alleges that Volpone disregarded the termination letter and continued to manufacture and distribute Nolan Ryan merchandise.

On August 16, 1999, Volpone commenced an action against Ryan, Merola and Mattgo in New York State Supreme Court asserting claims of breach of contract and fraud. Plaintiff commenced the present action in this Court on August 24, 1999.

Plaintiff . . . moves for a preliminary injunction pursuant to Fed. R. Civ. P. 65(a) enjoining Volpone from continuing to manufacture, sell, distribute and otherwise market Nolan Ryan products. It also moves this Court to direct Defendant to certify its compliance and account for its sales and revenue relating to Nolan Ryan items. . . .

V. NEW YORK CIVIL RIGHTS LAW CLAIM

Defendant has also moved to dismiss Plaintiff's second and eighth causes of action for failure to state a claim upon which relief can be granted.

A. Second Claim for Relief

In his second cause of action, Ryan alleges violations of N.Y. Civil Rights Law §§50 and 51. [Section] 50 creates a statutory right of privacy making it a misdemeanor for "[a] person, firm or corporation that uses for advertising purposes, or for the purposes of trade, the name, portrait or picture of any living person without having first obtained the written consent of such person." N.Y. Civil Rights Law §50 (McKinney 2000). [Section] 51 affords the right to bring an equitable action to "[a]ny person whose name, portrait, picture or voice is used within this state for advertising purposes or for the purposes of trade without the written consent first obtained." N.Y. Civil Rights Law §51 (McKinney 2000). A plaintiff asserting an action pursuant to this statute may be awarded injunctive relief, compensatory damages and, if the defendant knowingly violated the right of privacy, exemplary damages.

There is no dispute that Volpone used Ryan's name within New York State for advertising or trade purposes. However, Defendant maintains that Ryan consented to such use by entering into the licensing agreements. Volpone also argues that Ryan's alleged injury is not to his privacy, but rather to his purse. Defendant is correct that Ryan's right to privacy, as that concept is generally understood, has not been violated. Plaintiff actively sought to exploit the commercial use of his own name, signature and likeness which has substantial value as a result of his accomplishments on the baseball field. Defendant is also correct that New York has not created a statutory right of publicity nor does it recognize a common law right of publicity, in contrast to numerous other states. *See* Stephano v. News Group Publications, Inc., 474 N.E.2d 580 (1984).

Nevertheless, although New York's statutory right of privacy originated as a means to protect private individuals from unwanted publicity, the New York Court of Appeals has held that the statute is not limited to such situations. "By its terms the statute applies to any use of a person's picture or portrait for advertising or trade purposes whenever the defendant has not obtained the person's written consent to do so. It would therefore apply, and recently has been held to apply, in cases where the plaintiff generally seeks publicity, or uses his name, portrait or picture, for commercial purposes but has not given written consent for a particular use." Thus, the reason New York does not recognize a separate right of publicity is not because it has deemed such interest unworthy of legal protection, but rather because the right of publicity is already subsumed in the statutory right of privacy. . . .

Defendant cites Wrangell v. C.F. Hathaway Co., 253 N.Y.S.2d 41 (1st Dept. 1964), for the proposition that once consent to the use of one's name or photograph has been granted, the right of privacy is relinquished and subsequent disputes over the scope of the consent are merely matters of contract. In *Wrangell*, plaintiff had consented to the use of his photograph in the connection with the advertisement of men's shirts. When defendant began using the photo to advertise women's shirts as well, plaintiff sued, arguing that such use extended beyond the consent given. The court dismissed the cause of action, holding that "it is apparent that plaintiff's grievance is not the breach of his right to privacy, which he does not particularly seek, but the alleged unauthorized use of his photograph in a special way without extra compensation therefor. By his contract of employment and his consent to defendant's use of his photograph in its trademark, plaintiff relinquished his right to privacy."

Although *Wrangell* does support Volpone's argument, it appears that the reasoning adopted by the court in that case is no longer valid. *Wrangell* predated by twenty years the New York Court of Appeals holding in *Stephano* that the statutory right of privacy protects not only privacy, but an individual's so-called right of publicity as well. Therefore, the mere fact that the plaintiff in *Wrangell* was not concerned with an invasion of privacy should not have been fatal to the cause of action. If Wrangell could prove that his consent was limited to using the photo for the advertisement of men's shirts, it would seem that he had stated a cause of action under N.Y. Civil Rights Law §51.

Ryan alleges that he terminated the licensing agreements and thereby revoked his consent to the continued use by Volpone of his name, likeness and signature. Plaintiff notified Defendant of the termination and demanded that it cease and desist from any further use of his name. Volpone allegedly ignored these warnings. Seemingly in direct contrast to the holding in *Wrangell*, the New York Court of Appeals has held:

> [W]here the written consent to use the plaintiff's name or picture for advertising or trade purposes has expired or the defendant has otherwise exceeded the limitations of the consent, the plaintiff may seek damages or other relief under the statute, even though he might properly sue for breach of contract. The right which the statute permits the plaintiff to vindicate in such a case may, perhaps, more accurately be described as a right of publicity.

Stephano, 474 N.E.2d 580 (internal citations omitted). Viewing the allegations in the light most favorable to the Plaintiff, it would appear that Volpone used Ryan's name for commercial purposes without his consent in violation of New York's Civil Rights law. Additional case law supports Ryan's position.

In Nutrivida, Inc. v. Inmuno Vital, Inc., 1997 WL 1106569 (S.D. Fla. 1997), the parties had entered an agreement whereby Nutrivida would distribute a vitamin supplement product supplied by Inmuno. In connection with advertising the product, Nutrivida began to use the name of a Mexican actor, Andres Garcia Garcia, whose cancer was cured using the vitamin supplement. Garcia had consented expressly to Inmuno's use of his name, but not Nutrivida. Subsequently, a dispute arose and Nutrivida and Inmuno terminated the distribution agreement. Nevertheless, Nutrivida continued to run the Garcia advertisements.

In the suit that followed, Inmuno as exclusive licensee of the use of Garcia's name counter-claimed for a violation of its right of publicity under N.Y. Civil Rights Law §§50 and 51. Although there was a question whether Nutrivida ever had consent to use Garcia's name by virtue of its agreement with Inmuno, a question left to the jury, the court held that any such consent expired when the agreement was terminated. Thus, it concluded that "Nutrivida is liable as a matter of law because the consent to use Garcia's name, if there was any, expired after Garcia's counsel sent Nutrivida a cease and desist letter." *Nutrivida*, 1997 WL 1106569 at 6. In the case at bar, Ryan sent a termination notice and a cease and desist letter which Defendant disregarded. While Volpone may contest the validity of the termination, Ryan has certainly stated a viable cause of action.

A similar conclusion was reached in Welch v. Mr. Christmas Inc., 440 N.E.2d 1317 (1982). There the plaintiff agreed to appear in a television commercial which would run for only a limited time. However, Defendant continued to air the commercial even after the contractual time period had expired. Defendant argued that in light of plaintiff's written consent, Welch could only seek relief for breach of contract. Unpersuaded, the court held that "Plaintiff's statutory action is not foreclosed by the previously effective but now expired consent." *Id.* at 974, 440 N.E.2d 1317. As a result, Volpone's defense must amount to more than showing that Ryan had previously consented to the use of his name. That is not in dispute. Whether Ryan's consent remained in effect after the alleged termination is.

For the reasons stated above Ryan has stated a viable claim under New York's Civil Rights law. Accordingly, the motion to dismiss Plaintiff's second cause of action for failure to state a claim is denied.

B. Eighth Claim for Relief

In his eighth cause of action, Ryan alleges that Defendant "threatens to impair and dilute the value of plaintiff's celebrity, persona and image." Consequently, he seeks injunctive relief barring Defendant from continuing to exploit his name, signature and likeness without his consent. Volpone argues that this is an attempt to assert a common law right of publicity. Ryan responds that the "eighth cause of action is simply a claim for injunctive relief under common law, statutory and equitable principles." Plaintiff does not elaborate on the applicable common law that supposedly affords him the requested relief.

As previously discussed, *see* discussion *supra* Part V.A., New York does not recognize a common law right of publicity. However, injunctive relief is an available remedy under N.Y. Civil Rights Law §51. Since Plaintiff did not make an express prayer for injunctive relief as part of his second cause of action, the eighth count of the complaint is not redundant so as to require dismissal. Nevertheless, to the extent the claim is made pursuant to common law, the cause of action is dismissed. Plaintiff's basis for injunctive relief arises out of Defendant's alleged violations of the Lanham Act and/or reasons of wise judicial administration" in "exceptional" circumstances. . . .

VII. PRELIMINARY INJUNCTION

Having disposed of Defendant's various motions, I now turn to Plaintiff's motion for a preliminary injunction.

Plaintiff moves for a preliminary injunction pursuant to the Lanham Act, 15 U.S.C. §1116 and §51 of the New York Civil Rights law. "A preliminary injunction should be granted where the moving party demonstrates (1) irreparable harm and (2) either (a) a probability of success on the merits or (b) sufficiently serious questions going to the merits to make them fair grounds for litigation and a balance of hardships tipping decidedly in the moving party's favor." Church of Scientology International v. Elmira Mission of the Church of Scientology, 794 F.2d 38, 41 (2d Cir. 1986).

A. Probability of Success on the Merits

In order to prevail on the New York Civil Rights law claim, Plaintiff need only show that his name was used for commercial purposes without his consent. [The] claim[] depend[s] on Plaintiff's purported termination of the licensing agreements.

If the termination was proper, any use of Ryan's name, likeness or signature thereafter was without his consent violating N.Y. Civil Rights law §§50 and 51. Volpone does not directly attack the validity of Plaintiff's termination of the licensing agreements. Rather, Defendant argues that Ryan breached the agreements, specifically by licensing his name to others in violation of the exclusivity provision and by failing to honor his alleged obligation to protect Volpone against third party infringers, thereby justifying Volpone's refusal to continue to pay royalties. As previously explained, a party to a contract may respond to the other party's breach in one of two ways: the non-breaching party may stop performance and sue for total breach, or continue to perform and sue for partial breach. What the non-breaching party cannot do is avoid its obligations under the contract and yet continue to reap the benefits. S & R Corporation v. Jiffy Lube International, Inc., 968 F.2d 371, 376 (3d Cir. 1992). . . .

In the case at bar, the Master Agreement provides "[i]n the event of nonpayment of the minimum guarantee by the due date specified in the agreement, Licensor will have 60 days to cure the default. If the default is not cured after 60 days then the agreement is terminated and all sub-license agreements revert to Mattgo, without further notice." It is undisputed that Defendant stopped making royalty payments. As a result Plaintiff sent a notice dated August 10, 1999 terminating the agreement and ordering Volpone to cease and desist from continuing to manufacture, produce, distribute or sell any Nolan Ryan products. Given the 60-day cure period and since the payments were originally due on June 30, 1999, termination on August 10, 1999 might have been premature. Nevertheless, by the time Plaintiff sent the second cease and desist letter dated October 7, 1999, more than 60 days had passed without payment. The Master Agreement is clear that failure to cure nonpayment of royalties within the proscribed time period results in automatic termination of the license.

Volpone does not dispute that it continued to sell Nolan Ryan products through December 31, 1999, the date the agreements would have expired had Plaintiff not terminated them. Defendant also concedes that it continued to post a number of licensed items for sale on certain websites as recently as mid-March 2000 and that a number of licensed goods were sold after December 31, 1999. Thus, although Volpone might ultimately prevail on its breach of contract claims, it has, by its own admission, continued to market Nolan Ryan products after Plaintiff terminated the agreement and in spite of two cease and desist letters. Having withdrawn his consent by terminating the licensing agreements, there is a likelihood that Plaintiff will succeed on the merits of his New York Civil Rights law claim.

There being two bases for granting a preliminary injunction, New York Civil Rights law and the Lanham Act and having shown a probability of success on the merits of the former, Plaintiff need not show a probability of success on the latter to merit injunctive relief. . . .

B. Irreparable Harm

In order to warrant injunctive relief, Plaintiff must also demonstrate that it will suffer irreparable harm absent such relief. There is no doubt that Plaintiff has satisfied this requirement, for a finding of irreparable harm necessarily follows from the discussion above. . . .

Nolan Ryan earns substantial revenue through the licensing of his name and image. However, if companies such as Volpone can exploit his celebrity without his consent, his years of accomplishments on the baseball field will quickly lose their commercial value off the field. "For, in an age where star athletes make tenfold more from their endorsement contracts than from their team salaries, it denies reality to believe other than that an individual's persona can constitute valuable economic property. Moreover, the nature of that property is such that its value is diluted by unauthorized use." Jim Henson Productions, Inc. v. John T. Brady & Assoc., Inc., 867 F. Supp. 175, 189 (S.D.N.Y. 1994). . . .

For the aforementioned reasons, Plaintiff has demonstrated irreparable harm and the motion for a preliminary injunction is granted.

VIII. CONCLUSION

Defendant's motion to dismiss count eight of the complaint for failure to state a cause of action is granted to the extent the claim is based on common law. Count eight of the complaint states a viable cause of action to the extent it is based on N.Y. Civil Rights law §51.

FACENDA v. N.F.L. FILMS, INC.

542 F.3d 1007 (3d Cir. 2008)

AMBRO, Circuit Judge.

John Facenda, a Philadelphia broadcasting legend, provided his voice to many productions of NFL Films, Inc. before his death in 1984. More than two decades after Facenda's death, NFL Films used small portions of his voice-over work in a cable-television production about the football video game "Madden NFL 06." That production, entitled "The Making of Madden NFL 06," sparked this controversy.

Facenda's Estate ("the Estate") sued NFL Films, the National Football League, and NFL Properties (which we refer to collectively, where appropriate, as "the NFL") in the United States District Court for the Eastern District of Pennsylvania. The Estate claims that the program's use of Facenda's voice falsely suggested that Facenda endorsed the video game, violating the federal Lanham Act. The Estate also claims that the program was an unauthorized use of Facenda's name or likeness in violation of Pennsylvania's "right of publicity" statute. In its defense the NFL argued that its copyrights in the original NFL Films productions that Facenda narrated gave it the exclusive right to use portions of those productions' soundtracks as it saw fit.

I. FACTS

Facenda won national acclaim for his NFL Films work. His Estate credits that fame to the special qualities of his voice. In various depositions, several representatives for NFL Films described Facenda's deep baritone voice as "distinctive," "recognizable," [and] "legendary."

For decades, Facenda worked on a session-by-session basis under an oral agreement, receiving a per-program fee. But shortly before he died in 1984, Facenda signed a "standard release" contract stating that NFL Films enjoys "the unequivocal rights to use the audio and visual film sequences recorded of me, or any part of them . . . in perpetuity and by whatever media or manner NFL Films . . . sees fit, provided, however, such use does not constitute an endorsement of any product or service."

In 2005, NFL Films produced "The Making of Madden NFL 06" about the soon-to-be released annual update of the video game that simulates NFL games. This production is 22 minutes long and was shown on the NFL Network eight times in a three-day span leading up to the release of the video game to retail stores. It featured interviews with NFL players, the game's producers, and others. The end of the program featured a countdown to the video game's release. The District Court found that not a single critical observation was made in this video regarding Madden NFL 06; all the commentary was positive.

The program used sound recordings, taken from earlier NFL Films' productions, of three sentences read by Facenda: (1) "Pro Football, the game for the ear and the eye," (2) "This sport is more than spectacle, it is a game for all seasons," and (3) "X's and O's on the blackboard are translated into aggression on the field." These excerpts from his NFL Films work total 13 seconds of the program. The producers of the program used the excerpts in a slightly altered form. The sound waves in the original recording of Facenda's voice were digitally filtered to sound more like the synthesized speech one might hear from a computer.

The NFL has an agreement with EA Sports, the makers of Madden NFL 06, which provides the NFL with royalty revenue in return for the use of the NFL's intellectual property. Various e-mail messages in the record suggest that NFL Films sought to create the television program as a promotion for Madden NFL 06, describing it as the "Madden Promo" or as "the Advertisements" in actors' release forms. But in their depositions, many NFL Films executives testified that the program was a documentary and denied that it was a commercial. . . .

V. FALSE ENDORSEMENT UNDER THE LANHAM ACT

The Estate alleges that the use of sound samples of Facenda's voice in "The Making of Madden NFL 06" falsely implied that the Estate had agreed to endorse the video game. This false endorsement, they argue, violates §43(a)(1)(A) of the Lanham Act. To prove a violation of §43(a)(1)(A) in a false endorsement case, a plaintiff must show that: (1) its mark is legally protectable; (2) it owns the mark; and (3) the defendant's use of the mark to identify its goods or services is likely to create confusion concerning the plaintiff's sponsorship or approval of those goods or services. Our case [] focuses on the third prong: whether the NFL's use of Facenda's voice was "likely to cause confusion" among consumers by suggesting that Facenda's Estate has an "affiliation, connection, or association" with EA Sports's video game implying that the Estate "sponsor[s]" or "approve[s] of" that product.

A. The Legal Standard for Likelihood of Confusion in False Endorsement Claims Brought Under §43(a) of the Lanham Act

The NFL contends that the District Court applied the wrong legal standard under §43(a)(1) to the Estate's false endorsement claim. It also argues that our Constitution's First Amendment right to free speech prohibited application of the Lanham Act to its television production. Because the NFL's First Amendment defense presents a threshold issue that would affect how we apply trademark law, we address that argument first.

1. First Amendment Limits on the Lanham Act

The NFL argues that its production constitutes informational expression, artistic expression, or both, and is thus protected by the First Amendment. It asks our Court to adopt the balancing test of the Second Circuit Court of Appeals' decision in *Rogers v. Grimaldi*, which weighs "the public interest in avoiding consumer confusion" against "the public interest in free expression." Under the *Rogers* test, the proper balance between trademark law and free expression "will normally not support application of the [Lanham] Act unless the title [1] has no artistic relevance to the underlying work whatsoever, or . . . [2] the title explicitly misleads as to the source or the content of the work."

Before considering whether either prong of the *Rogers* test applies, we must decide whether the television production is a "work[ ] of artistic expression," as understood in the context of construing the Lanham Act narrowly to avoid a conflict with the First Amendment. The NFL posits that its program, taken as a whole, is a work of artistic expression, and that the use of the particular sound clips represented an artistic choice. The NFL [also] argues that its program cannot be mere commercial speech, which is defined as "speech that does no more than propose a commercial transaction." The NFL [] argues that, even if the program has promotional aspects they are "inextricably intertwined" with the artistic and informational elements, meaning that we must treat the program as "fully protected speech."

The Estate contends that the program is commercial speech, and we agree. Our Court has "three factors to consider in deciding whether speech is commercial: (1) is the speech an advertisement; (2) does the speech refer to a specific product or service; and (3) does the speaker have an economic motivation for the speech." The first factor presents a novel issue, because the program is not a traditional 30- or 60-second television advertisement. But ultimately the question is not close. The Estate's comparison of the program to an "infomercial" is apt. Like an infomercial, the program focuses on one product, explaining both how it works and the source of its innovations, all in a positive tone. The second factor is easily satisfied because the program's sole subject is Madden NFL 06. The show does not refer to other video games. The third factor is satisfied by NFL's licensing agreement with EA Sports, which gives the NFL a direct financial interest in sales of the video game.

Because we hold that "The Making of Madden NFL 06" is commercial speech rather than artistic expression, we need not reach the issue whether our Court will adopt the *Rogers* test. We acknowledge that commercial speech does receive some First Amendment protection. Yet the Lanham Act customarily avoids violating the First Amendment, in part by enforcing a trademark only when consumers are likely to be misled or confused by the alleged infringer's use. Thus, we reject the NFL's First Amendment defense and proceed to analyze the Estate's false endorsement claim.

2. Tailoring the Lapp Factors to False Endorsement Claims

The Estate claims that the NFL violated §43(a)(1)(A) of the Lanham Act by falsely implying that Facenda had endorsed Madden NFL 06. This claim is considered a trademark claim because Facenda's voice is a distinctive mark, the Estate owns the mark, and "The Making of Madden NFL 06" allegedly creates a likelihood of confusion that Facenda's Estate has an "affiliation, connection, or association" with the Madden NFL 06 video game implying that the Estate "sponsor[s]" or "approve[s] of" that game.

Section 43(a)(1)(A) covers more than just false endorsement claims. In fact, false endorsement claims are rare enough that our Court has not previously announced the legal standard that applies to them. A more typical claim under §43(a)(1)(A) involves one company accusing another company of using the first company's unregistered mark. We therefore must determine whether the District Court analyzed the Estate's Lanham Act claim under a standard suitably tailored to the false endorsement context.

Our Court evaluates §43(a)(1)(A) claims under the ten-factor test outlined in Interpace Corp. v. Lapp, Inc., 721 F.2d 460, 463 (3d Cir. 1983). We subsequently adapted Lapp slightly to accommodate cases involving either directly competing or non-competing goods. . . . But this makes Lapp an uncomfortable fit in a false-endorsement case like this one. This case presents the question whether the NFL used the Estate's mark (i.e., Facenda's voice) in a way that falsely implied that the Estate endorsed a video game. Rather than protecting its mark with respect to a particular product, the Estate seeks to reserve the exclusive right to grant or deny permission to those who wish to use Facenda's voice to promote unspecified products in the future.

To address this disconnect between Lapp and false-endorsement claims, the District Court concluded that under §43(a)(1)(A) the traditional Lapp factors apply in a modified form specifically crafted for false-endorsement cases by the Ninth Circuit Court of Appeals:

> (1) the level of recognition that the plaintiff has among the segment of the society for whom the defendant's product is intended; (2) the relatedness of the fame or success of the plaintiff to the defendant's product; (3) the similarity of the likeness used by the defendant to the actual plaintiff; (4) evidence of actual confusion; (5) marketing channels used; (6) likely degree of purchaser care; (7) defendant's intent [in] selecting the plaintiff; and (8) likelihood of expansion of the product lines.

Although these are all factors that are appropriate for consideration in determining the likelihood of confusion, they are not necessarily of equal importance, nor do they necessarily apply to every case. We substantially agree with the District Court's approach to tailoring the Lapp factors, emphasiz[ing] that this formulation [] applies only to false endorsement claims.

3. Distinguishing Between Subsections of Section 43(a)(1)

Under the modified Lapp test, evidence of actual confusion among consumers about whether Facenda's Estate had agreed to endorse Madden NFL 06 is one factor to consider among eight. A common way of providing such evidence of actual confusion is to conduct a survey, but the Estate did not conduct one. The District Court held that the lack of survey evidence was "not fatal." Weighing all the factors, the District Court held that a likelihood of confusion did exist about whether Facenda's Estate agreed to endorse Madden NFL 06.

The NFL . . . argues that subsections (a)(1)(A) and (a)(1)(B) have the same standard, which distinguishes impliedly false endorsements from expressly false endorsements. It also contends that claims of impliedly false endorsement like the Estate's—as opposed to, for example, an expressly false endorsement consisting of sound clips of Facenda's voice digitally stitched together to say "I think you should buy Madden NFL 06"—must be proven with evidence that the program actually confused consumers.

We reject the NFL's arguments about the proper legal standard. The *Lapp* factors apply, modified for false endorsement cases as described above, and no single factor is dispositive. Our Court has made the difference in the standards under (a)(1)(A) and (a)(1)(B) explicit:

> Some actions brought under the Lanham Act require proof of actual confusion and others do not. In an action brought under sections 32 and 43(a) of the Lanham Act for trademark infringement . . . plaintiff need not provide proof of actual confusion; he need only show likelihood of confusion. In an action brought under another part of section 43(a) of the Lanham Act for false advertising, 15 U.S.C. §1125(a)(1)(B), plaintiff need not prove the challenged advertising misled the public if he can show it was literally false. However, if his claim is not that the advertising was false but that it was misleading, he must prove the public was actually misled or confused by it.

For claims brought under subsection (a)(1)(A), only a likelihood of confusion is required. The statutory text of the two subsections differs; only subsection (a)(1)(A) includes the phrase "likely to cause confusion." 15 U.S.C. §1125(a)(1)(A). The case law also differs; our Court has long applied the *Lapp* factors in (a)(1)(A) cases but not in (a)(1)(B) cases.

B. Application to the Estate's Claim

With the legal standard under §43(a)(1)(A) settled, we turn to the application of that standard to the facts of the Estate's claim. First, we briefly explain the limited significance of the standard release contract between Facenda and NFL Films, signed shortly before his death. Second, we evaluate whether summary judgment for the Estate on its Lanham-Act false-endorsement claim was appropriate.

1. The Standard Release Contract

A threshold inquiry is whether the "standard release" contract that Facenda signed serves as a "complete defense" to the Estate's claims. The contract states that the NFL can use its recordings featuring Facenda's voice as it sees fit, "provided, however, such use does not constitute an endorsement of any product or service." The District Court rejected the NFL's defense. It concluded that "The Making of Madden NFL 06" is "commercial in nature"—i.e., that it constitutes an endorsement of the video game—and does not fall within the terms of the contract.

In interpreting the language of the contract, we would not focus on whether the program as a whole constitutes an endorsement. Instead, we would ask whether the use of Facenda's voice within the program constitutes an endorsement. The significance of the contract is that Facenda did not waive the right to bring a claim under the Lanham Act for false endorsement.

VI. UNAUTHORIZED USE OF NAME OR LIKENESS
UNDER PENNSYLVANIA LAW

Pennsylvania law grants individuals the exclusive right to their name and likeness, which includes voice. The District Court held that the NFL violated this statute with its use of Facenda's voice because (a) his voice's commercial value was not disputed, (b) the NFL used his voice for a commercial purpose, and (c) the standard release Facenda signed did not consent to the use of his voice in endorsements. We agree that the NFL has violated §8316 on its face. On appeal, the NFL [] focuses on [the] argument . . . that copyright law preempts the Estate's right-of-publicity.

A. The NFL's Copyright in the Sound Clips

A threshold issue for the NFL's preemption defense is whether the NFL has a valid copyright in the sound recordings of Facenda's voice. The NFL notes that it excerpted the sound clips at issue from copyrighted productions of NFL Films. Moreover, the sound clips represent Facenda's readings of copyrighted NFL scripts, making the clips "derivative works" in which a distinct copyright exists. The NFL is correct that copyright law, taken in isolation, gives it the exclusive right to use the sound recordings of Facenda's voice in the way that it did. The question for us is how the NFL's (federal) copyright relates to Facenda's (state-law) right of publicity. Put another way, does federal copyright law preempt the right of publicity claim under Pennsylvania law?

B. Express Preemption

The Copyright Code has an express preemption provision, which provides that all legal or equitable rights that [1] are equivalent to any of the exclusive rights within the general scope of copyright as specified by section 106 in [2] works of authorship that are fixed in a tangible medium of expression and come within the subject matter of copyright as specified by sections 102 and 103 . . . are governed exclusively by this title. 17 U.S.C. §301(a). In other words, for a state-law claim to be preempted by copyright law, it must protect (1) an exclusive right in (2) a work within copyright's subject matter.

1. Equivalent to an Exclusive Right?

The Estate's claim seeks to block the NFL from exercising its exclusive rights under to reproduce, distribute, perform, and make derivative works from sound recordings in which it owns the copyrights. Under the first prong of express copyright preemption analysis, some courts have looked to the elements of a state-law cause of action. The presence of an "additional element" . . . renders the state-law cause of action not equivalent to a copyright. Pennsylvania's right-of-publicity statute requires a showing of commercial value, defined as a "[v]aluable interest in a natural person's name or likeness that is developed through the investment of time, effort and money." The requirement under the statute that Facenda's voice have "commercial value" provides an additional element beyond what a copyright-infringement claim requires. Because the Estate's right-of-publicity claim relied on an element not equivalent to any of the exclusive rights granted to federal copyright holders, we hold that the first prong of §301(a) is not satisfied here.

2. Copyrightable Subject Matter?

Looking to the second prong, does Facenda's voice fall under the subject matter of copyright? The Court of Appeals for the Ninth Circuit has stated, in the context of vocal imitations, that "[a] voice is not copyrightable. The sounds are not 'fixed.' What is put forward [for protection] is more personal than any work of authorship." One can fix Facenda's voice in a tangible medium by recording it, but one cannot divorce his distinctive voice itself from the Facenda identity. We hold that Facenda's voice is outside the subject matter of copyright. Thus, the second prong of §301(a) is not satisfied [and, therefore, conclude] that copyright's express preemption provision does not bar the Estate's right-of-publicity claim.

C. Conflict Preemption

We also consider whether federal copyright law impliedly preempts the Estate's right-of-publicity claim. In some situations the right of publicity clashes with the exploitation of a defendant's copyright. Unlike the plaintiffs in cases involving vocal imitations, Facenda collaborated with the NFL to create the copyrighted sound recordings at issue. In our view, this gives the NFL a stronger preemption defense than the vocal-imitation defendants. Where a defendant in a right-of-publicity claim obtained a copyright in a work featuring the plaintiff, courts must separate legitimate exploitations of what Congress intended to be a copyright holder's exclusive rights from particular uses that infringe the right of publicity. Otherwise, few copyright holders would be safe from suits by performers who agreed to appear in the holders' works.

Conflict preemption is a particular species of implied preemption that "renders state law 'without effect' when, without 'express congressional command,' state law conflicts with federal law." Here we are concerned with the conflict between copyright law and the right of publicity. When does the right of individuals to avoid commercial exploitation of their identities interfere with the rights of copyright owners to exploit their works? In addition, we must confront the role of the standard release contract. Does a contract acknowledging a right-of-publicity for defendant's copyright in a work containing a plaintiff's identity mean that the defendant may use that work in any way it sees fit?

David Nimmer has proposed a two-part framework for handling cases at the intersection of copyright, the right of publicity, and contract. First, we look to how the copyrighted work featuring the plaintiff's identity is used. Surveying the case law, Nimmer finds that when defendants use the work "for the purposes of trade," such as in an advertisement, plaintiffs' right-of-publicity claims have not been held to be preempted. On the other hand, when defendants' uses constitute "expressive works," right-of-publicity claims have been preempted. The NFL used the sound recordings of Facenda's voice in a television production promoting the video game Madden NFL 06. This kind of use, in what amounts to a 22-minute promotional piece akin to advertising, does not count as an expressive work. Following the case law, this suggests that conflict preemption is inappropriate in our case.

The second part of Nimmer's framework addresses the way that contracts affect the preemption analysis. Nimmer proposes that courts should examine the purpose of the use to which the plaintiff initially consented when signing over the copyright in a contract. He argues that the proper question in cases involving advertising and a contract is whether the plaintiff "collaborated in the creation of a copyrighted advertising product." If the plaintiff did collaborate, then the party holding the copyright is in a very strong position to contend that allowing the plaintiff to assert a right of publicity against use of its likeness in advertising would interfere with the rights it acquired. If the plaintiff did not collaborate specifically in the creation of advertising content, then the plaintiff is in a strong position to assert continuing control over the use of his image.

Nimmer suggests that preemption is not appropriate [in our case]. Facenda consented to participation in films documenting NFL games, not an advertisement for a football video game. The release form Facenda signed did not implicitly waive his right to publicity, the core of which is the right not to have one's identity used in advertisements. In fact, the release specifically preserved that right by carving out endorsements. We hold that neither express nor implied conflict preemption bars the Estate's right-of-publicity claim under Pennsylvania law. We affirm the District Court's grant of summary judgment to the Estate on that claim.

MILLER v. GLENN MILLER PRODS., INC.
318 F. Supp. 2d 923 (C.D. Cal. 2004)

MATZ, District Judge.

This matter is before the Court on Plaintiffs' Motion for Summary Adjudication and Defendant's Motion for Summary Judgment.

FACTUAL BACKGROUND

The principal facts of this case are either undisputed or not genuinely disputed. Glenn Miller was a popular musician and band leader who formed the Glenn Miller Orchestra in 1938. During the 1930s and 1940s, Glenn Miller recorded and released sound recordings using his name and the name "Glenn Miller Orchestra." On December 15, 1944, Glenn Miller was aboard an armed services airplane that crashed in the English Channel. One year later, he was pronounced dead. Glenn Miller's last will and testament did not contain an express provision bequeathing his publicity rights, trademarks or other intellectual property rights. His widow, Helen Miller, inherited the residue of his will, which would include whatever intellectual property rights he had.

On either April 20, 1956 or April 23, 1956, David Mackay, Sr. (Glenn Miller's close friend and lawyer during his lifetime) incorporated Glenn Miller Productions, Inc. ("GMP"). GMP's Certificate of Incorporation specifies that among GMP's many purposes were:

> (c) To manufacture, purchase, sell and generally to trade and deal in and with goods, wares, products and merchandise of every kind, nature and description. . . .
>
> (e) To organize, own, operate, manage, direct, and control, directly or through others, one or more orchestras or musical organizations and to acquire by loan, hiring, purchase, agreement, or other lawful means, the right to use and deal in or with and to authorize others to use and deal in or with the name, likeness, music, scores, arrangements and musical style of others heretofore or hereafter engaged in the field of music. . . .
>
> (i) To acquire copyrights, licenses or other rights to or in plays, films, dramas, dramatizations, musical compositions and intellectual properties of all kinds.

Despite the broad grant of authority conferred by GMP's Certificate of Incorporation, at GMP's first Board of Director's meeting on April 25, 1956, David Mackay, Sr. stated that "the main business of the corporation would be to own and operate a traveling orchestra."

At the first Board of Director's meeting, David Mackay, Sr. was elected President of GMP and he remained president until his death in 1980. Helen Miller was elected Vice President of GMP and she served in that role until her death in 1966. GMP also employed Helen Miller as a technical advisor. David Mackay, Sr. and Helen Miller each owned 50% of the shares of GMP until the times of their respective deaths.

Sometime between April 25, 1956 and June 6, 1956 (in any case, shortly after GMP was incorporated), Helen Miller executed a written license agreement (the "1956 license agreement") in favor of GMP. The agreement consisted of one paragraph which read, in its entirety:

> For and in consideration of the sum of ONE AND NO 100THS ($1.00) DOLLAR and other good and valuable consideration, the undersigned, individually and as Executrix of the estate of Glenn Miller deceased, hereby grants to Glenn Miller Productions, Inc. the right and license to use the name and likeness of Glenn Miller and the library of music belonging to the Estate of Glenn Miller and/or the undersigned in connection with the business activities of Glenn Miller Productions, Inc.

Notwithstanding the amount of consideration (*i.e.*, $1.00) specified in the 1956 license agreement, the minutes of a June 6, 1956 GMP Board meeting state that the Board agreed to pay Helen Miller $13,000 per year in return for permission to use Glenn Miller's name, likeness and library of music (the same rights conveyed by the 1956 license agreement).

Sometime after the 1956 license agreement was executed, GMP began operating an orchestra called the Glenn Miller Orchestra and engaging in a variety of promotional activities. GMP entered into a written contract for the Glenn Miller Orchestra to perform at Washington & Lee University on June 6, 1956. In addition, the minutes of a June 2, 1961 GMP Board meeting indicate that in 1961, GMP authorized a zero-interest $30,000 loan to a production company to produce a television show on CBS titled "Glenn Miller Time" featuring the Glenn Miller Orchestra. The minutes also reflect that the production company received the rights to "use the Glenn Miller name, picture, likeness, music and arrangements in connection with the television show, and usual accompanying promotion and publicity." There is no evidence in the record that Helen Miller objected to this licensing of Glenn Miller's name, likeness and publicity rights. Finally, minutes from an August 26, 1971 GMP Board meeting indicate that in 1971, GMP's Board of Directors ratified GMP's agreement to purchase 1,000 copies of a book entitled "Glenn Miller Discography" in order to support its publication.

In 1965, GMP obtained a federal trademark registration for the "Glenn Miller Orchestra" mark, which it renewed in 1985.

Helen Miller died on June 2, 1966. Helen Miller's will established a testamentary trust containing her GMP shares. The will named David Mackay, Sr. as the trustee. In his capacity as trustee, David Mackay, Sr. later sold Helen Miller's GMP shares to GMP for $115,000. Upon Helen Miller's death, David Mackay, Jr. (the son of David Mackay, Sr.) was appointed vice president of GMP (Helen Miller's former position).

Like her deceased husband's will, Helen Miller's will did not contain an express provision which bequeathed any of Glenn Miller's publicity rights, trademarks or other intellectual property rights that she may have inherited. Her two adopted children, Steven Miller and Jonnie Soper Miller, would have inherited any such rights only through the residue of Helen Miller's will. . . .

On May 12, 1980, David Mackay, Sr. died. Upon his death, David Mackey, Jr. became the president of GMP.

Since at least the 1980s, an ensemble calling itself the Glenn Miller Orchestra has performed at many events and festivals, including at the yearly Glenn Miller Birthplace Society Festival in Iowa and the yearly Dancing on the Plains festival in Colorado. Since 1981, GMP has operated one regular Glenn Miller Orchestra band, as well as "special units" of the Glenn Miller Orchestra which supplement the regular Glenn Miller Orchestra band during times of high demand. These "special units" are comprised of different band leaders and musicians hired and supervised by GMP, and they work on a performance-by-performance basis. Since 1988, the regular Glenn Miller Orchestra has been led by Larry O'Brien. Between the 1990s and the present, Steven Miller has attended approximately 6 Glenn Miller Orchestra performances, all of which he believes were led by Larry O'Brien.

Also since 1988, GMP has sub-licensed to third parties the right to operate orchestras called the Glenn Miller Orchestra. These sub-licensees have operated Glenn Miller Orchestras in the United States, Canada, Germany and the United Kingdom. Currently, GMP has two sub-licensees: Schmidt & Salden GmbH & Co., which operates in Germany, and Ray McVay, who operates in the United Kingdom. Both sub-license agreements set forth detailed "performance standards" which provide, for example, that the orchestra shall consist of at least 16 musicians plus a leader and one male and one female vocalist, that the sub-licensee's bandstands must be similar to that used by the Glenn Miller Orchestra operated by GMP, that the orchestra shall consist of a particular number of various types of instruments, and that the orchestra "shall at all times behave and be groomed in accordance with the highest standards of the Glenn Miller Orchestra." The sub-license agreements also provide that a failure to conform to those standards constitutes a default. Finally, the sub-license agreements provide that they are not assignable or transferable. Counsel for GMP represented at the hearing on these motions that David Mackay, Jr. assures that the sub-licensees are complying with the terms of the sub-license agreements by observing their performances and monitoring their bookings.

Beginning in 1983, GMP also has been selling merchandise, including cassette tapes, videotapes, CDs, DVDs, t-shirts and polo shirts bearing the "Glenn Miller Orchestra" mark or the "GMO" logo. This merchandise is sold primarily at GMO performances. During each performance, an announcement is made regarding the sale of merchandise, and a table displaying merchandise is set up in a prominent location. Since September of 1998, merchandise has also been available on GMP's website, (*www.glennmillerorchestra.com*). Counsel for GMP represented at the hearing that GMP's annual worldwide revenue is approximately $2 million dollars.

During the 1980s and 1990s, counsel for Steven and Jonnie Miller sent at least eight cease and desist letters to third parties who were not authorized to use or otherwise exploit Glenn Miller's name or likeness, but who were, nevertheless, apparently doing so. Although most of these letters were sent to alleged infringers in the United States, one letter was sent to a man in the Republic of South Africa who had allegedly formed an unauthorized Glenn Miller Society in South Africa. However, the Millers never sent any cease and desist letters to GMP.

Indeed, before they filed this lawsuit, the Millers had never communicated with GMP regarding any qualitative aspect of GMP's business activities, such as its operation of the Glenn Miller Orchestra, its sub-licensing to third parties of the right to operate a Glenn Miller Orchestra, or its sale of merchandise bearing the "Glenn Miller Orchestra" mark. . . .

In 1994, the Millers hired the Roger Richman Agency, for a period of two years, to be their exclusive licensing agent for use of the Glenn Miller name "in connection with all video recording and tapes; look-alikes; sound-alikes; advertising; commercials; theater and other dramatic uses; animation; newspaper; book and magazine syndication; endorsements; promotions; premiums; sale of merchandise and/or use in all services." However, excluded from the grant of rights to the Roger Richman Agency were rights previously granted by GMP to certain third parties, including "Orchestras of Glenn Miller Productions, Inc., a New York Corporation." In 1996, the Millers hired Plaintiff CMG Worldwide, Inc. ("CMG") to be their exclusive licensing agent, subject to the same exclusion for the pre-existing rights of "Orchestras of Glenn Miller Productions, Inc., a New York Corporation. . . ."

Steven Miller claims that he first learned in 2000 or 2001 that there was more than one functioning Glenn Miller Orchestra, although he does not specify how he learned. Steven Miller also claims that he did not learn until April 2003 (after filing this lawsuit) that GMP has entered into sub-license agreements with third parties to use Glenn Miller's name and likeness in the United States and in foreign countries. The record does not indicate when Steven Miller learned that GMP has been selling merchandise bearing the Glenn Miller Orchestra mark.

On June 22, 2003, Steven Miller, Jonnie Miller, and CMG Worldwide, Inc. (collectively "Plaintiffs") filed this action against GMP, asserting eleven claims for relief: (1) breach of written contract; (2) termination of written contract; (3) infringement of statutory right of publicity; (4) violation of 15 U.S.C. §1125(a); (5) intentional interference with economic advantage; (6) federal statutory dilution; (7) state statutory dilution; (8) violation of Cal. Business & Professions Code §17200; (9) conversion; (10) accounting; and (11) declaratory relief, all based on GMP's sale of merchandise bearing Glenn Miller's name, likeness and identity, and GMP's sub-licensing to third parties of the right to operate orchestras named the Glenn Miller Orchestra.

Plaintiffs currently move for summary adjudication of one narrow issue in this case. They seek a ruling from the Court that GMP may not sub-license any intellectual property rights conveyed to it pursuant to the 1956 license agreement without express permission from the licensors (now the Millers), and therefore that GMP's admitted sub-licensing constitutes a material breach of the 1956 license agreement. Defendant has filed a cross-motion for summary judgment, contending that the 1956 license agreement and 1980 settlement agreement give GMP the right to sell merchandise and to operate and sub-license multiple bands[.]

ANALYSIS

B. Plaintiffs' Motion for Summary Adjudication: May GMP Sub-License Intellectual Property Rights Without Plaintiffs' Permission?

It is well established in patent and copyright law that a patent or copyright licensee may not sub-license his licensed intellectual property rights without express permission from the licensor. *See* Gardner v. Nike, Inc., 279 F.3d 774 (9th Cir. 2002); Everex Systems v. Cadtrak Corp.,

89 F.3d 673, 679 (9th Cir. 1996). (The Court will henceforth refer to this rule as "the sub-licensing rule.") Although the Ninth Circuit has not addressed whether the sub-licensing rule applies to trademark licenses, the courts that have addressed the issue have uniformly held it does, and thus that a trademark licensee may not sub-license a mark without express permission from the licensor. *See* Tap Publications, Inc. v. Chinese Yellow Pages (New York), Inc., 925 F. Supp. 212, 218 (S.D.N.Y. 1996) [citations omitted]. The reasoning behind the courts' extension of the sub-licensing rule to the trademark context is that, "[s]ince the licensor-trademark owner has the duty to control the quality of goods sold under its mark, it must have the right to pass upon the abilities of new potential licensees. . . ."

In Plaintiffs' motion for summary adjudication, Plaintiffs ask the Court to apply the sub-licensing rule (previously recognized by courts in *Tap, Travelot* and *Raufast*) to trademark licenses. Plaintiffs also ask the Court to extend the sub-licensing rule to licenses of publicity rights.[1] Finally, Plaintiffs seek a ruling that because the 1956 license agreement did not grant GMP express permission to sub-license, GMP does not have the right to sub-license any intellectual property rights it obtained under the 1956 license agreement.

1. Defendant's Threshold Arguments That the 1956 Agreement Did Not Convey a License

Defendant argues, first, that as a matter of contract law, the 1956 agreement between Helen Miller and GMP did not convey a license. Defendant also argues that even if the parties did intend the agreement to convey a license, at the time, there were no existing trademark rights that could be licensed.

a. The only reasonable interpretation of the 1956 agreement is that it conveys to GMP both a trademark license and a license of Glenn Miller's publicity rights

The threshold question is: what rights did the 1956 licensing agreement convey to GMP? Plaintiffs argue that the license agreement conveyed a trademark license to GMP. GMP first argues in opposition that the 1956 agreement did not convey a trademark license, but instead a license of Glenn Miller's right to publicity. In Plaintiffs' reply brief, Plaintiffs contend (somewhat inconsistently with their opening brief) that the 1956 agreement "transfers a bundle of rights, including trademark rights and publicity rights." In any case, Plaintiffs contend in their reply brief that the exact categorization of the rights conveyed by the 1956 licensing agreement is not relevant because the sub-licensing rule should apply to *all* areas of intellectual property. However, if Plaintiffs are wrong about the scope of the rights conveyed to GMP

---

1. Fundamentally, the right of publicity "is the inherent right of every human being to control the commercial use of his or her identity." *See* J. McCarthy, *The Rights of Publicity and Privacy*, §28:3. California law recognizes both a statutory and common law right of publicity. The statutory right of publicity is codified in Cal. Civil Code §3344, which provides in relevant part: "Any person who knowingly uses another's name, voice, signature, photograph, or likeness, in any manner, . . . for purposes of advertising or selling, . . . without such person's prior consent . . . shall be liable for any damages sustained by the person or persons injured as a result thereof." California's common-law right of publicity protects an individual's name and likeness from appropriation for either commercial or non-commercial purposes. *See* Wendt v. Host Int'l, Inc., 125 F.3d 806, 811 (9th Cir. 1997). The right to publicity extends 70 years beyond an individual's death. *See* McCarthy, *supra*, §28:27; Cal. Civ. Code §3344.1.

by the 1956 agreement, the Court would not have to address whether the sub-licensing rule should be extended to licenses of trademarks and publicity rights.

Courts apply general principles of contract interpretation when interpreting the terms and scope of a licensing agreement. [Citations omitted.] Under California law, "[t]he test of admissibility of extrinsic evidence to explain the meaning of a written instrument is not whether it appears to the court to be plain and unambiguous on its face, but whether the offered evidence is relevant to prove a meaning to which the language of the instrument is reasonably susceptible." [Citations omitted.] Because California law recognizes that the words of a written instrument often lack a clear meaning apart from the context in which the words were written, courts may preliminarily consider any extrinsic evidence offered by the parties. "If the court decides, after consideration of this evidence, that the language of a contract, in the light of all the circumstances, is 'fairly susceptible of either one of the two interpretations contended for,' extrinsic evidence relevant to prove either of such meanings is admissible." [Citations omitted.] Extrinsic evidence includes testimony regarding the circumstances in which a contract was written, the subsequent conduct of the parties, and the common usage of particular terms in a given industry. [Citations omitted.]

If, after considering the language of the contract and any admissible extrinsic evidence, the meaning of the contract is unambiguous, a court may properly interpret it on a motion for summary judgment. [Citation omitted.] However, if the interpretation turns upon the credibility of conflicting extrinsic evidence, or if "construing the evidence in the nonmovant's favor, the ambiguity can be resolved consistent with the nonmovant's position," summary judgment is inappropriate. [Citations omitted.]

The 1956 license agreement conveyed to GMP "the right and license to use the name and likeness of Glenn Miller . . . in connection with the business activities of [GMP]." The license agreement does not explicitly convey to GMP either the right to license any existing Glenn Miller trademark or Glenn Miller's publicity rights, or both. However, the terms "name" and/or "likeness" are found in both the Lanham Act definition of a trademark and in the definitions of California's statutory and common law rights to publicity. Because the 1956 agreement is ambiguous on its face and is reasonably susceptible to multiple interpretations, extrinsic evidence is admissible to prove the parties' intent when they executed the agreement.

It is undisputed that Helen Miller executed the 1956 license agreement shortly after incorporating GMP. The proximity of the two events, the undisputed fact that after its formation and until the execution of the license agreement, GMP did not conduct any business beyond electing officers and drafting bylaws, and GMP's use of the name "Glenn Miller" in its own name, strongly suggest that GMP was incorporated for the specific purpose of conducting business related to Glenn Miller, notwithstanding that the Certificate of Incorporation speaks more generally about its purposes. In addition, as described above, GMP's Certificate of Incorporation provided that GMP was authorized to "manufacture, purchase, sell and generally to trade and deal in and with goods, wares, products and merchandise of every kind, nature and description" as well as to "organize, own, operate, manage, direct and control, directly or through others, one or more orchestras or musical organizations." It is hard to imagine that GMP would be able to sell and trade merchandise and operate orchestras bearing the Glenn Miller mark without exploiting Glenn Miller's identity or likeness for promotional purposes. Likewise, it is hard to imagine that GMP could exploit Glenn Miller's publicity rights without using a trademark containing the Glenn Miller name. Therefore, the Court finds that 1956 agreement is susceptible to only one reasonable interpretation — that it conveys both a trademark license and a license of Glenn Miller's publicity rights. . . .

3. The Same Policies Also Support an Extension of the Sub-licensing Rule to Licenses of Publicity Rights

Plaintiffs [] argue that the sub-licensing rule should apply to licenses of an individual's publicity rights. Plaintiffs cite no authority for this proposition. . . .

Although trademarks and publicity rights share many common features, they are also dissimilar in several ways. For example, while trademark laws protect the trademark owner by fortifying the public's expectation regarding the source and quality of goods and services, the right of publicity protects an individual's "persona" from commercial exploitation by others. However, the distinction most relevant for the purposes of this motion is that a licensor of an individual's publicity rights, unlike a trademark licensor, lacks an affirmative statutory or common law duty to police its license and to ensure that the licensee is maintaining sufficient quality controls. Therefore, one of the two policy rationales supporting the extension of the sub-licensing rule to trademark licenses — that unfettered sub-licensing will prevent the licensor from satisfying his obligation to supervise the licensee — does not apply to licenses of publicity rights.

Nevertheless, a licensor of publicity rights may, in many instances — indeed, in probably *all* instances and respects — have a powerful incentive to supervise the licensee's use of those rights. The facts of this case are instructive. If GMP were permitted to sub-license Glenn Miller's publicity rights without notifying or obtaining permission from the owner of those rights — Plaintiffs, as this Court has found — it could sub-license Glenn Miller's publicity rights to a third party who used his name or photograph or likeness to promote fascism or pornography. Such use presumably would horrify Glenn Miller if he were alive; it also would adversely affect the image of Glenn Miller that Plaintiffs (successors to their mother, the original licensor) may wish to preserve. However, absent a sub-licensing rule, Plaintiffs would have no ability to prevent GMP from sullying their father's name (and, in fact, would have no right to even know that GMP was doing so). In addition, any disputes about whether GMP could sub-license Glenn Miller's right of publicity to a particular third party, or whether a third party sub-licensee was acting beyond the scope of the original license, would trigger litigation. These are undesirable results.

Moreover, in practice, many licenses convey both trademark rights and publicity rights. In such cases, "the special rules of trademark licensing must be followed in order to preserve the trademark significance of the licensed identity or persona." Again, the facts of this case help illustrate this principle. If, without Plaintiffs' knowledge or permission, GMP could sub-license the Glenn Miller mark to third parties who use the mark to sell products or causes at odds with what Glenn Miller stood for, the public's image of Glenn Miller's persona surely would become tainted in a manner that Plaintiffs did not intend. Conversely, if GMP could sub-license Glenn Miller's publicity rights to third parties who use his name or photograph or likeness to sell a wide variety of products whose quality is not controlled, then the Glenn Miller mark may become diluted. For these reasons, at least in cases such as this one in which a license conveys both trademark and publicity rights, the sub-licensing rule should be extended to cover publicity rights.

For these reasons, if a jury were to find that at the time Helen Miller executed the 1956 license agreement, she actually had a trademark in Glenn Miller's name to convey, then because the 1956 license agreement does not expressly grant GMP unilateral authority to sub-license the mark, GMP may not do so. In addition, because the 1956 license agreement does not grant GMP express permission to unilaterally sub-license Glenn Miller's publicity rights, GMP may not do so. . . .

C. Defendant's Motion for Summary Judgment

GMP has filed a cross-motion for summary judgment, contending that: (1) the 1956 license agreement and 1980 settlement agreement grant GMP the right to sell merchandise bearing the Glenn Miller Orchestra mark; (2) the same two agreements grant GMP the right to operate and sub-license multiple bands; (3) because GMP has the right to sell merchandise and to operate and sub-license multiple bands, all of Plaintiffs' eleven claims for relief necessarily fail; and (4) all of Plaintiffs' claims are barred by the doctrine of laches. Although the Court rejects GMP's first three contentions, it agrees that Plaintiffs' claims are barred by laches. The Court also finds that Plaintiffs are estopped from enforcing the terms of any trademark license Helen Miller conveyed to GMP in the 1956 agreement.

1. GMP Lacks the Unilateral Right to Sub-License Multiple Ensembles Using the Name "The Glenn Miller Orchestra"

GMP argues that the only reasonable interpretation of the 1956 license agreement and the 1980 settlement agreement is that they permit GMP to sub-license to an unlimited number of third parties the right to operate orchestras named the Glenn Miller Orchestra. However, because the Court has already ruled that a trademark and publicity rights licensee (such as GMP) may not sub-license those rights without the express permission of the licensor, and because it is undisputed that the two agreements do not expressly authorize GMP to sub-license, as a matter of law, GMP lacks the unilateral authority to sub-license its right to operate a band named the Glenn Miller Orchestra.

2. There Are Fact Issues Concerning Any Right of GMP to Directly Operate "Special Units" of the Glenn Miller Orchestra and to Sell Merchandise

GMP also argues that the only reasonable interpretation of the 1956 license agreement and the 1980 settlement agreement shows that Helen Miller and Plaintiffs actually granted to GMP the right to itself operate more than one ensemble named the Glenn Miller Orchestra, such as ensembles referred to as "special units," and to sell merchandise bearing the Glenn Miller Orchestra mark, including cassette tapes, videotapes, CDs, DVDs, t-shirts and polo shirts. GMP relies on the following undisputed evidence in support of its interpretation:

1. GMP's Certificate of Incorporation provides that GMP is authorized to "organize, operate, manage, direct, and control, directly or through others, one or more orchestras or musical organizations," and to "manufacture, purchase, sell and generally to trade and deal in and with goods, wares, products and merchandise of every kind, nature and description. . . ."

2. At the time Helen Miller executed the 1956 license agreement, she was a 50% shareholder in GMP.

3. The 1956 license agreement grants GMP the right to use Glenn Miller's name and likeness "in connection with the business activities of Glenn Miller Productions, Inc."

4. At GMP's first Board of Directors meeting on April 25, 1956, David Mackay, Sr. (the then-chairman) stated: "The main business of the corporation would be to own and operate a traveling orchestra."

5. During Helen Miller's lifetime, GMP sought and successfully obtained trademark protection for the "Glenn Miller Orchestra" name, and there is no evidence that Helen Miller objected.

6. The 1980 settlement agreement contains a non-compete clause which provides that Steven and Jonnie Miller "agree not to directly or indirectly organize and/or operate or cause to be organized and/or operate a band or orchestra using the name of Glenn Miller or any facsimile thereof."

7. GMP has operated "special units" of the Glenn Miller Orchestra since 1981 and Plaintiffs never objected.

8. GMP has openly sold merchandise bearing the Glenn Miller Orchestra mark at concerts since 1983 (six of which Steven Miller attended), and has sold merchandise on its website since September 1998. However, Plaintiffs never objected.

In contrast to the foregoing facts, which definitely do constitute powerful evidence favoring GMP, the record also shows that for at least 25 years after the execution of the 1956 license agreement (and during the entirety of Helen Miller and David Mackay, Sr.'s respective lifetimes), GMP did not operate more than one Glenn Miller Orchestra or sell merchandise bearing the Glenn Miller Orchestra mark. This lengthy history, which is consistent with the language of item 4, above ("a traveling orchestra"), would at least permit a jury to infer that Helen Miller's intent in executing the 1956 license agreement, and the intent of GMP and the Millers when they entered into the 1980 settlement agreement, was to have only one orchestra. Accordingly, the Court DENIES summary adjudication of this issue. . . .

CONCLUSION

For the foregoing reasons, the Court concludes that as a matter of contract law, in the 1956 agreement Helen Miller conveyed both a trademark license and a license to the right of publicity. It concludes that as a matter of trademark law, Helen Miller was in a position to convey a trademark license and that a jury could reasonably find facts establishing that she did. And it concludes that the sub-licensing rule applies to both such conveyances — *i.e.*, trademark and rights of publicity. However, despite having found that Plaintiffs have legal claims that the law could recognize, the Court nevertheless GRANTS IN WHOLE Defendant's motion for summary judgment and dismisses the complaint because under the doctrines of laches, Plaintiffs waited too long to assert those claims. Alternatively, the Court rules that Plaintiffs are estopped from enforcing the terms of any trademark that they licensed to GMP because Plaintiffs have failed to affirmatively supervise and control GMP's use of the license. In light of these latter rulings, Plaintiffs' motion for summary adjudication is, for technical reasons and to provide clarity to the docket, DENIED as moot.

O'BANNON v. NATIONAL COLLEGIATE ATHLETIC ASSOCIATION

802 F.3d 1049 (9th Cir. 2015)

BYBEE, Circuit Judge.

Section 1 of the Sherman Antitrust Act of 1890, 15 U.S.C. §1, prohibits "[e]very contract, combination . . . , or conspiracy, in restraint of trade or commerce." For more than a century, the National Collegiate Athletic Association (NCAA) has prescribed rules governing the eligibility of athletes at its more than 1,000 member colleges and universities. Those rules prohibit student-athletes from being paid for the use of their names, images, and likenesses (NILs). The question presented in this momentous case is whether the NCAA's rules are subject to the antitrust laws and, if so, whether they are an unlawful restraint of trade.

After a bench trial and in a thorough opinion, the district court concluded that the NCAA's compensation rules were an unlawful restraint of trade. It then enjoined the NCAA from prohibiting its member schools from giving student-athletes scholarships up to the full cost of attendance at their respective schools and up to $5,000 per year in deferred compensation, to be held in trust for student-athletes until after they leave college. As far as we are aware, the district court's decision is the first by any federal court to hold that any aspect of the NCAA's amateurism rules violate the antitrust laws, let alone to mandate by injunction that the NCAA change its practices.

We conclude that the district court's decision was largely correct. Although we agree with the Supreme Court and our sister circuits that many of the NCAA's amateurism rules are likely to be procompetitive, we hold that those rules are not exempt from antitrust scrutiny; rather, they must be analyzed under the Rule of Reason. Applying the Rule of Reason, we conclude that the district court correctly identified one proper alternative to the current NCAA compensation rules—i.e., allowing NCAA members to give scholarships up to the full cost of attendance—but that the district court's other remedy, allowing students to be paid cash compensation of up to $5,000 per year, was erroneous. We therefore affirm in part and reverse in part.

I

A. The NCAA

The NCAA has grown to include some 1,100 member schools, organized into three divisions: Division I, Division II, and Division III. Division I schools are those with the largest athletic programs—schools must sponsor at least fourteen varsity sports teams to qualify for Division I—and they provide the most financial aid to student-athletes. Division I has about 350 members.

B. The Amateurism Rules

One of the NCAA's earliest reforms of intercollegiate sports was a requirement that the participants be amateurs. . . . But the NCAA, still a voluntary organization, lacked the ability to enforce this requirement effectively, and schools continued to pay their athletes under the table in a variety of creative ways; a 1929 study found that 81 out of 112 schools surveyed provided some sort of improper inducement to their athletes.

The NCAA began to strengthen its enforcement capabilities in 1948, when it adopted what became known as the "Sanity Code" — a set of rules that prohibited schools from giving athletes financial aid that was based on athletic ability and not available to ordinary students. The Sanity Code also created a new "compliance mechanism" to enforce the NCAA's rules — "a Compliance Committee that could terminate an institution's NCAA membership."

In 1956, the NCAA departed from the Sanity Code's approach to financial aid by changing its rules to permit its members, for the first time, to give student-athletes scholarships based on athletic ability. These scholarships were capped at the amount of a full "grant in aid," defined as the total cost of "tuition and fees, room and board, and required course-related books." Student-athletes were prohibited from receiving any "financial aid based on athletics ability" in excess of the value of a grant-in-aid, on pain of losing their eligibility for collegiate athletics. Student-athletes could seek additional financial aid not related to their athletic skills; if they chose to do this, the total amount of athletic and nonathletic financial aid they received could not exceed the "cost of attendance" at their respective schools.

In August 2014, the NCAA announced it would allow athletic conferences to authorize their member schools to increase scholarships up to the full cost of attendance. The 80 member schools of the five largest athletic conferences in the country voted in January 2015 to take that step, and the scholarship cap at those schools is now at the full cost of attendance.

In addition to its financial aid rules, the NCAA has adopted numerous other amateurism rules that limit student-athletes' compensation and their interactions with professional sports leagues. An athlete can lose his amateur status, for example, if he signs a contract with a professional team, enters a professional league's player draft, or hires an agent. And, most importantly, an athlete is prohibited — with few exceptions — from receiving any "pay" based on his athletic ability, whether from boosters, companies seeking endorsements, or would-be licensors of the athlete's name, image, and likeness (NIL).

C. The O'Bannon and Keller Litigation

In 2008, Ed O'Bannon, a former All–American basketball player at UCLA, visited a friend's house, where his friend's son told O'Bannon that he was depicted in a college basketball video game produced by Electronic Arts (EA), a software company that produced video games based on college football and men's basketball from the late 1990s until around 2013. The friend's son turned on the video game, and O'Bannon saw an avatar of himself — a virtual player who visually resembled O'Bannon, played for UCLA, and wore O'Bannon's jersey number, 31. O'Bannon had never consented to the use of his likeness in the video game, and he had not been compensated for it.

In 2009, O'Bannon sued the NCAA and the Collegiate Licensing Company (CLC), the entity which licenses the trademarks of the NCAA and a number of its member schools for commercial use, in federal court. The gravamen of O'Bannon's complaint was that the NCAA's amateurism rules, insofar as they prevented student-athletes from being compensated for the use of their NILs, were an illegal restraint of trade under Section 1 of the Sherman Act, 15 U.S.C. §1.

Around the same time, Sam Keller, the former starting quarterback for the Arizona State University and University of Nebraska football teams, separately brought suit against the NCAA,

CLC, and EA. Keller alleged that EA had impermissibly used student-athletes' NILs in its video games and that the NCAA and CLC had wrongfully turned a blind eye to EA's misappropriation of these NILs. The complaint stated a claim under Indiana's and California's right of publicity statutes, as well as a number of common-law claims.

The two cases were consolidated during pretrial proceedings. The defendants moved to dismiss Keller's right-of-publicity claims on First Amendment grounds. The district court denied the motion to dismiss, and we affirmed that decision, holding that "[u]nder California's trans-formative use defense, EA's use of the likenesses of college athletes like Samuel Keller in its video games is not, as a matter of law, protected by the First Amendment." In re NCAA Student-Athlete Name & Likeness Licensing Litig. ("Keller"), 724 F.3d 1268, 1284 (9th Cir.2013).

In November 2013, the district court granted the plaintiffs' motion for class certification. The court held that certification of a damages class under Rule 23(b)(3) was inappropriate, but it certified the following class under Rule 23(b)(2) for injunctive and declaratory relief:

> All current and former student-athletes residing in the United States who compete on, or competed on, an NCAA Division I (formerly known as "University Division" before 1973) college or university men's basketball team or on an NCAA Football Bowl Subdivision (formerly known as Division I–A until 2006) men's football team and whose images, likenesses and/or names may be, or have been, included or could have been included (by virtue of their appearance in a team roster) in game footage or in videogames licensed or sold by Defendants, their co-conspirators, or their licensees.

After class certification was granted, the plaintiffs voluntarily dismissed their damages claims with prejudice. The plaintiffs also settled their claims against EA and CLC, and the district court preliminarily approved the settlement. O'Bannon and Keller were deconsolidated, and in June 2014, the antitrust claims against the NCAA at issue in O'Bannon went to a bench trial before the district court.

D. The District Court's Decision

After a fourteen-day bench trial, the district court entered judgment for the plaintiffs, concluding that the NCAA's rules prohibiting student-athletes from receiving compensation for their NILs violate Section 1 of the Sherman Act.

1. The Markets

The court began by identifying the markets in which the NCAA allegedly restrained trade. It identified two markets that were potentially affected by the challenged NCAA rules.

a. The College Education Market

First, the court found that there is a "college education market" in which FBS football and Division I basketball schools compete to recruit the best high school players by offering them "unique bundles of goods and services" that include not only scholarships but also coaching, athletic facilities, and the opportunity to face high-quality athletic competition. The court found that very few athletes talented enough to play FBS football or Division I basketball opt not to attend an FBS/Division I school; hardly any choose to attend an FCS, Division II, or Division III school or to compete in minor or foreign professional sports leagues, and athletes are not allowed to join either the NFL or the NBA directly from high school. Thus, the court concluded, the market specifically for FBS football and Division I basketball scholarships is cognizable under the antitrust laws because "there are no professional [or college] football or basketball leagues capable of supplying a substitute for the bundle of goods and services that FBS football and Division I basketball schools provide."

b. The Group Licensing Market

The second market identified by the district court was a "group licensing market" in which, but for the NCAA's compensation rules, college football and basketball athletes would be able to sell group licenses for the use of their NILs. The court broke this "group licensing market" down into three submarkets in which players' NILs could be profitably licensed: (1) live game telecasts, (2) sports video games, and (3) game rebroadcasts, advertisements, and other archival footage. With respect to live game telecasts, the court noted that the TV networks that broadcast live college football and basketball games "often seek to acquire the rights to use" the players' NILs, which the court concluded "demonstrate[s] that there is a demand for these rights" on the networks' part. With respect to video games, the court found that the use of NILs increased the attractiveness of college sports video games to consumers, creating a demand for players' NILs. And with respect to archival footage, the court noted that the NCAA had licensed footage of student-athletes—including current athletes—to a third-party licensing company, T3Media, proving that there is demand for such footage.

2. The Rule of Reason

Having concluded that the NCAA's compensation rules potentially restrained competition in these two markets, the court proceeded to analyze the legality of the challenged NCAA rules with respect to those markets, applying the Rule of Reason. The district court found that the NCAA's rules have an anticompetitive effect in the college education market but not in the group licensing market. It then concluded that the rules serve procompetitive purposes. Finally, it determined that the procompetitive purposes of the rules could be achieved by less restrictive alternative restraints and that the current rules were therefore unlawful.

a. Anticompetitive Effects

At the first step of the Rule of Reason, the court found that the NCAA's rules have an anticompetitive effect on the college education market. Were it not for those rules, the court explained, schools would compete with each other by offering recruits compensation exceeding the cost of attendance, which would "effectively lower the price that the recruits must pay for the combination of educational and athletic opportunities that the schools provide." The rules prohibiting compensation for the use of student-athletes' NILs are thus a price-fixing agreement: recruits pay for the bundles of services provided by colleges with their labor and their NILs, but the "sellers" of these bundles—the colleges—collectively "agree to value [NILs] at zero." Under this theory, colleges and universities behave as a cartel—a group of sellers who have colluded to fix the price of their product.

The court found in the alternative that the college education market can be thought of as a market in which student-athletes are sellers rather than buyers and the schools are purchasers of athletic services. In the court's alternative view, the college education market is a monopsony—a market in which there is only one buyer (the NCAA schools, acting collectively) for a particular good or service (the labor and NIL rights of student-athletes), and the colleges' agreement not to pay anything to purchase recruits' NILs causes harm to competition.

By contrast, the court found that the NCAA's rules do not have an anticompetitive effect on any of the submarkets of the group licensing market. The court explained that although these submarkets exist, there would be no competition in any of them if the challenged NCAA rules were abolished. The court reasoned that the value of an NIL license to a live game broadcaster or a video game company would depend on the licensee's acquiring every other NIL license that was available. A live game broadcaster, for example, would need to acquire a license from every team or player whose games it might telecast. Similarly, a video game producer would want to acquire NIL rights for all of the teams it needed to include in the game. Given these requirements, the court deemed it highly unlikely that groups of student-athletes would compete with each other to sell their NIL rights; on the contrary, they would have an incentive to cooperate to make sure that the package of NIL rights sold to buyers was as complete as possible. With respect to archival footage, meanwhile, the court found that the NCAA's licensing arrangement with T3Media did not deprive student-athletes of any compensation they might otherwise receive because T3Media is prohibited from licensing footage of current athletes and must obtain the consent of any former athlete whose NIL appears in its footage.

b. Procompetitive Purposes

At the second step of the Rule of Reason, the NCAA proffered four procompetitive purposes for its rules prohibiting student-athletes from receiving compensation for the use of their NILs: (1) preserving "amateurism" in college sports; . . . (3) integrating academics and athletics[.]

(1) Amateurism.

The NCAA argued to the district court that restrictions on student-athlete compensation are "necessary to preserve the amateur tradition and identity of college sports." It contended that amateurism had been one of the NCAA's core principles since its founding and that amateurism is a key driver of college sports' popularity with consumers and fans.

The district court rejected the NCAA's contention that it had a "longstanding commitment to amateurism," concluding instead that the NCAA's definition of amateurism was "malleable," changing frequently over time in "significant and contradictory ways." . . . It thus concluded that amateurism was not, in fact, a "core principle[ ]" of the NCAA.

The district court was not persuaded that amateurism is the primary driver of consumer demand for college sports—but it did find that amateurism serves some procompetitive purposes. The court first concluded that consumers are primarily attracted to college sports for reasons unrelated to amateurism, such as loyalty to their alma mater or affinity for the school in their region of the country. . . .

But the district court ultimately found that the NCAA's "current understanding of amateurism" plays some role in preserving "the popularity of the NCAA's product." It found that the

NCAA's current rules serve a procompetitive benefit by promoting this understanding of amateurism, which in turn helps preserve consumer demand for college sports. . . .

(3) Integrating Academics and Athletics.

The NCAA's third procompetitive justification for its restraints on student-athlete compensation was that these restraints integrate academics and athletics and thereby "improve the quality of educational services provided to student-athletes." According to the NCAA, student-athletes derive long-term benefits from participating fully in academic life at their schools, which the compensation rules encourage them to do.

The district court found that this was a viable procompetitive justification for the NCAA's regulating the college education market, but it concluded that most of the benefits of academic and athletic "integration" are not the result of the NCAA's rules restricting compensation. Rather, these benefits are achieved by other NCAA rules — such as those requiring student-athletes to attend class, prohibiting athletes-only dorms, and forbidding student-athletes to practice more than a certain number of hours per week. The court explained that the only way in which the compensation rules might facilitate the integration of athletics and academics is that, by prohibiting student-athletes from being paid large sums of money not available to ordinary students, the rules prevent the creation of a social "wedge" between student-athletes and the rest of the student body. It held, however, that even though the avoidance of such a "wedge" is a legitimate procompetitive goal, it does not justify a total, "sweeping prohibition" on paying student-athletes for the use of their NILs.

c. Less Restrictive Alternatives

Having found that the NCAA had presented two procompetitive justifications for "circumscribed" limits on student-athlete compensation — i.e., increasing consumer demand for college sports and preventing the formation of a "wedge" between student-athletes and other students — the court proceeded to the third and final step of the Rule of Reason, where it considered whether there were means of achieving the NCAA's procompetitive purposes that were "substantially less restrictive" than a total ban on compensating student-athletes for use of their NILs.

The court held that the plaintiffs had identified two legitimate, less restrictive alternatives to the current NCAA rules: (1) allowing schools to award stipends to student-athletes up to the full cost of attendance, thereby making up for any "shortfall" in their grants-in-aid, and (2) permitting schools to hold a portion of their licensing revenues in trust, to be distributed to student-athletes in equal shares after they leave college. The court determined that neither of these alternatives to the total ban on NIL compensation would undermine the NCAA's procompetitive purposes. The court also held that it would be permissible for the NCAA to prohibit schools from funding these stipends or trusts with anything other than revenue derived from the use of players' NILs.

After entering judgment for the plaintiffs on their antitrust claims, the district court permanently enjoined the NCAA from prohibiting its member schools from (1) compensating FBS football and Division I men's basketball players for the use of their NILs by awarding them grants-in-aid up to the full cost of attendance at their respective schools, or (2) paying up to $5,000 per year in deferred compensation to FBS football and Division I men's basketball players for the use of their NILs, through trust funds distributable after they leave school. The NCAA timely appealed. . . .

III

On appeal, the NCAA contends that the plaintiffs' Sherman Act claim fails on the merits. . . . We find none of these [] arguments persuasive.

A. Board of Regents *Did Not Declare the NCAA's Amateurism Rules "Valid as a Matter of Law"*

We consider, first, the NCAA's claim that, under *Board of Regents*, all NCAA amateurism rules are "valid as a matter of law."

Board of Regents concerned the NCAA's then-prevailing rules for televising college football games. The rules allowed television networks to negotiate directly with schools and conferences for the right to televise games, but they imposed caps on the total number of games that could be broadcast on television each year and the number of games that any particular school could televise. The University of Oklahoma and the University of Georgia challenged this regime as an illegal restraint of trade under Section 1.

The Court observed that the television rules resembled two kinds of agreements that are ordinarily considered per se unlawful when made among horizontal competitors in the same market: a price-fixing agreement (in that the rules set a minimum aggregate price that the television networks were required to pay the NCAA's members) and an output-restriction agreement (in that the rules artificially capped the number of televised game licenses for sale). But it concluded that applying a per se rule of invalidity to the NCAA's television rules would be "inappropriate" because college football is "an industry in which horizontal restraints on competition are essential if the product is to be available at all."

The Court held that the NCAA's rules should therefore be analyzed under the Rule of Reason. Applying the Rule of Reason, the Court struck down the television rules on the ground that they did not serve any legitimate procompetitive purpose. It then concluded its opinion by stating:

> The NCAA plays a critical role in the maintenance of a revered tradition of amateurism in college sports. There can be no question but that it needs ample latitude to play that role, or that the preservation of the student-athlete in higher education adds richness and diversity to intercollegiate athletics and is entirely consistent with the goals of the Sherman Act. But consistent with the Sherman Act, the role of the NCAA must be to preserve a tradition that might otherwise die; rules that restrict output are hardly consistent with this role. Today we hold only that the record supports the District Court's conclusion that by curtailing output and blunting the ability of member institutions to respond to consumer preference, the NCAA has restricted rather than enhanced the place of intercollegiate athletics in the Nation's life.

Quoting heavily from the language in *Board of Regents* that we have emphasized, the NCAA contends that any Section 1 challenge to its amateurism rules must fail as a matter of law because the *Board of Regents* Court held that those rules are presumptively valid. We disagree.

The *Board of Regents* Court certainly discussed the NCAA's amateurism rules at great length, but it did not do so in order to pass upon the rules' merits, given that they were not before the Court. Rather, the Court discussed the amateurism rules for a different and particular purpose: to explain why NCAA rules should be analyzed under the Rule of Reason, rather than held to be illegal per se. The point was a significant one. Naked horizontal agreements among competitors to fix the price of a good or service, or to restrict their output, are usually condemned as per se unlawful. The *Board of Regents* Court decided, however, that because college sports could not exist without certain horizontal agreements, NCAA rules should not be held per se unlawful even when — like the television rules in *Board of Regents* — they appear to be pure "restraints on the ability of member institutions to compete in terms of price and output."

Board of Regents, in other words, did not approve the NCAA's amateurism rules as categorically consistent with the Sherman Act. Rather, it held that, because many NCAA rules (among them, the amateurism rules) are part of the "character and quality of the [NCAA's] 'product,' " no NCAA rule should be invalidated without a Rule of Reason analysis. The Court's long encomium to amateurism, though impressive-sounding, was therefore dicta. . . .

To say that the NCAA's amateurism rules are procompetitive, as *Board of Regents* did, is not to say that they are automatically lawful; a restraint that serves a procompetitive purpose can still be invalid under the Rule of Reason if a substantially less restrictive rule would further the same objectives equally well. . . .

In sum, we accept *Board of Regents* 'guidance as informative with respect to the pro-competitive purposes served by the NCAA's amateurism rules, but we will go no further than that. The amateurism rules' validity must be proved, not presumed. . . .

C. The Plaintiffs Demonstrated that the Compensation Rules Cause Them Injury in Fact

The NCAA's last argument antecedent to the merits is that the plaintiffs' Section 1 claim fails at the threshold because the plaintiffs have failed to show that they have suffered "anti-trust injury." Antitrust injury is a heightened standing requirement that applies to private parties suing to enforce the antitrust laws. To satisfy the antitrust-injury requirement, a plaintiff must show "injury of the type the antitrust laws were intended to prevent and that flows from that which makes defendants' acts unlawful."

Although the NCAA purports to be making an antitrust-injury argument, it is mistaken. The NCAA has not contended that the plaintiffs' injuries are not "of the type the antitrust laws were intended to prevent." Rather, the NCAA has made a garden-variety standing argument: it alleges that the plaintiffs have not been injured in fact by the compensation rules because those rules do not deprive them of any NIL compensation they would otherwise receive. Addressing each of the potential markets for NIL rights that the district court identified, the NCAA argues that (1) there are no legally-recognized NIL rights for participants in live game broadcasts; (2) the NCAA's compensation rules do not deprive the plaintiffs of compensation for use of their NILs in video games because the NCAA no longer permits college sports video games to be made and has a separate policy forbidding the use of student-athletes' NILs in video games; and (3) the NCAA's licensing agreement for archival footage with T3Media does not deprive athletes of NIL compensation for archival footage because it prevents T3Media from licensing student-athletes' NILs while they are in school and requires the company to obtain consent once student-athletes have left school.

We conclude that the plaintiffs have shown that they are injured in fact as a result of the NCAA's rules having foreclosed the market for their NILs in video games. We therefore do not reach the thornier questions of whether participants in live TV broadcasts of college sporting events have enforceable rights of publicity or whether the plaintiffs are injured by the NCAA's current licensing arrangement for archival footage.

1. Absent the NCAA's Compensation Rules, Video Game Makers Would Negotiate with Student-Athletes for the Right to Use Their Nils

As we have explained, the district court found that, if permitted to do so, video game makers such as EA would negotiate with college athletes for the right to use their NILs in video games because these companies want to make games that are as realistic as possible. The district court noted that EA currently negotiates with the NFL and NBA players' unions for the right to use their members' NILs in pro sports video games. The plaintiffs also put into evidence a copy of a 2005 presentation by EA representatives to the NCAA, which stated that EA's inability to use college athletes' NILs was the "number one factor holding back NCAA video game growth." . . .

Because the plaintiffs have shown that, absent the NCAA's compensation rules, video game makers would likely pay them for the right to use their NILs in college sports video games, the plaintiffs have satisfied the requirement of injury in fact and, by extension, the requirement of antitrust injury.

IV

Having rejected all of the NCAA's preliminary legal arguments, we proceed to review the plaintiffs' Section 1 claim on the merits. . . . [W]e are persuaded . . . that the appropriate rule is the Rule of Reason. Like the district court, we follow the three-step framework of the Rule of Reason[.]

A. Significant Anticompetitive Effects Within a Relevant Market

. . . . [The District Court's] findings have substantial support in the record.

. . . . [The] NCAA makes three modest arguments about why the compensation rules do not have a significant anticompetitive effect. First, it argues that because the plaintiffs never showed that the rules reduce output in the college education market, the plaintiffs did not meet their burden of showing a significant anticompetitive effect. Second, it argues that the rules have no anticompetitive effect because schools would not pay student-athletes anything for their NIL rights in any event, given that those rights are worth nothing. And finally, the NCAA argues that even if the district court was right that schools would pay student-athletes for their NIL rights, any such payments would be small, which means that the compensation rules' anticompetitive effects cannot be considered significant.

We can dispose of the first two arguments quickly. First, the NCAA's contention that the plaintiffs' claim fails because they did not show a decrease in output in the college education market is simply incorrect. . . . Although output reductions are one common kind of anticompetitive effect in antitrust cases, a "reduction in output is not the only measure of anticompetitive effect."

The "combination[s] condemned by the [Sherman] Act" also include "price-fixing . . . by purchasers" even though "the persons specially injured . . . are sellers, not customers or consumers." At trial, the plaintiffs demonstrated that the NCAA's compensation rules have just this kind of anticompetitive effect: they fix the price of one component of the exchange between school and recruit, thereby precluding competition among schools with respect to that component. The district court found that although consumers of NCAA football and basketball may not be harmed directly by this price-fixing, the "student-athletes themselves are harmed by the price-fixing agreement among FBS football and Division I basketball schools." The athletes accept grants-in-aid, and no more, in exchange for their athletic per-formance, because the NCAA schools have agreed to value the athletes' NILs at zero, "an anticompetitive effect." This anticompetitive effect satisfied the plaintiffs' initial burden under the Rule of Reason.

Second, the NCAA's argument that student-athletes' NILs are, in fact, worth nothing is simply a repackaged version of its arguments about injury in fact, which we have rejected.

Finally, we reject the NCAA's contention that any NIL compensation that student-athletes might receive in the absence of its compensation rules would be de minimis and that the rules therefore do not significantly affect competition in the college education market. This "too small to matter" argument is incompatible with the Supreme Court [precedent].

The NCAA's compensation rules . . . "extinguish[ ] one form of competition" among schools seeking to land recruits. . . . [A]n antitrust court should not dismiss an anticompetitive price-fixing agreement as benign simply because the agreement relates only to one component of an overall price. That proposition finds further support in *Board of Regents*: in *Board of Regents*, a Rule of Reason case, the Court held that the NCAA's television plan had "a significant potential for anticompetitive effects" without delving into the details of exactly how much the plan restricted output of televised games or how much it fixed the price of TV contracts. While the precise value of NIL compensation is uncertain, . . . we conclude that the plaintiffs have met their burden at the first step of the Rule of Reason by showing that the NCAA's compensation rules fix the price of one component (NIL rights) of the bundle that schools provide to recruits.

Because we agree with the district court that the compensation rules have a significant anticompetitive effect on the college education market, we proceed to consider the procom-petitive justifications the NCAA proffers for those rules.

B. Procompetitive Effects

As discussed above, the NCAA offered the district court four procompetitive justifications for the compensation rules, [two of which the court accepted]: (1) promoting amateurism, and (3) integrating student-athletes with their schools' academic community[.] . . .

The district court acknowledged that the NCAA's current rules promote amateurism, which in turn plays a role in increasing consumer demand for college sports. The NCAA does not challenge that specific determination, but it argues to us that the district court gave the ama-teurism justification short shrift, in two respects. First, it claims that the district court erred by focusing solely on the question of whether amateurism increases consumers' (i.e., fans') demand for college sports and ignoring the fact that amateurism also increases choice for student-athletes by giving them "the only opportunity [they will] have to obtain a college education while playing competitive sports as students." Second, it faults the district court for being inappropriately skeptical of the NCAA's historical commitment to amateurism. Although we might have credited the depth of the NCAA's devotion to amateurism differently, these arguments do not persuade us that the district court clearly erred.

The NCAA is correct that a restraint that broadens choices can be procompetitive. The Court in *Board of Regents* observed that the difference between college and professional sports "widen[s]" the choices "available to athletes." But we fail to see how the restraint at issue in this particular case — i.e., the NCAA's limits on student-athlete compensation — makes college sports more attractive to recruits, or widens recruits' spectrum of choices in the sense that *Board of Regents* suggested. As the district court found, it is primarily "the opportunity to earn a higher education" that attracts athletes to college sports rather than professional sports and that opportunity would still be available to student-athletes if they were paid some compensation in addition to their athletic scholarships. Nothing in the plaintiffs' prayer for compensation would make student-athletes something other than students and thereby impair their ability to become student-athletes.

Indeed, if anything, loosening or abandoning the compensation rules might be the best way to "widen" recruits' range of choices; athletes might well be more likely to attend college, and stay there longer, if they knew that they were earning some amount of NIL income while they were in school.

We therefore reject the NCAA's claim that, by denying student-athletes compensation apart from scholarships, the NCAA increases the "choices" available to them.

The NCAA's second point has more force — the district court probably underestimated the NCAA's commitment to amateurism. But the point is ultimately irrelevant. Even if the NCAA's concept of amateurism had been perfectly coherent and consistent, the NCAA would still need to show that amateurism brings about some procompetitive effect in order to justify it under the antitrust laws. The NCAA cannot fully answer the district court's finding that the compensation rules have significant anticompetitive effects simply by pointing out that it has adhered to those rules for a long time. Nevertheless, the district court found, and the record supports that there is a concrete procompetitive effect in the NCAA's commitment to amateurism: namely, that the amateur nature of collegiate sports increases their appeal to consumers. We therefore conclude that the NCAA's compensation rules serve the two procompetitive purposes identified by the district court: integrating academics with athletics, and "preserving the popularity of the NCAA's product by promoting its current understanding of amateurism." . . . We thus turn to the final inquiry — whether there are reasonable alternatives to the NCAA's current compensation restrictions.

C. Substantially Less Restrictive Alternatives

The third step in the Rule of Reason analysis is whether there are substantially less restrictive alternatives to the NCAA's current rules. We bear in mind that — to be viable under the Rule of Reason — an alternative must be "virtually as effective" in serving the procompetitive purposes of the NCAA's current rules, and "without significantly increased cost." We think that plaintiffs must make a strong evidentiary showing that its alternatives are viable here. Not only do plaintiffs bear the burden at this step, but the Supreme Court has admonished that we must generally afford the NCAA "ample latitude" to superintend college athletics.

The district court identified two substantially less restrictive alternatives: (1) allowing NCAA member schools to give student-athletes grants-in-aid that cover the full cost of attendance; and (2) allowing member schools to pay student-athletes small amounts of deferred cash compensation for use of their NILs.

1. Capping the Permissible Amount of Scholarships at the Cost of Attendance

The district court did not clearly err in finding that allowing NCAA member schools to award grants-in-aid up to their full cost of attendance would be a substantially less restrictive alternative to the current compensation rules. All of the evidence before the district court indicated that raising the grant-in-aid cap to the cost of attendance would have virtually no impact on amateurism: Dr. Mark Emmert, the president of the NCAA, testified at trial that giving student-athletes scholarships up to their full costs of attendance would not violate the NCAA's principles of amateurism because all the money given to students would be going to cover their "legitimate costs" to attend school. Other NCAA witnesses agreed with that assessment. Nothing in the record, moreover, suggested that consumers of college sports would become less interested in those sports if athletes' scholarships covered their full cost of attendance, or that an increase in the grant-in-aid cap would impede the integration of student-athletes into their academic communities. . . .

Thus, in holding that setting the grant-in-aid cap at student-athletes' full cost of attendance is a substantially less restrictive alternative under the Rule of Reason, we are not declaring that courts are free to micromanage organizational rules or to strike down largely beneficial market restraints with impunity. Rather, our affirmance of this aspect of the district court's decision should be taken to establish only that where, as here, a restraint is patently and inexplicably stricter than is necessary to accomplish all of its procompetitive objectives, an antitrust court can and should invalidate it and order it replaced with a less restrictive alternative. . . . The district court's determination that the existing compensation rules violate Section 1 of the Sherman Act was correct and its injunction requiring the NCAA to permit schools to provide compensation up to the full cost of attendance was proper.

2. Allowing Students to Receive Cash Compensation for Their NILs

In our judgment, however, the district court clearly erred in finding it a viable alternative to allow students to receive NIL cash payments untethered to their education expenses. . . . We cannot agree that a rule permitting schools to pay students pure cash compensation and a rule forbidding them from paying NIL compensation are both equally effective in promoting amateurism and preserving consumer demand. Both we and the district court agree that the NCAA's amateurism rule has procompetitive benefits. But in finding that paying students cash compensation would promote amateurism as effectively as not paying them, the district court ignored that not paying student-athletes is precisely what makes them amateurs. . . .

The difference between offering student-athletes education-related compensation and offering them cash sums untethered to educational expenses is not minor; it is a quantum leap. Once that line is crossed, we see no basis for returning to a rule of amateurism and no defined stopping point; we have little doubt that plaintiffs will continue to challenge the arbitrary limit imposed by the district court until they have captured the full value of their NIL. . . . [W]e think it is clear the district court erred in concluding that small payments in deferred compensation are a substantially less restrictive alternative restraint. We thus vacate that portion of the district court's decision and the portion of its injunction requiring the NCAA to allow its member schools to pay this deferred compensation.

V

By way of summation, we wish to emphasize the limited scope of the decision we have reached and the remedy we have approved. Today, we reaffirm that NCAA regulations are subject to antitrust scrutiny and must be tested in the crucible of the Rule of Reason. When those regulations truly serve procompetitive purposes, courts should not hesitate to uphold them. But the NCAA is not above the antitrust laws, and courts cannot and must not shy away from requiring the NCAA to play by the Sherman Act's rules. In this case, the NCAA's rules have been more restrictive than necessary to maintain its tradition of amateurism in support of the college sports market. The Rule of Reason requires that the NCAA permit its schools to provide up to the cost of attendance to their student athletes. It does not require more.

We vacate the district court's judgment and permanent injunction insofar as they require the NCAA to allow its member schools to pay student-athletes up to $5,000 per year in deferred compensation. DISSENT omitted.

MARSHALL v. ESPN INC.
111 F. Supp. 3d 815 (M.D. Tenn. 2015)

KEVIN H. SHARP, District Judge.

This is a putative class action brought by current and former Student Athletes who played National Collegiate Athletic Association ("NCAA") football (at the Football Bowl Subdivision "FBS" level) or Division I college basketball. Named as Defendants are a host of conferences, networks, and licensors who allegedly profited from the broadcast and use of those Student Athletes' names, likenesses and images without permission. Pending before the Court are Motions to Dismiss filed on behalf of all Defendants. [F]or the reasons that follow, [the Court] will grant the Motions.

I. BACKGROUND

Plaintiffs are eight former college football players and two former college basketball players.

Defendants are more than two dozen separate entities that fall into three camps. The assorted athletic conferences (collectively, the "Conference Defendants") manage athletic competition among teams and sell the rights to broadcast conference games. The networks (the "Network Defendants") purchase media content, including college sports from content owners, or produce it internally, and then telecast that content to television viewers. The licensing agencies (collectively, the "Licensing Defendants") offer brand development and management and act as a conduit in licensing college teams' intellectual property.

Plaintiffs have filed a 194-paragraph, 39-page Complaint, the essence of which is that they "and other similarly situated current and former FBS football and NCAA Division I basketball Student Athletes . . . have been foreclosed from the market for the licensing, use, and sale of their names, images, and likenesses [.]" The Complaint alleges:

5. Defendants' collective action of excluding Student Athletes from the marketplace of their own names, images, and likenesses has caused the unlawful result of fixing the amount that current and former Student Athletes are paid for the licensing and sale of their names, images, and likeness at zero or, at most, their "cost of attendance."

6. Defendants' use of Student Athletes' names, images, and likenesses is unauthorized because Student Athletes have not legally assigned their publicity rights to Defendants, the NCAA, or third parties acting on behalf of the NCAA.

* * *

8. Broadcast Defendants have conspired to fix the amount Student Athletes are paid for the licensing, use, and sale of their names, images, and likenesses at zero or, at most, a portion of the cost of attendance, by colluding with the NCAA and Conference Defendants. Broadcast Defendants, to their own commercial advantage, refuse to negotiate or enter into contracts with Student Athletes. In so doing, Broadcast Defendants have adopted and implemented the restrictive bylaws and rules of the NCAA and Conference Defendants.

9. Licensing Defendants have conspired to fix the amount Student Athletes are paid for the licensing, use, and sale of their names, images, and likenesses at zero or, at most, a portion of the cost of attendance, by colluding with the NCAA and Conference Defendants. Licensing Defendants refuse to negotiate or enter into contracts with Student Athletes. In so doing, Licensing Defendants have adopted and implemented the restrictive rules and bylaws of the NCAA and Conference Defendants.

10. The conspiracy between and among the Broadcast Defendants, Licensing Defendants, Conference Defendants and the NCAA has created . . . an anticompetitive marketplace in which all Defendants commercially exploit the substantial value of each Student Athletes' images.

Though the NCAA is alleged to be a part of the conspiracy, it not named as a Defendant in this action. Nevertheless, Plaintiffs' tacitly concede that any discussion of the alleged unlawfulness must acknowledge it existence and the role it plays in college sports.

According to the Complaint, the NCAA was founded in 1906 and "is an unincorporated association consisting of more than 1,200 colleges, universities, and athletic conferences" in the United States and "serves as the governing body of its member schools and athletic conferences." The fundamental purpose of the NCAA is to:

maintain intercollegiate athletics as an integral part of the education program and the athlete as an integral part of the educational program and the athlete as a part of the student body and, by so doing, retain a clear line of demarcation between intercollegiate athletics and professional sports.

In accordance with NCAA rules, intercollegiate sports are limited to participation of "amateur" athletes:

Student-athletes shall be amateurs in intercollegiate sport, and their participation should be motivated primarily by education and by the physical, mental and social benefits to be derived. Student participation in intercollegiate athletics is an avocation, and student-athletes should be protected from commercial exploitation by professional and commercial enterprises.

A Student Athlete may lose his or her amateur status if he or she, [among other things]:

> a. Uses his or her athletics skill (directly or indirectly) for pay in any form in that sport;
>
> b. Accepts a promise of pay even if such pay is to be received following completion of intercollegiate athletics participation; . . .
>
> d. Receives, directly or indirectly, a salary, reimbursement of expenses or any other form of financial assistance from a professional sports organization based on athletics skill or participation, except as permitted by NCAA rules and regulations[.] . . .

In order to participate in NCAA sports, Student Athletes are required to sign a "Form 08–3a," that "allows the NCAA to use the Student Athlete's name or picture to 'generally promote' NCAA championships or other NCAA events, activities or programs." Plaintiffs allege that "Student Athletes desiring to extend their athletic careers beyond high school are left with no comparable alternative to accepting a scholarship from an FBS football or Division I basketball school," because "[b]oth the National Football League ('NFL') and the National Basketball Association ('NBA') prohibit high school players from entering their leagues directly after high school." As a consequence, in order to play at a competitive level, Student Athletes have little or no choice but to accept a scholarship and sign Form 08–3a, making the Form "a contract of adhesion and unenforceable."

Plaintiffs claim that the NCAA and Defendants have "multi-billion dollar agreements," yet "the Student Athlete, receives nothing or, at most, the cost of attendance." The restrictive NCAA and Conference rule which "even go as far as to place quotas on the number of meals a Student Athlete may eat," allegedly "have deprived Student Athletes from realizing the commercial value of their images." That is, while the NCAA "purports to protect Student Athletes from commercial exploitation, [it] has conspired with Defendants to create an anti-competitive market where Student Athletes are powerless to realize the commercial value of their names, images and likenesses." . . .

Plaintiffs' Complaint contains [several] Causes of Action. The first two Causes, against all Defendants, allege a statutory violation of the right of publicity under Tenn. Code Ann. §47–25–1105 (First Cause) and a violation of the right to publicity under Tennessee common law (Second Cause); [and] the Fourth Cause, again against all Defendants, alleges a violation of Section 1 of the Sherman Antitrust Act[.] . . .

II. APPLICATION OF LAW

A. Right of Publicity — First And Second Causes of Action

Tennessee's common law acknowledges a "property right in the use of one's name, photograph or likeness." In addition to the right of publicity under the common law, Tennessee provides statutory protection to that right. "The Tennessee Legislature codified the right of publicity in 1984 when it enacted the Tennessee Personal Rights Protection Act ('TPRPA')." The TPRPA "was intended to 'create an inheritable property right for those people who use their names or likenesses in a commercial manner, such as an entertainer or sports figure — someone who uses his or her name for endorsement purposes.'"

Defendants argue that the TPRPA supplants whatever right to publicity that may exist under the common law. For two reasons, this Court agrees.

First, at least two courts in Tennessee have indicated that the statutory and common law rights to publicity are "co-extensive." The term "'[c]oextensive' means 'extending over the same space or time; corresponding exactly in extent.'"

Second, Plaintiffs cite no case from any court in Tennessee that recognizes a right to publicity in sports broadcasts. Even if they could point to such a case, the Tennessee Supreme Court has stated that "'[w]hen there is a conflict between the common law and a statute, the provision[s] of the statute must prevail.'"

It is no answer, as Plaintiffs argue, that (1) "at least seven years earlier than the enactment of the TPRPA," courts recognized the existence of a common law right to publicity; (2) "where a common law tort has been recognized by courts prior to the enactment of a companion statute, 'the Legislature is presumed aware of this prior recognition'"; (3) "'where the remedies subsequently provided by the [Act] are not expressly stated to be exclusive, then the statutory remedies must be considered cumulative'"; and (4) "the TPRPA states that the remedies it provides 'are cumulative and shall be in addition to any others provided by law.'" The very case on which Plaintiffs rely prefaces its remarks by indicating that the "primary task in construing a statute is to give effect to the intent and purpose of the General Assembly 'without unduly restricting or expanding a statute's coverage beyond its intended scope.'" Furthermore, State ex rel. Presley, on which Plaintiffs rely for the proposition that the common law right to publicity existed years before enactment of the TPRPA, acknowledged that "[w]hile Tennessee's courts are capable of defining the parameters of the right of publicity on a case by case basis, the General Assembly also has the prerogative to define the scope of this right [and] undertook to do so in 1984 when it enacted" the TPRPA. In exercising that prerogative, the General Assembly specifically defined the right of publicity as it relates to sports broadcast (as discussed in more detail below), something which apparently had not been addressed by the courts in this state before.

Even if Tennessee's common law and statutory rights to publicity are not coextensive as that term is commonly understood, and even if the General Assembly did not effectively delimit the law regarding the right to publicity of sports broadcast, the first two Causes of Action in Plaintiff's Complaint are bound to be dismissed. This is because Plaintiffs' allegations do not set forth a plausible claim for relief, either under the common law or the TPRPA.

As noted, Plaintiffs' cite no Tennessee authority for the proposition that participants in sporting events have a right to publicity under the common law. This is unsurprising since it appears virtually all courts in jurisdictions that have decided the matter under their respective laws have held to the contrary for a variety of reasons.

The sole exception to this line of authority appears to be In re NCAA Student-Athlete Name and Likeness Litig., 37 F. Supp. 3d 1126 (N.D. Cal. 2014), which Plaintiffs cite for the proposition that "[r]ecent precedent specifically affirms that collegiate athletes have recognizable right of publicity related to sports broadcasts." The only value that case has for present purposes, however, is that there might be a right of publicity under Minnesota law for sports broadcast, itself a dubious proposition given a more recent interpretation of that state's case law.

In re NCAA Student-Athlete involved 23 current and former student athletes who played at the Division I level beginning in 1953. The sole issue presented in that opinion was whether the NCAA violated federal antitrust law by conspiring to restrain competition in the market for the commercial use of the players' names, images and likeness. In addressing that issue, the court found it necessary to "discuss the scope of student-athletes' publicity rights" in the context of "whether those rights could, absent the challenged restraint, give rise to a market for group licensing," but pointedly repeated that "[t]he court does not analyze the viability of Right-of-Publicity Plaintiffs' claims which remain stayed[.]" Nevertheless, the court noted that "the NCAA has not shown that each of the named Plaintiffs is, in fact, domiciled in a state that refuses to recognize an athlete's right of publicity in live broadcasts of sporting events," that two of the named plaintiffs "are domiciled in Minnesota," and that "recent case law suggests that athletes may bring such claims under Minnesota law to recover for the unauthorized use of their names and images in at least certain kinds of broadcast footage."

The court's statements in In re NCAA Student-Athlete about the right to publicity in sports broadcasts are clearly dicta. Moreover, Plaintiffs' right of publicity claims here are based exclusively on Tennessee law, and Defendants argue (and Plaintiffs do not dispute) that the plaintiffs in *In re NCAA Student-Athlete* conceded that Tennessee recognizes no right of publicity in sports broadcasts. Additionally, the Dryer court issued a subsequent opinion in which it held that plaintiffs did not establish that the NFL's use of video footage in television productions violated their publicity rights under Minnesota law, nor, for that matter under New York, New Jersey, California, or Texas law. Thus, the decision in *In re NCAA Student-Athlete* is of no real help to Plaintiffs in establishing an individual participant's right of publicity in a sports broadcast under any state's laws, let alone under Tennessee law.

Plaintiffs' statutory claim fares no better. In general, the TPRPA provides:

> Any person who knowingly uses or infringes upon the use of another individual's name, photograph, or likeness in any medium, in any manner directed to any person other than such individual, as an item of commerce for purposes of advertising products, merchandise, goods, or services . . . without such individual's prior consent, or, in the case of a minor, the prior consent of such minor's parent or legal guardian . . . shall be liable to a civil action.

Tenn. Code Ann. §47–25–1105(a).

Tellingly, the TPRPA speaks in terms of the use of an individual's name, photograph, or likeness "for purposes of advertising products, merchandise goods or services." The Act also specifically states that "[i]t is deemed a fair use and no violation of an individual's rights shall be found, for purposes of this part, if the use of a name, photograph, or likeness is in connection with any news, public affairs, or sports broadcast or account." Thus, the TPRPA clearly confers no right of publicity in sports broadcast, or with respect to any advertisement if the advertisement is in connection with such a broadcast. . . .

Thus far, the Court has concluded that the statutory and common law right to publicity are co-extensive under Tennessee law, that the common law in Tennessee does not recognize an individual participant's right to publicity in sports broadcasts, and that, in any event, the TPRPA circumscribes whatever rights may exist under the common law insofar as sports broadcast are concerned. Nevertheless, a couple of further points need to be addressed in order to give full consideration to Plaintiffs' right to publicity arguments.

Plaintiffs rely on Zacchini v. Scripps–Howard Broad. Co., 433 U.S. 562 (1977) and Wisconsin Interscholastic Athl. Ass'n v. Gannett Co., Inc., 658 F.3d 614 (7th Cir. 2011) to support their right of publicity claims, and to defend against any contention that the First Amendment bars such claims in the context of sports broadcasts. They argue that, like the plaintiff in *Zacchini*, they do "'not seek to enjoin the broadcast of [their] performance but simply want[ ] to be paid for it[.]'" The key to those cases, Plaintiffs insist, is the distinction drawn between reporting about sports events, as opposed to broadcasting entire sporting events with the former being protected as newsworthy and of public interest, and the latter not.

There is no doubt that *Zacchini* and *Wisconsin Interscholastic* draw the distinction made by Plaintiffs in this case, and the court in *In re NCAA Student–Athlete* relied on that distinction in holding that "the First Amendment does not guarantee media organizations an unlimited right to broadcast entire college football and basketball games." But, stating that the First Amendment does not guarantee unlimited broadcast rights does not mean that it correspondingly establishes a right to publicity by the athletic participants when entire games are broadcast. Moreover, just as with all cases, *Zacchini* and *Wisconsin Interscholastic* must be read in context and, when so read, are inapposite.

Hugo Zacchini was a "human cannonball" who performed the feat of being shot from a cannon into a net 200 feet away. In the summer of 1972, he performed his act at a county fair in Ohio and, over his protest, a local new reporter filmed the entire 15-second performance, which was then broadcast on the local eleven o'clock news. Mr. Zacchini brought an "action for damages, alleging that he is 'engaged in the entertainment business,'" and asserted that defendant "'showed and commercialized the film of his act without his consent,' and that such conduct was an 'unlawful appropriation of [his] professional property.'"

Unlike the situation here, Mr. Zacchini was not only a performer, he was also the producer of his one-man show and, as a consequence, "Ohio's decision to protect [his] right of publicity here rests on more than a desire to compensate the performer for the time and effort invested in his act; the protection provides an economic incentive for him to make the investment required to produce a performance of interest to the public." The Supreme Court went on to observe that "[t]his same consideration underlies the patent and copyright laws long enforced by this Court," laws that "were 'intended definitely to grant valuable, enforceable rights' in order to afford greater encouragement to the production of works of benefit to the public." It is a mistake, the Court believes, to read *Zacchini* as supporting a right of publicity by anyone who performs in an event produced by someone else.

Wisconsin Interscholastic involved a high school athletic association's challenge to the streaming of a tournament game by news organizations in violation of exclusive licensing agreements entered into between the association (which sponsored the tournaments) and a video production company. On its face that case does not aid Plaintiffs because the Seventh Circuit affirmed the association's right to enter into exclusive contracts for broadcasting entire games, noting that "tournament games are a performance product of [the association] which it has a right to control." True, the court stated that "[t]he distinction between coverage or reporting on the one hand, and broadcast of an 'entire' act on the other hand, was central to *Zacchini*," but the court also observed that *Zacchini* stands for a second proposition:

"*Zacchini* makes clear that the producer of entertainment is entitled to charge a fee in exchange for consent to broadcast; the First Amendment does not give the media the right to appropriate, without consent or remuneration, the products of others."

Here, Plaintiffs are the players in broadcast football and basketball games. The networks are the producers and the games are their products.

In light of this Court's conclusion that Plaintiffs fail to state a claim under either Tennessee's common law or the TPRPA, the Court declines to consider the matter.

B. Section One of the Sherman Act — Fourth Cause of Action

Under the Sherman Act, "[e]very contract, combination in the form of trust or otherwise, or conspiracy, in restraint of trade or commerce . . . is declared to be illegal." 15 U.S.C. §1. "For a plaintiff to successfully bring an antitrust claim under Section 1 of the Sherman Act, the plaintiff must establish that the defendant's actions constituted an unreasonable restraint of trade which caused the plaintiff to experience an antitrust injury." Plaintiffs have failed to adequately allege either element.

"A Section One complaint will survive a Rule 12(b)(6) motion to dismiss if it alleges facts sufficient to raise a plausible inference of an unlawful agreement to restrain trade." "To plead unlawful agreement, a plaintiff may allege either an explicit agreement to restrain trade, or 'sufficient circumstantial evidence tending to exclude the possibility of independent conduct.'"

In the Complaint, Plaintiffs attack the NCAA amateurism rules, describing them as anti-competitive agreements. . . . The Conference Defendants are alleged to "jointly enforce this clear demarcation between Student Athletes and professional athletes by permitting only 'amateur' Student Athletes to participate in intercollegiate sports," and have not only approved the NCAA's rules, but have mandated that its members follow those rules. The claim against the Network Defendants is more attenuated, with the allegation being those Defendants have entered into lucrative contracts with the NCAA and Conference Defendants which "effectively adopt and implement" the restrictive rules and bylaws of the NCAA. The claim against the Licensing Defendants is thinner still, alleging that "[t]he agreements between the Licensing Defendants and NCAA member institutions purportedly encompass the commercial value of Student Athletes' rights of publicity, yet Licensing Defendants refuse to negotiate or enter into agreements with Student Athletes to obtain such rights."

By necessarily linking their antitrust claims to the NCAA amateurism rules and attacking those rules, Plaintiffs are faced with a fundamental problem, notwithstanding that the NCAA is not a Defendant in this action. Their attack runs counter to a line of cases which have addressed the amateurism rules in a variety of circumstances, including NCAA v. Board of Regents, 468 U.S. 85 (1984), decided more than thirty years ago. . . .

Board of Regents has recently been read to mean that "most [NCAA] regulations will be 'a justifiable means of fostering competition among amateur athletic teams,' and are therefore procompetitive." It also has been read as giving courts "a license to find certain NCAA bylaws that 'fit into the same mold' as those discussed in *Board of Regents* to be procompetitive 'in the twinkling of an eye,' — that is, at the motion-to-dismiss stage." "Accordingly, when an NCAA bylaw is clearly meant to help maintain the 'revered tradition of amateurism in college sports' or the 'preservation of the student-athlete in higher education,' the bylaw will be presumed procompetitive, since [a court] must give the NCAA 'ample latitude to play that role.'" . . .

Right or wrong, under NCAA rules, other than the requirement that an athlete be a student, there can be no more basic eligibility rule for amateurism than that the athlete not be paid for playing his or her sport.

Notwithstanding the allegations in the Complaint, Plaintiffs argue in their response brief to the Licensing Defendants' Motion to Dismiss that "the amateurism rules that preclude Student Athlete Compensation are not the restraint at issue." Rather, "the restraints at issue include, but are not limited to, the multi-million dollar broadcast contract and multi-media agreements that purport to transfer the right to use the [names and likeness] of Student Athletes." Their attempt to distance themselves from a fundamental, underlying premise of their case only trades one problem for another.

To have standing to pursue any claim, an aggrieved party must suffer an injury-in-fact. "A plaintiff suffers an 'injury in fact' when his legally protected interest has been invaded[.]" Here, Plaintiffs claim injuries because of their exclusion from a broadcasting marketplace in which they do not (or did not) get paid. However, the Court has concluded that, as a matter of law, Plaintiffs do not have a right to publicity in sports broadcasts. Because Plaintiffs do not have a right to publicity under Tennessee law—the very basis of their claim that they have a right to be paid for appearing in television broadcasts of games and in advertisements for such broadcasts—they cannot plead any antitrust injury. And, they cannot have been injured by a purported conspiracy to deny them the ability to sell non-existent rights.

Moreover, "[b]ecause protecting competition is the sine qua non of the antitrust laws," "[a] private antitrust plaintiff, in addition to having to show injury-in-fact and proximate cause, must allege, and eventually prove, 'antitrust injury.'" Antitrust injury is an "injury of the type the antitrust laws were intended to prevent" and one "that flows from that which makes defendants' acts unlawful."

"[T]he antitrust injury doctrine is designed to ensure that 'the injury should reflect the anticompetitive effect either of the violation or of anticompetitive acts made possible by the violation.'" "'The Supreme Court has further explained the requirement as ensur[ing] that the harm claimed by the plaintiff corresponds to the rationale for finding a violation of the antitrust laws in the first place,' and, more specifically, it 'ensures that a plaintiff can recover only if the loss stems from a competition-reducing aspect or effect of the defendant's behavior.'" "The Sixth Circuit, it is fair to say, has been reasonably aggressive in using the antitrust injury doctrine to bar recovery where the asserted injury, although linked to an alleged violation of the antitrust laws, flows directly from conduct that is not itself an antitrust violation."

Undoubtedly, there is stiff competition among the conferences to secure air time for games, among the networks to broadcast those games, and among the licensors to market college games, and Plaintiffs' allegations suggests as much. Maybe a market where players get paid would result in more competition, or at least vastly different competition. However, Plaintiffs fail to show how Defendants' behavior (most particularly that of Network and Broadcast Defendants), in complying with NCAA rules, can be said to be the cause of reduced competition and any concomitant antitrust injury.

Accordingly, Plaintiffs' antitrust claim under Section One of the Sherman Act must be dismissed. . . .

III. CONCLUSION

[T]he Court's sole task is to determine whether present Plaintiffs have alleged sufficient facts or stated a viable claim that they are entitled to monetary compensation because they play in televised games. The Court finds that Plaintiffs have not done so under any of the theories that they set forth. Accordingly, the Motions to Dismiss filed by the Network Defendants, the Conference Defendants, and the Licensing Defendants will be granted. Said dismissal will be with prejudice.

III. PROBLEMS

1. ABC Sport Restaurants is the exclusive licensee of Strike/B.B. Player's name and likeness for a southern style restaurant in the Detroit metropolitan area. The license provides the following:

> Strike hereby grants to ABC, and ABC hereby accepts from Strike, the exclusive right and license in the Detroit metropolitan area to use the Name directly or through a partnership, joint venture or other entity of which ABC is a partner, joint venturer, owner, or other equity holder (a "Restaurant Entity") to own and operate the Restaurant Business.
>
> The restaurant license agreement further stated that Strike "will not take any action or enter into any new agreements in the restaurant industry that in any manner violates or interferes with the rights granted to ABC by Strike." The agreement also provides that during the term of the Restaurant License Agreement neither Strike nor any of its affiliates shall grant, sell, assign or otherwise entitle any person, firm, corporation or other entity the right to open any restaurant based on the Name within the Detroit metropolitan area.
>
> ABC employed Gibson to manage the restaurant. Gibson has made plans with B.B. Player directly to open a new restaurant in a nearby Detroit location using the Name. Without informing ABC, Gibson caused an easement to be recorded concerning a nearby property on which the new restaurant would sit. In addition to the easement, Gibson has taken the following actions with respect to the new restaurant: He initiated a "whispering campaign" regarding the opening of the new restaurant in Detroit; he released information to the media regarding the opening of the new restaurant; and he and B.B. Player strategically selected the location to benefit from its proximity to the sports stadium where B.B. Player and his team play their home games. Gibson and B.B. Player plan to utilize the Name in the following ways: by having B.B. Player personally appear to promote the new restaurant; by displaying B.B. Player's name on a publicly displayed billboard inside the restaurant; and by making B.B. Player's vehicles, many of which bear vanity license plates, "clearly visible" outside the new restaurant when B.B. Player is visiting. ABC has not consented to the use of the Name in connection with any restaurant other than the one it operates.

   Even though an exclusive licensee has a license agreement to exploit a celebrity's right of publicity, does that same licensee also have standing to sue for the misappropriation of the right of publicity if a third party and the celebrity use the name to open up the new restaurant?

2. Your client visits your office with a proposed new project. Specifically, she is a journalist and intends to write a series of articles for the *LA Times* about celebrity spouses and their daily problems and challenges with the media and the paparazzi. Your client inquires whether she is required to seek licenses to use the names and likenesses of the spouses to add context to the series of articles. What advice will you provide your client regarding the need to seek licenses for your client's proposed uses? What options might your client exploit if the spouses insist on withholding permission to use their respective rights of publicity?

3. Topps obtained rights of publicity from baseball players by means of individual contracts for exclusive licenses. The contracts assigned to Topps the exclusive right to publish the players' names, pictures, signatures, and biographical sketches "to be sold either alone or in combination with chewing gum, candy and confection, or any of them." The Major League Baseball Players Association (MLBPA) also contracted with baseball players to merchandise their publicity rights. Virtually all players, once they become members of a major league team, sign a commercial authorization agreement with the MLBPA. This agreement grants the MLBPA the exclusive right to convey group licenses to others to use the player's name, signature, and picture. The agreement excluded group-licensing contracts with merchandisers for rights covered by players' contracts respecting competitive products like the Topps contract. By virtue of its contract, does the MLBPA have the authority to license to any merchandiser the right to sell baseball cards alone or in combination with chewing gum, candy and confection? Is a licensor able to enter into multiple exclusive licenses? In what context would multiple exclusive licenses be permissible? *See* Topps Chewing Gum, Inc. v. Fleer Corp., 799 F.2d 851 (2d Cir. 1986).

4. In *Miller v. Glenn Miller Prods., Inc.*, Helen Miller executed a 1956-written license agreement with GMP for consideration of $1.00. In addition to this agreement, Helen Miller was elected to the Board of Directors of GMP and owned 50 percent of the shares of GMP. Ostensibly, Helen Miller received $13,000 per year in return for her permission for GMP to use Miller's right of publicity.

   Critique the structure of the license agreement and the method, manner, and documentation of payments to Helen Miller. Would you have structured the deal in the same way the case reflects? If not, how would you have structured the 1956 agreement and the payments to Helen Miller? When responding to these questions, consider the structure of the following NFL Player Contract:

   > 4. . . . (b) Player . . . hereby assigns to the NFLPA (National Football League Players Association) and its licensing affiliates, if any, the exclusive right to use and to grant to persons, firms or corporations (collectively "licensees") the right to use his name, signature facsimile, voice, picture, photograph, likeness, and/or biographical information (collectively "image") in group licensing programs. Group licensing programs are defined as those licensing programs in which a licensee utilizes a total of six (6) or more NFL player images on products that are sold at retail or used as promotional or premium items. . . .
   >
   > The assignment in this paragraph shall expire on December 31 of the later of (a) the third year following the execution of this contract, or (b) the year in which this contract expires.

22. . . . LAW. This contract is made under and shall be governed by the laws of the State of Tennessee.

23. In exchange for the assignment in paragraph 4, Player receives a signing bonus in the amount of $3,000.00.

5. Conference USA intends to work with its 20 member schools to develop better relations with their students-athletes by proposing new initiatives that will benefit student-athletes by offering athletic aid to cover the full cost of attendance, provide multi-year grants, and encourage former student athletes to continue their education by providing athletic aid.

The conference will need its member schools to present their student-athletes with the maximum amount of athletic aid allowed by NCAA bylaws, according to the release; grant student athletes with multi-year scholarships throughout the entirety of their eligibility; and award former student athletes with athletic aid if they leave their respective school before they meet their degree requirements.

In exchange, Conference USA mandates that all student-athletes sign the following release:

> Student-Athlete Name and Likeness Release Form
>
> I hereby grant and assign to Conference USA the right to publish, duplicate, print, broadcast or otherwise use in any manner or media, my name, photograph, likeness or other image of myself for any purpose Conference USA determines, in its sole discretion, as in the interest of Conference USA, including without limitation uses in promotional and marketing materials and uses by CBS Sports Network, FOX Sports Networks, American Sports Network and ESPN. All such uses shall be consistent with all applicable NCAA and Conference USA rules and regulations. I agree that neither I nor my heirs shall be entitled to any compensation for the use of my name, photograph, likeness or other image of myself.

What are the implications for student-athletes who agree to sign the release?

What are the implications for student-athletes who refuse to sign the release?

Assuming the NCAA does not consider this exchange a violation of amateurism rules, are these new initiatives responsive to the tensions between and among student-athletes, educational institutions, athletic conferences, television networks, and licensing agencies?

IV. DRAFTING EXERCISES

1. Big Kahuna Surf Magazine is running a contest for the best surf pictures of the month. Big Kahuna requires prospective entrants to comply with the following content submission provision, which states:

> All submissions must include: the Photographic Content; your name, mailing address, and email address; a statement that you are the creator of the

Photographic Content, if true; and a statement that you have obtained model releases for the subjects of the Photographic Content, if you have obtained such releases.

Your newest client, a fine print photographic artist, asks for your assistance to draft a one-paragraph model release agreement that she can use in connection with Big Kahuna's content submission requirements but that can also be used to satisfy future content submission requirements. Your client photographs many individuals, both adults and minors, involved in water sports, such as surfing, swimming, and body boarding. Below is a boilerplate model release provision that your law firm has used on several occasions.

I give _____ permission to record my image and give all rights to use my image in any medium for advertising purposes consistent with the business of print photography. I agree that all rights to the images belong to _____.

You may use this boilerplate as a starting point or you may choose to draft the model release form from scratch.

2. Using the information from and your responses to the questions in Problem 4, draft the right of publicity license grant and royalty provisions to compensate Helen Miller and then draft a bequest of Helen Miller's interest in Glenn Miller's post-mortem rights of publicity for the benefit of the children, Jonnie and Steven Miller.

3. The elements of a Lanham Act false endorsement claim are similar to the elements of a right of publicity claim under many state laws. In fact, one legal scholar has said that the Lanham Act false endorsement claim is the federal equivalent of the rights of publicity. *See* Bruce P. Keller, *The Right of Publicity: Past, Present, and Future*, 1207 PLI CORP. LAW AND PRAC. HANDBOOK 159, 170 (October 2000). Following upon this suggestion, use the language of §43(a) of the Lanham Act and the state statutory examples below to guide you in drafting a proposed federal right of publicity statute. How would you account for the modified *Lapp* factors in drafting your proposed federal statute? *See* Facenda v. N.F.L. Films, Inc., 542 F.3d 1007 (3d Cir. 2008).

• The Lanham Act (False Endorsement), §43(a) provides:

(a) Civil action
    (1) Any person who, on or in connection with any goods or services, or any container for goods, uses in commerce any word, term, name, symbol, or device, or any combination thereof, or any false designation of origin, false or misleading description of fact, or false or misleading representation of fact, which —

    (A) is likely to cause confusion, or to cause mistake, or to deceive as to the affiliation, connection, or association of such person with another person, or as to the origin, sponsorship, or approval of his or her goods, services, or commercial activities by another person, or

(B) in commercial advertising or promotion, misrepresents the nature, characteristics, qualities, or geographic origin of his or her or another person's goods, services, or commercial activities,

shall be liable in a civil action by any person who believes that he or she is or is likely to be damaged by such act.

- The California Civil Code, §3344 provides, in part:

(a) Any person who knowingly uses another's name, voice, signature, photograph, or likeness, in any manner, on or in products, merchandise, or goods, or for purposes of advertising or selling, or soliciting purchases of, products, merchandise, goods or services, without such person's prior consent, or, in the case of a minor, the prior consent of his parent or legal guardian, shall be liable for any damages sustained by the person or persons injured as a result thereof.

- The Tennessee Code Annotated, §47-25-1105 provides, in part:

(a) Any person who knowingly uses or infringes upon the use of another individual's name, photograph, or likeness in any medium, in any manner directed to any person other than such individual, as an item of commerce for purposes of advertising products, merchandise, goods, or services, or for purposes of fund raising, solicitation of donations, purchases of products, merchandise, goods, or services, without such individual's prior consent, or, in the case of a minor, the prior consent of such minor's parent or legal guardian, or in the case of a deceased individual, the consent of the executor or administrator, heirs, or devisees of such deceased individual, shall be liable to a civil action.

4. Using the information from your responses to the questions in Problem 5, assume you are an athletics compliance officer at a Division I school within Conference USA. In your position, you are required to obtain updated student-athlete signatures after first providing a presentation to all student-athletes of the new release form from Conference USA and the new initiatives. What information will you include in your presentation to the student-athletes? Explain.

PATENT LICENSING

I. OVERVIEW OF PATENT LICENSING

A. Introduction

Patentees can be individuals, small businesses, universities, partnerships, or corporations that hold a patent or patents. To benefit from their patents, many patentees manufacture and market products based on their patents. Most other patentees, however, do not have the resources or expertise to do this. These patentees can still benefit by selling the patent, assigning a portion of it, or granting an exclusive or non-exclusive license to a third party.

Patent licensing arrangements occur in various business transactions, corporate structures, and litigation settlements:

- Dr. James A. Thomson of the University of Wisconsin was the first to isolate human embryonic stem cells. The Wisconsin Alumni Research Foundation, which handles the University of Wisconsin's technology transfers, holds the important patents on stem cells discovered by Dr. Thomson. Dr. Thomson's work was financed by the Geron Corporation, a biotechnology company based in Menlo Park, California. The Foundation granted Geron Corporation an exclusive patent license to three types of cells made from the embryonic cells: neural cells, heart cells, and pancreatic islet cells, which produce insulin.
- Philips, Sony, and Ricoh pool their patents relating to rewritable compact discs, and the companies together license the patent pool to third-party entities that want to manufacture CD-RWs.
- Qimonda's bankruptcy estate consisted of some 10,000 patents. Qimonda cross-licensed its patents to competitors. Cross-licensing is a common strategy in the semiconductor industry to avoid infringement risks caused by the "patent thicket," a dense web of overlapping patent rights of some 420,000 patents in the semiconductor industry.

- The W.L. Gore Company sells its ubiquitous "Gore-tex" technology in the United States. The Company holds a number of patents related to the breathable, synthetic fabric beloved by sports enthusiasts. The Company formed a wholly owned subsidiary, Gore Enterprise Holdings ("Holdings"), in Delaware as a holding company for its patents. The Company transferred to Holdings all of its patents in return for Holdings' stock. Holdings then exclusively licensed those patents back to the Company. The royalty rate was set at 7.5 percent of the sales price of all products the Company makes and sells in the United States.
- Entity A holds a broad patent and grants Company B a license to use the patent. Company B will most likely make improvements on the patent and render the technology covered by the patent obsolete. The license agreement provides that Company B gives Entity A non-exclusive "grant backs" to practice the improvements and Company B retains title and all rights in the improvements.
- Hitachi, Ltd., headquartered in Tokyo, Japan, is a leading global electronics company. In 2003, Hitachi and Mitsubishi Electric Corporation established Renesas Technology Corporation as a joint-venture to design and manufacture highly integrated semiconductor system solutions for mobile, networking, automotive, industrial, and digital home electronics markets. Renesas Technology is one of the largest semiconductor companies in the world and microcontroller suppliers globally. Hitachi/Renesas became embroiled in patent litigation with International Rectifier Corporation in the United States and Japan. In 2004, the companies settled all outstanding litigation in the United States and Japan. The agreement provided for a patent cross-license agreement among the companies, recognizing the value of each party's intellectual property rights.

The examples above illustrate that patent licensing today has become increasingly complex as it crosses national borders and as it traverses numerous legal regimes, from contract to antitrust, bankruptcy, and tax law.

B. Assignment Versus License of Patents

A patent holder can either assign or license patents to others. An assignment usually means the transfer of the owner's legal title and all rights in the patent to the assignee. The assignee can now do whatever it wants with the patent within the confines of the law. The assignee can bring suit and enjoin others from infringement of the patents. If the patentee decides not to assign all of its legal rights and title in the patents, the patentee may choose to license the patents. Can an owner of a patent with several claims assign a single claim, so as to convey the legal title, or enable the assignee to sue thereon in his own name? Such an assignment is a mere license. See Pope Mfg. Co. v. Gormully & Jeffery Mfg. Co., 144 U.S. 248 (1892).

A license grant generally conveys the patentee's permission to enjoy exclusively or non-exclusively some or all of the statutory exclusionary rights under 35 U.S.C. §271 for a limited time and purpose, within a geographic area, and in a certain distribution channel. The licensee has no fear of an infringement and breach of contract suit from the patentee, as long as the licensee's conduct is within the scope of the license grant. Can a licensee unilaterally bring an infringement suit against a third party? A mere licensee does not have all rights in the patent to confer standing to bring an infringement suit without including the patentee as co-plaintiff.

Whether a transfer is an assignment or a license is important to the parties to the contract. The assignment severs the patentee's ownership in the patent. Under a license, the patentee still owns the patent. Additionally, the parties to a patent transfer are concerned about whether the transfer is an assignment or a license for tax and bankruptcy reasons. *See* Chapters 14 and 15.

In the employment context, if an employee was hired to research and develop a product or a process, the employee is required to assign his or her invention to the employer. *See* United States v. Dubilier Condenser Corp., 289 U.S. 178 (1933). If the employment, however, is general in scope but covers a field of labor and effort in the performance of which the employee conceived the invention for which he or she later obtained a patent, the employee is not required to assign the patent to the employer. Some states have statutes protecting employees and their rights in inventions. California Labor Code §2870 (West 2017) provides that employee invention assignment agreements may not require assignment of inventions that the employee developed entirely on his or her own time without using the employer's equipment, supplies, facilities, or trade secret information "except for those inventions" that either (1) relate to the employer's business, research or development; or (2) result from the work performed by the employee for the employer.

The employee, however, must grant the employer a "shop right" or a royalty-free, non-exclusive license to use the invention when the circumstances demand it, under principles of equity and fairness. *See* McElmurry v. Arkansas Power & Light Co., 995 F.2d 1576 (Fed. Cir. 1993) (holding the power company had acquired "shop right" in patented level detector developed by its employee at the company's expense). The employer may transfer the "shop right" as part of a transfer of the business, but may not separately assign or license the "shop right" to others. *See* Pure Oil Co. v. Hyman, 95 F.2d 22 (Ct. Cust. App. 1938); Tripp v. United States, 406 F.2d 1066 (Ct. Cl. 1969).

C. Patent License Grant

A patent holder is free to decide what it wants to include in the license grant, as long as the law permits it. There are multiple ways the patent holder can "slice and dice" its patents in license agreements for economic reasons and strategic partnership alliances, as long as the law permits. It may want to license the patents for use only in a particular territory, such as in the United States or the European Union assuming that it owns patents in the relevant countries. It may permit the licensee to use the patents only in defined fields of use and reserve its rights in the remainder. It may wish to provide an exclusive or non-exclusive license, charge a certain royalty rate or license royalty-free, reserve the right to use any improvements on the licensed patents subsequently created by the licensee, and set the length of the license term, among other possibilities.

Below is a sample provision of an exclusive license to use the licensed patents within a specific territory and for a specific field of use.

Licensor grants Licensee an exclusive right and sublicense to utilize the Patent Rights, in the United States, in the production, manufacture, and sale of trophies and trophy component parts.

Numerous factors may influence the patent holder's decision on the scope of the license grant with a potential licensee. For example, a research institution may decline to grant an exclusive license of a fundamental patent because it wants more individuals and entities to gain access to the patented inventions for further scientific and educational research purposes. A patentee may entice a well-financed licensee to enter into a long-term license arrangement by granting the licensee the exclusive license to use and exploit the patent. A different patentee may decide to have several non-exclusive licensees to exploit its patent because it does not want to be in an exclusive license arrangement where the licensee fails to commercialize the patent.

Generally, an exclusive license is a license to practice the patented invention accompanied by the patentee's promise that "others shall be excluded from practicing it within the field of use wherein the licensee is given leave." Textile Prods., Inc. v. Mead Corp., 134 F.3d 1481, 1484 (Fed. Cir. 1998). Therefore, an exclusive license gives the licensee the status of being the only party that receives the license grant from the licensor. If the license is exclusive, it may be tantamount to an assignment of the patent. *See* Group One, Ltd. v. Hallmark Cards, Inc., 254 F.3d 1041, 1053 (Fed. Cir. 2001). An exclusive licensee of all substantial rights, including the right to sue, may bring an infringement action against a third party without the need to include the licensor as a co-plaintiff. An exclusive license is generally recorded with the Patent Office. An exclusive license agreement may be transferable without authorization from the licensor.

A non-exclusive license means that the licensor does not grant its rights in the patents to only one licensee. The licensor has the right to either exercise its exclusive rights or license rights to a third party. The licensor and/or the third party can use the rights in the same area where the non-exclusive licensee is operating. The economic rationale for a non-exclusive licensing arrangement is to force the non-exclusive licensee to drive down its profit margin, creating competition among the non-exclusive licensees and generating more licensed products to be sold, and thereby increasing the patentee's profit. A non-exclusive patent license is often viewed either as an agreement to forebear from suit or a covenant not to sue.

Here are two examples of non-exclusive patent license provisions.

1. Licensor grants Licensee a non-transferable, non-exclusive license under Licensed Patents to make, use, and sell Licensed Products in the Field and in the Territory.
2. Licensor grants Licensee non-exclusive, non-transferable, royalty-free, worldwide licenses under Licensor Patents and Licensor Patent Applications to make, to have made, to use, to sell (either directly or indirectly), to lease, and to otherwise dispose of Licensed Products.

D. Patent License Misuse and Antitrust

Parties to a patent license have lots of flexibility in putting together the most beneficial and advantageous license arrangement. However, not all terms in the license agreement will be enforced. The bright line rule established under Brulotte v. Thys Co., 379 U.S. 29 (1964) prohibits a patent holder from collecting royalties pursuant to contract after the patent term has expired. Freedom of contract is not a defense to established public policies embodied in patent misuse and antitrust laws. If a patent misuse or antitrust violation is established, the license arrangement will be unenforceable.

Patent misuse practices themselves do not violate any law, but are equitable defenses to patent infringement. It is often raised if the patentee claims that the licensee has exceeded the scope of the license or to comply with a license-related obligation. The patent misuse doctrine originated to restrain a variety of abuses of the patent monopoly. See Princo v. ITC, 616 F.3d 1318 (Fed. Cir. 2010) (en banc), which is included in the Materials section of this chapter.

Patent misuse occurs when the patentee has impermissibly broadened the "physical or temporal scope" of the patent grant with anticompetitive effect. The policy of the patent misuse doctrine is to prevent the patentee from abusing its patent monopoly to obtain market benefit beyond what the patent statute provides. In 1988, the patent misuse statute, 35 U.S.C. §271(d), was amended, providing that in the absence of market power, conduct such as tying arrangements and refusals to license patents to others may not be characterized as patent misuse. What are the factors courts apply in analyzing whether the patentee's practice, including license arrangements, impose an unreasonable restraint on competition? See Princo v. ITC, 616 F.3d 1318 (Fed Cir. 2010) (en banc) (providing a comprehensive review of patent misuse doctrine development).

In addition to patent misuse, a license arrangement may be subject to scrutiny under antitrust law principles. See Princo v. ITC below in the Materials section. With respect to antitrust violations stemming from a patent license arrangement, if a patentee licenses its patents in ways that extend the patentee's dominance and monopoly in an industry, the license arrangement may run afoul of antitrust laws. Also, if the patentee, through licensing arrangements, seeks to control the conduct of the licensee by fixing prices and illegal tying, the license arrangement may face antitrust scrutiny. Ownership of a patent, in and of itself, does not confer market power on the patentee who uses the patent in a "tying" arrangement. See Illinois Tool Works Inc. v. Independent Ink, Inc., 547 U.S. 28 (2006). In the Illinois Tool Works case the patentees manufactured and marketed printing systems that included a patented printhead and ink container, and unpatented ink. The patentees sold to original equipment manufacturers who agreed that they would purchase ink exclusively from the patentees and that neither they nor their customers would refill the patented containers with ink of any kind. The Supreme Court held that in these tying arrangements, the plaintiff of the antitrust claim must prove that the defendant patentee has market power in the tying product. There is no presumption of market power from the ownership of the patent alone.

Additionally, it is not uncommon for the licensee to allege patent misuse or an antitrust violation to avoid compliance with other provisions in the patent license agreement or to assert it as a defense in breach of contract and infringement actions brought by the licensor. Also, a defendant may assert patent misuse or an antitrust violation as an affirmative defense in an infringement action brought by the licensor and licensee co-plaintiffs.

In 1995, the U.S. Department of Justice and the Federal Trade Commission jointly issued the Antitrust Guidelines for the Licensing of Intellectual Property. The Guidelines outline the United States government's antitrust enforcement policy with respect to the licensing of patents, copyrights, and trade secrets. The Guidelines address a number of licensing practices such as patent pooling, cross-licensing, and grant backs. The purpose of the Guidelines is to assist concerned parties "who need to predict whether the Agencies will challenge a practice as anticompetitive." The Materials section of this chapter provides a pointer to the latest update to these Guidelines.

E. Standards and Patents

Countless new technologies communicate with each other in myriad ways that enhance the user's experience and increase productivity. In fact, users have learned to expect compatibility and connectivity every time they purchase or use a new device, service or technology. Licensing plays a key role in achieving the compatibility and connectivity of technologies through standard setting involving patents. Standard-setting issues are of global concern as patents are owned by companies across borders and technologies are produced for users worldwide. WIPO has the following comments on Standards and Patents:

> Standards are essential for the wide adoption of new technologies in the marketplace. The potential for conflict between patents and standards arises when the implementation of the standard necessitates the use of technology protected by one or more patents. Although the objective of a standard setting body (SSB) as well as of participating companies is to establish standardized technology that can be used as widely as possible, rightholders may have a commercial interest in pushing for the adoption of their own patented technology in the framework of the standard, so that they could benefit from royalties. If a patent owner can, however, block the implementation of the standard by refusing a license or claiming unreasonably high royalties, this would obviously be against the objective of the technical standardization process.
>
> In order to minimize this risk of conflict and to assure a smooth and wide dissemination of standardized technology, most SSBs have established their own patent policy. For example, many SSBs require the parties involved in the standard-setting process to disclose information regarding relevant patents (and, sometimes, also patent applications), in order to include the relevant information into the standard-setting process. If any relevant patent (or patent application) exists, many SSBs require the patentee to agree on specific licensing conditions, such as that the license must be granted under reasonable and non-discriminatory terms (RAND license) or that the

license must be royalty free (RF). However, in general, the SSBs are not involved in either arrangements related to patents (such as license agreements) or in settling disputes in respect of the validity and scope of the relevant patents. As with any other policy issues, if the patent policy has not been drafted in a clear and unambiguous manner, different interpretations may be the source of disputes among the parties with respect to their obligations.

One way to address the situation where different patentees own a number of patents relevant to the standard is to set up a patent pool. Although each patent pool may be different, typically, a pool enables participating patentees to use the pooled patents, provides a standard license in respect of the pooled patents for licensees who are not members of the pool, and allocates to each member of the pool a portion of the licensing fees in accordance with the agreement. Patent pool agreements may provide competitive benefits through, for example, bundling patented technologies, removing patent-blockages or avoiding the need to conclude multiple licenses. On the other hand, certain types of patent pool agreements, for example, where they include patents that are substitutes for each other, may raise concerns as to their effect on competition.

As anticipated, disputes relating standards and patent licensing have become the subject of litigation around the world. In India, for example, there are many ongoing court cases on standard essential patents on Fair, Reasonable and Non-Discriminatory (FRAND) terms in the mobile phone industry. In the United States, there are also many pending disputes at the district court level. In recent years, some cases have reached the appellate courts. Microsoft v. Motorola, Inc., 795 F.3d 1024 (9th Cir. 2015) is illustrative of disputes involving RAND license terms.

F. Restrictions, Conditions, and Patent Exhaustion

In a license arrangement, the patent licensor can narrow the scope of the license grant by imposing restrictions on the license. The restrictions may include, for example, "territorial restrictions" and "fields of use" restrictions. *See* 35 U.S.C. §261; General Talking Pictures Corp. v. Western Elec. Co., 304 U.S. 124, 127 (1938).

End users and remanufacturers typically do not like restrictions or conditions imposed on their use or resale of patented products. The Supreme Court in three recent cases on patent exhaustion has greatly limited the patent licensor's ability to impose these types of restrictions or conditions in license agreements. *See* Quanta Computer, Inc. v. LG Electronics, Inc., 553 U.S. 617 (2008); Bowman v. Monsanto, 133 S. Ct. 1761, 1766 (2013); Impression Products, Inc. v. Lexmark International Inc., 137 S. Ct. 1523 (2017).

Under the patent exhaustion doctrine, when a patentee authorizes the sale of a patented product, the patentee cannot use patent law remedies to impose post-sale conditions or restrictions on use or resale of the patented product. Once the patent holder sells an item, the patent holder cannot use patent law to prohibit a consumer or dealer from using or reselling that item as it chooses. Patent exhaustion marks the transition where patent rights yield to the personal property rights of the purchaser of a patented product. Can the sale of a product that does not fully practice the invention still trigger "patent exhaustion"? What if the product covers the essential features of the patent, "substantially embodies the patent," and the product's "only and intended use" is to practice the patent? What if the sale is unauthorized? See the excerpt of Quanta Computer, Inc. v. LG Electronics, Inc., 553 U.S. 617 (2008), below in the Materials section.

In a recent case, Impression Products, Inc. v. Lexmark International Inc., the Supreme Court held that Lexmark's decision to sell its printer cartridges "exhausts all of its patent rights in that item, regardless of any restrictions the patentee purports to impose or the location of the sale." Thus, Lexmark could not use patent law remedies to enforce the single-use/no-resale provision accompanying its Return Program printer cartridges. However, Lexmark could resort to contract or tort law remedies to enforce its single-use/no resale provision. An excerpt of the *Impression Products* opinion is included in the Materials section of this chapter.

The patent exhaustion doctrine, however, only limits a patentee's ability to control use or resale of a particular article sold. That means the patentee still has the "ability to prevent a buyer from making new copies of the patented item." *See* Bowman v. Monsanto, 133 S. Ct. 1761, 1766 (2013), which is contained in the Materials section of Chapter 1. In Bowman v. Monsanto, Co., Monsanto placed restrictions on reproduction of its patented soybeans. Under Monsanto's license agreement, a grower could plant the licensed seeds in one and only one season but could not save any of the harvested seeds for replanting. Bowman, in violation of the license agreement, asserted a defense of patent exhaustion. The Court rejected Bowman's defense, explaining:

> Under the patent exhaustion doctrine, Bowman could resell the patented soybeans he purchased from the grain elevator; so too he could consume the beans himself or feed them to his animals. Monsanto, although the patent holder, would have no business interfering in those uses of Roundup Ready beans. But the exhaustion doctrine does not enable Bowman to make additional patented soybeans without Monsanto's permission (either express or implied). And that is precisely what Bowman did. He took the soybeans he purchased home; planted them in his fields at the time he thought best; applied glyphosate to kill weeds (as well as any soy plants lacking the Roundup Ready trait); and finally harvested more (many more) beans than he started with. That is how "to 'make' a new product," to use Bowman's words, when the original product is a seed. Because Bowman thus reproduced Monsanto's patented invention, the exhaustion doctrine does not protect him.

In light of recent Supreme Court decisions on patent exhaustion, licensors must think carefully about drafting restrictions and conditions in patent license agreements. Often, post-sale restrictions or conditions on patented products will not be enforceable using patent law remedies, so the patentee must consider whether contract or tort remedies will suffice.

G. Litigation Issues in Patent Licensing

1. Standing and Jurisdiction

The patentee may bring an action for patent infringement. A licensee is generally not entitled to bring suit in its own name as a patentee, unless the licensee holds "all substantial rights" under the patent. Ortho Pharm. Corp. v. Genetics Inst., Inc., 52 F.3d 1026, 1034 (Fed. Cir. 1995) (stating that bare licensees have no standing to bring suit); Vaupel Textilmaschinen KG v. Meccanica Euro Italia s.p.a., 944 F.2d 870, 875 (Fed. Cir. 1991). The Supreme Court recognized one exception to the general rule and permitted the exclusive licensee who did not have all the substantial rights the standing to bring suit where it is "necessary to prevent an absolute failure of justice, as where the patentee is the infringer, and cannot sue himself." Waterman v. Mackenzie, 138 U.S. 252, 255 (1891). *See also* Ortho Pharm. Corp. v. Genetics Inst., Inc., 52 F.3d 1026, 1030 (Fed. Cir. 1995).

In a dispute between the licensor and licensee relating to the patent license agreement, which forum, federal or state, is appropriate to resolve the dispute? The Supreme Court has long observed that the federal courts do not have jurisdiction over an action by a patentee for royalties under a license or assignment or for any remedy arising from a license permitting use of the patent. *See* Luckett v. Delpark, Inc., 270 U.S. 496, 502-09 (1926) (analyzing cases). On the other hand, the federal courts do have subject matter jurisdiction if the dispute between the licensor and the licensee is dependent on questions arising under patent law. For example, in U.S. Valves, Inc. v. Dray, 212 F.3d 1368 (Fed. Cir. 2000), the Federal Circuit held that the district court had jurisdiction in a case where the patentee granted the exclusive right to manufacture, use, sell, advertise, and distribute the patented invention. *Dray*, 212 F.3d at 1370. Subsequently, the parties' relationship strained and the licensee sued the patentee, alleging breach of contract due to the patentee's manufacture and sale of products covered by the license agreement. The Federal Circuit in *Dray* concluded that the licensee's breach of contract claim raised substantial issues of patent law because the success of the claim depended on demonstrating that the valves sold by the patentee were within the scope of the subject patents.

Generally, when a case involves substantive issues of patent law, the Court of Appeals for the Federal Circuit has the appellate jurisdiction to adjudicate the case. The Federal Circuit's jurisdiction does not attach when the patent issue is raised for the first time in a defendant's counterclaim. Appellate jurisdiction in such a case is with the other federal circuit courts. For example, in Schinzing v. Mid-States Stainless, Inc., 415 F.3d 807 (8th Cir. 2005), the Eighth Circuit maintained the appellate jurisdiction in a case where the plaintiff brought an action in state court against the defendant for breach of the license agreement by failing to pay royalties on washers after the termination of the license agreement. The defendant removed the case to federal court and counterclaimed for a declaratory judgment of patent invalidity and non-infringement. *Schinzing*, 415 F.3d at 807. Since the patent issues arose solely from the defendant's counterclaim, the *Schinzing* court concluded that it had jurisdiction over the case.

2. Licensee Estoppel Defense

Before the Supreme Court's ruling in Lear, Inc. v. Adkins, 395 U.S. 653, 655 (1969), a licensee was estopped from denying the validity of the licensed patent in a suit for royalties under the license agreement. The rationale behind the doctrine of licensee estoppel was that the licensee should not be allowed to assert that the underlying patent is invalid while it was enjoying the benefits of the license agreement. *Lear* overruled the doctrine of licensee estoppel, holding that a licensee may challenge the validity of the patent and that if the licensee is successful in establishing invalidity, it does not need to pay the royalties accrued under the license agreement. The holding encourages licensees to challenge the validity of patents, and it ensures that the public interest is served when only inventions which meet the rigorous requirements of patentability should be granted the monopoly and kept from the public domain for the term of the patent. *See Lear*, 395 U.S. at 653, 655.

Under the *Lear* doctrine, not every licensee in any circumstance has the right to challenge the validity of the licensed patent. In several instances, the Federal Circuit has either limited or declined to apply the *Lear* doctrine. *See, e.g.*, Flex-Foot, Inc. v. CRP, Inc., 238 F.3d 1362, 1368-70 (Fed. Cir. 2001); Studiengesellschaft Kohle, mbH v. Shell Oil Co., 112 F.3d 1561, 1567-68 (Fed. Cir. 1997), which is included in the Materials section of this chapter.

A licensee seeking a declaratory judgment of patent invalidity is not required to terminate or breach the patent license agreement prior to filing for the declaratory judgment action. MedImmune, Inc. v. Genentech, Inc., 549 U.S. 118 (2007). The *MedImmune* decision overturned the Federal Circuit's ruling in Gen-Probe Inc. v. Vysis, Inc., 359 F.3d 1376 (2004), which had held that a patent licensee in good standing cannot establish a declaratory judgment action with regard to validity, enforceability, or scope of the patent because the license agreement "obliterate[s] any reasonable apprehension" that the licensee will be sued for infringement. *MedImmune*, 549 U.S. at 122. The *MedImmune* Court reasoned that "[p]romising to pay royalties on patents that have not been held invalid does not amount to a promise *not to seek* a holding of their invalidity." *Id.* at 135. When a licensee seeks a declaratory judgment against the patentee licensor that there is no infringement, the burden of proving infringement remains with the patentee. Medtronic, Inc. v. Mirowski Family Ventures, LLC, 134 S. Ct. 843 (2014).

H. International Issues in Patent Licensing

International patent licensing arrangements often involve a host of challenging legal and non-legal issues, including parallel imports, compulsory licensing, antitrust, export controls, and taxation. *See* LaserDynamics, Inc. v. Quanta Computer, Inc., 694 F.3d 51 (2012), which is included in the Materials section of this chapter. The patent exhaustion doctrine, as emphasized in Impression Products v. Lexmark International, 137 S. Ct. 1523 (2017), eliminates the use of patent law remedies to enforce post-sale restrictions or conditions on patented products regardless of their location. An authorized sale of patented products outside the United States exhausts all of the patentee's rights everywhere. Even if the patentee has expressly prohibited reuse and resale of the patented products, patent exhaustion doctrine does not permit the patentee to sue remanufacturers for patent infringement if they import refurbished patented products into the United States. Any enforcement would have to come from a suit for breach of contract.

Parallel imports or "gray market" goods are goods that have been marketed outside the United States with authorization of the intellectual property owners and are then imported back into the United States without the owner's consent. The goods are distinct from counterfeits, which have been manufactured without the authorization of the intellectual property owners. Price discrimination and free-riding have been identified as the two main reasons for parallel importing. Parallel importation allows a country to seek and obtain lower prices for the same patented product from anywhere in the global market. In countries where parallel imports are permitted it means that patent rights are exhausted once the patented products are marketed the first time with the authorization of the patent owner. The exhaustion is "global."

In the United States, parallel imports or "gray market" goods covered by patents are not permitted. *See* Shubha Ghosh, *State Creation of Gray Markets as a Limit on Patent Rights*, 14 FLA. J. INT'L L. 217, 221 (2002) (noting that U.S. patent law offers the strongest protection against the gray market, but gray markets covered by patents in the United States are extremely rare). With respect to parallel imports of patented products between countries, the European Union has adopted community exhaustion for goods covered by patents, copyrights, and trademarks. That means that parallel imports of such goods between countries inside the EU are permitted, but not from outside the EU. Many developing countries, however, do not restrict parallel imports of goods covered by intellectual property.

The lack of resources and access to drugs to treat deadly diseases such as AIDS has forced countries who are members of the World Trade Organization to rely on "compulsory licensing" under the TRIPS (Trade-Related Aspects of Intellectual Property Rights) Agreement. According to Article 31 of the TRIPS Agreement, compulsory licensing is the "use of subject matter without the authorization of the right holder." That means WTO members can use patented drugs without authorization of the patentee if the uses, as described in Article 31(b), are: (i) a "national emergency or other circumstances of extreme urgency"; and (ii) a "public non-commercial use." Relying on Article 31 of the TRIPS Agreement, a government would authorize local companies to produce generic versions of the patented drugs for the treatment of diseases such as AIDS where the disease has become an epidemic. *See* Carlos M. Correa, *Investment Protection in Bilateral and Free Trade Agreements: Implications for the Granting of Compulsory Licenses*, 26 MICH. J. INT'L L. 331 (2004) (describing disputes between the United States and South Africa and Brazil with respect to compulsory licenses of the AIDS drugs).

Many governments of developing countries have been afraid of economic and political ramifications if they dared to exercise compulsory licenses under Article 31.

In November 2001, the WTO issued the Doha Declaration to address this concern. The Doha Declaration states "[the] TRIPS Agreement *does not* and *should not* prevent members from taking measures to protect public health . . . [and it] should be interpreted and implemented in a manner supportive of WTO members' right to protect public health and, in particular, to promote access to medicines for all" (emphasis added). The Doha Declaration also reaffirms WTO member countries' rights to use compulsory licenses, to determine what constitutes a national emergency, and to determine their own regime for the exhaustion of intellectual property rights.

In addition, patentees engaging in international patent licensing must be aware of competition and antitrust laws in various countries. Freedom of contract allows parties from different countries to engage in licensing arrangements; however, it does not mean that the parties can engage in conduct or include terms in the license agreement contrary to law and public policy. Competition laws in other countries are different from U.S. laws and impose different requirements relating to licensing. For example, in 1989, the Japanese Fair Trade Commission (JFTC) promulgated rules governing restrictions in international patent licensing agreements. Also, the Japan Antimonopoly Act imposes a filing requirement to ensure that international licensing agreements do not contain illegal restrictive provisions. The notification and a copy of patents and other technology-based agreements are required to be filed with the government within 30 days of the execution of the agreement. Failure to file will result in fines. The JFTC reviews the filings for possible violations of Japanese antitrust laws. Likewise, the European Union has its Competition and Antitrust laws, and its regulators ensure that patent licensing arrangements are in compliance with the laws. *See* James F. Rill & Mark C. Schechter, *International Antitrust and Intellectual Property Harmonization of the Interface*, 34 LAW & POL'Y INT'L BUS. 783 (2003) (discussing the disparity between the United States and other jurisdictions, like the EU, Japan, and Taiwan, on antitrust laws relating to patents).

II. MATERIALS

This Materials section includes excerpts from several cases. In the first case, Princo v. ITC, 616 F.3d 1318 (Fed. Cir. 2010) (en banc), you will read about the pooling and packaging of patents for licensing arrangements. In this rare en banc decision, the Federal Circuit addresses whether the patent licensing arrangements at issue violate patent misuse and antitrust laws. The Federal Circuit restricts patent misuse to situations in which a patentee has used a particular patent to leverage its power beyond the scope of that patent. Exclusionary use of a separate patent as part of a licensing agreement involving the patent-in-suit, on the other hand, may violate antitrust laws without patent misuse.

Next come three cases, Speedplay, Inc. v. Bebop, Inc., 211 F.3d 1245 (Fed. Cir. 2000), Studiengesellschaft Kohle, mbH v. Shell Oil Co., 112 F.3d 1561 (Fed. Cir. 1997), and Kimble v. Marvel Entertainment, 135 S. Ct. 2401 (2015). *Speedplay* centers on whether the licensee has standing to bring a patent infringement action against a third party. *Studiengesellschaft Kohle* explains when the licensee can challenge the validity of the licensed patent, and whether or not the licensee must cease royalty payments under the license agreement before it can invoke the protection under *Lear* doctrine. *Kimble* focuses on whether the bright line rule under *Brulotte* that prohibits patent holders to charge royalties for the use of patents after the patent term has expired should be overturned and discusses how patent licenses can be structured to avoid the concerns of *Brulotte*.

Next, Texas Instruments, Inc. v. Tessera, Inc., 231 F.3d 1325 (Fed. Cir. 2000), provides an example of a contract dispute wherein the parties disagreed over the contractual interpretation of the patent license agreement, specifically the governing law and venue provisions. Intel Corp. v. Negotiated Data Solutions, Inc., 703 F.3d 1360 (Fed. Cir. 2012), focuses on whether the scope of the patent license grant covers the reissue patents that are derived from the licensed patents. JP Morgan Chase Bank, N.A. v. Data Treasury Corp., 823 F.3d 1006 (5th Cir. 2016), is a case of first impression on "most favored licensee" clause, offering a valuable lesson on careful drafting of license terms.

Two important Supreme Court cases address patent exhaustion and license restrictions. Quanta Computer, Inc. v. LG Electronics, Inc., 553 U.S. 617 (2008), is an example of patent exhaustion in a complex downstream licensing context. Impression Products, Inc. v. Lexmark International, 137 S. Ct. 1523 (2017), addresses the enforceability of post-sale restrictions on patented products in both domestic and international transactions.

Next is Microsoft v. Motorola, Inc., 795 F.3d 1024 (9th Cir. 2015), which is a good example of patent licensing in the context of technological standard setting. The disputes in the case center on RAND license arrangements and a licensor's breach its obligation of good faith and fair dealing.

To illustrate the collision between the global movement of goods and cross-border patent license arrangements, you will find LaserDynamics, Inc. v. Quanta Computer, Inc., 694 F.3d 51 (2012). *LaserDynamics* illustrates that today's final products are made by multiple parties involving outsourcing arrangements, implied licensing, and "have made" rights. *See also* Impression Products, 137 S. Ct. 1523 (ruling patent exhaustion applied to international sale of patented products).

Finally, the Materials provide a pointer to the Antitrust Guidelines for the Licensing of Intellectual Property. The U.S. Department of Justice and the Federal Trade Commission first issued the Guidelines on April 6, 1995, setting forth the U.S. government's enforcement policy with respect to the licensing of intellectual property. The Justice Department and Federal Trade Commission issued new guidelines in 2017.

PRINCO v. ITC

616 F.3d 1318 (Fed. Cir. 2010) (en banc)

BRYSON, Circuit Judge.

This case requires us to consider the scope of the doctrine of patent misuse. Patent misuse developed as a nonstatutory defense to claims of patent infringement. In the licensing context, the doctrine limits a patentee's right to impose conditions on a licensee that exceed the scope of the patent right. Because patent misuse is a judge-made doctrine that is in derogation of statutory patent rights against infringement, this court has not applied the doctrine of patent misuse expansively. In this case, we adhere to that approach, and we sustain the decision of the International Trade Commission that the doctrine of patent misuse does not bar the intervenor, U.S. Philips Corporation, from enforcing its patent rights against the appellants Princo Corporation and Princo America Corporation (collectively, "Princo").

I

A

This case has a lengthy history, which we will recite only in pertinent part. The technology at issue concerns two types of digital storage devices — recordable compact discs ("CD-Rs") and rewritable compact discs ("CD-RWs"). Those devices were developed in the 1980s and 1990s. The companies that developed the CD-R/RW technology generated technical standards to ensure that discs made by different manufacturers would be compatible and playable on machines that were designed to read the earlier generation compact discs ("CDs") and "read-only" compact discs ("CD-ROMs"). The standards that were generated for CD-Rs and CD-RWs were collected in a publication entitled "Recordable CD Standard," informally known as the "Orange Book." The CD-R/RW technology was developed principally by Philips and Sony Corporation, working in collaboration. Philips and Sony also jointly developed the Orange Book standards.

One aspect of the CD-R/RW technology — and the corresponding Orange Book standards — is at issue in this case. In the course of their work, the Sony and Philips engineers had to address the problem of how to encode position information in the disc so that a consumer's CD reader/writer could maintain proper positioning while writing data to the disc. Philips and Sony proposed different solutions to that problem. Philips's solution was to use an analog method of modulating the frequency of the "groove" on the disc so as to add location codes to the disc. One of Sony's proposed solutions was to use a digital method to encode location codes into the disc groove. Philips's approach was later set forth in two of the patents at issue in this case, referred to as the "Raaymakers patents." Sony's approach was set forth in one of its own patents, referred to as the "Lagadec patent."

After reviewing the competing solutions, the Sony and Philips engineers agreed that they would use the Raaymakers approach to solving the problem, not the Lagadec approach. The engineers from both companies agreed that the Raaymakers approach "was simple and . . . worked very well." By contrast, as the Commission found in the course of this litigation, the Lagadec approach was "prone to error" and would have been "very difficult" to implement. Philips and Sony therefore incorporated the Raaymakers approach in the Orange Book as the standard for manufacturing CD-R/RW discs.

Philips and Sony sought to commercialize their technology by offering licenses to the patents that were required to manufacture CD-R/RW discs in accordance with the Orange Book standards. Administering the licensing program, Philips offered several different "package" licenses to the Philips and Sony patents (and those of several other patent holders). Philips included in the patent packages those patents that it regarded as potentially necessary to make Orange-Book–compliant CD-R or CD-RW discs, including the Raaymakers and Laga-dec patents. The package licenses contained a "field of use" restriction, limiting the licensees to using the licensed patents to produce discs according to the Orange Book standards. After 2001, Philips offered additional package options, grouping the patents into two categories, denominated "essential" and "nonessential," for producing compact discs that complied with the technology standards set forth in the Orange Book.

In the late 1990s, Princo sought to manufacture discs and import them into this country, and it entered into a package license agreement with Philips. Soon after entering the agreement, however, Princo stopped paying the licensing fees required by the agreement. Philips then filed a complaint with the International Trade Commission, alleging that Princo (along with several other parties) was violating section 337(a)(1)(B) of the Tariff Act of 1930, 19 U.S.C. §1337(a)(1)(B), by importing CD-Rs and CD-RWs that infringed Philips's patents.

[The case went through several rounds prior to the en banc decision. *See* U.S. Philips Corp. v. Int'l Trade Comm'n (Philips I), 424 F.3d 1179 (Fed. Cir. 2005), and Princo Corp. v. Int'l Trade Comm'n, 563 F.3d 1301 (Fed. Cir. 2009).]

II

A

The doctrine of patent misuse has its origins in a series of Supreme Court cases, beginning with the 1917 decision in Motion Picture Patents Co. v. Universal Film Manufacturing Co., 243 U.S. 502 (1917). In that case, which involved a patent on a motion picture projector, the Court addressed whether a patentee could require that the projector be used only with certain films, by "prescrib[ing] by notice attached to a patented machine the conditions of its use and the supplies which must be used in the operation of it, under pain of infringement of the patent." *Id.* at 509. The Court concluded that such a restriction imposed on the purchasers of the patented projectors was invalid because

> a film is obviously not any part of the invention of the patent in suit; because it is an attempt, without statutory warrant, to continue the patent monopoly in this particular character of film after it has expired, and because to enforce it would be to create a monopoly in the manufacture and use of moving picture films, wholly outside of the patent in suit and of the patent law as we have interpreted it.

Id. at 518. Since the Court regarded the requirement to use particular films as beyond the legitimate scope of the patent, it held that the patent could not be enforced against a purchaser who used the patented projector with unsanctioned films.

Fourteen years later, in Carbice Corp. of America v. American Patents Development Corp., 283 U.S. 27 (1931), the Court held that it was improper for the owner of a patent on "refrigerating transportation packages" for transporting and storing dry ice to insist that licensees of that patent purchase their dry ice from the patent owner or its affiliates. The Court stated that the patentee "may not exact as the condition of a license that unpatented materials used in connection with the invention shall be purchased only from the licensor." 283 U.S. at 31. The seller of dry ice, the Court stated, "has no right to be free from competition in the sale of solid carbon dioxide. Control over the supply of such unpatented material is beyond the scope of the patentee's monopoly." *Id.* at 33. Accordingly, the Court ruled that the party that had supplied dry ice to one of the patentee's licensees could not be held liable for contributory infringement of the patent.

In a third case, Morton Salt Co. v. G.S. Suppiger Co., 314 U.S. 488 (1942), the patentee owned a patent on a machine used to add salt to canned foods. The patented machines were leased to canners on the condition that the canners would use salt tablets purchased from the patentee. When one of the patentee's lessees used the machine with its own salt tablets, the patentee sued for infringement. The Supreme Court held that the patent was unenforceable on the ground that the patentee had unlawfully used the patent "to secure an exclusive right or limited monopoly not granted by the Patent Office and which it is contrary to public policy to grant." *Id.* at 492.

In those cases, and several others in the same line of authority, the Supreme Court established the basic rule of patent misuse: that the patentee may exploit his patent but may not "use it to acquire a monopoly not embraced in the patent." Transparent-Wrap Mach. Corp. v. Stokes & Smith Co., 329 U.S. 637, 643 (1947). As for the most common form of patent misuse — requiring the purchase of an unpatented product as a condition for obtaining a license to the patent, the Court observed, "He who uses his patent to obtain protection from competition in the sale of unpatented materials extends by contract his patent monopoly to articles as respects which the law sanctions neither monopolies nor restraints of trade." *Id.* at 644.

The Court applied the same reasoning to licenses requiring the payment of licensing fees after the expiration of the licensed patent and thus having the effect of extending the life of the patent beyond the statutory period. In Brulotte v. Thys Co., 379 U.S. 29 (1964), the Court explained that a patent "empowers the owner to exact royalties as high as he can negotiate with the leverage of that monopoly. But to use that leverage to project those royalty payments beyond the life of the patent is analogous to an effort to enlarge the monopoly of the patent by tieing the sale or use of the patented article to the purchase or use of unpatented ones." *Id.* at 33.

As applied to patent licensing agreements, the Supreme Court put the matter succinctly in *Zenith*, 395 U.S. at 136:

> [T]here are established limits which the patentee must not exceed in employing the leverage of his patent to control or limit the operations of the licensee. Among other restrictions upon him, he may not condition the right to use his patent on the licensee's agreement to purchase, use, or sell, or not to purchase, use, or sell, another article of commerce not within the scope of his patent monopoly.

In our cases applying the Supreme Court's patent misuse decisions, we have characterized patent misuse as the patentee's act of "impermissibly broaden[ing] the 'physical or temporal scope' of the patent grant with anticompetitive effect." Windsurfing Int'l, Inc. v. AMF, Inc., 782 F.2d 995, 1001 (Fed. Cir. 1986). When the patentee has used restrictive conditions on licenses or sales to broaden the scope of the patent grant, we have held that an accused infringer may invoke the doctrine of patent misuse to defeat the patentee's claim.

In B. Braun Medical, Inc. v. Abbott Laboratories, 124 F.3d 1419 (Fed. Cir. 1997), and Mallinckrodt, Inc. v. Medipart, Inc., 976 F.2d 700 (Fed. Cir. 1992), we explained the rationale underlying the doctrine. As a general matter, the unconditional sale of a patented device exhausts the patentee's right to control the purchaser's use of the device thereafter, on the theory that the patentee has bargained for, and received, the full value of the goods. That "exhaustion" doctrine does not apply, however, to a conditional sale or license, where it is more reasonable to infer that a negotiated price reflects only the value of the "use" rights conferred by the patentee. Thus, express conditions accompanying the sale or license of a patented product, such as field of use limitations, are generally upheld. See Gen. Talking Pictures Corp. v. W. Elec. Co., 304 U.S. 175, 181 (1938) ("Patent owners may grant licenses extending to all uses or limited to use in a defined field."). When those contractual conditions violate public policy, however, as in the case of price-fixing conditions and tying restraints, the underlying patents become unenforceable, and the patentee loses its right to sue for infringement or breach of contract. B. Braun, 124 F.3d at 1426; Mallinckrodt, 976 F.2d at 706.

The doctrine of patent misuse is thus grounded in the policy-based desire to "prevent a patentee from using the patent to obtain market benefit beyond that which inheres in the statutory patent right." Mallinckrodt, 976 F.2d at 704. It follows that the key inquiry under the patent misuse doctrine is whether, by imposing the condition in question, the patentee has impermissibly broadened the physical or temporal scope of the patent grant and has done so in a manner that has anticompetitive effects. B. Braun, 124 F.3d at 1426. Where the patentee has not leveraged its patent beyond the scope of rights granted by the Patent Act, misuse has not been found. See Monsanto, 363 F.3d at 1341 ("In the cases in which the restriction is reasonably within the patent grant, the patent misuse defense can never succeed."); Virginia Panel, 133 F.3d at 869 (particular practices by the patentee "did not constitute patent misuse because they did not broaden the scope of its patent, either in terms of covered subject matter or temporally").

In determining whether a particular licensing condition has the effect of impermissibly broadening the patent grant, courts have noted that the patentee begins with substantial rights under the patent grant — "includ[ing] the right to suppress the invention while continuing to prevent all others from using it, to license others, or to refuse to license, . . . to charge such royalty as the leverage of the patent monopoly permits," and to limit the scope of the license to a particular "field of use." United States v. Studiengesellschaft Kohle, m.b.H., 670 F.2d 1122, 1127, 1133 (D.C. Cir. 1981). Given that the patent grant entitles the patentee to impose a broad range of conditions in licensing the right to practice the patent, the doctrine of patent misuse "has largely been confined to a handful of specific practices by which the patentee seemed to be trying to 'extend' his patent grant beyond its statutory limits." USM Corp. v. SPS Techs., Inc., 694 F.2d 505, 510 (7th Cir. 1982).

Recognizing the narrow scope of the doctrine, we have emphasized that the defense of patent misuse is not available to a presumptive infringer simply because a patentee engages in some kind of wrongful commercial conduct, even conduct that may have anticompetitive effects. See C.R. Bard, Inc. v. M3 Sys., Inc., 157 F.3d 1340, 1373 (Fed. Cir. 1998) ("Although the defense of patent misuse . . . evolved to protect against 'wrongful' use of patents, the catalog of practices labeled 'patent misuse' does not include a general notion of 'wrongful' use."). Other courts have expressed the same view. See Kolene Corp. v. Motor City Metal Treating, Inc., 440 F.2d 77, 84-85 (6th Cir. 1971) (There is no such thing as "misuse in the air. The misuse must be of the patent in suit. An antitrust offense does not necessarily amount to misuse merely because it involves patented products or products which are the subject of a patented process." (citations omitted)); McCullough Tool Co. v. Well Surveys, Inc., 395 F.2d 230, 238-39 (10th Cir. 1968) (the defense of patent misuse has been allowed "only where there had been a misuse of the patent in suit"). While proof of an antitrust violation shows that the patentee has committed wrongful conduct having anticompetitive effects, that does not establish misuse of the patent in suit unless the conduct in question restricts the use of that patent and does so in one of the specific ways that have been held to be outside the otherwise broad scope of the patent grant.

Although patent misuse has been mainly a judicially created defense, Congress has not been entirely silent about the doctrine. However, instead of saying what patent misuse is, Congress has said what it is not. Thus, section 271(d) of the Patent Act sets forth five types of conduct that may not provide the basis for finding "misuse or illegal extension of the patent right." The last two of the five, which were added in 1988, are

> (4) refus[ing] to license or use any rights to the patent; or (5) condition[ing] the license of any rights to the patent or the sale of the patented product on the acquisition of a license to rights in another patent or purchase of a separate product, unless, in view of the circumstances, the patent owner has market power in the relevant market for the patent or patented product on which the license or sale is conditioned. 35 U.S.C. §271(d).

Importantly, Congress enacted section 271(d) not to broaden the doctrine of patent misuse, but to cabin it. The 1988 amendment in particular was designed to confine patent misuse, with respect to certain licensing practices, to conduct having anticompetitive effects. See Ill. Tool Works Inc. v. Indep. Ink, Inc., 547 U.S. 28, 41 (2006); S. Rep. No. 100-492, at 9 (1988) (explaining that purpose of the amendment was to narrow the patent misuse doctrine, which "punish[es] innovators engaged in procompetitive distribution and licensing practices"); id. at 14 ("The lack of clarity and predictability in application of the patent misuse doctrine and that doctrine's potential for impeding procompetitive arrangements are major causes for concern."); 134 Cong. Rec. 32,471 (1988) (statement of Sen. Patrick Leahy) ("Reform of patent misuse will ensure that the harsh misuse sanction of unenforceability is imposed only against those engaging in truly anticompetitive conduct."); id. at 32,295 (statement of Rep. Robert Kastenmeier) ("[T]he proposed modifications should have a procompetitive effect, insofar as they require some linkage between patent licensing practice and anti-competitive conduct.").

Section 271(d) is not directly implicated in this case because the conduct here at issue does not fall within any of the five statutorily defined categories. Nonetheless, the statute is pertinent because, as both the text and the legislative history of the 1988 amendment to section 271(d) make clear, Congress was concerned about the open-ended scope of the doctrine and sought to confine it to anticompetitive conduct by patentees who leverage their patents to obtain economic advantages outside the legitimate scope of the patent grant.

B

This case presents a completely different scenario from the cases previously identified by the Supreme Court and by this court as implicating the doctrine of patent misuse. Philips is not imposing restrictive conditions on the use of the Raaymakers patents to enlarge the physical or temporal scope of those patents. Instead, the alleged act of patent misuse that the panel focused on was the claimed horizontal agreement between Philips and Sony to restrict the availability of the Lagadec patent—an entirely different patent that was never asserted in the infringement action against Princo. Even if such an agreement were shown to exist, and even if it were shown to have anticompetitive effects, a horizontal agreement restricting the availability of Sony's Lagadec patent would not constitute misuse of Philips's Raaymakers patents or any of Philips's other patents in suit.

Reduced to its simplest elements, the question in this case comes down to this: When a patentee offers to license a patent, does the patentee misuse that patent by inducing a third party not to license its separate, competitive technology? Princo has not pointed to any authority suggesting that such a scenario constitutes patent misuse, and nothing in the policy underlying the judge-made doctrine of patent misuse would support such a result. Such an agreement would not have the effect of increasing the physical or temporal scope of the patent in suit, and it therefore would not fall within the rationale of the patent misuse doctrine as explicated by the Supreme Court and this court.

What patent misuse is about, in short, is "patent leverage," i.e., the use of the patent power to impose overbroad conditions on the use of the patent in suit that are "not within the reach of the monopoly granted by the Government." *Zenith*, 395 U.S. at 136-38. What that requires, at minimum, is that the patent in suit must "itself significantly contribute[ ] to the practice under attack." *Kolene Corp.*, 440 F.2d at 85. Patent misuse will not be found when there is "no connection" between the patent right and the misconduct in question, see Republic Molding Corp. v. B.W. Photo Utils., 319 F.2d 347, 351 (9th Cir. 1963), or no "use" of the patent, see *Virginia Panel*, 133 F.3d at 870. In this case, there is no such link between the putative misconduct and the Raaymakers patents.

Princo makes several arguments in its effort to bring this case within the scope of the traditional patent misuse doctrine. First, Princo contends that Philips "leveraged" its patents, as that term has been used in patent misuse cases, because it used the proceeds of its highly successful licensing program to fund royalty payments to Sony and because those payments gave Sony the incentive to enter into the alleged agreement to suppress the Lagadec patent. However, the use of funds from a lawful licensing program to support other, anticompetitive behavior is not the kind of "leveraging" that the Supreme Court and this court have referred to in discussing the leveraging of a patent that constitutes patent misuse. See *C.R. Bard*, 157 F.3d at 1373 ("Although the law should not condone wrongful commercial activity, the body of misuse law and precedent need not be enlarged into an open-ended pitfall for patent-supported commerce."). Even if such use of funds were to be deemed misconduct, it does not place any conditions on the availability of Philips's patents to any potential licensees, so it is not the power of Philips's patent right that is being misused.

Princo also argues that the Supreme Court has not required conventional "leveraging" of a patent in order to establish patent misuse. For that proposition, however, Princo relies on antitrust cases in which the Court stated that a patentee is not immunized against an antitrust violation by the privilege of a patent; those cases did not involve patent misuse or the enforceability of the defendants' patents. See United States v. U.S. Gypsum Co., 333 U.S. 364, 396-400 (1948) (finding unlawful price fixing and control of distribution of gypsum board); Standard Oil Co. (Ind.) v. United States, 283 U.S. 163, 174 (1931) ("[T]he limited monopolies granted to patent owners do not exempt them from the prohibitions of the Sherman Act."). That is a different issue altogether from the issue before us, which is whether an infringing party can obtain immunity against a valid charge of patent infringement by showing an unrelated antitrust violation. Although the Lagadec patent and the Raaymakers patents were all included together in the Orange Book package licenses offered by Philips, those package licenses are independent of the antitrust violation that is now being alleged, i.e., a separate agreement between Philips and Sony to suppress the availability of the Lagadec technology.

In theory, the reason an agreement with Sony has value to Philips is because suppressing potential competition with the Raaymakers technology makes the Philips licenses more valuable. But that value does not derive from the fact that Sony is a co-licensor with Philips or the fact that the Lagadec patent is included in the package licenses. If the Lagadec patent were owned by an independent third party and not included in the Philips-Sony package licenses at all, an agreement between Philips and the third party to suppress the Lagadec technology would have exactly the same economic impact on Philips and Princo as the hypothesized agreement with Sony. That agreement might be vulnerable to challenge under the antitrust laws, but it could not reasonably be characterized as misuse of the Raaymakers patents. Thus, it does not follow from the possible existence of an antitrust violation with respect to Sony's Lagadec patent that Philips is guilty of patent misuse with respect to the Raaymakers patents.

The dissent does not find fault with the terms of the licensing agreements between Philips and its licensees, but instead focuses its full attention on the purported horizontal agreement between Philips and Sony to suppress the Lagadec technology. The dissent then characterizes that agreement as invoking the doctrine of patent misuse because it is "part and parcel" of the licensing agreements between Philips and its licensees. That characterization, however, is incorrect. The Orange Book licensing agreements control what the licensees may do; the purported agreement between Philips and Sony controls what Sony may do. At bottom, Princo's complaint is not that its license to the Raaymakers patents is unreasonably conditioned, but that the Lagadec patent has not been made available for non–Orange-Book uses. And that is not patent misuse under any court's definition of the term.

The purported agreement between Philips and Sony has none of the features that courts have characterized as constituting patent misuse. In particular, it does not leverage the power of a patent to exact concessions from a licensee that are not fairly within the ambit of the patent right. Although the dissent contends that using the leverage of a patent against licensees is not a necessary component of patent misuse, every one of the "patent misuse" cases cited by the dissent for that proposition have that very fact pattern (except for the *Compton* case, discussed above, in which the patentee agreed to place restrictions on his own right to compete). If the purported agreement between Philips and Sony not to license the Lagadec technology is unlawful, that can only be under antitrust law, not patent misuse law; nothing about that agreement, if it exists, constitutes an exploitation of the Raaymakers patents against Philips's licensees.

The *Morton Salt* case, which the dissent cites in support of its broad characterization of the doctrine of patent misuse, is a typical "tying" case in which the patentee leveraged its patent to a machine by insisting that its licensees purchase unpatented goods, to be used in connection with the machine, from the patentee. It was because of the unlawful condition on the patent license that the Court in *Morton Salt* declined to enforce the patent. Significantly, the Court explained that its ruling was based on the use of the patent "as a means of restraining competition with the patentee's sale of an unpatented product," and that the successful prosecution of an infringement action "is a powerful aid to the maintenance of the attempted monopoly of the unpatented product," thus "thwarting the public policy underlying the grant of the patent." 314 U.S. at 493. There is no such exploitation of the Raaymakers patents in this case.

In sum, this is not a case in which conditions have been placed in patent licenses to require licensees to agree to anticompetitive terms going beyond the scope of the patent grant. Rather, in this case the assertion of misuse arises not from the terms of the license itself but rather from an alleged collateral agreement between Sony and Philips. In that setting, the doctrine of patent misuse does not immunize Princo against the legal effect of its acts of infringement.

C

Apart from Princo's failure to show that Philips unlawfully leveraged its Raaymakers patents, a finding of patent misuse is unwarranted in this case because Princo failed to establish that the alleged agreement to suppress the Lagadec technology had anticompetitive effects. Whether viewed as a matter of patent misuse or in light of general antitrust principles, Princo's claim regarding the alleged agreement fails because Philips and Sony acted legitimately in choosing not to compete against their own joint venture. Princo also failed to show that the asserted agreement had any anticompetitive effects because, as the Commission found, the Lagadec technology was not a viable potential competitor to the technology embodied in the Raaymakers patents.

At the outset, Princo urges us to overrule the line of authority in this court holding that patent misuse requires a showing that the patentee's conduct had anticompetitive effects. We decline to do so. This court has observed that "[t]o sustain a misuse defense involving a licensing arrangement not held to have been per se anticompetitive by the Supreme Court, a factual determination must reveal that the overall effect of the license tends to restrain competition unlawfully in an appropriately defined relevant market." *Windsurfing*, 782 F.2d at 1001-02. We have consistently adhered to that requirement. See, e.g., *Philips I*, 424 F.3d at 1184; *Monsanto*, 363 F.3d at 1341; *Virginia Panel*, 133 F.3d at 868; *B. Braun*, 124 F.3d at 1426; *Mallinckrodt*, 976 F.2d at 708. Our position is consistent with the traditional characterization of the defense of patent misuse by the Supreme Court, see *Ill. Tool Works*, 547 U.S. at 38 (describing the patent misuse doctrine as applying "when a patentee uses its patent 'as the effective means of restraining competition with its sale of an unpatented article'"); the decisions of other circuits, see County Materials Corp. v. Allan Block Corp., 502 F.3d 730, 736 (7th Cir. 2007); Carpet Seaming Tape Licensing Corp. v. Best Seam Inc., 616 F.2d 1133, 1142 (9th Cir. 1980); and the 1988 amendment to 35 U.S.C. §271(d), which makes clear that Congress intended to limit patent misuse to practices having anticompetitive effects.

Turning from patent misuse law to antitrust principles, Princo contends that the hypothesized agreement between Philips and Sony not to license the Lagadec technology for non–Orange-Book purposes was a naked restraint of trade with no procompetitive justification, and that Philips's conduct in entering into that agreement should render its Orange Book patents unenforceable. For the reasons set forth below, we disagree.

Although joint ventures can be used to facilitate collusion among competitors and are therefore subject to antitrust scrutiny, see NCAA v. Bd. of Regents of the Univ. of Okla., 468 U.S. 85, 113 (1984), research joint ventures such as the one between Philips and Sony can have significant procompetitive features, and it is now well settled that an agreement among joint venturers to pool their research efforts is analyzed under the rule of reason. See Addamax Corp. v. Open Software Found., Inc., 152 F.3d 48, 52 (1st Cir. 1998) (Joint venture research enterprises, "unless they amount to complete shams, are rarely susceptible to per se treatment. Where the venture is producing a new product . . . there is patently a potential for a productive contribution to the economy, and conduct that is strictly ancillary to this productive effort . . . is evaluated under the rule of reason."); see generally Am. Needle, Inc. v. Nat'l Football League, 560 U.S. 183 (2010) (rule of reason generally applied to joint venture agreements); 15 U.S.C. §4302 (conduct of research joint ventures is "not deemed illegal per se," but is "judged on the basis of its reasonableness, taking into account all relevant factors affecting competition"); FTC & Dep't of Justice, Antitrust Guidelines for Collaborations Among Competitors §3.31(a), at 14 (2000) (most research joint venture agreements "are procompetitive, and they typically are analyzed under the rule of reason"); ABA, Antitrust Law Developments 445-46 (6th ed. 2007) ("joint research ventures are typically analyzed under the rule of reason").

Collaboration for the purpose of developing and commercializing new technology can result in economies of scale and integrations of complementary capacities that reduce costs, facilitate innovation, eliminate duplication of effort and assets, and share risks that no individual member would be willing to undertake alone, thereby "promot[ing] rather than hinder[ing] competition." Dep't of Justice & FTC, Antitrust Guidelines for the Licensing of Intellectual Property §§5.1, at 24; 5.5, at 28 (Apr. 6, 1995); see also Herbert Hovenkamp, Antitrust Law ¶2115a, at 110 ("[J]oint innovation often produces significant social benefits in relation to costs.").

In particular, as we explained in *Philips I*, research joint ventures that seek to develop industry-wide standards for new technology can have decidedly procompetitive effects. The absence of standards for new technology can easily result in a "Tower of Babel" effect that increases costs, reduces utility, and frustrates consumers. As a leading treatise has noted, cooperation by competitors in standard-setting "can provide procompetitive benefits the market would not otherwise provide, by allowing a number of different firms to produce and market competing products compatible with a single standard." Herbert Hovenkamp et al., IP & Antitrust §35.2b (2010). Those benefits include greater product interoperability, including the promotion of price competition among interoperable products; positive network effects, including an increase in the value of products as interoperable products become more widely used; and incentives to innovate by establishing a technical baseline for further product improvements. Congress has recognized those procompetitive features and has directed that the activities of a "standards development organization while engaged in a standards development activity" [are] subject to the rule of reason. See Standards Development Organization Advancement Act of 2004, Pub. L. No. 108-237 §104, 118 Stat. 661, 663.

The "ancillary restraints" that are often important to collaborative ventures, such as agreements between the collaborators not to compete against their joint venture, are also assessed under the rule of reason. . . . Moreover, those ancillary restraints are not viewed in isolation, but in the context of the joint venture or other collaborative effort. Thus, agreements not to compete that might be suspect standing alone are regarded as reasonable when they are ancillary to "a larger endeavor whose success they promote." *Polk Bros.*, 776 F.2d at 189.

Princo does not contend that the selection of the Raaymakers technology, rather than the Lagadec technology, for the Orange Book standard was a violation of the public policy in favor of free competition, nor did the panel so find. Instead, the panel focused on whether Sony and Philips agreed to suppress competition between the technology represented by the Orange Book standard and technology that fell outside the Orange Book standard, i.e., the Lagadec digital encoding technology. The Commission did not answer that question because the question was never squarely presented to it. Nor do we need to decide whether there was any such agreement between Sony and Philips. That is because the Commission's factual findings make it clear that even if there was such an agreement, it did not have the effect of suppressing potentially viable technology that could have competed with the Orange Book standards.

The Commission found that "there has been no showing that the Lagadec '565 patent competes with another patent in the pool, no showing that the pool licensors would have competed in the technology licensing market absent the pooling arrangement, and no showing of the anti-competitive effect required under a rule of reason analysis." The Commission supported that general finding with a series of specific findings based on the record before it.

First, the Commission noted that the evidence before the administrative law judge showed that the Lagadec technology "does not work well according to the Orange Book standards." The Commission added that the administrative law judge "credited testimony that the Lagadec approach is prone to errors and 'did not provide a scheme that would work and was reliable.'" Those findings were not limited to the unsuitability of using Lagadec to produce Orange-Book–compliant discs, as Princo argues. Instead, as is clear from the testimony on which those findings were based, the findings applied more generally to the technical problems presented by the Lagadec technology. The administrative law judge referred to testimony by Philips's expert explaining that there is "a real problem" with the Lagadec digital approach and that "it is very difficult to carry out a decoding of this particular approach." The expert added that "[a]s a result, Philips and Sony dismissed the Lagadec approach because this is a very difficult problem to solve and Lagadec just did not provide a scheme that would work and was reliable. . . . [F]rom basic physics, you can just see that this is not a good solution, and it really wouldn't work well."

The Commission also noted that Princo had not pointed to any evidence "that the Lagadec approach is a commercially viable technological alternative to the technology of [the Raaymakers patents]." By way of explanation, the Commission commented that "the commercial viability of a method that is prone to errors, unreliable, and unworkable is doubtful." Based on the Commission's use of the term "commercial viability," Princo argues that the Commission used the wrong standard in evaluating the Lagadec technology. According to Princo, instead of addressing the commercial viability of that technology, the Commission should have limited its inquiry to whether Lagadec had "the technical potential to develop as a workable alternative."

The Commission, however, addressed both technical feasibility and commercial potential, and it found the Lagadec approach lacking in both respects.

Second, the Commission rejected the argument that Philips "included Sony in the [patent] pool not because Sony brought anything necessary to the CD-R/RW technology, but rather because Sony is a major player in the industry, whose cooperation Philips wanted." The Commission found that assertion to be baseless and contrary to the testimony of several witnesses that Philips "partnered with Sony for technical reasons." Thus, although Princo argues at length that the pooling arrangement was not designed as a joint technical project between Philips and Sony, but rather as a means of allowing Philips to share its royalties with Sony in exchange for Sony's agreement not to compete against the Orange Book standard, the Commission found to the contrary.

Finally, with respect to Princo's related argument that including the Lagadec patent in the package licenses enabled Philips to avoid competition from non–Orange-book discs, the Commission stated that Princo had "not identified evidence establishing that, if Sony's [Lagadec patent] were not included in the licenses, Sony likely would have developed technologies that competed against the Orange Book standard in a relevant market." The Commission added that there was no evidence in the record that Sony "would have entered and survived to become a significant competitive force" in the CD-R/RW market with the Lagadec technology or that, absent the pooling arrangements, the pool licensors would have competed with the Orange Book technology.

Likewise, there was no evidence that any potential licensee might develop the Lagadec technology to compete with the Orange Book discs. Princo did not show that any potential disc manufacturer had ever been refused a license to the Lagadec patent for purposes of producing non–Orange-Book discs, or had even sought to explore that possibility. Nor has Princo pointed to any evidence that the Lagadec patent was anything more than a theoretical solution, or that the unavailability of a separate license to Lagadec for non–Orange-Book purposes resulted in some realistic foreclosure of competition.

While the suppression of nascent threats can be construed as anticompetitive behavior under certain circumstances, see United States v. Microsoft Corp., 253 F.3d 34, 79 (D.C. Cir. 2001) (en banc), Princo had the burden of showing that the hypothesized agreement had an actual adverse effect on competition in the relevant market. . . .

What Princo had to demonstrate was that there was a "reasonable probability" that the Lagadec technology, if available for licensing, would have matured into a competitive force in the storage technology market. See United States v. Penn-Olin Chem. Co., 378 U.S. 158, 175-76 (1964) (requiring a finding that there was a reasonable probability that the competing companies would have "entered the market" or "remained a significant potential competitor"). It was not enough that there was some speculative possibility that Lagadec could have overcome the barriers to its technical feasibility and commercial success and become the basis for competing disc technology. The Commission found that Princo failed to show that the Lagadec technology had technical or commercial prospects that could enable it to compete with the Orange Book technology. Those findings wholly undermine Princo's contention that this is a case in which the patents in suit have been used as part of an overall horizontal agreement with the effect of keeping a viable competitor out of the relevant market.

The dissenting opinion seeks to sidestep the Commission's adverse factual findings by arguing that the burden of proof should have been placed on Philips, not Princo. The dissent acknowledges that an agreement among joint venturers who would otherwise be competitors is judged by the rule of reason. Within that framework, however, the dissent advocates a "quick look" rule of reason analysis on the ground that any agreement not to compete is inherently suspect and that competitive harm therefore should be presumed.

Quick-look analysis applies to "naked restraint[s] on price and output" where a detailed market analysis is unnecessary to conclude that the arrangements in question have anti-competitive effects. *Cal. Dental*, 526 U.S. at 769-70. In those circumstances, only a quick look is necessary because the arrangement is "so plainly anticompetitive that courts need undertake only a cursory examination before imposing antitrust liability." *Dagher*, 547 U.S. at 7 n. 3. However, the Supreme Court has cautioned that presumptions of anticompetitiveness should not be lightly invoked. *Broad. Music*, 441 U.S. at 8-9. Rather, the Court has stated:

> [B]efore a theoretical claim of anticompetitive effects can justify shifting to a defendant the burden to show empirical evidence of procompetitive effects, as quick-look analysis in effect requires, there must be some indication that the court making the decision has properly identified the theoretical basis for the anticompetitive effects and considered whether the effects actually are anticompetitive. Where, as here, the circumstances of the restriction are somewhat complex, assumption alone will not do. *Cal. Dental*, 526 U.S. at 775 n. 12.

A quick-look approach might be justified if the joint venture in this case were a sham, or if the alleged agreement were a naked restraint, i.e., not reasonably necessary to achieve the efficiency-enhancing benefits of the joint venture. See Major League Baseball Props., Inc. v. Salvino, Inc., 542 F.3d 290, 338 (2d Cir. 2008) (Sotomayor, J., concurring). The Commission, however, rejected the contention that the joint venture between Philips and Sony was a sham. And, as we have discussed, an agreement among joint venturers not to compete against the joint venture is not a naked restraint, because it provides assurance that the resources invested by one joint venturer will not be undermined or competitively exploited to the sole benefit of the other. See id. at 340 (noting that exclusivity and profit-sharing provisions are reasonably necessary to prevent the free-rider problem). Particularly when the purpose of the joint venture is to set standards for an industry, and choices must be made as to which technologies to promote and which to suppress, those choices must be supported equally by all participants to the standard-setting body in order to achieve successful creation and adoption of the standard. See generally Rambus Inc. v. Infineon Techs. AG, 318 F.3d 1081 (Fed. Cir. 2003).

In sum, Princo has failed to show that the putative agreement between Sony and Philips not to license the Lagadec technology for non–Orange-Book purposes had any market effect at all — actual or prospective. The record, and the findings of the Commission, make clear that the Lagadec technology lacked both the technical and the commercial prospects that would have made it a possible basis for a product that could compete with Orange-Book–compliant discs in the data storage market. For that reason, Princo failed to demonstrate that any agreement not to license Lagadec would have had the anticompetitive effects necessary to condemn that agreement under rule-of-reason analysis.

Accordingly, we conclude that even if Philips and Sony engaged in an agreement not to license the Lagadec patent for non–Orange-Book purposes, that hypothesized agreement had no bearing on the physical or temporal scope of the patents in suit, nor did it have anti-competitive effects in the relevant market. The asserted agreement between Philips and Sony therefore did not constitute patent misuse and cannot justify rendering all of Philips's Orange Book patents unenforceable.

AFFIRMED.

[Concurring and dissenting opinions omitted.]

SPEEDPLAY, INC. v. BEBOP, INC.

211 F.3d 1245 (Fed. Cir. 2000)

BRYSON, Circuit Judge.

Serious bicyclists often use pedal assemblies that enable them to secure their feet to the bicycle pedals. The effect of such assemblies is to allow the bicyclists to increase the power transmitted to the wheels by simultaneously applying a downward, pushing force with one foot and an upward, pulling force with the other. Clipless pedal and cleat assemblies offer one method of performing that function. With clipless pedals and cleats, a rider can attach his feet securely to the pedals yet release them easily, in contrast to earlier systems using straps or cages. The cleats attach to the rider's shoes and engage the pedals, which are specially designed to interact with the cleats. In most clipless pedal systems, the rider attaches his foot to the pedal by stepping straight down on the pedal until the cleat engages with the pedal. The rider typically releases his foot by rotating his foot to the side, which disengages the cleat from the pedal.

Richard Bryne, the chief executive officer and founder of Speedplay, Inc., is the inventor and primary designer of Speedplay's bicycle pedals. He obtained U.S. Patent No. 4,942,778 (the '778 patent) on a clipless pedal and cleat system, and in 1992 entered the market with a product based on that patent. Shortly thereafter, Bryne was issued U.S. Patent No. 5,213,009 (the '009 patent), which claims a multilayered cleat design. Within two years of its founding, Speedplay entered into two agreements with Bryne. The first granted Speedplay a license under the '778 patent and improvements thereon, while the second assigned to Speedplay all of Bryne's bicycle-related inventions made during his employment with the company. Steven Zoumaras, who held a 50% interest in the '778 patent in return for financing its procurement, was also a party to the license, but he assigned his entire interest to Speedplay during the course of the trial.

John Steinberg, the president and founder of Bebop, Inc., is the inventor of the Bebop bicycle pedals. In 1989, Steinberg conceived the basic idea for the Bebop pedal, which features a hollow, cylindrical body. Over the next few years, Steinberg refined the concept, obtained a patent on the invention, and marketed two Bebop pedal designs. Shortly after Bryne saw a Bebop prototype in 1993, the parties clashed over intellectual property and commercial tort issues. The dispute led to the present lawsuit, in which Speedplay claimed that Bebop was infringing the '778 and '009 patents by manufacturing and marketing the Bebop clipless bicycle pedals. . . .

Bebop raises a threshold issue concerning Speedplay's right to bring an action for infringement of the '778, '009, and '894 patents in its own name. The trial judge concluded that Bryne had transferred "all right, title, and interest to the inventions" to Speedplay, thereby securing to Speedplay the right to sue individually for infringement of the patents. We agree that Speedplay has standing to maintain this suit.

A party may bring an action for patent infringement only if it is the "patentee," i.e., if it owns the patent, either by issuance or by assignment. See 35 U.S.C. §§100(d), 261, 281. A party that has been granted all substantial rights under the patent is considered the owner regardless of how the parties characterize the transaction that conveyed those rights. Thus, in Vaupel Textilmaschinen KG v. Meccanica Euro Italia S.P.A., 944 F.2d 870, 874, 873-76 (Fed. Cir. 1991), this court held that the proper focus is on "the substance of what was granted," and that the grantee of an exclusive license could sue in its own name without joining the grantor if the license had the effect of conveying all substantial rights in the patent to the licensee.

Speedplay asserts that it obtained all substantial rights in the '778, '009, and '894 patents from Bryne, and that it may therefore sue for infringement in its own name. To support that assertion, Speedplay must produce a written instrument documenting the transfer of proprietary rights in the patents. See 35 U.S.C. §261; Enzo APA & Son, Inc. v. Geapag A.G., 134 F.3d 1090, 1093 (Fed. Cir. 1998). Speedplay relies on two documents, a Contribution and License Agreement and a Confidentiality and Inventions Agreement, to support its assertion of patent rights. Bebop contends that those two documents are insufficient to allow Speedplay to sue in its own name.

Through the Contribution and License Agreement (CLA), Speedplay issued common stock to Bryne and Zoumaras in exchange for broad rights in Bryne's initial pedal technology. The CLA defines two categories of rights. First, it defines "Licensed Product" as follows:

Bryne and Zoumaras are the owners of a design for a clipless bicycle pedal system as described and claimed in the United States Letters Patent 4,942,778, issued July 24, 1990 to Richard M. Bryne and entitled CLIPLESS BICYCLE PEDAL SYSTEM ("Licensed Product"). . . .

Second, it defines "Licensed Patents" as follows:

Bryne is the inventor and title holder of United States Letters Patent 4,522,221, and related foreign patent applications (collectively, the "Licensed Patents"). . . .

Based on those definitions, the grant to Speedplay consists of an "exclusive worldwide, royalty-free, right and license under and to the Licensed Patents and the exclusive rights and license to manufacture, have manufactured, distribute, market, use and sell the Licensed Product and any other apparatus, instrument, device or product covered in whole or in part by the Licensed Patents." In addition, the agreement permits Speedplay to exercise its granted rights through agents and sublicensees. All rights under the CLA terminate with the last to expire of the Licensed Patents, unless terminated earlier for various specified reasons such as breach or insolvency.

The primary problem with the CLA derives from the patent number cited in the definition of Licensed Patents. Although naming Bryne as the inventor, the definition refers to U.S. Patent No. 4,522,221, which is an unrelated patent on unrelated technology issued and assigned to some unknown third parties. Speedplay asserted at oral argument that the reference to that patent was a scrivener's error and that a reference to the '778 patent was intended. That contention finds support in the portion of the CLA that refers to "the Licensed Product and any other apparatus . . . covered . . . by the Licensed Patents," which indicates that the term Licensed Patents was meant to refer to patents that covered the Licensed Product. In addition, another provision of the CLA requires Speedplay to mark each Licensed Product with a notice "identifying by U.S. patent number the Licensed Patent." Because a Licensed Product is a pedal system "described and claimed" by the '778 patent, the CLA could not logically require such a product to be marked with any patent number other than 4,942,778. Consequently, we agree with Speedplay that despite the patent number erroneously set forth in the CLA, the explicitly defined Licensed Patents must be construed to mean the '778 and related foreign patents.

The conclusion that Licensed Patents include the '778 patent undermines Bebop's main argument that the CLA did not transfer all substantial patent rights to Speedplay because Speedplay did not receive the right to enforce the '778 patent. Under the CLA, Speedplay has the "sole right to enforce the Licensed Patents," which we construe as giving Speedplay the right to enforce the '778 patent.

Bebop argues in the alternative that Bryne and Zoumaras retained other substantial rights in the '778 patent that would prevent Speedplay from suing on that patent in its own name. Bebop's strongest argument on this point derives from the following language of the CLA: "In the event that [Speedplay] fails to halt an infringement . . . within three (3) months," then "Bryne and/or Zoumaras shall have the option to initiate appropriate legal proceedings in his/their own name." Relying on Abbott Laboratories v. Diamedix Corp., 47 F.3d 1128 (Fed. Cir. 1995), Bebop claims that the grantors' retention of that option is dispositive. We disagree.

In *Abbott*, the licensor retained an option to sue an infringer if the exclusive licensee did not. Even if the licensee brought suit, it could not manage the action in a manner that would compromise the licensor's rights in the patent and could not prevent the licensor from participating in the suit. In addition, the grant to the licensee was subject to prior-granted licenses and to a limited right of the licensor to make, use, and sell products embodying the patented invention. Finally, the licensee could not freely assign its license. Considering all the rights retained by the licensor, the court concluded that the licensor was a necessary party to the infringement action brought by the licensee. *Abbott*, 47 F.3d at 1132.

Abbott does not control this case. Unlike in *Abbott*, the license grant was not subject to any prior-granted licenses or to any retained rights by the licensor to practice the patent. Moreover, the CLA does not grant Bryne and Zoumaras the right to participate in an infringement action brought by Speedplay, nor does it limit Speedplay's management of any such action. In addition, Bryne and Zoumaras's right to sue an infringer if Speedplay does not is illusory, because Speedplay can render that right nugatory by granting the alleged infringer a royalty-free sublicense. Although the licensee in *Abbott* could grant sublicenses, its right to do so was not unfettered, because it was liable for annual royalties on the sales of the sublicensees. *Abbott*, 47 F.3d at 1129. Speedplay thus controls enforcement of the '778 patent for all practical purposes. Even though Bryne and Zoumaras retained the right to sue, that right would not hinder Speedplay's enjoyment of the patent rights in any meaningful way.

Bebop next contends that under the CLA Speedplay cannot assign its interest in the license without the consent of Bryne and Zoumaras, and that Speedplay's rights in the patent are therefore curtailed. To be sure, the licensee's inability to assign its interest was a factor important to the holding in *Abbott*. But again the factual differences between *Abbott* and this case dictate a different outcome. The licensor in *Abbott* had an absolute right to veto any assignment proposed by the licensee, other than to a successor in business. *Abbott*, 47 F.3d at 1132. Under the CLA, however, Bryne and Zoumaras's consent to an assignment "shall not be withheld unreasonably." Bryne and Zoumaras's only reasonable basis for refusing consent would be the impairment of their consideration for entering the CLA. As we held in *Vaupel*, 944 F.2d at 875, a licensor does not retain a substantial right in a patent merely by reserving a reversion in the patent contingent upon the licensee's financial distress or the licensee's cessation of production of machines embodying the patented invention. In effect, the *Vaupel* termination provision simply protected the licensor's consideration, which consisted in part of an ongoing royalty stream. Although the form of the protective mechanism differs in this case, the principle of *Vaupel* compels a conclusion that the consent requirement does not significantly restrict the scope of Speedplay's rights in the '778 patent.

Bebop next argues that the "Improvements" clause of the CLA leaves a significant right in Bryne and Zoumaras. The CLA defines an "improvement" to include "any invention or development that falls within the fair scope of any of the claims of the Licensed Patent." If Speedplay makes improvements during the term of the agreement, it is required to "assign to Bryne and Zoumaras, as tenants in common, all right, title and interest in and to the Improvements," including any related patents and patent applications. That right of Bryne and Zoumaras is limited, however, by the further provision of the CLA that "[t]he Improvements shall become part of the Licensed Patent for purposes of this Agreement." As a consequence of that provision, any party's successful effort to improve the pedal technology covered by the '778 patent during the term of the agreement would redound to Speedplay's exclusive benefit for that term. The Improvements clause thus serves to protect Bryne and Zoumaras's reversionary interest in any improvements, but not to limit Speedplay's proprietary interests in improvements made during the pendency of the agreement.

Finally, Bebop claims that Bryne and Zoumaras retain two additional substantial rights in the '778 patent. The CLA requires Speedplay to mark products intended for foreign sale "in accordance with written instructions" from Bryne and Zoumaras. The right to dictate the markings on products sold abroad may or may not be significant as a practical matter, but the right is certainly not one that interferes with the rights in a U.S. patent, which are limited in reach to the United States. *See Vaupel*, 944 F.2d at 875, 20 U.S.P.Q.2d at 1049 (finding that the licensor's right to obtain foreign patents did not affect the patent-standing inquiry). The CLA also requires Speedplay to allow Bryne and Zoumaras to inspect Speedplay's books and records regarding the exercise of rights under the agreement. Given the CLA's provision for termination upon the insolvency of Speedplay, which is consistent with *Vaupel*'s provision for termination upon bankruptcy, the inspection provision constitutes a policing mechanism, not a substantial proprietary right. Accordingly, we conclude that Bryne and Zoumaras retained no substantial rights in the '778 patent, and that Speedplay therefore may sue in its own name for infringement of that patent.

STUDIENGESELLSCHAFT KOHLE, MBH v. SHELL OIL CO.

112 F.3d 1561 (Fed. Cir. 1997)

RADER, Circuit Judge.

SGK is the licensing arm of a famous, non-profit research and educational organization in Germany — the Max-Planck Institute for Coal Research. The '698 patent is part of a family of patents filed by Professor Karl Ziegler, a Nobel laureate and past director of the Max-Planck Institute, and various co-inventors. Ziegler and his co-workers initially discovered that combinations of reducing agents (most notably organoaluminum compounds) and heavy metal compounds would polymerize ethylene to form high molecular plastics. Ziegler extended this discovery to the polymerization of higher members of the ethylene series, such as propylene and butene. Ziegler, et al. filed the 770,484 application, which matured into the '698 patent, on October 29, 1958.

Shell and SGK first entered into an agreement involving the Ziegler family of patents in 1974. . . . In 1987, after several disputes over this license, Shell and SGK renegotiated the license only with regard to the '698 patent. The new terms provided Shell a paid-up license to produce 450 million pounds of polypropylene per year, with a 1.5% running royalty on any polypropylene sales in excess of 450 million pounds.

In 1987, Shell also began producing polypropylene by an alleged new process in Seadrift, Texas (the Seadrift Process). Because Shell contended that the '698 patent did not cover the Seadrift Process, Shell did not pay royalties on polypropylene produced by that process. Moreover, in its yearly accountings to SGK, Shell did not disclose its production of polypropylene by the Seadrift Process.

Ultimately, SGK terminated Shell's license and brought an action for unpaid royalties from 1987 through 1993. Additionally, SGK set forth claims for infringement of the '698 patent for the period 1993 through 1995. Shell moved for summary judgment of invalidity of claims. . . .

IV.

According to the 1987 licensing agreement, Shell agreed to pay SGK a 1.5% running royalty on the sale of any polypropylene, produced with a heavy metal catalyst as defined in claim 1 of the '698 patent in excess of 450 million pounds per year. Further, as discussed above, this agreement obligated Shell to give a yearly accounting of its entire polypropylene production, specifying "the amount of Polypropylene produced which it considers as falling outside of the license." The agreement obligated Shell to provide SGK with sufficient information to allow independent evaluation of whether its production falls outside the scope of the license. The record shows that Shell breached this contract by producing polypropylene under the Seadrift Process, without either paying royalties or reporting the production as outside of the license.

Nothing in this license made payment of royalties contingent upon the validity of the '698 patent. Setting aside momentarily both federal patent law and policy, this contract — regardless of the patent's validity — obligates Shell to pay royalties on polypropylene produced in accordance with claim 1 of the '698 patent. In other words, contract law governs the enforcement of the license. Enforcement of these contract terms is not contingent upon validity of the patent which defines the subject matter of the license. Assuming that the Seadrift Process infringes claim 1 of the '698 patent and thus fits within the terms of the license, Shell breached the license by failing to pay royalties. Enforcement of the license, if the Seadrift Process infringes the '698 patent, would require Shell to pay back royalties.

With a patent licensing agreement at stake, this court examines the contract for rare, but potential, conflicts between state contract law and federal patent law. For example, in *Lear v. Adkins*, the Supreme Court prevented the enforcement of a valid royalty payment agreement to facilitate a determination of patent validity. Specifically, the Supreme Court declined to estop a patent licensee from contesting the validity of the licensed patent. In tones that echo from a past era of skepticism over intellectual property principles, the Court in *Lear* feared that

> [l]icensees may often be the only individuals with enough economic incentive to challenge the patentability of an inventor's discovery. If they are muzzled, the public may continually be required to pay tribute to would-be monopolists without need or justification. We think it plain that the technical requirements of contract doctrine must give way before the demands of the public interest. . . .

Lear, 395 U.S. at 670. Thus, in examining the interface between national patent policy and state contracts, the Supreme Court requires this court to consider "whether overriding federal policies would be significantly frustrated" by enforcing the license. *Id.* This court encountered the *Lear* test when an assignor-inventor and his company sought to defend against an infringement action by challenging the validity of the assigned patents. See Diamond Scientific v. Ambico, Inc., 848 F.2d 1220 (Fed. Cir. 1988). With careful consideration of the Lear test and policies, this court nonetheless estopped the assignor from challenging the validity of the patent:

> To allow the assignor to make that representation [of the worth of the patent] at the time of the assignment (to his advantage) and later to repudiate it (again to his advantage) could work an injustice against the assignee. . . . [D]espite the public policy encouraging people to challenge potentially invalid patents, there are still circumstances in which the equities of the contractual relationships between the parties should deprive one party . . . of the right to bring that challenge.

Diamond Scientific, 848 F.2d at 1224-5.

As in *Diamond Scientific*, this court detects no significant frustration of federal patent policy by enforcing the 1987 license agreement between Shell and SGK, to the extent of allowing SGK to recover royalties until the date Shell first challenged the validity of the claims. First, as in *Diamond Scientific*, Shell executed a contractual agreement which produced significant benefits for the corporation and attested to the worth of the patent. Under the agreement (with its provision for Shell to notify SGK of all polypropylene production), Shell had the benefits of producing polypropylene insulated from unlicensed competition, insulated from investigations of infringement, and even insulated from royalties (until SGK's discovery of the Seadrift Process). To these benefits, Shell now seeks to add the benefit of abrogating its agreement and avoiding its breach of the contract. Following the reasoning of *Diamond Scientific*, this court must prevent the injustice of allowing Shell to exploit the protection of the contract and patent rights and then later to abandon conveniently its obligations under those same rights.

Just as important, however, Shell's apparent breach of its duty to notify under the agreement is itself more likely to frustrate federal patent policy than enforcement of the contract. As already noted, *Lear* focused on the "full and free use of ideas in the public domain." *Lear*, 395 U.S. at 674. By abrogating its notification duty, Shell delayed a timely challenge to the validity of the '698 patent and postponed the public's full and free use of the invention of the '698 patent. Shell enjoyed the protection of the license from 1987 until SGK became aware of the Seadrift Process. Upon SGK's discovery of its Seadrift process, Shell suddenly seeks the protection of the *Lear* policies it flaunted for many years. However, a licensee, such as Shell, cannot invoke the protection of the *Lear* doctrine until it (i) actually ceases payment of royalties, and (ii) provides notice to the licensor that the reason for ceasing payment of royalties is because it has deemed the relevant claims to be invalid. Other circuits addressing this issue have arrived at the same conclusion. [Citations omitted.] In this factual setting, therefore, enforcement of the license according to its terms, even if this entails a determination of whether the Seadrift Process infringes a now-invalidated patent, does not frustrate federal patent policy. Accordingly, this court remands this case to the district court for enforcement of the license (prior to the date Shell first challenged the validity of the claims) and, if necessary, computation of back royalties.

KIMBLE v. MARVEL ENTERTAINMENT
135 S. Ct. 2401 (2015)

KAGAN, Justice.

In Brulotte v. Thys Co., 379 U.S. 29 (1964), this Court held that a patent holder cannot charge royalties for the use of his invention after its patent term has expired. The sole question presented here is whether we should overrule *Brulotte*.

I

In 1990, petitioner Stephen Kimble obtained a patent on a toy that allows children (and young-at-heart adults) to role-play as "a spider person" by shooting webs — really, pressurized foam string — "from the palm of [the] hand." U.S. Patent No. 5,072,856, Abstract (filed May 25, 1990). Respondent Marvel Entertainment, LLC (Marvel) makes and markets products featuring Spider-Man, among other comic-book characters. Seeking to sell or license his patent, Kimble met with the president of Marvel's corporate predecessor to discuss his idea for web-slinging fun. Soon afterward, but without remunerating Kimble, that company began marketing the "Web Blaster" — a toy that, like Kimble's patented invention, enables would-be action heroes to mimic Spider-Man through the use of a polyester glove and a canister of foam.

Kimble sued Marvel in 1997 alleging, among other things, patent infringement. The parties ultimately settled that litigation. Their agreement provided that Marvel would purchase Kimble's patent in exchange for a lump sum (of about a half-million dollars) and a 3% royalty on Marvel's future sales of the Web Blaster and similar products. The parties set no end date for royalties, apparently contemplating that they would continue for as long as kids want to imitate Spider-Man (by doing whatever a spider can).

And then Marvel stumbled across *Brulotte*, the case at the heart of this dispute. In negotiating the settlement, neither side was aware of *Brulotte*. But Marvel must have been pleased to learn of it. *Brulotte* had read the patent laws to prevent a patentee from receiving royalties for sales made after his patent's expiration. So the decision's effect was to sunset the settlement's royalty clause 2. On making that discovery, Marvel sought a declaratory judgment in federal district court confirming that the company could cease paying royalties come 2010 — the end of Kimble's patent term. The court approved that relief, holding that *Brulotte* made "the royalty provision . . . unenforceable after the expiration of the Kimble patent." 692 F. Supp. 2d 1156, 1161 (D. Ariz. 2010). The Court of Appeals for the Ninth Circuit affirmed, though making clear that it was none too happy about doing so. "[T]he *Brulotte* rule," the court complained, "is counterintuitive and its rationale is arguably unconvincing." 727 F.3d 856, 857 (2013).

II

Patents endow their holders with certain superpowers, but only for a limited time. In crafting the patent laws, Congress struck a balance between fostering innovation and ensuring public access to discoveries. While a patent lasts, the patentee possesses exclusive rights to the patented article — rights he may sell or license for royalty payments if he so chooses. But a patent typically expires 20 years from the day the application for it was filed. And when the patent expires, the patentee's prerogatives expire too, and the right to make or use the article, free from all restriction, passes to the public.

This Court has carefully guarded that cut-off date, just as it has the patent laws' subject-matter limits: In case after case, the Court has construed those laws to preclude measures that restrict free access to formerly patented, as well as unpatentable, inventions. In one line of cases, we have struck down state statutes with that consequence. By virtue of federal law, we reasoned, "an article on which the patent has expired," like an unpatentable article, "is in the public domain and may be made and sold by whoever chooses to do so." *Sears*, 376 U.S. at 231. In a related line of decisions, we have deemed unenforceable private contract provisions limiting free use of such inventions. Allowing even a single company to restrict its use of an expired or invalid patent, we explained, "would deprive . . . the consuming public of the advantage to be derived" from free exploitation of the discovery. And to permit such a result, whether or not authorized "by express contract," would impermissibly undermine the patent laws. *Id.*, at 255-256; Lear, Inc. v. Adkins, 395 U.S. 653, 668-675 (1969) (refusing to enforce a contract requiring a licensee to pay royalties while contesting a patent's validity).

Brulotte was brewed in the same barrel. There, an inventor licensed his patented hop-picking machine to farmers in exchange for royalties from hop crops harvested both before and after his patents' expiration dates. The Court (by an 8-1 vote) held the agreement unenforceable — "unlawful per se" — to the extent it provided for the payment of royalties "accru[ing] after the last of the patents incorporated into the machines had expired." 379 U.S. at 30, 32. To arrive at that conclusion, the Court began with the statutory provision setting the length of a patent term. Emphasizing that a patented invention "become[s] public property once [that term] expires," the Court then quoted from *Scott Paper*: Any attempt to limit a licensee's post-expiration use of the invention, "whatever the legal device employed, runs counter to the policy and purpose of the patent laws." 379 U.S. at 31. In the *Brulotte* Court's view, contracts to pay royalties for such use continue "the patent monopoly beyond the [patent] period," even though only as to the licensee affected. 379 U.S. at 33. And in so doing, those agreements conflict with patent law's policy of establishing a "post-expiration . . . public domain" in which every person can make free use of a formerly patented product.

The *Brulotte* rule, like others making contract provisions unenforceable, prevents some parties from entering into deals they desire. As compared to lump-sum fees, royalty plans both draw out payments over time and tie those payments, in each month or year covered, to a product's commercial success. And sometimes, for some parties, the longer the arrangement lasts, the better—not just up to but beyond a patent term's end. A more extended payment period, coupled (as it presumably would be) with a lower rate, may bring the price the patent holder seeks within the range of a cash-strapped licensee. (Anyone who has bought a product on installment can relate.) Or such an extended term may better allocate the risks and rewards associated with commercializing inventions—most notably, when years of development work stand between licensing a patent and bringing a product to market. As to either goal, *Brulotte* may pose an obstacle.

Yet parties can often find ways around *Brulotte*, enabling them to achieve those same ends. To start, *Brulotte* allows a licensee to defer payments for pre-expiration use of a patent into the post-expiration period; all the decision bars are royalties for using an invention after it has moved into the public domain. A licensee could agree, for example, to pay the licensor a sum equal to 10% of sales during the 20-year patent term, but to amortize that amount over 40 years. That arrangement would at least bring down early outlays, even if it would not do everything the parties might want to allocate risk over a long timeframe. And parties have still more options when a licensing agreement covers either multiple patents or additional non-patent rights. Under *Brulotte*, royalties may run until the latest-running patent covered in the parties' agreement expires. Too, post-expiration royalties are allowable so long as tied to a non-patent right—even when closely related to a patent. That means, for example, that a license involving both a patent and a trade secret can set a 5% royalty during the patent period (as compensation for the two combined) and a 4% royalty afterward (as payment for the trade secret alone). Finally and most broadly, *Brulotte* poses no bar to business arrangements other than royalties—all kinds of joint ventures, for example—that enable parties to share the risks and rewards of commercializing an invention.

Contending that such alternatives are not enough, Kimble asks us to abandon *Brulotte* in favor of "flexible, case-by-case analysis" of post-expiration royalty clauses "under the rule of reason." Used in antitrust law, the rule of reason requires courts to evaluate a practice's effect on competition by "taking into account a variety of factors, including specific information about the relevant business, its condition before and after the [practice] was imposed, and the [practice's] history, nature, and effect." State Oil Co. v. Khan, 522 U.S. 3, 10 (1997). Of primary importance in this context, Kimble posits, is whether a patent holder has power in the relevant market and so might be able to curtail competition.

III

Overruling precedent is never a small matter. Stare decisis—in English, the idea that today's Court should stand by yesterday's decisions—is "a foundation stone of the rule of law." Application of that doctrine, although "not an inexorable command," is the "preferred course because it promotes the evenhanded, predictable, and consistent development of legal principles, fosters reliance on judicial decisions, and contributes to the actual and perceived integrity of the judicial process." Payne v. Tennessee, 501 U.S. 808, 827-828 (1991). It also reduces incentives for challenging settled precedents, saving parties and courts the expense of endless relitigation.

Respecting stare decisis means sticking to some wrong decisions. The doctrine rests on the idea, as Justice Brandeis famously wrote, that it is usually "more important that the applicable rule of law be settled than that it be settled right." Burnet v. Coronado Oil & Gas Co., 285 U.S. 393, 406 (1932). Indeed, stare decisis has consequence only to the extent it sustains incorrect decisions; correct judgments have no need for that principle to prop them up. Accordingly, an argument that we got something wrong — even a good argument to that effect — cannot by itself justify scrapping settled precedent. Or otherwise said, it is not alone sufficient that we would decide a case differently now than we did then. To reverse course, we require as well what we have termed a "special justification" — over and above the belief "that the precedent was wrongly decided." Halliburton Co. v. Erica P. John Fund, Inc., 134 S. Ct. 2398, 2407 (2014).

What is more, stare decisis carries enhanced force when a decision, like *Brulotte*, interprets a statute. Then, unlike in a constitutional case, critics of our ruling can take their objections across the street, and Congress can correct any mistake it sees. That is true, contrary to the dissent's view, see post, at 2417-2418 (opinion of ALITO, J.), regardless whether our decision focused only on statutory text or also relied, as *Brulotte* did, on the policies and purposes animating the law. Indeed, we apply statutory stare decisis even when a decision has announced a "judicially created doctrine" designed to implement a federal statute. All our interpretive decisions, in whatever way reasoned, effectively become part of the statutory scheme, subject (just like the rest) to congressional change. Absent special justification, they are balls tossed into Congress's court, for acceptance or not as that branch elects.

And Congress has spurned multiple opportunities to reverse *Brulotte* — openings as frequent and clear as this Court ever sees. *Brulotte* has governed licensing agreements for more than half a century. During that time, Congress has repeatedly amended the patent laws, including the specific provision (35 U.S.C. §154) on which *Brulotte* rested. *Brulotte* survived every such change. Indeed, Congress has rebuffed bills that would have replaced *Brulotte* 's per se rule with the same antitrust-style analysis Kimble now urges. Congress's continual reworking of the patent laws — but never of the *Brulotte* rule — further supports leaving the decision in place.

Nor yet are we done, for the subject matter of *Brulotte* adds to the case for adhering to precedent. *Brulotte* lies at the intersection of two areas of law: property (patents) and contracts (licensing agreements). And we have often recognized that in just those contexts — "cases involving property and contract rights" — considerations favoring stare decisis are "at their acme." E.g., *Payne*, 501 U.S., at 828; *Khan*, 522 U.S., at 20. That is because parties are especially likely to rely on such precedents when ordering their affairs. To be sure, Marvel and Kimble disagree about whether *Brulotte* has actually generated reliance. Marvel says yes: Some parties, it claims, do not specify an end date for royalties in their licensing agreements, instead relying on *Brulotte* as a default rule. Overturning *Brulotte* would thus upset expectations, most so when long-dormant licenses for long-expired patents spring back to life. Not true, says Kimble: Unfair surprise is unlikely, because no "meaningful number of [such] license agreements . . . actually exist." To be honest, we do not know (nor, we suspect, do Marvel and Kimble). But even uncertainty on this score cuts in Marvel's direction. So long as we see a reasonable possibility that parties have structured their business transactions in light of *Brulotte*, we have one more reason to let it stand.

As against this superpowered form of stare decisis, we would need a superspecial justification to warrant reversing *Brulotte*. But the kinds of reasons we have most often held sufficient in the past do not help Kimble here. If anything, they reinforce our unwillingness to do what he asks.

First, *Brulotte*'s statutory and doctrinal underpinnings have not eroded over time. When we reverse our statutory interpretations, we most often point to subsequent legal developments — "either the growth of judicial doctrine or further action taken by Congress" — that have removed the basis for a decision. *Patterson*, 491 U.S. at 173 (calling this "the primary reason" for overruling statutory precedent). But the core feature of the patent laws on which *Brulotte* relied remains just the same: Section 154 now, as then, draws a sharp line cutting off patent rights after a set number of years. And this Court has continued to draw from that legislative choice a broad policy favoring unrestricted use of an invention after its patent's expiration. *Scott Paper* — the decision on which *Brulotte* primarily relied — remains good law. So too do this Court's other decisions refusing to enforce either state laws or private contracts constraining individuals' free use of formerly patented (or unpatentable) discoveries. *Brulotte*, then, is not the kind of doctrinal dinosaur or legal last-man-standing for which we sometimes depart from stare decisis. To the contrary, the decision's close relation to a whole web of precedents means that reversing it could threaten others. If *Brulotte* is outdated, then (for example) is *Scott Paper* too? We would prefer not to unsettle stable law.

And second, nothing about *Brulotte* has proved unworkable. The decision is simplicity itself to apply. A court need only ask whether a licensing agreement provides royalties for post-expiration use of a patent. If not, no problem; if so, no dice. *Brulotte*'s ease of use appears in still sharper relief when compared to Kimble's proposed alternative. Recall that he wants courts to employ antitrust law's rule of reason to identify and invalidate those post-expiration royalty clauses with anti-competitive consequences. But whatever its merits may be for deciding antitrust claims, that "elaborate inquiry" produces notoriously high litigation costs and unpredictable results. For that reason, trading in *Brulotte* for the rule of reason would make the law less, not more, workable than it is now. Once again, then, the case for sticking with long-settled precedent grows stronger: Even the most usual reasons for abandoning stare decisis cut the other way here.

IV

Lacking recourse to those traditional justifications for overruling a prior decision, Kimble offers two different ones. He claims first that *Brulotte* rests on a mistaken view of the competitive effects of post-expiration royalties. He contends next that *Brulotte* suppresses technological innovation and so harms the nation's economy. We consider the two claims in turn, but our answers to both are much the same: Kimble's reasoning may give Congress cause to upset *Brulotte*, but does not warrant this Court's doing so.

A

According to Kimble, we should overrule *Brulotte* because it hinged on an error about economics: It assumed that post-patent royalty "arrangements are invariably anticompetitive."

That is not true, Kimble notes; indeed, such agreements more often increase than inhibit competition, both before and after the patent expires. As noted earlier, a longer payment period will typically go hand-in-hand with a lower royalty rate. During the patent term, those reduced rates may lead to lower consumer prices, making the patented technology more competitive with alternatives; too, the lesser rates may enable more companies to afford a license, fostering competition among the patent's own users. And after the patent's expiration, Kimble continues, further benefits follow: Absent high barriers to entry, the licensee's continuing obligation to pay royalties encourages new companies to begin making the product, figuring that they can quickly attract customers by undercutting the licensee on price. In light of those realities, Kimble concludes, "the *Brulotte* per se rule makes little sense."

We do not join issue with Kimble's economics — only with what follows from it. A broad scholarly consensus supports Kimble's view of the competitive effects of post-expiration royalties, and we see no error in that shared analysis. Still, we must decide what that means for *Brulotte*. Kimble, of course, says it means the decision must go. Positing that *Brulotte* turned on the belief that post-expiration royalties are always anticompetitive, he invokes decisions in which this Court abandoned antitrust precedents premised on similarly shaky economic reasoning. But to agree with Kimble's conclusion, we must resolve two questions in his favor. First, even assuming Kimble accurately characterizes *Brulotte*'s basis, does the decision's economic mistake suffice to overcome stare decisis? Second and more fundamentally, was *Brulotte* actually founded, as Kimble contends, on an analysis of competitive effects?

If *Brulotte* were an antitrust rather than a patent case, we might answer both questions as Kimble would like. This Court has viewed stare decisis as having less-than-usual force in cases involving the Sherman Act. Congress, we have explained, intended that law's reference to "restraint of trade" to have "changing content," and authorized courts to oversee the term's "dynamic potential." Business Electronics Corp. v. Sharp Electronics Corp., 485 U.S. 717, 731-732 (1988). We have therefore felt relatively free to revise our legal analysis as economic understanding evolves and (just as Kimble notes) to reverse antitrust precedents that misperceived a practice's competitive consequences. Moreover, because the question in those cases was whether the challenged activity restrained trade, the Court's rulings necessarily turned on its understanding of economics. Accordingly, to overturn the decisions in light of sounder economic reasoning was to take them "on [their] own terms." *Halliburton*, 134 S. Ct., at 2410.

But *Brulotte* is a patent rather than an antitrust case, and our answers to both questions instead go against Kimble. To begin, even assuming that *Brulotte* relied on an economic misjudgment, Congress is the right entity to fix it. By contrast with the Sherman Act, the patent laws do not turn over exceptional law-shaping authority to the courts. Accordingly, statutory stare decisis — in which this Court interprets and Congress decides whether to amend — retains its usual strong force. And as we have shown, that doctrine does not ordinarily bend to "wrong on the merits"-type arguments; it instead assumes Congress will correct whatever mistakes we commit. Nor does Kimble offer any reason to think his own "the Court erred" claim is special. Indeed, he does not even point to anything that has changed since *Brulotte* — no new empirical studies or advances in economic theory. On his argument, the *Brulotte* Court knew all it needed to know to determine that post-patent royalties are not usually anticompetitive; it just made the wrong call. That claim, even if itself dead-right, fails to clear stare decisis 's high bar.

And in any event, *Brulotte* did not hinge on the mistake Kimble identifies. Although some of its language invoked economic concepts, the Court did not rely on the notion that post-patent royalties harm competition. Nor is that surprising. The patent laws — unlike the Sherman Act — do not aim to maximize competition (to a large extent, the opposite). And the patent term — unlike the "restraint of trade" standard — provides an all-encompassing bright-line rule, rather than calling for practice-specific analysis. So in deciding whether post-expiration royalties comport with patent law, *Brulotte* did not undertake to assess that practice's likely competitive effects. Instead, it applied a categorical principle that all patents, and all benefits from them, must end when their terms expire. Or more specifically put, the Court held, as it had in *Scott Paper*, that Congress had made a judgment: that the day after a patent lapses, the formerly protected invention must be available to all for free. And further: that post-expiration restraints on even a single licensee's access to the invention clash with that principle. *See Brulotte*, 379 U.S. at 31-32 (a licensee's obligation to pay post-patent royalties conflicts with the "free market visualized for the post-expiration period" and so "runs counter to the policy and purpose of the patent laws." That patent (not antitrust) policy gave rise to the Court's conclusion that post-patent royalty contracts are unenforceable — utterly "regardless of a demonstrable effect on competition." 1 Hovenkamp §3.2d, at 3-10.

Kimble's real complaint may go to the merits of such a patent policy — what he terms its "formalis[m]," its "rigid[ity]", and its detachment from "economic reality." But that is just a different version of the argument that *Brulotte* is wrong. And it is, if anything, a version less capable than the last of trumping statutory stare decisis. For the choice of what patent policy should be lies first and foremost with Congress. So if Kimble thinks patent law's insistence on unrestricted access to formerly patented inventions leaves too little room for pro-competitive post-expiration royalties, then Congress, not this Court, is his proper audience.

B

Kimble also seeks support from the wellspring of all patent policy: the goal of promoting innovation. *Brulotte*, he contends, "discourages technological innovation and does significant damage to the American economy." Recall that would-be licensors and licensees may benefit from post-patent royalty arrangements because they allow for a longer payment period and a more precise allocation of risk. If the parties' ideal licensing agreement is barred, Kimble reasons, they may reach no agreement at all. And that possibility may discourage invention in the first instance. The bottom line, Kimble concludes, is that some "breakthrough technologies will never see the light of day."

Maybe. Or, then again, maybe not. While we recognize that post-patent royalties are sometimes not anticompetitive, we just cannot say whether barring them imposes any meaningful drag on innovation. As we have explained, *Brulotte* leaves open various ways — involving both licensing and other business arrangements — to accomplish payment deferral and risk-spreading alike. Those alternatives may not offer the parties the precise set of benefits and obligations they would prefer. But they might still suffice to bring patent holders and product developers together and ensure that inventions get to the public. Neither Kimble nor his amici have offered any empirical evidence connecting *Brulotte* to decreased innovation; they essentially ask us to take their word for the problem. And the United States, which acts as both a licensor and a licensee of patented inventions while also implementing patent policy, vigorously disputes that *Brulotte* has caused any "significant real-world economic harm." Truth be told, if forced to decide that issue, we would not know where or how to start.

Which is one good reason why that is not our job. Claims that a statutory precedent has "serious and harmful consequences" for innovation are (to repeat this opinion's refrain) "more appropriately addressed to Congress." *Halliburton*, 134 S. Ct., at 2413. That branch, far more than this one, has the capacity to assess Kimble's charge that *Brulotte* suppresses technological progress. And if it concludes that *Brulotte* works such harm, Congress has the prerogative to determine the exact right response — choosing the policy fix, among many conceivable ones, that will optimally serve the public interest. As we have noted, Congress legislates actively with respect to patents, considering concerns of just the kind Kimble raises. In adhering to our precedent as against such complaints, we promote the rule-of-law values to which courts must attend while leaving matters of public policy to Congress.

V

What we can decide, we can undecide. But stare decisis teaches that we should exercise that authority sparingly. Cf. S. Lee and S. Ditko, Amazing Fantasy No. 15: "Spider-Man," p. 13 (1962) ("[I]n this world, with great power there must also come — great responsibility"). Finding many reasons for staying the stare decisis course and no "special justification" for departing from it, we decline Kimble's invitation to overrule *Brulotte*.

For the reasons stated, the judgment of the Court of Appeals is affirmed.

TEXAS INSTRUMENTS, INC. v. TESSERA, INC.
231 F.3d 1325 (Fed. Cir. 2000)

RADER, Circuit Judge.

In the United States District Court for the Central District of California, Texas Instruments Incorporated (TI) sought to enjoin Tessera, Inc. (Tessera) from continued participation in an International Trade Commission (ITC) infringement action that Tessera had initiated. The district court denied TI's motion. Because the license agreement between TI and Tessera requires any litigation, including ITC proceedings under Section 337 of the Tariff Act of 1930, to occur in the State of California, this court vacates and remands to the district court to re-entertain TI's preliminary injunction motion.

I.

On November 1, 1996, TI entered into a "Limited TCC License Agreement" with Tessera. The license agreement covers technology claimed in several of Tessera's United States patents. The technology relates to chip scale packaging, a semiconductor package with connections between the semiconductor chip and a circuit board underneath the chip, within the periphery of the chip itself. Tessera designates this type of chip package with the brand name "TCC," for Tessera Compliant Chip. TCCs occupy less space on a circuit board than conventionally packaged chips, a feature which is particularly attractive in applications such as cellular phones.

The license agreement between Tessera and TI contains a clause that governs the law and venue that applies to the agreement:

> Governing Law. This Agreement shall be governed, interpreted and construed in accordance with the laws of the States [sic] of California as if without regard to its provisions with respect to conflicts of Laws. Both parities [sic] shall use their best efforts to resolve by mutual agreement any disputes, controversies, claims or difference which may arise from, under, out of or in connection with this Agreement. If such disputes, controversies, claims or differences cannot be settled between the parties, any litigation between the parties relating to this Agreement shall take place in California. The parties hereby consent to personal jurisdiction and venue in the state and federal courts of California. (Emphasis added.)

In April 1999, Tessera requested royalties for a class of TI imports known as "MicroStar BGA." Tessera sought royalties under its United States Patents. . . . After negotiations, TI and Tessera could not agree on whether the license agreement covered the accused TI products. Therefore, on January 17, 2000, Tessera notified TI of its termination of the license agreement. In response to Tessera's notice of termination, TI filed an action for declaratory judgment of invalidity and non-infringement in the United States District Court for the Central District of California on February 1, 2000.

On March 28, 2000, Tessera filed a complaint with the ITC, under Section 337 of the Tariff Act of 1930, charging that TI's importation of the MicroStar BGA products and certain importations by others infringe the patents. See 19 U.S.C. §1337 (1994).

On April 4, 2000, TI applied for a Temporary Restraining Order (TRO) and an order requesting an expedited preliminary injunction hearing in the California district court. TI requested the court to restrain Tessera "from pursuing any disputes, controversies, claims or differences . . . against TI that arise from, under, out of or in connection with" the license agreement, in any place outside California. TI asserted that because the ITC tribunal is located in Washington, D.C., Tessera's ITC complaint violated the license agreement. TI further explained that the ITC determines whether to initiate an investigation within thirty days of the filing of a complaint. TI considered its request for an expedited preliminary injunction hearing warranted because Tessera could not simply withdraw its complaint once the ITC initiated an investigation. The district court denied TI's application for a TRO and set the preliminary injunction hearing date for May 1, 2000.

On April 27, 2000, the ITC instituted an investigation into the allegedly infringing imports. See In the Matter of Certain Semiconductor Chips with Minimized Chip Package Size and Products Containing Same, Investigation No. 337-TA-432 (April 27, 2000). The ITC's Notice of Investigation named TI, Sharp Corporation, and Sharp Electronics Corporation as respondents. Id. That same day, the ITC made a motion, under Fed. R. Civ. P. 24, for leave to intervene in the preliminary injunction hearing at the district court "for the purpose of opposing [TI's] motion to enjoin [Tessera] from pursuing claims . . . through the ITC."

On May 2, 2000, the district court granted ITC's motion to intervene and denied TI's motion for a preliminary injunction. . . . TI appeals, invoking this court's jurisdiction of interlocutory appeals under 28 U.S.C. §1292(c)(1) (1994).

II.

TI's preliminary injunction motion was a request for the district court to enjoin Tessera from continued participation in an ITC proceeding. This court has exclusive appellate jurisdiction over ITC determinations made under section 337 of the Tariff Act of 1930. See 28 U.S.C. §1295(a)(6) (1994). Thus, TI's appeal relates to a procedural matter arising from substantive issues in an area of law within the unique jurisdiction of this circuit. This circuit's procedural law, therefore, applies to the district court's order under review. Under Federal Circuit law, this court sustains a grant or denial of a preliminary injunction unless the district court abused its discretion, or based its decision on an erroneous legal standard or clearly erroneous findings of fact.

The district court's order denying TI's motion for a preliminary injunction also presents an issue concerning interpretation of a license agreement. General contract interpretation is not within the exclusive jurisdiction of the Federal Circuit. The Supreme Court has held that "[t]he interpretation of private contracts is ordinarily a question of state law." Volt Info. Sci., Inc. v. Bd. of Tr. of Leland Stanford Junior Univ., 489 U.S. 468, 474 (1989). Furthermore, the governing law clause of the license agreement requires interpretation of the agreement "in accordance with the laws of the States [sic] of California." This court will, therefore, apply California state law to interpret the license agreement. Under California state law, contracts are interpreted without deference on appeal. Plaza Freeway Ltd. P'ship v. First Mountain Bank, 81 Cal. App. 4th 616, 620 (2000).

According to this circuit's law, a party seeking an injunction must show: (1) a reasonable likelihood of success on the merits; (2) irreparable harm; (3) a balance of hardships in its favor; and (4) a public interest in favor of the injunction. See *Chrysler Motors Corp.*, 908 F.2d at 952, 15 U.S.P.Q.2d at 1470. The United States Court of Appeals for the Ninth Circuit applies the same test. See Am. Motorcyclist Ass'n v. Watt, 714 F.2d 962, 965 (9th Cir. 1983). . . .

The Cal. Civ. Code supplies basic rules for contract interpretation: (1) "clear and explicit" language which does not produce an absurdity will govern, Cal. Civ. Code §1638; (2) ambiguous terms receive the meaning "which the promisor believed, at the time of making it, that the promisee understood," Cal. Civ. Code §1649; and (3) ambiguity persisting beyond the application of the previous rule will be resolved against "the party who caused the uncertainty to exist," Cal. Civ. Code §1654. In sum, "the mutual intention of the parties at the time the contract is formed governs interpretation." AIU Ins. Co. v. Superior Court, 799 P.2d 1253, 1264 (1990).

When interpreting a contract provision, a court gives the contract terms their ordinary and popular meaning unless the contracting parties use them in a technical or a special sense. *Id.* at 822.

As noted above, contracts in California rely for meaning predominantly upon the mutual intention of the parties at the time of contracting. The district court did not make any findings as to the parties' understanding of the term "litigation" at the time of contracting. The license agreement at issue in this suit governs a very specific form of business arrangement, namely the licensing of patented technology. Both Tessera and TI are sophisticated corporations with experience in patent licensing. The United States Patent and Trademark Office Patent Bibliographic Database lists Tessera as the assignee of over 110 patents, TI of over 8000 patents. These corporations necessarily regularly apply the basic tenets of patent practice. Each is well aware of available remedies for patentees and defenses for accused infringers. Thus, these contracting parties would have negotiated the clauses of the patent license agreement with knowledge of patent law, including available remedies for patent law violations.

Patent law affords a patentee several alternative remedies against a purported infringer. For alleged domestic infringement, a patentee can file an action in a district court. For alleged infringement through importation, a patentee can also file an action in a district court or in the ITC. See 19 U.S.C. §1337. In fact, a patentee can bring suit both in a district court and in the ITC against an alleged infringer who is importing an allegedly infringing product.

The two forums offer a patentee different types of remedies. In a district court, a patentee can seek an injunction and damages. With respect to infringing imports, however, the patentee must take the additional step of requesting the U.S. Customs Service to enforce the district court judgment by seizing the offending goods. In the ITC, the patentee may not seek money damages, Bio-Tech. Gen. Corp. v. Genentech, Inc., 80 F.3d 1553, 1564 (Fed. Cir. 1996), but the ITC automatically enforces its judgment by directing the U.S. Customs Service to seize any infringing imports.

Thus, when TI and Tessera negotiated the terms of their licensing agreement, this court attributes to them adequate knowledge of the basic patent law actions and remedies available to litigants, including the available forums and venues. Both parties would have been fully aware of the forums of the district courts and the ITC for resolution of future controversies arising from the license agreement. With this in mind, this court next examines the parties' intentions in using the word "litigation" in the governing law clause of their agreement. As mentioned earlier, the district court determined the meaning of "litigation" based on the California Code of Civil Procedure Title for "Vexatious Litigants." The definition of "litigation" in that title does not govern this licensing agreement for Tessera patents. In the first place, the Cal. Code Civ. Proc., section 391, states: "As used in this title . . . 'Litigation' means. . . ." Thus, the California Code limits its definition to use in that particular title. This limitation hardly suggests that TI and Tessera would have incorporated that meaning from the California "Vexatious Litigants" section into their license agreement on patented technology. In the field of patent law, which is more relevant to the meaning of this license, "litigation" does not exclude ITC proceedings under section 337. Section 337 proceedings are inter partes actions initiated by the filing of a complaint and including discovery, filing of briefs and motions, and testimony and arguments at a hearing before an administrative law judge. See 19 U.S.C. §1337(c). In section 337 proceedings relevant to patent infringement, the ITC follows Title 35 of the United States Code and the case law of this court. In sum, this court has consistently treated section 337 patent infringement proceedings as litigation.

Indeed, the ITC itself refers to its section 337 proceedings as "litigation." See, e.g., ITC R. Prac. & P., 19 C.F.R. §210.27 (1999) (referring to the "cost of litigation" and "issues at stake in the litigation" with respect to ITC discovery rules); see also U.S. International Trade Commission Fiscal Year 1996 Annual Report, 1997 ITC Lexis 410 (August 1997) ("The ITC's Administrative Law Judges (ALJs) direct litigation, hold hearings, and make initial determinations in investigations under section 337 of the Tariff Act of 1930."). Moreover, practitioners, commentators, and scholars in the areas of both intellectual property and trade law also refer to section 337 investigations as litigation.

Therefore, section 337 proceedings at the ITC are recognized as litigation. As noted earlier, this court attributes knowledge of patent law and its language and usages to both parties at the time of contracting. In interpreting contracts, words are given their "clear and explicit" meaning in the field of the agreement unless it is clearly shown that the parties intended a different meaning. See Cal. Civ. Code §1638; see also Cal. Civ. Code §1649. Thus, the term "litigation" in the governing law clause of the license agreement includes section 337 proceedings at the ITC. The governing law clause, therefore, requires any litigation between the parties, including ITC proceedings, to take place in California. Because ITC actions cannot be brought in California, it follows that the parties did not agree to the ITC as a forum for litigation.

This court further notes that the governing law clause of the license agreement is not limited to license related issues such as the amount of royalty due, term of agreement, and cross-licensing. The governing law clause lists "disputes, controversies, claims or difference[s] which may arise from, under, out of or in connection with this Agreement." . . . Patent infringement disputes do arise from license agreements. There may be an issue, as here, of whether certain goods are covered by the licensed patents; or the licensee may elect to challenge the validity of the licensed patents. Thus, the governing law clause in the present case, as in any patent license agreement, necessarily covers disputes concerning patent issues.

The district court denied TI's preliminary injunction motion based on a finding that TI was not likely to succeed on its claim that the governing law clause includes ITC proceedings. Because this court has determined that the governing law clause does encompass ITC proceedings under section 337, this court reverses the district court's finding on this preliminary injunction factor.

Following a combination of Ninth Circuit and California state law, the district court only examined TI's likelihood of success on the merits in denying the motion for preliminary judgment. TI I, 192 F.R.D. at 640 ("Moreover, because the test for a preliminary injunction is in the conjunctive, the Court does not proceed with the other elements."). Because the district court did not make any relevant findings on the other preliminary injunction factors, this court does not have any record on which to review the irreparable harm and public policy factors. This court, therefore, vacates the district court's denial of TI's preliminary injunction motion and remands to the district court to make findings on the other factors and re-entertain TI's motion.

III.

In light of its interpretation of the term "litigation" in the license agreement, this court also observes that the district court erred in assessing the implications of enforcing the license agreement. Because the governing law clause encompasses ITC section 337 proceedings, Tessera breached this provision of the license agreement by bringing an action against TI at the ITC (which is in Washington, D.C.), rather than in a court in California, as mandated by the agreement. Thus, TI may have been prejudiced by Tessera's breach, for TI had already filed suit in California and would now be obliged to defend a second action in a Washington, D.C., forum. In effect, Tessera is attempting to compel TI to fight infringement battles on two fronts.

More important, TI's preliminary injunction motion will not and cannot enjoin the ITC action. TI has not sought to enjoin the ITC directly, but only to enjoin Tessera from participating in the ITC proceedings against TI. The ITC, intervening in this appeal, advised that the action will continue, even without Tessera's participation with respect to TI. The ITC's investigation of Tessera's complaint includes Sharp Corporation and Sharp Electronics Corporation as respondents in addition to TI. Tessera, therefore, will still participate in the overall ITC proceeding, even if TI's preliminary injunction request is ultimately granted. Any potential injunction would simply implement the governing law clause and any litigation between Tessera and TI will occur in a California district court.

CONCLUSION

This court reverses the district court's judgment that TI would not be likely to succeed in proving that Tessera's action before the ITC is covered by the governing law clause. This court, therefore, vacates the district court's denial of TI's preliminary injunction motion and remands to the district court to reconsider the preliminary injunction motion on the remaining preliminary injunction factors.

VACATED and REMANDED.

LOURIE, Circuit Judge, dissenting.

I respectfully dissent.

Everyone familiar with patent litigation knows that ITC proceedings are considered "litigation." However, our job is to construe a particular provision of a license agreement by determining the intentions of the parties to that agreement. I conclude that ITC proceedings were not intended to be within the scope of the venue provision at issue. Because ITC litigation is part of the patent world, as the majority clearly agrees, I believe that if the parties had intended that ITC proceedings be part of this paragraph, they would have so stated. I believe the limitation to California was intended to mean California, and not Texas or Delaware. The indication of California is a geographic limitation, not one indicating the type of forum. It did not state that litigation should be in a district court, rather than at the ITC.

Moreover, the provision relates to disputes "in connection with the agreement." Disputes in connection with a license agreement are most often disputes about the scope of licensed subject matter, amount of royalty due, term of agreement, cross-licensing, the meaning of other provisions, etc., rather than concerning the validity or infringement of the patent. The whole point of a license is not to exclude, as a patent does, but to legitimize the licensee under the patent. While obviously disputes can arise concerning validity and infringement, I believe that the language indicates that the parties meant questions most likely to arise under the contract, i.e., those that can be resolved by invoking California contract law. License agreements are construed under state law, in which case the particular venue might matter, thus supporting the idea that the parties intended one state as the venue, not another state. Moreover, the parties could not have intended that California law would govern the question of whether or not ITC proceedings are litigation, as California law has nothing relevant to offer on that issue. In addition, enjoining Tessera, even though it would not enjoin the Commission, would potentially impede and complicate the Commission's opportunity to pursue its own statutory duty to investigate possible violations of the Tariff Act. Any subpoena issued to Tessera would create a conflict with the district court's injunction. Such conflicts are to be abhorred and avoided if at all possible. Although it was pointed out at oral argument that Tessera could still prosecute its complaint against Sharp, any district court injunction would not be binding against TI. Thus, we might have the situation in which both parties to this appeal are in the ITC action, with TI having the opportunity to assist Sharp in its attack on Tessera's patent, but Tessera would have one hand tied behind its back, not being able to proceed against TI. That likelihood does not argue for the resolution adopted by the majority. Practicality supports affirmance.

Finally, we review a denial of an injunction on an abuse of discretion standard. Although contract interpretation is a question of law, I believe some reluctance should still exist in overthrowing a district court's denial of the injunction. I do not believe the facts of this case and the language of this contract justify reversal of the trial court.

INTEL CORP. v. NEGOTIATED DATA SOLUTIONS, INC.

703 F.3d 1360 (Fed. Cir. 2012)

LINN, Circuit Judge.

Negotiated Data Solutions, Inc. ("N-Data") appeals from the district court's grant of summary judgment of license and noninfringement in favor of Intel Corp. ("Intel"). Because Intel is licensed to practice the patents-in-suit pursuant to a licensing agreement with N-Data's predecessor in interest, National Semiconductor Corp. ("National"), this court affirms.

I. BACKGROUND

By the 1970s both Intel and National were actively developing semiconductor technology. On June 1, 1976, Intel and National entered into a patent cross-licensing agreement. Agreement between Intel Corp. and National Semiconductor Corp. (June 8, 1976) (J.A. 284) ("National Agreement" or "Agreement"). The Agreement gave Intel "non-exclusive, non-transferrable, royalty-free, world-wide licenses under NATIONAL PATENTS and NATIONAL PATENT APPLICATIONS to make, to have made, to use, to sell (either directly or indirectly), to lease and to otherwise dispose of LICENSED PRODUCTS," for the life or lives of the patents. The Agreement defined "NATIONAL PATENTS" ("National Patents") as:

> all classes or types of patents and utility models of all countries of the world, applications for which have a first effective filing date in any country prior to the date of expiration or termination of this Agreement, in respect of which, as of the EFFECTIVE DATE, or thereafter during the term of this Agreement, NATIONAL owns or controls . . . [or has] the right to grant licenses of the scope granted herein. . . .

The Agreement gave National similar rights in Intel's patents. The parties extended the five year agreement three times, finally allowing it to expire on December 31, 2003.

In 1998, National assigned U.S. Patents No. 5,361,261 ("'261 Patent"), No. 5,533,018 ("'018 Patent"), No. 5,566,169 ("'169 Patent"), No. 5,594,734 ("'734 Patent") (collectively the "Original Patents"), and others to Vertical Networks, Inc. ("Vertical"), a corporation consisting partially of former National engineers. Each one of the Original Patents was indisputably a National Patent under the Agreement. Then between 1998 and 1999 Vertical filed broadening reissue applications with the United States Patent and Trademark Office ("PTO") for the latter three of the Original Patents. In filing these reissue applications, Vertical increased the total number of claims in the three patents from 77 to 378. In 2003 and 2005, Vertical assigned the Original Patents and their corresponding reissue applications to N-Data. In 2005 and 2006, well after the Agreement had expired, the PTO issued to N-Data U.S. Reissue Patents RE38,820 ("RE'820 Patent"), RE39,216 ("RE'216 Patent"), and RE39,395 ("RE'395 Patent") (collectively the "Reissue Patents") corresponding to the '018, '734, and '169 Patents, respectively.

On December 13, 2006, N-Data sued Dell, Inc. ("Dell"), one of Intel's customers, in the United States District Court for the Eastern District of Texas, alleging infringement of several patents, including the Reissue Patents. Negotiated Data Solutions v. Dell, Inc., 2:06–cv–528 (E.D. Tx. July 13, 2009) ("*Dell*"), ECF No. 1. Intel intervened in N-Data's suit against Dell. On August 15, 2008, Intel filed a complaint seeking a declaratory judgment that under the National Agreement Intel and its customers are licensed to the National Patents and all reissue patents owned by N-Data that are derived from any of the National Patents. Intel Corp. v. Negotiated Data Solutions, LLC, No. 2:08–cv–319 (E.D. Tx. Mar. 18, 2010). N-Data counterclaimed alleging infringement against Intel and other Intel customers. Dell and N-Data ultimately settled, leaving Intel's declaratory judgment action and N-Data's counter-claim against Intel pending. Agreed Order of Dismissal with Prejudice, *Dell*, ECF No. 250.

II. DISCUSSION

The National Agreement is governed by California law, "under which the district court's interpretation . . . presents a question of law that we review de novo." Alfred E. Mann Found. For Scientific Research v. Cochlear Corp., 604 F.3d 1354, 1359 (Fed. Cir. 2010).

B. Analysis

The parties here ask this court to determine whether the National Agreement, which licenses National Patents to Intel, automatically extends to any reissue patents that are derived from those licensed National Patents.

1. 35 U.S.C. §252

N-Data contends that 35 U.S.C. §252 as a whole defines a nuanced arrangement where only substantially identical claims reach back to the date of the original patent and argues that the Agreement expressly covers only patents owned or controlled by National during the term of the license. Thus, according to N-Data, while the Agreement covered the Original Patents, it does not cover the Reissue Patents, which were each issued directly to N-Data after the Agreement had expired. According to N-Data, "upon surrender at reissue, '[t]he original claims are dead,'" Appellant's Br. 27, and the resulting reissue patent is a distinct property right that does not simply replace the original patent in an existing agreement.

Intel, however, focuses on §252's language that "every reissued patent shall have the same effect and operation in law, on the trial of actions for causes thereafter arising, as if the same had been originally granted in such amended form." According to Intel, when a cause of action arises after reissue, §252 provides that the reissue patent takes the place of the original patent *nunc pro tunc*, as if the reissued patent had been issued at the time of, and instead of, the original. *See* 35 U.S.C. §252. Intel points to language nearly identical to this portion of §252 in the statutes governing certificates of correction, 35 U.S.C. §§254 and 255, and argues that this court has held that in that context, this same language indicates that the corrected patent replaces the original *nunc pro tunc.* Thus, under Intel's reading of §252, the Reissue Patents should be treated as the Original Patents; because the Original Patents were indisputably licensed to Intel, the Reissue Patents are licensed as well.

Intel's focus on selected portions of the text of §252 ignores the specific language of the statute that grants intervening rights to those who may infringe only new claims added by reissue. In this important aspect alone, it is clear that a reissue patent does not simply replace an original patent *nunc pro tunc.* Intel's argument also fails to recognize that certificates of correction are not generally available to change the scope of coverage of a patent in the same way as a reissue, are not intended to remedy the same kinds of defects, and have different standards in implementation. Intel's attempt to draw parallels between §252 and the statutes governing certificates of correction thus falls short.

At bottom, the scheme set forth in §252 does not support Intel's simplistic proposition that a reissue patent replaces the original patent *nunc pro tunc.* The question remains, however, whether the National Agreement itself is properly interpreted, under California law, to extend the license granted thereunder to the Reissue Patents.

2. The Agreement

N-Data's primary argument is quite straightforward: the Agreement only covers National Patents, National Patents are patents that issued directly to National during the term of the Agreement, the Reissue Patents issued directly to N-Data after the Agreement had expired, and thus, the Reissue Patents are not covered by the grant in the Agreement. N-Data further contends that California law requires that the Agreement be interpreted in light of the parties' intent while contracting, and "the parties' general intent must be informed and limited by the particular provisions of the National License." Appellant's Br. 14. N-Data argues that the district court erred by discounting *Intergraph*'s interpretation of the National Agreement and *Altvater*'s proscription on rewriting a private contract to include a patent that did not exist at the time the parties formed the contract. N-Data also points to 35 U.S.C. §261, which makes any interest in a patent assignable, and McCoy v. Mitsuboshi Cutlery, Inc., 67 F.3d 917, 920 (Fed. Cir. 1995), to argue that National's interest in any potential reissue patents could have been licensed by contract, but here, was not. Finally, N-Data disagrees with the district court's conclusion that excluding reissue patents from licenses like the Agreement will allow for manipulation of the parties' intentions; here N-Data's Reissue Patents are broader than the Original Patents, and Intel therefore never had any rights under the new reissue claims. Thus, there is no way N-Data's conduct manipulates the system.

Intel agrees that under California law, a contract must be interpreted to give effect to the parties' mutual intent. *See* Cal. Civ. Code §1636. Intel contends, however, that in order to realize the parties' intention to avoid future patent infringement litigation, the Agreement broadly licensed all of National's patent rights; the Agreement did not license specific claims of any patents. Instead, the reissued patent covers "the" licensed invention from "the" original patent. *See* Oral Arg. at 22:55-23:50, *available at http://www.cafc.uscourts.gov/oral -argument-recordings/2011-1448/all/intel.html.* Thus, according to Intel, the district court correctly interpreted the contract as granting Intel a license to not only original patents, but also to any reissue patents that were derived therefrom and were directed to the inventions disclosed therein.

As the district court correctly noted, the key question in this case is not whether the Reissue Patents *are* National Patents under the definition set forth in the Agreement, but whether the Agreement evinces an intent on the part of the parties that Reissue Patents *should be treated as* National Patents under the Agreement. In this regard *Intergraph* is inapposite — that case only dealt with whether or not the National Agreement covered patent applications held momentarily by National as part of a corporate transaction in which a subsidiary possessed the applications but then immediately sold them, such that the applications never issued as National Patents. *See Intergraph*, 241 F.3d at 1355-56.

Nor does *Altvater* compel the conclusion that the Reissue Patents are not covered by the National Agreement. 319 U.S. 359. The issue that the Supreme Court considered in *Altvater* was whether there was a controversy between the parties when the district court found that there was not a valid license between the parties. 319 U.S. at 364-66. The language facially supporting N-Data's position is a restatement of the district court's findings, not a holding of the Supreme Court. The Court in *Altvater* was not deciding whether the license agreement between the parties terminated *because of* surrender and reissue. *Altvater* cannot mean that reissue of certain National Patents terminates the National Agreement; *Altvater* has no bearing on whether the National Agreement grants to Intel rights to reissue patents derived from National Patents and it does not compel adoption of the sweeping rule N-Data derives from it.

Section 251, which at the time the Agreement was signed provided in relevant part:

> [w]henever any patent is, through error without any deceptive intention, deemed wholly or partly inoperative or invalid, by reason of a defective specification or drawing, or by reason of the patentee claiming more or less than he had a right to claim in the patent, the Commissioner shall, on the surrender of such patent . . . reissue *the patent for the invention disclosed in the original patent*, and in accordance with a new and amended application, for the unexpired part of the term of the original patent. *No new matter shall be introduced into the application for reissue.*

35 U.S.C. §251 (1976) (emphasis added).

Section 251 does not refer to issuance of "a" reissue patent for "an" invention; it specifically refers to reissue of "the" inoperative or invalid patent for "the" invention disclosed in the original patent. 35 U.S.C. §251. The statute prohibits addition of new matter via reissue and indicates that "the" reissued patent will be effective for the remainder of the unexpired term of the original patent. Thus, the text of §251 suggests to a potential licensee that — in the absence of contrary language in the licensing agreement — a license under the patent that is not directed to any specific claims, field of use, or other limited right will extend to the full extent of protection provided by law to the invention which is the subject of that patent. Because the patent laws provide for the grant of reissue patents under specified circumstances, it is reasonable to conclude that the parties' mutual intent at the time of contracting was that the broad and unrestricted grant of license under National Patents extended to any reissues thereof.

This court's decisions in TransCore v. Electronic Transaction Consultants Corp., 563 F.3d 1271 (Fed. Cir. 2009), and General Protecht Group, Inc. v. Leviton Manufacturing Co., 651 F.3d 1355 (Fed. Cir. 2011), while not controlling, lend support to the interpretation made by the district court and affirmed by us here. In both of those cases this court analyzed a licensee's rights when the patent holder received a continuation patent that, if asserted against the licensee, would derogate from the licensee's right to practice the previously licensed patents.

Specifically, in *General Protecht* we observed that "the newly asserted continuations are based on the same disclosure as the previously licensed patents and that, by definition, *the continuations can claim no new invention not already supported in the earlier issued patents.*" 651 F.3d at 1361 (emphasis added). The "same inventive subject matter was disclosed" in the continuation patents as in the licensed patents, and "[i]f Leviton did not intend its license of these products to extend to claims presented in continuation patents, it had an obligation to make that clear." *Id.*

TransCore and *General Protecht* recognized that allowing the patent holder to sue on subsequent patents, when those later patents contain the same inventive subject matter that was licensed, risks derogating rights for which the licensee had paid consideration. In situations where the full extent of an invention disclosed in a patent is licensed, the concerns raised in *General Protecht* and *TransCore* are equally relevant, regardless of whether the case involves reissue patents or continuation patents.

N-Data repeatedly argues that "it has made and will make no assertion of infringement based on reissue claims that existed in any form prior to 2005," Appellant's Br. 9, thus there is no chance that N-Data will derogate from Intel's bargained for rights under the National Agreement. As support, N-Data cites to its counterclaim, where it alleged that Intel's acts exceed the scope of its license coverage, and to its motion for summary judgment of non-infringement of newly issued claims of the Reissue Patents. Intel disagrees, stating that N-Data has broadly asserted the Reissue Patents, including claims that were not new claims specific to the Reissue Patents. Appellee's Br. 9 ("N-Data asserted . . . original claims of the reissued patents (e.g., RE39,395 claims 1, 3, 7 and 14, RE39,216 claim 15, and RE38,820 claims 8, 30, 34). . . ."). Ultimately it is irrelevant which claims were asserted and when they were asserted. The district court granted summary judgment to Intel because the Agreement reflects the intent of the parties to license not only the literally described patents and patent applications, but also the reissue progeny of those licensed patents and patent applications from which the reissues were derived. This court agrees.

The National Agreement does not explicitly discuss reissue patents, but the grant of license under the National Patents is without limitation and without reference to any specific claims. The Agreement thus evinces the parties' intent that the license so granted extend not only to the claims then in existence but also to the full scope of any coverage available by way of reissue for the invention disclosed. To interpret the Agreement otherwise would allow the unilateral act of the licensor to place the licensee, which sought to eliminate any infringement risk and effect a global peace with the licensor for all claims in all patents, in a position of being exposed to further risk relating to the exact same inventions that were subject to the license. 35 U.S.C. §261 is not inconsistent with this conclusion. That a patent owner has the ability to assign (or reserve) any interest in its patent says nothing about interpreting a contract that does not expressly discuss that interest.

CONCLUSION

For the foregoing reasons, the judgment of the district court is affirmed.

JP MORGAN CHASE BANK, N.A. v. DATATREASURY CORP.
823 F.3d 1006 (5th Cir. 2016)

DAVIS, Circuit Judge:

In this case we review the district court's interpretation of a most favored licensee ("MFL") clause in a license agreement which allows Plaintiff-Appellee JP Morgan Chase Bank, N.A. ("JPMC") to use Defendant-Appellant DataTreasury Corporation's ("DTC") patented check processing technology. The negotiated license agreement granted JPMC unlimited use of the patented technology both as to time and volume of use for a lump sum, which JPMC paid in installments under the agreement. In its suit against DTC for breach of contract, JPMC invoked its rights under the MFL clause based on DTC's granting a similar unlimited license to another entity for a lesser lump sum than JPMC paid.

I. FACTUAL BACKGROUND AND PROCEDURAL HISTORY

DTC holds several patents applicable to electronic check-processing systems. In the late 1990s, the head of DTC reportedly met with several banks to discuss the use of DTC's patented technology, but the banks declined and instead created their own check-processing system. DTC sued JPMC and several other banks, including Bank One Corporation ("BOC"), which soon merged into JPMC, alleging willful patent infringement. Facing substantial potential liability, JPMC was the first bank to reach a settlement agreement with DTC in 2005.

As part of the settlement, JPMC entered into a consent judgment in which it admitted the patents were valid and enforceable and that JPMC had infringed them. It also entered into a license agreement permitting JPMC unlimited use of DTC's patented technology going forward. To protect JPMC from the risk that DTC would enter into a more favorable license with a later settling defendant, the license agreement included a most-favored licensee ("MFL") clause (also referred to as a most favored nations, or "MFN," clause), which forms the basis for this dispute. The settlement allowed both DTC and JPMC to avoid the risks and costs of litigation, drastically reduced JPMC's potential liability, and paved the way for DTC to settle with the other banks. DTC later obtained several hundred million dollars through the various settlements.

In the district court's superseding memorandum opinion and order in this case, entered February 5, 2015, it set out the relevant facts more fully as follows:

> On June 28, 2005, JPMC and BOC each entered into settlement agreements with DTC resolving patent infringement claims arising from certain of DTC's patents. The parties also entered into the License Agreement, allowing JPMC to use DTC's patents for a total consideration of $70 million. Although the $70 million altogether was a lump-sum payment for unlimited use of DTC's patents and not a "running royalty" paid per-use, the parties agreed to payment in installments: $25 million in 2005 under the BOC Settlement and Release Agreement; $5 million in 2005 under the JPMC Settlement and Release Agreement; and $5.5 million each year from 2006 to 2011, with a

final $7 million payment in 2012. Together, these payments are the full consideration for JPMC's use of DTC's patents.

Section 10.8 of the License Agreement provided that breaches of the agreement by either party generally could be cured, "other than the failure of JPMC to make the payments required by the Settlement and Release Agreement between DTC and JPMC," which breach "shall result in a termination of the licenses and rights granted to JPMC and its Subsidiaries in this Agreement." Thus, JPMC committed to pay the entire $70 million royalty from the outset and could not decide to stop paying even if it no longer desired to use DTC's patents. Under the unambiguous terms of the License Agreement, JPMC was required to pay the full $70 million or lose the license entirely. The district court continued:

Section 9 of the License Agreement contains the MFL at issue, which states:

9. Most Favored Licensee

If DTC grants to any other Person a license to any of the Licensed Patents, it will so notify JPMC, and JPMC will be entitled to the benefit of any and all more favorable terms with respect to such Licensed Patents. JPMC agrees that $.02 to $.05 per Transaction is a reasonable royalty under the license granted herein, and JPMC makes no representation as to what pro-rata share of such royalty is attributable to any portion or sub-part of such Transaction. The notification required under this Section shall be provided by DTC to JPMC in writing within thirty (30) days of the execution of any such third party license and shall be accompanied by a copy of the third party license agreement, which may be redacted by DTC if necessary to comply with any judicial order or other confidentiality obligation. The MFN shall be applied within thirty (30) days from the date this provision is recognized in accordance with Section 10.7.

Section 10.1 requires notices to be by fax and express delivery to both JPMC's Office of General Counsel and to outside counsel at Skadden, Arps, Slate, Meagher & Flom LLP (Skadden). Section 10.7 is a choice of law and forum clause requiring that the License Agreement be construed under Texas law, and that jurisdiction and venue exist solely in the United States District Court for the Eastern District of Texas, Texarkana Division.

After entering into the License Agreement, DTC separately entered into several other licensing agreements (the Subsequent Licenses) involving the same patents but at different lump sum price terms. Notably here, on October 1, 2012, DTC entered into such a license agreement with non-party Cathay General Bancorp (Cathay). The lump sum price term for Cathay's sole use (i.e., not extending to any after-acquired entities) was $250,000. However, as discussed below, the full consideration under the Cathay license also required additional payments under an established formula for any additional entities Cathay acquired later. No such provision exists in the JPMC-DTC License Agreement.

On November 29, 2012, JPMC filed the instant lawsuit for breach of contract against DTC, alleging that DTC had failed to notify JPMC of the Subsequent Licenses and that "many of the Subsequent Licenses were granted on terms substantially more favorable than those afforded to JPMC." Of note, the Cathay license agreement had not been noticed to JPMC, but was produced after JPMC initiated this lawsuit.

In its instant motion for summary judgment, JPMC seeks the benefit of the isolated price term granted to Cathay, and summary judgment on DTC's affirmative defenses and counterclaims. To obtain that benefit, JPMC contends that its $70 million lump-sum price term must be retroactively replaced with Cathay's $250,000 lump-sum price term and the balance refunded. JPMC also moved to dismiss DTC's counterclaims. . . .

[T]he district court entered a final judgment . . . in favor of JPMC in the amount of $69 million (the $70 million JPMC paid under its original license less the $1 million total it owed under the retroactively applied terms of the Cathay license). DTC timely filed a notice of appeal.

II. APPLICABLE LAW

B. Contract Interpretation Rules

The parties agree that Texas law applies to this dispute. The Fifth Circuit has summarized Texas's rules for contract interpretation as follows, citing opinions of the Texas Supreme Court:

Our first task is to determine whether the contract is enforceable as written, without resort to parol evidence. The primary objective of the reviewing court is to ascertain the intentions of the parties as expressed in the contract. To achieve this objective, the court should examine the entire contract in order to "harmonize and give effect to all of its provisions so that none will be rendered meaningless." A contract is unambiguous if it can be given a definite or certain legal meaning. Ambiguity does not arise because of a "simple lack of clarity," or because the parties proffer different interpretations of the contract. Rather, a contract is ambiguous only if it is subject to two or more reasonable interpretations after applying the pertinent canons of construction. If the contract is ambiguous, courts may consider parol evidence for the purpose of ascertaining the parties' intent.

The parol evidence rule is particularly important to this appeal because nearly all of DTC's arguments — and several of the dissent's points of contention — depend on parol evidence, not on the plain language of the MFL clause.

C. MFL Clauses, Royalties, and the Licenses at Issue

This dispute concerns an MFL clause, particularly DTC's primary contention that, as a matter of law, an MFL clause cannot be applied retroactively, i.e., to obtain a refund of amounts previously paid.

The licenses granted to JPMC and Cathay are identical in most respects. Both are paid-up lump-sum licenses granting unlimited use of the patent. That is to say, neither of the licenses involves periodic royalty payments covering discrete periods of time or per-transaction royalty payments; neither is subject to any cap on the number of transactions; and neither has language tying the lump-sum payment for the unlimited license to either the anticipated number of transactions or the asset size of the licensee.

Based on the plain language of the licenses, the only material differences in payment terms are as follows: (1) JPMC's lump-sum license cost $70 million, while Cathay's cost only $250,000; and (2) Cathay's license required it to pay up to $250,000 as an additional paid-up lump-sum license for each entity it later acquired. Although the $70 million owed under the JPMC license was paid in installments while the Cathay license was apparently made in a single payment, that difference is not material. As noted above, JPMC was required to pay the full amount, and its failure to make any payment "shall result in a termination of the licenses and rights granted to JPMC and its Subsidiaries in this Agreement" under the Settlement and Release Agreement between DTC and JPMC. Thus, the JPMC license was all-or-nothing with respect to both the payment owed and the right to use DTC's patents, just like the Cathay license.

III. ANALYSIS

A. The MFL Clause Applies Retroactively and Permits Refunds.

DTC primarily argues that the MFL clause cannot apply retroactively, only prospectively from the date the new terms are recognized, citing what it calls the forward-looking language of the MFL clause (e.g., "The MFN shall be applied . . ."). DTC claims that the clause allows JPMC to escape only future payments still owed under the license at the time the MFL clause is recognized.

DTC's argument is based on the MFL clause's silence regarding retroactivity, but that silence favors JPMC. The major problem with DTC's interpretation is that it would render the MFL clause effectively meaningless in this case and in other cases involving two otherwise paid-up lump-sum licenses, differing only in the total license cost. Under DTC's interpretation, once the first licensee had fully paid its license fee (even if it paid the full amount at the outset), it could receive no practical benefit from invoking the MFL clause.

JPMC made the final installment payment on its $70 million paid-up lump-sum license in 2012 prior to DTC granting Cathay an unlimited-use license for $250,000. Under DTC's interpretation of the MFL clause, refunds would be precluded. Thus, although the MFL clause would, by its plain terms, allow JPMC to apply the benefit of the terms of the Cathay license, the substitution of terms would mean nothing because JPMC could never get back its $69 million overpayment under the newly applicable terms. Indeed, under DTC's interpretation, if JPMC had simply made a single $70 million payment in 2005 rather than spreading that amount out over several years of installment payments, JPMC never would have been able to invoke the MFL clause to obtain a better price term.

As the dissent argues, DTC's prospective-only interpretation would not render the MFL clause wholly without meaning because it might still give JPMC some relief — the ability to skip future payments — if DTC entered into a more favorable license before JPMC finished paying. But DTC's interpretation finds no support in the plain language of the MFL clause or in the nature of JPMC's payment obligation. As we explained above, although the $70 million payment was broken into scheduled installments, it was treated as a single amount in every material way. JPMC's failure to make any payment would terminate the entire license; it was required to pay the full amount or lose any benefits thereunder. DTC's interpretation, then, arbitrarily treats as divisible the fundamentally indivisible $70 million payment for the paid-up lump-sum license. The $70 million was effectively an indivisible lump sum, and we must treat it as such.

We conclude DTC's interpretation reaches an unreasonable result. Thus, it does not satisfy Texas law for contract interpretation. The district court reached the same result for similar reasons. . . .

Under Texas law, common sense, the plain language of the MFL clause, and the commentary quoted above, we conclude that the district court correctly held that the MFL clause requires the court to apply the MFL clause retroactively and grant a refund.

We also conclude that DTC has failed to cite any analogous contrary authority. . . .

Neither the parties nor this court can find a single MFL clause case involving a switch from an initial paid-up lump-sum license to a later more favorable paid-up lump-sum license, as is present in this case. Even though the issue appears to be one of first impression in case law, it is actually simpler than most MFL clause cases. First, DTC has never cited any authority holding that amounts paid for a paid-up lump-sum license are nonrefundable, only cases stating that running royalties are nonrefundable. . . .

[T]wo paid-up lump-sum licenses are much closer to an apples-to-apples comparison than a running royalty license and a paid-up lump-sum license or two running royalty licenses with incommensurable terms. The biggest material difference between two paid-up lump-sum licenses is the total cost. An MFL clause would mean virtually nothing if it did not allow the earlier licensee to obtain a lower license cost, which in turn means nothing if the earlier licensee cannot receive a refund in the amount of the overpayment.

In sum, DTC's interpretation leads to an unreasonable result, and it has not cited any apposite legal authority in support of that interpretation. The district court correctly held that the MFL clause may be applied retroactively and that JPMC is entitled to a refund for the amount it overpaid under the retroactive terms of the Cathay license, i.e., $69 million.

B. The MFL Clause Does Not Permit an Analysis of Different Licenses Based on Check Volume.

Next, DTC argues that the district court erred by not considering the different levels of usage by JPMC and Cathay. DTC claims the MFL clause ties the total cost of the JPMC license to a per-transaction royalty estimate, based on the second sentence of the MFL clause: "JPMC agrees that $.02 to $.05 per Transaction is a reasonable royalty under the license granted herein, and JPMC makes no representation as to what pro-rata share of such royalty is attributable to any portion or sub-part of such Transaction." That argument has no merit.

The plain language of the MFL clause does not support DTC's interpretation because it does not, on its face, contain any language limiting the MFL clause. The district court reasoned that the second sentence is essentially disconnected:

> the second sentence of the MFL clause unambiguously provides JPMC's representation of a reasonable royalty rate in exchange for inclusion of the MFL clause. See Frost Nat'l Bank v. L & F Distribs., Ltd., 165 S.W.3d 310, 312 (Tex.2005) (encouraging courts to consider the business purpose a contract serves). The second sentence has no bearing here and neither party has argued otherwise.

DTC does assert on appeal that the second sentence limits application of the MFL clause by creating a per-transaction rate, but it has no support for that point. First, there is no question that the license at issue is a paid-up lump-sum license which allows unlimited use. It does not include a per-transaction royalty. As other courts have explained, "there is no basis in fact for the conversion of a lump sum rate of royalty into a rate of per cent of selling price royalty," or vice versa. The two types of royalties are fully distinct; "[t]he former is a true alternative to the latter and must be so treated in determining the rights of [the parties] in respect to royalty provisions."

Second, even if there were a factual basis for calculating the effective running royalty rate of the lump-sum royalty at issue here, it would be far from two to five cents per transaction. DTC claims JPMC processes approximately five billion check images each year. At two cents per transaction, JPMC's running royalty would amount to approximately $100 million per year. Considering JPMC entered into the license agreement in 2005, the total amount JPMC would have paid by 2012 under a per-transaction royalty agreement presumably would have exceeded $1 billion even at two cents per transaction, more than an order of magnitude greater than what it paid for the lump-sum license permitting unlimited use.

If anything, the presence of the "$.02 to $.05 per Transaction" clause undermines DTC's position. It indicates that the parties expected the MFL to apply to pricing terms in future licenses; if they thought about the possibility that some contracts could employ a running royalty method of payment, presumably they also anticipated the possibility that future contracts could use a lump-sum-payment method, as their contract in fact did. It is not entirely evident why the individual parties agreed to include the "$.02 to $.05 per Transaction" clause. JPMC contends it was designed to benefit DTC in other litigation, which DTC strongly disputes. Nevertheless, given the difficulties inherent in comparing lump-sum payments to running royalties, the purpose likely was to set a rate that JPMC would consider reasonable (i.e., not more favorable) in any running royalty contracts that DTC made. Obviously, the agreement already provided a point of comparison for lump-sum agreements — the $70 million fee.

Third and finally, there is no language in any relevant document (the settlement agreements, the JPMC license, or the Cathay license) explaining how the parties arrived at the lump-sum amounts paid by either JPMC or Cathay. Given that the contractual language is clear and unambiguous and supports only JPMC's interpretation, Texas law precludes parol evidence such as the relative asset sizes and check volumes of JPMC and Cathay.

This result is required by the plain language of the contract, but it could have been avoided with more careful drafting by DTC, as the district court explained:

> Having considered these problematic issues, the Court notes that Professor Dratler discusses ways to improve an MFL clause:
>
> Case law suggests two ways to improve the standard, broadly-drafted clause. The first is to make specific provision for situations that experience has shown are most likely to cause difficulties. The most common of these are infringement settlement licenses, cross-licenses, and lump-sum licenses and volume or production limits. . . .
>
> A second means of reducing the risk of most-favored-licensee clause from the licensor's standpoint is to require the favored licensee to accept all the terms of any later license, good and bad, as a condition of receiving the benefit of any more favorable terms. Although the law generally requires this in any event, explicit contractual language to that effect may avoid unnecessary litigation.

2 Jay Dratler, Licensing of Intellectual Property, §9.05[1]-[2] (2014) (footnotes omitted, bolded emphasis added); cf., Federal Judicial Center, Manual for Complex Litigation, Fourth, at §13.23 (2004), which states:

[MFL] clauses have several drawbacks: (1) the potential liability under them is indeterminate, making them risky; (2) the additional recovery they may produce for some
plaintiffs without any effort by their attorneys makes it difficult to fix fees; and (3) the
factors that induce parties to settle with different parties for different amounts, such as
the time of settlement and the relative strength of claims, are nullified. Such clauses
can provide an incentive for early settlement as well as an obstacle to later settlements.
To limit their prejudicial impact, such clauses should terminate after a specified length
of time (to prevent one or more holdouts from delaying final implementation), impose
ceilings on payments, and allow flexibility to deal with changed circumstances or with
parties financially unable to contribute proportionately. The judge may have to consider voiding or limiting them if enforcement becomes inequitable. If this determination involves disputed questions of fact, an evidentiary hearing and possibly additional
discovery may be necessary.

Here, the MFL clause was sparsely defined, very broadly worded, contained no specific limitations or provisions for difficult situations, included no language of termination, and appears not
to have contemplated the effect of a later license agreement, particularly one based on a
lump-sum payment of the type at issue here. The impact of a less than well-defined MFL
clause is clearly seen in this litigation.

We fully agree. The potential problems with a broadly worded and open-ended MFL clause
(most of which affect the licensor), are fairly obvious, and the means of avoiding potential
problems as experienced above are simple. DTC failed to include any such restriction, such as
limiting the effective period of JPMC's right under the MFL clause, capping the total volume of
check-clearing transactions under the Cathay license, tying the amount paid for the paid-up
lump-sum licenses to the licensee's asset size in either license, or stating that the amount paid
was tied to the remaining life of the patent. Any or all of those restrictions could have been
reasonable, as DTC argues, but the MFL clause contains none of them. Because the language
of the MFL clause is clear and unambiguous, we must apply it as written. DTC may not
introduce parol evidence, including the relative check volumes and asset sizes of JPMC
and Cathay, to change the plain language.

IV. CONCLUSION

We affirm the district court's final judgment for the reasons set out above and for the
reasons set out in the district court's careful memorandum opinion and order.

QUANTA COMPUTER, INC. v. LG ELECTRONICS, INC.
553 U.S. 617 (2008)

Justice **THOMAS** delivered the opinion of the Court.

Respondent LG Electronics, Inc. (LGE), purchased a portfolio of computer technology
patents in 1999, including the three patents at issue here: U.S. Patent Nos. 4,939,641
('641); 5,379,379 ('379); and 5,077,733 ('733) (collectively LGE Patents). The main functions of a computer system are carried out on a microprocessor, or central processing unit,
which interprets program instructions, processes data, and controls other devices in the system. A set of wires, or bus, connects the microprocessor to a chipset, which transfers data

between the microprocessor and other devices, including the keyboard, mouse, monitor, hard drive, memory, and disk drives.

The data processed by the computer are stored principally in random access memory, also called main memory. Frequently accessed data are generally stored in cache memory, which permits faster access than main memory and is often located on the microprocessor itself. When copies of data are stored in both the cache and main memory, problems may arise when one copy is changed but the other still contains the original "stale" version of the data. The '641 patent addresses this problem. It discloses a system for ensuring that the most current data are retrieved from main memory by monitoring data requests and updating main memory from the cache when stale data are requested.

The '379 patent relates to the coordination of requests to read from, and write to, main memory. Processing these requests in chronological order can slow down a system because read requests are faster to execute than write requests. Processing all read requests first ensures speedy access, but may result in the retrieval of outdated data if a read request for a certain piece of data is processed before an outstanding write request for the same data. The '379 patent discloses an efficient method of organizing read and write requests while maintaining accuracy by allowing the computer to execute only read outstanding write request. Upon receiving such a read request, the computer executes pending write requests first and only then returns to the read requests so that the most up-to-date data are retrieved.

The '733 patent addresses the problem of managing the data traffic on a bus connecting two computer components, so that no one device monopolizes the bus. It allows multiple devices to share the bus, giving heavy users greater access. This patent describes methods that establish a rotating priority system under which each device alternately has priority access to the bus for a preset number of cycles and heavier users can maintain priority for more cycles without "hogging" the device indefinitely. LGE licensed a patent portfolio, including the LGE Patents, to Intel Corporation (Intel). The cross-licensing agreement (License Agreement) permits Intel to manufacture and sell microprocessors and chipsets that use the LGE Patents (the Intel Products). The License Agreement authorizes Intel to "'make, use, sell (directly or indirectly), offer to sell, import or otherwise dispose of'" its own products practicing the LGE Patents. Notwithstanding this broad language, the License Agreement contains some limitations. Relevant here, it stipulates that no license "'is granted by either party hereto . . . to any third party for the combination by a third party of Licensed Products of either party with items, components, or the like acquired . . . from sources other than a party hereto, or for the use, import, offer for sale or sale of such combination.'"

The License Agreement purports not to alter the usual rules of patent exhaustion, however, providing that, "'[n]otwithstanding anything to the contrary contained in this Agreement, the parties agree that nothing herein shall in any way limit or alter the effect of patent exhaustion that would otherwise apply when a party hereto sells any of its Licensed Products.'"

In a separate agreement (Master Agreement), Intel agreed to give written notice to its own customers informing them that, while it had obtained a broad license "'ensur[ing] that any Intel product that you purchase is licensed by LGE and thus does not infringe any patent held by LGE,'" the license "'does not extend, expressly or by implication, to any product that you make by combining an Intel product with any non-Intel product.'" The Master Agreement also provides that "'a breach of this Agreement shall have no effect on and shall not be grounds for termination of the Patent License.'"

Petitioners, including Quanta Computer (collectively Quanta), are a group of computer manufacturers. Quanta purchased microprocessors and chipsets from Intel and received the notice required by the Master Agreement. Nonetheless, Quanta manufactured computers using Intel parts in combination with non-Intel memory and buses in ways that practice the LGE Patents. Quanta does not modify the Intel components and follows Intel's specifications to incorporate the parts into its own systems.

LGE filed a complaint against Quanta, asserting that the combination of the Intel Products with non-Intel memory and buses infringed the LGE Patents. The Court of Appeals for the Federal Circuit . . . concluded that exhaustion did not apply because LGE did not license Intel to sell the Intel Products to Quanta for use in combination with non-Intel products. 453 F.3d, at 1370.

II

The longstanding doctrine of patent exhaustion provides that the initial authorized sale of a patented item terminates all patent rights to that item. . . .

This Court most recently discussed patent exhaustion in *Univis*, 316 U.S. 241. Univis Lens Company, the holder of patents on eyeglass lenses, licensed a purchaser to manufacture lens blanks by fusing together different lens segments to create bi- and tri-focal lenses and to sell them to other Univis licensees at agreed-upon rates. Wholesalers were licensed to grind the blanks into the patented finished lenses, which they would then sell to Univis-licensed prescription retailers for resale at a fixed rate. Finishing retailers, after grinding the blanks into patented lenses, would sell the finished lenses to consumers at the same fixed rate. The United States sued Univis under the Sherman Act, 15 U.S.C. §§1, 3, 15, alleging unlawful restraints on trade. Univis asserted its patent monopoly rights as a defense to the antitrust suit. The Court determine[d] whether Univis' patent monopoly survived the sale of the lens blanks by the licensed manufacturer and therefore shielded Univis' pricing scheme from the Sherman Act.

The Court assumed that the Univis patents containing claims for finished lenses were practiced in part by the wholesalers and finishing retailers who ground the blanks into lenses, and held that the sale of the lens blanks exhausted the patents on the finished lenses. The Court explained that the lens blanks "embodi[ed] essential features of the patented device and [were] without utility until . . . ground and polished as the finished lens of the patent." *Id.*, at 249. The Court noted that:

> "where one has sold an uncompleted article which, because it embodies essential features of his patented invention, is within the protection of his patent, and has destined the article to be finished by the purchaser in conformity to the patent, he has sold his invention so far as it is or may be embodied in that particular article." *Id.*, at 250-251.

In sum, the Court concluded that the traditional bar on patent restrictions following the sale of an item applies when the item sufficiently embodies the patent — even if it does not completely practice the patent — such that its only and intended use is to be finished under the terms of the patent.

With this history of the patent exhaustion doctrine in mind, we turn to the parties' arguments.

III

[We reject LGE's argument that method claims, as a category, are never exhaustible.]

B

We next consider the extent to which a product must embody a patent in order to trigger exhaustion. Quanta argues that, although sales of an incomplete article do not necessarily exhaust the patent in that article, the sale of the microprocessors and chipsets exhausted LGE's patents in the same way the sale of the lens blanks exhausted the patents in *Univis*. Just as the lens blanks in *Univis* did not fully practice the patents at issue because they had not been ground into finished lenses, Quanta observes, the Intel Products cannot practice the LGE Patents—or indeed, function at all—until they are combined with memory and buses in a computer system. If, as in *Univis*, patent rights are exhausted by the sale of the incomplete item, then LGE has no postsale right to require that the patents be practiced using only Intel parts. Quanta also argues that exhaustion doctrine will be a dead letter unless it is triggered by the sale of components that essentially, even if not completely, embody an invention. Otherwise, patent holders could authorize the sale of computers that are complete with the exception of one minor step—say, inserting the microprocessor into a socket—and extend their rights through each downstream purchaser all the way to the end user. . . .

We agree with Quanta that *Univis* governs this case. As the Court there explained, exhaustion was triggered by the sale of the lens blanks because their only reasonable and intended use was to practice the patent and because they "embodie[d] essential features of [the] patented invention." 316 U.S., at 249-251. Each of those attributes is shared by the microprocessors and chipsets Intel sold to Quanta under the License Agreement. . . .

C

Having concluded that the Intel Products embodied the patents, we next consider whether their sale to Quanta exhausted LGE's patent rights. Exhaustion is triggered only by a sale authorized by the patent holder. *Univis*, 316 U.S. at 249.

LGE argues that there was no authorized sale here because the License Agreement does not permit Intel to sell its products for use in combination with non-Intel products to practice the LGE Patents. It cites General Talking Pictures Corp. v. Western Elec. Co., 304 U.S. 175 (1938), and General Talking Pictures Corp. v. Western Elec. Co., 305 U.S. 124 (1938), in which the manufacturer sold patented amplifiers for commercial use, thereby breaching a license that limited the buyer to selling the amplifiers for private and home use. The Court held that exhaustion did not apply because the manufacturer had no authority to sell the amplifiers for commercial use, and the manufacturer "could not convey to petitioner what both knew it was not authorized to sell." *General Talking Pictures*, at 181. LGE argues that the same principle applies here: Intel could not convey to Quanta what both knew it was not authorized to sell, i.e., the right to practice the patents with non-Intel parts.

LGE overlooks important aspects of the structure of the Intel-LGE transaction. Nothing in the License Agreement restricts Intel's right to sell its microprocessors and chipsets to purchasers who intend to combine them with non-Intel parts. It broadly permits Intel to "'make, use, [or] sell'" products free of LGE's patent claims. To be sure, LGE did require Intel to give notice to its customers, including Quanta, that LGE had not licensed those customers to practice its patents. But neither party contends that Intel breached the agreement in that respect. In any event, the provision requiring notice to Quanta appeared only in the Master Agreement, and LGE does not suggest that a breach of that agreement would constitute a breach of the License Agreement. Hence, Intel's authority to sell its products embodying the LGE Patents was not conditioned on the notice or on Quanta's decision to abide by LGE's directions in that notice.

LGE points out that the License Agreement specifically disclaimed any license to third parties to practice the patents by combining licensed products with other components. But the question whether third parties received implied licenses is irrelevant because Quanta asserts its right to practice the patents based not on implied license but on exhaustion. And exhaustion turns only on Intel's own license to sell products practicing the LGE Patents.

Alternatively, LGE invokes the principle that patent exhaustion does not apply to postsale restrictions on "making" an article. But this is simply a rephrasing of its argument that combining the Intel Products with other components adds more than standard finishing to complete a patented article. As explained above, making a product that substantially embodies a patent is, for exhaustion purposes, no different from making the patented article itself. In other words, no further "making" results from the addition of standard parts—here, the buses and memory—to a product that already substantially embodies the patent.

The License Agreement authorized Intel to sell products that practiced the LGE Patents. No conditions limited Intel's authority to sell products substantially embodying the patents. Because Intel was authorized to sell its products to Quanta, the doctrine of patent exhaustion prevents LGE from further asserting its patent rights with respect to the patents substantially embodied by those products.[1]

IV

The authorized sale of an article that substantially embodies a patent exhausts the patent holder's rights and prevents the patent holder from invoking patent law to control postsale use of the article. Here, LGE licensed Intel to practice any of its patents and to sell products practicing those patents. Intel's microprocessors and chipsets substantially embodied the LGE Patents because they had no reasonable noninfringing use and included all the inventive aspects of the patented methods. Nothing in the License Agreement limited Intel's ability to sell its products practicing the LGE Patents. Intel's authorized sale to Quanta thus took its products outside the scope of the patent monopoly, and as a result, LGE can no longer assert its patent rights against Quanta. Accordingly, the judgment of the Court of Appeals is reversed.

It is so ordered.

---

1. We note that the authorized nature of the sale to Quanta does not necessarily limit LGE's other contract rights. LGE's complaint does not include a breach-of-contract claim, and we express no opinion on whether contract damages might be available even though exhaustion operates to eliminate patent damages. See Keeler v. Standard Folding Bed Co., 157 U.S. 659, 666 (1895) ("Whether a patentee may protect himself and his assignees by special contracts brought home to the purchasers is not a question before us, and upon which we express no opinion. It is, however, obvious that such a question would arise as a question of contract, and not as one under the inherent meaning and effect of the patent laws").

IMPRESSION PRODUCTS, INC. v. LEXMARK INTERN. INC.
137 S. Ct. 1523 (2017)

Chief Justice ROBERTS delivered the opinion of the Court.

The underlying dispute in this case is about laser printers — or, more specifically, the cartridges that contain the powdery substance, known as toner, that laser printers use to make an image appear on paper. Respondent Lexmark International, Inc. designs, manufactures, and sells toner cartridges to consumers in the United States and around the globe. It owns a number of patents that cover components of those cartridges and the manner in which they are used.

When toner cartridges run out of toner they can be refilled and used again. This creates an opportunity for other companies — known as remanufacturers — to acquire empty Lexmark cartridges from purchasers in the United States and abroad, refill them with toner, and then resell them at a lower price than the new ones Lexmark puts on the shelves.

Not blind to this business problem, Lexmark structures its sales in a way that encourages customers to return spent cartridges. It gives purchasers two options: One is to buy a toner cartridge at full price, with no strings attached. The other is to buy a cartridge at roughly 20-percent off through Lexmark's "Return Program." A customer who buys through the Return Program still owns the cartridge but, in exchange for the lower price, signs a contract agreeing to use it only once and to refrain from transferring the empty cartridge to anyone but Lexmark. To enforce this single-use/no-resale restriction, Lexmark installs a microchip on each Return Program cartridge that prevents reuse once the toner in the cartridge runs out.

Lexmark's strategy just spurred remanufacturers to get more creative. Many kept acquiring empty Return Program cartridges and developed methods to counteract the effect of the microchips. With that technological obstacle out of the way, there was little to prevent the remanufacturers from using the Return Program cartridges in their resale business. After all, Lexmark's contractual single-use/no-resale agreements were with the initial customers, not with downstream purchasers like the remanufacturers.

Lexmark, however, was not so ready to concede that its plan had been foiled. In 2010, it sued a number of remanufacturers, including petitioner Impression Products, Inc., for patent infringement with respect to two groups of cartridges. One group consists of Return Program cartridges that Lexmark sold within the United States. Lexmark argued that, because it expressly prohibited reuse and resale of these cartridges, the remanufacturers infringed the Lexmark patents when they refurbished and resold them. The other group consists of all toner cartridges that Lexmark sold abroad and that remanufacturers imported into the country. Lexmark claimed that it never gave anyone authority to import these cartridges, so the remanufacturers ran afoul of its patent rights by doing just that.

Eventually, the lawsuit was whittled down to one defendant, Impression Products, and one defense: that Lexmark's sales, both in the United States and abroad, exhausted its patent rights in the cartridges, so Impression Products was free to refurbish and resell them, and to import them if acquired abroad. Impression Products filed separate motions to dismiss with respect to both groups of cartridges. The District Court granted the motion as to the domestic Return Program cartridges, but denied the motion as to the cartridges Lexmark sold abroad. Both parties appealed.

The Federal Circuit considered the appeals en banc and ruled for Lexmark with respect to both groups of cartridges.

We granted certiorari to consider the Federal Circuit's decisions with respect to both domestic and international exhaustion.

II

A

First up are the Return Program cartridges that Lexmark sold in the United States. We conclude that Lexmark exhausted its patent rights in these cartridges the moment it sold them. The single-use/no-resale restrictions in Lexmark's contracts with customers may have been clear and enforceable under contract law, but they do not entitle Lexmark to retain patent rights in an item that it has elected to sell.

The Patent Act grants patentees the "right to exclude others from making, using, offering for sale, or selling [their] invention[s]." 35 U.S.C. §154(a). For over 160 years, the doctrine of patent exhaustion has imposed a limit on that right to exclude. See Bloomer v. McQuewan, 14 L.Ed. 532 (1853). The limit functions automatically: When a patentee chooses to sell an item, that product "is no longer within the limits of the monopoly" and instead becomes the "private, individual property" of the purchaser, with the rights and benefits that come along with ownership. A patentee is free to set the price and negotiate contracts with purchasers, but may not, "by virtue of his patent, control the use or disposition" of the product after ownership passes to the purchaser. United States v. Univis Lens Co., 316 U.S. 241, 250 (1942). The sale "terminates all patent rights to that item." Quanta Computer, Inc. v. LG Electronics, Inc., 553 U.S. 617, 625 (2008).

This well-established exhaustion rule marks the point where patent rights yield to the common law principle against restraints on alienation. The Patent Act "promote[s] the progress of science and the useful arts by granting to [inventors] a limited monopoly" that allows them to "secure the financial rewards" for their inventions. *Univis*, 316 U.S., at 250. But once a patentee sells an item, it has "enjoyed all the rights secured" by that limited monopoly. Keeler v. Standard Folding Bed Co., 157 U.S. 659, 661 (1895). Because "the purpose of the patent law is fulfilled . . . when the patentee has received his reward for the use of his invention," that law furnishes "no basis for restraining the use and enjoyment of the thing sold." *Univis*, 316 U.S. at 251.

We have explained in the context of copyright law that exhaustion has "an impeccable historic pedigree," tracing its lineage back to the "common law's refusal to permit restraints on the alienation of chattels." Kirtsaeng v. John Wiley & Sons, Inc., 568 U.S. 519, 538 (2013). As Lord Coke put it in the 17th century, if an owner restricts the resale or use of an item after selling it, that restriction "is voide, because . . . it is against Trade and Traffique, and bargaining and contracting betweene man and man." 1 E. Coke, *Institutes of the Laws of England* §360, p. 223 (1628); *see* J. Gray, *Restraints on the Alienation of Property* §27, p. 18 (2d ed. 1895) ("A condition or conditional limitation on alienation attached to a transfer of the entire interest in personalty is as void as if attached to a fee simple in land").

This venerable principle is not, as the Federal Circuit dismissively viewed it, merely "one common-law jurisdiction's general judicial policy at one time toward anti-alienation restrictions." 816 F.3d, at 750. Congress enacted and has repeatedly revised the Patent Act against the backdrop of the hostility toward restraints on alienation. That enmity is reflected in the exhaustion doctrine. The patent laws do not include the right to "restrain [ ] . . . further alienation" after an initial sale; such conditions have been "hateful to the law from Lord Coke's day to ours" and are "obnoxious to the public interest." Straus v. Victor Talking Machine Co., 243 U.S. 490, 501 (1917). "The inconvenience and annoyance to the public that an opposite conclusion would occasion are too obvious to require illustration." *Keeler*, 157 U.S. at 667.

But an illustration never hurts. Take a shop that restores and sells used cars. The business works because the shop can rest assured that, so long as those bringing in the cars own them, the shop is free to repair and resell those vehicles. That smooth flow of commerce would sputter if companies that make the thousands of parts that go into a vehicle could keep their patent rights after the first sale. Those companies might, for instance, restrict resale rights and sue the shop owner for patent infringement. And even if they refrained from imposing such restrictions, the very threat of patent liability would force the shop to invest in efforts to protect itself from hidden lawsuits. Either way, extending the patent rights beyond the first sale would clog the channels of commerce, with little benefit from the extra control that the patentees retain. And advances in technology, along with increasingly complex supply chains, magnify the problem.

This Court accordingly has long held that, even when a patentee sells an item under an express restriction, the patentee does not retain patent rights in that product. In Boston Store of Chicago v. American Graphophone Co., for example, a manufacturer sold graphophones — one of the earliest devices for recording and reproducing sounds — to retailers under contracts requiring those stores to resell at a specific price. 246 U.S. 8, 17–18 (1918). When the manufacturer brought a patent infringement suit against a retailer who sold for less, we concluded that there was "no room for controversy" about the result: By selling the item, the manufacturer placed it "beyond the confines of the patent law, [and] could not, by qualifying restrictions as to use, keep [it] under the patent monopoly." *Id.* at 20, 25.

Two decades later, we confronted a similar arrangement in United States v. Univis Lens Co. There, a company that made eyeglass lenses authorized an agent to sell its products to wholesalers and retailers only if they promised to market the lenses at fixed prices. The Government filed an antitrust lawsuit, and the company defended its arrangement on the ground that it was exercising authority under the Patent Act. We held that the initial sales "relinquish [ed] . . . the patent monopoly with respect to the article[s] sold," so the "stipulation . . . fixing resale prices derive[d] no support from the patent and must stand on the same footing" as restrictions on unpatented goods. 316 U.S. at 249–251.

It is true that *Boston Store* and *Univis* involved resale price restrictions that, at the time of those decisions, violated the antitrust laws. But in both cases it was the sale of the items, rather than the illegality of the restrictions, that prevented the patentees from enforcing those resale price agreements through patent infringement suits. And if there were any lingering doubt that patent exhaustion applies even when a sale is subject to an express, otherwise lawful restriction, our recent decision in Quanta Computer, Inc. v. LG Electronics, Inc. settled the matter. In that case, a technology company — with authorization from the patentee — sold microprocessors under contracts requiring purchasers to use those processors with other parts that the company manufactured. One buyer disregarded the restriction, and the patentee sued for infringement. Without so much as mentioning the lawfulness of the contract, we held that the patentee could not bring an infringement suit because the "authorized sale . . . took its products outside the scope of the patent monopoly." 553 U.S., at 638.

Turning to the case at hand, we conclude that this well-settled line of precedent allows for only one answer: Lexmark cannot bring a patent infringement suit against Impression Products to enforce the single-use/no-resale provision accompanying its Return Program cartridges. Once sold, the Return Program cartridges passed outside of the patent monopoly, and whatever rights Lexmark retained are a matter of the contracts with its purchasers, not the patent law.

B

The Federal Circuit reached a different result largely because it got off on the wrong foot. The "exhaustion doctrine," the court believed, "must be understood as an interpretation of" the infringement statute, which prohibits anyone from using or selling a patented article "without authority" from the patentee. 816 F.3d, at 734 (quoting 35 U.S.C. §271(a)). Exhaustion reflects a default rule that a patentee's decision to sell an item "presumptively grant[s] 'authority' to the purchaser to use it and resell it." 816 F.3d, at 742. But, the Federal Circuit explained, the patentee does not have to hand over the full "bundle of rights" every time. If the patentee expressly withholds a stick from the bundle — perhaps by restricting the purchaser's resale rights — the buyer never acquires that withheld authority, and the patentee may continue to enforce its right to exclude that practice under the patent laws.

The misstep in this logic is that the exhaustion doctrine is not a presumption about the authority that comes along with a sale; it is instead a limit on "the scope of the patentee's rights." United States v. General Elec. Co., 272 U.S. 476, 489 (1926). The right to use, sell, or import an item exists independently of the Patent Act. What a patent adds — and grants exclusively to the patentee — is a limited right to prevent others from engaging in those practices. Exhaustion extinguishes that exclusionary power. As a result, the sale transfers the right to use, sell, or import because those are the rights that come along with ownership, and the buyer is free and clear of an infringement lawsuit because there is no exclusionary right left to enforce.

The Federal Circuit also expressed concern that preventing patentees from reserving patent rights when they sell goods would create an artificial distinction between such sales and sales by licensees. Patentees, the court explained, often license others to make and sell their products, and may place restrictions on those licenses. A computer developer could, for instance, license a manufacturer to make its patented devices and sell them only for noncommercial use by individuals. If a licensee breaches the license by selling a computer for commercial use, the patentee can sue the licensee for infringement. And, in the Federal Circuit's view, our decision in General Talking Pictures Corp. v. Western Elec. Co., 304 U.S. 175 (1938), established that — when a patentee grants a license "under clearly stated restrictions on post-sale activities" of those who purchase products from the licensee — the patentee can also sue for infringement those purchasers who knowingly violate the restrictions. If patentees can employ licenses to impose post-sale restrictions on purchasers that are enforceable through infringement suits, the court concluded, it would make little sense to prevent patentees from doing so when they sell directly to consumers.

The Federal Circuit's concern is misplaced. A patentee can impose restrictions on licensees because a license does not implicate the same concerns about restraints on alienation as a sale. Patent exhaustion reflects the principle that, when an item passes into commerce, it should not be shaded by a legal cloud on title as it moves through the marketplace. But a license is not about passing title to a product, it is about changing the contours of the patentee's monopoly: The patentee agrees not to exclude a licensee from making or selling the patented invention, expanding the club of authorized producers and sellers. See *General Elec. Co.*, 272 U.S., at 489–490. Because the patentee is exchanging rights, not goods, it is free to relinquish only a portion of its bundle of patent protections.

A patentee's authority to limit licensees does not, as the Federal Circuit thought, mean that patentees can use licenses to impose post-sale restrictions on purchasers that are enforceable through the patent laws. So long as a licensee complies with the license when selling an item, the patentee has, in effect, authorized the sale. That licensee's sale is treated, for purposes of patent exhaustion, as if the patentee made the sale itself. The result: The sale exhausts the patentee's rights in that item. See Hobbie v. Jennison, 149 U.S. 355, 362–363 (1893). A license may require the licensee to impose a restriction on purchasers, like the license limiting the computer manufacturer to selling for non-commercial use by individuals. But if the licensee does so — by, perhaps, having each customer sign a contract promising not to use the computers in business — the sale nonetheless exhausts all patent rights in the item sold. See Motion Picture Patents Co. v. Universal Film Mfg. Co., 243 U.S. 502, 506–507, 516 (1917). The purchasers might not comply with the restriction, but the only recourse for the licensee is through contract law, just as if the patentee itself sold the item with a restriction.

General Talking Pictures involved a fundamentally different situation: There, a licensee "knowingly ma[de] . . . sales . . . outside the scope of its license." 304 U.S. at 181–182. We treated the sale "as if no license whatsoever had been granted" by the patentee, which meant that the patentee could sue both the licensee and the purchaser — who knew about the breach — for infringement. General Talking Pictures Corp. v. Western Elec. Co., 305 U.S. 124, 127 (1938). This does not mean that patentees can use licenses to impose post-sale restraints on purchasers. Quite the contrary: The licensee infringed the patentee's rights because it did not comply with the terms of its license, and the patentee could bring a patent suit against the purchaser only because the purchaser participated in the licensee's infringement. *General Talking Pictures*, then, stands for the modest principle that, if a patentee has not given authority for a licensee to make a sale, that sale cannot exhaust the patentee's rights.

In sum, patent exhaustion is uniform and automatic. Once a patentee decides to sell — whether on its own or through a licensee — that sale exhausts its patent rights, regardless of any post-sale restrictions the patentee purports to impose, either directly or through a license.

III

Our conclusion that Lexmark exhausted its patent rights when it sold the domestic Return Program cartridges goes only halfway to resolving this case. Lexmark also sold toner cartridges abroad and sued Impression Products for patent infringement for "importing [Lexmark's] invention into the United States." 35 U.S.C. §154(a). Lexmark contends that it may sue for infringement with respect to all of the imported cartridges — not just those in the Return Program — because a foreign sale does not trigger patent exhaustion unless the patentee "expressly or implicitly transfer[s] or license[s]" its rights. The Federal Circuit agreed, but we do not. An authorized sale outside the United States, just as one within the United States, exhausts all rights under the Patent Act.

This question about international exhaustion of intellectual property rights has also arisen in the context of copyright law. Under the "first sale doctrine," which is codified at 17 U.S.C. §109(a), when a copyright owner sells a lawfully made copy of its work, it loses the power to restrict the purchaser's freedom "to sell or otherwise dispose of . . . that copy." In Kirtsaeng v. John Wiley & Sons, Inc., we held that this "'first sale' [rule] applies to copies of a copyrighted work lawfully made [and sold] abroad." 568 U.S. at 525. We began with the text of §109(a), but it was not decisive: The language neither "restrict[s] the scope of [the] 'first sale' doctrine geographically," nor clearly embraces international exhaustion. *Id.* at 528-533. What helped tip the scales for global exhaustion was the fact that the first sale doctrine originated in "the common law's refusal to permit restraints on the alienation of chattels." *Id.* at 538. That "common-law doctrine makes no geographical distinctions." *Id.* at 539. The lack of any textual basis for distinguishing between domestic and international sales meant that "a straight-forward application" of the first sale doctrine required the conclusion that it applies overseas. *Id.* at 540.

Applying patent exhaustion to foreign sales is just as straightforward. Patent exhaustion, too, has its roots in the antipathy toward restraints on alienation, and nothing in the text or history of the Patent Act shows that Congress intended to confine that borderless common law principle to domestic sales. In fact, Congress has not altered patent exhaustion at all; it remains an unwritten limit on the scope of the patentee's monopoly. And differentiating the patent exhaustion and copyright first sale doctrines would make little theoretical or practical sense: The two share a "strong similarity . . . and identity of purpose," Bauer & Cie v. O'Donnell, 229 U.S. 1, 13 (1913), and many everyday products—"automobiles, microwaves, calculators, mobile phones, tablets, and personal computers"—are subject to both patent and copyright protections, *see Kirtsaeng*, 568 U.S. at 545. There is a "historic kinship between patent law and copyright law," Sony Corp. of America v. Universal City Studios, Inc., 464 U.S. 417, 439 (1984), and the bond between the two leaves no room for a rift on the question of international exhaustion.

Lexmark sees the matter differently. The Patent Act, it points out, limits the patentee's "right to exclude others" from making, using, selling, or importing its products to acts that occur in the United States. 35 U.S.C. §154(a). A domestic sale, it argues, triggers exhaustion because the sale compensates the patentee for "surrendering [those] U.S. rights." A foreign sale is different: The Patent Act does not give patentees exclusionary powers abroad. Without those powers, a patentee selling in a foreign market may not be able to sell its product for the same price that it could in the United States, and therefore is not sure to receive "the reward guaranteed by U.S. patent law." Absent that reward, says Lexmark, there should be no exhaustion. In short, there is no patent exhaustion from sales abroad because there are no patent rights abroad to exhaust.

The territorial limit on patent rights is, however, no basis for distinguishing copyright protections; those protections "do not have any extraterritorial operation" either. 5 M. Nimmer & D. Nimmer, Copyright §17.02, p. 17–26 (2017). Nor does the territorial limit support the premise of Lexmark's argument. Exhaustion is a separate limit on the patent grant, and does not depend on the patentee receiving some undefined premium for selling the right to access the American market. A purchaser buys an item, not patent rights. And exhaustion is triggered by the patentee's decision to give that item up and receive whatever fee it decides is appropriate "for the article and the invention which it embodies." *Univis*, 316 U.S. at 251. The patentee may not be able to command the same amount for its products abroad as it does in the United States. But the Patent Act does not guarantee a particular price, much less the price from selling to American consumers. Instead, the right to exclude just ensures that the patentee receives one reward—of whatever amount the patentee deems to be "satisfactory compensation," *Keeler*, 157 U.S. at 661—for every item that passes outside the scope of the patent monopoly.

This Court has addressed international patent exhaustion in only one case, Boesch v. Graff, decided over 125 years ago. All that case illustrates is that a sale abroad does not exhaust a patentee's rights when the patentee had nothing to do with the transaction. *Boesch*—from the days before the widespread adoption of electrical lighting—involved a retailer who purchased lamp burners from a manufacturer in Germany, with plans to sell them in the United States. The manufacturer had authority to make the burners under German law, but there was a hitch: Two individuals with no ties to the German manufacturer held the American patent to that invention. These patentees sued the retailer for infringement when the retailer imported the lamp burners into the United States, and we rejected the argument that the German manufacturer's sale had exhausted the American patentees' rights. The German manufacturer had no permission to sell in the United States from the American patentees, and the American patentees had not exhausted their patent rights in the products because they had not sold them to anyone, so "purchasers from [the German manufacturer] could not be thereby authorized to sell the articles in the United States." 133 U.S. 697, 703 (1890).

Our decision did not, as Lexmark contends, exempt all foreign sales from patent exhaustion. Rather, it reaffirmed the basic premise that only the patentee can decide whether to make a sale that exhausts its patent rights in an item. The American patentees did not do so with respect to the German products, so the German sales did not exhaust their rights.

Finally, the United States, as an amicus, advocates what it views as a middle-ground position: that "a foreign sale authorized by the U.S. patentee exhausts U.S. patent rights unless those rights are expressly reserved." Its position is largely based on policy rather than principle. The Government thinks that an overseas "buyer's legitimate expectation" is that a "sale conveys all of the seller's interest in the patented article," so the presumption should be that a foreign sale triggers exhaustion. But, at the same time, "lower courts long ago coalesced around" the rule that "a patentee's express reservation of U.S. patent rights at the time of a foreign sale will be given effect," so that option should remain open to the patentee.

The Government has little more than "long ago" on its side. In the 1890s, two circuit courts—in cases involving the same company—did hold that patentees may use express restrictions to reserve their patent rights in connection with foreign sales. *See* Dickerson v. Tinling, 84 F. 192, 194–195 (C.A.8 1897); Dickerson v. Matheson, 57 F. 524, 527 (C.A.2 1893). But no "coalesc[ing]" ever took place: Over the following hundred-plus years, only a smattering of lower court decisions mentioned this express-reservation rule for foreign sales. *See, e.g.*, Sanofi, S.A. v. Med–Tech Veterinarian Prods., Inc., 565 F. Supp. 931, 938 (D.N.J. 1983). And in 2001, the Federal Circuit adopted its blanket rule that foreign sales do not trigger exhaustion, even if the patentee fails to expressly reserve its rights. *Jazz Photo*, 264 F.3d, at 1105. These sparse and inconsistent decisions provide no basis for any expectation, let alone a settled one, that patentees can reserve patent rights when they sell abroad.

The theory behind the Government's express-reservation rule also wrongly focuses on the likely expectations of the patentee and purchaser during a sale. Exhaustion does not arise because of the parties' expectations about how sales transfer patent rights. More is at stake when it comes to patents than simply the dealings between the parties, which can be addressed through contract law. Instead, exhaustion occurs because, in a sale, the patentee elects to give up title to an item in exchange for payment. Allowing patent rights to stick remora-like to that item as it flows through the market would violate the principle against restraints on alienation. Exhaustion does not depend on whether the patentee receives a premium for selling in the United States, or the type of rights that buyers expect to receive. As a result, restrictions and location are irrelevant; what matters is the patentee's decision to make a sale.

The judgment of the United States Court of Appeals for the Federal Circuit is reversed, and the case is remanded for further proceedings consistent with this opinion.

It is so ordered.

GINSBURG, Justice, concurring in part and dissenting in part.

I concur in the Court's holding regarding domestic exhaustion — a patentee who sells a product with an express restriction on reuse or resale may not enforce that restriction through an infringement lawsuit, because the U.S. sale exhausts the U.S. patent rights in the product sold. I dissent, however, from the Court's holding on international exhaustion. A foreign sale, I would hold, does not exhaust a U.S. inventor's U.S. patent rights.

Patent law is territorial. When an inventor receives a U.S. patent, that patent provides no protection abroad. *See* Deepsouth Packing Co. v. Laitram Corp., 406 U.S. 518, 531 (1972) ("Our patent system makes no claim to extraterritorial effect."). *See also* 35 U.S.C. §271(a) (establishing liability for acts of patent infringement "within the United States" and for "import[ation] into the United States [of] any patented invention"). A U.S. patentee must apply to each country in which she seeks the exclusive right to sell her invention. Microsoft Corp. v. AT & T Corp., 550 U.S. 437, 456 (2007) ("[F]oreign law alone, not United States law, currently governs the manufacture and sale of components of patented inventions in foreign countries."). See also Convention at Brussels, An Additional Act Modifying the Paris Convention for the Protection of Industrial Property of Mar. 20, 1883, Dec. 14, 1900, Art. I, 32 Stat. 1940 ("Patents applied for in the different contracting States . . . shall be independent of the patents obtained for the same invention in the other States."). And patent laws vary by country; each country's laws "may embody different policy judgments about the relative rights of inventors, competitors, and the public in patented inventions." *Microsoft*, 550 U.S. at 455.

Because a sale abroad operates independently of the U.S. patent system, it makes little sense to say that such a sale exhausts an inventor's U.S. patent rights. U.S. patent protection accompanies none of a U.S. patentee's sales abroad — a competitor could sell the same patented product abroad with no U.S.-patent-law consequence. Accordingly, the foreign sale should not diminish the protections of U.S. law in the United States.

The majority disagrees, in part because this Court decided, in Kirtsaeng v. John Wiley & Sons, Inc., 568 U.S. 519, 525 (2013), that a foreign sale exhausts U.S. copyright protections. Copyright and patent exhaustion, the majority states, "share a strong similarity." I dissented from our decision in *Kirtsaeng* and adhere to the view that a foreign sale should not exhaust U.S. copyright protections. *See* 568 U.S. at 557.

But even if I subscribed to *Kirtsaeng's* reasoning with respect to copyright, that decision should bear little weight in the patent context. Although there may be a "historical kinship" between patent law and copyright law, Sony Corp. of America v. Universal City Studios, Inc., 464 U.S. 417, 439 (1984), the two "are not identical twins," *id.* at 439, n. 19. The Patent Act contains no analogue to 17 U.S.C. §109(a), the Copyright Act first-sale provision analyzed in Kirtsaeng. More importantly, copyright protections, unlike patent protections, are harmonized across countries. Under the Berne Convention, which 174 countries have joined, members "agree to treat authors from other member countries as well as they treat their own." Golan v. Holder, 565 U.S. 302, 308 (2012). The copyright protections one receives abroad are thus likely to be similar to those received at home, even if provided under each country's separate copyright regime.

For these reasons, I would affirm the Federal Circuit's judgment with respect to foreign exhaustion.

MICROSOFT v. MOTOROLA, INC.
795 F.3d 1024 (9th Cir. 2015)

BERZON, Circuit Judge:

We live in an age in which the interconnectivity of a wide range of modern technological products is vital. To achieve that interconnection, patent-holders often join together in compacts requiring licensing certain patents on reasonable and non-discriminatory ("RAND") terms. Such contracts are subject to the common-law obligations of good faith and fair dealing.

At issue in this appeal are two patent portfolios, formerly owned by Appellants Motorola, Inc., Motorola Mobility, Inc., and General Instrument Corp., ("Motorola"), both of which are subject to RAND agreements. Appellee Microsoft, a third-party beneficiary to Motorola's RAND commitments, sued Motorola for breach of its obligation to offer RAND licenses to its patents in good faith. Motorola, meanwhile, brought infringement actions in a variety of fora to enjoin Microsoft from using its patents without a license.

We previously upheld, in an interlocutory appeal, an anti-suit injunction preventing Motorola from enforcing in a German action any injunction it might obtain against Microsoft's use of certain contested patents. Microsoft Corp. v. Motorola, Inc., 696 F.3d 872 (9th Cir. 2012) ("Microsoft I"). We did so after determining that there was, in the "sweeping promise" of Motorola's RAND agreements, "at least arguably a guarantee that the patent-holder will not take steps to keep would-be users from using the patented material, such as seeking an injunction, but will instead proffer licenses consistent with the commitment made." *Id.* at 884.

After our decision, a jury determined that Motorola had indeed breached its RAND good faith and fair dealing obligations in its dealings with Microsoft. In this appeal, we address (1) whether the district court overstepped its bounds by determining, at a bench trial preceding the jury trial on breach of contract, a reasonable and non-discriminatory rate, as well as a range of rates, for Motorola's patents; (2) whether the court erred in denying Motorola's motions for judgment as a matter of law on the breach of contract issue; (3) whether the court erred in awarding Microsoft attorneys' fees as damages in connection with Motorola's pursuit of injunctions against infringement; and (4) whether the district court abused its discretion in two contested evidentiary rulings.

I. BACKGROUND

A. Standard–Setting Organizations and Standard–Essential Patents

When we connect to WiFi in a coffee shop, plug a hairdryer into an outlet, or place a phone call, we owe thanks to standard-setting organizations ("SSOs"). SSOs set technical specifications that ensure that a variety of products from different manufacturers operate compatibly. Without standards, there would be no guarantee that a particular set of headphones, for example, would work with one's personal music player.

Standardization provides enormous value to both consumers and manufacturers. It increases competition by lowering barriers to entry and adds value to manufacturers' products by encouraging production by other manufacturers of devices compatible with them. But because SSO standards often incorporate patented technology, all manufacturers who implement a standard must obtain a license to use those standard-essential patents ("SEPs").

The development of standards thereby creates an opportunity for companies to engage in anti-competitive behavior. Most notably, once a standard becomes widely adopted, SEP holders obtain substantial leverage over new product developers, who have little choice but to incorporate SEP technologies into their products. Using that standard-development leverage, the SEP holders are in a position to demand more for a license than the patented technology, had it not been adopted by the SSO, would be worth. The tactic of withholding a license unless and until a manufacturer agrees to pay an unduly high royalty rate for an SEP is referred to as "hold-up." Ericsson, Inc. v. D–Link Sys., Inc., 773 F.3d 1201, 1209 (Fed. Cir. 2014). "Royalty stacking" refers to the risk that many holders of SEPs will engage in this behavior, resulting in excessive royalty payments such that (1) the cumulative royalties paid for patents incorporated into a standard exceed the value of the feature implementing the standard, and (2) the aggregate royalties obtained for the various features of a product exceed the value of the product itself.

To mitigate the risk that a SEP holder will extract more than the fair value of its patented technology, many SSOs require SEP holders to agree to license their patents on "reasonable and nondiscriminatory" or "RAND" terms. Under these agreements, an SEP holder cannot refuse a license to a manufacturer who commits to paying the RAND rate.

For example, International Telecommunications Union ("ITU"), one of the SSOs at issue in this case, has established a Common Patent Policy. That Policy provides that "a patent embodied fully or partly in a [standard] must be accessible to everybody without undue constraints." Any holder of a patent under consideration for incorporation into an ITU standard is required to submit a declaration of its commitment to "negotiate licenses with other parties on a non-discriminatory basis on reasonable terms and conditions." "If a 'patent holder is not willing to comply' with the requirement to negotiate licenses with all seekers, then the standard 'shall not include provisions depending on the patent.'"

The two standards underlying this case are the H.264 video-coding standard set by the ITU and the 802.11 wireless local area network standard set by the Institute of Electrical and Electronics Engineers ("IEEE"). The H.264 standard pertains to an efficient method of video compression. The 802.11 standard regards the wireless transfer of information using radio frequencies, commonly referred to as "WiFi." The H.264 standard is incorporated into Microsoft's Windows operating system and into its Xbox video game console. The 802.11 WiFi network standard is incorporated into Xbox.

B. History of the Present Dispute

In October 2010, Microsoft sued Motorola in both the U.S. International Trade Commission ("ITC") 3 and the Western District of Washington for alleged infringement of certain smartphone patents. The parties thereupon engaged in a series of discussions concerning, among other matters, the possibility of a cross-licensing agreement granting Motorola licenses to Microsoft's smartphone patents in exchange for licenses to any of Motorola's patents Microsoft's products may have been infringing.

On October 21st and 29th, Motorola sent Microsoft two letters offering to license its 802.11 and H.264 SEP portfolios at 2.25% of the price of the end product—no matter the manufacturer—incorporating the patents. In other words, Microsoft would pay Motorola 2.25% of the selling price of an Xbox game console or of any computer running Microsoft Windows. The two offer letters, identical in all material terms, represented that the offer was in keeping with Motorola's RAND commitments.

Soon after receiving Motorola's letters, in November 2010, Microsoft filed a diversity action in the Western District of Washington, alleging that Motorola had breached its RAND commitments to the IEEE and ITU.5 Microsoft alleged that Motorola's offer letters constituted a refusal to license Motorola's SEPs on RAND terms. The next day, Motorola filed suit against Microsoft in the Western District of Wisconsin seeking to enjoin Microsoft from using its H.264 patents. The cases were consolidated before Judge James Robart in the Western District of Washington.

Motorola also filed patent-enforcement suits with the ITC, seeking an exclusion order against importing Microsoft's Xbox products into the United States, and with a German court, seeking an injunction against sales of Microsoft's H.264-compliant products. The German action was particularly threatening to Microsoft, as its European distribution center for all Windows and Xbox products was in Germany. To guard against the economic loss that would result if an injunction against use of Motorola's two German H.264 patents were granted, Microsoft swiftly relocated its distribution center to the Netherlands. At the same time, Microsoft sought and obtained from the district court, in April 2012, an "anti-suit injunction" barring Motorola from enforcing any injunction it might obtain in a German court against Microsoft's use of Motorola's H.264 SEPs until the district court could "determine whether injunctive relief is an appropriate remedy for Motorola to seek." Microsoft I, 696 F.3d at 880. We affirmed the anti-suit injunction order in September 2012. Meanwhile, the German court had ruled that Motorola was entitled to an injunction.

Proceedings in the district court continued apace. Microsoft amended its complaint to allege that Motorola's filing of injunctive actions constituted a breach of contract, because the obligation to offer RAND licenses to all seekers prohibited Motorola from seeking injunctions for violations of patents subject to that obligation. The court granted a joint motion to stay all the patent-infringement claims in the consolidated cases pending the outcome on the RAND issues.

In a series of orders, Judge Robart held that (1) "RAND commitments create enforceable contracts between Motorola and the respective SSO"; (2) "Microsoft — as a standard-user — can enforce these contracts as a third-party beneficiary"; (3) "Motorola's commitments to the ITU and IEEE . . . requir[e] initial offers by Motorola to license its SEPs to be made in good faith," but that "initial offers do not have to be on RAND terms so long as a RAND license eventually issues"; and (4) Motorola was not entitled to injunctive relief on its H.264 or 802.11 patents.

In November 2012, Judge Robart conducted a bench trial to determine a RAND rate and range for Motorola's H.264 and 802.11 patents. Such determination was necessary, the court reasoned, because "[w]ithout a clear understanding of what RAND means, it would be difficult or impossible to figure out if Motorola breached its obligation to license its patents on RAND terms." After taking testimony from eighteen witnesses, the court issued a 207-page order setting forth its findings of fact and conclusions of law on RAND-rate-related issues. The court concluded that the RAND royalty for Motorola's H.264 portfolio was .555 cents per end-product unit, with an upper bound of 16.389 cents per unit, and that the rate for Motorola's 802.11 portfolio was 3.71 cents per unit, with a range of .8 cents to 19.5 cents.

The case then proceeded to a jury trial on the breach of contract claim. Over Motorola's objection, Microsoft was permitted to introduce the RAND rates determined at the bench trial through witness testimony. Microsoft also introduced, again over Motorola's objection, testimony that the FTC had previously investigated Motorola and its then-parent company, Google Inc., for failing to license patents relating to smartphones, tablets, and video gaming systems on RAND terms. As damages for the asserted breach of contract, Microsoft sought its attorneys' fees and costs in defending the injunctive actions Motorola had brought. Microsoft also sought as damages the cost of relocating its distribution facility from Germany to the Netherlands.

In September 2013, the jury returned a verdict for Microsoft in the amount of $14.52 million: $11.49 million for relocating its distribution center and $3.03 million in attorneys' fees and litigation costs. The verdict form asked both the general question whether Motorola "breached its contractual commitment [s]" to the IEEE and ITU and, specifically, for the purpose of damages, whether Motorola's "conduct in seeking injunctive relief, apart from Motorola's general course of conduct, violated Motorola's dut[ies] of good faith and fair dealing with respect to Motorola's contractual commitment[s]." The jury answered "yes" to all questions, unanimously.

Motorola moved for judgment as a matter of law both at the close of evidence and at the close of Microsoft's case-in-chief. After the jury's verdict, the court denied Motorola's motions in a joint order, concluding that (1) the evidence was sufficient for the jury reasonably to conclude that Motorola breached its duty of good faith and fair dealing by making offers far above the RAND rates and by seeking injunctions against Microsoft, and (2) the damages award was proper. The court granted Microsoft's motion for entry of final judgment on the breach of contract jury verdict.

Motorola then appealed from the judgment on the breach of contract claim to the Federal Circuit. On Microsoft's motion, the Federal Circuit transferred the appeal to this court. Microsoft Corp. v. Motorola, Inc., 564 Fed. Appx. 586 (Fed. Cir. 2014).

II. DISCUSSION

B. The RAND Bench Trial

. . .

2. The District Court's RAND Determination

Motorola contends that on its merits, the district court's RAND analysis violated Federal Circuit patent damages law. Specifically, Motorola cites to the damages provision of the Patent Act, 25 U.S.C. §284, which provides that a court shall award damages "adequate to compensate for the infringement, but in no event less than a reasonable royalty rate for the use made of the invention by the infringer," and to Federal Circuit cases calculating damages under that provision.

We reiterate that this is not a patent law action. Still, the Federal Circuit's patent law methodology can serve as guidance in contract cases on questions of patent valuation. The district court's analysis properly adapted that guidance to the current context.

a. The Hypothetical Agreement

Neither the IEEE nor the ITU provide a specific formula for setting the terms of a RAND license. At trial, both parties offered expert testimony as to the appropriate method for calculating a RAND rate. After trial, Judge Robart invited the parties to submit post-trial briefs and proposed findings of fact and conclusions of law. He then considered each party's submissions and adopted a framework sensitive to the circumstances and objectives of RAND agreements.

The framework settled on was "generally [consistent] with Motorola's approach." Applying that approach, the district court sought to approximate the royalty rates upon which the parties would have agreed by setting up a hypothetical negotiation between the parties. In doing so, the court carefully thought through the "factors an SEP owner and implementer would consider" in an actual negotiation directed at licensing a patent subject to RAND commitments. The court then discussed each of Motorola's fifteen H.264 patents and eleven 802.11 patents, considering the objective value each contributed to each standard, given the quality of the technology and the available alternatives as well as the importance of those technologies to Microsoft's business. Finally, the court performed a meticulous analysis of the testimony of eighteen witnesses, including executives, economists, and technology experts, to sort out which evidence to rely upon in determining the RAND royalty rate. Generally, the court credited Motorola's experts; where it did not, it provided reasoned explanations for not doing so.

Motorola's challenge to the district court's exhaustive analysis centers on its interpretation of Georgia-Pacific Corp. v. U.S. Plywood Corp., 318 F. Supp. 1116 (S.D.N.Y. 1970), a patent-infringement case whose hypothetical agreement framework for determining infringement damages has since been widely adopted by district courts and "sanctioned" by the Federal Circuit. *See* LaserDynamics, Inc. v. Quanta Computer, Inc., 694 F.3d 51, 60 n. 2 (Fed. Cir.2 012). *Georgia-Pacific* set out fifteen factors for courts to consider in arriving at a royalty rate the parties might have agreed upon in a hypothetical negotiation. Factor fifteen directs courts to set the hypothetical negotiation at "the time the infringement began." *Georgia-Pacific*, 318 F. Supp. at 1120.

Motorola's central RAND-rate merits contention is that Judge Robart's analysis failed to meet *Georgia-Pacific*'s factor fifteen criterion, as interpreted and applied by the Federal Circuit, and so constituted error. Several portions of the court's findings of fact and conclusions of law do indicate that the court did to an extent take into account the present-day value to Microsoft of Motorola's patents. For example, the court noted that a third-party valuation of Motorola's 802.11 SEPs was only somewhat probative because, at the time of the valuation, "Motorola's 802.11 SEP portfolio" was much larger than the portfolio "as it exists today."

This partial present-day focus did not, however, render the district court's RAND-rate determination invalid. First, the Federal Circuit has "never described the *Georgia-Pacific* factors as a talisman for royalty rate calculations." *Ericsson*, 773 F.3d at 1230. Instead, outside the RAND context, the Federal Circuit has recognized that, although "courts often parrot all 15 factors to the jury," some of the factors "clearly are not relevant" to every case. *Id.* And in the context of RAND agreements, the Federal Circuit in *Ericsson* cited Judge Robart's opinion in support of the proposition that many of the *Georgia-Pacific* factors are "contrary to RAND principles." *Id.* at 1229. *Ericsson* recognized, for example, as did Judge Robart, that factor four — "'[t]he licensor's established policy and marketing program to maintain his patent monopoly by not licensing others to use the invention or by granting licenses under special conditions designed to preserve that monopoly'" — is contrary to the RAND purpose of preventing monopolies. *Id.* at 1230.

Factor fifteen is another factor that merits modification in some RAND contract contexts. An element of Microsoft's claim is that Motorola maintained its demand of a 2.25% royalty rate throughout the proceedings, and also pressed its injunction suits even after Motorola was on notice that its actions were in tension with its RAND obligations. Given Microsoft's argument that Motorola's breach was ongoing, the district court could reasonably have concluded that it was appropriate to include the present-day value of Motorola's SEPs as a factor in calculating the RAND rate-and-range for use in the breach-of-contract proceeding.

Second, Motorola never specifies the past date the district court should have used. In pointing to "the time the infringement began," *Georgia-Pacific*, and subsequent cases applying its framework, referred to the date of the manufacturer's first unlicensed use of the patented technology. 318 F. Supp. at 1120; *see also Lucent Techs.*, 580 F.3d at 1324. But, as Motorola acknowledges, the "infringement" at issue in this case is Motorola's breach of contract, not Microsoft's use of Motorola's patents. Motorola mentions both "the date Motorola sent the [offer] letters" and "the time right before Microsoft's first [patent] infringement began" as possible hypothetical negotiation dates the court could have used, without specifying which is correct. Motorola did not mention either date in putting forth its version of the hypothetical negotiation analysis in its post-trial brief. To assume the correct date would have been the date the breach of contract began is of no help, as the alleged breach of contract was not tied to any specific date. The jury could have found a breach of contract based on Motorola's offer letters, its seeking a number of injunctions, or its overall course of conduct.

Third, it would have been impracticable for the court to consider only such evidence as could pinpoint the value of Motorola's patents to Microsoft at a precise point in time. Both parties introduced volumes of data — as to, for example, the parties' market share and the valuation of similar patents — all meant to approximate the value of Motorola's patents. Notably, Motorola itself urged the district court to rely on several studies and reports, from

2011 and 2012, that would not have been available to the parties at an earlier-dated hypothetical negotiation, and one of the "historical licenses" Motorola asked the court to consider — and now argues the court erred in failing to consider — dates from December 2011. As the data presented was not pinpointed to a past date, the district court's approximation from that data also could not be tied to a specific historical moment.

Finally, Motorola has not shown — nor has it even argued — that it was prejudiced by the court's analysis. *See* Brown & Williamson Tobacco Corp. v. Philip Morris Inc., 229 F.3d 1120, 1131 (Fed. Cir. 2000). As Motorola acknowledges, the purpose of the hypothetical agreement approach is to take account of the situation of the parties and of the value each places on the patents in question. Motorola has pointed to just one material change in the parties' positions since the dispute began that could be relevant to the court's analysis: In 2012, Google bought Motorola. Judge Robart considered Google's broad commercial interests, not just Motorola's, when he estimated as part of his RAND-rate analysis the likely benefits from inclusion in the patent pools. But Motorola has not explained how it was prejudiced by consideration of Google's interests. In fact, Microsoft maintains, persuasively, that Motorola benefitted from the court's conflation of Google and Motorola, as Google, a "sophisticated, substantial technology firm[ ] with [a] vast array[ ] of technologically complex products," would obtain more value from the pool than would Motorola as an independent entity.

In sum, given the need for flexibility in determining a royalty rate for a RAND-encumbered patent, *see Ericsson*, 773 F.3d at 1230–31, and given that Motorola has not shown that the court's consideration of the companies' circumstances at the time of the bench trial prejudiced it, *see Brown & Williamson Tobacco Corp.*, 229 F.3d at 1131, the district court's RAND order properly applied the hypothetical agreement approach.

b. Patent Pools and Historical Licenses as Indicators

In addition to challenging the district court's legal analysis, Motorola objects to the court's factual conclusions that (a) the rates charged by two patent pools are relevant indicators of the RAND rate for Motorola's patents; and (b) Motorola's historical licenses are not. Motorola's argument is that the district court gave too much weight to the former evidence and not enough to the latter, leading to a decision "fatal[ly]" unsupported by the evidence in the record.

Patent pools are collections of two or more SEP owners that package and license their SEPs collectively. Royalties are distributed amongst the contributors to the patent pool on a per-patent basis, generally by valuing each patent in the pool equally. Typically, pool members contributing their patents to the pool also become licensees of the pool's patent package.

For Motorola's 802.11 portfolio, the court regarded the VIA Licensing 802.11 pool as somewhat probative of the RAND rate and range. The 802.11 pool did not achieve widespread use of the covered standard. But it was designed with that objective in mind and was otherwise a reasonably reliable indicator of the RAND royalty rate. For Motorola's H.264 portfolio, the court found the royalty rate charged by the MPEG LA H.264 patent pool a reliable indicator of the RAND rate. That pool's objectives mirrored the objectives of RAND agreements, namely "includ[ing] advanced technology to create valuable standards, while at the same time . . . ensuring widespread adoption."

In both instances, the court credited testimony from Motorola's experts that patent pools generally license at lower rates than might be achieved in a bilateral agreement, because a company receives value from pool membership that goes beyond royalty payments — principally, grant-back licenses and promotion of the standard. To account for those benefits, the court multiplied the pool rates by three.

Motorola contends that a rate set by a pool arrangement is too different from the rate that might have been agreed upon bilaterally by the parties to serve as an appropriate RAND-rate indicator, even if the pool rate is multiplied by three. For the 802.11 patents, however, the district court used the pool rate just as one relevant data point in its overall analysis. The RAND rate the court ultimately settled on was an amalgamation of a number of considerations, the pool rate evidence being the most favorable to Motorola.

As to the H.264 patent, the district court provided a reasoned explanation for its conclusion that the H.264 pool was a reliable indicator: The pool's patents and Motorola's patents were essential to the same technical standards, and Motorola provided no evidence that its patents were more valuable than the other patents in the pool. If anything, the record indicates that Motorola's patents were on average less valuable than other H.264 patents. Many of the Motorola patents apply only to interlaced rather than (the more advanced) progressive video. Motorola offered some evidence suggesting that interlaced video coding was still valuable to Microsoft, but it did not show that support for interlaced video was more important to Microsoft than other video-coding capabilities. Motorola therefore was not prejudiced by the court's assumption that its patents were of roughly equal value to those in the pool, as they probably were worth less.

Instead of the patent pools, Motorola argues, the court should have considered several licensing agreements that included licenses to Motorola's H.264 and 802.11 patent portfolios as probative of the RAND rate. The agreements Motorola put forth provided for royalty rates close or equal to the 2.25% it offered Microsoft.

Georgia-Pacific suggests that the royalties a patent owner receives in other licensing agreements for the patents at issue can be relevant in determining a hypothetical royalty agreement. See 318 F. Supp. at 1120. In the current context, however, it was not clear error to reject the past licenses as too contextually dissimilar to be useful to the RAND rate calculation.

The district court found Motorola's license with VTech Communications, Inc. not probative of a RAND rate for Motorola's 802.11 and H.264 patents because those portfolios were licensed as part of a broader agreement that settled infringement claims Motorola held against VTech for use of its cell phone patents. VTech indicated in an email to Motorola that its interest in taking a license was to avoid a potential infringement lawsuit, and it paid only trivial royalties to Motorola under the 802.11 and H.264 licenses — an amount totaling a tiny fraction of the value of the broader agreement. The district court reasonably concluded that the 802.11 and H.264 VTech licenses were not reliable indicators of the RAND royalty rate.

In Motorola's RIM agreement, the 802.11 and H.264 SEPs were packaged with several other patents. Motorola and RIM entered into a broad cross-licensing agreement whereby, in exchange for a license to the Motorola SEPs RIM used in its mobile devices, RIM provided Motorola a license to its own SEPs, paid Motorola a large lump sum, and agreed to pay as a royalty rate a percentage of the net sales price of any mobile device it sold, subject to an annual royalty cap. The royalty rate represented a blended rate for all the Motorola patents included in RIM's products, including non-standard-essential patents. The district court concluded that, for that reason, it would be impracticable to isolate, or apportion the value of the 802.11 and H.264 SEPs, particularly given the evidence that Motorola's cell phone patent portfolio was highly valuable and likely dictated the terms of the agreement. In fact, an earlier agreement between Motorola and RIM provided for the same royalty rate but did not include rights to Motorola's 802.11 and H.264 patents, suggesting that the value of the 802.11 and H.264 patents was zero or negligible. Finally, the RIM agreement was subject to a royalty cap and was, like the VTech agreement, entered into to resolve an ongoing infringement dispute between the parties, further diminishing its trustworthiness as an indicator of a free-standing RAND rate.

Lastly, the district court also reasonably concluded that Motorola's three license agreements with Symbol Technologies were not relevant. Two of the agreements were formed under threat of litigation, included monetary caps, and provided licenses for Motorola patents that expired before Motorola and Microsoft's hypothetical agreement would have occurred. The third agreement also included patents that expired before October 2010, and it required a total payment amount much less than what Motorola would have obtained in seeking a 2.25% royalty rate from Microsoft.

The district court provided reasonable explanations for giving the Motorola bilateral licenses little to no weight. Motorola does not address any of those explanations.

In sum, in determining the RAND rate and range for each SEP portfolio, the district court engaged in a thoughtful and detailed analysis, giving careful consideration to the parties' briefing and evidentiary submissions, and to the testimony. Although Motorola criticizes the district court's approach, it provides no alternative other than strict adherence to the *Georgia-Pacific* factors, without accounting for the particulars of RAND agreements — a rigid approach disapproved of by the Federal Circuit in *Ericsson*. We conclude that the court's RAND determination was not based on a legal error or on a clearly erroneous view of the facts in light of the evidence.

. . .

[Attorneys, Fees]

The RAND context is analogous to these various circumstances in which attorneys' fees expended in earlier litigation are collectible as damages for a proven legal injury. As the district court reasoned, treating fees in separate lawsuits as damages where the RAND commitment is breached "makes particular sense in light of the purpose of the RAND commitment, which is to encourage widespread adoption of the standard." That purpose would be substantially defeated if adopting the standard "would expose [potential implementors] to bad faith injunctive relief claims and they were forced to absorb the cost of defending themselves."

. . . The prospect of an award of attorneys' fees for filing an infringement injunction action would encourage a licensor instead to negotiate directly with the potential licensee in furtherance of the public interest in promoting the standard. *See Apple Inc.*, 757 F.3d at 1332. The very purpose of the RAND agreement is to promote adoption of a standard by decreasing the risk of hold-up. If every SEP holder could force standard implementers into court to defend against injunctive actions without consequence, it would expose those implementers to a flood of litigation, and could discourage such implementers from adhering to standards in the future.

Enforcing the implied covenant of good faith and fair dealing in commercial contracts through tort-like remedies, including attorneys' fees, is appropriate where, as here, the contract is "characterized by elements of public interest." . . . The purposes to be served by awarding

Microsoft the fees incurred defending against Motorola's infringement suits mirror the purposes for which Washington courts have awarded attorneys' fees as damages.

In sum, we agree with the district court that, where a party's injunctive actions to enforce a RAND-encumbered patent violate the duty of good faith and fair dealing, Washington courts would allow the damages awarded to include the attorneys' fees and costs expended to defend against the injunction action.

. . .

III. CONCLUSION

With the parties' consent, the district court conducted a lengthy, thorough bench trial on the RAND rate and range. The court analyzed that evidence in its exhaustive findings of fact and conclusions of law, in a manner consistent with the Federal Circuit's recent approach to establishing damages in the RAND context. The court's factual findings were properly admitted at the jury trial. The jury's verdict was supported by substantial evidence, and its damages award was proper.

The judgment of the district court is affirmed.

LASERDYNAMICS, INC. v. QUANTA COMPUTER, INC.

694 F.3d 51 (2012)

REYNA, Circuit Judge.

I. BACKGROUND

A. The Patented Technology and the Optical Disc Drive Industry

LaserDynamics, Inc. ("LaserDynamics") is the owner of U.S. Patent No. 5,587,981 ("the '981 Patent"), which was issued in 1996. The patent is directed to a method of optical disc discrimination that essentially enables an optical disc drive ("ODD") to automatically identify the type of optical disc—e.g., a compact disc ("CD") versus a digital video disc ("DVD")—that is inserted into the ODD. Claim 3, which was asserted at trial, is representative:

> 3. An optical disk reading method comprising the steps of:
>
> processing an optical signal reflected from encoded pits on an optical disk until total number of data layers and pit configuration standard of the optical disk is identified;
>
> collating the processed optical signal with an optical disk standard data which is stored in a memory; and
>
> settling modulation of servomechanism means dependent upon the optical disk standard data which corresponds with the processed optical signal;
>
> (c) [sic] the servomechanism means including:
>
> a focusing lens servo to modulate position of a focusing lens; and
>
> a tracking servo to modulate movement of a pickup.

This automated process saves the user from having to manually identify the kind of disc being inserted into the ODD before the ODD can begin to read the data on the disc. The patented technology is alleged to be particularly useful in laptop computers where portability, convenience, and efficiency are essential. At least as early as 2006, a laptop computer was not commercially viable unless it included an ODD that could automatically discriminate between optical discs.

Yasuo Kamatani is the sole inventor of the '981 Patent. In 1998, viewing DVD technology as the next major data and video format, Mr. Kamatani founded LaserDynamics and assigned the '981 Patent to the company. Mr. Kamatani is the sole employee of LaserDynamics, which is exclusively in the business of licensing Mr. Kamatani's patents to ODD and consumer electronics manufacturers.

When LaserDynamics was founded, the DVD market had reached few mainstream consumers, and there was some skepticism among electronics companies as to the likely success of this technology compared with the established VHS format. By 2000, however, DVD sales and the ODD market were sharply rising. By 2003, most homes had DVD players and nearly every computer had an ODD. An ODD having automatic disc discrimination capability quickly became the industry standard for DVD players and computers.

B. LaserDynamics' Licensing History of the '981 Patent

According to LaserDynamics, it was initially difficult to generate interest in licensing the '981 Patent, due to the novelty of the technology and LaserDynamics' limited operating capital and bargaining power. Nevertheless, LaserDynamics entered into sixteen licensing agreements from 1998 to 2001. These licenses were granted to well known electronics and ODD manufacturers such as Sony, Philips, NEC, LG, Toshiba, Hitachi, Yamaha, Sanyo, Sharp, Onkyo, and Pioneer. All of the licenses were nonexclusive licenses granted in exchange for one time lump sum payments ranging from $57,000 to $266,000. There is no evidence that these licenses recited the lump sum amounts as representing a running royalty applied over a certain period of time or being calculated as a percentage of revenues or profits.

Several other lump sum licenses were granted by LaserDynamics between 1998 and 2003 to other ODD and electronics manufacturers via more aggressive licensing efforts involving actual or threatened litigation by LaserDynamics.

On February 15, 2006, LaserDynamics (and Mr. Kamatani) entered into a license agreement with BenQ Corporation to settle a two-year long litigation for a lump sum of $6 million.

Finally, in 2009 and 2010, LaserDynamics entered into license agreements with ASUSTeK Computer and Orion Electric Co., Ltd., respectively, for lump sum payments of $1 million or less. These two licenses were admitted into evidence in the second trial.

In total, twenty-nine licenses were entered into evidence in the second damages trial. With the exception of the $6 million BenQ license, all twenty-nine licenses were for lump sum amounts of $1 million or less.

C. Quanta Computer Inc. and Quanta Storage Inc.

Quanta Storage, Inc. ("QSI") is a manufacturer of ODDs that was incorporated in 1999. QSI is headquartered in Taiwan and is a partially-owned subsidiary of Quanta Computer, Inc. ("QCI"), with which it shares some common officers, directors, and facilities. QCI's corporate headquarters are also located in Taiwan, and its factories are located in China. QCI holds a minority share in QSI and does not control QSI's operations.

QCI assembles laptop computers for its various customers, which include name brand computer companies such as Dell, Hewlett Packard ("HP"), Apple, and Gateway. QCI does not manufacture ODDs, but will install ODDs into computers as instructed by its customers. QCI will sometimes purchase ODDs directly from ODD manufacturers such as Sony, Panasonic, Toshiba, or QSI, as directed by QCI's customers. Predominantly, however, QCI will be required to purchase the ODDs from the customer for whom QCI is assembling the laptop computer. In other words, QCI's typical practice is to buy ODDs from Dell, HP, Apple, or Gateway, which in turn purchased the ODDs from the ODD manufacturers. Because QCI eventually sells the fully assembled laptop computers — including the ODDs — to its customers, this process is called a "buy/sell" arrangement. When QCI purchases ODDs from one of its customers in a buy/sell context, it buys the ODDs for an artificially high "mask price" set by the customer and designed to hide the actual lower price of the ODDs from the customer's competitors. Thus, the mask price is always higher than the actual price to the customer.

QSI first sold its ODDs for integration into laptop computers in the United States in 2001. In 2002, LaserDynamics offered QSI a license under the '981 Patent, but QSI disputed whether its ODDs were within the scope of the '981 Patent and declined the offer. QCI sold its first computer in the United States using an ODD from QSI in 2003. It was not until August 2006 that LaserDynamics offered a license to QCI concurrently with the filing of this lawsuit. To date, neither QSI nor QCI has entered into a licensing agreement with LaserDynamics relating to the '981 Patent.

D. ODDs Made by Philips and Sony/NEC/Optiarc

Just as computer sellers Dell, HP, Apple, and Gateway outsource the assembly of their computers to companies like QCI, some sellers of ODDs outsource the assembly of their ODDs. QSI assembles ODDs for Philips and Sony/NEC/Optiarc — two of the largest sellers of ODDs. As discussed above, Philips and Sony/NEC/Optiarc are licensed by LaserDynamics to make and sell ODDs within the scope of the '981 Patent. Under the license agreements, both Philips and Sony/NEC/Optiarc also enjoy "have made" rights that permit them to retain companies like QSI to assemble ODDs for them.

When QCI purchases ODDs directly from Philips or Sony/NEC/Optiarc — i.e., not under a buy/sell arrangement — QCI has no knowledge of which entity assembled the ODDs. QCI pays Philips or Sony/NEC/Optiarc directly for the ODDs, which are not sold under the QSI brand name even if assembled by QSI.

ANALYSIS

. . .

B. QCI Has an Implied License to Assemble Laptops Using ODDs from QSI via Philips and Sony/NEC/Optiarc

QCI contends that it has an implied license to assemble laptop computers for its customers that include the accused ODDs assembled by QSI for Philips or Sony/NEC/Optiarc, pursuant to Philips's and Sony/NEC/Optiarc's "have made" rights under their patent license agreements with LaserDynamics. The QSI-assembled ODDs at issue are sold by Philips or Sony/NEC/Optiarc either directly to QCI or indirectly to QCI via QCI's customers such as Dell and HP, as directed by QCI's customers. "The existence vel non of an implied license is a question of law that we review de novo." Anton/Bauer, Inc. v. PAG, Ltd., 329 F.3d 1343, 1348 (Fed. Cir. 2003).

At oral argument before this court, counsel for QCI explained that the vast majority of the allegedly infringing ODDs would be covered under QCI's implied license theory, and that QCI's arguments concerning patent exhaustion pertain to only those same ODDs. Because we find that QCI has an implied license, we do not reach QCI's patent exhaustion arguments.

The district court relied solely on E.I. du Pont de Nemours & Co. v. Shell Oil Co., 498 A.2d 1108 (Del. 1985), in finding that "the Quanta defendants do not have an implied license with respect to drives that are manufactured by QSI and eventually sold to QCI (or another Quanta entity), notwithstanding the fact that those drives are sold through Philips or Sony/NEC/ Optiarc, two of [LaserDynamics'] licensees." According to the district court, "[t]he effect of such transactions is to grant an impermissible sublicense." Id. We disagree.

In du Pont, E.I. Du Pont de Nemours and Company, Inc. ("Du Pont") had entered into a license agreement with Shell Oil Company ("Shell") permitting Shell to "make, have made, use and sell for use or resale" an insecticide product covered by Du Pont's patent. 498 A.2d at 1110. The license agreement expressly prohibited any sublicensing by Shell. Union Carbide Agricultural Corporation, Inc. ("Union Carbide") later sought permission from Shell to produce the patented insecticide, but Shell declined due to the prohibition on sublicensing in its licensed agreement with Du Pont. Instead, Shell and Union Carbide came up with the following arrangement: (1) Union Carbide would manufacture the insecticide under the "have made" provision of the license agreement between Shell and Du Pont, then (2) Shell would immediately sell back the insecticide to Union Carbide pursuant to Shell's right to "sell for use or resale." Id. at 1111. The minimum amounts of insecticide that Union Carbide agreed to make and the minimum amounts that Shell agreed to sell back to Union Carbide were identical. The Supreme Court of Delaware deemed this arrangement an impermissible sublicense, rather than a permissible exercise of Shell's "have made" and "sell" rights, because "ultimately, Union Carbide was producing [the insecticide], not for Shell, but rather for itself." Id. at 1115 (citing Carey v. United States, 326 F.2d 975, 979 (Ct. Cl. 1964) (explaining that "the test is, whether the production is by or for the use of the original licensee or for the sublicensee himself or for someone else")).

The case before us presents a different situation from that in du Pont. The ODDs provided to QCI via Philips and Sony/NEC/Optiarc were undoubtedly assembled by QSI for Philips and Sony/NEC/Optiarc, not for QSI or QCI. Even though the ODDs made by QSI were in reality shipped directly from QSI to QCI, the substance of the transactions make clear that QSI's manufacture of the ODDs was limited to the needs and requests of Philips and Sony/NEC/ Optiarc. QSI had no unfettered ability to make more ODDs than were ordered from it. Nothing in the record suggests that this overall arrangement is designed to circumvent the terms of the patent licenses between LaserDynamics and Philips or Sony/NEC/Optiarc. Indeed, the shipping and manufacturing arrangements involved in this case reflect typical on-time delivery logistics of modern industrial reality.

The apposite precedent is our decision in Cyrix Corp. v. Intel Corp., 77 F.3d 1381 (Fed. Cir. 1996). That case involved Cyrix Corporation ("Cyrix"), a designer and seller of microprocessors, contracting with other companies to manufacture integrated circuit chips containing the Cyrix-designed microprocessors, then selling the chips back to Cyrix. Cyrix used manufacturers that were licensed under patents owned by Intel, including SGS-Thomson Microelectronics, Inc. ("ST"). ST had acquired by assignment a license from Intel "to make, have made . . . [and] sell" the patented chips. ST could not itself fulfill Cyrix's orders, however, and, relying on its "have made" rights, arranged for its Italian non-subsidiary affiliate company ("ST-Italy") to manufacture the chips, which ST then sold to Cyrix. The district court distinguished this situation from that in *du Pont* and held that ST did not exceed its rights under the Intel license by having ST-Italy make the chips for ST to sell to Cyrix. Cyrix and ST were both found to not infringe Intel's patents on this basis.

We affirmed, rejecting Intel's argument that the arrangement among ST, ST-Italy, and Cyrix was a mere paper transaction — a "sham" designed to circumvent Intel's license to ST. We endorsed the district court's reasoning that, unlike in *du Pont*, "[t]he production of the [chips] is for the use of ST, the original licensee, and not for the use of ST-Italy." *Id.* at 1387. As we explained, "[i]f the facts in this case had been that Cyrix made the product for ST under ST's 'have made' rights and then ST sold the product back to Cyrix, then they would have been analogous to those in *du Pont*, but those are not our facts." *Id.* at 1388.

This case likewise presents no "sham" transaction as in *du Pont*. QSI made the ODDs at issue here to fulfill bona fide orders from licensees Philips and Sony/NEC/Optiarc. The ODDs were then sold to QCI by the licensees. QCI did not make the ODDs for Philips or Sony/NEC/Optiarc and then immediately purchase the ODDs back so as to effectively receive a sub-license and obtain as many ODDs as it wanted. Rather, as in *Cyrix*, the manufacture of the ODDs by QSI and their eventual sale to QCI for incorporation into laptop computers, all via Philips and Sony/NEC/Optiarc, were legitimate and separate business transactions that did not expand or circumvent the patent licenses. *Id.* at 1387-88 ("The two agreements, one permitting ST-Italy to manufacture microprocessors for ST and the other providing for ST's sale of microprocessors to Cyrix, were separate business transactions."). Both the manufacture and sale of the ODDs were valid exercises of the "have made" and "sell" rights, respectively, under the license agreements in this case. We therefore conclude that QCI has an implied license to the '981 Patent with respect to the ODDs made by QSI and sold to QCI via Philips or Sony/NEC/Optiarc.

* * *

THE ANTITRUST GUIDELINES FOR THE LICENSING OF INTELLECTUAL PROPERTY

The U.S. Department of Justice and the Federal Trade Commission issued the Antitrust Guidelines for the Licensing of Intellectual Property protected by patents, copyright, and trade secret law, and of know-how. The Guidelines are helpful in predicting whether the Agencies will challenge a practice as anticompetitive. The Agencies first issued the Guidelines on April 6, 1995. The Agencies later revised the Guidelines and issued a new version on January 12, 2017. The new Guidelines are available at https://www.justice.gov/atr/IPguidelines/download. Due to the length of the new Guidelines and the limited space available in this book, we will not include an excerpt in this chapter.

III. PROBLEMS

1. State Paving Corporation (State Paving) constructed a set of sound barrier walls for the Florida Department of Transportation (FDOT). Subsequently, State Paving applied for patent protection for its inventions.

   State Paving entered into an agreement to transfer the inventions to State Contracting. The relevant contract specifies that State Paving "sells, assigns, and transfers" to State Contracting the "entire right title and interest in the inventions" relating to an Integrated Column & Pile, "to any component part and subassemblies thereof, and to any improvements in the foregoing Integrated Column & Pile, component part and subassemblies thereof, including, but not limited to subject matter disclosed in the two patents." The contract omits language explicitly assigning the patents and that it does not transfer all rights in the patents. State Paving retained the right to sue for future infringement, having expressly granted the right to sue only for past and present infringement.

   Thereafter, State Contracting sued FDOT and several highway construction contractors for infringement of the two patents. State Contracting alleged that FDOT had improperly incorporated the inventions into subsequent requests for bids and that the contractors had then infringed the patents when they carried out the construction contracts that resulted from those bids.

   Is the transfer between State Paving and State Contracting a license or an assignment? Does State Contracting have standing to bring the patent infringement suit?

2. Licensor and Licensee entered into a license agreement. The license covered both patent and trade secrets for keyholder design. The agreement provided for a royalty of 5 percent of keyholder sales for as long as the sales continued, but it also provided for a reduction of royalties to 2.5 percent if no patent was issued within five years. Because no patent was issued during the five-year period, the licensor reduced the royalty rate per the license agreement. Twenty-two years after the execution of the license agreement, the licensee sought to invalidate the agreement because it was beyond the 20-year patent term. Is the license agreement enforceable under patent and state laws?

3. ABI and EPT entered into a supply agreement wherein EPT agreed to distribute early pregnancy test (e.p.t.) products manufactured by ABI. The agreement contained an indemnification clause which required ABI to defend, indemnify, and hold EPT harmless from claims "arising out of or resulting from the use of the Patents or Know-how . . . in connection with the manufacture, use and sale of the e.p.t. test®." Subsequently, EPT faced a patent infringement suit brought by Armkel. EPT requested that ABI indemnify EPT for the patent infringement suit. ABI refused, and EPT defended, itself in the patent infringement suit, settled the case with Amkel and

subsequently brought a third-party complaint against ABI for breach of the indemnification provision of the agreement between ABI and EPT. ABI argued that it was not required to indemnify EPT and that EPT violated the procedures as stated in the indemnification provisions by settling the patent infringement claims with Armkel without ABI's prior written consent. Who should prevail?

4. PatentCo entered into a patent license agreement with DellCo to "make, use, or sell" certain inventions related to microprocessors and chipsets. In the license agreement, PatentCo requires DellCo to notify buyers of the microprocessors that they do not receive licensing rights for use of the DellCo microprocessors together with non-DellCo components. Thereafter, DellCo manufactured and sold microprocessors and chipsets to Vendors, and DellCo notified Vendors of the restrictions PatentCo placed on the microprocessors. Vendors proceeded to make and sell computer systems by combining DellCo's microprocessors and other non-DellCo components; PatentCo then sued Vendors for patent infringement. You are the attorney for Vendors. Does PatentCo's claim have any merit? What arguments can you make regarding the application of the doctrine of patent exhaustion to these patents? Who should prevail? *See* Quanta v. LG Electronics, 553 U.S. 617 (2008).

5. The Court in Impression Products v. Lexmark equates the patent exhaustion and copyright first sale doctrines. Evaluate the merits of that equivalency and its impact on copyright and software licensing. Does the Court leave the door open at all for the use of patent remedies to enforce license restrictions or conditions?

IV. DRAFTING EXERCISES

1. You are the attorney for State Contracting in the patent transaction between State Contracting and State Paving, discussed above in Problem 1. How would you have drafted the "Patent Grant Provision" of the agreement so as to avoid subsequent challenges by defendants in future infringement suits? Submit the new grant provision.

2. You are the attorney for PatentCo in the patent licensing transaction between PatentCo and DellCo, discussed above in Problem 4. How would you have drafted the "Patent Grant Provision" of the agreement so as to avoid subsequent buyers of the DellCo microprocessors from combining them with non-DellCo components and selling them (as Vendors did)? Submit your new grant provision. *See* Quanta v. LG Electronics, 553 U.S. 617 (2008).

3. Re-draft the "Governing Law" provision to avoid disputes similar to that seen in Texas Instruments, Inc. v. Tessera, Inc., 231 F.3d 1325 (Fed. Cir. 2000).

4. You represent N-Data in Intel Corp. v. Negotiated Data Solutions, Inc., 703 F.3d 1360 (Fed. Cir. 2012). Re-draft the License Grant and the definition for "National Patents" on behalf of N-Data to exclude any reissued patents in the license grant scope.

5. Adam is the inventor and holder of certain patents. He would like to enter into a license agreement with Big Company. Big Company drafted the license agreement, which includes the Warranty provision below. Adam is concerned because he does not know whether his patents infringe on others' patents. Adam wants you to markup the Warranty provision.

WARRANTY

A. LICENSOR represents and warrants that it is the owner of the entire right, title and interest in and to the Licensed Patents, that it has the right and power to grant the licenses granted herein, that there are no other agreements with any other party in conflict with such grant and that it knows of no prior art which would invalidate the Licensed Patents.

B. LICENSOR further represents and warrants that LICENSEE's contemplated use of the Licensed Patents as represented to LICENSOR does not infringe any valid rights of any third party, and that there are no infringement actions against LICENSOR with respect to items it manufactures and sells embodying the invention of the Licensed Patents in the United States.

---

6. You are responsible for drafting an important cross-license agreement for your client. The other party to the cross-license agreement is IntelCo. You are currently drafting the Indemnification provisions. The client wants IntelCo to provide the indemnity; IntelCo wants your client to provide the indemnity. Draft an acceptable indemnification agreement for your client. Below are some old sample Indemnification provisions that may be of assistance to you.

Sample 1

Licensor has all right, title and ownership to the Licensor Technology and Licensor Deliverables including any patents, copyrights, mask works, trade secrets, trademarks, and other intellectual property rights pertaining to the Licensor Technology and Licensor Deliverables including, without limitation, the right to grant the license herein to Licensee and it will take no action which would in any way impair the foregoing.

Licensor will indemnify Licensee based on a claim that the Licensor Technology or Licensor Deliverables, respectively, alone and not in combination with any other products, infringe any patent, copyright, trade secret, or other intellectual property right of a third party.

Neither Licensor nor Licensee shall settle or otherwise resolve any claim or potential claim, action or proceeding relating to the products without the prior written consent of the other party, which consent shall not be unreasonably withheld.

Sample 2

[FAAC] shall defend, indemnify and hold MSI, its officers, directors, agents, employees and customers harmless from any and all claims, liabilities, costs and damages (including attorneys' fees) arising from or in connection with any claims that the design, manufacture, sale or use of the System, any Deliverables, or portions thereof, or the services provided by [FAAC] hereunder infringe any patent, copyright, trade secret or other proprietary right of any third party. MSI will promptly notify [FAAC] of the existence of any such claim. [FAAC's] indemnification obligation will survive termination of this Agreement.

Sample 3

CENTRIX shall defend KERR, at Centrix' [sic] expense, against any claim, action or other proceedings ("all hereinafter the Action") brought against Kerr for patent infringement with regard to the use or sale of the Products, even if the allegations in the Action are groundless, false or fraudulent. In addition, CENTRIX shall indemnify KERR for any and all liability, damages, judgments incurred by KERR as a result of any such patent infringement Action.

· CHAPTER ·

7

TRADE SECRET LICENSING

I. OVERVIEW OF TRADE SECRET LICENSING

A. Introduction

Trade secrets represent a unique category of intellectual property. In the United States, trade secrets were primarily the domain of state common law and statutes up until the passage of the Defend Trade Secrets Act of 2016 ("DTSA"), Pub. L. No. 114-153, 130 Stat 376 (codified at 18 U.S.C. §§1831-1839 (2016)). The DTSA is the first federal law to create a civil cause of action for trade secret misappropriation. It amends the Economic Espionage Act to allow private citizens owning trade secrets to seek civil remedies, as long as the secret is "related to a product or service used in, or intended for use in, interstate or foreign commerce," 18 U.S.C. §1836(b)(1); *see also* §1839(4) (defining "owner"). The DTSA gives the United States district courts original jurisdiction over these actions, but does not preempt individuals from bringing claims in state courts under state trade secret laws, except against whistleblowers.

The drafters of The Uniform Trade Secrets Act (UTSA), 14 U.L.A. 433, 434-35 (2000), along with the many states that have enacted it, chose to define trade secrets very broadly. According to these sources of law a trade secret is

> information, including a formula, pattern, compilation, program, device, method, technique, or process, that: (i) derives independent economic value, actual or potential, from not being generally known to, and not being readily ascertainable by proper means by, other persons who can obtain economic value from its disclosure or use, and (ii) is the subject of efforts that are reasonable under the circumstances to maintain its secrecy.

The DTSA's definition of "trade secret" closely resembles the UTSA's definition. The broad definition of trade secrets means that it can cover everything from mundane customer lists to the most interesting and spectacular innovations envisioned by the high technology or computer software industries.

To give context to trade secrets, it is helpful to contrast them with other forms of intellectual property, specifically patents and copyrights. First, trade secrets derive their economic value from being secret. Second, trade secrets only provide for limited exclusivity, as there is no restriction on a third party's ability to derive independently the subject matter of the holder's secret, nor are there restrictions on a third party's efforts to legitimately reverse engineer a holder's secret. Third, to reap trade secret protection, the holder must establish measures to maintain secrecy, ensure nondisclosure, and prevent unauthorized use. Fourth, trade secret protection is expansive because there is no need to meet novelty and non-obviousness requirements. Finally, trade secret protection can extend into perpetuity, so long as the secret is maintained.

Exploiting the value of trade secrets through licensing has long been a common practice. Arguably, no other form of intellectual property is more dependent on licensing than trade secrets. Various license instruments convey the benefits embodied by the trade secret while still protecting and creating incentives for the labor and effort expended on marshalling of the trade secret. Without the licensing mechanism, inventors who are unable to take advantage of the patent system would be unwilling to share the product of their trade secrets with the public for fear that the trade secret would be disclosed and used without compensation. *See* Kewanee Oil Co. v. Bicron Corp., 416 U.S. 470, 486 (1974); Aronson v. Quick Point Pencil Co., 440 U.S. 257 (1979). As such, there is a significant public interest in the licensing of trade secrets. For example,

- Until very recently, Procter & Gamble guarded its technological secrets and know how in products such as Tide, Crest, and Pringles. P&G decided to license its trade secrets in hopes of maximizing its annual $1.7 billion investment in research and development by developing relationships with other companies to venture into new product areas to respond to sewage treatment and oil drilling and spills;
- Coca-Cola continues to vigilantly guard its secret soda beverage formula, but it has recently made efforts to license its patents on vending machines, drink dispensers, and packaging to other beverage companies;
- Prior to entering into licensing agreements with competitors, Ford Motor Company maintained for itself the trade secrets to a switch mechanism that allowed drivers to deactivate air bags as well as its adjustable pedals that aid the comfort of short drivers;
- Trade secrets are also integral to the online romance business. Match.com subpoenaed nine former employees who defected to True.com, an upstart competitor, to find out whether the former employees breached confidentiality agreements by disclosing secrets about proprietary information and a 12 million-person customer portfolio; and
- As discussed in Chapter 9, the licensing of trade secret source code is critical to innovation in the software industry.

Paradoxically, this beneficial sharing of trade secrets through licensing jeopardizes the very existence of trade secret protection. The greater the sharing, the greater the practical danger that the trade secrets will be revealed to the public, and public disclosure ends trade secret protection. Therefore, trade secret licenses obligate the licensee to take measures designed to maintain the secrecy of the licensed information. The nature of these confidentiality measures varies, from specific instructions about marking and storing material, to a general admonition to treat material as carefully as the licensee treats its own trade secret information.

Trade secret license agreements come in a variety forms. Some are stand-alone licenses focused on a particular document or set of information. Other trade secret licenses are but one part of a complex licensing transaction covering multiple types of intellectual property. The most common trade secret licenses come under the label "nondisclosure agreement" or "NDA." Given their ubiquity in trade secret licensing, two sample NDAs can be found later in this Overview.

B. Assignment Versus Licensing of Trade Secrets

An assignment of a trade secret transfers the right to use the trade secret as well as the right to prevent unauthorized disclosure of the trade secret. *See* E.I. du Pont de Nemours & Co. v. United States, 288 F.2d 904, 911-12 (Ct. Cl. 1961). In order for a transfer of a trade secret to meet the sale requirement, the transferor must convey his or her most important rights — the right to prevent unauthorized disclosure and the right to prevent further use of the trade secret by all others. A transfer of anything less results in a transaction that is not an assignment. *See* Stalker Corp. v. United States, 209 F. Supp. 30 (D. Mich. 1962). The right to prevent disclosure is the competitive advantage gained as a result of the assignment of a trade secret. The value lies in the rights they give to their owners for monopolistic exploitation. A party may pay the owner of a trade secret for its disclosure and use. That party may also pay for the residual right possessed by the holder — the right to continue to prevent unauthorized disclosure and use.

C. Exclusive and Non-Exclusive Trade Secret Licenses

An exclusive trade secret license is a promise by the licensor neither to practice within the scope of the license nor to grant further licenses to others within the scope of the exclusive license. In order for the licensor to retain a property interest in the trade secret, the licensor must expressly reserve any rights it wants to keep. For example,

> Licensor grants Licensee the exclusive right to manufacture baseball bats based on the proprietary techniques and know how contained in Licensor's technical manual entitled "Building Bats Under the SlugFast Process."

A non-exclusive license grants rights in a trade secret to multiple licensees. It is routinely referred to as a promise not to sue. Non-exclusive licenses in the trade secret context are common because dissemination of trade secret subject matter on this basis enables the licensor to most fully exploit its secret information or technology. While licensors are in the business of exploiting their trade secrets, the reality of having multiple non-exclusive licensees increases the risk of unauthorized or accidental disclosures. And, once the secrecy of the subject matter is destroyed, indefinite trade secret protection dissolves. The licensor must balance the desire for market penetration through cooperative non-exclusive license agreements with licensees against the costs associated with protecting the trade secret from disclosure. For example,

> The Foundation hereby grants to Licensee a non-exclusive right and license to use the Strain and Know How to make, have made, use, and sell the Vaccine in the Contract Territory. The "Contract Territory" is "the countries of Europe." "Know How" is defined as: Without limitation, all technical information and know how regarding preparation and propagation of the Strain and commercial production of the Vaccine, which are presently in the possession of the Foundation or are acquired hereafter by the Foundation during the term of this Agreement.

This license grant expressly identifies the license as non-exclusive and establishes the boundaries of the grant. The boundaries are important because a pharmaceutical licensor relies on many potential licensees in order to achieve market penetration. Any licensee would know from this agreement that other licensees exist and that they are operating in different territories. The license grant also provides non-exclusive access and use of present and future know how that can assist licensees in preparing and propagating the compound.

D. Nondisclosure Agreements

A nondisclosure agreement ("NDA") is a contract in which the parties promise to protect the confidentiality of secret information that is disclosed during employment or in the course of a business transaction. An NDA creates a confidential relationship between a person who owns a trade secret and someone who desires access to the trade secret. NDAs contain a variety of confidentiality measures designed to guard the secrecy of trade secrets. Even though the focus of the NDA seems to be on *non*disclosure of information (as the name suggests), the NDA is fundamentally a trade secret license. Bear this permission-granting purpose in mind as you study the NDAs below.

NDAs usually come in two forms: mutual agreements and one-way agreements. A mutual NDA is one in which both parties are exchanging confidential information, while a one-way agreement is used when only one party is making a disclosure. The basic elements of an NDA include a definition of the confidential information; exclusions from confidential information, for example, public domain information;

obligations and duties of receiving parties or dual obligations in the case of mutual agreements; duration of the access to and use of the trade secret; and other miscellaneous provisions such as severability provisions or addendums.

SAMPLE NONDISCLOSURE AGREEMENT (ONE-WAY)

WHEREAS, [YOUR NAME] agrees to furnish _____ certain confidential information relating to ideas, inventions or products for the purposes of determining an interest in developing, manufacturing, selling and/or joint venturing; WHEREAS, _____ agrees to review, examine, inspect or obtain such confidential information only for the purposes described above, and to otherwise hold such information confidential pursuant to the terms of this Agreement. BE IT KNOWN, that [YOUR NAME] has or shall furnish to _____ certain confidential information and may further allow _____ the right to discuss or interview representatives of [YOUR NAME] on the following conditions:

1. _____ agrees to hold confidential or proprietary information or trade secrets ("confidential information") in trust and confidence and agrees that it shall be used only for the contemplated purposes, shall not be used for any other purpose, or disclosed to any third party.
2. No copies will be made or retained of any written information or prototypes supplied without the permission of [YOUR NAME].
3. At the conclusion of any discussions, or upon demand by [YOUR NAME], all confidential information, including prototypes, written notes, photographs, sketches, models, memoranda or notes taken shall be returned to [YOUR NAME].
4. Confidential information shall not be disclosed to any employee, consultant or third party unless they agree to execute and be bound by the terms of this Agreement, and have been approved by [YOUR NAME].
5. This Agreement and its validity, construction and effect shall be governed by the laws of [insert jurisdiction].

---

* * *

SAMPLE NONDISCLOSURE AGREEMENT (MUTUAL)

This Nondisclosure Agreement ("Agreement") is made and entered into as of the later of the two signature dates below.

[Company]   [Company]
Signature:_____   Signature:_____
Printed Name:_____   Printed Name:_____
Title:_____   Title:_____
Signature Date:_____   Signature Date:_____
Address: Address:

1. Definition and Use of Confidential Information

(a) "Confidential Information" means nonpublic information in any form that a party
     to this Agreement ("Disclosing Party") designates as being confidential to the
     party that receives such information ("Receiving Party") or which, under the cir-
     cumstances surrounding disclosure ought to be treated as confidential by the
     Receiving Party. It may relate to, without limitation, information about released or
     pre-release software or hardware products, the marketing or promotion of pro-
     ducts, business policies or practices, and information received from others that
     Disclosing Party is obligated to treat as confidential. Confidential Information shall
     not include any information, however designated, that: (i) is or subsequently
     becomes publicly available without Receiving Party's breach of any obligation
     owed Disclosing Party; (ii) became known to Receiving Party prior to Disclosing
     Party's disclosure of such information to Receiving Party pursuant to the terms of
     this Agreement; (iii) became known to Receiving Party from a source other than
     Disclosing Party other than by the breach of an obligation of confidentiality owed
     to Disclosing Party; (iv) is independently developed by Receiving Party; or
     (v) constitutes Feedback (as defined in this Agreement).

(b) The Receiving Party may use Confidential Information for [*describe purpose*];
     otherwise, Receiving Party receives no right or license under any Disclosing
     Party patents, copyrights, trademarks, or trade secret information. Disclosing Party
     reserves without prejudice the ability to protect its rights under any such patents,
     copyrights, trademarks, or trade secrets except as expressly described above. All
     Confidential Information is and shall remain the property of Disclosing Party.

(c) The terms of confidentiality under this Agreement shall not be construed to limit
     either the Disclosing Party or the Receiving Party's right to independently develop
     or acquire products without use of the other party's Confidential Information.
     Further, the Receiving Party shall be free to use for any purpose the residuals
     resulting from access to or work with the Confidential Information of the Dis-
     closing Party, provided that the Receiving Party shall not disclose the Confidential
     Information except as expressly permitted pursuant to the terms of this Agree-
     ment. The term "residuals" means information in intangible form, which is
     retained in memory by persons who have had access to the Confidential Infor-
     mation, including ideas, concepts, know how or techniques contained therein.
     The Receiving Party shall not have any obligation to limit or restrict the assignment
     of such persons or to pay royalties for any work resulting from the use of residuals.

However, this sub-paragraph shall not be deemed to grant to the Receiving Party a license under the Disclosing Party's copyrights or patents.

2. Disclosure to Affiliates

Except as otherwise indicated in this Agreement, the term "Disclosing Party" and the term "Receiving Party" also includes all Affiliates. An "Affiliate" means any person, partnership, joint venture, corporation or other form of enterprise, domestic or foreign that directly or indirectly, control, are controlled by, or are under common control with a party. Prior to the time that any Confidential Information is shared with an Affiliate who has not signed this Agreement, the Receiving Party that executed this Agreement (the "Signatory Receiving Party") must enter into an appropriate written agreement with that Affiliate sufficient to enable the Disclosing Party and/or the Signatory Receiving Party to enforce all of the provisions of this Agreement against such Affiliate.

3. Obligations to Protect Confidential Information

(a) Receiving Party shall:

    (i) Refrain from disclosing any Confidential Information of the Disclosing Party to third parties for five (5) years following the date that Disclosing Party first discloses such Confidential Information to Receiving Party, except as expressly provided in Sections 3(b) and 3(c) of this Agreement;

    (ii) Take reasonable security precautions to keep confidential the Confidential Information of the Disclosing Party, at least as great as the precautions it takes to protect its own confidential information, but no less than reasonable care;

    (iii) Refrain from disclosing, reproducing, summarizing and/or distributing Confidential Information of the Disclosing Party except in pursuance of Receiving Party's business relationship with Disclosing Party, and only as otherwise provided hereunder; and

    (iv) Refrain from reverse engineering, decompiling or disassembling any software code and/or pre-release hardware devices disclosed by Disclosing Party to Receiving Party under the terms of this Agreement, except as expressly permitted by applicable law.

(b) Receiving Party may disclose Confidential Information of Disclosing Party in accordance with a judicial or other governmental order, provided that Receiving Party either (i) gives the Disclosing Party reasonable notice prior to such disclosure to allow Disclosing Party a reasonable opportunity to seek a protective order or equivalent, or (ii) obtains written assurance from the applicable judicial or governmental entity that it will afford the Confidential Information the highest level of protection afforded under applicable law or regulation. Notwithstanding the foregoing, the Receiving Party shall not disclose any computer source code that contains Confidential Information of the Disclosing Party in accordance with a judicial or other governmental order unless it complies with the requirement set forth in sub-section (i) of this Section 3(b).

(c) The Receiving Party may disclose Confidential Information only to Receiving Party's employees and consultants on a need-to-know basis. The Receiving Party will have executed or shall execute appropriate written agreements with its employees and consultants sufficient to enable Receiving Party to enforce all the provisions of this Agreement.

(d) Receiving Party shall notify the Disclosing Party immediately upon discovery of any unauthorized use or disclosure of Confidential Information or any other breach of this Agreement by Receiving Party and its employees and consultants, and will cooperate with Disclosing Party in every reasonable way to help Disclosing Party regain possession of the Confidential Information and prevent its further unauthorized use or disclosure.

(e) Receiving Party shall, at Disclosing Party's request, return all originals, copies, reproductions and summaries of Confidential Information and all other tangible materials and devices provided to the Receiving Party as Confidential Information, or at Disclosing Party's option, certify destruction of the same.

4. Remedies

The parties acknowledge that monetary damages may not be a sufficient remedy for unauthorized disclosure of Confidential Information and that Disclosing Party shall be entitled, without waiving any other rights or remedies, to such injunctive or equitable relief as may be deemed proper by a court of competent jurisdiction.

5. Miscellaneous

(a) The parties agree to comply with all applicable international and national laws that apply to (i) any Confidential Information, or (ii) any product (or any part thereof), process or service that is the direct product of the Confidential Information, including the U.S. Export Administration Regulations, as well as end-user, end-use and destination restrictions issued by the U.S. and other governments. For additional information on exporting [my company] products, see *http://www.[my company].com/[export control]/*.

(b) None of the provisions of this Agreement shall be deemed to have been waived by any act or acquiescence on the part of Disclosing Party, the Receiving Party, their agents, or employees, but only by an instrument in writing signed by an authorized employee of Disclosing Party and the Receiving Party. No waiver of any provision of this Agreement shall constitute a waiver of any other provision(s) or of the same provision on another occasion.

(c) If either Disclosing Party or the Receiving Party employs attorneys to enforce any rights arising out of or relating to this Agreement, the prevailing party shall be entitled to recover reasonable attorneys' fees and costs. This Agreement shall be construed and controlled by the laws of the State of [state], and the parties further consent to exclusive jurisdiction and venue in the federal courts sitting in [county] County, [state], unless no federal subject matter jurisdiction exists, in which case the parties consent to the exclusive jurisdiction and venue in the Superior Court of

[county] County, [state]. Company waives all defenses of lack of personal jurisdiction and forum *non conveniens*. Process may be served on either party in the
manner authorized by applicable law or court rule.

(d) This Agreement shall be binding upon and inure to the benefit of each party's
respective successors and lawful assigns; provided, however, that neither party
may assign this Agreement (whether by operation of law, sale of securities or assets,
merger or otherwise), in whole or in part, without the prior written approval of the
other party. Any attempted assignment in violation of this Section shall be void.

(e) If any provision of this Agreement shall be held by a court of competent jurisdiction to be illegal, invalid or unenforceable, the remaining provisions shall remain
in full force and effect.

(f) This Agreement shall remain in effect perpetually, except either party may terminate this Agreement with or without cause upon ninety (90) days prior written
notice to the other party sent to the address listed above. All sections of this
Agreement relating to the rights and obligations of the parties concerning use and
protection of Confidential Information disclosed during the term of the Agreement shall survive any such termination.

(g) This Agreement shall not be modified except by a written agreement dated
subsequent to the date of this Agreement and signed by both parties.

(h) This Agreement constitutes the entire agreement between the parties with
respect to the subject matter hereof and supersedes all prior and contemporaneous non-disclosure agreements or communications. It shall not be modified
except by a written agreement dated subsequent to the date of this Agreement
and signed on behalf of the parties by their respective duly authorized
representatives.

6. Suggestions and Feedback

The Receiving Party may from time to time, in its sole discretion, provide suggestions,
comments or other feedback ("Feedback") to the Disclosing Party with respect to
Confidential Information provided originally by the Disclosing Party. Feedback, even if
designated as confidential by the party offering the Feedback, shall not, absent a
separate written agreement, create any confidentiality obligation for the receiver of the
Feedback. The receiver of the Feedback shall be free to use, disclose, reproduce,
license or otherwise distribute, and exploit the Feedback provided to it without
obligation or restriction of any kind on account of intellectual property rights.

E. Non-Compete Agreements

In some cases, trade secret owners will insist upon executing covenants not to
compete, especially if the owners anticipate that former employees will commence

competitive operations upon terminating employment with trade secrets owners. *See* PepsiCo, Inc. v. Redmond, 54 F.3d 1262 (7th Cir. 1995) in the Materials section of this chapter. A non-compete agreement provides additional insurance above and beyond the employee's promise not to disclose trade secrets. In cases where covenants are breached, trade secret owners/former employers will sue for breach of contract and trade secret misappropriation. In such cases, courts may grant injunctive relief in such form that would temporarily restrict a former employee's employment with a competitor.

However, jurisdictions vary as to the validity and enforceability of provisions in contracts that restrict the ability of an employee to compete with the former employer. In some jurisdictions, covenants not to compete are considered void or voidable, except under certain circumstances. For example, California specifically makes such provisions invalid and unenforceable, except in certain narrow situations, such as unfair competition. *See* Cal. Bus. & Prof. Code §16600; *see also* Colo. Rev. Stat. §8-2-113(2). In those jurisdictions allowing covenants not to compete, the restrictions must be reasonable in, among other factors, time and geography. Specifically, the covenant must be for the purpose of protecting the trade secret and it must be reasonably limited in scope to the protection of those trade secrets. Regardless of their enforceability in certain jurisdictions, opposition to non-compete agreements may arise if such agreements are considered a pretext for restricting lawful competition.

Even with legal and equitable remedies for breach claims and misappropriation, there is a balancing that courts must undertake to protect an employee's right to pursue his or her livelihood versus accomplishing the goals of trade secret law. Accordingly, any non-compete agreement must consider that restrictions on future employment cannot be excessive or permanent. In addition, while jurisdictions may recognize a prospective claim, like the *threat* of misappropriation, the general skill and knowledge that an employee acquires during his or her tenure of employment, i.e., residuals, should not, in fairness, be the basis for such a claim.

F. Litigation Issues in Trade Secret Licensing

1. Standing and Jurisdiction

A trade secret owner who licenses a trade secret relies on nondisclosure agreements, which typically provide that the licensee will maintain the secrecy. If the licensee breaches the agreement by allowing an unauthorized party to have access to the trade secret, the licensee is liable for trade secret misappropriation. To have standing under the breach of contract cause of action, the licensor need only point to the trade secret license it has with the licensee. But to maintain a tort action, the licensor must demonstrate that it has a confidential relationship with the licensee.

While an exclusive licensee will likely have standing to sue for trade secret misappropriation, at least one court has held that a non-exclusive licensee does not have standing. This conclusion rests on analysis of the plain language of the Uniform Trade Secrets Act, as adopted, which contemplates that the "owner," not a non-exclusive licensee, of a trade secret is responsible for preventing its unauthorized disclosure. Thus, in general,[1] where a plaintiff is a non-exclusive licensee but not the owner of the trade secret involved in a lawsuit, the non-exclusive licensee does not have standing to sue for misappropriation of that secret. *See* RMS Software Dev., Inc. v. LCS, Inc., 1998 WL 74245 (Tex. App.-Hous. (1 Dist.) Feb. 19, 1998).

Generally, the law of the jurisdiction with "the most significant relationship to the transaction and the parties," as set forth in Section 188 of the *Restatement (Second) of Conflict of Laws*, is controlling. Choice of law can be a very important issue when an employee non-compete agreement is at stake because state policies differ on whether and to what extent such agreements should be enforced. A reasonable choice of controlling law will be enforced by the courts. If no choice of law provision is included in the license, the court in which an action is brought will follow the existing choice of law rules of the forum state to select the law that controls the interpretation and enforceability of the license. Many states apply a grouping of contacts approach to contract and quasi-contract claims. *See* Lazard Freres & Co. v. Protective Life Ins. Co., 108 F.3d 1531, 1539 (2d Cir. 1997). Courts consider such contacts as places of contracting, negotiation, performance, location of the subject matter, and domicile or place of business of the contracting parties. In a diversity case, a district court ordinarily determines the applicable state law by reference to the choice of law rules of the forum state.

2. Defenses

Trade secret law does not preclude a third party from using a trade secret that was properly obtained. Unlike other intellectual property, trade secrets do not possess the characteristic of absolute exclusivity because others are able to use what an owner may deem his or her trade secret if such use was by proper means. Thus, a third party who obtains a trade secret properly may use it as a trade secret or disclose it if that party so desires.

Trade secret law recognizes independent development and reverse engineering as defenses to claims of trade secret misappropriation. The independent development and reverse engineering defenses are effective because, unlike patent protection, trade secret protection only provides a limited negative right. This negative right allows the trade secret owner to prevent others from practicing the secret only if the secret was

---

1. In a small number of cases, non-exclusive licensees have been able to satisfy standing requirements in trade secret misappropriation cases. These cases typically involve exceptional circumstances, where the trade secret was misappropriated directly from the non-exclusive licensee, and where various circumstances existed that would have barred the trade secret owner from obtaining relief on behalf of the injured licensee. *See, e.g.,* DTM Research, L.L.C. v. AT & T Corp., 245 F.3d 327, 332 (4th Cir. 2001); Faiveley Transp. USA, Inc. v. Wabtec Corp., 758 F. Supp. 2d 211, 220 (S.D.N.Y. 2010); Metso Minerals Indus. v. FLSmidth-Excel LLC, 733 F. Supp. 2d 969, 972 (E.D. Wis. 2010). In general, however, there is a very strong presumption that a non-exclusive licensee does not have standing to maintain a cause of action for misappropriation.

obtained through improper means. This negative right is not enforceable against one who is in proper possession of the trade secret, as through independent development or proper reverse engineering. *See* Sony Computer Entm't v. Connectix Corp., 203 F.3d 596 (9th Cir. 2000); *see also* Sega Enters., Ltd. v. Accolade, Inc., 977 F.2d 1510 (9th Cir. 1993). However, license agreements that prohibit reverse engineering have been upheld by courts in the United States, although some commentators disagree with this result.[2] Blizzard Entertainment v. Jung in the Materials section of Chapter 1 and Bowers v. Baystate in the Materials section of Chapter 9 are examples of such cases.

3. Protective Orders

One of the unique aspects of litigation over a trade secret license concerns how the parties can effectively share secret information in the context of the litigation without sharing the secrets in a manner that discloses them to the public at large. Litigants use an agreement called a protective order to solve this dilemma. A protective order describes who can look at the trade secret information and for what purpose, and, outside of that, places the information under seal (i.e., keeps it out of the public record). For example, the protective order may only permit the court, outside counsel, select corporate counsel, and expert witnesses to view the secret information. *See* Stipulated Protective Order in Microsoft v. Kai-Fu Lee and Google, Inc., in the Materials section of this chapter.

To address the protection of trade secrets during litigation, some courts have adopted tiered levels of protective orders. The lowest tier is designated as confidential. This designation is used for pending litigation. The intermediate tier protective order is designated "attorneys and client representatives." This designation allows counsel to access trade secrets for purposes of litigation and more restricted access to client representatives. The most restrictive designation allows legal counsel to access trade secrets on an "attorneys' eyes only" basis. The party seeking the most restrictive designation often bears the burden of proving that documents so labeled warrant the restriction.

4. Remedies

An injured party has the right to seek damages and injunctive relief for breach of a trade secret license. Remedies play out in some unique ways, however, in the context of trade secrets. One issue relates to injunctive relief. Once the trade secret has been disclosed, is injunctive relief to stop further disclosure effective? In other words, if a secret formula has been disclosed in an Internet chat room, for example, will injunctive relief be an effective remedy? In some cases where limited copies were disclosed to a

---

2. *See, e.g.*, Daniel Laster, *The Secret Is Out: Patent Law Preempts Mass Market License Terms Barring Reverse Engineering for Interoperability Purposes*, 58 BAYLOR L. REV. 621 (2006); David A Rice, *Copyright and Contract: Preemption After* Bowers v. Baystate, 9 ROGER WILLIAMS U. L. REV. 595 (2004).

limited audience the answer may be "yes," but in many other cases (such as the latter example) the answer will be "no."

Another remedies-related issue has to do with damages. In many cases a party will suffer no direct damages as a result of the disclosure; for instance, there is no replacement cost for the secret in the sense that the secret cannot be replaced like a product. Thus, consequential damages may be the only viable remedy for breach of the trade secret license. This means that drafters of trade secret licenses should stop and ponder before including a disclaimer of consequential damages in their agreements.

Pursuant to the UTSA and DTSA, damages are awarded for any actual loss related to the trade secret's misappropriation plus unjust enrichment caused by the misappropriation that is not addressed in the actual loss award. Alternatively, reasonable royalties may be awarded in lieu of damages. Should the trade secret be "willfully and maliciously misappropriated," exemplary damages equal up to two times the damages amount may be awarded. Lastly, the prevailing party can receive attorney's fees upon showing willful and malicious appropriation.

The DTSA also provides discretion to courts to seize trade secrets misappropriated by improper means when necessary "to prevent the propagation or dissemination of the trade secret," but only "upon ex parte application [and] in extraordinary circumstances." "Extraordinary circumstances" is not defined, but according to the legislative history, seizure is meant for situations where a defendant is going to flee the country, immediately disclose the secret, or is otherwise uncooperative with the court's directives. Nonetheless, the statute does delineate several factors that must be met in order to grant the seizure. These include:

- a preliminary injunction, temporary restraining order, or other equitable relief would be inadequate;
- without seizure, "immediate and irreparable injury will occur;"
- harm to the applicant through denial outweighs the harm to other parties should the seizure be granted;
- the applicant is likely to succeed in showing the information is a trade secret and the person(s) against whom seizure is sought misappropriated it;
- the person(s) against whom seizure is sought actually possesses the secret;
- the application reasonably describes what is to be seized and, if possible, where it is;
- if the applicant provided seizure notice, the other parties "would destroy, move, hide, or otherwise make such matter inaccessible to the court,"
- "the applicant has not publicized the requested seizure."

Seizure orders must be narrow, seizing only what is necessary. The orders must also give law enforcement executing the seizure specific guidance, and set a hearing date within seven days from when issued. The court must also establish protective measures, such as to avoid disclosure of the seized property, and to require the applicant to provide a security deposit to pay for damages should the seizure be deemed wrongful or excessive.

An important provision of the DTSA provides whistleblower immunity. Individuals will not be held civilly or criminally liable for confidentially disclosing trade secrets to government officials or to attorneys either for investigating or reporting law violations or if the disclosure is made under seal in a court proceeding. Immunity is also available should an individual need to disclose a trade secret against an employer in an anti-retaliation lawsuit, as long as it remains under seal. Employers must notify employees entering into contracts or agreements governing confidential information or trade secret use of this immunity. Not providing notice could lead an employer to forfeit attorneys' fees or exemplary damages in an action against an employee. The term "employee" specifically includes "individual[s] performing work as a contractor or consultant for an employer."

G. International Issues in Trade Secret Licensing: Export Controls and Enforcement Issues

The United States has maintained extensive controls on the export and re-export of sensitive goods and technologies. Various U.S. laws limit the entities with which U.S. companies may do business and the goods in which they may trade. The export control regulations are complex and can present difficult compliance obligations and responsibilities. Furthermore, export control laws frequently change due to national security interests, controls, and boycotts. Because compliance with export controls is a necessity and because failure to comply may result in loss of export privileges, trade secret licenses must effectively anticipate the uses of the trade secret in a foreign country by non-U.S. individuals and business entities.

The laws and the approach taken by the U.S. Commerce Department with respect to trade are constantly evolving. The Commerce Department's Bureau of Industry and Security (BIS) administers the Export Administration Regulations (EAR), which control exports and re-exports of certain "dual use" (i.e., items used for commercial as well as military applications) goods, software, or technology. The factors listed below affect the application of EAR controls:

- the nature of the item at issue and its classification under the EAR;
- the ultimate destination of any applicable shipment; and
- the end use or end user of the product and the possible licensing requirements.

See 15 C.F.R. §730.1 (2002).

The BIS regulations also control the release or disclosure of technology or software source code to foreign nationals located anywhere in the world, including foreign employees of U.S. companies in the United States. *See* 15 C.F.R. §734.2(b)(1). When technology or software is released to a foreign national who is not a permanent resident of the United States or a "protected individual" under the Immigration and Naturalization Act, that release is treated as an export to the national's home country under the "deemed export" rule. *See* 15 C.F.R. §734.2(b)(2)(ii) (2002).

The Directorate of Defense Trade Controls (DDTC) of the U.S. Department of State administers the International Traffic in Arms Regulations (ITAR). These regulations control exports, re-exports, retransfers, and temporary imports of "defense articles" and "defense services," which are items on the U.S. Munitions Lists or goods and technologies specially designed or modified for military applications. *See* 22 C.F.R. §120.3 (2002) A list of export activities controlled by U.S. law appears below:

- doing business with certain countries without a license;
- doing business with certain people and other entities;
- exporting certain types of goods without a license;
- exporting or re-exporting certain types of goods to certain countries without a license; and
- complying with, or agreeing to comply with, one country's prohibitions on sales or services (i.e., a boycott) to a country that is friendly to the United States.

II. MATERIALS

The materials in this section provide examples of the value of trade secrets in the context of business development and the crucial role that trade secret licensing plays in protecting against disclosure of trade secrets and the potential loss of competitive advantage or streams of royalty income. The ever-relevant "Listerine" case, Warner-Lambert Pharm., Co. v. John R. Reynolds, Inc., 178 F. Supp. 655 (S.D.N.Y. 1959), exemplifies the role that trade secret licensing plays in establishing and maintaining a successful business model to protect and grow market share in an industry. This case also explores important issues regarding royalty structures and payments under trade secret licenses.

Concepts of federalism also loom large in determining the continued vitality of trade secret licenses. The U.S. Supreme Court impacted the future of trade secret licensing with its decision in Aronson v. Quick Point Pencil Co., 440 U.S. 257 (1979). In *Aronson* the Supreme Court examined whether federal patent law preempted trade secret licenses governed by state contract law. The Supreme Court recognized that states are free to regulate the use of intellectual property in a manner not inconsistent with federal law.

One significant mechanism to protect trade secrets from misappropriation is the use of employer-employee confidentiality agreements. Courts have been required to look at whether employees departing from an employer to work for a competitor threaten the trade secrets of the former employer and whether an employee's move to a competitor will result in a breach of a confidentiality agreement. In PepsiCo, Inc. v. Redmond, 54 F.3d 1262 (7th Cir. 1995), the threat of misappropriation, as opposed to actual misappropriation, is discussed as harm worthy of injunctive relief pursuant to the inevitable disclosure doctrine. While *PepsiCo* adopted the so-called "inevitable disclosure" doctrine, other jurisdictions — California, for example — have expressly rejected the doctrine based on the public policy against restricting an employee's employment mobility. Accordingly, in Edwards v. Arthur Andersen LLP, 44 Cal. 4th 937 (2008), the California Supreme Court rejected the Ninth Circuit's narrow-restraint exception when deciding that Arthur Andersen's attempt to enforce a non-compete agreement ran afoul of California's strong public policy against precluding one from engaging in a lawful profession, trade, or business.

The full impact of the Defend Trade Secrets Act (DTSA) has yet to be measured by the decisions of the federal courts. Since the enactment of the DTSA, federal courts have granted injunctive relief by applying existing state and federal law that predated the DTSA. Federal courts have focused on traditional application of the Federal Rules of Civil Procedure's injunctive relief provision and infrequently performed even a dual state-law/DTSA analysis. The case Henry Schein, Inc. v. Cook, No. 191 F. Supp. 3d 1072 (N.D. Cal. Jun. 22, 2016), is one of only a handful of cases analyzing claims of trade secrets misappropriation brought under both the DTSA and California Uniform Trade Secrets Act ("CUTSA"). In making its decision, the court analyzed both the DTSA and CUTSA claims simultaneously. The materials conclude with the Stipulated Protective Order in Microsoft v. Kai-Fu Lee and Google, Inc., which illustrates the judicial measures that will be taken to protect trade secrets during litigation.

WARNER-LAMBERT PHARM., CO. v. JOHN R. REYNOLDS, INC.
178 F. Supp. 655 (S.D.N.Y. 1959)

BRYAN, District Judge.

Plaintiff sues under the Federal Declaratory Judgment Act, 28 U.S.C. 2201 and 2202, for a judgment declaring that it is no longer obligated to make periodic payments to defendants based on its manufacture or sale of the well known product "Listerine," under agreements made between Dr. J.J. Lawrence and J.W. Lambert in 1881, and between Dr. Lawrence and Lambert Pharmacal Company in 1885. Plaintiff also seeks to recover the payments made to defendants pursuant to these agreements since the commencement of the action.

Plaintiff is a Delaware corporation which manufactures and sells Listerine, among other pharmaceutical products. It is the successor in interest to Lambert and Lambert Pharmacal Company which acquired the formula for Listerine from Dr. Lawrence under the agreements in question. Defendants are the successors in interest to Dr. Lawrence. Jurisdiction is based on diversity of citizenship.

For some seventy-five years plaintiff and its predecessors have been making the periodic payments based on the quantity of Listerine manufactured or sold which are called for by the agreements in suit. The payments have totalled more than twenty-two million dollars and are presently in excess of one million five hundred thousand dollars yearly.

All of the defendants move to dismiss the second amended complaint, pursuant to Rule 12(b)(6), F.R. Civ. P., 28 U.S.C.A., for failure to state a claim upon which relief can be granted, or, in the alternative, for summary judgment, pursuant to Rule 56, F.R. Civ. P.

As will become apparent from the discussion which follows, I find no genuine issue as to any material fact which requires a trial. Such issues of fact between the parties as may exist are peripheral only and are not material to the basic questions to be determined. In my view the defendants, upon the undisputed facts, are entitled to judgment as a matter of law.

In the early 1880's Dr. Lawrence, a physician and editor of a medical journal in St. Louis, Missouri, devised a formula for an antiseptic liquid compound which was given the name "Listerine." The agreement between Lawrence and J.W. Lambert made in 1881, and that between Lawrence and Lambert Pharmacal Company made in 1885, providing for the sale of the Lawrence formula, were entered into in that city. Lambert, and thereafter his corporation, originally engaged in the manufacture and sale of Listerine and other pharmaceutical preparations on a modest scale there. Through the years the business prospered and grew fantastically and Listerine became a widely sold and nationally known product. The Lambert Pharmacal Company, with various changes in corporate structure and name which are not material here, continued the manufacture and sale of Listerine and other preparations until March 31, 1955, when it was merged into Warner-Hudnut, Inc., a Delaware corporation, and the name of the merged corporation was changed to Warner-Lambert Pharmaceutical Company, Inc. The plaintiff in this action is the merged corporation which continues the manufacture and sale of Listerine.

Plaintiff's second amended complaint in substance alleges the following:

Prior to April 20, 1881 Dr. Lawrence furnished Lambert with an unnamed secret formula for the antiseptic compound which came to be known as "Listerine," and on or about that date Lambert executed the first of the documents with which we are concerned here. This document, in its entirety, reads as follows:

> Know all men by these presents, that for and in consideration of the fact, that Dr. J.J. Lawrence of the city of St Louis Mo has furnished me with the formula of a medicine called Listerine to be manufactured by me, that I Jordan W. Lambert, also of the city of St Louis Mo, hereby agree for myself, my heirs, executors and assigns to pay monthly to the said Dr. J.J. Lawrence his heirs, executors or assigns, the sum of twenty dollars for each and every gross of said Listerine hereafter sold by myself, my heirs, executors or assigns. In testimony whereof, I hereunto set my hand and seal, Done at St Louis Mo. this the 20th day of April, 1881 Jordan W. Lambert (Seal)

On or about May 2, 1881 Lambert began the manufacture of the formula and adopted the trademark "Listerine." The agreed payments under the 1881 agreement were reduced on October 21, 1881 by the following letter addressed to Lambert by Lawrence:

> I hereby reduce my royalty on Listerine from twenty dollars pr gross to twelve dollars pr gross on the condition that a statement of your sales made each preceding month be rendered to me promptly on or before the 10th of each month, and payment of the amount due me on said royalty be made to me or my heirs at the same time. I also hereby waive any demands of royalty on you preceding the 1st of October 1881 —

They were again reduced on March 23, 1883 by a similar letter reading as follows:

> I hereby reduce my royalty on Listerine from ten percent on gross amount of sales to six dollars pr gross, the same reduction is hereby made on my royalty on Renalia. Wishing you great prosperity.

Thereafter Lambert assigned his rights to Listerine and other Lawrence compounds to the Lambert Pharmacal Company and this company on January 2, 1885 executed an instrument assuming Lambert's obligations under these agreements with Lawrence and other obligations on account of other formulas which Lawrence had furnished, in the following language:

> J.J. Lawrence of St Louis Mo, having originated & heretofore sold to J.W. Lambert, the formulae & processes for the manufacture of two medical preparations, known as Listerine and Lithiated Hydrangea, with all the rights & benefits accruing therefrom and has received therefor a monthly royalty from J.W. Lambert, and J.W. Lambert having sold said formulae of Listerine & Lithiated Hydrangea to the Lambert Pharmacal Company, a corporation organized under the laws of the State of Missouri, and doing business in St Louis, and furthermore said J.J. Lawrence having sold to said Corporation his sole & exclusive right to the formulae & processes originated by him for making two preparations called "Dugongol" & Menthated Camphor, therefore know all men by these presents that for & in consideration of these facts, the said Lambert Pharmacal Co. hereby agrees and contracts for itself & assigns to pay to the said J.J. Lawrence, his heirs, executors & assigns, six dollars on each & every gross of Listerine & Lithiated Hydrangea manufactured or sold by the said Lambert Pharmacal Co. or its assigns, and ten per cent (10%) on gross amount of sales of the said Dugongol & Menthated Camphor, and all other goods which said Lambert Pharmacal Co. or its assigns may hereafter manufacture or sell on formulae furnished by said J.J. Lawrence, account of sales to be rendered & payment of said royalty to be made on the tenth day of each month. In testimony whereof said Lambert Pharmacal Co. has caused these presents to be sealed with its corporate seal and signed by its President & Secretary this second day of January 1885.

The agreements between the parties contemplated, it is alleged, "the periodic payment of royalties to Lawrence for the use of a trade secret, to wit, the secret formula for" Listerine. After some modifications made with Lawrence's knowledge and approval, the formula was introduced on the market. The composition of the compound has remained the same since then and it is still being manufactured and sold by the plaintiff.

It is then alleged that the "trade secret" (the formula for Listerine) has gradually become a matter of public knowledge through the years following 1881 and prior to 1949, and has been published in the United States Pharmacopoia, the National Formulary and the Journal of the American Medical Association, and also as a result of proceedings brought against plaintiff's predecessor by the Federal Trade Commission. Such publications were not the fault of plaintiff or its predecessors.

The complaint recites the chains of interest running respectively from Lambert to the present plaintiff and from Lawrence to the defendants, and concludes with a prayer for a declaration that plaintiff is "no longer liable to the defendants" for any further "royalties."

Despite the mass of material before me the basic issue between the parties is narrow. The plaintiff claims that its obligation to make payments to the defendants under the Lawrence-Lambert agreements was terminated by the public disclosure of the Listerine formula in various medical publications. The defendants assert that the obligation continued and has not been terminated.

The plaintiff seems to feel that the 1881 and 1885 agreements are indefinite and unclear, at least as to the length of time during which they would continue in effect. I do not find them to be so. These agreements seem to me to be plain and unambiguous.

In the 1881 agreement Lambert, for himself, his heirs, executors or assigns, agrees to pay Lawrence, his heirs, executors and assigns, "twenty dollars for each & every gross of said Listerine hereafter sold by myself my heirs executors or assigns." By the 1885 agreement the Lambert Pharmacal Company "agrees and contracts for itself & assigns to pay . . . J.J. Lawrence, his heirs executors & assigns, six dollars on each & every gross of Listerine . . . manufactured or sold by the said Lambert Pharmacal Co. or its assigns. . . ."

There is no ambiguity or uncertainty in this language. Nor can I ascertain any alternative or hidden meanings lurking within it.

The payments to Lawrence and his successors are conditioned upon the sale (in the 1881 agreement) and the manufacture or sale (in the 1885 agreement) of the medical preparation known as Listerine which Lawrence conveyed to Lambert. The obligation to pay on each and every gross of Listerine continues as long as this preparation is manufactured or sold by Lambert and his successors. It comes to an end when they cease to manufacture or sell the preparation. There is nothing which compels the plaintiff to continue such manufacture and sale. No doubt Lambert and his successors have been and still are free at any time, in good faith and in the exercise of sound business discretion, to stop manufacturing and selling Listerine. The plain meaning of the language used in these agreements is simply that Lambert's obligation to pay is co-extensive with manufacture or sale of Listerine by him and his successors.

The plaintiff, however, claims that despite the plain language of the agreement it may continue to manufacture and sell without making the payments required by the agreements because the formula which its predecessors acquired is no longer secret. To sustain this position plaintiff invokes the shade, if not the substance, of the traditional common law distaste for contractual rights and duties unbounded by definite limitations of time and argues that absent a construction that the obligation to pay is co-extensive only with the secrecy of the formula, it must be a forbidden "perpetuity" which the law will not enforce. I find no support for the plaintiff's theory either in the cases which it cites or elsewhere.

The word "perpetuity" is often applied very loosely to contractual obligations. Indiscriminate application of the term serves only to confuse. The mere fact that an obligation under a contract may continue for a very long time is no reason in itself for declaring the contract to exist in perpetuity or for giving it a construction which would do violence to the expressed intent of the parties.

There are contracts in which the promisor's obligation has been expressly fixed to last forever. Such cases mainly arise in the field of real property and are governed by various considerations of public policy which have no pertinence here. See 3 Corbin on Contracts, 533. The agreement in the case at bar does not fall within this category.

Contracts which omit any point of time or any condition which would terminate the promisor's liability are somewhat different. Town of Readsboro v. Hoosac Tunnel & W.R. Co., [6 F.2d 733 (2d Cir. 1925)]. Where it appears that the parties did in fact intend that the obligation terminate at an ascertainable time, the courts, in effect, will supply the missing clause and construe the contract accordingly. On the other hand, if it appears that no termination date was within the contemplation of the parties, or that their intention with respect thereto cannot be ascertained, the contract will be held to be terminable within a reasonable time or revocable at will, dependent upon the circumstances. Zimco Restaurants, Inc. v. Bartenders & Culinary Workers, 165 Cal. App. 2d 235, 331 P.2d 789.

In such cases the courts are loathe to find that the absence of a terminal point indicates an intention to contract for the indefinite future, and a perpetual obligation will not usually be inferred from the absence of a terminating date or condition. While there is no hard and fast rule, the terminal date or condition of termination will be that to be ascertained from the actual though unexpressed intention of the parties or as a remedy for their neglect. If the parties intend that the obligation be perpetual they must expressly say so. *Paisley v. Lucas, supra; Town of Readsboro v. Hoosac Tunnel & W.R. Co., supra.* As Judge Learned Hand says in *Readsboro*:

> [The contract] was in terms unlimited in time, and the plaintiff apparently reasons that the defendant is bound forever to pay. . . . This seems to us untenable. Had the parties expressed the intention to make a promise . . . perpetual . . . we should, of course, have nothing to say; their words would be conclusive. But they did not, and, as no time is expressly fixed, we must look to the circumstances to learn what they meant. Their purpose is pretty evident.

Contracts which provide no fixed date for the termination of the promisor's obligation but condition the obligation upon an event which would necessarily terminate the contract are in quite a different category and it is in this category that the 1881 and 1885 Lambert Lawrence agreements fall. On the face of the agreements the obligation of Lambert and its successors to pay is conditioned upon the continued manufacture or sale of Listerine. When they cease manufacturing or selling Listerine the condition for continued payment comes to an end and the obligation to pay terminates. This is the plain meaning of the language which the parties used. . . .

The obligation here is conditioned upon an event arising out of the very arrangement between the parties which is the subject matter of the contract. . . .

In Cammack v. J. B. Slattery & Bros., 241 N.Y. 39, 148 N.E. 781, plaintiff had furnished defendant with a secret process. Defendant's liability to make payments therefor depended upon use. There was held to be no uncertainty as to the term of the contract nor any perpetuity of obligation, but that the obligation to pay continued as long as the defendant used the secret process which it had acquired. The court expressly rejected the defendant's contention that the contract was terminable at will because it provided no fixed termination date.

In the case at bar the obligation to continue payments as long as Lambert or his successors continue to manufacture or sell Listerine is plain from the language of the agreements and is implicit in their terms. There is no need to "construe" these contracts so as to import a condition or date of termination other than that expressed by the parties themselves in the agreements which they made. Courts must "concern (themselves) with what the parties intended, but only to the extent that they evidenced what they intended by what they wrote." Raleigh Associates v. Henry, 302 N.Y. 467, 473, 99 N.E.2d 289, 291. An attempt to write new terms into this plain and simple agreement would be unwarranted and gratuitous. "We may not now imply a condition which the parties chose not to insert in their contract. . . ." Nor is there any need to resort to extrinsic evidence in order to ascertain what the intention of the parties was, or what the termination date of the obligation to pay would be, for the agreements themselves indicate the condition upon which the obligation terminates.

There is nothing unreasonable or irrational about imposing such an obligation. It is entirely rational and sensible that the obligation to make payments should be based upon the business which flows from the formula conveyed. Whether or not the obligation continues is in the control of the plaintiff itself. For the plaintiff has the right to terminate its obligation to pay whenever in good faith it desires to cease the manufacture or sale of Listerine.

However, plaintiff urges with vigor that the agreement must be differently construed because it involved the conveyance of a secret formula. The main thrust of its argument is that despite the language which the parties used the court must imply a limitation upon Lambert's obligation to pay measured by the length of time that the Listerine formula remained secret.

To sustain this theory plaintiff relies upon a number of cases involving the obligations of licensees of copyrights or patents to make continuing payments to the owner or licensor, and argues that these cases are controlling here.

One of these is April Productions, Inc. v. G. Schirmer, Inc., 308 N.Y. 366, 126 N.E.2d 283. There plaintiff's predecessor had licensed defendant publisher to publish certain music and defendant agreed to "pay . . . royalties for each and every copy sold. . . ." The publisher copyrighted the music in accordance with the custom of the trade. At the expiration of the original term of the copyright it was renewed by a third party who, the court assumed, was under no obligation to permit the defendant to continue publication of the music under the original license agreement. *See* Miller Music Corp. v. Daniels, 158 F. Supp. 188 (S.D.N.Y.), *aff'd*, 265 F.2d 925 (2d Cir.), *cert. granted*, 80 S. Ct. 77. In fact the defendant had entered into new agreements with the owner of the renewed copyright and was paying royalties to the renewal owner under it. Plaintiff contended that since the original license agreement mentioned no specific term, did not speak of copyright, and, in fact, did not convey an existing copyright, the defendant was obligated under the license to continue making payments to it as long as it published the music, despite the fact that the original copyright had expired. The court found that the entire background of the agreement was that of copyright since absent statutory copyright protection, the first publication would have put the music in the public domain. The court therefore applied the usual rule in patent and copyright cases that a license agreement under a patent or copyright, in the absence of express language to the contrary, is construed to require the payment of royalties only until the expiration of the underlying grant.

Such a construction of the license is in all likelihood in accord with the unexpressed or imperfectly expressed intention of the parties. As the court said:

Certainly, these experienced firms could not have contemplated continuation of royalty payments after the rights granted to Schirmer (the defendant licensee) had expired and the exclusive right to publish the music had vested in a third party. To accept plaintiff's position, we would have to ascribe to the parties an intent, not only that Schirmer be required to pay multiple royalties during the renewal term, . . . but also that . . . (the licensor) be entitled to exact royalties after the copyrights had actually expired and the works had entered the public domain. In our view, such an interpretation would be indefensible. The thought behind the phrase proclaims itself misread when the outcome of the reading is injustice or absurdity.

Thus, all *April Productions* holds, in accord with many other cases, is that when parties agree upon a license under a patent or copyright the court will assume, in the absence of express language to the contrary, that their actual intention as to the term is measured by the definite term of the underlying grant fixed by statute. . . .

There are other cases on which the plaintiff relies which hold that when a patent or copyright is held to be invalid before the expiration of the statutory term of the grant the obligation to pay royalties under a license terminates. This is but another aspect of the same principle. The rationale of this line of cases is stated in Bottlers' Seal Co. v. Rainey, 225 N.Y. 369, 372-373, 122 N.E. 200, 201, as follows:

> The covenanted payments are for the right to manufacture, use, and sell free from interference. The licensor, in law, undertakes merely that it will not sue for infringement during the period covered by the agreement. . . . In legal contemplation, the enjoyment of the undisturbed use of the patent, not the mere execution of the grant, is the consideration for the royalties.

Paralleling the concept that the licensing of a patent or copyright contracts only for the statutory monopoly granted in such cases is the concept not so frequently expressed that public policy may require a termination of the obligation to pay when the patent or copyright term is ended. As the Supreme Court said in Scott Paper Co. v. Marcalus Co., 326 U.S. 249, 255-256:

> If a manufacturer or user could restrict himself, by express contract, or by any action which would . . . (prevent him) from using the invention of an expired patent, he would deprive himself and the consuming public of the advantage to be derived from his free use of the disclosures. The public has invested in such free use by the grant of a monopoly to the patentee for a limited time. Hence any attempted reservation or continuation in the patentee or those claiming under him of the patent monopoly, after the patent expires, whatever the legal device employed, runs counter to the policy and purpose of the patent laws.

I see nothing in any of the cases which the plaintiff cites dealing with patents and copyrights which supports the theory which plaintiff advances here. Plaintiff has not cited a single case in which the rules of these cases have been applied to a contract involving the conveyance of a secret formula or a trade secret.

The sole common denominator between these cases and the case at bar is that both deal with contracts involving periodic payments and the term of such payments. The considerations which lead the courts in the patent and copyright cases cited to limit the obligation to the term of the patent or copyright have no application here. Nor can they be invoked to alter the terms of agreements such as those at bar involving quite different subject matter and which are clear and plain on their face.

In the patent and copyright cases the parties are dealing with a fixed statutory term and the monopoly granted by that term. This monopoly, created by Congress, is designed to preserve exclusivity in the grantee during the statutory term and to release the patented or copyrighted material to the general public for general use thereafter. This is the public policy of the statutes in reference to which such contracts are made and it is against this background that the parties to patent and copyright license agreements contract.

Here, however, there is no such public policy. The parties are free to contract with respect to a secret formula or trade secret in any manner which they determine for their own best interests. A secret formula or trade secret may remain secret indefinitely. It may be discovered by someone else almost immediately after the agreement is entered into. Whoever discovers it for himself by legitimate means is entitled to its use.

But that does not mean that one who acquires a secret formula or a trade secret through a valid and binding contract is then enabled to escape from an obligation to which he bound himself simply because the secret is discovered by a third party or by the general public. I see no reason why the court should imply such a term or condition in a contract providing on its face that payment shall be co-extensive with use. To do so here would be to rewrite the contract for the parties without any indication that they intended such a result.

It may be noted that here the parties themselves made no reference to secrecy in either the 1881 or the 1885 agreements. The word "secret" is not used anywhere in either of them. It is true that I have assumed during this discussion that the plaintiff is correct in its contention that what Lambert bargained for was a "secret" formula. But that in no way justifies the further assumption that he also bargained for continuing secrecy or that there would be failure of consideration if secrecy did not continue.

The argument that there was failure of consideration in 1931 after the agreement had been in force for some forty-five years because of disclosure then, is wholly devoid of merit. The plaintiff does not question that the conveyance to it of the "secret formula" furnished consideration for the contract. Once a contract is supported by consideration its terms are up to the parties. Whether the consideration is adequate or not is no concern of the court. The parties are free to fix their own terms and they have done so here. Plaintiff's argument goes only to adequacy of consideration. There is no question of failure of consideration.

One who acquires a trade secret or secret formula takes it subject to the risk that there be a disclosure. The inventor makes no representation that the secret is non-discoverable. All the inventor does is to convey the knowledge of the formula or process which is unknown to the purchaser and which in so far as both parties then know is unknown to any one else. The terms upon which they contract with reference to this subject matter are purely up to them and are governed by what the contract they enter into provides.

If they desire the payments or royalties should continue only until the secret is disclosed to the public it is easy enough for them to say so. But there is no justification for implying such a provision if the parties do not include it in their contract, particularly where the language which they use by fair intendment provides otherwise.

The case at bar illustrates what may occur in such cases. As the undisputed facts show, the acquisition of the Lawrence formula was the base on which plaintiff's predecessors built up a very large and successful business in the antiseptic or germicide field. Even now, twenty-five or more years after it is claimed that the trade secret was disclosed to the public, plaintiff retains more than 50% of the national market in these products.

Plaintiff lays stress on the large sums which have been spent in advertising and promoting the product, and there is no doubt that this and the business acumen of plaintiff's predecessors have contributed greatly to the success of the business. But it may be noted that the advertising and promotional material is primarily based on what are claimed to be the extraordinary merits of the formula for Listerine which plaintiff's predecessors acquired from Dr. Lawrence. Plaintiff and its predecessors have proclaimed for many years through the widest variety of advertising and promotional media the unique, indeed, almost magical properties of the formula from which Listerine is still made which is the formula conveyed by Lawrence to Lambert.

At the very least plaintiff's predecessors, through the acquisition of the Lawrence formula under this contract, obtained a head start in the field of liquid antiseptics which has proved of incalculable value through the years. There is nothing novel about business being transacted only in a small way at the outset of a contract relationship and thereafter growing far beyond what was anticipated when the contract was made. Because the business has prospered far beyond anticipations affords no basis for changing the terms of the contract the parties agreed upon when the volume was small.

There is nothing in this contract to indicate that plaintiff's predecessors bargained for more than the disclosure of the Lawrence formula which was then unknown to it. Plaintiff has pointed to no principle of law or equity which would require or permit the court gratuitously to rewrite the contract which its predecessors made for these considerations.

If plaintiff wishes to avoid its obligations under the contract it is free to do so, and, indeed, the contract itself indicates how this may be done. The fact that neither the plaintiff nor its predecessors have done so, and that the plaintiff continues to manufacture and sell Listerine under the Lawrence formula with great success, indicates how valuable the rights under the contract are and how unjust it would be to permit it to have its cake and eat it too.

Thus, I hold that under the agreements in suit plaintiff is obligated to make the periodic payments called for by them as long as it continues to manufacture and sell the preparation described in them as Listerine. . . . Defendants' motions for summary judgment are in all respects granted. Judgment for defendants dismissing the second amended complaint will be entered accordingly.

ARONSON v. QUICK POINT PENCIL CO.
440 U.S. 257 (1979)

BURGER, Chief Justice.

We granted certiorari to consider whether federal patent law pre-empts state contract law so as to preclude enforcement of a contract to pay royalties to a patent applicant, on sales of articles embodying the putative invention, for so long as the contracting party sells them, if a patent is not granted.

In October 1955 the petitioner, Mrs. Jane Aronson, filed an application, Serial No. 542677, for a patent on a new form of keyholder. Although ingenious, the design was so simple that it readily could be copied unless it was protected by patent. In June 1956, while the patent application was pending, Mrs. Aronson negotiated a contract with the respondent, Quick Point Pencil Co., for the manufacture and sale of the keyholder.

The contract was embodied in two documents. In the first, a letter from Quick Point to Mrs. Aronson, Quick Point agreed to pay Mrs. Aronson a royalty of 5% of the selling price in return for "the exclusive right to make and sell keyholders of the type shown in your application, Serial No. 542677." The letter further provided that the parties would consult one another concerning the steps to be taken "[i]n the event of any infringement."

The contract did not require Quick Point to manufacture the keyholder. Mrs. Aronson received a $750 advance on royalties and was entitled to rescind the exclusive license if Quick Point did not sell a million keyholders by the end of 1957. Quick Point retained the right to cancel the agreement whenever "the volume of sales does not meet our expectations." The duration of the agreement was not otherwise prescribed.

A contemporaneous document provided that if Mrs. Aronson's patent application was "not allowed within five (5) years, Quick Point Pencil Co. [would] pay . . . two and one half percent (2%) of sales . . . so long as you [Quick Point] continue to sell same."

In June 1961, when Mrs. Aronson had failed to obtain a patent on the keyholder within the five years specified in the agreement, Quick Point asserted its contractual right to reduce royalty payments to 2% of sales. In September of that year the Board of Patent Appeals issued a final rejection of the application on the ground that the keyholder was not patentable, and Mrs. Aronson did not appeal. Quick Point continued to pay reduced royalties to her for 14 years thereafter.

The market was more receptive to the keyholder's novelty and utility than the Patent Office. By September 1975 Quick Point had made sales in excess of $7 million and paid Mrs. Aronson royalties totaling $203,963.84; sales were continuing to rise. However, while Quick Point was able to pre-empt the market in the earlier years and was long the only manufacturer of the Aronson keyholder, copies began to appear in the late 1960's. Quick Point's competitors, of course, were not required to pay royalties for their use of the design. Quick Point's share of the Aronson keyholder market has declined during the past decade.

In November 1975 Quick Point commenced an action in the United States District Court for a declaratory judgment, pursuant to 28 U.S.C. §2201, that the royalty agreement was unenforceable. Quick Point asserted that state law which might otherwise make the contract enforceable was preempted by federal patent law. This is the only issue presented to us for decision.

Both parties moved for summary judgment on affidavits, exhibits, and stipulations of fact. The District Court concluded that the "language of the agreement is plain, clear and unequivocal and has no relation as to whether or not a patent is ever granted." Accordingly, it held that the agreement was valid, and that Quick Point was obliged to pay the agreed royalties pursuant to the contract for so long as it manufactured the keyholder.

The Court of Appeals reversed, one judge dissenting. It held that since the parties contracted with reference to a pending patent application, Mrs. Aronson was estopped from denying that patent law principles governed her contract with Quick Point. Although acknowledging that this Court had never decided the precise issue, the Court of Appeals held that our prior decisions regarding patent licenses compelled the conclusion that Quick Point's contract with Mrs. Aronson became unenforceable once she failed to obtain a patent. The court held that a continuing obligation to pay royalties would be contrary to "the strong federal policy favoring the full and free use of ideas in the public domain," Lear, Inc. v. Adkins, 395 U.S. 653,

674 (1969). The court also observed that if Mrs. Aronson actually had obtained a patent, Quick Point would have escaped its royalty obligations either if the patent were held to be invalid or upon its expiration after 17 years, *see* Brulotte v. Thys Co., 379 U.S. 29 (1964). Accordingly, it concluded that a licensee should be relieved of royalty obligations when the licensor's efforts to obtain a contemplated patent prove unsuccessful.

On this record it is clear that the parties contracted with full awareness of both the pendency of a patent application and the possibility that a patent might not issue. The clause de-escalating the royalty by half in the event no patent issued within five years makes that crystal clear. Quick Point apparently placed a significant value on exploiting the basic novelty of the device, even if no patent issued; its success demonstrates that this judgment was well founded. Assuming, *arguendo*, that the initial letter and the commitment to pay a 5% royalty was subject to federal patent law, the provision relating to the 2% royalty was explicitly independent of federal law. The cases and principles relied on by the Court of Appeals and Quick Point do not bear on a contract that does not rely on a patent, particularly where, as here, the contracting parties agreed expressly as to alternative obligations if no patent should issue.

Commercial agreements traditionally are the domain of state law. State law is not displaced merely because the contract relates to intellectual property which may or may not be patentable; the states are free to regulate the use of such intellectual property in any manner not inconsistent with federal law. Kewanee Oil Co. v. Bicron Corp., 416 U.S. 470, 479 (1974). In this as in other fields, the question of whether federal law pre-empts state law "involves a consideration of whether that law 'stands as an obstacle to the accomplishment and execution of the full purposes and objectives of Congress.' Hines v. Davidowitz, 312 U.S. 52, 67 (1941)." If it does not, state law governs.

In *Kewanee Oil Co.*, we reviewed the purposes of the federal patent system. First, patent law seeks to foster and reward invention; second, it promotes disclosure of inventions, to stimulate further innovation and to permit the public to practice the invention once the patent expires; third, the stringent requirements for patent protection seek to assure that ideas in the public domain remain there for the free use of the public.

Enforcement of Quick Point's agreement with Mrs. Aronson is not inconsistent with any of these aims. Permitting inventors to make enforceable agreements licensing the use of their inventions in return for royalties provides an additional incentive to invention. Similarly, encouraging Mrs. Aronson to make arrangements for the manufacture of her keyholder furthers the federal policy of disclosure of inventions; these simple devices display the novel idea which they embody wherever they are seen.

Quick Point argues that enforcement of such contracts conflicts with the federal policy against withdrawing ideas from the public domain and discourages recourse to the federal patent system by allowing states to extend "perpetual protection to articles too lacking in novelty to merit any patent at all under federal constitutional standards," Sears, Roebuck & Co. v. Stiffel Co., 376 U.S. 225, 232 (1964).

We find no merit in this contention. Enforcement of the agreement does not withdraw any idea from the public domain. The design for the keyholder was not in the public domain before Quick Point obtained its license to manufacture it. In negotiating the agreement, Mrs. Aronson disclosed the design in confidence. Had Quick Point tried to exploit the design in breach of that confidence, it would have risked legal liability. It is equally clear that the design entered the public domain as a result of the manufacture and sale of the keyholders under the contract.

Requiring Quick Point to bear the burden of royalties for the use of the design is no more inconsistent with federal patent law than any of the other costs involved in being the first to introduce a new product to the market, such as outlays for research and development, and marketing and promotional expenses. For reasons which Quick Point's experience with the Aronson keyholder demonstrate, innovative entrepreneurs have usually found such costs to be well worth paying.

Finally, enforcement of this agreement does not discourage anyone from seeking a patent. Mrs. Aronson attempted to obtain a patent for over five years. It is quite true that had she succeeded, she would have received a 5% royalty only on keyholders sold during the 17-year life of the patent. Offsetting the limited terms of royalty payments, she would have received twice as much per dollar of Quick Point's sales, and both she and Quick Point could have licensed any others who produced the same keyholder. Which course would have produced the greater yield to the contracting parties is a matter of speculation; the parties resolved the uncertainties by their bargain.

No decision of this Court relating to patents justifies relieving Quick Point of its contract obligations. We have held that a state may not forbid the copying of an idea in the public domain which does not meet the requirements for federal patent protection. Compco Corp. v. Day-Brite Lighting, Inc., 376 U.S. 234 (1964). Enforcement of Quick Point's agreement, however, does not prevent anyone from copying the keyholder. It merely requires Quick Point to pay the consideration which it promised in return for the use of a novel device which enabled it to pre-empt the market.

In Lear, Inc. v. Adkins, 395 U.S. 653 (1969), we held that a person licensed to use a patent may challenge the validity of the patent, and that a licensee who establishes that the patent is invalid need not pay the royalties accrued under the licensing agreement subsequent to the issuance of the patent. Both holdings relied on the desirability of encouraging licensees to challenge the validity of patents, to further the strong federal policy that only inventions which meet the rigorous requirements of patentability shall be withdrawn from the public domain. Accordingly, neither the holding nor the rationale of Lear controls when no patent has issued, and no ideas have been withdrawn from public use.

Enforcement of the royalty agreement here is also consistent with the principles treated in Brulotte v. Thys Co., 379 U.S. 29 (1964). There, we held that the obligation to pay royalties in return for the use of a patented device may not extend beyond the life of the patent. The principle underlying that holding was simply that the monopoly granted under a patent cannot lawfully be used to "negotiate with the leverage of that monopoly." The Court emphasized that to "use that leverage to project those royalty payments beyond the life of the patent is ana-logous to an effort to enlarge the monopoly of the patent. . . . Here the reduced royalty which is challenged, far from being negotiated "with the leverage" of a patent, rested on the con-tingency that no patent would issue within five years.

No doubt a pending patent application gives the applicant some additional bargaining power for purposes of negotiating a royalty agreement. The pending application allows the inventor to hold out the hope of an exclusive right to exploit the idea, as well as the threat that the other party will be prevented from using the idea for 17 years. However, the amount of leverage arising from a patent application depends on how likely the parties consider it to be that a valid patent will issue. Here, where no patent ever issued, the record is entirely clear that the parties assigned a substantial likelihood to that contingency, since they specifically provided for a reduced royalty in the event no patent issued within five years.

This case does not require us to draw the line between what constitutes abuse of a pending application and what does not. It is clear that whatever role the pending application played in the negotiation of the 5% royalty, it played no part in the contract to pay the 2% royalty indefinitely.

Our holding in *Kewanee Oil Co.* puts to rest the contention that federal law pre-empts and renders unenforceable the contract made by these parties. There we held that state law forbidding the misappropriation of trade secrets was not pre-empted by federal patent law. We observed:

> Certainly the patent policy of encouraging invention is not disturbed by the existence of another form of incentive to invention. In this respect the two systems [patent and trade secret law] are not and never would be in conflict.

Enforcement of this royalty agreement is even less offensive to federal patent policies than state law protecting trade secrets. The most commonly accepted definition of trade secrets is restricted to confidential information which is not disclosed in the normal process of exploitation. *See Restatement of Torts §757*, Comment *b*, p. 5 (1939). Accordingly, the exploitation of trade secrets under state law may not satisfy the federal policy in favor of disclosure, whereas disclosure is inescapable in exploiting a device like the Aronson keyholder.

Enforcement of these contractual obligations, freely undertaken in arm's-length negotiation and with no fixed reliance on a patent or a probable patent grant, will

> encourage invention in areas where patent law does not reach, and will prompt the independent innovator to proceed with the discovery and exploitation of his invention. Competition is fostered and the public is not deprived of the use of valuable, if not quite patentable, invention. (Footnote omitted.)

The device which is the subject of this contract ceased to have any secrecy as soon as it was first marketed, yet when the contract was negotiated the inventiveness and novelty were sufficiently apparent to induce an experienced novelty manufacturer to agree to pay for the opportunity to be first in the market. Federal patent law is not a barrier to such a contract. REVERSED.

PEPSICO, INC. v. REDMOND

54 F.3d 1262 (7th Cir. 1995)

FLAUM, Circuit Judge.

Plaintiff PepsiCo, Inc., sought a preliminary injunction against defendants William Redmond and the Quaker Oats Company to prevent Redmond, a former PepsiCo employee, from divulging PepsiCo trade secrets and confidential information in his new job with Quaker and from assuming any duties with Quaker relating to beverage pricing, marketing, and distribution. The district court agreed with PepsiCo and granted the injunction. We now affirm that decision.

I.

The facts of this case lay against a backdrop of fierce beverage-industry competition between Quaker and PepsiCo, especially in "sports drinks" and "new age drinks." Quaker's sports drink, "Gatorade," is the dominant brand in its market niche. PepsiCo introduced its Gatorade rival, "All Sport," in March and April of 1994, but sales of All Sport lag far behind those of Gatorade. Quaker also has the lead in the new-age-drink category. Although PepsiCo has entered the market through joint ventures with the Thomas J. Lipton Company and Ocean Spray Cranberries, Inc., Quaker purchased Snapple Beverage Corp., a large new-age-drink maker, in late 1994. PepsiCo's products have about half of Snapple's market share. Both companies see 1995 as an important year for their products: PepsiCo has developed extensive plans to increase its market presence, while Quaker is trying to solidify its lead by integrating Gatorade and Snapple distribution. Meanwhile, PepsiCo and Quaker each face strong competition from Coca Cola Co., which has its own sports drink, "PowerAde," and which introduced its own Snapple-rival, "Fruitopia," in 1994, as well as from independent beverage producers.

William Redmond, Jr., worked for PepsiCo in its Pepsi-Cola North America division ("PCNA") from 1984 to 1994. Redmond became the General Manager of the Northern California Business Unit in June, 1993, and was promoted one year later to General Manager of the business unit covering all of California, a unit having annual revenues of more than 500 million dollars and representing twenty percent of PCNA's profit for all of the United States.

Redmond's relatively high-level position at PCNA gave him access to inside information and trade secrets. Redmond, like other PepsiCo management employees, had signed a confidentiality agreement with PepsiCo. That agreement stated in relevant part that he w[ould] not disclose at any time, to anyone other than officers or employees of [PepsiCo], or make use of, confidential information relating to the business of [PepsiCo] . . . obtained while in the employ of [PepsiCo], which shall not be generally known or available to the public or recognized as standard practices.

Donald Uzzi, who had left PepsiCo in the beginning of 1994 to become the head of Quaker's Gatorade division, began courting Redmond for Quaker in May 1994. Redmond met in Chicago with Quaker officers in August 1994, and on October 20, 1994, Quaker, through Uzzi, offered Redmond the position of Vice President — On Premise Sales for Gatorade. Redmond did not then accept the offer but continued to negotiate for more money. Throughout this time, Redmond kept his dealings with Quaker secret from his employers at PCNA.

On November 8, 1994, Uzzi extended Redmond a written offer for the position of Vice President — Field Operations for Gatorade and Redmond accepted. Later that same day, Redmond called William Bensyl, the Senior Vice President of Human Resources for PCNA, and told him that he had an offer from Quaker to become the Chief Operating Officer of the combined Gatorade and Snapple company but had not yet accepted it. Redmond also asked whether he should, in light of the offer, carry out his plans to make calls upon certain PCNA customers. Bensyl told Redmond to make the visits.

Redmond also misstated his situation to a number of his PCNA colleagues, including Craig Weatherup, PCNA's President and Chief Executive Officer, and Brenda Barnes, PCNA's Chief Operating Officer and Redmond's immediate superior. As with Bensyl, Redmond told them that he had been offered the position of Chief Operating Officer at Gatorade and that he was leaning "60/40" in favor of accepting the new position.

On November 10, 1994, Redmond met with Barnes and told her that he had decided to accept the Quaker offer and was resigning from PCNA. Barnes immediately took Redmond to Bensyl, who told Redmond that PepsiCo was considering legal action against him.

True to its word, PepsiCo filed this diversity suit on November 16, 1994, seeking a temporary restraining order to enjoin Redmond from assuming his duties at Quaker and to prevent him from disclosing trade secrets or confidential information to his new employer. The district court granted PepsiCo's request that same day but dissolved the order *sua sponte* two days later, after determining that PepsiCo had failed to meet its burden of establishing that it would suffer irreparable harm. The court found that PepsiCo's fears about Redmond were based upon a mistaken understanding of his new position at Quaker and that the likelihood that Redmond would improperly reveal any confidential information did not "rise above mere speculation."

From November 23, 1994, to December 1, 1994, the district court conducted a preliminary injunction hearing on the same matter. At the hearing, PepsiCo offered evidence of a number of trade secrets and confidential information it desired protected and to which Redmond was privy. First, it identified PCNA's "Strategic Plan," an annually revised document that contains PCNA's plans to compete, its financial goals, and its strategies for manufacturing, production, marketing, packaging, and distribution for the coming three years. Strategic Plans are developed by Weatherup and his staff with input from PCNA's general managers, including Redmond, and are considered highly confidential. The Strategic Plan derives much of its value from the fact that it is secret and competitors cannot anticipate PCNA's next moves. PCNA managers received the most recent Strategic Plan at a meeting in July, 1994, a meeting Redmond attended. PCNA also presented information at the meeting regarding its plans for Lipton ready-to-drink teas and for All Sport for 1995 and beyond, including new flavors and package sizes.

Second, PepsiCo pointed to PCNA's Annual Operating Plan ("AOP") as a trade secret. The AOP is a national plan for a given year and guides PCNA's financial goals, marketing plans, promotional event calendars, growth expectations, and operational changes in that year. The AOP, which is implemented by PCNA unit General Managers, including Redmond, contains specific information regarding all PCNA initiatives for the forthcoming year. The AOP bears a label that reads "Private and Confidential — Do Not Reproduce" and is considered highly confidential by PCNA managers.

In particular, the AOP contains important and sensitive information about "pricing architecture" — how PCNA prices its products in the marketplace. Pricing architecture covers both a national pricing approach and specific price points for given areas. Pricing architecture also encompasses PCNA's objectives for All Sport and its new age drinks with reference to trade channels, package sizes and other characteristics of both the products and the customers at which the products are aimed. Additionally, PCNA's pricing architecture outlines PCNA's customer development agreements. These agreements between PCNA and retailers provide for the retailer's participation in certain merchandising activities for PCNA products. As with other information contained in the AOP, pricing architecture is highly confidential and would be extremely valuable to a competitor. Knowing PCNA's pricing architecture would allow a competitor to anticipate PCNA's pricing moves and underbid PCNA strategically whenever and wherever the competitor so desired. PepsiCo introduced evidence that Redmond had detailed knowledge of PCNA's pricing architecture and that he was aware of and had been involved in preparing PCNA's customer development agreements with PCNA's California and California-based national customers. Indeed, PepsiCo showed that Redmond, as the General Manager for California, would have been responsible for implementing the pricing architecture guidelines for his business unit.

PepsiCo also showed that Redmond had intimate knowledge of PCNA "attack plans" for specific markets. Pursuant to these plans, PCNA dedicates extra funds to supporting its brands against other brands in selected markets. To use a hypothetical example, PCNA might budget an additional $500,000 to spend in Chicago at a particular time to help All Sport close its market gap with Gatorade. Testimony and documents demonstrated Redmond's awareness of these plans and his participation in drafting some of them.

Finally, PepsiCo offered evidence of PCNA trade secrets regarding innovations in its selling and delivery systems. Under this plan, PCNA is testing a new delivery system that could give PCNA an advantage over its competitors in negotiations with retailers over shelf space and merchandising. Redmond has knowledge of this secret because PCNA, which has invested over a million dollars in developing the system during the past two years, is testing the pilot program in California.

Having shown Redmond's intimate knowledge of PCNA's plans for 1995, PepsiCo argued that Redmond would inevitably disclose that information to Quaker in his new position, at which he would have substantial input as to Gatorade and Snapple pricing, costs, margins, distribution systems, products, packaging and marketing, and could give Quaker an unfair advantage in its upcoming skirmishes with PepsiCo. Redmond and Quaker countered that Redmond's primary initial duties at Quaker as Vice President — Field Operations would be to integrate Gatorade and Snapple distribution and then to manage that distribution as well as the promotion, marketing and sales of these products. Redmond asserted that the integration would be conducted according to a pre-existing plan and that his special knowledge of PCNA strategies would be irrelevant. This irrelevance would derive not only from the fact that Redmond would be implementing pre-existing plans but also from the fact that PCNA and Quaker distribute their products in entirely different ways: PCNA's distribution system is vertically integrated (i.e., PCNA owns the system) and delivers its product directly to retailers, while Quaker ships its product to wholesalers and customer warehouses and relies on independent distributors. The defendants also pointed out that Redmond had signed a confidentiality agreement with Quaker preventing him from disclosing "any confidential information belonging to others," as well as the Quaker Code of Ethics, which prohibits employees from engaging in "illegal or improper acts to acquire a competitor's trade secrets." Redmond additionally promised at the hearing that should he be faced with a situation at Quaker that might involve the use or disclosure of PCNA information, he would seek advice from Quaker's in-house counsel and would refrain from making the decision.

PepsiCo responded to the defendants' representations by pointing out that the evidence did not show that Redmond would simply be implementing a business plan already in place. On the contrary, as of November, 1994, the plan to integrate Gatorade and Snapple distribution consisted of a single distributorship agreement and a two-page "contract terms summary." Such a basic plan would not lend itself to widespread application among the over 300 independent Snapple distributors. Since the integration process would likely face resistance from Snapple distributors and Quaker had no scheme to deal with this probability, Redmond, as the person in charge of the integration, would likely have a great deal of influence on the process. PepsiCo further argued that Snapple's 1995 marketing and promotion plans had not necessarily been completed prior to Redmond's joining Quaker, that Uzzi disagreed with portions of the Snapple plans, and that the plans were open to re-evaluation. Uzzi testified that the plan for integrating Gatorade and Snapple distribution is something that would happen in the future. Redmond would therefore likely have input in remaking these plans, and if he did, he would inevitably be making decisions with PCNA's strategic plans and 1995 AOP in mind. Moreover, PepsiCo continued, diverging testimony made it difficult to know exactly what Redmond would be doing at Quaker. Redmond described his job as "managing the entire sales effort of Gatorade at the field level, possibly including strategic planning," and at least at one point considered his job to be equivalent to that of a Chief Operating Officer. Uzzi, on the other hand, characterized Redmond's position as "primarily and initially to restructure and integrate our distribution systems for Snapple and for Gatorade, as per our distribution plan" and then to "execute marketing, promotion and sales plans in the marketplace." Uzzi also denied having given Redmond detailed information about any business plans, while Redmond described such a plan in depth in an affidavit and said that he received the information from Uzzi. Thus, PepsiCo asserted, Redmond would have a high position in the Gatorade hierarchy, and PCNA trade secrets and confidential information would necessarily influence his decisions. Even if Redmond could somehow refrain from relying on this information, as he promised he would, his actions in leaving PCNA, Uzzi's actions in hiring Redmond, and the varying testimony regarding Redmond's new responsibilities, made Redmond's assurances to PepsiCo less than comforting.

On December 15, 1994, the district court issued an order enjoining Redmond from assuming his position at Quaker through May, 1995, and permanently from using or disclosing any PCNA trade secrets or confidential information. The court entered its findings of fact and conclusions of law on January 26, 1995, *nunc pro tunc*, December 15, 1994. The court, which completely adopted PepsiCo's position, found that Redmond's new job posed a clear threat of misappropriation of trade secrets and confidential information that could be enjoined under Illinois statutory and common law. The court also emphasized Redmond's lack of forthrightness both in his activities before accepting his job with Quaker and in his testimony as factors leading the court to believe the threat of misappropriation was real. This appeal followed.

II.

Both parties agree that the primary issue on appeal is whether the district court correctly concluded that PepsiCo had a reasonable likelihood of success on its various claims for trade secret misappropriation and breach of a confidentiality agreement. We review the district court's legal conclusions in issuing a preliminary injunction *de novo* and its factual determinations and balancing of the equities for abuse of discretion. SEC v. Cherif, 933 F.2d 403, 408 (7th Cir. 1991).

A.

The Illinois Trade Secrets Act ("ITSA"), which governs the trade secret issues in this case, provides that a court may enjoin the "actual or threatened misappropriation" of a trade secret. 765 ILCS 1065/3(a); George S. May Int'l Co. v. Int'l Profit Associates, 256 Ill. App. 3d 779, 195 Ill. Dec. 183, 189, 628 N.E.2d 647, 653 (1st Dist. 1993), *appeal denied*, 156 Ill. 2d 557, 202 Ill. Dec. 921, 638 N.E.2d 1115 (1994). A party seeking an injunction must therefore prove both the existence of a trade secret and the misappropriation. The defendants' appeal focuses solely on misappropriation; although the defendants only reluctantly refer to PepsiCo's marketing and distribution plans as trade secrets, they do not seriously contest that this information falls under the ITSA.[3]

The question of threatened or inevitable misappropriation in this case lies at the heart of a basic tension in trade secret law. Trade secret law serves to protect "standards of commercial morality" and "encourage [] invention and innovation" while maintaining "the public interest in having free and open competition in the manufacture and sale of unpatented goods." Yet that same law should not prevent workers from pursuing their livelihoods when they leave their current positions. American Can Co. v. Mansukhani, 742 F.2d 314, 329 (7th Cir. 1984). It has been said that federal age discrimination law does not guarantee tenure for older employees. Partington v. Broyhill Furniture Industries, Inc., 999 F.2d 269, 271 (7th Cir. 1993). Similarly, trade secret law does not provide a reserve clause for solicitous employers. *Cf.* Flood v. Kuhn, 407 U.S. 258 (1972).

This tension is particularly exacerbated when a plaintiff sues to prevent not the actual misappropriation of trade secrets but the mere threat that it will occur. While the ITSA plainly permits a court to enjoin the threat of misappropriation of trade secrets, there is little law in Illinois or in this circuit establishing what constitutes threatened or inevitable misappropriation.[4] Indeed, there are only two cases in this circuit that address the issue: Teradyne, Inc. v. Clear Communications Corp., 707 F. Supp. 353 (N.D. Ill. 1989), and AMP Inc. v. Fleischhacker, 823 F.2d 1199 (7th Cir. 1987).

In *Teradyne*, Teradyne alleged that a competitor, Clear Communications, had lured employees away from Teradyne and intended to employ them in the same field. In an insightful opinion, Judge Zagel observed that "[t]hreatened misappropriation can be enjoined under Illinois law" where there is a "high degree of probability of inevitable and immediate . . . use of . . . trade secrets." Judge Zagel held, however, that Teradyne's complaint failed to state a claim because Teradyne did not allege "that defendants have in fact threatened to use Teradyne's secrets or that they will inevitably do so." Teradyne's claims

---

3. Under the ITSA, trade secret "means information, including but not limited to, technical or non-technical data, a formula, pattern, compilation, program, device, method, technique, drawing, process, financial data, or list of actual or potential customers that:

  (1) is sufficiently secret to derive economic value, actual or potential, from not generally being known to other persons who can obtain economic value from its disclosure or use; and
  (2) is the subject of efforts that are reasonable under the circumstances to maintain its secrecy or confidentiality.

4. The ITSA definition of misappropriation relevant to this discussion is "the disclosure or use of a trade secret of a person without express or implied consent by another person who . . . at the time of disclosure or use, knew or had reason to know that the knowledge of the trade secret was . . . acquired under circumstances giving rise to a duty to maintain its secrecy. . . ." 765 ILCS 1065/2(b).

would have passed Rule 12(b)(6) muster had they properly alleged inevitable disclosure, including a statement that Clear intended to use Teradyne's trade secrets or that the former Teradyne employees had disavowed their confidentiality agreements with Teradyne, or an allegation that Clear could not operate without Teradyne's secrets. However, [t]he defendants' claimed acts, working for Teradyne, knowing its business, leaving its business, hiring employees from Teradyne and entering the same field (though in a market not yet serviced by Teradyne) do not state a claim of threatened misappropriation. All that is alleged, at bottom, is that defendants could misuse plaintiff's secrets, and plaintiffs fear they will. This is not enough. It may be that little more is needed, but falling a little short is still falling short.

In *AMP*, we affirmed the denial of a preliminary injunction on the grounds that the plaintiff AMP had failed to show either the existence of any trade secrets or the likelihood that defendant Fleischhacker, a former AMP employee, would compromise those secrets or any other confidential business information. AMP, which produced electrical and electronic connection devices, argued that Fleishhacker's new position at AMP's competitor would inevitably lead him to compromise AMP's trade secrets regarding the manufacture of connectors. In rejecting that argument, we emphasized that the mere fact that a person assumed a similar position at a competitor does not, without more, make it "inevitable that he will use or disclose . . . trade secret information" so as to "demonstrate irreparable injury."

It should be noted that *AMP*, which we decided in 1987, predates the ITSA, which took effect in 1988. The ITSA abolishes any common law remedies or authority contrary to its own terms. The ITSA does not, however, represent a major deviation from the Illinois common law of unfair trade practices. Elmer Miller, Inc. v. Landis, 253 Ill. App. 3d 129, 192 Ill. Dec. 378, 381, 625 N.E.2d 338, 341 (1st Dist. 1993), *appeal denied*, 154 Ill. 2d 559, 197 Ill. Dec. 485, 631 N.E.2d 707 (1994). The ITSA mostly codifies rather than modifies the common law doctrine that preceded it. Thus, we believe that *AMP* continues to reflect the proper standard under Illinois's current statutory scheme.[5]

The ITSA, *Teradyne*, and *AMP* lead to the same conclusion: a plaintiff may prove a claim of trade secret misappropriation by demonstrating that defendant's new employment will inevitably lead him to rely on the plaintiff's trade secrets. The defendants are incorrect that Illinois law does not allow a court to enjoin the "inevitable" disclosure of trade secrets. Questions remain, however, as to what constitutes inevitable misappropriation and whether PepsiCo's submissions rise above those of the *Teradyne* and *AMP* plaintiffs and meet that standard. We hold that they do.

PepsiCo presented substantial evidence at the preliminary injunction hearing that Redmond possessed extensive and intimate knowledge about PCNA's strategic goals for 1995 in sports drinks and new age drinks. The district court concluded on the basis of that presentation that unless Redmond possessed an uncanny ability to compartmentalize information, he would necessarily be making decisions about Gatorade and Snapple by relying on his

---

5. The ITSA has overruled *AMP*'s implications regarding the durability of an agreement to protect trade secrets. *AMP* followed a line of Illinois cases questioning the validity of agreements to keep trade secrets confidential where those agreements did not have durational or geographical limits. The ITSA, in reversing those cases, provides that "a contractual or other duty to maintain secrecy or limit use of a trade secret shall not be deemed to be void or unenforceable solely for lack of durational or geographical limitation on the duty." 765 ILCS 1065/8(b)(1).

knowledge of PCNA trade secrets. It is not the "general skills and knowledge acquired during his tenure with" PepsiCo that PepsiCo seeks to keep from falling into Quaker's hands, but rather "the particularized plans or processes developed by [PCNA] and disclosed to him while the employer-employee relationship existed, which are unknown to others in the industry and which give the employer an advantage over his competitors." The *Teradyne* and *AMP* plaintiffs could do nothing more than assert that skilled employees were taking their skills elsewhere; PepsiCo has done much more.

Admittedly, PepsiCo has not brought a traditional trade secret case, in which a former employee has knowledge of a special manufacturing process or customer list and can give a competitor an unfair advantage by transferring the technology or customers to that competitor. PepsiCo has not contended that Quaker has stolen the All Sport formula or its list of distributors. Rather PepsiCo has asserted that Redmond cannot help but rely on PCNA trade secrets as he helps plot Gatorade and Snapple's new course, and that these secrets will enable Quaker to achieve a substantial advantage by knowing exactly how PCNA will price, distribute, and market its sports drinks and new age drinks and being able to respond strategically. This type of trade secret problem may arise less often, but it nevertheless falls within the realm of trade secret protection under the present circumstances.

Quaker and Redmond assert that they have not and do not intend to use whatever confidential information Redmond has by virtue of his former employment. They point out that Redmond has already signed an agreement with Quaker not to disclose any trade secrets or confidential information gleaned from his earlier employment. They also note with regard to distribution systems that even if Quaker wanted to steal information about PCNA's distribution plans, they would be completely useless in attempting to integrate the Gatorade and Snapple beverage lines.

The defendants' arguments fall somewhat short of the mark. Again, the danger of misappropriation in the present case is not that Quaker threatens to use PCNA's secrets to create distribution systems or co-opt PCNA's advertising and marketing ideas. Rather, PepsiCo believes that Quaker, unfairly armed with knowledge of PCNA's plans, will be able to anticipate its distribution, packaging, pricing, and marketing moves. Redmond and Quaker even concede that Redmond might be faced with a decision that could be influenced by certain confidential information that he obtained while at PepsiCo. In other words, PepsiCo finds itself in the position of a coach, one of whose players has left, playbook in hand, to join the opposing team before the big game. Quaker and Redmond's protestations that their distribution systems and plans are entirely different from PCNA's are thus not really responsive.

The district court also concluded from the evidence that Uzzi's actions in hiring Redmond and Redmond's actions in pursuing and accepting his new job demonstrated a lack of candor on their part and proof of their willingness to misuse PCNA trade secrets, findings Quaker and Redmond vigorously challenge. The court expressly found that:

> Redmond's lack of forthrightness on some occasions, and out and out lies on others, in the period between the time he accepted the position with defendant Quaker and when he informed plaintiff that he had accepted that position leads the court to conclude that defendant Redmond could not be trusted to act with the necessary sensitivity and good faith under the circumstances in which the only practical

verification that he was not using plaintiff's secrets would be defendant Redmond's word to that effect.

The facts of the case do not ineluctably dictate the district court's conclusion. Redmond's ambiguous behavior toward his PepsiCo superiors might have been nothing more than an attempt to gain leverage in employment negotiations. The discrepancy between Redmond's and Uzzi's comprehension of what Redmond's job would entail may well have been a simple misunderstanding. The court also pointed out that Quaker, through Uzzi, seemed to express an unnatural interest in hiring PCNA employees: all three of the people interviewed for the position Redmond ultimately accepted worked at PCNA. Uzzi may well have focused on recruiting PCNA employees because he knew they were good and not because of their confidential knowledge. Nonetheless, the district court, after listening to the witnesses, determined otherwise. That conclusion was not an abuse of discretion.

That conclusion also renders inapposite the defendants' reliance on Cincinnati Tool Steel Co. v. Breed, 136 Ill. App. 3d 267, 90 Ill. Dec. 463, 482 N.E.2d 170 (2d Dist. 1985). In *Cincinnati Tool*, the court held that the defendant's "express denial that she had disclosed or would disclose any confidential information or that she even possessed such information" left the plaintiff without a case, one that could not be saved "merely by offering evidence that defendant used customer and price data in her work while employed by plaintiff." In the instant case, the district court simply did not believe the denials and had reason to do so.

Thus, when we couple the demonstrated inevitability that Redmond would rely on PCNA trade secrets in his new job at Quaker with the district court's reluctance to believe that Redmond would refrain from disclosing these secrets in his new position (or that Quaker would ensure Redmond did not disclose them), we conclude that the district court correctly decided that PepsiCo demonstrated a likelihood of success on its statutory claim of trade secret misappropriation. . . .

C.

For the same reasons we concluded that the district court did not abuse its discretion in granting the preliminary injunction on the issue of trade secret misappropriation, we also agree with its decision on the likelihood of Redmond's breach of his confidentiality agreement should he begin working at Quaker. Because Redmond's position at Quaker would initially cause him to disclose trade secrets, it would necessarily force him to breach his agreement not to disclose confidential information acquired while employed in PCNA.

Quaker and Remond do not assert that the confidentiality agreement is invalid; such agreements are enforceable when supported by adequate consideration. Rather, they argue that "inevitable" breaches of these contracts may not be enjoined. The case on which they rely, however, R.R. Donnelley & Sons Co. v. Fagan, 767 F. Supp. 1259 (S.D.N.Y. 1991) (applying Illinois law), says nothing of the sort. The *R.R. Donnelley* court merely found that the plaintiffs had failed to prove the existence of any confidential information or any indication that the defendant would ever use it. The threat of misappropriation that drives our holding with regard to trade secrets dictates the same result here.

III.

Finally, Redmond and Quaker have contended in the alternative that the injunction issued against them is overbroad. They disagree in particular with the injunction's prohibition against Redmond's participation in the integration of the Snapple and Gatorade distribution systems. The defendants claim that whatever trade secret and confidential information Redmond has, that information is completely irrelevant to Quaker's integration task. They further argue that, because Redmond would only be implementing a plan already in place, the injunction is especially inappropriate. A district court ordinarily has wide latitude in fashioning injunctive relief, and we will restrict the breadth of an injunction only where the district court has abused its discretion. Nonetheless, a court abuses its discretion where the scope of injunctive relief "exceed[s] the extent of the plaintiff's protectible rights."

While the defendants' arguments are not without some merit, the district court determined that the proposed integration would require Redmond to do more than execute a plan someone else had drafted. It also found that Redmond's knowledge of PCNA's trade secrets and confidential information would inevitably shape that integration and that Redmond could not be trusted to avoid that conflict of interest. If the injunction permanently enjoined Redmond from assuming these duties at Quaker, the defendants' argument would be stronger. However, the injunction against Redmond's immediate employment at Quaker extends no further than necessary and was well within the district court's discretion.

For the foregoing reasons, we affirm the district court's order enjoining Redmond from assuming his responsibilities at Quaker through May, 1995, and preventing him forever from disclosing PCNA trade secrets and confidential information. AFFIRMED.

EDWARDS v. ARTHUR ANDERSEN LLP

44 Cal. 4th 937, 189 P.3d 285, 81 Cal. Rptr. 3d 282 (2008)

CHIN, J.

We granted review to address the validity of noncompetition agreements in California and the permissible scope of employment release agreements. [The Supreme Court presented two issues, only one of which is presented in this case excerpt. The Supreme Court addressed the following issue:] (1) To what extent does Business and Professions Code section 16600 prohibit employee noncompetition agreements. . . .

We conclude that section 16600 prohibits employee noncompetition agreements unless the agreement falls within a statutory exception. . . . We therefore affirm in part . . . the Court of Appeal judgment.

FACTS

In January 1997, Raymond Edwards II (Edwards), a certified public accountant, was hired as a tax manager by the Los Angeles office of the accounting firm Arthur Andersen LLP (Andersen). Andersen's employment offer was made contingent upon Edwards's signing a noncompetition agreement, which prohibited him from working for or soliciting certain Andersen clients for limited periods following his termination. The agreement was required of all managers, and read in relevant part: "If you leave the Firm, for eighteen months after release or resignation, you agree not to perform professional services of the type you provided for any client on which you worked during the eighteen months prior to release or resignation. This does not prohibit you from accepting employment with a client. [¶] For twelve months after you leave the Firm, you agree not to solicit (to perform professional services of the type you provided) any client of the office(s) to which you were assigned during the eighteen months preceding release or resignation. [¶] You agree not to solicit away from the Firm any of its professional personnel for eighteen months after release or resignation." Edwards signed the agreement.

Between 1997 and 2002, Edwards continued to work for Andersen, moving into the firm's private client services practice group, where he handled income, gift, and estate tax planning for individuals and entities with large incomes and net worth. Over this period he was promoted to senior manager and was on track to become a partner. In March 2002, the United States government indicted Andersen in connection with the investigation into Enron Corporation, and in June 2002, Andersen announced that it would cease its accounting practices in the United States. In April 2002, Andersen began selling off its practice groups to various entities. In May 2002, Andersen internally announced that HSBC USA, Inc. (a New York-based banking corporation), through a new subsidiary, Wealth and Tax Advisory Services (WTAS), would purchase a portion of Andersen's tax practice, including Edwards's group.

In July 2002, HSBC offered Edwards employment. Before hiring any of Andersen's employees, HSBC required them to execute a "Termination of Non-compete Agreement" (TONC) in order to obtain employment with HSBC. Among other things, the TONC required employees to, *inter alia*, (1) voluntarily resign from Andersen; (2) release Andersen from "any and all" claims, including "claims that in any way arise from or out of, are based upon or relate to Employee's employment by, association with or compensation from" defendant; (3) continue indefinitely to preserve confidential information and trade secrets except as otherwise required by a court or governmental agency; (4) refrain from disparaging Andersen or its related entities or partners; and (5) cooperate with Andersen in connection with any investigation of, or litigation against, Andersen. In exchange, Andersen would agree to accept Edwards's resignation, agree to Edwards's employment by HSBC, and release Edwards from the 1997 noncompetition agreement.

HSBC required that Andersen provide it with a completed TONC signed by every employee on the "Restricted Employees" list before the deal went through. At least one draft of the Restricted Employees list contained Edwards's name. Andersen would not release Edwards, or any other employee, from the noncompetition agreement unless that employee signed the TONC.

Edwards signed the HSBC offer letter, but he did not sign the TONC. In response, Andersen terminated Edwards's employment and withheld severance benefits. HSBC withdrew its offer of employment to Edwards.

PROCEDURAL HISTORY

On April 30, 2003, Edwards filed a complaint against Andersen, HSBC and WTAS for intentional interference with prospective economic advantage and anticompetitive business practices under the Cartwright Act (Bus. & Prof. Code, §16720 et seq.). Edwards alleged that the Andersen noncompetition agreement violated section 16600, which states "[e]xcept as provided in this chapter, every contract by which anyone is restrained from engaging in a lawful profession, trade, or business of any kind is to that extent void."

Edwards settled with all parties except Andersen. The trial court . . . denied Andersen's subsequent motion for summary adjudication on Edwards's intentional interference with prospective economic advantage cause of action, after concluding that triable issues of fact existed on the meaning of the agreements, and whether the agreements protected trade secrets. . . . The court dismissed all claims against Andersen, except for those relating to intentional interference with prospective economic advantage, which it concluded presented pure questions of law.

The trial court heard argument from both parties, but took no evidence. The court determined all issues of law in favor of Andersen on the merits, and entered judgment in its favor. The court specifically decided that (1) the noncompetition agreement did not violate section 16600 because it was narrowly tailored and did not deprive Edwards of his right to pursue his profession. . . . Edwards appealed the trial court's decision. . . .

In the published part of its opinion, the Court of Appeal held . . . the noncompetition agreement was invalid under section 16600.

DISCUSSION

A. Section 16600

Under the common law, as is still true in many states today, contractual restraints on the practice of a profession, business, or trade, were considered valid, as long as they were reasonably imposed. This was true even in California [where there was a relaxing of the original common law rule that all restraints on trade were invalid in recognition of increasing population and competition in trade]. However, in 1872 California settled public policy in favor of open competition, and rejected the common law "rule of reasonableness," when the Legislature enacted the Civil Code, [currently] enacted as Bus. & Prof. Code, §16600. Today in California, covenants not to compete are void, subject to several exceptions discussed briefly below.

Section 16600 states: "Except as provided in this chapter, every contract by which anyone is restrained from engaging in a lawful profession, trade, or business of any kind is to that extent void." The chapter excepts noncompetition agreements in the sale or dissolution of corporations (§16601), partnerships (*ibid.*; §16602), and limited liability corporations (§16602.5). In the years since its original enactment as Civil Code section 1673, our courts have consistently affirmed that section 16600 evinces a settled legislative policy in favor of open competition and employee mobility. The law protects Californians and ensures "that every citizen shall retain the right to pursue any lawful employment and enterprise of their choice." It protects "the important legal right of persons to engage in businesses and occupations of their choosing."

This court has invalidated an otherwise narrowly tailored agreement as an improper restraint under section 16600 because it required a former employee to forfeit his pension rights on commencing work for a competitor. In Muggill v. Reuben H. Donnelley Corp., 62 Cal. 2d 239, 398 P.2d 147, 42 Cal. Rptr. 107, the court reviewed an adverse judgment against a company's retired employee whose pension plan rights were terminated after the former employee commenced work for a competitor. [The Court] held that, with exceptions not applicable here, section 16600 invalidates provisions in employment contracts and retirement pension plans that prohibit "an employee from working for a competitor after completion of his employment or imposing a penalty if he does so unless they are necessary to protect the employer's trade secrets."[6] In sum, following the Legislature, this court generally condemns noncompetition agreements.

Under the statute's plain meaning, therefore, an employer cannot by contract restrain a former employee from engaging in his or her profession, trade, or business unless the agreement falls within one of the exceptions to the rule. Andersen, however, asserts that we should interpret the term "restrain" under section 16600 to mean simply to "prohibit," so that only contracts that totally prohibit an employee from engaging in his or her profession, trade, or business are illegal. It would then follow that a mere limitation on an employee's ability to practice his or her vocation would be permissible under section 16600, as long as it is reasonably based.

Andersen contends that some California courts have held that section 16600 (and its predecessor statutes, Civil Code former sections 1673, 1674, and 1675) are the statutory embodiment of prior common law, and embrace the rule of reasonableness in evaluating competitive restraints. . . . Andersen claims that these cases show that section 16600 "prohibits only broad agreements that prevent a person from engaging entirely in his chosen business, trade or profession. Agreements that do not have this broad effect — but merely regulate some aspect of post-employment conduct, e.g., to prevent raiding [employer's personnel] — are not within the scope of [s]ection 16600."

As Edwards observes, however, the cases Andersen cites to support a relaxation of the statutory rule simply recognize that the statutory exceptions to section 16600 reflect the same exceptions to the rule against noncompetition agreements that were implied in the common law. For example, *South Bay Radiology* acknowledged the general prohibition against restraints on trade while applying the specific partnership dissolution exception of section 16602 to the facts of its case. In that case, the covenant not to compete was set forth in a partnership agreement to which appellant doctor was a party. When appellant's partnership with several other doctors dissolved due to his inability to work following an accident, he challenged the noncompete clause. The court found the partnership exception to section 16600 applicable.

As the present Court of Appeal recognized, "Fairly read, the foregoing authorities suggest section 16600 embodies the original, strict common law antipathy toward restraints of trade, while the section 16601 and 16602 exceptions incorporated the later common law 'rule of reasonableness' in instances where those exceptions apply."

We conclude that Andersen's noncompetition agreement was invalid. As the Court of Appeal observed, "The first challenged clause prohibited Edwards, for an 18-month period, from performing professional services of the type he had provided while at Andersen, for any client on whose account he had worked during 18 months prior to his termination. The second

---

6. We do not here address the applicability of the so-called trade secret exception to section 16600, as Edwards does not dispute that portion of his agreement or contend that the provision of the noncompetition agreement prohibiting him from recruiting Andersen's employees violated section 16600.

challenged clause prohibited Edwards, for a year after termination, from 'soliciting,' defined by the agreement as providing professional services to any client of Andersen's Los Angeles office." The agreement restricted Edwards from performing work for Andersen's Los Angeles clients and therefore restricted his ability to practice his accounting profession. The noncompetition agreement that Edwards was required to sign before commencing employment with Andersen was therefore invalid because it restrained his ability to practice his profession.

B. Ninth Circuit's Narrow-Restraint Exception

Andersen asks this court to adopt the limited or "narrow-restraint" exception to section 16600 that the Ninth Circuit discussed in Campbell v. Trustees of Leland Stanford Jr. Univ. (9th Cir. 1987) 817 F.2d 499 and that the trial court relied on in this case in order to uphold the noncompetition agreement. In *Campbell*, the Ninth Circuit acknowledged that California has rejected the common law "rule of reasonableness" with respect to restraints upon the ability to pursue a profession, but concluded that section 16600 "only makes illegal those restraints which preclude one from engaging in a lawful profession, trade, or business." The court remanded the case to the district court in order to allow the employee to prove that the noncompetition agreement at issue completely restrained him from practicing his "profession, trade, or business within the meaning of section 16600."

The confusion over the Ninth Circuit's application of section 16600 arose in a paragraph in *Campbell*, in which the court noted that some California courts have excepted application of section 16600 "'where one is barred from pursuing only a small or limited part of the business, trade or profession.'" The Ninth Circuit cited two California cases that it believed may have carved out such an exception to section 16600. See Boughton v. Socony Mobil Oil Co. (1964) 231 Cal. App. 2d 188, 41 Cal. Rptr. 714 (interpreting deed restriction on land use) and King v. Gerold (1952) 109 Cal. App. 2d 316, 240 P.2d 710 (rejecting manufacturer's argument that clause not to produce its product after license expiration was not an illegal restraint under section 16600) Andersen relies on those cases, citing them as the underpinnings of the Ninth Circuit's exception to section 16600, and urges the court to adopt their reasoning here.

As the Court of Appeal observed, however, the analyses in *Boughton* and *King* do not provide persuasive support for adopting the narrow-restraint exception. In *Boughton*, the restriction was not upon the plaintiff's practice of a profession or trade, but took the form of a covenant in a deed to a parcel of land that specified the land could not be used as a gasoline service station for a specified time period. Because the case involved the use of the land, section 16600 was not implicated. Of note is the fact that *Boughton* relied on *King*, an unfair competition case in which the court applied a trade secret exception to the statutory rule against noncompetition clauses. In *King*, the plaintiff was not simply engaged in the manufacture and sale of goods (house trailers) but was allegedly using a trailer design substantially similar to his former employer's, the inventor of the design.

Andersen is correct, however, that *Campbell* has been followed in some recent Ninth Circuit cases to create a narrow-restraint exception to section 16600 in federal court. For example, International Business Machines Corp. v. Bajorek (9th Cir. 1999) 191 F.3d 1033, upheld an agreement mandating that an employee forfeits stock options if employed by a competitor within six months of leaving employment. General Commercial Packaging v. TPS Package (9th Cir. 1997) 126 F.3d 1131 held that a bargained-for contractual provision barring one party from courting a specific named customer was not an illegal restraint of trade prohibited by section 16600, because it did not "entirely preclude[ ]" the party from pursuing its trade or business.

Contrary to Andersen's belief, however, California courts have not embraced the Ninth Circuit's narrow-restraint exception. Indeed, no reported California state court decision has endorsed the Ninth Circuit's reasoning, and we are of the view that California courts "have been clear in their expression that section 16600 represents a strong public policy of the state which should not be diluted by judicial fiat."[7] Section 16600 is unambiguous, and if the Legislature intended the statute to apply only to restraints that were unreasonable or over-broad, it could have included language to that effect. We reject Andersen's contention that we should adopt a narrow-restraint exception to section 16600 and leave it to the Legislature, if it chooses, either to relax the statutory restrictions or adopt additional exceptions to the prohibition-against-restraint rule under section 16600.

DISPOSITION

We hold that the noncompetition agreement here is invalid under section 16600, and we reject the narrow-restraint exception urged by Andersen. Noncompetition agreements are invalid under section 16600 in California even if narrowly drawn, unless they fall within the applicable statutory exceptions of sections 16601, 16602, or 16602.5. AFFIRMED IN PART.

HENRY SCHEIN, INC. v. COOK
191 F. Supp. 3d 1072 (N.D. Cal. 2016)

ORDER GRANTING IN PART AND DENYING IN PART PLAINTIFFS' APPLICATION FOR TEMPORARY RESTRAINING ORDER AND DENYING REQUEST FOR EXPEDITED DISCOVERY WITHOUT PREJUDICE

TIGAR, J.

Plaintiff Henry Schein, Inc. ("HSI") has applied for a temporary restraining order ("TRO"), alleging that Defendant and former HSI employee Jennifer Cook stole confidential data in violation of trade secret law and employment agreements. HSI requests a TRO preventing Cook from accessing, using, or sharing any of this data, as well as early discovery against Cook and her new, non-party employer. The Court will grant the requested TRO and deny the request for early discovery.

---

7. As noted, the Ninth Circuit's reading of *Boughton* and *King* may be the source of that Circuit's narrow-restraint exception to section 16600. We are not persuaded that *Boughton* or *King* provides any guidance on the issue of noncompetition agreements, largely because neither involved noncompetition agreements in the employment context. However, to the extent they are inconsistent with our analysis, we disapprove *Boughton* and *King*.

I. BACKGROUND

According to Plaintiff's allegations, Plaintiff HSI "is in the business of marketing, distributing, and selling medical, dental and veterinary supplies and equipment, and other healthcare products, to medical, dental, and veterinary practitioners, and other healthcare professionals and organizations." Defendant Cook was hired as a "Field Sales Consultant" with HSI in April 2005, and entered into a Confidentiality and Non-Solicitation Agreement in 2005, as well as a Letter Agreement in 2011 that required her to hold "in strictest confidence" any confidential information "concerning the products, processes, services, business, suppliers, and customers of HSI," and to "neither copy nor take any such material upon leaving Company's employ." Cook resigned from HSI on May 13, 2016, and began working for one of HSI's competitors, Patterson Dental ("Patterson").

Plaintiff alleges that prior to leaving HSI, Cook "began to loot HSI's confidential, proprietary, and trade secret documents and information with the apparent goal of diverting HSI's customers." On May 10, Cook forwarded from her work email account, to her personal email, "several comprehensive, confidential HSI customer practice reports that were produced using HSI's proprietary software," which all "contained a wide array of confidential and trade secret information." On May 12, 2016, the day before she resigned, Cook forwarded "numerous additional customer-related reports, including an equipment inventory report, price quotations for prospective customers, and equipment proposals on which HSI was working." On May 13, Cook "logged into HSI's system with HSI's proprietary 'FSC' computer program," which "had the effect of 'updating' onto Cook's laptop, substantial, specific, customer related sales and ordering data from the HSI computer system." She then failed to return her laptop to HSI for two weeks. On May 14, the day after she resigned, Cook "unlawfully accessed the HSI computer system, this time using a web-based 'iPad app' and her company credentials." This type of access "would enable Cook to obtain on her iPad, large amounts of ordering and purchase data for each of the HSI customers that had been assigned to her."

Cook also attempted to erase the e-mails that she sent from her HSI computer. Before her resignation, Cook "also attempted to divert HSI customers to Patterson," and "visited the offices of certain HSI customers, deleted the HSI product ordering icon from their computer systems and destroyed HSI catalogues and business cards."

On June 9, 2016, the same day HSI applied for a TRO, Plaintiff filed a complaint alleging eight causes of action: (1) Misappropriation of Trade Secrets Under the Defend Trade Secrets Act (DTSA), 18 U.S.C. §1836, et seq.; (2) Misappropriation of Trade Secrets Under the California Uniform Trade Secrets Act (CUTSA), Cal. Civ. Code §3426, et seq.; (3) Breach of Fiduciary Duty and Duty of Loyalty; (4) Breach of Written Contract; (5) Breach of Implied Covenant of Good Faith and Fair Dealing; (6) Tortious Interference with Prospective Economic Advantage; (7) Violation of California Unfair Competition Law (UCL); (8) Violation of California Penal Code §502. Plaintiff also filed a declaration stating it attempted service of the complaint and application for TRO by e-mailing a copy to Cook's personal e-mail address and causing copies to be hand-delivered to Cook's last known home address.

II. JURISDICTION

This Court has jurisdiction over this action pursuant to the DTSA and 28 U.S.C. §1331, and supplemental jurisdiction over Plaintiff's remaining claims pursuant to 28 U.S.C. §1367. Further, a federal district court may issue an injunction to preserve the status quo even when subject matter jurisdiction is disputed or unclear.

III. LEGAL STANDARD

The same legal standard applies to a motion for a temporary restraining order and a motion for a preliminary injunction. A plaintiff seeking either remedy "must establish that he is likely to succeed on the merits, that he is likely to suffer irreparable harm in the absence of preliminary relief, that the balance of equities tips in his favor, and that an injunction is in the public interest." Injunctive relief is "an extraordinary remedy that may only be awarded upon a clear showing that the plaintiff is entitled to such relief."

To grant preliminary injunctive relief, a court must find that "a certain threshold showing is made on each factor." Provided that this has occurred, in balancing the four factors, " 'serious questions going to the merits' and a balance of hardships that tips sharply towards the plaintiff can support issuance of a preliminary injunction, so long as the plaintiff also shows that there is a likelihood of irreparable injury and that the injunction is in the public interest."

In addition, a movant seeking the issuance of an ex parte TRO must satisfy Federal Rule of Civil Procedure 65(b), which requires a showing "that immediate and irreparable injury, loss, or damage will result to the movant before the adverse party can be heard in opposition" and certification of "efforts made to give notice and the reasons why it should not be required."

IV. DISCUSSION

Plaintiff requests a TRO that prevents Cook from "accessing, using, disclosing, or making available" any of HSI's confidential data, from violating any of her agreements with HSI, and from soliciting, contacting, or accepting business from any HSI customers assigned to her while she was employed by Plaintiff. In addition, Plaintiff also requests that Cook be ordered to preserve all evidence related to this case pursuant to Fed. R. Civ. Pro. 26(d)(1) and be enjoined from altering, destroying, or disposing of any materials related to this action, including any confidential information she obtained from HSI. Finally, Plaintiff requests, both in its proposed TRO and as a motion for expedited discovery, that it be allowed to obtain "mirrors" of all data stored on Cook's personal devices, and to subpoena the Patterson entities and obtain other discovery from Cook. The Court will grant Plaintiff's first two requests but deny without prejudice its request to obtain mirrors from Cook and early discovery.

A. TRO

1. Likelihood of Irreparable Injury

Plaintiff contends there is a likelihood of irreparable injury by virtue of Defendant's "exploiting or disclosing HSI's trade secret and other confidential information; violating her confidentiality obligation to HSI; or soliciting business from HSI's customers whose accounts she was assigned while at HSI." They allege that Cook had access to, and downloaded, "information related to HSI's customers, products, margins, profit percentages, credit profiles, preferences and markets, particularly with respect to the customers assigned to her," and that this data was created "using proprietary HSI software." They further allege that Cook has used this information and made other efforts to divert customers from HSI to her new employer, Patterson.

Customer information such as sales history and customer needs and preferences constitute trade secrets. Further, "[e]vidence of threatened loss of prospective customers or goodwill certainly supports a finding of the possibility of irreparable harm." Here, Plaintiff has shown there is a likelihood that it will lose established customer relationships as well as the economic value of its accumulated data on current and prospective customers. These harms would likely be irreparable. In addition, it appears this loss may occur before Cook may be heard in opposition, as Plaintiff has alleged that Cook has already misappropriated HSI's customer information and sought to solicit and divert customers.

Accordingly, Plaintiff has demonstrated a likelihood of irreparable harm.

2. Likelihood of Success on the Merits

Plaintiff has brought claims under the DTSA, CUTSA, UCL, and for breach of contract, among other claims. It contends that Defendant has used "improper means" to obtain its protected customer-related information as defined by both the DTSA and CUTSA. *See* 18 U.S.C. §1839(6) (defining "improper means" as "theft, bribery, misrepresentation, breach or inducement of a breach of a duty to maintain secrecy, or espionage through electronic or other means"); Cal. Civ. Code §3426.1(a) (defining "improper means" as "theft, bribery, misrepresentation, breach or inducement of a breach of a duty to maintain secrecy, or espionage through electronic or other means").

Plaintiff has alleged that Defendant e-mailed and downloaded, to her personal devices, confidential information from HSI before leaving her employment to work at a competitor. It has also provided copies of a Confidential and Non-Solicitation Agreement and a Letter Agreement with provisions for confidentiality and non-solicitation, both of which appear to be signed by Cook, as exhibits to its complaint. In light of these contentions, the Court concludes that Plaintiff is likely to succeed on the merits.

3. Balance of Hardships

Plaintiff contends that it "has suffered and will continue to suffer irreparable harm if Cook is allowed to continue to try to divert its customers using HSI's own confidential, proprietary, and trade secret documents and information." "By contrast, Cook will suffer no undue hardship" because she would not be prohibited from "engaging in activity that is proper." Notably, HSI has not requested that Cook be enjoined from soliciting any and all business, but rather only from soliciting HSI customers to which she was assigned — conduct that is already prohibited under the provisions of the Confidentiality and Non-Solicitation Agreement. Accordingly, the Court concludes the balance of equities tips in favor of granting the TRO.

4. Public Interest

Similarly, the public interest is served when defendant is asked to do no more than abide by trade laws and the obligations of contractual agreements signed with her employer. Public interest is also served by enabling the protection of trade secrets.

Accordingly, the Court concludes that all four factors for a TRO have been met and will grant the requested TRO prohibiting Defendant from accessing or using HSI information and from contacting or soliciting HSI customers. Plaintiff argues that no bond should be required because the TRO will not cause any damage to Cook's legitimate business, and further because she agreed, in her employment agreements with HSI, that HSI may seek injunctive relief without a bond. The Court agrees, and concludes no bond is required.

B. Document Preservation and Early Discovery

Plaintiff has also made several requests in regards to preserving materials that Cook allegedly misappropriated from HSI and evidence of this misappropriation, and to preventing Cook from attempting to destroy this evidence. First, they request that the Court order Cook to preserve all documents, data, tangible things, and other materials relating to the case, and further that she not alter, destroy, or dispose of any evidence or materials related to this case. This is a reasonable request—indeed, litigants are generally obligated to maintain and preserve all documents, data, and tangible things that may be related to the litigation, pursuant to Fed. R. Civ. Pro. 26(a) and 37(e). Accordingly, the Court will grant this request.

CONCLUSION

The Court hereby GRANTS IN PART Plaintiff's ex parte application for a temporary restraining order as follows:

1. Pursuant to Federal Rule of Civil Procedure 26(d)(1), Defendant shall immediately preserve all documents, data, tangible things, and other materials relating to this case, including, without limitation, emails, data, data bases, cloud storage, and paper and electronic data and documents, including any and all metadata, and shall take all steps necessary to do so.

2. Defendant, and all those acting in concert or participation with her, are hereby enjoined from altering, destroying, or disposing of any evidence or other materials, in any form, relating to this action and the issues raised herein, including, without limitation, all devices, electronic media, cloud storage, and all copies of any and all documents, media and/or other materials, containing, identifying, describing, reflecting or referencing HSI's confidential, proprietary, or trade secret information, and any and all documents, data and information which was obtained by Cook from, or by virtue of her employment with, HSI, including all current or archived media, emails, chats, texts, documents, electronic logs, metadata, storage and directories.

3. Defendant, and all those acting in concert or participation with her, are hereby enjoined from directly or indirectly accessing, using, disclosing, or making available to any person or entity other than Plaintiff, any of HSI's confidential, proprietary, or trade secret documents, data or information.

4. Defendant, and all those acting in concert or participation with her, are hereby enjoined from directly or indirectly violating or interfering with the confidentiality obligations of her agreements with HSI.

5. Defendant, and all those acting in concert or participation with her, are hereby enjoined from, directly or indirectly, soliciting, continuing to solicit, initiating contact

with, or accepting business from, any HSI customers whose accounts were assigned to her while she was employed by HSI.

6. The Court concludes that no bond need by posted by HSI.

7. The Court denies Plaintiff's request for a TRO directing a forensics expert to obtain mirrors of Plaintiff's data and personal devices. It denies without prejudice Plaintiff's request for expedited discovery. . . .

IT IS SO ORDERED.

SAMPLE PROTECTIVE ORDER

HONORABLE STEVEN GONZALEZ

IN THE SUPERIOR COURT OF THE STATE OF WASHINGTON
IN AND FOR THE COUNTY OF KING

MICROSOFT CORPORATION, a
Washington corporation,

No. 05-2-23561-6 SEA

                                           Plaintiff,

STIPULATED PROTECTIVE ORDER[6]

          v.

KAI-FU LEE and GOOGLE INC.,
a Delaware corporation,
                              Defendants.

Stipulation

IT IS HEREBY STIPULATED by and among Defendants Kai-Fu Lee and Google Inc. (the Defendant "Party" and collectively all are termed the "Parties"), of record, that this Court may enter the following "Stipulated Order") to safeguard confidential and attorneys' eyes only information as disclosed in this litigation. This Order is necessary because this case concerns Microsoft's alleged confidential, proprietary and trade secret information. Microsoft and Google may make requests for information that would call for each others' confidential, proprietary and trade secret information, and this information could lose its value if disclosed to the public or improperly used outside of this litigation. It is also likely that the Parties' confidential, proprietary and trade secret information will be submitted to the court to assist in ruling on various motions. This information could lose its value if disclosed to the public.

---

6. The stipulated protective order in *Microsoft v. Kai-Fu Lee and Google, Inc.* was amended on August 29, 2005. To view the order amending the stipulated protective order, visit the King County, Washington, government Web site at *http://www.metrokc.gov/kcsc/rulings/msgoog.htm.*

Protective Order

IT IS HEREBY ORDERED that the following Protective Order be entered in this matter and that the Parties shall follow the procedures set forth below with respect to information, documents, or things produced in this litigation:

To protect the confidentiality of proprietary and trade secret information contained in documents produced, and other information disclosed in this litigation, the Court orders as follows:

(1) This Protective Order shall be applicable to and govern all depositions, documents, information or things produced in response to requests for production of documents, answers to interrogatories, responses to requests for admissions and all other discovery taken pursuant to the Washington Civil Rules, as well as testimony adduced at trial or other hearings, matters in evidence and other information which the disclosing party designates as "CONFIDENTIAL" or "ATTORNEYS' EYES ONLY" hereafter furnished, directly or indirectly, by or on behalf of any party or any non-party witness in connection with this action. As used herein, "disclosing party" shall refer to the parties to this action and to third parties who give testimony or produce documents or other information.

(2) The following information may be designated as "CONFIDENTIAL": any trade secret or other confidential research, design, development, financial, or commercial information (as defined by Washington State law) contained in any document, discovery response or testimony;

(3) The following information may be designated as "ATTORNEYS' EYES ONLY": any trade secret or other confidential research, design, development, or commercial information contained in any document, discovery response, or deposition testimony as such terms are used in Rule 26I(7) of the Washington Rules of Civil Procedure and any applicable case law interpreting Rule 26(c)(7) that is entitled to a higher level of protection due to its commercial sensitivity.

(4) A disclosing party may also designate materials as "CONFIDENTIAL" or "ATTORNEYS' EYES ONLY" if it contains information that the disclosing party, in good faith, believes is confidential or proprietary to a third-party. Material designated "CONFIDENTIAL" or "ATTORNEYS' EYES ONLY" shall be used by the parties to this litigation solely for the purpose of conducting this litigation, and the litigation commenced in Santa Clara County Superior Court, Case No. 105-CV-045586, and removed to the United States District Court, Northern District of California, Case No. CV 05-0309 5RMW (hereinafter referred to as the "California Litigation"), but not for any other purpose whatsoever.

(5) Disclosing parties shall designate "CONFIDENTIAL" or "ATTORNEYS' EYES ONLY" information as follows:

    (a) In the case of discovery responses and the information contained therein, designation shall be made by placing the following legend on every page of any such document prior to production: "CONFIDENTIAL" or "ATTORNEYS' EYES ONLY." In the event that a party inadvertently fails to stamp or otherwise designate a document or other information as "CONFIDENTIAL" or "ATTORNEYS' EYES ONLY" at the time of its production, that party shall have five (5) business days after such production to so stamp or otherwise designate the document or other information.

(b) The parties agree to produce electronic or paper copies of responsive documents absent good cause shown to designate documents for inspection only. In the case of documents or other material to be produced for inspection, all original documents produced for inspection shall be treated as "ATTORNEYS' EYES ONLY" for a period not to exceed five (5) business days after the receiving party inspecting the documents has indicated the documents it desires to be copied. After a receiving party inspecting the documents has indicated the documents it desires to be copied, and before such copies are provided to the requesting party, the producing party shall have a reasonable time, not to exceed the aforementioned five (5) business days, to review the copied documents and designate them as "CONFIDENTIAL" or "ATTORNEYS' EYES ONLY" pursuant to the terms of this Order.

(c) In the case of depositions, designation of the portion of the transcript (including exhibits) which contains CONFIDENTIAL or ATTORNEYS' EYES ONLY information shall be made by a statement to such effect on the record in the course of the deposition or, upon review of such transcript, by counsel for the party to whose CONFIDENTIAL or ATTORNEYS' EYES ONLY information the deponent has had access. If a party wishes to designate portions of a deposition transcript under this Order after a deposition, that party's counsel shall make such designation within five (5) business days after counsel's receipt of the transcript. Counsel shall list on a separate piece of paper the numbers of the pages of the transcript containing CONFIDENTIAL or ATTORNEYS' EYES ONLY information, inserting the list at the end of the transcript, and mailing copies of the list to counsel for all parties so that it may be affixed to the face of the transcript and each copy thereof. Pending such designation by counsel, the entire deposition transcript, including exhibits, shall be deemed CONFIDENTIAL, unless counsel during the deposition states that the information is ATTORNEYS' EYES ONLY, in which case it shall be deemed ATTORNEYS' EYES ONLY. If no designation is made during the deposition or within five (5) business days after receipt of the transcript, the transcript shall be considered not to contain any CONFIDENTIAL or ATTORNEYS' EYES ONLY information.

(d) Transcripts of depositions will not be filed with the Court unless it is necessary to do so for purposes of preliminary injunction hearings, trial, motions for summary judgment, or other matters. If a deposition transcript is filed and if it contains CONFIDENTIAL or ATTORNEYS' EYES ONLY information the transcript shall bear the appropriate legend on the caption page and shall be filed under seal.

(e) Any CONFIDENTIAL or ATTORNEYS' EYES ONLY information produced in a non-paper media (e.g., videotape, audiotape, computer disk, etc.) may be designated as such by labeling the outside of such non-paper media as "CONFIDENTIAL" or "ATTORNEYS' EYES ONLY." In the event such non-paper media is transmitted via email the producing party may designate the information produced as "CONFIDENTIAL" or "ATTORNEYS' EYES ONLY" by so identifying such media in the email. In the event a receiving party generates any "hard copy," transcription, or printout from any such designated non-paper media, such party must stamp each page "CONFIDENTIAL" or "ATTORNEYS' EYES ONLY" and the hard copy, transcription or printout shall be treated as it is designated.

(6) If any information designated CONFIDENTIAL or ATTORNEYS' EYES ONLY is filed or submitted to the Court, it shall be produced in sealed envelopes or containers indicating the following:

(a) the case caption;

(b) the nature of the contents therein; or

(c) the words "CONFIDENTIAL [or ATTORNEYS' EYES ONLY] — NOT TO BE OPENED EXCEPT BY ORDER OF THE COURT."

(7) All CONFIDENTIAL information shall be used solely for the purposes of this litigation between the parties hereto, and the California Litigation, including discovery, motions, trial and hearing preparation and during trial or hearings and not for any other purpose.

(8) Disclosure of all CONFIDENTIAL information shall be limited to:

(a) The outside attorneys working on this action, and the California Litigation, on behalf of any party, and any paralegal assistants, stenographic and clerical employees working under the direct supervision of such counsel;

(b) Two in-house counsel and one in-house paralegal for both sides directly working on the litigation, as follows: For Microsoft, _____; for Google, _____, provided they execute and deliver to the other side in advance of any review of documents subject to this Order a declaration in the form attached as Exhibit B, and sign the undertaking attached as Exhibit A;

(c) Officers of the Court and supporting personnel or officers of any appellate court to which an appeal may be taken in this litigation or the California Litigation or in which review is sought, including necessary stenographic and clerical personnel (e.g. court reporters);

(d) Other qualified reporters taking and videographers recording testimony involving such information and necessary stenographic and clerical personnel thereof;

(e) Any person of whom testimony is taken regarding the CONFIDENTIAL information, except that such person may only be shown copies of CONFIDENTIAL information during his/her testimony, and may not retain a copy of such CONFIDENTIAL information;

(f) Any person who is expressly retained or sought to be retained by any outside attorney described in paragraph 8(a) to assist in preparation of this action for trial, who is not employed by, affiliated with (whether as a consultant or otherwise), controlled by, agents of, or materially interested in any party or any competitor of any party, with disclosure only to the extent necessary to perform such work;

(g) The individual defendant, and the employees of Microsoft and Google who are required to work directly on this litigation, and the California Litigation, with disclosures only to the extent necessary to perform such work.

(9) Information designated as "ATTORNEYS' EYES ONLY" shall be used solely for the purposes of this litigation between the parties hereto, and the California Litigation. "ATTORNEYS' EYES ONLY" information shall not be disclosed, except by the prior written consent of the disclosing party or third party, or pursuant to an order of this Court, to any person other than the following:

(a) The outside attorneys working on this action on behalf of any party, and the California Litigation, and any paralegal assistants, stenographic and clerical employees working under the direct supervision of such counsel;

(b) Two in-house counsel and one in-house paralegal for both sides directly working on the litigation, as follows: For Microsoft, (1) Rosemary Lumpkins, (2) Tom Burt, and (3) Erica Couch; for Google, (1) Amy J. Lambert, (2) reserved to be designated, and (3) reserved to be designated, provided they execute and deliver to the other side in advance of any review of documents subject to this Order an affidavit in the form attached as Exhibit B, and sign the undertaking attached as Exhibit A;

(c) Officers of the Court and supporting personnel or officers of any appellate court to which any appeal may be taken in this litigation or the California Litigation or in which review is sought, including necessary stenographic and clerical personnel (e.g. court reporters);

(d) Other qualified reporters taking and videographers recording testimony involving such information and necessary stenographic and clerical personnel thereof;

(e) Any person who is an author or recipient of "ATTORNEYS' EYES ONLY" material or an employee of the party producing such materials may be shown copies of such material during his or her testimony, but may not retain a copy of such information following the deposition;

(f) Any person who is expressly retained or sought to be retained by any outside attorney described in paragraph 9(a) to assist in preparation of this action for trial, who is not employed by, affiliated with (whether as a consultant or otherwise), controlled by, agents of, or materially interested in any party or any competitor of any party, with disclosure only to the extent necessary to perform such work;

(g) The individual defendant, with disclosures only to the extent necessary to aid in the defense.

(10) Nothing herein shall restrict the use of CONFIDENTIAL or ATTORNEYS' EYES ONLY information of the disclosing party by the disclosing party.

(11) Prior to disclosure of any CONFIDENTIAL information to any persons in paragraphs 8(d), 8(e), 8(f) and 8(g), and prior to disclosure of any ATTORNEYS' EYES ONLY information to any persons in paragraphs 9(d) and 9(f) the procedure set forth in paragraph 12 shall be followed.

(12) Prior to the disclosure of CONFIDENTIAL or ATTORNEYS' EYES ONLY information to persons in paragraph 8(d), 8(e), 8(f), 8(g), 9(d) or 9(f), the outside counsel in this litigation or the California Litigation for the party making the disclosure shall advise each person that the information is CONFIDENTIAL or ATTORNEYS' EYES ONLY, can only be discussed with persons authorized by this Protective Order to view the material and can only be used for purposes of this litigation, and the California Litigation. Counsel shall retain, but need not disclose, a copy of a signed undertaking of each person to whom disclosure is made under paragraphs 8(d), 8(e), 8(f), and 8(g). Counsel shall retain and disclose to the other party a copy of a signed undertaking of each person to whom disclosure is made under paragraphs 9(d) and 9(f). The written undertaking, which shall be in the form as illustrated in Exhibit A hereto, shall acknowledge that he or she has read and understands this Protective Order, agrees to comply with this Protective Order, agrees that the CONFIDENTIAL or ATTORNEYS' EYES ONLY information will be used only to assist in this litigation or in the California Litigation, and agrees not to disclose or discuss CONFIDENTIAL or ATTORNEYS' EYES ONLY information with any person other than those authorized by this Order to view the material and to use it only for the purposes of this litigation, and the California Litigation.

(13) A party shall not be obligated to challenge the propriety of a CONFIDENTIAL or ATTORNEYS' EYES ONLY designation at the time made, and failure to do so shall not preclude a subsequent challenge thereto. In the event that any party to this litigation disagrees at any stage of these proceedings with such designation, such party shall provide to the producing party written notice of its disagreement with the designation. The parties shall first try to dispose of such dispute in good faith on an informal basis. If the dispute cannot be resolved, the party challenging the designation may request appropriate relief from the Court, but in any event, such relief from the Court shall not be requested before five (5) business days after the producing party is served with said written notice.

(14) Failure of counsel to designate or mark any document, thing, or testimony as CONFIDENTIAL or ATTORNEYS' EYES ONLY information as provided above shall not preclude the disclosing party from thereafter in good faith making such designation and requesting the receiving party to so mark and treat such documents and things so designated even after the expiration of the "five (5) business days" designation period described in paragraph 5(a). The receiving party, however, shall incur no liability for disclosures made prior to notice of such designations.

(15) If CONFIDENTIAL or ATTORNEYS' EYES ONLY information is disclosed to any person other than in the manner authorized by this Protective Order, the person responsible for the disclosure shall immediately bring all pertinent facts relating to such disclosure to the attention of counsel for all parties, without prejudice to other rights and remedies of any party, and shall make every effort to prevent further disclosure by it or by the person who was the recipient of such information.

(16) The Clerk of the Court is directed to maintain under seal all documents and all transcripts of deposition testimony filed with this Court in this litigation by any party which are, in whole or in part, designated as CONFIDENTIAL or ATTOR-NEYS' EYES ONLY, including all pleadings, deposition transcripts, exhibits, discovery responses or memoranda purporting to reproduce or paraphrase such information. The person filing such material shall designate to the Clerk that all or a designated portion thereof is subject to this Protective Order and is to be kept under seal, except that upon the failure of the filing party to so designate, any party may do so.

(17) In the event that any CONFIDENTIAL or ATTORNEYS' EYES ONLY information is used in any court proceeding in connection with this litigation, it shall not lose its CONFIDENTIAL or ATTORNEYS' EYES ONLY status through such use, and the parties shall take all steps reasonably required to protect its confidentiality during such use.

(18) The inadvertent production in the course of discovery in this action of any document or information (whether designated as confidential or not) shall not be deemed to waive whatever attorney-client privilege, work product protection or other privilege or immunity that would otherwise attach to the document or information produced or to other documents or information, as long as the producing party or person, promptly after discovery, notifies the other party or parties of the claim of privilege or other protection or immunity. Upon such notice, the other party or parties shall promptly destroy all copies of the documents or information referred to and notify the producing party that it has done so. Such destruction and notice shall not constitute an acknowledgment that the claimed document or information is in fact privileged or entitled to protection or immunity.

(19) Within 60 days after the later of the final termination of this litigation and the final termination of the California Litigation, counsel for each Party shall return to the originating source, or certify in writing the destruction of, all CONFIDENTIAL and ATTORNEYS' EYES ONLY information and all copies thereof and work product created therefrom; provided, however, counsel of record for each party may petition the Court to retain one copy of each document, for good cause shown.

(20) Nothing herein shall prevent any party from moving the court for modification of this Protective Order for good cause. No party shall cite this Order, or any provision thereof, as evidence, or in support of any argument, regarding the

merits of this litigation, or for any purpose other than seeking to enforce the terms of this Order.

(21) Except as specifically provided herein, the terms, conditions, and limitations of this Protective Order shall survive the termination of this action.

(22) Nothing herein shall be deemed to constitute a waiver of any objection a producing party may have to any request for production of documents or other requested discovery. Nothing herein shall prevent any party from objecting to production of documents or objecting to other discovery requests on any available grounds, or from seeking alternative protective orders from the Court.

IT IS SO STIPULATED this _____ day of August, 2005.

[Signatures for parties' attorneys]

IT IS SO ORDERED this _____ day of August, 2005.

                                        _____
                                        HONORABLE STEVEN GONZALEZ

Paragraph 23 to Stipulated Protective Order:

The court has approved the above Stipulated Protective Order among Microsoft Corporation, Dr. Kai-Fu Lee and Google, Inc. on the following conditions:

Each time restrictions on access to hearings or records from hearings are sought, the court must follow these steps: First, the proponent of closure and/or sealing must make a sufficient showing of the need therefor; second, the intervenors and anyone present when a sealing or closure motion is made must be given an opportunity to object; third, the court, proponents and objectors should carefully analyze whether the requested method for curtailing access would be both the least restrictive means available and effective in protecting the interests threatened; fourth, the court must weigh competing interests of parties and the public and consider the alternative or less restrictive methods; and fifth, the order must be no broader in its application or duration than necessary to serve its purpose. Seattle Times Co. v. Ishikawa, 97 Wash. 2d 30, 640 P.2d 716 (Wash. 1982); Dreiling v. Jain, 151 Wash. 2d 900 (2004). Therefore, while the parties are free to designate any document, deposition, or other thing not filed with the courts as "sealed" or "confidential" or "protected" or "attorneys' eyes only" and limit its dissemination and use, each thing filed with the court must be subject to the above analysis and treatment and a court order reflecting the same and authorizing sealing must be obtained no later than the hearing in connection with which it is filed. This may be done by motion noted without oral argument and may be based on a report and recommendation from the discovery master, as previously ordered. The burden is on the party proposing that the document be sealed to provide the needed information so that the court can determine whether all, a portion or none of the documents may be filed under seal.

_____
Dated

_____
Judge Steven González

EXHIBIT A

Undertaking

I acknowledge that I, _____ (Name), of _____ (Place and Position of Employment), am about to receive confidential information supplied by _____ (Party). I certify that I understand that such confidential information will be provided to me pursuant to the terms and restrictions of the PROTECTIVE ORDER of _____, 2005, in *Microsoft Corporation v. Kai-Fu Lee and Google Inc.*, Civil Action No. 05-2-23561-6 SEA in the Superior Court of the State of Washington for the County of King. I further represent that I have been given a copy of and have read that PROTECTIVE ORDER, and that I agree to be bound by all of its applicable terms. I also understand that documents and/or information having any CONFIDENTIAL or ATTORNEYS' EYES ONLY designation, and all copies, summaries, notes and other records that may be made regarding such documents and/or information, shall be disclosed to no one other than persons qualified under the PROTECTIVE ORDER to have access to such information.

I understand and acknowledge that violation of this Undertaking or the PROTECTIVE ORDER may be punishable by Contempt of Court.

DATED this _____ day of _____, 2005.

By: _____

EXHIBIT B

Declaration of Inside Counsel/Paralegal I, _____, state and declare as follows:

(1) I am employed as an attorney (or paralegal) at <insert party name> and my title is <insert title>. My general job responsibilities are <insert>.

(2) I am not involved in competitive business decision making or patent prosecution with regard to the subject areas at issue in this case. More specifically, I do not participate in prosecuting patents or advise <insert company name> on competitive business decisions about the following: search technologies, business plans to market and monetize search products, natural language processing, speech research, machine learning concepts, strategies for the China market, or strategies to compete with <insert adverse party's name>.

(3) I further agree not to assume any responsibility for competitive business decision making or patent prosecution with regard to the subject areas at issue in this case (described in paragraph 2 above) for at least twelve months following the earlier of: (a) the conclusion of this case and the California Litigation (whichever is later), or (b) my leaving <insert party name>'s employment.

(4) I have reviewed the Stipulated Protective Order. I understand the obligations the Protective Order imposes on anyone who is given access to Confidential or Attorneys' Eyes Only information and I will fulfill those obligations.

(5) If I leave <insert party name>'s employ, I agree to destroy or return to outside counsel for <insert party name> all confidential information obtained by virtue of my access to materials as in-house counsel (or paralegal) for <insert party name> under the protective order in this case.

I hereby declare, under penalty of perjury under the laws of the State of Washington, that the foregoing is true and correct.

EXECUTED at _____ [CITY], _____ [STATE].

DATED:_____   _____
                                       [Signature]

III. PROBLEMS

1. Penalty Strike conceived of a beverage label marketing and production process known as "Magic Windows." Magic Windows consisted of the following: a scrambled message on the inside of a beverage container label that could be decoded and read only after the beverage container was emptied. The message would be read through a colored filter printed on a label on the opposite side of the container, directly across from the coded message. Representatives from Penalty Strike met with the Carmel Cola Company (CCC) to demonstrate Magic Windows. Penalty Strike orally advised CCC representatives that the information concerning Magic Windows was confidential, and the representatives regarded it as such. Penalty Strike also advised CCC that Penalty Strike was pursuing global patent protection on Magic Windows, and thus would be in a position to provide CCC the exclusive rights to the Magic Windows marketing tool. The parties executed a *Non-Disclosure Agreement* in which each agreed not to disclose to any third party any confidential information shared during discussions regarding Magic Windows. However, the agreement went on to provide:

> [T]here is no obligation to maintain in confidence any information that:
>
> (i) at the time of disclosure is available to the public;
> (ii) after disclosure, becomes available to the public by publication or otherwise;
> (iii) is in [CCC's or its subsidiaries' or affiliates' possession], at the time of disclosure [];
> (iv) is rightfully received from a third party; [or] . . .
> (v) CCC can establish was subsequently developed independently by [CCC or its subsidiaries or affiliates] independently of any disclosure hereunder.

After the execution of the agreement, CCC drafted a *Development and License Agreement* in which, among other things, CCC proposed to pay Penalty Strike $1 million and a per label royalty for a global license giving CCC the exclusive right to use Magic Windows. Along with sending its proposed license agreement, however, CCC undertook an intellectual property review of Penalty Strike's patent applications. In the course of that review, CCC unearthed a copy of the Virtual Image patent application revealing the two main concepts of Magic Windows — using a colored filter to decode a disguised message and placing the filter on the side of a bottle label opposite the coded message — already existed in prior art. In view of this development CCC terminated all negotiations.

CCC met with its regular printer for labels used on CCC's products in Argentina to discuss a windows label promotion in Argentina. CCC discussed the concept of the window label in general terms, showed the printer a mock-up of a bottle with a label, and asked about the capability of manufacturing such a label. The printer informed CCC it could produce the label and it set out to do so.

The printer independently determined the type of printing press, inks, color sequences, and production processes needed; constructed the scrambled text on the label; planned the print formula; selected the film to use as a substrate for the label; chose the color to use on the filter; figured out how to block the scrambled message from being read from the outside; picked the weight and tone of the ink; established the printing setup; and decided whether to print on the surface or reverse print the label. CCC subsequently used the label in an Argentinean marketing promotion.

Penalty Strike learned of the Argentinean promotion. After viewing one of the CCC bottles, Penalty Strike was alarmed by (what it perceived to be) the striking similarity between its Magic Windows label and the bottle label developed by CCC's printer. Penalty Strike contacted CCC to determine whether CCC had used the information Penalty Strike had shared to help create the CCC label. When CCC denied any wrongdoing, Penalty Strike filed suit.

1.1 Did Carmel Cola Co. misappropriate Penalty Strike's trade secret? Why or why not?

1.2 Will CCC be able to persuade the trier of fact that Penalty Strike's confidential information was in fact available to the public? *See* Penalty Kick Mgmt., Ltd. v. Coca-Cola Co., 318 F.3d 1284 (11th Cir. 2003).

1.3 If Penalty Strike and CCC had executed the license agreement and CCC exceeded the scope of the license, would Penalty Strike be limited to an action for breach of contract or would Penalty Strike also be able to maintain a claim for trade secret misappropriation? *See* McRoberts Software, Inc. v. Media 100, Inc., 2001 WL 1224727 (S.D. Ind. 2001).

2. Problem 1 demonstrates trade secret misappropriation in the context of two private parties. Consider trade secret misappropriation in the context where one party happens to be the U.S. Government. Generally, the U.S. Government enjoys sovereign immunity arising from certain torts committed by federal employees in the scope of their employment. In addition, even if the U.S. Government has waived sovereign immunity pursuant to the Federal Tort Claims Act (FTCA), *see* 28 U.S.C. §§1346(b), 2674 (2000), the U.S. Government continues to enjoy exceptions to liability, namely the discretionary function exception and the intentional tort exception. *See* 28 U.S.C. §2680. Despite sovereign immunity and potential exceptions to tort liability pursuant to the FTCA, will the U.S. Government be liable for trade secret misappropriation and breach of a confidential relationship if it induces trade secret disclosure and then divulges that information to others? *See* Jerome Stevens Pharms., Inc. v. Food & Drug Admin., 402 F.3d 1249 (D.C. Cir. 2005).

3. Papier Copy Co. (PCC) entered into a license agreement with M. Louis, an inventor of paper collating machines. The license agreements gave PCC the right to manufacture and sell paper-handling machines. In exchange, Louis received the right to royalties on each machine manufactured and sold. Louis applied for a patent on the machine that was the subject of the license agreement. PCC was the sole and exclusive licensee and it began manufacturing the paper handling

machines before the eventual issuance of Louis's patent. The license specifically provided that PCC was to begin manufacture and development of the machines solely by virtue of Louis's disclosure to it of the principles of the technical and manufacturing know how necessary for the commercial production of the machines. In addition PCC could not assign or sublicense the manufacture of the machines, unless such manufacturer agreed in writing to keep secret all confidential information relating to the machine, its parts, or its attachments.

3.1 Does the license agreement anticipate licensing patent rights only, trade secret rights only, or both?

3.2 Assume the license agreement is silent as to post-patent expiration royalty payments, should Louis continue to receive royalty payments for PCC's continued manufacture of the machines?

3.3 What factors could Louis raise to persuade a court that he was not engaged in patent misuse and, therefore, should be entitled to post-patent expiration royalty payments? *See* Pitney Bowes, Inc. v. Mestre, 701 F.2d 1365 (11th Cir. 1983).

4. Jurisdictions vary as to the validity and enforceability of provisions in contracts that restrict the ability of an employee to compete with the former employer. Some states allow such restrictions provided they are reasonable. California law, however, specifically makes such provisions invalid and unenforceable, except in certain narrow situations, like unfair competition. *See* Cal. Bus. & Prof. Code §16600 (stating, "Except as provided in this chapter, every contract by which anyone is restrained from engaging in a lawful profession, trade, or business of any kind is to that extent void.").

Consider the Confidentiality and Non-Compete agreements that follow:

Confidentiality Agreement

You recognize that the Company's Confidential Information is extremely valuable to it and that disclosure or use of Confidential Information outside the Company could irreparably damage the Company. You therefore agree that you will not use any Confidential Information for any purpose other than to benefit the Company. In furtherance of that commitment you will disclose Confidential Information to other persons within the Company only if they have a need to know the information in order to perform their job responsibilities for the Company and will not disclose Confidential Information to any person outside the Company. . . . You understand and agree that your confidentiality obligations under this paragraph will continue after termination of your employment with the Company, regardless of the reason for the termination, as long as the information is not generally known to the public.

Non-Compete Agreement

You recognize that the Company's business is very competitive and that to protect its Confidential Information the Company expects you not to compete with it for a period of time. You therefore agree that during your employment with the Company, and for a period of twelve (12) months after termination of your employment with the Company, regardless of the reason for the termination, you will not work for or otherwise actively participate in any business on behalf of any Competitor in which you could benefit the Competitor's business or harm the Company's business by using or disclosing Confidential Information. This restriction shall apply only in the geographic areas for which you had work-related responsibility during the last twelve (12) months of your employment by the Company and in any other geographic area in which you could benefit the Competitor's business through the use or disclosure of Confidential Information.

Are the above provisions enforceable? Why or why not? *See* Estee Lauder Cos., Inc. v. Batra, 2006 WL 1188183 (S.D.N.Y. 2006). (Courts must weigh the need to protect the employer's legitimate business interests against the employee's concern regarding the possible loss of livelihood, a result strongly disfavored by public policy in New York. A covenant that is reasonable in time and geographic scope shall be enforced to the extent necessary "(1) to prevent an employee's solicitation or disclosure of trade secrets, (2) to prevent an employee's release of confidential information regarding the employer's customers, or (3) in those cases where the employee's services to the employer are deemed special or unique.")

4.1 What public policy concerns are various states addressing by generally making non-compete agreements invalid or unenforceable? *See* Whyte v. Schlage Lock Co., 125 Cal. Rptr. 2d 277, 101 Cal. App. 4th 1443 (2002) (holding, "The inevitable disclosure doctrine, in which a plaintiff may prove a claim of trade secret misappropriation by demonstrating that defendant's new employment will inevitably lead him to rely on the plaintiff's trade secrets, is not the law in California; the doctrine creates a de facto covenant not to compete and runs counter to the strong public policy favoring employee mobility, and when a confidentiality agreement is in place, the inevitable disclosure doctrine in effect converts the confidentiality agreement into such a covenant not to compete after the employment contract is made, and therefore alters the employment relationship without the employee's consent.").

4.2 If some jurisdictions are guided by California's view that the inevitable disclosure doctrine is not recognized because it results in an unenforceable covenant not to complete, why might these same jurisdictions consider implementing an exception for the protection of trade secrets? *See* Merck & Co., Inc. v. Lyon, 941 F. Supp. 1443, 1460 (M.D.N.C. 1996) (holding that the inevitable disclosure theory can be applied under North Carolina law, where (1) injunction is limited to protecting specifically defined trade secrets and (2) the trade secret is clearly identified and of significant value). Will California courts change their approach in not recognizing the inevitable disclosure doctrine in light of DTSA?

4.3 Does *Edwards v. Arthur Andersen LLP* leave unanswered the issue whether a non-compete or non-solicitation provision can be enforced if its purpose is to protect trade secrets? Short of proposing additional legislative exceptions to section 16600, how should employers approach drafting employment agreements with prospective employees? *See* Retirement Group v. Galante, 176 Cal. App. 4th 1226, 1238, 98 Cal. Rptr. 3d 585, 593 (Cal. App. 2009) and Dowell v. Biosense Webster, Inc., 179 Cal. App. 4th 564, 575, 102 Cal. Rptr. 3d 1, 8 (Cal. App. 2009).

5. Review the sample long-form Nondisclosure Agreement (Mutual) in the Overview section of this chapter.

    5.1 Is this agreement sufficient to protect trade secrets, while still facilitating the sharing of confidential information? Is the NDA too onerous for this purpose? Is it too porous?

    5.2 With respect to the residuals clause at 1(c), determine whether the clause adequately protects the trade secret owner from inadvertent disclosure of the trade secret.

    5.3 Which provisions of the NDA grant permission to use trade secrets? Why is this perspective important?

6. MellowWare is a small software company operating out of a block of rented apartments in North Bend, Washington. MellowWare prides itself on its relaxed culture. Employees come and go as they please, often telecommute, and can be found brainstorming ideas and writing code at local coffee houses as well as at their quarterly off-site "think retreats." Not only does this culture allow MellowWare to attract bright employees in a competitive job market, it is one of the keys to its cutting edge creativity and nimbleness. BestComputer is a large computer hardware corporation with headquarters in a tall office building in Boston, Massachusetts. BestComputer prides itself on its professional, organized, and efficient culture. All employees keep a black leather bound copy of *The Best Practices* on their desks as a constant reminder of BestComputer's rigorous policies and procedures, including its trade secret protection policy.

    The companies would like to collaborate on new mobile phone technology and must agree on appropriate measures to protect trade secrets that might be exchanged in the course of their business relationship. BestComputer insists that all confidential materials must be marked "CONFIDENTIAL" and that all buildings must be limited to employee card key access only. Should MellowWare agree to these measures? Are any compromises possible and advisable?

7. Review the sample protective order in the Materials section of this chapter.

    7.1 Does the protective order adequately facilitate the sharing of information with outside counsel?

    7.2 Under the protective order, which individuals should have access to the trade secrets in the event of litigation?

IV. DRAFTING EXERCISES

1. You are the attorney for Louis in the license transaction between Louis and PCC discussed in Problem 3 above. Draft a license provision(s) that will protect the

vitality of the royalty payments to be received for use of the trade secret even after the expiration of the patent.

2. You are in-house counsel for Omnipotent Pharmacal Co. (OPC), the nation's fastest growing pharmaceutical research and development for-profit corporation. Your supervising attorney has asked you to review the company's standard license grant provision for licensees and sub-licensees of OPC. In particular, you are told that OPC will begin research and distribution collaborations internationally in the next quarter. Your supervising attorney has also communicated that in-house researchers are eager to learn how various licensees might advance the processes of preparing related Vaccines. Evaluate the license grant provision and provide feedback in the form of comments as to what should be added or deleted from the standard provision. The provision follows:

> Omnipotent Pharmacal Company ("OPC") grants to "Licensee" an exclusive right and license to use the "Strain/Process" and "related Know How" to make, have made, use, and sell the Drug Vaccine in all domestic markets. "Know How" is defined as technical information, formulas, and processes regarding preparation and propagation of the "Strain/Drug" and commercial production of the Vaccine, which are presently in the possession of OPC.

3. To beat your supervising attorney to the punch, you decide to re-draft the trade secret license grant provision in anticipation of OPC's entry into international markets. Draft the trade secret license grant provision that will accompany your comments to Drafting Exercise 2. Make sure to consider OPC's access to improvements upon the original trade secret and keep in mind whether or not the improvements are the subject matter of trade secret protection or some other form of intellectual property.

4. Re-draft the "residuals" clause in the Nondisclosure Agreement (Mutual) in the Overview section of this chapter so that it provides greater trade secret protection for the trade secret owner.

5. Add additional confidential protection measures to the Nondisclosure Agreement (Mutual) in the Overview section of this chapter so that it provides greater trade secret protection for the trade secret owner.

· CHAPTER ·

8

COPYRIGHT LICENSING

I. OVERVIEW OF COPYRIGHT LICENSING

A. Introduction

The creation and distribution of copyrighted works often involve copyright licenses. Copyright licenses are used in countless scenarios from fine arts, music, theatre, motion pictures, books, software, cloud services, and Web site designs to advertising and marketing materials. Copyright licensing can be a relatively simple or a very complex arrangement, depending on the circumstances. For example, Charlie Brown and the other Peanuts characters are now owned and licensed by a partnership between the Iconix Brand Group and Charles Schulz's family.

Various terms are used for "copyright license." A film producer seeks *cover* for various songs and recordings used in a movie. An author obtains a *clearance* to include an excerpt from an existing novel in her manuscript. A magazine receives a *waiver* from a photographer for the use of a photograph accompanying a soon to be published article.

Copyright licenses also come in various forms. Once upon a time, in Hollywood, copyright license agreements were often oral because the "[m]oviemakers do lunch, not contracts" and are "too absorbed in developing joint creative endeavors to focus on the legal niceties of copyright licenses." Effects Associates, Inc. v. Cohen, 908 F.2d 555, 558 (9th Cir. 1990). Instead of an oral agreement, today's movie producers rely on written contracts. A movie producer may enter into a one-page letter agreement granting a non-exclusive license to use a photograph in a particular film. Or the same movie producer may enter into a complicated licensing agreement where various rights are granted for use in the manufacture of different products based on the film's characters to be distributed in different markets. The movie producer may decide to reserve its rights for future technologies because the rapid changes in technology may open new fields of use and distribution channels.

B. Assignment Versus License of Copyrights

The ownership of a copyright may be transferred in whole or in part; such transfer must be executed in writing and signed by the copyright holder. *See* 17 U.S.C. §204. This is called an assignment of the copyright. The recordation of a copyright transfer with the Copyright Office is voluntary. If the transfer is not recorded, the new holder may lose its priority in the ownership of the copyright to a subsequent bona fide purchaser who records the transfer, pays for value, and has no notice of the holder's earlier transfer. *See* 17 U.S.C. §205. Unlike patent and trademark laws, copyright law provides reversion of copyright assignments. The assignee can terminate a copyright assignment after a certain period of time by following the required procedure as set in the statutory provision. *See* Baldwin v. EMI Fesit Catalog, Inc., 805 F.3d 18 (2d. Cir. 2015), which is included in the Materials section.

Copyright assignments are used in many contexts, but one common use is to re-allocate ownership of commissioned works because these works may be owned, upon creation, by the independent contractor (as opposed to the person who paid for the work) under the work for hire doctrine. For example, in the sample provision below, the parties anticipate that copyrighted works may be developed in the context of creating advertisements. The sample provision addresses work for hire ownership and assignment:

> **OWNERSHIP OF ADVERTISEMENTS.** All layouts, sketches, and copy used in advertisements ("Advertising Materials") placed or to be placed by Licensee or third parties on Licensee's behalf concerning Licensed Products and the Property shall be considered specially commissioned "Works Made for Hire" and shall become the exclusive property of Licensor upon expiration or termination of this Agreement. In the event that the Advertising Materials are not copyrightable subject matter or for any reason are deemed not to be Works Made For Hire, then and in such event, by this Agreement Licensee hereby assigns all right, title, and interest to said Advertising Materials to Licensor and agrees to execute all documents required to evidence such assignment. Thereafter Licensor shall have the full and free right to use any and all such Advertising Materials in any way deemed by Licensor to be necessary or advisable, either directly or through agents or otherwise without payment of any compensation to Licensee.

The holder of a copyright can license to others the exclusive or non-exclusive right to use the copyright. For example, the author of a novel can grant the exclusive right to make movies based on the novel to a producer worldwide and the merchandising right based on the characters in the novel to a third party outside the United States. In some cases, granting an exclusive license of the statutory rights may be deemed as a transfer of copyright ownership. *See* Radio Televisión Española v. New World Entertainment, Ltd., 183 F.3d 922 (9th Cir. 1999).

Below is a sample provision of a copyright license grant:

> During the term, in the Territory, on the terms and subject to the conditions hereinafter set forth, Licensor hereby grants to Licensee the exclusive right to use and reproduce, and Licensee hereby undertakes to use and reproduce the Designs in connection with the manufacture, distribution, marketing, and sale of the Products.

A copyright holder may decide to license a copyright on a non-exclusive basis to several licensees. A copyright holder may prefer non-exclusive arrangements because the holder will not have to rely on only one licensee to exploit the copyright. The holder may believe that non-exclusive arrangements with several licensees will widen the reach of the copies of the copyrighted work. Generally, a non-exclusive licensee has no standing to bring an infringement action; it must join the holder as co-plaintiff in such suit. *See* Radio Televisión Española v. New World Entertainment, Ltd., 183 F.3d 922 (9th Cir. 1999); Konigsberg Int'l Inc. v. Rice, 16 F.3d 355, 356-57 (9th Cir. 1994); Effects Assocs., Inc. v. Cohen, 908 F.2d 555, 556-58 (9th Cir. 1990).

Below is a provision for a non-exclusive license to copy and create derivative works for internal use. In this provision the parties agree that the licensor will own the copyright in both the original and the derivative works:

> Licensor hereby grants Licensee a non-exclusive right to copy certain materials described in Attachment A (the "Material"), in whole or in part, and to incorporate the Material, in whole or in part, into other works (the "Derivative Works") for Licensee's internal use only. All right, title, and interest in the Material, including without limitation, any copyright, shall remain with Licensor. Licensor shall own the copyright in the Derivative Works.

C. New Medium of Expression and Derivative Works

Similar to the licensing of other types of intellectual property, the scope of the license grant is the most important aspect of the copyright license agreement. The licensor and the licensee must determine the proper boundaries of the grant. The boundaries consist of the duration, licensed territory, new works to be created, and which exclusive right(s) will be granted. Complicating the construction of the boundaries is that a copyrighted work can be expressed in different media currently known or available in the future. The rapid change in technology facilitates the growth in mediums such as records, tapes, videocassettes, CDs, DVDs, television, motion picture, and Web-based and digital hardware devices, among others. Problems arise when parties to a licensing arrangement seek to ascertain whether the licensed work is authorized to be copied, distributed, or broadcast in a new medium that was not specified in the license agreement.

In some cases, the new-use licensing turns on the foreseeability of the new channels of distribution at the time of contracting. For example, in *Boosey & Hawkes Music Publishers, Ltd. v. Walt Disney Co.*, the Second Circuit explained that the license agreement extended to video format distribution because the "new-use license hinges on the foreseeability of the new channels of distribution at the time of contracting . . . [and that] Disney has proffered unrefuted evidence that a nascent market for home viewing of feature films existed by 1939." 145 F.3d 481, 486 (2d Cir. 1998). In other cases, the courts will take the approach that license grants should not extend beyond permissions expressly granted and clearly understood on the effective date of the license.

D. Statutory Termination of Copyright Licenses

Generally, a copyright license agreement contains a duration provision and expires at the end of the duration. When the licensor is an individual author, the copyright statute has a termination provision that allows the individual author licensor a window period to terminate existing license agreement with indefinite duration. Section 203 of the Copyright Act relieves individual authors of the consequences of "ill-advised and unremunerative grants that had been made before the author had a fair opportunity to appreciate the true value of the work by permitting the authors to terminate existing license agreements." Mills Music, Inc. v. Snyder, 469 U.S. 153, 172-73 & n.39 (1985). The author can terminate exclusive or non-exclusive licenses and recapture their rights at any time during the five-year period beginning 35 years after the date of the grant. If the grant covers the right of publication, the termination period begins at the end of 35 years from the date of publication of the work or at the end of 40 years from the date of execution of the grant, whichever term ends earlier. Circuit courts are split on the issue of whether Section 203 imposes a minimum term of 35 years on licenses of indefinite duration that would otherwise be subject to earlier termination under state contract law. See Korman v. HBC Florida, Inc., 182 F.3d 1291, 1293-94 (11th Cir. 1999); compare Baldwin v. EMI Fesit Catalog, Inc., 805 F.3d 18 (2d Cir. 2015).

Procedurally, notice to terminate the grant must be served on the grantee during the period of two to ten years prior to the effective date of termination. The notice must contain the effective date of termination and such date must fall within the five-year period provided under the statute. A copy of the notice to terminate must be recorded with the Copyright Office prior to the effective date of termination.

In the event that a derivative work had been prepared under authority of the license before the termination occurs, the derivative work may continue per the terms of the license grant after its termination. However, after the termination, such privilege does not extend to the preparation of other derivative works based upon the copyrighted work covered by the terminated grant.

E. Copyright Compulsory Licenses

When Congress enacted the Copyright Act of 1909, it was concerned that exclusivity with respect to musical compositions would give rise to "a great music monopoly." H.R. Rep. No. 2222, 60th Cong., 2d Sess. 6 (1909). It enacted a compulsory license provision which required the copyright owner to license the right to record songs on phonograph records. We call these "mechanical licenses," and that name continues despite drastic changes in recording technology since 1909.

The compulsory mechanical license concept was later embodied in Section 115 of the Copyright Act of 1976. Section 115 permits anyone who would like to record a copyrighted nondramatic musical work to do so by paying the statutory payments and strictly observing the statutory requirements. The licensee, under the compulsory license provision, does not have to seek the consent of the copyright owner. There is no fear of copyright infringement, as long as the potential licensee observes the strict requirements under the compulsory license provision. If the licensee fails to follow the requirements described in the compulsory licensing provision under copyright law, the licensee's use of the song is an act of copyright infringement. *See* 24/7 Records, Inc. v. Sony Music Entertainment, Inc., 429 F.3d 39 (2d Cir. 2005) (noting that the licensee foreclosed the possibility of obtaining a compulsory license because it mailed the notice of intent to obtain a compulsory license to Sony two days after the distribution of the Ketchup Song).

F. Copyright Licensing, Misuse, and Antitrust

A copyright holder has the right to license or not to license its copyrights to others. The refusal to license its copyrights to others in and of itself does not amount to an antitrust violation. Image Technical Services, Inc. v. Eastman Kodak Co., 125 F.3d 1195, 1216 (9th Cir. 1997).

Though the copyright holder is free to use its copyright in whatever ways it wishes, the copyright holder cannot use its copyright in a manner contrary to public policy embodied in the grant of copyright. For example, the copyright holder may be found in violation of the copyright misuse doctrine where its license to use the copyrights prohibits the licensee from creating competing products. *See* Lasercomb America, Inc. v. Reynolds, 911 F.2d 970, 979 (4th Cir. 1990) (holding the copyright holder misused its copyright by including in licensing agreements a provision that neither the licensee company nor its officers and employees could develop competing goods for the term of the agreement, plus 99 years). The *Lasercomb* case can be found in the Materials section of Chapter 9.

The doctrine of copyright misuse provides a defense to copyright infringement. A finding of copyright misuse, however, does not invalidate the underlying copyright, but precludes copyright enforcement until the misuse has been purged. Also, a defendant in a copyright infringement suit need not prove an antitrust violation to prevail on a copyright misuse defense. *See* Practice Management Information Corp. v. American Medical Association, 121 F.3d 516 (9th Cir. 1997).

Compared to the patent misuse doctrine developed through both statutory and case law, the copyright misuse doctrine is not well developed. Further, some courts have expressed their skepticism in the copyright misuse doctrine. *See* Video Pipeline, Inc. v. Buena Vista Home Entertainment, Inc., 342 F.3d 191, 203 (3d Cir. 2003) ("Neither the Supreme Court nor this Court has affirmatively recognized the copyright misuse doctrine."). The *Video Pipeline* case can be found in the Materials section of Chapter 1. Apart from copyright misuse, the Supreme Court in *United States v. Paramount Pictures* condemned the conditioning of a copyright license where the licensor had market power. 334 U.S. 131, 156-58 (1948). The Court in that case focused on whether the copyright was used in arrangements that violated antitrust law (such as whether the licensing agreement is "reasonable"), but did not address whether a copyright was being used in a manner violative of the public policy embodied in the grant of a copyright. The Supreme Court has also upheld, against antitrust challenges, copyright licensing done by collective rights organizations such as ASCAP and BMI, as explained in the *Broadcast Music, Inc. v. Columbia Broadcast System, Inc.* case, which can be found in the Materials section of Chapter 1.

G. Litigation Issues in Copyright Licensing

1. Standing and Jurisdiction

Parties to a copyright license arrangement may want to know in advance whether the licensor or the licensee will bring an action against a third party in the event that infringement by the third party occurs. The licensee obviously does not want to see the infringement continue, particularly in a situation where the infringement directly impacts the licensee's market for the licensed products. Consequently, the licensor will receive less royalty income if the royalty scheme is dependent on the sales of licensed products.

Section 501(b) of the 1976 Copyright Act confers standing to sue for copyright infringement to "the legal or beneficial owner of an exclusive right under a copyright." 17 U.S.C. §501(b). Such owner can institute an action for infringement of the particular right while he or she is the owner of the right. *See* Righthaven LLC v. Hoehn, 716 F.3d 1166, 1170 (9th Cir. 2013) ("if a copyright owner grants an exclusive license of particular rights, only the exclusive licensee and not the original owner can sue for infringement of those rights"). A transferee without legal or beneficial interest in the copyright cannot bring an action for copyright infringement against a third party without the authorization from the copyright owner. In Silvers v. Sony Pictures Entertainment, Inc., 402 F.3d 881 (9th Cir. 2005), the court held that an assignee who holds an accrued claim for copyright infringement, but who has no legal or beneficial interest in the copyright itself, has no right to institute an action for infringement against others.

When the licensor and the licensee have a dispute related to the license arrangement, the parties will look to state contract law. The federal courts have exclusive jurisdiction over any civil action "arising under" any act of Congress relating to copyrights. Federal subject matter jurisdiction does not exist in all actions concerning a copyright; in determining whether the court has subject matter jurisdiction, the court may follow the rule outlined in T.B. Harms Co. v. Eliscu, 339 F.2d 823 (2d Cir. 1964).

2. Remedies

Generally, if a license is limited in scope and the licensee acts outside the scope of the license, the licensor can bring an action for copyright infringement. Injunctive relief is one of the most powerful remedies for infringement because it forces the licensee to stop using the works. In some cases where the breach is purely a matter of contract, the court will only find a breach of contract law, not an infringement of copyright. There are a number of remedies available to the licensor if it can establish that the licensee committed both copyright infringement and breach of contract. *See*

Kepner-Tregoe, Inc. v. Vroom, 186 F.3d 283, 289 (2d Cir. 1999), in the Materials section of this chapter.

Damages may be awarded by a court for breach of contract or copyright infringement. In rare cases, where the licensor has sufficient evidence to establish that the licensee willfully infringed the licensor's copyrights, the licensor is entitled to enhanced statutory damages. *See* MCA Television v. Feltner, 89 F.3d 766, 768 (11th Cir. 1996).

Damages are difficult to resolve in cases where damages are dependent "upon taste and fancy for success." Contemporary Mission v. Famous Music, 557 F.2d 918, 926 (2d Cir. 1977). For instance, in *Contemporary Mission* the plaintiff sued the record production company for failure to promote the records and for assigning the manufacture and distribution agreement to another entity without authorization from the plaintiff. The Second Circuit held that damages in the form of lost royalties, not lost profits, were available to the plaintiff.

H. International Issues in Copyright Licensing

1. Gray Market and First Sale

As in the international licensing of patented and trademarked goods, the importation of "parallel" or "gray" copyrighted goods has become a concern for copyright owners. A U.S. copyright owner does not want to see that copyrighted goods manufactured and distributed overseas pursuant to an agreement between the owner and the distributor become available for sale in the United States without its consent. Due to the price differential between overseas and U.S. goods, the imported goods often can be sold at lower prices through unauthorized retailers in the United States.

Section 602(a) of the Copyright Act prohibits importation into the United States of copyrighted goods manufactured and acquired outside of the United States without the authority of the owner of the copyright or its exclusive licensee. Such conduct amounts to an infringement of the exclusive right to distribute copies. The rights against the importation of "gray market" goods under Section 602(a) have some limitations. The copyright owner cannot prevent the distribution and sale of copyrighted products after the owner has completed the "first sale" of the products. For example, in Quality King Distributors, Inc. v. L'anza Research Int'l, Inc., 523 U.S. 135 (1998), the California manufacturer of hair care products made in the United States and affixed with copyrighted labels, sold its products to distributors for sale of the products in different geographic markets. The importer bought the hair care products from one of the manufacturer's overseas distributors and sold them in the United States. In other words, the products had made a roundtrip from the United States to overseas and back to the United States for retail sale. The Court held that the "first sale" exhaustion doctrine applied, allowing the gray marketer to import the goods lawfully made under U.S. copyright law back into the United States. Hence, there was no violation of the copyright owner's distribution right. *See also* Kirtsaeng v. John Wiley & Sons, Inc., 568 U.S. 519 (2013) (holding that the first sale rule applies to copies of a copyrighted work lawfully made and sold abroad).

2. Moral Rights

Another issue relating to international licensing of copyrights is moral rights. The European Union and other countries recognize moral rights of the copyright author. Moral rights exist independently of any copyright protection held in the work. They may not be contracted away in a license agreement. Countries provide varying degrees of moral rights protection. Moral rights may protect the author's personal, non-economic interests in receiving attribution for his or her work. Moral rights may protect the works from mutilation, thus preserving the original form of the copyrighted work, even after the work is sold or licensed to others. Additionally, some countries such as France recognize the right of disclosure and retraction.

The United States enacted the Visual Artists Rights Act (VARA), providing limited "moral rights" for authors of works of "visual art," but it is generally acknowledged that U.S. moral rights protection is at the low end of the range. *See* 17 U.S.C. §106A. Given the disparity in the recognition of moral rights, some copyright owners rely on contract law to protect the integrity of their copyrighted works. *See* Gilliam v. ABC, Inc., 538 F.2d 14 (2d Cir. 1976) ("courts have long granted relief for misrepresentation of an artist's work by relying on theories outside the statutory law of copyright, such as contract law.").

II. MATERIALS

The above Overview section provides you with a broad introduction to copyright licensing law and practice. The Materials below enable you to further understand how copyright law and contract law influence each other.

The first excerpt, from Rey v. Lafferty, 990 F.2d 1379 (1st Cir. 1993), illustrates how the change in technology impacts the medium of expression and distribution of the licensed copyright. The parties' dispute over whether or not the licensee's "video right" was covered by the license agreement was drafted when video technology was non-existent. The second case, Korman v. HBC Florida, Inc., 182 F.3d 1291 (11th Cir. 1999), concerns a copyright license agreement with an indefinite term. *Korman* is interesting because the license is an implied non-exclusive copyright license. The question becomes whether or not the licensor can terminate the license at will or in accordance with 17 U.S.C. §203. The next case, Baldwin v. EMI Fesit Catalog, Inc., 805 F.3d 18 (2d Cir. 2015), addresses termination of copyright assignment as provided under relevant copyright statutory provisions.

Smith v. Barnesandnoble.com, LLC, 839 F.3d 163 (2d Cir. 2016) determines the scope of the license in e-book publishing context. UMG Recordings, Inc. v. Augusto, 628 F.3d 1175 (9th Cir. 2011), focuses on whether promotional music CDs are copyright "licenses."

Similar to what you learned in Chapter 6 on the doctrine of patent misuse, the excerpt from Practice Management Information Corp. v. American Medical Ass'n, 121 F.3d 516 (9th Cir. 1997), focuses on when and how a copyright licensing arrangement can amount to copyright misuse.

The next two cases center on breach of a license agreement and violation of copyright law. Gilliam v. American Broadcasting Companies, Inc., 538 F.2d 14 (2d Cir. 1976), is an older case focusing on the concept of an author's moral rights and the licensee's unauthorized alterations of the licensor's copyrighted work. The next case is Kepner-Tregoe, Inc. v. Vroom, 186 F.3d 283 (2d Cir. 1999). It shows that when the licensee breaches the license agreement, the licensor often brings both breach of contract and copyright infringement claims against the licensee.

The last case illustrates cross-border copyright licensing arrangements and the "gray market" goods problem. Disenos Artisticos e Industriales, S.A. v. Costco Wholesale Corp., 97 F.3d 377 (9th Cir. 1996), will give you an opportunity to compare it with the "gray market" goods cases in the Patent Licensing and Trademark Licensing chapters.

REY v. LAFFERTY
990 F.2d 1379 (1st Cir. 1993)

CYR, Circuit Judge.

Margret Rey, who owns the copyright to the "Curious George" children's books, challenges an award of damages to Lafferty Harwood & Partners ("LHP") for Rey's withholding of approval of various ancillary products utilizing the "Curious George" character under their 1983 licensing agreement. LHP appeals the district court order awarding Rey damages and future royalties on certain other "Curious George" products.

BACKGROUND

"Curious George" is an imaginary monkey whose antics are chronicled in seven books, written by Margret and H.A. Rey, which have entertained readers since the 1940s. A mischievous personality consistently lands Curious George in amusing scrapes and predicaments. The more recent "monkey business"—leading to the present litigation—began in 1977 when Margret Rey granted Milktrain Productions an option to produce and televise 104 animated "Curious George" film episodes. The option agreement was contingent on Milktrain's obtaining financing for the film project, and adverted to a potential agreement to license "ancillary products," based on the "Curious George" character, once the 104 film episodes had been completed.

A. The Original Film Agreements

Milktrain approached LHP, a Canadian investment firm, to obtain financing for the project. LHP agreed to fund the venture by selling shares in the project to investors (hereinafter: the "Milktrain Agreement"); LHP and its investors were to divide a 50% share of Milktrain's profits on the films and on any future ancillary products.

With the financing commitment in place, Rey granted Milktrain and LHP a limited license "to produce (within a two-year period from the date of exercise) one hundred and four (104) four minute film episodes based on the ["Curious George"] character solely for broadcast on television" (hereinafter: the "Rey License"). Rey was to receive a fee for assisting with the editing and production of the episodes, and an additional royalty amounting to 10% of the revenues from any film telecasts. The Rey License made no mention of ancillary product rights. Nevertheless, LHP promoted the project to investors through a prospectus (hereinafter: the "1978 Private Placement Memorandum") which represented, inter alia, that "the production contract [with Rey] gives LHP the right to participate in the financing of . . . the option . . . to undertake the exploitation of other rights to 'Curious George' including manufacturing, food, licensing and other commercial areas of exploitation." . . .

On November 5, 1979, . . . a revised version of the Rey License (hereinafter: the "Revised Rey License" or "RRL") was executed, . . . and superseding the original Rey License. The RRL recited that the original Rey License had granted Milktrain and LHP the right to produce and distribute animated "Curious George" films "for television viewing," but made no mention of the "ancillary product" rights unsuccessfully sought by LHP.

C. The Ancillary Products Agreement

Production of the 104 TV episodes was completed in 1982. On January 3, 1983, an Ancillary Products Agreement (or "APA") was signed by Rey and LHP, granting LHP a general right to license "Curious George" in spin-off ("ancillary") products for a renewable term of five years. The APA defined "ancillary products" as:

> All tangible goods . . . excluding books, films, tapes, records, or video productions. . . . However, for stories already owned by [LHP] and which have been produced as 104 episodes under the license granted in the January, 1978 agreement and the November 5, 1979 revision of that agreement, [LHP] shall have the right to produce books, films, tapes, records and video productions of these episodes under this Agreement, subject to [Rey's] prior approval . . . which prior approval shall not be unreasonably withheld.

In return for these rights, Rey was to receive one-third of the royalties on the licensed products, with certain minimum annual payments guaranteed. Rey retained the right to disapprove any product, and to propose changes which would make a disapproved product acceptable to her. The APA provided, inter alia, that Rey's approval would not be withheld "unreasonably."

. . . Following the execution of the Ancillary Products Agreement, LHP assigned its licensing rights to a new subsidiary, Curgeo Enterprises, which turned its attention to licensing the "Curious George" character in various product forms. On March 27, 1984, Curgeo executed a contract with Houghton Mifflin Company to publish the 104 television film episodes in the form of a children's book series. . . . Pursuant to the contract, Houghton Mifflin published four books each year from 1984 through 1987. In 1987 . . . Houghton Mifflin extended its contract for the additional five-year term, publishing an additional four books in 1988 and again in 1989. It ceased publication of the book series in 1990, when Rey advised that the APA had been cancelled.

E. Other Product Licenses

Curgeo moved aggressively to license the "Curious George" character in other product areas as well. Beginning in 1983, the "Curious George" TV episodes were licensed to Sony Corporation, which transferred the images from the television film negatives to videotape. LHP takes the position that the Sony video license was entered pursuant to the RRL; Rey claims it is subject to the APA. . . .

When the APA came up for renewal in January 1988, LHP declined to exercise its option for an additional five-year term. Instead, the parties agreed to renew on a month-to-month basis, terminable by either party on one month's notice. Rey's royalty rate was increased to

50% (effective January 3, 1988), but with no guaranteed minimum payment. On April 10, 1989, Rey terminated the APA. LHP responded by advising that Curgeo would "continue to administer those licenses which [remained] outstanding and report to you from time to time accordingly." LHP thereupon continued to market the Sony videos and to publish the television films in book form under the Houghton Mifflin agreements. . . .

G. "Curious George" Goes to Court

On February 8, 1991, Rey filed suit against Lafferty, Curgeo and LHP, in connection with LHP's continuing, allegedly unauthorized production of the Houghton Mifflin books and Sony videos. Rey's complaint alleged violations of federal copyright, trademark and unfair-competition statutes, breach of contract, and violations of Mass. Gen. L. ch. 93A ("chapter 93A"); it sought to enjoin further violations and to recover unpaid royalties on the books and videos. . . . After a four-day bench trial, the district court found for Rey on her claims for breach of contract, ruling that the book and video licenses were governed by the APA and that Rey was entitled to recover $256,327 in royalties. . . .

DISCUSSION

A. "New Uses" and Copyright Law

For purposes of the present appeal, we accept the uncontested district court finding that the relevant video technology "was not in existence at the time that the rights" were granted under the RRL in January 1979. Consequently, it must be inferred that the parties did not specifically contemplate television "viewing" of the "Curious George" films in videocassette form at the time the RRL was signed. Such absence of specific intent typifies cases which address "new uses" of licensed materials, i.e., novel technological developments which generate unforeseen applications for a previously licensed work. See Melville B. Nimmer and David Nimmer, 3 NIMMER ON COPYRIGHT §10.10[B] at 10-85 (1992) ("NIMMER") ("the . . . fact that we are most often dealing with a later developed technological process (even if it were known in some form at the time of execution) suggests that the parties' ambiguous phraseology masks an absence of intent rather than a hidden intent which the court simply must 'find'").

Normally, in such situations, the courts have sought at the outset to identify any indicia of a mutual general intent to apportion rights to "new uses," insofar as such general intent can be discerned from the language of the license, the surrounding circumstances, and trade usage. See, e.g., Murphy v. Warner Bros. Pictures, Inc., 112 F.2d 746, 748 (9th Cir. 1940) (grant of "complete and entire" motion picture rights to licensed work held to encompass later-developed sound motion picture technology); Filmvideo Releasing Corp. v. Hastings, 446 F. Supp. 725 (S.D.N.Y. 1978) (author's explicit retention of "all" television rights to licensed work, in grant of motion picture rights predating technological advances permitting movies to be shown on television, included retention of right to show motion picture on television). Where no reliable indicia of general intent are discernible, however, courts have resorted to one of several interpretive methods to resolve the issue on policy grounds.

Under the "preferred" method, recently cited with approval in SAPC, Inc. v. Lotus Development Corp., 921 F.2d 360, 363 (1st Cir. 1990), the court will conclude, absent contrary indicia of the parties' intent, that "the licensee may properly pursue any uses which may reasonably be said to fall within the medium as described in the license." 3 NIMMER at 10-86. Under this interpretive method, the courts will presume that at least the possibility of nonspecific "new uses" was foreseeable by the contracting parties at the time the licensing agreement was drafted; accordingly, the burden and risk of drafting licenses whose language anticipates the possibility of any particular "new use" are apportioned equally between licensor and licensee.

An alternative interpretive method is to assume that a license of rights in a given medium (e.g., "motion picture rights") includes only such uses as fall within the unambiguous core meaning of the term . . . and excludes any uses which lie within the ambiguous penumbra (e.g., exhibition of motion picture film on television). Thus any rights not expressly (in this case meaning unambiguously) granted are reserved. See 3 Nimmer at 10-85. This method is intended to prevent licensees from "'reap[ing] the entire windfall' associated with the new medium," Cohen v. Paramount Pictures Corp., 845 F.2d 851, 854 (9th Cir. 1988), and is particularly appropriate in situations which involve overreaching or exploitation of unequal bargaining power by a licensee in negotiating the contract. It may also be appropriate where a particular "new use" was completely unforeseeable and therefore could not possibly have formed part of the bargain between the parties at the time of the original grant. Cohen, 845 F.2d at 854. Obviously, this method may be less appropriate in arm's-length transactions between sophisticated parties involving foreseeable technological developments; in such situations, narrow construction of license grants may afford an unjustifiable windfall to the licensor, who would retain blanket rights to analogous "new uses" of copyright material notwithstanding the breadth of the bargained-for grant. See generally 3 Nimmer at 10-85 ("it is surely more arbitrary and unjust to put the onus on the licensee by holding that he should have obtained a further clarification of a meaning which was already present than it is to hold that the licensor should have negated a meaning which the licensee might then or thereafter rely upon.").[1]

B. Video Technology as "New Use"

These fine-tuned interpretive methods have led to divergent results in cases considering the extension of television rights to new video forms. Thus, for example, in Rooney v. Columbia Pictures Industries, Inc., 538 F. Supp. 211 (S.D.N.Y.), aff'd, 714 F.2d 117 (2d Cir. 1982), the court determined that a series of contracts granting motion picture distributors a general license to exhibit plaintiffs' films "by any present or future methods or means" and "by any means now known or unknown" fairly encompassed the right to distribute the films by means of later-developed video technology. Similarly, in Platinum Record Co. v. Lucasfilm, Ltd., 566 F. Supp. 226, 227 (D.N.J. 1983), the court held that videocassette rights were encompassed by a broad synchronization license to "exhibit, distribute, exploit, market, and perform [a motion picture containing licensed musical composition] . . . perpetually throughout the world by any means or methods now or hereafter known." Again, the court rested its holding on the "extremely broad and completely unambiguous" contractual grant of general rights to

---

1. The problem becomes particularly acute when the analogous technology develops so rapidly as to supplant the originally contemplated application of the licensed work, rendering the parties' original bargain obsolete. Thus, for example, broad grants of "motion picture rights," made before technological advances permitted the combination of moving images with sound, later were held, typically, to encompass the rights to sound motion picture technology; a narrower holding would have left the original license virtually worthless, despite its broad language, and would have provided the licensor with an undeserved windfall.

applications of future technologies, which was held to "preclude[ ] any need in the Agreement for an exhaustive list of specific potential uses of the film." *Id.*

By contrast, in *Cohen*, 845 F.2d at 853-54, the Ninth Circuit concluded that a 1969 contract granting rights to "[t]he exhibition of [a] motion picture [containing a licensed work] . . . by means of television," but containing a broad restriction reserving to the licensor "all rights and uses in and to said musical composition, except those herein granted," did not encompass the right to revenues derived from sales of the film in videocassette form. After deciding that "[t]he general tenor of the [contract] section [in which the granting clause was found] contemplate[d] some sort of broadcasting or centralized distribution, not distribution by sale or rental of individual copies to the general public," see id. at 853, the court stressed that the playing of videocassettes, with their greater viewer control and decentralized access on an individual basis, did not constitute "exhibition" in the sense contemplated by the contract. Id. at 853-54.

Most recently, in Tele-Pac, Inc. v. Grainger, 570 N.Y.S.2d 521, *appeal dismissed*, 588 N.E.2d 99 (1991), the court held (one judge dissenting) that a license to distribute certain motion pictures "for broadcasting by television or any other similar device now known or hereafter to be made known" did not encompass the videocassette film rights. "Transmission of sound and images from a point outside the home for reception by the general public . . . is implicit in the concept of 'broadcasting by television.' Conversely, while one may speak of 'playing,' 'showing,' 'displaying,' or even perhaps 'exhibiting' a videotape, we are unaware of any usage of the term 'broadcasting' in that context." Id. 570 N.Y.S.2d at 523. . . .

C. Video Rights and the RRL

Although the question is extremely close, under the interpretive methodology outlined above we conclude that the RRL's grant of rights to the 104 film episodes "for television viewing" did not encompass the right to distribute the "Curious George" films in videocassette form. First, unlike the contracts in *Rooney* and *Lucasfilm*, the RRL contained no general grant of rights in technologies yet to be developed, and no explicit reference to "future methods" of exhibition. Compare *Lucasfilm*, 566 F. Supp. at 227; *Rooney*, 538 F. Supp. at 228. Rather, the RRL appears to contemplate a comparatively limited and particular grant of rights, encompassing only the 104 film episodes and leaving future uses of "Curious George" to later negotiation in the ancillary products agreement. Although the RRL conversely contains no "specific limiting language," compare *Cohen*, 845 F.2d at 853, we believe such limitation is reasonably inferable from the situation of the parties and the "general tenor of the section" in which the "television viewing" rights were granted.

Second, as properly noted in *Cohen*, "television viewing" and "videocassette viewing" are not coextensive terms. Even though videocassettes may be, and often are, viewed by means of VCRs on home television screens, see, e.g., Sony Corp. of America v. Universal City Studios, Inc., 464 U.S. 417, 429 (1984) (noting prevalent use of videocassette recorders for "time-shifting" of commercial television programming); *Rooney*, 538 F. Supp. at 228 ("whether the exhibition apparatus is a home videocassette player or a television station's broadcast transmitter, the films are 'exhibited' as images on home television screens"), still, as the Ninth Circuit pointed out, a "standard television set capable of receiving television signals" is not strictly required for videocassette viewing. *Cohen*, 845 F.2d at 854. "[I]t is only necessary to have a monitor capable of displaying the material on the magnetized tape." Id. Indeed, a number of non-television monitors recently marketed in the United States permit videocassette viewing on computer screens, flat-panel displays, and the like. Thus, we find insufficient reliable indicia of a contrary mutual intent on the part of Rey and LHP to warrant disturbing the district court's implicit determination that the language of the RRL is not broad enough to cover the new use.

Finally, any lingering concerns about the correctness of the district court's interpretation are dispelled by the evidence that the RRL (including its "television viewing" clause) was drafted and proposed by LHP, a professional investment firm accustomed to licensing agreements. Rey, an elderly woman, does not appear to have participated in its drafting, and, indeed, does not appear to have been represented by counsel during the larger part of the transaction. Under these circumstances, as noted supra p. 1388, ambiguities in the drafting instrument are traditionally construed against the licensor and the drafter. See also NIMMER at 10-71 ("ambiguities [in licensing agreements] will generally be resolved against the party preparing the instrument of transfer"); U.S. Naval Institute v. Charter Communications, Inc., 875 F.2d 1044, 1051 (2d Cir. 1989) (interpreting ambiguous copyright assignment against sophisticated drafting party); see generally, e.g., Merrimack Valley Nat'l Bank v. Baird, 363 N.E.2d 688, 690 (1977) ("as a general rule, a writing is construed against the author of the doubtful language . . . if the circumstances surrounding its use and the ordinary meaning of the words do not indicate the intended meaning of the language").

Accordingly, as the Sony videocassette sales were not encompassed by the RRL, but governed exclusively by the APA, we find no conflict between the terms of the documents, and we affirm the award of royalties to Rey under the APA.

KORMAN v. HBC FLORIDA, INC.
182 F.3d 1291 (11th Cir. 1999)

CARNES, Circuit Judge.

Mimi Korman sued HBC Florida, Inc. ("HBC") for copyright infringement. The basis of her complaint was that WQBA-AM ("WQBA"), a radio station owned by HBC, continued to play one of the jingles she had written for it during their business relationship, even after that relationship ended and she insisted that the station stop.

I. FACTS

During the 1970s, Mimi Korman wrote and produced a number of jingles for WQBA, even though she and the station never had any written agreement. In 1978, Korman wrote the lyrics for a jingle entitled "Yo Llevo a Cuba La Voz," which translates as "I Convey the Voice to Cuba." WQBA liked the jingle enough to use it as a station identifier, and it did so with her permission, at least at the time. Neither party remembers how much WQBA paid Korman for this jingle, but they have stipulated that "WQBA paid Korman a fee for her work in writing the lyrics to the Jingle. No royalties or residuals were ever paid to Korman for the Jingle." In 1979, Korman terminated her relationship with WQBA. Korman argues to us that she told WQBA, either at the beginning of their relationship or during its existence, that the license she was granting it to use her jingles would terminate when she ended her relationship with the station. However, her attorney conceded to the district court that there is no evidence indicating any understanding about the duration of the implied license. We hold her to that concession.

In 1993, Korman heard WQBA playing "Yo Llevo a Cuba La Voz," and left a message for its general manager, saying that the jingle was her property and the station should stop using the jingle unless it was willing to negotiate with her. She never heard from the station. Thereafter, she applied for and received a certificate of copyright registration for the jingle.

In May 1995, Korman again heard the jingle being played by WQBA, and she wrote the station a letter. In her letter, Korman referred to the copyright certificate she had obtained for the jingle, accused the station of violating her copyright in the jingle, and offered to negotiate about the use of that and other jingles, which she had written "on a freelance basis" during her previous relationship with the station. Despite Korman's letter, WQBA continued to play the jingle even though no agreement was reached between the station and Korman. Korman then sued HBC, WQBA's current owner, for copyright infringement.

II. DISCUSSION

A. Did Korman Grant WQBA a Nonexclusive License?

Initially, Korman challenges the district court's holding that she granted WQBA a nonexclusive license to use the jingle. We reject that challenge. While an exclusive license to use copyrighted material must be written, a nonexclusive license can be granted orally or can be implied from the conduct of the parties. See 17 U.S.C. §204; Jacob Maxwell, Inc. v. Veeck, 110 F.3d 749, 751-52 (11th Cir. 1997). HBC does not contend that Korman orally gave it an explicit license to use the jingle; HBC argues instead that Korman's conduct gave it an implied license.

[T]he conduct of the parties in this case establishes that a nonexclusive license was granted. Korman wrote jingles for WQBA for seven years, and during that time she allowed the station to air those jingles, including the one at issue in this case. Given that conduct, she "cannot reasonably deny" that she granted WQBA a nonexclusive license to use her jingle.

B. Does 17 U.S.C. §203 Prevent Korman from Terminating the License?

After determining that Korman had granted a nonexclusive license to WQBA, the district court decided she could not terminate the license. The court based its decision on two premises: (1) the implied license came within the scope of 17 U.S.C. §203, the termination provision of the Copyright Act; and (2) section 203 prevented Korman from terminating the license for 35 years. We agree with the first premise, but not the second.

1. Does 17 U.S.C. §203 Apply to Implied Nonexclusive Licenses?

17 U.S.C. §203 applies to "the exclusive or nonexclusive grant of a transfer or license of copyright . . . executed by the author on or after January 1, 1978. . . ." 17 U.S.C. §203(a). As we have already determined, this case involves a nonexclusive grant of a license. The plain language of section 203 covers all nonexclusive grants of a license that are executed after the specified date, and nothing in the statute excludes those that are implied.

Korman argues that section 203 does not apply to implied licenses because they are not "executed," as required by that provision. They are not executed, she says, because they are not in writing. As a basis for her contention that licenses must be in writing in order to be executed, she points to 17 U.S.C. §204, which states that one of the requirements for a valid transfer of copyright ownership is that the transfer be written. See 17 U.S.C. §204(a). Korman's reliance on section 204 is misplaced, because that provision applies only to transfers of copyright ownership; it has no application to nonexclusive licenses, which do not transfer ownership. See Bateman v. Mnemonics, Inc., 79 F.3d 1532, 1537 n.12 (11th Cir. 1996) (noting that Copyright Act's definition of "transfer of copyright ownership" excludes nonexclusive licenses).

The existence of a writing requirement in section 204 cuts against Korman's position that section 203 only applies to written licenses, because it shows that Congress knows how to impose such a requirement when it wants to do so. Congress did not do so in section 203. "Executed" means "carried into full effect," see *Black's Law Dictionary* 567 (6th ed. 1990), and nothing in section 203 or elsewhere in the Copyright Act requires that nonexclusive licenses be in writing before they can be carried into full effect. The nonexclusive license involved in this case went into effect when Korman permitted WQBA to use the jingle notwithstanding the absence of a writing. She did that after January 1, 1978, the date of applicability set out in section 203, so that section does apply to this license. With that holding of the district court we are in full agreement.

2. Where No Termination Date Has Been Specified, Does 17 U.S.C. §203 Prevent Termination of a License Before 35 Years Have Elapsed?

The holding with which we disagree concerns the applicability of section 203 to the grant of a license like the one in this case. The district court held that, unless the parties agree to a shorter duration, section 203 imposes a minimum term of 35 years for copyright licenses. After finding that Korman and WQBA had not agreed to a shorter duration, the district court held that section 203 prevented Korman from terminating the license until 35 years had passed. The issue of whether section 203 imposes a minimum term of 35 years on licenses of indefinite duration has caused a split among the other circuits. Compare Walthal v. Rusk, 172 F.3d 481, 484-85 (7th Cir. 1999) (section 203 does not create a minimum term of 35 years for licenses of indefinite duration), with Rano v. Sipa Press, Inc., 987 F.2d 580, 585 (9th Cir. 1993) (section 203 does create a minimum term of 35 years for licenses of indefinite duration). After reviewing the text and legislative history of section 203 and considering the views of the other circuits, we conclude that section 203 does not create a minimum term for licenses of indefinite duration.

Section 203 provides: "Termination of the grant [of a transfer or license] may be effected at any time during a period of five years beginning at the end of thirty-five years from the date of execution of the grant." 17 U.S.C. §203(a)(3). The plain language of this provision gives the author of a work the right to terminate any copyright transfer or license still in effect after 35 years, provided she exercises that right after 35 and before 40 years have elapsed. See also 17 U.S.C. §203(a)(5) ("Termination of the grant may be effected notwithstanding any agreement to the contrary. . . ."). But the issue before us is not about what happens during that five-year period, which begins after 35 years. Instead, the issue is about what happens, or what can happen, before 35 years have passed.

Both circuits to speak to this aspect of section 203 have recognized that it does not prevent the parties from creating by agreement a license that lasts for less than 35 years. See *Walthal*, 172 F.3d at 485 (license for 10 years would be terminable at the end of the 10-year period);

Rano, 987 F.2d at 585 ("[L]icensing agreements . . . are terminable at the will of the author only during a five[-]year period beginning at the end of thirty-five years from the date of execution of the license unless they explicitly specify an earlier termination date.") The House and Senate Reports accompanying the Copyright Act clearly indicate that section 203 was not intended to preclude or affect the duration of licensing agreements made for terms of less than 35 years. See H.R. Rep. No. 94-1476, at 128 (1976), reprinted in 1976 U.S.C.C.A.N. 5659, 5743 ("Nothing contained in this section or elsewhere in this legislation is intended to extend the duration of any license, transfer or assignment made for a period of less than thirty-five years. If, for example, an agreement provides an earlier termination date or lesser duration, or if it allows the author the right of cancelling or terminating the agreement under certain circumstances, the duration is governed by the agreement."); S. Rep. No. 94-473, at 111 (1975) ("Nothing contained in this section or elsewhere in this legislation is intended to extend any license or transfer made for a period of less than thirty-five years."). In other words, the parties are free to agree to a license that is of definite duration, including one for a period of less than 35 years. That is clear.

The more interesting issue is whether section 203 imposes a 35-year term for a license of indefinite duration that would otherwise be subject to earlier termination under state contract law. In *Rano*, the Ninth Circuit ruled that section 203 does impose such a term and therefore preempts state law. See *Rano*, 987 F.2d at 585. In *Walthal*, which was decided after the district court's decision in this case, the Seventh Circuit disagreed with *Rano* and held that section 203 does not impose a minimum 35-year term on licenses of indefinite duration and thus does not preempt state law. See *Walthal*, 172 F.3d at 484-85. After reviewing the text and legislative history of section 203, we agree with the Seventh Circuit.

The first, and most important, step in statutory construction is to examine the language of the provision itself. See, e.g., United States v. Steele, 147 F.3d 1316, 1318 (11th Cir. 1998) (en banc). Section 203 does not say that copyright licenses of indefinite duration cannot be terminated for 35 years. What it says, in subsection (a)(3), is: "Termination of the grant may be effected at any time during a period of five years beginning at the end of thirty-five years from the date of execution of the grant." 17 U.S.C. §203(a)(3). That is not the same thing as saying termination "may only be effected at any time during a period of five years beginning at the end of thirty-five years. . . ." The *Rano* decision reads into the language of the statute the word "only," a word that changes the meaning of the provision, and a word Congress did not put there.

Before we get to a discussion of congressional intent, however, it is worth noting that the *Rano* court's rewriting of section 203 extends beyond insertion of the word "only." By recognizing that parties could agree to make a license with a shorter duration, the court essentially interpreted section 203 to impose a 35-year term as a default rule. See *Rano*, 987 F.2d at 585. Under this interpretation, the language of the provision would become (with the words that must be added underscored): "Termination of the grant may *only* be effected at any time during a period of five years beginning at the end of thirty-five years from the date of execution of the grant *unless the parties agree to a specific shorter term*." One alteration begets another. See 3 Melville B. Nimmer & David Nimmer, Nimmer on Copyright §11.01[B], at 11-9 (1994) ("[H]ad Section 203 been designed, as interpreted by the [*Rano*] court, to prevent terminations earlier than thirty-five years after execution, then a contrary agreement by the parties would be a nullity, in contrast to the court's conclusion."). It is not the business of courts to rewrite statutes, and our interpretation of section 203 requires no rewriting. We take the provision as Congress wrote it, and neither add words to nor subtract them from it.

Our reading of section 203 furthers, instead of defeats, the manifest congressional intent behind that section — the protection of authors. Characterizing section 203 as "a provision safeguarding authors against unremunerative transfers," the House Report states that "[a] provision of this sort is needed because of the unequal bargaining position of authors, resulting in part from the impossibility of determining a work's value until it has been exploited." H.R. REP. No. 94-1476, at 124 (1976), reprinted in 1976 U.S.C.C.A.N. 5659, 5740. The Senate Report contains the same language. See S. REP. No. 94-473, at 108 (1975).

The Supreme Court has recognized that the purpose of section 203 is to help authors, not publishers or broadcasters or others who benefit from the work of authors. See Mills Music, Inc. v. Snyder, 469 U.S. 153, 172-73 & n.39 (1985).

Giving the other side of the issue its due, we recognize that one provision of section 203 could be read to support the Rano court's conclusion. Section 203(b)(6) states: "Unless and until termination is effected under this section, the grant, if it does not provide otherwise, continues in effect for the term of copyright provided by this title." 17 U.S.C. §203(b)(6). We think, though, that section 203(b)(6) does not provide much support for the holding in Rano, and it certainly does not compel that holding. The reason is that state laws governing contracts of indefinite duration, which are read into a contract, do "provide otherwise" within the meaning of section 203(b)(6). It is a well-established principle that state law is read into and becomes part of a contract. . . .

As the Seventh Circuit, in rejecting the Rano decision, explained:

> [A] contract which implicitly provides for termination, as this one does under Illinois law, presents no conflict with §203. This contract does not differ in any meaningful way from a contract which specifies a term of, for instance, 10 years, which would be terminable at the end of the 10-year period.

Walthal, 172 F.3d at 485. We join the Seventh Circuit in rejecting Rano's conversion of "casual oral permission into a thirty-five year straitjacket." 3 NIMMER ON COPYRIGHT §11.01[B], at 11-9 (1994). We hold that if state law provides that licenses of indefinite duration may be terminated in less than 35 years, it is state law and not section 203 that governs the question of termination before 35 years. We leave it to the district court on remand to determine state law.

BALDWIN v. EMI FEIST CATALOG, INC.
805 F.3d 18 (2d Cir. 2015)

LIVINGSTON, Circuit Judge.

This appeal involves a dispute over the copyright in the musical composition "Santa Claus Is Comin' to Town" (the "Song"), a classic Christmas song written by J. Fred Coots and Haven Gillespie in the 1930s. Coots and Gillespie sold the Song and "the right to secure copyright therein" to EMI's predecessor Leo Feist, Inc. ("Feist") in an agreement dated September 5, 1934 (the "1934 Agreement"). In the 1934 Agreement, Feist agreed to "publish [the Song] in saleable form . . . within one (1) year," and to pay Coots and Gillespie certain royalties generated by the Song. On September 27, 1934, Feist registered its copyright in the Song with the Copyright Office.

At the time, the Copyright Act of 1909 (the "1909 Act") was in effect. Under the 1909 Act, authors were entitled to copyright in their work for an initial twenty-eight-year period beginning on the date the work was published. They then had the right to renew their copyright for an additional twenty-eight-year "renewal term," a right that they could exercise even if they had granted their rights in the initial copyright term to a publisher. Thus, "[t]he renewal term permit[ted] the author, originally in a poor bargaining position, to renegotiate the terms of the grant once the value of the work ha[d] been tested." Stewart v. Abend, 495 U.S. 207, 218-19 (1990). Unless the author died before the renewal term began—in which case his renewal rights vested in his statutory heirs, notwithstanding his assignment of an expectancy in those rights—a grant of renewal rights ensured that the publisher would own the copyright for the entire fifty-six-year period provided by the 1909 Act.

While many authors sold their rights in the initial term and the renewal term simultaneously, Coots granted his renewal rights separately, in the 1951 Agreement. The 1951 Agreement assigned to Feist a number of "musical compositions" by Coots, including the Song, "and all renewals and extensions of all copyrights therein," in exchange for certain royalties to be paid "during all renewal periods of the United States copyright in each of said compositions." Feist renewed its copyright in the Song on September 27, 1961, at which point its rights were set to expire fifty-six years after copyright was originally registered—i.e., on September 27, 1990.

In 1976, Congress enacted a major overhaul of U.S. copyright law (the "1976 Act"), several aspects of which are central to this appeal. For works created on or after January 1, 1978, the 1976 Act did away with the 1909 Act's dual-term structure, replacing it with a single copyright term lasting for the life of the author plus fifty years. By contrast, for works created before January 1, 1978, the 1976 Act retained the 1909 Act's dual-term structure, and for works (like the Song) already in their renewal term, it extended the renewal term to "seventy-five years from the date copyright was originally secured." Id. §304(b). After the passage of the 1976 Act, the rights in the Song that Coots had granted to Feist were scheduled to expire in 2009.

Although the 1976 Act extended copyright protection for works already in their renewal term, it contained a mechanism for giving authors and their families, as opposed to publishers who had come to own the renewal term rights, an opportunity to benefit from the extended term. See 3 Melville B. Nimmer & David Nimmer, NIMMER ON COPYRIGHT §11.05[B][1] (2013) [hereinafter "Nimmer"]. To this end, §304(c) of the statute permitted authors—or, if the author had died, certain statutory heirs designated in §304(c)(2)—to terminate "the exclusive or nonexclusive grant of a transfer or license of the renewal copyright . . . executed before January 1, 1978." 17 U.S.C. §304(c). Because the parties' dispute implicates the intricacies of this section, we quote the relevant portions at length:

> (3) Termination of the grant may be effected at any time during a period of five years beginning at the end of fifty-six years from the date copyright was originally secured, or beginning on January 1, 1978, whichever is later.

(4) The termination shall be effected by serving an advance notice in writing upon the grantee or the grantee's successor in title. . . .

> (A) The notice shall state the effective date of the termination, which shall fall within the five-year period specified by clause (3) of this subsection, . . . and the notice shall be served not less than two or more than ten years before that date. A copy of the notice shall be recorded in the Copyright Office before the effective date of termination, as a condition to its taking effect.

> (B) The notice shall comply, in form, content, and manner of service, with requirements that the Register of Copyrights shall prescribe by regulation.

(5) Termination of the grant may be effected notwithstanding any agreement to the contrary, including an agreement to make a will or to make any future grant.

(6) . . . In the case of a grant executed by one or more of the authors of the work, all of a particular author's rights under this title that were covered by the terminated grant revert, upon the effective date of termination, to that author or, if that author is dead, to [his statutory heirs]. In all cases the reversion of rights is subject to the following limitations:

> . . .

> (B) The future rights that will revert upon termination of the grant become vested on the date the notice of termination has been served as provided by clause (4) of this subsection.

> . . .

> (D) A further grant, or agreement to make a further grant, of any right covered by a terminated grant is valid only if it is made after the effective date of the termination. As an exception, however, an agreement for such a further grant may be made between the author . . . and the original grantee or such grantee's successor in title, after the notice of termination has been served as provided by clause (4) of this subsection.

> . . .

> (F) Unless and until termination is effected under this subsection, the grant, if it does not provide otherwise, continues in effect for the remainder of the extended renewal term.

17 U.S.C. §304(c).

In addition to this §304(c) termination right for pre-1978 grants, the 1976 Act granted authors (or their statutory heirs) the right to terminate grants "executed by the author on or after January 1, 1978." 17 U.S.C. §203. This §203 termination right can be exercised during a five-year period "beginning at the end of thirty-five years from the date of execution of the grant," but if the grant "covers the right of publication of the work," that five-year period begins at the earlier of (1) thirty-five years from the work's publication or (2) forty years from the execution of the grant. *Id.* §203(a)(3). As with termination under §304(c), termination under §203 "may be effected notwithstanding any agreement to the contrary." *Id.* §203(a)(5).

Under the first of the termination provisions just described, §304(c), the 1951 Agreement was, as a pre-1978 grant, subject to termination starting on September 27, 1990, so Coots could serve a termination notice as early as ten years before that date. 17 U.S.C. §304(c)(3),

(4). Between service of the notice and the date of termination, he could reach an agreement for a further grant of the terminated rights with Feist or its successor in title, but no one else. *Id.* §304(c)(6)(D). In fact, on September 24, 1981, Coots served on Feist's successor, Robbins Music Corporation ("Robbins"), a termination notice naming October 23, 1990, as the termination date for the 1951 Agreement (the "1981 Termination Notice"). Coots's attorney, William Krasilovsky, sent a copy of the 1981 Termination Notice to the Register of Copyrights on November 25, 1981. He then set about negotiating with Robbins on Coots's behalf, culminating in the 1981 Agreement, which was signed on December 15, 1981.

The 1981 Agreement recited that Coots (the "Grantor") had transferred his rights in the Song's renewal term to Feist in the 1951 Agreement; that Feist had renewed the copyright; that Congress had extended the renewal term in the 1976 Act; and that "the parties hereto desire to insure that [Robbins (the "Grantee")] shall, for the balance of the period of copyright [in the Song], be possessed of all United States copyright interest therein." Coots agreed as follows:

> Grantor hereby sells, assigns, grants, transfers and sets over to Grantee . . . all rights and interests whatsoever now or hereafter known or existing, heretofore or at any time or times hereafter acquired or possessed by Grantor in and to [the Song and various derivative works], under any and all renewals and extensions of all copyrights therein and all United States reversionary and termination interests in copyright now in existence or expectant, including all rights reverted, reverting or to revert to Grantor[,] his heirs, executors, administrators or next of kin by reason of the termination of any transfers or licenses covering any extended renewal term of copyright pursuant to Section 304 of the Copyright Act of 1976, together with all renewals and extensions thereof.

Further, he made a series of representations, including that he had served on Robbins "and recorded in the Copyright Office" a termination notice, which, the parties agreed:

> shall for the purposes of this agreement and Section 304(c)(6)(D) of the Copyright Act of 1976 be deemed to have been served upon Grantee, in advance of any further grant of rights hereunder, and shall be deemed to take effect at the earliest date possible under the Copyright Act of 1976 and the regulations prescribed by the Register of Copyrights.

Robbins agreed to pay both a $100,000 "non-recoupable bonus" to Coots's children in annual installments from 1981 to 1995, and royalties "as specified in the [1951 Agreement]" for "the period of the Extended Renewal Term of Copyright," a phrase that the 1981 Agreement did not define. Coots's four children — Clayton Coots, Gloria Coots Baldwin, Patricia Coots Chester, and John Coots, Jr. — also signed the 1981 Agreement. "As an inducement to [Robbins] to enter into the . . . agreement," they assigned to Robbins all of their rights and interests in the Song "for the extended renewal term thereof."

On May 26, 1982, Krasilovsky received a letter from the Copyright Office stating: "Pursuant to our telephone conversation of March 1, 1982, we are returning" the 1981 Termination Notice "to you unrecorded." There is no explanation for this decision either in the letter or elsewhere in the record. At his deposition in this case, Krasilovsky could not recall why the notice was returned or what had transpired in the "telephone conversation" mentioned in the letter. The parties agree that the 1981 Termination Notice was never actually recorded, although EMI (Robbins's successor) claims it was not aware of the non-recordation of the notice until 2011.

As noted, when the 1981 Agreement was signed, the copyright in the Song was scheduled to subsist until December 31, 2009, the end of the year seventy-five years after copyright was initially secured. See supra note 1. The parties therefore did not anticipate that §203 termination—which is available only against grants executed after January 1, 1978 and lasting longer than thirty-five years—would be available against the 1981 Agreement, which they thought would come to an end in 2009, less than thirty-five years later. Things changed in 1998, however, when Congress passed the Sonny Bono Copyright Term Extension Act (the "1998 Act"). For copyrights still in their renewal term at that time, the 1998 Act extended the renewal term to last "95 years from the date copyright was originally secured." 17 U.S.C. §304(b). Because the Song's copyright was secured in 1934, its copyright was now set to expire on December 31, 2029.

The 1998 Act also added a new termination right to allow authors and their heirs to extract value from the new twenty-year extension of the renewal term. For copyrights still in their renewal term, authors (or their statutory heirs) could effect termination in the same general way as under §304(c) if "the termination right provided in [§304(c)] has expired by such date" and "the author or owner of the termination right has not previously exercised such termination right." 17 U.S.C. §304(d). Termination pursuant to §304(d) can "be effected at any time during a period of 5 years beginning at the end of 75 years from the date copyright was originally secured," Id. §304(d)(2)—in the Song's case, starting on September 27, 2009.

The possibilities created by the 1998 Act led to a flurry of activity by Coots's statutory heirs, who sought to take advantage of the termination rights that Congress had afforded, but were forced to contend with uncertainty stemming from the fact that the 1981 Termination Notice was never recorded. In 2004, Coots's heirs served on EMI (Robbins's successor) and recorded in the Copyright Office a §304(d) termination notice with an effective date of September 27, 2009 (the "2004 Termination Notice"). Evidently, the 2004 Termination Notice was based on the related premises that EMI still owned its rights under the 1951 Agreement (a pre-1978 grant), and that Coots had not already exercised his §304(c) termination rights. Under the impression that the 1981 Agreement was operative, EMI personnel were confused by the 2004 Termination Notice; they ran a search for a prior §304(c) termination notice, which came up empty. EMI prepared a draft affidavit to "refute" the 2004 Termination Notice, but this was never sent. Instead, in 2006, EMI began negotiating with Krasilovsky, who was now representing Coots's heirs.

EMI and Krasilovsky agreed that in light of the 1981 Agreement, EMI's rights in the Song were more appropriately terminated under §203. Accordingly, in early 2007, Coots's statutory heirs served and recorded the 2007 Termination Notice, which indicated that the 1981 Agreement would terminate pursuant to §203 on December 15, 2016. Krasilovsky then began negotiating to sell the to-be-terminated rights back to EMI. EMI offered Coots's statutory heirs $2.75 million for those rights, an offer that was rejected as insufficient. At that point, EMI's efforts to acquire the rights appear to have stalled.

Two years later, in 2009, Warner-Chappell Music, which had been acting as copyright administrator for a Coots family venture called Toy Town Toons, wrote to EMI claiming the copyright in the Song under the 2004 Termination Notice—apparently having returned to the position that termination of the 1951 Agreement had never taken place. EMI responded to this letter through outside counsel, asserting that its copyright "has not been and cannot be terminated" and would expire in 2029. EMI claimed that §304(d) termination was unavailable because Coots had already exercised his §304(c) termination right in the 1981 Agreement, and that §304(d) "does not provide a second right to terminate where the right of termination has already been exercised."

In 2012, Coots's statutory heirs served and recorded the 2012 Termination Notice. Like the 2007 Termination Notice, the 2012 Termination Notice cited §203, not §304(d), as the source of the heirs' right to terminate the 1981 Agreement. But "in an abundance of caution," the 2012 Termination Notice assumed that the 2007 Termination Notice was premature, on the theory (which Coots's statutory heirs anticipated EMI might advance) that the 1981 Agreement was a grant "cover[ing] the right of publication of the work," 17 U.S.C. §203(a)(3), and that the "publication" of the Song under the 1981 Agreement, which resulted in EMI's owning the nineteen years' worth of rights spanning from 1990 to 2009, took place in 1990. On that potentially available theory, the 1981 Agreement could not be terminated until December 15, 2021 — i.e., forty years after the agreement's execution.

On December 16, 2011, Plaintiffs sued EMI in the United States District Court for the Southern District of Florida, seeking a declaration that the 2004 Termination Notice had terminated EMI's rights in the Song on December 31, 2009, or, alternatively, that the 2007 Termination Notice would terminate EMI's rights on December 15, 2016. The Florida court granted EMI's motion to dismiss for lack of personal jurisdiction, and Plaintiffs brought this action in the Southern District of New York on December 21, 2012. Plaintiffs now seek a declaration that the 2007 Termination Notice will terminate EMI's rights on December 15, 2016, or, alternatively, that the 2012 Termination Notice will terminate EMI's rights on December 16, 2021.

[T]he district court concluded that EMI's rights would survive until 2029. Judgment was entered on December 17, 2013, and Plaintiffs timely appealed.

DISCUSSION

I

The first question we must address is whether EMI owns its rights in the Song under the 1951 Agreement or, instead, under the 1981 Agreement. The 2007 Termination Notice and the 2012 Termination Notice purported to terminate EMI's rights pursuant to 17 U.S.C. §203, but §203 termination rights are not available against pre-1978 grants. See 17 U.S.C. §203(a). Accordingly, if the 1951 Agreement is the source of EMI's rights, Plaintiffs cannot terminate those rights under §203. Plaintiffs argue that the 1981 Agreement superseded the 1951 Agreement and, upon doing so, became the operative source of EMI's rights. EMI responds that the 1981 Agreement did not supersede the 1951 Agreement, and that Coots's failure to record the 1981 Termination Notice means that the 1951 Agreement was never terminated and therefore remains in effect.

A.

Some preliminary discussion is necessary to understand the parties' dispute fully. As noted, §304(c)(6)(D) provides that "[a] further grant, or agreement to make a further grant, of any right covered by a terminated grant is valid only if it is made after the effective date of the termination. As an exception, however, an agreement for such a further grant may be made between the author [or his statutory heirs] and the original grantee . . . after the notice of termination has been served as provided by" §304(c)(4). We will refer to the exception permitting pre-termination, post-notice agreements with the original grantee as the "existing-grantee exception." This existing-grantee exception was included in the 1976 Act to give the grantee "some advantage over others in obtaining the terminated rights." NIMMER §11.08 [A].

When an author or his statutory heirs serves a termination notice, the grantee's previously undivided copyright interest is effectively split into three pieces, one owned by the author or his statutory heirs and two owned by the grantee. The author (or his statutory heirs) holds a future interest in the copyright. *See* 17 U.S.C. §304(c)(6) (providing that the "rights under this title that were covered by the terminated grant revert, upon the effective date of termination, to th[e] author" or his statutory heirs); Mills Music, Inc. v. Snyder, 469 U.S. 153, 162 (1985) (labeling the post-termination interest a "reversion"). This future interest, however (unlike an author's renewal right under the 1909 Act), "become[s] vested on the date the notice of termination has been served," 17 U.S.C. §304(c)(6); *see* Range Road Music, Inc. v. Music Sales Corp., 76 F.Supp.2d 375, 381 (S.D.N.Y. 1999), which gives the grantee confidence, in negotiations under the existing-grantee exception, that the grantor actually has something to convey.

Although an author's (or his statutory heirs') interest vests immediately upon service of a termination notice, it becomes possessory—i.e., it entitles the author (or his statutory heirs) to ownership of the copyright—only if the notice is recorded before the termination date. *See* 17 U.S.C. §304(c)(4)(A) ("A copy of the notice shall be recorded in the Copyright Office before the effective date of termination, as a condition to its taking effect."). In other words, even after a notice is served, the interest that vests upon service may be divested if the notice is not recorded, and the grantee will continue to own the copyright through the end of the extended renewal term. *See Id.* §304(c)(6)(F) ("Unless and until termination is effected under this subsection, the grant, if it does not provide otherwise, continues in effect for the remainder of the extended renewal term."); 3 NIMMER §11.06[B] ("Recordation . . . is not a condition precedent to vesting, but a failure to record prior to the effective date of termination constitutes failure to satisfy a condition subsequent, and therefore results in invalidation."). So upon being served with a termination notice, the grantee—by virtue of the existing grant—holds both a present interest scheduled to terminate on the notice's effective date and a contingent future interest that will vest on that date and entitle the grantee to possession if the notice goes unrecorded. (In common law property terms, these two interests are analogous to a term of years and a contingent remainder, respectively. *See, e.g.*, Jesse Dukeminier et al., PROPERTY 274 (7th ed. 2010)).

With this background in mind, in the prototypical agreement contemplated by the existing-grantee exception, the author or his statutory heirs convey only the future interest that vested in them upon service of the termination notice—that is, the only interest they hold at the time the notice is served. In effect, EMI claims that the 1981 Agreement is such a prototypical agreement, and that Coots conveyed to EMI only the vested future interest scheduled to revert to him upon termination. From this premise, EMI argues that the 1951 Agreement remained in place as the source of EMI's other two interests in the Song—i.e., the present interest that would have terminated in 1990 had the notice been recorded and the future interest contingent on the non-recordation of the 1981 Termination Notice. When the notice's effective date passed without its being recorded, EMI urges, EMI's contingent future interest vested and entitled it to ownership of the Song's copyright. Accordingly, on EMI's view that that contingent interest arises from the 1951 Agreement, which remains in place, it claims that it currently owns the Song's copyright under the 1951 Agreement. We disagree.

B.

The 1981 Agreement not only granted EMI the future interest scheduled to revert to Coots upon termination, it also replaced the 1951 Agreement as the source of EMI's existing rights in the Song. "[W]here the parties have clearly expressed or manifested their intention that a subsequent agreement supersede or substitute for an old agreement, the subsequent agreement extinguishes the old one." Northville Indus. Corp. v. Fort Neck Oil Terminals Corp., 474 N.Y.S.2d 122, 125 (1984). The question is simply whether the parties intended for the new contract to substitute for the old one, and that intention, if otherwise clear, need not be articulated explicitly in the new agreement.

The parties to the 1981 Agreement "clearly . . . manifested" an intention to replace the 1951 Agreement and not merely to convey to EMI Coots's future interest in the nineteen-year statutory renewal term extension. The relevant language is contained in §1 of the 1981 Agreement, which reads as follows:

> Grantor hereby sells, assigns, grants, transfers and sets over to Grantee . . . [1] *all rights and interests* whatsoever now or hereafter known or existing, *heretofore* or at any time or times hereafter *acquired or possessed by Grantor in and to [the Song]* . . . *under any and all renewals and extensions of all copyrights therein and* [2] all United States reversionary and termination interests in copyright now in existence or expectant, including all rights reverted, reverting or to revert to Grantor . . . by reason of the termination of any transfers or licenses covering any extended renewal term of copyright pursuant to Section 304 of the Copyright Act of 1976, together with all renewals and extensions thereof.

It is quite clear from the first half of the quoted language that Coots was granting more than the vested future interest scheduled to revert to him or his statutory heirs upon termination; he was also granting "all rights and interests . . . heretofore . . . acquired or possessed by [him] . . . under any and all renewals and extensions." Ignoring the bedrock principle that "[a] contract 'should be read to give effect to all its provisions,'" God's Battalion of Prayer Pentecostal Church, Inc. v. Miele Assocs., LLP, 845 N.E.2d 1265, 1267 (2006), EMI makes no effort to explain why EMI and Coots would have included the first half of §1 had they not meant for it to have some effect. But to give any effect to this language at all, we must read it as replacing the 1951 Agreement, creating a new conveyance of all of Coots's interest in the copyright at once, and not merely as a piecemeal conveyance of his reversionary interest. Put simply, it would make no sense to have two grants of the same exact rights be operative at the same time; if the first half of §1 were not meant to replace the 1951 agreement, there would be no reason for the parties to have included it.

. . .

II

Our conclusion that the 1981 Agreement—a post-1978 agreement—is the source of EMI's rights in the Song means that Plaintiffs can terminate the 1981 Agreement under §203. The only remaining question, then, is whether the 1981 Agreement will be terminated by the 2007 Termination Notice or, instead, by the 2012 Termination Notice. We conclude that the 2007 Termination Notice will terminate the 1981 Agreement in 2016.

As noted, termination under §203 is available for grants "executed by the author on or after January 1, 1978." 17 U.S.C. §203(a). Where the author is dead, termination may be effected by individuals holding more than half of the author's termination interest as set forth in the statute. *Id.* §203(a)(1), (2). Ordinarily, these individuals may effect termination "at any time during a period of five years beginning at the end of thirty-five years from the date of execution of the grant." *Id.* §203(a)(3). In this case, that period would begin in 2016. But "if the grant covers the right of publication of the work," an alternative calculation method applies: termination may be effected in the five-year period beginning "thirty-five years from the date of publication of the work under the grant or . . . forty years from the date of execution of the grant, whichever term ends earlier." *Id.* A termination notice may be served between two and ten years before the termination date. *Id.* §203(a)(4)(A). The notice must "state the effective date of the termination," be recorded in the Copyright Office "as a condition to its taking effect," and comply with various other formalities prescribed by regulation. *Id.* §203(a)(4); *see* 37 C.F.R. §201.10.

. . .

In sum: EMI does not dispute that the 1981 Agreement was executed on December 15, 1981. Because that grant was "executed by the author" and does not "cover the right of publication," it is terminable under §203 starting on December 15, 2016—which is the effective date of termination stated in the 2007 Termination Notice. Accordingly, we conclude that the 2007 Termination Notice will terminate the 1981 Agreement on that date.

SMITH v. BARNESANDNOBLE.COM, LLC
839 F.3d 163 (2d Cir. 2016)

JACOBS, Circuit Judge:

Plaintiff Cheryl Smith appeals from the judgment of the United States District Court for the Southern District of New York, dismissing her complaint on summary judgment. Smith alleged direct and contributory copyright infringement by defendant Barnesandnoble.com, LLC ("Barnes & Noble" or "defendant"). The defendant, under license, uploads books and book samples to digital "lockers" that the defendant maintains for its individual customers. When the license granted by Smith was terminated, the defendant did not delete a sample of Smith's book. Because the allegedly infringing conduct was authorized by the contracts at issue, we affirm the district court.

BACKGROUND

The plaintiff is the widow of Louis K. Smith, who authored and copyrighted a book entitled The Hardscrabble Zone ("Hardscrabble"). In 2009, Mr. Smith contracted with Smashwords, Inc. ("Smashwords"), an online ebook distributor, to market his book. One relevant term of the agreement provided:

6d. Promotional Rights. Smashwords shall have the right to distribute samples of the Work in any form of media, including printed media, in order to promote (a) the author or author's Work and/or (b) the Smashwords service. These samples will be licensed for free, non-commercial use, duplication and sharing, and will comply with the sample percentage authorized by the Author.

The agreement contemplated robust rights in digital samples: it recognized that "uninhibited sampling and sharing" had the potential to "dramatically increase" an author's "total audience and sales opportunities." At the same time, the contract provided that end-users who acquired a "free work" (defined to include "sample works") had a license to "duplicate, share and reproduce" the sample, but only for "non-commercial purposes" and only "during the time the price is set at zero." While these arrangements contemplate that a customer's right to share and duplicate a free sample could be terminated, the agreement did not provide that a customer's right to use a validly obtained sample (or the entire work) would terminate, even if the entire distribution agreement was canceled. The agreement gave notice that "Smashwords does not publish works containing digital rights management schemes that limit the customer's ability to consume Author's Work as they see fit."

In accordance with this contract (and with Mr. Smith's permission), Smashwords provided Hardscrabble for sale and sampling to its retail partners, including Barnes & Noble, which listed the book for sale on bn.com and made free samples available.

Apparently disappointed with the sales figures (none were sold), Mr. Smith terminated his agreement with Smashwords in October 2011. Despite the termination, the book erroneously remained listed by Barnes & Noble on bn.com. The book was de-listed on April 20, 2012, and the dispositive issue is whether any customers acquired a sample while it was listed without a distribution agreement in place. Prior to termination of the agreement, a single customer of Barnes & Noble acquired a digital sample of Mr. Smith's book. No other customer bought a copy or obtained a sample, before or after the distribution agreement was cancelled.

The sample was stored through Barnes & Noble's digital locker system. When a Barnes & Noble customer downloads a free sample (or purchases an ebook) the content is stored through a digital locker associated with the customer's account. The system, effectively the user's bookshelf for digital products, is cloud-based. Cloud computing uses remote servers and networks for data storage which may be accessed using web-enabled devices, such as computers, tablets, or smart phones.

There is no dispute that the single customer's initial access to the sample was authorized under the contract and occurred before the agreement was terminated. After Mr. Smith cancelled the agreement with Smashwords, that same customer twice accessed the sample in his or her cloud-based account. Those two instances of access form the basis of the plaintiff's claim that Barnes & Noble infringed the copyright. There is no record evidence that any other customer accessed a sample after the agreement was cancelled; and there is no record evidence that any person ever purchased the entire work from Barnes & Noble. The plaintiff's theory of liability is that Barnes & Noble was no longer permitted to provide its customers with access to the sample after the agreement was terminated.

DISCUSSION

A claim of direct copyright infringement requires proof that (1) the plaintiff had a valid copyright in the work, and (2) the defendant infringed the copyright by violating one of the exclusive rights that 17 U.S.C. §106 bestows upon the copyright holder. Island Software & Computer Serv., Inc. v. Microsoft Corp., 413 F.3d 257, 260 (2d Cir. 2005). There is no dispute in this case that the plaintiff has a valid copyright, but the plaintiff must also be able to demonstrate that the copying was unauthorized. Where, as here, the existence of the license is undisputed, and the only contested issue is its scope, the copyright owner bears the burden of proving that the defendant's conduct was unauthorized under the license. See Bourne v. Walt Disney Co., 68 F.3d 621, 631 (2d Cir. 1995).

The plaintiff had a distribution agreement that explicitly permitted the distribution of samples as promotional material. The plaintiff concedes that digital sampling as a method of distribution was permitted under the distribution agreement's phrase "any form of media."

After the agreement was canceled, the one customer who had already validly obtained a sample was permitted to access the sample in the customer's cloud-based account two more times; the plaintiff contends that these two instances of access amount to copyright infringement. However, the agreement provides for the distribution of samples with a license "for free, noncommercial use, duplication and sharing," without provision to terminate the license for samples already distributed in the event the distribution agreement itself is terminated. Significantly, the distribution agreement authorizes paper samples as well as digital samples, and treats them alike. Since a customer who has a paper sample may obviously keep it, reread it, and make additional paper copies of it for noncommercial use at will, it follows that the agreement does not provide or imply that a person who obtained a digital sample would lose the license for free access upon termination of the distribution agreement. Cf. Boosey & Hawkes Music Publishers, Ltd. v. Walt Disney Co., 145 F.3d 481, 486 (2d Cir. 1998) (explaining that licensees "may properly pursue any uses which may reasonably be said to fall within the medium as described in the license." . . .) To the contrary, the agreement contemplated robust sampling rights, and Smashwords prohibited authors from using digital rights management schemes that would limit a customer's ability to consume the author's work "as they see fit." The plaintiff does not argue that a customer who purchased the book itself would lose cloud-based access to it upon termination of a distribution agreement; the license to access the (free) sample is no more restrictive or limited than the license to access the book itself after purchase. Once the customer acquired the cloud-based sample, the service that Barnes & Noble provided was no longer distribution; the service provided was access. The cloud-based digital locker system permitted the customers to put ebooks or samples into their accounts, which books and samples they could then download to their devices whenever and wherever they wanted.

Because the agreement does not provide for the license in the sample to terminate after the sample has been distributed, the plaintiff cannot sustain her burden to prove that providing cloud-based access to validly obtained samples is beyond the scope of the license agreement. Accordingly, the district court was correct to grant defendants' motion for summary judgment, and we affirm the judgment, albeit on different grounds.

UMG RECORDINGS, INC. v. AUGUSTO

628 F.3d 1175 (9th Cir. 2011)

CANBY, Circuit Judge:

The material facts of the case are undisputed. UMG is among the world's largest music companies. One of its core businesses is the creation, manufacture, and sale of recorded music, or phonorecords, the copyrights of which are owned by UMG. These phonorecords generally take the form of compact discs ("CDs").

Like many music companies, UMG ships specially-produced promotional CDs to a large group of individuals ("recipients"), such as music critics and radio programmers, that it has selected. There is no prior agreement or request by the recipients to receive the CDs. UMG does not seek or receive payment for the CDs, the content and design of which often differs from that of their commercial counterparts. UMG ships the promotional CDs by means of the United States Postal Service and United Parcel Service. Relatively few of the recipients refuse delivery of the CDs or return them to UMG, and UMG destroys those that are returned.

Most of the promotional CDs in issue in this case bore a statement (the "promotional statement") similar to the following:

> This CD is the property of the record company and is licensed to the intended recipient for personal use only. Acceptance of this CD shall constitute an agreement to comply with the terms of the license. Resale or transfer of possession is not allowed and may be punishable under federal and state laws.

Some of the CDs bore a more succinct statement, such as "Promotional Use Only—Not for Sale."

Augusto was not among the select group of individuals slated to receive the promotional CDs. He nevertheless managed to acquire numerous such CDs, many of which he sold through online auctions at eBay.com. Augusto regularly advertised the CDs as "rare . . . industry editions" and referred to them as "Promo CDs."

After several unsuccessful attempts at halting the auctions through eBay's dispute resolution program, UMG filed a complaint against Augusto in the United States District Court for the Central District of California, alleging that Augusto had infringed UMG's copyrights in eight promotional CDs for which it retained the "exclusive right to distribute." The district court granted summary judgment in favor of Augusto, and UMG appealed.

DISCUSSION

. . . Although UMG, as the owner of the copyright, has exclusive rights in the promotional CDs, "[e]xemptions, compulsory licenses, and defenses found in the Copyright Act narrow [those] rights." Wall Data Inc. v. Los Angeles Cnty. Sheriff's Dept., 447 F.3d 769, 777 (9th Cir. 2006). Augusto invokes the "first sale" doctrine embodied in §109(a) of the Act. 17 U.S.C. §109(a). He argues that the circumstances attending UMG's distribution of the discs effected a "sale" (transfer of ownership) of the discs to the original recipients and that, under the "first sale" doctrine, the recipients and subsequent owners of those particular copies were permitted to sell or otherwise dispose of those copies without authorization by the copyright holder.

UMG, on the other hand, contends that the promotional statement effected a license with the recipients and, because the recipients were not owners but licensees of the CDs, neither they nor Augusto were entitled to sell or otherwise transfer the CDs. See Quality King Distribs., Inc. v. L'anza Research Int'l, Inc., 523 U.S. 135, 146-47 (1998) ("[B]ecause the protection afforded by §109(a) is available only to the 'owner' of a lawfully made copy . . . , the first sale doctrine would not provide a defense to . . . any nonowner such as a bailee, a licensee, a consignee, or one whose possession of the copy was unlawful.").

The Distribution of the Promotional CDs Effected a Sale

The first sale doctrine provides that "the owner of a particular copy or phonorecord lawfully made under [the Act], or any person authorized by such owner, is entitled, without the authority of the copyright owner, to sell or otherwise dispose of the possession of that copy or phonorecord." 17 U.S.C. §109(a). Notwithstanding its distinctive name, the doctrine applies not only when a copy is first sold, but when a copy is given away or title is otherwise transferred without the accouterments of a sale. The seminal illustration of the principle is found in Bobbs-Merrill Co. v. Straus, 210 U.S. 339, 341 (1908), where a copyright owner unsuccessfully attempted to restrain the resale of a copyrighted book by including in it the following notice: "The price of this book at retail is $1 net. No dealer is licensed to sell it at a less price, and a sale at less price will be treated as an infringement of the copyright." Id. The Court noted that the statutory grant to a copyright owner of the "sole right of vending" the work did not continue after the first sale of a given copy. Id. at 349-50. "The purchaser of a book, once sold by authority of the owner of the copyright, may sell it again, although he could not publish a new edition of it." Id. at 350. The attempt to limit resale below a certain price was therefore held invalid. Id. at 351.

The rule of *Bobbs-Merrill* remains in full force, enshrined as it is in §109(a) of the Act: a copyright owner who transfers title in a particular copy to a purchaser or donee cannot prevent resale of that particular copy. We have recognized, however, that not every transfer of possession of a copy transfers title. Particularly with regard to computer software, we have recognized that copyright owners may create licensing arrangements so that users acquire only a license to use the particular copy of software and do not acquire title that permits further transfer or sale of that copy without the permission of the copyright owner. Our most recent example of that rule is Vernor v. Autodesk, Inc., 621 F.3d 1102 (9th Cir. 2010). . . . . All of these cases dealt with the question whether arrangements with consumers amounted to sales of copies, or succeeded in awarding only licenses. They recognized that the mere labeling of an arrangement as a license rather than a sale, although it was a factor to be considered, was not by itself dispositive of the issue. See, e.g., *Vernor*, 621 F.3d at 1109.

The same question is presented here. Did UMG succeed in creating a license in recipients of its promotional CDs, or did it convey title despite the restrictive labeling on the CDs? We conclude that, under all the circumstances of the CDs' distribution, the recipients were entitled to use or dispose of them in any manner they saw fit, and UMG did not enter a license agreement for the CDs with the recipients. Accordingly, UMG transferred title to the particular copies of its promotional CDs and cannot maintain an infringement action against Augusto for his subsequent sale of those copies.

Our conclusion that the recipients acquired ownership of the CDs is based largely on the nature of UMG's distribution. First, the promotional CDs are dispatched to the recipients without any prior arrangement as to those particular copies. The CDs are not numbered, and no attempt is made to keep track of where particular copies are or what use is made of them. As explained in greater detail below, although UMG places written restrictions in the labels of the CDs, it has not established that the restrictions on the CDs create a license agreement.

There are additional reasons for concluding that UMG's distribution of the CDs did not involve a consensual licensing operation. Some of the statements on the CDs and UMG's purported method of securing agreement to licenses militate against a conclusion that any licenses were created. The sparest promotional statement, "Promotional Use Only—Not for Sale," does not even purport to create a license. But even the more detailed statement is flawed in the manner in which it purports to secure agreement from the recipient. The more detailed statement provides:

> This CD is the property of the record company and is licensed to the intended recipient for personal use only. Acceptance of this CD shall constitute an agreement to comply with the terms of the license. Resale or transfer of possession is not allowed and may be punishable under federal and state laws.

It is one thing to say, as the statement does, that "acceptance" of the CD constitutes an agreement to a license and its restrictions, but it is quite another to maintain that "acceptance" may be assumed when the recipient makes no response at all. This record reflects no responses. Even when the evidence is viewed in the light most favorable to UMG, it does not show that any recipients agreed to enter into a license agreement with UMG when they received the CDs.

Because the record here is devoid of any indication that the recipients agreed to a license, there is no evidence to support a conclusion that licenses were established under the terms of the promotional statement. Accordingly, we conclude that UMG's transfer of possession to the recipients, without meaningful control or even knowledge of the status of the CDs after shipment, accomplished a transfer of title.

Return of possession is not invariably required in a license, however. We have since read *Wise* and our software licensing cases "to prescribe three considerations that we may use to determine whether a software user is a licensee, rather than an owner of a copy. First, we consider whether the copyright owner specifies that a user is granted a license. Second, we consider whether the copyright owner significantly restricts the user's ability to transfer the software. Finally, we consider whether the copyright owner imposes notable use restrictions." *Vernor*, 621 F.3d at 1110-11 (footnote omitted).

This formulation, however, applies in terms to software users, and software users who order and pay to acquire copies are in a very different position from that held by the recipients of UMG's promotional CDs. As we have already explained, UMG has virtually no control over the unordered CDs it issues because of its means of distribution, and it has no assurance that any recipient has assented or will assent to the creation of any license or accept its limitations. UMG also does not require the ultimate return of the promotional CDs to its possession. Although the failure to require return of the CDs may not, by itself, conclusively establish a sale under our precedent, it is one more indication that UMG had no control over the promotional CDs once it dispatched them. UMG thus did not retain "sufficient incidents of ownership" over the promotional copies "to be sensibly considered the owner of the cop[ies]." Krause v. Titleserv, Inc., 402 F.3d 119, 124 (2d Cir. 2005).

Because we conclude that UMG's method of distribution transferred the ownership of the copies to the recipients, we have no need to parse the remaining provisions in UMG's purported licensing statement; UMG dispatched the CDs in a manner that permitted their receipt and retention by the recipients without the recipients accepting the terms of the promotional statements. UMG's transfer of unlimited possession in the circumstances present here effected a gift or sale within the meaning of the first sale doctrine, as the district court held.

PRACTICE MANAGEMENT INFORMATION CORP. v. AMERICAN MED. ASS'N
121 F.3d 516 (9th Cir. 1997)

BROWNING, Circuit Judge.

Practice Management Information Corporation ("Practice Management") appeals from a partial summary judgment and preliminary injunction forbidding it from publishing a medical procedure code copyrighted by the American Medical Association ("the AMA").

I.

Over thirty years ago, the AMA began the development of a coding system to enable physicians and others to identify particular medical procedures with precision. These efforts culminated in the publication of the Physician's Current Procedural Terminology ("the CPT"), on which the AMA claims a copyright.

The current edition of the CPT identifies more than six thousand medical procedures and provides a five-digit code and brief description for each. The CPT is divided into six sections — evaluation, anesthesia, surgery, radiology, pathology, and medicine. Within each section, procedures are arranged to enable the user to locate the code number readily. In the anesthesia section, procedures are grouped according to the body part receiving the anesthetic; in the surgical section, the procedures are grouped according to the body system, such as the digestive or urinary system, on which surgery is performed. The AMA revises the CPT each year to reflect new developments in medical procedures.

In 1977, Congress instructed the Health Care Financing Administration ("HCFA") to establish a uniform code for identifying physicians' services for use in completing Medicare and Medicaid claim forms. See 42 U.S.C. §1395w-4(c)(5). Rather than creating a new code, HCFA contracted with the AMA to "adopt and use" the CPT. Agreement ¶1. The AMA gave HCFA a "non-exclusive, royalty free, and irrevocable license to use, copy, publish and distribute" the CPT. Id. ¶3(a). In exchange, HCFA agreed "not to use any other system of procedure nomenclature . . . for reporting physicians' services" and to require use of the CPT in programs administered by HCFA, by its agents, and by other agencies whenever possible. Id. ¶1.

Practice Management, a publisher and distributor of medical books, purchases copies of the CPT from the AMA for resale. After failing to obtain the volume discount it requested, Practice Management filed this lawsuit seeking a declaratory judgment that the AMA's copyright in the CPT was invalid for two reasons: (1) the CPT became uncopyrightable law when HCFA adopted the regulation mandating use of CPT code numbers in applications for Medicaid reimbursement, and (2) the AMA misused its copyright by entering into the agreement that HCFA would require use of the CPT to the exclusion of any other code. The district court granted partial summary judgment for the AMA and preliminarily enjoined Practice Management from publishing the CPT. Practice Management appeals. . . .

Practice Management argues that the AMA misused its copyright by negotiating a contract in which HCFA agreed to use the CPT exclusively. See Lasercomb America, Inc. v. Reynolds, 911 F.2d 970, 977-79 (4th Cir. 1990) (defense of copyright misuse "forbids the use of the copyright to secure an exclusive right or limited monopoly not granted by the Copyright Office"); see also DSC Communications Corp. v. DGI Techs., Inc., 81 F.3d 597, 601 (5th Cir. 1996) (same). We have implied in prior decisions that misuse is a defense to copyright infringement. We now adopt that rule.

On the undisputed facts in the record before us, we conclude the AMA misused its copyright by licensing the CPT to HCFA in exchange for HCFA's agreement not to use a competing coding system. The AMA argues it did not insist HCFA use only the CPT; rather, HCFA decided to use a single code to take advantage of natural efficiencies. However, the plain language of the AMA's licensing agreement requires HCFA to use the AMA's copyrighted coding system and prohibits HCFA from using any other. The exclusivity requirement is a part of the consideration in exchange for which the AMA agreed to grant HCFA a "non-exclusive, royalty-free, and irrevocable license to use, copy, publish and distribute" the CPT. Although HCFA apparently had nothing to gain from inclusion of the exclusivity provision, which side urged its inclusion is of no consequence. Cf. Anchor Serum Co. v. Federal Trade Comm., 217 F.2d 867, 870 (7th Cir. 1954) (rejecting argument that exclusive dealing contract did not violate section 3 of the Clayton Act because buyer initiated negotiations and seller did not impose the contract terms on buyer). The controlling fact is that HCFA is prohibited from using any other coding system by virtue of the binding commitment it made to the AMA to use the AMA's copyrighted material exclusively. The absence of the agreement would not preclude HCFA from doing what the AMA suggests would be proper — deciding on its own to use only the AMA's system. What offends the copyright misuse doctrine is not HCFA's decision to use the AMA's coding system exclusively, but the limitation imposed by the AMA licensing agreement on HCFA's rights to decide whether or not to use other forms as well. Conditioning the license on HCFA's promise not to use competitors' products constituted a misuse of the copyright by the AMA.

The adverse effects of the licensing agreement are apparent. The terms under which the AMA agreed to license use of the CPT to HCFA gave the AMA a substantial and unfair advantage over its competitors. By agreeing to license the CPT in this manner, the AMA used its copyright "in a manner violative of the public policy embodied in the grant of a copyright." Lasercomb, 911 F.2d at 977.

The AMA argues the copyright misuse defense fails because Practice Management did not establish an antitrust violation. We agree with the Fourth Circuit that a defendant in a copyright infringement suit need not prove an antitrust violation to prevail on a copyright misuse defense. See Lasercomb, 911 F.2d at 978.

We also reject the AMA's argument that the *Noerr-Pennington* doctrine immunized its actions. Because Practice Management need not establish an antitrust violation, we need not consider the AMA's antitrust defenses. Moreover, because the AMA did not lobby HCFA to adopt the CPT, the AMA's First Amendment right to petition the government is not at stake.

IV.

We affirm the district court's ruling that the AMA did not lose its copyright when use of the CPT was required by government regulations, but reverse the ruling with respect to copyright misuse. We hold that Practice Management established its misuse defense as a matter of law, vacate the preliminary injunction, and remand for entry of judgment in favor of Practice Management.

GILLIAM v. AMERICAN BROADCASTING CO., INC.

538 F.2d 14 (2d Cir. 1976)

LUMBARD, Circuit Judge

Plaintiffs, a group of British writers and performers known as "Monty Python," appeal from a denial by Judge Lasker in the Southern District of a preliminary injunction to restrain the American Broadcasting Company (ABC) from broadcasting edited versions of three separate programs originally written and performed by Monty Python for broadcast by the British Broadcasting Corporation (BBC).

Since its formation in 1969, the Monty Python group has gained popularity primarily through its thirty-minute television programs created for BBC as part of a comedy series entitled "Monty Python's Flying Circus." In accordance with an agreement between Monty Python and BBC, the group writes and delivers to BBC scripts for use in the television series. This scriptwriters' agreement recites in great detail the procedure to be followed when any alterations are to be made in the script prior to recording of the program. The essence of this section of the agreement is that, while BBC retains final authority to make changes, appellants or their representatives exercise optimum control over the scripts consistent with BBC's authority and only minor changes may be made without prior consultation with the writers. Nothing in the scriptwriters' agreement entitles BBC to alter a program once it has been recorded. The agreement further provides that, subject to the terms therein, the group retains all rights in the script.

Under the agreement, BBC may license the transmission of recordings of the television programs in any overseas territory. . . . In October 1973, Time-Life Films acquired the right to distribute in the United States certain BBC television programs, including the Monty Python series. Time-Life was permitted to edit the programs only "for insertion of commercials, applicable censorship or governmental . . . rules and regulations, and National Association of Broadcasters and time segment requirements." No similar clause was included in the scriptwriters' agreement between appellants and BBC. Prior to this time, ABC had sought to acquire the right to broadcast excerpts from various Monty Python programs in the spring of 1975, but the group rejected the proposal for such a disjoined format. Thereafter, in July 1975, ABC agreed with Time-Life to broadcast two ninety-minute specials each comprising three thirty-minute Monty Python programs that had not previously been shown in this country.

Correspondence between representatives of BBC and Monty Python reveals that these parties assumed that ABC would broadcast each of the Monty Python programs "in its entirety." On September 5, 1975, however, the group's British representative inquired of BBC how ABC planned to show the programs in their entirety if approximately 24 minutes of each 90-minute program were to be devoted to commercials. BBC replied on September 12, "we can only reassure you that ABC have decided to run the programmes 'back to back,' and that there is a firm undertaking not to segment them."

ABC broadcast the first of the specials on October 3, 1975. Appellants did not see a tape of the program until late November and were allegedly "appalled" at the discontinuity and "mutilation" that had resulted from the editing done by Time-Life for ABC. Twenty-four minutes of the original 90 minutes of recording had been omitted. Some of the editing had been done in order to make time for commercials; other material had been edited, according to ABC, because the original programs contained offensive or obscene matter.

In early December, Monty Python learned that ABC planned to broadcast the second special on December 26, 1975. The parties began negotiations concerning editing of that program and a delay of the broadcast until Monty Python could view it. These negotiations were futile, however, and on December 15 the group filed this action to enjoin the broadcast and for damages. . . .

. . . The rationale for finding infringement when a licensee exceeds time or media restrictions on his license — the need to allow the proprietor of the underlying copyright to control the method in which his work is presented to the public — applies equally to the situation in which a licensee makes an unauthorized use of the underlying work by publishing it in a truncated version. Whether intended to allow greater economic exploitation of the work, as in the media and time cases, or to ensure that the copyright proprietor retains a veto power over revisions desired for the derivative work, the ability of the copyright holder to control his work remains paramount in our copyright law. We find, therefore, that unauthorized editing of the underlying work, if proven, would constitute an infringement of the copyright in that work similar to any other use of a work that exceeded the license granted by the proprietor of the copyright.

If the broadcast of an edited version of the Monty Python program infringed the group's copyright in the script, ABC may obtain no solace from the fact that editing was permitted in the agreements between BBC and Time-Life or Time-Life and ABC. BBC was not entitled to make unilateral changes in the script and was not specifically empowered to alter the recordings once made; Monty Python, moreover, had reserved to itself any rights not granted to BBC. Since a grantor may not convey greater rights than it owns, BBC's permission to allow Time-Life, and hence ABC, to edit appears to have been a nullity.

. . . Finally, ABC contends that appellants must have expected that deletions would be made in the recordings to conform them for use on commercial television in the United States. ABC argues that licensing in the United States implicitly grants a license to insert commercials in a program and to remove offensive or obscene material prior to broadcast. According to the network, appellants should have anticipated that most of the excised material contained scatological references inappropriate for American television and that these scenes would be replaced with commercials, which presumably are more palatable to the American public.

The proof adduced up to this point, however, provides no basis for finding any implied consent to edit. Prior to the ABC broadcasts, Monty Python programs had been broadcast on a regular basis by both commercial and public television stations in this country without interruption or deletion. Indeed, there is no evidence of any prior broadcast of edited Monty Python material in the United States. These facts, combined with the persistent requests for assurances by the group and its representatives that the programs would be shown intact belie the argument that the group knew or should have known that deletions and commercial interruptions were inevitable.

Several of the deletions made for ABC, such as elimination of the words "hell" and "damn," seem inexplicable given today's standard television fare. If, however, ABC honestly determined that the programs were obscene in substantial part, it could have decided not to broadcast the specials at all, or it could have attempted to reconcile its differences with appellants. The network could not, however, free from a claim of infringement, broadcast in a substantially altered form a program incorporating the script over which the group had retained control.

Our resolution of these technical arguments serves to reinforce our initial inclination that the copyright law should be used to recognize the important role of the artist in our society and the need to encourage production and dissemination of artistic works by providing adequate legal protection for one who submits his work to the public. We therefore conclude that there is a substantial likelihood that, after a full trial, appellants will succeed in proving infringement of their copyright by ABC's broadcast of edited versions of Monty Python programs. In reaching this conclusion, however, we need not accept appellants' assertion that any editing whatsoever would constitute infringement. Courts have recognized that licensees are entitled to some small degree of latitude in arranging the licensed work for presentation to the public in a manner consistent with the licensee's style or standards. That privilege, however, does not extend to the degree of editing that occurred here especially in light of contractual provisions that limited the right to edit Monty Python material.

It also seems likely that appellants will succeed on the theory that, regardless of the right ABC had to broadcast an edited program, the cuts made constituted an actionable mutilation of Monty Python's work. This cause of action, which seeks redress for deformation of an artist's work, finds its roots in the continental concept of *droit moral*, or moral right, which may generally be summarized as including the right of the artist to have his work attributed to him in the form in which he created it.

American copyright law, as presently written, does not recognize moral rights or provide a cause of action for their violation, since the law seeks to vindicate the economic, rather than the personal, rights of authors. Nevertheless, the economic incentive for artistic and intellectual creation that serves as the foundation for American copyright law, cannot be reconciled with the inability of artists to obtain relief for mutilation or misrepresentation of their work to the public on which the artists are financially dependent. Thus courts have long granted relief for misrepresentation of an artist's work by relying on theories outside the statutory law of copyright, such as contract law, Granz v. Harris, 198 F.2d 585 (2d Cir. 1952) (substantial cutting of original work constitutes misrepresentation), or the tort of unfair competition, Prouty v. National Broadcasting Co., 26 F. Supp. 265 (D. Mass. 1939). Although such decisions are clothed in terms of proprietary right in one's creation, they also properly vindicate the author's personal right to prevent the presentation of his work to the public in a distorted form. See Gardella v. Log Cabin Products Co., 89 F.2d 891, 895-96 (2d Cir. 1937). . . .

Complete relief for the alleged infringement and mutilation complained of may be accorded between Monty Python and ABC, which alone broadcast the programs in dispute. If ABC is ultimately found liable to appellants, a permanent injunction against future broadcasts and a damage award would satisfy all of appellants' claims. ABC's assertion that failure to join BBC and Time-Life may leave it subject to inconsistent verdicts in a later action against its licensors may be resolved through the process of impleader, which ABC has thus far avoided despite a suggestion from the district court to use that procedure. . . . For these reasons we direct that the district court issue the preliminary injunction sought by the appellants.

KEPNER-TREGOE, INC. v. VROOM
186 F.3d 283 (2d Cir. 1999)

MOTLEY, District Judge.

This is an appeal of a civil judgment against Professor Victor H. Vroom (Dr. Vroom) for breach of contract and copyright infringement relating to an exclusive licensing agreement between Dr. Vroom and Kepner-Tregoe, Inc. (K-T). The licensing agreement provided K-T with the exclusive use of executive leadership training materials co-authored by Dr. Vroom in return for the payment of royalties to Dr. Vroom. The two issues presented by this appeal are (1) whether the district court's finding of liability against Dr. Vroom for intentional copyright infringement and breach of contract should be upheld, and (2) whether the district court properly assessed damages in the amount of $219,855.21 plus attorneys' fees.

BACKGROUND

In 1972, Dr. Vroom, a professor at Yale University's School of Organization and Management, entered into a licensing agreement with K-T, an international management training company. (Joint Appendix (JA) at 1575-79). This agreement granted K-T the exclusive worldwide rights to specific copyrighted materials co-authored by Dr. Vroom. These materials, known as the Vroom-Yetton model, were used to teach managers how to make better decisions. In return, K-T agreed to pay Dr. Vroom and his co-author, Dr. Philip W. Yetton, royalties based on its exclusive use of the licensed materials. (JA at 1575). The licensing agreement also included a teaching clause that allowed Dr. Vroom to retain non-assignable rights to use the licensed materials for his "own teaching and private consultation work." (JA at 1575, ¶2(c)).

In the mid-1980s, Dr. Vroom created a more sophisticated software program, entitled "Managing Participation in Organizations" (MPO), which partially overlapped with the materials licensed to K-T. (JA at 1515). Dr. Vroom used the MPO program to conduct management training seminars for corporate executives at Yale University and other college campuses. (JA at 1516). Upon learning of Dr. Vroom's use of the copyrighted materials, K-T initiated this lawsuit in 1989. (JA at 1512).

K-T alleges that Dr. Vroom's use of the MPO program in his teaching of executives in the university setting infringes on its copyrights and constitutes a breach of the licensing agreement. It further alleges that Dr. Vroom breached the licensing agreement by assigning the rights to the MPO program, which infringed K-T's licensed materials, to Leadership Software Inc. (LSI), a Texas company founded by Dr. Vroom and his colleague, Dr. Arthur Jago. LSI was created to market the MPO program.

In 1990, K-T initiated a separate lawsuit against LSI and Dr. Jago in federal district court in Texas. Dr. Vroom was not a defendant in the suit because personal jurisdiction was unavailable. (JA at 1515). In that case, K-T alleged copyright infringement based on LSI's sales of the MPO program, which contained substantial similarities to the Vroom-Yetton model, the copyrighted materials exclusively licensed to K-T. The Texas district court found in favor of K-T and awarded it $46,000 in actual damages as well as injunctive relief. The Fifth Circuit modified the injunction entered by the district court, but affirmed its finding of liability. See *Kepner-Tregoe, Inc.*, 12 F.3d at 540.

After a five-day bench trial in April 1997, the district court in the present action held that Dr. Vroom's use of the licensed materials, including the infringing MPO program, in his teaching of executives in the university setting was not permitted under the teaching clause of the licensing agreement. (JA at 1527-28). The trial court found that the teaching clause was ambiguous as written and looked to other contemporaneous documentary evidence for clarification of the parties' intentions. (JA at 1534). The lower court interpreted the teaching clause to mean that Dr. Vroom was only allowed to use the copyrighted materials for his teaching of bona fide enrolled graduate and undergraduate students. (JA at 1541). Moreover, the district court found that Dr. Vroom willfully infringed the copyrighted material licensed to K-T and breached his contract with K-T when he taught the exclusively licensed materials to large groups of executives in the university setting. (JA at 1530, 1536). The court below also found that Dr. Vroom violated the licensing agreement when he assigned his rights to the licensed materials to LSI. (JA at 1532).

Awarding K-T the maximum statutory damages of $100,000, the district court found that Dr. Vroom's continued use of the MPO program in his executive training seminars, despite his knowledge of two federal court decisions in Texas that held the MPO program infringed K-T's copyrights, constituted willful infringement. (JA at 1538-39). The district court further held that K-T was entitled to attorneys' fees and costs under the Copyright Act, 17 U.S.C. §505. (JA at 1539-40). The trial court issued an injunction prohibiting Dr. Vroom from using the MPO program or other materials exclusively licensed to K-T in any proscribed manner. The lower court also awarded K-T $119,855.21 in compensatory damages on its breach of contract claim. (JA at 1539). The contractual damage award reflected the costs K-T incurred in litigating the Texas suit, which the district court found to be a direct consequence of Dr. Vroom's breach of the licensing agreement.

DISCUSSION

There is no dispute between the parties that the MPO program contains elements of the materials exclusively licensed to K-T. Rather, the only issues on appeal are (1) whether Dr. Vroom's use of the MPO program and other licensed materials in his executive training workshops on campus falls within the teaching clause of the licensing agreement, and (2) whether the district court properly assessed damages. Dr. Vroom contends that the district court erred in rejecting his acquiescence and public domain defenses to the copyright infringement claim. He further argues that the damage award constitutes a double recovery for a single injury. We will address the issue of copyright infringement before turning to Dr. Vroom's appeal of the damage award.

I. Copyright Infringement & Breach of Contract Claims

The central issue in this case involves the proper interpretation of the teaching clause of the licensing agreement, which allows Dr. Vroom to use the licensed materials in the course of his "own teaching and private consultation work." We find that the district court did not err in finding the teaching clause ambiguous. It properly looked to prior negotiations between the parties to determine the parties' intentions regarding the interpretation of the clause. Furthermore, credible evidence was presented at trial that supported the lower court's interpretation of the teaching clause so as to limit Dr. Vroom's teaching to only bona fide enrolled undergraduate and graduate students.

A. Interpretation of Teaching Clause

Dr. Vroom argues that the district court effectively rewrote the clear and unambiguous language of the licensing agreement by restricting his teaching of the licensed materials to only students. Dr. Vroom contends that the parties intended to allow him to retain broad and unlimited rights to use the licensed materials in his teaching, including his teaching of executives in the university setting. Dr. Vroom also claims that the trial court's decision will virtually deprive him of his right to earn a living because he is enjoined from using the MPO program in his courses for executives at Yale and other colleges.

We review the district court's construction of the text of the licensing contract de novo. To begin with, we agree with the district court that the teaching clause was ambiguous. K-T contends that this clause was only intended to allow the teaching of undergraduate and graduate students; Dr. Vroom argues that this clause, which also allowed "private consulting," also permitted him to teach classes to large groups of executives. We hold, as did the district court, that in the context of the agreement the word "teaching" was susceptible to the interpretation advanced by either Dr. Vroom or K-T. Accordingly, the district court was entitled to consider extrinsic evidence to interpret the contractual language.

We also affirm the district court's holding limiting the clause to the teaching of enrolled graduate and undergraduate students. The communications of the parties during the negotiation of the licensing agreement support this interpretation. K-T wrote a memorandum to Dr. Vroom in January of 1972, stating that it wanted to prevent "mass" teaching of the materials. Dr. Vroom produced no evidence at trial that he ever contradicted K-T's interpretation of the teaching clause in any communications with K-T throughout the remainder of the negotiations. The district court properly relied on this evidence to conclude that the teaching clause did not extend beyond the teaching of enrolled graduate and undergraduate students.

B. Acquiescence

Contrary to Dr. Vroom's contention, the district court materially addressed the acquiescence argument in the context of its discussion of breach of contract and the proper interpretation of the teaching clause. We find that the district court properly rejected this defense, for which Dr. Vroom bore the burden of proof. See Corning Glass Works v. Southern New England Tel. Co., 835 F.2d 451, 452 (2d Cir. 1987) (per curiam). Dr. Vroom presented no evidence that K-T knew he was using licensed materials in his executive training seminars. K-T only knew Dr. Vroom was teaching executive seminars on campus. (Pl.'s Br. at 24). Since Dr. Vroom presented no evidence that suggested that K-T had knowledge that he was using the copyrighted materials and failed to object, we hold that the district court did not err in rejecting Dr. Vroom's acquiescence defense.

C. Public Domain

Finally, Dr. Vroom alleges that the licensed materials entered the public domain in December of 1971, when he published the Vroom-Yetton model in an article in *Novus*, a publication of Carnegie-Mellon University. This article was distributed without any notice of copyright. We reject this contention.

These events are governed by the 1909 Copyright Act. Under the 1909 Act, an unpublished expression was protected only by a common law copyright. If the expression was then published in compliance with the Act, including notice of copyright, it received statutory copyright protection; if it was published without notice, the common law copyright was forfeited, and the material entered the public domain. See Sanga Music, Inc. v. EMI Blackwood Music, Inc., 55 F.3d 756, 758-59 (2d Cir. 1995); see also Shoptalk, Ltd. v. Concorde-New Horizons Corp., 168 F.3d 586, 590 (2d Cir.), cert. denied, 527 U.S. 1038 (1999) ("Under the 1909 Act, the publication of a work, with a proper notice, secured statutory copyright protection."). Once a statutory copyright was acquired by publication with notice, this common law forfeiture could not occur.

In this case, Dr. Vroom's first publication of the Vroom-Yetton model, as stated on his copyright application was on August 12, 1971. Registration was obtained in October of 1971. The *Novus* article did not appear until December of 1971, after statutory protection had been secured, and it did not result in forfeiture of the copyright. Moreover, the district court, relying on evidence of the extensive subsequent measures taken by Dr. Vroom to protect his copyright, properly found that Dr. Vroom did not intend to abandon the copyright by publication of the model in *Novus*.

II. Damages

A. Maximum Statutory Award Is Justified in Light of Dr. Vroom's Willful Infringement

Dr. Vroom also appeals the district court's finding of willfulness. He alleges that he had a reasonable and good faith belief that his use of the licensed materials was protected under the licensing agreement. Dr. Vroom contends that he did not knowingly violate the Copyright Act since he had a good faith belief that his activities fell within the teaching clause, which the district court found to be ambiguous. K-T, on the other hand, argues that Dr. Vroom knowingly used the MPO program after two federal courts found it to be infringing, which justifies the enhanced statutory damages and attorneys' fees award. It further argues that the district court's willfulness finding was amply supported by the record.

This court reviews the district court's finding of willfulness and resulting enhanced statutory damages for clear error. See Knitwaves, Inc. v. Lollytogs Ltd., 71 F.3d 996, 1010 (2d Cir. 1995). The standard for willfulness is "whether the defendant had knowledge that [his] conduct represented infringement or perhaps recklessly disregarded the possibility." Twin Peaks Prods., Inc. v. Publications Int'l, Ltd., 996 F.2d 1366, 1382 (2d Cir. 1993).

The $100,000 statutory copyright infringement damages were justified in this case since the district court's finding that Dr. Vroom willfully violated the agreement was supported by the evidence presented at trial. (JA at 1518-24, 1527, 1530, 1532-33). Dr. Vroom continued to use the MPO program even after a Texas district court and the Fifth Circuit found that the MPO program infringed K-T's copyrights and entered an injunction against LSI's use of the MPO program. (JA at 1538-39). Dr. Vroom was clearly aware of these decisions, evidenced by his 50% ownership in LSI, the defendant in the Texas suit, and his financing of LSI's unsuccessful appeal to the Fifth Circuit. (JA at 97, 1530). However, Dr. Vroom chose to ignore the injunction and continued to use the MPO program in his executive training workshops. (JA at 1517, 1538-39). Dr. Vroom also knowingly assigned his rights to the licensed materials to a third party in direct violation of the licensing agreement. (JA at 1527, 1532-33). Each of these acts justifies a finding of willful infringement.

The court's award of attorney fees under the Copyright Act, 17 U.S.C. §505, is also justified based on the court's finding of willfulness and is in line with the statutory goal of deterrence. See Fogerty v. Fantasy, Inc., 510 U.S. 517, 534 n. 19 (1994). Thus, as the district court noted, Dr. Vroom's egregious conduct in continuing to use the MPO program following the Texas court's injunction was the "antithesis of innocence" and fully justified the district court's award of maximum statutory damages as well as its award of attorneys' fees. (A1538-40).

B. Breach of Contract Damages

Dr. Vroom further contends that the district court erred in awarding a double recovery to K-T. Dr. Vroom argues that K-T is being compensated twice for the same alleged injury under two legal theories, copyright infringement and breach of contract. K-T objects to this ground for appeal, claiming that Dr. Vroom did not raise this issue in the district court.

The district court's damage award does not represent a double recovery. The fact that Dr. Vroom did not raise this issue in his Post-Trial Memorandum does not preclude this court from addressing the issue. Dr. Vroom cannot be said to have reasonably anticipated that the lower court would make an allegedly double damage award. However, this court finds that the district court did not award K-T double damages as Dr. Vroom contends. The approximately $120,000 in contract damages represents the cost of litigating the Texas suit, which was found to be a direct consequence of Dr. Vroom's breach of the licensing agreement. Such damages are permissible under Ingersoll Milling Mach. Co. v. M/V Bodena, 829 F.2d 293, 309 (2d Cir. 1987), which allowed for the recovery of counsel fees and other litigation expenses incurred in a prior suit to enforce contract rights against a third party.

Thus, there are two distinct categories of damages based on two separate acts. The $100,000 statutory damage award stems from Dr. Vroom's willful acts of copyright infringement after the Texas court enjoined the sale or use of the infringing MPO program. The approximately $120,000 contractual damage award represents K-T's consequential damages of having to litigate a suit in Texas to enforce its copyright rights stemming from Dr. Vroom's breach of the licensing agreement when he assigned the rights to the MPO to a third party. Thus, the two elements of the district court's damage award are permissible and do not constitute a double recovery.

CONCLUSION

Having considered all of defendant's grounds for appeal, we find no basis for reversing the district court's findings. Therefore, the decision of the district court is affirmed.

DISENOS ARTISTICOS E INDUSTRIALES, S.A. v. COSTCO WHOLESALE CORP.
97 F.3d 377 (9th Cir. 1996)

KLEINFELD, Circuit Judge.

This is a copyright case involving importation of Lladro figurines. We conclude that the defendant was entitled to summary judgment because the undisputed facts established implied authority for the importation.

FACTS

The copyrighted objects at issue in this case are Lladro figurines. These are decorative figurines designed for collection and display. They are copyrighted by the lead plaintiff, Disenos Artisticos e Industriales, S.A. (DAISA), a Spanish Corporation.

DAISA, the copyright owner, is part of a group of related corporations. Lladro Comercial, S.A. is the parent corporation, and through intermediaries, wholly owns DAISA. Lladro USA's business strategy in the United States is to market the figurines only to select up-scale retailers. It spends considerable money on marketing to promote the reputation of the brand as high quality collectors' items and supports auctions establishing a secondary market for the figurines.

DAISA, the copyright owner, does not manufacture the figurines itself. Nor does the parent corporation. Instead, DAISA licenses the copyright to four Spanish corporations, all affiliated with the Lladro group, and contracts with them to manufacture the figurines.

The manufacturers are licensed not only to produce, but also to sell the figurines "to all countries of the world, without the existence of any limitations or exclusions of territory." DAISA does not restrict its licensees at all with respect to distribution. The licensed manufacturers do not, however, take advantage of their license from DAISA to sell to all countries of the world. Instead, each has a contract with the parent corporation, Lladro Comercial, to sell the entire output of figurines to the parent corporation. The parent corporation then distributes the figurines throughout the world. The manufacturers' contracts with the parent corporation provide that the parent corporation controls the means of sale, "selecting the appropriate category of the places to sell as well as the distributors and representatives."

The parent corporation then sells the figurines, directly to retailers in some countries, and to distributors in others. In its contract with Lladro USA, the parent corporation promises not to export the figurines to anyone but Lladro USA within the fifty states of the United States. The parent further covenants that it "shall not knowingly cause any third party to sell the Product in the Territory," "nor shall authorize any other party to distribute the Product within the Territory."

Lladro Comercial has at least three arrangements regarding re-export. It has contracts with some distributors prohibiting commercial re-export and even sales of large quantities to other retailers who might themselves export. Other distributors are prohibited only from "carry[ing] out an active marketing policy of the product outside the territory," as by "publicity" or starting a subsidiary. In a third arrangement, Lladro Comercial directly or through distributors sells to retailers without any contractual restrictions at all.

The defendant, Costco, operates a chain of retail stores throughout the United States. During the years relevant to this case, 1990 through 1994, it sold Lladro figurines in its stores. None of the figurines were pirated copies or fakes. All were genuine and were manufactured pursuant to the manufacturing license granted by DAISA. Lladro USA has not sold figurines to Costco, or authorized Costco to sell them.

Costco did not import any of the figurines. All of the figurines in question were purchased from various other sources within the United States. Most of the boxes in the Costco stores had a portion of the box sliced off. Lladro's detective work suggested the likelihood that Costco's figurines were distributed within Spain, and ultimately wound up in the United States through chains of distribution other than those Lladro Comercial intended, and definitely not through Lladro USA. Some came from countries where they were sold directly to retailers without contractual restrictions. For example, some were imported by an American company from a store in Mexico that went out of business. The Mexican store had no contractual agreement with any Lladro affiliate restricting its right to market inventory in the United States or anywhere else.

DAISA and Lladro USA filed a complaint in federal district court alleging that Costco's sale of Lladro figurines was unauthorized and in violation of section 602(a) of the Copyright Act. On cross motions for summary judgment, the district court granted summary judgment in favor of Lladro USA and DAISA, on the theory that the sales to Costco were not authorized.

ANALYSIS

We begin with the statute upon which DAISA and Lladro rely, which prohibits importation of copyrighted goods into the United States "without the authority of the owner of copyright":

> Importation into the United States, without the authority of the owner of the copyright under this title, of copies or phonorecords of a work that has been acquired outside the United States is an infringement of the exclusive right to distribute copies. . . .

17 U.S.C. §602(a). This statute is part of the legislative scheme for dealing with pirated and "gray market" goods. In the trademark context, "[a] gray-market good is a foreign-manufactured good, bearing a valid United States trademark, that is imported without the consent of the United States trademark holder." Kmart Corporation v. Cartier, Inc., 486 U.S. 281, 285, 108 S. Ct. 1811, 1814, 100 L. Ed. 2d 313 (1988). Copyright and trademark owners fought a lengthy and intense legislative battle over the degree to which they would be able to use the customs service and federal law to control the flow of gray market goods. Melville B. Nimmer & David Nimmer, NIMMER ON COPYRIGHT §8.11 [B] (1992). Copyright and trademark law are not the only means of protecting the integrity of a distributorship network, of course. To the extent that the copyright owner has enough market power to obtain and enforce them, it can use contractual restrictions on resale. It can also buy back unsold inventory, as chewing gum and magazine distributors typically do. Wholesalers and retailers may bargain for the right to sell back unsold inventory, or the freedom to liquidate it however they can. We should not put our thumb on the legislative scale. A court construing a statute should avoid adding to or detracting from the benefits Congress accorded to any of the competing interests.

Costco did not import any of the figurines, so on its face, the statutory prohibition of "importation into the United States" might be understood not to have any application.

DAISA argues that under Parfums Givenchy, Inc. v. Drug Emporium, Inc., 38 F.3d 477, 482 (9th Cir. 1994), a retailer can violate section 602(a)'s importation restriction even if it does not import into the United States. Costco offers arguments which would factually distinguish and limit *Parfums Givenchy*.

DAISA concedes that under its interpretation of section 602(a) and *Parfums Givenchy*, every little gift shop in America would be subject to copyright penalties for genuine goods purchased in good faith from American distributors, where unbeknownst to the gift shop proprietor, the copyright owner had attempted to arrange some different means of distribution several transactions back. DAISA suggests that the answer to this problem is for each gift shop proprietor to obtain from the copyright owner (not his seller) a certification that the importation into the United States was authorized.

Costco also argues that the first sale doctrine, at common law or as codified in 17 U.S.C. §109(a), which limits the right of a copyrighter to control disposition of a genuine copy after the first sale of that copy, supplies a defense in this case because DAISA obtained the benefit of its copyright at the time of its first lawful sale abroad. DAISA argues, based on *Parfums Givenchy* and BMG Music v. Perez, 952 F.2d 318 (9th Cir. 1991), that the first sale doctrine does not provide a defense to copyright infringement until there is an authorized first sale in the United States.

The impracticality of the burden DAISA would have us impose on the retailers gives us pause about whether its reading of *Parfums Givenchy* and *BMG Music* is correct. But we do not reach either issue in our disposition. We thus have no occasion to decide whether Costco as a non-importer can be liable for importation under section 602(a), or whether the first sale doctrine applies in this case. Unlike *Givenchy* and *BMG Music*, this case is resolved on whether the importation was authorized.

Under section 602(a), the only authorization that counts is authorization by "the owner of the copyright." DAISA owns the copyright, not Lladro Comercial or Lladro USA. It is true that DAISA is a subsidiary of Lladro Comercial, but that does not mean that the parent owns the copyright. Lladro Comercial would have us pierce its own corporate veil. But a corporation is not entitled to establish and use its affiliates' separate legal existence for some purposes, yet have their separate corporate existence disregarded for its own benefit against third parties. Generally, the corporate veil can be pierced only by an adversary of the corporation, not by the corporation itself for its own benefit. United Continental Tuna Corp. v. United States, 550 F.2d 569, 573 (9th Cir. 1977); Harry G. Henn & John R. Alexander, Laws of Corporations and Other Business Enterprises §149, at 347 ("corporateness is rarely disregarded" for the benefit of the shareholders).

Because DAISA owned the copyright, we determine whether importation was "without the authority of the owner" by examining the conduct of DAISA. DAISA's arrangements were with its licensees only. DAISA authorized its licensee manufacturers to sell the figurines to "all countries of the world." It did not require its licensees to restrict the sales in any way. So far as DAISA's contracts provided, any of the manufacturers could distribute any of the figurines directly or indirectly into the United States.

Costco argues this express grant of authority flows downstream to all subsequent purchasers, so, as a subsequent purchaser, Costco has express authority under section 602(a). DAISA argues that because Lladro USA has the only express grant of authority to import into the United States, Costco's liability for infringement cannot be avoided on the basis of express authority. We do not decide whether the grant of express authority by the copyright owners, DAISA, to its licensee manufacturers to sell "all countries of the world" amounts to an express authorization for "importation into the United States." Implied authority is plain enough, so that we need not reach the question of express authority.

In Effects Associates, Inc. v. Cohen, 908 F.2d 555 (9th Cir. 1990), we held that a party's "conduct created an implied license" to use copyrighted material. Id. at 558. The statutory language supports this interpretation of "authority" in 17 U.S.C. §602(a) to include implied authority. In at least two other copyright statutes, Congress uses the phrase "except with the express consent of the copyright owner." See, e.g., 17 U.S.C. §112(e); 17 U.S.C. §115(a)(2). In the trademark law analogous to 17 U.S.C. §602(a), importation of marked merchandise is generally prohibited "unless written consent of the owner of such trademark is produced at the time of making entry." 43 U.S.C. §1526(a). When Congress resolved the gray market battle between retailers and copyright owners under section 602(a), it did not do it with the words "express consent" or "written consent." Instead it said "authority," which ordinarily includes implied authority. Cf. Thomas v. INS, 35 F.3d 1332, 1339 (9th Cir. 1994); In re Nelson, 761 F.2d 1320, 1322 (9th Cir. 1985).

The authority to export to the United States must necessarily imply the authority to import into the United States, commercially as well as logically. Lladro USA's evidence on summary judgment shows how a secondary market supports a higher price:

> Lladro USA manages the Lladro Collectors Society and publishes Expressions Magazine, both of which are dedicated to serving the needs of collectors of Lladro figurines. Lladro USA has also published two high quality "art" books devoted to the study of Lladro figurines.
>
> Lladro USA promotes two annual auctions in the United States at which investors in Lladro figurines may buy and sell their figurines. Because of Lladro's high quality, high prestige reputation, many people are able to realize a return several times their investment at these auctions.

Likewise, the existence of a liquidation market could be expected to support a higher wholesale price. When a purchaser of Lladro figurines from Lladro Comercial bargains for the right to export them outside its territory, it can afford to pay more for them, because of the larger market for liquidation of excess inventory. Some of the Costco figurines were derived from a Mexican store which had closed. That store had purchased its figurines with no restriction upon its right to resell them. Had Lladro Comercial bargained with that store owner for a prohibition upon his right to sell them into the United States, then the store owner would have had to consider the smaller market available for liquidation when she considered how much money she could afford to commit to Lladro inventory. The right to export would be valueless if it did not imply a right to import.

Costco argues that authority for importation into the United States has to be inferred from DAISA's authorization to its licensee manufacturers to sell the figurines anywhere in the world. DAISA and Lladro Comercial argue that only Lladro USA had express authority to import, and it was plain from the distribution scheme organized by Lladro Comercial that Lladro USA was intended to be the only authorized importer. Because DAISA owned the copyright, and authorized export into the United States, we find Costco's argument to be the persuasive one.

Lladro Comercial correctly points out that the manufacturers did not export the figurines into the United States, but sold all of them to Lladro Comercial, whose intent was to make Lladro USA the exclusive United States distributor. This is irrelevant for purposes of section 602(a), because Lladro Comercial was not the copyright owner. Lladro Comercial owned the goods, was the parent company of the company which copyrighted them, and was indirectly the United States distributor, but it did not own the copyright. Section 602(a) confers power only on the "owner of the copyright." Where the owner of the goods is a separate firm from the owner of the copyright, it cannot use Section 602(a) to control its distribution network.

Authorization by a copyright owner to export goods to anywhere in the world necessarily implies authority to import the goods into the United States. So do sales without restriction on export into the United States. No written or express authorization to import is required by 17 U.S.C. §602(a). Therefore, absence of written authorization to import does not establish the element of a claim under 17 U.S.C. §602(a), that the importation is "without the authority of the owner," at least where other words or conduct imply authority. Accordingly, in this case, the copyright owner, DAISA, and Lladro USA failed to establish that the importation into the United States was "without the authority of the owner of the copyright." Because the undisputed facts establish absence of that element, Costco was entitled to summary judgment.

Costco and Appellees both seek attorneys' fees for this appeal under 17 U.S.C. §505. We have discretion to award them. Attorneys' fees are awarded in favor of Costco, in an amount to be determined by the district court.

The judgment of the district court is REVERSED, and on REMAND judgment should be entered in favor of Costco.

III. PROBLEMS

1. New World is a Delaware corporation that produces and distributes television programs. Televisión Española is a Spanish company that acquires rights to broadcast television programs throughout Spain.

   In April 1994, the two companies met at a television market in Cannes, France, where Televisión Española alleges there was an oral agreement for an exclusive license for two of New World's animated programs, *Spiderman* and *Marvel Action Hour*. After the Cannes meeting, New World informed Televisión Española that any licensing of *Spiderman* would have to be accompanied by deals for *Marvel Action Hour* and two other programs, *Tales from the Crypt* and *The Extraordinary*.

   The parties engaged in further negotiations and faxed each other memos discussing details concerning regional affiliates, format of the programs, price, and quantity. The first fax sent by New World to Televisión Española did not set forth the terms of any license agreement regarding *Spiderman* or *Marvel Action Hour*. The second fax from New World to Televisión Española stated that the *Spiderman* program should be "divided into two contracts which will be issued together and will provide as" stated in the rest of the fax. New World apparently authorized the division of the contracts, but they would "have to be done by year" and "the package cannot be broken up." The fax concludes: "[w]ith nothing further at this time, awaiting the contracts. . . ."

Not until May 26, 1995, did Televisión Española finally deliver the written proposed licensing contracts to New World. New World, however, never signed the contracts.

Was there a valid exclusive license agreement between the parties? *See* 17 U.S.C. §204(a) and 17 U.S.C. §101 (providing definition for "transfer of copyright ownership").

2. Bartsch granted to MGM "motion picture rights throughout the world, in and to a certain musical play . . . together with the sole and exclusive right to . . . copyright, vend, license and exhibit such motion picture photoplays throughout the world." Thereafter, MGM made a television adaptation of the play and Bartsch's estate sued, alleging that the original grant did not include the television rights.

How would you defend MGM?

3. The parties entered into an agreement that contains the following grant provision:

> The Author hereby grants and assigns solely and exclusively to the Publisher throughout the world during the full term of copyright and all renewals thereof on the terms set out in the Agreement, the book and volume publishing right in the English language throughout the world in *Evidence of Love* along with the following rights; abridgement, syndication, radio broadcasting, television, mechanical recording and rendition, projection, Braille, microfilm, translation, dramatic, and motion pictures; ancillary commercial promotion rights, together with the right to grant licenses for the exercise of and/or to dispose of any or all of the rights granted.

Does the grant cover "video distribution right"?

4. Adobe is one of the leading software development and publishing companies in the United States. Some of its copyrighted software products include Adobe Illustrator, Adobe Pagemaker, and Adobe Acrobat. Adobe also makes "Educational" versions of its software packages available for license to students and educators at a discount. Adobe Educational distributors are licensed to transfer Educational software only to resellers who have signed Off- or On-Campus Educational Reseller Agreements ("OCRA") with Adobe.

Stargate is a discount software distributor. Stargate is not an authorized distributor of Adobe products. In 1997, Stargate began acquiring software from two businesses, Dallas Computer and D.C. Micro, with the majority of the software being Adobe Educational software. Adobe contends that Stargate's suppliers acquired Adobe Educational software from Adobe Educational distributor Douglas Stewart Co. pursuant to valid OCRAs. However, Stargate alleges that all of the Adobe software products that Stargate sold were purchased through either D.C. Micro, Inc. or Dallas Computers, Inc.

Between March 1998 and April 1999, Stargate purchased between 1795-2189 packages of "Educational" software produced by Adobe. Stargate distributed this Educational software at below-market prices to retail customers and unauthorized resellers through magazine advertisements, trade shows, action Web sites, and its Web site "*www.stargatesoftware.com.*" Adobe alleges that Stargate infringed Adobe's copyrights by obtaining and selling Educational versions of Adobe software without Adobe's authorization. Stargate contends that it was the rightful owner of the Adobe software products and therefore did not infringe Adobe's copyright by reselling those products, pursuant to the "first sale" doctrine.

Does the manufacturer's distribution of copies of its software to licensed distributors constitute "first sale" of copies?

5. Can a district court issue a preliminary injunction under the Federal Arbitration Act when the parties to the copyright license agreement have agreed that arbitration "shall be the sole and exclusive remedy for resolving any disputes between the parties arising out of or involving the Agreement" sued upon? Is preliminary injunctive relief available even though the dispute between the licensor and the licensee is the subject of mandatory arbitration?

IV. DRAFTING EXERCISES

1. Identify potential problems in the following grant provision and re-draft it to fix the problems:

> Scholastics grants Barnes and Noble the exclusive right to publish the paperback edition of "The Hunger Games" not sooner than October 2010.

2. The following provision purports to give ownership of derivative works to the licensor. Does it? Re-draft the provision to make sure that the licensor gets ownership.

> Licensor hereby grants Licensee a non-exclusive right to copy certain materials described in Attachment A (the "Material"), in whole or in part, and to incorporate the Material, in whole or in part, into other works (the "Derivative Works") for Licensee's internal use only. All right, title, and interest in the Material, including without limitation, any copyright, shall remain with Licensor. Licensor shall own the copyright in the Derivative Works.

3. Consider the non-exclusive license below. Identify potential problems and re-draft the grant provision.

> Licensor grants to Licensee the non-exclusive right to use, duplicate, and disclose, in whole or in part, such materials in any manner for any purpose whatsoever.

4. Sometimes the copyright holder may not know whether it has all the bundle of rights under copyright law and whether all of the copyrighted works are outside of the public domain. As the copyright term of protection is long and lasts beyond the life of the individual author, the new copyright holder is then the heir or the estate.

Imagine that the new copyright holder is the estate of a known prolific artist, and the copyright holder may not know what the artist had done to various rights in his or her works. The copyright holder would like to enter into a license agreement with a licensee. Draft the license agreement to address the above problems. The copyright holder has heard about carving out potential liability in the "Representations and Warranties" provision of the license agreement.

PART THREE

LICENSING IN BUSINESS
AND INDUSTRY

9

SOFTWARE LICENSING

I. OVERVIEW OF SOFTWARE LICENSING

A. Introduction

Licensing is important in all aspects of the software industry, from the development and distribution of software, to its end use. With a license, a software developer can provide the same code to diverse users for diverse uses: A developer might grant one person the right to create unlimited derivative works, another the right to fix bugs, another the right to examine the inner-workings of the software in order to create interoperable software, another the right to distribute the code in packaged product form, another the right to distribute the code preinstalled on computers, and another the right simply to use the software. Licensing underlies all these possibilities.

This Overview begins by describing the various forms of software. This is important because software licenses do not normally grant rights to "software" but delineate rights based on the various forms that software takes. Next, the Overview provides a brief history of software licensing. Then, it describes the wide variety of software licenses and some of the significant issues that arise in the context of each type of licensing.

B. The Forms of Software

The term "software" came into general usage around 1960. *See* Fredrick P. Brooks, Jr., THE MYTHICAL MAN MONTH: ESSAYS ON SOFTWARE ENGINEERING 4 (1975). A software developer would probably say that software comes in two forms: source code and object code. "Source code" refers to the code written by software programmers in a computer language such as Basic, C, or Java. Source code is human readable code — it can be understood by any programmer proficient in the language in which it is written.

"Object code" is derived from source code using a software tool called a compiler. It consists of a series of ones and zeroes so it is sometimes called "binary code." Object code executes (i.e., runs) on the computer hardware. Because of this, it is sometimes referred to as "executable code." Object code is machine readable code — only computers can make sense of it.

Apart from object code and source code, another way to describe software is by its output. What do we see when it runs? We see the visual displays that the software generates. In the early days of computing most displays were character-based but now most are graphical.

Another way to describe software is by its functionality — what does it do when it runs? People often put software into categories such as servers, operating systems, applications, middleware, utilities, and developer tools. They also talk about a particular program's function vis-à-vis the overall program, so they may refer to code as a file system, a kernel, a directory, a library, an interface, a header file, a driver, or a plug-in. These categories change over time; the boundaries may blur or vanish and new categories often appear.

A recent trend is to talk about software in terms of the user experience or the service it provides. Software publishers sometimes call this "software as a service." Tim Berners-Lee, father of the World Wide Web, predicts that someday software will be embedded in so many devices so ingeniously that its presence will be nearly invisible to the user. *See* Tim Berners-Lee, *Raising the Full Potential of the Web*, W3C, *at http://www.w3.org/1998/02/Potential.html* (Dec. 3, 1997).

C. Brief History of Software Licensing

1. The Early Days

The use of licenses has a long history in the software industry. Many of the early software developers were scientists, academics, or hobbyists. It was common for them to share code. In sharing code, the programmers either gave express or implied permission to copy and distribute the code as well as to create derivatives of it. *See generally* Martin Campbell-Kelly, A History of the Software Industry: From Airline Reservations to Sonic the Hedgehog (2003). This practice is licensing, although often it was done without any awareness of the label.

Initially, software came bundled with the computer hardware it ran on. Hardware and software were packaged together and thought of as a unitary product, with software being one component. *See* Michael A. Cusumano, The Business of Software (2004). Firms such as AT&T, IBM, and Digital Equipment Corporation sold complete systems of computer hardware and software, often together with maintenance and support.

The focus of licensing at this stage was on granting permission to share and collaborate. To the extent licenses were directed to the end users of software, the audience was the software programmers employed by the end users to allow them to fix, adapt, support, and maintain the software.

2. A Software Industry Emerges

Over time, however, firms began to offer software as a separate product. The first software entrepreneurs worked as defense contractors for the U.S. government in the 1950s, with civilian uses following in the 1960s. These firms wrote specially designed software for a particular purpose and end user. For example, a programmer might write software to run an automatic bank teller machine or an online airline reservations service. This type of custom software development continues to this day.

3. Mass Market Software

The software industry blossomed in the 1970s spurred by IBM's decision to un-bundle the hardware and software for the IBM PC. Firms such as Ashton-Tate, Lotus, Microsoft, Novell, and WordPerfect emerged to produce software for the personal computers produced by IBM and IBM PC "compatibles." The personal computer revolution put software in the hands of millions of people. Few of them had any expertise or interest in software programming. They simply wanted to use the software in object code form. This led to the creation of a variety of distribution licensing models to deliver software to the mass market and to the use of standard form end user licenses.

4. Enterprise Software

Lying somewhere between custom software and mass market software is enterprise software. Enterprise software forms the backbone of business enterprises by handling fundamental tasks such as storing data, facilitating communications, managing customer accounts, tracking inventory, billing, and accounting. Enterprise software tends to have prefabricated components which are then customized for the particular customer. Companies such as SAP, Oracle, and IBM provide enterprise software with licenses tailored to the needs of enterprise customers.

5. Digital Convergence

It used to be easy to distinguish between sound recordings, motion pictures, literary works, and software. That is no longer true. Many software products contain elements from some or all these formerly discrete product categories. These products are sometimes known as multimedia products.

A major challenge of this convergence, from a licensing perspective, is that the producers of these formerly discrete product categories — movie studios, record companies, print publishers, and software developers — all have different licensing models, both for product production and distribution. In other words, licensing models are colliding at the same time as digital media are converging. Chapter 11 explores some of these issues.

6. Embedded Software

Software now runs on more devices than the ones traditionally we have called "computers." Software powers everything from coffeemakers and telephones to car brakes, air traffic control systems, and sophisticated medical imaging equipment. This software often comes embedded in the hardware. The decision about whether to embed software or provide it on a disk comes down to a series of engineering trade-offs between speed, size, and flexibility. However, the form often has a substantive impact on end user licensing: Users may expect to see a license in certain forms (e.g., on disks) but not others (embedded). It may also affect which contract law applies to the transaction because, at least on the face of it, one form (e.g., on disks) appears to be a license of software governed by the common law and the other (e.g., embedded) a sale of goods governed by UCC Article 2.

7. Networked Environment

Computer networks, especially the Internet, have had several important effects on software licensing. Networking allows software developers to collaborate and share code on a massive scale. It has eased and increased the number of ways to distribute software. It has also enabled users to download and run software from and store data on remote sites — this hosted software model, sometimes called "cloud computing" or "software as a service," allows users to outsource software maintenance, support, and storage to third parties. Finally, it has increased the need for software programs to interoperate with one another over networks. Standards organizations often provide the forum for the software industry to come together to collaborate on interoperable systems.

8. Multiple Rights

As discussed in Chapter 1, a software program may be covered by a variety of intellectual property rights. Initially, trade secret rights and copyrights were the most important, but now patents and trademarks are important as well. A software license, therefore, must take account of all these rights. For each software license, the parties must analyze which rights should be licensed. Will the license grant rights under copyright? How about patent, trademark, or trade secret rights? Within each category of proprietary rights, which of the particular exclusive rights should be licensed (e.g., copying, derivative works) and under what conditions and within which parameters?

D. The Landscape of Software Licensing

There are a wide variety of license transactions in the software industry. The transactions fall into four main categories: licenses to build products; licenses to create customer solutions; licenses to distribute software; and licenses that describe usage. The former two categories are often called upstream licenses; the latter two are called downstream licenses.

1. Upstream Licenses

Mass market end user software licenses are ubiquitous in modern commerce. Their sheer volume gives the impression that most licensing law and practice is concerned with them. It is not. Instead, upstream licenses make up the lion's share of a licensing lawyer's practice.

a. Licenses to Build Products

Sometimes a programmer develops software alone and from scratch. If so, the programmer owns the rights in the code. If an employee develops the code in the course of employment, in the United States the employer owns the copyright in the code as a "work made for hire." The *Aymes v. Bonelli* case in the Materials section of this chapter explores the parameters of the work for hire doctrine in the context of software development.

It is common practice, however, for a programmer to collaborate with many others in creating a software program. The *Ashton-Tate v. Ross* case in the Materials section of this chapter illustrates one such collaboration. Large software projects contain code and digital content from many individuals and firms. Although the Microsoft Windows and GNU/Linux operating systems differ in many ways, both systems incorporate an array of code that is created by third parties other than (as the case may be) Microsoft or Linus Torvalds. The programmers may jointly own rights in the code. However, software developers typically use licenses to apportion the rights between the various contributors in a way that makes the most sense under the circumstances. In other words, software developers use licenses as the legal tool to build their software products.

b. Licenses to Create Solutions

In the early days of the software industry, users received all necessary computer technology from one source. Companies such as IBM provided complete packages of computer hardware, software, and services and support. Today this sort of one-stop shopping is less common. A simple personal computer system contains components from a variety of sources: The microprocessor may come from Intel, the hard disk drive from Fujitsu, the CPU from Lenovo, the monitor from Samsung, the keyboard from Hewlett-Packard, the mouse from Logitec, the printer from Canon, the operating system from Microsoft, Google, Apple, or Red Hat, and other software from Adobe, Autodesk, Electronic Arts, Facebook, Monta Vista, Mozilla, Novell, Oracle,

SendMail, Valve, and Symantec. In order for these components to work together, the different developers often need to exchange rights. They do so in the form of licenses.

For example, for the assortment of computer hardware and software described above to be useful for a user, the following licenses may need to be exchanged:

- License under patents from the microprocessor firm to the computer hardware manufacturer;
- Licenses between the operating system developer and the keyboard, mouse, and monitor manufacturers to create and distribute device driver software;
- License between the operating system developer and the printer manufacturer for font and page description software;
- License to application programming interface (API) information or source code between the applications developer and the systems software developer;
- License from the systems software developer to hardware and microprocessor manufacturers to study and modify systems software source code in order to tune the computer hardware or microprocessor so that it runs most effectively;
- Licenses to protocol information to enable communication over the Internet.

c. Source Code Licensing

Source code licensing plays an important role in collaborations to build products and create customer solutions. Sometimes the license involves rights to use confidential source code; other times the license is to use non-confidential source code that is available in the mass market either in a software development kit licensed by a commercial software developer or available as free or open source software.

Confidential Source Code. It is standard industry practice for software developers to hold some or all of their source code as a trade secret. *See, e.g.,* McRoberts Software Inc. v. Media 100, Inc., 329 F.3d 557 (7th Cir. 2003); Dun & Bradstreet Software Services v. Grace Consulting, Inc., 307 F.3d 197 (3d Cir. 2002). Even so, software developers need to share their confidential source code in order to collaborate with others in building their product or making it work with other hardware or software components to create a viable customer solution. Consequently, confidential source code licensing is a common form of licensing in the software industry. The Materials section of this chapter contains a sample confidential source code license. These licenses combine the characteristics of a copyright and trade secret license. The copyright license grant is carefully tailored to the licensee's particular uses of the source code and the license contains a series of measures to protect the confidentiality of the code.

Free and Open Source Software. Not all software development takes place using confidential source code. Some programmers believe that source code always should be shared on a non-confidential basis. This is known as "free" or "open source" software ("FOSS" for short). The underlying rationale for this belief differs. Some believe that code sharing is a good engineering practice to create high quality software. Others maintain that code sharing increases competition in the software industry. Still others contend that freely sharing code is akin to free speech.

Regardless of the rationale, the developers of FOSS have shaken up the traditional commercial software industry. Originally FOSS was made and used primarily by programmers; now FOSS is prominent in many venues. A FOSS program called SendMail routes most of the e-mail in the Internet, BIND displays Internet addresses in readable form, Apache runs many Web servers, and the Linux kernel is the basis of operating systems running on computers large and small. FOSS burst onto the public stage when Netscape decided to release the source code to its popular browser software under an open source license. Companies such as Red Hat, MontaVista, and IBM have based successful businesses on FOSS. Many governments have adopted or are considering the adoption of FOSS. The traditional commercial software industry has not stood still either. Many companies are licensing source code more broadly and trying to convince customers that the total cost of owning traditional software is lower than FOSS.

To be clear, the term "free software" refers to freedom, not price. As Richard Stallman, founder of the Free Software Foundation, likes to say: "Think 'free speech' not 'free beer.'" Free software refers to software licensed with certain rights espoused by the Free Software Foundation: to study the source code; run the software for any purpose; change the software in any manner; distribute the software and any changes. The term "open source software" was created to avoid the perceived anti-commercial connotation of the "free software" label. *See* Open Source Initiative, *History of the OSI*, at *http://www.opensource.org/docs/history.php/*. Open source software is based on principles embodied in the Open Source Definition published by an organization known as the Open Source Initiative. The Open Source Definition is provided in the Materials section of this chapter.

The terms "free" and "open" lead some people to believe that the software is in the public domain or provided as a copyright first sale free of charge. However, a copyright in the code, combined with a license of the code, provides the legal framework. A copyright first sale is an inadequate transaction model because it does not provide the rights to make multiple copies or create derivative works. Free software developers do not place code in the public domain because they want to ensure that the code and derivatives will always be available for the creation of further derivatives, and this can only be accomplished by controlling the terms of use via a license.

There are many standard form licenses that meet the goals of free and open source software. In fact, there are so many that some fear this license proliferation causes confusion which hinders the adoption of FOSS. In practice, there are two predominant standard form licenses: the General Public License ("GPL") and the BSD-style license ("BSD License"). Both license forms are in the Materials section of this chapter.

The University of California at Berkeley created the original BSD License to accompany its distribution of the UNIX operating system known as the Berkeley Software Distribution (hence "BSD"). *See* Marshall McKusick, *Twenty Years of Berkeley UNIX: From AT&T-Owned to Freely Redistributable*, in Open Sources: Voices from the Open Source Revolution (Chris DiBona et al. eds., 1999). Variations of this license are used with popular software programs such as the Apache Web server. The GPL was created by Richard Stallman of the Free Software Foundation. *See* Richard Stallman, *The GNU Operating System and the Free Software Movement*, in

OPEN SOURCES: VOICES FROM THE OPEN SOURCE REVOLUTION (Chris DiBona et al. eds., 1999). The GPL is widely viewed as the free software movement's constitution.

There are a number of differences between the GPL and BSD License. *See* Robert W. Gomulkiewicz, *De-Bugging Open Source Software Licensing*, 64 U. PITT. L. REV. 75 (2002). The most fundamental difference is in the grant of rights. The BSD License grants the licensee the right to do anything with the source code, including creating derivative source code that may be held as a trade secret. The GPL, by contrast, conditions its license grant in such a way that if a licensee creates a derivative and then distributes it, then the licensee must provide the source code and full rights to do anything with it to all parties. This is called a "copyleft" — reversing the exclusive rights under copyright by licensing them out forever. There are also a number of similarities between the GPL and BSD License, including the disclaimer of all warranties and limitation of all damages.

Other Source Code Licenses.   A substantial amount of source code is licensed under licenses that do not meet the definitions of free or open source software, yet grant substantial derivative works rights and do not hold the source code as a trade secret.

Examples of these licenses include:

- Software development kits (SDKs).

    SDKs contain a collection of software and documentation licensed by system software publishers to developers who want to write applications software or middleware to run on top of the systems software platform.
- Device driver kits (DDKs).

    DDKs contain a collection of software and documentation licensed by system software publishers to device manufacturers so that the manufacturer's device, such as a printer or keyboard, will work with the systems software. DDKs often contain sample drivers in source code form that the device manufacturer can use as a starting point to create its own driver.
- Developer tools.

    Developer tool products contain software and documentation that enable a developer to write code in a certain computer language, such as Basic, Java, or C. These tool products contain libraries of code that can be used as pre-fabricated building blocks in developing a software program.

Other examples of source code licensing exist as well. The main point is that source code licensing comes in a variety of forms. Although confidential source code licensing and free and open source licensing are prominent, there are many other flavors of source code licensing.

2. Downstream Licenses

a. Licenses to Distribute Software

Copyright law gives the software developer the right to control distribution of its software. One of the defining characteristics of software is that it is distributable in many ways: on diskettes in shrink-wrapped boxes, on CD-ROMs in plastic jewel cases, pre-installed on computer hard disk drives, uploaded to a server and downloaded to a local computer, posted on a server and accessed from and executed on the server, or sent as an e-mail attachment. It often makes economic sense for the software developer to rely on third parties to distribute software products. These may be retail stores (bricks and mortar or Internet), distributors, original equipment manufacturers (OEMs) who make PCs and other devices, or value added resellers (VARs) who provide custom hardware/software packages. Distribution licenses enable these third parties to distribute the developer's software.

b. Licenses that Describe Usage

Software often comes with a license directed to the end user that describes how the user may use the software. Software developers call these "end user license agreements" or "EULAs." EULAs come in two basic varieties: relatively custom licenses and standard form mass market licenses.

"Custom" End User Licenses. Sometimes software is developed specifically for a certain end user's needs. If the developer retains ownership, the parties will negotiate the customer's use rights. Outside of this context, however, few end user licenses are truly custom, negotiated licenses. Most of the time a software developer begins with a standard form license which may present various options for certain terms, such as quantity, price, and product support. Whether the developer will negotiate any other license agreement provision such as warranties, indemnification, or choice of law depends on the parties' interests and bargaining power.

Mass Market Standard Form End User Licenses ("EULAs"). When most people think about software licensing, they think about standard form mass market EULAs. These come in a variety of forms with a variety of colorful names such as "shrink wrap," "boot screen," "click wrap," or "browse wrap" (or, less charitably, as "sneak wrap") licenses. Why do software developers use EULAs in the mass market?

One of the chief benefits is that they promote efficient software transactions: Like all standard form contracts, uniform terms facilitate high volume distribution without the cost of negotiating individual licenses. Beyond that, EULAs educate unsophisticated end users about what may and may not be done with software. EULAs also contain important terms and conditions about warranties and limitations of liability.

The most important value, however, lies in their ability to provide software users with various collections of rights at various price points. For example, a software publisher might license word processing software to business users for one price, to home users for a lower price, to academic institutions for an even lower price, and to charitable organizations free of charge. The publisher may grant the user the right to make an extra copy of the word processing software for a laptop computer or the right to create derivative works of clip art.

Despite their usefulness and ubiquity, EULAs are quite controversial. Over a hundred law review articles have been written condemning them on various grounds. *See, e.g.,* Jean Braucher, *Amended Article 2 and the Decision to Trust the Courts: The Case*

Against Enforcing Delayed Mass-Market License Terms, Especially for Software, 2004 WIS. L. REV. 752 (2004). Some believe that the contract formation process is inadequate to form a binding contract. Some challenge the fairness or legality of various EULA terms, such as limitations on use, choice of law, or prohibitions on reverse engineering. Others contend that the use of standard form EULAs in the mass market tips the balance in intellectual property laws too far in favor of software developers.

Despite the criticism, beginning with the Seventh Circuit Court of Appeal's decision in ProCD v. Zeidenberg, 86 F.3d 1447 (7th Cir. 1996), most courts have held that EULAs are enforceable as a general proposition.[1] That is not to say that all EULAs are enforceable in all circumstances. Courts have now moved on to address whether a EULA or EULA provision is enforceable in a particular fact pattern. *See* Robert W. Gomulkiewicz, *Getting Serious About User Friendly Mass Market Licensing for Software*, 12 GEO. MASON L. REV. 687 (2004) (discussing the evolution of the EULA debates). The *Specht v. Netscape* case in the Materials section of this chapter provides a good example.

"No Reverse Engineering" Clauses.   As discussed previously, many software developers treat their source code as a trade secret. A complication arises in maintaining trade secret protection for software distributed to the mass market. When software is distributed in object code form, the secrecy of the source code is maintained because the conversion of source to object code transforms source code so that its secrets are obscured. Many of the secrets can be discovered, however, if a programmer runs the object code through a tool that reverses the compilation or assembly process. *See generally* Andrew Johnson-Laird, *Software Reverse Engineering in the Real World*, 19 U. DAYTON L. REV. 843 (1994). Most courts hold that reverse engineering the object code to discover the unprotectable ideas in the underlying source code may be a copyright fair use. *See, e.g.*, Sega Enters. v. Accolade, Inc., 977 F.2d 1510 (9th Cir. 1992). Therefore, software publishers who want to protect the secrecy of their source code must do so using a contract—the EULA.

These "no reverse engineering" clauses have two primary effects. First, as mentioned, they protect programming secrets, thereby depriving other software developers of an easy head start in making a clone product. The Bowers v. Baystate case in the

1. *See* Mark A. Lemley, *Terms of Use*, 91 MINN. L. REV. 459, 459-60 (2006) ("Every court to consider the issue has found 'clickwrap' licenses . . . enforceable. A majority of courts in the past ten years have enforced 'shrinkwrap' licenses. . . . Finally, and more recently, an increasing number of courts have enforced 'browsewrap' licenses.") *See, e.g.*, Apple, Inc. v. Psystar Corp., 658 F.3d 1150 (9th Cir. 2011); Vernor v. Autodesk, 621 F.3d 1102 (9th Cir. 2010); MDY Indus. v. Blizzard Entm't, 629 F.3d 928 (9th Cir. 2010); Bowers v. Baystate Techs., Inc., 320 F.3d 1317 (Fed. Cir. 2003); Specht v. Netscape Commc'ns Corp., 306 F.3d 17 (2d Cir. 2002); Micro Star v. Formgen Inc., 154 F.3d 1107 (9th Cir. 1998); ProCD, Inc. v. Zeidenberg, 86 F.3d 1447, 1455 (7th Cir. 1996); Adobe Sys., Inc. v. Stargate Software, Inc., 216 F. Supp. 2d 1051 (N.D. Cal. 2002); i.LAN Sys., Inc. v. Netscout Serv. Level Corp., 183 F. Supp. 2d 328 (D. Mass. 2002); Storm Impact, Inc. v. Software of the Month Club, 13 F. Supp. 2d 782 (N.D. Ill. 1998); Ariz. Retail Sys., Inc. v. Software Link, Inc., 831 F. Supp. 759 (D. Ariz. 1993); I-A Equip. Co. v. I-Code, Inc., 43 U.C.C. Rep. Serv. 2d 807 (Mass. Dist. Ct. 2000); M.A. Mortenson Co. v. Timberline Software Corp., 140 Wash. 2d 568, 998 P.2d 305 (2000).

Materials section of this chapter provides a good example.[2] Second, they may have the effect of preventing interoperability between software products. For example, for one server to share information with another server or for a client program to share information with a server, the programmers need to know certain protocol or interface information. The Blizzard Entertainment v. Jung case in the Materials section of Chapter 1 describes this scenario. Prohibitions on reverse engineering have been challenged on various grounds, although U.S. courts have usually enforced them as they did in the Bowers v. Baystate and Blizzard Entertainment v. Jung cases.

E. Boundaries Around Software Licenses

As discussed in Chapter 1, not all licenses or license provisions are fair game. The law places a number of boundaries around what can and cannot be done in a software license. These boundaries fall into several categories:

1. Antitrust Law

Antitrust law is one of the most important bodies of law placing a boundary around software licenses. For example, in United States v. Microsoft, 253 F.3d 34 (D.C. Cir. 2001), the court held that several of Microsoft's licensing practices had been used illegally to maintain its Windows operating system monopoly. The *Microsoft* case can be found in the Materials section of this chapter. In a related case, the European Union ordered Microsoft to license Windows operating system protocol information, source code, and a version of its Windows operating system without the media player.

2. Misuse

The doctrine of "misuse" can be employed by courts to prevent software developers from using licenses to unfairly extend intellectual property monopolies. For example, in Lasercomb America, Inc. v. Reynolds, 911 F.2d 970 (4th Cir. 1990), the "misuse" arose from use of a standard form license purporting to restrict licensees from developing competing products for a period of 99 years. *See also* Apple, Inc. v. Psystar Corp., 658 F.3d 1150 (9th Cir. 2011) (rejecting a misuse challenge to a license grant use restriction and observing that the court has "applied the doctrine sparingly"). Misuse does not invalidate the software copyright, but it does prevent the copyright holder from enforcing it until the misuse has been purged. The *Laserscomb* and *Psystar* cases can be found in the Materials section of this chapter.

---

2. *See generally* Robert W. Gomulkiewicz, *Fostering the Business of Innovation: The Untold Story of Bowers v. Baystate Technologies*, 7 WASH. J.L. TECH. & ARTS 44 (2012).

3. Copyright and Patent Law Preemption

A software license is fundamentally a contract about intellectual property, particularly copyrights and often patents. As such, a software license represents an intersection between state contract law and federal intellectual property law. Federal intellectual property laws preempt any state laws that provide equivalent rights. Do software licenses provide equivalent rights? Provisions of software licenses have been challenged on this basis. A successful challenge to the license on this basis would allow a party to avoid abiding by a term of a license, such as a condition on a license grant or a prohibition on reverse engineering the software, or limit the causes of action in a lawsuit. The Blizzard Entertainment v. Jung case in Chapter 1 explores these preemption issues.

As a general proposition, breach of contract claims are not preempted. More specifically, challenges to certain software license provisions have been rejected by the courts, such as challenges to limitations on an end user's scope of use. *See* National Car Rental v. Computer Assocs. Int'l, Inc., 991 F.2d 426 (8th Cir. 1993). In other cases, however, courts have upheld preemption challenges, particularly when a litigant attempts to recover damages under both intellectual property laws and state laws such as conversion and misappropriation. *See* Kabehie v. Zoland, 102 Cal. App. 4th 513, 124 Cal. Rptr. 2d 721 (2002) (discussing a variety of preemption cases).

4. Fundamental Public Policy

There may be instances where a fundamental public policy outweighs the parties' private contractual terms. The *Restatement (Second) of Contracts* §178 summarizes this principle as follows: "A promise or other term of an agreement is unenforceable on grounds of public policy if legislation provides that it is unenforceable or the interest in its enforcement is clearly outweighed in the circumstances by a public policy against enforcement of such terms." Uniform Computer Information Transactions Act §105 contains a similar provision.

5. European Software Directive

In 1991, the European Union passed a significant directive on legal protection for computer software ("Software Directive"). COUNCIL DIRECTIVE 91/250/EEC ON THE LEGAL PROTECTION OF SOFTWARE PROGRAMS (May 14, 1991). The Software Directive can be found in the Materials section of this chapter. One part of the Software Directive addresses the issue of "reverse engineering." The Software Directive provides that if a software developer needs to discover information about another software program to interoperate with it and the information is not otherwise available, the programmer may reverse engineer the software to learn how to interoperate with it even if a EULA prohibits this act.

6. Fair Use

Under the Copyright Act certain uses of copyrighted works, though technically infringing, are socially beneficial and thus constitute "fair uses." 17 U.S.C. §107. A party asserts its right to a "fair use" as a defense to a suit for copyright infringement. In the context of software, a fair use defense is often raised by defendants who have decompiled or reverse engineered software to discover unprotectable ideas to create a compatible or competing product. Absent a license, courts have consistently held that such reverse engineering to discover unprotectable ideas is a fair use. *See, e.g.,* Sony Computer Entertainment, Inc. v. Connectix Corp., 203 F.3d 596 (9th Cir. 2000). If a license prohibits reverse engineering, however, several cases have upheld this limitation. *See, e.g.,* Blizzard Entertainment v. Jung, 422 F.3d 630 (8th Cir. 2005); Bowers v. Baystate Tech., 320 F.3d 1317 (Fed. Cir. 2003).

7. Unconscionability

Courts can strike down license terms that are "unconscionable." Unconscionability provides an important boundary around software licenses, particularly mass market EULAs. It allows courts to guard against abusive contract terms (substantive unconscionability) and contracting practices (procedural unconscionability). For example, courts have stricken down binding arbitration and exclusive venue provisions in computer-related transactions as unconscionable under the circumstances. *See, e.g.,* Comb v. PayPal, Inc., 218 F. Supp. 2d 1165 (N.D. Cal. 2002) (binding arbitration); America Online, Inc. v. Superior Court, 90 Cal. App. 4th 1, 108 Cal. Rptr. 2d 699 (2001) (exclusive forum).

II. MATERIALS

These Materials enable you to explore some of the software-related issues and transaction models that are described in the Overview. The first set of items show licensing in the context of software development. 17 U.S.C. §101 defines "works for hire" and "joint works" in U.S. copyright law. Aymes v. Bonelli, 980 F.2d 857 (2d Cir. 1992), involves the hiring of a programmer to develop software for a business and determines whether the software created should be classified as a work made for hire under copyright law. Ashton-Tate Corp. v. Ross, 916 F.2d 516 (9th Cir. 1990), also involves software development, but this case examines whether the software constitutes a work of joint authorship under copyright law.

Next comes a set of items that will allow you to explore source code licensing. The Materials contain a sample confidential source code license. The Materials also contain several items related to FOSS licensing. GNU General Public License (GPL) 2.0 is the most important so-called "copyleft" license, and GPL 3.0 is the latest version of the GPL. Linus Torvalds's famous "NOTE!" regarding use of the GPL with Linux is an interesting amendment to GPL 2.0. The "Open Source Definition" promulgated by the Open Source Initiative organization defines so-called "open source" software, and the BSD License is one of the most prominent open source licenses. In addition, you will find Jacobsen v. Katzer, 535 F.3d 1373 (Fed. Cir. 2008), which enforced an open source license and describes the importance of non-monetary remedies in this setting.

Following that case is a collection of items that explore two prominent software license transactions: mass market end user licensing and distribution. Specht v. Netscape Communications Corp., 306 F.3d 17 (2d Cir. 2002), examines the enforceability of mass market end user licenses in general as well as particular licensing practices that may or may not contribute to creating an enforceable license. Adobe Systems, Inc. v. Stargate Software, Inc., 216 F. Supp. 2d 1051 (N.D. Cal. 2002), discusses distribution licensing and examines the difference between "license" and "first sale" in this context. Note that the Vernor v. Autodesk case in the Materials section of Chapter 1 also addresses the "license" versus "first sale" distinction in a software end user license context.

Finally, you will find a set of cases that examine the boundaries of licenses. An excerpt from United States v. Microsoft Corp., 253 F.3d 34 (D.C. Cir. 2001), looks at the role antitrust law plays in putting a boundary around licensing practices. Lasercomb America v. Reynolds, 991 F.2d 970 (4th Cir. 1990), and Apple, Inc. v. Psystar Corp., 658 F.3d 1150 (9th Cir. 2011), examine copyright misuse in the context of software licensing. Bowers v. Baystate, 320 F.3d 1317 (Fed. Cir. 2003), addresses the enforceability of contractual restrictions on reverse engineering, and the European Union Council Directive on Legal Protection of Computer Programs 91/250/EEC provides the European perspective on the matter.

UNITED STATES CODE ANNOTATED: TITLE 17. COPYRIGHTS

§101. Definitions

A "joint work" is a work prepared by two or more authors with the intention that their contributions be merged into inseparable or interdependent parts of a unitary whole. A "work made for hire" is —

(1) a work prepared by an employee within the scope of his or her employment; or

(2) a work specially ordered or commissioned for use as a contribution to a collective work, as a part of a motion picture or other audiovisual work, as a translation, as a supplementary work, as a compilation, as an instructional text, as a test, as answer material for a test, or as an atlas, if the parties expressly agree in a written instrument signed by them that the work shall be considered a work made for hire. For the purpose of the foregoing sentence, a "supplementary work" is a work prepared for publication as a secondary adjunct to a work by another author for the purpose of introducing, concluding, illustrating, explaining, revising, commenting upon, or assisting in the use of the other work, such as forewords, afterwords, pictorial illustrations, maps, charts, tables, editorial notes, musical

arrangements, answer material for tests, bibliographies, appendixes, and indexes, and an "instructional text" is a literary, pictorial, or graphic work prepared for publication and with the purpose of use in systematic instructional activities.

AYMES v. BONELLI

980 F.2d 857 (2d Cir. 1992)

ALTIMARI, Circuit Judge:

Clifford Scott Aymes, proceeding pro se. . . .

BACKGROUND

In May 1980, Aymes was hired by defendant-appellee Jonathan Bonelli, the president and chief executive officer of Island, to work as a computer programmer. Island operated a chain of retail stores selling swimming pools and related supplies. Aymes, who received a graduate degree from Cornell University's School of Engineering in 1981, worked with Island's computer systems from 1980 to 1982.

Aymes did most of his programming at the Island office, where he had access to Island's computer hardware. He generally worked alone, without assistants or co-workers, and enjoyed considerable autonomy in creating CSALIB. This autonomy was restricted only by Bonelli who directed and instructed Aymes on what he wanted from the program. Bonelli was not, however, sufficiently skilled to write the program himself.

Although Aymes worked semi-regular hours, he was not always paid by the hour and on occasion presented his bills to Bonelli as invoices. At times, Aymes would be paid by the project and given bonuses for finishing the project on time. It is undisputed that Aymes never received any health or other insurance benefits from Island. It is similarly undisputed that Island never paid an employer's percentage of Aymes's payroll taxes and never withheld any of his salary for federal or state taxes. In fact, Aymes was given an Internal Revenue Service 1099 Non-Employee Compensation form instead of the standard employee W-2 form.

DISCUSSION

Under the Copyright Act of 1976, copyright ownership "vests initially in the author or authors of the work." 17 U.S.C. §201(a) (1988). Although the author is generally the party who actually creates the copyrightable work, the Act provides:

In the case of a work made for hire, the employer or other person for whom the work was prepared is considered the author for purposes of this title, and, unless the parties have expressly agreed otherwise in a written instrument signed by them, owns all of the rights comprised in the copyright.

It is undisputed that Aymes and Bonelli never signed a written agreement assigning ownership rights in CSALIB. We must therefore consider whether the program was a work prepared by Aymes as an employee within the scope of his employment. If so, CSALIB qualifies as a "work made for hire" whose copyright belongs to Island as Aymes's employer.

The Copyright Act does not define the terms "employee" or "employment," and, conse-quently, the application of these terms is left to the courts. In *Reid*, the Supreme Court addressed the question of when an individual is an employee under the work for hire doctrine. Community for Creative Non-Violence v. Reid, 490 U.S. 730 (1989). Relying extensively on the legislative history of the Copyright Act, the Court concluded that to "determine whether a work is for hire under the Act, a court first should ascertain, using principles of the general common law of agency, whether the work was prepared by an employee or an independent contractor." Id. at 751. The Court then set forth the factors to be used in making this determination:

> In determining whether a hired party is an employee under the general common law of agency, we consider the hiring party's right to control the manner and means by which the product is accomplished. Among the other factors relevant to this inquiry are the skill required, the source of the instrumentalities and tools, the location of the work; the duration of the relationship between the parties, whether the hiring party has the right to assign additional projects to the hired party; the extent of the hired party's discretion over when and how long to work; the method of payment; the hired party's role in hiring and paying assistants; whether the work is part of the regular business of the hiring party; whether the hiring party is in business; the provision of employee benefits, and the tax treatment of the hired party.

I. Application of the Reid Test . . .

We begin our analysis by noting that the *Reid* test can be easily misapplied, since it consists merely of a list of possible considerations that may or may not be relevant in a given case. *Reid* established that no one factor was dispositive, but gave no direction concerning how the factors were to be weighed. It does not necessarily follow that because no one factor is dispositive all factors are equally important, or indeed that all factors will have relevance in every case. The factors should not merely be tallied but should be weighed according to their significance in the case.

For example, the factors relating to the authority to hire assistants will not normally be relevant if the very nature of the work requires the hired party to work alone. In such a case, that factor should be accorded no weight in applying the *Reid* test. Having the authority to hire assistants, however, might have great probative value where the individual claiming to be an independent contractor does exercise authority to enlist assistants without prior approval of the party that hired him. In the latter case, this show of authority would be highly indicative that the hired party was acting as an independent contractor.

Some factors, therefore, will often have little or no significance in determining whether a party is an independent contractor or an employee. In contrast, there are some factors that will be significant in virtually every situation. These include: (1) the hiring party's right to control the manner and means of creation; (2) the skill required; (3) the provision of employee benefits; (4) the tax treatment of the hired party; and (5) whether the hiring party has the right to assign additional projects to the hired party. These factors will almost always be relevant and should be given more weight in the analysis, because they will usually be highly probative of the true nature of the employment relationship.

Although the *Reid* test has not yet received widespread application, other courts that have interpreted the test have in effect adopted this weighted approach by only addressing those factors found to be significant in the individual case. We begin by addressing those factors bearing most significantly in our analysis.

a. The Right to Control

The district court did not specifically address whether Aymes or Island Swimming had the right to control the manner of CSALIB's creation. Even without a specific finding, it is clear from the record that Bonelli and Island had the right to control the manner in which CSALIB was created. Aymes disputed Bonelli's purported skill at programming, but even without such knowledge Bonelli was capable of directing Aymes on CSALIB's necessary function. Aymes was not working entirely alone. He received significant input from Bonelli in programming CSALIB, and worked under programming limitations placed by Bonelli. Consequently, this factor weighs heavily in favor of finding that Aymes was an employee.

b. The Level of Skill

The district court found that although Aymes's ability as a programmer required skills "beyond the capacity of a layman, it required no peculiar expertise or creative genius." We disagree. Aymes's work required far more than merely transcribing Bonelli's instructions. Rather, his programming demanded that he use skills developed while a graduate student at Cornell and through his experience working at a family run company. Other courts that have addressed the level of skill necessary to indicate that a party is an independent contractor have held architects, photographers, graphic artists, drafters, and indeed computer programmers to be highly-skilled independent contractors.

We therefore conclude that the district court erred in relying on Aymes's relative youth and inexperience as a professional computer programmer. Rather, the court should have examined the skill necessary to perform the work. In this case, Aymes was clearly a skilled craftsman. Consequently, this factor weighs heavily in his favor.

c./d. The Employee Benefits and Tax Treatment

The district court found that Aymes received no employee benefits from Island, but disregarded this factor as merely being an indication that Aymes was an employee who worked "off the books." It is undisputed that Aymes was not provided with health, unemployment, or life insurance benefits. Similarly, it is uncontested that Island did not pay a share of Aymes's social security taxes and did not withhold federal or state income taxes.

The failure of Island to extend Aymes any employment benefits or to pay any of his payroll taxes is highly indicative that Aymes was considered an outside independent contractor by Island. Indeed, these two factors constitute virtual admissions of Aymes's status by Bonelli himself. Moreover, they also point out a basic inequity in Aymes's treatment. Island benefitted from treating Aymes like an independent contractor when it came to providing benefits and paying a percentage of his payroll taxes. Island should not in one context be able to claim that Aymes was an independent contractor and ten years later deny him that status to avoid a copyright infringement suit.

These two factors are given even greater weight because they are undisputed in this case. During the ten years in which this case has been litigated, all the other issues have been hotly contested. But for purposes of benefits and taxes, Island definitely and unequivocally chose not to treat Aymes as an employee. Island deliberately chose to deny Aymes two basic attributes of employment it presumably extended to its workforce. This undisputed choice is completely inconsistent with their defense.

The importance of these two factors is underscored by the fact that every case since *Reid* that has applied the test has found the hired party to be an independent contractor where the hiring party failed to extend benefits or pay social security taxes.

e. The Right to Assign Other Projects

The district court found that Bonelli had the right to and did assign Aymes other projects in addition to the creation of CSALIB. This is fairly strong evidence that Aymes was an employee, since independent contractors are typically hired only for particular projects. However, this factor carries less weight than those evaluated above, because the delegation of additional projects to Aymes is not inconsistent with the idea that he was Island's independent trouble shooter who might be asked to intervene as computer problems arose. Accordingly, this factor weighs fairly strongly but not conclusively for Island.

f. Remaining Factors

The remaining factors are relatively insignificant or negligible in weight because they are either indeterminate or inapplicable to these facts.

On balance, application of the *Reid* test requires that we find Aymes to be an independent contractor when he was creating CSALIB for Island. Consequently, we hold that CSALIB is not a work for hire. Aymes therefore owns the copyright as author of the program.

ASHTON-TATE CORP. v. ROSS

916 F.2d 516 (9th Cir. 1990)

CHOY, Circuit Judge.

BACKGROUND

In September 1984 appellant Richard Ross (Ross) decided to collaborate with Randy Wigginton (Wigginton) on the development of a computer spreadsheet program for the Apple Macintosh computer. Ross alleged that he and Wigginton agreed that Ross would work on the "engine," or computational component of the program, and Wigginton would work on the user interface portion. During September 1984 through February of 1985, Ross and Wigginton worked on their respective portions of the program. They also met on at least two occasions to discuss ideas and concepts for the program. At one of these meetings, Ross gave Wigginton a handwritten list of user commands he felt the interface should contain. The actual writing of the user interface portion of the program was done by Wigginton, however. Ross did all the writing of the computational half of the program.

In April 1985 Wigginton [went] to work for Ashton-Tate. He and his company, "Encore," continued to work on the user interface and adapted it for use with a new engine from a program called "Alembic," which Ashton-Tate already had an interest in. Eventually, the combination of Wigginton's user interface and the adapted Alembic engine became the "Full Impact" spreadsheet program released by Ashton-Tate. Meanwhile, Ross worked on his spreadsheet program. By June of 1986, he completed work on a user interface to combine with his engine and published "MacCalc."

DISCUSSION

II. Copyright Ownership of Full Impact

A. Are intention and ideas enough?

[A] "joint work" is "a work prepared by two or more authors with the intention that their contributions be merged into inseparable or interdependent parts of a unitary whole." 17 U.S.C. §101 (1977). The authors of a joint work are co-owners of the copyright in that work. 17 U.S.C. §201(a). The question presented by Appellants' first theory, where Ross claims authorship on the basis of an alleged agreement to collaborate combined with his noncopyrightable contribution to the interface, is what satisfies the requirements for joint authorship.

The district court held that "[b]ecause Ross only contributed ideas to the Full Impact interface, which by themselves are not protectable, the program is not a 'joint work' between Ross and Wigginton." The rule expressed by the district court—that only contributors of copyrightable material can be authors of a work—is not entirely settled, but is consistent with the direction our circuit has taken.

Academic authorities split on what type of "contribution" the copyright law requires for joint authorship purposes. The Nimmers argue that:

> If authors A and B work in collaboration, but if A's contribution is limited to plot ideas which standing alone would not be copyrightable, and B weaves the ideas into a completed literary expression, it would seem that A and B are joint authors of the resulting work.

M. & D. Nimmer, 1 Nimmer on Copyright §6.07, p. 6-18 (1989). Conversely, Goldstein in *Copyright: Principles, Law and Practice*, takes a different view: A collaborator's contribution will not produce a joint work, and a contributor will not obtain a co-ownership interest, unless the contribution represents original expression that could stand on its own as the subject matter of copyright. P. Goldstein, Copyright: Principles, Law and Practice, §4.2.1 p. 379 (1989).

The district court adopted the view championed by Professor Goldstein. This court recently adopted the same position in S.O.S. Inc. v. Payday Inc., 886 F.2d 1081, 1086-87 (9th Cir. 1989). We held in Payday that "[t]o be an author, one must supply more than mere direction or ideas; one must 'translate[] an idea into a fixed tangible expression entitled to copyright protection.' Community for Creative Non-Violence v. Reid, 490 U.S. 730 (1989)." Id.

Payday involved a dispute over a commissioned work. The *Reid* decision quoted in *Payday* stated the general rule that a person must translate ideas into copyrightable expression to receive copyright protection as an author of a work. *Reid* also pointed out, however, that the Copyright Act carves out an important exception for works made for hire. 109 S. Ct. at 2171. Further, *Reid* left undecided whether joint authorship is another exception to the general rule that to be an author one must make an independently copyrightable contribution to a work.

Even though this issue is not completely settled in the case law, our circuit holds that joint authorship requires each author to make an independently copyrightable contribution. Thus the district court properly decided this issue against Appellants.

B. Was Ross's contribution to the user interface copyrightable?

Appellants argue that the handwritten list of user commands Ross gave to Wigginton was a fixed expression of Ross's ideas, and as such was entitled to copyright protection. They contend that this list was used by Wigginton to help develop the user interface and therefore, Ross is a joint author of the interface portion of Full Impact. This argument is meritless for the reasons given in the district court's order. The list simply does not qualify for copyright protection.

C. Did Ross's copyrightable contribution to the MacCalc prototype make him a joint author of full impact?

Appellants also claim that Ross is a joint author of the Full Impact program on the basis of his contribution to the MacCalc prototype. They argue that because Ross contributed copyrightable expression to the MacCalc prototype by writing the engine portion of the program, he is a joint author of the prototype and that this gave him an undivided ownership interest in the entire prototype. Hence, they argue, Full Impact's use of the user interface portion of the MacCalc prototype made Ross a joint author of that program as well.

The district court focused on the user interface and Ross's contributions to it when determining appellants' joint authorship claim. This made sense, because this was the theory pushed by Appellants, and at the time the contribution requirement for authorship of joint works was not settled in this circuit. It is possible, however, to conceive of the entire MacCalc prototype as a joint work. Indeed, if Ross and Wigginton intended to create a joint work, and both contributed copyrightable material to the resulting work (the MacCalc prototype), then they may have both obtained an undivided interest in the entire work. 17 U.S.C. §201(a); 1 Nimmer on Copyright, §6.03 (1989).

In other words, Ross may have obtained a one-half ownership interest in the user interface and Wigginton may have obtained a one-half interest in the engine. We need not decide this issue now, however. Even assuming, arguendo, that Ross does have a one-half interest in the interface written by Wigginton, it does not follow that Ross is a joint author of the Full Impact program because its interface is derived from his and Wigginton's joint work. The Second Circuit's decision in Weissmann v. Freeman, 868 F.2d 1313 (2d Cir.), cert. denied, 493 U.S. 883 (1989), is a clear refutation of this position. Joint authorship in a prior work is insufficient to make one a joint author of a derivative work: "[i]f such were the law, it would eviscerate the independent copyright protection that attaches to a derivative work that is wholly independent of the protection afforded the preexisting work." Id. at 1317. The analysis in Weissmann is sound, and we adopt its reasoning on this point.

Interestingly, the court in Weissmann also discussed the situation where a joint work is utilized or licensed for use in a derivative work by one of the co-authors of the joint work. In such a situation, no cause of action for infringement exists, "because an individual cannot infringe his own copyright. The only duty joint owners have is to account for profits from [the joint work's] use." Id. at 1318.

[I]t appears that Appellants have misframed the type of relief they could litigate with any possibility of success. While an author of a joint work does not acquire an authorship interest in derivative works that utilize part of the joint work, that author may be entitled to compensation for the use of the original joint work. The problem for Appellants in this appeal, however, is that such a claim for compensation is not a copyright claim. Furthermore, the claim would have to be against the alleged "co-author" Wigginton, because he was the person who allegedly allowed Ashton-Tate to use the user interface portion of the joint work for use in Full Impact.

SOURCE CODE AGREEMENT

This Source Code License Agreement ("Agreement") is an agreement between Pipsqueak Software, Inc. ("Company") and _____ ("You"), effective this _____ day of _____, 20___ ("Effective Date").

Recitals

A. Company created the HoundPup browser software.

B. Company wants You to create an enhanced version of HoundPup.

You and Company agree as follows:

Agreement

1. DEFINITIONS

   1.1 "HoundPup" means Company's HoundPup browser software as that software exists on the Effective Date.

   1.2 "Pup Source Code" means HoundPup in its source code form, including source code comments, build and installation scripts, and documentation.

   1.3 "New Code" means software developed by You to create and implement in HoundPup the features described in Attachment A. New Code includes software in object and source code forms, build and installation scripts, and documentation.

   1.4 "NewHoundPup" means a version of HoundPup containing New Code.

2. PROTECTING CONFIDENTIAL INFORMATION

   2.1 The Pup Source Code is confidential information and a trade secret of Company.

   2.2 When You get Pup Source Code, You agree to:

   - never disclose it to anyone else (unless a court or the government orders You to);
   - keep it secret as You would Your most sensitive confidential information;
   - provide access to Your employees only on a need to know basis;
   - use it only as described in the Agreement;
   - have agreements in place with Your employees that protect its secrecy.

   2.3 If a court or the government orders You to disclose Pup Source Code, You must give Company prompt notice of the order so that Company can seek an appropriate protective order (or equivalent).

2.4 Company does not consider certain information about the Pup Source Code to be confidential or a trade secret. If You legally received information from someone other than Company and that person was entitled to share the information with You and did not obligate You to keep it secret, You do not need to keep that information secret. The same holds true for information Company disclosed to You or someone else without an obligation to keep it secret or information that You develop independently.

2.5 For purpose of this Section 2, Pup Source Code shall include New Code in source code form.

3. LICENSE GRANT. Company hereby grants You a personal, limited license, under all of Company's applicable intellectual property rights, to make, use, reproduce, and create derivative works of the Pup Source Code for the sole purpose of creating NewHoundPup. All other rights are reserved by Company.

4. ASSIGNMENT OF RIGHTS. You hereby assign to Company all right, title, and interest in and to New Code, including all rights under copyright, patent, and trade secret law.

5. DELIVERY OF NEW CODE. Immediately upon completion of New Code or at any time when Company requests, You shall provide New Code to Company on CD-ROM or on any other medium requested by Company.

6. NO WARRANTIES. COMPANY PROVIDES PUP SOURCE CODE TO YOU, AND YOU PROVIDE NEW CODE TO COMPANY, WITHOUT ANY EXPRESS, IMPLIED OR STATUTORY WARRANTY, NOT EVEN THE IMPLIED WARRANTY OF MERCHANT-ABILITY OR FITNESS FOR A PARTICULAR PURPOSE, OR THE WARRANTY OF TITLE OR NON-INFRINGEMENT.

7. LIMITATION OF LIABILITY. YOU AND COMPANY AGREE THAT NEITHER PARTY WILL BE LIABLE UNDER THIS AGREEMENT FOR ANY INDIRECT, CONSEQUENTIAL, SPECIAL, INCIDENTAL OR PUNITIVE DAMAGES.

8. TERM & TERMINATION

8.1 This Agreement is in effect until the earlier of 3 years from the Effective Date or completion of New Code.

8.2 Company may end this Agreement at any time in its sole discretion upon notice to You.

8.3 When Your license to any Pup Source Code ends, You must immediately return to Company or destroy all copies of the Pup Source Code. If Company asks, You agree that an executive of Your company will provide Company with a letter stating that all copies of the Pup Source Code have been returned or destroyed.

8.4 When this Agreement ends, the following terms remain in effect: [list terms].

9. NOTICES

    9.1 If You or Company need to send a notice under the Agreement, the notice will be considered given when delivered to a commercial courier service or deposited in the United States of America mails, postage prepaid, certified or registered, return receipt requested. All notices must be addressed as follows:

To You:	To Company:
_____	Pipsqueak Software, Inc.
[street address]	[street address]
[city], [state], [zip]	[city], [state] [zip]
Attention: _____	Attention: _____
Phone: _____	Phone: _____
Fax: _____	Fax: _____
Email: _____	Email: _____
Copy to:	Copy to:

    9.2 Either You or Company may change these addresses by giving notice of the change.

10. GOVERNING LAW/VENUE/ATTORNEY FEES. The Agreement shall be governed by the laws of the State of Delaware USA, excluding its conflicts of laws. All claims brought relating to the Agreement shall be brought exclusively in the state or federal courts in Delaware. If either You or Company use attorneys to enforce rights relating to the Agreement, the prevailing party shall be entitled to recover its reasonable attorney fees and litigation costs.

11. OUTCOME IF SOME SECTIONS ARE INVALID. If a part of the Agreement, other than Sections 2, 4, 6, or 7 is held by a competent court to be unenforceable, the rest shall remain in effect. If Sections 2, 4, 6, or 7 are held by a competent court to be unenforceable, the Agreement ends immediately.

12. YOU CANNOT ASSIGN THE AGREEMENT. You may not assign the Agreement and if You attempt to assign the Agreement for any reason, the Agreement ends immediately. As used in the Agreement, the term "assign" includes: (a) any change of ownership of beneficial interest in Your company where greater than a twenty percent (20%) interest is transferred (whether in a single or a series of transactions); (b) a merger of Your company with another party, whether or not Your company is the surviving entity; (c) the acquisition of more than twenty percent (20%) of any class of Your company's voting stock (or any class of non-voting security convertible into voting stock) by another party (whether in a single transaction or a series of transactions); or (d) the sale of more than fifty percent (50%) of Your company's assets (whether in a single transaction or series of transactions).

13. GOVERNMENT APPROVALS AND RESTRICTED RIGHTS.

    13.1 You must, at Your expense, obtain and maintain any government approvals, consents, licenses, authorizations, declarations, filings, and registrations as may be necessary or advisable for Your performance under the Agreement. You must also pay (and indemnify Company if it gets charged) for any sales taxes, use taxes and any other taxes imposed by any jurisdiction as a result of the entry into this Agreement, the performance of any of its provisions, or the transfer of any property or rights under it.

13.2 Any software provided to the U.S. Government pursuant to solicitations issued on or after December 1, 1995 is provided with the rights and restrictions described elsewhere herein. Any software provided to the U.S. Government pursuant to solicitations issued prior to December 1, 1995 is provided with "Restricted Rights" as provided for in FAR, 48 CFR 52.227-14 (JUNE 1987) or DFAR, 48 CFR 252.227-7013 (OCT 1988), as applicable. You are responsible for ensuring that any Pup Source Code or New Code source code is marked with the "Restricted Rights Notice" or "Restricted Rights Legend," as required.

14. EXPORT RESTRICTIONS. The Pup Source Code is of United States-origin. You must comply with all applicable international and national laws that apply to it, including the United States Export Administration Regulations, as well as end-user, end-use and country destination restrictions issued by United States and other governments. For information on exporting Company products, see *http://www.pipsqueaksoftware.com/export control/*.

15. ENTIRE AGREEMENT. The Agreement is the only agreement between You and Company covering the subject matter of this Agreement. It supersedes all other prior or contemporaneous agreements and communications on the subject. The Agreement shall not be modified unless You and Company sign an amendment after the Effective Date. Neither You nor Company waives the right to claim breach of contract unless the waiver is in a signed, written document. A waiver only applies to things described in that document; it does not apply to other breaches of contract.

We agree to everything in the Agreement.

Pipsqueak Software, Inc.   [Name of Company]

_____   _____
By   By

_____   _____
Name (print)   Name (print)

_____   _____
Title   Title

_____   _____
Date   Date

Attachment A: New Features for HoundPup

---

* * *

GNU GENERAL PUBLIC LICENSE (GPL), VERSION 2

Copyright © 1989, 1991 Free Software Foundation, Inc.
59 Temple Place, Suite 330, Boston, MA 02111-1307 USA

Preamble

The licenses for most software are designed to take away your freedom to share and change it. By contrast, the GNU General Public License is intended to guarantee your freedom to share and change free software — to make sure the software is free for all its users. This General Public License applies to most of the Free Software Foundation's software and to any other program whose authors commit to using it. (Some other Free Software Foundation software is covered by the GNU Library General Public License instead.) You can apply it to your programs, too.

When we speak of free software, we are referring to freedom, not price. Our General Public Licenses are designed to make sure that you have the freedom to distribute copies of free software (and charge for this service if you wish), that you receive source code or can get it if you want it, that you can change the software or use pieces of it in new free programs; and that you know you can do these things.

To protect your rights, we need to make restrictions that forbid anyone to deny you these rights or to ask you to surrender the rights. These restrictions translate to certain responsibilities for you if you distribute copies of the software, or if you modify it.

For example, if you distribute copies of such a program, whether gratis or for a fee, you must give the recipients all the rights that you have. You must make sure that they, too, receive or can get the source code. And you must show them these terms so they know their rights.

We protect your rights with two steps: (1) copyright the software, and (2) offer you this license which gives you legal permission to copy, distribute and/or modify the software.

Also, for each author's protection and ours, we want to make certain that everyone understands that there is no warranty for this free software. If the software is modified by someone else and passed on, we want its recipients to know that what they have is not the original, so that any problems introduced by others will not reflect on the original authors' reputations.

Finally, any free program is threatened constantly by software patents. We wish to avoid the danger that redistributors of a free program will individually obtain patent licenses, in effect making the program proprietary. To prevent this, we have made it clear that any patent must be licensed for everyone's free use or not licensed at all.

The precise terms and conditions for copying, distribution and modification follow.

Terms and Conditions for Copying, Distribution and Modification

0. This License applies to any program or other work which contains a notice placed by the copyright holder saying it may be distributed under the terms of this General Public License. The "Program," below, refers to any such program or work, and a "work based on the Program" means either the Program or any derivative work under copyright law: that is to say, a work containing the Program or a portion of it, either verbatim or with modifications and/or translated into another language. (Hereinafter, translation is included without limitation in the term "modification.") Each licensee is addressed as "you."

Activities other than copying, distribution and modification are not covered by this License; they are outside its scope. The act of running the Program is not restricted, and the output from the Program is covered only if its contents constitute a work based on the Program (independent of having been made by running the Program). Whether that is true depends on what the Program does.

1. You may copy and distribute verbatim copies of the Program's source code as you receive it, in any medium, provided that you conspicuously and appropriately publish on each copy an appropriate copyright notice and disclaimer of warranty; keep intact all the notices that refer to this License and to the absence of any warranty; and give any other recipients of the Program a copy of this License along with the Program.

You may charge a fee for the physical act of transferring a copy, and you may at your option offer warranty protection in exchange for a fee.

2. You may modify your copy or copies of the Program or any portion of it, thus forming a work based on the Program, and copy and distribute such modifications or work under the terms of Section 1 above, provided that you also meet all of these conditions:

These requirements apply to the modified work as a whole. If identifiable sections of that work are not derived from the Program, and can be reasonably considered independent and separate works in themselves, then this License, and its terms, do not apply to those sections when you distribute them as separate works. But when you distribute the same sections as part of a whole which is a work based on the Program, the distribution of the whole must be on the terms of this License, whose permissions for other licensees extend to the entire whole, and thus to each and every part regardless of who wrote it.

Thus, it is not the intent of this section to claim rights or contest your rights to work written entirely by you; rather, the intent is to exercise the right to control the distribution of derivative or collective works based on the Program.

In addition, mere aggregation of another work not based on the Program with the Program (or with a work based on the Program) on a volume of a storage or distribution medium does not bring the other work under the scope of this License.

(a) You must cause the modified files to carry prominent notices stating that you changed the files and the date of any change.

(b) You must cause any work that you distribute or publish, that in whole or in part contains or is derived from the Program or any part thereof, to be licensed as a whole at no charge to all third parties under the terms of this License.

(c) If the modified program normally reads commands interactively when run, you must cause it, when started running for such interactive use in the most ordinary way, to print or display an announcement including an appropriate copyright notice and a notice that there is no warranty (or else, saying that you provide a warranty) and that users may redistribute the program under these conditions, and telling the user how to view a copy of this License. (Exception: if the Program itself is interactive but does not normally print such an announcement, your work based on the Program is not required to print an announcement.)

3. You may copy and distribute the Program (or a work based on it, under Section 2) in object code or executable form under the terms of Sections 1 and 2 above provided that you also do one of the following:

The source code for a work means the preferred form of the work for making modifications to it. For an executable work, complete source code means all the source code for all modules it contains, plus any associated interface definition files, plus the scripts used to control compilation and installation of the executable. However, as a special exception, the source code distributed need not include anything that is normally distributed (in either source or binary form) with the major components (compiler, kernel, and so on) of the operating system on which the executable runs, unless that component itself accompanies the executable.

If distribution of executable or object code is made by offering access to copy from a designated place, then offering equivalent access to copy the source code from the same place counts as distribution of the source code, even though third parties are not compelled to copy the source along with the object code.

(a) Accompany it with the complete corresponding machine-readable source code, which must be distributed under the terms of Sections 1 and 2 above on a medium customarily used for software interchange; or,

(b) Accompany it with a written offer, valid for at least three years, to give any third party, for a charge no more than your cost of physically performing source distribution, a complete machine-readable copy of the corresponding source code, to be distributed under the terms of Sections 1 and 2 above on a medium customarily used for software interchange; or,

(c) Accompany it with the information you received as to the offer to distribute corresponding source code. (This alternative is allowed only for noncommercial distribution and only if you received the program in object code or executable form with such an offer, in accord with Subsection b above.)

4. You may not copy, modify, sublicense, or distribute the Program except as expressly provided under this License. Any attempt otherwise to copy, modify, sublicense or distribute the Program is void, and will automatically terminate your rights under this License. However, parties who have received copies, or rights, from you under this License will not have their licenses terminated so long as such parties remain in full compliance.

5. You are not required to accept this License, since you have not signed it. However, nothing else grants you permission to modify or distribute the Program or its derivative works. These actions are prohibited by law if you do not accept this License. Therefore, by modifying or distributing the Program (or any work based on the Program), you indicate your acceptance of this License to do so, and all its terms and conditions for copying, distributing or modifying the Program or works based on it.

6. Each time you redistribute the Program (or any work based on the Program), the recipient automatically receives a license from the original licensor to copy, distribute or modify the Program subject to these terms and conditions. You may not impose any further restrictions on the recipients' exercise of the rights granted herein. You are not responsible for enforcing compliance by third parties to this License.

7. If, as a consequence of a court judgment or allegation of patent infringement or for any other reason (not limited to patent issues), conditions are imposed on you (whether by court order, agreement or otherwise) that contradict the conditions of this License, they do not excuse you from the conditions of this License. If you cannot distribute so as to satisfy simultaneously your obligations under this License and any other pertinent obligations, then as a consequence you may not distribute the Program at all. For example, if a patent license would not permit royalty-free redistribution of the Program by all those who receive copies directly or indirectly through you, then the only way you could satisfy both it and this License would be to refrain entirely from distribution of the Program.

If any portion of this section is held invalid or unenforceable under any particular circumstance, the balance of the section is intended to apply and the section as a whole is intended to apply in other circumstances.

It is not the purpose of this section to induce you to infringe any patents or other property right claims or to contest validity of any such claims; this section has the sole purpose of protecting the integrity of the free software distribution system, which is implemented by public license practices. Many people have made generous contributions to the wide range of software distributed through that system in reliance on consistent application of that system; it is up to the author/donor to decide if he or she is willing to distribute software through any other system and a licensee cannot impose that choice.

This section is intended to make thoroughly clear what is believed to be a consequence of the rest of this License.

8. If the distribution and/or use of the Program is restricted in certain countries either by patents or by copyrighted interfaces, the original copyright holder who places the Program under this License may add an explicit geographical distribution limitation excluding those countries, so that distribution is permitted only in or among countries not thus excluded. In such case, this License incorporates the limitation as if written in the body of this License.

9. The Free Software Foundation may publish revised and/or new versions of the General Public License from time to time. Such new versions will be similar in spirit to the present version, but may differ in detail to address new problems or concerns.

Each version is given a distinguishing version number. If the Program specifies a version number of this License which applies to it and "any later version," you have the option of following the terms and conditions either of that version or of any later version published by the Free Software Foundation. If the Program does not specify a version number of this License, you may choose any version ever published by the Free Software Foundation.

10. If you wish to incorporate parts of the Program into other free programs whose distribution conditions are different, write to the author to ask for permission. For software which is copyrighted by the Free Software Foundation, write to the Free Software Foundation; we sometimes make exceptions for this. Our decision will be guided by the two goals of preserving the free status of all derivatives of our free software and of promoting the sharing and reuse of software generally.

NO WARRANTY

11. BECAUSE THE PROGRAM IS LICENSED FREE OF CHARGE, THERE IS NO WARRANTY FOR THE PROGRAM, TO THE EXTENT PERMITTED BY APPLICABLE LAW. EXCEPT WHEN OTHERWISE STATED IN WRITING THE COPYRIGHT HOLDERS AND/OR OTHER PARTIES PROVIDE THE PROGRAM "AS IS" WITHOUT WARRANTY OF ANY KIND, EITHER EXPRESSED OR IMPLIED, INCLUDING, BUT NOT LIMITED TO, THE IMPLIED WARRANTIES OF MERCHANTABILITY AND FITNESS FOR A PARTICULAR PURPOSE. THE ENTIRE RISK AS TO THE QUALITY AND PERFORMANCE OF THE PROGRAM IS WITH YOU. SHOULD THE PROGRAM PROVE DEFECTIVE, YOU ASSUME THE COST OF ALL NECESSARY SERVICING, REPAIR OR CORRECTION.

12. IN NO EVENT UNLESS REQUIRED BY APPLICABLE LAW OR AGREED TO IN WRITING WILL ANY COPYRIGHT HOLDER, OR ANY OTHER PARTY WHO MAY MODIFY AND/OR REDISTRIBUTE THE PROGRAM AS PERMITTED ABOVE, BE LIABLE TO YOU FOR DAMAGES, INCLUDING ANY GENERAL, SPECIAL, INCIDENTAL OR CONSEQUENTIAL DAMAGES ARISING OUT OF THE USE OR INABILITY TO USE THE PROGRAM (INCLUDING BUT NOT LIMITED TO LOSS OF DATA OR DATA BEING RENDERED INACCURATE OR LOSSES SUSTAINED BY YOU OR THIRD PARTIES OR A FAILURE OF THE PROGRAM TO OPERATE WITH ANY OTHER PROGRAMS), EVEN IF SUCH HOLDER OR OTHER PARTY HAS BEEN ADVISED OF THE POSSIBILITY OF SUCH DAMAGES.

* * *

NOTE BY LINUS TORVALDS FOUND IN LINUX ALONG WITH GPL 2.0:

"NOTE! This copyright does not cover user programs that use kernel services by normal system calls — this is merely considered normal use of the kernel, and does not fall under the heading of 'derived work.' Also note that the GPL below is copyrighted by the Free Software Foundation, but the instance of the code that it refers to (the Linux Kernel) is copyrighted by me and others who actually wrote it."

* * *

GNU GENERAL PUBLIC LICENSE (GPL), VERSION 3

Copyright © 2007 Free Software Foundation, Inc. *<http://fsf.org/>*
Everyone is permitted to copy and distribute verbatim copies of this license document, but changing it is not allowed.

Preamble

The GNU General Public License is a free, copyleft license for software and other kinds of works.

The licenses for most software and other practical works are designed to take away your freedom to share and change the works. By contrast, the GNU General Public License is intended to guarantee your freedom to share and change all versions of a program — to make sure it remains free software for all its users. We, the Free Software

Foundation, use the GNU General Public License for most of our software; it applies also to any other work released this way by its authors. You can apply it to your programs, too.

When we speak of free software, we are referring to freedom, not price. Our General Public Licenses are designed to make sure that you have the freedom to distribute copies of free software (and charge for them if you wish), that you receive source code or can get it if you want it, that you can change the software or use pieces of it in new free programs, and that you know you can do these things.

To protect your rights, we need to prevent others from denying you these rights or asking you to surrender the rights. Therefore, you have certain responsibilities if you distribute copies of the software, or if you modify it: responsibilities to respect the freedom of others.

For example, if you distribute copies of such a program, whether gratis or for a fee, you must pass on to the recipients the same freedoms that you received. You must make sure that they, too, receive or can get the source code. And you must show them these terms so they know their rights.

Developers that use the GNU GPL protect your rights with two steps: (1) assert copyright on the software, and (2) offer you this License giving you legal permission to copy, distribute and/or modify it.

For the developers' and authors' protection, the GPL clearly explains that there is no warranty for this free software. For both users' and authors' sake, the GPL requires that modified versions be marked as changed, so that their problems will not be attributed erroneously to authors of previous versions.

Some devices are designed to deny users access to install or run modified versions of the software inside them, although the manufacturer can do so. This is fundamentally incompatible with the aim of protecting users' freedom to change the software. The systematic pattern of such abuse occurs in the area of products for individuals to use, which is precisely where it is most unacceptable. Therefore, we have designed this version of the GPL to prohibit the practice for those products. If such problems arise substantially in other domains, we stand ready to extend this provision to those domains in future versions of the GPL, as needed to protect the freedom of users.

Finally, every program is threatened constantly by software patents. States should not allow patents to restrict development and use of software on general-purpose computers, but in those that do, we wish to avoid the special danger that patents applied to a free program could make it effectively proprietary. To prevent this, the GPL assures that patents cannot be used to render the program non-free.

The precise terms and conditions for copying, distribution and modification follow.

Terms and Conditions

0. Definitions.

"This License" refers to version 3 of the GNU General Public License.

"Copyright" also means copyright-like laws that apply to other kinds of works, such as semiconductor masks.

"The Program" refers to any copyrightable work licensed under this License. Each licensee is addressed as "you". "Licensees" and "recipients" may be individuals or organizations.

To "modify" a work means to copy from or adapt all or part of the work in a fashion requiring copyright permission, other than the making of an exact copy. The resulting work is called a "modified version" of the earlier work or a work "based on" the earlier work.

A "covered work" means either the unmodified Program or a work based on the Program.

To "propagate" a work means to do anything with it that, without permission, would make you directly or secondarily liable for infringement under applicable copyright law, except executing it on a computer or modifying a private copy. Propagation includes copying, distribution (with or without modification), making available to the public, and in some countries other activities as well.

To "convey" a work means any kind of propagation that enables other parties to make or receive copies. Mere interaction with a user through a computer network, with no transfer of a copy, is not conveying.

An interactive user interface displays "Appropriate Legal Notices" to the extent that it includes a convenient and prominently visible feature that (1) displays an appropriate copyright notice, and (2) tells the user that there is no warranty for the work (except to the extent that warranties are provided), that licensees may convey the work under this License, and how to view a copy of this License. If the interface presents a list of user commands or options, such as a menu, a prominent item in the list meets this criterion.

1. Source Code.

The "source code" for a work means the preferred form of the work for making modifications to it. "Object code" means any non-source form of a work.

A "Standard Interface" means an interface that either is an official standard defined by a recognized standards body, or, in the case of interfaces specified for a particular programming language, one that is widely used among developers working in that language.

The "System Libraries" of an executable work include anything, other than the work as a whole, that (a) is included in the normal form of packaging a Major Component, but which is not part of that Major Component, and (b) serves only to enable use of the work with that Major Component, or to implement a Standard Interface for which an implementation is available to the public in source code form. A "Major Component", in this context, means a major essential component (kernel, window system, and so on) of the specific operating system (if any) on which the executable work runs, or a compiler used to produce the work, or an object code interpreter used to run it.

The "Corresponding Source" for a work in object code form means all the source code needed to generate, install, and (for an executable work) run the object code and to modify the work, including scripts to control those activities. However, it does not include the work's System Libraries, or general-purpose tools or generally available free programs which are used unmodified in performing those activities but which are not part of the work. For example, Corresponding Source includes interface definition files associated with source files for the work, and the source code for shared libraries and dynamically linked subprograms that the work is specifically designed to require, such as by intimate data communication or control flow between those subprograms and other parts of the work.

The Corresponding Source need not include anything that users can regenerate automatically from other parts of the Corresponding Source.

The Corresponding Source for a work in source code form is that same work.

2. Basic Permissions.

All rights granted under this License are granted for the term of copyright on the Program, and are irrevocable provided the stated conditions are met. This License explicitly affirms your unlimited permission to run the unmodified Program. The output from running a covered work is covered by this License only if the output, given its content, constitutes a covered work. This License acknowledges your rights of fair use or other equivalent, as provided by copyright law.

You may make, run and propagate covered works that you do not convey, without conditions so long as your license otherwise remains in force. You may convey covered works to others for the sole purpose of having them make modifications exclusively for you, or provide you with facilities for running those works, provided that you comply with the terms of this License in conveying all material for which you do not control copyright. Those thus making or running the covered works for you must do so exclusively on your behalf, under your direction and control, on terms that prohibit them from making any copies of your copyrighted material outside their relationship with you.

Conveying under any other circumstances is permitted solely under the conditions stated below. Sublicensing is not allowed; section 10 makes it unnecessary.

3. Protecting Users' Legal Rights From Anti-Circumvention Law.

No covered work shall be deemed part of an effective technological measure under any applicable law fulfilling obligations under article 11 of the WIPO copyright treaty adopted on 20 December 1996, or similar laws prohibiting or restricting circumvention of such measures.

When you convey a covered work, you waive any legal power to forbid circumvention of technological measures to the extent such circumvention is effected by exercising rights under this License with respect to the covered work, and you disclaim any intention to limit operation or modification of the work as a means of enforcing, against the work's users, your or third parties' legal rights to forbid circumvention of technological measures.

4. Conveying Verbatim Copies.

You may convey verbatim copies of the Program's source code as you receive it, in any medium, provided that you conspicuously and appropriately publish on each copy an appropriate copyright notice; keep intact all notices stating that this License and any non-permissive terms added in accord with section 7 apply to the code; keep intact all notices of the absence of any warranty; and give all recipients a copy of this License along with the Program.

You may charge any price or no price for each copy that you convey, and you may offer support or warranty protection for a fee.

5. Conveying Modified Source Versions.

You may convey a work based on the Program, or the modifications to produce it from the Program, in the form of source code under the terms of section 4, provided that you also meet all of these conditions:

(a) The work must carry prominent notices stating that you modified it, and giving a relevant date.

(b) The work must carry prominent notices stating that it is released under this License and any conditions added under section 7. This requirement modifies the requirement in section 4 to "keep intact all notices".

(c) You must license the entire work, as a whole, under this License to anyone who comes into possession of a copy. This License will therefore apply, along with any applicable section 7 additional terms, to the whole of the work, and all its parts, regardless of how they are packaged. This License gives no permission to license the work in any other way, but it does not invalidate such permission if you have separately received it.

(d) If the work has interactive user interfaces, each must display Appropriate Legal Notices; however, if the Program has interactive interfaces that do not display Appropriate Legal Notices, your work need not make them do so.

A compilation of a covered work with other separate and independent works, which are not by their nature extensions of the covered work, and which are not combined with it such as to form a larger program, in or on a volume of a storage or distribution medium, is called an "aggregate" if the compilation and its resulting copyright are not used to limit the access or legal rights of the compilation's users beyond what the individual works permit. Inclusion of a covered work in an aggregate does not cause this License to apply to the other parts of the aggregate.

6. Conveying Non-Source Forms.

You may convey a covered work in object code form under the terms of sections 4 and 5, provided that you also convey the machine-readable Corresponding Source under the terms of this License, in one of these ways:

(a) Convey the object code in, or embodied in, a physical product (including a physical distribution medium), accompanied by the Corresponding Source fixed on a durable physical medium customarily used for software interchange.

(b) Convey the object code in, or embodied in, a physical product (including a physical distribution medium), accompanied by a written offer, valid for at least three years and valid for as long as you offer spare parts or customer support for that product model, to give anyone who possesses the object code either (1) a copy of the Corresponding Source for all the software in the product that is covered by this License, on a durable physical medium customarily used for software interchange, for a price no more than your reasonable cost of physically performing this conveying of source, or (2) access to copy the Corresponding Source from a network server at no charge.

(c) Convey individual copies of the object code with a copy of the written offer to provide the Corresponding Source. This alternative is allowed only occasionally and noncommercially, and only if you received the object code with such an offer, in accord with subsection 6b.

(d) Convey the object code by offering access from a designated place (gratis or for a charge), and offer equivalent access to the Corresponding Source in the same way through the same place at no further charge. You need not require recipients to copy the Corresponding Source along with the object code. If the place to copy the object code is a network server, the Corresponding Source may be on a different server (operated by you or a third party) that supports equivalent copying facilities, provided you maintain clear directions next to the object code saying where to find the Corresponding Source. Regardless of what server hosts the Corresponding Source, you remain obligated to ensure that it is available for as long as needed to satisfy these requirements.

(e) Convey the object code using peer-to-peer transmission, provided you inform other peers where the object code and Corresponding Source of the work are being offered to the general public at no charge under subsection 6d.

A separable portion of the object code, whose source code is excluded from the Corresponding Source as a System Library, need not be included in conveying the object code work.

A "User Product" is either (1) a "consumer product", which means any tangible personal property which is normally used for personal, family, or household purposes, or (2) anything designed or sold for incorporation into a dwelling. In determining whether a product is a consumer product, doubtful cases shall be resolved in favor of coverage. For a particular product received by a particular user, "normally used" refers to a typical or common use of that class of product, regardless of the status of the particular user or of the way in which the particular user actually uses, or expects or is expected to use, the product. A product is a consumer product regardless of whether the product has substantial commercial, industrial or non-consumer uses, unless such uses represent the only significant mode of use of the product.

"Installation Information" for a User Product means any methods, procedures, authorization keys, or other information required to install and execute modified versions of a covered work in that User Product from a modified version of its Corresponding Source. The information must suffice to ensure that the continued functioning of the modified object code is in no case prevented or interfered with solely because modification has been made.

If you convey an object code work under this section in, or with, or specifically for use in, a User Product, and the conveying occurs as part of a transaction in which the right of possession and use of the User Product is transferred to the recipient in perpetuity or for a fixed term (regardless of how the transaction is characterized), the Corresponding Source conveyed under this section must be accompanied by the Installation Information. But this requirement does not apply if neither you nor any third party retains the ability to install modified object code on the User Product (for example, the work has been installed in ROM).

The requirement to provide Installation Information does not include a requirement to continue to provide support service, warranty, or updates for a work that has been modified or installed by the recipient, or for the User Product in which it has been modified or installed. Access to a network may be denied when the modification itself materially and adversely affects the operation of the network or violates the rules and protocols for communication across the network.

Corresponding Source conveyed, and Installation Information provided, in accord with this section must be in a format that is publicly documented (and with an implementation available to the public in source code form), and must require no special password or key for unpacking, reading or copying.

7. Additional Terms.

"Additional permissions" are terms that supplement the terms of this License by making exceptions from one or more of its conditions. Additional permissions that are applicable to the entire Program shall be treated as though they were included in this License, to the extent that they are valid under applicable law. If additional permissions apply only to part of the Program, that part may be used separately under those permissions, but the entire Program remains governed by this License without regard to the additional permissions.

When you convey a copy of a covered work, you may at your option remove any additional permissions from that copy, or from any part of it. (Additional permissions may be written to require their own removal in certain cases when you modify the work.) You may place additional permissions on material, added by you to a covered work, for which you have or can give appropriate copyright permission.

Notwithstanding any other provision of this License, for material you add to a covered work, you may (if authorized by the copyright holders of that material) supplement the terms of this License with terms:

(a) Disclaiming warranty or limiting liability differently from the terms of sections 15 and 16 of this License; or

(b) Requiring preservation of specified reasonable legal notices or author attributions in that material or in the Appropriate Legal Notices displayed by works containing it; or

(c) Prohibiting misrepresentation of the origin of that material, or requiring that modified versions of such material be marked in reasonable ways as different from the original version; or

(d) Limiting the use for publicity purposes of names of licensors or authors of the material; or

(e) Declining to grant rights under trademark law for use of some trade names, trademarks, or service marks; or

(f) Requiring indemnification of licensors and authors of that material by anyone who conveys the material (or modified versions of it) with contractual assumptions of liability to the recipient, for any liability that these contractual assumptions directly impose on those licensors and authors.

All other non-permissive additional terms are considered "further restrictions" within the meaning of section 10. If the Program as you received it, or any part of it, contains a notice stating that it is governed by this License along with a term that is a further restriction, you may remove that term. If a license document contains a further restriction but permits relicensing or conveying under this License, you may add to a covered work material governed by the terms of that license document, provided that the further restriction does not survive such relicensing or conveying.

If you add terms to a covered work in accord with this section, you must place, in the relevant source files, a statement of the additional terms that apply to those files, or a notice indicating where to find the applicable terms.

Additional terms, permissive or non-permissive, may be stated in the form of a separately written license, or stated as exceptions; the above requirements apply either way.

8. Termination.

You may not propagate or modify a covered work except as expressly provided under this License. Any attempt otherwise to propagate or modify it is void, and will automatically terminate your rights under this License (including any patent licenses granted under the third paragraph of section 11).

However, if you cease all violation of this License, then your license from a particular copyright holder is reinstated (a) provisionally, unless and until the copyright holder explicitly and finally terminates your license, and (b) permanently, if the copyright holder fails to notify you of the violation by some reasonable means prior to 60 days after the cessation.

Moreover, your license from a particular copyright holder is reinstated permanently if the copyright holder notifies you of the violation by some reasonable means, this is the first time you have received notice of violation of this License (for any work) from that copyright holder, and you cure the violation prior to 30 days after your receipt of the notice.

Termination of your rights under this section does not terminate the licenses of parties who have received copies or rights from you under this License. If your rights have been terminated and not permanently reinstated, you do not qualify to receive new licenses for the same material under section 10.

9. Acceptance Not Required for Having Copies.

You are not required to accept this License in order to receive or run a copy of the Program. Ancillary propagation of a covered work occurring solely as a consequence of using peer-to-peer transmission to receive a copy likewise does not require acceptance. However, nothing other than this License grants you permission to propagate or modify any covered work. These actions infringe copyright if you do not accept this License. Therefore, by modifying or propagating a covered work, you indicate your acceptance of this License to do so.

10. Automatic Licensing of Downstream Recipients.

Each time you convey a covered work, the recipient automatically receives a license from the original licensors, to run, modify and propagate that work, subject to this License. You are not responsible for enforcing compliance by third parties with this License.

An "entity transaction" is a transaction transferring control of an organization, or substantially all assets of one, or subdividing an organization, or merging organizations. If propagation of a covered work results from an entity transaction, each party to that transaction who receives a copy of the work also receives whatever licenses to the work the party's predecessor in interest had or could give under the previous paragraph, plus a right to possession of the Corresponding Source of the work from the predecessor in interest, if the predecessor has it or can get it with reasonable efforts.

You may not impose any further restrictions on the exercise of the rights granted or affirmed under this License. For example, you may not impose a license fee, royalty, or other charge for exercise of rights granted under this License, and you may not initiate litigation (including a cross-claim or counterclaim in a lawsuit) alleging that any patent claim is infringed by making, using, selling, offering for sale, or importing the Program or any portion of it.

11. Patents.

A "contributor" is a copyright holder who authorizes use under this License of the Program or a work on which the Program is based. The work thus licensed is called the contributor's "contributor version".

A contributor's "essential patent claims" are all patent claims owned or controlled by the contributor, whether already acquired or hereafter acquired, that would be infringed by some manner, permitted by this License, of making, using, or selling its contributor version, but do not include claims that would be infringed only as a consequence of further modification of the contributor version. For purposes of this definition, "control" includes the right to grant patent sublicenses in a manner consistent with the requirements of this License.

Each contributor grants you a non-exclusive, worldwide, royalty-free patent license under the contributor's essential patent claims, to make, use, sell, offer for sale, import and otherwise run, modify and propagate the contents of its contributor version.

In the following three paragraphs, a "patent license" is any express agreement or commitment, however denominated, not to enforce a patent (such as an express permission to practice a patent or covenant not to sue for patent infringement). To "grant" such a patent license to a party means to make such an agreement or commitment not to enforce a patent against the party.

If you convey a covered work, knowingly relying on a patent license, and the Corresponding Source of the work is not available for anyone to copy, free of charge and under the terms of this License, through a publicly available network server or other readily accessible means, then you must either (1) cause the Corresponding Source to be so available, or (2) arrange to deprive yourself of the benefit of the patent license for this particular work, or (3) arrange, in a manner consistent with the requirements of this License, to extend the patent license to downstream recipients. "Knowingly relying" means you have actual knowledge that, but for the patent license, your conveying the covered work in a country, or your recipient's use of the covered work in a country, would infringe one or more identifiable patents in that country that you have reason to believe are valid.

If, pursuant to or in connection with a single transaction or arrangement, you convey, or propagate by procuring conveyance of, a covered work, and grant a patent license to some of the parties receiving the covered work authorizing them to use, propagate, modify or convey a specific copy of the covered work, then the patent license you grant is automatically extended to all recipients of the covered work and works based on it.

A patent license is "discriminatory" if it does not include within the scope of its coverage, prohibits the exercise of, or is conditioned on the non-exercise of one or more of the rights that are specifically granted under this License. You may not convey a covered work if you are a party to an arrangement with a third party that is in the business of distributing software, under which you make payment to the third party based on the extent of your activity of conveying the work, and under which the third party grants, to any of the parties who would receive the covered work from you, a discriminatory patent license (a) in connection with copies of the covered work conveyed by you (or copies made from those copies), or (b) primarily for and in connection with specific products or compilations that contain the covered work, unless you entered into that arrangement, or that patent license was granted, prior to 28 March 2007.

Nothing in this License shall be construed as excluding or limiting any implied license or other defenses to infringement that may otherwise be available to you under applicable patent law.

12. No Surrender of Others' Freedom.

If conditions are imposed on you (whether by court order, agreement or otherwise) that contradict the conditions of this License, they do not excuse you from the conditions of this License. If you cannot convey a covered work so as to satisfy simultaneously your obligations under this License and any other pertinent obligations, then as a consequence you may not convey it at all. For example, if you agree to terms that obligate you to collect a royalty for further conveying from those to whom you convey the Program, the only way you could satisfy both those terms and this License would be to refrain entirely from conveying the Program.

13. Use with the GNU Affero General Public License.

Notwithstanding any other provision of this License, you have permission to link or combine any covered work with a work licensed under version 3 of the GNU Affero General Public License into a single combined work, and to convey the resulting work. The terms of this License will continue to apply to the part which is the covered work, but the special requirements of the GNU Affero General Public License, section 13, concerning interaction through a network will apply to the combination as such.

14. Revised Versions of this License.

The Free Software Foundation may publish revised and/or new versions of the GNU General Public License from time to time. Such new versions will be similar in spirit to the present version, but may differ in detail to address new problems or concerns.

Each version is given a distinguishing version number. If the Program specifies that a certain numbered version of the GNU General Public License "or any later version" applies to it, you have the option of following the terms and conditions either of that numbered version or of any later version published by the Free Software Foundation. If the Program does not specify a version number of the GNU General Public License, you may choose any version ever published by the Free Software Foundation.

If the Program specifies that a proxy can decide which future versions of the GNU General Public License can be used, that proxy's public statement of acceptance of a version permanently authorizes you to choose that version for the Program.

Later license versions may give you additional or different permissions. However, no additional obligations are imposed on any author or copyright holder as a result of your choosing to follow a later version.

15. Disclaimer of Warranty.

THERE IS NO WARRANTY FOR THE PROGRAM, TO THE EXTENT PERMITTED BY APPLICABLE LAW. EXCEPT WHEN OTHERWISE STATED IN WRITING THE COPYRIGHT HOLDERS AND/OR OTHER PARTIES PROVIDE THE PROGRAM "AS IS" WITHOUT WARRANTY OF ANY KIND, EITHER EXPRESSED OR IMPLIED, INCLUDING, BUT NOT LIMITED TO, THE IMPLIED WARRANTIES OF MERCHANT-ABILITY AND FITNESS FOR A PARTICULAR PURPOSE. THE ENTIRE RISK AS TO THE QUALITY AND PERFORMANCE OF THE PROGRAM IS WITH YOU. SHOULD THE PROGRAM PROVE DEFECTIVE, YOU ASSUME THE COST OF ALL NECESSARY SER-VICING, REPAIR OR CORRECTION.

16. Limitation of Liability.

IN NO EVENT UNLESS REQUIRED BY APPLICABLE LAW OR AGREED TO IN WRITING WILL ANY COPYRIGHT HOLDER, OR ANY OTHER PARTY WHO MODIFIES AND/OR CONVEYS THE PROGRAM AS PERMITTED ABOVE, BE LIABLE TO YOU FOR DAMAGES, INCLUDING ANY GENERAL, SPECIAL, INCIDENTAL OR CONSE-QUENTIAL DAMAGES ARISING OUT OF THE USE OR INABILITY TO USE THE PROGRAM (INCLUDING BUT NOT LIMITED TO LOSS OF DATA OR DATA BEING RENDERED INACCURATE OR LOSSES SUSTAINED BY YOU OR THIRD PARTIES OR A FAILURE OF THE PROGRAM TO OPERATE WITH ANY OTHER PROGRAMS), EVEN IF SUCH HOLDER OR OTHER PARTY HAS BEEN ADVISED OF THE POSSIBILITY OF SUCH DAMAGES.

17. Interpretation of Sections 15 and 16.

If the disclaimer of warranty and limitation of liability provided above cannot be given local legal effect according to their terms, reviewing courts shall apply local law that most closely approximates an absolute waiver of all civil liability in con-nection with the Program, unless a warranty or assumption of liability accompanies a copy of the Program in return for a fee.

* * *

THE BSD LICENSE

Redistribution and use in source and binary forms, with or without modification, are permitted provided that the following conditions are met:

- Redistributions of source code must retain the above copyright notice, this list of conditions and the following disclaimer.

- Redistributions in binary form must reproduce the above copyright notice, this list of conditions and the following disclaimer in the documentation and/or other materi-als provided with the distribution.

- Neither the name of the <ORGANIZATION> nor the names of its contributors may be used to endorse or promote products derived from this software without specific prior written permission.

THIS SOFTWARE IS PROVIDED BY THE COPYRIGHT HOLDERS AND CONTRIBUTORS "AS IS" AND ANY EXPRESS OR IMPLIED WARRANTIES, INCLUDING, BUT NOT LIMITED TO, THE IMPLIED WARRANTIES OF MERCHANTABILITY AND FITNESS FOR A PARTICULAR PURPOSE ARE DISCLAIMED. IN NO EVENT SHALL THE COPYRIGHT OWNER OR CONTRIBUTORS BE LIABLE FOR ANY DIRECT, INDIRECT, INCIDENTAL, SPECIAL, EXEMPLARY, OR CONSEQUENTIAL DAMAGES (INCLUDING, BUT NOT LIMITED TO, PROCUREMENT OF SUBSTITUTE GOODS OR SERVICES; LOSS OF USE, DATA, OR PROFITS; OR BUSINESS INTERRUPTION) HOWEVER CAUSED AND ON ANY THEORY OF LIABILITY, WHETHER IN CONTRACT, STRICT LIABILITY, OR TORT (INCLUDING NEGLIGENCE OR OTHERWISE) ARISING IN ANY WAY OUT OF THE USE OF THIS SOFTWARE, EVEN IF ADVISED OF THE POSSIBILITY OF SUCH DAMAGE.

* * *

THE OPEN SOURCE DEFINITION

Introduction

Open source doesn't just mean access to the source code. The distribution terms of open-source software must comply with the following criteria:

1. Free Redistribution

The license shall not restrict any party from selling or giving away the software as a component of an aggregate software distribution containing programs from several different sources. The license shall not require a royalty or other fee for such sale.

2. Source Code

The program must include source code, and must allow distribution in source code as well as compiled form. Where some form of a product is not distributed with source code, there must be a well-publicized means of obtaining the source code for no more than a reasonable reproduction cost — preferably, downloading via the Internet without charge. The source code must be the preferred form in which a programmer would modify the program. Deliberately obfuscated source code is not allowed. Intermediate forms such as the output of a preprocessor or translator are not allowed.

3. Derived Works

The license must allow modifications and derived works, and must allow them to be distributed under the same terms as the license of the original software.

4. Integrity of the Author's Source Code

The license may restrict source code from being distributed in modified form *only* if the license allows the distribution of "patch files" with the source code for the purpose of modifying the program at build time. The license must explicitly permit distribution of software built from modified source code. The license may require derived works to carry a different name or version number from the original software.

5. No Discrimination Against Persons or Groups

The license must not discriminate against any person or group of persons.

6. No Discrimination Against Fields of Endeavor

The license must not restrict anyone from making use of the program in a specific field of endeavor. For example, it may not restrict the program from being used in a business, or from being used for genetic research.

7. Distribution of License

The rights attached to the program must apply to all to whom the program is redistributed without the need for execution of an additional license by those parties.

8. License Must Not Be Specific to a Product

The rights attached to the program must not depend on the program's being part of a particular software distribution. If the program is extracted from that distribution and used or distributed within the terms of the program's license, all parties to whom the program is redistributed should have the same rights as those that are granted in conjunction with the original software distribution.

9. License Must Not Restrict Other Software

The license must not place restrictions on other software that is distributed along with the licensed software. For example, the license must not insist that all other programs distributed on the same medium must be open-source software.

10. License Must Be Technology-Neutral

No provision of the license may be predicated on any individual technology or style of interface.

JACOBSEN v. KATZER

535 F.3d 1373 (Fed. Cir. 2008)

HOCHBERG, District Judge, sitting by designation.

BACKGROUND

Copyright holder filed action against competitor alleging infringement of copyright to computer programming code and also sought declaratory judgment that patent issued to defendant was not infringed by copyright holder and was invalid. The United States District Court for the Northern District of California, Jeffrey S. White, J., 2007 WL 2358628, denied holder's request for preliminary injunction. Holder appealed.

DISCUSSION

We consider here the ability of a copyright holder to dedicate certain work to free public use and yet enforce an "open source" copyright license to control the future distribution and modification of that work. Appellant Robert Jacobsen ("Jacobsen") appeals from an order denying a motion for preliminary injunction. Jacobsen v. Katzer, No. 06-CV-01905 JSW, 2007 WL 2358628 (N.D. Cal. Aug. 17, 2007). Jacobsen holds a copyright to computer programming code. He makes that code available for public download from a website without a financial fee pursuant to the Artistic License, an "open source" or public license. Appellees Matthew Katzer and Kamind Associates, Inc. (collectively "Katzer/Kamind") develop commercial software products for the model train industry and hobbyists. Jacobsen accused Katzer/Kamind of copying certain materials from Jacobsen's website and incorporating them into one of Katzer/Kamind's software packages without following the terms of the Artistic License. Jacobsen brought an action for copyright infringement and moved for a preliminary injunction.

The District Court held that the open source Artistic License created an "intentionally broad" nonexclusive license which was unlimited in scope and thus did not create liability for copyright infringement. The District Court reasoned:

> The plaintiff claimed that by modifying the software the defendant had exceeded the scope of the license and therefore infringed the copyright. Here, however, the JMRI Project license provides that a user may copy the files verbatim or may otherwise modify the material in any way, including as part of a larger, possibly commercial software distribution. The license explicitly gives the users of the material, any member of the public, "the right to use and distribute the [material] in a more-or-less customary fashion, plus the right to make reasonable accommodations." The scope of the nonexclusive license is, therefore, intentionally broad. The condition that the user insert a prominent notice of attribution does not limit the scope of the license. Rather, Defendants' alleged violation of the conditions of the license may have constituted a breach of the nonexclusive license, but does not create liability for copyright infringement where it would not otherwise exist.

Jacobsen, 2007 WL 2358628 at *7 (internal citations omitted).

On this basis, the District Court denied the motion for a preliminary injunction. We vacate and remand.

I.

Jacobsen manages an open source software group called Java Model Railroad Interface ("JMRI"). Through the collective work of many participants, JMRI created a computer programming application called DecoderPro, which allows model railroad enthusiasts to use their computers to program the decoder chips that control model trains. DecoderPro files are available for download and use by the public free of charge from an open source incubator website called SourceForge; Jacobsen maintains the JMRI site on SourceForge. The downloadable files contain copyright notices and refer the user to a "COPYING" file, which clearly sets forth the terms of the Artistic License.

Katzer/Kamind offers a competing software product, Decoder Commander, which is also used to program decoder chips. During development of Decoder Commander, one of Katzer/Kamind's predecessors or employees is alleged to have downloaded the decoder definition files from DecoderPro and used portions of these files as part of the Decoder Commander software. The Decoder Commander software files that used DecoderPro definition files did not comply with the terms of the Artistic License. Specifically, the Decoder Commander software did not include (1) the authors' names, (2) JMRI copyright notices, (3) references to the COPYING file, (4) an identification of SourceForge or JMRI as the original source of the definition files, and (5) a description of how the files or computer code had been changed from the original source code. The Decoder Commander software also changed various computer file names of DecoderPro files without providing a reference to the original JMRI files or information on where to get the Standard Version.[3]

Jacobsen moved for a preliminary injunction, arguing that the violation of the terms of the Artistic License constituted copyright infringement and that, under Ninth Circuit law, irreparable harm could be presumed in a copyright infringement case. The District Court reviewed the Artistic License and determined that "Defendants' alleged violation of the conditions of the license may have constituted a breach of the nonexclusive license, but does not create liability for copyright infringement where it would not otherwise exist." Id. at *7. The District Court found that Jacobsen had a cause of action only for breach of contract, rather than an action for copyright infringement based on a breach of the conditions of the Artistic License. Because a breach of contract creates no presumption of irreparable harm, the District Court denied the motion for a preliminary injunction.

Jacobsen appeals the finding that he does not have a cause of action for copyright infringement. Although an appeal concerning copyright law and not patent law is rare in our Circuit, here we indeed possess appellate jurisdiction. In the district court, Jacobsen's operative complaint against Katzer/Kamind included not only his claim for copyright infringement, but also claims seeking a declaratory judgment that a patent issued to Katzer is not infringed by Jacobsen and is invalid. Therefore the complaint arose in part under the patent laws. See 28 U.S.C. §2201(a); Golan v. Pingel Enter., 310 F.3d 1360, 1367 (Fed. Cir. 2002) (explaining that "[i]n the context of a complaint seeking a declaration of noninfringement, the action threatened by the declaratory defendant . . . would be an action for patent infringement," and "[s]uch an action clearly arises under the patent laws"). Thus the district court's jurisdiction was based, at least in part, on 28 U.S.C. §1338(a) as *it relates to the patent laws*, and we have appellate jurisdiction under 28 U.S.C. §1292(c)(1).

II.

This Court looks to the interpretive law of the regional circuit for issues not exclusively assigned to the Federal Circuit. Hutchins v. Zoll Med. Corp., 492 F.3d 1377, 1383 (Fed. Cir. 2007). Under Ninth Circuit law, an order granting or denying a preliminary injunction will be reversed only if the district court relied on an erroneous legal premise or abused its discretion. Wright v. Rushen, 642 F.2d 1129, 1132 (9th Cir. 1981). A district court's order denying a preliminary injunction is reversible for factual error only when the district court rests its conclusions on clearly erroneous findings of fact. Sports Form, Inc. v. United Press Int'l, Inc., 686 F.2d 750, 753 (9th Cir. 1982).

---

3. Katzer/Kamind represents that all potentially infringing activities using any of the disputed material have been voluntarily ceased. The district court held that it could not find as a matter of law that Katzer/Kamind's voluntary termination of allegedly wrongful activity renders the motion for preliminary injunction moot because it could not find as a matter of law that it is absolutely clear that the alleged behavior could not recur. *Jacobsen*, 2007 WL 2358628 at *5. We agree that this matter is not moot. *See also* Adarand Constructors, Inc. v. Slater, 528 U.S. 216, 222, 120 S. Ct. 722, 145 L. Ed. 2d 650 (2000) ("Voluntary cessation of challenged conduct moots a case . . . only if it is *absolutely* clear that the allegedly wrongful behavior could not reasonably be expected to recur." (emphasis in original)).

In determining whether to issue a preliminary injunction, the Ninth Circuit requires demonstration of (1) a combination of probability of success on the merits and the possibility of irreparable harm; or (2) serious questions going to the merits where the balance of hardships tips sharply in the moving party's favor. Perfect 10, Inc. v. Amazon.com, Inc., 487 F.3d 701, 713-14 (9th Cir. 2007); Dep't of Parks & Recreation v. Bazaar Del Mundo, Inc., 448 F.3d 1118, 1123 (9th Cir. 2006). In cases involving copyright claims, where a copyright holder has shown likelihood of success on the merits of a copyright infringement claim, the Ninth Circuit has held that irreparable harm is presumed. LGS Architects, Inc. v. Concordia Homes of Nev., 434 F.3d 1150, 1155-56 (9th Cir. 2006). *But see* MGM Studios, Inc. v. Grokster, Ltd., 518 F. Supp. 2d 1197, 1212 (C.D. Cal. 2007) (noting that "the longstanding rule that irreparable harm can be a presumed after a showing of likelihood of success for purposes of a copyright preliminary injunction motion may itself have to be reevaluated in light of *eBay* [Inc. v. MercExchange, L.L.C., 547 U.S. 388, 126 S. Ct. 1837, 164 L. Ed. 2d 641 (2006)]"). Thus, for a preliminary injunction to issue, Jacobsen must either show (1) a likelihood of success on the merits of his copyright infringement claim from which irreparable harm is presumed; or (2) a fair chance of success on the merits and a clear disparity in the relative hardships that tips sharply in his favor.

A.

Public licenses, often referred to as "open source" licenses, are used by artists, authors, educators, software developers, and scientists who wish to create collaborative projects and to dedicate certain works to the public. Several types of public licenses have been designed to provide creators of copyrighted materials a means to protect and control their copyrights. Creative Commons, one of the amici curiae, provides free copyright licenses to allow parties to dedicate their works to the public or to license certain uses of their works while keeping some rights reserved.

Open source licensing has become a widely used method of creative collaboration that serves to advance the arts and sciences in a manner and at a pace that few could have imagined just a few decades ago. For example, the Massachusetts Institute of Technology ("MIT") uses a Creative Commons public license for an OpenCourseWare project that licenses all 1800 MIT courses. Other public licenses support the GNU/Linux operating system, the Perl programming language, the Apache web server programs, the Firefox web browser, and a collaborative web-based encyclopedia called Wikipedia. Creative Commons notes that, by some estimates, there are close to 100,000,000 works licensed under various Creative Commons licenses. The Wikimedia Foundation, another of the amici curiae, estimates that the Wikipedia website has more than 75,000 active contributors working on some 9,000,000 articles in more than 250 languages.

Open Source software projects invite computer programmers from around the world to view software code and make changes and improvements to it. Through such collaboration, software programs can often be written and debugged faster and at lower cost than if the copyright holder were required to do all of the work independently. In exchange and in consideration for this collaborative work, the copyright holder permits users to copy, modify and distribute the software code subject to conditions that serve to protect downstream users and to keep the code accessible.[4] By requiring that users copy and restate the license and attribution information, a copyright holder can ensure that recipients of the redistributed computer code know the identity of the owner as well as the scope of the license granted by the original owner. The Artistic License in this case also requires that changes to the computer code be tracked so that downstream users know what part of the computer code is the original code created by the copyright holder and what part has been newly added or altered by another collaborator.

Traditionally, copyright owners sold their copyrighted material in exchange for money. The lack of money changing hands in open source licensing should not be presumed to mean that there is no economic consideration, however. There are substantial benefits, including economic benefits, to the creation and distribution of copyrighted works under public licenses that range far beyond traditional license royalties. For example, program creators may generate market share for their programs by providing certain components free of charge. Similarly, a programmer or company may increase its national or international reputation by incubating open source projects. Improvement to a product can come rapidly and free of charge from an expert not even known to the copyright holder. The Eleventh Circuit has recognized the economic motives inherent in public licenses, even where profit is not immediate. *See* Planetary Motion, Inc. v. Techsplosion, Inc., 261 F.3d 1188, 1200 (11th Cir. 2001) (Program creator "derived value from the distribution [under a public license] because he was able to improve his Software based on suggestions sent by end-users. . . . It is logical that as the Software improved, more end-users used his Software, thereby increasing [the programmer's] recognition in his profession and the likelihood that the Software would be improved even further.").

B.

The parties do not dispute that Jacobsen is the holder of a copyright for certain materials distributed through his website.[5] Katzer/Kamind also admits that portions of the DecoderPro software were copied, modified, and distributed as part of the Decoder Commander software. Accordingly, Jacobsen has made out a prima facie case of copyright infringement. Katzer/Kamind argues that they cannot be liable for copyright infringement because they had a license to use the material. Thus, the Court must evaluate whether the use by Katzer/Kamind was outside the scope of the license. *See LGS Architects*, 434 F.3d at 1156. The copyrighted materials in this case are downloadable by any user and are labeled to include a copyright notification and a COPYING file that includes the text of the Artistic License. The Artistic License grants users the right to copy, modify, and distribute the software:

> provided that [the user] insert a prominent notice in each changed file stating how and when [the user] changed that file, and provided that [the user] do at least ONE of the following:

---

4. For example, the GNU General Public License, which is used for the Linux operating system, prohibits downstream users from charging for a license to the software. *See* Wallace v. IBM Corp., 467 F.3d 1104, 1105-06 (7th Cir. 2006).

5. Jacobsen's copyright registration creates the presumption of a valid copyright. *See, e.g.*, Triad Sys. Corp. v. SE Exp. Co., 64 F.3d 1330, 1335 (9th Cir. 1995).

a) place [the user's] modifications in the Public Domain or otherwise make them Freely Available, such as by posting said modifications to Usenet or an equivalent medium, or placing the modifications on a major archive site such as ftp.uu.net, or by allowing the Copyright Holder to include [the user's] modifications in the Standard Version of the Package.

b) use the modified Package only within [the user's] corporation or organization.

c) rename any non-standard executables so the names do not conflict with the standard executables, which must also be provided, and provide a separate manual page for each nonstandard executable that clearly documents how it differs from the Standard Version, or

d) make other distribution arrangements with the Copyright Holder.

The heart of the argument on appeal concerns whether the terms of the Artistic License are conditions of, or merely covenants to, the copyright license. Generally, a "copyright owner who grants a nonexclusive license to use his copyrighted material waives his right to sue the licensee for copyright infringement" and can sue only for breach of contract. Sun Microsystems, Inc., v. Microsoft Corp., 188 F.3d 1115, 1121 (9th Cir. 1999); Graham v. James, 144 F.3d 229, 236 (2d Cir. 1998). If, however, a license is limited in scope and the licensee acts outside the scope, the licensor can bring an action for copyright infringement. See S.O.S., Inc. v. Payday, Inc., 886 F.2d 1081, 1087 (9th Cir. 1989); NIMMER ON COPYRIGHT, §1015[A] (1999).

Thus, if the terms of the Artistic License allegedly violated are both covenants and conditions, they may serve to limit the scope of the license and are governed by copyright law. If they are merely covenants, by contrast, they are governed by contract law. See Graham, 144 F.3d at 236-37 (whether breach of license is actionable as copyright infringement or breach of contract turns on whether provision breached is condition of the license, or mere covenant); Sun Microsystems, 188 F.3d at 1121 (following Graham; independent covenant does not limit scope of copyright license). The District Court did not expressly state whether the limitations in the Artistic License are independent covenants or, rather, conditions to the scope; its analysis, however, clearly treated the license limitations as contractual covenants rather than conditions of the copyright license.[6]

Jacobsen argues that the terms of the Artistic License define the scope of the license and that any use outside of these restrictions is copyright infringement. Katzer/Kamind argues that these terms do not limit the scope of the license and are merely covenants providing contractual terms for the use of the materials, and that his violation of them is neither compensable in damages nor subject to injunctive relief. Katzer/Kamind's argument is premised upon the assumption that Jacobsen's copyright gave him no economic rights because he made his computer code available to the public at no charge. From this assumption, Katzer/Kamind argues that copyright law does not recognize a cause of action for non-economic rights, relying on Gilliam v. ABC, 538 F.2d 14, 20-21 (2d Cir. 1976) ("American copyright law, as presently

---

6. The District Court held that "Defendants' alleged violation of the conditions of the license may have constituted a breach of the nonexclusive license . . . [and] the Court finds that Plaintiff's claim properly sounds in contract." *Jacobsen*, 2007 WL 2358628 at *7. Thus, despite the use of the word "conditions," the District Court treated the terms of the Artistic License as contractual covenants which did not limit the scope of the license.

written, does not recognize moral rights or provide a cause of action for their violation, since the law seeks to vindicate the economic, rather than the personal rights of authors."). The District Court based its opinion on the breadth of the Artistic License terms, to which we now turn.

III.

The Artistic License states on its face that the document creates conditions: "The intent of this document is to state the *conditions* under which a Package may be copied." (Emphasis added.) The Artistic License also uses the traditional language of conditions by noting that the rights to copy, modify, and distribute are granted "*provided that*" the conditions are met. Under California contract law, "provided that" typically denotes a condition. *See, e.g.*, Diepenbrock v. Luiz, 159 Cal. 716, 115 P. 743 (1911) (interpreting a real property lease reciting that when the property was sold, "this lease shall cease and be at an end, *provided that* the party of the first part shall then pay [certain compensation] to the party of the second part"; considering the appellant's "interesting and ingenious" argument for interpreting this language as creating a mere covenant rather than a condition; and holding that this argument "cannot change the fact that, attributing the usual and ordinary signification to the language of the parties, a *condition* is found in the provision in question") (emphases added).

The conditions set forth in the Artistic License are vital to enable the copyright holder to retain the ability to benefit from the work of downstream users. By requiring that users who modify or distribute the copyrighted material retain the reference to the original source files, downstream users are directed to Jacobsen's website. Thus, downstream users know about the collaborative effort to improve and expand the SourceForge project once they learn of the "upstream" project from a "downstream" distribution, and they may join in that effort.

The District Court interpreted the Artistic License to permit a user to "modify the material in any way" and did not find that any of the "provided that" limitations in the Artistic License served to limit this grant. The District Court's interpretation of the conditions of the Artistic License does not credit the explicit restrictions in the license that govern a downloader's right to modify and distribute the copyrighted work. The copyright holder here expressly stated the terms upon which the right to modify and distribute the material depended and invited direct contact if a downloader wished to negotiate other terms. These restrictions were both clear and necessary to accomplish the objectives of the open source licensing collaboration, including economic benefit. Moreover, the District Court did not address the other restrictions of the license, such as the requirement that all modification from the original be clearly shown with a new name and a separate page for any such modification that shows how it differs from the original.

Copyright holders who engage in open source licensing have the right to control the modification and distribution of copyrighted material. As the Second Circuit explained in Gilliam v. ABC, 538 F.2d 14, 21 (2d Cir. 1976), the "unauthorized editing of the underlying work, if proven, would constitute an infringement of the copyright in that work similar to any other use of a work that exceeded the license granted by the proprietor of the copyright." Copyright licenses are designed to support the right to exclude; money damages alone do not support or enforce that right. The choice to exact consideration in the form of compliance with the open source requirements of disclosure and explanation of changes, rather than as a dollar-denominated fee, is entitled to no less legal recognition. Indeed, because a calculation of damages is inherently speculative, these types of license restrictions might well be rendered meaningless absent the ability to enforce through injunctive relief.

In this case, a user who downloads the JMRI copyrighted materials is authorized to make modifications and to distribute the materials "provided that" the user follows the restrictive terms of the Artistic License. A copyright holder can grant the right to make certain modifications, yet retain his right to prevent other modifications. Indeed, such a goal is exactly the purpose of adding conditions to a license grant.[7] The Artistic License, like many other common copyright licenses, requires that any copies that are distributed contain the copyright notices and the COPYING file. *See, e.g.*, 3-10 NIMMER ON COPYRIGHT §10.15 ("An express (or possibly an implied) condition that a licensee must affix a proper copyright notice to all copies of the work that he causes to be published will render a publication devoid of such notice without authority from the licensor and therefore, an infringing act.").

It is outside the scope of the Artistic License to modify and distribute the copyrighted materials without copyright notices and a tracking of modifications from the original computer files. If a downloader does not assent to these conditions stated in the COPYING file, he is instructed to "make other arrangements with the Copyright Holder." Katzer/Kamind did not make any such "other arrangements." The clear language of the Artistic License creates conditions to protect the economic rights at issue in the granting of a public license. These conditions govern the rights to modify and distribute the computer programs and files included in the downloadable software package. The attribution and modification transparency requirements directly serve to drive traffic to the open source incubation page and to inform downstream users of the project, which is a significant economic goal of the copyright holder that the law will enforce. Through this controlled spread of information, the copyright holder gains creative collaborators to the open source project; by requiring that changes made by downstream users be visible to the copyright holder and others, the copyright holder learns about the uses for his software and gains others' knowledge that can be used to advance future software releases.

IV.

For the aforementioned reasons, we vacate and remand. While Katzer/Kamind appears to have conceded that they did not comply with the aforedescribed conditions of the Artistic License, the District Court did not make factual findings on the likelihood of success on the merits in proving that Katzer/Kamind violated the conditions of the Artistic License. Having determined that the terms of the Artistic License are enforceable copyright conditions, we

---

7. Open source licensing restrictions are easily distinguished from mere "author attribution" cases. Copyright law does not automatically protect the rights of authors to credit for copyrighted materials. *See Gilliam*, 538 F.2d at 20-21 ("American copyright law, as presently written, does not recognize moral rights or provide a cause of action for their violation, since the law seeks to vindicate the economic, rather than the personal rights of authors."); *Graham*, 144 F.3d at 236. Whether such rights are protected by a specific license grant depends on the language of the license. *See* County of Ventura v. Blackburn, 362 F.2d 515, 520 (9th Cir. 1966) (copyright infringement found where the county removed copyright notices from maps licensed to it where the license granted the county "the right to obtain duplicate tracings" from photographic negatives that contained copyright notices).

remand to enable the District Court to determine whether Jacobsen has demonstrated (1) a likelihood of success on the merits and either a presumption of irreparable harm or a demonstration of irreparable harm; or (2) a fair chance of success on the merits and a clear disparity in the relative hardships and tipping in his favor.[8]

The judgment of the District Court is vacated and the case is remanded for further proceedings consistent with this opinion.

VACATED and *REMANDED*.

SPECHT v. NETSCAPE COMMUNICATIONS CORP.
306 F.3d 17 (2d Cir. 2002)

SOTOMAYOR, Circuit Judge.

In the time period relevant to this litigation, Netscape offered on its website various software programs, including Communicator and SmartDownload, which visitors to the site were invited to obtain free of charge. It is undisputed that five of the six named plaintiffs—Michael Fagan, John Gibson, Mark Gruber, Sean Kelly, and Sherry Weindorf—downloaded Communicator from the Netscape website. These plaintiffs acknowledge that when they proceeded to initiate installation of Communicator, they were automatically shown a scrollable text of that program's license agreement and were not permitted to complete the installation until they had clicked on a "Yes" button to indicate that they accepted all the license terms. If a user attempted to install Communicator without clicking "Yes," the installation would be aborted. All five named user plaintiffs expressly agreed to Communicator's license terms by clicking "Yes." The Communicator license agreement that these plaintiffs saw made no mention of SmartDownload or other plug-in programs, and stated that "[t]hese terms apply to Netscape Communicator and Netscape Navigator" and that "all disputes relating to this Agreement (excepting any dispute relating to intellectual property rights)" are subject to "binding arbitration in Santa Clara County, California."

Although Communicator could be obtained independently of SmartDownload, all the named user plaintiffs, except Fagan, downloaded and installed Communicator in connection with downloading SmartDownload. Each of these plaintiffs allegedly arrived at a Netscape webpage captioned "SmartDownload Communicator" that urged them to "Download With Confidence Using SmartDownload!" At or near the bottom of the screen facing plaintiffs was the prompt "Start Download" and a tinted button labeled "Download." By clicking on the button, plaintiffs initiated the download of SmartDownload. Once that process was complete, SmartDownload, as its first plug-in task, permitted plaintiffs to proceed with downloading and installing Communicator, an operation that was accompanied by the clickwrap display of Communicator's license terms described above.

The signal difference between downloading Communicator and downloading SmartDownload was that no clickwrap presentation accompanied the latter operation. Instead, once plaintiffs Gibson, Gruber, Kelly, and Weindorf had clicked on the "Download" button located at or near the bottom of their screen, and the downloading of SmartDownload was

---

8. At oral argument, the parties admitted that there might be no way to calculate any monetary damages under a contract theory.

complete, these plaintiffs encountered no further information about the plug-in program or the existence of license terms governing its use. The sole reference to SmartDownload's license terms on the "SmartDownload Communicator" webpage was located in text that would have become visible to plaintiffs only if they had scrolled down to the next screen.

Had plaintiffs scrolled down instead of acting on defendants' invitation to click on the "Download" button, they would have encountered the following invitation: "Please review and agree to the terms of the Netscape SmartDownload software license agreement before downloading and using the software." Plaintiffs Gibson, Gruber, Kelly, and Weindorf averred in their affidavits that they never saw this reference to the SmartDownload license agreement when they clicked on the "Download" button. They also testified during depositions that they saw no reference to license terms when they clicked to download SmartDownload, although under questioning by defendants' counsel, some plaintiffs added that they could not "remember" or be "sure" whether the screen shots of the SmartDownload page attached to their affidavits reflected precisely what they had seen on their computer screens when they downloaded SmartDownload.

In sum, plaintiffs Gibson, Gruber, Kelly, and Weindorf allege that the process of obtaining SmartDownload contrasted sharply with that of obtaining Communicator. Having selected SmartDownload, they were required neither to express unambiguous assent to that program's license agreement nor even to view the license terms or become aware of their existence before proceeding with the invited download of the free plug-in program. Moreover, once these plaintiffs had initiated the download, the existence of SmartDownload's license terms was not mentioned while the software was running or at any later point in plaintiffs' experience of the product.

Even for a user who, unlike plaintiffs, did happen to scroll down past the download button, SmartDownload's license terms would not have been immediately displayed in the manner of Communicator's clickwrapped terms. Instead, if such a user had seen the notice of Smart-Download's terms and then clicked on the underlined invitation to review and agree to the terms, a hypertext link would have taken the user to a separate webpage entitled "License & Support Agreements." The first paragraph on this page read, in pertinent part:

> The use of each Netscape software product is governed by a license agreement. You must read and agree to the license agreement terms BEFORE acquiring a product. Please click on the appropriate link below to review the current license agreement for the product of interest to you before acquisition. For products available for download, you must read and agree to the license agreement terms BEFORE you install the software. If you do not agree to the license terms, do not download, install or use the software.

Below this paragraph appeared a list of license agreements, the first of which was "License Agreement for Netscape Navigator and Netscape Communicator Product Family (Netscape Navigator, Netscape Communicator and Netscape SmartDownload)." If the user clicked on that link, he or she would be taken to yet another webpage that contained the full text of a license agreement that was identical in every respect to the Communicator license agreement except that it stated that its "terms apply to Netscape Communicator, Netscape Navigator, and

Netscape SmartDownload." The license agreement granted the user a nonexclusive license to use and reproduce the software, subject to certain terms:

> BY CLICKING THE ACCEPTANCE BUTTON OR INSTALLING OR USING NETSCAPE COMMUNICATOR, NETSCAPE NAVIGATOR, OR NETSCAPE SMARTDOWNLOAD SOFTWARE (THE "PRODUCT"), THE INDIVIDUAL OR ENTITY LICENSING THE PROD-UCT ("LICENSEE") IS CONSENTING TO BE BOUND BY AND IS BECOMING A PARTY TO THIS AGREEMENT. IF LICENSEE DOES NOT AGREE TO ALL OF THE TERMS OF THIS AGREEMENT, THE BUTTON INDICATING NON-ACCEPTANCE MUST BE SELECTED, AND LICENSEE MUST NOT INSTALL OR USE THE SOFTWARE.

Among the license terms was a provision requiring virtually all disputes relating to the agreement to be submitted to arbitration:

> Unless otherwise agreed in writing, all disputes relating to this Agreement (excepting any dispute relating to intellectual property rights) shall be subject to final and binding arbitration in Santa Clara County, California, under the auspices of JAMS/EndDispute, with the losing party paying all costs of arbitration.

Unlike the four named user plaintiffs who downloaded SmartDownload from the Netscape website, the fifth named plaintiff, Michael Fagan, claims to have downloaded the plug-in program from a "shareware" website operated by ZDNet, an entity unrelated to Nets-cape. Shareware sites are websites, maintained by companies or individuals, that contain libraries of free, publicly available software. The pages that a user would have seen while downloading SmartDownload from ZDNet differed from those that he or she would have encountered while downloading SmartDownload from the Netscape website. Notably, instead of any kind of notice of the SmartDownload license agreement, the ZDNet pages offered only a hypertext link to "more information" about SmartDownload, which, if clicked on, took the user to a Netscape webpage that, in turn, contained a link to the license agreement. Thus, a visitor to the ZDNet website could have obtained SmartDownload, as Fagan avers he did, without ever seeing a reference to that program's license terms, even if he or she had scrolled through all of ZDNet's webpages.

The sixth named plaintiff, Christopher Specht, never obtained or used SmartDownload, but instead operated a website from which visitors could download certain electronic files that permitted them to create an account with an internet service provider called WhyWeb. Specht alleges that every time a user who had previously installed SmartDownload visited his website and downloaded WhyWeb-related files, defendants intercepted this information. Defendants allege that Specht would receive a representative's commission from WhyWeb every time a user who obtained a WhyWeb file from his website subsequently subscribed to the WhyWeb service. Thus, argue defendants, because the "Netscape license agreement conferred on each user the right to download and use both Communicator and SmartDownload software," Specht received a benefit under that license agreement in that SmartDownload "assisted in obtaining the WhyWeb file and increased the likelihood of success in the download process." This benefit, defendants claim, was direct enough to require Specht to arbitrate his claims pursuant to Netscape's license terms. Specht, however, maintains that he never received any commissions based on the WhyWeb files available on his website.

III. WHETHER THE USER PLAINTIFFS HAD REASONABLE NOTICE OF AND MANIFESTED ASSENT TO THE SMARTDOWNLOAD LICENSE AGREEMENT

Whether governed by the common law or by Article 2 of the Uniform Commercial Code ("UCC"), a transaction, in order to be a contract, requires a manifestation of agreement between the parties. See Windsor Mills, Inc. v. Collins & Aikman Corp., 25 Cal. App. 3d 987, 991 (1972) ("[C]onsent to, or acceptance of, the arbitration provision [is] necessary to create an agreement to arbitrate."); see also Cal. Com. Code §2204(1) ("A contract for sale of goods may be made in any manner sufficient to show agreement, including conduct by both parties which recognizes the existence of such a contract."). Mutual manifestation of assent, whether by written or spoken word or by conduct, is the touchstone of contract. Binder v. Aetna Life Ins. Co., 75 Cal. App. 4th 832, 848 (1999); cf. *Restatement (Second) of Contracts* §19(2) (1981) ("The conduct of a party is not effective as a manifestation of his assent unless he intends to engage in the conduct and knows or has reason to know that the other party may infer from his conduct that he assents.").

Although an onlooker observing the disputed transactions in this case would have seen each of the user plaintiffs click on the SmartDownload "Download" button, see Cedars Sinai Med. Ctr. v. Mid-West Nat'l Life Ins. Co., 118 F. Supp. 2d 1002, 1008 (C.D. Cal. 2000) ("In California, a party's intent to contract is judged objectively, by the party's outward manifestation of consent."), a consumer's clicking on a download button does not communicate assent to contractual terms if the offer did not make clear to the consumer that clicking on the download button would signify assent to those terms, see *Windsor Mills*, 25 Cal. App. 3d at 992 ("[W]hen the offeree does not know that a proposal has been made to him this objective standard does not apply."). California's common law is clear that "an offeree, regardless of apparent manifestation of his consent, is not bound by inconspicuous contractual provisions of which he is unaware, contained in a document whose contractual nature is not obvious." Id.; see also Marin Storage & Trucking, Inc. v. Benco Contracting & Eng'g, Inc., 89 Cal. App. 4th 1042, 1049, (2001) (same).

Downloadable software, however, is scarcely a "tangible" good, and, in part because software may be obtained, copied, or transferred effortlessly at the stroke of a computer key, licensing of such Internet products has assumed a vast importance in recent years. Recognizing that "a body of law based on images of the sale of manufactured goods ill fits licenses and other transactions in computer information," the National Conference of Commissioners on Uniform State Laws has promulgated the Uniform Computer Information Transactions Act ("UCITA"), a code resembling UCC Article 2 in many respects but drafted to reflect emergent practices in the sale and licensing of computer information. UCITA, prefatory note (rev. ed. Aug. 23, 2001) (available at *www.ucitaonline.com/ucita.html*). UCITA—originally intended as a new Article 2B to supplement Articles 2 and 2A of the UCC but later proposed as an independent code—has been adopted by two states, Maryland and Virginia. See Md. Code Ann. Com. Law §§22-101 et seq.; Va. Code Ann. §§59.1-501.1 et seq.

We need not decide today whether UCC Article 2 applies to Internet transactions in downloadable products. The district court's analysis and the parties' arguments on appeal show that, for present purposes, there is no essential difference between UCC Article 2 and the common law of contracts. We therefore apply the common law, with exceptions as noted.

Arbitration agreements are no exception to the requirement of manifestation of assent. "This principle of knowing consent applies with particular force to provisions for arbitration."

Windsor Mills, 101 Cal. Rptr. at 351. Clarity and conspicuousness of arbitration terms are important in securing informed assent. "If a party wishes to bind in writing another to an agreement to arbitrate future disputes, such purpose should be accomplished in a way that each party to the arrangement will fully and clearly comprehend that the agreement to arbitrate exists and binds the parties thereto." Commercial Factors Corp. v. Kurtzman Bros., 280 P.2d 146, 147-48 (1955) (internal quotation marks omitted). Thus, California contract law measures assent by an objective standard that takes into account both what the offeree said, wrote, or did and the transactional context in which the offeree verbalized or acted.

A. The Reasonably Prudent Offeree of Downloadable Software

Defendants argue that plaintiffs must be held to a standard of reasonable prudence and that, because notice of the existence of SmartDownload license terms was on the next scrollable screen, plaintiffs were on "inquiry notice" of those terms. We disagree with the proposition that a reasonably prudent offeree in plaintiffs' position would necessarily have known or learned of the existence of the SmartDownload license agreement prior to acting, so that plaintiffs may be held to have assented to that agreement with constructive notice of its terms. See CAL. CIV. CODE §1589 ("A voluntary acceptance of the benefit of a transaction is equivalent to a consent to all the obligations arising from it, so far as the facts are known, or ought to be known, to the person accepting."). It is true that "[a] party cannot avoid the terms of a contract on the ground that he or she failed to read it before signing." *Marin Storage & Trucking*, 89 Cal. App. 4th at 1049. But courts are quick to add: "An exception to this general rule exists when the writing does not appear to be a contract and the terms are not called to the attention of the recipient. In such a case, no contract is formed with respect to the undisclosed term." Id.; cf. Cory v. Golden State Bank, 95 Cal. App. 3d 360, 364 (1979) ("[T]he provision in question is effectively hidden from the view of money order purchasers until after the transactions are completed. Under these circumstances, it must be concluded that the Bank's money order purchasers are not chargeable with either actual or constructive notice of the service charge provision, and therefore cannot be deemed to have consented to the provision as part of their transaction with the Bank.").

We are not persuaded that a reasonably prudent offeree in these circumstances would have known of the existence of license terms. Plaintiffs were responding to an offer that did not carry an immediately visible notice of the existence of license terms or require unambiguous manifestation of assent to those terms. Thus, plaintiffs' "apparent manifestation of . . . consent" was to terms "contained in a document whose contractual nature [was] not obvious." *Windsor Mills*, 25 Cal. App. 3d at 992.

ADOBE SYSTEMS INC. v. STARGATE SOFTWARE INC.

216 F. Supp. 2d 1051 (N.D. Cal. 2002)

WARE, District Judge.

I. INTRODUCTION

Plaintiff, Adobe Systems Inc., ("Adobe") filed this action against Defendant, Stargate Systems Inc., ("Stargate") for copyright infringement of Adobe's educational software.

II. BACKGROUND

Adobe is one of the leading software development and publishing companies in the United States. Some of its copyrighted software products include Adobe Illustrator, Adobe Pagemaker, and Adobe Acrobat. Adobe contends that it distributes its software products under license to a network of distributors and original equipment manufacturers. These distributors sign license agreements that permit them to engage in limited re-distribution to entities or individuals authorized by Adobe. Adobe claims all Adobe software products are subject to a shrink-wrap End User License Agreement ("EULA") that prohibits copying or commercial re-distribution.

Adobe also makes "Educational" versions of its software packages available for license to students and educators at a discount. Adobe Educational distributors are licensed to transfer Educational software only to resellers who have signed Off or On Campus Educational Reseller Agreements ("OCRA") with Adobe. In turn, the OCRA requires that re-distribution of Educational software be limited to students and educators. Adobe claims that the Educational versions are prominently marked "Education Version — Academic ID Required" and include the legend, "Notice to users: Use of the enclosed software is subject to the license agreement contained in the package."

Stargate is a discount software distributor wholly owned by Leonid Kelman. Neither Stargate nor Mr. Kelman are authorized distributors of Adobe products. In 1995, Mr. Kelman co-founded a software distribution company called Action Software with Alexander Belfer. Together they incorporated Stargate Software Inc. In 1997, Stargate began acquiring software from two businesses, Dallas Computer and D.C. Micro, with the majority of the software being Adobe Educational software. Adobe contends that Stargate's suppliers acquired Adobe Educational software from Adobe Educational distributor Douglas Stewart Co. pursuant to valid OCRAs. However, Stargate alleges that all of the Adobe software products that Stargate sold were purchased through either D.C. Micro, Inc. or Dallas Computers, Inc.

Between March 1998 and April 1999, Stargate, purchased between 1795-2189 packages of "Educational" software produced by Adobe. Stargate distributed this Educational software at below-market prices to retail customers and unauthorized resellers through magazine advertisements, trade shows, action websites and its website *"www.stargatesoftware .com."* Adobe learned of this practice, made a trap purchase of the Educational software in April 1999, and filed suit in this Court against Stargate and Mr. Kelman soon thereafter.

Adobe alleges that Stargate infringed Adobe's copyrights by obtaining and selling Educational versions of Adobe software without Adobe's authorization. Stargate contends that it was the rightful owner of the Adobe software products and therefore did not infringe Adobe's copyright by reselling those products, pursuant to the "first sale" doctrine, codified at 17 U.S.C. §109.

IV. DISCUSSION

A. Copyright Infringement Claim

Section 106 of the Copyright Act (the "Act") outlines the exclusive rights enjoyed by owners of a copyright including the exclusive right "to distribute copies or phonorecords of the copyrighted work to the public by sale or other transfer of ownership, or by rental, lease, or lending." 17 U.S.C. §106(3). Under this provision, the copyright owner would have the "right to control the first public distribution of an authorized copy or phonorecord of his work, whether by sale, gift, loan, or some rental or lease arrangement." 17 U.S.C. §106(3). Section 109(a) of the Act, makes clear that "the copyright owner's rights under §106(3) cease with respect to a particular copy or phonorecord once he has parted with ownership of it." 17 U.S.C. §109(a) (emphasis added). Also pursuant to §109(a), "the owner of a particular copy or phonorecord lawfully made under this title, or any person authorized by such owner, is entitled without the authority of the copyright owner, to sell or otherwise dispose of the possession of that copy or phonorecord." 17 U.S.C. §109(a) (emphasis added). One significant effect of §109(a) is to limit the exclusive right to distribute copies to their first voluntary disposition, and thus negate copyright owner control over further or "downstream" transfer to a third party. Quality King Distrib. v. L'anza Research Int'l, Inc., 523 U.S. 135, 118 (1998). Thus, under the first sale doctrine, "a sale of a lawfully made copy terminates a copyright holder's authority to interfere with subsequent sales or distribution of that particular copy." Parfums Givenchy, Inc. v. Drug Emporium, Inc., 38 F.3d 477, 480 (9th Cir. 1994). "[T]he copyright owner is entitled to realize no more and no less than full value of each copy or phonorecord upon its disposition." Parfums Givenchy, Inc. v. C & C Beauty Sales, Inc., 832 F. Supp. 1378 (C.D. Cal. 1993).

B. Sale or License

The issue before the Court is whether Adobe, through its OCRA and EULA, transferred ownership of each particular copy of its software to its distributors D.C. Micro and Dallas Computers. Having transferred such ownership would bar Adobe from claiming copyright infringement by Stargate under the first sale doctrine. An issuance via license, however, would not. Rather, the establishment of a license by Adobe would protect Adobe under the first sale doctrine.

Implicably, Stargate concedes that Adobe retains title to the objective coded software of the intellectual property contained on the CD-ROM. Nevertheless, Stargate claims, however, that whenever there is a sale, Adobe has parted with title to that particular copy of its copyrighted intellectual property, thereby divesting itself of the exclusive right to vend that particular copy. In essence, Stargate contends that each time Adobe is paid by a distributor or reseller for a package of software, it has "received its rewards" for that package and has parted with title to that particular copy. Stargate argues that after examining the "economic realities" of the initial transaction between Adobe and its distributors, Adobe's distribution of its educational software constitutes a sale, rather than a license of each particular copy.

Stargate further alleges that nowhere in either the OCRA or in the EULA, does Adobe purport in any manner to retain title to that particular copy of its software, that is, the package including a CD-ROM on which the program is stored, and any manuals or other materials included within it. Therefore, Stargate argues that further transfers of that package do not infringe Adobe's copyright.

Adobe contends, on the other hand, that "a common method of distribution for software products is through licensing agreements, which permit the copyright holder to place restrictions upon the distribution of its products." Adobe Systems, Inc. v. One Stop Micro, 84

F. Supp. 2d 1086, 1092 (N.D. Cal. 2000). Adobe alleges that Mr. Kelman, Stargate's sole owner, was aware that Adobe's software is distributed pursuant to licensing agreements. Kelman Deposition at 223:1-13. Specifically, Kelman testified that, "I've seen that there was a licensing agreement (in the software box)." Kelman Deposition at 233:9-13. Furthermore it was Adobe's intent to license the software rather than to make an outright sale. According to Adobe, "Adobe does not sell its software. Instead, Adobe distributes its software products under license to a network of distributors . . ." Navarro Declaration ¶¶3-4, Exhibits A and B.

Adobe also argues that under the Act, the first sale doctrine does not turn on whether the copyright owner "received its reward" for a particular piece of software, but whether the software has been sold. In this case, Adobe has elected to distribute its products via license rather than sale. Adobe alleges that their OCRA and EULA are clearly licenses. According to Adobe, multiple restrictions on title are placed on each distributor through the express terms of its OCRA. Additionally, Adobe asserts that it was their intention to affect a license agreement, through their OCRAs, rather than a sale.

1. The Term "Software"

In this case, it is important to draw a distinction between the objective code "software" and the medium and packaging through which it is sold on the market. Section 202 of the Act recognizes a distinction between tangible property rights in copies of the work and intangible property rights in the creation itself. "Ownership of a copyright, or of any of the exclusive rights under a copyright, is distinct from ownership of any material object in which the work is embodied." 17 U.S.C. §202. In this case, both Parties are in agreement that Adobe is the rightful owner of the intangible portion of the software, i.e. the intellectual property.

The dispute arises, however, as to who is the rightful owner of the package, or physical manifestation of this intellectual property. The CD-ROM itself is worth not much more than a nominal amount, and it is the code that justifies the purchase price of the product. That being the case, the economic reality of this transaction is that a consumer is ultimately paying for the software contained on the CD-ROM, rather than the CD-ROM itself. Despite this fact, this case is still based on the ownership of each particular copy of software distributed by Adobe. The determination of ownership in turn is based primarily on an examination of the OCRA, the agreement between Adobe and its distributors.

2. The OCRA

The Court looks to the language, content, and intent of the OCRA, in determining whether its terms affect a sale or license of the software. In the OCRA, Adobe contends that "Adobe is the owner and developer of Adobe Educational Software Products." See Bloch Declaration ¶7, Exhibit F: ("OCRA"), preamble. According to the OCRA, "Educational Software Products," consist of "the respective software program in object code ('Software'), supporting documentation ('Documentation'), and all other related material, if any, supplied to Reseller in a commercial package." OCRA ¶1(d). Adobe characterizes each transaction it concluded throughout the entire stream of commerce relevant to this action as a license. Accordingly,

Adobe argues that it retains ownership of its software, the accompanying documentation, and all other related materials pursuant to the OCRA.

a. Terminology

[T]he Court in this case also concludes that the language in Adobe's OCRA is evidence of a license, rather than a sale. Although the OCRA contains language such as "repurchase" and "owned," additional language indicates that the OCRA only confers a license. For instance, Paragraph 9 of the OCRA is titled, "Ownership of Proprietary Rights and Nondisclosure" (Referring to Adobe) OCRA ¶9. Under that same paragraph, the OCRA furthers states, "Reseller acknowledges that the structure and organization of the Software is proprietary to Adobe and that Adobe retains exclusive ownership of the Software and Trademarks." OCRA, ¶9 (emphasis added). The OCRA further states, "Reseller . . . to protect Adobe's proprietary rights in the Educational Software Products. Except as provided herein, reseller is not granted any rights to patents, copyrights, trade secrets, trade names, trademarks (whether registered or unregistered), or any other rights, franchises, or licenses with respect to the Software or Educational Software Products." OCRA, ¶9. As explained by the Court in One Stop, "evidence of trade usage demonstrates that it is commonplace for sales terminology to be used in connection with software licensing agreements." *One Stop Micro*, 84 F. Supp. 2d at 1091. This Court concurs.

b. Content

After examining the contents of the OCRA, as well as its express terms, it is clear that the agreement outlines numerous restrictions on title that are imposed upon the reseller regarding the distribution of its software. For example in the OCRA, ¶3, Adobe premises their restrictions with the following statement, "Reseller shall have the right to purchase Educational Software Products from Adobe or authorized Adobe distributors who carry the Educational Software Products and to distribute the Educational Software Products so long as it remains in compliance with all of the following conditions." OCRA, ¶3.

The Court in *One Stop* stated, "These numerous restrictions imposed by Adobe indicate a license rather than a sale because they undeniably interfere with the reseller's ability to further distribute the software." *One Stop Micro*, 84 F. Supp. 2d at 1091. The Court in *One Stop* found the following restriction set forth in Adobe's OCRA in ¶3(a)(ii) particularly compelling: "Reseller distributes pursuant to the terms and conditions of the then current applicable Software Product [EULA]." OCRA ¶3(a)(ii).

As explained by the court in *One Stop*, supra, the EULA is a shrink-wrap license agreement which accompanies every Adobe software product. The EULA states that "Adobe grants to you a nonexclusive license to use the Software and Documentation," provided that the user agrees to certain restrictions. EULA, preamble. The Court in *One Stop* concluded that under the EULA, the end user was only granted a license to use the software. Adobe's specific incorporation of the EULA into the OCRA indicates that the reseller obtains a license, rather than actual ownership of the product in question. The Court in *One Stop* stated, "It would be incongruous to conclude that educational resellers are owners of the Adobe educational versions, while the end users who the resellers distribute to are granted a mere license." *One Stop Micro*, 84 F. Supp. 2d at 1091.

Similar to the OCRA at issue in *One Stop*, the OCRA in this case contains multiple restrictions that limit the reseller's ability to distribute Adobe's software. Specifically, pursuant to the terms of the OCRA, the Reseller promises to:

(1) Not distribute outside the country in which its principal place of business is located. OCRA, ¶3(a)(i);

(2) Distribute solely to Educational End Users at Reseller's Outlet or through Reseller's direct sales force. OCRA, ¶3(a)(iii);

(3) Require each Educational End User to provide identification as follows: (1) in the case of a purchase by an individual, a valid photo ID or such other identification as is used by the educational institution for faculty, staff, or students, or (2) in the case of a purchase by an entity, an official purchase order indicating the name of the entity. OCRA, ¶3(a)(iv);

(4) Distribute the Educational Software Products solely in the form obtained from Adobe. OCRA, ¶3(a)(v);

(5) Provide adequate service and support in connection with the distribution of the Educational Software Products. OCRA, ¶3(a)(vi);

(6) Agree not to distribute the Educational Software Products other than pursuant to the provisions of the EULA and, by way of illustration but not of limitation, shall not be entitled to grant any form of site license for Education Software Products. Reseller agrees not to distribute the Educational Software Products without prior written approval from Adobe (i) by mail order, (ii) by rental or lease, (iii) in bulk for redistribution, (iv) with knowledge or reason to know that the Educational Software Products will be transported outside the country in which a Software Product is provided to an Educational End User, or (v) to other Educational Resellers or other dealers, resellers, or redistributions. OCRA, ¶3(b); and

(7) Promises that the reseller's rights in Educational Software Products used for demonstration purposes shall be subject to the terms and conditions of the respective EULA, which are hereby incorporated by reference. OCRA, ¶3(c).

In light of the fact that the OCRA in this case is substantially similar to the OCRA in *One Stop*, this Court agrees that the OCRA in the present case contains numerous restrictions on title that are imposed on the reseller, limiting the reseller's ability to re-distribute Adobe software, and thereby conferring a license between Adobe and the reseller. It is clear to the Court that the terms of the OCRA substantially and undeniably interfere with a reseller's ability to distribute and/or convey title to the products in question. 17 U.S.C. §106.

c. Softman v. Adobe

Stargate, however, cites Softman Products Company v. Adobe Systems Inc., 171 F. Supp. 2d 1075 (C.D. Cal. 2001) for the proposition that the OCRA in this case constitutes a sale, rather than a license. In *Softman*, a case arising out of the United States District Court for the Central District of California, Softman, a computer software distributor brought an action against Adobe. Adobe counterclaimed, alleging copyright infringement. Adobe claimed that Softman distributed unauthorized copies of Adobe software, including Adobe's Educational software and illegally unbundled Adobe "Collections." The court stated, "If a transaction involves a single payment giving the buyer an unlimited period in which it has a right to possession, the transaction is a sale." Id. at 1086. The *Softman* court held the nature of the transaction between Adobe and its distributor was a sale and Softman was thus protected by the first sale doctrine.

This Court respectfully declines to adopt the *Softman* analysis. Although the court in *Softman*, stated, "The Court understands fully why licensing has many advantages for software publishers," it concluded that the transaction between the parties constituted a sale. Id. at 1087. In this case, however, the Court reaches a different conclusion.

The facts involved in *Softman* are distinguishable from this case. The court in *Softman* dealt with the question of whether the purchaser of a retail collection of Adobe software can re-distribute the collection's constituent parts. *Softman*, 171 F. Supp. 2d at 1079-80. In *Softman*, the court noted that the terms of the Adobe EULA prohibited licensees from transferring or assigning any individual Adobe product that was originally distributed as part of a Collection, unless it was transferred with all the software contained in that original Collection. *Softman Products*, 171 F. Supp. 2d at 1083. In *Softman*, it was uncontested by the Parties that the constituent parts were re-distributed in that prohibited manner. In contrast, the present case involves the re-distribution of Adobe software, with no substantial evidence of adulteration or the illegal unbundling of software.

Furthermore, this Court notes that, within the context of this case, when a "single payment" is made for a particular copy of software, the payment is being made for the value of the objective code that is burned on the CD-ROM. Absent this "valuable" information and intellectual property, a CD-ROM would be almost worthless. The true economic value of the product is derived from the intellectual property embodied within it.

This Court notes that software is unique from other forms of copyrighted information. Technology and software, in particular, has radically transformed the way information is created and exchanged. Software fundamentally differs from more traditional forms of medium, such as print or phonographic materials, in that software can be both, more readily and easily copied on a mass scale in an extraordinarily short amount of time and relatively inexpensively. One of the primary advantages of software, its ability to record, concentrate and convey information with unprecedented ease and speed, makes it extraordinarily vulnerable to illegal copying and piracy. This Court finds that it is important to acknowledge these special characteristics of the software industry and provide enhanced copyright protection for its inventors and developers.

Lastly, as a matter of general principle, this Court finds that no colorable reason exists in this case as to why Adobe and its distributors should be barred from characterizing the transaction that has been forged between them as a license. In light of the restrictions on title that have been incorporated into the OCRA, as well as the Parties' free and willing consent to enter into and execute its terms, the Parties should be free to negotiate and/or set a price for the product being exchanged, as well as set the terms by which the product is exchanged. Gray v. American Exp. Co., 743 F.2d 10 (D.C. Cir. 1984). Fundamental to any free society is the liberty of its members to formulate contracts in accordance with the terms that they agree and consent to mutually execute. "The right to contract freely with the expectation that the contract shall endure according to its terms is as fundamental to the society as the right to write and to speak without restraint." Blount v. Smith, 231 N.E.2d 301 (1967). While exceptions are made in the case of unfair or exploitive contracts, or where an inequitable end results as a result of the agreement, commercial parties are generally free to contract as they desire. Mellon Bank, N.A. v. Aetna Business Credit, Inc., 619 F.2d 1001 (3d Cir. 1980).

3. The EULA

Furthermore, the Court finds that Adobe's EULA contains significant restrictions on title that provides additional evidence that the relevant transaction between Adobe and its distributors is a license, rather than a sale. For example, the EULA states the following:

(1) "THIS IS A CONTRACT. BY OPENING THIS PACKAGE YOU ACCEPT ALL THE TERMS AND CONDITIONS OF THIS AGREEMENT." EULA, preamble.
(2) "This package contains software ('Software') and related explanatory written materials ('Documentation')." EULA, preamble.
(3) "Adobe grants to you a nonexclusive license to use the Software and Documentation, provided that you agree to the following." EULA, preamble.
(4) "The Software is owned by Adobe and its suppliers." EULA, ¶(2).

This Court in *One Stop* stated that, ". . . under the EULA the end user is only granted a license to use the software. Adobe's specific incorporation of the EULA indicates that the reseller obtains a license. It would be incongruous to conclude that educational resellers are owners of the Adobe educational versions, while the end users who the resellers distribute to are granted a mere license." *One Stop Micro*, 84 F. Supp. 2d at 1091.

Due to the substantially similar nature and terms of the EULA in both cases, this Court adopts the analysis used in *One Stop*. Like the EULA in *One Stop*, the EULA in this case maintains numerous restrictions on title with respect to the end user. Furthermore, it clearly states at the top of the agreement that it is a license agreement. Though, the EULA is packaged inside the box, the end user is given the opportunity to return the package if he or she is not in agreement with the terms of the contract. It is clear that Adobe, through the express terms of its EULA, intended and attempted openly and in good faith to maintain proprietary ownership over its product, as well as preserve its rights to title.

The Court, therefore, concludes that based on the clear and unambiguous language of the relevant contracts, coupled with the multiple restrictions on title placed on the reseller in the above agreements, the transaction should be characterized as a license, rather than a sale.

UNITED STATES v. MICROSOFT CORPORATION
253 F.3d 34 (D.C. Cir. 2001)

PER CURIAM. . . .

II. MONOPOLIZATION

Section 2 of the Sherman Act makes it unlawful for a firm to "monopolize." 15 U.S.C. §2. The offense of monopolization has two elements: "(1) the possession of monopoly power in the relevant market and (2) the willful acquisition or maintenance of that power as distinguished from growth or development as a consequence of a superior product, business acumen, or historic accident." United States v. Grinnell Corp., 384 U.S. 563, 570-71 (1966). . . .

We turn to the question whether [Microsoft] maintained this power through anticompetitive means.

B. Anticompetitive Conduct

As discussed above, having a monopoly does not by itself violate §2. A firm violates §2 only when it acquires or maintains, or attempts to acquire or maintain, a monopoly by engaging in exclusionary conduct "as distinguished from growth or development as a consequence of a superior product, business acumen, or historic accident." Grinnell, 384 U.S. at 571, see also United States v. Aluminum Co. of Am., 148 F.2d 416, 430 (2d Cir. 1945) (Hand, J.) ("The successful competitor, having been urged to compete, must not be turned upon when he wins.").

Whether any particular act of a monopolist is exclusionary, rather than merely a form of vigorous competition, can be difficult to discern: the means of illicit exclusion, like the means of legitimate competition, are myriad. The challenge for an antitrust court lies in stating a general rule for distinguishing between exclusionary acts, which reduce social welfare, and competitive acts, which increase it.

From a century of case law on monopolization under §2, however, several principles do emerge. First, to be condemned as exclusionary, a monopolist's act must have an "anticompetitive effect." That is, it must harm the competitive process and thereby harm consumers. In contrast, harm to one or more competitors will not suffice. "The [Sherman Act] directs itself not against conduct which is competitive, even severely so, but against conduct which unfairly tends to destroy competition itself." Spectrum Sports, Inc. v. McQuillan, 506 U.S. 447, 458 (1993); see also Brooke Group Ltd. v. Brown & Williamson Tobacco Corp., 509 U.S. 209, 225 (1993) ("Even an act of pure malice by one business competitor against another does not, without more, state a claim under the federal antitrust laws. . . .").

Second, the plaintiff, on whom the burden of proof of course rests, see, e.g., Monsanto Co. v. Spray-Rite Serv. Corp., 465 U.S. 752, 763 (1984), must demonstrate that the monopolist's conduct indeed has the requisite anticompetitive effect. See generally Brooke Group, 509 U.S. at 225-26. In a case brought by a private plaintiff, the plaintiff must show that its injury is "of 'the type that the statute was intended to forestall,'" Brunswick Corp. v. Pueblo Bowl-O-Mat, Inc., 429 U.S. 477, 487-88, 97 S. Ct. 690 (1977) (quoting Wyandotte Transp. v. United States, 389 U.S. 191, 202 (1967)); no less in a case brought by the Government, it must demonstrate that the monopolist's conduct harmed competition, not just a competitor.

Third, if a plaintiff successfully establishes a prima facie case under §2 by demonstrating anticompetitive effect, then the monopolist may proffer a "procompetitive justification" for its conduct. See Eastman Kodak, 504 U.S. at 483. If the monopolist asserts a procompetitive justification—a nonpretextual claim that its conduct is indeed a form of competition on the merits because it involves, for example, greater efficiency or enhanced consumer appeal—then the burden shifts back to the plaintiff to rebut that claim. Cf. Capital Imaging Assocs., P.C. v. Mohawk Valley Med. Assocs., Inc., 996 F.2d 537, 543 (2d Cir. 1993).

Fourth, if the monopolist's procompetitive justification stands unrebutted, then the plaintiff must demonstrate that the anticompetitive harm of the conduct outweighs the procompetitive benefit. In cases arising under §1 of the Sherman Act, the courts routinely apply a similar balancing approach under the rubric of the "rule of reason." The source of the rule of reason is Standard Oil Co. v. United States, 221 U.S. 1 (1911), in which the Supreme Court used that term to describe the proper inquiry under both sections of the Act. See *id.* at 61-62, 31 S. Ct. 502 ("[W]hen the second section [of the Sherman Act] is thus harmonized with . . . the first, it becomes obvious that the criteria to be resorted to in any given case for the purpose of ascertaining whether violations of the section have been committed, is the rule of reason guided by the established law. . . ."). As the Fifth Circuit more recently explained, "[i]t is clear . . . that the analysis under section 2 is similar to that under section 1 regardless whether the rule of reason label is applied. . . ." Mid-Texas Communications Sys., Inc. v. AT & T, 615 F.2d 1372, 1389 n.13 (5th Cir. 1980) (citing Byars v. Bluff City News Co., 609 F.2d 843, 860 (6th Cir. 1979)).

Finally, in considering whether the monopolist's conduct on balance harms competition and is therefore condemned as exclusionary for purposes of §2, our focus is upon the effect of that conduct, not upon the intent behind it. Evidence of the intent behind the conduct of a monopolist is relevant only to the extent it helps us understand the likely effect of the monopolist's conduct. See, e.g., Chicago Bd. of Trade v. United States, 246 U.S. 231, 238 (1918) ("knowledge of intent may help the court to interpret facts and to predict consequences"); Aspen Skiing Co. v. Aspen Highlands Skiing Corp., 472 U.S. 585, 603 (1985).

a. Anticompetitive Effect of the License Restrictions

The restrictions Microsoft places upon Original Equipment Manufacturers are of particular importance in determining browser usage share because having an OEM pre-install a browser on a computer is one of the two most cost-effective methods by far of distributing browsing software. (The other is bundling the browser with internet access software distributed by an IAP.) Findings of Fact ¶145. The District Court found that the restrictions Microsoft imposed in licensing Windows to OEMs prevented many OEMs from distributing browsers other than IE. Conclusions of Law, at 39-40. In particular, the District Court condemned the license provisions prohibiting the OEMs from: (1) removing any desktop icons, folders, or "Start" menu entries; (2) altering the initial boot sequence; and (3) otherwise altering the appearance of the Windows desktop. Findings of Fact ¶213.

The District Court concluded that the first license restriction — the prohibition upon the removal of desktop icons, folders, and Start menu entries — thwarts the distribution of a rival browser by preventing OEMs from removing visible means of user access to IE. Id. ¶203. The OEMs cannot practically install a second browser in addition to IE, the court found, in part because "[p]re-installing more than one product in a given category . . . can significantly increase an OEM's support costs, for the redundancy can lead to confusion among novice users." Id. ¶159; see also id. ¶217. That is, a certain number of novice computer users, seeing two browser icons, will wonder which to use when and will call the OEM's support line. Support calls are extremely expensive and, in the highly competitive original equipment market, firms have a strong incentive to minimize costs. Id. ¶210.

Microsoft denies the "consumer confusion" story; it observes that some OEMs do install multiple browsers and that executives from two OEMs that do so denied any knowledge of consumers being confused by multiple icons.

Other testimony, however, supports the District Court's finding that fear of such confusion deters many OEMs from pre-installing multiple browsers.

As noted above, the OEM channel is one of the two primary channels for distribution of browsers. By preventing OEMs from removing visible means of user access to IE, the license restriction prevents many OEMs from pre-installing a rival browser and, therefore, protects Microsoft's monopoly from the competition that middleware might otherwise present. Therefore, we conclude that the license restriction at issue is anticompetitive. We defer for the moment the question whether that anticompetitive effect is outweighed by Microsoft's proffered justifications.

The second license provision at issue prohibits OEMs from modifying the initial boot sequence — the process that occurs the first time a consumer turns on the computer. Prior to the imposition of that restriction, "among the programs that many OEMs inserted into the boot sequence were Internet sign-up procedures that encouraged users to choose from a list of IAPs assembled by the OEM." Findings of Fact ¶210. Microsoft's prohibition on any alteration of the boot sequence thus prevents OEMs from using that process to promote the services of IAPs, many of which — at least at the time Microsoft imposed the restriction — used Navigator rather than IE in their internet access software. See id. ¶212; GX 295, reprinted in 12 J.A. at 14533 (Upon learning of OEM practices including boot sequence modification, Microsoft's Chairman, Bill Gates, wrote: "Apparently a lot of OEMs are bundling non-Microsoft browsers and coming up with offerings together with [IAPs] that get displayed on their machines in a FAR more prominent way than MSN or our Internet browser."). Microsoft does not deny that the prohibition on modifying the boot sequence has the effect of decreasing competition against IE by preventing OEMs from promoting rivals' browsers. Because this prohibition has a substantial effect in protecting Microsoft's market power, and does so through a means other than competition on the merits, it is anticompetitive. Again the question whether the provision is nonetheless justified awaits later treatment.

Finally, Microsoft imposes several additional provisions that, like the prohibition on removal of icons, prevent OEMs from making various alterations to the desktop: Microsoft prohibits OEMs from causing any user interface other than the Windows desktop to launch automatically, from adding icons or folders different in size or shape from those supplied by Microsoft, and from using the "Active Desktop" feature to promote third-party brands. These restrictions impose significant costs upon the OEMs; prior to Microsoft's prohibiting the practice, many OEMs would change the appearance of the desktop in ways they found beneficial. See, e.g., Findings of Fact ¶214; GX 309, reprinted in 22 J.A. at 14551 (March 1997 letter from Hewlett-Packard to Microsoft: "We are responsible for the cost of technical support of our customers, including the 33% of calls we get related to the lack of quality or confusion generated by your product. . . . We must have more ability to decide how our system is presented to our end users. If we had a choice of another supplier, based on your actions in this area, I assure you [that you] would not be our supplier of choice.").

The dissatisfaction of the OEM customers does not, of course, mean the restrictions are anticompetitive. The anticompetitive effect of the license restrictions is, as Microsoft itself recognizes, that OEMs are not able to promote rival browsers, which keeps developers focused upon the APIs in Windows. Findings of Fact ¶212 (quoting Microsoft's Gates as writing, "[w]inning Internet browser share is a very very important goal for us," and emphasizing the need to prevent OEMs from promoting both rival browsers and IAPs that might use rivals' browsers); see also 01/13/99 Tr. at 305-06 (excerpts from deposition of James Von Holle of Gateway) (prior to restriction Gateway had pre-installed non-IE internet registration icon that was larger than other desktop icons). This kind of promotion is not a zero-sum game; but for the restrictions in their licenses to use Windows, OEMs could promote multiple IAPs and browsers. By preventing the OEMs from doing so, this type of license restriction, like the first two restrictions, is anticompetitive: Microsoft reduced rival browsers' usage share not by improving its own product but, rather, by preventing OEMs from taking actions that could increase rivals' share of usage.

b. Microsoft's Justifications for the License Restrictions

Microsoft argues that the license restrictions are legally justified because, in imposing them, Microsoft is simply "exercising its rights as the holder of valid copyrights." Appellant's Opening Br. Microsoft also argues that the licenses "do not unduly restrict the opportunities of Netscape to distribute Navigator in any event." Id.

Microsoft's primary copyright argument borders upon the frivolous. The company claims an absolute and unfettered right to use its intellectual property as it wishes: "[I]f intellectual property rights have been lawfully acquired," it says, then "their subsequent exercise cannot give rise to antitrust liability." Appellant's Opening Br. at 105. That is no more correct than the proposition that use of one's personal property, such as a baseball bat, cannot give rise to tort liability. As the Federal Circuit succinctly stated: "Intellectual property rights do not confer a privilege to violate the antitrust laws." In re Indep. Serv. Orgs. Antitrust Litig., 203 F.3d 1322, 1325 (Fed. Cir. 2000).

Although Microsoft never overtly retreats from its bold and incorrect position on the law, it also makes two arguments to the effect that it is not exercising its copyright in an unreasonable manner, despite the anticompetitive consequences of the license restrictions discussed above. In the first variation upon its unqualified copyright defense, Microsoft cites two cases indicating that a copyright holder may limit a licensee's ability to engage in significant and deleterious alterations of a copyrighted work. See Gilliam v. ABC, 538 F.2d 14, 21 (2d Cir. 1976); WGN Cont'l Broad. Co. v. United Video, Inc., 693 F.2d 622, 625 (7th Cir. 1982). The relevance of those two cases for the present one is limited, however, both because those cases involved substantial alterations of a copyrighted work, see Gilliam, 538 F.2d at 18, and because in neither case was there any claim that the copyright holder was, in asserting its rights, violating the antitrust laws, see WGN Cont'l Broad., 693 F.2d at 626; see also Cmty. for Creative Non-Violence v. Reid, 846 F.2d 1485, 1498 (D.C. Cir. 1988) (noting, again in a context free of any antitrust concern, that "an author [] may have rights against" a licensee that "excessively mutilated or altered" the copyrighted work).

The only license restriction Microsoft seriously defends as necessary to prevent a "substantial alteration" of its copyrighted work is the prohibition on OEMs automatically launching a substitute user interface upon completion of the boot process. See Findings of Fact ¶211 ("[A] few large OEMs developed programs that ran automatically at the conclusion of a new PC system's first boot sequence. These programs replaced the Windows desktop either with a user interface designed by the OEM or with Navigator's user interface."). We agree that a shell that automatically prevents the Windows desktop from ever being seen by the user is a drastic alteration of Microsoft's copyrighted work, and outweighs the marginal anticompetitive effect of prohibiting the OEMs from substituting a different interface automatically upon completion of the initial boot process. We therefore hold that this particular restriction is not an exclusionary practice that violates §2 of the Sherman Act.

In a second variation upon its copyright defense, Microsoft argues that the license restrictions merely prevent OEMs from taking actions that would reduce substantially the value of Microsoft's copyrighted work: that is, Microsoft claims each license restriction in question is necessary to prevent OEMs from so altering Windows as to undermine "the principal value of Windows as a stable and consistent platform that supports a broad range of applications and that is familiar to users." Appellant's Opening Br. at 102. Microsoft, however, never substantiates this claim, and, because an OEM's altering the appearance of the desktop or promoting programs in the boot sequence does not affect the code already in the product, the practice does not self-evidently affect either the "stability" or the "consistency" of the platform. See Conclusions of Law, at 41; Findings of Fact ¶227. Microsoft cites only one item of evidence in support of its claim that the OEMs' alterations were decreasing the value of Windows. Defendant's Trial Exhibit ("DX") 2395 at MSV0009378A, reprinted in 19 J.A. at 12575. That document, prepared by Microsoft itself, states: "there are quality issues created by OEMs who are too liberal with the pre-install process," referring to the OEMs' installation of Windows and additional software on their PCs, which the document says may result in "user concerns and confusion." To the extent the OEMs' modifications cause consumer confusion, of course, the OEMs bear the additional support costs. See Findings of Fact ¶159. Therefore, we conclude Microsoft has not shown that the OEMs' liberality reduces the value of Windows except in the sense that their promotion of rival browsers undermines Microsoft's monopoly—and that is not a permissible justification for the license restrictions.

Apart from copyright, Microsoft raises one other defense of the OEM license agreements: It argues that, despite the restrictions in the OEM license, Netscape is not completely blocked from distributing its product. That claim is insufficient to shield Microsoft from liability for those restrictions because, although Microsoft did not bar its rivals from all means of distribution, it did bar them from the cost-efficient ones.

In sum, we hold that with the exception of the one restriction prohibiting automatically launched alternative interfaces, all the OEM license restrictions at issue represent uses of Microsoft's market power to protect its monopoly, unredeemed by any legitimate justification. The restrictions therefore violate §2 of the Sherman Act.

LASERCOMB AMERICA, INC. v. REYNOLDS

991 F.2d 970 (4th Cir. 1990)

SPROUSE, Circuit Judge.

FACTS AND PROCEEDINGS BELOW

Appellants and defendants below are Larry Holliday, president and sole shareholder of Holiday Steel Rule Die Corporation (Holiday Steel), and Job Reynolds, a computer programmer for that company. Appellee is Lasercomb America, Inc. (Lasercomb), the plaintiff below. Holiday Steel and Lasercomb were competitors in the manufacture of steel rule dies that are used to cut and score paper and cardboard for folding into boxes and cartons. Lasercomb developed a software program, Interact, which is the object of the dispute between the parties. Using this program, a designer creates a template of a cardboard cutout on a computer screen and the software directs the mechanized creation of the conforming steel rule die.

In 1983, before Lasercomb was ready to market its Interact program generally, it licensed four prerelease copies to Holiday Steel which paid $35,000 for the first copy, $17,500 each for the next two copies, and $2,000 for the fourth copy. Lasercomb informed Holiday Steel that it would charge $2,000 for each additional copy Holiday Steel cared to purchase. Apparently ambitious to create for itself an even better deal, Holiday Steel circumvented the protective devices Lasercomb had provided with the software and made three unauthorized copies of Interact which it used on its computer systems. Perhaps buoyed by its success in copying, Holiday Steel then created a software program called "PDS-1000," which was almost entirely a direct copy of Interact, and marketed it as its own CAD/CAM die-making software. These infringing activities were accomplished by Job Reynolds at the direction of Larry Holliday.

There is no question that defendants engaged in unauthorized copying, and the purposefulness of their unlawful action is manifest from their deceptive practices. For example, Lasercomb had asked Holiday Steel to use devices called "chronoguards" to prevent unauthorized access to Interact. Although defendants had deduced how to circumvent the chronoguards and had removed them from their computers, they represented to Lasercomb that the chronoguards were in use. Another example of subterfuge is Reynolds' attempt to modify the PDS-1000 program output so it would present a different appearance than the output from Interact.

Holliday and Reynolds raise several issues on appeal. They do not dispute that they copied Interact, but they contend that Lasercomb is barred from recovery for infringement by its concomitant culpability. They assert that, assuming Lasercomb had a perfected copyright, it impermissibly abused it. This assertion of the "misuse of copyright" defense is based on language in Lasercomb's standard licensing agreement, restricting licensees from creating any of their own CAD/CAM die-making software.

II.

Misuse of Copyright Defense

A successful defense of misuse of copyright bars a culpable plaintiff from prevailing on an action for infringement of the misused copyright. Here, appellants claim Lasercomb has misused its copyright by including in its standard licensing agreement clauses which prevent the licensee from participating in any manner in the creation of computer-assisted die-making software. The offending paragraphs read:

> D. Licensee agrees during the term of this Agreement that it will not permit or suffer its directors, officers and employees, directly or indirectly, to write, develop, produce or sell computer assisted die making software.
> E. Licensee agrees during the term of this Agreement and for one (1) year after the termination of this Agreement, that it will not write, develop, produce or sell or assist others in the writing, developing, producing or selling computer assisted die making

software, directly or indirectly without Lasercomb's prior written consent. Any such activity undertaken without Lasercomb's written consent shall nullify any warranties or agreements of Lasercomb set forth herein.

The "term of this Agreement" referred to in these clauses is ninety-nine years.

Defendants were not themselves bound by the standard licensing agreement. Lasercomb had sent the agreement to Holiday Steel with a request that it be signed and returned. Larry Holliday, however, decided not to sign the document, and Lasercomb apparently overlooked the fact that the document had not been returned. Although defendants were not party to the restrictions of which they complain, they proved at trial that at least one Interact licensee had entered into the standard agreement, including the anticompetitive language.

A. Does a "Misuse of Copyright" Defense Exist?

The misuse of a patent is a potential defense to suit for its infringement, and both the existence and parameters of that body of law are well established. Although there is little case law on the subject, courts from time to time have intimated that the similarity of rationales underlying the law of patents and the law of copyrights argues for a defense to an infringement of copyright based on misuse of the copyright. E.g., United States v. Loew's, Inc., 371 U.S. 38, 44-51 (1962); United States v. Paramount Pictures, Inc., 334 U.S. 131, 157-59 (1948); Mitchell Bros. Film Group v. Cinema Adult Theater, 604 F.2d 852, 865 & n.27 (5th Cir. 1979), cert. denied, 445 U.S. 917 (1980). The origins of patent and copyright law in England, the treatment of these two aspects of intellectual property by the framers of our Constitution, and the later statutory and judicial development of patent and copyright law in this country per-suade us that parallel public policies underlie the protection of both types of intellectual property rights. We think these parallel policies call for application of the misuse defense to copyright as well as patent law. . . .

3. The "Misuse of Copyright" Defense

Although the patent misuse defense has been generally recognized since *Morton Salt*, it has been much less certain whether an analogous copyright misuse defense exists. This uncertainty persists because no United States Supreme Court decision has firmly established a copyright misuse defense in a manner analogous to the establishment of the patent misuse defense by Morton Salt. The few courts considering the issue have split on whether the defense should be recognized, and we have discovered only one case which has actually applied copyright misuse to bar an action for infringement. M. Witmark & Sons v. Jensen, 80 F. Supp. 843 (D. Minn. 1948), appeal dismissed, 177 F.2d 515 (8th Cir. 1949).

We are of the view, however, that since copyright and patent law serve parallel public interests, a "misuse" defense should apply to infringement actions brought to vindicate either right. As discussed above, the similarity of the policies underlying patent and copyright is great and historically has been consistently recognized. Both patent law and copyright law seek to increase the store of human knowledge and arts by rewarding inventors and authors with the exclusive rights to their works for a limited time. At the same time, the granted monopoly power does not extend to property not covered by the patent or copyright. *Morton Salt*, 314 U.S. at 492; cf. Baker v. Selden, 101 U.S. 99 (1880).

Thus, we are persuaded that the rationale of *Morton Salt* in establishing the misuse defense applies to copyrights. In the passage from *Morton Salt* quoted above, the phraseology adapts easily to a copyright context:

> The grant to the [author] of the special privilege of a [copyright] carries out a public policy adopted by the Constitution and laws of the United States, "to promote the Progress of Science and useful Arts, by securing for limited Times to [Authors] . . . the exclusive Right . . ." to their ["original" works]. United States Constitution, Art. I, §8, cl. 8, [17 U.S.C.A. §102]. But the public policy which includes [original works] within the granted monopoly excludes from it all that is not embraced in the [original expression]. It equally forbids the use of the [copyright] to secure an exclusive right or limited monopoly not granted by the [Copyright] Office and which it is contrary to public policy to grant.

Having determined that "misuse of copyright" is a valid defense, analogous to the misuse of patent defense, our next task is to determine whether the defense should have been applied by the district court to bar Lasercomb's infringement action against the defendants in this case.

B. The District Court's Finding That the Anticompetitive Clauses Are Reasonable

Lasercomb undoubtedly has the right to protect against copying of the Interact code. Its standard licensing agreement, however, goes much further and essentially attempts to suppress any attempt by the licensee to independently implement the idea which Interact expresses. The agreement forbids the licensee to develop or assist in developing any kind of computer-assisted die-making software. If the licensee is a business, it is to prevent all its directors, officers and employees from assisting in any manner to develop computer-assisted die-making software. Although one or another licensee might succeed in negotiating out the noncompete provisions, this does not negate the fact that Lasercomb is attempting to use its copyright in a manner adverse to the public policy embodied in copyright law, and that it has succeeded in doing so with at least one licensee. See supra note 8 and accompanying text. Cf. Berlenbach v. Anderson & Thompson Ski Co., 329 F.2d 782, 784-85 (9th Cir.), cert. denied, 379 U.S. 830 (1964).

The language employed in the Lasercomb agreement is extremely broad. Each time Lasercomb sells its Interact program to a company and obtains that company's agreement to the noncompete language, the company is required to forego utilization of the creative abilities of all its officers, directors and employees in the area of CAD/CAM die-making software. Of yet greater concern, these creative abilities are withdrawn from the public. The period for which this anticompetitive restraint exists is ninety-nine years, which could be longer than the life of the copyright itself.

We previously have considered the effect of anticompetitive language in a licensing agreement in the context of patent misuse. Compton v. Metal Products, Inc., 453 F.2d 38 (4th Cir. 1971), cert. denied, 406 U.S. 968 (1972). Compton had invented and patented coal auguring equipment. He granted an exclusive license in the patents to Joy Manufacturing, and the license agreement included a provision that Compton would not "engage in any business or activity relating to the manufacture or sale of equipment of the type licensed hereunder" for as long as he was due royalties under the patents. Suit for infringement of the Compton patents was brought against Metal Products, and the district court granted injunctive relief and damages. On appeal we held that relief for the infringement was barred by the misuse defense, stating:

> The need of Joy to protect its investment does not outweigh the public's right under our system to expect competition and the benefits which flow therefrom, and the total withdrawal of Compton from the mining machine business . . . everywhere in the world for a period of 20 years unreasonably lessens the competition which the public has a right to expect, and constitutes misuse of the patents.

Id. at 45. Cf. *Berlenbach*, supra (applying misuse doctrine where license to sell patented ski bindings prohibited licensee from manufacturing or selling any competing ski binding).

We think the anticompetitive language in Lasercomb's licensing agreement is at least as egregious as that which led us to bar the infringement action in *Compton*, and therefore amounts to misuse of its copyright. Again, the analysis necessary to a finding of misuse is similar to but separate from the analysis necessary to a finding of antitrust violation. The misuse arises from Lasercomb's attempt to use its copyright in a particular expression, the Interact software, to control competition in an area outside the copyright, i.e., the idea of computer-assisted die manufacture, regardless of whether such conduct amounts to an antitrust violation.

C. The Effect of Appellants Not Being Party to the Anticompetitive Contract

In its rejection of the copyright misuse defense, the district court emphasized that Holiday Steel was not explicitly party to a licensing agreement containing the offending language. However, again analogizing to patent misuse, the defense of copyright misuse is available even if the defendants themselves have not been injured by the misuse. In *Morton Salt*, the defendant was not a party to the license requirement that only Morton-produced salt tablets be used with Morton's salt-depositing machine. Nevertheless, suit against defendant for infringement of Morton's patent was barred on public policy grounds. Similarly, in *Compton*, even though the defendant Metal Products was not a party to the license agreement that restrained competition by Compton, suit against Metal Products was barred because of the public interest in free competition. See also *Hensley Equip. Co.*, 383 F.2d at 261; cf. *Berlenbach*, 329 F.2d at 784-85.

Therefore, the fact that appellants here were not parties to one of Lasercomb's standard license agreements is inapposite to their copyright misuse defense. The question is whether Lasercomb is using its copyright in a manner contrary to public policy, which question we have answered in the affirmative.

In sum, we find that misuse of copyright is a valid defense, that Lasercomb's anticompetitive clauses in its standard licensing agreement constitute misuse of copyright, and that the defense is available to appellants even though they were not parties to the standard licensing agreement. Holding that Lasercomb should have been barred by the defense of copyright misuse from suing for infringement of its copyright in the Interact program, we reverse the injunction and the award of damages for copyright infringement.

Because of this holding, we do not reach the other defenses to copyright infringement advanced by appellants.

Although we find misuse of copyright, we reject the contention of appellants — that they should recover attorney fees from Lasercomb under 17 U.S.C. §505 because Lasercomb brought this action in bad faith. Given the conduct of defendants and the obscurity of their defenses, we find such a position completely untenable.

APPLE, INC. v. PSYSTAR CORP.

658 F.3d 1150 (9th Cir. 2011)

SCHROEDER, Circuit Judge.

. . .

I. BACKGROUND

Apple launched its Macintosh line of personal computers in 1984. This line of computers has included Mac Pro, iMac, Mac Mini, MacBook, MacBook Air, and MacBook Pro. Apple launched its Mac OS X operating system in 2001. Apple now sells all Mac computers with a preinstalled, licensed copy of Mac OS X. Apple's Software License Agreement ("SLA") requires that the Mac OS X be used exclusively on Apple computers. Apple also separately distributes Mac OS X in a stand-alone, retail-packaged DVD with licensed software for the sole purpose of enabling Apple's existing customers to upgrade their Mac computers to the latest version of the operating system. Apple owns a registered copyright for each version of its operating system and the SLA for each requires the system to be used only on Apple computers.

In addition to the SLA and the copyrights, Apple uses lock-and-key technological measures to prevent Mac OS X from operating on non-Apple computers. This involves the use of a "kernel" extension, which is software that is executed and becomes part of the operating system on an Apple computer. The kernel extension communicates with other kernel extensions to locate the decryption keys in Apple hardware, and to unlock the encrypted files.

In April 2008, Psystar began manufacturing and selling personal computers — originally named "OpenMac" and then renamed "Open Computers." Psystar's Open Computers can run a variety of operating systems, but Psystar has chosen to sell Open Computers with Mac OS X. To do so, Psystar purchased a copy of Mac OS X, installed this copy of Mac OS X on a Mac Mini computer, and downloaded various software updates, using the automatic-update feature of Mac OS X. Psystar then imaged the Mac Mini with the OS X software, i.e., made a copy of the software, and transferred the copy to a non-Apple computer used as an imaging station. Psystar then added its own bootloader and kernel extensions to the Mac OS X on the imaging station, and this copy became the "master image." Psystar used this imaging station to reproduce the master image and install it on Open Computers for sale to the general public. Finally, Psystar shipped Open Computers with a copy of the master image installed, and with an unopened copy of Mac OS X, which Psystar purchased from Apple or third-party vendors such as Amazon, in the box. The unopened copy enabled Psystar to maintain it had purchased a copy of Mac OS X for each computer it sold, but the computer actually was to run on the copy of the altered Mac OS X installed in the Psystar computer.

On July 3, 2008, Apple filed this action against Psystar in the Northern District of California, alleging breach and induced breach of its SLA for Mac OS X, direct and contributory copyright infringement, trademark and trade dress infringement, and violation of state and common law unfair competition laws. Apple later amended its complaint to add a DMCA claim arising from Psystar's circumvention of the technological protection measures employed by Apple to prevent unauthorized access to and copying of Mac OS X.

Psystar asserted a counterclaim for a declaratory judgment that Apple was misusing its copyright in Mac OS X by requiring purchasers to run their copies only on Apple computers. The district court dismissed an earlier antitrust counterclaim that Psystar filed with its initial answer to the original complaint. That ruling is not appealed.

In August of 2009, Apple released its next version of Mac OS X — Mac OS X Snow Leopard ("Snow Leopard"); Psystar, in turn, released a new version of Open Computers, Rebel EFI, which was capable of running Snow Leopard. On August 27, Psystar sued Apple in the Southern District of Florida, alleging new antitrust claims and seeking a declaratory judgment that its products did not infringe Apple's intellectual property in Snow Leopard.

Both parties then filed cross motions for summary judgment. On November 13, 2009 the district court granted Apple's motion for summary judgment, finding that 1) Psystar's production process and hard drive imaging did not constitute fair use of Apple's operating system; 2) Psystar infringed Apple's exclusive right to create derivative works; 3) Apple's licensing agreement was not unduly restrictive and thus did not constitute copyright misuse; and 4) Psystar's use of decryption software to obtain access to operating system violated the DMCA.

The district court then, in a second published opinion, issued a permanent injunction against Psystar, enjoining all current and future infringement of Apple's Mac OS X software and the manufacture or sale of any device to circumvent Apple's software production. *See Apple II*, 673 F. Supp. 2d at 948-49. The court ruled in favor of Apple in its legal argument on copyright infringement and found that Apple would suffer irreparable harm if an injunction did not issue. The court found that the Apple software did not work well on Psystar computers and was causing Apple a loss of business reputation. "With respect to its brand, business reputation, and goodwill, Apple has put forth significant evidence, undisputed by Psystar, that its investment in and commitment to high standards of quality control and customer service would be irreparably harmed if Psystar's illegal activities were allowed to continue." *Id.*

This appeal by Psystar followed. The principal issue is whether the district court erred when it rejected Psystar's defense of copyright misuse.

II. PSYSTAR'S AFFIRMATIVE DEFENSE OF COPYRIGHT MISUSE

Psystar contends that Apple misused its copyright in Mac OS X in two ways. Psystar first contends that Apple misused its copyright by asserting invalid claims of copyright infringement in this case. We find this contention entirely unpersuasive, however, given that Psystar does not appeal the district court's findings of infringement of Apple's valid copyright in Mac OS X.

Psystar's main contention of misuse is aimed at Apple's requirement that licensees of Mac OS X run their copies only on Apple computers. The relevant section of Apple's SLA for Mac OS X provides,

> This License allows you to install, use and run one (1) copy of the Apple Software on a single-Apple-labeled computer at a time. You agree not to install, use or run the Apple Software on any non-Apple labeled computer, or to enable others to do so.

Psystar contends that this language barring use of the Apple software on non-Apple computers impermissibly extends the reach of Apple's copyright and constitutes misuse. We conclude that the district court correctly ruled that Apple had not engaged in copyright misuse. As we will explain, this is principally because its licensing agreement was intended to require the operating system to be used on the computer it was designed to operate, and it did not prevent others from developing their own computer or operating systems. These licensing agreements were thus appropriately used to prevent infringement and control use of the copyrighted material.

A. Software licensing agreements, rather than sales, have become ubiquitous in the software industry because they enable the licensor to control the use of the copyrighted material

To understand why license agreements, rather than sales, have become the predominate form of the transfer of rights to use copyrighted software material, it is necessary to understand the legal principle that applies when copyrighted works are not licensed, but sold: the "first sale doctrine." The first sale doctrine allows owners of copies of copyrighted works to resell their copies without restriction.

The doctrine was first recognized by the Supreme Court in Bobbs-Merrill Co. v. Straus, 210 U.S. 339, 28 S. Ct. 722, 52 L. Ed. 1086 (1908). At issue in *Bobbs-Merrill* was the exclusive right of a copyright owner to restrict the resale terms of its copyrighted material. The Supreme Court interpreted the then copyright statute's "sole right to vend" to bar a publisher from restricting future sales of a book by placing a notice on the book's cover that limited resale to $1 or more. *Id.* at 350, 28 S. Ct. 722. Congress codified the first sale doctrine in the 1909 Copyright Act, *see* 17 U.S.C. §41 (1909), and then refined the doctrine in the 1976 Copyright Act and its subsequent amendments. *See* 17 U.S.C. §109 (2008). As currently constituted, the doctrine exempts subsequent owners who then sell a legitimate copy of a copyrighted work from claims of infringing the original owner's exclusive distribution rights:

> Notwithstanding the provisions of Section 106(3), the owner of a particular copy or phonorecord lawfully made under this title, or any person authorized by such owner, is entitled, without the authority of the copyright owner, to sell or otherwise dispose of the possession of that copy or phonorecord.

Id. at §109(a). Thus, once a publisher sells a valuable, vellum-bound volume, for example, it forfeits its exclusive distribution privilege and enables the buyer, the new owner of the volume, to resell the copy to another buyer. *See* 2 Melville B. Nimmer & David Nimmer, Nimmer on Copyright §8.12[B][1][d] (rev. ed. 2010).

The statute specifically excludes the doctrine's application, however, when the copy is transferred through "rental, lease, loan, or otherwise, without acquiring ownership of it." 17 U.S.C. at §109(d). Thus, the first sale doctrine does not apply to a licensee. *See* Vernor v. Autodesk, Inc., 621 F.3d 1102, 1107-08 (9th Cir. 2010) ("The first sale doctrine does not apply to a person who possesses a copy of the copyrighted work without owning it, such as a licensee.").

Our court's application of §109(d) in *Vernor* not only reconciled our prior cases and avoided a possible disagreement with the Federal Circuit, but also constituted a significant validation of license restrictions on transfer and use of software.

B. Licensees have reacted to the proliferation of software licensing agreements by asking the courts to apply copyright misuse defense to limit the scope of such agreements

Copyright misuse is a judicially crafted affirmative defense to copyright infringement, derived from the long-standing existence of such a defense in patent litigation. The patent misuse defense was originally recognized by the Supreme Court in 1942, in holding that the owner of the patent on a salt tablet machine could not require licensees to use only un-patented salt tablets sold by the patent owner. Morton Salt Co. v. G.S. Suppiger Co., 314 U.S. 488, 62 S. Ct. 402, 86 L. Ed. 363 (1942). The Court held that this improper tying of a patented product and an unpatented product constituted misuse, and prohibited the patent holder from maintaining infringement actions until the patent holder ceased misuse of the patent. *Id.* at 493.

In 1990, the Fourth Circuit became the first federal circuit to extend the misuse rationale to copyrights. *See* Lasercomb Am., Inc. v. Reynolds, 911 F.2d 970, 972 (4th Cir. 1990).

Subsequently, our court recognized the existence of a copyright misuse doctrine. *See, e.g.,* Altera Corp. v. Clear Logic, Inc., 424 F.3d 1079, 1090 (9th Cir. 2005); Practice Mgmt. Info. Corp. v. Am. Med. Ass'n, 121 F.3d 516, 521 (9th Cir. 1997), *amended by* 133 F.3d 1140 (9th Cir. 1998). In *Altera*, we made it clear that the defense is not a defense to state law claims, and in A&M Records v. Napster, Inc., 239 F.3d 1004 (9th Cir. 2001), we rejected the appli-cability of the defense on the merits, upholding, in the circumstances of that case, the district court's conclusion that there was actionable copyright infringement.

We have thus applied the doctrine sparingly. The doctrine did not apply in *Altera* when there had been no allegation of copyright infringement. 424 F.3d at 1090. In *Napster*, we observed that the plaintiffs who sought to enjoin unlicensed use of copyrighted works were entitled to do so because they were not seeking to extend a copyright monopoly to other products or works. We described the purpose of the defense as preventing holders of copy-rights "from leveraging their limited monopoly to allow them control of areas outside the monopoly." *Napster*, 239 F.3d at 1026.

Our decision in *Practice Management* is the only case in which we upheld a copyright misuse defense. We did so because the copyright licensor in that case prevented the licensee from using any other competing product. 121 F.3d at 520-21. In *Practice Management*, a publisher and distributor of medical books was using a coding system developed by the American Medical Association ("AMA") to enable physicians and others to identify particular medical procedures with precision. *Id.* Practice Management sued the AMA for a declaratory judgment that the AMA's copyright in its coding system, the Physician's Current Procedural Terminology ("CPT"), was not valid. *Id.* at 518. The CPT had become an industry standard, and the AMA had a licensing agreement that allowed the Health Care Financing Administration ("HCFA") to use the AMA system. The agreement provided, however, that HCFA use only the AMA system. *Id.* at 520-21 (the agreement required "HCFA to use the AMA's copyrighted coding system and prohibit[ed] HCFA from using any other.").

We held this was copyright misuse, because the AMA was not entitled to use the license agreement to prevent the use of all competitor's [*sic*] products. *Id.* at 521 ("Conditioning the license on HCFA's promise not to use competitors' products constituted a misuse of the copyright by the AMA."). In recognizing clear abuse of the copyright, we observed that the AMA's misuse was its limitation on the HCFA's right to decide whether or not to use other systems as well. It was not necessary to decide whether the limitation, in the antitrust context, would have been reasonable or not. We said that "a defendant in a copyright infringement suit need not prove an antitrust violation to prevail on a copyright misuse defense." *Id.* (citing *Lasercomb*, 911 F.2d at 978).

No such limitation existed in Triad Sys. Corp. v. Se. Express Co., 64 F.3d 1330 (9th Cir. 1995). We therefore rejected a copyright misuse defense and upheld the software licensing agreement. *Id.* at 1337. We held that there was no abuse where the copyright license did not prevent the licensee from developing competing software. *Triad* has significance for this case because we there adopted the Fourth Circuit's view in *Lasercomb* that copyright misuse involves restraining development of competing products. *See* 911 F.2d at 978.

Triad, a hardware and software producer, brought a copyright infringement action against Southeastern, an independent service organization that services Triad hardware. Triad licensed its copyrighted operating and diagnostic software for use by its licensees in the operation of Triad computers. 64 F.3d at 1333. Triad's software license agreement prohibited the licensee from making copies of the software and from allowing third parties to use the software. *Id.* Triad alleged that Southeastern infringed Triad's copyrights when Southeastern's technicians serviced a licensees' [*sic*] computers, because, during servicing, Southeastern copied Triad's operating and service software and loaded it into Southeastern memory. *Id.*

Triad sought to enjoin Southeastern from servicing its computers because of the infringement. Southeastern asserted a copyright misuse defense, claiming Triad was trying to monopolize its computer maintenance. By restricting third-party use of its software, "Triad ha[d] used its intellectual property monopoly over Triad software to leverage its position in the Triad computer maintenance market." Triad Sys. Corp. v. Southeastern Exp. Co., 1994 WL 446049, *3 n. 1 (N.D. Cal. Mar. 18, 1994). The district court rejected this argument and this court affirmed on appeal, holding that there was no attempt to stifle competition in the service software market. "Triad did not attempt to prohibit Southeastern or any other [independent service operator] from developing its own service software to compete with Triad." *Triad*, 64 F.3d at 1337.

To the extent that *Triad* held that copying of software for purposes of servicing the computer was unlawful, it has been legislatively overruled. *See* 17 U.S.C. §117(c); *see also* Melissa A. Bogden, Note, *Fixing Fixation: The RAM Copy Doctrine*, 43 Ariz. St. L.J. 181, 196-97 (2011). To the extent that its reasoning requires rejection of a misuse defense in contexts other than maintenance, its reasoning remains the law of the circuit. A software licensing agreement may reasonably restrict use of the software as long as it does not prevent the development of competing products.

C. Psystar's misuse defense fails because it is an attempt to apply the first sale doctrine to a valid licensing agreement

Psystar attempts to distinguish *Triad* from the present case by invoking the first sale doctrine. Psystar argues that Apple, unlike Triad, attempts to control the use of Mac OS X software after it has been sold, because Psystar purchased retail-packaged copies of the operating software. Psystar contends that while the copyright owner can refuse to sell copies, it cannot control their subsequent use. This argument falsely assumes that Apple transferred ownership of Mac OS X when it sold a retail-packaged DVD containing software designed to enable Apple's existing customers to upgrade to the latest version of the operating system. The buyers of that DVD purchased the disc. They knew, however, they were not buying the software. Apple's SLA clearly explained this.

The DVD purchasers were licensees, not owners, of the software. The Mac OS X SLA[] states that the software is "licensed, not sold, to [the customer] by Apple Inc. (Apple) for use only under the terms of this License." Thus the SLA provides that Apple "retain[s] ownership of the Apple Software itself." The SLA also imposes significant use and transfer restrictions, providing, *inter alia*, that a licensee may only run one copy and "may not rent, lease, lend, redistribute or sublicense the Apple Software." *Cf. Wall Data*, 447 F.3d at 785 ("Generally, if the copyright owner makes it clear that she or he is granting only a license to the copy of software and imposes significant restrictions on the purchaser's ability to redistribute or transfer that copy, the purchaser is considered a licensee, not an owner, of the software."). The license thus satisfied *Vernor*'s three-factor test for demonstrating the existence of a licensor/licensee relationship. 621 F.3d at 1111.

Contrary to Psystar's assertion, such licensing arrangements are also firmly rooted in the history of copyright law. While copyright owners may choose to simply exclude others from their work, i.e. not to transfer their rights, *see* Stewart v. Abend, 495 U.S. 207, 228-29, 110 S. Ct. 1750, 109 L. Ed. 2d 184 (1990); Fox Film Corp. v. Doyal, 286 U.S. 123, 127, 52 S. Ct. 546, 76 L. Ed. 1010 (1932), courts have long held that copyright holders may also use their limited monopoly to leverage the right to use their work on the acceptance of specific conditions, *see, e.g.*, Metro-Goldwyn-Mayer Distrib. Corp. v. Bijou Theatre Co., 59 F.2d 70, 77 (1st Cir. 1932) (holding that if a motion picture license is subject to the condition that its exhibition must occur at specified times and places, the licensee's exhibitions at other times and places is without authority from the licensor and therefore constitutes copyright infringement).

. . .

The copyright misuse doctrine does not prohibit using conditions to control use of copyrighted material, but it does prevent copyright holders from using the conditions to stifle competition.

AFFIRMED in part, **REMANDED** in part. Costs are awarded to Apple.

BOWERS v. BAYSTATE TECHNOLOGIES, INC.
320 F.3d 1317 (Fed. Cir. 2003)

RADER, Circuit Judge.

Harold L. Bowers (Bowers) created a template to improve computer aided design (CAD) software, such as the CADKEY tool of Cadkey, Inc. Mr. Bowers filed a patent application for his template on February 27, 1989. On June 12, 1990, United States Patent No. 4,933,514 ('514 patent) issued from that application.

Generally, a CAD software program has many commands that the software presents to the user in nested menus many layers deep. The layering often makes it difficult for a user to find quickly a desired command. To address this problem, the claimed template works with a CAD system as illustrated in Fig. 1 of the '514 patent. In that figure, the '514 patent template lies on top of the digitizing tablet of a CAD computer. The user selects data from the template with a pointing device. The template places the many CAD commands in a claimed visual and logical order.

In 1989, Mr. Ford offered Mr. Bowers an exclusive license to his Geodraft software. Mr. Bowers accepted that offer and bundled Geodraft and Cadjet together as the Designer's Toolkit. Mr. Bowers sold the Designer's Toolkit with a shrink-wrap license that, *inter alia*, prohibited any reverse engineering.

In 1989, Baystate also developed and marketed other tools for CADKEY. One of those tools, Draft-Pak version 1 and 2, featured a template and GD & T software. In 1988 and 1989, Mr. Bowers offered to establish a formal relationship with Baystate, including bundling his template with Draft-Pak. Baystate rejected that offer, however, telling Mr. Bowers that it believed it had "the in-house capability to develop the type of products you have proposed."

In 1990, Mr. Bowers released Designer's Toolkit. By January 1991, Baystate had obtained copies of that product. Three months later, Baystate introduced the substantially revised Draft-Pak version 3, incorporating many of the features of Designer's Toolkit. Although Draft-Pak version 3 operated in the DOS environment, Baystate later upgraded it to operate with Microsoft Windows®.

Baystate's introduction of Draft-Pak version 3 induced intense price competition between Mr. Bowers and Baystate. To gain market share over Baystate, Mr. Bowers negotiated with Cadkey, Inc., to provide the Designer's Toolkit free with CADKEY. Mr. Bowers planned to recoup his profits by selling software upgrades to the users that he hoped to lure to his products. Following pressure from Baystate, however, Cadkey, Inc., repudiated its distribution agreement with Mr. Bowers. Eventually, Baystate purchased Cadkey, Inc., and eliminated Mr. Bowers from the CADKEY network—effectively preventing him from developing and marketing the Designer's Toolkit for that program.

On May 16, 1991, Baystate sued Mr. Bowers for declaratory judgment that 1) Baystate's products do not infringe the '514 patent, 2) the '514 patent is invalid, and 3) the '514 patent is unenforceable. Mr. Bowers filed counterclaims for copyright infringement, patent infringement, and breach of contract.

Following trial, the jury found for Mr. Bowers and awarded $1,948,869 for copyright infringement, $3,831,025 for breach of contract, and $232,977 for patent infringement. The district court, however, set aside the copyright damages as duplicative of the contract damages and entered judgment for $5,270,142 (including pre-judgment interest). Baystate filed timely motions for judgment as a matter of law (JMOL), or for a new trial, on all of Mr. Bowers' claims. Baystate appeals the district court's denial of its motions for JMOL or a new trial, while Mr. Bowers appeals the district court's denial of copyright damages. This court has jurisdiction under 28 U.S.C. §1295(a)(1) (2000).

A.

Baystate contends that the Copyright Act preempts the prohibition of reverse engineering embodied in Mr. Bowers' shrink-wrap license agreements. Swayed by this argument, the district court considered Mr. Bowers' contract and copyright claims coextensive. The district court instructed the jury that "reverse engineering violates the license agreement only if Baystate's product that resulted from reverse engineering infringes Bowers' copyright because it copies protectable expression." Mr. Bowers lodged a timely objection to this instruction. This court holds that, under First Circuit law, the Copyright Act does not preempt or narrow the scope of Mr. Bowers' contract claim.

Courts respect freedom of contract and do not lightly set aside freely-entered agreements. Beacon Hill Civic Ass'n v. Ristorante Toscano, 422 Mass. 318, 662 N.E.2d 1015, 1017 (1996). Nevertheless, at times, federal regulation may preempt private contract. Cf. Nebbia v. New York, 291 U.S. 502, 523, 54 S. Ct. 505, 78 L. Ed. 940 (1934) ("Equally fundamental with the private right is [the right] of the public to regulate [the private right] in the common interest."). The Copyright Act provides that "all legal or equitable rights that are equivalent to any of the exclusive rights within the general scope of copyright . . . are governed exclusively by this title." 17 U.S.C. §301(a) (2000). The First Circuit does not interpret this language to require preemption as long as "a state cause of action requires an extra element, beyond mere copying, preparation of derivative works, performance, distribution or display." Data Gen. Corp. v. Grumman Sys. Support Corp., 36 F.3d 1147, 1164, 32 USPQ2d 1385, 1397 (1st Cir. 1994) (quoting Gates Rubber Co. v. Bando Chem. Indus., 9 F.3d 823, 847, 28 USPQ2d 1503, 1520 (10th Cir. 1993)); see also Computer Assoc. Int'l, Inc. v. Altai, Inc., 982 F.2d 693, 716 (2d Cir. 1992) ("But if an 'extra element' is 'required instead of or in addition to the acts of reproduction, performance, distribution or display, in order to constitute a state-created cause of action, then the right does not lie "within the general scope of copyright," and there is no preemption.' ") (quoting 1 NIMMER ON COPYRIGHT §1.01[B] at 1-15). Nevertheless, "[n]ot every 'extra element' of a state law claim will establish a qualitative variance between the rights protected by federal copyright law and those protected by state law." Id.

In Data General, Data General alleged that Grumman misappropriated its trade secret software. 36 F.3d at 1155. Grumman obtained that software from Data General's customers and former employees who were bound by confidentiality agreements to refrain from disclosing the software. Id. at 1154-55. In defense, Grumman argued that the Copyright Act preempted Data General's trade secret claim. Id. at 1158, 1165. The First Circuit held that the Copyright Act did not preempt the state law trade secret claim. Id. at 1165. Beyond mere copying, that state law claim required proof of a trade secret and breach of a duty of confidentiality. Id. These additional elements of proof, according to the First Circuit, made the trade secret claim qualitatively different from a copyright claim. Id. In contrast, the First Circuit noted that claims might be preempted whose extra elements are illusory, being "mere label[s] attached to the same odious business conduct." Id. at 1165 (quoting Mayer v. Josiah Wedgwood & Sons, Ltd., 601 F. Supp. 1523, 1535, 225 USPQ 776, 784 (S.D.N.Y. 1985)). For example, the First Circuit observed that "a state law misappropriation claim will not escape preemption . . . simply because a plaintiff must prove that copying was not only unauthorized but also commercially immoral." Id.

The First Circuit has not addressed expressly whether the Copyright Act preempts a state law contract claim that restrains copying. This court perceives, however, that Data General's rationale would lead to a judgment that the Copyright Act does not preempt the state contract action in this case. Indeed, most courts to examine this issue have found that the Copyright Act does not preempt contractual constraints on copyrighted articles. See, e.g., ProCD, Inc. v.

Zeidenberg, 86 F.3d 1447, 39 USPQ2d 1161 (7th Cir. 1996) (holding that a shrink-wrap license was not preempted by federal copyright law); Wrench LLC v. Taco Bell Corp., 256 F.3d 446, 457, 59 USPQ2d 1434, 1441-42 (6th Cir. 2001) (holding a state law contract claim not preempted by federal copyright law); Nat'l Car Rental Sys., Inc. v. Computer Assocs. Int'l, Inc., 991 F.2d 426, 433, 26 USPQ2d 1370, 1376 (8th Cir. 1993); Taquino v. Teledyne Monarch Rubber, 893 F.2d 1488, 1501 (5th Cir. 1990); Acorn Structures v. Swantz, 846 F.2d 923, 926, 6 USPQ2d 1810, 1812 (4th Cir. 1988); *but see* Lipscher v. LRP Publs., Inc., 266 F.3d 1305, 1312, 60 USPQ2d 1468, 1473 (11th Cir. 2001).

In *ProCD*, for example, the court found that the mutual assent and consideration required by a contract claim render that claim qualitatively different from copyright infringement. 86 F.3d at 1454. Consistent with *Data General's* reliance on a contract element, the court in *ProCD* reasoned: "A copyright is a right against the world. Contracts, by contrast, generally affect only their parties; strangers may do as they please, so contracts do not create 'exclusive rights.'" *Id.* Indeed, the Supreme Court recently noted "[i]t goes without saying that a contract cannot bind a nonparty." EEOC v. Waffle House, Inc., 534 U.S. 279, 122 S. Ct. 754, 764, 151 L. Ed. 2d 755 (2002). This court believes that the First Circuit would follow the reasoning of *ProCD* and the majority of other courts to consider this issue. This court, therefore, holds that the Copyright Act does not preempt Mr. Bowers' contract claims.

In making this determination, this court has left untouched the conclusions reached in *Atari Games v. Nintendo* regarding reverse engineering as a statutory fair use exception to copyright infringement. Atari Games Corp. v. Nintendo of America, Inc., 975 F.2d 832, 24 USPQ2d 1015 (Fed. Cir. 1992). In *Atari*, this court stated that, with respect to 17 U.S.C. §107 (fair use section of the Copyright Act), "[t]he legislative history of section 107 suggests that courts should adapt the fair use exception to accommodate new technological innovations." *Atari*, 975 F.2d at 843. This court noted "[a] prohibition on all copying whatsoever would stifle the free flow of ideas without serving any legitimate interest of the copyright holder." *Id.* Therefore, this court held "reverse engineering object code to discern the unprotectable ideas in a computer program is a fair use." *Id.* Application of the First Circuit's view distinguishing a state law contract claim having additional elements of proof from a copyright claim does not alter the findings of *Atari*. Likewise, this claim distinction does not conflict with the expressly defined circumstances in which reverse engineering is not copyright infringement under 17 U.S.C. §1201(f) (section of the Digital Millennium Copyright Act) and 17 U.S.C. §906 (section directed to mask works).

Moreover, while the Fifth Circuit has held a state law prohibiting all copying of a computer program is preempted by the federal Copyright Act, Vault Corp. v. Quaid Software, Ltd., 847 F.2d 255 (5th Cir. 1988), no evidence suggests the First Circuit would extend this concept to include private contractual agreements supported by mutual assent and consideration. The First Circuit recognizes contractual waiver of affirmative defenses and statutory rights. *See* United States v. Spector, 55 F.3d 22, 24-5 (1st Cir. 1995) (holding that a contractual waiver of the statute of limitations defense constitutes an "effective waiver of defendant's rights under the statute of limitations" if the agreement were properly executed, and the "waiver is made knowingly and voluntarily."); Tompkins v. United Healthcare of New England, 203 F.3d 90, 97 (1st Cir. 2000) (stating that "in some circumstances contractual waiver of statutory rights is permissible," citing Canal Elec. Co. v. Westinghouse Elec. Corp., 406 Mass. 369, 548 N.E.2d

182, 187 (Mass. 1990) ("a contractual waiver of statutory rights is permissible when the statute's purpose is the 'protection of the property rights of individual parties . . . rather than . . . the protection of the general public.'")). Thus, case law indicates the First Circuit would find that private parties are free to contractually forego the limited ability to reverse engineer a software product under the exemptions of the Copyright Act. Of course, a party bound by such a contract may elect to efficiently breach the agreement in order to ascertain ideas in a computer program unprotected by copyright law. Under such circumstances, the breaching party must weigh the benefits of breach against the arguably de minimus damages arising from merely discerning non-protected code.

This court now considers the scope of Mr. Bowers' contract protection. Without objection to the choice of law, the district court applied Massachusetts contract law. Accordingly, contract terms receive "the sense and meaning of the words which the parties have used; and if clear and free from ambiguity the words are to be taken and understood in their natural, usual and ordinary sense." Farber v. Mutual Life Ins. Co., 250 Mass. 250, 253, 145 N.E. 535 (Mass. 1924); see also Kelly v. Marx, 428 Mass. 877, 881, 705 N.E.2d 1114 (Mass. 1999) ("The proper course is to enforce contracts according to their plain meaning and not to undertake to be wiser than the parties.") (quoting Guerin v. Stacy, 175 Mass. 595, 597, 56 N.E. 892 (1900) (Holmes, C.J.)).

In this case, the contract unambiguously prohibits "reverse engineering." That term means ordinarily "to study or analyze (a device, as a microchip for computers) in order to learn details of design, construction, and operation, perhaps to produce a copy or an improved version." *Random House Unabridged Dictionary* (1993); see also *The Free On-Line Dictionary of Computing* (2001), at *http://wombat.doc.ic.ac.uk/foldoc/foldoc.cgi?reverse+engineering* (last visited Jul. 17, 2002). Thus, the contract in this case broadly prohibits any "reverse engineering" of the subject matter covered by the shrink-wrap agreement.

The record amply supports the jury's finding of a breach of that agreement. As discussed above, the district court erred in instructing the jury that copyright law limited the scope of Mr. Bowers' contract protection. Notwithstanding that error, this court may affirm the jury's breach of contract verdict if substantial record evidence would permit a reasonable jury to find in favor of Mr. Bowers based on a correct understanding of the law. Larch v. Mansfield Mun. Elec. Dept., 272 F.3d 63, 69 (1st Cir. 2001). The shrink-wrap agreements in this case are far broader than the protection afforded by copyright law. Even setting aside copyright violations, the record supports a finding of breach of the agreement between the parties. In view of the breadth of Mr. Bowers' contracts, this court perceives that substantial evidence supports the jury's breach of contract verdict relating to both the DOS and Windows versions of Draft-Pak.

The record indicates, for example, that Baystate scheduled two weeks in Draft-Pak's development schedule to analyze the Designer's Toolkit. Indeed, Robert Bean, Baystate's president and CEO, testified that Baystate generally analyzed competitor's products to duplicate their functionality.

The record also contains evidence of extensive and unusual similarities between Geodraft and the accused Draft-Pak — further evidence of reverse engineering. James Spencer, head of mechanical engineering and integration at the Space and Naval Warfare Systems Center, testified that he examined the relevant software programs to determine "the overall structure of the operating program" such as "how the operating programs actually executed the task of walking a user through creating a [GD&T] symbol." Mr. Spencer concluded: "In the process of taking the [ANSI Y14.5M] standard and breaking it down into its component parts to actually create a step-by-step process for a user using the software, both Geodraft and Draft-Pak [for DOS] use almost the identical process of breaking down that task into its individual pieces, and it's organized essentially identically." This evidence supports the jury's verdict of a contract breach based on reverse engineering.

Mr. Ford also testified that he had compared Geodraft and Draft-Pak. When asked to describe the Draft-Pak interface, Mr. Ford responded: "It looked like I was looking at my own program [i.e., Geodraft]." Both Mr. Spencer and Mr. Ford explained in detail similarities between Geodraft and the accused Draft-Pak. Those similarities included the interrelationships between program screens, the manner in which parameter selection causes program branching, and the manner in which the GD&T symbols are drawn.

Both witnesses also testified that those similarities extended beyond structure and design to include many idiosyncratic design choices and inadvertent design flaws. For example, both Geodraft and Draft-Pak offer "straightness tolerance" menu choices of "flat" and "cylindric," unusual in view of the use by ANSI Y14.5M of the terms "linear" and "circular," respectively. As another example, neither program requires the user to provide "angularity tolerance" secondary datum to create a feature control frame — a technical oversight that causes creation of an incomplete symbol. In sum, Mr. Spencer testified: "Based on my summary analysis of how the programs function, their errors from the standard and their similar nomenclatures reflecting nonstandard items, I would say that the Draft-Pak [for DOS] is a derivative copy of a Geodraft product."

Mr. Ford and others also demonstrated to the jury the operation of Geodraft and both the DOS and Windows versions of the accused Draft-Pak. Those software demonstrations undoubtedly conveyed information to the jury that the paper record on appeal cannot easily replicate. This court, therefore, is especially reluctant to substitute its judgment for that of the jury on the sufficiency and interpretation of that evidence. In any event, the record fully supports the jury's verdict that Baystate breached its contract with Mr. Bowers.

Baystate does not contest the contract damages amount on appeal. Thus, this court sustains the district court's award of contract damages. Mr. Bowers, however, argues that the district court abused its discretion by dropping copyright damages from the combined damage award. To the contrary, this court perceives no abuse of discretion.

The shrink-wrap license agreement prohibited, *inter alia*, all reverse engineering of Mr. Bowers' software, protection encompassing but more extensive than copyright protection, which prohibits only certain copying. Mr. Bowers' copyright and contract claims both rest on Baystate's copying of Mr. Bowers' software. Following the district court's instructions, the jury considered and awarded damages on each separately. This was entirely appropriate. The law is clear that the jury may award separate damages for each claim, "leaving it to the judge to make appropriate adjustments to avoid double recovery." Britton v. Maloney, 196 F.3d 24, 32 (1st Cir. 1999) (citing Spectrum Sports, Inc. v. McQuillan, 506 U.S. 447, 451 n.3, 113 S. Ct. 884, 122 L. Ed. 2d 247 (1993)); *see also* Data Gen. Corp. v. Grumman Sys. Support Corp., 825 F. Supp. 340, 346 (D. Mass. 1993) ("So long as a plaintiff is not twice compensated for a single injury, a judgment may be comprised of elements drawn from separate . . .

remedies."), *aff'd in relevant part*, 36 F.3d 1147 (1st Cir. 1994). In this case, the breach of contract damages arose from the same copying and included the same lost sales that form the basis for the copyright damages. The district court, therefore, did not abuse its discretion by omitting from the final damage award the duplicative copyright damages. Because this court affirms the district court's omission of the copyright damages, this court need not reach the merits of Mr. Bowers' copyright infringement claim.

DYK, Circuit Judge, concurring in part and dissenting in part.

I join the majority opinion except insofar as it holds that the contract claim is not preempted by federal law. Based on the petition for rehearing and the opposition, I have concluded that our original decision on the preemption issue, reaffirmed in today's revision of the majority opinion, was not correct. By holding that shrinkwrap licenses that override the fair use defense are not preempted by the Copyright Act, 17 U.S.C. §§101 *et seq.*, the majority has rendered a decision in conflict with the only other federal court of appeals decision that has addressed the issue — the Fifth Circuit decision in Vault Corp. v. Quaid Software Ltd., 847 F.2d 255 (5th Cir. 1988). The majority's approach permits state law to eviscerate an important federal copyright policy reflected in the fair use defense, and the majority's logic threatens other federal copyright policies as well. I respectfully dissent.

I

Congress has made the Copyright Act the exclusive means for protecting copyright. The Act provides that "all legal or equitable rights that are equivalent to any of the exclusive rights within the general scope of copyright . . . are governed exclusively by this title." 17 U.S.C. §301(a) (2000). All other laws, including the common law, are preempted. "[N]o person is entitled to any such right or equivalent right in any such work under the common law or statutes of any State." *Id.*

The test for preemption by copyright law, like the test for patent law preemption, should be whether the state law "substantially impedes the public use of the otherwise unprotected" material. Bonito Boats, Inc. v. Thunder Craft Boats, Inc., 489 U.S. 141, 157, 167, 109 S. Ct. 971, 103 L. Ed. 2d 118 (1989) (state law at issue was preempted because it "substantially restrict[ed] the public's ability to exploit ideas that the patent system mandates shall be free for all to use."); Sears, Roebuck & Co. v. Stiffel Co., 376 U.S. 225, 231-32, 84 S. Ct. 784, 11 L. Ed. 2d 661 (1964). *See also* Eldred v. Ashcroft, 537 U.S. 186, 123 S. Ct. 769, 154 L. Ed. 2d 683 (2003) (applying patent precedent in copyright case). In the copyright area, the First Circuit has adopted an "equivalent in substance" test to determine whether a state law is preempted by the Copyright Act. Data Gen. Corp. v. Grumman Sys. Support Corp. 36 F.3d 1147, 1164-65 (1st Cir. 1994). That test seeks to determine whether the state cause of action contains an additional element not present in the copyright right, such as scienter. If the state cause of action contains such an extra element, it is not preempted by the Copyright Act. *Id.* However, "such an action is equivalent in substance to a copyright infringement claim [and thus preempted by the Copyright Act] where the additional element merely concerns *the extent to which* authors and their licensees can prohibit unauthorized copying by third parties." *Id.* at 1165 (emphasis in original).

II

The fair use defense is an important limitation on copyright. Indeed, the Supreme Court has said that "[f]rom the infancy of copyright protection, some opportunity for fair use of copyrighted materials has been thought necessary to fulfill copyright's very purpose, '[t]o promote the Progress of Science and useful Arts. . . .' U.S. Const., Art. I, §8, cl. 8." Campbell v. Acuff-Rose Music, Inc., 510 U.S. 569, 575, 114 S. Ct. 1164, 127 L. Ed. 2d 500 (1994). The protective nature of the fair use defense was recently emphasized by the Court in the *Eldred* case, in which the Court noted that "copyright law contains built-in accommodations," including "the 'fair use' defense [which] allows the public to use not only facts an ideas contained in the copyrighted work, but also expression itself in certain circumstances." *Id.* at, 123 S. Ct. 769.

We correctly held in Atari Games Corp. v. Nintendo of America, Inc., 975 F.2d 832, 843 (Fed. Cir. 1992), that reverse engineering constitutes a fair use under the Copyright Act. The Ninth and Eleventh Circuits have also ruled that reverse engineering constitutes fair use. Bateman v. Mnemonics, Inc., 79 F.3d 1532, 1539 n.18 (11th Cir. 1996); Sega Enters. Ltd. v. Accolade, Inc., 977 F.2d 1510, 1527-28 (9th Cir. 1992). No other federal court of appeals has disagreed.

We emphasized in *Atari* that an author cannot achieve protection for an idea simply by embodying it in a computer program. "An author cannot acquire patent-like protection by putting an idea, process, or method of operation in an unintelligible format and asserting copyright infringement against those who try to understand that idea, process, or method of operation." 975 F.2d at 842. Thus, the fair use defense for reverse engineering is necessary so that copyright protection does not "extend to any idea, procedure, process, system, method of operation, concept, principle, or discovery, regardless of the form in which it is described, explained, illustrated, or embodied in such work," as proscribed by the Copyright Act. 17 U.S.C. §102(b) (2000).

III

A state is not free to eliminate the fair use defense. Enforcement of a total ban on reverse engineering would conflict with the Copyright Act itself by protecting otherwise unprotectable material. If state law provided that a copyright holder could bar fair use of the copyrighted material by placing a black dot on each copy of the work offered for sale, there would be no question but that the state law would be preempted. A state law that allowed a copyright holder to simply label its products so as to eliminate a fair use defense would "substantially impede" the public's right to fair use and allow the copyright holder, through state law, to protect material that the Congress has determined must be free to all under the Copyright Act. *See Bonito Boats*, 489 U.S. at 157, 109 S. Ct. 971.

I nonetheless agree with the majority opinion that a state can permit parties to contract away a fair use defense or to agree not to engage in uses of copyrighted material that are permitted by the copyright law, if the contract is freely negotiated. *See, e.g.*, Nat'l Car Rental Sys., Inc. v. Computer Assocs. Int'l, Inc., 991 F.2d 426 (8th Cir. 1993); Acorn Structures v. Swantz, 846 F.2d 923, 926 (4th Cir. 1988). *See also* Taquino v. Teledyne Monarch Rubber, 893 F.2d 1488 (5th Cir. 1990). *But see* Wrench LLC v. Taco Bell Corp., 256 F.3d 446, 457

(6th Cir. 2001) ("If the promise amounts only to a promise to refrain from reproducing, performing, distributing or displaying the work, then the contract claim is preempted."). A freely negotiated agreement represents the "extra element" that prevents preemption of a state law claim that would otherwise be identical to the infringement claim barred by the fair use defense of reverse engineering. *See Data Gen.*, 36 F.3d at 1164-65.

However, state law giving effect to shrinkwrap licenses is no different in substance from a hypothetical black dot law. Like any other contract of adhesion, the only choice offered to the purchaser is to avoid making the purchase in the first place. *See* Fuentes v. Shevin, 407 U.S. 67, 95, 92 S. Ct. 1983, 32 L. Ed. 2d 556 (1972). State law thus gives the copyright holder the ability to eliminate the fair use defense in each and every instance at its option. In doing so, as the majority concedes, it authorizes "shrinkwrap agreements . . . [that] are far broader than the protection afforded by copyright law."

IV

There is, moreover, no logical stopping point to the majority's reasoning. The amici rightly question whether under our original opinion the first sale doctrine and a host of other limitations on copyright protection might be eliminated by shrinkwrap licenses in just this fashion. *See* Brief for Electric Frontier Foundation et al. as *Amici Curiae* 10. If by printing a few words on the outside of its product a party can eliminate the fair use defense, then it can also, by the same means, restrict a purchaser from asserting the "first sale" defense, embodied in 17 U.S.C. §109(a), or any other of the protections Congress has afforded the public in the Copyright Act. That means that, under the majority's reasoning, state law could extensively undermine the protections of the Copyright Act.

V

The Fifth Circuit's decision in *Vault* directly supports preemption of the shrinkwrap limitation. The majority states that *Vault* held that "a state law prohibiting all copying of a computer program is preempted by the federal Copyright Act" and then states that "no evidence suggests the First Circuit would extend this concept to include private contractual agreements supported by mutual assent and consideration." But, in fact, the Fifth Circuit held that the specific provision of state law that authorized contracts prohibiting reverse engineering, decompilation, or disassembly of computer programs was preempted by federal law because it conflicted with a portion of the Copyright Act and because it "'touche[d] upon an area' of federal copyright law." 847 F.2d at 269-70 (quoting *Sears, Roebuck*, 376 U.S. at 229, 84 S. Ct. 784). From a preemption standpoint, there is no distinction between a state law that explicitly validates a contract that restricts reverse engineering (*Vault*) and general common law that permits such a restriction (as here). On the contrary, the preemption clause of the Copyright Act makes clear that it covers "any such right or equivalent right in any such work *under the common law or statutes of any State.*" 17 U.S.C. §301(a) (2000) (emphasis added).

I do not read ProCD, Inc. v. Zeidenberg, 86 F.3d 1447 (7th Cir. 1996), the only other court of appeals shrinkwrap case, as being to the contrary, even though it contains broad language stating that "a simple two-party contract is not 'equivalent to any of the exclusive rights within the general scope of copyright.'" *Id.* at 1455. In *ProCD*, the Seventh Circuit validated a shrink-wrap license that restricted the use of a CD-ROM to non-commercial purposes, which the defendant had violated by charging users a fee to access the CD-ROM over the Internet. The court held that the restriction to non-commercial use of the program was not equivalent to any rights protected by the Copyright Act. Rather, the "contract reflect[ed] private ordering, essential to efficient functioning of markets." *Id.* at 1455. The court saw the licensor as legit-imately seeking to distinguish between personal and commercial use. "ProCD offers software and data for two prices: one for personal use, a higher prices for commercial use," the court said. The defendant "wants to use the data without paying the seller's price." *Id.* at 1454. The court also emphasized that the license "would not withdraw any information from the public domain" because all of the information on the CD-ROM was publicly available. *Id.* at 1455.

The case before us is different from *ProCD*. The Copyright Act does not confer a right to pay the same amount for commercial and personal use. It does, however, confer a right to fair use, 17 U.S.C. §107, which we have held encompasses reverse engineering.

ProCD and the other contract cases are also careful not to create a blanket rule that all contracts will escape preemption. The court in that case emphasized that "we think it prudent to refrain from adopting a rule that anything with the label 'contract' is necessarily outside the preemption clause." 86 F.3d at 1455. It also noted with approval another court's "recogni[tion of] the possibility that some applications of the law of contract could interfere with the attain-ment of national objectives and therefore come within the domain" of the Copyright Act. *Id.* The Eighth Circuit too cautioned in *National Car Rental* that a contractual restriction could impermissibly "protect rights equivalent to the exclusive copyright rights." 991 F.2d at 432.

I conclude that *Vault* states the correct rule; that state law authorizing shrinkwrap licenses that prohibit reverse engineering is preempted; and that the First Circuit would so hold because the extra element here "merely concerns *the extent to which* authors and their licensees can prohibit unauthorized copying by third parties." *Data Gen.*, 36 F.3d at 1165 (emphasis in original). I respectfully dissent.

EUROPEAN UNION LEGISLATION

Council Directive of 14 May 1991 on the legal protection of computer programs (91/250/EEC)

ARTICLE 6

Decompilation

1. The authorization of the rightholder shall not be required where reproduction of the code and translation of its form within the meaning of Article 4(a) and (b) are indispensable to obtain the information necessary to achieve the interoperability of an independently created computer program with other programs, provided that the following conditions are met:

(a) these acts are performed by the licensee or by another person having a right to use a copy of a program, or on their behalf by a person authorized to to so;

(b) the information necessary to achieve interoperability has not previously been readily available to the persons referred to in subparagraph (a); and

(c) these acts are confined to the parts of the original program which are necessary to achieve interoperability.

2. The provisions of paragraph 1 shall not permit the information obtained through its application:

(a) to be used for goals other than to achieve the interoperability of the independently created computer program;

(b) to be given to others, except when necessary for the interoperability of the independently created computer program; or

(c) to be used for the development, production or marketing of a computer program substantially similar in its expression, or for any other act which infringes copyright.

3. In accordance with the provisions of the Berne Convention for the protection of Literary and Artistic Works, the provisions of this Article may not be interpreted in such a way as to allow its application to be used in a manner which unreasonably prejudices the right holder's legitimate interests or conflicts with a normal exploitation of the computer program.

III. PROBLEMS

1. The following problems deal with custom software development.

1.1 Sayoko is a student at Carnegie Mellon University studying computer science. During the summer she worked for the Kirkland Little League organization (KLL), where she used to play fast pitch softball. She has developed a software program for KLL to assist with player registration. The software allows a parent or guardian to register a child to play using KLL's Web site. As a parent or guardian completes the registration form online, the information about the child gets stored in a database. As the day for try-outs approaches, a notification goes out via e-mail.

Sayoko designed her software to work with the software KLL uses for its player try-outs and draft. For example, the try-out scores must be recorded in the database created by Sayoko. The same e-mail notification system that notifies parents about the tryouts must also notify parents about what team has drafted their child.

Sayoko's classmate, Slava, specializes in user interface design. One summer while visiting Sayoko, Slava designed the user interface for the registration software. It incorporated some original ideas and designs that Slava had developed as part of his senior honors project which, in turn, is part of a larger research project being done by one of his professors.

Sayoko wrote most of the source code on her laptop but she did most of the testing on KLL's servers at KLL's site. Slava designed the user interface on one of Sayoko's old laptops. Both Sayoko and Slava worked closely with a KLL parent volunteer who works as the computer system administrator for KLL. KLL paid Sayoko a lump sum stipend for her work, but Slava did his work as a favor to Sayoko although he did get unlimited, free use of a batting cage run by KLL.

Who owns the software written by Sayoko? Who owns the software written by Slava? Is either the software written by Sayoko or Slava a "work made for hire" under United States copyright law? Is any software a joint work? If Sayoko or Slava owns the software, what licenses should the KLL get for the software? If KLL owns the software, what licenses should Sayoko and Slava get? What rights does Carnegie Mellon University or Slava's professor have? What licenses should they get if they do not own the rights?

1.2 Assume that Slava worked on enhancements and bug fixes to his user interface software the following summer when he worked as a contractor for Google and into the autumn when he had a permanent job at Amazon. In his development work, Slava used his own laptop, PCs at KLL, and various computers at Google and Amazon. He consulted on the design frequently with folks from the KLL and got advice from his mangers at Google and Amazon. How does this change the ownership equation? What licenses would you advise to properly allocate rights?

2. The following problem deals with collaboration on a new software and hardware platform.

Dependable Computing Company (DCC) is an established player in the computer industry. Its mini-computer, the Dependable2, is one of the leading computers used by large corporate end users. DCC created all aspects of the Dependable2, including the microprocessor, the operating system, the developer tools, and the applications software. However, personal computers ("PCs") are fast becoming as powerful as mini-computers, doing many things the Dependable2 can do at a fraction of the price.

DCC distributes PCs running PCSoft's GUIDuck operating system, but these computers are only good enough for running personal productivity applications, not heavy duty applications like e-mail routing, transaction processing, or database management. However, PCSoft is developing a new industrial strength operating system called MightyOS that is designed to run industrial strength applications. One of the advantages of MightyOS is that it is easily portable to different microprocessors, such as DCC's newly created Mars processor.

The executives from DCC and PCSoft met to discuss collaboration. They agreed on the following deal points:

- DCC will port MightyOS source code to the Mars processor with assistance from PCSoft.
- DCC will distribute MightyOS on DCC's PCs.
- DCC and PCSoft will jointly develop a compiler for creating applications for MightyOS running on Mars, using PCSoft's existing C/C++ "front end" user interface and DCC's "back end" code generator, and PCSoft will distribute the compiler as part of its C/C++ developer tool product.
- PCSoft will port its popular GoodStuff personal productivity software (word processor, spreadsheet, and presentation graphics) to the MightyOS/Mars platform.
- DCC will port its e-mail system to the MightyOS/Mars platform.

Describe the licenses for each deal point. Discuss the types of intellectual property being licensed, and within each type of intellectual property, what rights would be granted. Discuss license parameters such as scope of use and duration. Discuss any materials that need to be exchanged (e.g., documentation).

3. The following problems deal with distribution and use.

   3.1 Blast Software Ltd. (Blast) has developed advanced language translation software known as "Libero." It allows a user to speak his or her native language into a handheld computer or cell phone, and the software will translate the input on the fly and "speak" the foreign language in the user's own voice tone. The Libero software comes with five base languages: English, Japanese, German, French, and Mandarin. Other languages may be added via add-on modules. Blast has created some of these modules, but others have been created by third parties whose software plugs into the Libero system by calling certain application programming interfaces (APIs).

   Blast intends to distribute its products both preinstalled on hardware devices and via download from retail Web sites such as eBay and Amazon.com. In terms of its pricing, it is considering several different tiers: an expensive, full-featured product for the corporate market; a lower priced product for the consumer market; and an even lower priced product for the education market. In addition, Blast would like to provide its product to international relief agencies and human rights organizations free of charge. Blast is concerned about price arbitrage: someone acquiring a free or low-priced version of the product who then distributes it into a different market.

   Outline Blast's end user licensing strategy based on the facts, including whether a EULA is needed at all. What provisions would be in the EULA? Should it prohibit reverse engineering? As a small start-up venture, Blast would like to provide its software with no warranties, limit its liability to the extent possible, and litigate any case in Houston, Texas, because it fears being subject to litigation around the globe. Would these provisions be enforceable in a standard form EULA?

   3.2 How should the EULA be presented to the end user? Write a best practices memo to your client for an enforceable EULA. How do you expect the client to react to your memo? How would you work with your client to resolve the client's concerns? Does it depend on the method of distribution?

   3.3 Blast's President requests the addition of the following provision to its EULA:

   > Licensee agrees that it shall not use any information from the software that allows the Licensee to compete with Libero for the term of this EULA. Licensee understands and agrees that this provision is part of the consideration for the license granted hereunder.

   What would you advise as counsel for Blast? If you were a court reviewing the provision, what are the different approaches that you could take to eliminate the possible improper effects of the provision?

   3.4 Assume the provision in Problem 3.3 was contained in a license with software developers who were using Blast software tools and information to write add-on language software. Would that change your analysis of the provision?

3.5 In ten years Blast has become the dominant provider of language translation software, with over 70 percent of the U.S. market and 60 percent of the market in Europe. Blast's core Libero product now consists of ten languages, including Spanish. The Spain-based subsidiary of a Mexican software company, DigaMe Co., has complained to the European Union authorities about the inclusion of a Spanish-language module in the base Libero product. DigaMe's Spanish-language add-on product currently has 80 percent of the market for add-on products in the United States and Europe as well as 95 percent in Latin America. DigaMe challenged the fact that Blast now charges developers a fee for API information. It has also challenged the following provisions in an exclusive distribution license that Blast has with Samsung:

> Libero shall be the only translation software pre-installed on Samsung's head-sets which it distributes in the European and Latin American markets.
>
> Blast has provided Samsung with certain trade secret information about Libero interfaces and therefore Samsung shall not develop any software that competes with Libero for the term of the Agreement and five years thereafter.
>
> Upon the initial start up of the Samsung headset models listed in Attachment 1, the headset shall display a banner advertisement promoting Blast's language module add-on software. This banner advertisement shall be the exclusive advertisement for language translation software on these models.
>
> In the event Samsung displays a banner advertisement promoting Blast's language module add-on software for the Samsung headset models listed in Attachment 2, Samsung shall receive a discount of 5% off the royalties due in the Agreement.

Analyze DigaMe's claims. Would the analysis change if DigaMe controlled a smaller percentage of the U.S., European, or Latin American markets for Spanish-language add-ons? A larger percentage? Should worldwide market share matter? What actions would you advise Blast to take in response to DigaMe's compaints?

4. The following question deals with open source licensing.

   4.1 Pipsqueak Software, a Canadian company, has developed an Internet browser designed especially for users under 12 years of age. This browser, known as HoundPup, was derived from a browser that is licensed under the GPL 2.0. The first version (v1) of the HoundPup software was distributed on CDs, which were enclosed in various children's breakfast cereal boxes. Then, Pipsqueak entered into an agreement with Samsung to embed another version of HoundPup (v2) in a Linux-based cell phone made especially for kids. Pipsqueak arranged for a third version (v3) to be distributed pre-installed on the hard drive of an inexpensive PC, which will be distributed by the United Nations to orphanages around the world. HoundPup v3 was substantially re-written and now contains less than 5 percent of the original browser code, although it now relies increasingly on calls to functionality provided by the GNU/Linux operating system (also licensed under the GPL with

Torvalds's clarifying "NOTE," which can be found in the Materials section of this chapter).

Now that HoundPup has become popular among young computer users, Sony has approached Pipsqueak about forming a joint venture to distribute HoundPup on a variety of Sony hardware devices. As part of the joint venture agreement, Sony will create a layer of code to enable HoundPup to run on Sony devices (this is called "port code"). Sony anticipates that this port code can be derived from other port code that Sony has written in the past. Sony considers its port code to be very proprietary because it reveals trade secret information about Sony's hardware.

Pipsqueak, for its part, has agreed to redesign the HoundPup user interface and re-write HoundPup as needed to run on the port code. Pipsqueak will also design some software that will enable HoundPup to interact well with a planned Internet gaming site that Sony plans as part of the joint venture. Portions of that software will be incorporated into the browser, but other portions will run on the server. The software uses some routines, algorithms, and ideas from HoundPup.

In which, if any, scenarios will Pipsqueak and/or Sony be required to release the source code of its software under the GPL 2.0.? If the parties' goal is to minimize the release of source code, what strategies could they employ?

4.2 Pipsqueak is considering the use of a new plain language implementation of GPL 2.0 known as the Simple Public License (SimPL):

Simple Public License (SimPL) 2.0

Preamble
This Simple Public License 2.0 (SimPL for short) is a plain language implementation of GPL 2.0. The words are different, but the goal is the same — to guarantee for all users the freedom to share and change software. If anyone wonders about the meaning of the SimPL, they should interpret it as consistent with GPL 2.0.

License
The SimPL applies to the software's source and object code and comes with any rights that I have in it (other than trademarks). You agree to the SimPL by copying, distributing, or making a derivative work of the software.

You get the royalty-free right to:

- Use the software for any purpose;
- Make derivative works of it (this is called a "Derived Work");
- Copy and distribute it and any Derived Work.

If you distribute the software or a Derived Work, you must give back to the community by:

- Prominently noting the date of any changes you make;
- Leaving other people's copyright notices, warranty disclaimers, and license terms in place;
- Providing the source code, build scripts, installation scripts, and interface definitions in a form that is easy to get and best to modify;
- Licensing it to everyone under SimPL, or substantially similar terms (such as GPL 2.0), without adding further restrictions to the rights provided;
- Conspicuously announcing that it is available under that license.

There are some things that you must shoulder:

- You get NO WARRANTIES. None of any kind;
- If the software damages you in any way, you may only recover direct damages up to the amount you paid for it (that is zero if you did not pay anything). You may not recover any other damages, including those called "consequential damages." (The state or country where you live may not allow you to limit your liability in this way, so this may not apply to you).

The SimPL continues perpetually, except that your license rights end automatically if:

- You do not abide by the "give back to the community" terms (your licensees get to keep their rights if they abide);
- Anyone prevents you from distributing the software under the terms of the SimPL.

It is important to Pipsqueak, from a marketing point of view, that any license that it uses complies with the Open Source Definition. Does the SimPL comply?

4.3 Pipsqueak asks your advice on choosing the best open source license for its browser software. Explain the advantages and disadvantages of choosing the BSD License, the SimPL, GPL 2.0, and GPL 3.0.

5. The following questions deal with contract law as it pertains to software licenses.

5.1 Do you think that UCC 2 or the common law of contracts provides the best contract law for software licenses? What about UCITA? The courts in *ProCD v. Zeidenberg* and *Specht v. Netscape* seemed to think that the choice of contract law mattered very little in the case before them. When would it matter?

5.2 How do UCC 2 implied and gap filler warranties mesh with the GPL and the BSD License? Should contract law allow open source EULAs to disclaim warranties and limit liability in ways that other EULAs cannot?

5.3 *Jacobsen v. Katzer* highlights the distinction between license conditions and pure contractual covenants. To what extent can license drafters choose whether a particular provision is a pure covenant or a license condition? Is a license infinitely malleable or should the law limit drafting flexibility in some manner? *See* MDY Industries LLC v. Blizzard Entertainment, Inc., 629 F.3d 928 (9th Cir. 2010) in the Materials section of Chapter 1. For a critique of the court's approach in the *MDY Industries* case, *see* Robert W. Gomulkiewicz, *Enforcing Open Source Software Licenses: The MDY Trio's Inconvenient Complications*, 14 Yale J.L. & Tech. 106 (2011).

6. The *Lasercomb* court draws on patent law to formulate a misuse defense for copyright. Do you agree that a misuse defense is as necessary for copyright as it is for patent law? The court in *Psystar* suggests that the copyright misuse defense should be applied sparingly. Do you agree, and if not, can you think of contexts in which courts should apply the misuse defense more liberally?

7. Looking back on the *United States v. Microsoft* case with 20/20 hindsight, how would you evaluate the court's decision? What do you think about antitrust enforcement as a tool to police anticompetitive behavior in technology markets?

IV. DRAFTING EXERCISES

1. Go back and look at the facts in Problem 1. Write a license grant from Sayoko that: 1) grants KLL the right to use the software for its operations; 2) permits KLL to grant rights to other youth softball and baseball organizations to use the software for their operations; 3) grants KLL the right to fix bugs and adapt the software; and 4) retains all other rights for Sayoko.

2. Draft the license grants for the deal points described in Problem 2.

3. Draft the license grant in Problem 3.1 for Libero's distribution license with a hardware device OEM and with an Internet retailer.

4. Go back and look at the facts in Problem 3. Draft the following provisions for Libero's EULA: license grant; limitation of liability; disclaimer of warranty; choice of venue; and prohibition on reverse engineering.

5. Revise the provision in Problem 3.3 so that it would survive a copyright misuse challenge yet meet Blast's business objectives.

6. Revise the license grant of the GPL 2.0 so that, in keeping with Linus Torvalds's NOTE!, it clearly provides that the use of kernel services do not require an application programmer to release the source code of an application that calls and uses kernel services.

7. Retaining the same intent, write a plain language version of the license grant sections of GPL 3.0.

8. Revise GPL 2.0 so that Sections 6 and 8 become license conditions rather than pure covenants.

9. Fill in the surviving terms in Section 8 of the Source Code License Agreement from the Materials section of this chapter.
10. Revise Section 6 of the Source Code License Agreement from the Materials section of this chapter so that the parties provide reciprocal warranties of non-infringement to one another.

· CHAPTER ·
10

INFORMATION AND DATABASE
LICENSING

I. OVERVIEW OF INFORMATION AND DATABASE
LICENSING

A. Introduction

Information, the facts representing knowledge of something, and data, the useful format into which information is processed for analysis or searching, are crucial to conducting business in the global economy. Collecting, analyzing, and classifying enormous volumes of information and raw data equate to huge profits for those businesses able to harness its power through information and data processing. Every day, Wal-Mart uploads 20 million point-of-sale transactions to a computer system with myriad processors running a centralized database. Wal-Mart rapidly turns this raw data into significant insights about its customers and markets to guide marketing, supply chain management, and other strategic aspects of its business.

Wal-Mart is not alone. Businesses and other organizations that sell or use electronic information and databases pervade the modern economy. For example:

- The NASDAQ stock exchange conducts its transactions using computers rather than by using human floor traders. NASDAQ's computer system processes the information necessary for traders to buy and sell millions of shares of stock on an hourly basis. Not only does NASDAQ earn revenue from processing stock trades, it earns revenue from selling real-time access to the stock prices themselves;
- Westlaw and Lexis/Nexis sell electronic access to large databases of public domain cases, statutes, and regulations;

- *Consumer Reports* sells electronic access to its product reviews and rating information;
- Hospitals, doctors' offices, and pharmacies create and control large databases of patient information. This information is often shared amongst them in the course of patient treatment. Sometimes it is shared with insurance companies for billing purposes. Sometimes it is shared with researchers for medical and epidemiological research;
- eBay's Web site contains information about thousands of products for sale in its auctions and stores. It also provides systems for traders to bid in auctions and pay for items purchased;
- The Sloan Digital Sky Survey is building an electronic database of all the stars, planets, and other bodies in the galaxies of the universe. This database will allow scientists to conduct research in many fields, including astrophysics, astronomy, and computer science;
- A small venture in Suriname gathers electronic consumer data through various means and sells its lists to spammers; and
- 7-Eleven convenience stores share customer data with their suppliers to keep inventory at optimal levels.

Individuals also use electronic information. Electronic information has become key to performing many routine tasks of everyday life. Just think about what you do before you leave for law classes in the morning — you surf the Internet to get your news and the weather, you pay your overdue credit card bills by phone or through Internet bill pay services, you grab your laptop, cardkey, and cell phone or personal digital assistant (PDA) as you whisk through the door, you listen to XM stereo or a news program while driving to class, and you use your prepaid meal card to grab a coffee and a muffin to keep you company while you sit in class resisting the urge to check e-mail or send a text message to your moot court partner. All of these routine tasks that you accomplish during the day in some way rely upon the use of electronic information or data.

Turn now to a common personal transaction — purchasing a reliable used car. How will a prospective car buyer determine what to buy? S/he might purchase a copy of *Consumer Reports* magazine from the newsstand, visit the library to consult a variety of car-related publications, and visit several car dealers in the area. The modern consumer, however, might decide to get free product reviews from the Carpoint Web site and purchase information on high/low car prices for certain car models from Consumer Reports' electronic service. S/he might use one of several information aggregation Web sites that allow for the purchase of compiled data about specific vehicles, like Carfax® or Edwards®. Upon narrowing the choices to a few models, the consumer browses the online inventories of several dealers that include a picture of the car, video "tours" of the car's interior, descriptions of its features, and pricing information. When the consumer is sufficiently armed with information, s/he might avoid the pressure tactics of an in-person visit to the car dealer by conducting the negotiations over e-mail. If the consumer does not get a good price, s/he might try purchasing a car in an online auction.

B. Incentive to Enter the Information Digitization and Aggregation Business

The Internet has made it possible to distribute electronic information as described above. The Internet has also facilitated new ways to package and repackage information goods for consumption. In fact, the Internet and new distribution methods have generated strong incentives to develop business models based upon aggregation and disaggregation of information goods.

Before discussing incentives, let's define information aggregation and disaggregation. "Information aggregation is a service that gathers relevant information from multiple sources to provide convenience and add value by analyzing that aggregated information for specific objectives. . . ." *See* Hongwei Zhu, Michael D. Siegel & Stuart E. Madnick, *Information Aggregation—A Value-Added E-Service*, Paper 106 (June 2001). Information disaggregation is the extraction of small bits of previously bundled digitized information or data.

Now, what are the incentives for entering the business of information aggregation and disaggregation? One incentive derives from the near-zero marginal costs associated with networking, processing, and storing information, all of which make information aggregation goods and post-aggregation services profitable. Another incentive draws from the ability to extract or disaggregate information to achieve perfect price discrimination that maximizes an information seller's profits. Perfect price discrimination allows a seller of information to capture an individual consumer's interest in extracted or disaggregated information. For example, a seller of information may find a profitable niche in selling small units of information, for limited periods of time, to a limited audience. Thus, instead of having to purchase an entire newspaper to read just one article, the Internet and digitization make it possible to enter a transaction to access the one story the consumer would like to read without committing to purchasing the entire newspaper.

C. The Impact of Privatizing Information and Data

Roughly speaking, two parties, at times having disparate interests, are involved in the information industry. At one end of the spectrum is the data subject, an individual exercising control over the flow of her personal information and, in many cases, expecting freedom from violations of information privacy caused by unauthorized secondary uses of personal information collected for an authorized primary use. At the other end of the spectrum are data aggregators who collect, use, and disclose the personal information of others for commercial purposes. In response to balancing the interests between these two parties, several approaches for protection of information have surfaced. One such approach is the information market-based approach.

The information market-based approach seeks to privatize information by promoting information as a property right. The impact of privatization from the perspective of the data subject is being aware of the collection of personal information and making a choice about disclosure and whether to proceed in a primary transaction.

If disclosure for the primary transaction is made, the data subject expects protection from secondary use disclosures that s/he has not agreed to, either implicitly or explicitly. The effect of information privatization at the data subject level is the subject's retention of the right of transfer of personal information and the attendant complexities relating to negotiation and enforcement of the property right in transactions with data users and aggregators.

With respect to information users and aggregators, the market-based approach also recognizes their interests in collecting and aggregating information. Typically, aggregators collect information for the primary purpose of completing a transaction with data subjects, but aggregators also profit from the business generated by secondary uses of information, i.e., providing third-party access to aggregated information. The drawback associated with information privatization at the data user/aggregator level is the cost associated with private, self-regulation of secondary uses of a subject's personal information and the management of the possessory rights transferred from the data subject to the data user/aggregator. What additional concerns are raised by the privatization of information and data? *See* section G of this Overview.

D. Legal Protection for Information: Limited U.S. Protection

As explained above, there are strong incentives for entering the information and data aggregation business and, in fact, these incentives have created a colossal, powerful information industry. Despite this huge industry, legal protections and related policies for digital information, data, and databases remain tenuous. The United States has avoided enacting general data protection rules in favor of specific sectoral laws governing, for example, video rental records and financial privacy. In such cases, enforcement is achieved through a range of mechanisms. A major drawback with this approach is that it requires that new legislation be introduced with each new technology. For example, the U.S. Copyright Act does not generally protect raw data or even aggregated information. The Supreme Court, in Feist Publ'ns, Inc. v. Rural Tel. Serv. Co., 499 U.S. 340 (1991), interpreted the Copyright Act and concluded that databases and collections of information qualify for only thin copyright protection — the copyright only applies to the original selection, coordination, or arrangement of facts. The *Feist* decision is no comfort to database makers and information aggregators who invest millions in hopes of earning millions more from their information products.

Even with thin or no copyright protection, the U.S. Congress has yet to enact comprehensive, generally applicable legislation to protect collections of information or databases; instead, possessors of these assets must rely on a patchwork of U.S. laws that are fragmented in nature with each law having application only to a specific sector. For example, the federal judiciary has decided that there is limited protection against the misappropriation of so-called "hot news." *See* International News Service v. Associated Press, 248 U.S. 215 (1918) (holding that the news originally collected by Associated Press was not copyrightable, but defendant's copying of AP's compiled news constituted free riding, which supported the conclusion that INS violated unfair competition law), and National Basketball Ass'n v. Motorola, 105 F.3d 841 (2d Cir. 1997) (recognizing and affirming "hot news" misappropriation as a valid claim against free riding and the direct competitive use of another's information gathered at significant cost in support of an ongoing business). In certain cases, state law claims of trespass to chattels have been effective in protecting the investment in information where taking the information causes injury to the information processing systems. *See* eBay, Inc. v. Bidder's Edge, Inc., 100 F. Supp. 2d 1058 (N.D. Cal. 2000) (relying on trespass to chattels doctrine to prevent the defendant's computer bots from crawling eBay's auction Web site for the purpose of using eBay's data along with data from other auction Web sites to yield a larger aggregate auction Web site); *but see* Intel Corp. v. Hamidi, 30 Cal. 4th 1342, 71 P.3d 296, 1 Cal. Rptr. 3d 32 (2003) (denying Intel's request for injunction premised upon a trespass to chattels theory because the Supreme Court of California concluded that Intel did not present evidence that a former employee's unsolicited e-mails interfered with the efficient functioning of Intel's computer system).

In addition, possessors of information assets have looked to federal legislation to protect information and databases in certain contexts. For example, the Computer Fraud and Abuse Act (CFAA), §1030(g) provides for both criminal and civil actions. With respect to the civil right of action, the CFAA prohibits unauthorized access to a protected computer; the prohibition extends to obtaining information from a protected computer. In order to maintain an action under the CFAA, the prohibition rests on unauthorized conduct involving interstate or foreign communication and requires damage or loss to be incurred in the amount of at least $5,000. Furthermore, the No Electronic Theft Act (Net Act), Pub. L. No. 105-147, 111 Stat. 2678 (1978), which amended 17 U.S.C. §506, increased the severity of the criminal penalty for infringement of copyright or protected material undertaken willfully (1) for purposes of commercial advantage or private financial gain; or (2) by the reproduction or distribution, within a certain time period, of one or more copies or phonorecords of one or more copyrighted works, which have a total value of more than $1,000.

E. European Union Protections

1. European Union Directive on the Legal Protection of Databases

In many countries, there is a general law that governs the collection, use, and dissemination of personal information by both the public and private sectors. This is the model for most countries adopting data protection laws and was adopted by the European Union to ensure compliance with its data protection regime. Thus, in contrast to the United States approach of fragmented legal protection, the European Union has taken the position, through its Database Directive, that protection for databases and collections of information under a generally applicable regulatory scheme will facilitate the proper functioning of internal markets. *See* Directive 96/9/EC of the European Parliament and of the Council of 11 March 1996 on the Legal Protection of Databases, OJ L 77, 27.3.1996, 20-28.

The EU Database Directive creates a legal framework that establishes the ground rules for the protection of a wide variety of databases: (1) a harmonized level of protection of "original" databases under copyright for the structure of a database — but not its contents — by reason of its arrangement and selection; and (2) the introduction of a new *sui generis* right to protect investments in databases, specifically, protecting against unauthorized extraction of all or a substantial part, considered quantitatively or qualitatively, of the contents of any database produced through substantial investment. The Directive also provides for certain exceptions. Any "lawful user" may use "insubstantial parts" of the contents of a database without incurring liability. Permitted uses include extraction for "private purposes" (from the contents of a "non-electronic database"), as well as extraction for purposes of teaching, scientific research, public security, and administrative or judicial procedure. The extraction right, however, does not give control over the information, but merely over the right to restrict access to the information from the particular resource.

Despite EU goals to provide broad protection for databases and collections of information, the European Court of Justice has narrowly applied the Directive to protect only the collection, verification, and presentation of data for use in databases. This narrow reading of the Directive, therefore, extends protection only to the obtaining of existing data in order to assemble the contents of a database. *See* British Horse-racing Board Ltd. v. William Hill, 2004 WL 2709083, [2005] C.E.C. 68, [2005] 1 C.M.L.R. 15, [2004] ECR I-10415, [2005] Info. T.L.R. 157, [2005] R.P.C. 13, [2005] E.C.D.R. 1, Celex No. 602J0203, EU: Case C-203/02, ECJ (Nov. 09, 2004) (holding that investments protected by the *sui generis* right are the resources expended in gathering information and collecting that information into a database, not in developing or creating a process to generate data itself.). This case can be found in the Materials section of this chapter.

2. European Union General Data Protection Regulation

The General Data Protection Regulation (GDPR) is the European Union's (EU's) new omnibus law adopted on April 27, 2016, and entering into force on May 25, 2018.[1] The Regulation is intended to strengthen and unify data protection for individuals in the EU. When the Regulation enters into force, it will replace Directive 95/46/EC of the European Parliament and of the Council of October 24, 1995, on the protection of individuals with regard to the processing of personal data.

The purpose of the Regulation is to "ensure an equivalent level of protection of natural persons and the free flow of personal data throughout the Union[.]" The Regulation acknowledges that, although not absolute, "the protection of natural persons in relation to the processing of personal data is a fundamental right." Specifically,

---

1. Regulation 2016/679 of the European Parliament and of the Council of 27 March 2016 on the Protection of Natural Persons with Regard to the Processing of Personal Data and on the Free Movement of Such Data, and Repealing Directive 95/46/EC (General Data Protection Regulation), 2016 O.J. (L 119) 1 [hereinafter *GDPR*]; *id.* art. 99, at 87.

Article 1(2) states: the Regulation "protects the fundamental rights and freedoms of natural persons and in particular their right to the protection of personal data." At the same time, Article 1(3) balances the interests of controllers and processors by providing "[t]he free movement of personal data within the Union shall be neither restricted nor prohibited for reasons connected with the protection of natural persons with regard to the processing of personal data."

The Regulation covers professional and commercial activities, not the processing of personal data by a natural person in the course of purely personal or household activity. In regard to the latter, "[t]he Regulation applies to the processing of personal data in the context of the activities of an establishment of a controller or processor in the Union, regardless of whether the processing takes place in the Union or not."

Pursuant to the Regulations, the standard for processing is that it be lawful, fair, and transparent (LFT) in relation to the data subject and collected for specified, explicit, and legitimate purposes and not further processed in an incompatible manner. The Regulation establishes general rights of the data subject and further articulates heightened rights for special categories of individuals, for example, children. Rights include, but are not limited to, information and access to personal data, rectification and erasure, restrictions on processing of personal data, portability of data, and lodging objections.

The Regulation obligates controller and processors, among other things, to implement data protection policies, adhere to approved codes of conduct, implement data protection by design and by default, maintain records of processing activities, implement proportional security measures to protect personal data, provide breach notices and communications, carryout data protection impact assessments, and designate data protection officers. The Regulation brings into its purview the transfer of personal data undergoing processing or intended for processing after transfer to a third country or to an international organization — inclusive of onward transfers of personal data to additional countries or international organizations. The Regulation allows such transfers to take place only if, subject to other provisions of the Regulation, controllers and processors comply with the conditions in Chapter V of the Regulation. Even more notable, Article 68 of the Regulation establishes the European Data Protection Board as a body of the Union that acts independently when performing its tasks or exercising its power and authority to ensure the consistent application of the Regulation. Significantly, the Regulation provides for remedies and the imposition of liability, fines, and penalties.

3. The Fall of the Safe Harbor Framework and the Rise of the Privacy Shield

Cross-border transfer of data from the European Union to the United States is vital to the information economy. Harmonizing EU and US privacy laws have presented significant challenges for businesses in the information economy. As illustrated above, the EU has strong privacy protection for natural persons, and it deems current U.S. protections inadequate primarily because the US lacks a comprehensive federal data protection framework. To transfer personal information, such as information relating to customers, vendors, and employees, from the EEA and Switzerland to affiliates or service providers in inadequate countries, organizations must either: (1) put an EU-approved transfer mechanism in place; or (2) qualify for a statutory exception.

In July 2000, the EU Commission approved the EU-US Safe Harbor Framework as a method of providing adequate protection for data transfers to the US under Commission Decision 2000/520/EC. Thousands of US companies used the Safe Harbor to support cross-border data transfers from the EU. However, on October 6, 2015, the ECJ issued an opinion in Maximillian Schrems v. Data Protection Commissioner, in which it declared Decision 2000/520/EC invalid and, therefore, invalidated the Safe Harbor Framework (Case C-362/14).

Prior to *Schrems*, the EU and US were already in negotiations to adopt a replacement framework. That new framework is the EU-US Privacy Shield, which supports cross-border personal information data transfers by businesses from EU member states to the US.

The EU-U.S. Privacy Shield (Privacy Shield) was designed by the U.S. Department of Commerce (DOC) and the European Commission (Commission) to provide companies on both sides of the Atlantic with a mechanism to comply with data protection requirements when transferring personal data from the European Union (EU) to the United States in support of transatlantic commerce. On July 12, 2016, the Commission deemed the Privacy Shield adequate to enable data transfers under EU law, and on August 1, 2016, the DOC began accepting self-certifications from U.S. companies to join the program, which is voluntary.

To be eligible to participate in the Privacy Shield program, the organization must be subject to the jurisdiction of the FTC or DOT. By self-certifying, a company is committing itself publicly to complying with the Privacy Shield Principles (including Supplemental Principles), which commitment is enforceable under U.S. law through either the Federal Trade Commission (FTC) or Department of Transportation (DOT).

The Privacy Shield serves as a bridge between two very different data protection regimes influenced by significant cultural differences in their conception of privacy. The Privacy Shield Principles incorporate many core EU data protection principles and some of them go far beyond generally accepted and customary privacy practices in the U.S.

Below is a summary of the Privacy Shield Principles:

- Notice. Notice to individuals must be timely provided in *clear and conspicuous* language. It also must contain certain prescribed information about the organization's privacy practices, including its participation in Privacy Shield and, in the event of a dispute, *the individual's right to use an independent dispute resolution provider free of charge and to invoke binding arbitration.*
- Choice. Organizations must provide individuals the opportunity to choose (opt-out) whether their personal information is to be disclosed to a third party or to be used for a purpose that is materially different from the purpose(s) for which it was originally collected. For *sensitive information* (i.e., personal information specifying medical or health conditions, racial or ethnic origin, political opinions, religious or philosophical beliefs, trade union membership or information

specifying the sex life of the individual), organizations must obtain *affirmative express consent* (opt-in) from individuals before disclosing such information to a third party or using it for a purpose other than those for which it was originally collected.

- Accountability for Onward Transfer. If an organization transfers personal information to a third party, the organization and the third party must enter into a contract that provides that the data may only be processed for limited and specific purposes consistent with the consent of the individual.
- Security. Organizations must use reasonable and appropriate measures, proportional to the risks involved in processing and the nature of the data, to protect personal information from loss, misuse and unauthorized access, disclosure, alteration, and destruction.
- Data Integrity and Purpose Limitation. Collection of personal information must be limited to the information that is relevant for the purpose of processing, and an organization may not process such information in a way that is *incompatible* with the purposes for which it has been collected.
- Access. Individuals must have access to personal information about them and be able to correct, amend, or delete that information where it is inaccurate or has been processed in violation of the Principles, except where the burden or expense of doing so is disproportionate to the risks to the individual's privacy in the case in question or where the rights of persons other than the individual would be violated.
- Recourse, Enforcement, and Liability. Organizations must put in place robust mechanisms to assure compliance with the Principles and consequences for the organization when the Principles are not followed, including at a minimum, *independent recourse mechanisms* by which each individual's complaints and disputes are investigated and expeditiously resolved, at no cost to the individual and by reference to the Principles, and damages awarded where the applicable law or private-sector initiatives so provide. In addition, if an individual invokes his right to binding arbitration, the organization is obligated to arbitrate the claim in accordance with the arbitration procedures set forth in Annex 1 of the Privacy Shield. In the context of an onward transfer, an organization *is* liable if its third party agent processes personal information in a manner inconsistent with the Principles, *unless* the organization *proves* that it is not responsible for the event giving rise to the damage.

The Privacy Shield Supplemental Principles, which are equally binding, augment the Principles and address the requirements for implementing the program for an organization based on the type of information being collected, stored, disclosed, or processed.[2]

---

2. These sixteen principles are: Sensitive Data; Journalistic Exceptions; Secondary Liability; Performing Due Diligence and Conducting Audits; the Role of the Data Protection Authorities; Access; Self-Certification; Verification; Human Resources Data; Obligatory Contracts for Onward Transfers; Dispute Resolution and Enforcement; Choice—Timing of Opt-Out; Travel Information; Pharmaceutical and Medical Products; Public Record and Publicly Available Information; and Access Requests by Public Authorities.

Currently, there is uncertainty about the interplay between the Privacy Shield and the General Data Protection Regulation. Among other things, the GDPR will expand the number of options for organizations that conduct cross border data transfers, including: binding corporate rules, standard contractual clauses, approved certification mechanisms, and/or DPA authorized contractual clauses.

It is not clear how Privacy Shield and the GDPR will work together, or even if they have to work together. During the Privacy Shield negotiations, the DOC and Commission were aware of and considered the GDPR. But there are significant gaps between the Privacy Shield and the GDPR. For example, the GDPR contains provisions relating to notification to regulators and EU citizens in the event of a data breach. The Privacy Shield Principles, however, are completely silent on the subject of data breach notification, even though such obligations have been widely accepted and incorporated into federal and state laws and regulations in the U.S.

Despite these questions, firms are self-certifying as being compliant with the Privacy Shield. To join the Privacy Shield Framework, a U.S.-based company will be required to self-certify to the Department of Commerce and publicly commit to comply with the Framework's requirements. While joining the Privacy Shield Framework will be voluntary, once an eligible company makes the public commitment to comply with the Framework's requirements, the commitment will become enforceable under U.S. law.

F. Licensing: The Legal Source for Business Models to Profit from Information

According to many data users and aggregators, the current legal landscape for protecting the proprietary interests in information and data leaves them wanting. Even in Europe protection appears relatively limited in light of the *British Horseracing* decision. Because of the general uncertainty in the United States, Europe, and now Asia regarding information and database protection, the question is "What law or legally recognized transactional models will provide adequate protection for these assets? As well, what protection regime(s) will respond to the needs of users and aggregators in the information industry who continue to invest in the creation of information goods and services for consumption by businesses, governments, universities, and individuals?" The answer increasingly has been the licensing model. In the context of information and databases, licensing generally accomplishes what copyright law does not — the creation of contractual rights. But businesses and their license drafters must recognize that information and data should be categorized in a very sophisticated manner. As one practitioner has observed, "some data will constitute personally identifiable information, some will be protected by intellectual property laws, some will belong to third parties and be subject to license restrictions, and some will be public domain."[3] Bearing this in mind, information "should be assigned to

---

3. William A. Tanenbaum, *Sharing Business Information in a High-Risk World*, 912 PLI/Pat 127 (2007).

different legal categories, using multiple axes of analysis, and [license drafters] should then apply the appropriate laws and policies to the relevant categories."[4] Multiple categories of data and their corresponding laws for protection and enforcement require license drafters to "drive data protection down to the data level."[5] This means that the drafter must exercise best practices in identifying data, isolating its uses, and determining the applicable law and policies in order to establish enforceable contractual rights in information and data. Below are several typical information licensing models.

1. Access/Site License for Information Browsing

Some Web sites simply provide information that is available for browsing. Examples of this type of Web site are yahoo.com and slate.com. An access or site license, also known as an unlimited use license, permits access to and use of digital information at a specific site. *See* Madison River Mgmt. Co. v. Business Mgmt. Software Corp., 387 F. Supp. 2d 521, 529 (M.D.N.C. 2005). The Uniform Computer and Information Transactions Act (UCITA), §611(a)(4), defines an access contract as "a contract to obtain by electronic means access to, or information from, an information processing system of another person, or the equivalent of such access." As applied to informational content, an access contract grants a licensee the right to obtain access to the articles, images, personal financial information, or other information located on a site. An example of a site or access license allowing for access and use for a limited purpose of information follows:

> Boeing Store, Inc. grants you a limited license to make personal use only of the Site. Such grant does not include, without limitation: (a) any resale or commercial use of the Site or content therein; (b) the collection and use of any product listings or descriptions; (c) making derivative uses of the Site and its contents; or (d) use of any data mining, robots, or similar data gathering and extraction methods. Except as noted above, you are not conveyed any right or license by implication, estoppel, or otherwise in or under any patent, trademark, copyright, or proprietary right of Boeing, Boeing Store, Inc., or any third party.

A more sophisticated version of an information access license would be the license a stockbroker might enter into to acquire real-time stock quotes from the NASDAQ stock exchange.

2. Online Content License

Certain Web sites provide access to content, such as photos, text, video, audio, and software. The user is invited to view the content and often download it. An example of a content Web site is corbis.com. An online content license agreement describes the

---

4. *Id.*
5. *Id.*

conditions, obligations, and payment structures under which a licensee is permitted to access or download the content. An example of an online content license agreement follows:

LICENSE

Through our Services, you will be provided with objects including their API's as well as images, photographs, templates, animations, video, audio, music, text and "applets," and "online" or electronic documentation (together called the "Digital Content"). You may use, modify and publish the Digital Content in accordance with the terms of this License Agreement. Any supplemental software code and supporting materials provided to you as part of support services for the Digital Content shall be considered part of the Digital Content and are subject to the terms and conditions of this License Agreement. The copyright and all other rights to the Digital Content shall remain with our licensors.

PERMITTED USE OF DIGITAL CONTENT

You may incorporate the Digital Content into your own original work and publish your work in a website provided that: The Digital Content is incorporated for viewing purposes only and no permission is given to download or save the Digital Content for any reason; and You continue to pay for the Service.

3. Database License

A database simply is a structured collection of data. *See* NAACP v. Acusport Corp., 210 F.R.D. 268 (E.D.N.Y. 2002) (explaining the general principles of databases). An example of a licensed electronic database is Westlaw or Lexis/Nexis. A database license agreement describes the conditions, obligations, and payment structures under which a licensee is permitted access to or use of a licensor's database. An example of a database license agreement follows:

Pursuant to the terms and conditions set forth in this Database License, Accessible grants Licensee a non-exclusive, non-transferable, limited license to use any or all Accessible databases ("Database") purchased by Licensee. Accessible shall make the Database available to the Licensee for use only by faculty, staff, students of the entity of which Licensee is a part, and/or walk-in users who are physically present in Licensee's buildings ("Users"). Persons affiliated with Licensee as students, faculty, or employees may have access to the Database off site. Such use shall be on the terms and conditions set forth in this On-Line Database License Agreement. Access to the Database shall be controlled by Accessible through the use of IP addresses and/or passwords.

4. Information and Transactions License

Some Web sites provide information but also enable transactions or other services. Examples of this type of site are eBay.com and Ticketmaster.com. The license agreement governing use of these sites must not only describe permitted uses of information on the site but the rules for conducting transactions on the site. The following is an example from eBay.com:

While using the Site, you will not:

- post content or items in an inappropriate category or areas on the Site;
- violate any laws, third party rights, or our policies such as the Prohibited and Restricted Items policies;
- use the Site if you are not able to form legally binding contracts, are under the age of 18, or are temporarily or indefinitely suspended from our Site;
- fail to deliver payment for items purchased by you, unless the seller has materially changed the item's description after you bid, a clear typographical error is made, or you cannot authenticate the seller's identity;
- fail to deliver items purchased from you, unless the buyer fails to meet the posted terms, or you cannot authenticate the buyer's identity;
- manipulate the price of any item or interfere with other user's listings;
- circumvent or manipulate our fee structure, the billing process, or fees owed to eBay;
- post false, inaccurate, misleading, defamatory, or libelous content (including personal information);
- take any action that may undermine the feedback or ratings systems (such as displaying, importing or exporting feedback information off of the Site or for using it for purposes unrelated to eBay);
- transfer your eBay account (including feedback) and User ID to another party without our consent;
- distribute or post spam, chain letters, or pyramid schemes;
- distribute viruses or any other technologies that may harm eBay, or the interests or property of eBay users;
- copy, modify, or distribute content from the Site and eBay's copyrights and trademarks; or
- harvest or otherwise collect information about users, including email addresses, without their consent.

Additionally, you agree that you will not:

- take any action that imposes or may impose (in our sole discretion) an unreasonable or disproportionately large load on our infrastructure;
- copy, reproduce, modify, create derivative works from, distribute, or publicly display any content (except for Your Information) from the Site without the prior expressed written permission of eBay and the appropriate third party, as applicable;
- interfere or attempt to interfere with the proper working of the Site or any activities conducted on the Site; or
- bypass our robot exclusion headers or other measures we may use to prevent or restrict access to the Site.

5. Information Sharing Licenses

It is common for businesses and non-profit entities to share information for a variety of productive purposes. This ranges from the sharing of patient data between a hospital, primary care doctor, and pharmacists, to the sharing of customer data between Wal-Mart and its suppliers. Each of these exchanges of information is governed by a license that describes the permitted uses of the information. For example, the American Cancer Society describes specific uses of the data it collects on its Web site. Its privacy policy provides for internal and external uses of data. Its policy states:

DATA USE

We limit the use of information provided to us on our Web site to the following:

Internal Use

1. If you do not make a service request, donation, purchase, or otherwise identify yourself, we will have no personally identifiable information about you. We will only use aggregate information derived, in part, from your use of our site to improve our site and our service to you.

2. If you provide personal information, we may enter your name into our constituent database and contact you in order to:

   - Complete voluntary surveys seeking feedback for quality and service improvement purposes.

   - Supply you with information including cancer related health news, ACS programs, events and services.

   - Request voluntary time or monetary contributions to ACS.

   - Request your participation in an ACS research study.

3. We collect the email addresses of those who communicate with us by email. Inquiries may be forwarded to the appropriate ACS department for response and may be entered into our constituent database. If your name is entered into the database, we may contact you (see (2) above).

External Use

Your health-related information is privileged and confidential and will not be shared or released to any organization or business entity other than those affiliated with or working in conjunction with ACS as follows:

1. We use third parties to provide you with the following services:
   a. **Cancer Profiler:** Disclosure of personal information is optional when using the cancer profiler. Additional services offered by NexCura are covered by their privacy policy and may require payment and disclosure.

b. **Clinical Trials:** If you are considering clinical trial participation and would like to seek a clinical trial match to your condition through EmergingMed (EM), you must create an ID and password, then answer medical questions. If you request a trial referral from ACS and EM, then ACS and EM will share your information with each other as part of the matching process. ACS will then contact you to discuss the details or provide further information.

2. We occasionally make our constituent names and postal addresses available to other reputable non-profit organizations. We have found this to be the most cost-effective method of increasing our database of potential constituents and hope that you value the information they send you. Your name is only made available to these carefully screened organizations through third-party mailing agents for a limited use. Other organizations will not have continued access to your name and address unless you choose to respond to their initial mailing. We do not share email addresses or health related data. Information gathered as part of Cancer Profiler or Clinical Trials (above) is not shared.

3. We occasionally hire other companies to provide limited services on our behalf. We will only provide those companies the information they need to deliver the service and prohibit them from using that information for any other purpose.

4. We have relationships with companies that conduct charitable sales promotions and commercial co-ventures that support us in our mission and activities. If you provide us with your mailing address, we may pass your contact information to these companies so that they may ask you if you are interested in receiving their services. Your choice to use their services will benefit us; the amount of money we receive from these entities as a result of your participation is disclosed at the time you are contacted about the service. You are under no obligation to respond and the companies are restricted from using your contact information for any other purpose. Information gathered as part of Cancer Profiler or Clinical Trials (above) is not shared.

---

6. Licenses for Supplying Information

In many cases businesses want to acquire information to include in their products or on their Web sites. Examples include information to include in an electronic encyclopedia or weather or traffic information to display on a Web site. A license agreement governs this acquisition of information and describes its permitted uses, pricing, and other terms.

G. Issues Surrounding Information and Data Licenses

Reliance on licenses has become a necessity for the information industry; however, there are a number of concerns related to the use of contracts to control use of and access to data and information. *See, e.g.*, Assessment Technologies of WI, LLC v. WIREdata, Inc., 350 F.3d 640 (7th Cir. 2003) (determining that the plaintiff's copyright infringement suit to protect its software, database, and the underlying data was an attempt to secrete the data in its copyrighted program — a program the existence of which reduced the likelihood that the data would be retained in a form in which they would have been readily accessible). This case can be found in the Materials section of this chapter. One concern relates to the contracting process itself. Are those who license information giving potential licensees a meaningful opportunity to review terms and manifest assent? Are licensors using the electronic format of licenses to hide terms or set up contracting schemes that are unfair, such as by allowing the licensor to amend terms simply by posting the amendment on a Web site that the licensee is required to check periodically? *Cf.* Ticketmaster L.L.C. v. RMG Tech., Inc., 507 F. Supp. 2d 1096 (C.D. Cal. 2007).

Other fundamental issues exist as well. Some question whether a party should have the right to control use of or access to information via contract. They reason that this information is in the public domain and therefore no one has the right to control it through any legal mechanism. A related point is that permitting control of data via contract disrupts the balance in the Copyright Act between subject matter entitled to exclusive rights and subject matter available for public use such as ideas, or by virtue of First Amendment rights of free expression. Courts by and large, however, have permitted use of licenses to govern use of someone's particular collection of information. *See* ProCD v. Zeidenberg, 86 F.3d 1447 (7th Cir. 1996).

Additional concerns arise when the data or information pertains to individuals, consumers, or patients. At the heart of these concerns are questions about what personal information is considered private and what uses of the information are considered improper. These concerns raise the all too important concern of a data subject's protection against violations of information privacy. In these instances, laws such as the Health Insurance Portability and Accountability Act (HIPAA)[6] and other privacy-related statutes

---

6. Title II of HIPAA defines numerous offenses relating to health care and sets civil and criminal penalties for them. It also creates several programs to control fraud and abuse within the health care system. The most significant provisions of Title II are its Administrative Simplification rules. Title II requires the Department of Health and Human Services (HHS) to draft rules aimed at increasing the efficiency of the health care system by creating standards for the use and dissemination of health care information. *See* 42 U.S.C. §1320a-7c; 45 C.F.R. 164.501. The Privacy Rule establishes regulations for the use and disclosure of Protected Health Information (PHI). PHI is any information about health status, provision of health care, or payment for health care that can be linked to an individual. This is interpreted rather broadly and includes any part of a patient's medical record or payment history. Covered entities must disclose PHI to the individual within 30 days upon request. A covered entity may disclose PHI to facilitate treatment, payment, or health care operations if the covered entity has obtained authorization from the individual. However, when a covered entity discloses any PHI, it must make a reasonable effort to disclose only the minimum necessary information required to achieve its purpose. The Privacy Rule gives individuals the right to request that a covered entity correct any inaccurate PHI. It also requires covered entities to take reasonable steps to ensure the confidentiality of communications with individuals. The Privacy Rule requires covered entities to notify individuals of uses of their PHI. Covered entities must also keep track of disclosures of PHI and document privacy policies and procedures. An individual who believes that the Privacy Rule is not being upheld can file a complaint with the Department of Health and Human Services Office for Civil Rights (OCR).

are invoked; but the question remains whether these laws adequately protect against violations of information privacy.

The significance of privacy policies in the area of licensing should not be underestimated. Now, more than ever, privacy issues are central to licensing practice, particularly with respect to online transactions and advertising. Growing fears over the use of consumer tracking and targeting practices in the field of online advertising have led to a formal complaint to the U.S. Federal Trade Commission (FTC) by two leading public-interest advocacy groups in the United States, the Center for Digital Democracy (CDD) and the U.S. Public Interest Research Group (US PIRG).

The groups launched the formal complaint on November 1, 2006, in response to what they view as the growing threat to consumer privacy posed by the new generation of online advertising and interactive marketing. These groups described as "unfair and deceptive online marketing practices," technologies that "aggressively track" Internet users wherever they go. The main cause for complaint is that consumers are not advised that their information is being collected to enable online advertisers to target consumers more effectively. While many of the advertising networks do not per se collate personal information (i.e., names and addresses), they do have sufficient information to track a user's every move.

The FTC faces significant challenges in policing this type of mass marketing, which is taking on an increasingly personalized angle. Advertisers and marketers now benefit from detailed analysis of consumers' Web-browsing behavior to deliver tailored campaigns to a more specific audience. Some privacy advocates have criticized the lack of market incentives that have as their object the protection of consumer privacy. The FTC has cited the "growing media universe" as the major obstacle to monitoring online marketing and advertising effectively and has recommended that companies themselves should play a more active role in ensuring consumer protection. That protection may include companies providing more clarity to consumers and a greater level of choice regarding the use of their data. *See* Ruth Hill Bro, *Government Enforcement and the Risks of Privacy Noncompliance*, 902 PLI/Pat 235 (2007).

The various unauthorized uses of an individual's information, of which society has been made painfully aware, i.e., data surveillance, data mining, identity theft, theft of computers and hard drives containing sensitive compiled information, data exchange, and data gathering, suggest that protection mechanisms, either legal or technical, are not adequate. These practices result in a data subject's personal information being exchanged or transferred without consent and often leads to the development of hidden information, such as consumer patterns, that may not even be conceived by the data subject. Most reputable actors in the information industry will provide data subjects and consumers with easy access to their online privacy policies. The question is, however, whether there is equal bargaining power between an individual seeking to protect personal information and businesses seeking further growth in the information industry. The intersection between contract, intellectual property, privacy, and constitutional law, among others, are explored in the Problems for this chapter.

II. MATERIALS

The materials in this section illustrate the various legal mechanisms relied upon by data users and aggregators to protect their interests in aggregated and disaggregated information. In particular, Ticketmaster Corp. v. Tickets.com, Inc., 2003 WL 21408289 (C.D. Cal.), 2003 Corp. L. Dec. ¶28,607, discusses the various theories for protecting information, such as breach of contract, trespass to chattels, and copyright infringement. *Ticketmaster* is of significant import for its analysis of the use of licenses to regulate conduct vis-à-vis employing terms of use license agreements to regulate commercial use of Internet-accessible information between two businesses.

Register.com, Inc. v. Verio, Inc., 356 F.3d 393 (2d Cir. 2004), another terms of use license case, examines breach of contract claims based upon unauthorized secondary uses of public access information. Specifically, this case analyzes the contract formation issue of whether there was acceptance of the terms of use prohibiting certain secondary uses of information in exchange for access to that information. The *Verio* case explains that the defendant's conduct of repeated online accessing of information is a manifestation of the intent to be bound by the plaintiff's terms of use license agreement.

Another important issue for information licensors and licensees is the access to public domain data. In Assessment Technologies of WI, LLC v. WIREdata, Inc., 350 F.3d 640 (7th Cir. 2003), the court dealt with a compilation copyright owner's attempt to prevent its licensees from disclosing public domain data to a third party on the basis that the data was bundled with the licensor's copyright protected software program. An example of an information disaggregation or extraction case, *Assessment Technologies* distinguishes between infringement copying of database items embedded in a program versus copying for the purpose of extracting noncopyrighted materials for a non-competing commercial use.

The European Court of Justice case, British Horseracing Board v. William Hill Org. Ltd, 2004 WL 2709083, EU: Case C-203/02, ECJ, Nov. 09, 2004, interprets the European Union Database Directive Article 7 regarding unauthorized extraction and/ or re-utilization of all or a substantial part of the contents of a database. The case represents the seminal European Court of Justice interpretation of the Directive, which narrowly construes the Directive as applying the *sui generis* right only to protect the substantial investment in collecting, verifying, and presenting existing material to be included in a database, as opposed to protecting the investment in creating underlying data generated from a database process. And finally, In the Matter of Decusoft, L.L.C. complaint and decision and order illustrate the Federal Trade Commission's approach to enforcing provisions of the Privacy Shield for the benefit of protecting EU citizens whose personal data is being transferred by companies from the European Union to the United States in support of transatlantic commerce.

TICKETMASTER CORP. v. TICKETS.COM, INC.

2003 WL 21406289 (C.D. Cal.), 2003 Corp. L. Dec. ¶28,607

HUPP, J.

This motion by defendant Tickets.com, Inc. (hereafter TX) for summary judgment on plaintiffs Ticketmaster Corporation and Ticket Online-CitySearch, Inc. (hereafter collectively TM), intellectual property issues is denied as to the contract claim of TM and granted as to the copyright and trespass to chattels claims, which are dismissed by this minute order.

Many of the factual items are not contested, although the legal result of applying the law to the uncontested facts is heavily contested. Among the uncontested facts are the following: Both TM and TX are in the business of selling tickets to all kinds of "events" (sports, concerts, plays, etc.) to the public. They are in heavy competition with one another, but operate in distinctive ways. TM is the largest company in the industry. It sells tickets by the four methods of ticket selling—venue box office, retail outlets, by telephone, and over the internet. Telephone and internet sales require the customer to establish credit with the ticket seller (usually by credit card). Internet sales have been the fastest growing segment of the industry. TX at the time of the events considered in this motion was primarily (but not exclusively) an internet seller. Both TM and TX maintain a web page reachable by anyone with an internet connection. Each of their web pages has many subsidiary (or interior) web pages which describe one event each and provide such basic information as to location, date, time, description of the event, and ticket prices. The TM interior web pages each have a separate electronic address or Uniform Resource Locator ("URL") which, if possessed by the internet user, allows the user to reach the web page for any particular event by by-passing the "home" web page and proceeding past the index to reach the interior web page for the event in question. The TM interior web pages provide telephone numbers for customers or allow the customer to order tickets to the event by interactive computer use. A charge is made for the TM service.

TM principally does business by exclusive contracts with the event providers or their producers, and its web pages only list the events for which TM is the exclusive ticket seller. TX also sells tickets to a number of events for which it is the ticket seller. At one point, its web pages attempted to list all events for which tickets were available whether or not TX sold the tickets. Its interior web pages also listed the event, the date, time, ticket prices, and provided for internet purchase if TX could sell the tickets. When TX could not sell the tickets, it listed ticket brokers who sold at premium prices. In early 2000, TX discontinued this practice of listing events with tickets sold by other ticket brokers. Until early 2000, in situations where TM was the only source of tickets, TX provided a "deep link" by which the customer would be transferred to the interior web page of TM's web site, where the customer could purchase the ticket from TM. This process of "deep linking" is the subject of TM's complaint in this action, of which there is now left the contract, copyright, and trespass theories.

Starting in 1998 and continuing to July 2001, when it stopped the practice, TX employed an electronic program called a "spider" or "crawler" to review the internal web pages (available to the public) of TM. The "spider" "crawled" through the internal web pages to TM and electronically extracted the electronic information from which the web page is shown on the user's computer. The spider temporarily loaded this electronic information into the Random Access Memory ("RAM") of TX's computers for a period of from 10-15 seconds. TX then extracted the factual information (event, date, time, tickets prices, and URL) and discarded the rest (which consisted of TM identification, logos, ads, and other information which TX did not intend to use; much of this discarded material was protected by copyright). The factual information was then organized in the TX format to be displayed on the TX internal web page. The TX internal web page carried no TM identification and had only the factual information about the event on it which was taken from TM's interior web page but rearranged in TX format plus any information or advertisement added by TX. From March 1998, to early 2000, the TX user was provided the deep linking option described above to go directly from the TX web site to the relevant TM interior web page. This option stopped (or was stopped by TM) in early 2000. For an unknown period afterward, the TX customer was given the option of linking to the TM home page, from which the customer could work his way to the interior web page in which he was interested.

The contract aspect of the case derives from a notice placed on the home page of the TM web site which states that anyone going beyond that point into the interior web pages of the web site accepts certain conditions, which include, relevant to this case, that all information obtained from the website is for the personal use of the user and may not be used for commercial purposes.

Earlier in this case (and at the time of the motion for preliminary injunction) the notice was placed at the bottom of the home page of the TM web site, so that a user without an especially large screen would have to scroll down the page to read the conditions of use. Since then, TM has placed in a prominent place on the home page the warning that proceeding further binds the user to the conditions of use. As one TX executive put it, it could not be missed. At the time of the preliminary injunction motion, the court commented that there was no evidence that the conditions of use were known to TX. Since then, there has been developed evidence that TX was fully familiar with the conditions TM claimed to impose on users, including a letter from TM to TX which quoted the conditions (and a reply by TX stating that it did not accept the conditions). Thus, there is sufficient evidence to defeat summary judgment on the contract theory if knowledge of the asserted conditions of use was had by TX, who nevertheless continued to send its spider into the TM interior web pages, and if it is legally concluded that doing so can lead to a binding contract. For reasons dealing with the desirability of clear unmistakable evidence of assent to the conditions on trial of such issues, the court would prefer a rule that required an unmistakable assent to the conditions easily provided by requiring clicking on an icon which says "I agree" or the equivalent. Such a rule would provide certainty in trial and make it clear that the user had called to his attention the conditions he or she accepted when using the web site. . . . The principle has long been established that no particular form of words is necessary to indicate assent — the offeror may specify that a certain action in connection with his offer is deemed acceptance, and ripens into a contract when the action is taken. Thus, as relevant here, a contract can be formed by proceeding into the interior web pages after knowledge (or, in some cases, presumptive knowledge) of the conditions accepted when doing so. In *Specht*, 306 F.3d 17 (2d Cir. 2002), the court found that there was no mutual assent when a notice of the existence of license terms governing the use of software was visible to internet users only if they scrolled down the screen. That case is distinguishable from the facts at hand on the grounds that in *Specht*, the plaintiff's terms of use were not plainly visible or known to defendants. Moreover, *Specht* involved a different set of circumstances, that of consumers invited to download free software from an internet site that did not contain a plainly visible notice of license terms. As a result, the TX motion for summary judgment on the contract issue is denied.

The trespass to chattels issue requires adapting the ancient common law action to the modern age. No cases seem to have reached the appellate courts although there appears to be a number of district court cases. [T]here have been a number of district court cases discussing the chattel theory (some published and some not). These cases tend to support the proposition that mere invasion or use of a portion of the web site by a spider is a trespass (leading at least to nominal damages), and that there need not be an independent showing of direct harm either to the chattel (unlikely in the case of a spider) or tangible interference with the use of the computer being invaded. However, scholars and practitioners alike have criticized the extension of the trespass to chattels doctrine to the internet context, noting that this doctrinal expansion threatens basic internet functions (i.e., search engines) and exposes the flaws inherent in applying doctrines based in real and tangible property to cyberspace. Pending appellate guidance, this court comes down on the side of requiring some tangible interference with the use or operation of the computer being invaded by the spider. *Restatement (Second) of Torts* §219 requires a showing that "the chattel is impaired as to its condition, quality, or value." Therefore, unless there is actual dispossession of the chattel for a substantial time (not present here), the elements of the tort have not been made out. Since the spider does not cause physical injury to the chattel, there must be some evidence that the use or utility of the computer (or computer network) being "spiderized" is adversely affected by the use of the spider. No such evidence is presented here. This court respectfully disagrees with other district courts' finding that mere use of a spider to enter a public[ly] available web site to gather information, without more, is sufficient to fulfill the harm requirement for trespass to chattels.

TM complains that the information obtained by the use of the spider was valuable (and even that it was sold by TX), and that it spent time and money attempting to frustrate the spider, but neither of these items shows damage to the computers or their operation. One must keep in mind that we are talking about the common law tort of trespass, not damage from breach of contract or copyright infringement. The tort claim may not succeed without proof of tort-type damage. Plaintiff TM has the burden to show such damage. None is shown here. The motion for summary judgment is granted to eliminate the claim for trespass to chattels. This minute order is the order eliminating that claim. This approach to the tort of trespass to chattels should hurt no one's policy feelings; after all, what is being attempted is to apply a medieval common law concept in an entirely new situation which should be disposed of by modern law designed to protect intellectual property interests.

The copyright issues are more difficult. They divide into three issues. The first is whether the momentary resting in the TX computers of all of the electronic signals which are used to form the video representation to the viewer of the interior web pages of the TX computer constitutes actionable copyright infringement. The second is whether the URLs, which were copied and used by TX, contain copyrightable material. The third is whether TX's deep-linking caused the unauthorized public display of TM event pages. In examining these questions, we must keep in mind a prime theorem of copyright law—facts, as such, are not subject to copyright protection. What is subject to copyright protection is the manner or mode of expression of those facts. Thus, addresses and telephone numbers contained in a directory do not have copyright protection (*Feist Publications*, 499 U.S. 350), despite the fact that time, money, and effort went into compiling the information. Similarly, in this case, the existence of the event, its date and time, and its ticket prices, are not subject to copyright. Anyone is free to print (or show on the internet) such information. Thus, if TX had sat down a secretary at the computer screen with instructions manually to go through TM's web sites and pick out and write down purely factual information about the events, and then feed it into the TX web pages (using the TX distinctive format only), no one could complain. The objection is that the same thing was done with an electronic program. However, the difference is that the spider picks up all of the electronic symbols which, if it had been put on a monitor with the right software, would duplicate the TM web page. However, this is not the way it was done. The spider picks up the electronic symbols and loads them momentarily (for 10 to 15 seconds) into the RAM of the TX computers, where a program picks up the factual data (not protected), places same into the TX format for its web pages, and immediately discards the balance, which may consist of TM logos, TM advertisements, TM format for presentation of the material, and other material which is copyrightable. Thus, the actual copying (if it can be called that) is momentary while the non-protected material, all open to the public, is extracted. Is this momentary resting of the electronic symbols from which a TM web page could be (but is not) constructed fair use where the purpose is to obtain non-protected facts? The court thinks the answer is "yes." There is not much law [o]n point. However, there are two Ninth Circuit cases which shed light on the problem. They are *Sony Computer Entertainment*, 203 F.3d 596 (9th Cir. 2000) and *Sega*, 977 F.2d 1510 (9th Cir. 1992). In each of these cases, the alleged infringer attempted to get at non-protected source code by reverse engineering of the plaintiff's copyrighted software. In doing so, the necessary method was to copy the software and work backwards to derive the unprotected source code. The copied software was then destroyed. In each case, this was held to be fair use since it was necessary to temporarily copy the software to obtain the non-protected material. There may be a difference with this case, however, at least TM claims so. It asserts in its points and authorities that taking the temporary copy in this case was not the only way to obtain the unprotected information, and that TX was able to, and in actuality did purchase such information from certain third-parties. Both *Sony* and *Sega* stated that the fair use was justified because reverse engineering (including taking a temporary copy) was the only way the unprotected information could be obtained. Although this court recognizes that the holdings of *Sony* and *Sega* were limited to the specific context of "disassembling" copyrighted object code in order to access unprotected elements contained in the source code, this court believes that the "fair use" doctrine can be applied to the current facts.

Taking the temporary copy of the electronic information for the limited purpose of extracting unprotected public facts leads to the conclusion that the temporary use of the electronic signals was "fair use" and not actionable. In determining whether a challenged use of copyrighted material is fair, a court must keep in mind the public policy underlying the Copyright Act: to secure a fair return for an author's creative labor and to stimulate artistic creativity for the general good. This court sees no public policy that would be served by restricting TX from using spiders to temporarily download TM's event pages in order to acquire the unprotected, publicly available factual event information. The rest of the event page information (which consisted of TM identification, logos, ads, and other information) was discarded and not used by TX and is not exposed to the public by TX. In temporarily downloading TM's event pages to its

RAM through the use of spiders, TX was not exploiting TM's creative labors in any way: its spiders gathered copyrightable and non-copyrightable information alike but then immediately discarded the copyrighted material. It is unlikely that the spiders could have been programmed to take only the factual information from the TM web pages without initially downloading the entire page.

Consideration of the fair use factors listed in 17 USC §106 supports this result. First, TX operates its site for commercial purposes, and this fact tends to weigh against a finding of fair use. *Campbell*, 510 U.S. 569, 585 (1994). TX's use of the data gathered from TM's event pages was only slightly transformative. As for the second factor, the nature of the copyrighted work, the copying that occurred when spiders download the event page, access the source code for each page, and extract the factual data embedded in the code, is analogous to the process of copying that the *Sony* court condoned (however, the Court recognizes that the fair use holding from that decision does not fit perfectly onto the facts at hand). Third, because TX's final product—the TX web site—did not contain any infringing material, the "amount and substantiality of the portion used" is of little weight. *Connectix*, 203 F.3d at 606 (9th Cir. 2000). The fourth factor (the effect on the market value of the copyrighted work) is, of course nil, and weighs towards finding fair use. TM's arguments and evidence regarding loss of advertising revenue, as well as the loss of potential business with Volt Delta, are not persuasive.

Accordingly, summary judgment is granted on the copyright claims of TM and it is eliminated from this action.

REGISTER.COM, INC. v. VERIO, INC.

356 F.3d 393 (2d Cir. 2004)

LEVAL, Circuit Judge.

Defendant, Verio, Inc. ("Verio") appeals from an order of the United States District Court for the Southern District of New York granting the motion of plaintiff Register.com, Inc. ("Register") for a preliminary injunction.

BACKGROUND

This plaintiff Register is one of over fifty companies serving as registrars for the issuance of domain names on the world wide web. As a registrar, Register issues domain names to persons and entities preparing to establish web sites on the Internet. Web sites are identified and accessed by reference to their domain names.

Register was appointed a registrar of domain names by the Internet Corporation for Assigned Names and Numbers, known by the acronym "ICANN." ICANN is a private, non-profit public benefit corporation which was established by agencies of the U.S. government to administer the Internet domain name system. To become a registrar of domain names, Register was required to enter into a standard form agreement with ICANN, designated as the ICANN Registrar Accreditation Agreement, November 1999 version (referred to herein as the "ICANN Agreement").

Applicants to register a domain name submit to the registrar contact information, including at a minimum, the applicant's name, postal address, telephone number, and electronic mail address. The ICANN Agreement, referring to this registrant contact information under the rubric "WHOIS information," requires the registrar, under terms discussed in greater detail below, to preserve it, update it daily, and provide for free public access to it through the Internet as well as through an independent access port, called port 43. *See* ICANN Agreement §II.F.1.

In compliance with §II.F.1 of the ICANN Agreement, Register updated the WHOIS information on a daily basis and established Internet and port 43 service, which allowed free public query of its WHOIS information. An entity making a WHOIS query through Register's Internet site or port 43 would receive a reply furnishing the requested WHOIS information, captioned by a legend devised by Register, which stated,

> By submitting a WHOIS query, you agree that you will use this data only for lawful purposes and that under no circumstances will you use this data to . . . support the transmission of mass unsolicited, commercial advertising or solicitation via email.

The terms of that legend tracked §II.F.5 of the ICANN Agreement in specifying the restrictions Register imposed on the use of its WHOIS data. Subsequently, as explained below, Register amended the terms of this legend to impose more stringent restrictions on the use of the information gathered through such queries.

In addition to performing the function of a registrar of domain names, Register also engages in the business of selling web-related services to entities that maintain web sites. These services cover various aspects of web site development. In order to solicit business for the services it offers, Register sends out marketing communications. Among the entities it solicits for the sale of such services are entities whose domain names it registered. However, during the registration process, Register offers registrants the opportunity to elect whether or not they will receive marketing communications from it.

The defendant Verio, against whom the preliminary injunction was issued, is engaged in the business of selling a variety of web site design, development and operation services. In the sale of such services, Verio competes with Register's web site development business. To facilitate its pursuit of customers, Verio undertook to obtain daily updates of the WHOIS information relating to newly registered domain names. To achieve this, Verio devised an automated software program, or robot, which each day would submit multiple successive WHOIS queries through the port 43 accesses of various registrars. Upon acquiring the WHOIS information of new registrants, Verio would send them marketing solicitations by email, telemarketing and direct mail. To the extent that Verio's solicitations were sent by email, the practice was inconsistent with the terms of the restrictive legend Register attached to its responses to Verio's queries.

In the meantime, Register changed the restrictive legend it attached to its responses to WHOIS queries. While previously the legend conformed to the terms of §II F.5, which authorized Register to prohibit use of the WHOIS information for mass solicitations "via email," its new legend undertook to bar mass solicitation "via direct mail, electronic mail, or by telephone." Section II.F.5 of Register's ICANN Agreement, as noted above, required Register to permit use of the WHOIS data "for any lawful purpose except to . . . support the transmission of mass unsolicited solicitations via email (spam)." Thus, by undertaking to prohibit Verio from using the WHOIS information for solicitations "via direct mail . . . or by telephone," Register was acting in apparent violation of this term of its ICANN Agreement.

Register wrote to Verio demanding that it cease using WHOIS information derived from Register not only for email marketing, but also for marketing by direct mail and telephone. Verio ceased using the information in email marketing, but refused to stop marketing by direct mail and telephone.

Register brought this suit on August 3, 2000, and moved for a temporary restraining order and a preliminary injunction. Register asserted, among other claims, that Verio was (a) causing confusion among customers, who were led to believe Verio was affiliated with Register; (b) accessing Register's computers without authorization, a violation of the Computer Fraud and Abuse Act, 18 U.S.C. §1030; and, (c) trespassing on Register's chattels in a manner likely to harm Register's computer systems by the use of Verio's automated robot software programs. On December 8, 2000, the district court entered a preliminary injunction. Verio appeals from that order.

DISCUSSION

(a) Verio's Enforcement of the Restrictions Placed on Register by the ICANN Agreement

Verio conceded that it knew of the restrictions Register placed on the use of the WHOIS data and knew that, by using Register's WHOIS data for direct mail and telemarketing solicitations, it was violating Register's restrictions. Verio's principal argument is that Register was not authorized to forbid Verio from using the data for direct mail and telemarketing solicitation because the ICANN Agreement prohibited Register from imposing any "terms and conditions" on use of WHOIS data, "except as permitted by ICANN-adopted policy," which specified that Register was required to permit "any lawful purpose, except . . . mass solicitation[] via email."

Register does not deny that the restrictions it imposed contravened this requirement of the ICANN Agreement. Register contends, however, that the question whether it violated §II.F.5 of its Agreement with ICANN is a matter between itself and ICANN, and that Verio cannot enforce the obligations placed on Register by the ICANN Agreement. Register points to §II.S.2 of the ICANN Agreement, captioned "No Third-Party Beneficiaries," which, as noted, states that the agreement is not to be construed "to create any obligation by either ICANN or Registrar to any non-party." Register asserts that Verio, a non-party, is asking the court to construe §II.F.5 as creating an obligation owed by Register to Verio, and that the Agreement expressly forbids such a construction.

We are persuaded by the arguments Register and ICANN advance. It is true Register incurred a contractual obligation to ICANN not to prevent the use of its WHOIS data for direct mail and telemarketing solicitation. But ICANN deliberately included in the same contract that persons aggrieved by Register's violation of such a term should seek satisfaction within the framework of ICANN's grievance policy, and should not be heard in courts of law to plead entitlement to enforce Register's promise to ICANN. As experience develops in the fast changing world of the Internet, ICANN, informed by the various constituencies in the Internet community, might well no longer consider it salutary to enforce a policy which it earlier expressed in the ICANN Agreement. For courts to undertake to enforce promises made by registrars to

ICANN at the instance of third parties might therefore be harmful to ICANN's efforts to develop well-informed and sound Internet policy.

Verio's invocation of the ICANN Agreement necessarily depends on its entitlement to enforce Register's promises to ICANN in the role of third party beneficiary. The ICANN Agreement specified that it should be deemed to have been made in California, where ICANN is located. Under §1559 of the California Civil Code, a "contract, made expressly for the benefit of a third person, may be enforced by him." CAL. CIV. CODE §1559. For Verio to seek to enforce Register's promises it made to ICANN in the ICANN Agreement, Verio must show that the Agreement was made for its benefit. *See* Am. Home Ins. Co. v. Travelers Indemnity Co., 175 Cal. Rptr. 826, 834 (1981). Verio did not meet this burden. To the contrary, the Agreement expressly and intentionally excluded non-parties from claiming rights under it in court proceedings.

(b) Verio's Assent to Register's Contract Terms

Verio's next contention assumes that Register was legally authorized to demand that takers of WHOIS data from its systems refrain from using it for mass solicitation by mail and telephone, as well as by email. Verio contends that it nonetheless never became contractually bound to the conditions imposed by Register's restrictive legend because, in the case of each query Verio made, the legend did not appear until after Verio had submitted the query and received the WHOIS data. Accordingly, Verio contends that in no instance did it receive legally enforceable notice of the conditions Register intended to impose. Verio therefore argues it should not be deemed to have taken WHOIS data from Register's systems subject to Register's conditions.

Verio's argument might well be persuasive if its queries addressed to Register's computers had been sporadic and infrequent. If Verio had submitted only one query, or even if it had submitted only a few sporadic queries, that would give considerable force to its contention that it obtained the WHOIS data without being conscious that Register intended to impose conditions, and without being deemed to have accepted Register's conditions. But Verio was daily submitting numerous queries, each of which resulted in its receiving notice of the terms Register exacted. Furthermore, Verio admits that it knew perfectly well what terms Register demanded. Verio's argument fails.

Each day Verio repeatedly enters Register's computers and takes that day's new WHOIS data. Each day upon receiving the requested data, Verio receives Register's notice of the terms on which it makes the data available — that the data not be used for mass solicitation via direct mail, email, or telephone. Verio acknowledges that it continued drawing the data from Register's computers with full knowledge that Register offered access subject to these restrictions. Verio is no[t] free to take Register's data without being bound by the terms on which Register offers it[.]

Verio seeks support for its position from cases that have dealt with the formation of contracts on the Internet. An excellent example, although decided subsequent to the submission of this case, is Specht v. Netscape Communications Corp., 306 F.3d 17 (2d Cir. 2002). The dispute was whether users of Netscape's software, who downloaded it from Netscape's web site, were bound by an agreement to arbitrate disputes with Netscape, where Netscape had posted the terms of its offer of the software (including the obligation to arbitrate disputes) on the web site from which they downloaded the software. We ruled against Netscape and in favor of the users of its software because the users would not have seen the terms Netscape exacted without scrolling down their computer screens, and there was no reason for them to do so. The evidence did not demonstrate that one who had downloaded Netscape's software had necessarily seen the terms of its offer.

Verio, however, cannot avail itself of the reasoning of *Specht*. In *Specht*, the users in whose favor we decided visited Netscape's web site one time to download its software. Netscape's posting of its terms did not compel the conclusion that its downloaders took the software subject to those terms because there was no way to determine that any down-loader had seen the terms of the offer. There was no basis for imputing to the downloaders of Netscape's software knowledge of the terms on which the software was offered. This case is crucially different. Verio visited Register's computers daily to access WHOIS data and each day saw the terms of Register's offer; Verio admitted that, in entering Register's computers to get the data, it was fully aware of the terms on which Register offered the access.

Verio's next argument is that it was not bound by Register's terms because it rejected them. Even assuming Register is entitled to demand compliance with its terms in exchange for Verio's entry into its systems to take WHOIS data, and even acknowledging that Verio was fully aware of Register's terms, Verio contends that it still is not bound by Register's terms because it did not agree to be bound. In support of its claim, Verio cites a district court case from the Central District of California, Ticketmaster Corp. v. Tickets.com, Inc., No. CV99-7654, 2000 WL 1887522 (C.D. Cal. Aug. 10, 2000), in which the court rejected Ticketmaster's application for a preliminary injunction to enforce posted terms of use of data available on its website against a regular user. Noting that the user of Ticket-master's web site is not required to check an "I agree" box before proceeding, the court concluded that there was insufficient proof of agreement to support a preliminary injunc-tion. *Id.* at *5.

We acknowledge that the *Ticketmaster* decision gives Verio some support, but not enough. In the first place, the *Ticketmaster* court was not making a definitive ruling rejecting Ticketmaster's contract claim. It was rather exercising a district court's discretion to deny a preliminary injunction because of a doubt whether the movant had adequately shown like-lihood of success on the merits.

But more importantly, we are not inclined to agree with the *Ticketmaster* court's analysis. There is a crucial difference between the circumstances of *Specht*, where we declined to enforce Netscape's specified terms against a user of its software because of inadequate evidence that the user had seen the terms when downloading the software, and those of Ticketmaster, where the taker of information from Ticketmaster's site knew full well the terms on which the information was offered but was not offered an icon marked, "I agree," on which to click. Under the circumstances of *Ticketmaster*, we see no reason why the enforceability of the offeror's terms should depend on whether the taker states (or clicks), "I agree."

We recognize that contract offers on the Internet often require the offeree to click on an "I agree" icon. And no doubt, in many circumstances, such a statement of agreement by the offeree is essential to the formation of a contract. But not in all circumstances. While new commerce on the Internet has exposed courts to many new situations, it has not fundamentally changed the principles of contract. It is standard contract doctrine that when a benefit is offered subject to stated conditions, and the offeree makes a decision to take the benefit with knowledge of the terms of the offer, the taking constitutes an acceptance of the terms, which accordingly become binding on the offeree. *See, e.g., Restatement (Second) of Contracts* §69(1)(a) (1981) ("[S]ilence and inaction operate as an acceptance . . . [w]here an offeree takes the benefit of offered services with reasonable opportunity to reject them and reason to know that they were offered with the expectation of compensation.")[.]

[T]he defendant in *Ticketmaster* and Verio in this case [e]ach was offered access to information subject to terms of which they were well aware. Their choice was either to accept the offer of contract, taking the information subject to the terms of the offer, or, if the terms were not acceptable, to decline to take the benefits.

We find that the district court was within its discretion in concluding that Register showed likelihood of success on the merits of its contract claim.

(d) Trespass to Chattels

Verio also attacks the grant of the preliminary injunction against its accessing Register's computers by automated software programs performing multiple successive queries. This prong of the injunction was premised on Register's claim of trespass to chattels. Verio contends the ruling was in error because Register failed to establish that Verio's conduct resulted in harm to Register's servers and because Verio's robot access to the WHOIS database through Register was "not unauthorized." We believe the district court's findings were within the range of its permissible discretion.

"A trespass to a chattel may be committed by intentionally . . . using or intermeddling with a chattel in the possession of another," *Restatement (Second) of Torts* §217(b) (1965), where "the chattel is impaired as to its condition, quality, or value," *id.* §218(b); *see also* City of Amsterdam v. Goldreyer Ltd., 882 F. Supp. 1273, 1281 (E.D.N.Y. 1995) (citing the *Restatement* definition as New York law).

The district court found that Verio's use of search robots, consisting of software programs performing multiple automated successive queries, consumed a significant portion of the capacity of Register's computer systems. While Verio's robots alone would not incapacitate Register's systems, the court found that if Verio were permitted to continue to access Register's computers through such robots, it was "highly probable" that other Internet service providers would devise similar programs to access Register's data, and that the system would be overtaxed and would crash. We cannot say these findings were unreasonable.

Nor is there merit to Verio's contention that it cannot be engaged in trespass when Register had never instructed it not to use its robot programs. As the district court noted, Register's complaint sufficiently advised Verio that its use of robots was not authorized and, according to Register's contentions, would cause harm to Register's systems.

CONCLUSION

The ruling of the district court is hereby AFFIRMED, with the exception that the court is directed to delete the reference to "first step on the web" from paragraph one of its order.

ASSESSMENT TECHNOLOGIES OF WI, LLC v. WIREDATA, INC.
350 F.3d 640 (7th Cir. 2003)

POSNER, Circuit Judge.

This case is about the attempt of a copyright owner to use copyright law to block access to data that not only are neither copyrightable nor copyrighted, but were not created or obtained by the copyright owner. The owner is trying to secrete the data in its copyrighted program — a program the existence of which reduced the likelihood that the data would be retained in a form in which they would have been readily accessible. It would be appalling if such an attempt could succeed.

Assessment Technologies (AT, we'll call it) brought suit for copyright infringement and theft of trade secrets against WIREdata, and the district court after an evidentiary hearing issued a permanent injunction on the basis of AT's copyright claim alone, without reaching the trade secret claim.

The copyright case seeks to block WIREdata from obtaining noncopyrighted data. AT claims that the data can't be extracted without infringement of its copyright. The copyright is of a compilation format, and the general issue that the appeal presents is the right of the owner of such a copyright to prevent his customers (that is, the copyright licensees) from disclosing the compiled data even if the data are in the public domain.

WIREdata, owned by Multiple Listing Services, Inc., wants to obtain, for use by real estate brokers, data regarding specific properties — address, owner's name, the age of the property, its assessed valuation, the number and type of rooms, and so forth — from the southeastern Wisconsin municipalities in which the properties are located. The municipalities collect such data in order to assess the value of the properties for property-tax purposes. Ordinarily they're happy to provide the data to anyone who will pay the modest cost of copying the data onto a disk. Indeed, Wisconsin's "open records" law, WIS. STAT. §§19.31-.39; State ex rel. Milwaukee Police Ass'n v. Jones, 237 Wis. 2d 840, 615 N.W.2d 190, 194-96 (2000), which is applicable to data in digital form, see *id.* at 195-96; WIS. STAT. §19.32(2), requires them to furnish such data to any person who will pay the copying cost. However, three municipalities refused WIREdata's request. They (or the contractors who do the actual tax assessment for them) are licensees of AT. The open-records law contains an exception for copyrighted materials, *id.*, and these municipalities are afraid that furnishing WIREdata the requested data would violate the copyright. WIREdata has sued them in the state courts of Wisconsin in an attempt to force them to divulge the data, and those suits are pending. Alarmed by WIREdata's suits, AT brought the present suit to stop WIREdata from making such demands of the municipalities and seeking to enforce them by litigation.

The data that WIREdata wants are collected not by AT but by tax assessors hired by the municipalities. The assessors visit the property and by talking to the owner and poking around the property itself obtain the information that we mentioned in the preceding paragraph — the age of the property, the number of rooms, and so forth. AT has developed and copyrighted a computer program, called "Market Drive," for compiling these data. The assessor types into a computer the data that he has obtained from his visit to the property or from other sources of information and then the Market Drive program, in conjunction with a Microsoft database program (Microsoft Access), automatically allocates the data to 456 fields (that is, categories of information) grouped into 34 master categories known as tables. Several types of data relating to a property, each allocated to a different field, are grouped together in a table called "Income Valuations," others in a table called "Residential Buildings," and so on. The data collected by the various assessors and inputted in the manner just described are stored in an electronic file, the database. The municipality's tax officials can use various queries in Market Drive or Market Access to view the data in the file.

WIREdata's appeal gets off on the wrong foot, with the contention that Market Drive lacks sufficient originality to be copyrightable. Copyright law unlike patent law does not require substantial originality. Feist Publications, Inc. v. Rural Telephone Service Co., 499 U.S. 340, 345-48 (1991). In fact, it requires only enough originality to enable a work to be distinguished from similar works that are in the public domain. This modest requirement is satisfied by Market Drive because no other real estate assessment program arranges the data collected by the assessor in these 456 fields grouped into these 34 categories, and because this structure is not so obvious or inevitable as to lack the minimal originality required.

So AT has a valid copyright; and if WIREdata said to itself, "Market Drive is a nifty way of sorting real estate data and we want the municipalities to give us their data in the form in which it is organized in the database, that is, sorted into AT's 456 fields grouped into its 34 tables," and the municipalities obliged, they would be infringing AT's copyright because they are not licensed to make copies of Market Drive for distribution to others; and WIREdata would be a contributory infringer (subject to a qualification concerning the fair-use defense to copyright infringement, including contributory infringement, that we discuss later). But WIREdata doesn't want the compilation as structured by Market Drive. It isn't in the business of making tax assessments, which is the business for which Market Drive is designed. It only wants the raw data, the data the assessors inputted into Market Drive. Once it gets those data it will sort them in accordance with its own needs, which have to do with providing the information about properties that is useful to real estate brokers as opposed to taxing authorities.

But how are the data to be extracted from the database without infringing the copyright? Or, what is not quite the same question, how can the data be separated from the tables and fields to which they are allocated by Market Drive? One possibility is to use tools in the Market Drive program itself to extract the data and place it in a separate electronic file; this can be done rapidly and easily with just a few keystrokes. But the municipalities may not have the program, because the inputting of the data, which did of course require its use, was done by assessors employed by firms to do this work as independent contractors of the municipalities. And if the municipalities do have the program, still their license from AT forbids them to disseminate the data collected by means of it — a restriction that may or may not be in violation of the state's open-records law, a question we come back to later. A second extraction possibility, which arises from the fact that the database is a Microsoft file accessible by Microsoft Access, is to use Access to extract the data and place it in a new file, bypassing Market Drive. But there is again the scope of the license to be considered and also whether the method of extraction is so cumbersome that it would require more effort than the open-records law requires of the agencies subject to it. It might take a programmer a couple of days to extract the data using Microsoft Access, and the municipalities might lack the time, or for that matter the programmers, to do the extraction. But that should not be a big problem, because WIREdata can hire programmers to extract the data from the municipalities' computers at its own expense.

From the standpoint of copyright law all that matters is that the process of extracting the raw data from the database does not involve copying Market Drive, or creating, as AT mysteriously asserts, a derivative work; all that is sought is raw data, data created not by AT but by the assessors, data that are in the public domain. A derivative work is a translation or other transformation of an original work and must itself contain minimum originality for the same evidentiary reason that we noted in discussing the requirement that a copyrighted work be original. Pickett v. Prince, 207 F.3d 402, 405 (7th Cir. 2000). A work that merely copies uncopyrighted material is wholly unoriginal and the making of such a work is therefore not an infringement of copyright. The municipalities would not be infringing Market Drive by extracting the raw data from the databases by either method that we discussed and handing those data over to WIREdata; and since there would thus be no direct infringement, neither would there be contributory infringement by WIREdata. It would be like a Westlaw licensee's copying the text of a federal judicial opinion that he found in the Westlaw opinion database and giving it to someone else. Westlaw's compilation of federal judicial opinions is copyrighted and copyrightable because it involves discretionary judgments regarding selection and arrangement. But the opinions themselves are in the public domain (federal law forbids assertion of copyright in federal documents, 17 U.S.C. §105), and so Westlaw cannot prevent its licensees from copying the opinions themselves as distinct from the aspects of the database that are copyrighted. See Matthew Bender & Co. v. West Publishing Co., 158 F.3d 693 (2d Cir. 1998).

AT would lose this copyright case even if the raw data were so entangled with Market Drive that they could not be extracted without making a copy of the program. The case would then be governed by Sega Enterprises Ltd. v. Accolade, Inc., 977 F.2d 1510, 1520-28 (9th Cir. 1992). Sega manufactured a game console, which is a specialized computer, and copyrighted the console's operating system, including the source code. Accolade wanted to make computer games that would be compatible with Sega's console, and to that end it bought a Sega console and through reverse engineering reconstructed the source code, from which it would learn how to design its games so that they would activate the operating system. For technical reasons, Accolade had to make a copy of the source code in order to be able to obtain this information. It didn't want to sell the source code, produce a game-console operating system, or make any other use of the copyrighted code except to be able to sell a noninfringing product, namely a computer game. The court held that this "intermediate copying" of the operating system was a fair use, since the only effect of enjoining it would be to give Sega control over noninfringing products, namely Accolade's games. *See also* Sony Computer Entertainment, Inc. v. Connectix Corp., 203 F.3d 596, 602-08 (9th Cir. 2000). Similarly, if the only way WIREdata could obtain public-domain data about properties in southeastern Wisconsin would be by copying the data in the municipalities' databases as embedded in Market Drive, so that it would be copying the compilation and not just the compiled data only because the data and the format in which they were organized could not be disentangled, it would be privileged to make such a copy, and likewise the municipalities. For the only purpose of the copying would be to extract noncopyrighted material, and not to go into competition with AT by selling copies of Market Drive. We emphasize this point lest AT try to circumvent our decision by reconfiguring Market Drive in such a way that the municipalities would find it difficult or impossible to furnish the raw data to requesters such as WIREdata in any format other than that prescribed by Market Drive. If AT did that with that purpose it might be guilty of copyright misuse. . . .

AT argues that WIREdata doesn't need to obtain the data in digital form because they exist in analog form, namely in the handwritten notes of the assessors, notes that all agree are not covered by the Market Drive copyright. But we were told at argument without contradiction that some assessors no longer make handwritten notes to copy into a computer at a later time. Instead they take their laptop to the site and type the information in directly. So WIREdata could not possibly obtain all the data it wants (all of which data are in the public domain, we emphasize) from the handwritten notes. But what is more fundamental is that since AT has no ownership or other legal interest in the data collected by the assessor, it has no legal ground for making the acquisition of that data more costly for WIREdata. AT is trying to use its copyright to sequester uncopyrightable data, presumably in the hope of extracting a license fee from WIREdata.

We are mindful of pressures, reflected in bills that have been pending in Congress for years to provide legal protection to the creators of databases, as Europe has already done. (Ironically, considering who owns WIREdata, the multiple-listing services are pressing for such protection. Ron Eckstein, "The Database Debate," *Legal Times*, Jan. 24, 2000, p. 16.) The creation of massive electronic databases can be extremely costly, yet if the database is readily searchable and the data themselves are not copyrightable (and we know from *Feist* that mere data are indeed not copyrightable) the creator may find it difficult or even impossible to recoup the expense of creating the database. Legal protection of databases as such (as distinct from programs for arranging the data, like Market Drive) cannot take the form of copyright, as the Supreme Court made clear in *Feist* when it held that the copyright clause of the Constitution does not authorize Congress to create copyright in mere data. But that is neither here nor there; what needs to be emphasized in this case is that the concerns that actuate the legislative proposals for database protection have no relevance because AT is not the collector of the data that go into the database. All the data are collected and inputted by the assessors; it is they, not AT, that do the footwork, the heavy lifting.

AT points to the terms of its license agreements with the municipalities, which though ambiguous might be interpreted to forbid the licensees to release the raw data, even without the duplication, or revelation of any copyrighted feature, of Market Drive. But AT is not suing for breach of the terms of the agreements — it can't, since WIREdata is not a party to them. Nor is it suing for intentional interference with contract, Frandsen v. Jensen-Sundquist Agency, Inc., 802 F.2d 941, 947-48 (7th Cir. 1986) (Wisconsin law), which would be the logical route for complaining about WIREdata's inviting the municipalities that are AT's licensees to violate the terms of their license. The licenses do nothing for AT in this case.

So it is irrelevant that ProCD, Inc. v. Zeidenberg, 86 F.3d 1447, 1453-55 (7th Cir. 1996), holds that a copyright owner can by contract limit copying beyond the right that a copyright confers. See also Bowers v. Baystate Technologies, Inc., 320 F.3d 1317, 1323-26 (Fed. Cir. 2003). Like other property rights, a copyright is enforceable against persons with whom the owner has no contractual relations; so a property owner can eject a trespasser even though the trespasser had not contractually bound himself to refrain from entering the property. That is why AT is suing WIREdata for copyright infringement rather than for breach of contract. The scope of a copyright is given by federal law, but the scope of contractual protection is, at least prima facie, whatever the parties to the contract agreed to. But our plaintiff did not create the database that it is seeking to sequester from WIREdata; or to be more precise, it created only an empty database, a bin that the tax assessors filled with the data. It created the compartments in the bin and the instructions for sorting the data to those compartments, but those were its only innovations and their protection by copyright law is complete. To try by contract or otherwise to prevent the municipalities from revealing *their own* data, especially when, as we have seen, the complete data are unavailable anywhere else, might constitute copyright misuse.

The doctrine of misuse "prevents copyright holders from leveraging their limited monopoly to allow them control of areas outside the monopoly." A & M Records, Inc. v. Napster, Inc., 239 F.3d 1004, 1026-27 (9th Cir. 2001); see Alcatel USA, Inc. v. DGI Technologies, Inc., 166 F.3d 772, 792-95 (5th Cir.1999); Lasercomb America, Inc. v. Reynolds, 911 F.2d 970, 976-79 (4th Cir. 1990). The data in the municipalities' tax-assessment databases are beyond the scope of AT's copyright. It is true that in Reed-Union Corp. v. Turtle Wax, Inc., 77 F.3d 909, 913 (7th Cir.1996), we left open the question whether copyright misuse, unless it rises to the level of an antitrust violation, is a defense to infringement; our earlier decision in Saturday Evening Post Co. v. Rumbleseat Press, Inc., 816 F.2d 1191, 1200 (7th Cir.1987), had intimated skepticism. No effort has been made by WIREdata to show that AT has market power merely by virtue of its having a copyright on one system for compiling valuation data for real estate tax assessment purposes. Cases such as *Lasercomb*, however, cut misuse free from antitrust, pointing out that the cognate doctrine of patent misuse is not so limited, 911 F.2d at 977-78, though a difference is that patents tend to confer greater market power on their owners than copyrights do, since patents protect ideas and copyrights, as we have noted, do not. The argument for applying copyright misuse beyond the bounds of antitrust, besides the fact that confined to antitrust the doctrine would be redundant, is that for a copyright owner to use an infringement suit to obtain property protection, here in data, that copyright law clearly does not confer, hoping to force a settlement or even achieve an outright victory over an opponent that may lack the resources or the legal sophistication to resist effectively, is an abuse of process.

We need not run this hare to the ground, nor decide whether the licenses interpreted as AT would have us interpret them — as barring municipalities from disclosing noncopyrighted data — would violate the state's open-records law. WIREdata is not a licensee of AT, and AT is not suing to enforce any contract it might have with WIREdata. It therefore had no cause to drag the licenses before us. But since it did, we shall not conceal our profound skepticism concerning AT's interpretation. If accepted, it would forbid municipalities licensed by AT to share the data in their tax-assessment databases with each other even for the purpose of comparing or coordinating their assessment methods, though all the data they would be exchanging would be data that their assessors had collected and inputted into the databases. That seems an absurd result.

To summarize, there are at least four possible methods by which WIREdata can obtain the data it is seeking without infringing AT's copyright; which one is selected is for the municipality to decide in light of applicable trade-secret, open-records, and contract laws. The methods are: (1) the municipalities use Market Drive to extract the data and place it in an electronic file;

(2) they use Microsoft Access to create an electronic file of the data; (3) they allow programmers furnished by WIREdata to use their computers to extract the data from their database— this is really just an alternative to WIREdata's paying the municipalities' cost of extraction, which the open-records law requires; (4) they copy the database file and give it to WIREdata to extract the data from. The judgment is reversed with instructions to vacate the injunction and dismiss the copyright claim.

BRITISH HORSERACING BOARD v. WILLIAM HILL ORGANIZATION LTD.
2004 WL 2709083, EU: Case C-203/02, ECJ, Nov. 09, 2004

THE COURT (Grand Chamber).

Composed of: V. Skouris, President, P. Jann, C.W.A. Timmermans, A. Rosas and K. Lenaerts (Rapporteur), (Presidents of Chambers), J.P. Puissochet, R. Schintgen, N. Colneric and J.N. Cunha Rodrigues, Judges, after hearing the Opinion of the Advocate General at the sitting on 8 June 2004, gives the following Judgment:

GROUNDS

1. This reference for a preliminary ruling concerns the interpretation of Article 7 and Article 10(3) of Directive 96/9/EC of the European Parliament and of the Council of 11 March 1996 on the legal protection of databases (OJ 1996 L 77, p. 20, the directive).

2. The reference was made in the course of proceedings brought by The British Horseracing Board Ltd, the Jockey Club and Weatherbys Group Ltd (the BHB and Others) against William Hill Organization Ltd (William Hill). The litigation arose over the use by William Hill, for the purpose of organising betting on horse racing, of information taken from the BHB database.

3. The directive, according to Article 1(1) thereof, concerns the legal protection of databases in any form. A database is defined, in Article 1(2), as a collection of independent works, data or other materials arranged in a systematic or methodical way and individually accessible by electronic or other means.

4. Article 3 provides for copyright protection for databases which, by reason of the selection or arrangement of their contents, constitute the author's own intellectual creation.

5. Article 7 provides for a sui generis right in the following terms:

OBJECT OF PROTECTION

1. Member States shall provide for a right for the maker of a database which shows that there has been qualitatively and/or quantitatively a substantial investment in either the obtaining, verification or presentation of the contents to prevent extraction and/or re-utilisation of the whole or of a substantial part, evaluated qualitatively and/or quantitatively, of the contents of that database.

2. For the purposes of this Chapter:

(a) extraction shall mean the permanent or temporary transfer of all or a substantial part of the contents of a database to another medium by any means or in any form;

(b) re-utilisation shall mean any form of making available to the public all or a substantial part of the contents of a database by the distribution of copies, by renting, by on-line or other forms of transmission. The first sale of a copy of a database within the Community by the rightholder or with his consent shall exhaust the right to control resale of that copy within the Community; public lending is not an act of extraction or re-utilisation.

3. The right referred to in paragraph 1 may be transferred, assigned or granted under contractual licence.

4. The right provided for in paragraph 1 shall apply irrespective of the eligibility of that database for protection by copyright or by other rights. Moreover, it shall apply irrespective of eligibility of the contents of that database for protection by copyright or by other rights. Protection of databases under the right provided for in paragraph 1 shall be without prejudice to rights existing in respect of their content.

5. The repeated and systematic extraction and/or re-utilisation of insubstantial parts of the contents of the database implying acts which conflict with a normal exploitation of that database or which unreasonably prejudice the legitimate interests of the maker of the database shall not be permitted.

6. Article 8(1) provides:

The maker of a database which is made available to the public in whatever manner may not prevent a lawful user of the database from extracting and/or re-utilising insubstantial parts of its contents, evaluated qualitatively and/or quantitatively, for any purposes whatsoever. Where the lawful user is authorised to extract and/or re-utilise only part of the database, this paragraph shall apply only to that part.

7. Under Article 9 Member States may stipulate that lawful users of a database which is made available to the public in whatever manner may, without the authorisation of its maker, extract or re-utilise a substantial part of its contents:

in the case of extraction for private purposes of the contents of a non-electronic database;
in the case of extraction for the purposes of illustration for teaching or scientific research, as long as the source is indicated and to the extent justified by the non-commercial purpose to be achieved;
in the case of extraction and/or re-utilisation for the purposes of public security or an administrative or judicial procedure. . . .

10. The BHB and Others manage the horse racing industry in the United Kingdom and in various capacities compile and maintain the BHB database which contains a large amount of information supplied by horse owners, trainers, horse race organisers and others involved in the racing industry. The database contains information on inter alia the pedigrees of some one million horses, and prerace information on races to be held in the United Kingdom. That information includes the name, place and date of the race concerned, the distance over which the race is to be run, the criteria for eligibility to enter the race, the date by which entries must be received, the entry fee payable and the amount of money the racecourse is to contribute to the prize money for the race.

11. Weatherbys Group Ltd, the company which compiles and maintains the BHB database, performs three principal functions, which lead up to the issue of pre-race information.

12. First, it registers information concerning owners, trainers, jockeys and horses and records the performances of those horses in each race.

13. Second, it decides on weight adding and handicapping for the horses entered for the various races.

14. Third, it compiles the lists of horses running in the races. This activity is carried out by its own call centre, manned by about 30 operators. They record telephone calls entering horses in each race organised. The identity and status of the person entering the horse and whether the characteristics of the horse meet the criteria for entry to the race are then checked. Following those checks the entries are published provisionally. To take part in the race, the trainer must confirm the horse's participation by telephone by declaring it the day before the race at the latest. The operators must then ascertain whether the horse can be authorised to run the race in the light of the number of declarations already recorded. A central computer then allocates a saddle cloth number to each horse and determines the stall from which it will start. The final list of runners is published the day before the race.

15. The BHB database contains essential information not only for those directly involved in horse racing but also for radio and television broadcasters and for bookmakers and their clients. The cost of running the BHB database is approximately €4 million per annum. The fees charged to third parties for the use of the information in the database cover about a quarter of that amount.

16. The database is accessible on the internet site operated jointly by BHB and Weatherbys Group Ltd. Some of its contents are also published each week in the BHB's official journal. The contents of the database, or of certain parts of it, are also made available to Racing Pages Ltd, a company jointly controlled by Weatherbys Group Ltd and the Press Association, which then forwards data to its various subscribers, including some bookmakers, in the form of a Declarations Feed, the day before a race. Satellite Information Services Limited (SIS) is authorised by Racing Pages to transmit data to its own subscribers in the form of a raw data feed (RDF). The RDF includes a large amount of information, in particular, the names of the horses running in the races, the names of the jockeys, the saddle cloth numbers and the weight for each horse. Through the newspapers and the Ceefax and Teletext services, the names of the runners in a particular race are made available to the public during the course of the afternoon before the race.

17. William Hill, which is a subscriber to both the Declarations Feed and the RDF, is one of the leading providers of offcourse bookmaking services in the United Kingdom, to both UK and international customers. It launched an on-line betting service on two internet sites. Those interested can use these sites to find out what horses are running in which races at which racecourses and what odds are offered by William Hill.

18. The information displayed on William Hill's internet sites is obtained, first, from newspapers published the day before the race and, second, from the RDF supplied by SIS on the morning of the race.

19. [T]he information displayed on William Hill's internet sites represents a very small proportion of the total amount of data on the BHB database, given that it concerns only the

following matters: the names of all the horses in the race, the date, time and/or name of the race and the name of the racecourse where the race will be held. Also according to the order for reference, the horse races and the lists of runners are not arranged on William Hill's internet sites in the same way as in the BHB database.

20. In March 2000 the BHB and Others brought proceedings against William Hill in the High Court of Justice of England and Wales, Chancery Division, alleging infringement of their sui generis right. They contend, first, that each day's use by William Hill of racing data taken from the newspapers or the RDF is an extraction or re-utilisation of a substantial part of the contents of the BHB database, contrary to Article 7(1). Secondly, they say that even if the individual extracts made by William Hill are not substantial they should be prohibited under Article 7(5).

21. The High Court of Justice ruled in a judgment of 9 February 2001 that the action of BHB and Others was well founded. William Hill appealed to the referring court. . . .

23. Article 7(1) provides for specific protection, called a sui generis right, for the maker of a database within the meaning of Article 1(2), provided that it shows that there has been qualitatively and/or quantitatively a substantial investment in either the obtaining, verification or presentation of the contents.

24. [T]he referring court seeks an interpretation of the concept of investment in the obtaining and verification of the contents of a database within the meaning of Article 7(1).

25. Article 7(1) authorises a maker of a database protected by a sui generis right to prevent extraction and/or re-utilisation of the whole or of a substantial part of its contents. Article 7(5) also prohibits the repeated and systematic extraction and/or re-utilisation of insubstantial parts of the contents of the database implying acts which conflict with a normal exploitation of that database or which unreasonably prejudice the legitimate interests of the maker of the database. . . .

29. Article 7(1) reserves the protection of the sui generis right to databases which meet a specific criterion, namely to those which show that there has been qualitatively and/or quantitatively a substantial investment in the obtaining, verification or presentation of their contents.

30. [The purpose of the directive] is to promote and protect investment in data storage and processing systems which contribute to the development of an information market against a background of exponential growth in the amount of information generated and processed annually in all sectors of activity. It follows that the expression investment in . . . the obtaining, verification or presentation of the contents of a database must be understood, generally, to refer to investment in the creation of that database as such.

31. [T]he expression investment in . . . the obtaining . . . of the contents of a database must . . . be understood to refer to the resources used to seek out existing independent materials and collect them in the database, and not to the resources used for the creation as such of independent materials. The purpose of the protection by the sui generis right . . . is to promote the establishment of storage and processing systems for existing information and not the creation of materials capable of being collected subsequently in a database.

32. That interpretation is backed up by the 39th recital of the preamble to the directive, according to which the aim of the sui generis right is to safeguard the results of the financial and professional investment made in obtaining and collection of the contents[] of a

database. As the Advocate General notes in points 41 to 46 of her Opinion, despite slight variations in wording, all the language versions of the 39th recital support an interpretation which excludes the creation of the materials contained in a database from the definition of obtaining. . . .

34. The expression investment in . . . the . . . verification . . . of the contents of a database must be understood to refer to the resources used, with a view to ensuring the reliability of the information contained in that database, to monitor the accuracy of the materials collected when the database was created and during its operation. The resources used for verification during the stage of creation of data or other materials which are subsequently collected in a database, on the other hand, are resources used in creating a database and cannot therefore be taken into account in order to assess whether there was substantial investment in the terms of Article 7(1).

35. In that light, the fact that the creation of a database is linked to the exercise of a principal activity in which the person creating the database is also the creator of the materials contained in the database does not, as such, preclude that person from claiming the protection of the sui generis right, provided that he establishes that the obtaining of those materials, their verification or their presentation, in the sense described in paragraphs 31 to 34 of this judgment, required substantial investment in quantitative or qualitative terms, which was independent of the resources used to create those materials.

36. Thus, although the search for data and the verification of their accuracy at the time a database is created do not require the maker of that database to use particular resources because the data are those he created and are available to him, the fact remains that the collection of those data, their systematic or methodical arrangement in the database, the organisation of their individual accessibility and the verification of their accuracy throughout the operation of the database may require substantial investment in quantitative and/or qualitative terms within the meaning of Article 7(1).

37. [T]he referring court seeks to know whether the investments described in paragraph 14 of this judgment can be considered to amount to investment in obtaining the contents of the BHB database. The plaintiffs in the main proceedings stress, in that connection, the substantial nature of the above investment.

38. However, investment in the selection, for the purpose of organising horse racing, of the horses admitted to run in the race concerned relates to the creation of the data which make up the lists for those races which appear in the BHB database. It does not constitute investment in obtaining the contents of the database. It cannot, therefore, be taken into account in assessing whether the investment in the creation of the database was substantial.

39. Admittedly, the process of entering a horse on a list for a race requires a number of prior checks as to the identity of the person making the entry, the characteristics of the horse and the classification of the horse, its owner and the jockey.

40. However, such prior checks are made at the stage of creating the list for the race in question. They thus constitute investment in the creation of data and not in the verification of the contents of the database.

41. It follows that the resources used to draw up a list of horses in a race and to carry out checks in that connection do not represent investment in the obtaining and verification of the contents of the database in which that list appears. . . .

43. [T]he referring court seeks essentially to know whether use such as that made by William Hill of a database constitutes extraction and/or re-utilisation within the meaning of Article 7. The referring court asks, inter alia, whether the protection conferred by the sui generis right also covers the use of data which, although derived originally from a protected database, were obtained by the user from sources other than that database.

44. The protection of the sui generis right provided for by Article 7(1) gives the maker of a database the option of preventing the unauthorised extraction and/or re-utilisation of all or a substantial part of the contents of that database, according to the 41st recital of the preamble to the directive. Furthermore, Article 7(5) prohibits, under certain conditions, the unauthorised extraction and/or re-utilisation of insubstantial parts of the contents of a database.

45. The terms extraction and re-utilisation must be interpreted in the light of the objective pursued by the sui generis right. It is intended to protect the maker of the database against acts by the user which go beyond [the] legitimate rights and thereby harm the investment of the maker. . . .

46. According to the 48th recital of the preamble to the directive, the sui generis right has an economic justification, which is to afford protection to the maker of the database and guarantee a return on his investment in the creation and maintenance of the database.

47. Accordingly, it is not relevant, in an assessment of the scope of the protection of the sui generis right, that the act of extraction and/or re-utilisation is for the purpose of creating another database, whether in competition with the original database or not, and whether the same or a different size from the original, nor is it relevant that the act is part of an activity other than the creation of a database. The 42nd recital of the preamble to the directive confirms, in that connection, that the right to prohibit extraction and/or re-utilisation of all or a substantial part of the contents relates not only to the manufacture of a parasitical competing product but also to any user who, through his acts, causes significant detriment, evaluated qualitatively or quantitatively, to the investment. . . .

49. In Article 7(2)(a), extraction is defined as the permanent or temporary transfer of all or a substantial part of the contents of a database to another medium by any means or in any form, while in Article 7(2)(b), re-utilisation is defined as any form of making available to the public all or a substantial part of the contents of a database by the distribution of copies, by renting, by on-line or other forms of transmission.

50. The reference to a substantial part in the definition of the concepts of extraction and re-utilisation gives rise to confusion given that, according to Article 7(5), extraction or re-utilisation may also concern an insubstantial part of a database. As the Advocate General observes, the reference in Article 7(2) to the substantial nature of the extracted or re-utilised part does not concern the definition of those concepts as such but must be understood to refer to one of the conditions for the application of the sui generis right laid down by Article 7(1).

51. The use of expressions such as by any means or in any form and any form of making available to the public indicates that the Community legislature intended to give the concepts of extraction and re-utilisation a wide definition. In the light of the objective pursued by the directive, those terms must therefore be interpreted as referring to any act of appropriating and making available to the public, without the consent of the maker of

the database, the results of his investment, thus depriving him of revenue which should have enabled him to redeem the cost of the investment.

52. Against that background, and contrary to the argument put forward by William Hill and the Belgian and Portuguese Governments, the concepts of extraction and re-utilisation cannot be exhaustively defined as instances of extraction and re-utilisation directly from the original database at the risk of leaving the maker of the database without protection from unauthorised copying from a copy of the database. That interpretation is confirmed by Article 7(2)(b), according to which the first sale of a copy of a database within the Community by the rightholder or with his consent is to exhaust the right to control resale, but not the right to control extraction and re-utilisation of the contents, of that copy within the Community.

53. Since acts of unauthorised extraction and/or re-utilisation by a third party from a source other than the database concerned are liable, just as much as such acts carried out directly from that database are, to prejudice the investment of the maker of the database, it must be held that the concepts of extraction and re-utilisation do not imply direct access to the database concerned.

54. However, it must be stressed that the protection of the sui generis right concerns only acts of extraction and re-utilisation as defined in Article 7(2). That protection does not, on the other hand, cover consultation of a database.

55. Of course, the maker of a database can reserve exclusive access to his database to himself or reserve access to specific people. However, if he himself makes the contents of his database or a part of it accessible to the public, his sui generis right does not allow him to prevent third parties from consulting that base.

56. The same applies where the maker of the database authorises a third party to re-utilise the contents of his database, in other words, to distribute it to the public. According to the definition of re-utilisation in Article 7(2)(b), read in conjunction with the 41st recital of the preamble thereto, the authorisation of the maker for the re-utilisation of the database or a substantial part of it implies that he consents to his database or the relevant part of it being made accessible to the public by the third party to whom he gave that authorisation. In authorising re-utilisation, the maker of the database thus creates an alternative means of access to the contents of and of consultation of his database for those interested.

57. The fact that a database can be consulted by third parties through someone who has authorisation for re-utilisation from the maker of the database does not, however, prevent the maker from recovering the costs of his investment. It is legitimate for the maker to charge a fee for the re-utilisation of the whole or a part of his database which reflects, inter alia, the prospect of subsequent consultation and thus guarantees him a sufficient return on his investment.

58. On the other hand, a lawful user of a database, in other words, a user whose access to the contents of a database for the purpose of consultation results from the direct or indirect consent of the maker of the database, may be prevented by the maker, under the sui generis right provided for by Article 7(1), from then carrying out acts of extraction and/or re-utilisation of the whole or a substantial part of the database. The consent of the maker of the database to consultation does not entail exhaustion of the sui generis right.

59. That analysis is confirmed, as regards extraction, by the 44th recital of the preamble to the directive, according to which, when on-screen display of the contents of a database

necessitates the permanent or temporary transfer of all or a substantial part of such contents to another medium, that act should be subject to authorisation by the rightholder. Similarly, as regards re-utilisation, the 43rd recital of the preamble to the directive states that in the case of on-line transmission, the right to prohibit re-utilisation is not exhausted either as regards the database or as regards a material copy of the database or of part thereof made by the addressee of the transmission with the consent of the rightholder.

60. It should, however, be emphasised that the prohibition in Article 7(1) concerns only extraction and/or re-utilisation of the whole or of a substantial part of a database whose creation required a substantial investment. According to Article 8(1), apart from in the cases referred to in Article 7(5), the sui generis right does not prevent a lawful user from extracting and re-utilising insubstantial parts of the contents of a database.

61. It follows from the foregoing that acts of extraction, in other words, the transfer of the contents of the database to another medium, and acts of reutilisation, in other words, the making available to the public of the contents of a database, which affect the whole or a substantial part of the contents of a database require the authorisation of the maker of the database, even where he has made his database, as a whole or in part, accessible to the public or authorised a specific third party or specific third parties to distribute it to the public.

62. The directive contains an exception to the principle set out in the previous paragraph. Article 9 defines exhaustively three cases in which Member States may stipulate that lawful users of a database which is made available to the public in whatever manner may, without the authorisation of its maker, extract or re-utilise a substantial part of the contents of that database. Those cases are: extraction for private purposes of the contents of a non-electronic database, extraction for the purposes of illustration for teaching or scientific research and extraction and/or re-utilisation for the purposes of public security or an administrative or judicial procedure.

63. [T]he order for reference states that the data concerning horse races which William Hill displays on its internet site and which originate in the BHB database are obtained, first, from newspapers published the day before the race and, second, from the RDF supplied by SIS.

64. [T]he information published in the newspapers is supplied to the press directly by Weatherbys Group Ltd, the company which maintains the BHB database. As regards William Hill's other source of information, it must be borne in mind that SIS is authorised by Racing Pages Ltd, which is partly controlled by Weatherbys Group Ltd, to supply information concerning horse races in the form of RDF to its own members, which include William Hill. The data in the BHB database concerning horse races have thus been made accessible to the public for the purpose of consultation with the authorisation of BHB.

65. Although William Hill is a lawful user of the database made accessible to the public, at least as regards the part of that database representing information about races, it appears from the order for reference that it carries out acts of extraction and re-utilisation within the meaning of Article 7(2). First, it extracts data originating in the BHB database by transferring them from one medium to another. It integrates those data into its own electronic system. Second, it re-utilises those data by then making them available to the public on its internet site in order to allow its clients to bet on horse races.

66. [T]hat extraction and re-utilisation was carried out without the authorisation of BHB and Others. Since the present case does not fall within any of the cases described in Article 9, acts such as those carried out by William Hill could be prevented by BHB and Others under their sui generis right provided that they affect the whole or a substantial part of the contents of the BHB database within the meaning of Article 7(1). If such acts affected insubstantial parts of the database they would be prohibited only if the conditions in Article 7(5) were fulfilled. . . .

68. [T]he referring court raises the question of the meaning of the terms substantial part and insubstantial part of the contents of a database as used in Article 7. [I]t also seeks to know whether materials derived from a database do not constitute a part, substantial or otherwise, of that database, where their systematic or methodical arrangement and the conditions of their individual accessibility have been altered by the person carrying out the extraction and/or re-utilisation.

69. In that connection, it must be borne in mind that protection by the sui generis right covers databases whose creation required a substantial investment. Against that background, Article 7(1) prohibits extraction and/or re-utilisation not only of the whole of a database protected by the sui generis right but also of a substantial part, evaluated qualitatively or quantitatively, of its contents. According to the 42nd recital of the preamble to the directive, that provision is intended to prevent a situation in which a user through his acts causes significant detriment, evaluated qualitatively or quantitatively, to the investment. It appears from that recital that the assessment, in qualitative terms, of whether the part at issue is substantial, must, like the assessment in quantitative terms, refer to the investment in the creation of the database and the prejudice caused to that investment by the act of extracting or re-utilising that part.

70. The expression substantial part, evaluated quantitatively, of the contents of a database within the meaning of Article 7(1) refers to the volume of data extracted from the database and/or re-utilised, and must be assessed in relation to the volume of the contents of the whole of that database. If a user extracts and/or re-utilises a quantitatively significant part of the contents of a database whose creation required the deployment of substantial resources, the investment in the extracted or re-utilised part is, proportionately, equally substantial.

71. The expression substantial part, evaluated qualitatively, of the contents of a database refers to the scale of the investment in the obtaining, verification or presentation of the contents of the subject of the act of extraction and/or re-utilisation, regardless of whether that subject represents a quantitatively substantial part of the general contents of the protected database. A quantitatively negligible part of the contents of a database may in fact represent, in terms of obtaining, verification or presentation, significant human, technical or financial investment.

72. It must be added that, as the existence of the sui generis right does not, according to the 46th recital of the preamble to the directive, give rise to the creation of a new right in the works, data or materials themselves, the intrinsic value of the materials affected by the act of extraction and/or re-utilisation does not constitute a relevant criterion for the assessment of whether the part at issue is substantial.

73. It must be held that any part which does not fulfill the definition of a substantial part, evaluated both quantitatively and qualitatively, falls within the definition of an insubstantial part of the contents of a database.

74. In that regard, it appears from the order for reference that the materials displayed on William Hill's internet sites, which derive from the BHB database, represent only a very small proportion of the whole of that database, as stated in paragraph 19 of this judgment. It must therefore be held that those materials do not constitute a substantial part, evaluated quantitatively, of the contents of that database.

75. According to the order for reference, the information published by William Hill concerns only the following aspects of the BHB database: the names of all the horses running in the race concerned, the date, the time and/or the name of the race and the name of the racecourse, as also stated in paragraph 19 of this judgment.

76. In order to assess whether those materials represent a substantial part, evaluated qualitatively, of the contents of the BHB database, it must be considered whether the human, technical and financial efforts put in by the maker of the database in obtaining, verifying and presenting those data constitute a substantial investment.

77. BHB and Others submit, in that connection, that the data extracted and re-utilised by William Hill are of crucial importance because, without lists of runners, the horse races could not take place. They add that those data represent a significant investment, as demonstrated by the role played by a call centre employing more than 30 operators.

78. However, it must be observed, first, that the intrinsic value of the data affected by the act of extraction and/or re-utilisation does not constitute a relevant criterion for assessing whether the part in question is substantial, evaluated qualitatively. The fact that the data extracted and re-utilised by William Hill are vital to the organisation of the horse races which BHB and Others are responsible for organising is thus irrelevant to the assessment whether the acts of William Hill concern a substantial part of the contents of the BHB database.

79. Next, it must be observed that the resources used for the creation as such of the materials included in a database cannot be taken into account in assessing whether the investment in the creation of that database was substantial, as stated in paragraphs 31 to 33 of this judgment.

80. The resources deployed by BHB to establish, for the purposes of organising horse races, the date, the time, the place and/or name of the race, and the horses running in it, represent an investment in the creation of materials contained in the BHB database. Consequently, and if, as the order for reference appears to indicate, the materials extracted and re-utilised by William Hill did not require BHB and Others to put in investment independent of the resources required for their creation, it must be held that those materials do not represent a substantial part, in qualitative terms, of the BHB database. . . .

83. [T]he referring court seeks to know what type of act is covered by the prohibition laid down by Article 7(5). It also seeks to know whether acts such as those carried out by William Hill are covered by that prohibition.

84. On that point, it appears from Article 8(1) and from the 42nd recital of the preamble to the directive that, as a rule, the maker of a database cannot prevent a

lawful user of that database from carrying out acts of extraction and re-utilisation of an insubstantial part of its contents. Article 7(5), which authorises the maker of the database to prevent such acts under certain conditions, thus provides for an exception to that general rule.

85. Common Position (EC) No. 20/95 adopted by the Council on 10 July 1995 (OJ 1995 C 288, p. 14) states, under point 14 of the Council's statement of reasons: to ensure that the lack of protection of the insubstantial parts does not lead to their being repeatedly and systematically extracted and/or re-utilised, paragraph 5 of this article in the common position introduces a safeguard clause.

86. It follows that the purpose of Article 7(5) is to prevent circumvention of the prohibition in Article 7(1). Its objective is to prevent repeated and systematic extractions and/or re-utilisations of insubstantial parts of the contents of a database, the cumulative effect of which would be to seriously prejudice the investment made by the maker of the database just as the extractions and/or re-utilisations referred to in Article 7(1) would.

87. The provision therefore prohibits acts of extraction made by users of the database which, because of their repeated and systematic character, would lead to the reconstitution of the database as a whole or, at the very least, of a substantial part of it, without the authorisation of the maker of the database, whether those acts were carried out with a view to the creation of another database or in the exercise of an activity other than the creation of a database.

88. Similarly, Article 7(5) prohibits third parties from circumventing the prohibition on re-utilisation laid down by Article 7(1) by making insubstantial parts of the contents of the database available to the public in a systematic and repeated manner.

89. Under those circumstances, acts which conflict with a normal exploitation of [a] database or which unreasonably prejudice the legitimate interests of the maker of the database refer to unauthorised actions for the purpose of reconstituting, through the cumulative effect of acts of extraction, the whole or a substantial part of the contents of a database protected by the sui generis right and/or of making available to the public, through the cumulative effect of acts of re-utilisation, the whole or a substantial part of the contents of such a database, which thus seriously prejudice the investment made by the maker of the database.

90. [I]t is clear, in the light of the information given in the order for reference, that the acts of extraction and re-utilisation carried out by William Hill concern insubstantial parts of the BHB database, as stated in paragraphs 74 to 80 of this judgment. [T]hey are carried out on the occasion of each race held. They are thus of a repeated and systematic nature.

91. However, such acts are not intended to circumvent the prohibition laid down in Article 7(1). There is no possibility that, through the cumulative effect of its acts, William Hill might reconstitute and make available to the public the whole or a substantial part of the contents of the BHB database and thereby seriously prejudice the investment made by BHB in the creation of that database.

92. [A]ccording to the order for reference, the materials derived from the BHB database which are published daily on William Hill's internet sites concern only the races for that day and are limited to the information mentioned in paragraph 19 of this judgment.

93. As explained in paragraph 80 of this judgment, . . . the presence, in the database of the claimants, of the materials affected by William Hill's actions did not require investment by BHB and Others independent of the resources used for their creation.

94. It must therefore be held that the prohibition in Article 7(5) does not cover acts such as those of William Hill. . . .

UNITED STATES OF AMERICA
BEFORE THE FEDERAL TRADE COMMISSION
COMMISSIONERS: Maureen K. Ohlhausen, Acting Chairman
Terrell McSweeny

In the Matter of	)	
	)	
Decusoft, LLC,	)	**DOCKET NO. C-**
a limited liability company.	)	
	)	
	)	
	)	

COMPLAINT

The Federal Trade Commission ("FTC"), having reason to believe that Decusoft, LLC, a limited liability company, has violated the Federal Trade Commission Act ("FTC Act"), and it appearing to the Commission that this proceeding is in the public interest, alleges:

1. Respondent Decusoft, LLC is a New Jersey limited liability company with its principal office or place of business at 70 Hilltop Road, Suite 1003, Ramsey, New Jersey 07446.

2. Respondent develops software for use in human resources applications.

3. The acts and practices of respondent as alleged in this complaint have been in or affecting commerce, as "commerce" is defined in Section 4 of the FTC Act.

4. Respondent has set forth on its website, http://www.decusoft.com/privacy-policy, privacy policies and statements about its practices, including statements related to its participation in the Privacy Shield frameworks agreed upon by the U.S. government and the European Commission ("EU-U.S. Privacy Shield") and the U.S. and Switzerland ("Swiss-U.S. Privacy Shield").

5. In fact, respondent has not been certified to participate in either the EU-U.S. Privacy Shield framework or the Swiss-U.S. Privacy Shield framework.

Privacy Shield

6. The EU-U.S. Privacy Shield framework ("Privacy Shield") was designed by the U.S. Department of Commerce ("Commerce") and the European Commission to provide companies on both sides of the Atlantic with a mechanism to comply with European Union ("EU") data protection requirements when transferring personal data from the EU to the United States in support of transatlantic commerce.

7. Privacy Shield provides a mechanism for U.S. companies to transfer personal data outside of the EU that is consistent with the requirements of the European Union Directive on Data Protection. Enacted in 1995, the Directive sets forth EU requirements for privacy and the protection of personal data. Among other things, it requires EU Member States to implement legislation that prohibits the transfer of personal data outside the EU, with exceptions, unless the European Commission has made a determination that the recipient jurisdiction's laws ensure the protection of such personal data. This determination is referred to commonly as meeting the EU's "adequacy" standard.

8. To satisfy the EU adequacy standard for certain commercial transfers, Commerce and the European Commission negotiated the EU-U.S. Privacy Shield framework, which went into effect in July 2016. The EU-U.S. Privacy Shield framework allows companies to transfer personal data lawfully from the EU to the United States. To join the EU-U.S. Privacy Shield framework, a company must self-certify to Commerce that it complies with the Privacy Shield Principles and related requirements that have been deemed to meet the EU's adequacy standard.

9. Companies under the jurisdiction of the FTC, as well as the U.S. Department of Transportation, are eligible to join the EU-U.S. Privacy Shield framework. A company under the FTC's jurisdiction that claims it has self-certified to the Privacy Shield Principles, but failed to self-certify to Commerce, may be subject to an enforcement action based on the FTC's deception authority under Section 5 of the FTC Act.

10. The Swiss-U.S. Privacy Shield framework is identical to the EU-U.S. Privacy Shield framework and is consistent with the requirements of the Swiss Federal Act on Data Protection. The Swiss-U.S. Privacy Shield framework went into effect in April 2017.

11. Commerce maintains a public website, https://www.privacyshield.gov/welcome, where it posts the names of companies that have self-certified to the EU-U.S. and/or Swiss-U.S. Privacy Shield framework. The listing of companies, https://www.privacyshield.gov/list, indicates whether the company's self-certification is current.

Violations of Section 5 of the FTC Act

12. Respondent has disseminated or caused to be disseminated privacy policies and statements on the http://www.decusoft.com/privacy-policy/website, including, but not limited to, the following statements:

> Decusoft participates in and has certified its compliance with the EU-U.S. Privacy Shield Framework and the Swiss-U.S. Privacy Shield Framework. We are committed to subjecting all personal data received from European Union (EU) member countries, in reliance on the Privacy Shield Framework, to the Framework's applicable Principles. To learn more about the Privacy Shield Framework, visit the U.S. Department of Commerce's Privacy Shield List, https://www.privacyshield.gov/list.

13. Through the means described in Paragraph 12, respondent represents, expressly or by implication, that it is a participant in both the EU-U.S. Privacy Shield framework and the Swiss-U.S Privacy Shield framework.

14. In truth and in fact, although respondent initiated an application to Commerce for Privacy Shield certification, it did not complete the steps necessary to participate in either the EU-U.S. or the Swiss-U.S. Privacy Shield frameworks. Therefore, the representation set forth in Paragraph 13 is false and misleading.

15. The acts and practices of respondent as alleged in this complaint constitute deceptive acts or practices, in or affecting commerce, in violation of Section 5(a) of the Federal Trade Commission Act.

THEREFORE, the Federal Trade Commission this twentieth day of November, 2017, has issued this complaint against respondent.

By the Commission.

Donald A. Clark
Secretary

UNITED STATES OF AMERICA
BEFORE THE FEDERAL TRADE COMMISSION
COMMISSIONERS: Maureen K. Ohlhausen, Acting Chairman
Terrell McSweeny

In the Matter of	)	**DOCKET NO. C-**
	)	
Decusoft, LLC,	)	**DECISION AND ORDER**
a limited liability company.	)	
	)	
	)	
	)	

DECISION

The Federal Trade Commission ("Commission") initiated an investigation of certain acts and practices of the Respondent named above in the caption. The Commission's Bureau of Consumer Protection ("BCP") prepared and furnished to Respondent a draft Complaint. BCP proposed to present the draft Complaint to the Commission for its consideration. If issued by the Commission, the draft Complaint would charge Respondent with violation of the Federal Trade Commission Act.

Respondent and BCP thereafter executed an Agreement Containing Consent Order ("Consent Agreement"). The Consent Agreement includes: 1) statements by Respondent that it neither admits nor denies any of the allegations in the Complaint, except as specifically stated in this Decision and Order, and that only for purposes of this action, it admits the facts necessary to establish jurisdiction; and 2) waivers and other provisions as required by the Commission's Rules.

The Commission considered the matter and determined that it had reason to believe that Respondent has violated the Federal Trade Commission Act, and that a Complaint should issue stating its charges in that respect. The Commission accepted the executed Consent Agreement and placed it on the public record for a period of 30 days for the receipt and consideration of public comments. The Commission duly considered any comments received from interested persons pursuant to Section 2.34 of its Rules, 16 C.F.R. §2.34. Now, in further conformity with the procedure prescribed in Rule 2.34, the Commission issues its Complaint, makes the following Findings, and issues the following Order:

Findings

1. Respondent Decusoft, LLC is a New Jersey limited liability company with its principal office or place of business at 70 Hilltop Road, Suite 1003, Ramsey New Jersey 07446.
2. The Commission has jurisdiction over the subject matter of this proceeding and over Respondent, and the proceeding is in the public interest.

ORDER

Definitions

For purposes of this Order, the following definitions apply:

1. "Respondent" means Decusoft, LLC, a limited liability company and its successors and assigns.

Provisions

I. Prohibition Against Misrepresentations About Participation in Privacy or Security Programs

IT IS ORDERED that Respondent and its officers, agents, employees, and attorneys, and all other persons in active concert or participation with any of them, who receive actual notice of this order, whether acting directly or indirectly, in connection with the advertising, marketing, promotion, offering for sale, or sale of any product or service must not misrepresent in any manner, expressly or by implication, the extent to which Respondent is a member of, adheres to, complies with, is certified by, is endorsed by, or otherwise participates in any privacy or security program sponsored by a government or any self-regulatory or standard-setting organization, including but not limited to the EU-U.S. Privacy Shield framework and the Swiss-U.S. Privacy Shield framework.

II. Acknowledgments of the Order

IT IS FURTHER ORDERED that Respondent obtain acknowledgments of receipt of this Order:

A. Respondent, within 10 days after the effective date of this Order, must submit to the Commission an acknowledgment of receipt of this Order.

B. For twenty (20) years after the issuance date of this Order, Respondent must deliver a copy of this Order to: (1) all principals, officers, directors, and LLC managers and members; (2) all employees, agents, and representatives with responsibilities related to the subject matter of the Order; and (3) any business entity resulting from any change in structure as set forth in the Provision titled Compliance Report and Notices. Delivery must occur within ten (10) days after the effective date of this Order for current personnel. For all others, delivery must occur before they assume their responsibilities.

C. From each individual or entity to which Respondent delivered a copy of this Order, Respondent must obtain, within thirty (30) days, a signed and dated acknowledgment of receipt of this Order.

III. Compliance Report and Notices

IT IS FURTHER ORDERED that Respondent make timely submissions to the Commission:

A. Sixty (60) days after the issuance date of this Order, Respondent must submit a compliance report, sworn under penalty of perjury, in which Respondent must: (a) identify the primary physical, postal, and email address and telephone number, as designated points of contact, which representatives of the Commission, may use to communicate with Respondent; (b) identify all of Respondent's businesses by all of their names, telephone numbers, and physical, postal, email, and Internet addresses; (c) describe the activities of each business; (d) describe in detail whether and how Respondent is in compliance with each Provision of this Order; and (e) provide a copy of each Acknowledgment of the Order obtained pursuant to this Order, unless previously submitted to the Commission.

B. Respondent must submit a compliance notice, sworn under penalty of perjury, within 14 days of any change in the following: (1) any designated point of contact; or (2) the structure of Respondent or any entity that Respondent has any ownership interest in or controls directly or indirectly that may affect compliance obligations arising under this Order, including: creation, merger, sale, or dissolution of the entity or any subsidiary, parent, or affiliate that engages in any acts or practices subject to this Order.

C. Respondent must submit notice of the filing of any bankruptcy petition, insolvency proceeding, or similar proceeding by or against Respondent within 14 days of its filing.

D. Any submission to the Commission required by this Order to be sworn under penalty of perjury must be true and accurate and comply with 28 U.S.C. §1746, such as by concluding: "I declare under penalty of perjury under the laws of the United States of America that the foregoing is true and correct. Executed on: _____" and supplying the date, signatory's full name, title (if applicable), and signature.

E. Unless otherwise directed by a Commission representative in writing, all submissions to the Commission pursuant to this Order must be emailed to Debrief@ftc.gov or sent by overnight courier (not the U.S. Postal Service) to: Associate Director of Enforcement, Bureau of Consumer Protection, Federal Trade Commission,

600 Pennsylvania Avenue, N.W., Washington, D.C. 20580. The subject line must begin: In re *Decusoft, LLC*, FTC File No. 1723173.

IV. Recordkeeping

IT IS FURTHER ORDERED that Respondent must create certain records for twenty (20) years after the issuance date of the Order, and retain each such record for 5 (five) years. Specifically, Respondent must create and retain the following records:

A. accounting records showing the revenues from all goods or services sold;

B. personnel records showing, for each person providing services, whether as an employee or otherwise, that person's: name; addresses; telephone numbers; job title or position; dates of service; and (if applicable) the reason for termination;

C. all records necessary to demonstrate full compliance with each provision of this Order, including all submissions to the Commission; and

D. a copy of each unique advertisement, promotional material, or other marketing material making any representation subject to this Order, and all materials that were relied upon in making the representation.

V. Compliance Monitoring

IT IS FURTHER ORDERED that, for the purpose of monitoring Respondent's compliance with this Order:

A. Within ten (10) days of receipt of a written request from a representative of the Commission, Respondent must: submit additional compliance reports or other requested information, which must be sworn under penalty of perjury, and produce records for inspection and copying.

B. For matters concerning this Order, representatives of the Commission are authorized to communicate directly with Respondent. Respondent must permit representatives of the Commission to interview anyone affiliated with Respondent who has agreed to such an interview. The interviewee may have counsel present.

C. The Commission may use all other lawful means, including posing through its representatives as consumers, suppliers, or other individuals or entities, to Respondent or any individual or entity affiliated with Respondent, without the necessity of identification or prior notice. Nothing in this Order limits the Commission's lawful use of compulsory process, pursuant to Sections 9 and 20 of the FTC Act, 15 U.S.C. §§49, 57b-1.

VI. Order Effective Dates

IT IS FURTHER ORDERED that this Order is final and effective upon the date of its publication on the Commission's website (ftc.gov) as a final order. This Order will terminate twenty (20) years from the date of its issuance (which is stated at the end of this Order, next to the Commission's seal), or twenty (20) years from the most recent date that the United States or the Commission files a complaint (with or without an accompanying settlement) in federal court alleging any violation of the Order, whichever comes later; *provided, however*, that the filing of such a complaint will not affect the duration of:

> A. any Provision in this Order that terminates in less than twenty (20) years;
>
> B. this Order's application to any Respondent that is not named as a defendant in such complaint; and
>
> C. this Order if such complaint is filed after the order has terminated pursuant to this Provision. If such complaint is dismissed or a federal court rules that Respondent did not violate any provision of the Order, and the dismissal or ruling is either not appealed or upheld on appeal, then the Order as to Respondent will terminate according to this Provision as though the complaint had never been filed, except that the Order will not terminate between the date such complaint is filed and the later of the deadline for appealing such dismissal or ruling and the date such dismissal or ruling is upheld on appeal.

By the Commission.

Donald S. Clark
Secretary

III. PROBLEMS

1. Would a refusal to license database content or information be considered a misuse or an unlawful extension of a monopoly? Why or why not? *See* Rural Tel. Serv. Co. v. Feist Publ'ns, 737 F. Supp. 610, 622 (Kan. 1990).

2. Would a provision in a license agreement restricting the disclosure of raw data compiled by a database software program be enforceable against a disclosing licensee to a third party not bound by the license agreement? If the raw data were segregable but intertwined with a copyrighted database software program, would your response be the same? What if the raw data could not be segregated from the copyrighted program without great expense to the licensor? What if the database program were a trade secret as opposed to copyrighted and the raw data were segregably intertwined but with substantial risk of disclosure of the trade secret to the detriment of the licensor?

3. What is the theory supporting the concept of public domain information? Should there be a statute outlawing licenses that lock up public domain materials? Would this solve the tension created by the use of licensing to govern parties' rights to use public domain or uncopyrightable materials? *See* U.S. Copyright Act, 17 U.S.C. §§102-103.

4. If a market-based approach to information were completely adopted as the model for balancing the interests between information privacy of a data subject and accessible information for aggregation or disaggregation by the information industry, what would be the impact on the market for this information? What legal

mechanisms or regulations would be required to support the market-based approach to information? What would be the impact on subsequent competition and innovation in the information industry if information were privatized?

5. With respect to EU database protection, do the governing provisions give ownership rights to data or information? Why or why not? Is the ECJ's *British Horseracing Board* decision harmful to the interests of organizations creating collections of information or databases? Practically, should these organizations create databases separate and apart from the collection of the raw data contained in the database? Would such a strategy make any difference in the protection afforded to both the database itself and the content or subject matter of the database? When will systematic extraction of insubstantial parts of the database amount to infringement under Article 7(5) and the *British Horseracing Board* decision? Does *British Horseracing Board's* interpretation of Article 7(5) broaden or limit the scope of infringement? What advice would you give to your clients engaged in both creation of databases and content for databases to maximize protection of their investments?

6. What opportunities for U.S. businesses are presented by the Department of Commerce's Privacy Shield Framework and the Federal Trade Commission's enforcement authority? What are the challenges? *See* https://www.privacyshield.gov /article?id = Benefits-of-Participation. What, if any, connections should be drawn between the EU General Data Protection Regulation and the Privacy Shield? How should a third party licensee protect itself from unintended data breaches, implicating the personal data of EU citizens: By its own activities or the activities of a licensor?

IV. DRAFTING EXERCISES

1. You represent Cable Entertainment (CE), a local cable company in the State of Hawai'i. ABC Video has approached your client seeking access to and use of CE's proprietary customer database. Draft a license grant provision that will allow ABC Video access to and use of CE's customer information and database for ABC's promotions for one year. When drafting the license grant provision, consider customer privacy issues, primary and secondary uses of information, i.e., third-party access and use of information, and any modifications, updates, and limitations necessary to protect your client's interests in the customer database and its ability to continue to use and build its database. Use the sample provision below to address in your drafting of the license grant the balance that must be struck in protecting the interest of data subjects who have provided your client information and your client's business incentives to maximize profit but also maintain its reputation in the marketplace for protecting data subject privacy.

> CE is committed to respecting Your privacy and the confidentiality of Your personal data. The "Privacy Policy" that is published on the CE Web site at

www.sampleprivacypolicy.com applies to the use of Your personal data, the traffic data as well as the content contained in Your communication(s). We do not sell or rent Your personal information to third parties for their marketing purposes without Your explicit consent and we use Your information only as described in the Privacy Policy. We store and process Your information on computers that may be located outside Your country, and that are protected by physical as well as technological security devices. You can access and modify the information You provide in accordance with the Privacy Policy. If You object to Your information being transferred or used in this way please do not use our services.

2. Based on the license grant provision in Drafting Exercise 1, draft a warranty provision that will protect your client from liability for inaccurate information or data contained in the database. Use the sample provision below to assist you in drafting the warranty provision(s).

> No warranties. THE INFORMATION AND DATABASE ARE PROVIDED "AS IS", WITH NO WARRANTIES WHATSOEVER; CE DOES NOT, EITHER EXPRESSED, IMPLIED OR BY STATUTE, MAKE ANY WARRANTIES, CLAIMS OR REPRESENTATIONS WITH RESPECT TO THE CE CONTENT AND DATABASE, INCLUDING, WITHOUT LIMITATION, WARRANTIES OF QUALITY, PERFORMANCE, NON-INFRINGEMENT, MERCHANTABILITY, OR FITNESS FOR USE OR A PARTICULAR PURPOSE.

3. Based on the license grant provision in Drafting Exercise 1, draft an indemnification provision that will protect your client from liability for unauthorized access to and disclosure of an individual's raw data and personal information.

> Indemnification. You agree to indemnify, defend and hold CE, Affiliates and the CE Staff harmless from and against any and all liability and costs, including reasonable attorneys' fees incurred by said parties, in connection with or arising out of this agreement.

4. Information and database license drafters often insist upon including acknowledgments in license agreements that require the licensee to contractually affirm the licensor's ownership of the information or database by express terms. You represent the licensee, MTV and Viacom. The licensor, Blockbuster, wants to grant a non-exclusive license to your client to use certain proprietary information, specifically customer names and addresses and demographic data. How would you re-draft this license to protect your client from agreeing to a contract acknowledgment that is too broad? In re-drafting this provision, consider the Supreme Court's decision in *Feist*.

> SECTION XX. OWNERSHIP OF CUSTOMER DATABASE. All information contained in the Customer Database, including any copies, translations or compilations of all or any part thereof, and any revisions, modifications or additions thereto made by Blockbuster or MTV, or an Affiliate of Viacom, as the case may be, are and shall remain the sole exclusive property of Blockbuster, except for any additions thereto which are made solely by MTV, or an Affiliate of Viacom, as the case may be, which MTV or an Affiliate of Viacom, as the case may be, shall own and shall make

available to Blockbuster for its use in conducting its business. This Section XX shall survive the termination of this Agreement.

5. Draft a gap-filling provision that would respond to the existence of GDPR requirements relating to notification to regulators and EU citizens in the event of a data breach on the one hand and the absence of breach notifications in the Privacy Shield on the other hand.

MULTIMEDIA LICENSING

I. OVERVIEW OF MULTIMEDIA LICENSING

A. Nature of Multimedia Products

We call certain products "multimedia products." The "multi" part of the term refers to the fact that these products contain multiple types of works: text, sounds, music, photographs, drawings, paintings, motion pictures, and data.[1] Multimedia products combine these works in digital form and utilize computer technology. This allows authors to combine works that could not otherwise be easily combined. Computers also allow users to easily manipulate information and provide them with an interactive user experience — the user does something with information and then it "replies" by producing new information or visual displays to which the user can relate and react.

Many types of products can be considered multimedia products, including the following:

- video games;
- interactive reference works, such as electronic encyclopedias;
- interactive training materials or tutorials;
- interactive television;
- virtual worlds;
- multiplayer games hosted online.

As technology evolves, the distinctiveness of the "multimedia" label may diminish. Works that we have always thought of as a "software program," "book," or "movie"

---

1. The term "multi*media*" is a bit of a misnomer because, rather than containing many types of *media*, multimedia products combine multiple *works* on one medium, such as a CD-ROM.

now appear more like a multimedia work. For example, word processing software no longer serves simply as a tool to manipulate plain text. It also gives the user an ability to display and manipulate data, sound, and images. It may contain "help files" that provide assistance to the user via the written or spoken word, aided by pictures, photos, or graphics, with music playing in the background. Another example is the telephone. At one time, a telephone could only take keystroke input (dialing) and manipulate sounds. Now the user can use a phone to store, manipulate, and display text and data, as well as record, play, and display sounds, music, and still and moving images.

At what point has word processing software or the telephone become a multimedia product? The answer may simply be that so many products now contain multiple works in digital form running on computer technology that the distinctive category of "multimedia product" has become obsolete. Perhaps "multimedia-ness" has become the expected form rather than a unique form of expression.

B. Creating a Multimedia Product

As described above, one of the defining characteristics of a multimedia product is its rich content. The amount of original content created by the author of a multimedia product varies, from complete authorship to serving simply as an assembler of third-party content. Most multimedia products contain at least some and most contain a great deal of third-party content. In many instances the third-party content is crucial to the success of the product. The multimedia product may be based on a popular character or movie, contain famous works of art, or be set to certain music. Without the third-party content, the product would not be worth producing.

This means that the developer of a multimedia work must obtain a variety of rights from a variety of sources. Indeed, the richer the content of the work, the more licenses the developer will need. The process of licensing these rights is often called "clearing the rights" or obtaining "waivers."

There are three distinct challenges in this licensing: identifying the rights to be licensed; identifying who can grant the rights; and determining whether it is economically feasible to create the product due to the cost of licensing the third-party content. This chapter focuses on the first two challenges. However, it is important to be aware that many great ideas for multimedia products have failed in the marketplace because the cost of obtaining multiple licenses did not translate into a reasonable purchase price for the multimedia product. In fact, the more creative and interesting the proposed multimedia product due to the richness of the content, the more likely it is that acquiring the rights will be too costly (without a clever business arrangement).

1. Rights and Rights Holders

a. Text

Multimedia products often use text from literary works. Literary works of both fiction and nonfiction may be protected by copyright. However, there may be times when text is not protected by copyright. Ideas, stock scenes, individual facts, and short words or phrases are not copyrightable. *See* 17 U.S.C. §102(b); 37 C.F.R. §202.1 (addressing short words and phrases). Some text is in the public domain or has been licensed for general usage. Still other text may be used without permission because its use is a "fair use" under the Copyright Act. 17 U.S.C. §107.

b. Music and Sound

Both the musical notes and the lyrics of a song may be protected by copyright law. The copyrights in a musical composition are owned at the outset by the music's composer and, if the lyrics are written by someone other than the composer, the copyright in the lyrics is owned by the lyricist. Often composers and lyricists assign their rights to music publishers or recording companies. The rights to non-dramatic public performances are often licensed to one of the performing rights societies such as American Society of Composers, Authors, and Publishers (ASCAP), Broadcast Music Inc. (BMI), or Society of European Stage Authors and Composers (SESAC). These organizations license rights via standard form licenses, such as a mechanical license (for sound recordings) and a sync license (for combining music with an audiovisual work).

In addition to the copyright in the musical work, the recording of a particular rendition of a musical work by a performer or performers may be protected by a sound recording copyright. A sound recording copyright applies to a particular performance of a work as recorded on a "phonogram."[2] Recordings of a compilation of public domain sounds are also copyrightable in a sound recording. A sound recording copyright grants the exclusive right to copy, distribute, and adapt the work but not the right to control public performance.[3]

Several authors may contribute to a sound recording, primarily the performers and the producer of the sound recording. At the outset, the copyright in the recording is jointly owned by the performers and the producer. In practice, the record companies usually acquire the rights to the sound recording copyright from the other contributors.

On top of copyright protection, performers have the right to control the distinctive sound of their voice through their publicity rights. In several cases, courts have prevented sound-a-like recordings of singers with distinct voices. *See, e.g.*, Midler v. Ford Motor Co., 849 F.2d 460 (9th Cir. 1988) (Bette Midler); Waits v. Frito-Lay, Inc., 978 F.2d 1093 (9th Cir. 1992) (Tom Waits).

c. Still Images

Still images protectable by copyright include photographs, drawings, paintings, ornamental designs and patterns, architectural plans and blueprints, puzzles, and maps. In addition to copyright, trademark law can protect the use of designs, pictures,

---

2. This term is the origin of the circle "p" as the marking for a sound recording copyright.

3. The Digital Performance Right in Sound Recording Act grants an exclusive right to publicly perform a copyrighted sound recording via a "digital audio transmission" subject to a number of exceptions. The exceptions limit coverage of the right essentially to digital audio transmissions that are part of an interactive or subscription service.

and symbols. If a still image contains the image of a person, that person's right of publicity or privacy may also be implicated.

One of the most efficient ways to license still images is through stock photo houses such as Getty Images or Corbis. In many cases, these firms own the copyright in the images or have the right to license them, but in other cases the firm only has a copy of the image and cannot adequately trace its rights in the underlying copyright. The actual rights held by the stock photo house will be revealed in the license grant, which simply grants whatever rights it has (which may be "none"), or when a request for a copyright warranty or indemnification is refused by the photo house.

d. Moving Images

Copyright protects audiovisual works that are "works that consist of a series of related images which are intrinsically intended to be shown by the use of machines . . . together with accompanying sounds, if any." 17 U.S.C. §101 (definition of audiovisual works). Audiovisual works include filmstrips, slide shows, videos, television shows, and motion pictures. In addition to copyrights, performers in audiovisual works such as motion pictures have the right to control their name and likeness through their publicity right. *See, e.g.,* Ventura v. Titan Sports, Inc., 65 F.3d 725 (8th Cir. 1995) (color commentary by former pro wrestler and governor Jesse "The Body" Ventura).

Sorting out the rights holders for audiovisual works can be challenging. A motion picture, for instance, may contain rights from multiple copyright holders, including writers, actors and actresses, musicians, composers, and artists. Normally, the production company owns the copyright in the motion picture or television program (that is, the work as a whole). It is also likely to own the copyright, as a work for hire or by assignment, in many of the elements of the motion picture, such as the script, the performances, animation or special effects, and the accompanying musical sound track. This is not always the case, however, because independent producers, famous performers, and popular writers may retain all or certain rights.

Licensing rights in motion pictures or film clips is complicated by the fact that the custom and practice in the motion picture industry is not to carefully track rights. *See* Effects Assocs. Inc. v. Cohen, 908 F.2d 555 (9th Cir. 1990) ("movie makers do lunch, not contracts"). In addition, some film producers are reluctant to license portions of their work, believing that this degrades the integrity of the work as a whole.

e. Data

Although individual facts are not protected under the copyright law, original arrangements of facts may be. Feist Publ'ns, Inc. v. Rural Tel. Serv. Co., 499 U.S. 340 (1991). In addition, data may be protected in Europe under the Database Directive (and in other jurisdictions with similar measures). Contracts may also limit use of a particular database. *See* Register.com v. Verio, Inc., 356 F.3d 393 (2d Cir. 2004).

In terms of seeking permission to use facts, on the one hand, facts are in the public domain, available for anyone to take and use. On the other hand, gathering facts, assembling and arranging them, and hosting and providing a useful means to access facts takes time, effort, and expense. Thus, the decision to license data usually arises out of simple economics: It is more cost effective to use the product of someone else's work than repeat the effort. The decision to license is not driven by exclusive intellectual property rights but by expediency.

f. Characters

Copyright law protects fictional characters. Sometimes characters are depicted visually in a book, magazine, movie, or television program. Examples include the Mickey Mouse and Donald Duck characters in cartoons, the Peanuts characters in comic strips, the Superman character in comic books, and the Paddington bear character in children's books. On other occasions characters are depicted by actors in movies or television, such as Darth Vader, the fallen Jedi knight, and the droids R2-D2 and C-3PO depicted in the *Star Wars* movies; James Bond, the British secret agent; and Rocky, the "Italian Stallion" boxer depicted in the *Rocky* movies. Other characters are not shown visually but are described in literature. Characters in this context may be protected if they are sufficiently well developed by the author. For example, a court held that the Tarzan character from *Tarzan of the Apes* had been developed well enough to qualify for copyright protection. *See* Burroughs v. Metro-Goldwyn-Mayer, Inc., 519 F. Supp. 388, 391 (S.D.N.Y. 1981), *aff'd*, 683 F.2d 610 (2d Cir. 1982). *But see* Rice v. Fox Broad. Co., 148 F. Supp. 2d 1029 (2001) ("mystery magician" character not deserving of copyright protection).

Trademark law and the law of unfair competition also protect fictional characters when they are used to designate the source of a good or service. Characters used in this manner include the Pink Panther character, Charles M. Schulz's Peanuts characters, and several of Dr. Seuss's fictional characters.

2. Is Permission Needed?

As described above, clearing third-party content can be a significant undertaking. Is the author of a multimedia product required to seek permission to use every bit of content produced by a third party? The answer, of course, is "no" — content may be in the public domain or permission may be excused as a "fair use" under copyright or trademark law or permitted under the First Amendment. In certain cases, the author may have a preexisting license for the content that seems to grant permission to use the content in a multimedia product. However, it takes skilled legal analysis to know when to seek permission and when to forge ahead without it, and the decisions are seldom clear-cut. An approach that seeks any and all arguable permissions may be costly, time consuming, and stir up disputes that would have otherwise remained dormant; an approach that seeks minimal permissions may expose the producer of a multimedia product to damages and an injunction.

C. Creating a Multimedia Platform or Service

Some multimedia products are individual products, such as a multimedia encyclopedia, enjoyed by individual end users. Other multimedia products aim to provide a platform on top of which other products operate. The platform can provide hardware functionality, software functionality, or both. A classic example is a videogame console that provides hardware and software on which games created by third parties can run.

For the creator of the platform to make money, however, sometimes it must restrict the manner in which third parties can access the services of the platform. Access to the services of the platform is controlled in various ways, such as by use of trade secret information, patents, trademarks, anti-circumvention technology (backed up by the Digital Millennium Copyright Act), and contracts.

Two lines of cases have arisen out of the attempts of multimedia platform producers to enforce restrictions. The first line of cases involves the attempts of developers of applications and enhancements for the platform to tie into the platform without permission. In order to do this, these developers must reverse engineer crucial information about the platform and, in the process, make copies of software. Courts have permitted these efforts in most cases. For example, the court in *Lewis Galoob Toys, Inc. v. Nintendo of America, Inc.*, upheld the sale of a hardware device that speeded up the rate of play of a computer game. 964 F.2d 965 (9th Cir. 1992). The court in *Sega Enterprises, Ltd. v. Accolade, Inc.*, ruled that making copies of software in the process of reverse engineering to discover unprotectable ideas was a fair use under copyright law. 977 F.2d 1510 (9th Cir. 1993). *See also* Assessment Techs. v. WIREdata, Inc., 350 F.3d 640 (7th Cir. 2003).

The second line of cases involves emulation technology. Emulators allow products written for one platform to run on a different platform. In order to create the emulator, someone must reverse engineer software and, in the process, make copies. The court in *Sony Computer Entertainment, Inc. v. Connectix Corp.* ruled that it was a fair use to repeatedly copy Sony's BIOS to gain access to functional information in order to create an emulator that would allow personal computer users to play games written for the Sony PlayStation console. 203 F.3d 596 (9th Cir. 2000).

The exception to these lines of cases arises when the party who performed the reverse engineering had agreed to a contract prohibiting this activity. License restrictions on reverse engineering have been upheld in several cases including, most notably in the multimedia context, a restriction on discovering information to interoperate with a gaming Web site in Blizzard Entertainment v. Jung, 422 F.3d 630 (8th Cir. 2005). This case can be found in the Materials section of Chapter 1. In that case, Blizzard Entertainment distributed a CD-ROM version of its game. In addition to the copy of the game, the end user acquired the right to access and use a Web site that facilitated playing the game in a multiplayer format. To use the Web site, the user had to assent to Terms of Use that prohibited "reverse engineering." When a group of programmers created a competing Web site by discovering crucial protocol information via reverse engineering, Blizzard sued for breach of the license, and the court enforced the license against the programmers who had manifested assent to it.

D. Licensing End Users of Multimedia Products

Once a multimedia product is created, the creator must choose a transaction model for providing the product to customers. Some producers of multimedia products come from the software industry, others from the movie, record, or publishing industries, and still others come with ties to none of them. Each industry has developed its unique transaction models for providing products to end users. Software publishers often license their products to end users. Movie producers typically rent copies or sell copies to end users as a copyright "first sale." The publishers of books, magazines, and records typically sell copies of their works to end users. To complicate matters, the choice to use a first sale or to rent or license may be influenced by a retailer, distributor, or computer hardware manufacturer if the multimedia product is distributed through these channels.

What is the proper end user transaction model for a multimedia product? The model chosen often simply mirrors the industry practice of the producer's industry of origin. A first principles approach, however, would ask the following questions:

Is There a Reason Not to Use a First Sale? The reason to begin with this question is that a first sale transaction is simple and efficient. It does not require a sophisticated or costly contracting process or written document. A first sale automatically gives the user the right to use the copy purchased in any manner for which it is capable of being used and to dispose of the copy. The user simply pays money for a copy or copies, and the rest of the transaction is governed by the Copyright Act and default rules of contract law.

Is There a Need to Describe a Particular Scope of Usage? In some ways this is the flip side of the prior question. If the multimedia product producer needs to place parameters around use of the copy, to grant rights beyond those that are available via a copyright first sale (e.g., the right to create a derivative work), or describe some other creative usage arrangement, then a license may be the appropriate transaction model. For example, a license would be useful to achieve the following arrangements:

- a multimedia product that is only intended for home or education usage;
- allowing the user to make multiple copies, modify the work (or portions of it), or publicly perform or display it (even in certain proscribed venues or for certain audiences); and
- providing a product that includes both a work on fixed media and an online service, such as a multiplayer gaming Internet service.

Will a Copy of the Work Be Provided? If the multimedia product consists of a service streamed over the Internet then the end user is not purchasing a copy, so no copyright first sale transaction may be implicated. An example of this is the Neopets virtual world that is popular among children where users acquire, trade, tend to, and chat about various fantasy pets.

Is There a Need to Prohibit Reverse Engineering of Software or Protocols That Provide Access to a Service? As explained above, some multimedia producers rely on a business model in which they control access to a software platform or service. To enforce this business model, the multimedia producer may need to rely on a contractual provision to prohibit reverse engineering.

Is There a Need to Give or Disclaim Warranties or Limit Liability?   As mentioned in Chapter 1, some courts have applied UCC 2's default warranties to software products. If the multimedia producer would like to provide additional or different warranties or to disclaim UCC 2's implied warranties, a license agreement is a vehicle for doing this. The same is true for contractual limitations of liability such as a disclaimer of consequential damages.

II. MATERIALS

These Materials will help you explore issues in multimedia licensing in various settings. First is an excerpt from the definitions section of the U.S. Copyright Act, 17 U.S.C. §101, which contains several definitions relevant to multimedia licensing, such as audiovisual works, motion pictures, literary works, phonorecords, joint works, collective works, compilations, and computer programs. Next is a set of cases pointing up issues that arise when licenses must deal with mixed media and new media. New York Times v. Tasini, 533 U.S. 483 (2001), deals with how to treat copyrighted text created by freelance journalists as newspapers move from hard copy to the Internet. Simon & Schuster, Inc. v. Qintex Entertainment, Inc., 1990 U.S. Dist. LEXIS 19987 (C.D. Cal. Feb. 12, 1990), and Boosey & Hawkes Music Publishers Ltd. v. Walt Disney Co., 145 F.3d 481 (2d Cir. 1998), show the challenges of interpreting license grant terms, such as "electronic rights" and "video format," as the meaning of terms changes as technology changes. Landham v. Lewis Galoob Toys, Inc., 227 F.3d 619 (6th Cir. 2000), raises issues concerning licensing of the right of publicity, and MAI Photo News Agency, Inc. v. American Broadcasting Co., Inc., 2001 WL 180020 (S.D.N.Y. Feb. 22, 2001), addresses distribution rights and the issue of attribution.

Following these excerpts are two cases dealing with video games. Data East v. Epyx, 862 F.2d 204 (9th Cir. 1988), examines copyright protection for the visual images in video games and when a license is or is not needed to copy the appearance, compilation, and sequence of the audiovisual display of a video game. Sony v. Connectix, 203 F.3d 586 (9th Cir. 2000), addresses the issue of whether it is proper to engage in reverse engineering to create a competing or different video game platform.

Finally, the Materials contain an "Agreement" between Apple Computer and Apple Corps that settled a dispute in the early 1990s over use of the Apple trademark. When Apple Computer began to sell music through its iTunes service, this agreement became the subject of a lawsuit. That suit has settled now, but the agreement is still instructive.

17 U.S.C. §101 DEFINITIONS

"Audiovisual works" are works that consist of a series of related images which are intrinsically intended to be shown by the use of machines, or devices such as projectors, viewers, or electronic equipment, together with accompanying sounds, if any, regardless of the nature of the material objects, such as films or tapes, in which the works are embodied.

A "collective work" is a work, such as a periodical issue, anthology, or encyclopedia, in which a number of contributions, constituting separate and independent works in themselves, are assembled into a collective whole.

A "compilation" is a work formed by the collection and assembling of preexisting materials or of data that are selected, coordinated, or arranged in such a way that the resulting work as a whole constitutes an original work of authorship. The term "compilation" includes collective works.

A "computer program" is a set of statements or instructions to be used directly or indirectly in a computer in order to bring about a certain result.

"Motion pictures" are audiovisual works consisting of a series of related images which, when shown in succession, impart an impression of motion, together with accompanying sounds, if any.

A "joint work" is a work prepared by two or more authors with the intention that their contributions be merged into inseparable or interdependent parts of a unitary whole.

"Literary works" are works, other than audiovisual works, expressed in words, numbers, or other verbal or numerical symbols or indicia, regardless of the nature of the material objects, such as books, periodicals, manuscripts, phonorecords, film, tapes, disks, or cards, in which they are embodied.

The term "motion picture exhibition facility" means a movie theater, screening room, or other venue that is being used primarily for the exhibition of a copyrighted motion picture, if such exhibition is open to the public or is made to an assembled group of viewers outside of a normal circle of a family and its social acquaintances.

"Phonorecords" are material objects in which sounds, other than those accompanying a motion picture or other audiovisual work, are fixed by any method now known or later developed, and from which the sounds can be perceived, reproduced, or otherwise communicated, either directly or with the aid of a machine or device. The term "phonorecords" includes the material object in which the sounds are first fixed.

* * *

NEW YORK TIMES v. TASINI
533 U.S. 483 (2001)

Justice **GINSBURG** delivered the opinion of the court:

This copyright case concerns the rights of freelance authors and a presumptive privilege of their publishers. The litigation was initiated by six freelance authors and relates to articles they contributed to three print periodicals (two newspapers and one magazine). Under agreements with the periodicals' publishers, but without the freelancers' consent, two computer database companies placed copies of the freelancers' articles — along with all other articles from the periodicals in which the freelancers' work appeared — into three databases. Whether written by a freelancer or staff member, each article is presented to, and retrievable by, the user in isolation, clear of the context the original print publication presented.

The freelance authors' complaint alleged that their copyrights had been infringed by the inclusion of their articles in the databases. The publishers, in response, relied on the privilege of reproduction and distribution accorded them by §201(c) of the Copyright Act, which provides:

> Copyright in each separate contribution to a collective work is distinct from copyright in the collective work as a whole, and vests initially in the author of the contribution. In the absence of an express transfer of the copyright or of any rights under it, the owner of copyright in the collective work is presumed to have acquired only the privilege of reproducing and distributing the contribution as part of that particular collective work, any revision of that collective work, and any later collective work in the same series. 17 U.S.C. §201(c).

Specifically, the publishers maintained that, as copyright owners of collective works, *i.e.*, the original print publications, they had merely exercised "the privilege" §201(c) accords them to "reproduc[e] and distribut[e]" the author's discretely copyrighted contribution.

The 1976 Act rejected the doctrine of indivisibility, recasting the copyright as a bundle of discrete "exclusive rights," 17 U.S.C. §106 (1994 ed. and Supp. V), each of which "may be transferred and owned separately," §201(d)(2). Congress also provided, in §404(a), that "a single notice applicable to the collective work as a whole is sufficient" to protect the rights of freelance contributors. And in §201(c), Congress codified the discrete domains of "[c]opyright in each separate contribution to a collective work" and "copyright in the collective work as a whole." Together, §404(a) and §201(c) "preserve the author's copyright in a contribution even if the contribution does not bear a separate notice in the author's name, and without requiring any unqualified transfer of rights to the owner of the collective work." H.R. Rep. 122, U.S. Code Cong. & Admin. News 1976, pp. 5659, 5738.

In the instant case, the Authors wrote several Articles and gave the Print Publishers permission to publish the Articles in certain newspapers and magazines. It is undisputed that the Authors hold copyrights and, therefore, exclusive rights in the Articles. It is clear, moreover, that the Print and Electronic Publishers have exercised at least some rights that §106 initially assigns exclusively to the Authors: LEXIS/NEXIS' central discs and UMI's CD-ROMs "reproduce . . . copies" of the Articles, §106(1); UMI, by selling those CD-ROMs, and LEXIS/NEXIS, by selling copies of the Articles through the NEXIS Database, "distribute copies" of the Articles "to the public by sale," §106(3); and the Print Publishers, through contracts licensing the production of copies in the Databases, "authorize" reproduction and distribution of the Articles, §106.

Against the Authors' charge of infringement, the Publishers do not here contend the Authors entered into an agreement authorizing reproduction of the Articles in the Databases. See *supra,* at 2385, n.1. Nor do they assert that the copies in the Databases represent "fair use" of the Authors' Articles. See 17 U.S.C. §107 ("fair use of a copyrighted work . . . is not an infringement"; four factors identified among those relevant to fair use determination).

Instead, the Publishers rest entirely on the privilege described in §201(c). Each discrete edition of the periodicals in which the Articles appeared is a "collective work," the Publishers agree. They contend, however, that reproduction and distribution of each Article by the Databases lie within the "privilege of reproducing and distributing the [Articles] as part of . . . [a] revision of that collective work," §201(c). The Publishers' encompassing construction of the §201(c) privilege is unacceptable, we conclude, for it would diminish the Authors' exclusive rights in the Articles.

In determining whether the Articles have been reproduced and distributed "as part of" a "revision" of the collective works in issue, we focus on the Articles as presented to, and perceptible by, the user of the Databases. See §102 (copyright protection subsists in original works fixed in any medium "from which they can be perceived, reproduced, or otherwise communicated"). In this case, the three Databases present articles to users clear of the context provided either by the original periodical editions or by any revision of those editions. The Databases first prompt users to search the universe of their contents: thousands or millions of files containing individual articles from thousands of collective works (*i.e.*, editions), either in one series (the Times, in NYTO) or in scores of series (the sundry titles in NEXIS and GPO). When the user conducts a search, each article appears as a separate item within the search result. In NEXIS and NYTO, an article appears to a user without the graphics, formatting, or other articles with which the article was initially published. In GPO, the article appears with the other materials published on the same page or pages, but without any material published on other pages of the original periodical. In either circumstance, we cannot see how the Database perceptibly reproduces and distributes the article "as part of" either the original edition or a "revision" of that edition.

One might view the articles as parts of a new compendium — namely, the entirety of works in the Database. In that compendium, each edition of each periodical represents only a miniscule fraction of the ever-expanding Database. The Database no more constitutes a "revision" of each constituent edition than a 400-page novel quoting a sonnet in passing would represent a "revision" of that poem. "Revision" denotes a new "version," and a version is, in this setting, a "distinct form of something regarded by its creator or others as one work." *Webster's Third New International Dictionary* 1944, 2545 (1976). The massive whole of the Database is not recognizable as a new version of its every small part.

Alternatively, one could view the Articles in the Databases "as part of" no larger work at all, but simply as individual articles presented individually. That each article bears marks of its origin in a particular periodical (less vivid marks in NEXIS and NYTO, more vivid marks in GPO) suggests the article was *previously* part of that periodical. But the markings do not mean the article is *currently* reproduced or distributed as part of the periodical. The Databases' reproduction and distribution of individual Articles — simply *as individual Articles* — would invade the core of the Authors' exclusive rights under §106.

The Publishers press an analogy between the Databases, on the one hand, and microfilm and microfiche, on the other. We find the analogy wanting. Microforms typically contain continuous photographic reproductions of a periodical in the medium of miniaturized film. Accordingly, articles appear on the microforms, writ very small, in precisely the position in which the articles appeared in the newspaper. The Times, for example, printed the beginning of Blakely's "Remembering Jane" Article on page 26 of the Magazine in the

September 23, 1990, edition; the microfilm version of the Times reproduces that same Article on film in the very same position, within a film reproduction of the entire Magazine, in turn within a reproduction of the entire September 23, 1990, edition. True, the microfilm roll contains multiple editions, and the microfilm user can adjust the machine lens to focus only on the Article, to the exclusion of surrounding material. Nonetheless, the user first encounters the Article in context. In the Databases, by contrast, the Articles appear disconnected from their original context. In NEXIS and NYTO, the user sees the "Jane" Article apart even from the remainder of page 26. In GPO, the user sees the Article within the context of page 26, but clear of the context of page 25 or page 27, the rest of the Magazine, or the remainder of the day's newspaper. In short, unlike microforms, the Databases do not perceptibly reproduce articles as part of the collective work to which the author contributed or as part of any "revision" thereof.

Invoking the concept of "media neutrality," the Publishers urge that the "transfer of a work between media" does not "alte[r] the character of" that work for copyright purposes. Brief for Petitioners 23. That is indeed true. See 17 U.S.C. §102(a) (copyright protection subsists in original works "fixed in any tangible medium of expression"). But unlike the conversion of newsprint to microfilm, the transfer of articles to the Databases does not represent a mere conversion of intact periodicals (or revisions of periodicals) from one medium to another. The Databases offer users individual articles, not intact periodicals. In this case, media neutrality should protect the Authors' rights in the individual Articles to the extent those Articles are now presented individually, outside the collective work context, within the Databases' new media.

For the purpose at hand—determining whether the Authors' copyrights have been infringed—an analogy to an imaginary library may be instructive. Rather than maintaining intact editions of periodicals, the library would contain separate copies of each article. Perhaps these copies would exactly reproduce the periodical pages from which the articles derive (if the model is GPO); perhaps the copies would contain only typescript characters, but still indicate the original periodical's name and date, as well as the article's headline and page number (if the model is NEXIS or NYTO). The library would store the folders containing the articles in a file room, indexed based on diverse criteria, and containing articles from vast numbers of editions. In response to patron requests, an inhumanly speedy librarian would search the room and provide copies of the articles matching patron-specified criteria.

Viewing this strange library, one could not, consistent with ordinary English usage, characterize the articles "as part of" a "revision" of the editions in which the articles first appeared. In substance, however, the Databases differ from the file room only to the extent they aggregate articles in electronic packages (the LEXIS/NEXIS central discs or UMI CD-ROMs), while the file room stores articles in spatially separate files. The crucial fact is that the Databases, like the hypothetical library, store and retrieve articles separately within a vast domain of diverse texts. Such a storage and retrieval system effectively overrides the Authors' exclusive right to control the individual reproduction and distribution of each Article, 17 U.S.C. §§106(1), (3). Cf. Ryan v. Carl Corp., 23 F. Supp. 2d 1146 (N.D. Cal. 1998) (holding copy shop in violation of §201(c)).

The Publishers claim the protection of §201(c) because users can manipulate the Databases to generate search results consisting entirely of articles from a particular periodical edition. By this logic, §201(c) would cover the hypothetical library if, in response to a request, that library's expert staff assembled all of the articles from a particular periodical edition.

However, the fact that a third party can manipulate a database to produce a noninfringing document does not mean the database is not infringing. Under §201(c), the question is not whether a user can generate a revision of a collective work from a database, but whether the database itself perceptibly presents the author's contribution as part of a revision of the collective work. That result is not accomplished by these Databases.

We conclude that the Electronic Publishers infringed the Authors' copyrights by reproducing and distributing the Articles in a manner not authorized by the Authors and not privileged by §201(c). We further conclude that the Print Publishers infringed the Authors' copyrights by authorizing the Electronic Publishers to place the Articles in the Databases and by aiding the Electronic Publishers in that endeavor. We therefore affirm the judgment of the Court of Appeals.

SIMON & SCHUSTER, INC. v. QINTEX ENTM'T, INC.

1990 U.S. Dist. LEXIS 19987 (C.D. Cal. Feb. 12, 1990)

HUPP, District Judge.

ORDER:

The motion for partial summary judgment is granted in part as to defendant Dove and continued as to defendant Qintex as set forth below. The motion for preliminary injunction is granted in part as to defendant Dove and denied as to defendant Qintex. The Qintex motion to file a third amended complaint and an amended counterclaim is granted.

1. Larry McMurtry (LM) authored a book *Lonesome Dove* (LD) which had substantial success. In 1984, he contracted with Simon & Schuster (SS) for publication of the work. The contract granted all rights for printing as a book to SS, and in addition, granted the following "electronic rights":

> . . . sole and exclusive right to use and adapt . . . [LD] or any portion thereof, as a basis for . . . audio . . . recording. . . .

From this grant, there were excluded motion picture, educational picture, and television rights. LM later granted motion picture and television rights to Motown, and they were eventually assigned to Qintex Entertainment (QE), who produced a mini-series based on the book which was played on CBS television in February, 1989. QE granted to Dove Books-On-Tape (Dove) (without warranty that it had such rights) the right to market audio cassettes of the sound track from the mini-series. Dove then produced in audio cassette form the soundtrack from the television series, and started to market the cassettes, until stopped by this court's temporary restraining order in April, 1989, subsequently carried into a preliminary injunction in August, 1989.

SS now seeks partial summary judgment, adjudicating for the purposes of this action that it has exclusive rights to produce and sell audio cassettes based on LD.

b. The motion must be granted in part, determining that the grant language in the LM-SS contract is unambiguous and, therefore, not subject to extrinsic evidence about its meaning or effect, and that the electronics rights granted to SS are superior to any rights granted to Dove by assignment from QE. The SS contract is prior in time and the contract was properly registered in the Copyright Office long before rights were created, if any, by the LM contract with Motown (assigned to QE, and then to Dove with respect to audio cassettes). Dove suggests that the exclusion for television and movie rights is sufficiently ambiguous to form a basis for the argument that the sound track from the television version is a separate item from the grant of rights to place the book or excerpts from it on audio tape, and that the reservation to LM of the right to assign television and movie rights includes the right to convey rights to use the soundtrack from the same for sale in audio cassettes. The court does not agree. This interpretation would nullify the rights clearly granted. Nothing in the agreement supports the interpretation.

The suggestion that the "allied rights" to the movie or television rights, reserved to LM to grant, could reasonably include rights to market in cassette form the soundtrack is also made. That this cannot be true is shown by the definition of such "allied rights" so as to allow advertising for the movie or television program (to which SS raised no protest). The further suggestion is made that the right to distribute the audio tape was retained in the "movie" exclusion which referred to LM's retention of the right to "use to authorize others to use . . . the Literary Work . . . for the purpose of making motion pictures primarily for exhibition in regular commercial channels." This argument, however, fails to appreciate that this clause is not present in the "television" exclusion. Since the mini-series was a television production, this clause in the "movie" exclusion seems inapplicable. Even if it is assumed that the "movie" clause applies, the argument would still falter, however, because the distribution of the audio tape involves a completely different product from the mini-series which is aimed at a different market. Thus, distribution of the audio-tape does not fit within the "for the purpose of making motion pictures" portion of the clause.

The contract is clear and unambiguous and, as a result, SS has superior rights to Dove to market audio cassette versions of LD. It is acknowledged that the Dove version is substantially similar to the book version, and, indeed, is based on it. Access is admitted.

c. Dove has argued that there is substantial evidence of contemporaneous interpretation by LM and SS which is inconsistent with the idea that audio cassette rights were intended to be granted. There is, indeed, such evidence, although it is not uncontradicted by SS. For example, LM granted the rights to an audio cassette book to Books-On-Tape (no relation to Dove) without protest by SS. Conversations with interested parties by LM and his agent clearly assume at certain times that LM retained the rights to authorize audio cassettes. Two SS executives made statements which are inconsistent with the concept that SS had the exclusive rights. Since the contract is clear and is not ambiguous, these pieces of evidence may not be used to change the meaning of the contract. (SS argues that this evidence is explainable as a simple mistake, but this explanation would not be relevant on a summary judgment motion, since it could not be weighed with that opposed to it.)

d. Dove also contends that some of the SS statements were relied on by it to its detriment and that such reliance raises an estoppel against SS to assert its prior rights against Dove. This raises a triable issue of fact. (SS argues that Dove did not in fact so rely and took no steps to determine the truth; again this cannot be determined on summary judgment, whose function is to determine whether triable issues of fact exist, not adjudicate them.) Since there is a triable issue on the estoppel question, the whole of this part of the case cannot be adjudicated at this time and the motion is granted only in part.

e. From the evidence recited above, and from other evidence concerning the manner in which the contract was prepared, Dove contends that the inclusion of the electronics rights clause in the original LM-SS contract was a mistake. However, it appears that neither LM nor SS have moved to correct the mistake, if mistake it be. In effect, it appears that Dove is attempting, as a non-party to the contract, to reform it at this late date. Dove cites no authority that it may do so (SS cites no authority that it may not). The court doubts that Dove has any standing to claim that the unambiguous electronic rights clause was inserted into the contract by mistake. Very preliminary research by the court's law clerk indicates that the predominant view is that a non-party to a contract (or one not in privity with a party) may not attempt to reform it. However, the court is not ready to decide this as a matter of law without giving the parties a chance to brief it.

f. This summary judgment is rendered as to defendant Dove only. The court will need confirmation that no bankruptcy stay exists which would inhibit the adjudication of these issues as to QE before proceeding to do so.

g. The preliminary injunction remains in effect.

2. The motion for preliminary injunction as to packaging issues: The motion for preliminary injunction as to packaging issues is granted in part and denied in part. The motion is denied as to QE, who is not shown to be involved in the cover for Dove's tapes. The issues involving the cover to SS's book and Dove's tape cassettes are entirely different and separate from the issues about the electronic clause in the LM-SS contract. The most probable finding after trial is that the title "Lonesome Dove" and the red line border and curlicues surrounding that title, have achieved secondary meaning in the hands of SS, so that it may prevent (on a Lanham Act theory) confusion of source from the substantially similar rendition of the same on the Dove cassette covers. In addition, it seems likely to be determined on trial that the artist, in granting rights to QE to use the artwork in connection with the television show, did not do so in connection with the audio cassettes, so that the subsequent grant of the same to SS (either just before or just after this lawsuit started) effectively granted the audio cassette rights for the artwork to SS, not Dove. This theory, however, would not cover Dove's use of the artwork for the cassettes already manufactured (being held pursuant to the injunction), since SS was not the owner until the grant from the artist. Thus, as to existing cassettes, any preliminary injunction would have to rest on a Lanham Act theory. Dove argues that the SS implied permission to use the artwork for the television show should carry over for the marketing of video cassettes of the soundtrack; the court cannot see why. SS could reasonably give its permission (if needed, as it surely was on Lanham Act if not copyright theory) to promote the television show, since it could conceive that to be consonant with its best interests, but not for the audio cassette marketing, since that was in competition to its own rights. No permission to Dove's use can be implied from the permission to QE for the television use. The picture used by Dove does not infringe, and its use will not be enjoined. Dove suggests that mere type face is not protected. True, but this is not mere type-face; it is instead an artistic creation involving the complex letters with their different shapes (in the capitals) and coloring. It is surely protectible. Accordingly, a limited preliminary injunction will issue enjoining Dove's use of the lettering style and associated features from LD's cover, including border and curlicues, but not enjoining the picture or color scheme. Plaintiff to provide form of preliminary injunction. Bond to be filed in the amount of $10,000.

3. The motions to file amended counterclaim and third party claim: QE asks permission to file an amended counterclaim against SS seeking declaratory relief as to whether the electronic rights clause includes video cassettes of the TV mini-series, and to file a third party complaint against LM requesting indemnity for damages QE may suffer by reason of any liability to SS in this action. These motions are granted; original pleadings in the form attached to the notice of motion are to be filed with the clerk this date. SS opposes the motion to file the third party complaint against LM on the ground that the motion is too late and that, in any event, it does not state a claim because LM owes no indemnity. The arguments are rejected. The "lateness" is adequately explained. And, the court cannot determine on this motion whether or not LM owes an indemnity to QE or not. The indemnity claim is based on the LM-Motown contract, with QE (the assignee of Motown by mense assignments) claiming that the grant of the television rights carried with it the right to market audio and video cassettes, even though not expressly set forth. QE and Dove advanced similar arguments in opposition to the motion for partial summary judgment. However, the argument was not there relevant, since if SS had prior rights, a subsequent grant of the same rights to Motown-QE-Dove would not aid Dove. The argument does become relevant as to LM-QE rights if SS prevails (as it has on the contract interpretation) in the lawsuit as a whole. Thus, the third party claim for indemnity is a proper one.

SS also resists the filing of an additional counterclaim as to it requesting declaratory relief as to video cassette rights as between QE and SS. QE alleges that it desires to market video cassettes, but that SS will not take a position one way or the other as to whether it contends that the electronic rights clause gives SS prior rights to market such. SS confirms in its opposition to the motion that it has not taken such a position. It suggests that there is not now a case or controversy on the subject.

The court disagrees and permits the filing of the amendment to the counterclaim. The same clause that controls the audio cassette rights also deals with video cassettes. This creates a "reasonable apprehension" on the part of Qintex as that term is used in the applicable case law. See, e.g., Grafor Corp. v. Hausermann, 602 F.2d 781 (7th Cir. 1979).

As to whether the same result follows or not, the court has no opinion, but surely there is sufficient doubt about the subject to warrant declaratory relief if QE, as it alleges, intends to market the video cassettes. In granting this permission to amend its claims, the court assumes that the automatic stay as to QE either has been or shortly will be lifted; there is a certain unfairness in allowing QE to make claims if its opponents may not.

BOOSEY & HAWKES MUSIC PUBLISHERS LTD. v. WALT DISNEY COMPANY
145 F.3d 481 (2d Cir. 1998)

LEVAL, Circuit Judge.

Boosey & Hawkes Music Publishers Ltd., an English corporation and the assignee of Igor Stravinsky's copyrights for "The Rite of Spring," brought this action alleging that the Walt Disney Company's foreign distribution in video cassette and laser disc format ("video format") of the film "Fantasia," featuring Stravinsky's work, infringed Boosey's rights. In 1939 Stravinsky licensed Disney's distribution of The Rite of Spring in the motion picture. Boosey, which acquired Stravinsky's copyright in 1947, contends that the license does not authorize distribution in video format.

The district court granted partial summary judgment to Boosey, declaring that Disney's video format release was not authorized by the license agreement. Disney appeals from that ruling.

I. BACKGROUND

During 1938, Disney sought Stravinsky's authorization to use The Rite of Spring (sometimes referred to as the "work" or the "composition") throughout the world in a motion picture.

Because under United States law the work was in the public domain, Disney needed no authorization to record or distribute it in this country, but permission was required for distribution in countries where Stravinsky enjoyed copyright protection. In January 1939 the parties executed an agreement (the "1939 Agreement") giving Disney rights to use the work in a motion picture in consideration of a fee to Stravinsky of $6,000.

The 1939 Agreement provided that

> In consideration of the sum of Six Thousand ($6,000.) Dollars, receipt of which is hereby acknowledged, [Stravinsky] does hereby give and grant unto Walt Disney Enterprises, a California corporation . . . the nonexclusive, irrevocable right, license, privilege and authority to record in any manner, medium or form, and to license the performance of, the musical composition herein below set out.

Under "type of use" in ¶3, the Agreement specified that

> The music of said musical composition may be used in one motion picture throughout the length thereof or through such portion or portions thereof as the Purchaser shall desire. The said music may be used in whole or in part and may be adapted, changed, added to or subtracted from, all as shall appear desirable to the Purchaser in its uncontrolled discretion. The title "Rites of Spring" or "Le Sacre de Printemps," or any other title, may be used as the title of said motion picture and the name of [Stravinsky] may be announced in or in connection with said motion picture.

The Agreement went on to specify in ¶4 that Disney's license to the work "is limited to the use of the musical composition in synchronism or timed-relation with the motion picture." Paragraph Five of the Agreement provided that

> The right to record the musical composition as covered by this agreement is conditioned upon the performance of the musical work in theatres having valid licenses from the American Society of Composers, Authors and Publishers, or any other performing rights society having jurisdiction in the territory in which the said musical composition is performed.

We refer to this clause, which is of importance to the litigation, as "the ASCAP Condition." Finally, ¶7 of the Agreement provided that "the licensor reserves to himself all rights and uses in and to the said musical composition not herein specifically granted" (the "reservation clause").

Disney released Fantasia, starring Mickey Mouse, in 1940. The film contains no dialogue. It matches a pantomime of animated beasts and fantastic creatures to passages of great classical music, creating what critics celebrated as a "partnership between fine music and animated film." The soundtrack uses compositions of Bach, Beethoven, Dukas, Schubert, Tchaikovsky, and Stravinsky, all performed by the Philadelphia Orchestra under the direction of Leopold Stokowski. As it appears in the film soundtrack, The Rite of Spring was shortened from its original 34 minutes to about 22.5; sections of the score were cut, while other sections were reordered. For more than five decades Disney exhibited The Rite of Spring in Fantasia under the 1939 license. The film has been re-released for theatrical distribution at least seven times since 1940, and although Fantasia has never appeared on television in its entirety, excerpts including portions of The Rite of Spring have been televised occasionally over the years. Neither Stravinsky nor Boosey has ever previously objected to any of the distributions.

In 1991 Disney first released Fantasia in video format. The video has been sold in foreign countries, as well as in the United States. To date, the Fantasia video release has generated more than $360 million in gross revenue for Disney. Boosey brought this action in February 1993.

II. DISCUSSION

We confront four questions on appeal. Disney challenges the summary judgment which declared that the 1939 Agreement does not authorize video distribution of The Rite of Spring. Boosey appeals three other rulings: the dismissal for forum non conveniens, and the grants of summary judgment on the claims for damages for violation of the Lanham Act and breach of contract.

A. Declaratory Judgment on the Scope of the License

Boosey's request for declaratory judgment raises two issues of contract interpretation: whether the general grant of permission under the 1939 Agreement licensed Disney to use The Rite of Spring in the video format version of Fantasia (on which the district court found in Disney's favor); and, if so, whether the ASCAP Condition barred Disney from exploiting the work through video format (on which the district court found for Boosey).

1. *Whether the "motion picture" license covers video format.* Boosey contends that the license to use Stravinsky's work in a "motion picture" did not authorize distribution of the motion picture in video format, especially in view of the absence of an express provision for "future technologies" and Stravinsky's reservation of all rights not granted in the Agreement. Disputes about whether licensees may exploit licensed works through new marketing channels made possible by technologies developed after the licensing contract—often called "new-use" problems—have vexed courts since at least the advent of the motion picture. See 3 Melville B. Nimmer and David Nimmer, NIMMER ON COPYRIGHT, §10.10[A] at 10-86 (hereinafter "NIMMER"); Kirke La Shelle Co. v. Paul Armstrong Co., 263 N.Y. 79, 188 N.E. 163 (1933) (deciding whether a license for a stage production also conveyed rights in sound motion pictures).

In Bartsch v. Metro-Goldwyn-Mayer, Inc., we held that "licensee[s] may properly pursue any uses which may reasonably be said to fall within the medium as described in the license." 391 F.2d 150, 155 (2d Cir. 1968) (Friendly, J.) (quoting NIMMER). We held in Bartsch that a license of motion picture rights to a play included the right to telecast the motion picture. We observed that "[i]f the words are broad enough to cover the new use, it seems fairer that the burden of framing and negotiating an exception should fall on the grantor," at least when the new medium is not completely unknown at the time of contracting. *Id.* at 154, 155.

The 1939 Agreement conveys the right "to record [the composition] in any manner, medium or form" for use "in [a] motion picture." We believe this language is broad enough to include distribution of the motion picture in video format. At a minimum, *Bartsch* holds that when a license includes a grant of rights that is reasonably read to cover a new use (at least where the new use was foreseeable at the time of contracting), the burden of excluding the right to the new use will rest on the grantor. 391 F.2d at 155; see also Bloom v. Hearst Entertainment Inc., 33 F.3d 518, 524-25 (5th Cir. 1994) (applying *Bartsch* to hold that a grant of movie and television rights to a book encompassed video rights as well). The license "to record in any manner, medium or form" doubtless extends to videocassette recording and we can see no reason why the grant of "motion picture" reproduction rights should not include the video format, absent any indication in the Agreement to the contrary. See Bourne v. Walt Disney Co., 68 F.3d 621, 630 (2d Cir. 1995); *Bloom*, 33 F.3d at 525. If a new-use license hinges on the foreseeability of the new channels of distribution at the time of contracting — a question left open in *Bartsch* — Disney has proffered unrefuted evidence that a nascent market for home viewing of feature films existed by 1939. The *Bartsch* analysis thus compels the conclusion that the license for motion picture rights extends to video format distribution.

We recognize that courts and scholars are not in complete accord on the capacity of a broad license to cover future developed markets resulting from new technologies. The NIMMER treatise describes two principal approaches to the problem. According to the first view, advocated here by Boosey, "a license of rights in a given medium (e.g., 'motion picture rights') includes only such uses as fall within the unambiguous core meaning of the term (e.g., exhibition of motion picture film in motion picture theaters) and exclude any uses that lie within the ambiguous penumbra (e.g., exhibition of motion picture on television)." NIMMER, §10.10[B] at 10-90; see also Cohen v. Paramount Pictures Corp., 845 F.2d 851, 853-54 (9th Cir. 1988) (holding that license to use musical score in television production does not extend to use in videocassette release); Rey v. Lafferty, 990 F.2d 1379, 1390-91 (1st Cir. 1993) (holding that license to portray Curious George in animations for "television viewing" does not extend to videocassette release). Under this approach, a license given in 1939 to "motion picture" rights would include only the core uses of "motion picture" as understood in 1939 — presumably theatrical distribution — and would not include subsequently developed methods of distribution of a motion picture such as television videocassettes or laser discs. See NIMMER §10.10[b] at 10-90.

The second position described by Nimmer is "that the licensee may properly pursue any uses that may reasonably be said to fall within the medium as described in the license." *Id.* at 10-91. NIMMER expresses clear preferences for the latter approach on the ground that it is "less likely to prove unjust." *Id.* As Judge Friendly noted in *Bartsch*, "[S]o do we." 391 F.2d at 155.

We acknowledge that a result which deprives the author-licensor of participation in the profits of new unforeseen channels of distribution is not an altogether happy solution. Nonetheless, we think it more fair and sensible than a result that would deprive a contracting party of the rights reasonably found in the terms of the contract it negotiates. This issue is too often, and improperly, framed as one of favoritism as between licensors and licensees. Because licensors are often authors — whose creativity the copyright laws intend to nurture — and are often impecunious, while licensees are often large business organizations, there is sometimes a tendency in copyright scholarship and adjudication to seek solutions that favor licensors over licensees. Thus in *Cohen*, 845 F.2d at 854, the Ninth Circuit wrote that a "license must be construed in accordance with the purpose underlying federal copyright law," which the court construed as the granting of valuable, enforceable rights to authors and the encouragement of the production of literary works. Asserting that copyright law "is enacted for the benefit of the composer," (quoting Jondora Music Publish. Co. v. Melody Recordings, Inc., 506 F.2d 392, 395 (3d Cir. 1974) (as amended)), the court concluded that it would "frustrate the purposes of the [copyright] Act" to construe the license as encompassing video technology, which did not exist when the license was granted. *Id.*; see also Warner Bros. Pictures v. Columbia Broadcasting System, 216 F.2d 945, 949 (9th Cir. 1954) ("Such doubt as there is should be resolved in favor of the composer. The clearest language is necessary to divest the author from the fruit of his labor."); William F. Patry, 1 Copyright Law and Practice 392 (1994) (arguing that "agreements should, wherever possible, be construed in favor of the copyright transferor," to reflect Congress's "policy judgment that copyright owners should retain all rights unless specifically transferred").

In our view, new-use analysis should rely on neutral principles of contract interpretation rather than solicitude for either party. Although *Bartsch* speaks of placing the "burden of framing and negotiating an exception . . . on the grantor," 391 F.2d at 155, it should not be understood to adopt a default rule in favor of copyright licensees or any default rule whatsoever. What governs under *Bartsch* is the language of the contract. If the contract is more reasonably read to convey one meaning, the party benefitted by that reading should be able to rely on it; the party seeking exception or deviation from the meaning reasonably conveyed by the words of the contract should bear the burden of negotiating for language that would express the limitation or deviation. This principle favors neither licensors nor licensees. It follows simply from the words of the contract.

The words of Disney's license are more reasonably read to include than to exclude a motion picture distributed in video format. Thus, we conclude that the burden fell on Stravinsky, if he wished to exclude new markets arising from subsequently developed motion picture technology, to insert such language of limitation in the license, rather than on Disney to add language that reiterated what the license already stated.

Other significant jurisprudential and policy considerations confirm our approach to new-use problems. We think that our view is more consistent with the law of contract than the view that would exclude new technologies even when they reasonably fall within the description of what is licensed. Although contract interpretation normally requires inquiry into the intent of the contracting parties, intent is not likely to be helpful when the subject of the inquiry is something the parties were not thinking about. See NIMMER, §10.10[B] at 10-90 (noting that usually "there simply was no intent at all at the time of execution with respect to whether the grant includes a new use developed at a later time"). Nor is extrinsic evidence such as past dealings or industry custom likely to illuminate the intent of the parties, because the use in question was, by hypothesis, new, and could not have been the subject of prior negotiations or established practice. See Michael R. Fuller, Hollywood Goes Interactive: Licensing Problems Associated with Re-Purposing Motion Pictures into Interactive Multimedia Videogames, 15 Loy. L.A. Ent. L.J. 599, 607 (1985). Moreover, many years after formation of the contract, it may well be impossible to consult the principals or retrieve documentary evidence to ascertain the parties' intent, if any, with respect to new uses. On the other hand, the parties or assignees of the contract should be entitled to rely on the words of the contract. Especially where, as here, evidence probative of intent is likely to be both scant and unreliable, the burden of justifying a departure from the most reasonable reading of the contract should fall on the party advocating the departure.

Neither the absence of a future technologies clause in the Agreement nor the presence of the reservation clause alters that analysis. The reservation clause stands for no more than the truism that Stravinsky retained whatever he had not granted. It contributes nothing to the definition of the boundaries of the license. See *Bartsch*, 391 F.2d at 154 n. 1. And irrespective of the presence or absence of a clause expressly confirming a license over future technologies, the burden still falls on the party advancing a deviation from the most reasonable reading of the license to insure that the desired deviation is reflected in the final terms of the contract. As we have already stated, if the broad terms of the license are more reasonably read to include the particular future technology in question, then the licensee may rely on that language.

Bartsch therefore continues to articulate our "preferred" approach to new-use questions, NIMMER, §10.10[B] at 10-91, and we hold that the district court properly applied it to find that the basic terms of Disney's license included the right to record and distribute Fantasia in video format.

LANDHAM v. LEWIS GALOOB TOYS, INC.
227 F.3d 619 (6th Cir. 2000)

BATCHELDER, Circuit Judge.

I. BACKGROUND

Landham is a fringe actor who has played supporting roles in several motion pictures, including *48 Hours*, *Action Jackson*, and *Maximum Force*, as well as several unrated, pornographic films. This suit concerns the role of "Billy, the Native American Tracker" that Landham portrayed in Fox's 1987 action film *Predator*. Landham's employment was initially memorialized in a March 3, 1986, "Standard Cast Deal Memo" ("Memo"), which detailed only the salary, starting date, and an agreement that Landham would pay for a bodyguard for himself. Fox later delivered a "Deal Player Employment Agreement" ("Agreement") which, among other things, assigned all merchandising rights for the Billy character to Fox. The Agreement was never signed, however, and there is a dispute between the parties as to how long after Landham left for filming in Mexico the Agreement was received by his agent in the United States. Landham testified that the only contractual understanding he had with Fox was that he would act in the movie for a specified amount of money and that he would be required to pay for the bodyguard. In 1995, Fox licensed to Galoob the rights to produce and market a line of its "Micro Machines" toys based on *Predator*. One of these three sets of toys contained a "Billy" action figure. Because the toy is only 1.5 inches tall and has no eyes or mouth, it bears no personal resemblance to Landham. Moreover, Eric Shank, the Galoob employee who designed the toy, purposefully avoided any such resemblance. Nonetheless, Landham argues that the toy violates his right of publicity under Kentucky law and amounts to a false endorsement under the Lanham Act. The district court disagreed, finding insufficient evidence to suggest that consumers would associate the toy with Landham. . . .

B. The Right of Publicity

The right of publicity is a creature of state common law and statute and originated as part of the common-law right of privacy. The Supreme Court has recognized its consistency with federal intellectual property laws and the First Amendment, *see generally* Zacchini v. Scripps-Howard Broadcasting Co., 433 U.S. 562, 97 S. Ct. 2849, 53 L. Ed. 2d 965 (1977), and Kentucky has long recognized the right of privacy, now embodied in the *Restatement (Second) of Torts*, §652A, from which the publicity right emanates.

Landham's claim is not preempted by the Copyright Act. The Supreme Court has recognized that rights of publicity are generally consistent with the Copyright Act. *See Zacchini,* 433 U.S. at 577. As long as a plaintiff states a claim of invasion of personal, state-law rights that are distinct from copyright protections, the claim will not be preempted. Unlike the baseball player-plaintiffs in Baltimore Orioles, Inc. v. Major League Baseball Players Assoc., 805 F.2d 663 (7th Cir. 1986), Landham is not claiming the right of publicity in order to gain rights in the telecast of his performance, or to contest Fox's right to create derivative works from its copyrighted work in general. Rather, he claims that the toy evokes his personal identity — an inchoate "idea" which is not amenable to copyright protection — to his emotional and financial detriment. Regardless of the merits of this claim, it does assert a right separate from those protected by the Copyright Act. *See Wendt,* 125 F.3d at 809 (claim that animatronic robots "look like" plaintiff and thereby evoke his identity in violation of his right of publicity is not preempted); *cf.* Midler v. Ford Motor Co., 849 F.2d 460, 462 (9th Cir. 1988) (distinctive sound of celebrity's voice is not protected by copyright). . . .

D. Contractual Assignment of Publicity Right

Fox argues that although Landham never signed the Agreement, its terms regarding merchandising should be enforced against him. Fox correctly argues that parties may be bound by the terms of an unsigned contract when their actions demonstrate assent to the agreement. *See* Cowden Mfg. Co., Inc. v. Systems Equip. Lessors, Inc., 608 S.W.2d 58, 61 (Ky. Ct. App. 1980). But Fox points only to Landham's presence on the set and hiring of the bodyguard as evidence of his assent to the Agreement. Those terms were included in the Memo, however, and therefore are not evidence of assent to the Agreement. Without such evidence, we cannot enforce the unsigned Agreement against Landham.

E. Commercial Value of Landham's Identity

The right of publicity is designed to reserve to a celebrity the personal right to exploit the commercial value of his own identity. *See* Carson v. Here's Johnny Portable Toilets, Inc., 698 F.2d 831, 835 (6th Cir. 1983) (noting that the right was meant to protect famous celebrities); McFarland v. Miller, 14 F.3d 912, 919 (3d Cir. 1994) (describing the heart of the right as the value of an association with the plaintiff's image). Landham correctly argues that he need not be a national celebrity to prevail. But in order to assert the right of publicity, a plaintiff must demonstrate that there is value in associating an item of commerce with his identity. *See Cheatham,* 891 F. Supp. at 386 (noting that plaintiffs do not need national celebrity but must show "significant 'commercial value' "); *Wendt*, 125 F.3d at 811; *McFarland*, 14 F.3d at 920 (noting that the right is worthless without an association); Lugosi v. Universal Pictures, 25 Cal. 3d 813, 160 Cal. Rptr. 323, 603 P.2d 425, 431 (1979) (per curiam) (same). The defendant's act of misappropriating the plaintiff's identity, however, may be sufficient evidence of commercial value.

To succeed, then, Landham must show that a merchant would gain significant commercial value by associating an article of commerce with him. He presented no such evidence to the district court. Landham argues vigorously on appeal that Galoob's use of Landham's identity is itself sufficient evidence of commercial value. But this argument assumes that by identifying its toy as "Billy," Galoob has evoked Landham's identity in the public mind.

F. Relationship Between the "Billy" Toy and Landham's Personal Identity

Although the right began as a protection for a celebrity's "name and likeness," *i.e.*, physical features, it is now generally understood to cover anything that suggests the plaintiff's personal identity. *See* Ky. Rev. Stat. §391.170(1) ("the right of publicity . . . is a right of protection from appropriation of *some element of an individual's personality*") (emphasis added); *Carson*, 698 F.2d at 835 ("If the celebrity's identity is commercially exploited, there has been an invasion of his right whether or not his 'name or likeness' is used. Carson's identity may be exploited even if his name . . . or his picture is not used."); *see also* Abdul-Jabbar v. General Motors Corp., 85 F.3d 407, 413-15 (9th Cir. 1996) (noting that to articulate exhaustively the protected ways in which one's identity may be exploited is to invite clever marketers to discover new ways); Motschenbacher v. R.J. Reynolds Tobacco Co., 498 F.2d 821 (9th Cir. 1974) (holding that slightly altered picture of well-known driver's race car was distinctive enough to suggest the plaintiff's identity, although the driver could not be seen); Ali v. Playgirl, Inc., 447 F. Supp. 723, 727 (S.D.N.Y. 1978) (finding drawing of a nude, black boxer identified as "The Greatest" evocative of Muhammad Ali's identity, even though the face was not clearly his and the figure was labeled "Mystery Man"); Hirsch v. S.C. Johnson & Son, Inc., 90 Wis. 2d 379, 280 N.W.2d 129, 137 (1979) (finding use of the name "Crazylegs" for female shaving gel violated the right of publicity of a professional football player known by that appellation).

What is not as clear, however, is the point at which the identity of a fictional character becomes so synonymous with the identity of the actor playing the role that the actor may challenge the character's exploitation. If the use of a fictional character also evokes the identity of the actor who played that character, he may challenge that use regardless of the fact that the actor's personal notoriety was gained exclusively through playing that role. *See Wendt*, 125 F.3d at 811 (reversing summary judgment against two actors from the TV series *Cheers* who challenged the use of animatronic bar patrons modeled after their characters in *Cheers*-themed airport bars); *McFarland*, 14 F.3d at 920 (reversing summary judgment against George McFarland, who played "Spanky" in *Our Gang*, in suit against owner of the restaurant "Spanky McFarland's"). Courts have generally been careful, however, to draw the line between the character's identity and the actor's, siding with plaintiffs only when it is shown that the two personalities are inseparable in the public's mind. *See Lugosi*, 160 Cal. Rptr. 323, 603 P.2d at 432 (Mosk, J., concurring) (explaining that actors have no inherent right in their roles, although those who play themselves or characters of their own creation may); *McFarland*, 14 F.3d at 920 (adopting J. Mosk's *Lugosi* concurrence and holding that "[w]here an actor's screen persona becomes so associated with him that it becomes inseparable from the actor's own public image, the actor obtains an interest in the image"); *Wendt*, 125 F.3d at 811 (describing the issue as whether the robots physically "look like" plaintiffs, since plaintiffs had conceded that they had no rights in the *Cheers* characters themselves); *Motschenbacher*, 498 F.2d at 827 (asking whether race car led viewers to believe that the plaintiff was in the ad, not simply that it reminded them of him). These cases, which appear to be accepted by the majority — if not all — of the courts to address the issue, make clear that although exploitation of a fictional character may, in some circumstances, be a means of evoking the actor's identity as well, the focus of any right of publicity analysis must always be on the actor's own persona and not the character's.

One case that may be read to depart significantly from this rule, and one upon which Landham heavily relies, is White v. Samsung Electronics America, Inc., 971 F.2d 1395 (9th Cir. 1992). There, an advertiser humorously evoked a futuristic version of the game show *Wheel of Fortune* through an animatronic replica of its hostess, Vanna White. The robot bore no facial resemblance to White, but it was adorned with a blond wig, jewelry and clothing similar to White's typical ensemble, and in her familiar pose turning the game board's letters. Although none of these factors individually suggested White, the court found that, taken together, they clearly evoked her identity. *See id.* at 1399. The dissenting judge argued that the majority had confused White, the person, with her TV role, and that the only element of the commercial that was unique to her was the *Wheel of Fortune* set, which was not part of her personal identity. *See id.* at 1404-05 (Alarcon, J., dissenting). Three other judges on the circuit agreed:

> Consider how sweeping this new right is. What is it about the ad that makes people think of White? It's not the robot's wig, clothes or jewelry; there must be ten million blond women (many of them quasi-famous) who wear dresses and jewelry like White's. It's that the robot is posed near the "Wheel of Fortune" game board. Remove the game board from the ad, and no one would think of Vanna White. . . . But once you include the game board, anybody standing beside it — a brunette woman, a man wearing women's clothes, a monkey in a wig and gown — would evoke White's image, precisely the way the robot did. It's the "Wheel of Fortune" set, not the robot's face or dress or jewelry that evokes White's image. The panel is giving White an exclusive right not in what she looks like or who she is, but in what she does for a living.

White v. Samsung Elecs. Am., Inc., 989 F.2d 1512, 1515 (9th Cir. 1993) (Kozinski, J., dissenting from denial of rehearing en banc). The judges warned of the dangers of overextending intellectual property laws, noting that it is impossible to evoke a movie or TV show without evoking the identities of its actors to some extent. *See generally id.* The Tenth Circuit has specifically adopted the reasoning of Judge Kozinski's dissent. *See* Cardtoons v. Major League Baseball Players Assoc., 95 F.3d 959, 970 (10th Cir. 1996).

We decline Landham's invitation to extend *White* to this case. First, the holding is factually distinguishable, as White used her own name in her television role, and also produced evidence that her identity was invoked and had commercial value. More importantly, we share, as we think the Kentucky courts would, Judge Kozinski's unwillingness to give every individual who appears before a television or movie camera, by occupation or happenstance, the right as a matter of law to compensation for every subtle nuance that may be taken by someone as invoking his identity without first being required to prove significant commercial value and identifiability. Such a holding would upset the careful balance that courts have gradually constructed between the right of publicity and the First Amendment and federal intellectual property laws, undermining the right's viability. We therefore decline to give Landham "an exclusive right not in what [he] looks like or who [he] is, but in what [he] does for a living." *White,* 989 F.2d at 1515. To the extent that *White* may be read to require a contrary result, we reject its reasoning.

In sum, Landham has not demonstrated — either through direct evidence or by virtue of Galoob's use of the "Billy" character — that his persona has "significant commercial value" or that the "Billy" toy invokes his own persona, as distinct from that of the fictional character. For these reasons, we affirm the district court's grant of summary judgment to Defendants on this claim.

G. Landham's Claim Under the Federal Lanham Act

A false designation of origin claim brought by an entertainer under §43(a) of the Lanham Act in a case such as this is equivalent to a false association or endorsement claim, *see Waits,* 978 F.2d at 1110, and the "mark" at issue is the plaintiff's identity. *See White,* 971 F.2d at 1399-1400. The underlying question to be answered is whether the plaintiff has shown "that the public believe[s] that 'the mark's owner sponsored or otherwise approved of the use of the trademark.'" *Wynn Oil Co. v. Thomas,* 839 F.2d 1183, 1186 (6th Cir. 1988).

Our findings on the right of publicity issue dictate the outcome of this claim as well. Noting that Landham had offered no evidence with regard to his name recognition among children, the district court correctly held that there was no genuine issue of fact material to the strength of Landham's mark, and that given "the general adult nature of [Landham's] past work, it does not appear that his mark possessed any significant degree of strength among that part of society relevant to this action" — the toy-buying public. Likewise, the factors accounting for the similarity of the marks, Defendants' intent, and expansion of the product lines weigh against Landham. The court correctly found that three factors — relatedness, marketing channels, and degree of purchaser care — weighed in Landham's favor. Our resolution of this claim, however, is not determined by numerical calculations or the weighted values of particular "factors." These are simply objective aids for reaching a subjective conclusion as to whether the consuming public is likely to be genuinely confused about whether Landham endorsed Galoob's "Billy" toy. For the same reasons that we found that Landham had not demonstrated the infringement of any right of publicity, we hold that he has not established a claim under the Lanham Act.

MAI PHOTO NEWS AGENCY, INC. v. AMERICAN BROADCASTING CO., INC.
2001 WL 180020 (S.D.N.Y. Feb. 22, 2001)

KNAPP, Sr. District Judge.

FACTUAL BACKGROUND

The facts of this case concern two video tapes which plaintiff Greg E. Mathieson ("Mathieson") licensed to Defendant American Broadcasting Company, Inc. ("ABC" or "defendant") to be used in ABC broadcasting specials about the relationship between the United States Central Intelligence Agency ("CIA") and Iraqi leader Saddam Hussein.

In the spring of 1997, ABC News producer Mark Atkinson ("Atkinson") was collecting materials for an ABC News special about Iraq and the CIA. Atkinson contacted Mathieson who runs plaintiff MAI Photo News Agency, Inc. ("MAI") regarding possible footage for the program. Mathieson told Atkinson that he had relevant footage, but that he was unwilling to send these tapes to Atkinson without an applicable contract, and Atkinson would have to travel to MAI's office, in Mathieson's home in Centreville, Virginia, to view the tapes.

Atkinson, together with his production associate Matthew Karatz ("Karatz"), made the trip to review various footage. They decided they were interested in two tapes. One was a two-hour "Hi-8" film cassette that Mathieson had recorded during a January 1993 trip through Northern Iraq ("Hi-8 Tape"). The second was a VHS film copy that contained footage of a Kurdish military offensive in the area of Kirkuk ("VHS Tape"). It was later revealed that the footage on the second tape was not taken by Mathieson, but that either in 1993 or 1995 he had received this tape from Kurdish fighters on a trip to Northern Iraq in either 1993 or 1995.

Atkinson informed Mathieson that he wanted to use these two tapes and that Mathieson should get in touch with ABC's Rights and Clearances Department which was responsible for negotiating licenses and payment contracts. Atkinson gave him the names of the individuals who should be contacted in that department.

On April 25, 1997, Mathieson sent the tapes to Atkinson, via Federal Express. Mathieson claims that when he sends such materials as these tapes he usually includes a printed form stating that the receiver: cannot copy the tapes; must insure them when returning them; and must use a courier service or special carrier that requires a signed receipt upon delivery.

After sending ABC the tapes, Mathieson negotiated a contract with ABC's Rights & Clearances Department. On May 9, 1997 ABC sent MAI a proposed license. Mathieson asked for certain changes to the terms of the proposed license. On May 19 Mathieson signed a final License Agreement which provides in part (License Agreement ¶1):

> Licensor (MAI) hereby grants to Licensee (ABC) a non-exclusive, non-transferable license to use two times . . . footage of the Iraqi Opposition, military training in Northern Iraq, Kurdish Parties, and the military offensive of the Iraqi Opposition ("the Footage"). Licensor hereby grants to Licensee the right to include the Footage in the ABC News program Peter Jennings Reporting ("the Program"), as distributed two times worldwide in all media now known and hereafter conceived or created. . . .

It also provides that ABC will pay MAI $40 per second of footage used, with a minimum payment of $2,400 whether or not the footage is used; that ABC is responsible for any additional costs incurred in the process of editing and integrating the footage into the production; that the footage is protected by copyright; and that ABC will give Mathieson and MAI end credit for its granting permission to use the footage, provided they run credits, but that any failure to run credits due to lack of time will not be deemed a breach of this agreement. (*Id.* ¶¶2, 4(b), and 6). Finally, the License Agreement states that it is an integrated contract, i.e. it contains the entire agreement of the parties and supersedes all prior agreements. (*Id.* ¶8).

On June 26, 1997 ABC aired "Peter Jennings Reporting: Unfinished Business—The CIA and Saddam Hussein" ("Unfinished Business"). At the end of the broadcast ABC announced that interested viewers could purchase a copy of the broadcast for $29.95 plus shipping and handling. A total of 248 copies of Unfinished Business were purchased after the broadcast, at least one of which was purchased by Mathieson.

The program was one hour in length and included 85 seconds of MAI's footage. ABC sent Mathieson a check for $3,400 (85 seconds times $40 per second). Mathieson received and cashed the check. Neither MAI nor Mathieson received end credit for the use of the footage provided to Unfinished Business. The only credit given at the end of the broadcast was "Special Thanks to Fred." According to Atkinson, Fred was a fictional character the Unfinished Business production team created for the purpose of discussing CIA operations, and this credit line was included at the end of the program as an inside joke.

On July 8, Karatz returned MAI's tapes through Airborne Express, a carrier that ABC regularly used. The package was correctly addressed and since Mathieson was not home at the time of delivery, the package was left at the front door to his home. Mathieson stated in his deposition that he never received the tapes. Mathieson demanded $576,000 ($40 per second times four hours) for the missing tapes. ABC sent Mathieson copies that had been made of the tapes. These were "working copies" that ABC made of the tapes in the process of incorporating the footage into Unfinished Business.

ABC re-edited Unfinished Business for a follow-up broadcast in December 1997. For this broadcast ABC omitted all of MAI's footage. Since Mathieson had complained and threatened to take legal action, ABC did not use any of his footage in the December broadcast.

DISCUSSION

We first address defendant's motion for summary judgment. For the purposes of this opinion we assume, contrary to the fact, that we had granted plaintiffs' motion to amend the Complaint and that such an amended complaint would have contained the claims alleged in the above mentioned subsequent action.

A. The Copyright Claims

Plaintiffs do not dispute that ABC had permission to use their footage pursuant to the License Agreement, but claim that ABC exceeded the scope of the License Agreement, thus infringing on plaintiffs' copyrights.

1. The License Agreement

As previously stated, the License Agreement permits ABC to distribute the program with plaintiffs' footage two times in all media for a period of two years. The Complaint states that ABC violated this provision by distributing multiple copies of Unfinished Business on home video and by making working copies of plaintiffs' tapes.

2. The Home Video Distribution

In his deposition, Mathieson said he interpreted "in all media" to relate to ABC's right to copy the tape from one format to another, for example, by copying the tapes from the VHS format to the Beta format, during its production of the television program. He did not understand the phrases "two distributions" and "in all media" to include producing multiple copies of the program for home video distribution.

Determining the scope of a license agreement present us with a question of contract interpretation. Bourne v. Walt Disney Co. (2d Cir. 1995) 68 F.3d 621, 631. In cases where only the scope of the license is at issue, it is the copyright owner's burden to prove that defendant's usage was unauthorized. *Id.* The Second Circuit has held that "licensees may properly pursue any uses which may reasonably be said to fall within the medium as described in the license." Boosey & Hawkes Music Publishers, Ltd. v. Walt Disney Co., 145 F.3d 481, 486 (2d Cir. 1998). The party seeking exception or deviation from the meaning reasonably conveyed by the terms of the license "should bear the burden of negotiating for language that would express the limitation or deviation." *Id.* at 487.

"In all media" seems to us to include authorization for ABC to distribute Unfinished Business on home video. NIMMER, one of the foremost authorities on intellectual property law, states that "a grant of the right to exhibit a motion picture by 'television' . . . includes any device by which the motion picture may be seen on television screens, including cable television and videocassette uses." 3 NIMMER §10.10[B] at 10-92. In *Boosey* the Second Circuit found that a license to include a musical composition in a motion picture included the authorization to distribute the motion picture in video format. 145 F.3d at 487. We therefore conclude that if plaintiffs wanted home video distribution excluded from the license they gave ABC to use the footage in the broadcast, it was up to them to specify such in the License Agreement.

Furthermore, defendants are correct in their assertion that plaintiffs' infringement argument in regard to the home video distribution would fail even if we were to adopt plaintiffs' interpretation of the license. The license allowed the footage to be used in "two distributions." The allegations of the Complaint only state that ABC used the footage twice, which is in accord with plaintiffs' construction; once in the television broadcast and once in the home video distribution.

Plaintiffs have alleged in their motion briefs and in the related case they subsequently filed that their footage was used in the December 1997 re-edited version of the television broadcast, although such allegation did not appear in the original Complaint. Since we have already found that the home video distribution of Unfinished Business could be included in the license to use the footage in the television broadcast of the same, ABC could have used the footage in the December 1997 broadcast and still have been within the terms of the License Agreement.

We therefore conclude that neither the home video distribution nor the alleged usage in the December 1997 broadcast violated the Licensing Agreement and therefore such usages do not constitute copyright infringement.

3. The Working Copies

Working copies of plaintiffs' tapes were made in the course of editing and producing Unfinished Business. The Complaint states that ABC went beyond the licensing agreement by making such copies. However, Mathieson conceded at his deposition that ABC had the right to copy the tapes from VHS to Beta format in order to prepare the footage for the broadcast. In addition, the License Agreement specifically anticipates such use. Furthermore, the License Agreement must be read to permit such uses as are necessary to accomplish the purposes of the agreement. See NIMMER §10.10[B] at 10-95. We therefore conclude that creating working copies did not violate the License Agreement and that doing so did not result in copyright violation.

B. The Contract Claims

The Complaint states the following two claims for breach of contract: (1) breach of ABC's implicit promise to return the tapes safely; and (2) breach of the License Agreement for failing to give plaintiffs end credit on the broadcast.

1. Implied Promise of Safe Return

The Complaint alleges that ABC "impliedly agreed" to return all of the tapes undamaged and to pay plaintiffs reasonable damages if it failed to return them. Although the Complaint fails to mention any actual contract entered into between plaintiffs and ABC to this effect, in their opposition papers plaintiffs refer to a "bailment contract" which they claim was included in the package when Mathieson sent ABC the tapes. This "bailment contract" is claimed to have consisted of a form statement which Mathieson states he routinely includes when lending out his tapes for use and provides that their return must be by an insured carrier requiring both insurance and a signature receipt for delivery. It is further claimed to have stated that loss or damage must be compensated by the bailee in the amount of $40 per second of footage on the tapes. The individuals who received the tapes at ABC deny having seen the form or assenting to its terms. Although at his deposition Mathieson admitted he does not specifically recall including the form with these tapes that he sent to ABC, plaintiffs contend that silently accepting and using the tapes constitutes acceptance of the terms of the "bailment contract." Therefore, plaintiffs allege that ABC breached this agreement by using Airborne Express, which did not require the recipient's signature as a receipt, for its carrier and thus owes plaintiffs $576,000 ($40 per second times four hours) for the tapes Mathieson never received as outlined in the "bailment contract."

Even if the "bailment contract" had in fact been enclosed in the package Mathieson sent to ABC its existence would not create an issue of material fact. The License Agreement is an integrated contract which was signed after the receipt of the tapes. The last paragraph of the License Agreement states: "[t]his agreement contains the entire agreement of the parties, [and] supercedes all prior agreements on this subject matter." (¶8). The "bailment contract," if it did in fact exist, was a prior agreement which became null once the License Agreement went into effect.

ABC does not deny its position as a bailee for mutual benefit and that it therefore was required to exercise that degree of care which a reasonably careful owner of similar goods would exercise under the same circumstances. 9 N.Y. Jur. 2d Bailments §111 (1980). ABC satisfied this duty by delivering the tapes to Airborne Express, a reasonably safe carrier, with correct instructions for return to Mathieson's home. In addition, as a courtesy, ABC sent Mathieson working copies that had been made of his tapes to help alleviate plaintiffs' loss.

2. Failure to Give End Credit

Plaintiffs allege that ABC breached the Licensing Agreement by failing to give MAI or Mathieson end credit for the footage used in Unfinished Business. The Licensing Agreement states:

Licensee [ABC] shall give Licensor an end credit ("Greg Mathieson/MAI Photo News Agency Inc.") for its granting permission to use the Footage, provided credits are run. Our failure to broadcast any credits . . . shall not be deemed a breach of this agreement (¶6).

Plaintiffs claim that by running "Special Thanks to Fred" at the end of the broadcast ABC did run end credits and therefore breached the License Agreement.

Other than listing those employees who created the broadcast, e.g. producers, reporters, etc., ABC did not run any other credits except for the special thanks given to Fred. ABC did not give end credit to any of the several outside sources used for the broadcast.

As stated in the Licensing Agreement, ABC had no obligation to run end credits and the decision not to do so does not amount to a breach of that agreement. The credit given to the fictitious "Fred" does not, in our opinion, constitute "end credit" that would have required end credit be given to plaintiffs. Including the "Special Thanks to Fred" was obviously a joke, although one lost on the Court, but does not amount to breach of contract.

Furthermore, the Complaint does not state any damages incurred by plaintiffs for the failure to be given end credit. Plaintiffs concede in their opposition papers that they do not allege any damages resulting directly from this claim. In order for such a claim to survive, plaintiffs must have asserted damages. Trademark Research Corp. v. Maxwell Online, Inc. (2d Cir. 1993) 995 F.2d 326, 332.

C. The Unfair Competition Claims

Plaintiffs make various unfair competition and Lanham Act claims, all of which are pre-empted by federal copyright laws. Computer Assocs. Int'l v. Altai, Inc., 982 F.2d 693, 717 (2d Cir. 1992) (common law "unfair competition and misappropriation claims grounded solely in the copying of a plaintiff's protected expression are preempted by section 301" of the Copyright Act); Lipton v. Nature Co. (2d Cir. 1995) 71 F.3d 464, 473 (Lanham Act claims are preempted by federal copyright laws; therefore a plaintiff cannot sustain a Lanham Act claim by merely alleging that defendant distributed plaintiff's work under defendant's copyright). There is no evidence that these images have indeed been broadcast before, or even if they had, that the public would recognize them and associate them with MAI.

For the foregoing reasons, defendant's motion for summary judgment is granted in its entirety and plaintiffs' Complaint is dismissed as without merit.

DATA EAST USA, INC. v. EPYX, INC.
862 F.2d 204 (9th Cir. 1988)

TROTT, Circuit Judge.

I. FACTS

Data East is a California corporation engaged in the design, manufacture, and sale of audio-visual works embodied in video games for coin-operated and home computer use. In July 1984, Data East commenced distribution in Japan of an arcade game entitled "Karate Champ" ("Arcade # 1"). In September 1984, Data East commenced distribution in Japan and later in the United States and Europe of an updated version of "Karate Champ" ("Arcade # 2" or more generally as "arcade game"). Finally, on October 12, 1985, Data East commenced distribution in the United States of a home computer game version of "Karate Champ" ("home game"). Data East applied for and received audio-visual copyright certificates for each game.

In November of 1985, System III Software, Ltd., an English company, commenced distribution in England of a home computer game entitled "International Karate." Epyx, a California corporation engaged in the development and distribution of audio-visual works for use on home computers, obtained a license agreement with System III and commenced distribution in the United States on April 30, 1986 of a Commodore-compatible version of "International Karate" under the name "World Karate Championship."

Each competing product, "Karate Champ" and "World Karate Championship," consists of the audio-visual depiction of a karate match or matches conducted by two combatants, one clad in a typical white outfit and the other in red. Successive phases of combat are conducted against varying stationary background images depicting localities or geographic scenes. The match is supervised by a referee who directs the beginning and end of each phase of combat and announces the winning combatant of each phase by means of a cartoon-style speech balloon. Each game has a bonus round where the karate combatant breaks bricks and dodges objects. Similarities also exist in the moves used by the combatants and the scoring method.

Data East alleged that the overall appearance, compilation, and sequence of the audio-visual display of the video game "World Karate Championship" infringed its copyright for "Karate Champ" as embodied in the arcade and home versions of the video game. Data East also charged Epyx with trademark and trade dress infringement. To establish copyright infringement, Data East must prove both ownership of a valid copyright and "copying" by Epyx of the copyrighted work. Sid & Marty Krofft Television Products, Inc. v. McDonald's Corp., 562 F.2d 1157, 1162 (9th Cir. 1977). It is undisputed that Data East is the registered copyright owner of the audio-visual work for each version of "Karate Champ." Thus we need only determine whether Epyx copied "Karate Champ." This sounds simple and straightforward. It is not. As in most infringement cases of this kind, no direct evidence was developed that System III Software or anybody else copied any version of Data East's product. There seldom is any direct evidence of copying in these matters. Therefore, copying may be established instead by circumstantial evidence of (1) the defendant's access to the copyrighted work prior to defendant's creation of its work, and (2) the substantial similarity of both the general ideas and expression between the copyrighted work and defendant's work. *Id.*; Baxter v. MCA, Inc., 812 F.2d 421, 423 (9th Cir. 1987), cert. denied, 484 U.S. 954 (1987). In essence, the question of copying becomes a matter of reasonable inferences. Because we find no substantial similarity, we decline to address the issue of access. . . .

B. Substantial Similarity

"To show that two works are substantially similar, plaintiff must demonstrate that the works are substantially similar in both ideas and expression." Frybarger v. International Business Machines Corp., 812 F.2d 525, 529 (9th Cir. 1987). Although plaintiff must first show that the ideas are substantially similar, the ideas themselves are not protected by copyright and therefore, cannot be infringed. It is an axiom of copyright law that copyright protects only an author's expression of an idea, not the idea itself. Mazer v. Stein, 347 U.S. 201, 217-18 (1954). There is a strong public policy corollary to this axiom permitting all to use freely ideas contained in a copyrightable work, so long as the protected expression itself is not appropriated. Landsberg v. Scrabble Crossword Game Players, Inc., 736 F.2d 485, 488 (9th Cir. 1984), cert. denied, 469 U.S. 1037 (1984). Thus, to the extent the similarities between plaintiff's and defendant's works are confined to ideas and general concepts, these similarities are noninfringing.

The Ninth Circuit has developed a two-step test for the purposes of determining substantial similarity. *McCulloch*, 823 F.2d at 319; *Krofft*, 562 F.2d at 1164. First, an "extrinsic" test is used to determine whether two ideas are substantially similar. This is an objective test which rests upon specific criteria that can be listed and analyzed. *Krofft*, id. Second, an "intrinsic" test is used to compare forms of expression. This is a subjective test which depends on the response of the ordinary reasonable person. *Id.*

Once an idea is found to be similar or identical, as in this case, the second or intrinsic step is applied to determine whether similarity of the expression of the idea occurs. This exists when the "total concept and feel of the works" is substantially similar. Aliotti v. R. Dakin & Co., 831 F.2d 898 (9th Cir. 1987). Analytic dissection of the dissimilarities as opposed to the similarities is not appropriate under this test because it distracts a reasonable observer from a comparison of the total concept and feel of the works. *Id.*

The rule in the Ninth Circuit, however, is that "[n]o substantial similarity of expression will be found when 'the idea and its expression are . . . inseparable,' given that 'protecting the expression in such circumstances would confer a monopoly of the idea upon the copyright owner.'" *Id.* Nor can copyright protection be afforded to elements of expression that necessarily follow from an idea, or to "scenes a faire," i.e., expressions that are "as a practical matter, indispensable or at least standard in the treatment of a given [idea]." *Aliotti*, 831 F.2d at 901.

To determine whether similarities result from unprotectable expression, analytic dissection of similarities may be performed. If this demonstrates that all similarities in expression arise from use of common ideas, then no substantial similarity can be found. *Id.*

The district court found that the visual depiction of karate matches is subject to the constraints inherent in the sport of karate itself. The number of combatants, the stance employed by the combatants, established and recognized moves and motions regularly employed in the sport of karate, the regulation of the match by at least one referee or judge, and the manner of scoring by points and half points are among the constraints inherent in the sport of karate. Because of these constraints, karate is not susceptible of a wholly fanciful presentation. Furthermore, the use of the Commodore computer for a karate game intended for home consumption is subject to various constraints inherent in the use of that computer. Among the constraints are the use of sprites, and a somewhat limited access to color, together with limitations upon the use of multiple colors in one visual image.

The fifteen features listed by the court "encompass the idea of karate." These features, which consist of the game procedure, common karate moves, the idea of background scenes, a time element, a referee, computer graphics, and bonus points, result from either constraints inherent in the sport of karate or computer restraints. After careful consideration and viewing of these features, we find that they necessarily follow from the idea of a martial arts karate combat game, or are inseparable from, indispensable to, or even standard treatment of the idea of the karate sport. As such, they are not protectable. "When idea and expression coincide, there will be protection against nothing other than identical copying." *Krofft*, 562 F.2d at 1168. A comparison of the works in this case demonstrates that identical copying is not an issue.

Accordingly, we hold that the court did not give the appropriate weight and import to its findings which support Epyx's argument that the similarities result from unprotectable expression. Consequently, it was clear error for the district court to determine that protectable substantial similarity existed based upon these facts.

The lower court erred by not limiting the scope of Data East's copyright protection to the author's contribution — the scoreboard and background scenes. In actuality, however, the backgrounds are quite dissimilar and the method of scorekeeping, though similar, is inconsequential. Based upon these two features, a discerning 17.5 year-old boy could not regard the works as substantially similar. Accordingly, Data East's copyright was not infringed on this basis either.

SONY COMPUTER ENTERTAINMENT, INC. v. CONNECTIX CORP.

203 F.3d 596 (9th Cir. 2000)

CANBY, Circuit Judge.

I. BACKGROUND

A. The Products

Sony is the developer, manufacturer and distributor of both the Sony PlayStation and Sony PlayStation games. Sony also licenses other companies to make games that can play on the PlayStation. The PlayStation system consists of a console (essentially a mini-computer), controllers, and software that produce a three-dimensional game for play on a television set. The PlayStation games are CDs that load into the top of the console. The PlayStation console contains both (1) hardware components and (2) software known as firmware that is written onto a read-only memory (ROM) chip. The firmware is the Sony BIOS. Sony has a copyright on the BIOS. It has claimed no patent relevant to this proceeding on any component of the PlayStation. PlayStation is a registered trademark of Sony.

Connectix's Virtual Game Station is software that "emulates" the functioning of the PlayStation console. That is, a consumer can load the Virtual Game Station software onto a computer, load a PlayStation game into the computer's CD-ROM drive, and play the PlayStation game. The Virtual Game Station software thus emulates both the hardware and firmware components of the Sony console. The Virtual Game Station does not play PlayStation games as well as Sony's PlayStation does. At the time of the injunction, Connectix had marketed its Virtual Game Station for Macintosh computer systems but had not yet completed Virtual Game Station software for Windows.

B. Reverse Engineering

Copyrighted software ordinarily contains both copyrighted and unprotected or functional elements. Sega Enters. Ltd. v. Accolade, Inc., 977 F.2d 1510, 1520 (9th Cir. 1992) (amended opinion); *see* 17 U.S.C. §102(b) (copyright protection does not extend to any "idea, procedure, process, system, method of operation, concept, principle, or discovery" embodied in the copyrighted work). Software engineers designing a product that must be compatible with a copyrighted product frequently must "reverse engineer" the copyrighted product to gain access to the functional elements of the copyrighted product. *See* Andrew Johnson-Laird, *Software Reverse Engineering in the Real World,* 19 U. Dayton L. Rev. 843, 845-46 (1994).

Reverse engineering encompasses several methods of gaining access to the functional elements of a software program. They include: (1) reading about the program; (2) observing "the program in operation by using it on a computer"; (3) performing a "static examination of the individual computer instructions contained within the program"; and (4) performing a "dynamic examination of the individual computer instructions as the program is being run on a computer." *Id.* at 846. Method (1) is the least effective, because individual software manuals often misdescribe the real product. *See id.* It would be particularly ineffective in this case because Sony does not make such information available about its PlayStation. Methods (2), (3), and (4) require that the person seeking access load the target program on to a computer, an operation that necessarily involves copying the copyrighted program into the computer's random access memory or RAM.

C. Connectix's Reverse Engineering of the Sony BIOS

Connectix began developing the Virtual Game Station for Macintosh on about July 1, 1998. In order to develop a PlayStation emulator, Connectix needed to emulate both the PlayStation hardware and the firmware (the Sony BIOS).

Connectix first decided to emulate the PlayStation's hardware. In order to do so, Connectix engineers purchased a Sony PlayStation console and extracted the Sony BIOS from a chip inside the console. Connectix engineers then copied the Sony BIOS into the RAM of their computers and observed the functioning of the Sony BIOS in conjunction with the Virtual Game Station hardware emulation software as that hardware emulation software was being developed by Connectix. The engineers observed the operation of the Sony BIOS through use of a debugging program that permitted the engineers to observe the signals sent between the BIOS and the hardware emulation software. During this process, Connectix engineers made additional copies of the Sony BIOS every time they booted up their computer and the Sony BIOS was loaded into RAM.

Once they had developed the hardware emulation software, Connectix engineers also used the Sony BIOS to "debug" the emulation software. In doing so, they repeatedly copied and disassembled discrete portions of the Sony BIOS.

Connectix also used the Sony BIOS to begin development of the Virtual Game Station for Windows. Specifically, they made daily copies to RAM of the Sony BIOS and used the Sony BIOS to develop certain Windows-specific systems for the Virtual Game Station for Windows. Although Connectix had its own BIOS at the time, Connectix engineers used the Sony BIOS because it contained CD-ROM code that the Connectix BIOS did not contain.

Early in the development process, Connectix engineer Aaron Giles disassembled a copy of the entire Sony BIOS that he had downloaded from the Internet. He did so for the purpose of testing a "disassembler" program he had written. The print-out of the source code was not used to develop the Virtual Game Station emulator. Connectix engineers initially used this copy of the Sony BIOS to begin the reverse engineering process, but abandoned it after realizing that it was a Japanese-language version.

During development of the Virtual Game Station, Connectix contacted Sony and requested "technical assistance" from Sony to complete the development of the Virtual Game Station. Connectix and Sony representatives met during September 1998. Sony declined Connectix's request for assistance.

II. DISCUSSION

To prevail on its motion for injunctive relief, Sony was required to demonstrate "either a likelihood of success on the merits and the possibility of irreparable injury or that serious questions going to the merits were raised and the balance of the hardships tip sharply in its favor." Cadence Design Sys., Inc. v. Avant! Corp., 125 F.3d 824, 826 (9th Cir. 1997) (omitted), *cert. denied*, 523 U.S. 1118 (1998). Connectix admits that it copied Sony's copyrighted BIOS software in developing the Virtual Game Station but contends that doing so was protected as a fair use under 17 U.S.C. §107.

A. Fair Use

The fair use issue arises in the present context because of certain characteristics of computer software. The object code of a program may be copyrighted as expression, 17 U.S.C. §102(a), but it also contains ideas and performs functions that are not entitled to copyright protection. *See* 17 U.S.C. §102(b). Object code cannot, however, be read by humans. The unprotected ideas and functions of the code therefore are frequently undiscoverable in the absence of investigation and translation that may require copying the copyrighted material. We conclude that, under the facts of this case and our precedent, Connectix's intermediate copying and use of Sony's copyrighted BIOS was a fair use for the purpose of gaining access to the unprotected elements of Sony's software.

The general framework for analysis of fair use is established by statute, 17 U.S.C. §107. We have applied this statute and the fair use doctrine to the disassembly of computer software in the case of Sega Enterprises Ltd. v. Accolade, Inc., 977 F.2d 1510 (9th Cir. 1992) (amended opinion). Central to our decision today is the rule set forth in *Sega*:

> [W]here disassembly is the *only way to gain access to the ideas and functional elements embodied in a copyrighted computer program* and where there is a legitimate reason for seeking such access, disassembly is a fair use of the copyrighted work, as a matter of law. *Id.* at 1527-28 (emphasis added).

In *Sega*, we recognized that intermediate copying could constitute copyright infringement even when the end product did not itself contain copyrighted material. *Id.* at 1518-19. But this copying nonetheless could be protected as a fair use if it was "necessary" to gain access to the functional elements of the software itself. *Id.* at 1524-26. We drew this distinction because the Copyright Act protects expression only, not ideas or the functional aspects of a software program. *See id.* at 1524 (citing 17 U.S.C. §102(b)). We also recognized that, in the case of computer programs, this idea/expression distinction poses "unique problems" because computer programs are "in essence, utilitarian articles — articles that accomplish tasks. As such, they contain many logical, structural, and visual display elements that are dictated by the function to be performed, by considerations of efficiency, or by external factors such as compatibility requirements and industry demands." *Id.* Thus, the fair use doctrine preserves public access to the ideas and functional elements embedded in copyrighted computer software programs. This approach is consistent with the "'ultimate aim [of the Copyright Act], to stimulate artistic creativity for the general public good.'" Sony Corp. of Am. v. Universal City Studios, Inc., 464 U.S. 417, 432 (1984).

We turn then to the statutory fair use factors, as informed by our precedent in *Sega*.

1. Nature of the Copyrighted Work

Under our analysis of the second statutory factor, nature of the copyrighted work, we recognize that "some works are closer to the core of intended copyright protection than others." Campbell v. Acuff-Rose Music, Inc., 510 U.S. 569, 586 (1994). Sony's BIOS lies at a distance from the core because it contains unprotected aspects that cannot be examined without copying. *See Sega*, 977 F.2d at 1526. We consequently accord it a "lower degree of protection than more traditional literary works." *Id.* As we have applied this standard, Connectix's copying of the Sony BIOS must have been "necessary" to have been fair use. *See id.* at 1524-26. We conclude that it was.

There is no question that the Sony BIOS contains unprotected functional elements. Nor is it disputed that Connectix could not gain access to these unprotected functional elements without copying the Sony BIOS. Sony admits that little technical information about the functionality of the Sony BIOS is publicly available. The Sony BIOS is an internal operating system that does not produce a screen display to reflect its functioning. Consequently, if Connectix was to gain access to the functional elements of the Sony BIOS it had to be through a form of reverse engineering that required copying the Sony BIOS onto a computer. Sony does not dispute this proposition.

The question then becomes whether the methods by which Connectix reverse-engineered the Sony BIOS were necessary to gain access to the unprotected functional elements within the program. We conclude that they were. Connectix employed several methods of reverse engineering (observation and observation with partial disassembly) each of which required Connectix to make intermediate copies of copyrighted material. Neither of these methods renders fair use protection inapplicable. *Sega* expressly sanctioned disassembly. *See id.* at 1527-28. We see no reason to distinguish observation of copyrighted software in an emulated computer environment. Both methods require the reverse engineer to copy protected as well as unprotected elements of the computer program. Because this intermediate copying is the gravamen of the intermediate infringement claim, *see* 17 U.S.C. §106(1); *Sega*, 977 F.2d at 1518-19, and both methods of reverse engineering require it, we find no reason inherent in these methods to prefer one to another as a matter of copyright law. Connectix presented evidence that it observed the Sony BIOS in an emulated environment to observe the functional aspects of the Sony BIOS. When this method of reverse engineering was unsuccessful, Connectix engineers disassembled discrete portions of the Sony BIOS to view directly the ideas contained therein. We conclude that intermediate copying in this manner was "necessary" within the meaning of *Sega*.

Sony contends that Connectix's reverse engineering of the Sony BIOS should be considered unnecessary on the rationale that Connectix's decision to observe the Sony BIOS in an emulated environment required Connectix to make more intermediate copies of the Sony BIOS than if Connectix had performed a complete disassembly of the program. Under this logic, at least some of the intermediate copies were not necessary within the meaning of *Sega*. This construction stretches *Sega* too far. The "necessity" we addressed in *Sega* was the necessity of the method, i.e., disassembly, not the necessity of the number of times that method was applied. *See* 977 F.2d at 1524-26. In any event, the interpretation advanced by Sony would be a poor criterion for fair use. Most of the intermediate copies of the Sony

BIOS were made by Connectix engineers when they booted up their computers and the Sony BIOS was copied into RAM. But if Connectix engineers had left their computers turned on throughout the period during which they were observing the Sony BIOS in an emulated environment, they would have made far fewer intermediate copies of the Sony BIOS (perhaps as few as one per computer). Even if we were inclined to supervise the engineering solutions of software companies in minute detail, and we are not, our application of the copyright law would not turn on such a distinction. Such a rule could be easily manipulated. More important, the rule urged by Sony would require that a software engineer, faced with two engineering solutions that each require intermediate copying of protected and unprotected material, often follow the *least efficient solution.* (In cases in which the solution that required the fewest number of intermediate copies was also the most efficient, an engineer would pursue it, presumably, without our urging.) This is precisely the kind of "wasted effort that the proscription against the copyright of ideas and facts . . . [is] designed to prevent." Feist Publications, Inc. v. Rural Tel. Serv. Co., 499 U.S. 340, 354 (1991) (internal quotation marks omitted). Such an approach would erect an artificial hurdle in the way of the public's access to the ideas contained within copyrighted software programs. These are "aspects that were expressly denied copyright protection by Congress." *Sega*, 977 F.2d at 1526 (citing 17 U.S.C. §102(b)). We decline to erect such a barrier in this case. If Sony wishes to obtain a lawful monopoly on the functional concepts in its software, it must satisfy the more stringent standards of the patent laws. *See* Bonito Boats, Inc. v. Thunder Craft Boats, Inc., 489 U.S. 141, 160-61 (1989); *Sega*, 977 F.2d at 1526. This Sony has not done. The second statutory factor strongly favors Connectix.

2. Amount and Substantiality of the Portion Used

With respect to the third statutory factor, amount and substantiality of the portion used in relation to the copyrighted work as a whole, Connectix disassembled parts of the Sony BIOS and copied the entire Sony BIOS multiple times. This factor therefore weighs against Connectix. But as we concluded in *Sega*, in a case of intermediate infringement when the final product does not itself contain infringing material, this factor is of "very little weight." *Sega*, 977 F.2d at 1526-27; *see also* Sony Corp. of Am. v. Universal City Studios, Inc., 464 U.S. 417, 449-50 (1984) (copying of entire work does not preclude fair use).

3. Purpose and Character of the Use

Under the first factor, purpose and character of the use, we inquire into whether Connectix's Virtual Game Station merely supersedes the objects of the original creation, or instead adds something new, with a further purpose or different character, altering the first with new expression, meaning, or message; it asks, in other words, whether and to what extent the new work is "transformative." Campbell v. Acuff-Rose Music, Inc., 510 U.S. 569, 579 (1994). As an initial matter, we conclude that the district court applied an erroneous legal standard; the district court held that Connectix's commercial purpose in copying the Sony BIOS gave rise to a "presumption of unfairness that . . . can be rebutted by the characteristics of a particular commercial use." Order at 14-15 (citing *Sega*, 977 F.2d at 1522). Since *Sega*, however, the

Supreme Court has rejected this presumption as applied to the first and fourth factor of the fair use analysis. *Acuff-Rose*, 510 U.S. at 584, 594. Instead, the fact that Connectix's copying of the Sony BIOS was for a commercial purpose is only a "separate factor that tends to weigh against a finding of fair use." *Id.* at 585.

We find that Connectix's Virtual Game Station is modestly transformative. The product creates a new platform, the personal computer, on which consumers can play games designed for the Sony PlayStation. This innovation affords opportunities for game play in new environments, specifically anywhere a Sony PlayStation console and television are not available, but a computer with a CD-ROM drive is. More important, the Virtual Game Station itself is a wholly new product, notwithstanding the similarity of uses and functions between the Sony PlayStation and the Virtual Game Station. The expressive element of software lies as much in the organization and structure of the object code that runs the computer as it does in the visual expression of that code that appears on a computer screen. *See* 17 U.S.C. §102(a) (extending copyright protection to original works of authorship that "can be perceived, repro-duced, or otherwise communicated, either directly or with the aid of a machine or device"). Sony does not claim that the Virtual Game Station itself contains object code that infringes Sony's copyright. We are therefore at a loss to see how Connectix's drafting of entirely new object code for its VGS program could not be transformative, despite the similarities in function and screen output.

Finally, we must weigh the extent of any transformation in Connectix's Virtual Game Station against the significance of other factors, including commercialism, that militate against fair use. *See Acuff-Rose*, 510 U.S. at 579. Connectix's commercial use of the copyrighted material was an intermediate one, and thus was only "indirect or derivative." *Sega*, 977 F.2d at 1522. Moreover, Connectix reverse-engineered the Sony BIOS to produce a product that would be compatible with games designed for the Sony PlayStation. We have recognized this purpose as a legitimate one under the first factor of the fair use analysis. *See id.* Upon weighing these factors, we find that the first factor favors Connectix.

4. Effect of the Use upon the Potential Market

We also find that the fourth factor, effect of the use upon the potential market, favors Connectix. Under this factor, we consider not only the extent of market harm caused by the particular actions of the alleged infringer, but also "whether unrestricted and widespread conduct of the sort engaged in by the defendant . . . would result in a substantially adverse impact on the potential market" for the original. *Acuff-Rose*, 510 U.S. at 590. Whereas a work that merely supplants or supersedes another is likely to cause a substantially adverse impact on the potential market of the original, a transformative work is less likely to do so. *See id.* at 591.

The district court found that "[t]o the extent that such a substitution [of Connectix's Virtual Game Station for Sony PlayStation console] occurs, Sony will lose console sales and profits." Order at 19. We recognize that this may be so. But because the Virtual Game Station is transformative, and does not merely supplant the PlayStation console, the Virtual Game Sta-tion is a legitimate competitor in the market for platforms on which Sony and Sony-licensed games can be played. *See Sega*, 977 F.2d at 1522-23. For this reason, some economic loss by Sony as a result of this competition does not compel a finding of no fair use. Sony understandably seeks control over the market for devices that play games Sony produces or licenses. The copyright law, however, does not confer such a monopoly. *See id.* at 1523-24 ("[A]n attempt to monopolize the market by making it impossible for others to compete runs counter to the statutory purpose of promoting creative expression and cannot constitute a strong equitable basis for resisting the invocation of the fair use doctrine."). This factor favors Connectix.

The four statutory fair use factors must be "weighed together, in light of the purposes of copyright." *Acuff-Rose*, 510 U.S. at 578. Here, three of the factors favor Connectix; one favors Sony, and it is of little weight. Of course, the statutory factors are not exclusive, *Harper & Row*, 471 U.S. at 560, but we are unaware of other factors not already considered that would affect our analysis. Accordingly, we conclude that Connectix's intermediate copying of the Sony BIOS during the course of its reverse engineering of that product was a fair use under 17 U.S.C. §107, as a matter of law. With respect to its claim of copyright infringement, Sony has not established either a likelihood of success on the merits or that the balance of hardships tips in its favor. *See* Cadence Design Sys., Inc. v. Avant! Corp., 125 F.3d 824, 826 (9th Cir. 1997), *cert. denied*, 523 U.S. 1118 (1998). Accordingly, we need not address defenses asserted by Connectix under 17 U.S.C. §117(a)(1) and our doctrine of copyright misuse. We reverse the district court's grant of a preliminary injunction on the ground of copyright infringement.

*   *   *

AGREEMENT BETWEEN APPLE COMPUTER, INC. AND APPLE CORPS LTD.

<u>AGREEMENT</u>

This Agreement is made the 9th day of October, 1991
Between:

    <u>APPLE CORPS LIMITED</u> an English Company with its principal
    place of business at 6 Stratton Street, London W1X 5FD, its
    Subsidiaries, and their respective successors in business
    and assigns, (collectively "Apple Corps"); and

    <u>APPLE COMPUTER, INC.</u> a California Corporation with its
    principal place of business at 20525 Mariani Avenue,
    Cupertino, California 95014, its Subsidiaries, and their
    respective successors in business and assigns (collectively
    "Apple Computer").

Whereas, the context in which this Agreement arises is the
parties' desire to reserve for Apple Corps' field of use for its
trademarks, the record business, The Beatles, Apple Corps'
catalog and artists and related material all as set forth in
section 1.3 herein and to reserve for Apple Computer's field of
use for its trademarks, the computer, data processing and telecommunications business as set forth in section 1.2 herein and to
coordinate the use of their respective trademarks in such fields
of use as set forth in section 4 herein.

<u>ACCORDINGLY, THE PARTIES AGREE AS FOLLOWS:</u>

1.   <u>DEFINITIONS</u>

    1.1.   "Apple Catalog" means the sound recordings, musical
          works, films and videos which now or hereafter cannot
          be released or published without Apple Corps' consent.

    1.2.   "Apple Computer Field of Use" means (i) electronic
          goods, including but not limited to computers,
          microprocessors and microprocessor controlled devices,
          telecommunications equipment, data processing
          equipment, ancillary and peripheral equipment, and
          computer software of any kind on any medium; (ii) data
          processing services, data transmission services,
          broadcasting services, telecommunications services;
          (iii) ancillary services relating to any of the
          foregoing, including without limitation, training,
          education, maintenance, repair, financing and
          distribution; (iv) printed matter relating to any of
          the foregoing goods or services; and (v) promotional
          merchandising relating to the foregoing.

1.3. "Apple Corps Field of Use" means (i) the Apple Musical
       Artists; the Apple Catalog; personalities or characters
       which appear in or are derived from the Apple Catalog;
       the names, likenesses, voices or musical sounds of the
       Apple Musical Artists; any musical works or per-
       formances of the Apple Musical Artists; (ii) any
       current or future creative works whose principal
       content is music and/or musical performances; regard-
       less of the means by which those works are recorded, or
       communicated, whether tangible or intangible;
       (iii) promotional merchandise relating to any of the
       foregoing; (iv) merchandising relating to the Apple
       Musical Artists and the Apple Catalog and the related
       subject matter set forth in subsection (i), including,
       without limitation, the commercial exploitation of
       personalities, characters, names, designs, images,
       words, photographs, drawings, or other materials
       through articles such as posters, toys, games
       (including computer games), novelties, figures,
       figurines and clothing; and (v) printed matter relating
       to any of the foregoing goods or services.

1.4. "Apple Computer Marks" means (i) any design, repro-
       duction or other depiction of an apple, in whole or in
       part, except for a whole green apple or a half apple
       (of any color(s)); and (ii) the word "Apple".

1.5   Apple Corps Marks" means (1) any design, reproduction
       or other depiction of an apple, in whole or in part,
       except a "rainbow" or multicolor striped apple (in
       whole or in part) or any apple (of any color(s)) with a
       "bite" removed; and (ii) the words "Apple", and
       "Zapple".

1.6. "Apple Corps Registrations" means all trade mark
       applications and registrations, current or future, of
       Apple Corps for the Apple Corps Marks.

1.7. "Apple Computer Registrations" means all trade mark
       applications and registrations, current or future, of
       Apple Computer for the Apple Computer Marks.

1.8. "Apple Musical Artists" means (i) The Beatles and
       (ii) any other musical recording artists whose works
       are now or in the future included in the Apple Catalog.

1.9. "Apple Corps Specification" shall mean the following
       wording (or its equivalent) for purposes of registra-
       tion of the Apple Corps Marks: sound records, video
       records and cinematographic films.

1.10. "The Beatles" means George Harrison, John Lennon, Paul McCartney and Richard Starkey and all or any of them whether performing together as members of The Beatles or otherwise.

1.11. "Subsidiary(ies)" means any company or corporate entity which is owned or controlled, directly or indirectly, by Apple Corps Limited or Apple Computer, Inc. (as the case may be).

2. PAYMENT

Apple Computer shall pay to Apple Corps the sum of One Hundred Thousand Dollars ($100,000) (exclusive of VAT), the receipt of which is hereby acknowledged by Apple Corps. Apple Computer shall be responsible for any VAT that may be levied as a consequence of such payment and will indemnify and hold harmless Apple Corps if any VAT is due but not paid and any attempt is made by the relevant authority to levy such upon Apple Corps. Apple Corps shall be responsible for any income or similar tax payable by Apple Corps as a consequence of the receipt of such payment and will indemnify and hold harmless Apple Computer if such tax is not paid and any attempt is made by the relevant fiscal authority to levy such upon Apple Computer. If there is any attempt to levy any VAT or income tax on the payment set forth herein, the indemnified party shall cooperate fully with the indemnifying party and the indemnifying party shall have the right to contest or control any proceeding arising in connection thereto.

3. REPRESENTATIONS AND WARRANTIES

3.1. Apple Corps represents and warrants that it has not and shall not enter into any licenses or other contracts or take any other action which conflicts with this Agreement.

3.2. Apple Computer represents and warrants that it has not and shall not enter into any licenses or other contracts or take any other action which conflicts with this Agreement.

3.3. Apple Corps represents and warrants that it has done everything necessary (including the passing of all necessary Board resolutions) to authorize the execution of this Agreement and that Neil Aspinall is duly authorized on behalf of Apple Corps to sign on its behalf and to bind it to the obligations herein.

3.4. Apple Computer represents and warrants that it has done everything necessary (including the passing of all necessary Board resolutions) to authorize the execution of this Agreement and that Joseph Graziano is duly authorized on behalf of Apple Computer to sign on its behalf and to bind it to the obligations herein.

4.   <u>RIGHTS TO USE TRADEMARKS</u>

4.1.   Apple Computer shall have the exclusive worldwide right, as between the parties, to use and authorize others to use the Apple Computer Marks on or in connection with goods and services within the Apple Computer Field of Use.

4.2.   Apple Corps shall have the exclusive worldwide right, as between the parties, to use and authorize others to use the Apple Corps Marks on or in connection with goods and services within the Apple Corps Field of Use.

4.3.   The parties acknowledge that certain goods and services within the Apple Computer Field of Use are capable of delivering content within the Apple Corps Field of Use. In such case, even though Apple Corps shall have the exclusive right to use or authorize others to use the Apple Corps Marks on or in connection with content within subsection 1.3(i) or (ii), Apple Computer shall have the exclusive right to use or authorize others to use the Apple Computer Marks on or in connection with goods or services within subsection 1.2 (such as software, hardware or broadcasting services) used to reproduce, run, play or otherwise deliver such content provided it shall not use or authorize others to use the Apple Computer Marks on or in connection with physical media delivering pre-recorded content within subsection 1.3(i) or (ii) (such as a compact disc of the Rolling Stones music).

4.4.   Notwithstanding Section 4.2, Apple Computer shall have the right to use or authorize others to use the Apple Computer Marks on or in connection with goods within Section 1.3(ii) (but not within Section 1.3(i)) which are not charged for separately (other than for costs of shipping and handling) for the bona fide purpose of training, advertising, promoting, or demonstrating the use of goods within the Apple Computer Field of Use.

4.5.   Except in connection with the other party's exclusive fields of use and as otherwise provided herein, either party may use and authorize the use of its Marks on or in connection with any goods or services, except where such use causes or is likely to cause confusion with the use of the other party's Marks. No such confusion shall in any way restrict either party's exclusive rights under subsections 4.1 and 4.2.

4.6   Both parties shall have the non-exclusive right to use and authorize others to use their respective Marks on or in connection with any current or future creative works whose principal subject matter is music or musical performances of artists or composers (provided, in the case of Apple Computer, that such works do not fall within either subsections 1.3(i) or (ii)).

4.7.   The rights of use contained in this Section 4 shall apply notwithstanding any registrations, trade marks or other rights of either party.

4.8.   Apple Corps agrees not to use or authorize others to use a "rainbow" or multicolor striped apple or any apple (of any color(s)) with a "bite" removed and Apple Computer agrees not to use or authorize others to use a whole green apple or a half apple (of any color(s)) or the word mark "Zapple."

4.9.   Except as provided in subsection 4.4, neither party shall use or authorize others to use their respective Marks on or in connection with the other party's exclusive field of use hereunder.

5.   <u>REGISTRATIONS</u>

5.1.   If any Apple Corps Registrations are now or in the future cited by any trademark authority against any Apple Computer application for any Apple Computer Marks, the parties agree to take the following steps:

5.1.1.   If such Apple Computer application includes any of the Apple Corps Specification, Apple Computer agrees to part-cancel or amend such application to exclude the Apple Corps Specification.

5.1.2.   If the procedure in subsection 5.1.1 fails to overcome the citation, Apple Corps shall, within twenty-eight (28) days of written request of Apple Computer, accompanied by all relevant documents in a form reasonably acceptable to Apple Corps' counsel and ready for execution, provide written consent to the registration of said Apple Computer application.

5.1.3.   If the procedure in subsection 5.1.2 fails to overcome the citation, upon written request, Apple Corps shall use best efforts to part-cancel or amend the cited Apple Corps Registrations to exclude all goods necessary to facilitate the registration provided that it shall have no obligation to exclude the Apple Corps Specification.

5.1.4.   If such part-cancellation or amendment is not allowed or if it shall fail to enable the registration of the Apple Computer application:

5.1.4.1.   Except as provided in subsection 5.1.4.3, for Apple Computer applications for computer hardware filed prior to the date of this Agreement in Spain only:

(a)   Apple Corps shall assign to Apple Computer the applicable cited Apple Corps Registration(s) within twenty-eight (28) days of Apple Computer's written request.

(b)   Thereafter, and to the extent allowed or possible under the trademark laws of the relevant jurisdiction, Apple Computer shall assign back to Apple Corps said Apple Corps Registration(s) no later than ninety (90) days after the issuance of Apple Computer's registration or if, as of the date of issuance, there is an outstanding action undertaken by Apple Computer under the assigned Apple Corps Registration(s) against a third party in the relevant jurisdiction, such reassignment shall take place no later than ninety (90) days after the final judgment in such action; _provided, however_, that if at such date Apple Computer shall be prohibited from making such reassignment, then it shall assign the said Registration back to Apple Corps within ninety (90) days after Apple Corps' written request subsequent to the

trademark laws being changed to
permit such re-assignment.

(c)   Apple Computer shall grant to Apple
Corps an exclusive, royalty-free
license in perpetuity to use or
authorize others to use the Apple
Corps Marks, pursuant to the
assigned Apple Corps Registration,
on or in connection with the Apple
Corps Field of Use in that
jurisdiction, in accordance with
the terms and conditions of this
Agreement, which license shall be
effective for so long as it holds
such Registration.

5.1.4.2.   Except as provided in subsection
5.1.4.3, for all other past and future
Apple Computer applications (including
without limitation computer software) in
all other countries:

(a)   Apple Computer shall assign to
Apple Corps the applicable Apple
Computer application(s). Apple
Corps shall provide Apple Computer
or its authorized agent with a
Power of Attorney to enable Apple
Computer to prosecute the Apple
Computer application(s) under Apple
Corps' name.

(b)   Upon the registration of the Apple
Computer application in the name of
Apple Corps, and to the extent
allowed or possible under the
trademark laws of the relevant
jurisdiction, Apple Corps shall
assign back to Apple Computer said
Apple Computer Registration(s), but
only insofar as such assignment may
be made without adversely affecting
Apple Corps' pre-existing registrations.

(c)   Apple Corps shall grant to Apple
Computer an exclusive, royalty free
license in perpetuity to use or
authorize others to use the Apple
Computer Marks, pursuant to the
assigned Apple Computer applica-

tion(s), on or in relation to the Apple Computer Field of Use in that jurisdiction, in accordance with the terms and conditions of this Agreement, which license shall be effective for so long as it holds such Registration.

5.1.4.3 For Apple Computer applications for computer hardware filed prior to the date of this Agreement in Sweden, Portugal and Brazil only the parties shall discuss whether the procedure set forth in subsection 5.1.3 and/or 5.1.4.2 would be sufficient for Apple Computer to secure registration and if it is agreed that such a course of action would succeed then the provisions of subsection 5.1.3 and/or 5.1.4.2 shall apply to such applications. If it is agreed that such a course of action would not succeed then the provisions of subsection 5.1.4.1 shall apply to such applications.

5.1.5. All actions undertaken pursuant to this Section 5.1 shall be at the expense of Apple Computer, which shall fully indemnify and hold harmless Apple Corps for all costs and expenses (including attorneys' fees) arising from such actions.

5.2. If any Apple Computer Registrations are now or in the future cited by any trademark authority against any Apple Corps application for any Apple Corps Marks, the parties agree to take the following steps:

5.2.1. Apple Corps agrees to part-cancel or amend such application to exclude all goods or services other than the Apple Corps Specification.

5.2.2. If the procedure in subsection 5.2.1 fails to overcome the citation, Apple Computer shall, within twenty-eight (28) days of written request of Apple Corps, accompanied by all relevant documents in a form reasonably acceptable to Apple Computer's counsel and ready for execution, provide written consent to the registration of said Apple Corps application.

5.2.3.   If the procedure in subsection 5.2.2 fails to overcome the citation, upon written request, Apple Computer shall use best efforts to part-cancel or amend the cited Apple Computer Registrations to exclude the goods set forth in the Apple Corps Specification.

5.2.4.   If such part-cancellation or amendment is not allowed or if it shall fail to enable the registration of the Apple Corps application(s):

5.2.4.1.   Apple Corps shall assign to Apple Computer the applicable Apple Corps application(s) or file such applications in the name of Apple Computer. Apple Computer shall provide Apple Corps or its authorized agent, with a Power of Attorney to enable Apple Corps to prosecute the Apple Corps application(s) under Apple Computer's name.

5.2.4.2.   Upon the registration of the Apple Corps application in the name of Apple Computer, and to the extent allowed or possible under the trademark laws of the relevant jurisdiction, Apple Computer shall assign back to Apple Corps said Apple Corps Registration(s) but only insofar as such assignment may be made without adversely affecting Apple Computer's pre-existing registrations.

5.2.4.3.   Apple Computer shall grant to Apple Corps an exclusive, royalty free license in perpetuity to use or authorize others to use the Apple Corps Marks, pursuant to the assigned Apple Corps application(s), on or in connection with the Apple Corps Field of Use in that jurisdiction, in accordance with the terms and conditions of this Agreement, which license shall be effective for so long as it holds such Registration.

5.2.5.   All actions undertaken pursuant to this Section 5.2 shall be at the expense of Apple Corps, which shall fully indemnify and hold harmless Apple Computer for all costs and expenses (including attorneys' fees) arising from such actions.

5.3. The assignee of any Registration pursuant to subsections 5.1.4.1(a), 5.1.4.2(a) or 5.2.4.1 shall permit the assignor to enforce its rights against third parties by virtue of such registration as if the assignor had remained the owner of the relevant registration; and the assignor shall indemnify and hold harmless the assignee for all liabilities, costs and expenses (including legal fees) arising from any such enforcement of the assignor's rights.

6. **NO CHALLENGE; LIMITS ON USE/RESTRICTIONS IN EEC**

6.1. Neither party shall challenge the other party's trademark registrations or applications for registration in any part of the world with respect to that other party's Field of Use.

6.2. Apple Corps' rights of use and the restrictions on Apple Computer's rights of use of their respective trade marks (including the restrictions on challenging Apple Corps' trademark registrations and applications for registration) hereunder shall cease in relation to the European Economic Community if within ninety (90) days of a reasonably grounded request from Apple Computer, Apple Corps fails to satisfy the following test of use. Apple Corps shall satisfy the test of use if Apple Corps or its authorized licensees has used the Apple Corps Marks or any of them on or in relation to goods or services within the Apple Corps Field of Use anywhere within the European Economic Community at any time during the five (5) year period ending with the date of the request.

6.3. Apple Computer's rights of use and the restrictions on Apple Corps' rights of use of their respective trade marks (including the restrictions on challenging Apple Computer's trademark registrations and applications for registration) hereunder shall cease in relation to the European Economic Community if within ninety (90) days of a reasonably grounded request from Apple Corps, Apple Computer fails to satisfy the following test of use. Apple Computer shall satisfy the test of use if Apple Computer or its authorized licensees has used the Apple Computer Marks or any of them on or in relation to goods or services within the Apple Computer Field of Use anywhere within the European Economic Community at any time during the five (5) year period ending with the date of the request.

6.4. Neither subsection 6.2 nor 6.3 shall be effective until the question of the relevant party's compliance with the test of use has been finally resolved by mutual

agreement or judgment by a court of competent
jurisdiction.

7.   NO LICENSE

This Agreement does not constitute a license.

8.   INTEGRATION

This Agreement represents the entire agreement between the
parties with respect to the subject matter hereof. This
Agreement may not be varied except by written agreement of the
parties.

9.   SEVERABILITY

If any part or parts of this Agreement shall be determined to be
void, invalid or unenforceable by any Court or competent authority in any jurisdiction, such determination shall not affect the
validity or enforceability of any other part or parts of this
Agreement all of which shall remain in full force and effect.
The part or parts of this Agreement rendered or declared void,
invalid or unenforceable shall be void, invalid or unenforceable
as the case may be in that jurisdiction only, and this Agreement
shall remain in full force and effect in all other jurisdictions.

10. CONFIDENTIALITY

This Agreement shall be deemed confidential and shall not be
disclosed by the parties except to their respective legal and/or
other professional advisers from time to time and except as may
be required under any applicable law or regulation or in order to
implement the terms of this Agreement in which event such disclosure shall be limited to the extent required. However, the
parties shall be permitted to disclose to their shareholders so
many of the terms of this Agreement as may be necessary or desirable. Notwithstanding the generality of the foregoing, nothing
herein shall preclude any party making any necessary disclosure
to their auditors or accountants or where necessary to prosecute
or defend any legal action concerning this Agreement or as
required by law or in litigation between the parties or any of
them or as otherwise ordered by a Court or Tribunal of competent
jurisdiction.

11. NOTICES

Notices required hereunder shall be in writing and shall be sent
by personal delivery or express courier to the following address
or as either party may subsequently designate.

11.1. To Apple Computer at 20525 Mariani Avenue, Cupertino, California 95014, U.S.A. for the attention of Chief Executive Officer and the General Counsel.

11.2. To Apple Corps at 6 Stratton Street, London W1X 5FD, England, with copies to Frere Cholmeley, 28 Lincoln's Inn Fields, London WC2A 3HH, England (attention Nicholas Valner) and Frank B. Dehn & Co., Imperial House, 15/19 Kingsway, London WC2B 6UZ, England (attention Michael Butler).

All notices shall be deemed to have been received when delivered (if by personal delivery) or on the third business day after dispatch (if by express courier).

12. ASSIGNMENTS

12.1. Apple Corps may assign or transfer all or any of its rights hereunder and any of its registrations, applications or other rights in respect of the Apple Corps Marks, provided that it shall first obtain from the intended assignee or transferee a binding undertaking to Apple Corps and Apple Computer to perform and be subject to all of the obligations of this Agreement (so far as the same have not already been discharged by performance). No such assignment or transfer by Apple Corps shall have effect or confer any rights upon the intended assignee or transferee unless and until such undertaking has been provided. The foregoing requirement to obtain an undertaking shall not apply to grants of licenses in the ordinary course of business other than licenses to companies whose principal activity is the computer or data processing business and not the record, film or video business.

12.2. Apple Computer may assign or transfer all or any of its rights hereunder and any of its registrations, applications or other rights in respect to the Apple Computer Marks provided that it shall first obtain from the intended assignee or transferee a binding undertaking to Apple Computer and Apple Corps to perform and be subject to all of the obligations of this Agreement (so far as the same have not already been discharged by performance). No such assignment or transfer by Apple Computer shall have effect or confer any rights upon the intended assignee or transferee unless and until such undertaking has been provided. The foregoing requirement to obtain an undertaking shall not apply to grants of licenses in connection with merchandising in the ordinary course of business.

13.   NOTIFICATION

13.1.   The parties shall as soon as possible after execution hereof jointly notify this Agreement to The Commission of the European Communities for negative clearance and/or exemption under Council Regulation 17 of 6th February 1962, and shall jointly take all reasonably necessary steps and cooperate with each other with a view to obtaining such clearance and/or exemption.

13.2.   No provision of this Agreement (including any agreement or arrangement of which it forms part) being a restriction by virtue of which this Agreement is subject to registration under Section 35 of the Restrictive Trade Practices Act 1976 shall take effect until the day after particulars of this Agreement have been furnished to the Director General of Fair Trading under that Act. Both parties shall use all reasonable endeavors to procure that the said particulars are so furnished as soon as possible after execution of this Agreement and, in any event, within three (3) months thereafter.

14.   IMPLEMENTATION

Except as provided in subsection 13.2, implementation of this Agreement is not subject to the fulfillment of any conditions of any kind.

      IN WITNESS WHEREOF, the duly authorized representatives of the parties have executed this Agreement on the date first above written.

Signed _____   Signed _____
       Name _____   Name _____
       Title _General Manager._   Title _EVP & CFO_

ON BEHALF OF APPLE CORPS   ON BEHALF OF APPLE COMPUTER,
LIMITED   INC.

III. PROBLEMS

1. Imagine that a software developer wants to create a baseball game called "Ken Griffey, Jr.'s Old Timer Major League Baseball." To create this product, the developer needs the following third-party content:

   - Ken Griffey, Jr.'s name and likeness, as well as the names and likenesses of other pro baseball players both past and present;
   - photos from *Sports Illustrated* and various newspapers;
   - music typically heard at a ballpark;
   - video content from ESPN, Fox, ABC, CBS, and NBC;
   - news articles from *The Sporting News* and various local newspapers;
   - Major League Baseball's logo;
   - data from Elias Sports Bureau;
   - baseball teams' names and logos;
   - the "look" of baseball stadiums;
   - audio recordings of crowd noise, baseballs striking bats and gloves, and other typical sounds heard at a baseball game;
   - user interface design;
   - video compression technology from a computer science professor;
   - Internet game hosting service secret log-in information and communications protocols;
   - audio with announcer Dave Neihaus's famous "My oh my!" and "That one will fly away!" calls.

   1.1 For each type of content, describe the intellectual property or other rights that must be licensed. For each particular type of intellectual property, which exclusive rights would be implicated? If you were representing the owner of the intellectual property or other rights, what conditions would you seek on use of his or her rights? Are there items that do not need to be licensed because they are in the public domain or usable as a "fair use"? If you were representing the software developer, what conditions could you accept and what conditions would be deal breakers?

   1.2 Describe the various ways in which the multimedia product developer could attempt to profit from its product. What transaction models could be used to support or create these opportunities? What are the advantages and disadvantages of various approaches?

   1.3 Assume the following license grant appears in a form license agreement from Major League Baseball:

   > Major League Baseball grants to Developer the worldwide right to use the Major League Baseball name and logo in conjunction with Developer's "Ken Griffey, Jr.'s Old Timer Major League Baseball" computer game.

   The second version of the game contains a feature that allows users to reconfigure the teams to play games as if they were national Olympic or World Baseball Classic teams. The feature allows the user to add players other than Major League Baseball players, such as collegiate players and players from international professional leagues. Would this be permissible under the license grant? If not, what cause of action could Major League Baseball bring and what remedies could it seek? What defenses could the product developer raise?

1.4 What type of music license would you seek and from whom?

2. If you were a policy maker who was attempting to create a contract statute that would cover contracts to make and distribute multimedia products but exclude music, movies, books, and magazines, how would you distinguish these works? *See* UCITA §103 and Official Comment *d*. What contract law(s) currently cover multimedia works? Are these a good fit? When might the applicable body of contract law matter?

IV. DRAFTING EXERCISES

1. Re-draft the license grant in Problem 1.3 so that it more clearly allows the multimedia product developer to create version 2 of the game as described.
2. Draft an exclusive license grant from *The Sporting News* to the multimedia product developer for use of certain *Sporting News* articles in the multimedia game.
3. Draft a warranty from the Associated Press to the multimedia product developer for some old AP stock baseball photos, which AP believes are in the public domain.
4. Re-draft the licenses in the Apple Computer/Apple Corps License Agreement to make it clearer that Apple Computer may use the Apple trademark in its iTunes and iPod businesses (and future related businesses).
5. Re-draft the license in the Simon & Schuster v. Qintex case to make it clear that Simon & Schuster has exclusive rights to produce and sell audio cassettes based on the *Lonesome Dove* book.
6. Re-draft the license in the Boosey & Hawkes Music Publishers v. Walt Disney Co. case to make it clear that Boosey & Hawkes does not have the right to distribute *The Rite of Spring* song in video format.

12

UNIVERSITY INTELLECTUAL
PROPERTY TRANSFERS

I. UNIVERSITIES AS CENTERS FOR KNOWLEDGE
AND COMPETING INTERESTS

Universities are sites of significant research and development. With the enactment of the Bayh-Dole Act in 1980, universities conducting research with federal funding can patent and transfer their technology to the commercial sector. Since 1980, research activities at universities have flourished and have contributed significantly to technological growth. For example, Stanford University developed and transferred the technology for the Google search engine and Carnegie Mellon University did the same for the Lycos search engine. Florida State University developed and transferred the technology for Taxol, the Bristol-Meyers Squibb cancer drug. The University of Texas at Arlington developed and obtained the software patent that the BlackBerry device infringed. *See UT System Wins $1.8M Settlement from the BlackBerry Maker*, Austin Bus. J., Aug. 1, 2005, *http://austin.bizjournals.com/austin/stories/2005/08/01/daily6.html*. Some universities have exploited their patent portfolios through active patent infringement litigation and licensing strategies.

These successes have generated publicity and monetary returns. The successes come with a great deal of complexity because the interests of various parties such as the professors, researchers, students, the university, the government, the funding foundation, and the industry may compete against one another. The professor highly values his or her academic research freedom and would like to maintain this independence without the restraint from the university and funding sources. The university has concerns about the reputation of the institution, fulfilling its public service mission, the demands on research space, and overhead costs.

Universities themselves do not have the financial resources to fund all of their researchers in their wide range of research projects. Outside sources are pivotal in funding research conducted at university sites. Outside sources have their own interests, which may not correspond to the interests of the university or the researchers. The industry often cares primarily about the commercial possibilities of the research development and may restrict the university and the professor from the disclosure of information or collaboration with others. The U.S. government has an interest as well when it funds research. Under the Bayh-Dole Act it has "march-in" rights in certain cases as well as a non-exclusive license for use within the government. *See* BethLynn Maxwell et al., *Overview of Licensing Technology from Universities,* 762 PLI/Pat 507 (2004) (discussing the effects of the Bayh-Dole Act on universities' rights in research funded by the government). An excerpt of this article appears below in section II.D of this chapter.

The competing interests of various parties may lead to disputes regarding inventorship, authorship, and ownership. Among the researchers collaborating on a research project that later becomes a patented invention, the researcher not listed as a co-inventor may bring an action to correct the problem. Inventorship disputes, however, are not merely about correction of the inventors, but also involve the economic rewards stemming from being a co-inventor of a technology that is the subject of an exclusive license arrangement with a third party. The dispute described in Chou v. University of Chicago, excerpted in the Materials section of this chapter, was brought by a post-doctoral research assistant whose name was not included as an inventor in several patents.

II. INTELLECTUAL PROPERTY AND MATERIALS TRANSFERS

Universities collaborate with industry in many ways, leading to commercialization by utilizing joint ventures and other licensing arrangements.

For instance, the university may have to grant exclusive licenses to the technology developed by the researchers to induce the necessary outside investment; it may offer royalty-bearing licenses to some and royalty-free licenses to others to foster further development. Some universities assign all the technology to a foundation, such as the Cornell Research Foundation for Cornell University, ARCH Development Corporation for the University of Chicago, and Wisconsin Alumni Research Foundation for the University of Wisconsin, to control and manage all technology transfers. The Wisconsin Alumni Research Foundation has wielded significant power over the direction of research related to human embryonic stem cells because it held the fundamental patents on such stem cells, with the invention first discovered by Dr. James A. Thomson of the University of Wisconsin.

Subsection A provides more detail about university intellectual property transfers and provides a look at university technology transfer policies that govern ownership of intellectual property created by professors, researchers, and students. Subsection B discusses materials transfer agreements that work hand in hand with certain intellectual property licenses.

A. Intellectual Property Transfers

1. Trademarks

Universities engage in trademark licensing to protect the integrity of the university's identifying marks, ensure that products bearing the marks are of good quality, ensure that each licensed use reflects positively on the institution, and generate revenues for the university. Some trademark licensing arrangements are quite lucrative. For example, the University of Florida receives about $9 million annually from PepsiCo for the license of the trademark Gatorade.

Some universities screen potential licensees before they decide to enter into a license agreement. For example, Michigan State University (MSU) posts an Application for Trademark License on its Web site so a potential vendor can apply for a license by providing certain information relating to the company, product samples, and an application processing fee. MSU then evaluates the application and, if it approves, contacts the vendor and subsequently executes a Trademark License Agreement with the vendor. The vendor is authorized to use MSU trademarks after it receives a fully executed Trademark License Agreement, its products and graphics have been approved by MSU, and the vendor has provided MSU with evidence of product liability insurance. *See http://licensing.msu.edu/ licapp.pdf. See also* University of Alabama Bd. of Trustees v. New Life Art, Inc., 683 F.3d 1266 (11th Cir. 2012), which is included in the Materials section of this chapter.

2. Copyrighted Works

University professors and researchers develop software, databases, Web sites, multimedia, instructional materials, and other copyrighted works that the university owns and may license to others for royalty-bearing or royalty-free use and distribution. For example, the University of Washington Technology Transfer Office reported in 2003 that licensing revenue generated from software and medical tutoring instructions was between $3 to $5 million per year. Many universities, however, do not own the copyrights in scholarly or educational materials, art works, musical compositions, or dramatic and non-dramatic literary works related to a faculty member's academic or professional field. The Molinelli-Freytes v. University of Puerto Rico case in the Materials section of this chapter addresses ownership of copyrighted works created by professors and the challenges presented by the Copyright Act's "work for hire" doctrine. Even if the university does not hold the copyright, it nonetheless may have a license to use the work. With respect to software, universities take different approaches. The University of Texas also does not assert ownership in software, except if the software is an invention. Northwestern University allows faculty members and researchers to own the copyright in software, but they must share with the university any revenue generated from the licensing of the software.

3. Inventions

Universities require that inventions by faculty members and researchers be promptly disclosed to the university technology transfer office. The university owns the inventions if they are produced by faculty members and researchers of the university. The inventors are required to cooperate and assist the university in all phases of the patent application process and must assign such applications or any patents resulting therefrom to the university. This is often spelled out in a university's technology transfer policy and implemented in various ways such as via assignment agreements or letters of employment. The Stanford University v. Roche case in the Materials provides a window into university technology transfer policies and highlights the challenges faced in implementing them. We provide an excerpt from Stanford University's tech transfer policy below along with an excerpt from the Massachusetts Institute of Technology (MIT) tech transfer policy for comparison.

Some inventions discovered by university faculty and research members are valuable as an income-generating source. Universities receive revenue and royalty income from sponsors and licensees for the inventions. Universities often share the income with the faculty members, researchers, or their academic unit. Universities adopt a variety of arrangements on the distribution of royalties from patents. Cornell University provides 33 percent of the total net royalty income (gross royalties received by the university less directly assignable expenses such as patent prosecution and licensing costs) to the inventors and another 33 percent to Cornell Research Foundation to cover its operating expenses. The remaining one third (33.3 percent) of the net royalty income is divided as follows: (a) 60 percent to the inventor's research budget, and (b) 40 percent to the University for general research support. By contrast, the University of Michigan distributes the revenue and royalty income as follows:

Up to $200,000
50% to the inventor(s)
17% to the originating unit(s)
18% to the originating school, college, division, or other responsible center(s)
15% to the central administration

Over $200,000 (and up to $2,000,000)
30% to the inventor(s)
20% to the originating unit(s)
25% to the originating school, college, division, or other responsible center(s)
25% to the central administration

Over $2,000,000
30% to the inventor(s)
35% to the originating school, college, division, or other responsible center(s)
35% to the central administration

Here are excerpts of Stanford's and MIT's policies for ownership of intellectual property created by professors, researchers, students, and staff:

STANFORD POLICY

All potentially patentable inventions conceived or first reduced to practice in whole or in part by members of the faculty or staff (including student employees) of the University in the course of their University responsibilities or with more than incidental use of University resources, shall be disclosed on a timely basis to the University. Title to such inventions shall be assigned to the University, regardless of the source of funding, if any.

Patent and Copyright Agreement for Personnel at Stanford

I understand that, consistent with applicable laws and regulations, Stanford University is governed in the handling of intellectual property by its official policies titled Inventions, Patents and Licensing and Copyright Policy (both published in the Research Policy Handbook), and I agree to abide by the terms and conditions of those policies, as they may be amended from time to time.

Pursuant to those policies, and in consideration of my employment by Stanford, the receipt of remuneration from Stanford, participation in projects administered by Stanford, access to or use of facilities or resources provided by Stanford and/or other valuable consideration, I hereby agree as follows:

1. I will disclose to Stanford all potentially patentable inventions conceived or first reduced to practice in whole or in part in the course of my University responsibilities or with more than incidental use of University resources. I hereby assign to Stanford all my right, title and interest in such patentable inventions and to execute and deliver all documents and do any and all things necessary and proper on my part to effect such assignment.

   (See Inventions, Patents and Licensing, particularly Section 2. D., for further clarification and discussion related to this paragraph.)

2. I am free to place my inventions in the public domain as long as in so doing neither I nor Stanford violates the terms of any agreements that governed the work done.

3. Stanford policy states that all rights in copyright shall remain with the creator unless the work:
   a. is a work-for-hire (and copyright therefore vests in the University under copyright law),
   b. is supported by a direct allocation of funds through the University for the pursuit of a specific project,
   c. is commissioned by the University,
   d. makes significant use of University resources or personnel, or
   e. is otherwise subject to contractual obligations.

> I hereby assign or confirm in writing to Stanford all my right, title and interest, including associated copyright, in and to copyrightable materials falling under a) through e), above.
>
> 4. I am now under no consulting or other obligations to any third person, organization or corporation in respect to rights in inventions or copyrightable materials which are, or could be reasonably construed to be, in conflict with this agreement.
>
>   NOTE: An alternative to this agreement may be appropriate for personnel with a prior existing and conflicting employment agreement that establishes a right to intellectual property in conflict with Stanford policies. Personnel in this situation should contact the office of the Vice Provost and Dean of Research.
>
> 5. I will not enter into any agreement creating copyright or patent obligations in conflict with this agreement.
>
> 6. This agreement is effective on the later of July 1, 2011 (on the one hand) or my date of hire, enrollment, or participation in projects administered by Stanford (on the other hand), and is binding on me, my estate, heirs and assigns.

*　*　*

> ## MIT POLICY
>
> ### 13.1.1 Ownership of Intellectual Property
>
> With the exception of student theses as described below in Section 13.1.3 (Ownership of Copyrights in Theses), rights in patentable inventions, mask works, tangible research property, trademarks, and copyrightable works, including software ("Intellectual Property"), made or created by MIT faculty, students, staff, and others participating in MIT programs, including visitors, are as follows:
>
> 1. Inventor(s)/author(s) will own Intellectual Property that is:
>   1. not developed in the course of or pursuant to a sponsored research or other agreement (the faculty advisor, administrative officer, or the Office of Sponsored Programs contracts administrator can advise on the terms of the agreements that apply to specific research); and
>   2. not created as a "work-for-hire" by operation of copyright law (a "work-for-hire" is defined, in part, as a work prepared by an employee within the scope of his or her employment) and not created pursuant to a written agreement with MIT providing for a transfer of copyright or ownership of Intellectual Property to MIT; and
>   3. not developed with the significant use of funds or facilities administered by MIT ("significant use" is discussed in Section 2.1.2 of the *Guide*).

2. Ownership of all other Intellectual Property will be as follows:
    1. ownership of Intellectual Property developed in the course of or pursuant to a sponsored research or other agreement will be determined according to the terms of such agreement;
    2. ownership of copyrightable works created as "works-for-hire" or pursuant to a written agreement with MIT providing for the transfer of any Intellectual Property or ownership to MIT will vest with MIT;
    3. ownership of Intellectual Property developed by faculty, students, staff, and others participating in MIT programs, including visitors, with the significant use of funds or facilities administered by MIT will vest with MIT.

Inventions and Proprietary Information Agreement

This agreement is made in consideration of the following:

(My) continuing or anticipated employment at the Massachusetts Institute of Technology ("M.I.T."); and/or my performance of research at M.I.T.; and/or opportunities made or to be made available to me to use M.I.T.'s funds, facilities or other resources.

In exchange for the consideration listed above: I will disclose promptly to and assign to, and I hereby assign to, M.I.T. all rights to all inventions, copyrightable materials, computer software, semiconductor mask works, tangible research property, and trademarks ("Intellectual Property") conceived, invented, reduced to practice, or authored by me, either solely or jointly with others, which: are developed in the course of or pursuant to a sponsored research or other agreement in which I am a participant as defined in Part 2 of the Technology Policy Guide; or result from the significant use of M.I.T. administered funds or M.I.T. facilities as defined in Paragraph 2.1.2. in the Technology Policy Guide; or result from a work-for-hire funded by M.I.T. as defined in Paragraph 2.1.3 of the Technology Policy Guide.

I will execute all necessary papers and otherwise provide proper assistance, promptly upon M.I.T.'s request and at M.I.T.'s expense, during and subsequent to the period of my M.I.T. affiliation, to enable M.I.T. to obtain, maintain, or enforce for itself or its nominees, patents, copyrights or other legal protection for such Intellectual Property.

I will prepare and maintain for M.I.T. adequate and current written records of all such M.I.T. Intellectual Property.

I will deliver promptly to M.I.T. when I leave M.I.T. for whatever reason, and at any other time as M.I.T. may request, copies of all written records referred to in Paragraph C. above as well as all related memoranda, notes, records, schedules, plans or other documents, and tangible research property made by, compiled by, delivered to, or manufactured, used, developed or investigated by M.I.T., which will at all times be the property of M.I.T.

I will not disclose to M.I.T. or use in my work at M.I.T. (unless otherwise agreed in writing with M.I.T.): any proprietary information of any of my prior employers or of any third party, such information to include, without limitation, any trade secrets or confidential information with respect to the business, work or investigations of such prior employer or other third party; or any ideas, writings, or Intellectual Property of my own which are not included in Paragraph A. above within the scope of this Agreement (please note that inventions previously conceived, even though a patent application has been filed or a patent issued, are subject to this Agreement if they are actually first reduced to practice under the circumstances included in Paragraph A. above).

This Agreement replaces all previous agreements relating in whole or in part to the same or similar matters that I may have entered into with M.I.T. It may not be modified or terminated, in whole or in part, except in writing signed by an authorized representative of M.I.T. Discharge of my undertakings in this Agreement will be an obligation of my executors, administrators, or other legal representatives or assignees.

Furthermore, I represent that, except as identified on pages attached hereto: (i) I have not executed any agreements with or incurred any obligations to others in conflict with the foregoing; and (ii) I will not, while bound by this Agreement, enter into any other agreements, or otherwise incur any obligations, that conflict with the foregoing.

B. Materials Transfers

In addition to the license and transfer of intellectual property, many universities have a policy on the transfer of research material such as cell lines and biological materials. A researcher who would like to obtain a sample of a particular cell line to conduct his or her own investigation requests the sample from the university and the appropriate researcher with the cell line. Some, but not all, cell lines are patented. The researcher would be required to sign a Materials Transfer Agreement (MTA). MTA is a contractual agreement entered into by a provider (institution, university) and a recipient (individual, institution or university) of research material. The purpose of the MTA is to protect the provider's intellectual property and other rights while further research conducted by the recipient with the material is authorized.

Generally there are three MTAs. The first covers materials transfers between academic institutions (when a researcher from University A requests research material from a colleague at University B), the second on transfers of research material from the industry to the university (when the university researcher requests research material samples from a company), and the third on transfers of research material out of the university to the industry (when a company requests a sample of research material). *See* sample MTAs in the Materials section of this chapter.

The use of MTAs, however, has generated concerns regarding the provider's potentially overreaching control of research materials. Typically, MTAs do not convey ownership of the physical materials, but require the recipient "to exercise care in the handling of the materials, to maintain control over the distribution of the materials, to acknowledge the provider in publications, and to follow relevant [Public Health Service] guidelines relating to recombinant DNA, protection of human subjects in research, and the use of animals." Sean O'Connor, *The Use of MTAs to Control Commercialization of Stem Cell Diagnostics and Therapeutics*, 21 BERKLEY TECH. J. 1017 (2006). Such requirements, which impose on the recipient the protection of the provider's interest in the biological research materials, are not based on patent rights. Professor O'Connor notes that the provider uses "their non-patent property rights to require recipient consent to arguably onerous MTAs" and, consequently, blocking a potential recipient's access to the research material and ultimately preventing the recipient from pursuing the research plan.

C. Overview of Applicable Laws

Contract law is the foundation for license agreements between a university as the licensor and other entities as the licensees. With respect to the licensing of trademarks, copyrights, databases, patents, and trade secrets, universities experience similar issues as discussed in preceding chapters. However, there are certain prominent issues and specific statutes and regulations unique to university transfers.

For example, issues arise because researchers work collaboratively. Collaborators may include primary investigators (who usually have his or her own lab), investigators who work under the primary investigators, and post-doctoral research assistants and outside researchers including researchers at other universities and corporate partners. In a collaboration on research that leads to inventions and patents, concerns relating to correct inventorship and ownership are often subject to disputes. Patent law and contract law issues must be sorted out in such disputes. *See* Chou v. University of Chicago, 254 F.3d 1347 (Fed. Cir. 2001), which can be found in the Materials section of this chapter.

In recent years, disputes between the research subject and the university have surfaced. Some research subjects have claimed ownership in the patented invention the university researcher has discovered based on work with the biological materials provided by the research subjects. *See* Moore v. Regents of the Univ. of Cal., 51 Cal. 3d 120 (Cal. 1990), holding that the patient plaintiff did not have a cause of action for conversion against defendant's physicians, the university, and its licensee, for the cell line developed from the patient's T-lymphocytes.

Another example is that universities have relied heavily in the recent past on the experimental use defense under patent law for their educational and experimental research. Relying on the defense, they failed to try to obtain permission to use patented research tools. What has complicated the defense is the changing reality that now many major research universities conduct research for commercial purposes as well as for experimental purposes. It is difficult to prevail with the experimental use defense when the research is for commercial pursuit. *See* Madey v. Duke University, 307 F.3d 1351 (Fed. Cir. 2002), which can be found in the Materials section of this chapter.

Additionally, the federal government's right in research projects funded by federal grants is unique to university transfers. Many university faculty and researchers receive federal funding for their works. Under the Bayh-Dole Act, universities have the option to retain the ownership of inventions funded by a federal grant. Universities are prohibited from assignments of the invention to a third party. The federal government, however, has a non-exclusive right to practice the invention and "march-in" rights that allow the government to require the university to license the technology to a third party for health and safety reasons and for noncommercialization. Furthermore, the Act requires that universities provide preference to small businesses (companies with less than 500 employees) in licensing transactions. If the patented products are to be distributed for sales in the United States, the products must be substantially manufactured in the United States. Also, the National Institutes of Health (NIH), as the federal agency sponsor of numerous research projects in the United States, requires that research materials generated from funded research are made available to other researchers. *See* BethLynn Maxwell et al., *Overview of Licensing Technology from Universities*, 762 PLI/Pat 507 (2004), an excerpt of which appears in the next section (II.D) of this chapter. Whether the Bayh-Dole Act vests title in the patent in the university employer or the inventor employee is an issue of great importance to all universities receiving federal grants. *See* Stanford University v. Roche Molecular Systems, Inc., 131 S. Ct. 2188 (2011), which is included in the Materials section of this chapter.

As state universities form separate entities, e.g., University of Florida Research Foundation, Wisconsin Alumni Research Foundation, to manage and monetize patent portfolios, new issues have emerged when the entities attempt to enforce patent license agreements. Contractual disputes brought by the universities against former licensees in state court face two potential challenges. The first challenge is the former licensee's removal of the contract suit from state court to federal court on the basis that the license relates to patents. The second challenge is the former licensee's petition to the Patent Trial and Appeal Board to invalidate the licensed patents. A successful response to the two challenges, as of the present time, is the defense of sovereign immunity under the Eleventh Amendment raised by the separate entities. These entities assert that they are an arm of the state and are entitled to Eleventh Amendment immunity from suit in a federal forum. Therefore, both the federal suit and PTAB proceeding must be dismissed and the breach of license case must be remanded back to state court. *See* University of Florida Research Foundation, Inc. v. Medtronic PLC, Medtronic, Inc., 2016 WL 3869877 (N.D. Florida July 15, 2016); Covidien v. University of Florida Research Foundation Incorporated (USPTO Patent Trial and Appeal Board, January 25, 2017), which are contained in the Materials section of this Chapter.

D. University Technology Transfer Office

When a university and an industry partner engage in a joint venture, the university's technology transfer office handles the transaction. A typical technology transfer office is responsible for all aspects relating to technology disclosures, intellectual property filings, and inbound and outbound technology transfers in compliance with federal law and regulations. Excerpts in the Materials section of this chapter from Stanford University v. Roche Molecular Systems, Inc., 131 S. Ct. 2188 (2011), AsymmetRx, Inc. v. Biocare Medical, LLC, 582 F.3d 1314 (Fed. Cir. 2009), and Wisconsin Alumni Research Foundation v. Xenon Pharmaceuticals, Inc., 591 F.3d 876 (7th Cir. 2010), provide a window into the transactions and issues handled by a university technology transfer office in its relationship with its own researchers and industry partners.

Consider the summary below of university technology transfers and federal laws along with NIH Guidelines.[1]

One would be hard-pressed to dispute the overwhelming success of university-industry technology transfer. Technology licensing, start-up company development, patenting and many other facets of intellectual property are now a fixture in most academic settings. University technology transfer has even spawned its own professional organization, the Association of University Technology Managers (AUTM: www.autm.net). AUTM was founded in 1974 and now counts over 3000 members representing over 1500 institutions and companies world-wide. AUTM conducts national and regional meetings and special workshops covering topics such as licensing negotiations and start-up company development. The latest annual survey of AUTM members (FY2001) shows that sponsored research programs and technology transfer in universities remains strong. Of the 198 institutions reporting, sponsored research expenditures were $31.7 billion, up 7.5% from fiscal year 2000. Those institutions received 13,569 disclosures of new inventions and filed 6,812 new U.S. Patent Applications, up 6.9% from the previous year. 4,058 new licenses and options were executed and 494 new companies were formed. The adjusted gross license income was $1.071 billion and running royalties on product sales were $845 million. AUTM reports that since 1980, at least 3,870 new companies have been initiated based on university technology transfer.

Of course these statistics are not the sole indicators of the success of university technology transfer. Universities advance the greater public good through education, research and service. Consequently, income generation is not the primary motivator of university technology transfer. There are many valuable university innovations that fail to generate substantial income returns but nevertheless advance the greater public good and are therefore commensurate with university missions.

---

1. BethLynn Maxwell et al., *Overview of Licensing Technology from Universities*, 762 PLI/Pat 507 (2004). Reprinted with permission.

University technology transfer had its biggest boost in the passage of the Bayh-Dole Act in 1980 (additional discussion of Bayh-Dole is found in Section V, infra). For the first time, the Bayh-Dole Act allowed recipients of federal funding to retain ownership of inventions created with federal funding. Prior to this Act, the federal government retained ownership of inventions and granted non-exclusive licenses to any party interested in practicing the patent. Companies were obviously reluctant to invest in the development of technologies that anyone could use and, as a consequence, many federally funded inventions went undeveloped. Since a large majority of university research was supported by federal funds, universities had little intellectual property to develop or offer to third parties.

Under the Bayh-Dole Act, universities now have the option to retain ownership of inventions and have the responsibility of ensuring that the inventions are used commercially. The federal government retains (1) a non-exclusive right to practice any invention created with federal funding, and (2) "march-in" rights that allow the government to require the owning party to license the technology to third parties for health and safety issues, for non-commercialization, or if other legal requirements are not met. In licensing transactions, universities are required to give preference to small business firms (firms that have less than 500 employees) and to require that any product that is to be sold in the U.S. be substantially manufactured in the U.S. Further, universities are not allowed to assign these inventions to third parties.

Since the passage of the Bayh-Dole Act, most universities have developed technology transfer offices to aid in the commercialization of inventions that are now owned by the university. The technology transfer process used from disclosure of an invention to licensing is not the same in all universities. In general, however, the process involves a researcher disclosing the invention to the college's technology transfer office. The technology transfer office is staffed with skilled personnel with a mix of scientific, business and legal backgrounds and degrees. The technology transfer office assesses the commercial potential of the invention and, if warranted, begins marketing the invention. If patent coverage enhances the marketing potential, a patent application (provisional or non-provisional) is filed. Universities generally prefer having a licensee in hand before a domestic patent application is converted to international filings. International filings can be expensive, and university patent budgets are usually insufficient to handle a large number of international patent filings. In some circumstances, a university may elect to file a PCT application naming the United States, therefore providing an eighteen-month window to find a licensee to cover the higher costs for national filings. The costs and expenses associated with the patent process are almost always recouped when the invention is licensed.

If a licensee is identified, the agreement is negotiated by the technology transfer office. Legal review follows, and the license is executed by the appropriate college official. In some cases the college legal department may take an active role in the license negotiations. Additionally, there are online license checklists to assist the university negotiator to conform to their specific policy and guidelines (See http:// www.utsystem.edu/ogc/intellectualproperty/liccklst.htm; and http://www.utsystem .edu/ogc/intellectualproperty/lcreview.htm).

In some cases the university decides to form a new entity to exploit the technology. The college and its faculty may be given equity in the new company instead of royalties. Additionally, if no commercial prospects are found, the invention is released back to the faculty member and in some cases with State universities, the university retains a portion of any consideration the faculty member realizes from his/her invention. There are several variations on this theme. Also, some universities have active patent committees that review the commercialization efforts and may even get involved in the commercialization. . . .

In 1994, the current NIH guidelines were released. NIH, *Developing Sponsored Research Agreements, Considerations for Recipients of NIH Research Grants and Contracts*, reprinted in 59 Fed. Reg. 55674-79 (Nov. 18, 1994). Although primarily directed at universities involved in sponsored research programs with industry (such as industrial sponsorship agreements (ISAs), otherwise known as SRAs), the NIH guidelines set forth basic tenets applicable to all university-industry interactions, including licensing.

Academic research freedom based upon social collaboration within the scientific community and the scrutiny of claims and beliefs by its members is at the heart of scientific advancement within the United States. Primarily through federal funding, academic institutions have contributed to fundamental knowledge and techniques upon which current and future scientific discoveries and technological innovations depend. Therefore, the preservation of academic freedom for Recipient institutions and researchers is of considerable concern to the NIH.

Recipients should be aware that their interest in the scientific endeavor covered by a sponsored research agreement and the interest of the industrial sponsor may not be totally consonant. As a result, in general, Recipients should ensure that sponsored research agreements preserve the freedom for academic researchers to select projects, collaborate with other scientists, determine the types of sponsored research activities in which they wish to participate, and communicate their research findings at meetings, and by publication and through other means. Academic researchers also should be made aware of any agreements executed by their institutions that may restrict their ability to pursue research activities and publish research results. Recipients also should maintain their independence to pursue their own mission without undue influence or restraint by their industrial sponsors. For example, an agreement which gives an industrial sponsor the ability to direct the research mission of a recipient would be inappropriate. *Id.*

NIH, however, does specifically tolerate some constraint of academic freedom to accommodate commercial concerns. In the current NIH guidelines, "NIH recognizes that there may be certain instances when it may be reasonable for a grantee institution to agree to minimally restrict a researcher from collaborating with another industrial partner when the subject matter of such collaboration overlaps with that of the sponsored research agreement." NIH, *Developing Sponsored Research Agreements, Considerations for Recipients of NIH Research Grants and Contracts*, reprinted in 59 Fed. Reg. 55674-79 (Nov. 18, 1994). For example, a sixty-day publication delay to allow the commercial sponsor to file patents is considered a "reasonable period" under these guidelines. *Id.*

While an industry sponsor may be granted preferential rights (right of first refusal) to intellectual property developed under an ISA, NIH forbids preexisting lock-ups. "Recipients should not enter into sponsored research agreements that permit a sponsor to tie up the development of a technology by acquiring exclusive licensing rights to the product of given research results before deciding whether or not it will actively develop and commercialize that product." *Id.* at 55676.

III. MATERIALS

The Materials in this section enhance your understanding of research universities as centers of intellectual property production. Chou v. University of Chicago, 254 F.3d 1347 (Fed. Cir. 2001), highlights the relationship between the university and its researchers, the relationship between a principal researcher and subordinates, and the inventorship problem. Molinelli-Freytes v. University of Puerto Rico, 792 F. Supp. 2d 164 (D.P.R. 2010), addresses ownership of copyrights in works created by university employees and the viability of the "teacher exception." Madey v. Duke University, 307 F.3d 1351 (Fed. Cir. 2002), explains the collaboration among researchers and between university and industry and the changing role of the university as a center for the commercialization of research results. The case addresses whether the experimental use defense is a viable one for such a research university.

The next three cases, Stanford University v. Roche Molecular Systems, Inc., 131 S. Ct. 2188 (2011), AsymmetRx, Inc. v. Biocare Medical, LLC, 582 F.3d 1314 (Fed. Cir. 2009), and Wisconsin Alumni Research Foundation v. Xenon Pharmaceuticals, Inc., 591 F.3d 876 (7th Cir. 2010), show how multiple issues, including ownership, standing to bring infringement suits, contract drafting, and patent statutory interpretations can arise in many university and industry collaborations.

University of Alabama Bd. of Trustees v. New Life Art, Inc., 683 F.3d 1266 (11th Cir. 2012), demonstrates how the initial license arrangement has turned into an uneasy relationship between a university's desire to control its image and monetize its brand and an artist's expression and First Amendment rights. And finally, University of Florida Research Foundation, Inc. v. Medtronic PLC, Medtronic, Inc., 2016 WL 3869877 (N.D. Florida July 15, 2016), and Covidien v. University of Florida Research Foundation Inc. (USPTO Patent Trial and Appeal Board, January 25, 2017) explore the issue of sovereign immunity in the context of state university ownership and licensing of intellectual property.

Following the cases is a sample Patent License Agreement between a university and its industry sponsor. The Agreement provides you an opportunity to examine the relationships among different players: the university licensor, the industry licensee, and the inventors.

Additionally, Materials Transfer Agreements (from the Association of University Technology Managers) for outgoing materials leaving the university and incoming materials coming into the university are included at the end of this Materials section.

CHOU v. UNIVERSITY OF CHICAGO

254 F.3d 1347 (Fed. Cir. 2001)

LOURIE, Circuit Judge.

Joany Chou appeals from the decision of the United States District Court for the Northern District of Illinois granting Bernard Roizman and Aviron Company's motions to dismiss her claims for correction of inventorship, declaratory judgment of inventorship, fraud, breach of fiduciary duty, unjust enrichment, breach of express contract, and breach of implied contract. Chou also seeks reinstatement of those same claims against the University of Chicago ("University").

BACKGROUND

Dr. Chou was a graduate student and subsequently a post-doctoral research assistant for Dr. Roizman at the University of Chicago's Department of Molecular Genetics and Cell Biology from 1983 to 1996. Roizman is named as the sole inventor on U.S. Patent 5,328,688 and a co-inventor on U.S. Patents 5,795,713 and 5,922,328, all of which relate to herpes simplex virus and its use in an avirulent vaccine.

Under University policy, inventors receive 25% of the gross royalties and up-front payments from licensing of the patents, as well as 25% of the stock of new companies that are based on their inventions. Chou allegedly told Roizman in February of 1991 that her discoveries should be patented, and he allegedly disagreed. At that time, however, Roizman had already filed the '688 patent application, which was allegedly directed to the same disputed invention, and had named himself as the sole inventor of that subject matter. During prosecution of that application, the United States Patent and Trademark Office ("PTO") cited two joint Chou-Roizman publications as prior art. In response, Roizman submitted a declaration stating that those publications were not available as prior art because he was the sole inventor of the work described therein and that she merely worked under his direction and supervision.

On July 14, 1992, Roizman assigned the '688 patent application to Institut Merieux, a French company that had supported the research. Just before that assignment, however, on July 1, 1992, it appears that Aviron had received an exclusive license to the herpes simplex virus technology from ARCH Development Corporation, a wholly owned affiliate of the University established to license and commercialize the University's technology and intellectual property. Institut Merieux later assigned the patent application to ARCH, which in turn licensed Aviron. ARCH and Roizman each own Aviron stock and have received licensing revenue from NeuroVir, the sublicensee of Aviron's rights.

DISCUSSION

Whether a putative inventor who lacks a potential ownership interest in a patent has standing to sue is a question of law that we decide *de novo*. We also review the grant of a motion to dismiss under FED. R. CIV. P. 12(b)(6) for failure to state a claim *de novo*.

A. Standing to Sue for Correction of Inventorship Under 35 U.S.C. §256

As a preliminary matter, we agree with the defendants that Chou was obligated to assign her inventions to the University. Although it is true that Chou never signed a contract with the University specifically obligating her to assign her inventions to the University, she accepted her academic appointment subject to the administrative policies of the University. We are not persuaded by Chou's argument that the University's administrative policies do not include its patent statutes. The Faculty Handbook refers to the patent statutes as patent policies within a section entitled "Academic Policies." The University's Patent Statute section 20 provides as follows:

> Every patentable invention or discovery that results from research or other activities carried out at the University, or with the aid of its facilities or funds administered by it, shall be the property of the University, and shall be assigned, as determined by the University, to the University, to an organization sponsoring the activities, or to an outside organization deemed capable of administering patents.

It is true that the Faculty Handbook contains the following statement: "The contents of this handbook do not create a contract or agreement between an individual and the University." That statement, however, must be read in light of the statement immediately following it: "The basic terms and conditions of the employment agreement are set out in the letter of appointment received from the Provost's Office." Chou's letter of appointment stated that the appointment was subject to "the administrative policies of the University," which include the obligation to assign inventions to the University. Illinois law, which governs our determination of Chou's assignment obligations, thus obligated Chou to assign her inventions to the University even though she never specifically agreed to do so. *See* Duldulao v. St. Mary of Nazareth Hosp. Ctr., 483 N.E.2d 956, 958 (1985) (holding that employee handbooks may impose enforceable obligations on employers and employees even if the terms of the handbook are not bargained for). Chou accepted her appointment, thereby assuming the obligations set out in the University's policies. Moreover, she did not dispute her obligation when she assigned to the University other inventions for which she was a recognized inventor. We therefore conclude that if Chou is indeed an inventor of the contested subject matter, she would be obligated to assign those inventions to the University.

That conclusion, however, does not defeat Chou's standing to sue for correction of inventorship under §256. Section 256 of title 35 provides a cause of action for judicial correction of inventorship:

> The error of omitting inventors or naming persons who are not inventors shall not invalidate the patent in which such error occurred if it can be corrected as provided in this section. The court before which such matter is called in question may order correction of the patent *on notice and hearing of all parties concerned* and the Director shall issue a certificate accordingly.

35 U.S.C. §256 (Supp. V 1999) (emphasis added).

We conclude that an expectation of ownership of a patent is not a prerequisite for a putative inventor to possess standing to sue to correct inventorship under §256. The statute imposes no requirement of potential ownership in the patent on those seeking to invoke it. We have previously interpreted §256 broadly as a "savings provision" to prevent patent rights from being extinguished simply because the inventors are not correctly listed. Pannu v. Iolab Corp., 155 F.3d 1344, 1349 (Fed. Cir. 1998). The same considerations apply here. Chou should have the right to assert her interest, both for her own benefit and in the public interest of assuring correct inventorship designations on patents. The interest of both inventors and the public are thus served by a broad interpretation of the statute.

Chou argues that a reputational interest alone is enough to satisfy the requirements of Article III standing. That assertion is not implausible. After all, being considered an inventor of important subject matter is a mark of success in one's field, comparable to being an author of an important scientific paper. Pecuniary consequences may well flow from being designated as an inventor. However, we need not decide that issue because Chou has alleged a concrete financial interest in the patent, albeit an interest less than ownership. Chou claims that the University is obligated to provide "[f]aculty, student and staff inventors . . . 25% of the gross royalties and up-front payments from licensing activities." She also claims the right to receive rights to 25% of the stock of new companies based on their inventions. If Chou has indeed been deprived of an interest in proceeds from licensing the invention and in stock ownership by the conduct that she alleges, then she will have suffered an injury-in-fact, i.e., the loss of those benefits. That loss would be directly traceable to Roizman's alleged conduct in naming himself as the sole inventor of discoveries that she at least partly made, and it would be redressable by an order from the district court to the Director of the PTO to issue a certificate naming Chou as an inventor, which would entitle her under the University's policy to a share of the licensing proceeds and stock already received by Roizman. We therefore determine that Chou is entitled to sue for correction of inventorship under §256.

We next address the question of which defendants Chou may sue under §256. The validity of a patent requires that the inventors be correctly named. It follows that parties with an economic stake in a patent's validity are entitled to be heard on inventorship issues once a putative inventor has sued to correct inventorship. Each of the defendants in this case has an economic stake in the validity of the patents involved and hence in the correct inventorship designations on the patents. The University/ARCH owns the '688 and '713 patents and derives royalty income therefrom. Aviron owns the '328 patent and possesses exclusive licenses under the '688 and '713 patents; it derives royalties from its sublicense of those patents to NeuroVir. Roizman similarly receives a portion of the royalty income and stock benefits from those patents based on the University's policy to reward inventors. All of those benefits would be jeopardized by a determination that the patents are invalid for improper inventorship. Roizman's share of the profits would also be affected by joinder of Chou. Thus, each of the defendants has an economic stake in a correct inventorship designation on the patents at issue and each may properly be named as a defendant in this §256 action.

Furthermore, our conclusion that Roizman is a proper defendant in Chou's §256 action also negates the University's argument that Chou cannot maintain her §256 action against the University based on her stipulation that the district court's order applies with equal force and effect to the University and ARCH as it does to Roizman. Chou's §256 claim against the University and ARCH should be reinstated.

Accordingly, we reverse the district court's conclusion that Chou has no standing to sue Roizman under 35 U.S.C. §256, and instruct that court to reinstate her §256 claim against the University and ARCH, and, if necessary, allow Chou leave to amend her §256 claim to add Aviron as a defendant. The district court will determine whether Chou should be named as the sole inventor or a co-inventor on the '688 patent or a co-inventor on the '713 and '328 patents.

MOLINELLI-FREYTES v. UNIVERSITY OF PUERTO RICO
792 F. Supp. 2d 164 (D.P.R. 2010)

DOMINGUEZ, District Judge.

I. PROCEDURAL HISTORY

Plaintiffs aver that they created an original manuscript ("the Proposal") during non-working hours while employed as professors at Defendant University of Puerto Rico ("UPR"). Plaintiffs also allege that Defendant Puerto Rico Council on Higher Education ("PRCHE") knowingly approved implementation of an unauthorized modified version of the Proposal and that UPR subsequently began to implement a Masters and Doctorate Program based upon the Proposal in violation of Plaintiffs' duly registered copyright.

On July 30, 2009, Plaintiffs filed a Motion Requesting Preliminary Injunction and on August 31, 2009, Defendants filed an Opposition to Preliminary Injunction Request. Subsequently, the Court held seven days of hearings regarding the injunction request and, ultimately, denied the preliminary injunction, noting in that order that a fundamental question of law remained unanswered as to the existence of a "teacher exception" to the work for hire defense raised by Defendants in the instant case. The Court then ordered further briefing of the matter in order to allow it to properly narrow the issues in the instant case for trial.

II. WORK FOR HIRE DOCTRINE AND THE COMMON LAW "TEACHER EXCEPTION"

At this juncture, the Court must assume the role of a legal historian in order to unearth the octogenarian common law roots of a "teacher exception" in order to determine if this relic has survived the years and silently incorporated itself into modern day copyright law. Accordingly, the Court shall begin its discussion at the birth of the "teacher exception" while the 1909 Copyright Act and common law of copyright were still the law of the land.

Although the 1909 precursor to the present Copyright Act mentioned a "work for hire" doctrine under which employers could qualify as "authors," the doctrine under that Act was not further defined and courts were left to apply this ambiguous doctrine without further guidance. See e.g. Cmty. for Creative Non-Violence v. Reid, 490 U.S. 730, 744 (1989). Ultimately, the courts of yesteryear determined that "the work for hire doctrine codified in [the 1909 Act] referred only to works made by employees in the regular course of their employment." *Id.*

It was under this framework that the first case recognizing an exception to the work for hire doctrine for professors' academic work, *Sherrill v. Grieves*, was decided. See 57 Wash. L. Rep. 286. In that case, a military instructor drafted a textbook of his own initiative and during his leisure time once he discovered that no textbook matching his course's curriculum existed. *Id.* at 290. Prior to publication of the textbook, the instructor authorized publication of a pamphlet which incorporated a portion of the book. *Id.* Later, the defendant incorporated portions of that pamphlet in two books which he authored and, once sued, claimed that the military instructor did not own the copyright to the pamphlet because it was produced for his military employer. *Id.* at 286-87. Ultimately, the Supreme Court for the District of Columbia held that the pamphlet was not a work for hire, stating that "[t]he court does not know of any authority holding that . . . a professor is obliged to reduce his lectures to writing or if he does so that they become the property of the institution employing him." *Id.* at 290. Thus the "teacher exception" was born.

The next case to apply the common law "teacher exception" prior to enactment of the 1976 Act was Williams v. Weisser, a California case. See 153 U.S.P.Q. 866, aff'd 273 Cal. App. 2d 726. In that case, decided under California's common law of copyrights in 1967 and appealed in 1969, the trial court once again held that a professor retained the copyright to his lectures, adding that this copyright also extends to other unspecified writings. 153 U.S.P.Q. at 868. Unlike the plaintiff in *Sherrill*, the plaintiff in *Williams* had not written the contents of his lectures in the form of a textbook; in fact, the plaintiff had not reduced his lectures to a written form at all. *Id.* at 867. Rather, defendant, a company that sold college notes, placed a note-taker in the plaintiff's class and subsequently printed and sold the notes taken by the note-taker during the plaintiff's lectures. *Id.*

When sued, the defendant countered by stating that the plaintiff had no standing to sue as the copyright to his lectures was held by the university, rather than by the professor himself. *Id.* at 866-67. Interestingly, the trial court placed great emphasis on a letter circulated by the university to its professors in which the university informed the professors that they, not the university, held copyright to their lectures under California common law. *Id.* at 867-68. The court in that case concluded that this letter constituted the "apparent relinquishment of any rights to such literary property by the university, if indeed it possessed any." *Id.*

Upon appeal, the court rejected defendant's assertion that the plaintiff was an employee whose work fell under the work for hire doctrine. 273 Cal. App. 2d at 734-35. Therein, the appeals court cited *Sherrill*, as well as several English and Scottish common law cases, to support its view that copyright lies with the person who produces or delivers a lecture. *Id.* at 736-39. Further, the appeals court stated that it considered lectures sui generis, particularly in light of the peripatetic nature of professors, and emphasized that "[n]o reason ha[d] been suggested why a university would want to retain the ownership in a professor's expression" in reaching its determination. *Id.* at 734-35. This case marks the second and last application of the common law "teacher exception" to date.

Before the Court moves on to discuss the 1976 Copyright Act and its consequences for the work for hire doctrine and the potential application of a "teacher exception," the Court finds it pertinent to note that, prior to the enactment of the 1976 Act, at least one case declined to apply a "teacher exception" to a professor's work product. See Manasa v. Univ. of Miami, 320 So. 2d 467. In the brief opinion rendered by the Florida appeals court, they distinguished that case, which centered around ownership of a copyright to a proposal for an academic program, from *Williams* based upon the type of document involved. *Id.* The court then decided that the proposal was created within the scope of the plaintiff's employment and, accordingly, that the professor was not entitled to recover for copyright infringement against the university for use of the proposal. *Id.*

When Congress enacted the 1976 Copyright Act, replacing the 1909 Act and abolishing all state common law regarding copyright, it set forth a more detailed outline of the work for hire doctrine than that contained in the 1909 Act. See 17 U.S.C. §301(a) (containing the expression of preemption); 17 U.S.C. §101 (containing the expanded definition of work for hire). Specifically, under the 1976 Act, a work for hire is defined as:

> (1) a work prepared by an employee within the scope of his or her employment; or
> (2) a work specially ordered or commissioned for use as a contribution to a collective work, as a part of a motion picture or other audiovisual work, as a translation, as a supplementary work, as a compilation, as an instructional text, as a test, as answer material for a test, or as an atlas, if the parties expressly agree in a written instrument signed by them that the work shall be considered a work made for hire.

17 U.S.C. §101. Thus, where a work falls within the scope of the work for hire doctrine, the employer, rather than the author, is deemed the owner of the copyright, "unless the parties have expressly agreed otherwise in a written instrument signed by them." 17 U.S.C. §201(b).

The question of whether the "teacher exception" created by *Sherrill* and *Williams* survived the enactment of the 1976 Act has provided much fodder for academic debate. However, case law regarding the potential applicability of the "teacher exception" in the wake of the 1976 Act's enactment is scant, and no reported opinion exists holding either that such an exception survived or that it was extinguished by the 1976 Act. Nevertheless, two cases from the Seventh Circuit, Weinstein v. Univ. of Ill., 811 F.2d 1091 (7th Cir. 1987), and Hays v. Sony Corp. of America, 847 F.2d 412 (7th Cir. 1988), have addressed the issue in dicta.

In *Weinstein*, an opinion authored by Circuit Judge Easterbrook for a panel on which Judge Posner sat, the Court noted that an "academic tradition [existing] since copyright law began" vests ownership of theorem, scholarly articles and an unspecified group of "other intellectual property" created by professors in the professors themselves, rather than in the universities that employ them. 811 F.2d at 1094. However, Judge Easterbrook also admitted that the applicable statute appears "general enough to make every academic article a 'work for hire' and therefore vest exclusive control in universities rather than scholars[,]" noting that many universities now adopt policies in order to relinquish ownership of certain works to the professors who create them. *Id.* at 1093-94. The court in that case did not base its ultimate decision regarding ownership upon application of a "teacher exception," but, rather, based its finding that the disputed work, an article co-authored by the plaintiff university professor, did not constitute a work for hire upon a reading of the employer-university's copyright policy and the custom within that university. *Id.* at 1094-95.

A year later, Judge Posner authored an influential opinion again discussing the common law "teacher exception." See *Hays*, 847 F.2d 412. In that case, high school teachers of business brought a copyright infringement claim against a corporation which, at the request of the teachers' school district, allegedly performed an illegal modification of a manual which the teacher-plaintiffs had authored. *Id.* at 413. The court in that case was thus tasked with rendering a determination of whether the manual constituted a work for hire. *Id.* at 416. The Court acknowledged that "it is widely believed that the 1976 Act abolished the teacher exception." *Id.* Further, the court admitted that "[t]o a literalist of statutory interpretation, the conclusion that the Act abolished the exception may seem inescapable" as there is no discussion of the "teacher exception" in the legislative history of the Act and as the exception was not included in the body of the Act itself. *Id.* However, Judge Posner, a professor himself, also stated that failure to recognize a "teacher exception" would wreak havoc on the "settled practices of academic institutions" and would run contrary to the usual practices of academia before determining that "if forced to decide the issue, [the court might] conclude that the exception had survived the enactment of the 1976 Act." *Id.* at 416-17. However, the discussion of the "teacher exception" in this opinion was, once again, dicta, as the court found that "even if the statute abolished the teacher exception this would not necessarily spell victory for" the defendant-corporation. *Id.* at 417.

In 1989, the Supreme Court broke new ground in *Reid*, a case which forever changed the work for hire analysis. See 490 U.S. 730. In that case, the Supreme Court established a three-step process for resolving whether a work constitutes a work for hire. 490 U.S. at 751-52. Under this new guideline for application of the work for hire doctrine, courts are directed to first "ascertain, using principles of general common law agency whether work was prepared by an employee or an independent contractor." *Id.* at 751. Next, courts are directed to the Act itself in order to make a determination of whether the work at dispute falls within the first or second category of works which the Act states constitute works for hire. *Id.* Finally, courts must apply the common law of agency to determine whether the work was created within the scope of employment. In reaching its holding, the Court explicitly rejected the argument that Congress silently intended "to incorporate a line of cases decided under the 1909 Act" which advocated a different method, noting that "Congress' silence is just that — silence." *Reid*, 490 U.S. at 748-49.

In the wake of *Reid*, courts appear to have abandoned the "teacher exception" and those which cite the earlier Seventh Circuit cases do so solely in the context of determining whether teachers' work-product falls within the scope of their employment. See Shaul v. Cherry Valley-Springfield Central School Dist., 363 F.3d 177, 185-86 (2d Cir. 2004) (applying the *Reid* guidelines for the work for hire doctrine to materials created by a teacher without addressing a "teacher exception"); see also Pavlica v. Behr, 397 F. Supp. 2d 519, 525-26 (S.D.N.Y. 2005) (discussing *Hays* while determining whether a genuine issue of material fact existed as to whether a manual created by a high school teacher was created within the scope of his employment). Additionally, this apparent abandonment of the "teacher exception" is chronicled in a September, 2010 treatise on copyright law, which concludes that the "teacher exception," if it ever indeed existed in federal law, perished with the enactment of the 1976 Act.

Although a state court's decisions are not binding upon this Court, the Court also notes that the one court which has squarely addressed the issue of whether the "teacher exception" survived until the present day answered that question in the negative. See Pittsburg State University/Kansas Nat'l Edu. Ass'n v. Kansas Board of Regents/Pittsburg State University, 280 Kan. 408, 421-24, 122 P.3d 336 (2005) (analyzing the potential application of a "teacher exception" to the 1976 Copyright Act work for hire doctrine in the wake of *Reid*). Thus, the Court concludes that the current trend in both high-level academia and in relevant jurisprudence is to forego application of the common law "teacher exception" and to determine whether a work prepared by a teacher or professor falls within the work for hire doctrine, utilizing the steps set forth by *Reid*.

Additionally, as Posner noted in *Hays*, there is no mention of a "teacher exception" in the legislative history of the 1976 Act. See *Hays*, 847 F.2d at 416. In light of the Supreme Court's subsequent decision in *Reid* that silence on the part of the legislature regarding inclusion of common law jurisprudence indicates that such jurisprudence should not apply under the 1976 Act, the Court finds that this silence weighs heavily towards a finding that no "teacher exception" remains in existence. See 490 U.S. at 748-49 (finding that legislative silence does not indicate legislative intent to include common law from prior to enactment of the 1976 Act and noting that, in other portions of the Act, where Congress intended to include prior case law, it did so explicitly). Accordingly, the legislative history weighs against finding that a "teacher exception" to the work for hire doctrine exists today, particularly following the Supreme Court's analysis thereof with reference to the work for hire doctrine in *Reid*.

Thus, only policy and historical custom weigh in favor of a finding that a "teacher exception" remains. Even if the Court were inclined to engage in the judicial lawmaking which would be required to resurrect the common law exception at this stage, the Court harbors serious reservations regarding the continued applicability of the policy and custom which traditionally upheld the exception. In *Williams*, the court placed emphasis on its view that universities had no reason to "want to retain the ownership in a professor's expression" in finding that a teacher exception applied. 273 Cal. App. 2d at 734-35. This rationale no longer rings as true as it once did, however. In an age of distance-learning and for-profit institutions of higher learning, universities stand to gain much by retaining ownership of certain works created by their employees. In fact, Plaintiffs admit as much in their brief when they argue that UPR wishes to use the Proposal for commercial, profit-maximizing reasons.

Additionally, the policy of continuing to apply the "teacher exception" so as to defer to the "settled practices of academic institutions" and the traditional "conditions of academic production" emphasized by Judge Posner in *Hays* no longer applies with the strength which it held in 1988. Most academic institutions today have already responded to the uncertainty regarding the "teacher exception" by enacting policies, returning ownership of works traditionally copyrighted by professors to the professors themselves. Thus, two decades from when Posner cited his concerns for preserving academic tradition by recognizing the "teacher exception," this concern has already become de minimis as universities have proactively created policies that grant professors ownership of copyrights which the "teacher exception" once ensured. Accordingly, the only remaining enunciated policy concerns involve the transient nature of university professors and Plaintiffs' speculative concerns that failure to recognize a "teacher exception" would cause a chilling in academic innovation. The Court will not find that a "teacher exception" continues to exist based solely upon these two potential concerns. Accordingly, the Court rules that no such exception survived the enactment of the 1976 Copyright Act and, accordingly, Plaintiffs may claim no such exception in relation to Defendants' work for hire defense.

Thus, the Court must resolve the instant case within the framework of the work for hire doctrine, utilizing the standard set forth in *Reid* as well as considering any relevant University regulations specifically recognizing professor or university ownership over certain works.

MADEY v. DUKE UNIVERSITY

307 F.3d 1351 (Fed. Cir. 2002)

GAJARSA, Circuit Judge.

Dr. John M.J. Madey ("Madey") appeals from a judgment of the United States District Court for the Middle District of North Carolina.

BACKGROUND

In the mid-1980s Madey was a tenured research professor at Stanford University. At Stanford, he had an innovative laser research program, which was highly regarded in the scientific community. An opportunity arose for Madey to consider leaving Stanford and take a tenured position at Duke. Duke recruited Madey, and in 1988 he left Stanford for a position in Duke's physics department. In 1989 Madey moved his free electron laser ("FEL") research lab from Stanford to Duke. The FEL lab contained substantial equipment, requiring Duke to build an addition to its physics building to house the lab. In addition, during his time at Stanford, Madey had obtained sole ownership of two patents practiced by some of the equipment in the FEL lab.

At Duke, Madey served for almost a decade as director of the FEL lab. During that time the lab continued to achieve success in both research funding and scientific breakthroughs. However, a dispute arose between Madey and Duke. Duke contends that, despite his scientific prowess, Madey ineffectively managed the lab. Madey contends that Duke sought to use the lab's equipment for research areas outside the allocated scope of certain government funding, and that when he objected, Duke sought to remove him as lab director. Duke eventually did remove Madey as director of the lab in 1997. The removal is not at issue in this appeal, however, it is the genesis of this unique patent infringement case. As a result of the removal, Madey resigned from Duke in 1998. Duke, however, continued to operate some of the equipment in the lab. Madey then sued Duke for patent infringement of his two patents, and brought a variety of other claims.

A. The Patents and Infringing Equipment

One of Madey's patents, U.S. Patent No. 4,641,103 ("the '103 patent"), covers a "Microwave Electron Gun" used in connection with free electron lasers. The other patent, U.S. Patent No. 5,130,994 ("the '994 patent"), is titled "Free-Electron Laser Oscillator For Simultaneous Narrow Spectral Resolution And Fast Time Resolution Spectroscopy." The details of these two patents are not material to the issues on appeal. Their use in the lab, however, as embodied in certain equipment, is central to this appeal. The equipment at the Duke FEL lab that practices the subject matter disclosed and claimed in the patents is set forth in the list below, which first lists the equipment and then the patent(s) it embodies.

- An infrared FEL called the "Mark III FEL," embodying the '994 patent and the '103 patent (by incorporating the microwave electron gun in the infrared FEL).
- A "Storage Ring FEL," embodying the same patents as the Mark III FEL because it incorporates a Mark III FEL.
- A "Microwave Gun Test Stand," embodying the '103 patent (by incorporating the microwave electron gun).

The three alleged infringing devices are the Mark III FEL, the Storage Ring FEL, and the Microwave Gun Test Stand. Although it is not clear from the record, perhaps because Duke defended by asserting experimental use and government license defenses, Duke seems to concede that the alleged infringing devices and methods read on the claims of the patents. Although the three devices were housed in Duke's physics facilities, the Microwave Gun Test Stand was not Duke's asset, but rather belonged to North Carolina Central University ("NCCU").

B. Duke's Relationship with NCCU

Madey and Duke built the Microwave Gun Test Stand as a subcontractor to NCCU after the government awarded NCCU a contract to study microwave guns (the "AFOSR Contract"). Professor Jones of NCCU was the principal investigator under this government project. The Microwave Gun Test Stand was built and housed in the Duke FEL lab. The AFOSR Contract listed the Microwave Gun Test Stand as NCCU's asset.

DISCUSSION

C. The District Court's Application of Experimental Use

The District Court Improperly Shifted the Burden to Madey

As a precursor to the burden-shifting issue, Madey argues that the experimental use defense is an affirmative defense that Duke must plead or lose. We disagree. Madey points to no source of authority for its assertion that experimental use is an affirmative defense. Indeed, we have referred to the defense in a variety of ways. *See Roche*, 733 F.2d at 862, 221 USPQ at 939-40 (referring to experimental use as both an exception and a defense). Given this lack of precise treatment in the precedent, Madey has no basis to support its affirmative defense argument. The district court and the parties in the present case joined the issue during the summary judgment briefing. We see no mandate from our precedent, nor any compelling reason from other considerations, why the opportunity to raise the defense if not raised in the responsive pleading should not also be available at the later stages of a case, within the procedural discretion typically afforded the trial court judge.

The district court held that in order for Madey to overcome his burden to establish actionable infringement, he must establish that Duke did not use the patent-covered free electron laser equipment solely for experimental or other non-profit purposes. *Summary Judgment Opinion* at 10. Madey argues that this improperly shifts the burden to the patentee and conflates the experimental use defense with the initial infringement inquiry.

We agree with Madey that the district court improperly shifted the burden to him. The district court folded the experimental use defense into the baseline assessment as to whether Duke infringed the patents. Duke characterizes the district court's holding as expressing the following sequence: first, the court recognized that Madey carried his burden of proof on infringement; second, the court held that Duke carried its burden of proof on the experimental use defense; and third, the court held that Madey was unable to marshal sufficient evidence to rebut Duke's shifting of the burden. We disagree with Duke's reading of the district court's opinion. *See Summary Judgment Opinion* at 8-14. The district court explicitly contradicts Duke's argument by stating that Madey failed to "meet its burden to establish patent infringement by a preponderance of the evidence." *Id.* at 13. This statement is an assessment of whether

Madey supported his initial infringement claim. It is not an assessment of which party carried or shifted the burden of evidence related to the experimental use defense. Thus, the district court did not conclude that Madey failed to rebut Duke's assertion of the experimental use defense. Instead, it erroneously required Madey to show as a part of his initial claim that Duke's use was not experimental. The defense, if available at all, must be established by Duke.

The District Court's Overly Broad Conception of Experimental Use

Madey argues, and we agree, that the district court had an overly broad conception of the very narrow and strictly limited experimental use defense. The district court stated that the experimental use defense inoculated uses that "were solely for research, academic, or experimental purposes," and that the defense covered use that "is made for experimental, non-profit purposes only." *Id.* at 9. Both formulations are too broad and stand in sharp contrast to our admonitions in *Embrex* and *Roche* that the experimental use defense is very narrow and strictly limited. In *Embrex*, we followed the teachings of *Roche* and *Pitcairn* to hold that the defense was very narrow and limited to actions performed "for amusement, to satisfy idle curiosity, or for strictly philosophical inquiry." *Embrex*, 216 F.3d at 1349. Further, use does not qualify for the experimental use defense when it is undertaken in the "guise of scientific inquiry" but has "definite, cognizable, and not insubstantial commercial purposes." *Id.* (quoting *Roche*, 733 F.2d at 863). The concurring opinion in *Embrex* expresses a similar view: use is disqualified from the defense if it has the "slightest commercial implication." *Id.* at 1353. Moreover, use in keeping with the legitimate business of the alleged infringer does not qualify for the experimental use defense. *See Pitcairn*, 547 F.2d at 1125-26.

Our precedent clearly does not immunize use that is in any way commercial in nature. Similarly, our precedent does not immunize any conduct that is in keeping with the alleged infringer's legitimate business, regardless of commercial implications. For example, major research universities, such as Duke, often sanction and fund research projects with arguably no commercial application whatsoever. However, these projects unmistakably further the institution's legitimate business objectives, including educating and enlightening students and faculty participating in these projects. These projects also serve, for example, to increase the status of the institution and lure lucrative research grants, students and faculty.

In short, regardless of whether a particular institution or entity is engaged in an endeavor for commercial gain, so long as the act is in furtherance of the alleged infringer's legitimate business and is not solely for amusement, to satisfy idle curiosity, or for strictly philosophical inquiry, the act does not qualify for the very narrow and strictly limited experimental use defense. Moreover, the profit or non-profit status of the user is not determinative.

In the present case, the district court attached too great a weight to the non-profit, educational status of Duke, effectively suppressing the fact that Duke's acts appear to be in accordance with any reasonable interpretation of Duke's legitimate business objectives.[2]

---

2. Duke's patent and licensing policy may support its primary function as an educational institution. *See Duke University Policy on Inventions, Patents, and Technology Transfer* (1996), available at *http://www.ors .duke.edu/policies/patpol.htm* (last visited Oct. 3, 2002). Duke, however, like other major research institutions of higher learning, is not shy in pursuing an aggressive patent licensing program from which it derives a not insubstantial revenue stream. *See id.*

On remand, the district court will have to significantly narrow and limit its conception of the experimental use defense. The correct focus should not be on the non-profit status of Duke but on the legitimate business Duke is involved in and whether or not the use was solely for amusement, to satisfy idle curiosity, or for strictly philosophical inquiry.

D. The District Court's Analysis of the Test Stand Gun Motion

In contrast to our conclusion that the district court erred in its dismissal-in-part of the alleged '103 patent infringement and its application of the experimental use defense, we find no error in the court's summary judgment conclusion that there is no genuine issue of material fact concerning Duke's non-use of the NCCU Microwave Gun Test Stand during the relevant time period.

Specifically, the district court found that NCCU, through the subcontractor agreement it had with Duke, owned the Microwave Gun Test Stand, and that Dr. Jones of NCCU controlled the gun with a key switch. Even though the gun was located on Duke's premises, Dr. Jones stated that no Duke faculty member or employee had used the gun during the relevant time period. This evidence of ownership, control, and no known Duke use, is sufficient to shift the summary judgment burden to Madey, who, in the district court's words, offers in response only bare allegations and speculation. Most of the response is testimony by Madey himself.

Madey contends that Duke and Dr. Jones have tacitly admitted to disputed questions of fact concerning whether Duke had any control or benefit over the Microwave Gun Test Stand. In addition, Madey contends that joint publications by Dr. Jones and Duke faculty, as well as research interests held by Duke faculty in areas potentially implicated by the Microwave Gun Test Stand, demonstrate disputed material facts about Duke's benefit and influence over the gun. Like the district court, we do not find that the record supports Madey's contentions, nor do we concur in the inferences in which Madey would have us draw. *See Anderson*, 477 U.S. at 248 (explaining that a party cannot create a genuine issue of material fact based on mere allegations, but must present actual evidence); Amgen, Inc. v. Chugai Pharm. Co., 927 F.2d 1200, 1206-07 (Fed. Cir. 1991) (explaining that the patent-holder's alleged inferences were mere speculation and thus not supportable).

In addition, we note that the record does not indicate that Madey plead any vicarious liability claims, such as alleging that Duke induced NCCU's infringement, or contributory infringement claims. To the extent that this was a strategic decision or tactical choice on Madey's part, he should not be allowed to overcome this choice now by acceptance of allegations and speculation as genuine issues of material fact.

Duke's Assertion of a Government License Defense

Before this court, Duke argued vehemently that even if we did not agree with the district court's application of the experimental use defense that we could affirm the district court's judgment on alternate grounds: that the government had a license to have the patents at issue practiced on its behalf. We disagree with Duke's assertion because it overstates the information contained in the record on appeal. The only concrete evidence Duke cites is the statements on each of the patents noting that the government has rights in the patents.

This, however, is insufficient because these short notations on the patents do not define the scope of the government's rights. None of the controlling contracts that would define the scope of such rights are provided in the record nor discussed by Duke in its arguments.

In addition, Duke discusses at length the Bayh-Dole Act, urging that this provides a basis to conclude that the scope of the rights granted to the government encompass Duke's use. Madey, however, notes that the provisions cited by Duke were enacted into law after Madey's two patents issued. Thus, some other provision may have generated the "government rights" notation on the two patents. In sum, this discussion serves to illustrate that the government license issue needs further development before the district court if it is to ultimately provide Duke the defense it seeks.

STANFORD UNIVERSITY v. ROCHE MOLECULAR SYSTEMS, INC.

131 S. Ct. 2188 (2011)

Chief Justice **ROBERTS** delivered the opinion of the Court.

Since 1790, the patent law has operated on the premise that rights in an invention belong to the inventor. The question here is whether the University and Small Business Patent Procedures Act of 1980—commonly referred to as the Bayh-Dole Act—displaces that norm and automatically vests title to federally funded inventions in federal contractors. We hold that it does not.

I

A

In 1985, a small California research company called Cetus began to develop methods for quantifying blood-borne levels of human immunodeficiency virus (HIV), the virus that causes AIDS. A Nobel Prize winning technique developed at Cetus—polymerase chain reaction, or PCR—was an integral part of these efforts. PCR allows billions of copies of DNA sequences to be made from a small initial blood sample.

In 1988, Cetus began to collaborate with scientists at Stanford University's Department of Infectious Diseases to test the efficacy of new AIDS drugs. Dr. Mark Holodniy joined Stanford as a research fellow in the department around that time. When he did so, he signed a Copyright and Patent Agreement (CPA) stating that he "agree[d] to assign" to Stanford his "right, title and interest in" inventions resulting from his employment at the University. App. to Pet. for Cert. 118a-119a.

At Stanford Holodniy undertook to develop an improved method for quantifying HIV levels in patient blood samples, using PCR. Because Holodniy was largely unfamiliar with PCR, his supervisor arranged for him to conduct research at Cetus. As a condition of gaining access to Cetus, Holodniy signed a Visitor's Confidentiality Agreement (VCA). That agreement stated that Holodniy "will assign and do[es] hereby assign" to Cetus his "right, title and interest in each of the ideas, inventions and improvements" made "as a consequence of [his] access" to Cetus. *Id.*, at 122a-124a.

For the next nine months, Holodniy conducted research at Cetus. Working with Cetus employees, Holodniy devised a PCR-based procedure for calculating the amount of HIV in a patient's blood. That technique allowed doctors to determine whether a patient was benefiting from HIV therapy.

Holodniy then returned to Stanford where he and other University employees tested the HIV measurement technique. Over the next few years, Stanford obtained written assignments of rights from the Stanford employees involved in refinement of the technique, including Holodniy, and filed several patent applications related to the procedure. Stanford secured three patents to the HIV measurement process.

In 1991, Roche Molecular Systems, a company that specializes in diagnostic blood screening, acquired Cetus's PCR-related assets, including all rights Cetus had obtained through agreements like the VCA signed by Holodniy. After conducting clinical trials on the HIV quantification method developed at Cetus, Roche commercialized the procedure. Today, Roche's HIV test "kits are used in hospitals and AIDS clinics worldwide." Brief for Respondents 10-11.

B

In 1980, Congress passed the Bayh-Dole Act to "promote the utilization of inventions arising from federally supported research," "promote collaboration between commercial concerns and nonprofit organizations," and "ensure that the Government obtains sufficient rights in federally supported inventions." 35 U.S.C. §200. To achieve these aims, the Act allocates rights in federally funded "subject invention[s]" between the Federal Government and federal contractors ("any person, small business firm, or nonprofit organization that is a party to a funding agreement"). §§201(e), (c), 202(a). The Act defines "subject invention" as "any invention of the contractor conceived or first actually reduced to practice in the performance of work under a funding agreement." §201(e).

The Bayh-Dole Act provides that contractors may "elect to retain title to any subject invention." §202(a). To be able to retain title, a contractor must fulfill a number of obligations imposed by the statute. The contractor must "disclose each subject invention to the [relevant] Federal agency within a reasonable time"; it must "make a written election within two years after disclosure" stating that the contractor opts to retain title to the invention; and the contractor must "file a patent application prior to any statutory bar date." §§202(c)(1)-(3). The "Federal Government may receive title" to a subject invention if a contractor fails to comply with any of these obligations. *Ibid.*

The Government has several rights in federally funded subject inventions under the Bayh-Dole Act. The agency that granted the federal funds receives from the contractor "a nonexclusive, nontransferrable, irrevocable, paid-up license to practice . . . [the] subject invention." §202(c)(4). The agency also possesses "[m]arch-in rights," which permit the agency to grant a license to a responsible third party under certain circumstances, such as when the contractor fails to take "effective steps to achieve practical application" of the invention. §203. The Act further provides that when the contractor does not elect to retain title to a subject invention, the Government "may consider and after consultation with the contractor grant requests for retention of rights by the inventor." §202(d).

Some of Stanford's research related to the HIV measurement technique was funded by the National Institutes of Health (NIH), thereby subjecting the invention to the Bayh-Dole Act.

Accordingly, Stanford disclosed the invention, conferred on the Government a nonexclusive, nontransferable, paid-up license to use the patented procedure, and formally notified NIH that it elected to retain title to the invention.

C

In 2005, the Board of Trustees of Stanford University filed suit against Roche Molecular Systems, Inc., Roche Diagnostics Corporation, and Roche Diagnostics Operations, Inc. (collectively Roche), contending that Roche's HIV test kits infringed Stanford's patents. As relevant here, Roche responded by asserting that it was a co-owner of the HIV quantification procedure, based on Holodniy's assignment of his rights in the Visitor's Confidentiality Agreement. As a result, Roche argued, Stanford lacked standing to sue it for patent infringement. 487 F. Supp. 2d 1099, 1111, 1115 (N.D. Cal. 2007). Stanford claimed that Holodniy had no rights to assign because the University's HIV research was federally funded, giving the school superior rights in the invention under the Bayh-Dole Act.

The District Court held that the "VCA effectively assigned any rights that Holodniy had in the patented invention to Cetus," and thus to Roche. *Id.*, at 1117. But because of the operation of the Bayh-Dole Act, "Holodniy had no interest to assign." *Id.*, at 1117, 1119. The court concluded that the Bayh-Dole Act "provides that the individual inventor may obtain title" to a federally funded invention "only after the government and the contracting party have declined to do so." *Id.*, at 1118.

The Court of Appeals for the Federal Circuit disagreed. First, the court concluded that Holodniy's initial agreement with Stanford in the Copyright and Patent Agreement constituted a mere promise to assign rights in the future, unlike Holodniy's agreement with Cetus in the Visitor's Confidentiality Agreement, which itself assigned Holodniy's rights in the invention to Cetus. See 583 F.3d 832, 841-842 (2009). Therefore, as a matter of contract law, Cetus obtained Holodniy's rights in the HIV quantification technique through the VCA. Next, the court explained that the Bayh-Dole Act "does not automatically void ab initio the inventors' rights in government-funded inventions" and that the "statutory scheme did not automatically void the patent rights that Cetus received from Holodniy." *Id.*, at 844-845. The court held that "Roche possesse[d] an ownership interest in the patents-in-suit" that was not extinguished by the Bayh-Dole Act, "depriv[ing] Stanford of standing." *Id.*, at 836-837. The Court of Appeals then remanded the case with instructions to dismiss Stanford's infringement claim. *Id.*, at 849.

II

A

Congress has the authority "[t]o promote the Progress of Science and useful Arts, by securing . . . to Authors and Inventors the exclusive Right to their respective Writings and Discoveries." U.S. Const. Art. I, §8, cl. 8. The first Congress put that power to use by enacting the Patent Act of 1790. That Act provided "[t]hat upon the petition of any person or persons . . . setting forth, that he, she, or they, hath or have invented or discovered" an invention, a patent could be granted to "such petitioner or petitioners" or "their heirs, administrators or assigns." Act of Apr. 10, 1790, §1, 1 Stat. 109-110. Under that law, the first patent was granted in 1790 to Samuel Hopkins, who had devised an improved method for making potash, America's first industrial chemical. U.S. Patent No. 1 (issued July 31, 1790).

Although much in intellectual property law has changed in the 220 years since the first Patent Act, the basic idea that inventors have the right to patent their inventions has not. Under the law in its current form, "[w]hoever invents or discovers any new and useful process, machine, manufacture, or composition of matter . . . may obtain a patent therefor." 35 U.S.C. §101. The inventor must attest that "he believes himself to be the original and first inventor of the [invention] for which he solicits a patent." §115. In most cases, a patent may be issued only to an applying inventor, or—because an inventor's interest in his invention is "assignable in law by an instrument in writing"—an inventor's assignee. §§151, 152, 261.

Our precedents confirm the general rule that rights in an invention belong to the inventor. See, *e.g.,* Gayler v. Wilder, 51 U.S. (10 How. 477), 493 (1851) ("the discoverer of a new and useful improvement is vested by law with an inchoate right to its exclusive use, which he may perfect and make absolute by proceeding in the manner which the law requires"); Solomons v. United States, 137 U.S. 342, 346 (1890) ("whatever invention [an inventor] may thus conceive and perfect is his individual property"); United States v. Dubilier Condenser Corp., 289 U.S. 178, 188 (1933) (an inventor owns "the product of [his] original thought"). The treatises are to the same effect. See, *e.g.,* 8 Chisum on Patents §22.01, p. 22-2 (2011) ("The presumptive owner of the property right in a patentable invention is the single human inventor").

It is equally well established that an inventor can assign his rights in an invention to a third party. See Dubilier Condenser Corp., *supra,* at 187 ("A patent is property and title to it can pass only by assignment"); 8 Chisum on Patents, *supra,* §22.01, at 22-2 ("The inventor . . . [may] transfer ownership interests by written assignment to anyone"). Thus, although others may acquire an interest in an invention, any such interest—as a general rule—must trace back to the inventor.

In accordance with these principles, we have recognized that unless there is an agreement to the contrary, an employer does not have rights in an invention "which is the original conception of the employee alone." Dubilier Condenser Corp., 289 U.S., at 189. Such an invention "remains the property of him who conceived it." *Ibid.* In most circumstances, an inventor must expressly grant his rights in an invention to his employer if the employer is to obtain those rights. See *id.,* at 187 ("The respective rights and obligations of employer and employee, touching an invention conceived by the latter, spring from the contract of employment").

B

Stanford and the United States as *amicus curiae* contend that the Bayh-Dole Act reorders the normal priority of rights in an invention when the invention is conceived or first reduced to practice with the support of federal funds. In their view, the Act moves inventors from the front of the line to the back by vesting title to federally funded inventions in the inventor's employer—the federal contractor. See Brief for Petitioner 26-27; Brief for United States as *Amicus Curiae* 6.

Congress has in the past divested inventors of their rights in inventions by providing unambiguously that inventions created pursuant to specified federal contracts become the property of the United States. For example, with respect to certain contracts dealing with nuclear material and atomic energy, Congress provided that title to such inventions "shall be vested in, and be the property of, the [Atomic Energy] Commission." 42 U.S.C. §2182. Congress has also enacted laws requiring that title to certain inventions made pursuant to contracts with the National Aeronautics and Space Administration "shall be the exclusive property of the United States," Pub. L. 111-314, §3, 124 Stat. 3339. 51 U.S.C. §20135(b)(1) and that title to certain inventions under contracts with the Department of Energy "shall vest in the United States." 42 U.S.C. §5908.

Such language is notably absent from the Bayh-Dole Act. Nowhere in the Act is title expressly vested in contractors or anyone else; nowhere in the Act are inventors expressly deprived of their interest in federally funded inventions. Instead, the Act provides that contractors may "elect to retain title to any subject invention." 35 U.S.C. §202(a). A "subject invention" is defined as "any invention of the contractor conceived or first actually reduced to practice in the performance of work under a funding agreement." §201(e).

Stanford asserts that the phrase "invention of the contractor" in this provision "is naturally read to include all inventions made by the contractor's employees with the aid of federal funding." Brief for Petitioner 32 (footnote omitted). That reading assumes that Congress subtly set aside two centuries of patent law in a statutory definition. It also renders the phrase "of the contractor" superfluous. If the phrase "of the contractor" were deleted from the definition of "subject invention," the definition would cover "any invention . . . conceived or first actually reduced to practice in the performance of work under a funding agreement." Reading "of the contractor" to mean "all inventions made by the contractor's employees with the aid of federal funding," as Stanford would, adds nothing that is not already in the definition, since the definition already covers inventions made under the funding agreement. That is contrary to our general "reluctan[ce] to treat statutory terms as surplusage." Duncan v. Walker, 533 U.S. 167, 174 (2001) (internal quotation marks omitted).

Construing the phrase to refer instead to a particular category of inventions conceived or reduced to practice under a funding agreement — inventions "of the contractor," that is, those owned by or belonging to the contractor — makes the phrase meaningful in the statutory definition. And "invention owned by the contractor" or "invention belonging to the contractor" are natural readings of the phrase "invention of the contractor." As we have explained, "[t]he use of the word 'of' denotes ownership." Poe v. Seaborn, 282 U.S. 101, 109 (1930); see Flores-Figueroa v. United States, 129 S. Ct. 1886, 1889 (2009) (treating the phrase "identification [papers] of another person" as meaning such items belonging to another person (internal quotation marks omitted)); Ellis v. United States, 206 U.S. 246, 259 (1907) (interpreting the phrase "works of the United States" to mean "works belonging to the United States" (internal quotation marks omitted)).

That reading follows from a common definition of the word "of." See Webster's Third New International Dictionary 1565 (2002) ("of" can be "used as a function word indicating a possessive relationship"); New Oxford American Dictionary 1180 (2d ed. 2005) (defining "of" as "indicating an association between two entities, typically one of belonging"); Webster's New Twentieth Century Dictionary 1241 (2d ed. 1979) (defining "of" as "belonging to").

Stanford's reading of the phrase "invention of the contractor" to mean "all inventions made by the contractor's employees" is plausible enough in the abstract; it is often the case that whatever an employee produces in the course of his employment belongs to his employer. No one would claim that an autoworker who builds a car while working in a factory owns that car. But, as noted, patent law has always been different: We have rejected the idea that mere employment is sufficient to vest title to an employee's invention in the employer. Against this background, a contractor's invention — an "invention of the contractor" — does not automatically include inventions made by the contractor's employees.

The Bayh-Dole Act's provision stating that contractors may "elect to *retain* title" confirms that the Act does not *vest* title. 35 U.S.C. §202(a) (emphasis added). Stanford reaches the opposite conclusion, but only because it reads "retain" to mean "acquire" and "receive." Brief for Petitioner 36 (internal quotation marks omitted). That is certainly not the common meaning of "retain." "[R]etain" means "to hold or continue to hold in possession or use." Webster's Third, *supra*, at 1938; see Webster's New Collegiate Dictionary 980 (1980) ("to keep in possession or use"); American Heritage Dictionary 1109 (1969) ("[t]o keep or hold in one's possession"). You cannot retain something unless you already have it. See Alaska v. United States, 545 U.S. 75, 104 (2005) (interpreting the phrase "the United States shall retain title to all property" to mean that "[t]he United States . . . retained title to *its* property located within Alaska's borders") (emphasis added). The Bayh-Dole Act does not confer title to federally funded inventions on contractors or authorize contractors to unilaterally take title to those inventions; it simply assures contractors that they may keep title to whatever it is they already have. Such a provision makes sense in a statute specifying the respective rights and responsibilities of federal contractors and the Government.

The Bayh-Dole Act states that it "take[s] precedence over any other Act which would require a disposition of rights in subject inventions . . . that is inconsistent with" the Act. 35 U.S.C. §210(a). The United States as *amicus curiae* argues that this provision operates to displace the basic principle, codified in the Patent Act, that an inventor owns the rights to his invention. See Brief for United States 21. But because the Bayh-Dole Act, including §210(a), applies only to "subject inventions" — "inventions of the contractor" — it does not displace an inventor's antecedent title to his invention. Only when an invention belongs to the contractor does the Bayh-Dole Act come into play. The Act's disposition of rights — like much of the rest of the Bayh-Dole Act — serves to clarify the order of priority of rights between the Federal Government and a federal contractor in a federally funded invention that already belongs to the contractor. Nothing more.

The isolated provisions of the Bayh-Dole Act dealing with inventors' rights in subject inventions are consistent with our construction of the Act. Under the Act, a federal agency may "grant requests for retention of rights by the inventor . . . [i]f a contractor does not elect to retain title to a subject invention." §202(d). If an employee inventor never had title to his invention because title vested in the contractor by operation of law — as Stanford submits — it would be odd to allow the Government to grant "requests for retention of rights by the inventor." By using the word "retention," §202(d) assumes that the inventor had rights in the subject invention at some point, undermining the notion that the Act automatically vests title to federally funded inventions in federal contractors.

The limited scope of the Act's procedural protections also bolsters our conclusion. The Bayh-Dole Act expressly confers on contractors the right to challenge a Government-imposed impediment to retaining title to a subject invention. §202(b)(4). As Roche correctly notes, however, "the Act contains not a single procedural protection for third parties that have neither sought nor received federal funds," such as cooperating private research institutions. Brief for Respondents 29. Nor does the Bayh-Dole Act allow inventors employed by federal contractors to contest their employer's claim to a subject invention. The Act, for example, does not expressly permit an interested third party or an inventor to challenge a claim that a particular invention was supported by federal funding. In a world in which there is frequent collaboration between private entities, inventors, and federal contractors, see Brief for Pharmaceutical Research and Manufacturers of America as *Amicus Curiae* 22-23, that absence would be deeply troubling. But the lack of procedures protecting inventor and third-party rights makes perfect sense if the Act applies only when a federal contractor has already acquired title to an inventor's interest. In that case, there is no need to protect inventor or third-party rights, because the only rights at issue are those of the contractor and the Government.

The Bayh-Dole Act applies to subject inventions "conceived *or* first actually reduced to practice in the performance of work" "funded in whole *or in part* by the Federal Government." 35 U.S.C. §§201(e), 201(b) (emphasis added). Under Stanford's construction of the Act, title to one of its employee's inventions could vest in the University even if the invention was conceived before the inventor became a University employee, so long as the invention's reduction to practice was supported by federal funding. What is more, Stanford's reading suggests that the school would obtain title to one of its employee's inventions even if only one dollar of federal funding was applied toward the invention's conception or reduction to practice.

It would be noteworthy enough for Congress to supplant one of the fundamental precepts of patent law and deprive inventors of rights in their own inventions. To do so under such unusual terms would be truly surprising. We are confident that if Congress had intended such a sea change in intellectual property rights it would have said so clearly — not obliquely through an ambiguous definition of "subject invention" and an idiosyncratic use of the word "retain." Cf. Whitman v. American Trucking Assns., Inc., 531 U.S. 457, 468 (2001) ("Congress . . . does not alter the fundamental details of a regulatory scheme in vague terms or ancillary provisions").

Though unnecessary to our conclusion, it is worth noting that our construction of the Bayh-Dole Act is reflected in the common practice among parties operating under the Act. Contractors generally institute policies to obtain assignments from their employees. See Brief for Respondents 34; Brief for Pharmaceutical Research and Manufacturers of America as *Amicus Curiae* 13-18. Agencies that grant funds to federal contractors typically expect those contractors to obtain assignments. So it is with NIH, the agency that granted the federal funds at issue in this case. In guidance documents made available to contractors, NIH has made clear that "[b]y law, an inventor has initial ownership of an invention" and that contractors should therefore "have in place employee agreements requiring an inventor to 'assign' or give ownership of an invention to the organization upon acceptance of Federal funds." NIH Policies, Procedures, and Forms, A "20-20" View of Invention Reporting to the National Institutes of Health (Sept. 22, 1995). Such guidance would be unnecessary if Stanford's reading of the statute were correct.

Stanford contends that reading the Bayh-Dole Act as not vesting title to federally funded inventions in federal contractors "fundamentally undermin[es]" the Act's framework and severely threatens its continued "successful application." Brief for Petitioner 45. We do not agree. As just noted, universities typically enter into agreements with their employees requiring the assignment to the university of rights in inventions. With an effective assignment, those inventions — if federally funded — become "subject inventions" under the Act, and the statute as a practical matter works pretty much the way Stanford says it should. The only significant difference is that it does so without violence to the basic principle of patent law that inventors own their inventions.

The judgment of the Court of Appeals for the Federal Circuit is affirmed.

WISCONSIN ALUMNI RESEARCH FOUNDATION v. XENON PHARMACEUTICALS, INC.

591 F.3d 876 (7th Cir. 2010)

SYKES, Circuit Judge.

This case arises out of a complex set of contractual relationships between the Wisconsin Alumni Research Foundation, the patent-management entity for the University of Wisconsin; certain research scientists at the University; and Xenon Pharmaceuticals, a Canadian drug company. . . .

I. BACKGROUND

Researchers at the University of Wisconsin became interested in an enzyme called Stearoyl CoA Desaturase ("SCD") because of its potential to help treat diabetes, obesity, and other diseases by lowering cholesterol. In 1999 the researchers discovered that suppressing SCD levels in the human body lowered cholesterol levels. Pursuant to University policy, the researchers disclosed their research results to the Foundation and in January 2000 signed a Memorandum Agreement assigning all their rights in the discovery to the Foundation. The next month, the Foundation filed a provisional patent application for the discovery.

Meanwhile, Xenon, a Canadian pharmaceutical company that was collaborating with the University on research into a separate enzyme, learned of the University's discoveries and expressed interest in jointly pursuing SCD research. The University and Xenon entered into a series of research agreements (referred to as Research Agreements 1, 2, and 3) in which Xenon agreed to jointly sponsor various SCD research projects with the University. Each research agreement identified the scope of the research, the principal researcher, the expected cost, and the period of performance. These agreements also referred to a separate Sponsor Option Agreement between the Foundation and Xenon that governed ownership of any discoveries arising from the joint research program. The Sponsor Option Agreement cross-referenced the contracts between the Foundation and the individual University researchers requiring the researchers to assign to the Foundation any property rights in the discoveries emanating from the research and gave Xenon an exclusive option to license any resulting technology. Attached to the Sponsor Option Agreement were the individual contracts between the Foundation and the University researchers.

At the same time that Xenon signed its first research agreement with the University, Xenon also entered into a series of short-term consulting agreements with individual researchers at the University who worked on SCD projects. In exchange for consulting fees, these scientists undertook specific research projects for Xenon and agreed to assign any discoveries arising from these consulting projects to Xenon.

In February 2001 Xenon and the Foundation filed a joint patent application deriving from the provisional patent application the Foundation had filed in 2000. The application covered, among other things, the SCD enzyme itself and a method (called an assay) of using the enzyme to identify compounds that lower SCD levels. A patent was issued for the assay, but the patent application covering the remaining claims is still pending. Also in February 2001, Xenon exercised its option under the Sponsor Option Agreement to an exclusive license for any discoveries arising from the Xenon-sponsored SCD research at the University. As a result Xenon and the Foundation entered into an Exclusive License Agreement giving Xenon an exclusive right to make, use, and sell patented products under the joint patent application within the field of human healthcare. In exchange for these exclusive rights, Xenon agreed to pay the Foundation a percentage of any product sales, royalties, or sublicense fees it received.

After receiving the exclusive license, Xenon worked with Discovery Partners, Inc., to help identify compounds that inhibit the SCD enzyme. Using the jointly patented assay, Discovery Partners screened thousands of compounds and identified a set of 20 (referred to as the PPA compounds) with the potential to suppress SCD levels. Xenon shipped the PPA compounds to Mark Gray-Keller, a University researcher with whom it had a consulting agreement, for confirmatory testing. Gray-Keller successfully confirmed the inhibitory potential of the PPA compounds and thereafter assigned any interest he had in the compounds to Xenon. In 2002 Xenon filed a patent application covering the PPA compounds.

The Foundation objected, claiming that it had an ownership interest in the PPA compounds under the various interlocking agreements among the parties. More specifically, the Foundation noted that Gray-Keller had assigned all his rights in SCD discoveries and any improvements to the Foundation in his 2000 Memorandum Agreement. The Foundation also noted that the Sponsor Option Agreement between it and Xenon specifically acknowledged that Gray-Keller was required to assign his interest in any inventions arising from the jointly sponsored research to the Foundation. Alternatively, the Foundation claimed it had title to the compounds under the Bayh-Dole Act, 35 U.S.C. §§200 et seq., because federal funds had been used in the research and development of the compounds.

Relations between Xenon and the Foundation continued to deteriorate in 2004 when Xenon signed a license agreement with Novartis Pharma AG ("Novartis"), a Swiss corporation. This agreement gave Novartis a license to the technology covered by the joint patent application and purported to transfer ownership of the PPA compounds. After learning of this agreement (via a press release), the Foundation demanded a percentage of the sublicense fees from Xenon under the terms of the Exclusive License Agreement. Xenon refused, claiming it had the right to license its undivided interest in the joint patent application without being subject to the terms of its license agreement with the Foundation.

The Foundation then brought this suit claiming that Xenon violated the terms of the Exclusive License Agreement and owed the Foundation a percentage of the sublicense fees it received from Novartis. The Foundation also claimed that it, not Xenon, owned Gray-Keller's interest in the PPA compounds. The Foundation sought damages and declaratory judgment. Xenon responded with counterclaims against the Foundation. The district court, on cross-motions for summary judgment, entered a series of rulings on all issues except damages. . . .

The case proceeded to a jury trial on the question of damages for Xenon's failure to pay royalties or sublicense fees. The jury awarded $1 million, but on Xenon's motion for remittitur the court reduced the award to $300,000, which the Foundation accepted. The parties cross-appealed from the judgment.

II. DISCUSSION

For organization and ease of discussion, we divide the issues on appeal into two groups: (1) those that relate to the rights of the parties under the Exclusive License Agreement, and (2) those that relate to the rights of the parties regarding the PPA compounds.

A. Exclusive License Agreement

1. Xenon's Transfer of Rights to Novartis

We begin by addressing Xenon's contention that it did not violate the terms of the Exclusive License Agreement when it licensed its interest in the joint patent application to Novartis without paying the Foundation its share of the licensing fee. As a threshold matter, Xenon argues that this dispute is resolved by federal patent law, not by contract law. The district court did not address the question whether Xenon retained a federal statutory right to freely license its interest without regard to the Foundation's contract rights. The court resolved the parties' disputes based solely on the terms of their various contracts, holding that Xenon effectively executed a sublicense with Novartis and that this transaction fell within the provision of the Exclusive License Agreement governing sublicenses. Xenon contends that federal law-specifically, 35 U.S.C. §262 gives it the right to freely license its undivided one-half interest in the joint patent application without accounting to the Foundation under the terms of the Exclusive License Agreement. We disagree.

Federal law provides that joint patent owners, like the Foundation and Xenon, have control over the entire property, and each co-owner may freely use the patented technology without regard to the other. We have previously observed that under this principle of patent law, "each co-owner is 'at the mercy' of the other in that the right of each to license independently 'may, for all practical purposes, destroy the monopoly and so amount to an appropriation of the whole value of the patent.' " Rail-Trailer Co. v. ACF Indus., Inc., 358 F.2d 15, 17 (7th Cir. 1966). This statutory rule is subject to an important exception, however: Joint patent owners may vary their rights by contract. The statute provides that "*[i]n the absence of any agreement to the contrary*, each of the joint owners of a patent may make, use, offer to sell, or sell the patented invention . . . without the consent of and without accounting to the other owners." 35 U.S.C. §262 (emphasis added). The statutory default rule therefore controls *unless* there is an agreement to the contrary.

Here, the Foundation and Xenon modified the statutory default rule by contract; the Exclusive License Agreement plainly qualifies as "an agreement to the contrary" for purposes of §262. That agreement provides: "[The Foundation] hereby grants to Xenon an exclusive license, limited to the [field of human healthcare,] . . . under the Licensed Patents to make, use and sell Products." In exchange Xenon agreed to pay the Foundation a percentage of any payments, royalties, or sublicense fees it received by commercializing the technology itself or sublicensing the technology to a third party to commercialize. Under the terms of the agreement, sublicenses are expressly permitted—*provided* Xenon pays the Foundation the specified percentage of any royalties or sublicense fees—but *assignments* are prohibited without the Foundation's prior written consent.

Xenon argues that nothing in the Exclusive License Agreement explicitly revokes its statutory right to license its interest freely. True, but the agreement's provision requiring that Xenon pay the Foundation a share of the fees derived from any sublicense plainly undermines Xenon's claim that it retained an unfettered right under §262 to transfer its interest in the technology to third parties. So does the agreement's provision prohibiting assignment of the license without the Foundation's consent. The bargained-for exchange between the parties provided that the Foundation would forego its right to separately license the patent in exchange for receiving a share of the profits from Xenon's commercialization of the technology—either directly or via a sublicense to a third party. Xenon received a significant benefit from the agreement—the exclusive right to exploit the technology protected by the joint patent application. Xenon cannot avoid paying royalties or sublicense fees to the Foundation simply by labeling the Novartis transaction a "license" rather than a "sublicense."

Accordingly, the terms of the Exclusive Licensing Agreement, not 35 U.S.C. §262, govern the parties' rights and responsibilities here. Under that agreement Xenon held an exclusive license to develop the SCD discovery for commercial purposes and a corresponding obligation to share proceeds with the Foundation. The agreement gives Xenon three options: (1) commercialize the technology directly and pay royalties to the Foundation; (2) sublicense the technology to a third party and pay a percentage of the sublicense fees to the Foundation; or (3) assign its exclusive licensing rights to a third party with the prior consent of the Foundation.

Xenon suggests in the alternative that it never actually gave Novartis a license to the Foundation's interest in the jointly patented technology. The district court properly rejected this argument. The Xenon-Novartis agreement provides that Xenon grants to Novartis an exclusive license to all Xenon technology in the field of human and animal healthcare. Xenon technology includes "Xenon's interest in all Patent Rights in the Field, as specifically described in Schedule B," and Schedule B prominently lists the joint patent application owned by Xenon and the Foundation—first out of four listed patents. Xenon argues unpersuasively that the phrase "patent rights" does not include rights it obtained through the Exclusive License Agreement. In the warranty clause of the Xenon-Novartis agreement, Xenon represents that "it is the owner *or licensee* of all rights, title and interest in and to the Xenon Patent Rights." (Emphasis added.) Accordingly, Xenon granted Novartis any interest it held in the joint patent application by specifically including it in Schedule B. Put another way, Xenon effectively sublicensed its exclusive license rights in the jointly patented technology. The district court correctly concluded that the Xenon-Novartis agreement is subject to the terms of the Exclusive License Agreement governing sublicenses.

2. Sublicense Fees

After concluding that Xenon granted Novartis a sublicense in the jointly patented technology, the district court held that Xenon violated the terms of the Exclusive License Agreement by failing to pay the Foundation a share of the sublicense fees. Xenon argues that it is not obligated to make payments to the Foundation until products are actually brought to market and sold as a result of the sublicense. Because no products have yet been sold, Xenon claims it does not owe the Foundation anything. Again, we disagree. The Exclusive License Agreement requires Xenon to pay the Foundation license fees, milestones, and royalty payments as soon as they are received.

Section 4 of the Exclusive License Agreement, titled "Consideration," lays out the payment details and schedule. Subsection (B)(i) of that section states: "For all Products *sold directly by Xenon*, Xenon shall pay to [the Foundation] . . . a royalty calculated as a percentage of the Selling Price of Products. . . ." (Emphasis added.) It goes on to specify that royalties are earned on either the date the product is actually sold, the date an invoice is sent, or the date the product is transferred to a third party for promotional reasons—whichever comes first. The next subsection—the provision most relevant to this dispute—states:

> For all Products sold by Xenon sublicensees, Xenon shall pay to [the Foundation] a percentage of any license fees, milestones, and royalty payments received by Xenon as consideration for the sublicense granted to such sublicensees under Section 2B. The percentage shall remain fixed at a rate of ten percent (10%) for years one (1) and two (2) of this Agreement and seven and one-half percent (7.5%) thereafter until this Agreement is terminated.

Because both subsections begin with the phrase "[f]or all Products *sold*" (emphasis added), Xenon argues that it does not owe the Foundation any payments for the Novartis sublicense until products are actually brought to market and sold.

We agree with the district court that Section 4, read as a whole, requires payment of the Foundation's share of the sublicense fee independent of any actual sales of products. The apparent point of the prefatory phrase "[f]or all Products sold" in each of the two subsections governing payment is to distinguish between payments required when Xenon commercialized the technology itself and payments required when Xenon issued a sublicense to a third party to do so. In the former circumstance, the payment due to the Foundation is a royalty based on products sold; in the latter circumstance, the payment due to the Foundation is a specified percentage of the sublicense fee Xenon receives, plus "milestones" and royalties. Because the Novartis transaction falls under the second subsection, payment is due on receipt of a sublicense fee, not on the occurrence of product sales.

This reading of the payment provision is the most plausible for several reasons. Although both subsections use the same introductory phrase, the first subsection also says that payment is due upon actual product sale while the second subsection—governing sublicenses—does not include similar language. Instead, the second subsection states that Xenon owes the Foundation a percentage of any license fees and "milestones," in addition to royalty payments, stemming from any sublicense. As the district court noted, sublicense fees and milestone payments are not contingent upon a sale; they are paid immediately or on an ongoing basis by a licensee or sublicensee in exchange for the right to make sales of products developed in the future. Finally, the parties agree that it generally takes about 15 years to bring a drug product to market. Yet the Exclusive License Agreement specifies that Xenon must pay the Foundation 10% of any license fees, milestones, and royalty payments received during the first two years of the agreement and 7.5% thereafter. This provision would make little sense if no payment was required on a sublicense until a product was brought to market. Accordingly, the district court properly concluded that Xenon breached the Exclusive Licensing Agreement by failing to pay the Foundation its share of the fee from the Novartis transaction.

B. PPA Compounds

A brief recap of the relevant facts is in order: Xenon, with the help of Discovery Partners, used the jointly patented assay to screen thousands of compounds for therapeutic potential. Xenon and Discovery Partners identified a set of 20 "PPA compounds" with the potential to lower SCD levels in the human body, and Xenon sent these compounds to Gray-Keller for confirmatory screening. Gray-Keller confirmed the cholesterol-inhibiting potential of the PPA compounds and in July 2003 purported to assign his rights to Xenon pursuant to the terms of his consulting agreement.

The Foundation contends that the interlocking network of contracts among the parties gives it ownership of Gray-Keller's interest in the PPA compounds, and therefore Gray-Keller's assignment is void. We agree. Under the Sponsor Option Agreement, all University researchers working on the Xenon-funded research program agreed to assign to the Foundation their rights to any inventions that they "conceived of or reduced to practice . . . whether solely or jointly with others." Each University researcher, including Gray-Keller, signed an individual Memorandum Agreement to that effect, and copies were attached to and incorporated as part of the Sponsor Option Agreement. The scope of the joint research program was defined by three separate research agreements—Research Agreements 1, 2, and 3.

The Foundation maintains that Gray-Keller's work on the PPA compounds fell within the scope of Research Agreement 2, and therefore Gray-Keller was required to assign his interest in the compounds to the Foundation. Research Agreement 2 generally covers research to identify compounds that will influence SCD levels in the human body for therapeutic effect on cholesterol levels. While the scientific language and acronyms keep the contract from being readily understandable to a layperson, the scope of the research program is clear enough. First, Exhibit A to Research Agreement 2 is titled "Stearoyl CoA Desaturase (SCD) as a Target for Elevation of HDL." It states that its overall goal is to "evaluate SCD as a target for the development of drugs that would increase the levels of HDL in plasma and decrease triglycerides (which should have a therapeutic impact on cardiovascular disease)." It then lists a handful of more specific goals, such as to "[s]creen and rank order substrates/inhibitors of SCD1 activity for impact on SCD1 transcription in vitro" and to "[e]valuate lead substrates/inhibitors from in vitro screen for their effect on SCD1 transcription, SCD1 enzyme activity and HDL metabolism in vivo."

Gray-Keller's work identifying and confirming the therapeutic potential of the PPA compounds derived from the SCD enzyme was expressly contemplated by Research Agreement 2, which broadly covered research "to validate SCD as a target for screening novel compounds that may elevate HDL levels in vivo." Gray-Keller performed his research on this project at the University using University resources and was required under his Memorandum

Agreement to assign his interest in any discoveries to the Foundation. The fact that his work was conducted partly under Xenon's sponsorship and at its behest is not dispositive. Under the Sponsor Option Agreement and each of the individual agreements attached to it, the Foundation was entitled to ownership of any discoveries "conceived of or reduced to practice" by the researchers under the joint research program; Xenon was entitled to an exclusive license to commercialize the discoveries. Accordingly, the district court erred in granting summary judgment to Xenon on the claims pertaining to the Foundation's ownership interest in the PPA compounds. Under the Sponsor Option Agreement, the Memorandum Agreement, and Research Agreement 2, the Foundation was entitled to a declaration of its ownership interest in the PPA compounds.

ASYMMETRX, INC. v. BIOCARE MEDICAL, LLC
582 F.3d 1314 (Fed. Cir. 2009)

LOURIE, Circuit Judge.

The dispute in this case is over the rights to anti-p63 monoclonal antibodies (the "p63 antibodies"), which can be used to detect malignant carcinoma, such as cervical, breast, and prostate cancer. Harvard owns U.S. Patents 6,946,256 ("the 256 patent") and 7,030,227 ("the 227 patent") by assignment. The patents relate to the p63 antibodies and methods for using them to detect malignant carcinoma.

In May 2002, Biocare approached Harvard seeking to license the p63 antibodies. Later that year, Harvard entered into a Biological Materials License Agreement with Biocare ("the Biocare License"), effective October 15, 2002, to make, use, and sell the p63 antibodies. Section 2.5 of the Biocare License stated, "The license granted by this Agreement does not include a license under any U.S. or foreign patents." The 256 and 227 patents were pending but had not issued prior to the effective date of the Biocare License. The Biocare License also defined a limited field of use, the life science research market, but did not actually limit the license grant to that field.

A few years later, Harvard entered into an agreement with AsymmetRx (the "AsymmetRx License"), effective June 30, 2004, that also concerned the p63 antibodies. Under the AsymmetRx License, AsymmetRx received "an exclusive commercial license" under the 256 and 227 patents and "a license" to use the p63 antibodies. The grant under the AsymmetRx License was limited to a field defined as the "[s]ale of clinical and diagnostic products and services based on detecting p63 expression or mutation." Under §3.2(b) of the AsymmetRx License, Harvard reserved the right to make and use the p63 antibodies for academic research purposes as well as the right to grant non-exclusive licenses for the p63 antibodies to other non-profit or governmental institutions for academic research purposes. In addition, §§3.2(d) and (e) stated that Harvard could render the AsymmetRx License non-exclusive if AsymmetRx did not meet certain benchmarks in terms of commercial use and availability to the public within three years or if AsymmetRx did not meet certain FDA filing milestones. Sections 3.4(f) and (g) indicated that, although AsymmetRx could grant sublicenses, the sublicensees could not further sublicense, and Harvard could suggest who received a sublicense; §4.4 stated that AsymmetRx was to pay a portion of the sublicense income to Harvard. Section 3.4(h) required AsymmetRx, during the period of exclusivity in the United States, to manufacture any licensed product produced for sale in the United States substantially in the United States unless a waiver was obtained by the U.S. National Institutes of Health.

In terms of patent filing and maintenance, §7.2 specified that Harvard and AsymmetRx were to cooperate fully in the preparation, filing, prosecution, and maintenance of Harvard's patents "so as to enable Harvard to apply for, to prosecute and to maintain patent applications in patents in Harvard's name in any country." With respect to infringement of the patents, §8.1 gave Asymm-metRx "the right to prosecute in its own name and at its own expense any infringement" within the commercial diagnostic field, so long as AsymmetRx still had an exclusive license at the time the action was commenced. Before commencing such an action, AsymmetRx was to "give careful consideration to the views of Harvard and to potential effects on the public interest in making its decision whether or not to sue." If AsymmetRx did commence such an action, §8.2 stated that Harvard "may, to the extent permitted by law, elect to join as a party in that action." If Harvard joined such an action, Harvard and AsymmetRx jointly controlled that action. Under §8.4, no settlement, consent judgment, or other voluntary final disposition of such an infringement suit could be entered into without the prior written consent of Harvard, which was not to be unrea-sonably withheld. In addition, §8.6 of the AsymmetRx License provided,

> If LICENSEE elects not to exercise its right to prosecute an infringement of the PATENT RIGHTS pursuant to this Article, HARVARD may do so at its own expense, controlling such action and retaining all recoveries therefrom. LICENSEE shall cooperate fully with HARVARD in connection with any such action.

On June 27, 2007, AsymmetRx sued Biocare for patent infringement, alleging that Biocare's sale of the p63 antibodies violated AsymmetRx's exclusive rights in the commercial diagnostic field. Biocare countered that the Biocare License placed no restrictions on the scope of Biocare's sales. The parties made cross-motions for summary judgment. The parties agreed that the issue before the district court involved matters of pure contract interpretation. . . . [F]inal judgment was entered in favor of Biocare.

DISCUSSION

The parties to this appeal have focused on whether the district court properly interpreted the language of the Biocare License in finding that Biocare did not infringe any patent rights of AsymmetRx. We believe, however, that this appeal must be resolved by addressing an antecedent question: whether AsymmetRx had the statutory right to bring an action for infringement without joining the patent owner, Harvard. Because we find that AsymmetRx may pursue its infringement action against Biocare only if Harvard also participates in that action, we conclude that the district court's decision must be vacated.

The issue of AsymmetRx's standing to bring suit without Harvard joining as a plaintiff was not raised by either party or by the district court. However, an appellate court must satisfy itself that it has standing and jurisdiction whether or not the parties have raised them.

A civil action for infringement may be brought by "a patentee." 35 U.S.C. §281. A "patentee" is defined by statute to include the party to whom the patent was issued and the successors in title to the patent. 35 U.S.C. §100(d). Accordingly, a suit for infringement ordinarily must be brought by a party holding legal title to the patent. See Abbott Labs. v.

Diamedix Corp., 47 F.3d 1128, 1130 (Fed. Cir. 1995). Parties not holding title to the patent have been accorded the right to sue, or "standing," only in certain limited circumstances.

Under Waterman v. Mackenzie, 138 U.S. 252 (1891) and its successors, the critical determination regarding a party's ability to sue in its own name is whether an agreement transferring patent rights to that party is, in effect, an assignment or a mere license. To determine whether an assignment of patent rights was made, we must "examine whether the agreement transferred all substantial rights" to the patents and "whether the surrounding circumstances indicated an intent to do so." Vaupel Textilmaschinen KG v. Meccanica Euro Italia S.P.A., 944 F.2d 870, 874 (Fed. Cir. 1991).

We have stated that the exclusive right to sue is "particularly dispositive" in cases where, as here, we are deciding whether a patent owner must be joined as a party. Vaupel, 944 F.2d at 875. Accordingly, we found in Abbott that the patent owner had retained too great an interest in the patents to enable the licensee to sue for infringement on its own. Those interests included "a limited right to make, use, and sell products embodying the patented inventions, a right to bring suit if [the licensee] declined to do so, and the right to prevent [the licensee] from assigning its rights under the license to any party other than a successor in business." Abbott, 47 F.3d at 1132. More specifically, the agreement stated that if the patent owner asked the licensee to bring suit against an alleged infringer and the licensee declined to do so, the patent owner had the right to bring its own infringement action. Thus, although the licensee had the option to initiate a suit for infringement, "it [did] not enjoy the right to indulge infringements, which normally accompanies a complete conveyance of the right to sue." Id. In addition, even if the licensee did exercise its option to sue for infringement, it was "obligated under the agreement not to 'prejudice or impair the patent rights in connection with such prosecution or settlement.'" Id.

In contrast, . . . in Speedplay, Inc. v. Bebop, Inc., 211 F.3d 1245 (Fed. Cir. 2000), we distinguished Abbott and found that a licensee had standing because "the license grant was not subject to any prior-granted licenses or to any retained rights by the licensor to practice the patent." Speedplay, 211 F.3d at 1251. Significantly, the license in Speedplay did not grant the original patent owners "the right to participate in an infringement action brought by [the licensee], nor [did] it limit [the licensee's] management of any action," in contrast to the agreement in Abbott. Id. In addition, and unlike in Abbott, a clause allowing the patent owners to bring their own infringement action if the licensee failed to do so within three months was an "illusory" retention of the right to sue because the licensee could "render that right nugatory by granting the alleged infringer a royalty-free sublicense." Id. Thus, in . . . Speedplay, the transfer was as if title had passed, at least for the purposes of standing to sue.

This case is more similar to Abbott than to . . . Speedplay in terms of what rights Harvard retained under the patents. Although the AsymmetRx License effected a broad conveyance of rights to AsymmetRx, Harvard retained substantial interests under the 256 and 227 patents, including the right to sue for infringement, and AsymmetRx therefore does not have the right to sue for infringement as a "patentee" under the patent statute.

Under the AsymmetRx License, Harvard also retained the right to make and use the p63 antibodies for its own academic research purposes, as well as the right to provide the p63 antibodies to non-profit or governmental institutions for academic research purposes. In addition, Harvard retained a great deal of control over aspects of the licensed products within the commercial diagnostic field, such as requiring AsymmetRx to meet certain commercial use, availability, and FDA filing benchmarks; specifying that manufacture had to take place in the United States during the period of exclusivity; and maintaining input on sublicensing and receiving a share of those royalties. AsymmetRx was required to grant sublicenses suggested by Harvard, provided they were not contrary to sound and reasonable business practices and materially increased the availability to the public of the licensed products. The agreement also specified that AsymmetRx was to cooperate with Harvard to maintain the patent rights, so as to enable Harvard to apply for, to prosecute, and to maintain patent applications and patents in Harvard's name. Retention of all of those rights is inconsistent with an assignment of the patents. See *Abbott*, 47 F.3d at 1132 (discussing the patent owner's retention of "the right to make and use, for its own benefit, products embodying the inventions claimed in the patents").

Moreover, although AsymmetRx was given the right of first refusal in suing alleged infringers, the AsymmetRx License provides that if AsymmetRx elects not to exercise its right to sue, Harvard has the right to bring its own infringement action. Thus, as in *Abbott*, although AsymmetRx has the option to initiate suit for infringement, "it does not enjoy the right to indulge infringements, which normally accompanies a complete conveyance of the right to sue." *Abbott*, 47 F.3d at 1132. In addition, even if AsymmetRx exercises its option to sue for infringement, it is obligated under the AsymmetRx License to consider Harvard's views and the public interest, and Harvard's approval is necessary for any settlement of suit. Such consideration of Harvard's views is akin to the licensee in Abbott being required "not to 'prejudice or impair the patent rights in connection with such prosecution or settlement.'" *Id.* Finally, if AsymmetRx does commence an infringement action, Harvard may elect to join as a party in that action and, if Harvard does join such an action, it jointly controls the suit with AsymmetRx. In short, Harvard did not convey the entire right to enforce the patents to AsymmetRx. When viewing the retention of the right to sue in conjunction with all of the other rights retained by Harvard, it is clear that Harvard conveyed less than all substantial rights under the 256 and 227 patents. While any of these restrictions alone might not have been destructive of the transfer of all substantial rights, their totality is sufficient to do so.

The provisions of the AsymmetRx License may all have met the respective needs of the parties; after all, they negotiated and executed the agreement. They may also reflect the perceived needs of a university attempting to balance the public interest with commercializing the results of its professors' research. Be that as it may, in attempting to meet these goals, the contractual result is that Harvard retained substantial control over the patent rights it was exclusively licensing, such that its agreement with AsymmetRx did not convey all substantial rights under the patents and thus did not make the license tantamount to an assignment. AsymmetRx must therefore be considered a licensee, not an assignee. Under *Waterman* and its successors, AsymmetRx does not have a sufficient interest in the 256 and 227 patents to sue, on its own, as the "patentee" entitled by 35 U.S.C. §281 to judicial relief from infringement. Harvard, by retaining the various rights to its patents, must join in any infringement suit its licensee chooses to bring.

Furthermore, the policies underlying Federal Rule of Civil Procedure 19, the federal joinder rule, argue for Harvard's joinder in this case. Rule 19(a) provides that a person who can be joined as a party should be joined if (1) the person's absence would make it impossible to grant complete relief to the parties, or (2) the person claims an interest in the subject matter of the action and is so situated that the disposition of the action in his absence could impede his ability to protect that interest or leave any of the parties subject to a substantial risk of incurring multiple inconsistent obligations. Harvard obviously retains an interest in the patents, and the disposition of AsymmetRx's suit against Biocare could either prejudice Harvard's interests or expose Biocare to the risk of multiple litigations. This is especially true because the Biocare License provides that, upon reasonable notice by Biocare, Harvard is obligated to help Biocare defend against any infringement suit by a third party. Harvard, by granting licenses to two parties involving the same subject matter, has potentially put itself in the conflicting position of having to aid two licensees opposed to each other. Complicating matters is the fact that Harvard is continuing to accept royalty payments from Biocare resulting from sales in the commercial diagnostic market that AsymmetRx asserts are infringing its patent rights. If anything, this added complication indicates that the purpose of Rule 19 to avoid multiple suits or incomplete relief arising from the same subject matter is best served by joinder of Harvard, which would permit the relationships between AsymmetRx, Biocare, and Harvard to all be resolved at the same time as well as solve the standing problem.

That is not to say that if Harvard declines to participate voluntarily, the action cannot go forward. "A patentee that does not voluntarily join an action prosecuted by its exclusive licensee can be joined as a defendant or, in a proper case, made an involuntary plaintiff if it is not subject to service of process." *Abbott*, 47 F.3d at 1133. For the purposes of this case, we need not decide the nature of Harvard's participation, as it is unclear whether Harvard was ever given the opportunity to join the action at the district court. We thus conclude that Harvard did not convey all substantial rights under the 256 and 227 patents to AsymmetRx in the AsymmetRx License, and, as a result, AsymmetRx lacks statutory standing, on its own, to bring an infringement suit against Biocare.

UNIVERSITY OF ALABAMA BD. OF TRUSTEES v. NEW LIFE ART, INC.
683 F.3d 1266 (11th Cir. 2012)

ANDERSON, Circuit Judge:
Since 1979, Daniel A. Moore has painted famous football scenes involving the University of Alabama (the "University" or "Alabama"). The paintings feature realistic portrayals of the University's uniforms, including helmets, jerseys, and crimson and white colors. Moore has reproduced his paintings as prints and calendars, as well as on mugs and other articles. . . .

From 1979 to 1990, Moore painted historical Alabama football scenes without any kind of formal or informal relationship with the University. From 1991 to 1999, Moore signed a dozen licensing agreements with the University to produce and market specific items, which would often include additional Alabama trademarks on the border or packaging, or would come with a certificate or stamp saying they were officially licensed products.

From 1991 to 2002, Moore produced other Alabama-related paintings and prints that were not the subject of any licensing agreements. He also continued to sell paintings and prints of images that had originally been issued before 1991. He did not pay royalties for any of these items, nor did the University request that he do so. Moore said that he would enter into a licensing agreement if he felt that it would help increase the sales of that particular product, or if he wanted the University—his alma mater—to benefit from royalties.

During this time, the University issued Moore press credentials so he could obtain material for his work. The University also asked Moore to produce an unlicensed painting on live television during a football game.

However, in January 2002, the University told Moore that he would need to license all of his Alabama-related products because they featured the University's trademarks. In particular, the University asserted that Moore needed permission to portray the University's uniforms, including the jersey and helmet designs and the crimson and white colors.

Moore contended that he did not need permission to paint historical events and that there was no trademark violation so long as he did not use any of the University's trademarks outside of the "image area" of the painting (i.e., outside the original painting). Despite this disagreement, the University still sold Moore's unlicensed calendars in its campus stores for several years. It also displayed unlicensed paintings at its Bryant Museum and athletic department office.

The parties were unable to reach a satisfactory resolution, and the University brought suit on March 18, 2005, in the Northern District of Alabama. The University contended that (1) Moore had breached several terms of his prior licensing agreements and (2) Moore's paintings, prints, calendars, mugs, and other objects violated the Lanham Act by infringing the University's trademark rights in its football uniforms. See 15 U.S.C. §1125(a). . . .

We believe that the simplest way to address all of the arguments in this appeal is to divide the opinion based on the two categories of objects produced by Moore. With respect to both categories, we address only objects which were never the subject of a specific, written licensing agreement. First we address the arguments of the respective parties with respect to a category of objects composed of paintings, prints, and calendars. Then we address the arguments of the parties with respect to a second category of objects composed of mugs and other "mundane products."

II. PAINTINGS, PRINTS, AND CALENDARS

The University first argues that it is unnecessary to reach the trademark issues in this appeal because the language of Moore's prior licensing agreements prohibits his unlicensed portrayal of the University's uniforms. We disagree.

A. Licensing Agreements

Through addenda, the parties renewed their 1995 licensing agreement ("1995 Agreement") annually through 2000. The 1995 Agreement states that it "cancels, terminates, and supersedes any prior agreement or understanding." Accordingly, for the sake of simplicity, we focus on the 1995 Agreement's language, although we note that previous licensing agreements used substantially similar language in most respects.

The University contends that even after the 1995 Agreement and its addenda expired, Moore had to obtain permission to use any of the University's "licensed indicia," which the University argues includes football uniforms, on any items he produced.

The 1995 Agreement's definition of "licensed indicia" is very broad:

"Licensed Indicia" means the names, symbols, designs, and colors of the [University], including without limitation, the trademarks, service marks, designs, team names, nicknames, abbreviations, city/state names in the appropriate context, slogans, logographics, mascots, seals and other symbols associated with or referring to the [University]. Licensed Indicia includes those in Appendix B and indicia adopted, used and approved for use by the [University]. Any newly adopted indicia shall be deemed to be additions to the Licensed Indicia in Appendix B and shall be subject to the terms and conditions of the Agreement.

The items listed in Appendix B are the phrases "University of Alabama," "Roll Tide," "Crimson Tide," "U of A," "Bama," and "Alabama." It also lists the colors "Crimson PMS 201" and "Gray PMS 429" and includes images of the University's official seal, an elephant wearing a sweater with an "A" on it, an "A" with an elephant charging through it, and an "A" with the University's official seal superimposed.

The design and colors of uniforms are not specifically mentioned anywhere in the 1995 Agreement, but the University contends that they are nonetheless covered by the broad language defining "licensed indicia" and the reference in Appendix B to the colors "Crimson PMS 201" and "Gray PMS 429" — the University's crimson and white colors.

The 1995 Agreement also requires that Moore "shall not use the Licensed Indicia for any purpose other than upon or in connection with" explicitly licensed items, and that the "terms and conditions of this Agreement necessary to protect the rights and interests of the [University] in [its] Licensed Indicia . . . shall survive the termination or expiration of this Agreement."

The University contends that these clauses, when taken together, clearly require Moore to obtain permission whenever he depicts the University's football uniforms in any of his products. The district court disagreed with the University and held that the parties did not intend "licensed indicia" to include colors on uniforms. The court concluded that the colors in Appendix B were listed only with respect to the logos and words actually shown in the appendix. Uniforms are not shown in the appendix, nor are they otherwise listed anywhere in the 1995 Agreement. Thus, the district court held as a matter of law that Moore's portrayal of the University's colors on uniforms in his paintings and other objects was not prohibited by the licensing agreements.

We believe that the 1995 Agreement is ambiguous on this issue. While the definition of "licensed indicia" is broad, there is also language indicating that it would not include the portrayal of uniforms in the content of a painting, print, or calendar. For instance, the 1995 Agreement repeatedly refers to products "bearing" "licensed indicia." Other sections refer to "licensed indicia" being used "on" products. Another provision instructs that Moore "shall not contract with any party for the production or application of Licensed Indicia by that party" without authorization. It seems unlikely that uniforms in a painting would be "produced" or "applied." This language implies that the parties intended "licensed indicia" to refer to the packaging or labels placed upon products, rather than uniforms depicted within the content of a painting, print, or calendar.

Also weighing in favor of ambiguity is a section indicating that there must be a circled "R" or the "TM" symbol beside all "licensed indicia." Under the University's view, this would apparently require that every player portrayed in a painting would need an "R" or "TM" symbol accompanying his uniform.

Additionally, the University's proffered interpretation of the 1995 Agreement would mean that, just in exchange for the right to label his annual calendars as officially sponsored, Moore had effectively indentured himself to the University, in that he would need to perpetually obtain permission to paint any historically accurate scenes from Alabama football games. Given the contradictions present in the 1995 Agreement, we conclude that it is ambiguous as to whether the parties intended that Moore would have to obtain permission to depict Alabama uniforms in his products.

However, for paintings, prints, and calendars, we can resolve this ambiguity on the basis of the parties' subsequent course of conduct. The 1995 Agreement states that it will be governed by Georgia law. In Georgia, where "the contract is ambiguous to such a degree that the question of the parties' intent in this regard cannot be ascertained as a matter of law by applying usual statutory rules of contract construction," courts should examine "the course of conduct and actions of the various parties" with the understanding that "the construction placed upon a contract by the parties thereto, as shown by their acts and conduct, is entitled to much weight and may be conclusive upon them." Am. Honda Motor Co. v. Williams & Assocs., Inc., 431 S.E.2d 437, 443 (1993). The most relevant evidence for this analysis would be the parties' behavior—active or passive—during and after the time when they were entering into licensing agreements (i.e., from 1991 until this litigation).

There is considerable evidence indicating that the parties did not intend that Moore's portrayal of the uniforms in unlicensed paintings, prints, and calendars would violate the licensing agreements. Between 1991 and 2002, Moore produced several new paintings and prints that ubiquitously featured the University's uniforms. He also continued to sell paintings and prints of works that had originally been issued before 1991. Despite the public notoriety of Moore's work, the University never requested (until this litigation) that he pay royalties on these unlicensed items.

From 2001 to 2004, the University sold over $12,000 worth of Moore's unlicensed calendars in its campus store. On at least one occasion, the University detached the images from an unlicensed calendar, then framed and sold them. The Bryant Museum, which is run by the University, displayed and sold unlicensed Moore prints and featured an unlicensed painting on the cover of its brochure.

In 2001, the University asked Moore to complete a sketch on live television during a nationally televised football game; this sketch was unlicensed and featured the University's football helmet. For many years, the University had displayed unlicensed Moore prints in its own athletic department office and had granted Moore press credentials so he could take photographs to be used as source material for paintings, many of which were never licensed.

The parties' course of conduct clearly indicates that they did not intend that Moore would need permission every time he sought to portray the University's uniforms in the content of his paintings, prints, and calendars. See Am. Honda Motor Co., 431 S.E.2d at 443. There is no genuine dispute on this issue, and accordingly we reject the University's argument that the licensing agreements end this appeal.

B. Trademark Claims

Because we find that the licensing agreements were not intended to prohibit Moore's depiction of the University's uniforms in unlicensed paintings, prints, or calendars, we proceed to address the University's trademark claims with respect to these items. The University's claim is that Moore's unlicensed paintings, prints, and calendars infringe on the University's trademarks because the inclusion in these products of the University's football uniforms (showing the University's crimson and white colors) creates a likelihood of confusion on the part of buyers that the University sponsored or endorsed the product.

The University argues that its uniforms are "strong" trademarks and that its survey provides strong evidence of confusion sufficient to establish a likelihood of confusion to sustain a Lanham Act violation by Moore. See 15 U.S.C. §1125(a); Two Pesos, Inc. v. Taco Cabana, Inc., 505 U.S. 763, 769 (1992). Contrary to the University's argument, the district court concluded there was a "weak mark and [merely] some likelihood of confusion." And contrary to the University's argument that its trademarks triggered the sales of Moore's products, the district court concluded with respect to the paintings and prints that "the plays and Moore's reputation established during a period when his art was agreeably not licensed are what predominantly trigger the sales." Similarly, with respect to the University's survey upon which the University relies to support likelihood of confusion, the district court concluded "that the survey lacks strength because of its manner of taking, the form of the questions, the nature of the surveyed customers, and the number of responders. It involved only one print. The questions are loaded with suggestions that there is a 'sponsor' other than the artist." We note that Moore's signature was prominent on the paintings, prints, and calendars, clearly telegraphing that he was the artist who created the work of art. We also note that the one print used in the survey was in fact specifically licensed, and thus had an actual, historical sponsorship association with the University. Although we are in basic agreement with the district court's evaluation of the mark and the degree of confusion as to the source and sponsorship of the paintings, prints, and calendars, we need not in this case settle upon a precise evaluation of the strength of the mark or the degree of likelihood of confusion. As our discussion below indicates, we conclude that the First Amendment interests in artistic expression so clearly outweigh whatever consumer confusion that might exist on these facts that we must necessarily conclude that there has been no violation of the Lanham Act with respect to the paintings, prints, and calendars.

The First Amendment's protections extend beyond written and spoken words. "[P]ictures, films, paintings, drawings, and engravings . . . have First Amendment protection[.]" Kaplan v. California, 413 U.S. 115 (1973).

The University argues that Moore's paintings, prints, and calendars "are more commercial than expressive speech and, therefore, entitled to a lower degree" of First Amendment protection. See Cent. Hudson Gas & Elec. Corp. v. Pub. Serv. Comm'n of N.Y., 447 U.S. 557, 562-63 (1980) ("The Constitution . . . accords a lesser protection to commercial speech than to other constitutionally guaranteed expression."). However, these items certainly do more than "propos[e] a commercial transaction." Id. at 562. Naturally, Moore sells these items for money, but it "is of course no matter that the dissemination [of speech] takes place under commercial auspices." Smith v. California, 361 U.S. 147, 150 (1959). Like other expressive speech, Moore's paintings, prints, and calendars are entitled to full protection under the First Amendment.

Thus, we must decide whether Moore's First Amendment rights will give way to the University's trademark rights. We are not the first circuit to confront this issue. In 1989, the Second Circuit decided Rogers v. Grimaldi, 875 F.2d 994 (2d Cir. 1989), which is the landmark case for balancing trademark and First Amendment rights. In Rogers, the defendant created a film about two fictional Italian dancers who were called "Ginger and Fred," which was the film's title. *Id.* at 996-97. Ginger Rogers, a famous dancer who often worked with Fred Astaire, sued under §43(a) of the Lanham Act, 15 U.S.C. §1125(a), arguing that the film's title falsely implied that she was endorsing or featured in the film. *Rogers*, 875 F.2d at 997.

The court noted that the purchaser of artistic works, "like the purchaser of a can of peas, has a right not to be misled as to the source of the product." *Id.* at 997-98. However, the court concluded that the Lanham Act should be read narrowly to avoid impinging on speech protected by the First Amendment. *Id.* at 998-1000. Thus, the court adopted a balancing test:

> We believe that in general the Act should be construed to apply to artistic works only where the public interest in avoiding consumer confusion outweighs the public interest in free expression. In the context of allegedly misleading titles using a celebrity's name, that balance will normally not support application of the Act unless the title has no artistic relevance to the underlying work whatsoever, or if it has some artistic relevance, unless the title explicitly misleads as to the source of the work. *Id.* at 999.

Under the facts of *Rogers*, the court concluded that "the slight risk that such use of a celebrity's name might implicitly suggest endorsement or sponsorship to some people is outweighed by the danger of restricting artistic expression." *Id.* at 1000. Accordingly, the court ruled in favor of the movie's producers because the title was artistically relevant to the film, there had been no evidence of explicit misleading as to source, and the risk of confusion was "so outweighed by the interests in artistic expression as to preclude application of the Lanham Act." *Id.* at 1001.

Circuit courts have also applied *Rogers* in cases where trademark law is being used to attack the content — as opposed to the title — of works protected by the First Amendment. . . .

Therefore, we have no hesitation in joining our sister circuits by holding that we should construe the Lanham Act narrowly when deciding whether an artistically expressive work infringes a trademark. This requires that we carefully "weigh the public interest in free expression against the public interest in avoiding consumer confusion." *Cliffs Notes*, 886 F.2d at 494. An artistically expressive use of a trademark will not violate the Lanham Act "unless the use of the mark has no artistic relevance to the underlying work whatsoever, or, if it has some artistic relevance, unless it explicitly misleads as to the source or the content of the work." *ESS Entm't*, 547 F.3d at 1099.

In this case, we readily conclude that Moore's paintings, prints, and calendars are protected under the *Rogers* test. The depiction of the University's uniforms in the content of these items is artistically relevant to the expressive underlying works because the uniforms' colors and designs are needed for a realistic portrayal of famous scenes from Alabama football history. Also there is no evidence that Moore ever marketed an unlicensed item as "endorsed" or "sponsored" by the University, or otherwise explicitly stated that such items were affiliated with the University. Moore's paintings, prints, and calendars very clearly are embodiments of artistic expression, and are entitled to full First Amendment protection. The extent of his use of the University's trademarks is their mere inclusion (their necessary inclusion) in the body of the image which Moore creates to memorialize and enhance a particular play or event in the University's football history. Even if "some members of the public would draw the incorrect inference that [the University] had some involvement with [Moore's paintings, prints, and calendars,] . . . that risk of misunderstanding, not engendered by any overt [or in this case even implicit] claim . . . is so outweighed by the interest in artistic expression as to preclude" any violation of the Lanham Act. *Rogers*, 875 F.2d at 1001.

Because Moore's depiction of the University's uniforms in the content of his paintings, prints, and calendars results in no violation of the Lanham Act, we affirm the district court with respect to paintings and prints, and reverse with respect to calendars.

III. MUGS AND OTHER "MUNDANE PRODUCTS"

We now proceed to the issues related to Moore's depiction of the University's uniforms on "mini-prints, mugs, cups, . . . flags, towels, t-shirts, or any other mundane products." Moore is appellant for these items, which we will refer to as "mugs and other 'mundane products.'"

A. Licensing Agreements

As with the paintings, prints, and calendars, the University argues that the licensing agreements dispositively determine its claim for royalties with respect to the mugs and other "mundane products." However, as discussed supra at Part II.A, the licensing agreements are ambiguous with respect to whether Moore needed permission to portray the University's uniforms. For paintings, prints, and calendars, we could resolve this ambiguity by looking to the parties' subsequent course of conduct.

However, for mugs and other "mundane products," we conclude that the record is not clear enough for us to resolve the ambiguity as a matter of law. There is a lack of evidence indicating how the parties viewed Moore's portrayal of the University's uniforms on mugs and other "mundane products." In thirty years, Moore has produced only three sets of mugs. The fact that two of the sets were licensed perhaps indicates that the parties thought that Moore would need permission to produce mugs portraying the University's uniforms. However, the fact that one set was not licensed implies the opposite. During the course of this litigation, the parties have focused almost exclusively on the paintings, prints, and calendars, with little attention paid to mugs and other objects.

The University observes that Moore once sought permission from the University before using a symbol on one of his mugs. The University contends that this shows that the parties believed that permission was required before Moore could use the University's colors and symbols, at least when reproduced on mugs. However, the symbol in question appears to be an "A" with an elephant charging through it, which was a symbol explicitly included in the 1995 Agreement's Appendix B. This provides no insight into how the parties viewed Moore's depiction of the University's uniforms on mugs and other "mundane products."

Because disputed issues of material fact remain, we reverse the grant of summary judgment to the University on this licensing issue.

B. Moore's Copyright Argument

Moore argues that because his original paintings do not infringe the University's trademarks, he has an unfettered right to produce derivative works featuring those paintings. We disagree with this broad contention. "[T]he defendant's ownership of or license to use a copyrighted image is no defense to a charge of trademark infringement. It should be remembered that a copyright is not a 'right' to use: it is a right to exclude others from using the copyrighted work." 1 J. Thomas McCarthy, McCarthy on Trademarks and Unfair Competition §6:14 (4th ed. 2011); see also Fed. Trade Comm'n v. Real Prods. Corp., 90 F.2d 617, 619 (2d Cir. 1937) ("A copyright is not a license to engage in unfair competition.").

If it were otherwise, a person could easily circumvent trademark law by drawing another's trademark and then placing that drawing on various products with impunity. Selling the copyrighted drawing itself may not amount to a trademark infringement, but its placement on certain products very well might. See, e.g., Nova Wines, Inc. v. Adler Fels Winery LLC, 467 F. Supp. 2d 965, 983 (N.D. Cal. 2006) (holding that the copyright holder of a Marilyn Monroe photograph could not use the photo on wine bottles because it would infringe the trademark rights of another winery that sold wine in bottles that prominently featured images of Monroe); McCarthy, supra, §6:14. Thus, we reject Moore's argument that his copyright in the paintings gives him an automatic defense to any trademark claims made by the University.

. . .

IV. CONCLUSION

As evidenced by the parties' course of conduct, Moore's depiction of the University's uniforms in his unlicensed paintings, prints, and calendars is not prohibited by the prior licensing agreements. Additionally, the paintings, prints, and calendars do not violate the Lanham Act because these artistically expressive objects are protected by the First Amendment, by virtue of our application of the *Rogers* balancing test. The uniforms in these works of art are artistically relevant to the underlying works, Moore never explicitly misled consumers as to the source of the items, and the interests in artistic expression outweigh the risk of confusion as to endorsement. Accordingly, we affirm the judgment of the district court with respect to the paintings and prints, and reverse with respect to the prints as replicated on calendars.

With respect to the licensing agreements' coverage of the mugs and other "mundane products," we reverse the district court because disputed issues of fact remain. Moore has not argued on appeal that his actions with respect to these items constituted fair use or were protected by the First Amendment, and therefore any such protection has been waived, and we need not address those issues with respect to the mugs and other "mundane products." We remand this case to the district court for further proceedings, consistent with this opinion.

AFFIRMED IN PART, REVERSED IN PART, AND REMANDED.

UNIVERSITY OF FLORIDA RESEARCH FOUNDATION, INC. v. MEDTRONIC PLC, MEDTRONIC, INC.

2016 WL 3869877 (N.D. Florida July 15, 2016)

MARK E. WALKER, United States District Judge.

Plaintiff, the University of Florida Research Foundation, Inc. ("UFRF") filed suit in state court against Defendants alleging breach of a licensing contract.

While this case was still in state court, Defendants brought a counterclaim seeking a declaratory judgment to the effect that they have not infringed the patent at the center of the licensing agreement. Under an odd new removal statute, this counterclaim could be an independent basis for removal. *See* 28 U.S.C. §1454 ("A civil action in which any party asserts a claim for relief arising under any Act of Congress relating to patents . . . may be removed to the district court of the United States for the district and division embracing the place where the action is pending. . . . The removal of an action under this section shall be made in accordance with section 1446, except that if the removal is based solely on this section . . . the action may be removed by any party.").

Defendants removed this case in late May, asserting all three of the aforementioned bases for removal. UFRF timely filed a motion to remand, arguing that (1) it is an arm of the State of Florida and therefore cannot be a "diverse" party for purposes of diversity jurisdiction, (2) its claims as pleaded in the amended complaint do not arise under federal law, and (3) Defendants' counterclaim does not form a basis for removal under §1454 because it is not a compulsory counterclaim and because UFRF enjoys Eleventh Amendment immunity from suit in federal court which cannot be overcome by §1454. UFRF also filed a motion to dismiss Defendants' counterclaim in which it argues more forcefully that it is entitled to Eleventh Amendment immunity.

If UFRF is entitled to Eleventh Amendment immunity, and if it has not waived that immunity, then this case must be remanded back to state court. For Eleventh Amendment immunity is, in part, an immunity from suit in federal court, not just an immunity from certain types of relief. When a state entity finds itself in federal court involuntarily, it may assert its Eleventh Amendment privilege to be free "from being compelled to appear in the courts of another sovereign against [its] will." McClendon v. Ga. Dep't of Cmty. Health, 261 F.3d 1252, 1256 (11th Cir. 2001).

Is UFRF Entitled to Eleventh Amendment Immunity?

In determining "whether [an] entity . . . is an arm of the state," the circumstances "must be assessed in light of the particular function in which the [entity] was engaged when taking the actions out of which liability is asserted to arise." Abusaid v. Hills-borough Cty. Bd. of Cty. Comm'rs, 405 F.3d 1298, 1303 (11th Cir. 2005) (quoting Manders v. Lee, 338 F.3d 1304, 1308 (11th Cir. 2003) (en banc)). "To determine whether [an entity], while engaged in the relevant function, acts as an arm of the state, we conduct a four-factor inquiry, taking into account (1) how state law defines the entity; (2) what degree of control the state maintains over the entity; (3) the source of the entity's funds; and (4) who bears financial responsibility for judgments entered against the entity." *Id.*

Here, the "relevant function" is the licensing of patents and the collection of royalties from those license agreements. UFRF undertakes this function "for the benefit of a state university in Florida" — namely, the University of Florida — and pursuant to a certification by the University of Florida Board of Trustees that it is "operating in a manner consistent with the goals of the university and in the best interest of the state." §1004.28(1)(a), Fla. Stat. (2015). And UFRF does not have free reign — "[t]he board of trustees, in accordance with rules and guidelines of the Board of Governors, . . . prescribe [s] by rule conditions with which [UFRF] must comply in order to use property, facilities, or personal services at any state university. Such rules . . . provide for budget and audit review and oversight by the board of trustees." *Id.* §1004.28(2)(b).

The University of Florida Board of Trustees has made such rules. For instance, it requires UFRF (and all other organizations of its kind) to "have Articles of Incorporation and Bylaws that together . . . [p]rovide that the chief executive officer or director . . . shall be selected and appointed by the governing board . . . with prior approval of the President of the University, and that the chief executive officer or director shall report to the President or a designee reporting directly to the President." Fla. Admin. Code R. 6C1-1.300. (2)(b).

UFRF's bylaws further limit its independence from the University and the State of Florida. For instance, the "annual operating budget . . . must be approved by . . . the President of the University or his or her designee who shall be a Vice President or other senior finance or business officer of the University reporting directly to the President or to a senior official who reports to the President." And "[a]ny Director may be removed for cause by the President of the University or his or her designee after consulting with the nonaffected Directors of the corporation or the Board's authorized designee acting in an executive capacity."

All of this suggests that UFRF is controlled by the state. Indeed, the Florida Supreme Court recently held that the University of Central Florida Athletics Association — like UFRF, an entity organized under §1004.28 — was entitled to limited sovereign immunity under §768.28, Florida Statutes as "an instrumentality of the state." Plancher v. UCF Athletics Ass'n, Inc., 175 So. 3d 724, 729 (Fla. 2015). In reaching this conclusion, the court relied on many of the same features that are present in this case, including the university's control over the entity's board of directors, and the university's control over the entity's bylaws. It's true that the court in Plancher was not determining the entity's Eleventh Amendment immunity, but, as it noted, its analysis of sovereign immunity under state law was similar to that employed in the Eleventh Amendment context; the "focus [in each case is] upon governmental control over the" entity.

The Plancher decision is important not only because of the parallels between the factual situation in that case and in this case — which bears on the "degree of control" factor — but also because it makes clear that entities like UFRF are considered arms of the state under state law. If UFRF would be afforded sovereign immunity under §768.28, that suggests that it is considered under Florida law to be an instrumentality of the state. It's true that "an entity may be a state establishment for purposes of the state constitution and state statutes, [but] may also exercise sufficient independence so that it cannot claim [E]leventh [A]mendment immunity as an arm of the state under federal law." Magula v. Broward Gen. Med. Ctr., 742 F. Supp. 645, 648 (S.D. Fla. 1990). But the state's characterization is still relevant to the Eleventh Amendment analysis.

There is not a tremendous amount of evidence in the record that bears on the other two factors. It appears that UFRF derives much of its income from "development and commercialization of University work products." In the patent context, this means that UFRF takes the inventions of UF researchers, profits from them, and then feeds some, perhaps most, of that money back into the school. So in a sense UFRF is "funded" by the state, in that it relies on the raw input of patents, etc. from state employees to make money. Admittedly, this is not state "funding" in the traditional sense — the state legislature does not appear to be appropriating money to fund UFRF. But it also involves more reliance on the state than the case of, say, a city or county school board that can raise revenue through bonds and taxes.

As for who would pay a money judgment against UFRF, there is simply no indication in the record. It should be said, though, that any financial harm to UFRF would harm the University of Florida, which is indisputably an arm of the state.

Putting all this together, this Court is convinced that UFRF is an arm of the state — at least for the purposes of this case — and that it is entitled to Eleventh Amendment immunity.

Has UFRF Waived Its Immunity?

The key question vis-à-vis waiver is whether UFRF is in federal court voluntarily. Clearly, UFRF did not file suit in a federal forum, nor did it remove this case to federal court. Either of these actions would have amounted to a waiver of UFRF's Eleventh Amendment immunity from suit in federal court, though not necessarily a waiver of its immunity from all forms of claims for relief.

Normally, this would settle the matter. But there's an odd twist in this case thanks to the recently-amended patent jurisdiction statutes. The problem is this: when a state entity files a patent suit in federal court, it waives any Eleventh Amendment immunity it might have to a compulsory counterclaim. Regents of Univ. of N.M. v. Knight, 321 F.3d 1111, 1125 (Fed. Cir. 2003). In this case, suit was filed in state court, but the state court doesn't have jurisdiction over the counterclaim under the new version of 28 U.S.C. §1338. Defendants argue that this leaves them in an untenable situation — the state court can't hear their counterclaim, but they'll lose it if they don't bring it, and the federal court can't hear the case at all if UFRF is allowed to raise an Eleventh Amendment immunity defense. The way out of this, they argue, is to treat UFRF as having waived its immunity from suit in federal court and from the counterclaim, just as it would have had it originally filed in federal court.

There's some force to this argument. If a state entity brings a claim in state court knowing that it will trigger a compulsory counterclaim that is outside the jurisdiction of the state court, then it has in some sense voluntarily availed itself of a federal forum by setting in motion a series of events that will inevitably lead it to federal court. If it were clear in this case that Defendants' counterclaim is compulsory, there might be good reason to treat the initial act of bringing the suit to be a waiver of immunity. But it's not clear — the parties, in fact, hotly dispute this. Under these circumstances, treating UFRF's conduct as a waiver of immunity seems almost as unfair as effectively shutting the door on Defendants' counterclaim. As UFRF points out, an automatic waiver rule even when a counterclaim is not clearly compulsory would effectively force state entities to waive Eleventh Amendment immunity in any case involving patents by allowing defendants to "fil[e] merit-less counterclaims that relate to 'patent issues' not presently raised or contested by the sovereign." . . .

In sum, if Defendants' counterclaim is not compulsory, then in no sense has UFRF voluntarily submitted to a federal forum, and it is entitled to raise Eleventh Amendment immunity from suit as a defense. If Defendants' counterclaim is compulsory, then at least under these circumstances — where the compulsory nature is not so evident as to raise an inference that UFRF knew the counterclaim would have to be brought, leading inevitably to federal court — UFRF still cannot be said to have voluntarily submitted to a federal forum. Furthermore, the unfairness that Defendants worry about will not come to pass, as the impossibility of bringing their counterclaim in state court will prevent their failure to do so from having claim preclusive effect in federal court.

This result may seem odd — after all, it prevents the state court from overseeing the litigation of a counterclaim that it would normally require to be litigated. But the "interest in judicial economy" underlying a state's compulsory counterclaim rules "is . . . local in scope." Chapman v. Aetna Finance Co., 615 F.2d 361, 363 (5th Cir. 1980). The concerns underlying both the Eleventh Amendment and the federal courts' exclusive jurisdiction over patent disputes must trump these local concerns when they come into conflict.

CONCLUSION

UFRF is an arm of the state and is entitled to Eleventh Amendment immunity from suit in a federal forum. UFRF is here involuntarily. Therefore, this case must be remanded back to state court.

COVIDIEN v. UNIVERSITY OF FLORIDA RESEARCH FOUNDATION INCORPORATED

(USPTO Patent Trial and Appeal Board, January 25, 2017)

Before **KRISTEN L. DROESCH, BRYAN F. MOORE**, and **FRANCES L. IPPOLITO**, Administrative Patent Judges.

IPPOLITO, Administrative Patent Judge.

I. INTRODUCTION

On June 28, 2016, Covidien LP (Petitioner) filed three petitions seeking inter partes review of claims 1-18 of U.S. Patent No. 7,062,251 B2 (Exhibit 1001, "the '251 patent") pursuant to 35 U.S.C. §§311-19. IPR2016-01274, ("Pet."); IPR2016-01275, IPR2016-01276. . . .

This Decision addresses the issue of whether Patent Owner UFRF is entitled to Eleventh Amendment immunity defense to the institution of an inter partes review of the '251 patent.

For the reasons discussed below, we determine that Patent Owner UFRF, as an arm of the State of Florida, is entitled to a sovereign immunity defense to the institution of an inter partes review of the challenged patent. Further, we dismiss Petitioner's Petitions in IPR2016-01274, -01275, and -01276 because UFRF has successfully raised this defense in these proceedings.

II. BACKGROUND

By way of background, Patent Owner filed an action in the Circuit Court of the Eighth Judicial District in Florida, against Petitioner alleging breach of a license contract between the parties involving the '251 patent. In that suit, Petitioner responded with a counterclaim seeking a declaratory judgment that it does not infringe the '251 patent. On this basis, Petitioner successfully removed the state court suit to the United States District Court for the Northern District of Florida. See Univ. of Fla. Res. Found., Inc. v. Medtronic PLC, 2016 WL 3869877 (N.D. Fla. July 15, 2016) ("UFRF v. Medtronic"). Separately, Petitioner also filed three petitions requesting inter partes review of the '251 patent.

Following removal of its dispute to district court, Patent Owner argued there that it is an arm of the State of Florida through the University of Florida. On this basis, UFRF argued that it is entitled to Eleventh Amendment immunity from Petitioner's declaratory judgment counter-claim in the federal court. The District Court agreed with Patent Owner and remanded the action back to state court.

III. ANALYSIS

a. Sovereign Immunity in Administrative Proceedings

The Eleventh Amendment of the United States Constitution provides that the "Judicial power of the United States shall not be construed to extend to any suit in law or equity, commenced or prosecuted against one of the United States by Citizens of another State, or by Citizens or Subjects of any Foreign State." U.S. CONST. amend. XI. The Supreme Court has interpreted this amendment to encompass a broad principle of sovereign immunity, whereby the Eleventh Amendment limits not only the judicial authority of the federal courts to subject a state to an unconsented suit, but also precludes certain adjudicative administrative proceedings, depending on the nature of those proceedings, from adjudicating complaints filed by a private party against a nonconsenting State. Fed. Mar. Comm'n v South Carolina State Ports Auth., 535 U.S. 743, 753–761 (2002) ("FMC"); see also Vas-Cath, Inc. v. Curators of Univ. of Missouri, 473 F.3d 1376, 1383 (Fed. Cir. 2007).

Of particular relevance to our inquiry is the Supreme Court's decision in *FMC*. In *FMC*, South Carolina Maritime Services, Inc., a cruise ship company, filed a complaint against the South Carolina State Ports Authority (SCSPA) with the Federal Maritime Commission (Commission) seeking damages and injunctive relief from the SCSPA's repeated denials of Maritime Services' requests for permission to berth a cruise ship in the port facilities in Charleston, South Carolina. FMC, 535 U.S. at 747-749.

Maritime Services' Complaint was referred to an administrative law judge (ALJ) at the Commission for review. SCPSA moved to dismiss Maritime Services' Complaint because the "Constitution prohibits Congress from passing a statute authorizing Maritime Services to file this Complaint before the Commission and, thereby sue the State of South Carolina for damages and injunctive relief." *Id.* at 749. The ALJ handling the matter agreed with SCPSA and dismissed Maritime Services' Complaint. *Id.*

The Commission then performed its own review of the ALJ's dismissal and found that the doctrine of state sovereign immunity "is meant to cover proceedings before judicial tribunals, whether Federal or State, not executive branch administrative agencies like the Commission." *Id.* at 750.

SCSPA appealed the Commission's findings to the Fourth Circuit Court of Appeals. *Id.* In reversing the Commission's decision, the Fourth Circuit Court of Appeals reviewed the "precise nature" of the procedures employed by the Commission and determined that "the Commission's proceeding walks, talks, and squawks very much like a lawsuit and . . . its placement within the Executive Branch cannot blind us to the fact that the proceeding is truly an adjudication." *Id.* at 750-751.

At the Supreme Court, in a 5-4 majority decision, with Justice Thomas writing for the majority, the Supreme Court began with the sentiment that "[t]he Framers, who envisioned a limited Federal Government, could not have anticipated the vast growth of the administrative state." FMC, 535 U.S. at 755. The Court further explained that, in these circumstances, a "Hans presumption" of sovereign immunity may apply where "the Constitution was not intended to raise up any proceedings against the States that were anomalous and unheard of when the Constitution was adopted." *Id.* (citing Hans v. Louisiana, 132 U.S. 1, 18 (1890)). To decide whether the "Hans presumption" applies, the Supreme Court examined the nature of the

Commission's adjudication proceedings to "determine whether they are the type of proceedings from which the Framers would have thought the States possessed immunity when they agreed to enter the Union." *Id.* at 756. The Court further noted generally that there are numerous common features shared by administrative adjudications and judicial proceedings:

> Federal administrative law requires that agency adjudication contain many of the same safeguards as are available in the judicial process. The proceedings are adversary in nature. They are conducted before a trier of fact insulated from political influence. A party is entitled to present his case by oral or documentary evidence, and the transcript of testimony and exhibits together with the pleadings constitute the exclusive record for decision. The parties are entitled to know the findings and conclusions on all of the issues of fact, law, or discretion presented on the record. Ibid. (citations omitted).

Id. at 756-757.

The Court further observed that the similarities between the Commission's proceedings and civil litigation were "overwhelming." FMC, 535 U.S. at 759. For example, the Court found that the Commission's Rules of Practice and Procedure "bear a remarkably strong resemblance to civil litigation in federal courts" (e.g., similarity between the Commission's rules governing pleadings and discovery and the Federal Rules of Civil Procedure). *Id.* at 757-58.

Additionally, the Court found that the role of the ALJ assigned to hear cases at the Commission was similar to that of an Article III judge. *Id.* at 758-59. In particular, the ALJ prescribed the order in which evidence shall be presented; disposed of procedural requests or similar matters; heard and ruled upon motions; administered oaths and affirmations; examined witnesses; directed witnesses to testify or produce evidence available to them; ruled upon offers of proof; and disposed of any other matter that normally and properly arose in the course of proceedings. The Court noted the ALJ fixed the time and manner of filing briefs and issued a decision that included a statement of findings and conclusions, "as well as the reasons or basis therefor, upon all the material issues presented on the record, and the appropriate rule, order, section, relief, or denial thereof." *Id.* at 759. The Court added that the ALJ's ruling subsequently becomes the final decision of the Commission unless a party appeals to the Commission or the Commission decides to review the ALJ's decision "on its own initiative." *Id.* at 759.

Based on these similarities between the Commission's proceeding and civil litigation, the Court held that state sovereign immunity barred the Commission from adjudicating complaints filed by a private party against a nonconsenting State. *Id.* at 760. In doing so, the Court commented that

> if the Framers thought it an impermissible affront to a State's dignity to be required to answer the complaints of private parties in federal courts, we cannot imagine that they would have found it acceptable to compel a State to do exactly the same thing before the administrative tribunal of an agency, such as the FMC. The affront to a State's dignity does not lessen when an adjudication takes place in an administrative tribunal as opposed to an Article III court. In both instances, a State is required to defend itself in an adversarial proceeding against a private party before an impartial federal officer. Moreover, it would be quite strange to prohibit Congress from exercising its Article I

powers to abrogate state sovereign immunity in Article III judicial proceedings but permit the use of those same Article I powers to create court-like administrative tribunals where sovereign immunity does not apply.

Id. at 760-761.

b. Whether the FMC Decision Applies to Inter Partes Review Proceedings

As a threshold issue, Petitioner argues that the *FMC* decision does not apply to inter partes reviews because these proceedings are a mechanism for the Office to take "'a second look at an earlier administrative grant of a patent' — a federally-issued property right that would not exist but for the statutory provisions in the Patent Act." Petitioner asserts the Office may issue a patent only if it appears that the applicant is entitled to a patent under standards defined by federal law because a patent is "created by the act of Congress; and no rights can be acquired in it unless authorized by statute, and in the manner the statute prescribes. Further, according to Petitioner, "a patent owner takes a patent subject to the Patent Office's authority to review that property grant."

In this regard, Petitioner contends that the patent grant is not a private right but a *public right* subject to all statutory conditions for its grant. Petitioner further relies on MCM Portfolio LLC v. Hewlett-Packard Co., 812 F.3d 1284, 1289 (Fed. Cir. 2015), for the proposition that "because patent rights are public rights, 'their validity is susceptible to review by an administrative agency.'" Petitioner adds that the Office has conducted proceedings that correct or cancel issued patents for decades without "any suggestion that this authority would be limited by sovereign immunity."

Petitioner's arguments are unpersuasive. Petitioner does not cite to any case law, or persuasive authority otherwise, supporting its position that a state's Eleventh Amendment immunity may be limited or abrogated by a public rights exception. In *MCM*, Petitioner MCM argued that inter partes reviews are unconstitutional because any action revoking a patent must be tried in an Article III court with the protections of the Seventh Amendment. *MCM*, 812 F.3d at 1288. Disagreeing with Petitioner MCM, the Federal Circuit noted that the public rights exception allows Congress to delegate disputes over public rights to non-Article III courts. *Id.* at 1289. The Federal Circuit further noted that prior Federal Circuit precedents have held that "the issuance of a valid patent is primarily a public concern and involves a 'right that can only be conferred by the government even though validity often is brought into question in disputes between private parties." MCM, 812 F.3d at 1291.

Nonetheless, although the *MCM* decision held that inter partes reviews do not violate Article III or the right to a jury trial under the Seventh Amendment, this decision did not address the particular issue before us, which is whether inter partes reviews implicate the immunity afforded to a state by the Eleventh Amendment. Thus, Petitioner's arguments based on the public rights exception are unpersuasive.

Next, Petitioner argues that sovereign immunity is irrelevant to inter partes reviews because these proceedings are directed to the patent itself, and are not suits or adjudications of a private claim against the state by another party. Petitioner points to the fact that a patent owner is not subject to a monetary judgment in an inter partes review and that the Office may continue an inter partes review without the petitioner's participation. Petitioner further describes the federal government as the acting party in an inter parte review, and argues that a state entity cannot use sovereignty to prevent the federal government from bringing an action against it. In a separate section of its Opposition, Petitioner additionally analogizes inter partes reviews to in rem bankruptcy actions "in which jurisdiction of the adjudicating court or agency is predicated on the property such that the owner's sovereign immunity is irrelevant." In this context, Petitioner argues that the Office does not exercise jurisdiction over a patent owner in an inter partes review and the identity of the patent owner is irrelevant.

We do not agree that the *FMC* decision is inapplicable to inter partes reviews on this basis. First, in FMC, the Court observed that the type of relief sought is irrelevant to the issue of whether a suit is barred by the Eleventh Amendment. FMC, 535 U.S. at 765 (citing Seminole Tribe, 517 U.S. 44, 58 (1996). "While state sovereign immunity serves the important function of shielding state treasuries . . . the doctrine's central purpose is to accord the States the respect owed them as joint sovereigns. **It is for this reason, for instance, that sovereign immunity applies regardless of whether a private plaintiff's suit is for monetary damages or some other type of relief.**" *Id.* (internal citations omitted) (emphasis added).

Second, we are not persuaded that an inter partes review is an in rem action directed only to the patent and not against the patent owner. Initially, we observe that the term inter partes means between the parties, which in itself captures the notion that the proceeding is directed to both parties over whom the Board exercises jurisdiction. The statutes and rules governing inter partes reviews are consistent with this view. To start, the patent owner must be served with the petition for the petition to be considered "complete" and accorded a filing date. 37 C.F.R. §42.105 ("The petition and supporting evidence must be served on the patent owner at the correspondence address of record for the subject patent. The petitioner may additionally serve the petition and supporting evidence on the patent owner at any other address known to the petitioner as likely to effect service."); 37 C.F.R. §42.106 ("A petition to institute inter partes review will not be accorded a filing date until the petition satisfies all of the following requirements . . . (2) Effects service of the petition on the correspondence address of record as provided in §42.105(a).").

Moreover, the statutory framework of Leahy-Smith America Invents Act, Pub. L. No. 112–29, 125 Stat. 284, 331 (2011) (AIA or Patent Act) includes procedural safeguards against the harassment of patent owners through successive petitions by the same or related parties. . . .

Third, Petitioner's reliance on bankruptcy actions, such as those described in Tennessee Student Assistance Corp. v. Hood, 541 U.S. 440 (2004), is misplaced. In *Hood*, the Supreme Court reiterated the principle that a "bankruptcy court's in rem jurisdiction permits it to determine all claims that anyone, whether named in the action or not, has to the property or thing in question. The proceeding is one against the world [and] . . . [b]ecause the court's jurisdiction is premised on the res, however, a nonparticipating creditor cannot be subjected to personal liability." *Id.* at 448. In contrast, an inter partes review is not a proceeding "against the world," but directed to evaluating the validity of the patent owner's patent. This distinction is shown, for example, by the estoppel provisions in 37 C.F.R. §42.73(d)(3)(i)–(ii) following an adverse judgment against the patent owner. Specifically, Rule 73(d)(3)(i)–(ii) provides:

> (3) Patent applicant or owner. A patent applicant or owner is precluded from taking action inconsistent with the adverse judgment, including obtaining in any patent:

     (i) A claim that is not patentably distinct from a finally refused or canceled claim; or

     (ii) An amendment of a specification or of a drawing that was denied during the trial proceeding, but this provision does not apply to an application or patent that has a different written description.

    The effect of estoppel in this instance extends beyond the challenged patent at issue in the inter partes review to "any patent" that the patent owner may seek to obtain. Thus, the estoppel arising from an adverse judgment applies to a particular patent owner, not the world at large or otherwise.

    Fourth, we are not persuaded that an inter partes review is an action brought by the federal government against a state. In general, any "person other than the owner of the patent may petition the PTO for [inter partes] re-view." St. Jude Med., Cardiology Div., Inc. v. Volcano Corp., 749 F.3d 1373, 1374 (Fed. Cir. 2014). A petition for inter partes review must identify "each claim challenged, the grounds on which the challenge to each claim is based, and the evidence that supports the grounds for the challenge to each claim." 35 U.S.C. §312(a)(3). The patent owner may file a response to the petition, and the PTO must decide within three months after receiving that response whether to institute an inter partes review. 35 U.S.C. §314(b). The PTO may not institute an inter partes review unless "there is a reasonable likelihood that the petitioner would prevail with respect to at least 1 of the claims challenged in the petition."

    35 U.S.C. §314(a). After instituting inter partes review, the Board conducts the review on the merits. Unless the review is dismissed, the Board "shall issue a final written decision" addressing the patentability of the claims at issue in the proceeding. 35 U.S.C. §318(a). In this capacity, the Board's role in the inter partes review is not unlike that of the Commission in FMC (see FMC, 535 U.S. at 764), which is to assess the merits of the arguments presented by the parties in an impartial manner.

    Thus, based on the foregoing, we determine that the analysis in FMC applies to the present issue before us. With the decision in FMC as guidance, we next examine whether an inter partes review is the type of proceeding from which the Framers would have thought the states possessed immunity.

c. FMC Analysis Applied to Inter Partes Review

    In its Motion, Patent Owner argues that an inter partes review is an adjudicatory agency proceeding that meets all the requirements evaluated in FMC for sovereign immunity to apply. Referring to legislative history, Patent Owner argues that when inter partes reviews replaced inter partes reexaminations, Congress intended to convert inter partes reexamination from an examinational to an adjudicative proceeding. Patent Owner adds that Congress required the Director to promulgate regulations for inter partes review proceedings that "enact many features common to judicial proceedings, including discovery, depositions, protective orders, the imposition of sanctions, and an oral hearing."

    Patent Owner argues that, under the enacted rules, inter partes review is similar to civil litigation for several reasons. This, according to Patent Owner, is because inter partes reviews are adversarial "contested cases between a patent owner and a petitioner in which the petitioner bears the burden of proof and initiates the proceeding by filing a petition requesting the institut[ion of] a trial.". Patent Owner argues that inter partes reviews are routinely held before panels of three impartial administrative patent judges (APJs), immune from political influence, who serve a role functionally comparable to that of an Article III judge, including ruling on proffers of evidence, regulating the course of the proceeding, exercising independent judgment and having the power to compel testimony.

Further, Patent Owner argues that inter partes reviews are governed by pleadings similar to those in civil litigation that include the petition, patent owner's preliminary response, and post-institution patent owner's response. Patent Owner notes that inter partes reviews provide for discovery through which parties "can seek subpoenas for documents and witness testimony, which are governed by the Federal Rules of Civil Procedure. Similarly, Patent Owner asserts that evidence provided in an inter partes review is governed by the Federal Rules of Evidence.

In its Opposition, Petitioner responds that there are several meaningful differences between inter partes review and civil litigation. Specifically, Petitioner argues inter partes review differs from district court litigation because: (1) the only remedy in an inter partes review is cancellation of claims; (2) there is no personal jurisdiction requirement over the patent owner; (3) an inter partes review may be requested by any person regardless of whether they have any stake in the outcome of the proceeding; (4) inter partes reviews are like patent examinations because a patent owner has an opportunity to amend its claims; (5) the discovery rights and obligations in inter partes review are limited compared to those available in district court litigation; (6) inter partes review and district court proceedings employ different stands of proof; and (7) the pleading standard of "reasonable likelihood" is higher in an inter partes review for the institution of a proceeding.

To start, we are not persuaded by Petitioner's argument that the absence of monetary and injunctive relief matters for our determination of whether sovereign immunity applies. "[S]overeign immunity applies regardless of whether a private plaintiff's suit is for monetary damages or some other type of relief." *FMC*, 535 U.S. at 766 (internal citations omitted) (emphasis added). We are also not persuaded by Petitioner's argument that there is no personal jurisdiction over the Patent Owner. As discussed above, an inter partes review is an action against the patent owner, who as a party, may suffer the consequences of an adverse judgment for failing to respond to the petition.

In considering the nature of an inter partes review in the context of the *FMC* analysis, we are not persuaded by Petitioner that the differences in pleadings, discovery, relief, standards, and jurisdictional and standing requirements effectively distinguish inter partes reviews from civil litigation for the purposes of applying sovereign immunity. As Patent Owner discerns, inter partes reviews are adversarial "contested cases between a patent owner and a petitioner in which the petitioner bears the burden of proof and initiates the proceeding by filing a petition requesting the institution of a trial." In 2011, Congress overhauled and expanded the PTO's processes for reconsidering the patentability of such claims. See AIA §6. Enacted in response to "a growing sense that questionable patents are too easily obtained and are too difficult to challenge," H.R. Rep. No. 98, 112th Cong., 1st Sess. Pt. 1, at 39 (2011) (2011 House Report), the AIA replaced inter partes reexamination with inter partes review, an adversarial proceeding before the new Patent Trial and Appeal Board (PTAB or Board). Congress created inter partes review to "establish a more efficient and streamlined patent system that will improve patent quality and limit unnecessary and counterproductive litigation costs." 2011 House Report at 40.

Moreover, we note that the Board rules and procedures governing inter partes review resemble civil litigation in federal courts. The petitioner takes the first step to initiate an inter partes review proceeding by requesting review of a challenged patent through the filing of a petition, which in nature is similar to a complaint filed in civil litigation, and not unlike that at issue in *FMC*. A petition for inter partes review must identify "each claim challenged, the grounds on which the challenge to each claim is based, and the evidence that supports the grounds for the challenge to each claim." 35 U.S.C. §312(a)(3). The patent owner may file a preliminary response to the petition, and, in some circumstances, may be permitted to file a motion to dismiss the petition (which was authorized in the instant proceeding) prior to the Board's decision on whether to institute an inter partes review. 35 U.S.C. §313; see 37 C.F.R. §42.5(a). Post-institution, a patent owner may file a patent owner's response to the petition addressing any ground for unpatentability not already denied. 37 C.F.R. §42.120.

After instituting inter partes review, the Board conducts a review on the merits. During the proceeding, the parties may conduct discovery and submit additional briefing that includes, for example, a patent owner response and petitioner's reply to the patent owner's response. See 37 C.F.R. §§42.23, 42.51–42.53, 42.120. The parties may also engage in motion practice whereby the parties must obtain authorization from the Board to file motions unless otherwise pre-authorized by the rules, statutes, etc. pertaining to the proceeding. 37 C.F.R. §42.20(b); 37 C.F.R. §42.64(c), 37 C.F.R. §42.121

In the way of discovery, the procedures of an inter partes review are similar, but limited in scope, to those in federal court litigation. The parties are entitled to "routine discovery" that includes production of "any exhibit cited in a paper or in testimony must be served with the citing paper or testimony," cross-examination of affidavit testimony prepared for the proceeding, and "information that is inconsistent with a position advanced by the party during the proceeding concurrent with the filing of the documents or things that contains the inconsistency." 37 C.F.R. §42.51 (1)(i)–(iii). "Additional discovery" may be obtained by agreement between the parties, or through a showing by a moving party that "such additional discovery is in the interests of justice." 37 C.F.R. §42.51(2).

Like civil litigation, discovery may be compelled in an inter partes review. 35 U.S.C. §24; see 37 C.F.R. §§42.52 (a), 42.53(a). Through §24, the Board may "issue a subpoena for any witness residing or being within such district, commanding him to appear and testify before an officer in such district authorized to take depositions and affidavits, at the time and place stated in the subpoena." 35 U.S.C. §24. Additionally, "[t]he provisions of the Federal Rules of Civil Procedure relating to the attendance of witnesses and to the production of documents and things shall apply to contested cases in the Patent and Trademark Office." *Id.* (emphasis added). Further, the Board may issue sanctions against a party for violation of discovery rules, procedures, and orders. See 37 C.F.R. §42.12. In addition, the Federal Rules of Evidence also apply to inter partes review with the exception of portions relating to criminal proceedings, juries, and other matters not relevant to proceedings under this subpart shall not apply. 37 C.F.R. §42.62(b).

Inter partes reviews, like civil litigation, also provide for the protection of confidential information covered by a protective order. 37 C.F.R. §42.54; see Practice Guide at 48,760 ("Confidential information: The rules identify confidential information in a manner consistent with Federal Rule of Civil Procedure 26(c)(1)(G), which provides for protective orders for trade secret or other confidential research, development, or commercial information.").

However, this protection is limited. If a final written decision in an inter partes review substantively relies on information in a sealed document, the document may be unsealed by an Order of the Board. If any sealed document contains no information substantively relied on in the final written decision, the document may be expunged from the record by an Order of the Board. 37 C.F.R. §42.56.

There are also notable similarities between the role of the APJs in an inter partes review and that of an Article III judge in civil litigation. In an inter partes review, APJs serve as impartial officers designated, on behalf of the Director, to review the petition and preliminary response (if submitted) to determine whether the petitioner has demonstrated a "reasonable likelihood" of prevailing on the grounds of unpatentability presented in the petition. See 35 U.S.C. §314. When an inter partes review is instituted, APJs issue a scheduling order setting due dates for each party to take action in the proceeding. During the course of the proceeding, APJs apply standards and procedures for discovery of relevant evidence; hear and rule upon motions; dispose of procedural requests or similar matters; prescribe, if necessary, sanctions for abuse of discovery, abuse of process, or any other improper use of the proceeding; and issue a final written decision with respect to the patentability of any patent claim challenged by the petitioner and any new claim added under section 316(d). 35 U.S.C. §§316, 318; see also 37 C.F.R. §42.20(a) ("Relief, other than a petition requesting the institution of a trial, must be requested in the form of a motion."), §42.21(a) ("The Board may require a party to file a notice stating the relief it requests and the basis for its entitlement to relief."), §42.21(b) ("The Board may set the times and conditions for filing and serving notices required under this section.").

On the whole, considering the nature of inter partes review and civil litigation, we conclude that the considerable resemblance between the two is sufficient to implicate the immunity afforded to the States by the Eleventh Amendment. Although there are distinctions, such as in the scope of discovery, we observe that there is no requirement that the two types of proceedings be identical for sovereign immunity to apply to an administrative proceeding. Further, we note that there are several similarities between civil litigation and inter partes review that are not unlike those compared in *Vas-Cath* for interferences. As discussed, in *Vas-Cath*, the Federal Circuit noted that:

> Like proceedings in the Federal Maritime Commission, contested interference proceedings in the PTO bear "strong similarities" to civil litigation, and the administrative proceeding can indeed be characterized as a lawsuit. **PTO interferences involve adverse parties, examination and cross- examination by deposition of witnesses, production of documentary evidence, findings by an impartial federal adjudicator, and power to implement the decision. See, e.g., 37 C.F.R. §1.651(a) (during an interference, "an administrative patent judge shall set a time for filing motions (§1.635), for additional discovery under §1.687(c) and testimony period for taking any necessary testimony."); §1.671(a) ("Evidence [for an interference] consists of affidavits, transcripts of depositions, documents and things."); §1.671(b) ("[T]he Federal Rules of Evidence shall apply to interference proceedings" except "[t]hose portions of the Federal Rules of Evidence relating to criminal actions, juries, and other matters not relevant to interferences.").**

Vas-Cath, 473 F.3d at 1382 (citation omitted) (emphasis added). While Petitioner contends that interference proceedings are "fundamentally" different from inter partes reviews, we, nevertheless, discern that the manner of discovery, adversarial nature of the proceeding, role of the APJ, and the applicability of the Federal Rules of Evidence in an inter partes review largely mirrors that involved in an interference proceeding. . . .

Petitioner additionally argues that "immunizing patents owned by alleged state entities from IPR proceedings would have harmful and far- reaching consequences." Here, Petitioner's arguments are three-fold. One, invalid patents would stand simply because they are assigned to a state entity. Two, a patent owned by a monetization foundation affiliated with a state university would be insulated from the inter partes review process. Three, determining whether an entity is entitled to sovereign immunity is a fact-intensive inquiry that the Patent Office is not designed to adjudicate.

With respect to the first two arguments, we are cognizant of the fact that applying an Eleventh Amendment immunity to inter partes review, absent waiver by the state entity, precludes the institution of inter partes review against a state entity entitled to Eleventh Amendment immunity.

This, indeed, is precisely the point of the Eleventh Amendment, which is the preservation of the dignity afforded to sovereign states. "The preeminent purpose of state sovereign immunity is to accord States the dignity that is consistent with their status as sovereign enti- ties." FMC, 535 U.S. at 760 (citing In re Ayers, 123 U.S. 443, 505 (1887)). When sovereign immunity conflicts with legislation, Congress may abrogate sovereign immunity if it has unequivocally expressed its intent to abrogate the immunity and has acted pursuant to a valid exercise of power. Seminole Tribe, 517 U.S. at 55. Petitioner does not point to, and we do not find there is, an unequivocal, express intent by Congress in the AIA to abrogate immunity for the purposes of inter partes review.

Further, we are not persuaded that an application of sovereign immunity to inter partes review will do violence to the patent system. The Supreme Court in Florida Prepaid Postse- condary Education Expense Board v. College Savings Bank, 527 U.S. 627 (1999) held that Congress does not have authority to abrogate Eleventh Amendment immunity with respect to patent infringement by the States, for "Congress identified no pattern of patent infringement by the States, let alone a pattern of constitutional violations." Id. at 640. Based on the record before us, there is no evidence that the harm to the patent system, described by the Petitioner, will come to pass, let alone exists as a basis to divest States of sovereign immunity.

Finally, we are not persuaded that our tribunal cannot perform the fact-finding duties that Petitioner alleges would be required to determine whether an entity is entitled to sovereign immunity. Our rules and procedures provide for discovery and motion practice which, at a minimum, would provide the parties an opportunity to present arguments and supporting evidence pertaining to sovereign immunity.

Thus, we are persuaded that Eleventh Amendment immunity bars the institution of an inter partes review against an unconsenting state that has not waived sovereign immunity.

d. UFRF is an Arm of the State of Florida

[In this section, the PTAB followed the analysis as seen in University of Florida Research Foundation, Inc. v. Medtronic PLC, Medtronic, Inc., 2016 WL 3869877 (N.D. Florida July 15, 2016)]

. . .

Thus, based on the facts before us, we agree with Patent Owner that the UFRF is an arm of the State of Florida.

IV. CONCLUSION

For the foregoing reasons, we conclude that Eleventh Amendment immunity applies to inter partes review proceedings, and that UFRF, having shown it is an arm of the State of Florida, is entitled to assert its sovereign immunity as a defense to the institution of an inter partes review of the '251 patent. Accordingly, the Petitions in IPR2016-01274, -01275, and -01276 are dismissed.

PATENT LICENSE AGREEMENT

THIS Agreement is between the Board of Regents ("Board") of The University of _____ System ("System"), an agency of the State of _____, whose address is _____ Texas, and _____, a _____ corporation having a principal place of business located at _____ ("Licensee").

Table of Contents

RECITALS

SIGNATURES

RECITALS

A. Board owns certain Patent Rights and Technology Rights related to Licensed Subject Matter, which were developed at The University of Texas _____ ("University"), a component institution of System.

B. Board desires to have the Licensed Subject Matter developed and used for the benefit of Licensee, Inventor, Board, and the public as outlined in Board's Intellectual Property Policy.

C. Licensee wishes to obtain a license from Board to practice Licensed Subject Matter.

NOW, THEREFORE, in consideration of the mutual covenants and premises herein contained, the parties agree as follows:

1. EFFECTIVE DATE

This Agreement is effective _____ ("Effective Date").

2. DEFINITIONS

As used in this Agreement, the following terms have the meanings indicated:

2.1 **"Affiliate"** means any business entity more than 50% owned by Licensee, any business entity which owns more than 50% of Licensee, or any business entity that is more than 50% owned by a business entity that owns more than 50% of Licensee.

2.2 **"Licensed Field"** means _____.

2.3 **"Licensed Product"** means any product Sold by Licensee comprising Licensed Subject Matter pursuant to this Agreement.

2.4 **"Licensed Subject Matter"** means inventions and discoveries covered by Patent Rights or Technology Rights within Licensed Field.

2.5 **"Licensed Territory"** means the _____.

2.6 **"Net Sales"** means the gross revenues received by Licensee from the Sale of Licensed Products less sales and/or use taxes actually paid, import and/or export duties actually paid, outbound transportation prepaid or allowed, and amounts allowed or credited due to returns (not to exceed the original billing or invoice amount).

2.7 **"Patent Rights"** means Board's rights in information or discoveries covered by patents and patent applications whether domestic or foreign, and all divisions, continuations, continuations-in-part, reissues, reexaminations or extensions thereof, and any letters patent that issue thereon, which name _____ as either sole or joint inventor ("Inventor") and which relate to the manufacture, use or sale of _____.

2.8 **"Sale, Sell or Sold"** means the transfer or disposition of a Licensed Product for value to a party other than Licensee.

2.9 **"Technology Rights"** means Board's rights in technical information, know-how, processes, procedures, compositions, devices, methods, formulas, protocols, techniques, software, designs, drawings or data created by _____

(Inventor) at University before the Effective Date relating to _____
(Name of Technology) which are not covered by Patent Rights but which are
necessary for practicing the invention covered by Patent Rights.

3. WARRANTY: SUPERIOR RIGHTS

3.1 Except for the rights, if any, of the Government of the United States, as set forth below, Board represents and warrants its belief that (i) it is the owner of the entire right, title, and interest in and to Licensed Subject Matter, (ii) it has the sole right to grant licenses thereunder, and (iii) it has not knowingly granted licenses thereunder to any other entity that would restrict rights granted to Licensee except as stated herein.

3.2 Licensee understands that the Licensed Subject Matter may have been developed under a funding agreement with the Government of the United States of America and, if so, that the Government may have certain rights relative thereto. This Agreement is explicitly made subject to the Government's rights under any agreement and any applicable law or regulation. If there is a conflict between an agreement, applicable law or regulation and this Agreement, the terms of the Government agreement, applicable law or regulation shall prevail.

3.3 Licensee understands and acknowledges that Board, by this Agreement, makes no representation as to the operability or fitness for any use, safety, efficacy, ability to obtain regulatory approval, patentability, and/or breadth of the Licensed Subject Matter. Board, by this Agreement, also makes no representation as to whether there are any patents now held, or which will be held, by others or by Board in the Licensed Field, nor does Board make any representation that the inventions contained in Patent Rights do not infringe any other patents now held or that will be held by others or by Board.

3.4 Licensee, by execution hereof, acknowledges, covenants and agrees that it has not been induced in any way by Board, System, University or its employees to enter into this Agreement, and further warrants and represents that (i) it has conducted sufficient due diligence with respect to all items and issues pertaining to this Article 3 and all other matters pertaining to this Agreement; and (ii) Licensee has adequate knowledge and expertise, or has utilized knowledgeable and expert consultants, to adequately conduct the due diligence, and agrees to accept all risks inherent herein.

4. LICENSE

4.1 Board hereby grants to Licensee a royalty-bearing, exclusive license under Licensed Subject Matter to manufacture, have manufactured, and/or sell Licensed Products within the Licensed Territory for use within Licensed Field. This grant is subject to the payment by Licensee to Board of all consideration as provided herein, and is further subject to rights retained by Board to:

    a. Publish the general scientific findings from research related to Licensed Subject Matter subject to the terms of Section 13, Confidential Information; and

b. Use Licensed Subject Matter for research, teaching and other educationally-related purposes.

4.2 Licensee may extend the license granted herein to any Affiliate if the Affiliate consents to be bound by this Agreement to the same extent as Licensee.

4.3 Licensee may grant sublicenses consistent with this Agreement if Licensee is responsible for the operations of its sublicensees relevant to this Agreement as if the operations were carried out by Licensee, including the payment of royalties whether or not paid to Licensee by a sublicensee. Licensee must deliver to Board a true and correct copy of each sublicense granted by Licensee, and any modification or termination thereof, within 30 days after execution, modification, or termination. When this Agreement is terminated, all existing sublicenses granted by Licensee must be assigned to Board.

5. PAYMENT AND REPORT

5.1 In consideration of rights granted by Board to Licensee under this Agreement, Licensee will pay Board the following:

a. A nonrefundable license documentation fee in the amount of $_____, due and payable when this Agreement is executed by Licensee;

b. An annual license reissue fee in the amount of $_____, due and payable on each anniversary of the Effective Date beginning on the first anniversary;

c. A running royalty equal to _____% of Net Sales for Licensed Products sold by Licensee and protected by a valid claim included within Patent Rights; and

d. A minimum yearly royalty of $_____ beginning 1 year after approval of the first Sale or offer for Sale of a Licensed Product by the Food and Drug Administration or a comparable foreign regulatory authority.

5.2 In consideration of rights granted by Board to Licensee under this Agreement, Licensee further agrees to pay Board the following after the execution of a sublicense hereunder:

a. Within 30 days after the execution of the sublicense, a sublicense fee of _____% of any up-front cash payment made to Licensee in consideration of the sublicense, excluding funds paid to Licensee for research and development purposes, or $_____, whichever is more;

b. Within 30 days after the execution of the sublicense, a sublicense fee constituting a cash payment equal to 10% of any non-cash consideration received by Licensee from a sublicensee, such consideration to include, without limitation, equity in other companies or equity investments in Licensee. The value of an equity investment will be calculated as the average market value of the class of stock involved for 5 consecutive days preceding the execution of the sublicense agreement. In cases where the sublicense agreement calls for payment to Licensee of a premium over the market value, Board will also share 10% of the premium paid to Licensee; and

c. One half of the gross revenue royalty payments received on Net Sales of Licensed Products received by Licensee from any sublicensee.

5.3 During the Term of this Agreement and for 1 year thereafter, Licensee agrees to keep complete and accurate records of its and its sublicensees' Sales and Net Sales of Licensed Products under the license granted in this Agreement in sufficient detail to enable the royalties payable hereunder to be determined. Licensee agrees to permit Board or its representatives, at Board's expense, to periodically examine its books, ledgers, and records during regular business hours for the purpose of and to the extent necessary to verify any report required under this Agreement. If the amounts due to Board are determined to have been underpaid, Licensee will pay the cost of the examination and accrued interest at the highest allowable rate.

5.4 Within 30 days after March 31, June 30, September 30, and December 31, beginning immediately after the Effective Date, Licensee must deliver to Board a true and accurate written report, even if no payments are due Board, giving the particulars of the business conducted by Licensee and its sublicensee(s), if any exist, during the preceding 3 calendar months under this Agreement as are pertinent to calculating payments hereunder. This report will include at least:

a. the quantities of Licensed Subject Matter that it has produced;

b. the total Sales;

c. the calculation of royalties thereon; and

d. the total royalties computed and due Board.

Simultaneously with the delivery of each report, Licensee must pay to Board the amount, if any, due for the period of each report.

5.5 On or before each anniversary of the Effective Date, irrespective of having a first Sale or offer for Sale, Licensee must deliver to Board a written progress report as to Licensee's (and any sublicensee's) efforts and accomplishments during the preceding year in diligently commercializing Licensed Subject Matter in the Licensed Territory and Licensee's (and, if applicable, sublicensee's) commercialization plans for the upcoming year.

5.6 All amounts payable here by Licensee must be paid in United States funds without deductions for taxes, assessments, fees, or charges of any kind. Checks must be payable to [Component name and address].

5.7 Licensee must reimburse Board for all its out-of-pocket expenses thus far incurred in filing, prosecuting, enforcing and maintaining exclusively licensed

Patent Rights and must pay all future expenses so long as and in the countries its license remains exclusive.

6. COMMON STOCK: EQUITY OWNERSHIP

[NOTE: We advise you to contact an outside counsel with expertise in corporate and securities law before completing this article.]

6.1 In consideration of the rights granted to Licensee by Board in this Agreement, Licensee will, upon execution of this Agreement, issue Board _____ fully paid, non-assessable shares of its common stock (equaling _____% of all shares of its common stock), at $_____ par value.

6.2 Board will name directors to serve on the board of directors of Licensee in proportion to the number of shares held by Board relative to the total number of issued shares, however Board will always have at least one seat on Licensee's board.

6.3 In addition, Licensee hereby grants Board a 1 year option, exercisable in its sole discretion, to purchase up to an additional _____ shares of its common stock at a fixed purchase price of $_____ per share upon the same general terms and conditions as are applicable to the other purchasers of the stock. Board may exercise its option to purchase all or part of the optioned shares, by providing Licensee 60 days written notice, specifying the number of shares it wants to purchase and the proposed date of purchase.

7. TERM AND TERMINATION

7.1 The term of this Agreement is from the Effective Date to the full end of the term or terms for which Patent Rights have not expired or, if only Technology Rights are licensed and no Patent Rights are applicable, for a term of 15 years.

7.2 Any time after 2 years from the Effective Date, Board and University have the right to terminate the exclusivity of this license in any national political jurisdiction in the Licensed Territory if Licensee, within 90 days after receiving written notice from University of intended termination of exclusivity, fails to provide written evidence satisfactory to University that Licensee or its sublicensees has commercialized or is actively attempting to commercialize a licensed invention in such jurisdiction(s).

7.3 Any time after 3 years from the Effective Date, Board and University have the right to terminate this license in any national political jurisdiction in the Licensed Territory if Licensee, within 90 days after receiving written notice from University of intended termination, fails to provide written evidence satisfactory to University that Licensee or its sublicensees has commercialized or is actively attempting to commercialize a licensed invention in such jurisdiction(s).

7.4 The following definitions apply to Article 7: (i) "Commercialize" means having Sales of Licensed Products in such jurisdiction; and (ii) "Active attempts to commercialize" means having Sales of Licensed Products or an effective, ongoing and active research, development, manufacturing, marketing or sales program as appropriate, directed toward obtaining regulatory approval, production or Sales of Licensed Products in any jurisdiction, and plans acceptable to University, in its sole discretion, to commercialize licensed inventions in the jurisdiction(s) that University intends to terminate.

7.5 This Agreement will earlier terminate:

a. automatically if Licensee becomes bankrupt or insolvent and/or if the business of Licensee is placed in the hands of a receiver, assignee, or trustee, whether by voluntary act of Licensee or otherwise; or

b. upon 30 days' written notice from Board if Licensee breaches or defaults on its obligation to make payments (if any are due) or reports, in accordance with the terms of Article 5, unless, before the end of the 30-day period, Licensee has cured the default or breach and so notifies Board, stating the manner of the cure; or

c. upon 90 days' written notice if Licensee breaches or defaults on any other obligation under this Agreement, unless, before the end of the 90-day period, Licensee has cured the default or breach and so notifies Board, stating the manner of the cure; or

d. at any time by mutual written agreement between Licensee, University and Board, upon 180 days' written notice to all parties and subject to any terms herein which survive termination; or

e. under the provisions of Paragraphs 7.2 and 7.3 if invoked.

7.6 If this Agreement is terminated for any cause:

a. nothing herein will be construed to release either party of any obligation matured prior to the effective date of the termination;

b. after the effective date of the termination, Licensee may sell all Licensed Products and parts therefor it has on hand at the date of termination, if it pays earned royalties thereon according to the terms of Article 5; and

c. Licensee will be bound by the provisions of Articles 11 (Indemnification), 12 (Use of Board and Component's Name), and 13 (Confidential Information) of this Agreement.

8. INFRINGEMENT BY THIRD PARTIES

8.1 Licensee, at its expense, must enforce any patent exclusively licensed hereunder against infringement by third parties and it is entitled to retain recovery from such enforcement. Licensee must pay Board a royalty on any monetary recovery if the monetary recovery is for damages or a reasonable royalty in lieu thereof. If Licensee does not file suit against a substantial infringer of a patent within 6 months of knowledge thereof, then Board may enforce any patent licensed hereunder on behalf of itself and Licensee, Board retaining all recoveries from such enforcement and/or reducing the license granted hereunder to non-exclusive.

8.2 In any infringement suit or dispute, the parties agree to cooperate fully with each other. At the request and expense of the party bringing suit, the other party will permit access to all relevant personnel, records, papers, information, samples, specimens, etc., during regular business hours.

9. ASSIGNMENT

Except in connection with the sale of substantially all of Licensee's assets to a third party, this Agreement may not be assigned by Licensee without the prior written consent of Board, which will not be unreasonably withheld.

10. PATENT MARKING

Licensee must permanently and legibly mark all products and documentation manufactured or sold by it under this Agreement with a patent notice as may be permitted or required under Title 35, United States Code.

11. INDEMNIFICATION AND INSURANCE

11.1 Licensee agrees to hold harmless and indemnify Board, System, University, its Regents, officers, employees and agents from and against any claims, demands, or causes of action whatsoever, including without limitation those arising on account of any injury or death of persons or damage to property caused by, or arising out of, or resulting from, the exercise or practice of the license granted hereunder by Licensee, its Affiliates or their officers, employees, agents or representatives.

11.2 In no event shall Board be liable for any indirect, special, consequential or punitive damages (including, without limitation, damages for loss of profits or expected savings or other economic losses, or for injury to persons or property) arising out of or in connection with this Agreement or its subject matter, regardless of whether Board knows or should know of the possibility of such damages.

11.3 Insurance

    a. Beginning at the time when any Licensed Subject Matter is being distributed or sold (including for the purpose of obtaining regulatory approvals) by Licensee or by a sublicensee, Licensee shall, at its sole cost and expense, procure and maintain commercial general liability insurance in amounts not less than $2,000,000 per incident and $2,000,000 annual aggregate, and Licensee shall use reasonable efforts to have the Board, System, University, its Regents, officers, employees and agents named as additional insureds. Such commercial general liability insurance shall provide (i) product liability coverage; (ii) broad form contractual liability coverage for Licensee's indemnification under this Agreement; and (iii) coverage for litigation costs. The minimum amounts of insurance coverage required shall not be construed to create a limit of Licensee's liability with respect to its indemnification under this Agreement.

b. Licensee shall provide Board with written evidence of such insurance upon Board's request. Licensee shall provide Board with written notice of at least fifteen (15) days prior to the cancellation, non-renewal or material change in such insurance.

c. Licensee shall maintain such commercial general liability insurance beyond the expiration or termination of this Agreement during (i) the period that any Licensed Subject Matter developed pursuant to this Agreement is being commercial distributed or sold by Licensee or by a sublicensee or agent of Licensee; and (ii) the five (5) year period immediately after such period.

12. USE OF BOARD AND COMPONENT'S NAME

Licensee may not use the name of University, System or Board without express written consent.

13. CONFIDENTIAL INFORMATION AND PUBLICATION

13.1 Board and Licensee each agree that all information contained in documents marked "confidential" and forwarded to one by the other (i) be received in strict confidence, (ii) be used only for the purposes of this Agreement, and (iii) not be disclosed by the recipient party, its agents or employees without the prior written consent of the other party, except to the extent that the recipient party can establish competent written proof that such information:

a. was in the public domain at the time of disclosure;

b. later became part of the public domain through no act or omission of the recipient party, its employees, agents, successors or assigns;

c. was lawfully disclosed to the recipient party by a third party having the right to disclose it;

d. was already known by the recipient party at the time of disclosure;

e. was independently developed by the recipient; or

f. is required by law or regulation to be disclosed.

13.2 Each party's obligation of confidence hereunder shall be fulfilled by using at least the same degree of care with the other party's confidential information as it uses to protect its own confidential information. This obligation shall exist while this Agreement is in force and for a period of 3 years thereafter.

13.3 University will submit its manuscript for any proposed publication of research related to Licensed Subject Matter to Licensee at least 30 days before publication, and Licensee shall have the right to review and comment upon the publication in order to protect Licensee's confidential information. Upon Licensee's request, publication will be delayed up to 60 additional days to enable Licensee to secure adequate intellectual property protection of Licensee's property that would be affected by the publication.

14. PATENTS AND INVENTIONS

14.1 If after consultation with Licensee, both parties agree that a patent application should be filed for Licensed Subject Matter, Board will prepare and file the appropriate patent applications, and Licensee will pay the cost of searching, preparing, filing, prosecuting and maintaining same. If Licensee notifies Board that it does not intend to pay the cost of an application, or if Licensee does not respond or make an effort to agree with Board on the disposition of rights in the subject invention, then Board may file an application at its own expense and Licensee will have no rights to the invention. Board will provide Licensee a copy of any patent application for which Licensee has paid the cost of filing, as well as copies of any documents received or filed with the respective patent office during the prosecution thereof.

15. ALTERNATIVE DISPUTE RESOLUTION

15.1 Any dispute or controversy arising out of or relating to this Agreement, its construction or its actual or alleged breach will be decided by mediation. If the mediation does not result in a resolution of such dispute or controversy, it will be finally decided by an appropriate method of alternative dispute resolution, including without limitation, arbitration, conducted in the city of _____, Texas in accordance with the Commercial Dispute Resolution Procedures of the American Arbitration Association. The arbitration panel will include members knowledgeable in the evaluation of _____ technology. Judgment upon the award rendered may be entered in the highest court or forum having jurisdiction, state or federal. The provisions of this Article 15 will not apply to decisions on the validity of patent claims or to any dispute or controversy as to which any treaty or law prohibits such arbitration. The decision of the arbitration must be sanctioned by a court of law having jurisdiction to be binding upon and enforceable by the parties.

16. GENERAL

16.1 This Agreement constitutes the entire and only agreement between the parties for Licensed Subject Matter and all other prior negotiations, representations, agreements, and understandings are superseded hereby. No agreements altering or supplementing the terms hereof may be made except by a written document signed by both parties.

16.2 Any notice required by this Agreement must be given by prepaid, first class, certified mail, return receipt requested and addressed to:
UNIVERSITY
[Address]

or in the case of Licensee to:_____
ATTENTION: _____
FAX: _____
PHONE: _____

or other addresses as may be given from time to time under the terms of this notice provision.

16.3 Licensee must comply with all applicable federal, state and local laws and regulations in connection with its activities pursuant to this Agreement.

16.4 This Agreement will be construed and enforced in accordance with the laws of the United States of America and of the State of Texas.

16.5 Failure of Board to enforce a right under this Agreement will not act as a waiver of that right or the ability to later assert that right relative to the particular situation involved.

16.6 Headings are included herein for convenience only and shall not be used to construe this Agreement.

16.7 If any part of this Agreement is for any reason found to be unenforceable, all other parts nevertheless remain enforceable.

IN WITNESS WHEREOF, parties hereto have caused their duly authorized representatives to execute this Agreement.

BOARD OF REGENTS OF THE
UNIVERSITY _____ SYSTEM

LICENSEE _____

_____

_____
Administrative Officer or Designee

_____

Approved as to Content:
By:_____
Name:_____
Date:_____

* * *

NIH Simple Letter Agreement for the Transfer of Materials (for Materials Leaving the University)

In response to the RECIPIENT's request for the MATERIAL [insert description] the PROVIDER asks that the RECIPIENT and the RECIPIENT SCIENTIST agree to the following before the RECIPIENT receives the MATERIAL:

1. The above MATERIAL is the property of the PROVIDER and is made available as a service to the research community.

2. THIS MATERIAL IS NOT FOR USE IN HUMAN SUBJECTS.

3. The MATERIAL will be used for teaching or not-for-profit research purposes only.

4. The MATERIAL will not be further distributed to others without the PROVIDER's written consent. The RECIPIENT shall refer any request for the MATERIAL to the PROVIDER. To the extent supplies are available, the PROVIDER or the PROVIDER SCIENTIST agree to make the MATERIAL available, under a separate Simple Letter Agreement to other scientists for teaching or not-for-profit research purposes only.

5. The RECIPIENT agrees to acknowledge the source of the MATERIAL in any publications reporting use of it.

6. Any MATERIAL delivered pursuant to this Agreement is understood to be experimental in nature and may have hazardous properties. THE PROVIDER MAKES NO REPRESENTATIONS AND EXTENDS NO WARRANTIES OF ANY KIND, EITHER EXPRESSED OR IMPLIED. THERE ARE NO EXPRESS OR IMPLIED WARRANTIES OF MERCHANTABILITY OR FITNESS FOR A PARTICULAR PURPOSE, OR THAT THE USE OF THE MATERIAL WILL NOT INFRINGE ANY PATENT, COPYRIGHT, TRADEMARK, OR OTHER PROPRIETARY RIGHTS. Unless prohibited by law, RECIPIENT assumes all liability for claims for damages against it by third parties which may arise from the use, storage or disposal of the MATERIAL except that, to the extent permitted by law, the PROVIDER shall be liable to the RECIPIENT when the damage is caused by the gross negligence or willful misconduct of the PROVIDER.

7. The RECIPIENT agrees to use the MATERIAL in compliance with all applicable statutes and regulations.

8. The MATERIAL is provided at no cost, or with an optional transmittal fee solely to reimburse the PROVIDER for its preparation and distribution costs. If a fee is requested, the amount will be indicated here: [insert fee] _____

The PROVIDER, RECIPIENT and RECIPIENT SCIENTIST must sign both copies of this letter and return one signed copy to the PROVIDER. The PROVIDER will then send the MATERIAL.

PROVIDER INFORMATION and AUTHORIZED SIGNATURE

Provider Scientist: _____
Provider Organization: _____

Address: _____

Name of Authorized Official: _____
Title of Authorized Official: _____

Certification of Authorized Official: This Simple Letter Agreement _____ has / _____ has not [check one] been modified. If modified, the modifications are attached.

_____   _____
Signature of Authorized Official   Date

RECIPIENT INFORMATION and AUTHORIZED SIGNATURE

Recipient Scientist: _____
Recipient Organization: _____

Address: _____

Name of Authorized Official: _____
Title of Authorized Official: _____

Signature of Authorized Official/Date Signed: _____
                                                    /_____

Certification of Recipient Scientist: I have read and understood the conditions outlined in this Agreement and I agree to abide by them in the receipt and use of the MATERIAL.
Recipient Scientist:
Date:

_____

*   *   *

Uniform BioMaterial Transfer Agreement
(for Materials Coming into the University)

UBMTA Implementing Letter

The purpose of this letter is to provide a record of the biological material transfer, to memorialize the agreement between the PROVIDER SCIENTIST (identified below) and the RECIPIENT SCIENTIST (identified below) to abide by all terms and conditions of the Uniform Biological Material Transfer Agreement ("UBMTA") March 8, 1995, and to certify that the RECIPIENT (identified below) organization has accepted and signed an unmodified copy of the UBMTA. The RECIPIENT organization's Authorized Official also will sign this letter if the RECIPIENT SCIENTIST is not authorized to certify on behalf of the RECIPIENT organization. The RECIPIENT SCIENTIST (and the Authorized Official of RECIPIENT, if necessary) should sign both copies of this letter and return one signed copy to the PROVIDER. The PROVIDER SCIENTIST will forward the material to the RECIPIENT SCIENTIST upon receipt of the signed copy from the RECIPIENT organization. This Implementing Letter is effective when signed by all parties. The parties executing this Implementing Letter certify that their respective organizations have accepted and signed an unmodified copy of the UBMTA, and further agree to be bound by its terms, for the transfer specified above. Please fill in all of the blank lines below:

- Original Material (Enter Description): [description]
- Optional Termination Date: [date]
- Optional Transmittal Fee (to reimburse the PROVIDER for preparation and distribution costs): [Amount]

- PROVIDER (Organization providing the ORIGINAL MATERIAL):

Name of Organization:
Street Address:
City/State/ZIP:

- PROVIDER SCIENTIST:

Name and Title:
Street Address:
City/State/ZIP:
Signature:
Date:

- RECIPIENT SCIENTIST:

Name and Title:
Street Address:
City/State/ZIP:
Signature:
Date:

- RECIPIENT ORGANIZATION CERTIFICATION (Organization receiving the ORIGINAL MATERIAL):

Name and Title:
Street Address:
City/State/ZIP:
Signature:
Date:

* * *

Upon execution of an Implementing Letter in the form attached which specifies the materials to be transferred, this organization agrees to be bound by the terms of the attached Uniform Biological Material Transfer Agreement ("UBMTA") published in the Federal Register on March 8, 1995.

Attachments:
UBMTA
Implementing Letter
Organization:
Address:
Authorized Official:
Title:
Signature:
Date:

Please return an executed copy of this Master Agreement to: The UBMTA Project, Association of University Technology Managers (AUTM), 111 Deer Lake Rd., Suite 100, Deerfield, IL 60015. AUTM will be maintaining signed originals and the official list of signatory organizations.

The Uniform Biological Material Transfer Agreement
March 8, 1995

I. Definitions:

1. PROVIDER: Organization providing the ORIGINAL MATERIAL. The name and address of this party will be specified in an implementing letter.
2. PROVIDER SCIENTIST: The name and address of this party will be specified in an implementing letter.
3. RECIPIENT: Organization receiving the ORIGINAL MATERIAL. The name and address of this party will be specified in an implementing letter.
4. RECIPIENT SCIENTIST: The name and address of this party will be specified in an implementing letter.
5. ORIGINAL MATERIAL: The description of the material being transferred will be specified in an implementing letter.
6. MATERIAL: ORIGINAL MATERIAL, PROGENY, and UNMODIFIED DERIVATIVES. The MATERIAL shall not include: (a) MODIFICATIONS, or (b) other substances created by the RECIPIENT through the use of the MATERIAL which are not MODIFICATIONS, PROGENY, or UNMODIFIED DERIVATIVES.
7. PROGENY: Unmodified descendant from the MATERIAL, such as virus from virus, cell from cell, or organism from organism.
8. UNMODIFIED DERIVATIVES: Substances created by the RECIPIENT which constitute an unmodified functional subunit or product expressed by the ORIGINAL MATERIAL. Some examples include: subclones of unmodified cell lines, purified or fractionated subsets of the ORIGINAL MATERIAL, proteins expressed by DNA/RNA supplied by the PROVIDER, or monoclonal antibodies secreted by a hybridoma cell line.
9. MODIFICATIONS: Substances created by the RECIPIENT which contain/incorporate the MATERIAL.
10. COMMERCIAL PURPOSES: The sale, lease, license, or other transfer of the MATERIAL or MODIFICATIONS to a for-profit organization. COMMERCIAL PURPOSES shall also include uses of the MATERIAL or MODIFICATIONS by any organization, including RECIPIENT, to perform contract research, to screen compound libraries, to produce or manufacture products for general sale, or to conduct research activities that result in any sale, lease, license, or transfer of the MATERIAL or MODIFICATIONS to a for-profit organization. However, industrially sponsored academic research shall not be considered a use of the MATERIAL or MODIFICATIONS for COMMERCIAL PURPOSES per se, unless any of the above conditions of this definition are met.
11. NONPROFIT ORGANIZATION(S): A university or other institution of higher education or an organization of the type described in section 501(c)(3) of the Internal Revenue Code of 1954 (26 U.S.C. 501(c)) and exempt from taxation under section 501(a) of the Internal Revenue Code (26 U.S.C. 501(a)) or any

nonprofit scientific or educational organization qualified under a state nonprofit organization statute. As used herein, the term also includes government agencies.

II. Terms and Conditions of This Agreement:

1. The PROVIDER retains ownership of the MATERIAL, including any MATERIAL contained or incorporated in MODIFICATIONS.
2. The RECIPIENT retains ownership of: (a) MODIFICATIONS (except that, the PROVIDER retains ownership rights to the MATERIAL included therein), and (b) those substances created through the use of the MATERIAL or MODIFICATIONS, but which are not PROGENY, UNMODIFIED DERIVATIVES or MODIFICATIONS (i.e., do not contain the ORIGINAL MATERIAL, PROGENY, UNMODIFIED DERIVATIVES). If either 2(a) or 2(b) results from the collaborative efforts of the PROVIDER and the RECIPIENT, joint ownership may be negotiated.
3. The RECIPIENT and the RECIPIENT SCIENTIST agree that the MATERIAL:
   (a) is to be used solely for teaching and academic research purposes;
   (b) will not be used in human subjects, in clinical trials, or for diagnostic purposes involving human subjects without the written consent of the PROVIDER;
   (c) is to be used only at the RECIPIENT organization and only in the RECIPIENT SCIENTIST's laboratory under the direction of the RECIPIENT SCIENTIST or others working under his/her direct supervision; and
   (d) will not be transferred to anyone else within the RECIPIENT organization without the prior written consent of the PROVIDER.
4. The RECIPIENT and the RECIPIENT SCIENTIST agree to refer to the PROVIDER any request for the MATERIAL from anyone other than those persons working under the [Page 12774] RECIPIENT SCIENTIST's direct supervision. To the extent supplies are available, the PROVIDER or the PROVIDER SCIENTIST agrees to make the MATERIAL available, under a separate implementing letter to this Agreement or other agreement having terms consistent with the terms of this Agreement, to other scientists (at least those at NONPROFIT ORGANIZATION(S)) who wish to replicate the RECIPIENT SCIENTIST's research; provided that such other scientists reimburse the PROVIDER for any costs relating to the preparation and distribution of the MATERIAL.
5. (a) The RECIPIENT and/or the RECIPIENT SCIENTIST shall have the right, without restriction, to distribute substances created by the RECIPIENT through the use of the ORIGINAL MATERIAL only if those substances are not PROGENY, UNMODIFIED DERIVATIVES, or MODIFICATIONS.
   (b) Under a separate implementing letter to this Agreement (or an agreement at least as protective of the PROVIDER's rights), the RECIPIENT may distribute MODIFICATIONS to NONPROFIT ORGANIZATION(S) for research and teaching purposes only.
   (c) Without written consent from the PROVIDER, the RECIPIENT and/or the RECIPIENT SCIENTIST may NOT provide MODIFICATIONS for

COMMERCIAL PURPOSES. It is recognized by the RECIPIENT that such COMMERCIAL PURPOSES may require a commercial license from the PROVIDER and the PROVIDER has no obligation to grant a commercial license to its ownership interest in the MATERIAL incorporated in the MODIFICATIONS. Nothing in this paragraph, however, shall prevent the RECIPIENT from granting commercial licenses under the RECIPIENT's intellectual property rights claiming such MODIFICATIONS, or methods of their manufacture or their use.

6. The RECIPIENT acknowledges that the MATERIAL is or may be the subject of a patent application. Except as provided in this Agreement, no express or implied licenses or other rights are provided to the RECIPIENT under any patents, patent applications, trade secrets or other proprietary rights of the PROVIDER, including any altered forms of the MATERIAL made by the PROVIDER. In particular, no express or implied licenses or other rights are provided to use the MATERIAL, MODIFICATIONS, or any related patents of the PROVIDER for COMMERCIAL PURPOSES.

7. If the RECIPIENT desires to use or license the MATERIAL or MODIFICATIONS for COMMERCIAL PURPOSES, the RECIPIENT agrees, in advance of such use, to negotiate in good faith with the PROVIDER to establish the terms of a commercial license. It is understood by the RECIPIENT that the PROVIDER shall have no obligation to grant such a license to the RECIPIENT, and may grant exclusive or non-exclusive commercial licenses to others, or sell or assign all or part of the rights in the MATERIAL to any third party(ies), subject to any pre-existing rights held by others and obligations to the Federal Government.

8. The RECIPIENT is free to file patent application(s) claiming inventions made by the RECIPIENT through the use of the MATERIAL but agrees to notify the PRO-VIDER upon filing a patent application claiming MODIFICATIONS or method(s) of manufacture or use(s) of the MATERIAL.

9. Any MATERIAL delivered pursuant to this Agreement is understood to be experimental in nature and may have hazardous properties. The PROVIDER MAKES NO REPRESENTATIONS AND EXTENDS NO WARRANTIES OF ANY KIND, EITHER EXPRESSED OR IMPLIED. THERE ARE NO EXPRESS OR IMPLIED WARRANTIES OF MERCHANTABILITY OR FITNESS FOR A PARTICULAR PURPOSE, OR THAT THE USE OF THE MATERIAL WILL NOT INFRINGE ANY PATENT, COPYRIGHT, TRADEMARK, OR OTHER PROPRIETARY RIGHTS.

10. Except to the extent prohibited by law, the RECIPIENT assumes all liability for damages which may arise from its use, storage or disposal of the MATERIAL. The PROVIDER will not be liable to the RECIPIENT for any loss, claim or demand made by the RECIPIENT, or made against the RECIPIENT by any other party, due to or arising from the use of the MATERIAL by the RECIPIENT, except to the extent permitted by law when caused by the gross negligence or willful misconduct of the PROVIDER.

11. This agreement shall not be interpreted to prevent or delay publication of research findings resulting from the use of the MATERIAL or the

MODIFICATIONS. The RECIPIENT SCIENTIST agrees to provide appropriate acknowledgement of the source of the MATERIAL in all publications.

12. The RECIPIENT agrees to use the MATERIAL in compliance with all applicable statutes and regulations, including Public Health Service and National Institutes of Health regulations and guidelines such as, for example, those relating to research involving the use of animals or recombinant DNA.

13. This Agreement will terminate on the earliest of the following dates: (a) when the MATERIAL becomes generally available from third parties, for example, though reagent catalogs or public depositories, or (b) on completion of the RECIPIENT's current research with the MATERIAL, or (c) on thirty (30) days' written notice by either party to the other, or (d) on the date specified in an implementing letter, provided that:

   (a) if termination should occur under 13(a), the RECIPIENT shall be bound to the PROVIDER by the least restrictive terms applicable to the MATERIAL obtained from the then-available resources; and

   (b) if termination should occur under 13(b) or (d) above, the RECIPIENT will discontinue its use of the MATERIAL and will, upon direction of the PRO-VIDER, return or destroy any remaining MATERIAL. The RECIPIENT, at its discretion, will also either destroy the MODIFICATIONS or remain bound by the terms of this agreement as they apply to MODIFICATIONS; and

   (c) in the event the PROVIDER terminates this Agreement under 13(c) other than for breach of this Agreement or for cause such as an imminent health risk or patent infringement, the PROVIDER will defer the effective date of termination for a period of up to one year, upon request from the RECIPIENT, to permit completion of research in progress. Upon the effective date of termination, or if requested, the deferred effective date of termination, RECIPIENT will discontinue its use of the MATERIAL and will, upon direction of the PROVIDER, return or destroy any remaining MATERIAL. The RECIPIENT, at its discretion, will also either destroy the MODIFICATIONS or remain bound by the terms of this agreement as they apply to MODIFICATIONS.

14. Paragraphs 6, 9, and 10 shall survive termination.

15. The MATERIAL is provided at no cost, or with an optional transmittal fee solely to reimburse the PROVIDER for its preparation and distribution costs. If a fee is requested by the PROVIDER, the amount will be indicated in an implementing letter.

IV. PROBLEMS AND DRAFTING EXERCISES

1. What are some concerns associated with a university granting exclusive licenses in patents to a third party? How would you draft the exclusive license grant provision to address the concerns?

2. How does the Bayh-Dole Act stimulate university research? Who owns the invention in government-funded research? How are benefits derived from inventions distributed among players?

3. Use the sample University Patent License Agreement in the Materials section above to answer these questions:

    3.1 Who owns the patents?

    3.2 Who pays for the procurement of patents?

    3.3 What is the duration of the license? What is the scope of the license?

    3.4 Does the Patent License Agreement address the university researcher's (the inventor's) rights and interests?

4. Why did Stanford University rely on the Bayh-Dole Act in its arguments for ownership of the patents in Stanford University v. Roche Molecular Systems, Inc.? Draft a new grant provision for the Stanford University's Copyright and Patent Agreement to avoid the problems faced by the university in Stanford University v. Roche Molecular Systems, Inc.

5. You are an attorney for Xenon Pharmaceutical, Inc. Xenon does not want to pay sublicensing fees to the University of Wisconsin. Draft a new grant provision for the Exclusive License Agreement between Wisconsin Alumni Research Foundation and Xenon Pharmaceuticals, Inc.

6. AsymmetRx learned a difficult lesson in AsymmetRx, Inc. v. Biocare Medical, LLC, 582 F.3d 1314 (Fed. Cir. 2009). You are an attorney for AsymmetRx. You negotiate with attorneys from Harvard for the exclusive rights in the commercial diagnostic field. You want to make sure that AsymmetRx can bring infringement litigation against others in the future. Draft a new grant provision for the patent agreement between Harvard and AssymetRx to avoid the problems that arose in the 2009 court decision.

7. Draft a new license agreement on behalf of the University of Alabama in its dealing with Mr. Moore. Please note that the University would like to avoid the problems discussed in University of Alabama v. New Life Arts, Inc.

8. Assume that no "teacher exception" exists to the Copyright Act's work for hire doctrine. Draft an assignment or license agreement that gives professors copyright ownership or rights equivalent to ownership of the professor's scholarly works.

· CHAPTER ·
13

INTELLECTUAL PROPERTY AND GOVERNMENT CONTRACTS

I. OVERVIEW OF GOVERNMENT CONTRACTS IN THE ACQUISITION OF INTELLECTUAL PROPERTY

A. Introduction

The federal government has a long history of partnering with the private sector to develop innovations and technology. In 1802, Thomas Jefferson on behalf of the government placed the first order for the domestic refining of saltpeter, an ingredient in gunpowder, with a new Delaware manufacturing company called E.I. du Pont. On or about September 9, 1908, at Fort Myer, Virginia, Orville Wright flew the first Wright plane made under a $25,000 government contract with the U.S. Army Signal Corps for 62 minutes, completing 57 circles at an altitude of 36.6 meters. Government contracts have also led to the development of items as diverse as Superglue, Tang, and the Internet.

Historically, when the federal government used tax dollars to pay for the creation of intellectual property, it demanded ownership of the intellectual property. This was due to the government's responsibility to enter into agreements as a trustee for the proper expenditure of taxpayer dollars. Over time, however, this requirement of government ownership became counterproductive. Many innovators avoided contracting with the government because they did not want to give up ownership of their intellectual property. The innovators were willing to give the government a license but not outright ownership. Accordingly, Congress re-drafted statutes and agencies re-drafted regulations to recalibrate the rights between the federal government and its contractors with respect to ownership and licensing of intellectual property. *See* Bayh-Dole Act, 35 U.S.C. §§200-212 (1980); 10 U.S.C. §§2320 and 2321; 41 U.S.C. §§2302 and 4703; *see also* Campbell Plastics Eng'g & Mfg., Inc. v. Brownlee, 389 F.3d 1243 (Fed. Cir. 2004) (this case can be found in the Materials section of this chapter).

Specifically, the U.S. Congress passed the Competition in Contracting Act, Pub. L. No. 98-369, 98 Stat. 1175 (1984), to reduce the economic risks historically encountered by federal contractors who performed work for the government involving intellectual property and technical data. *See generally* FAR Part 27 (governing procurements by civilian agencies) and DFARS Part 227 (governing procurements by defense agencies). In lieu of standard contract clauses and licenses that effectively stripped contractors of their rights and competitive positions with respect to their intellectual property, the federal government initiated greater use of nontraditional, flexible binding instruments to facilitate mutually beneficial partnerships for the development of dual use technologies.

While switching to more flexible contract and licensing vehicles is the federal government's policy, these agreements represent wholly distinct transactions than a standard commercial license for the use of intellectual property. Government contracts are comprised of a combination of standard and alternate provisions and contract clauses. The proper allocation of rights in intellectual property depends on (1) when the intellectual property was developed — either before the performance of a government contract or during the performance of a government contract (the standard applicable to procurements with civilian agencies); (2) whether the intellectual property was privately funded or funded in whole or in part at government expense (the standard applicable to procurements with defense agencies); (3) whether the intellectual property is available commercially (applicable to procurements with both civilian and defense agencies); (4) the type of licenses that correspond to the time of performance, the funding of intellectual property, and the commercial or noncommercial nature of the intellectual property (generally applicable to procurements with both civilian and defense agencies); and (5) at times, consideration of the respective interests of the government and its contractors.

B. Acquisition of Intellectual Property by the Government

The government may hold title to patents as well as seek to license/use patentable inventions. The government may also seek to license a contractor's technical data, thus allowing the government to access recorded information of a scientific, technical, or confidential nature to help it understand critical elements of procured technology. The government may also seek to license computer software. In seeking technical data and computer software, the government may also need to secure copyright assignments or permissions. Regardless of what the government seeks to acquire, its policy is to only obtain its minimum needs — nothing more and nothing less. Therefore, the government will balance its interests with those of its contractors by reviewing the type of intellectual property it needs, the method of funding of the intellectual property, and the commercial or noncommercial nature of the intellectual property. The following sections describe, in general terms, how ownership and licensing work in the government acquisition of rights in patents, technical data, computer software, and copyrighted works.

C. Patents

The policies, procedures, solicitation provisions, and contract clauses pertaining to inventions made in the performance of work under a Government contract or subcontract for experimental, developmental, or research work are found in the Federal Acquisition Regulation (FAR) 27.3 (provision) and 52.227-11 (contract clause). The FAR sets forth the government's policy to respect patent holders' rights in existing patents and also to promote the commercialization of patentable results made during the performance of a government contract by granting to all contractors the title to patents made, in whole or in part, with federal funds, in exchange for royalty-free use by or on behalf of the government. The government may hold title to a patent, may seek use of a patentable invention through licensing, or may grant authorization and consent for a government contractor to use another's patent for the benefit of the government. The latter two examples listed above represent voluntary and compulsory licensing, respectively.

The patent rights provisions and clauses grant the government license/use rights only if the invention is either conceived or first actually reduced to practice during contract performance. The exact time of invention and the public/private funding determination support the policy that the government should not have to pay royalties twice for its use of a patentable invention that tax dollars helped to develop. Regardless, if the government must use another's patent and no license/use rights exist, the government may authorize and consent to another contractor's patent infringement in order for the government to obtain desired goods, services, or research for the United States, with appropriate royalties paid to the patent holder in a suit against the government in the Court of Federal Claims for such a taking. *See* 28 U.S.C. §1498; *see also* Hutchinson Indus., Inc. v. Accuride Corp., 2010 WL 1379720 (D.N.J.) (this case can be found in the Materials section of this chapter).

Notwithstanding its license/use rights, the government may obtain title to an invention pursuant to its policy to disclose inventions in a timely manner as well as pursuant to its march-in rights. Along similar lines, to the extent provided in the patent rights clause, the government has the right to receive title to an invention when the contractor has not pursued invention disclosure or patent application filing. The government is entitled to exercise its march-in rights and receive title to an invention if the contractor refuses to practice an invention or license an invention after negotiation of reasonable terms. March-in rights are authorized to be exercised only after the contractor has been provided a reasonable time to present facts and show cause why the proposed agency action should not be taken, and afforded an opportunity to take appropriate action if the contractor wishes to dispute or appeal the proposed action. *See* FAR 27.302(f) (provision) and 52.227-11(h) (contract clause).

Once rights in the subject invention are established and the contractor retains title, the government has the right to a license to be used to further the public interest. The FAR exclusively governs the scope of the license grant for patents.[1] Specifically, the government must receive at least a non-exclusive, nontransferable, irrevocable, paid-up

---

1. With respect to patent regulations only, defense agencies follow FAR Part 27 and the various applicable contract clauses, which are supplemented by defense specific contract clauses found in DFARS 252.227.

license to practice, or have practiced for or on behalf of the United States, any subject invention throughout the world. In addition, it may, if provided in the contract, have additional rights to sub-license to any foreign government or international organization pursuant to existing treaties or agreements identified in the contract, or to otherwise effectuate such treaties or agreements. To illustrate, an abridged version of FAR 52.227-11 appears below:

PATENT RIGHTS – OWNERSHIP BY THE CONTRACTOR (May. 2014)

(a) As used in this clause –
"Invention" means any invention or discovery that is or may be patentable or otherwise protectable under title 35 of the U.S. Code, or any variety of plant that is or may be protectable under the Plant Variety Protection Act (7 U.S.C. 2321, *et seq.*)
"Made" means –

(1) When used in relation to any invention other than a plant variety, the conception or first actual reduction to practice of the invention; or

(2) When used in relation to a plant variety, that the Contractor has at least tentatively determined that the variety has been reproduced with recognized characteristics. . . .

"Practical application" means to manufacture, in the case of a composition of product; to practice, in the case of a process or method, or to operate, in the case of a machine or system; and, in each case, under such conditions as to establish that the invention is being utilized and that is benefits are, to the extent permitted by law or Government regulations, available to the public on reasonable terms.

"Subject invention" means any invention of the Contractor made in the performance of work under this contract.

(b) *Contractor's rights.*

(1) *Ownership.* The Contractor may retain ownership of each subject invention throughout the world in accordance with the provisions of this clause.

(2) *License.*

(i) The Contractor shall retain a nonexclusive royalty-free license throughout the world in each subject invention to which the Government obtains title, unless the Contractor fails to disclose the invention within the times specified in paragraph (c) of this clause. The Contractor's license extends to any domestic subsidiaries and affiliates within the corporate structure of which the Contractor is a part, and includes the right to grant sublicenses to the extent the Contractor was legally obligated to do so at contract award. The license is transferable only with the written approval of the agency, except when transferred to the successor of that part of the Contractor's business to which the invention pertains.

(ii) The Contractor's license may be revoked or modified by the agency to the extent necessary to achieve expeditious practical application of the subject invention in a particular country in accordance with the procedures in FAR 27.302(i)2 and 27.304(f).

(c) *Contractor's obligations.*

(1) The Contractor shall disclose in writing each subject invention to the Contracting Officer within 2 months after the inventor discloses it in writing to Contractor personnel responsible for patent matters. The disclosure shall identify the inventor(s) and this contract under which the subject invention was made. It shall be sufficiently complete in technical detail to convey a clear understanding of the subject invention. The disclosure shall also identify any publication, on sale (i.e., sale or offer for sale), or public use of the subject invention, or whether a manuscript describing the subject invention has been submitted for publication and, if so, whether it has been accepted for publication. In addition, after disclosure to the agency, the Contractor shall promptly notify the Contracting Officer of the acceptance of any manuscript describing the subject invention for publication and any on sale or public use.

(2) The Contractor shall elect in writing whether or not to retain ownership of any subject invention by notifying the Contracting Officer within 2 years of disclosure to the agency. However, in any case where publication, on sale, or public use has initiated the 1-year statutory period during which valid patent protection can be obtained in the United States, the period for election of title may be shortened by the agency to a date that is no more than 60 days prior to the end of the statutory period.

(3) The Contractor shall file either a provisional or a nonprovisional patent application or a Plant Variety Protection Application on an elected subject invention within 1 year after election. However, in any case where a publication, on sale, or public use has initiated the 1-year statutory period during which valid patent protection can be obtained in the United States, the Contractor shall file the application prior to the end of that statutory period. If the Contractor files a provisional application, it shall file a nonprovisional application within 10 months of the filing of the provisional application. The Contractor shall file patent applications in additional countries or international patent offices within either 10 months of the first filed patent application (whether provisional or nonprovisional) or 6 months from the date permission is granted by the Commissioner of Patents to file foreign patent applications where such filing has been prohibited by a Secrecy Order.

(4) The Contractor may request extensions of time for disclosure, election, or filing under paragraphs (c)(1), (c)(2), and (c)(3) of this clause.

(d) *Government's rights —*

(1) *Ownership.* The Contractor shall assign to the agency, on written request, title to any subject invention —

(i) If the Contractor fails to disclose or elect ownership to the subject invention within the times specified in paragraph (c) of this clause, or elects not to retain ownership; provided, that the agency may request title only within 60 days after learning of the Contractor's failure to disclose or elect within the specified times.

(ii) In those countries in which the Contractor fails to file patent applications within the times specified in paragraph (c) of this clause; provided, however, that if the Contractor has filed a patent application in a country after the times specified in paragraph (c) of this clause, but prior to its receipt of the written request of the agency, the Contractor shall continue to retain ownership in that country.

(iii) In any country in which the Contractor decides not to continue the prosecution of any application for, to pay the maintenance fees on, or defend in reexamination or opposition proceeding on, a patent on a subject invention.

(2) *License.* If the Contractor retains ownership of any subject invention, the Government shall have a nonexclusive, nontransferable, irrevocable, paid-up license to practice, or have practiced for or on its behalf, the subject invention throughout the world.

(e) *Contractor action to protect the Government's interest.*

(1) The Contractor shall execute or have executed and promptly deliver to the agency all instruments necessary to —

(i) Establish or confirm the rights the Government has throughout the world in those subject inventions in which the Contractor elects to retain ownership; and

(ii) Assign title to the agency when requested under paragraph (d) of this clause and to enable the Government to obtain patent protection and plant variety protection for that subject invention in any country.

(2) The Contractor shall require, by written agreement, its employees, other than clerical and nontechnical employees, to disclose promptly in writing to personnel identified as responsible for the administration of patent matters and in the Contractor's format, each subject invention in order that the Contractor can comply with the disclosure provisions of paragraph (c) of this clause, and to execute all papers necessary to file patent applications on subject inventions and to establish the Government's rights in the subject inventions. The disclosure format should require, as a minimum, the information required by paragraph (c)(1) of this clause. The Contractor shall instruct such employees, through employee agreements or other suitable educational programs, as to the importance of reporting inventions in sufficient time to permit the filing of patent applications prior to U.S. or foreign statutory bars.

(3) The Contractor shall notify the Contracting Officer of any decisions not to file a nonprovisional patent application, continue the prosecution of a patent application, pay maintenance fees, or defend in a reexamination or opposition proceeding on a patent, in any country, not less than 30 days before the expiration of the response or filing period required by the relevant patent office.

(4) The Contractor shall include, within the specification of any United States nonprovisional patent or plant variety protection application and any patent or plant variety protection certificate issuing thereon covering a subject invention, the following statement, "This invention was made with Government support under (identify the contract) awarded by (identify the agency). The Government has certain rights in the invention." . . .

(h) *March-in rights.* The Contractor acknowledges that, with respect to any subject invention in which it has retained ownership, the agency has the right to require licensing pursuant to 35 U.S.C. 203 and 210(c), and in accordance with the procedures in 37 CFR 401.6 and any supplemental regulations of the agency in effect on the date of contract award.

D. Technical Data

The government honors the rights in data resulting from private developments and limits its demands for such rights to those essential for government purposes. One type of deliverable that the government frequently acquires is technical data. Technical data is recorded information, regardless of the form or method of recording, of a scientific or technical nature.

Technical data is extremely important to the government, in particular to the Department of Defense (DOD),[2] because the government must be in the position to maintain and repair supplies, services, and construction that it obtains under government contracts. In fulfilling its mission, DOD must often secure all of the detailed design information for technologies in order to maximize the agency's ability to use the technology without delay or restriction. Access to technical data ensures interoperability and integration of legacy and cutting-edge systems, without suffering potential margins of error due to reliance on private contractor capability to ensure systems integration. In addition, access to technical data guarantees that DOD will have the technical and legal ability to maintain and repair systems in the event of emergencies and ensures that DOD can support its deployed technologies when commercial support is unavailable, thereby leading to longer lifecycles for technology. Finally, technical data accomplishes the government's policy goal to promote full and open competition. When the government possesses technical data it can conduct competitive reprocurements of supplies, services, and construction.

The FAR uses the general data rights clause to acquire use rights in noncommercial technical data when the procurement is with civilian agencies. *See* FAR 27.4 (provision) and 52.227-14 (contract clause). For government contracts with civilian agencies, the pivotal question in determining the government's license rights in the contractor's technical data will be whether the technical data was first produced during the performance of a government contract, as opposed to previously developed before performance of the government contract. Two types of license rights are envisioned under the FAR general data rights clause — unlimited rights and limited/restricted rights. Generally, the government receives an unlimited rights license in a civilian government contract governed by FAR 52.227-14 when the technical data is first produced in the performance of a government contract. Unlimited rights entitle the government to use,

---

2. Unlike the uniform regulations governing patents, civilian and defense agencies have their own respective regulations that apply to the acquisition and/or license of rights in technical data, computer software, and copyrights. The American Bar Association, Public Contract Law Section has criticized the lack of consistency, for example, between FAR regulations and DFARS regulations dealing with the government's policies on data rights.

disclose, reproduce, prepare derivative works, distribute copies to the public, and perform publicly and display publicly technical data, in any manner and for any purpose, and to have or permit others to do so. In contrast, previously developed technical data allows the contractor to withhold such data and restrict the government's use of limited rights data as prescribed by a government-contractor negotiated license grant provision.

The DFARS establishes a detailed matrix for what data rights clauses to use in defense contracts let by military agencies. *See* DFARS 227.7103-5 (provision). Pursuant to the DFARS, the pivotal questions that determine the government's license rights are (1) who funded the development of the item, component, or process to which the data relates and (2) whether the contractor's technical data is commercial or noncommercial. The standard license rights in noncommercial technical data that a contractor grants to the government are "unlimited rights," "government purpose rights," or "limited rights." In unusual circumstances, the standard rights may not satisfy the government's needs or the government may be willing to accept lesser rights in data in return for other consideration. In those cases, a special license may be negotiated.

When DOD obtains an unlimited rights license, it can use the contractor's technical data and permit others to use data to the same extent. When DOD and other contractors receive the data pursuant to unlimited rights, they have the right to use, disclose, reproduce, prepare derivative works, distribute copies to the public, and perform publicly and display publicly technical data, in any manner and for any purpose. *See* DFARS 227.7103-5(a) (provision) and 252.227-7013 (contract clause).

Generally, the government will obtain a government purpose rights license in technical data that was produced with mixed funding, i.e., both the government and the contractor contributed to the creation of the technical data relating to developmental items. When an item, component, or process is developed with mixed funding, the government may use, modify, release, reproduce, perform, display, or disclose the data pertaining to such items, components, or processes within the government without restriction, but may release or disclose the data outside the government only for government purposes. *See* DFARS 227.7103-5(b) (provision) and 252.227-7013 (contract clause). Once presumptively five years, now the period during which government purpose rights are effective is negotiable.

When technical data is produced at private expense, the contractor typically confines the government to receiving a limited rights license. Regulations define limited rights as the rights of the government in limited rights data. Data in which the government has limited rights may not be used, released, or disclosed outside the government without the permission of the contractor asserting the restriction except for a use, release, or disclosure that is necessary for emergency repair and overhaul; or to a foreign government when use, release, or disclosure is in the interest of the United States and is required for evaluation or information purposes. *See* DFARS 227.7103-5(c) (provision) and 252.227-7013 (contract clause).

Finally, pursuant to the DFARS, commercial items and the data pertaining to them are presumed to be developed at private expense. As such, the government's rights to technical data pertaining to commercial items are in line with the rights of the general public. Stated another way, when the government is procuring technical data in the commercial marketplace, it should be treated, to the maximum extent practicable, as just another commercial customer. *See* DFARS 227.7102-2 (provision) and 252.227-7015 (contract clause).

E. Computer Software

As with technical data, the regulations governing the procurement of computer software will differ between civilian and military agencies. The FAR, however, does not distinguish between technical data and computer software. Thus, both are governed by FAR 52.227-14 when determining the types of license rights the government will receive, i.e., unlimited rights or restricted rights in relation to either technical data or computer software (as a matter of semantics, the term restricted rights, as opposed to limited rights, is used in the regulations to express the rights in computer software).

In contrast to the FAR, the DFARS treats technical data and computer software in separate provisions; it specifically articulates definitions for computer software and expressly states the license rights that are available to the government based upon whether the computer software is identified as commercial or noncommercial. *See* DFARS 227.72 (general provisions), FAR 12.212 and DFARS 227-7202 (commercial computer software provisions, providing for licenses customarily provided to the public), and DFARS 252.227-7014 (noncommercial computer software contract clause). According to the DFARS, computer software means computer programs, source code, source code listings, object code listings, design details, algorithms, processes, flow charts, formulae, and related material that would enable the software to be reproduced, recreated, or recompiled. Computer software does not include computer databases or computer software documentation; again, these are treated as technical data.

The DFARS does not have any clauses governing acquisition of commercial computer software because DOD's policy is to take the same rights in commercial computer software that are offered to the general public. Commercial computer software means software developed or regularly used for nongovernmental purposes that has been sold, leased, or licensed to the public; has been offered for sale, lease, or license to the public; has not been offered, sold, leased, or licensed to the public but will be available for commercial sale, lease, or license in time to satisfy the delivery requirements of this contract; or satisfies one of the above criterion and would require only minor modification to meet the requirements of this contract. If the government has a need for rights not conveyed under the license customarily provided to the public, the government must negotiate with the contractor to determine if there are acceptable terms for transferring such rights. To illustrate the point that the government is a commercial customer, the DFARS, unlike the FAR,[3] does not have its own boilerplate contract clause covering its use rights in commercial computer software; instead, defense agencies are subject to the customary licenses offered to others in the commercial marketplace.

---

3. *See* FAR 52.227-19 (Commercial Computer Software License) (Dec. 2007).

By contrast, the DFARS specifically addresses noncommercial computer software. Again, the source of funding used to develop computer software will determine the type of license the government obtains. Similar to technical data, the standard license rights in computer software that a licensor grants to the government are "unlimited rights," "government purpose rights," or "restricted rights." In unusual situations, the standard rights may not satisfy the government's needs or the government may be willing to accept lesser rights in return for other consideration. In those cases, a special license may be negotiated. As with technical data, unlimited rights in noncommercial computer software means the right to use, modify, reproduce, release, perform, display, or disclose computer software in whole or in part, in any manner and for any purpose whatsoever, and to have or authorize others to do so. *See* DFARS 227.7203-5 (provision) and 252.227-7014 (contract clause).

The government obtains government purpose rights in noncommercial computer software developed with mixed funding. Government purpose can mean any activity in which the federal government is a party, including cooperative agreements with international or multinational defense organizations or sales or transfers by the U.S. government to foreign governments or international organizations. Government purposes include competitive procurement, but do not include the rights to use, modify, reproduce, release, perform, display, or disclose computer software for commercial purposes or authorize others to do so. Government purpose rights mean the rights to use, modify, reproduce, release, perform, display, or disclose computer software within the government without restriction, and release or disclose computer software outside the government and authorize persons to whom release or disclosure has been made to use, modify, reproduce, release, perform, display, or disclose the software for U.S. government purposes. *See* DFARS 227.7203-5(b) (provision) and 252.227-7014 (contract clause).

As with non-commercial technical data, the period during which government purpose rights are effective is negotiable, with no presumption of a length of five years. Either party may request a different period. The government purpose rights period commences upon execution of the contract, subcontract, letter contract (or similar contractual instrument), contract modification, or option that required development of the computer software. Upon expiration of the government purpose rights period, the government has unlimited rights in the software, including the right to authorize others to use the data for commercial purposes. The conversion from government purpose rights to unlimited use rights represents the underlying assumption that the contractor has diligently commercialized its software and established a market for the software, and after the expiration of the government purpose period, the government's increased use rights theoretically will not cause undue harm to the contractor with respect to the market for the software.

During the government purpose rights period, the government may not use, or authorize others to use, computer software marked with government purpose rights legends for commercial purposes. Legends and restrictive markings place the government on notice that the intellectual property of the contractor is being delivered with restrictions. The government may not release or disclose, or authorize others to release or disclose, computer software in which it has government purpose rights to any person unless the intended recipient is subject to use and nondisclosure agreements incorporated into the contract, or the intended recipient is a government contractor receiving access to the software for performance of a government contract that contains a Limitations on the Use or Disclosure of Government-Furnished Information Marked with Restrictive Legends clause. Contractors use restrictive legends to protect all types of intellectual property and confidential information delivered under contract or agreement to the government.

According to the DFARS, the government obtains restricted rights in noncommercial computer software to be delivered or otherwise provided to the government under a contract where the software was developed exclusively at private expense. Contractors are not required to provide the government additional rights in computer software delivered or otherwise provided to the government with restricted rights. *See* DFARS 227.7203-5(c) (provision) and 252.227-7014 (contract clause); *but see* 28 U.S.C. §1498 (affirmative defense to government contractors, acting without a license, who use a patented invention "for the government with its authorization and consent," without regard to what rights the government may ultimately hold in the invention).

F. Copyrights

The government must ensure that it has the right to use a copyrighted work that was not first produced under the government contract because it does not possess an inherent license to such work that was created independent of government funds. Therefore, the government requires that contractors obtain permission from copyright owners before including privately owned copyrighted works in data the government requires to be delivered under government contracts. Contractors are not to incorporate in data delivered under a contract any data that is not first produced under the contract and that is marked with the copyright notice of 17 U.S.C §401 or §402, without either acquiring for or granting to the government certain copyright license rights for the data, or obtaining permission from the contracting officer to do otherwise. *See* FAR 52.227-14(c) and DFARS 252.227-7013(d) and 7014(d) (contract clauses).

G. Summary

The regulations summarized above are simplified for this casebook; regardless, these regulations can be cumbersome and arcane. But consider that the federal government and the contractors making up the American industrial contractor base are responsible for some of the most cutting-edge technology innovations of the information age. Also consider that the U.S. federal procurement system is generally viewed as the world's best model for procurement transparency and integrity. Finally, consider that governments around the world are more often the largest purchasers of goods, services, and construction in the global economy. Realizing the significance of governments as purchasers and developers of intellectual property and technology innovations should make the study of government contracts and licensing a top priority.

II. MATERIALS

The Materials in this section illustrate the application of Federal Acquisition Regulation and Defense Federal Acquisition Regulation Supplement provisions and contract clauses to disputes between contractors and the federal government involving ownership and licensing of intellectual property, trade secrets, and confidential information.[4] The cases in this section were chosen over others because they provide a modern interpretation of the most current regulations that embody the federal government's policies toward intellectual property licensing under government contracts.

The seminal case dealing with a contractor's forfeiture of title to a patentable invention is Campbell Plastics Eng'g & Mfg., Inc. v. Brownlee, 389 F.3d 1243 (Fed. Cir. 2004). This case provides an example of the impact that the patent rights contract clauses have on ownership of a government funded invention. In *Campbell*, the federal government demanded title to a patentable invention upon its contractor's failure to comply with invention disclosure provisions required by the government contract. In contrast to forfeiture, the government will compensate a patent holder whose patent has otherwise been infringed by a contractor or subcontractor who, without the patent holder's permission, makes use of the patent on behalf of the U.S. government with its authorization and consent. The case updating the analysis relating to authorization and consent is Hutchison Indus., Inc. v. Accuride Corp., 2010 WL 1379720 (D.N.J.). Another seminal case in the technical data arena is Ervin & Associates, Inc. v. United States, 59 Fed. Cl. 267 (2004). This case interprets the FAR data rights clause to determine the scope of the federal government's use rights in a database and software program developed by a contractor during the performance of a government contract. Penultimately, In re General Atronics Corp., 2002 WL 450441, ASBCA No. 49196 (Mar. 19, 2002), demonstrates the significance of the requirement to mark intellectual property, computer software, trade secrets, or confidential information with restrictive legends before delivery to the federal government.

Finally, United States Marine, Inc. v. United States, 722 F.3d 1360 (Fed. Cir. 2013), presents issues involving jurisdiction over and remedies for the U.S. Government's misappropriation of a subcontractor's/third party beneficiary's trade secret. This case analyzes the interaction between the Federal Tort Claims Act (FTCA) and Tucker Act schemes, the former vesting exclusive jurisdiction in the district courts and the latter vesting exclusive jurisdiction in the U.S. Court of Federal Claims (COFC). Specifically, the case applies the *Woodbury* principle, which states: "where an action is essentially for breach of a contractual undertaking, and the liability, if any, depends wholly upon the government's alleged promise, the action must be under the

---

4. It should be noted that while the Materials in this chapter are drawn from federal sources, states, territories, and commonwealths of the United States have their own distinct state procurement laws and/or codes. Many states are currently dealing with complex issues involving acquisition of intellectual property; however, treatment of these issues are beyond the scope of this casebook. Regardless, the states, territories, and commonwealths have either adopted all or part of the FAR, the American Bar Association Model Procurement Code, or other acquisition rules and regulations for application within their respective jurisdictions. Accordingly, the FAR remains a source of guidance for these jurisdictions.

Tucker Act, and cannot be under the FTCA." Lastly, the case raises a currently unresolved issue regarding whether the Tucker Act embraces intellectual property takings claims asserted against the U.S. Government.

CAMPBELL PLASTICS ENG'G & MFG., INC. v. BROWNLEE
389 F.3d 1243 (Fed. Cir. 2004)

CLEVENGER, Circuit Judge.

Campbell Plastics Engineering & Mfg., Inc. ("Campbell Plastics") appeals the decision by the Armed Services Board of Contract Appeals ("ASBCA" or "Board") upholding an Administrative Contracting Officer's ("ACO's") demand for title to an invention developed pursuant to a contract between Campbell Plastics and the U.S. Army Chemical Research, Development and Engineering Center ("Army" or "government"). *See* In re Campbell Plastics Eng'g & Mfg. Inc., ASBCA No. 53319, 2003 WL 1518313 (Mar. 18, 2003). Because we conclude that Campbell Plastics failed to comply with the invention disclosure provisions of the contract, we affirm.

I

On September 25, 1992, Campbell Plastics entered into a cost-plus-fixed-fee contract, DAAA15-92-C-0082, with the Army to develop certain components of an aircrew protective mask, as part of a program for small disadvantaged business concerns pursuant to section 8(a) of the Small Business Act, 15 U.S.C. §637(a) (1988).

Section I of the contract incorporates numerous clauses from the Federal Acquisition Regulations ("FARs"), including a "Patent Rights—Retention by the Contractor" clause from 48 C.F.R. §52.227-11 (1991) ("FAR 52.227-11") that requires a contractor to disclose any subject invention developed pursuant to a government contract and sets forth certain substantive requirements for doing so. The clause further provides that the government may obtain title if the contractor fails to disclose the invention within two months from the date upon which the inventor discloses it in writing to contractor personnel responsible for patent matters. Section I also incorporates from 48 C.F.R. §252.227-7039 (1991) ("FAR 252.227-7039") a "Patents—Reporting of Subject Inventions" clause which requires the contractor to disclose subject inventions in interim reports furnished every twelve months and final reports furnished within three months after completion of the contracted work. Subsection H.11 of the contract, titled "Patent Rights Reports," requires the contractor to submit all "interim and final invention reports required by patent clause in Section I" on a "DD Form 882, Report of Inventions and Subcontracts."

On October 11, 1992, Mr. Richard Campbell, President of Campbell Plastics, submitted to the Army a DD Form 882 wherein he expressly stated "no inventions." At a post-award conference on November 17, an Army representative told Mr. Campbell that a DD form 882 was due at least once every twelve months from the date upon which the contract was awarded. Shortly thereafter, on December 14, Mr. Campbell faxed several handwritten drawings to Mr. Jeff Hoffman, an ACO Representative. One of the drawings identified a location for a "sonic weld or snap fit."

On December 19, 1992, Mr. Campbell faxed a handwritten letter to Mr. Hoffman seeking to "reopen the question of the sonic welding." The letter included an explanation of the advantages of sonic welding and the assembly concept. On January 20, 1993, Mr. Campbell provided Mr. Hoffman with two protective masks that had sonic-welded side ports.

On February 11, Mr. Campbell faxed Mr. Hoffman a drawing of a side port having a sonic weld. In a monthly progress report submitted on March 2, Campbell Plastics . . . reported that a "prototype mold is currently being fabricated to prove out the feasibility of sonic welding. . . ."

On March 19, 1993, Mr. Campbell faxed Mr. Hoffman a sketch of the side port voicemitter and the following note: "I am having this sketched up and a simple mold made to test Sonic Weld/Kapton Concept." On March 22 and 24, Mr. Campbell faxed various diagrams of the lens retaining system and the front voicemitter housing and speaking unit, and indicated that certain joints were to be sonic welded. In monthly progress reports dated April 29 and June 30, Campbell Plastics reported on its testing of the use of sonic welding. On July 8, Mr. Campbell faxed drawings of the lens retaining system to Mr. Hoffman and stated specifically that the assembly was sonic welded. On July 21 and August 5, Mr. Campbell submitted cost estimates and noted in each that the concept of sonic welding was "nearly complete."

On October 6, 1993, Mr. Joseph J. Stehlik, ACO, wrote to Mr. Campbell to remind him that an Interim Report of Inventions and Subcontracts, preferably on a DD Form 882, must be delivered at least every twelve months from the date of the contract, listing the subject inventions during the period and also certifying that the required procedures for identifying and disclosing subject inventions have been disclosed. In the letter, Mr. Stehlik requested that Campbell Plastics submit an interim report within ten days. On October 18, Mr. Campbell submitted a DD Form 882 but did not disclose an invention.

On September 15, Mr. Campbell submitted a DD Form 882 that again indicated that no invention had been developed under the contract. Campbell Plastics did not submit another DD Form 882 for the remainder of the contract period. . . . In monthly progress reports . . . Campbell Plastics reported continued work on the sonic welding process.

In August 1997, Campbell Plastics contacted an attorney who soon after drafted a patent application for a "Sonic Welded Gas Mask and Process." Campbell Plastics filed the application on October 9, 1997. The U.S. Patent and Trademark Office ("USPTO") made the application available to the Army for the limited purpose of making a secrecy determination pursuant to 35 U.S.C. §181 (1994).

The patent application issued on April 20, 1999, as U.S. Patent No. 5,895,537 ("the '537 patent"). The '537 patent expressly reserved for the government a paid-up license and "the right in limited circumstances to require the patent owner to license others on reasonable terms as provided for by the terms of Contract No. DAAA15-92-C-0082 awarded by The Army." On April 28, Campbell Plastics notified the Army in writing of the '537 patent.

After an exchange of letters between the parties regarding the Army's claim to joint own-ership of the subject invention, including one in which the Army admitted that it had, by June 1997, a report drafted by government employees that provided an enabling disclosure of the invention, the ACO ultimately concluded that Campbell Plastics forfeited title to the patent by failing to comply with FAR 52.227-11.

Campbell Plastics appealed the ACO's decision. Both parties filed cross-motions for sum-mary judgment. Though Campbell Plastics conceded in its motion that its disclosure was not in the form of a DD Form 882 as was required by the contract, Campbell Plastics argued that it disclosed all technical aspects of the invention to the Army and that the Army [had an enabling disclosure]. Campbell Plastics furthermore argued that forfeiture is not favored by law, especially where the government suffered no genuine harm.

In denying the appeal, the Board ruled that Campbell Plastics failed to satisfy its contractual obligation to inform the Army that it considered sonic welding to be an invention. The Board further ruled that any information the Army gleaned from its review of the patent application for secrecy determination purposes and its own June 1997 report was not provided by Campbell Plastics, and that forfeiture was appropriate under the circumstances. Finally, the Board recognized that FAR 52.227-11(d), vests the Army with some discretion in determining whether to take title. The Board found, however, that the Army had not abused its discretion. Campbell Plastics now appeals the Board's decision.

III

Because we have never before defined a contractor's obligation to disclose a "subject invention" under FAR 52.227-11, this case presents a matter of first impression for this court.

In 1980, Congress passed the Bayh-Dole Act, 35 U.S.C. §§200-212, the statutory scheme from which FAR 52.227-11 arises. With few exceptions, the Act allows nonprofit organizations and small business firms to elect to retain title to any invention by the contractor developed pursuant to a government contract. For purposes of the Act, Congress has termed these inventions "subject inventions." *See* 35 U.S.C. §201(d)-(e) (1988) (defining an "invention" to mean "any invention or discovery that is or may be patentable," and "subject invention" to mean "any invention of the contractor conceived or first actually reduced to practice in the performance of work under a funding agreement").

Congress required that each government contract entered into pursuant to the Act shall contain provisions that require the contractor to "disclose each subject invention to the Federal agency within a reasonable time after it becomes known to contractor personnel responsible for the administration of patent matters, and that the Federal Government may receive title to any subject invention not disclosed to it within such time." 35 U.S.C. §202(c)(1) (1988). The reasons for this are clear. Though the Act provides nonprofit organizations and small business firms the right to elect title to a subject invention, it also vests in the government the right to a paid-up license to practice the invention when the contractor elects to retain title, *id.* §202(c)(4), and the right to receive title to the invention in the United States or any other country in which the contractor has not filed a patent application on the invention prior to any pertinent statutory bar date, *id.* §202(c)(3). The disclosure provisions of section 202(c)(1) thus provide the government adequate means with which to protect these rights.

Subsection 1.53 of Campbell Plastics's contract incorporated the clause "Patent Rights — Retention by the Contractor" of FAR 52.227-11, which obligates the contractor to disclose "subject inventions" to the government and sets forth both substantive and formal requirements for the disclosure. The clause states in relevant part:

> **(c)** Invention disclosure, election of title, and filing of patent application by contractor.
>   **(1)** The Contractor will disclose each subject invention to the Federal agency within 2 months after the inventor discloses it in writing to Contractor personnel responsible for patent matters. The disclosure to the agency shall be in the form of a written report and shall identify the contract under which the invention was made

and the inventor(s). It shall be sufficiently complete in technical detail to convey a clear understanding to the extent known at the time of the disclosure, of the nature, purpose, operation, and the physical, chemical, biological or electrical characteristics of the invention. . . .

　　　(d) Conditions when the government may obtain title. The Contractor will convey to the Federal agency, upon written request, title to any subject invention —

　　　　　　(1) If the Contractor fails to disclose or elect title to the subject invention within the times specified in paragraph (c) of this clause. . . .

　　FAR 52.227-11.

　　Subsection H.11 of Campbell Plastics's contract, titled "Patent Rights Reports," requires the contractor to submit all interim and final invention reports "required by patent clause in Section I" on a DD Form 882, "Report of Inventions and Subcontracts," and Campbell Plastics does not dispute that the DD Form 882 is the contractual means for disclosing subject inventions pursuant to FAR 52.227-11(c)(1). In addition to the disclosure requirements of FAR 52.227-11(c)(1), the form also requires a contractor to report the title of the invention, whether it elects to file a patent application in either the United States or a foreign country, and any foreign country so elected.

　　The language of the Patent Rights Reports clause and the incorporated FAR [clauses] is clear and unambiguous. It affords the government the opportunity to take title to any invention by the contractor that is or may be patentable and was conceived or first actually reduced to practice in the performance of work under the contract if the contractor fails to disclose on a DD Form 882 the technical aspects of the invention, the inventor and the contract under which the invention was developed, within two months of disclosing the invention to contractor personnel responsible for patent matters.

　　This plain-meaning interpretation of the contract is buttressed by the policy considerations behind the Bayh-Dole Act. While Congress clearly intended "to promote the commercialization and public availability of inventions made in the United States by United States industry and labor," and "to encourage maximum participation of small business firms in federally supported research and development efforts," 35 U.S.C. §200 (2000), it also provided the government with certain aforementioned rights to the inventions and sought to ensure the safeguard of those rights by requiring government contractors to disclose subject inventions. . . . A single, written report containing the information required by FAR 52.227-11(c)(1) effectively provides such a safeguard.

　　Neither party disputes that Campbell Plastics first disclosed the method for fabricating a sonic welded gas mask to its patent counsel in August 1997, or that the method was indeed a "subject invention." At a minimum, then, the contract required Campbell Plastics to disclose on a DD Form 882 by October 1997, the technical aspects of its method for fabricating a sonic welded gas mask, the inventor[,] and the contract under which the invention was developed. Campbell Plastics admittedly did not do so, and instead indicated "no invention" and "none" on DD Form 882s that it did submit.

　　Campbell Plastics contends, however, that it continually disclosed all features of the invention throughout the contractual period. While it is at least debatable whether the various progress reports and drawings Campbell Plastics submitted to the Army together convey a clear understanding of the nature, purpose[,] and operation of the invention as well as the invention's physical, chemical, biological or electrical characteristics, we think the contract requirement of a single, easily identified form on which to disclose inventions is sound and needs to be strictly enforced. If we were to find Campbell Plastics's style of disclosure sufficient, methods of disclosure could vary widely from case to case. The government never would be sure of which piece of paper, or which oral statement, might be part of an overall invention disclosure. But we do not so find. The contract instead demands a single form for disclosure, which enables the contracting officials to direct the inventive aspects of the contract performance to the correct personnel in the agency for a determination of whether the government has an interest in the disclosed invention, and for the government to determine how best to protect its interest. Sound policy is promoted by the rule of strict compliance with the method of disclosure demanded by the contract.

Because Campbell Plastics's piecemeal submissions do not adequately disclose the subject invention under the parties' contract, the government may take title to the invention pursuant to FAR 52.227-11(d). The arguments Campbell Plastics advances in an attempt to avoid application of that subsection are unavailing. Campbell Plastics argues that the subsection refers only to the timing of the disclosure, and not to the substance of the disclosure itself. Under Campbell Plastics's interpretation, however, it could disclose anything under the sun in any form whatsoever and still avoid forfeiture, so long as it does so within two months of disclosing the subject invention to its personnel responsible for patent matters.

Campbell Plastics also argues that the government's possession of an enabling disclosure of the subject invention by June 1997, and its review of the patent application for secrecy determination purposes, satisfied Campbell Plastics's obligations under the contract. But whatever information the government had regarding the invention, it did not get it from Campbell Plastics in the form of a proper invention disclosure.

IV

The Board determined that because FAR 52.227-11(d) specifies when the government "may" obtain title to a subject invention, the decision to demand title is a discretionary matter. Although the Board did not understand Campbell Plastics to have specifically raised the issue of whether the ACO's decision to demand title to the patent in this case is within the bounds of discretion, the Board nonetheless addressed and decided the issue. We surmise that the Board took this step because while Campbell Plastics did not phrase its contention in the language of abuse of discretion, it clearly argued that when the government obtains a license to the patent and is not otherwise harmed, the penalty of forfeiture of title is unwarranted.

In deciding the abuse of discretion issue, the Board properly considered (1) evidence of whether the government official acted with subjective bad faith; (2) whether the official had a reasonable, contract-related basis for his decision; (3) the amount of discretion given to the official; and (4) whether the official violated a statute or regulation. *See* McDonnell Douglas Corp. v. United States, 182 F.3d 1319, 1326 (Fed. Cir. 1999). Ruling in favor of the government on each point, the Board concluded that the ACO did not abuse his discretion in demanding title to the subject invention and necessarily rejected Campbell Plastics's argument that when the government takes a license in the invention and is otherwise not harmed, the government cannot cause forfeiture of the patent.

On appeal, Campbell Plastics argu[es] directly that the ACO abused his discretion by demanding title in circumstances where the government suffered no harm. The government responds that it suffered harm from Campbell Plastics's failure to meet the notification requirements by putting the patent rights of the United States in foreign countries in jeopardy.

We agree with the Board that FAR 52.227-11(d) vests discretion in the government in determining whether to invoke forfeiture when an invention has not been correctly disclosed to it. We also agree that the test for abuse of discretion set forth in *McDonnell Douglas* is the test to be applied in this case. We hold that harm to the government is not a requirement in order for the ACO to insist on forfeiture. . . . Campbell Plastics points to nothing in its contract with the Army, or in the relevant statute or its legislative history, that requires the government to show harm to itself in order to invoke the remedy of forfeiture. . . . Because the Board correctly applied the proper test . . . , we reject Campbell Plastics's argument that an abuse of discretion occurred here. . . . The decision of the Board to deny Campbell Plastics's appeal is affirmed.

HUTCHINSON INDUS., INC. v. ACCURIDE CORP.
2010 WL 1379720 (D.N.J.)

WOLFSON, District Judge.

Plaintiffs Hutchinson Industries, Inc. and Hutchinson S.A. (collectively, "Plaintiffs") are holders of U.S. Patent No. 6,474,383 (the "'383 patent"), which describes an automotive wheel with an internal valve system. In the instant suit, Plaintiffs allege that Defendant Accuride Corp. ("Defendant") infringed on their '383 patent. Specifically, Plaintiffs allege that Defendant has made or had others make the allegedly infringing wheel, and that Defendant has offered for sale or sold the wheel within the United States. Defendant moves to dismiss, or in the alternative for summary judgment on, all counts of Plaintiffs' complaint. Defendant submits that its wheel was manufactured solely for the United States Government ("Government") with its authorization and consent, placing the alleged infringing conduct within the scope of 28 U.S.C. §1498, and that Defendant is thereby immune from suit in this patent infringement action.

I. BACKGROUND

Defendant has manufactured an automotive wheel with an internal valve system designed to operate in conjunction with a "central tire inflation system" ("CTIS"). A CTIS equipped vehicle allows the driver of the vehicle to adjust the tire pressure in all tires while driving, in order to select a tire pressure best suited for the terrain. A vehicle's CTIS can connect to CTIS-compatible wheels and tires. Defendant has supplied its wheels to three private companies: BAE Systems Ground Systems, Navistar Defense, and Oshkosh Corp. (collectively, the "Companies"). The Companies have used these wheels in conjunction with a CTIS in the manufacture of mine-resistant, ambush-protected, all-terrain vehicles ("M-ATVs"), which were built to bid on a Government contract (the "Solicitation"). The Solicitation requires any bidding party to provide prototype M-ATVs in order to remain eligible to be awarded the contract. The Solicitation also lists specifications the Government requires or prefers to be included as part of the M-ATVs. One of these specifications is a CTIS; [the specification states]: ("The vehicle shall be equipped with a Central Tire Inflation System (CTIS), which will allow the driver to adjust all vehicle tires to any one of four preset tire pressures, from a single control, corresponding to Emergency, Mud/Snow/Sand, Cross-Country, and Highway operation."). Two of the Companies used Defendant's wheel in their M-ATVs delivered as prototype vehicles, and the Government ordered three more vehicles from BAE Systems Ground Systems with Defendant's wheels.

Plaintiffs hold a patent for an automotive wheel designed to operate in conjunction with a CTIS. Specifically, Plaintiffs' '383 patent describes a wheel equipped with an internal valve system that connects a CTIS through the wheel rim to the tire. In addition to holding the patent, Plaintiffs manufacture and sell the wheel. Plaintiffs became aware of Defendant's wheel at some point during the Companies' delivery of prototype M-ATVs to the Government. Plaintiffs informed Defendant that its wheel with an internal valve system was similar or identical to that encompassed by the '383 patent, and thus infringed on the patent. Defendant disputed this assertion. Shortly thereafter, Plaintiffs filed a complaint in this Court alleging that Defendant infringed on the '383 patent.

Defendant moves to dismiss, or alternatively for summary judgment on, Plaintiffs' complaint on the basis that Defendant's wheel falls within the scope and protection of 28 U.S.C. §1498. Specifically, Defendant argues that because the alleged infringing wheel was made in response to bids on a Government contract, §1498 applies to shield Defendant from liability for patent infringement. Defendant further argues that under §1498, Plaintiffs' sole recourse for any alleged infringement is a claim against the United States Government in the United States Court of Federal Claims. . . .

III. DISCUSSION

This dispute turns solely on the nature and applicability of 28 U.S.C. §1498(a), which states:

> Whenever an invention described in and covered by a patent of the United States is used or manufactured by or for the United States without license of the owner thereof or lawful right to use or manufacture the same, the owner's remedy shall be by action against the United States in the United States Court of Federal Claims for the recovery of his reasonable and entire compensation for such use and manufacture. . . .

For the purposes of this section, the use or manufacture of an invention described in and covered by a patent of the United States by a contractor, a subcontractor, or any person, firm, or corporation for the Government and with the authorization or consent of the Government, shall be construed as use or manufacture for the United States.[5]

---

5. At oral argument, both parties conceded that §1498 is not a jurisdictional bar, but rather an affirmative defense. Moreover, the Federal Circuit has resolved any uncertainty in this regard: in "litigation between private parties . . . section 1498(a) acts as a codification of a defense and not as a jurisdictional statute." *Toxgon Corp.*, 312 F.3d at 1381 (quotations omitted); see also Madey v. Duke University, 307 F.3d 1351, 1360 (Fed. Cir. 2002) ("Because §1498(a) is not jurisdictional, . . . the basis for the district court's partial dismissal was improper."). Thus, because §1498 operates as an affirmative defense, a district court must resolve the matter through summary judgment. *Toxgon Corp.*, 312 F.3d at 1381.

In order for §1498(a) to shield a contractor or subcontractor from liability for patent infringement, the alleged infringing party must show that its conduct is both (1) "for the United States [Government]"; and (2) "with the authorization or consent of the Government." Thus, the sole issue before the Court is whether Defendant's manufacture and supply of an allegedly infringing wheel for the purpose of bidding on a Government contract falls within the scope of §1498.

To resolve this issue, the Court finds it helpful to review the underlying history and policy rationale of §1498. "The original purpose of §1498 was 'to stimulate contractors to furnish what was needed for the [First World] War, without fear of becoming liable themselves for infringements to inventors or the owners or assignees of patents.'" Madey v. Duke Univ., 413 F. Supp. 2d 601, 606 (M.D.N.C. 2006). This statute was enacted

> to relieve the contractor entirely from liability of every kind for the infringement of patents in manufacturing anything for the government, and to limit the owner of the patent . . . to suit against the United States in the Court of Claims for the recovery of his reasonable and entire compensation for such use and manufacture. The word "entire" emphasizes the exclusive and comprehensive character of the remedy provided.

Put another way, §1498 "deprives the owner of the patent of a remedy against the infringing private contractor for infringements thereof and makes the government indemnitor for its manufacturer or contractor in his infringements." Thus, it is clear that the purpose of §1498 is to remove the potential threat of a patent infringement suit from Government contractors, transferring it to the Government instead. This transfer of liability helps ensure that the Government's freedom in selecting contractors is not limited by a contractor's fear of becoming entangled in litigation. In this manner, §1498 "allows the Government to obtain what it needs from third parties, whether goods, services, or research, regardless of potential patent infringement, with compensation provided later to patent holders in a suit against the Government in the Court of Federal Claims for any patents infringed in the process." Lastly, "the coverage of §1498 should be broad because Congress intended 'to allow the Government to procure whatever it wished regardless of possible patent infringement.'"

The Court now turns to whether §1498(a) shields Defendant from liability here. Neither party disputes that, here, Defendant's product is "for the Government," as the wheel was manufactured solely for the Companies in response to the Solicitation. This falls within the generally understood definition of "for the Government." Instead, Plaintiffs claim that Defendant did not produce the wheel with the "authorization or consent of the Government." This Court disagrees.

For the purposes of §1498(a), the Government's authorization and consent can be either explicit or implied. Explicit authorization and consent occurs when the Government specifically includes in its contract a product or service that authorizes the contracting party to infringe on another's patent. Further, when a Government contract contains an explicit authorization and consent clause, the language of that clause, be it broad or narrow, is generally determinative of whether the Government consented to the contractor's alleged infringement in the performance of the contract.

In reviewing the cases that discuss explicit authorization and consent, it appears this issue primarily arises in circumstances where a Government contract has been awarded to a contractor, and not in the context of bidding. However, there are times when the Government does explicitly authorize and consent to infringement in the bidding context by inserting the authorizing language into the invitation to bid. See Stelma, Inc. v. Bridge Elecs. Co., 300 F.2d 761, 762 (3d Cir. 1962) (finding explicit authorization where "the invitation to bid specif[ied] that the subject matter of the contract was [the patented] 'Stelma, Inc.'s Model TDA-2S, or equal'"). The [present] Solicitation[ ] does not contain any express language that authorizes the Companies or their subcontractors to infringe on the '383 patent. Therefore, the Government has not explicitly consented to the infringement of the '383 patent to bid on the Solicitation; no contract has been awarded to Defendant, and the Solicitation only requests that the M-ATVs contain a CTIS, without reference to the '383 patent.

In addition to explicit authorization or consent, the Government can also implicitly give its authorization or consent. There are two general categories of cases in which courts have addressed the Government's implied authorization or consent: cases in which the contractor has entered into a contract with the Government, and cases in which the contractor is bidding on a contract with the Government.

In circumstances where a contractor has entered into a contract with the Government, and the patent holder's infringement claim turns on a product or method used in the contractor's execution of the contract, courts limit a finding of the Government's implied authorization and consent to certain conditions. The rationale for limiting implied authorization and consent once a contract exists is easily understood. Because the parties have agreed to the terms of the contract, including when the Government will be liable for the contractor's infringement, a court should be hesitant to impose additional liability on the Government through a finding of implied authorization and consent. Additionally, where the Government is the defendant in an infringement suit under §1498, any implied authorization or consent should be narrowly construed because "implied consent operates as a waiver of sovereign immunity."

Thus, where the Government and contractor have entered into a contract, the Government provides its explicit authorization and consent by the language of the contract, and its implied authorization and consent "'by contracting officer instructions, by specifications or drawings which impliedly sanction and necessitate infringement, [or] by post hoc intervention of the Government in pending infringement litigation against individual contractors.'" An example of implied consent under a contract with the Government is where "(1) the government expressly contracted for work to meet certain specifications; (2) the specifications cannot be met without infringing on a patent; and (3) the government had some knowledge of the infringement."

[A] case where the court did not find any implied authorization or consent by the Government [is Carrier]. [In Carrier, the court] held the Government not liable for the alleged infringing act of a contractor, the Government had entered into a services contract with a contractor to remove garbage from an Air Force base, [where] during the performance of the contract the contractor had allegedly used equipment that infringed on the plaintiff's patent. The plaintiff brought suit against the Government in Claims Court. The court found that the neither the services contract nor the Government contracting officer had ever requested or required use of the infringing equipment. For this reason, the court rejected the plaintiff's argument that the Government had implicitly authorized or consented to the contractor's use of infringing equipment in the performance of a contract. [T]he rationale in th[is] case[ ] does not apply to circumstances where no Government contract has been awarded, and the alleged infringer is merely bidding on the contract.

[In the bidding context], courts have broadly construed the Government's implied authorization and consent. The leading case addressing the applicability of §1498 to private parties bidding on a Government contract is *TVI Energy*. The issue before the *TVI Energy* court was, "whether a private party which infringes another's patent during Government bidding activities . . . is immune under 28 U.S.C. §1498 from a District Court infringement action for [a] test demonstration." *TVI Energy*, 806 F.2d at 1059. The court answered in the affirmative, holding that the "only purpose in demonstrating the [infringing] targets was to comply with the Government's bidding requirements. In these circumstances, [the court] can come to no other conclusion than that this demonstration fell within the scope of §1498 as being 'for the United States' and 'with its approval.' " Significantly, the court further held that the Government had impliedly authorized the bidding contractor's alleged infringement despite the fact the contract did not necessitate infringement. The *TVI Energy* court rejected the plaintiff's argument that there could be no authorization or consent because the Government did not provide the bidding party with a formal "authorization and consent letter." Instead, the court focused solely on the fact that the Government required parties bidding on the contract to provide products for demonstration purposes in order to remain eligible for the contract. This required demonstration, the *TVI Energy* court reasoned, carried with it the Government's implied authorization and consent to convey immunity under §1498 to the bidding parties.

Courts consistently construe the Government's authorization and consent broadly in the bidding context for the purposes of determining whether a private party is immune from suit under §1498. For example, in *W.L. Gore*, a private party sought relief from a previous injunction so that it could bid to become a subcontractor on a proposed Government contract. 842 F.2d at 1278. The court found it unnecessary to modify the injunction because §1498 unequivocally ensured the party "freedom to bid on and participate in the sale to the government of products which, or the process of making which, infringe [the other party's] patents." In *Trojan*, the Federal Circuit reaffirmed the broad nature of §1498 in the bidding context, and held that "a patent owner may not use its patent to cut the government off from sources of supply, either at the bid stage or during performance of a government contract." 885 F.2d 854, 856-57 (Fed. Cir. 1989).

Plaintiffs advance a number of challenges to Defendant's §1498(a) defense. For the reasons that follow, none of these challenges are sufficient to preclude the application of §1498 to Defendant's alleged conduct. To begin, Plaintiffs argue that the Government did not authorize Defendant's wheel because the wheel was not "directly related" to the technology requested by the Solicitation here. In this sense, Plaintiffs seek to distinguish *TVI Energy* on the ground that the defendant in that case was alleged to have infringed on a patent that embodied the specific technology requested by the Government. Put differently, Plaintiffs argue that because neither a CTIS-compatible wheel, nor the technology of Plaintiffs' patented wheel, is the subject matter of the Solicitation, *TVI Energy* does not extend to shield Defendant from liability. The Court does not read *TVI Energy* so narrowly. Indeed, the *TVI Energy* court stated that §1498 should be broadly interpreted: "[t]he coverage of §1498 should be broad so as not to limit the Government's freedom in procurement by considerations of private patent infringement." For these reasons, and the underlying purpose of §1498, the Court rejects Plaintiffs' argument.

Plaintiffs additionally argue that because the Government has included an "authorization and consent clause" in the Solicitation, that clause provides the exclusive means for determining the scope of the Government's authorization. Here, the Solicitation incorporates by reference Federal Acquisitions Regulation ("FAR") 52.227-1, which states that

> The Government authorizes and consents to all use and manufacture, in performing this contract or any subcontract at any tier, of any invention described in and covered by a United States patent . . .
>
> (2) Used in machinery, tools, or methods whose use necessarily results from compliance by the Contractor or a subcontractor with (i) specifications or written provisions forming a part of this contract or (ii) specific written instructions given by the Contracting Officer directing the manner of performance.

Plaintiffs claim that this clause limits the Government's authorization and consent to infringement only when it "necessarily results from compliance" with the Solicitation's specifications. Because the specifications did not expressly require an infringing wheel, Plaintiffs argue that the Government did not authorize or consent to Defendant's alleged infringement. Plaintiffs' argument is misplaced. Because Defendant's wheels have only been used in the bidding context, the Court is not constrained by an explicit authorization and consent analysis based on the language of the authorization and consent clause. Instead, the Court engages in an implied authorization and consent analysis based on whether Defendant supplied its wheels in connection with, and contemplated by, the Solicitation specifications, and whether the Government required demonstration of the products in order to be eligible to bid for the contract.

This is not to say that the Government's choice to include an authorization and consent clause in the Solicitation is immaterial to the Court's implied authorization and consent analysis. Rather, in the context of bidding, the Solicitation's authorization and consent clause serves as a reminder to those bidding on the contract that the Government is limiting its authorization and consent to the goods or services requested by the Solicitation. That is, the authorization and consent clause in the Solicitation signals to a bidder, like Defendant, that for the purposes of establishing the bidding party's immunity, the Government is providing its authorization and consent to bids that correspond to the specifications in the Solicitation.

Here, a CTIS is specified by the Solicitation, but no mention is made of what type of wheels to supply. Obviously, to supply a functional CTIS requires CTIS-compatible wheels — although not necessarily wheels embodied by Plaintiffs' patent. Thus, although infringement is not specified, CTIS-compatible wheels are necessarily required. Therefore, Defendant's wheels were supplied in connection with, and are encompassed by, the subject matter of the Solicitation specifications, and are subject to implied authorization and consent consideration in connection with this bid.

Conversely, a bidder would likely not obtain immunity in the bidding process for products not the subject matter of, or reasonably contemplated by the terms of, the Solicitation or its specifications, even considering that *TVI Energy* holds that an infringing product does not have to be required and specified in order for the bidder to be shielded under §1498. For example, if the Solicitation specifications did not require or request that the M-ATVs include any type of horn device, then a bidding party that supplied an infringing version of such a product would likely not be shielded by the above implied authorization and consent analysis — even under a broad reading of authorization and consent in the bidding context.

For the foregoing reasons, the Court finds that the Government implicitly authorized and consented to Defendant's bid-related activities. Because Defendant's alleged infringement occurred in the context of bidding on a Government contract, a broad construction of the Government's implied authorization and consent is appropriate. Under this construction, a potential Government contractor or subcontractor is immune from a patent infringement suit if: (1) it provides a product that the Government requests in a solicitation to bid on a contract, even if the request does not necessitate infringement; and (2) the Government requires parties bidding on the contract to provide these products for demonstration or testing purposes. Here, Defendant's activities were related and in response to the Solicitation specifications, and the Government required demonstration of the products in order to be eligible to bid for the contract. The Solicitation requested that the Companies' M-ATVs include a CTIS and thus, by necessity, CTIS-compatible wheels, and required that the Companies provide fully functional prototype vehicles to the Government to remain eligible in the bidding process. Further, it is immaterial as to whether the Solicitation requested or required a CTIS and its compatible wheels because *TVI Energy* holds that §1498(a) shields contractors and subcontractors bidding on Government contracts from patent infringement liability even if the solicitation to bid does not necessitate infringement. Because both parties concede that the manufacture and supply of Defendant's wheel was used solely for the purpose of the prime contractors bidding on the Solicitation, and Defendant has provided the Court with certified documentation linking Defendant's wheel to the M-ATVs and CTIS specification under the Solicitation, Defendant is entitled to immunity under §1498.

CONCLUSION

For the foregoing reasons, the Court treats Defendant's motion as one for summary judgment. Further, the Court finds that Defendant has proven it is entitled the protection of 28 U.S.C. §1498(a) because it has shown that its allegedly infringing wheels were produced for the United States with its implied authorization and consent as part of the bidding process on a Government contract. Defendant is thus immune from a patent infringement suit for these wheels. Accordingly, the Court GRANTS Defendant's motion for summary judgment.

ERVIN & ASSOCIATES, INC. v. UNITED STATES
59 Fed. Cl. 267 (2004)

BRADEN, Judge.

This government contracting case raises an important issue concerning the scope of the Federal Acquisition Regulation ("FAR") "Rights In Data-General" Clause. Since 1987, civilian federal contracts have included a standard "Rights In Data-General" Clause, which provides the federal government ("Government") with virtually "unlimited rights" in technical data and computer software. In fact, the "Rights In Data-General" Clause "does not provide any rights to the contractor, instead, these rights tend to limit rights that a contractor may have in data by requiring the license of the technology to the [G]overnment — effectively, a compulsory license. Indeed, in contrast to a patent or copyright, for which the [G]overnment may demand a license, the data rights regulations specifically require conditions under which a contractor must grant the [G]overnment specific, non-exclusive license rights."

RELEVANT FACTS

From 1993 through 1997, the relevant period in this case, the United States Department of Housing and Urban Development ("HUD") managed a portfolio of approximately 16,000 HUD-insured and HUD-held loans worth $50 billion, secured by over two million multifamily apartment projects located throughout the United States. Each year, owners of these loans were required to submit an audited annual financial statement ("AFS") in hard copy to HUD.

On July 21, 1993, HUD issued a Request for Proposals No. DV100C000018266 ("RFP"), seeking a contractor to collect and review AFS forms and provide draft follow-up letters to HUD.

The RFP's Statement of Work ("SOW") required that the successful contractor annually would review over 16,000 AFS forms and develop a "trend analysis" comparing the forms for the current year to those of the two previous years. The SOW also required that the successful contractor survey the Independent Public Accountants that audit HUD partnerships and provide HUD with a "plan to automate the financial statement that is compatible with HUD's automatic systems considering fully the capability of the IPA[s]." The purpose of this plan was to allow the AFS forms to be delivered to HUD electronically. In addition, the initial SOW incorporated by reference several HUD handbooks that provided information regarding HUD requirements for review and analysis of the AFS forms.

HUD issued a[n] amendment [to the solicitation] that added t[he] require[ment to] input certain data elements into HUD's Field Office Multifamily National System ("FOMNS"). . . . HUD [issued a] third amendment specifically request[ing] best and final offers ("BAFOs") from five companies that previously had submitted offers technically acceptable to HUD. . . . On December 7, 1993, HUD issued a fourth amendment eliminating the CLIN 0001 ("Trend Analysis Report") and 0008 ("Automation and Procedures") requirements. On December 23, 1993, HUD issued a sixth and final amendment.

In 1989, Ervin began a business to provide acquisition, management, disposition, and financing services to owners and lenders with multifamily loan portfolios. Ervin then began to develop and expand [a] centralized computer database system that it acquired to create the Ervin Multifamily Information Systems ("EMFIS").

HUD received 13 proposals in response to the initial RFP. Five, including Ervin's, were found to be technically acceptable. . . . Ervin's final BAFO was priced at $12,328,000, compared to an average price of approximately $22 million.

On February 14, 1994, HUD executed the AFS Contract Award. The AFS Contract Award included HUD's RFP, as amended, but prominently noted on the cover sheet that Ervin's "technical proposals, dated August 27, 1993, as amended September 24, 1993 and December 29, 1993, are hereby incorporated by reference and made part of this contract." John Ervin signed the AFS Contract Award ("AFS Contract").

The AFS Contract referenced the "Rights In Data-General" Clause. See 48 C.F.R. §52.227-14. The "Rights In Data-General" Clause provides the Government with "unlimited rights" in the following categories of data:

Except as provided in paragraph (c) of this clause regarding copyright, the Government shall have unlimited rights in —

(i) Data first produced in the performance of this contract;

(ii) Form, fit and function data delivered under this contract;

(iii) Data delivered under this contract (except for restricted computer software) that constitute manuals or instructional and training material for installation, operation, or routine maintenance and repair of items, components, or processes delivered or furnished for use under this contract; and

(iv) All other data delivered under this contract unless provided otherwise for limited rights data or restricted computer software in accordance with paragraph (g) of this clause.

In addition to the "Rights In Data-General" Clause, the AFS Contract also contained an additional provision affecting data rights that specified: "If additional software and computer applications are developed to present the data specified under the contract, then such will be considered property of the Department."

In early 1995, HUD decided to develop a database for multifamily housing that would include AFS data. This project was known within HUD as the "Data Warehouse." [A HUD] Report, evaluated Ervin's systems and, despite giving Ervin an excellent rating, recommended "replac[ing Ervin's systems] with a new, HUD-owned Asset Management system."

[Ervin was directed to provide AFS data for the Data Warehouse.] On June 27, 1995, Ervin delivered a high capacity Syquest disk cartridge containing a download of 1993 AFS data to HUD for use to test the Data Warehouse. . . . HUD takes the position that the AFS Contract required Ervin to provide "downloads of AFS Data."

According to John Ervin, [he was] assured that the data downloads provided HUD would only be used to test the Data Warehouse and would not be provided to Ervin's competitors. Ervin believed that it would not be competitively harmed by providing the data, so long as it was used only by HUD personnel. But Ervin later learned that [HUD was] establishing "[p]rocedures for providing databases to [third parties]," including the Data Warehouse. It was not until several months after Ervin provided data downloads to HUD that Ervin learned that several of its competitors had access to the Data Warehouse.

On November 20, 1995, Ervin filed a copyright registration on "certain aspects of its system." Ervin states that the "copyrighted features included the particular manner used to process individual AFSs . . . and the programs used for running competitive queries in multiple projects and assessing the performance of these projects." Ervin states that it applied for the copyright because it suspected that HUD was attempting to duplicate its computer system. . . .

On June 5, 1996, Ervin filed an action in the United States District Court for the District of Columbia[.] . . . HUD terminated the AFS Contract in February 1997. *See* Ervin & Assocs. v. United States, 44 Fed. Cl. 646, 648 (1999).

Based on its experience in the "affordable housing industry," Ervin claims to have identified and summarized 437 "conditions" that typically arise during review of an AFS form, such as missing or inaccurate information, "equity skimming," and indications of certain risks to HUD. [E]rvin wrote computer programs automatically to test the interrelationships of the data elements for each AFS. These tests produced "findings" or "conditions. . . ." Ervin assembled a compilation of these conditions into a three-ring binder ("Conditions Notebook").

On November 20, 1995, Ervin received a copyright on the July 17, 1995 version of the Conditions Notebook, which was distributed to HUD with the notice: "Copyright 1994, 1995 By Ervin and Associates, Incorporated." Ervin also applied and received a copyright [TXU 740-716] on the May 29, 1996 version of the Conditions Notebook. This is the version of the Conditions Notebook that is subject to Counts 6 and 7 of the Complaint in this action.

In a June 13, 1996 letter, Ervin offered to negotiate a copyright license with HUD to resolve a copyright infringement claim that was part of the lawsuit Ervin filed on June 5, 1996 in the United States District Court for the District of Columbia.

DISCUSSION

A. Jurisdiction

[A contractor must exhaust its administrative remedies by first seeking and obtaining a formal decision of the CO (Contracting Officer) before the United States Court of Federal Claims has jurisdiction to hear a breach of contract claim. See 41 U.S.C. §605(a). The United States Court of Federal Claims is authorized under the Tucker Act, 28 U.S.C. §1491(a)(1) (2000), to render judgment and money damages on any claim against the United States Under the CDA (Contract Disputes Act)].

B. Standard for Decision

Review of the contracting officer's decision

The CO's decision, although a prerequisite for the court's exercise of jurisdiction, nevertheless is entitled to no deference, and the contractor retains the burden of proof as to liability, causation, and injury. . . . The plain language of the CDA make[s] it clear that when suit is brought following a contracting officer's decision, the findings of fact in that decision are not binding upon the parties and are not entitled to any deference. The contractor has the burden of proving the fundamental facts of liability and damages *de novo. See* Servidone Constr. Corp. v. United States, 931 F.2d 860, 861 (Fed. Cir. 1991).

C. Issues Raised by the Parties for Summary Judgment

1. The Data Downloads Ervin Provided HUD Were Required by the AFS Contract

HUD claims, as a matter of law, that the data downloads Ervin provided HUD were required by the AFS Contract. Ervin claims the AFS Contract did not require the production or delivery of data downloads.

The record reflects that Ervin provided HUD with four or five separate data downloads during the time the AFS Contract was in effect. In 1994, Ervin voluntarily provided HUD with an extract "representing a sample of HUD projects, to allow HUD to validate the work of its Loan Loss Reserve contractor." HUD asserts that Ervin also delivered AFS Data to HUD "by June

1995," without "attempting to place any restriction on HUD's use." On June 27, 1995, Ervin provided HUD with a "Syquest" disk containing a download of AFS data that HUD requested to test its Data Warehouse. On July 20, 1995, Ervin delivered another Syquest disk to HUD. On or about September 21, 1995, Ervin also provided [government personnel] with a Syquest disk containing a copy of 1993 and 1994 AFS data, which then was inputted into the Data Warehouse and provided by HUD to Ervin's competitors, including Kerry, E & Y, and Hamilton Securities Group.

The AFS Contract specifically incorporated by reference the July 1993 RFP and six subsequent amendments, as well as each of Ervin's proposals, dated August 27, 1993, as amended on September 24, 1993 and December 29, 1993. The finalized SOW required that the selected contractor perform certain "task requirements" and provide specific "deliverables" concerning the AFS forms.

The court has reviewed each of Ervin's proposals, including the December 29, 1993 BAFO, and found that these documents, in large part, are a narrative of Ervin's capabilities. For example, in describing the comparative advantages of its proposal, Ervin advised HUD that:

> We are proposing to provide a full computerized review on all 16,000 financial statements at no additional cost to HUD [and] we also propose to complete a full inventory of all financial statement information instead of only the abbreviated review of the basic financial statements.

What Ervin proposed, however, was a "review" and an "inventory." This language did not specify what the format or manner of delivery for Ervin's "review" and "inventory" would be.

Likewise, Ervin stated that "we would expect to provide a ratio and trend analysis (on hard copy and diskette) for each and every project." A "draft format" of the type of analysis Ervin proposed was attached in an Exhibit B, however, that document also was marked "For Illustrative Purposes Only." In light of the illusory nature of Ervin's proposal regarding the ratio and trend analysis, such language would not support requiring Ervin to deliver ratio and trend reports by download, for each and every project (i.e., 100% of the projects). See RESTATEMENT (SECOND) OF CONTRACTS §2 comment e ("Words of promise which by their terms make performance entirely optional with the 'promisor' . . . do not constitute a promise.").

To illustrate this point, the court suggests a comparison with other portions of Ervin's proposal, where the language used is more definite:

- All information in any way related to the collection and review of annual financial statements will be collected and input (electronically or manually) into one of a series of relational databases residing in a single central location on our IBM AS/400 midrange system.
- Once all required information on a given project has been entered into the system and processed, it will be converted to a WordPerfect compatible format, and transferred to a 5.25″ diskette. This diskette will include the following: [a trend analysis of the project, mail ready draft audit letter, and three other HUD forms].
- Similarly, all information required to be loaded to FO-MNS and/or MIPS systems will be downloaded and converted to the required file type and layout and placed on whatever electronic media is most useful for HUD.

Therefore, the court must look elsewhere in the record to determine whether "Ervin was required by the contract to provide periodic downloads of the financial statement data to the Government." The AFS Contract has two provisions that provide such evidence.

First, the AFS Contract provides that the contractor is required to provide: "data tracking and all data from the Statement of Profit and Loss, Form HUD 92410, and current assets and liabilities from the Balance Sheet, owners equity, accounts payable (other than regular tenants), and accounts receivable (tenants) for downloading to the Field Office Multifamily National System (FOMNS) on a 5-1/4" floppy disc for all fiscal year 1993 financial statements along with the previous two years if not already loaded into the system." Second, the contractor is required to deliver "information required for entry into the Multifamily Insured Processing System ('MIPS') and/or other HUD automated data systems. . . . [But it] must be on HUD provided software." The court finds that these directives in the AFS Contract require Ervin to provide HUD with data from the AFS forms by downloading it in a manner that can be utilized by HUD's automated data systems.

The court also has considered the fact that HUD did not provide Ervin with the required software for the delivery of FOMNS data, as HUD has conceded. . . . HUD's failure to provide the software at issue, however, was not material to Ervin's ability to perform under the contract. *See* Stone Forest Industries, Inc. v. United States, 973 F.2d 1548, 1550 (Fed. Cir. 1992) (holding "not every departure from the literal terms of a contract is sufficient to be deemed a material breach of a contract, thereby allowing the non-breaching party to cease its performance and seek appropriate remedy."). Therefore, the court finds there was no breach that would relieve Ervin from its obligation to provide HUD with the data downloads, expressly as required by the AFS Contract.

There was no constructive change to the *AFS* contract

Ervin contends that HUD's demands for data downloads amounted to a constructive change to the AFS Contract. HUD counters that no changes were made to the AFS Contract and, in any event, Ervin never properly informed the CO that Ervin was being asked to perform extra-contractual work. *See* FAR §52.243-7, "Notification of Changes" Clause, incorporated into the AFS Contract, requiring notice to the CO.

Ervin does not contest that it failed to notify the CO of HUD's requests for allegedly extra-contractual data downloads. . . . Instead, Ervin claims it notified other HUD employees who were in a position to convey this information to the CO or the CO "either knew or should have known of Ervin's contention that the data downloads were not required."

In light of Ervin's representations regarding its experience as a government contractor with a significant prior working relationship with HUD, the court finds that it is Ervin that knew or should have known of the requirement to inform the CO directly of any issues regarding the contract. . . . [I]f there had been a request for work beyond that required by the AFS Contract, appropriate notification to the CO at least would have allowed HUD the opportunity to make an inquiry and address the situation. *See* Calfon Constr., Inc. v. United States, 18 Cl. Ct. 426, 439 (1989), *aff'd*, 923 F.2d 872 (Fed. Cir. 1990) ("[C]ontractors are duty bound to inform the contracting officer if official direction will result in claims against the Government.").

No separate implied-in-fact contract was created

Ervin alleges that a separate implied-in-fact contract arose from Ervin's September 21, 1995 transmittal letter, attached to the Syquest disk containing 1993 and 1994 AFS data, to which HUD did not respond. A related allegation is that HUD breached a second implied-in-fact contract requiring payment for HUD's use of the Conditions Notebooks.

[The] "Rights In Data-General" Clause was implemented in 1987 to provide specific guidance as to what intellectual property rights the Government was entitled when it contracts with private parties. *See* 48 C.F.R. §52.227-14. In addition, they were decided before this issue was addressed by the United States Court of Appeals for the Federal Circuit. *See* Atlas Corp. v. United States, 895 F.2d 745, 754 (Fed. Cir. 1990), *cert. denied*, 498 U.S. 811 (1990) ("The existence of an express contract precludes the existence of an implied contract dealing with the same subject, unless the implied contract is entirely unrelated to the express contract."). In this case, the data downloads and Conditions Notebook at issue were subject to an express contract.

2. The FAR "Rights In Data-General" Clause Provided HUD with "Unlimited Rights" to all Data "First Produced" Under the AFS Contract

HUD also seeks summary judgment that the "Rights In Data-General" Clause provided HUD with "unlimited rights" to information "first produced" under the AFS Contract. Ervin claims otherwise.

a. The AFS contract incorporated the "rights in data-general" clause

The AFS Contract refers to the standard FAR "Rights In Data-General" Clause, but there is no specific language that states that this provision is incorporated into the AFS Contract, in contrast to other provisions of FAR that were incorporated by explicit language. *Compare* Def. App. at 1070 (listing several FAR sections prefaced by the explanation: "This contract incorporates one or more clauses by reference with the same force and effect as if they were given in full text.") *with* Def. App. at 1080 (listing several FAR sections with no such explanation). In fact, it appears that the reference to the "Rights In Data-General" Clause in the AFS Contract was simply "cut and pasted" into the document, along with several other FAR sections.

The United States Court of Appeals for the Federal Circuit has held that the general rules of interpretation apply when the United States is a party to a contract. *See* Scott Timber Co. v. United States, 333 F.3d 1358, 1366 (Fed. Cir. 2003). The purpose of contract interpretation is to carry out the intent of the parties. *See* Gould, Inc. v. United States, 935 F.2d 1271, 1274 (Fed. Cir. 1991).

The isolated reference to FAR §52.227-14 in the AFS Contract can be analyzed two ways. First, if this issue is considered as a matter of missing language, the court may supply "a term which is reasonable under the circumstances" where such language provides "a reasonable meaning to all of [a contract's] . . . parts [which is] . . . preferred to one that leaves a portion of it useless, inexplicable, inoperative, void, insignificant, meaningless [or] superfluous[.]" *Gould, Inc.*, 935 F.2d at 1274. Accordingly, the court finds that the FAR provisions [listed] should be read as if the prefatory language found [to incorporate the other FAR clauses was also present].

On the other hand, if the absence of contract language is viewed as an issue of ambiguity, the court should first determine whether the ambiguity is patent or latent. In this case, the isolated reference to the "Rights In Data-General" Clause is patently ambiguous. The record contains numerous references to Ervin's prior contract expertise. Therefore, if there were any question regarding the applicability of the "Rights In Data-General" Clause, one would expect that an experienced government contractor, like Ervin, would make an inquiry, particularly in light of Ervin's view that the EMFIS, components thereof, and all resulting output was proprietary. Accordingly, under these circumstances, any ambiguity should not be construed against HUD, although sloppy drafting likely contributed to the confusion among HUD employees regarding what data rights HUD actually acquired under the AFS Contract.

The downloads HUD requested of Ervin were for data created in accordance with Ervin's proposals, which represented that all AFS data would be entered into Ervin's computer systems. Because that data did not exist until Ervin performed under the AFS Contract, necessarily they were "first produced in the performance of the contract." HUD, therefore, obtained unlimited rights in the data and the data downloads. *See* 48 C.F.R. §52.227-14(b)(1).

b. Ervin failed to protect its alleged proprietary data with the required limited rights or restricted rights notices

Under the FAR, "data" is defined as "recorded information, regardless of the form or media in which it may be recorded and includes both technical data and computer software." 48 C.F.R. §52.227-14(a). The Government can acquire data with "unlimited rights," "limited rights" or "restricted rights." *See* 48 C.F.R. §52.227-14(a). As a matter of law, the Government obtains "unlimited rights" in all data "first produced" under a government contract, but the contractor may assert that certain data is instead "limited rights" data or "restricted rights" computer software. *See* 48 C.F.R. §52.227-14(b)(iv), (g).

If the contract requires the delivery of "limited rights" data, the contractor may, however, provide the data with a prescribed "Limited Rights Notice" that sets forth the precise conditions under which the Government may disclose data to third parties, i.e., only if the third parties are prohibited from any further use and disclosure. *See* 48 C.F.R. §52.227-14(g) and Alt. II (Limited Rights Notice (June 1987)). "Technical Data" may be delivered with "limited rights," however, if challenged by the Government, the contractor must assert and establish that the data was "developed at private expense" and that the data "embody trade secrets" or are "commercial or financial" and "confidential or privileged." *See* 48 C.F.R. §52.227-14(a), (e). [If] the contractor does not provide the required notice, it must withhold delivery of the data and provide instead "form, fit, and function data." *See* 48 C.F.R. §52.227-14(g)(1).

If the contract requires the delivery of "restricted computer software," the contractor may affix a prescribed "Restricted Rights Notice," that sets forth the more limited conditions under which the Government may disclose data to third parties. *See* 48 C.F.R. §52.227-14(g) and Alt. III (Restricted Rights Notice (June 1987)). Computer software may be delivered with "restricted rights," but the contractor also must, if challenged by the Government, assert and establish that the software was "developed at private expense and [that] it is a trade secret; is commercial or financial and is confidential or privileged; or is published, copyrighted computer software." 48 C.F.R. §52.225-14(a); *see also* §52.225-14(e), (g).

Ervin asserts that it self-funded the creation of the EMFIS prior to the award of the AFS Contract, but upgraded its databases after the award. Ervin, however, did not specify what components of the EMFIS were developed at private expense. Ervin represents that it paid NHP for the rights in "NHP's systems." The record, however, reflects that Ervin, in fact, obtained a perpetual license but only for certain unspecified computer programs and software. In addition, Ervin also had considerable contracting experience with HUD prior to being awarded the AFS Contract and that the EMFIS was created, at least in part, in connection with Ervin's performance of the 1990 Co-Insurance Contract and 1993 Asset Management Contract. Any AFS data in the EMFIS that resulted from work performed under the 1990 Co-Insurance Contract and 1993 Asset Management Contract, however, still would be subject to the "Rights In Data-General" Clause, which has been in effect since June 1987. In addition, four interrelated databases were developed after the AFS Contract was awarded, i.e., the Project Information Database; Tracking Database; Financial Statement Database; and Draft Financial Statement Letter and Analysis Database.

In *Bell Helicopter Textron*, ASBCA No. 21,192, 85-3 BCA ¶18,415, 1985 WL 17050 (1985), the Board held that if no legend was affixed to data, the Government takes "unlimited rights" under the "Rights In Technical Data" Clause, but where the wrong legends were affixed, further inquiry is required to determine whether the data at issue was "limited rights data," i.e., data "developed at private expense." The Board, however, severely limited the potential scope of such data, finding that "[a]ny . . . [g]overnment reimbursement . . . as a direct or indirect cost, of some of the costs of developing an item, component, or process would mean that that item, component, or process was not developed 'at private expense.'" *Id.* at 92,423, 1985 WL 17050; *see also Megapulse, Inc.*, 1980 WL 17275 at *10.

Ervin did not establish that the EMFIS or its components were developed solely at private expense. First, the databases of AFS data were created per Ervin's proposals. Second, they did not exist until the performance began under the AFS Contract. Third, they were required under the AFS Contract, under which Ervin was paid for its services. Moreover, Ervin admitted in its AFS proposal that the EMFIS "currently maintains (prior to the award of the AFS Contract) financial data on over 400 annual financial statements, covering a period of three years or more[.]" Therefore at least a portion of the data at issue was developed at Government expense under the Co-Insurance Contract and Asset Management Contract. Based on this record, the court cannot conclude that the EMFIS or components thereof were developed at private expense.

Even if some databases at issue were developed at Ervin's expense and could qualify as "limited rights" data, as Ervin argues, Ervin was required under FAR to withhold the data after identifying it and furnishing "form, fit, and function data" in its place, or affix the specified notices. [*See*] 48 C.F.R. §52.227-14(g)(1) and Alt. II, III. Ervin never withheld any data and provided "form, fit, and function data" in its place. Moreover, Ervin did not deliver any of the data with either "limited rights" or "restricted rights" notices. Instead, Ervin claims that oral statements, letters, and e-mails to a variety of other HUD officials provided sufficient "limited rights" notice under the "Rights In Data-General" Clause. These communications did not comply with the manner of notice prescribed by FAR and therefore, even if the Government did not already have unlimited rights and even if Ervin's data and EMFIS were developed at private expense, the Government nonetheless acquired "unlimited rights" in all technical data and computer software delivered under the terms of the AFS Contract. In short, Ervin's warnings were both too late and too little.

3. There Was No Infringement of Ervin's System or Components Thereof

a. The EMFIS was not infringed

[T]he court holds that the EMFIS was not copyrightable and therefore, as a matter of law, was not infringed by HUD.

b. The components of the EMFIS were not infringed

At various places in Ervin's briefs and appendix references, Ervin asserts that its computer screens, computer programs, and/or computer databases were infringed. Therefore, each of these claims will be examined.

(i) Computer screens

[T]he court holds that Ervin's computer screens were not copyrightable and therefore, as a matter of law, could not be infringed by HUD.

(ii) Computer programs

In this case, however, a substantial similarity inquiry is not required because all of the computer programs in dispute were created to fulfill Ervin's obligations under the AFS Contract and were "first produced" to perform that work and therefore were subject to the "Rights In Data-General" Clause. See 48 C.F.R. §52.227-14(c)(2). Under this FAR provision, a contractor cannot incorporate copyrighted data "not first produced in the performance of this contract" into data "delivered under this contract" without the grant of an unlimited license to the Government. Id. (emphasis added). Therefore, even if elements of Ervin's computer programs, developed before the AFS Contract was awarded, were used in other programs to perform the AFS Contract, any pre-existing copyrightable interest in Ervin's programs was subject to the FAR. For these reasons, the court holds that any copyrightable elements of Ervin's computer programs were subject to the FAR, which does not permit the incorporation of prior copyrighted material without the permission of the CO or providing the Government with an unlimited license. See 48 C.F.R. §52.227-14(c)(2).

Moreover, although FAR affords "restricted computer software" special protection, it must be software that is "delivered at private expense and . . . a trade secret; is commercial or financial and is confidential or privileged; or is published copyrighted computer software, including minor modifications of such computer software." 48 C.F.R. §52.227-14(a). Arguably, any software that Ervin developed prior to entering into the AFS Contract on February 14, 1994 would be entitled to "restricted treatment," if it were a trade secret, confidential or copyrightable. For reasons previously discussed, however, the court need not make this determination since Ervin's computer software at issue in this case was not delivered at private expense.

(iii) Computer databases

Ervin also claims that it developed "databases of financial data on HUD's portfolio of multifamily mortgages," however, in its proposal, Ervin stated that: "The first step in this process will be to develop a series of four interrelated databases that will work together to collect all of the important information from each project, [i.e.,] . . . Project Information Database; Tracking Database; Financial Statement Database; and Draft Financial Statement Letter and Analysis Database."

[The] FAR does not authorize special protection for databases, but instead provides that: "limited rights data that are formatted as computer databases for delivery to the Government are to be treated as limited rights data and not restricted computer software." 48 C.F.R. §52.227-14(g). Accordingly, the contractor has the obligation to withhold a database, unless it is required to be delivered under the contract. *Id.* And, if the contractor seeks "limited rights" treatment it is required to provide the prescribed "Limited Rights Notice" at the time of delivery.

In this case, the AFS Contract required production of the databases that Ervin created, however, Ervin took none of the requisite steps to have its databases treated as "limited rights" data. *See* 48 C.F.R. §52.227-14(f)(1). For these reasons, the court holds that the computer databases at issue were not copyrightable and, in any event, were subject to the FAR's "limited rights" requirements, which Ervin did not follow. Therefore, as a matter of law, the databases could not be infringed by HUD.

4. The Conditions Notebook Was Not Infringed

The first version of the Conditions Notebook was provided to HUD in 1994 without limited rights or copyright notices. Therefore, HUD acquired this version with "unlimited rights." *See* 48 C.F.R. §52.227-14(b)(1)(iv) and (f)(1) [(granting the Government unlimited rights in "[a]ll other data delivered under this contract unless provided otherwise[,]" 48 C.F.R. §52.227-14(b)(1)(iv); and providing that "[d]ata delivered to the [G]overnment [without notice of limited rights or copyright] shall be deemed to have been furnished with unlimited rights[.]" 48 C.F.R. §52.227-14(f)(1))].

All three versions of the Conditions Notebook were "first produced in performance of [the AFS Contract]." The FAR provides, however, that "[t]he prior, express written permission of the [CO] is required to establish a claim to copyright subsisting in all . . . data first produced in the performance of the contract," other than certain articles for publication. 48 C.F.R. §52.227-14(c)(1). If permission is granted, the contractor must provide the Government with a "paid-up, nonexclusive, irrevocable worldwide license in such copyrighted data[.]" *Id.*

There is no evidence in the record that Ervin requested written permission from the CO prior to delivering the 1995 version of the Conditions Notebook to HUD with a copyright notice. Ervin also did not seek written permission from the CO before registering its copyright for the 1996 Conditions Notebook, but instead, after delivery, demanded that HUD either return all copies of the 1996 version or pay Ervin copyright royalties. Ervin's actions ignored FAR[ ] requirements.

Even if the Conditions Notebooks were not "first produced" in performance of the AFS Contract, they nonetheless were delivered thereunder as training material. *See* 48 U.S.C. §52.227-14(b)(1)(iii) (providing the Government with unlimited rights in "[d]ata delivered under . . . contract . . . that constitute manuals or instructional and training material for instal-lation, operation, or routine maintenance . . . of . . . processes delivered or furnished for use under this contract[.]"); *see also Litton Applied Technology, Corp.* Comp. Gen. Dec. B-227156, B-227090, 87-2 CPD ¶219, 1987 WL 102828 (holding that technological information in a manual could be used by the Government for any purpose since it was delivered with unlimited rights). Therefore, the Government had "unlimited rights" to the Conditions Notebooks, as training material delivered under the AFS Contract.

In addition, although Ervin included copyright notices with its delivery of the 1995 and 1996 Conditions Notebooks, the FAR also governs the copyright of data "not first produced in the performance of this contract" in relation to data "delivered" under contract. *See* 48 C.F.R. §52.227-14(c)(2). Under this provision, the contractor "shall not, without prior written permission of the Contracting Officer, incorporate in data delivered under this contract any data not first produced in the performance of this contract and which contains [a] copyright notice . . . unless the [c]ontractor identifies such data and grants to the Government, or acquires on its behalf, a license of the same scope as set forth in . . . (c)(1) of this clause." *Id.* The function of paragraphs (c)(1) and (c)(2) is to prevent a contractor from imposing potential copyright liability on the Government for data delivered under an existing contract.

The 1995 and 1996 version of the Conditions Notebook, while revised, retain much of the same information as the 1994 version, in which HUD had "unlimited rights." Although the 1995 and 1996 versions included a copyright notice, under the FAR, Ervin could not incorporate copyrighted data not "first produced" under the AFS Contract into data that was "delivered" under the AFS Contract, without the express permission of the CO. *Id.* Therefore, as a matter of law, HUD's "unlimited rights" in the 1995 and 1996 versions of the Conditions Notebook were not diminished by Ervin's copyright notices.

CONCLUSION

For the foregoing reasons, the Government's February 4, 2003 motion for summary judgment is hereby GRANTED in its entirety and Ervin's April 15, 2003 cross-motion for summary judgment is DENIED in its entirety. All counts of the March 19, 2001 complaint are dismissed. The Clerk of the Court is ordered to enter judgment consistent with this opinion.

IN RE GENERAL ATRONICS CORP.
2002 WL 450441, ASBCA No. 49196 (Mar. 19, 2002)

OPINION BY ADMINISTRATIVE JUDGE PAUL PURSUANT TO BOARD RULE 11

This is a timely appeal of a deemed denial by the contracting officer of appellant General Atronics Corporation's (GAC) claim in the amount of $327,000 for software license fees. The Contract Disputes Act (CDA), 41 U.S.C. §§601 et seq., is applicable; only issues of entitlement are before us for decision. The parties elected to submit the appeal on the record pursuant to Board Rule 11. Thereafter, each party filed two sets of briefs; the parties also submitted a voluminous "joint statement of facts as to which there is no genuine issue" (JSF).

FINDINGS OF FACT

1. On 30 October 1991, the Regional Contracting Department, Naval Supply Center (NSC), Norfolk, Virginia, issued a notice . . . stating an intent to "negotiate a fixed-price contract for the design, development, manufacture, and delivery of . . . AN/USQ-XXX Data Terminals

(DTs) with complete mounting hardware, mating connectors, and backshells, associated data, and support services."

2. On 10 April 1992, the Navy's contracting officer issued Solicitation No. N00189-92-R-0039 which stated a requirement for 194 DTs during the base year and four option years. The solicitation incorporated by reference several regulations, including DFARS 252.227-7027, DEFERRED ORDERING OF TECHNICAL DATA OR COMPUTER SOFTWARE (APR 1988) which provided:

> In addition to technical data or computer software specified elsewhere in this contract to be delivered hereunder, the Government may, at any time during the performance of this contract or within a period of three (3) years after acceptance of all items (other than technical data or computer software) to be delivered under this contract or the termination of this contract, order any technical data or computer software generated in the performance of this contract or any subcontract hereunder. When the technical data or computer software is ordered, the Contractor shall be compensated for converting the data or computer software into the prescribed form, for reproduction and delivery. The obligation to deliver the technical data of a subcontractor and pertaining to an item obtained from him shall expire three (3) years after the date the Contractor accepts the last delivery of that item from that subcontractor under this contract. The Government's rights to use said data or computer software shall be pursuant to the "Rights in Technical Data and Computer Software" clause of this contract.

3. The solicitation also incorporated DFARS 252.227-7013, "RIGHTS IN TECHNICAL DATA AND COMPUTER SOFTWARE (OCT 1988)," which provided, in pertinent part:

(a) Definitions.

(1) "Commercial computer software," as used in this clause, means computer software which is used regularly for other than Government purposes and is sold, licensed, or leased in significant quantities to the general public at established market or catalog prices.

(2) "Computer," as used in this clause, means a data processing device capable of accepting data, performing prescribed operations on the data, and supplying the results of these operations; for example, a device that operates on analog data by performing physical processes on the data.

(3) "Computer data base," as used in this clause, means a collection of data in a form capable of being processed and operated on by a computer.

(4) "Computer program," as used in this clause, means a series of instructions or statements in a form acceptable to a computer, designed to cause the computer to execute an operation or operations. Computer programs include operating systems, assemblers, compilers, interpreters, data management systems, utility programs, sort-merge programs, and ADPE maintenance/diagnostic programs, as well as applications programs such as payroll, inventory control, and engineering analysis programs. Computer programs may be either machine-dependent or machine-independent, and may be general-purpose in nature or be designed to satisfy the requirements of a particular user.

(5) "Computer software," as used in this clause, means computer programs and computer data bases. . . .

(c) Rights in Computer Software. —

(1) Restricted Rights.

(i) The Government shall have restricted rights in computer software, listed or described in a license agreement made a part of this contract, which the parties have agreed will be furnished with restricted rights. Notwithstanding any contrary provision in any such license agreement, the Government shall have the rights included in the definition of "restricted rights" in paragraph (a)(17) above. Unless the computer software is marked by the Contractor with the following legend:

Restricted Rights Legend

Use, duplication or disclosure is subject to restrictions stated in Contract No. _____ (Name of Contractor) and the related computer software documentation includes a prominent statement of the restrictions applicable to the computer software, the Government shall have unlimited rights in the software. The Contractor may not place any legend on computer software restricting the Government's rights in such software unless the restrictions are set forth in a license agreement made a part of this contract prior to the delivery date of the software. Failure of the Contractor to apply a restricted rights legend to the computer software shall relieve the Government of liability with respect to unmarked software.

(ii) Notwithstanding subparagraph (c)(1)(i) above, commercial computer software and related documentation developed at private expense and not in the public domain may be marked with the following legend:

Restricted Rights Legend

Use, duplication, or disclosure by the Government is subject to restrictions as set forth in subparagraph (c)(1)(ii) of the Rights In Technical Data and Computer Software clause at DFARS 252.227-7013.

_____

(Name of Contractor and Address). . . .

(2) Unlimited Rights. The Government shall have unlimited rights in:

(ii) Computer software required to be originated or developed under a Government contract, or generated as a necessary part of performing a contract;. . . .

(v) Computer software which is otherwise publicly available, or had been, or is normally released, or disclosed by the Contractor or subcontractor without restriction on further release or disclosure.

(d) Technical Data and Computer Software Previously Provided Without Restriction. Contractor shall assert no restriction on the Government's rights to use or disclose any data or computer software which the contractor has previously delivered to the Government without restriction. The limited or restricted rights provided for by this clause shall not impair the right of the Government to use similar or identical data or computer software acquired from other sources.

(e) Copyright.

(1) In addition to the rights granted under paragraphs (b) and (c), above, the contractor hereby grants to the Government a nonexclusive, paid-up license throughout the world, of the scope set forth below, under any copyright owned by the contractor, in any work of authorship prepared for or acquired by the Government under this contract, to reproduce the work in copies or phonorecords, to distribute copies or phonorecords to the public, to perform or display the work publicly, and to prepare derivative works thereof, and to have others do so for Government purposes. With respect to technical data and computer software in which the Government has unlimited rights the license shall be of the same scope as the rights set forth in the definition of "unlimited rights" in (a)(19) above. With respect to technical data in which the Government has limited rights, the scope of the license is limited to the rights set forth in the definition of "limited rights." With respect to computer software which the parties have agreed will be delivered with restricted rights, the scope of the license is limited to such rights. . . .

(f) Removal of Unjustified and Nonconforming Markings. . . .

(3) Unjustified and Nonconforming Computer Software Markings. Notwithstanding any provision of this contract concerning inspection and acceptance, the Government may correct, cancel, or ignore any marking not authorized by the terms of this contract on any computer software furnished hereunder if:

(i) The Contractor fails to respond within sixty (60) days to a written inquiry by the Government concerning the propriety of the markings; or

(ii) The Contractor's response fails to substantiate, within sixty (60) days after written notice, the propriety of the restricted rights markings.

In either case, the Government shall give written notice to the contractor of the action taken. . . .

(h) Limitation on Charges for Data and Computer Software. The Contractor recognizes that the Government is not obligated to pay, or to allow to be paid, any charges for data or computer software which the Government has a right to use and disclose to others without restriction and Contractor agrees to refund any such payments. This provision applies to contracts that involve payments by subcontractors and those entered into through the Military Assistance Program, in addition to U.S. Government prime contracts. It does not apply to reasonable reproduction, handling, mailing, and similar administrative costs. . . .

(k) Identification of Restrictions on Government Rights. Technical data and computer software shall not be tendered to the Government with other than unlimited rights, unless the technical data or computer software are identified in a list made part of this contract. This list is intended to facilitate review and acceptance of the technical data and computer software by the Government and does not change, waive, or otherwise modify the rights or obligations of the parties under the clause DFARS 252.227-7013. As a minimum, this list must —

(1) Identify the items, components, processes, or computer software to which the restrictions on the Government apply;

(2) Identify or describe the technical data or computer software subject to other than unlimited rights; and

(3) Identify and describe, as appropriate, the category or categories of Government Rights, the agreed-to time limitations, or any special restrictions on the use or disclosure of the technical data or computer software. . . .

5. GAC submitted the sole offer in response to the solicitation. This proposal, dated 10 July 1992, included several pertinent documents. Among them were: Volume I—Part A—Engineering; Volume I—Part C—Management; Appendix B—Software Development; and Appendix F—Bid Sample Manual.

6. GAC listed several "Deviations/Enhancements" in the engineering section of its technical proposal. Under this heading, it stated: "GAC takes no exceptions to the specification, but does offer some unique capabilities and enhancements not required by the specification." GAC described one such enhancement, the "Wireline/Digital Interface," in these terms:

Wireline/Digital Interface (Additional, Unspecified Feature). The proposed AN/USQ-XXX includes GAC's standard wireline/satellite 2400 bps, RS-232 digital data interface. This interface bypasses the HF modem sections of the DT and transmits and receives compatible Line-11 data at 2400 bps. This digital signal contains all the control codes, address codes, error correction and data frames used in conventional Line-11. It enables a DT to operate a variety of system applications and to interoperate with AN/USQ-76(V) and MX-512P DTs which have similar capabilities. These applications include:

a) Point-to-point, two-station digital net (1 unit is PKT; 1 unit is NCS). This can be used for digital transmission of Link-11 over UHS SATCOM, STU-III, DIAL-UP telephone lines, etc. It is particularly helpful in setting up a two-station net for Link-11 software validation with validation facilities (all of which have MX-512P or AN/USQ-76).

b) Mixed Mode (Multi-Media Gateway). Some PUs in a net operate as standard "audio/radio" PUs and some as "wireline/satellite" PUs. The DT, as an NCS, acts as a gateway and rebroadcasts data received on either medium over the other medium in real time. This is a multi-media mode. It has been standard in all GAC DTs for 12 years.

c) Translator. The MX-512PV can be used as a relay between two media such as the wireline and HF or UHF radio link. The DT functionally operates as a picket.

d) Split Mode. Two DTs are interconnected with the 2400 bps digital circuit and act together as a single PU. The "remote" DT functions as an HF modem and can be located at an unattended Ground Entry Station. The "local" DT manages the station and interfaces to the KG-40. It is usually at the OPS Center. In this way, a ground-based PU with a remote radio facility can meet the old MIL-STD-188-203-1 transmission and timeout standard (15 frames).

7. In late October 1992, representatives of the Navy and GAC met to discuss pricing of the optional items—or "enhancements"—contained in GAC's proposal. GAC provided the Navy with a "matrix" of these options on 29 October 1992 (attach. 1 to GAC's letter to the Board of 19 July 1994). The matrix clearly referred to the software packages associated with the wireline interface hardware as "Options." On 30 October 1992, the parties concluded their negotiations relating to the various options offered by GAC. The memorandum of negotiations treated the pricing of the options accepted by the Navy in great detail. However, the software

packages associated with the wireline interface hardware were not even mentioned as being among the optional items purchased by the Navy.

8. On 17 November 1992, NSC awarded fixed-price Contract No. N00189-93-C-0082 to GAC in the amount of $1,140,030. After award, the parties became engaged in a dispute as to whether GAC was required to provide certain of the software packages along with the wireline interface hardware. GAC supplied the software packages under protest and later submitted a certified claim in the amount of $203,684. In a decision issued on 16 August 1994, ASBCA No. 46784, 94-3 BCA ¶27,112, the Board ruled that NSC had not purchased the software packages and that they had been offered as options by GAC. We sustained the appeal.

9. As awarded, the contract incorporated various regulations, including DFARS 252.227-7027 (APR 1988) and DFARS 252.227-7013 (OCT 1988), which we have quoted at length. Viewed together, these provisions gave the Navy unlimited rights in GAC's wireline software unless GAC both marked the software with a specific "Restricted Rights Legend" and, under (c)(i), incorporated the restrictions in a licensing agreement "made a part of [the] contract prior to the delivery date of the software."

10. Further, the contractual requirements which we have cited make no distinction between computer software which is contained in a diskette and that, like the software at issue here, which is embedded in a memory device. DFARS 252.227-7013(a) defines computer software as "computer programs and computer data bases." Computer program is, in turn, defined very broadly to include software which is "either machine-dependent or machine-independent[.]" The imbedded wireline software supplied by GAC was "machine-dependent"; therefore, the legending requirements applied to it.

11. GAC's proposal contained the following proprietary language:

GENERAL ATRONICS PROPRIETARY

This proposal or quotation includes data that shall not be disclosed outside the Government and shall not be duplicated, used, or disclosed — in whole or in part — for any purpose other than to evaluate this proposal or quotation. If, however, a contract is awarded to this offerer or quoter as a result of — or in connection with — the submission of this data, the Government shall have the right to duplicate, use, or disclose the data to the extent provided in the resulting contract. This restriction does not limit the Government's right to use information contained in this data if it is obtained from another source without restriction. The data subject to this restriction is contained in sheets marked, "USE OR DISCLOSURE OF DATA CONTAINED ON THIS SHEET IS SUBJECT TO THE RESTRICTION ON THE TITLE PAGE OF THIS PROPOSAL OR QUOTATION."

The data subject to this restriction are contained in sheets ALL. (FAR 52.215-12, APR 1984)

Furthermore, the information contained in this Volume, including, without limitation, proposer's cost, financial and technical data, is subject to exemption from disclosure under the Freedom of Information Act, 5 USC Section 522, paragraphs (b)(4) and (b)(5). In addition, GAC placed the following language at the bottom of each page of its proposal: "Use or disclosure of data contained on this sheet is subject to the restriction on the title page of this proposal or quotation."

12. When GAC delivered the wireline interface software, it did not mark the software with any specific restricted rights legend. In addition, prior to the delivery date of the software, the parties did not execute a licensing agreement. In fact, GAC did not even propose to enter a licensing agreement until 12 October 1994, approximately 16 months after the first DT units had been delivered.

13. Although GAC failed to mark the wireline interface software with a restrictive legend, it did place the following legends on the display screen which comprised part of the DT system:

AN/USQ-125 VERSION 1.11
GENERAL ATRONICS CORPORATION 1995

However, these legends did not conform with the specific requirements of DFARS 252.227-7013. In addition, they did not even make reference to any proprietary rights on GAC's part.

14. During contractual performance, GAC forwarded to the Navy a document entitled "Firmware Update Procedure For The CP-2206/USQ-125 Processor." The first page of the document contained the following statement: "This document contains information proprietary to General Atronics Corporation. It shall not be published, reproduced, copied, or used, in whole or in part, for any purpose without the expressed [sic] written permission of a duly authorized agent of the company." This assertion did not make any reference to the wireline interface software. Nor did the document itself refer to the software.

15. The memory devices containing the wireline interface software contained the following alphanumeric markings: 20183-34116-V48 and 20183-34115-V47. These markings do not contain any restrictive legends, as prescribed by DFARS 252.227-7013.

16. Upon receipt of the Board's decision sustaining GAC's appeal that it had offered the interface wireline software as an option, ASBCA No. 46784, 94-3 BCA ¶27,112, the parties entered into settlement negotiations resulting in the execution of bilateral Modification No. P00020 to the contract on 20 March 1995. The Navy agreed to pay GAC $230,477 in [full] settlement of its claim. On 20 September 1994, GAC submitted a request for an equitable adjustment in the amount of $327,000 for license fees for the software applications. On 12 October 1994, GAC refiled its claim with a proper certification; however, the Navy's contracting officer never issued a final decision on this claim. In a decision issued on 25 September 1995, ASBCA No. 46784, 96-1 BCA ¶28,004, the Board ordered that GAC's appeal for license fees be given a new docket number. The appeal was subsequently docketed as ASBCA No. 49196.

DECISION

In formulating their arguments, both parties rely heavily on the Board's seminal decision in *Bell Helicopter Textron*, ASBCA No. 21192, 85-3 BCA ¶18,415. The contract at issue in that appeal contained a "Rights in Technical Data" clause, ASPR 7-104.9(a) (AUG 1969) which was almost identical with DFARS 252.227-7013 (OCT 1988), the provision which governs the present dispute. Appellant's subcontractor, Hughes Aircraft Company (Hughes), repeatedly placed the Government on notice that it considered data relating to a missile launching subsystem to be proprietary. Nevertheless, Hughes delivered 21 out of a total of 103 technical, engineering drawings to the Government without restrictive legends. Citing the specific requirements of the "Rights in Technical Data" clause, the Board ruled that, by failing to mark the drawings at issue with restrictive legends and by not seeking an express determination of limited rights, Hughes had given the Government unlimited rights in the technical data conveyed by the drawings. Accordingly, the Board rejected Hughes' estoppel argument. 85-3 BCA ¶18,415 at 92,409, 92,432-33.

Citing the *Bell Helicopter Textron* decision, GAC refers to its assertion of proprietary rights in its proposal and concludes that the Navy should be estopped from contending that it has unlimited rights in the wireline interface software. GAC's reliance on the decision is misplaced. It overlooks the fact that the Government in *Bell Helicopter Textron* was also aware of Hughes' assertion of proprietary rights. Perhaps more significantly, GAC does not emphasize that, like Hughes, it failed to comply with the regulation governing the effective assertion of proprietary rights. Specifically, GAC did not mark the wireline interface software with a restrictive legend. Moreover, it did not incorporate any restrictions into a licensing agreement "made a part of [the] contract prior to the delivery date of the software." Therefore, pursuant to DFARS 252.227-7013 (OCT 1988), the Navy acquired unlimited rights in the software.

GAC's subsidiary arguments do not detract from this conclusion. For example, it appears to contend that DFARS 252.227-7013 (OCT 1988) applies only to diskettes and not to software embedded in memory devices. GAC is mistaken. Subsection (a) of the regulation makes it clear that the term "computer software" refers to machine-dependent programs. The wireline interface software is embedded in memory devices and is, thus, machine-dependent. Therefore, the regulation's requirements are applicable to it (finding 10).

We are also not persuaded that various markings placed by GAC on other elements of the DTs such as the display screen, the firmware update document, or the memory devices themselves constituted restrictive legends. The requirements of the regulation are very specific, and GAC failed to comply with them (findings 13, 14, 15). Finally, GAC's belated attempt to place restrictive legends on the two diskettes which it delivered in September 1995 is unavailing. By this point in time, all of the DTs had been delivered and the Navy had gained unlimited rights in the technical data (finding 15). . . . The appeal is denied.

UNITED STATES MARINE, INC. v. UNITED STATES

722 F.3d 1360 (Fed. Cir. 2013)

United States Marine, Inc. (USM) sued the United States in the United States District Court for the Eastern District of Louisiana under the Federal Tort Claims Act (FTCA). Specifically, USM claimed that the United States Navy, which had lawfully obtained USM's proprietary technical drawings under a contract (to which USM was not a party), owed USM a duty of secrecy that it breached by disclosing those drawings to a rival private firm.

After the district court found the United States liable for trade-secret misappropriation and awarded USM damages, the United States Court of Appeals for the Fifth Circuit held that the district court lacked jurisdiction over USM's claims under the FTCA. The Fifth Circuit reasoned that (a) the Navy's liability and USM's recovery depended on the interpretation of a federal-government contract and (b) therefore the matter lay exclusively within the jurisdiction of the Court of Federal Claims under the Tucker Act, 28 U.S.C. §1491(a)(1).

Given the decision of the transfer question in this case by the Fifth Circuit, we do not decide the question afresh. We ask only whether the Fifth Circuit decision was clearly in error. Unable to say that it was, we affirm.

BACKGROUND

USM builds military boats. Sometime before mid-1993, working with VT Halter Marine, Inc., which was a subsidiary of Trinity Marine Group and also a shipbuilder, USM developed a design for a special-operations craft with a hull made out of composite materials. The companies developed the design — now called the "Mark V," — for VT Halter to use in competing for the "MK V Special Operations Craft and Transporter System Contract" with the United States Navy. Before VT Halter submitted a bid to the Navy, USM and VT Halter built a prototype of the special-operations craft. The district court in this case found that the design and development of the craft did not rely on government funds. VT Halter also designed a version of the craft with an aluminum hull. Although the working relationship between USM and VT Halter initially was informal, the companies shared ownership of the Mark V design.

As part of its bid for two development contracts with the Navy in 1993, VT Halter submitted technical drawings of both the aluminum and composite versions of the Mark V design. VT Halter stamped the drawings with a "Limited Rights Legend" that invoked a specific provision of the DFARS, namely, Section 252.227-7013(a)(15), which states limitations on the government's use and outside disclosure of certain information. VT Halter's proposal also stated that, if it were awarded the contracts, any design data would be furnished subject to restrictions on the government's use and disclosure as provided for in the contracts.

On August 6, 1993, the Navy, through its Special Operations Command, awarded VT Halter two contracts to develop prototypes of (respectively) the aluminum- and composite-hull crafts. The development contracts incorporated by reference all of DFARS §252.227-7013, which addresses "[r]ights in technical data and computer software." As required, VT Halter marked its submitted design drawings and technical data with a Limited Rights Legend as prescribed by the DFARS provision.

On November 30, 1994, after testing and evaluation of the prototypes, the Navy selected the Mark V aluminum-hull craft for actual construction and awarded VT Halter a production contract. VT Halter again submitted design drawings marked with the legend required by DFARS §252.227-7013; but for whatever reason, the production contract did not incorporate that provision. Pursuant to the production contract, VT Halter built and delivered twenty-four Mark V special-operations craft to the Navy.

In 2004, the Navy awarded a research grant to the University of Maine to improve the ride and handling capabilities of the Mark V craft. Between 2004 and late 2006, the Navy provided numerous, detailed design drawings of the Mark V craft to firms that were acting as contractors for Maine Marine Manufacturing LLC, a joint venture between the University of Maine and a private shipbuilder. Although the design drawings were stamped with the DFARS Limited Rights Legend, the Navy did not obtain VT Halter's consent for the Navy's disclosure to the firms.

When USM discovered that the Navy had disclosed its Mark V design information outside the government, it took pre-suit steps prescribed by the FTCA and then sued the United States for misappropriation of trade secrets in the federal district court in Louisiana. The FTCA expressly declares the United States subject to liability on certain tort claims — using relevant state law to define the torts — and vests jurisdiction over such claims exclusively in the district courts, thus waiving sovereign immunity for such claims. 28 U.S.C. §§1346(b)(1), 2674. In its complaint, USM alleged that the United States owed it a duty to maintain the secrecy of its Mark V design information and to limit its use because of the confidentiality provisions in the contracts and the legends stamped on the design drawings.

The government moved to dismiss USM's claim for lack of subject matter jurisdiction. Pointing to USM's allegation that the Navy's duty to protect the Mark V design information and drawings arose from the contracts between VT Halter and the Navy, the government argued that USM's claim should be treated as a claim of tortious breach of contract, which could be heard only by the Claims Court under the Tucker Act, 28 U.S.C. §1491(a)(1). The district court denied the government's motion.

After the district court also refused to find that VT Halter was a necessary party to the case, the government brought VT Halter into the case through a third-party complaint. In response, VT Halter filed a counterclaim against the United States, adding its own FTCA-based claim for trade-secret misappropriation to USM's. The government moved to dismiss VT Halter's counterclaim on the jurisdictional ground that it already had unsuccessfully invoked against USM's suit, but the district court denied the motion. Despite arguing that jurisdiction was proper in the Claims Court in both motions to dismiss, at no point during the litigation did the government request a transfer of the case to the Claims Court.

In January 2010, the district court held a bench trial on liability. On April 1, 2010, the court found that the Navy misappropriated Mark V design information by disclosing it to Maine Marine Manufacturing without VT Halter's or USM's authorization. Regarding the source of the restriction on the government's use of the design information — a necessary element of the tort — the court determined that "[b]oth the contractual provision and limited rights legends were sufficient notification to the government that disclosure of the [Mark V] design would violate a duty to its owners." After a separate bench trial on damages, the court held that USM and VT Halter were entitled to approximately $1.45 million in damages as a reasonable royalty for the government's use of the trade secrets.

The government appealed, challenging both the district court's jurisdiction over VT Halter's claim and the damages award. The government did not challenge the district court's jurisdiction over USM's claim.

The Fifth Circuit held that the district court lacked jurisdiction over VT Halter's counterclaim under the FTCA. U.S. Marine, Inc. v. United States, 478 Fed. Appx. 106 (5th Cir. 2012). Although VT Halter styled its counterclaim as a tort, the Fifth Circuit ruled that the Navy's alleged duty "stem[med] directly from the 'limited rights' provisions found in the VT Halter-Navy contracts," and the district court had necessarily interpreted those contract provisions in order to determine the Navy's duties with respect to using and disclosing the design information. Therefore, the Fifth Circuit reasoned, any claims stemming from the alleged breach of such provisions sounded in contract, not in tort, and were within the exclusive jurisdiction of the Claims Court.

Although the government did not appeal the district court's jurisdiction over USM's claim, and indeed stated at oral argument that the Claims Court would not have jurisdiction over USM's claim, the Fifth Circuit sua sponte held USM's claim barred from district court for the same reason as VT Halter's. A majority of the panel held that USM's claim, like VT Halter's, was based on the contract between VT Halter and the Navy and was therefore within the exclusive jurisdiction of the Claims Court:

> Like VT Halter's counterclaim, the "limited rights" provisions of the contracts provide the essential basis for USM[ ]'s claim. We can find no basis for the Navy's potential liability independent of those terms and the duties of non-disclosure they placed upon the Navy. . . . The Tucker Act explicitly forbids such interpretation of federal contracts by the district courts, and there is no potential liability in this case without it.

[T]he majority noted that the lack of privity between the Navy and USM might mean that USM would be denied the right to recover in the Claims Court. With no further analysis, the court left it to the Claims Court to consider whether USM qualified as an implied third-party beneficiary allowed to enforce the contracts' limited-rights provisions under the Tucker Act. The Fifth Circuit vacated the district court's judgment and remanded with instructions to transfer the case to the Claims Court under 28 U.S.C. §1631.

DISCUSSION

For the transfer order to be correct under 28 U.S.C. §1631, two conditions must be met, as the government expressly agrees: the district court must lack jurisdiction over USM's action, and the Claims Court must have jurisdiction over USM's action.

The Fifth Circuit is a coordinate court, not bound by any ruling this court might independently make on the question. If we were to disagree with that court's judgment requiring transfer, the case would seemingly be left without a forum, unless the Supreme Court intervened. In these circumstances, under the "law of the case" doctrine, we think that we must affirm the transfer order here unless we conclude that the Fifth Circuit's judgment requiring transfer was "clearly erroneous," i.e., was not even "plausible." Whatever result we would reach if we were considering the question de novo, we are not able to draw that conclusion.

If one were to look only at the statutory grants of jurisdiction, and start with the statute under which USM brought its claim, transfer here would be hard to support. That is so with regard to both requirements for the Section 1631 transfer: that the district court lack jurisdiction and the Claims Court have jurisdiction.

In the liability-imposing section of the FTCA, with exceptions not applicable here, Congress unequivocally imposed liability on the United States for torts, using state law to define the torts. There is no dispute here, and the Fifth Circuit recognized, that misappropriation of a trade secret is a form of liability-supporting tort that is recognized in the relevant state in this case. In 28 U.S.C. §1346(b)(1), Congress expressly granted district courts, like the district court here, jurisdiction to adjudicate such liability.

In contrast, the Claims Court cannot adjudicate USM's claim of tort liability for misappropriation of trade secrets. Congress committed the adjudication of Section 2674 liability to the "exclusive jurisdiction" of the district courts. Nothing on the face of the Claims Court's jurisdictional statute, 28 U.S.C. §1491, overrides that exclusive commitment.

In short, USM's expressly stated claim is an FTCA claim for liability based on the Virginia law of trade-secret misappropriation. That claim, on its face, is within the district court's jurisdiction and is not within the Claims Court's jurisdiction. Without further analysis, those conclusions would make the Fifth Circuit's order to transfer the case wrong on both of the premises required for transfer.

B

The basis for the Fifth Circuit's conclusion can be seen if one changes the analysis in two ways. The first is to begin with the Tucker Act, not with the FTCA. The second is to give prominence to the essential background principle of sovereign immunity and what it means for jurisdiction over claims against the United States.

As relevant here, the Tucker Act, in 28 U.S.C. §1491(a)(1), grants the Claims Court jurisdiction over a claim "founded . . . upon any express or implied contract with the United States . . . ," and where the claim is for $10,000 or more, the Tucker Act grants jurisdiction over such a claim only to the Claims Court.

[The Court then reviewed the purpose of the Tucker Act in light of the principles of sovereign immunity.]

Accordingly, if one begins with the Tucker Act grant, one must ask whether the matter at issue falls within that grant and, if so, whether another statute should be read to grant a district court jurisdiction over the matter despite the Tucker Act. A court must consider whether the matter is within the policy underlying the presumptive congressional commitment to Claims Court/Federal Circuit exclusivity, whether it is within another congressionally enacted policy, and whether the latter displaces the former if both apply.

The Fifth Circuit in this case started with the Tucker Act and proceeded down this analytic path. It held that USM's claim depends on an adjudication of the government's contract obligation, which the Tucker Act presumptively limits to the Claims Court for claims of this magnitude. USM does not dispute that characterization of its claim, which therefore brings into play the Tucker Act's forum policies. The Fifth Circuit must be understood as having then determined that there was no good enough reason to find a congressional displacement, for this case, of the Tucker Act's commitment of major contract-adjudication issues to particular forums.

C

In doing so, the Fifth Circuit followed a number of decisions, going back half a century, involving non-contract claims that arose out of conduct that also gave rise to contract claims. Those decisions hold that sometimes a party's tort claim in district court is so rooted in a contract-breach claim that its adjudication outside the Tucker Act's grant of jurisdiction would be an unjustified incursion on the presumptive commitment of contract matters to the forums designated in the Tucker Act. In those cases, any claim of liability under the FTCA, specifically

28 U.S.C. §2674, was necessarily displaced, because that claim cannot be heard in the Claims Court.

In Woodbury v. United States, the Ninth Circuit ruled that a claim against the United States for breach of fiduciary duty, though styled as a tort, should be treated as claim for a breach of contract properly within the jurisdiction of the Claims Court. 313 F.2d 291 (9th Cir. 1963). The district court dismissed [Woodbury's breach of fiduciary duty] claim for lack of jurisdiction, and the Ninth Circuit agreed.

According to the Ninth Circuit, where an "action is essentially for breach of a contractual undertaking, and the liability, if any, depends wholly upon the government's alleged promise, the action must be under the Tucker Act, and cannot be under the [FTCA]." The court explained:

> Many breaches of contract can also be treated as torts. But in cases such as this, where the "tort" complained of is based entirely upon breach by the government of a promise made by it in a contract, so that the claim is in substance a breach of contract claim, and only incidentally and conceptually also a tort claim, we do not think that the common law or local state law right to "waive the breach and sue in tort" brings the case within the Federal Tort Claims Act.

The Ninth Circuit added that a different result threatened "the long established policy that government contracts are to be given a uniform interpretation and application under federal law." The Ninth Circuit concluded that Mr. Woodbury's claim for breach of fiduciary duty had to be brought under the Tucker Act because liability depended entirely on the contractual promise by the federal agency and whether the agency breached it.

Other cases followed *Woodbury*.

[I]n those cases the plaintiffs necessarily lost the ability to pursue FTCA tort claims when the matters were routed to the Claims Court. The fact that transfer of USM's case to the Claims Court will cause it to lose its tort claim as pleaded, therefore, does not distinguish this case. The argument instead focuses on what claims would be meaningfully available in the Claims Court upon transfer.

In at least most of the cases in the *Woodbury* line, the plaintiffs had the kind of asserted privity of contract with the United States that readily permits litigation of the issues of contract breach, injury, and damages under the Tucker Act (subject to generally applicable requirements such as timeliness). In that circumstance, transfer to the Claims Court, while depriving the plaintiff of the ability to press an FTCA tort claim, seemingly leaves the plaintiff with a cause of action that permits recovery of compensation for contract-related harm caused by the United States. USM's case is challenging for application of the *Woodbury* principle precisely because of the arguable difference in that respect. But for two reasons together, we are not prepared to say that the Fifth Circuit's reliance on the *Woodbury* principle is clearly in error.

1

It is not clear whether a meaningful opportunity for recovery in the Claims Court is always a necessary requirement for application of the principle implemented in the *Woodbury* line of cases. The policy implicit in the Tucker Act's presumptive commitment of government-contract adjudications to the Claims Court (except for small claims) and to this court (for all claims) conceivably might be impaired by allowing another forum to construe a government-contract provision even if the Claims Court could not do so in the particular case. Such a construction might impair the government's interest in uniform construction of a provision, like a standard DFARS provision, that is widely used in the government's contracts. More broadly, appeals to the idea that wrongs presumptively have remedies, which often has great force in resolving genuine uncertainties in statutory interpretation, require special caution where the wrongdoer is the United States, which, by virtue of sovereign immunity, generally cannot be sued even for harm it wrongfully inflicts except where it consents to suit. For these reasons, we cannot easily dismiss (while we need not affirmatively embrace) the notion that an apparent congressional bar on adjudication of the United States' contractual duties outside the Tucker Act forums can prevail even when the result is to preclude recovery for harm.

2

This case, however, does not require us to adopt or to reject the starker potential view of a Tucker-Act-exclusivity principle, because we cannot say that USM itself lacks a meaningful remedy under the Tucker Act in the Claims Court. Unable to exclude the availability of a meaningful Tucker Act remedy for USM, we are not prepared to conclude that USM's position differs materially, in the respect USM rightly features as its strongest point, from that of most plaintiffs in the *Woodbury* line.

This is not because we recognize a meaningful possibility that USM can litigate a tort claim in the Claims Court. If a tort claim is brought under the FTCA, it plainly cannot be adjudicated in the Claims Court, because Section 1346(b)(1) gives the district court exclusive jurisdiction over such claims. . . . [H]istory counts strongly against allowing adjudication of any "tort" claims under the Tucker Act. . . . In any event, we are not prepared to initiate what would be a sea-change in Tucker Act law to find a tort claim cognizable in the Claims Court.

Instead, we rest our conclusion about the possibility of a meaningful Tucker Act remedy for USM on other grounds. The first is that it now appears that USM can pursue a contract claim, in the specific sense that it can proceed directly to litigate whether the government breached a contract-based obligation (regarding USM's trade secrets), the harm caused, and the appropriate quantification of damages. The Fifth Circuit expressly ruled that "USM[ ] was a subcontractor to VT Halter with respect to the VT Halter-Navy contracts," while noting that it would ultimately be for the Claims Court to decide what contract-enforcement rights USM had. That ruling is subject to the law-of-the-case doctrine, with its protections and limitations, as to both USM and the government.

In short, the government's argument for the Claims Court's jurisdiction (made here and in the district court, but not in the Fifth Circuit) legally acknowledges that USM is entitled to get to the breach, injury, and damages questions, having cleared the threshold of being among those with a right to recover upon satisfactory proof on those questions. And it follows that this court's action in now adopting the government's argument and affirming the transfer order, which depends on the Claims Court's having jurisdiction, establishes that right, as a matter of binding precedent and judicial estoppel. While USM has until now sought to deny its right to recover in contract in the Claims Court, it may well be able to do so once the case is transferred to the Claims Court based on the government's jurisdictional argument.

The second reason for our conclusion that USM may have a meaningful remedy in the Claims Court concerns the possibility that USM has a takings claim. The Supreme Court has held that a government use or disclosure of a trade secret can constitute a taking for which, under the Fifth Amendment, the United States must pay just compensation. Ruckelshaus v. Monsanto Co., 467 U.S. 986, 1001-04, 104 S. Ct. 2862, 81 L. Ed. 2d 815 (1984) (trade secrets protected by Takings Clause); *id.* at 1011-14, 104 S. Ct. 2862 (disclosure or use by the government contrary to restrictions under which the government received trade-secret information may be a compensable taking). The Tucker Act, in 28 U.S.C. §1491(a)(1), embraces takings claims within its coverage of claims "founded . . . upon the Constitution. . . . " In a recent non-precedential opinion, this court has recognized the point, reversing a dismissal of a takings claim involving trade secrets. Gal-Or v. United States, 470 Fed. Appx. 879 (Fed. Cir. 2012).

Under that authority, USM may have a claim for compensation under the Tucker Act. We do not say that USM has such a claim, because the case has not been pled in that form (the case not having been in a forum where such pleading was possible), and the issue therefore has not been explored. Nor do we say anything about the merits of such a claim if USM can assert it. We say only that such a claim may be available to USM; if so, the claim might provide USM a meaningful compensatory remedy for the wrong and injury it alleges.

If USM has a meaningful remedy in the Claims Court, USM's strongest argument for seeking to distinguish the *Woodbury* line of cases, and for criticizing the Fifth Circuit's resolution of the boundary problem for the FTCA and Tucker Act in this case, weakens substantially. On that premise, the transfer question does not depend on the stark and much more problematic assertion that the interest in uniform Claims Court (and Federal Circuit) adjudication of government-contract obligations, an interest embodied in the Tucker Act, is so strong as to justify stripping an injured party of any right to compensation, including the right Congress expressly granted in the FTCA's Section 2674. If USM has a meaningful remedy in the Claims Court, both of the congressionally declared interests — the forum-specificity interest and the compensation interest — can be meaningfully preserved. We are not prepared to conclude that this case clearly requires sacrifice of the compensation interest.

CONCLUSION

We need not say whether we would draw a conclusion different from that of the Fifth Circuit if we were freshly conducting the analysis of the interaction of the FTCA and Tucker Act schemes. When the general Tucker Act's reach overlaps with that of another statutory regime, it is certainly possible that the other regime is the one that takes precedence. But we cannot say that the Fifth Circuit's determination, that in this case it is the FTCA that gives way, is clearly wrong.

The Fifth Circuit ruling that the case must be transferred to the Claims Court is law of the case. Applying that doctrine, we affirm the resulting transfer order. In doing so, we necessarily hold that the Claims Court has jurisdiction over USM's suit, with all that entails under this court's precedents about the issues thereby resolved. At this point, this case presents even more than the usual reasons for litigation to proceed with expedition and with minimization of wasteful duplication.

AFFIRMED.

III. PROBLEMS

1. In contrast to the *Campbell* case cited in the Materials section of this chapter, the federal government's policy is generally to respect the patent rights of the owner of subject invention, particularly in the case of a preexisting invention. There are times, however, when the government will be required to induce infringement of a patented invention. In those instances, the federal government or its contractors should attempt to anticipate the required infringement and seek to include an authorization and consent clause from the FAR into a solicitation or a government contract.

   1.1 What would be the rationale for including an authorization and consent clause from FAR into a government contract with a contractor who is not the owner of the patented invention? *See* Madey v. Duke University, 413 F. Supp. 2d 601 (M.D.N.C. 2006).

   1.2 In what circumstance would the government want to include a broad, as opposed to a narrow or limited, authorization and consent clause?

   1.3 Compare the two clauses provided below and identify which is broad and which is limited:

Authorization and Consent #1

The Government hereby gives its authorization and consent for all use and manufacture of any invention described in and covered by a patent of the United States in the performance of this grant or any part hereof or any amendment hereto or any contract hereunder (including all lower-tier contracts hereunder). See FAR 27.201-2(b).

Authorization and Consent #2

The Government authorizes and consents to all use and manufacture in performing this contract or any subcontract at any tier of any invention described in and covered by a United States patent (1) embodied in the structure or composition of any article the delivery of which is accepted by the Government under this contract or (2) used in machinery, tools, or methods whose use necessarily results from compliance by the Contractor or subcontractor with (i) specifications or written provisions forming a part of this contract or (ii) specific written instructions given by the Contracting Officer directing the manner of performance. See FAR 27.201-2(a).

   1.4 With respect to Authorization and Consent #2, would a research proposal, which is subsequently funded by the federal government, allow the researcher to avoid liability for patent infringement where the government is not specifically aware of the infringement and has not specifically approved of such infringement in its specifications, directions, or other communications with the researcher/contractor? *See Madey*, 413 F. Supp. 2d 601 (M.D.N.C. 2006).

2. The *Ervin* case analyzes the civilian data rights provision governing the acquisition and use of contractor-developed intellectual property. In addition to the civilian

data rights clause, the federal government has seen fit to promulgate regulations governing military acquisition and use of technical data and computer software. Specifically, the DFARS has its own data rights provisions. These provisions can be found in several places — on the Internet, in legal research databases, and in the Code of Federal Regulations. If you were to compare the two provisions side-by-side, you would swiftly conclude that the provisions and contract clauses are starkly different. In fact, the military data rights clauses in the DFARS are significantly more detailed than those in the FAR.

2.1 What rationales would you put forth to explain the differences between the civilian and the military data rights provisions and contract clauses? Note that both civilian agencies and military agencies rely on the same patent rights provisions and contract clauses of the FAR.

2.2 How do you explain the federal government's approach to regulating technical data and computer software under one complex scheme while using a separate regulatory scheme for patent rights?

2.3 Should separate regulatory schemes be maintained for both civilian and military agencies for the acquisition of intellectual property?

2.4 Under the FAR data rights clause, 52.227-14, why are "government purpose rights" excluded from the use rights available to the federal government, especially considering that this use license appears in DFARS 227.7103-5(b) (provision) and 252.227-7013 (contract clause)?

3. You are lobbying the Congressional Joint Armed Services Committee for your client, a prominent military defense contractor that develops computer war-game simulators for use by the Army. Your client has explained to you that segregable components of the military software programs that it provides to the Army have previously been developed from commercial use applications. Will you lobby for regulations that unify the civilian and military data rights clauses, will you favor the varied approach to data rights regulations, or will you propose some different or hybrid treatment? *See generally* In re Appeal of Ship Analytics International, Inc., 2001 WL 66653, 01-1 BCA ¶31,253, ASBCA No. 50,914 (Jan. 11, 2001).

4. As the Federal Circuit noted in *U.S. Marine, supra*, the Federal Circuit and the numbered geographic circuits are coordinate courts. As a result, a decision by the Federal Circuit would not bind the Fifth Circuit, and the Fifth Circuit cannot bind the Federal Circuit. Yet the Federal Circuit has (in effect) exclusive jurisdiction over contract disputes when the United States is the defendant, while the geographic circuits have (in effect) exclusive jurisdiction over tort cases when the United States is the defendant.

In *U.S. Marine*, the plaintiff appears to have fully complied with the DFARS requirements for providing the government with restricted rights in technical data. When the government breached, U.S. Marine brought it to court, took the case to trial, and was awarded substantial damages only to have the Fifth Circuit rule that the case had been brought in the wrong forum, effectively forcing it to start over in the Court of Federal Claims. Could this outcome have been avoided? If so, how?

IV. DRAFTING EXERCISES

1. Meta Corporation is negotiating a grant with the National Institutes of Health and the Environmental Protection Agency. The scope of the prospective grant involves the development of new systems for the diagnosis and therapy of cardiovascular disease and potential methods for UV irradiation for pathogen inactivation in surface waters. The government intends to fund development of a lab at Meta Corporation to assist in the research for these two projects. The proposed period for funding is from October 1, 2010, to September 30, 2014. Specifically, you are called in to draft and negotiate the authorization and consent clause that will govern the grant. Meta informs you that not all of the research on the two projects can be done only by Meta researchers; rather, Meta will rely on both government researchers and outside researchers (from universities and other organizations) to achieve research results. List the considerations you will have to take into account before drafting the authorization and consent provision for inclusion in the funding agreement/contract with the federal government.

2. Now that you have listed the considerations, draft the authorization and consent provision for the funding agreement that will ensure Meta the greatest protection against liability for potential patent infringement while performing research and using the lab under the grant with NIH and EPA.

3. In the *Ervin* case, the Court of Federal Claims accused HUD of sloppy provision drafting regarding the General Data Rights Clause and the Statement of Work. Re-draft the data right provision such that it would assist practitioners in avoiding sloppy drafting and place both the government and the contractor in a position to understand their respective rights and obligations to the database and raw data.

LICENSES IN THE BUSINESS LIFE CYCLE: FROM FINANCING TO BANKRUPTCY

I. OVERVIEW

The majority of companies need financing to develop their technology and products or services for the market. How does a company receive its financing? The company may receive financing from investors who provide the capital in exchange for certain control of the company, such as ownership of the company's stock. The company may receive financing from creditors who advance the capital in exchange for security interest in the company's present and future technology, among other corporate assets. Sometimes the investors may demand both a share of the company's stock and a security interest in the company's present and future technology. A start-up company would very much like or more accurately dream of becoming a publicly traded company so it can receive the influx of capital from the stock issued, but until that day, the company relies on lenders and venture capitalists who, in turn, require stock or security interests from the company.

If the company's valuable assets are intellectual property and related licenses, the assets play an important role in the company's ability to receive financing. If the investors believe after their due diligence that the company's technology is worth the financing and the intellectual property is defensible, they will provide the necessary capital in exchange for equity in the company and other terms favorable to the investors. Traditional lenders, on the other hand, want to make loans or revolving credit lines available to the company if the company has some prospects of making the scheduled payments. If the company's sole assets are intellectual property, the lenders may demand to see a valuation of the company's intellectual property assets before they provide the financing. The royalty stream or expectation of income generated from the intellectual property assets is often used as a strong indicator in the valuation.

It is common for corporate entities to use their assets as security in obtaining financing from the more traditional creditors, such as lenders. The intellectual property and licenses are also used as security in financing. If the company is unable to make the scheduled payments, the secured creditor has certain rights under secured financing law against the debtor and others who have an interest in the intellectual property assets. Creditors who provide the financing would like to inform the world that they have taken a security interest in the intellectual property and licenses. Preferably, the secured creditors would want their interest to enjoy priority over other creditors, including the bankruptcy trustee.

In the competitive world, new businesses have a 50 percent survival rate in the first five years. Venture capitalists would claim that the survival rate for technology start-ups is about 10 percent. As financing runs out, the company faces liquidation. If the company faces liquidation, a common bankruptcy proceeding, the company's intellectual property and licenses become of great interest to various parties. Creditors want to see the intellectual property and licenses as part of the bankruptcy estate so the assets will be liquidated and the creditors may get some of their money back. Secured creditors would try to either foreclose on the intellectual property or claim priority in the intellectual property and proceeds. Existing licensees of the intellectual property would like to continue using the intellectual property because either their businesses depend on the technology or perhaps they do not want to see the intellectual property licenses assigned to a third party, especially a potential competitor. Existing licensors who had entered into license agreements with the company before liquidation now would like to collect unpaid royalties and terminate the agreements.

The life cycle of a company seems to run from obtaining financing for the development of technology to the date that the company is unable to obtain further financing and ends in liquidation. Of course the life cycle does not have to end at liquidation, if the company survives and prospers. On the path to prosperity, the company may wish to expand, and it would likely need financing for its expansion. Intellectual property and licenses continue to play an important role in each stage of the life cycle.

II. THE USE OF INTELLECTUAL PROPERTY AND LICENSES IN TRANSACTIONS

A. Secured Transactions

Companies can use their intellectual property assets and licenses as security in financing plans. That means companies grant creditors a security interest in the intellectual property assets and licenses. A security interest is an interest in personal property that secures payment or performance of an obligation.

B. Perfection and Priority of Security Interest
in Intellectual Property and Licenses

A creditor who provides financing to a debtor and takes a security interest in the debtor's intellectual property assets should know that its security interest in the intellectual property is not enforceable against the debtor or other third parties unless three requirements are satisfied. First, the debtor must have rights in the intellectual property or power to transfer rights in the assets. Second, the creditor must provide value (financing, loan, credit line) to the debtor. Third, the debtor must authenticate a written security agreement that describes the intellectual property as "general intangible" collateral. When all three requirements are fulfilled, the creditor's security interest in the asset collateral becomes "attached."

After attachment of the security interest, to protect its attached security interest against the rest of the world, the secured creditor must perfect it by employing an appropriate method of perfection. The most common method of perfection is filing the financing statement (UCC-1 statement) covering the collateral with an appropriate government office.

Intellectual property such as trademarks, copyrights, and patents do not fall into any category of intangibles and thus are in the residual category of general intangibles under Uniform Commercial Code Article 9. Perfection of a security interest in general intangibles is generally achieved by filing a financing statement covering the general intangibles with the office of the Secretary of State in the state where the debtor is located. With respect to perfection of intellectual property assets, there is a mixture of federal and state filings. For perfection of security interest in patents, patent applications, trademarks, and related licenses, the filing of a financing statement covering such intellectual property with the office of the Secretary of State where the debtor is deemed located achieves perfection. For registered copyrights, the filing of the security interest must be with the U.S. Copyright Office for perfection purposes, but for unregistered copyrights, perfection can only occur with the filing of the financing statement in the office of the Secretary of State. The mechanics for perfecting a security interest in registered copyrights are detailed in 17 U.S.C. §205. That statute provides a grace period of 30 days for filing if the grant of security interest in registered copyrights is executed in the United States. *See* 17 U.S.C. §205(d).

Perfection of a security interest is important to the priority of a party's interest in the intellectual property, particularly in case of bankruptcy. The secured creditor enjoys a superior right over the bankruptcy trustee if the debtor later is in bankruptcy. The secured creditor also enjoys priority over other junior creditors who take a security interest in the same intellectual property collateral. *See* In re Cybernetic Services, Inc., 252 F.3d 1039 (9th Cir. 2001) (the bank correctly perfected the security interest in the patents and had priority over the bankruptcy trustee), which can be found in the Materials section of this chapter; and In re World Auxiliary Power Co., 303 F.3d 1120 (9th Cir. 2002) (Silicon Valley Bank had priority over Aerocon in the unregistered copyrights), which can also be found in this chapter's Materials section.

III. THE INTELLECTUAL PROPERTY LICENSES AND BANKRUPTCY

A. Bankruptcy

The purpose of bankruptcy law is to provide the debtor with a chance to make a fresh start. Through bankruptcy, debts will be discharged and the debtor can begin anew. Bankruptcy law is federal, and the Bankruptcy Code is codified in Title 11 of the U.S. Code. Bankruptcy cases are often labeled in accordance with the "chapter" under which the case is filed. A bankruptcy filed under Chapter 7 is a liquidating proceeding wherein the trustee gathers all nonexempt assets, converts them to cash, and distributes the proceeds to creditors. A bankruptcy filed under Chapter 11 is a reorganization proceeding for businesses wherein assets are not liquidated and the business operation may continue during the reorganization process. The process enables the rehabilitated business to operate successfully in the future. The majority of bankruptcy cases fall under Chapter 7 liquidation. Chapter 9 governs municipal bankruptcy. Chapter 13 governs an individual's debt restructuring where the assets are not liquidated; the debtor instead proposes a plan to restructure the debts by extending payment schedules or reducing the principal amount of the old debt. Chapter 12 is similar to Chapter 13 but governs bankruptcies filed by farmers.

All bankruptcy cases are filed under one of the Chapters described above. A case originally brought under one Chapter can be converted to another Chapter. With the creation of the special bankruptcy courts located in each federal judicial district, all issues arising in a bankruptcy case can be adjudicated in one bankruptcy court.

Most bankruptcy cases are commenced voluntarily by the filing of a bankruptcy petition by the debtor. Some bankruptcy cases are involuntary and are filed by creditors. On the petition filing date, the bankruptcy estate is created. This section discusses the bankruptcy estate as well as the roles of the trustee and debtor in possession (DIP).

The trustee has many powers to fulfill its statutory and administrative duties. The trustee's principal duty is to collect and administer the property of the estate, dispose of the property, and distribute the cash proceeds to creditors in accordance with priority. Under Section 542 of the Bankruptcy Code, the trustee has possession of the estate assets. The trustee can take steps to secure or safeguard estate assets. The trustee can abandon property of the estate that is deemed to be burdensome or of little value and benefit to the estate. Under Section 363 of the Bankruptcy Code the trustee may use, sell, or lease property of the estate in the ordinary course of the debtor's business without court approval. Court approval will be required for sales of debtor's assets outside the ordinary course of business. In operating the debtor's business, the trustee may seek authority to incur debt or to use cash collateral, subject to the requirements of the applicable provisions of the Bankruptcy Code.

The trustee can assume and reject executory contracts and leases. Under numerous sections of the Bankruptcy Code, the trustee may avoid certain pre-petition and post-petition transfers of property of the estate, including the grant of a security interest in property, preferences, and fraudulent conveyances. An excerpt from In re Exide Technologies, 607 F.3d 957 (3d Cir. 2010), included in the Materials section of this chapter addresses whether an exclusive trademark license agreement is an executory contract.

B. The Licensor as Debtor and the Intellectual Property Licenses in Bankruptcy Act

Under Section 362 of the Bankruptcy Code, the commencement of a bankruptcy case automatically enjoins all actions and activities to obtain possession of or seize control over the property of the estate. When a petition is filed to commence a bankruptcy case, an "estate" is created and all property of the estate is protected from creditors while the case is pending. That means non-debtor parties (such as a non-debtor contracting party to an intellectual property license) are prohibited, without the bankruptcy court's authorization, from foreclosing on the debtor's collateral assets and, among other prohibitions, from terminating the license agreements, notwithstanding the fact that the agreements may provide such termination rights. The rights of non-debtor parties are not extinguished by the automatic stay; instead, they are held in abeyance to provide the debtor a breathing spell while it attempts to devise a satisfactory method of satisfying its debts.

Congress passed the Intellectual Property Licenses in Bankruptcy Act (IPLBA or the Act) in October 1988, in response to the Fourth Circuit Court of Appeals' decision in Lubrizol Enterprises, Inc. v. Richmond Metal Finishers, Inc., 756 F.2d 1043 (4th Cir. 1985), *cert. denied*, 475 U.S. 1057 (1986). The *Lubrizol* court authorized the debtor licensor's unilateral rejection of a license agreement concerning a metal coating process technology. Under then current bankruptcy law, the licensee could treat the rejection as a breach and seek a monetary damages remedy, but could not retain its license rights in the technology by specific performance. Essentially, the licensee's right to use the technology extinguished upon rejection. The denial of the right to use the technology license threatened the licensee's business. Indeed, the *Lubrizol* court even acknowledged that the consequences to the licensee were harsh and could have a chilling effect upon the willingness of licensees to contract at all with debtor licensors in financial difficulties. The harsh outcome led to congressional passage of the IPLBA.

The IPLBA (codified as 11 U.S.C. §365(n)) provides special protection to intellectual property licensees when the debtor licensor is in bankruptcy. The IPLBA permits a licensee to retain its right under a license even when the debtor licensor files a bankruptcy petition and decides to reject the license.

Under the IPLBA, intellectual property means: (a) trade secrets, (b) inventions, processes, designs, or plants protected under Title 35, (c) patent applications, (d) plant varieties, (e) works of authorship protected under Title 17, or (f) mask works protected under Chapter 9 of Title 17. The definition of intellectual property deliberately excludes trademarks.

Accordingly, when the debtor licensor files for bankruptcy and rejects the intellectual property license agreements, only licensees of patent license agreements, copyright license agreements, and trade secrets license agreements have statutory rights that would allow them to continue using the license. *See* In re Spansion, Inc., 2012 WL 6634899 (3d Cir. 2012), which is included in the Materials section of this chapter. In cross-border, international bankruptcy cases where debtor licensors are located in jurisdictions that do not afford patent licensees similar protection under Section 365(n), U.S. courts face a difficult and complex task in determining whether to allow a U.S. licensee the statutory protection or to apply other jurisdiction's law where the main bankruptcy proceeding occurs. *See* Jaffe v. Samsung, 737 F.3d 14 (4th Cir. 2013), which is also included in the Materials section.

Licensees of trademark license agreements, however, have no statutory right under Section 365(n) to elect the right to use the trademark license after the debtor licensor rejects the trademark license agreement. This may cause problems to licensees of both trademarks and other permissible intellectual property (patents, copyrights, trade secrets). The licensees have the license to use the technology but cannot use the trademark in connection with the use of the technology. *See* In re Tempnology LLC, 559 B.R. 809 (1st Cir. 2016), which is included in the Materials section.

C. Licensor as Creditor

An intellectual property holder may find itself in a situation where its licensee is in bankruptcy. The intellectual property holder as licensor may have several concerns. First, will the licensor receive the payments owed to it prior to the licensee filing the bankruptcy petition? Second, will the licensor get paid for the license used by the licensee debtor during the pending bankruptcy proceeding? Third, can the licensor prevent the assignment of the license by the trustee to a third party? *See* In re CFLC, Inc., 89 F.3d 673 (9th Cir. 1996) and In re Trump Entertainment Resorts, Inc., which are in the Materials. *Compare* In re Rooster, Inc., 100 B.R. 228 (Bankr. E.D. Pa. 1989) (permitting the assumption and assignment of trademark licenses), which can also be found in this chapter's Materials section. Some courts have taken a step further by prohibiting the assumption of executory license agreements, even though there was no contemplation of subsequent assignment of the license agreements to a third party.

IV. MATERIALS

The Materials consist of nine cases, providing you an opportunity to learn how intellectual property, contract, secured transaction, and bankruptcy laws influence one another. The first two cases focus on the perfection of security interests in different types of intellectual property assets. In re Cybernetic Services, Inc., 252 F.3d 1039 (9th Cir. 2001), explains how a security interest in patent collateral must be perfected. In re World Auxiliary Power Co., 303 F.3d 1120 (9th Cir. 2002), discusses the perfection of security interests in registered and unregistered copyright collaterals.

The third case—In re Exide Technologies, 607 F.3d 957 (3d Cir. 2010)—discusses whether an exclusive trademark license agreement is an executory contract subject to rejection by the debtor licensor.

The next set of cases address the rights of the intellectual property licensee and licensor when one of the parties to the license agreement is in bankruptcy. In re Tempnology LLC, 559 B.R. 809 (1st Cir. 2016), confronts the difficulties in addressing the licensee's right to use different types of intellectual property licenses in a situation where the debtor licensor is in bankruptcy.

In re Spansion Inc., 507 Fed. Appx. 125, 2012 WL 6634899 (3d Cir. 2012), is a brief case on whether a letter agreement is a patent license subject to Section 365(n) protection for the licensee. Jaffe v. Samsung, 737 F.3d 14 (4th Cir. 2013), turns on international, cross-border bankruptcy and addresses whether patent licensees have protection under Section 365(n) to use the patent when the international debtor licensor is in bankruptcy.

On the other spectrum, In re CFLC, Inc., 89 F.3d 673 (9th Cir. 1996), is a case about the debtor licensee's right in a patent license agreement when the debtor licensee is in bankruptcy. The case addresses whether the debtor licensee may assume and assign the patent license to a third party without the non-debtor licensor's consent. Next are a pair of cases, In re Trump Entertainment Resorts, Inc., 526 B.R. 116 (Bankr. D. Delaware 2015), and Rooster, Inc. 100 B.R. 228 (Bankr. E.D. Pa. 1989), focusing on whether the debtor licensee may assume and assign a trademark license agreement without the non-debtor licensor's consent.

IN RE CYBERNETIC SERVICES, INC.

252 F.3d 1039 (9th Cir. 2001)

GRABER, Circuit Judge.

As is often true in the field of intellectual property, we must apply an antiquated statute in a modern context. The question that we decide today is whether 35 U.S.C. §261 of the Patent Act, or Article 9 of the Uniform Commercial Code (UCC), as adopted in California, requires the holder of a security interest in a patent to record that interest with the federal Patent and Trademark Office (PTO) in order to perfect the interest as against a subsequent lien creditor. We answer "no"; neither the Patent Act nor Article 9 so requires. We therefore affirm the decision of the Bankruptcy Appellate Panel (BAP).

FACTUAL AND PROCEDURAL BACKGROUND

The parties stipulated to the relevant facts: Matsco, Inc., and Matsco Financial Corporation (Petitioners) have a security interest in a patent developed by Cybernetic Services, Inc. (Debtor). The patent is for a data recorder that is designed to capture data from a video signal regardless of the horizontal line in which the data is located. Petitioners' security interest in the patent was "properly prepared, executed by the Debtor and timely filed with the Secretary of State of the State of California," in accordance with the California Commercial Code. Petitioners did not record their interest with the PTO.

After Petitioners had recorded their security interest with the State of California, certain creditors filed an involuntary Chapter 7 petition against Debtor, and an order of relief was granted. The primary asset of Debtor's estate is the patent. Petitioners then filed a motion for relief from the automatic stay so that they could foreclose on their interest in the patent. The bankruptcy Trustee opposed the motion, arguing that Petitioners had failed to perfect their interest because they did not record it with the PTO.

The bankruptcy court ruled that Petitioners had properly perfected their security interest in the patent by following the provisions of Article 9. Furthermore, the court reasoned, because Petitioners had perfected their security interest before the filing of the bankruptcy petition, Petitioners had priority over the Trustee's claim in the patent and deserved relief from the stay. Accordingly, the bankruptcy court granted Petitioners' motion. The BAP affirmed. Petitioners then filed this timely appeal.

DISCUSSION

Article 9 of the UCC, as adopted in California, governs the method for perfecting a security interest in personal property. Article 9 applies to "general intangibles," a term that includes intellectual property.

[T]he Supreme Court has instructed clearly that the Patent Act does not preempt every state commercial law that touches on intellectual property. For example, in Aronson v. Quick Point Pencil Co., 440 U.S. 257, 262 (1979), the Supreme Court observed that commercial agreements "traditionally are the domain of state law. State law is not displaced merely because the contract relates to intellectual property which may or may not be patentable; the states are free to regulate the use of such intellectual property in any manner not inconsistent with federal law."

[The Court analyzed the relevant Patent provisions and provided the following summary:]

In summary, the statute's text, context, and structure, when read in the light of Supreme Court precedent, compel the conclusion that a security interest in a patent that does not involve a transfer of the rights of ownership is a "mere license" and is not an "assignment, grant or conveyance" within the meaning of 35 U.S.C. §261. And because §261 provides that only an "assignment, grant or conveyance shall be void" as against subsequent purchasers and mortgagees, only transfers of ownership interests need to be recorded with the PTO. . . .

The Trustee is not a subsequent "mortgagee," as that term is used in 35 U.S.C. §261, because the holder of a patent mortgage holds title to the patent itself. *Waterman*, 138 U.S. at 258. Instead, the Trustee is a hypothetical lien creditor. The Patent Act does not require parties to record documents in order to provide constructive notice to subsequent lien creditors who do not hold title to the patent. . . .

The Trustee argues that requiring lien creditors to record their interests with the PTO is in line with the general policy behind recording statutes. It may be, as the Trustee argues, that a national system of filing security interests is more efficient and effective than a state-by-state system. However, there is no statutory hook upon which to hang the Trustee's policy arguments. Moreover, we are not concerned with the policy behind recording statutes generally but, rather, with the policy behind 35 U.S.C. §261 specifically.

Title 35 U.S.C. §261, as we have demonstrated and as its label suggests, is concerned with patent ownership. . . .

The Patent Act was written long before the advent of the "unitary" Article 9 security interest. But we must interpret 35 U.S.C. §261 as Congress wrote it. The Constitution entrusts to Congress, not to the courts, the role of ensuring that statutes keep up with changes in financing practices. It is notable that Congress has revised the Patent Act numerous times since its enactment, most recently in 1999, see Pub. L. 106-113, but it has not updated the Act's recording provision. We decline the Trustee's invitation to do so in Congress' place.

The Trustee's second major argument is that Article 9 itself requires that a creditor file notice of a secured transaction with the PTO in order to perfect a security interest. California Commercial Code §9302(3)(a) states that the filing of a financing statement pursuant to Article 9 "is not necessary or effective to perfect a security interest in property subject to . . . [a] statute . . . which provides for a national or international registration . . . or which specifies a place of filing different from that specified in" Article 9. If §9302(3)(a) applies, then a party must utilize the federal registration system in order to perfect its security interest. Cal. Com. Code §9302(4).

The question, then, is whether the Patent Act is "[a] statute . . . which provides for a national or international registration . . . or which specifies a place of filing different from that specified in" Article 9. Cal. Com. Code §9302(3)(a). The Patent Act is clearly a statute that provides for a national registration. But that begs the more focused question: a national registration of what? Courts have tended to use the context of the statute to amplify the bare text and to answer the focused question: a national registration of security interests. For example, in Aerocon Engineering, Inc. v. Silicon Valley Bank (In re World Auxiliary Power Co.), 244 B.R. 149, 155 (1999), the bankruptcy court observed that §9302(3)(a), if read literally, would be absurd. It would provide that, whenever a particular type of collateral may be registered nationally, regardless of whether the federal statute specifies a place for filing a security interest different than that provided by the UCC, filing a UCC-1 financing statement would be neither necessary nor effective to perfect a security interest in the collateral.

Courts have thus read §9302(3)(a) as providing that federal filing is necessary only when there is a statute that "provides for" a national registration of security interests. See, e.g., Trimarchi v. Together Dev. Corp., 255 B.R. 606, 610 (D. Mass. 2000) (holding that §9302(3)(a) did not require the federal filing of a trademark because the Lanham Act does not provide for a national recording system of security interests). We agree with that interpretation. . . .

Under that more restrictive definition, it is clear that the Patent Act is outside the scope of §9302(3)(a). As we have explained, a transaction that grants a party a security interest in a patent but does not effect a transfer of title is not the type of "assignment, grant or conveyance" that is referred to in 35 U.S.C. §261. The transaction in this case did not transfer an ownership interest. Therefore, §9302(3)(a) did not require that Petitioners record their security interest with the PTO. . . .

Because 35 U.S.C. §261 concerns only transactions that effect a transfer of an ownership interest in a patent, the Patent Act does not preempt Article 9, and neither California

Commercial Code §9104(a) nor §9302(3) applies. Consequently, Petitioners perfected their security interest in Debtor's patent by recording it with the California Secretary of State. They have priority over the Trustee's claim because they recorded their interest before the filing of the bankruptcy petition.

IN RE WORLD AUXILIARY POWER CO.

303 F.3d 1120 (9th Cir. 2002)

KLEINFELD, Circuit Judge.

In this case we decide whether federal or state law governs priority of security interests in unregistered copyrights.

FACTS

Basically, this is a bankruptcy contest over unregistered copyrights between a bank that got a security interest in the copyrights from the owners and perfected it under state law, and a company that bought the copyrights from the bankruptcy trustees after the copyright owners went bankrupt. These simple facts are all that matters to the outcome of this case, although the details are complex.

Three affiliated California corporations — World Auxiliary Power, World Aerotechnology, and Air Refrigeration Systems — designed and sold products for modifying airplanes. The FAA must approve modifications of civilian aircraft by issuing "Supplemental Type Certificates." The three companies owned copyrights in the drawings, technical manuals, blue-prints, and computer software used to make the modifications. Some of these copyrighted materials were attached to the Supplemental Type Certificates. The companies did not register their copyrights with the United States Copyright Office.

The companies got financing from Silicon Valley Bank, one of the appellees in this case. Two of the companies borrowed the money directly, the third guaranteed the loan. The security agreement, as is common, granted the bank a security interest in a broad array of presently owned and after-acquired collateral. The security agreement covered "all goods and equipment now owned or hereafter acquired," as well as inventory, contract rights, general intangibles, blueprints, drawings, computer programs, accounts receivable, patents, cash, bank deposits, and pretty much anything else the debtor owned or might be "hereafter acquired." The security agreement and financing statement also covered "[a]ll copyright rights, copyright applications, copyright registrations, and like protections in each work of authorship and derivative work thereof, whether published or unpublished, now owned or hereafter acquired."

The bank perfected its security interest in the collateral, including the copyrights, pursuant to California's version of Article 9 of the Uniform Commercial Code, by filing UCC-1 financing statements with the California Secretary of State. The bank also took possession of the Supplemental Type Certificates and the attached copyrighted materials. But the copyrights still weren't registered with the United States Copyright Office, and the bank did not record any document showing the transfer of a security interest with the Copyright Office.

Subsequently, the three debtor companies filed simultaneous but separate bankruptcy proceedings. Their copyrights were among their major assets. Aerocon Engineering, one of their creditors (and the appellant in this case), wanted the copyrights. Aerocon was working on a venture with another company, Advanced Aerospace, and its President, Michael Gilsen, and an officer and director, Merritt Widen (all appellees in this case), to engineer and sell aircraft modifications using the debtors' designs. Their prospective venture faced a problem: Silicon Valley Bank claimed a security interest in the copyrights. To solve this problem, Aerocon worked out a deal with Gilsen, Widen, and a company named Erose Capital (not a party in this case) to buy the debtors' assets, including their copyrights, from the bankruptcy trustees along with the trustees' right to sue to avoid Silicon Valley Bank's security interest. Once Aerocon owned the copyrights, it planned to exercise the trustees' power to avoid Silicon Valley Bank's security interest so that the venture would own the copyrights free and clear.

The transaction to purchase the copyrights and the trustees' avoidance action worked as follows. First, Aerocon paid the bankruptcy trustees $90,000, $30,000 for each of the three bankruptcy estates. Then, the trustees, with the bankruptcy court's approval, sold the estates' assets and avoidance action to Erose Capital, Gilsen, and Widen. Gilsen and Widen then sold their two-thirds interest to their company, Advanced Aerospace.

After this transaction was completed, for reasons not relevant to this appeal, Aerocon's planned joint venture with Advanced Aerospace and Gilsen and Widen fell through. In the aftermath, Erose Capital sold its one-third interest to Aerocon and Advanced Aerospace sold its two-thirds interest to Airweld. These transactions meant that Aerocon and Airweld owned the debtors' copyrights and the trustees' avoidance action as tenants in common.

Meanwhile, Silicon Valley Bank won relief from the bankruptcy court's automatic stay and, based on its security interest, foreclosed on the copyrights. Then the bank sold the copyrights to Advanced Aerospace (Gilsen's and Widen's company) which then sold the copyrights to Airweld. Had Aerocon's joint venture with Gilsen and Widen gone through, buying off the trustees' and the bank's interests in the copyrights would have been a sensible, if expensive, way to ensure that the venture owned the copyrights free and clear. But, of course, the venture did not go through, and Gilsen and Widen's affiliations had changed. Thus Gilsen and Widen's purchase from the bank and sale to Airweld meant that Aerocon, which had paid $90,000 for the copyrights and had owned them as a tenant in common with Airweld, now had a claim adverse to Airweld's, which purportedly owned the copyrights in fee simple.

Aerocon brought an adversary proceeding in each of the three bankruptcy proceedings against Silicon Valley Bank, Advanced Aerospace, Gilsen, Widen, and Airweld. (These adversary proceedings were later consolidated.) Aerocon sued to avoid Silicon Valley Bank's security interest and to recover the copyrights or their value from subsequent transferees Advanced Aerospace, Gilsen, Widen, and Airweld. The bankruptcy court granted the subsequent transferees' motion to dismiss Aerocon's claims against them as time-barred. The bankruptcy court then granted summary judgment to Silicon Valley Bank on all of Aerocon's claims on the ground that the bank had perfected its security interest in the copyrights under California's version of Article 9 of the Uniform Commercial Code. Aerocon appealed to the Ninth Circuit Bankruptcy Appellate Panel. Silicon Valley Bank objected, and the appeal was transferred to the district court, which affirmed the bankruptcy court. Aerocon appeals from the district court's order.

ANALYSIS

Copyright and bankruptcy law set the context for this litigation, but the legal issue is priority of security interests. The bankruptcy trustees sold Aerocon their power to avoid any security interest "that is voidable by a creditor that extends credit to the debtor at the time of the commencement of the case, and that obtains, at such time and with respect to such credit, a judicial lien. . . ." Under this "strong-arm" provision, Aerocon has the status of an "ideal creditor" who perfected his lien at the last possible moment before the bankruptcy commenced, and if this hypothetical creditor would take priority over Silicon Valley Bank's lien, then Aerocon may avoid the bank's security interest.

Whether Aerocon's hypothetical lien creditor would take priority turns on whether federal or state law governs the perfection of security interests in unregistered copyrights. The bank did everything necessary to perfect its security interest under state law, so if state law governs, the bank has priority and wins. The bank did nothing, however, to perfect its interest under federal law, so if federal law governs, Aerocon's hypothetical lien creditor arguably has priority, although the parties dispute whether Aerocon might face additional legal hurdles.

We are assisted in deciding this case by two opinions, neither of which controls, but both of which are thoughtful and scholarly. The first is the bankruptcy court's published opinion in this case, Aerocon Engineering Inc. v. Silicon Valley Bank (In re World Auxiliary Power Co.), which we affirm largely for the reasons the bankruptcy judge gave. The second is a published district court opinion, National Peregrine, Inc. v. Capitol Federal Savings & Loan Association (In re Peregrine Entertainment, Ltd.), the holdings of which we adopt but, like the bankruptcy court, distinguish and limit.

Our analysis begins with the Copyright Act of 1976. Under the Act, "copyright protection subsists . . . in original works of authorship fixed in any tangible medium of expression. . . ." While an owner must register his copyright as a condition of seeking certain infringement remedies, registration is permissive, not mandatory, and is not a condition for copyright protection. Likewise, the Copyright Act's provision for recording "transfers of copyright ownership" (the Act's term that includes security interests) is permissive, not mandatory: "Any transfer of copyright ownership or other document pertaining to copyright may be recorded in the Copyright Office. . . ." The Copyright Act's use of the word "mortgage" as one definition of a "transfer" is properly read to include security interests under Article 9 of the Uniform Commercial Code.

Under the Copyright Act,

> [a]s between two conflicting transfers, the one executed first prevails if it is recorded, in the manner required to give constructive notice . . . within one month after its execution . . . or at any time before recordation . . . of the later transfer. Otherwise the later transfer prevails if recorded first in such manner, and if taken in good faith, for valuable consideration . . . and without notice of the earlier transfer.

The phrase "constructive notice" refers to another subsection providing that recording gives constructive notice

> but only if—
> (1) the document, or material attached to it, specifically identifies the work to which it pertains so that, after the document is indexed by the Register of Copyrights, it would

be revealed by a reasonable search under the title or registration number of the work; and

    (2) registration has been made for the work.

A copyrighted work only gets a "title or registration number" that would be revealed by a search if it's registered. Since an unregistered work doesn't have a title or registration number that would be "revealed by a reasonable search," recording a security interest in an unregistered copyright in the Copyright Office wouldn't give "constructive notice" under the Copyright Act, and, because it wouldn't, it couldn't preserve a creditor's priority. There just isn't any way for a secured creditor to preserve a priority in an unregistered copyright by recording anything in the Copyright Office. And the secured party can't get around this problem by registering the copyright, because the secured party isn't the owner of the copyright, and the Copyright Act states that only "the owner of copyright . . . may obtain registration of the copyright claim. . . ."

Aerocon argues that the Copyright Act's recordation and priority scheme exclusively controls perfection and priority of security interests in copyrights. First, *Aerocon* argues that state law, here the California U.C.C., by its own terms "steps back" and defers to the federal scheme. Second, whether or not the U.C.C. steps back, *Aerocon* argues that Congress has preempted the U.C.C. as it applies to copyrights. We address each argument in turn.

A. U.C.C. Step Back Provisions

To avoid conflict with the federal law, the U.C.C. has two "step-back provisions," by which state law steps back and out of the way of conflicting federal law. . . . Under the U.C.C.'s two step-back provisions, there can be no question that, when a copyright has been registered, a security interest can be perfected only by recording the transfer in the Copyright Office. As the district court held in *Peregrine*, the Copyright Act satisfies the broad U.C.C. step-back provision by creating a priority scheme that "governs the rights of parties to and third parties affected by transactions" in registered copyrights and satisfies the narrow step-back provision by creating a single "national registration" for security interests in registered copyrights. Thus, under these step-back provisions, if a borrower's collateral is a registered copyright, the secured party cannot perfect by filing a financing statement under the U.C.C. in the appropriate state office, or alternatively by recording a transfer in the Copyright Office. For registered copyrights, the only proper place to file is the Copyright Office. We adopt *Peregrine*'s holding to this effect.

However, the question posed by this case is whether the U.C.C. steps back as to unregistered copyrights. We, like the bankruptcy court in this case, conclude that it does not. As we've explained, there's no way for a secured creditor to perfect a security interest in unregistered copyrights by recording in the Copyright Office. The U.C.C.'s broader step-back provision says that the U.C.C. doesn't apply to a security interest "to the extent" that a federal statute governs the rights of the parties. The U.C.C. doesn't defer to the Copyright Act under this broad step-back provision because the Copyright Act doesn't provide for the rights of secured parties to unregistered copyrights; it only covers the rights of secured parties in registered copyrights. The U.C.C.'s narrow step-back provision says the U.C.C. doesn't apply if a federal statute "provides for a national . . . registration . . . or which specifies a place of filing different from that specified in this division for filing of the security interest." The U.C.C. doesn't defer to the Copyright Act under this narrow step-back provision because the Copyright Act doesn't provide a "national registration": unregistered copyrights don't have to be registered, and because unregistered copyrights don't have a registered name and number, under the Copyright Act there isn't any place to file anything regarding unregistered copyrights that makes any legal difference. So, as a matter of state law, the U.C.C. doesn't step back in deference to federal law, but governs perfection and priority of security interests in unregistered copyrights itself.

B. Federal Preemption

It wouldn't matter that state law doesn't step back, however, if Congress chose to knock state law out of the way by preemption. . . . We presume that federal law does not preempt "state law in areas traditionally regulated by the States." . . .

In the one instance where the Copyright Act conditions some action concerning a copyright on its registration — the right to sue for infringement — the Act makes that condition explicit. Nowhere does the Copyright Act explicitly condition the use of copyrights as collateral on their registration. Second, the Copyright Act contemplates that most copyrights will not be registered. Since copyright is created every time people set pen to paper, or fingers to keyboard, and affix their thoughts in a tangible medium, writers, artists, computer programmers, and web designers would have to have their hands tied down to keep them from creating unregistered copyrights all day every day. Moreover, the Copyright Act says that copyrights "may" be registered, implying that they don't have to be, and since a fee is charged and time and effort is required, the statute sets up a regime in which most copyrights won't ever be registered.

Though Congress must have contemplated that most copyrights would be unregistered, it only provided for protection of security interests in registered copyrights. There is no reason to infer from Congress's silence as to unregistered copyrights an intent to make such copyrights useless as collateral by preempting state law but not providing any federal priority scheme for unregistered copyrights. That would amount to a presumption in favor of federal preemption, but we are required to presume just the opposite. The only reasonable inference to draw is that Congress chose not to create a federal scheme for security interests in unregistered copyrights, but left the matter to States, which have traditionally governed security interests.

For similar reasons, we reject *Aerocon*'s argument that congressional intent to preempt can be inferred from conflict between the Copyright Act and the U.C.C. There is no conflict between the statutory provisions: the Copyright Act doesn't speak to security interests in unregistered copyrights, the U.C.C. does.

Nor does the application of state law frustrate the objectives of federal copyright law. The basic objective of federal copyright law is to "promote the Progress of Science and useful Arts" by "establishing a marketable right to the use of one's expression" and supplying "the economic incentive to create and disseminate ideas." *Aerocon* argues that allowing perfection under state law would frustrate this objective by injecting uncertainty in secured transactions involving copyrights. *Aerocon* conjures up the image of a double-crossing debtor who, having gotten financing based on unregistered copyrights, registers them, thus triggering federal law, and gets financing from a second creditor, who then records its interest with the Copyright Office and takes priority. We decline to prevent this fraud by drawing the unreasonable inference that Congress intended to render copyrights useless as collateral unless registered.

Prudent creditors will always demand that debtors disclose any copyright registrations and perfect under federal law and will protect themselves against subsequent creditors gaining priority by means of covenants and policing mechanisms. The several amici banks and banking association in this case argue that most lenders would lend against unregistered copyrights subject to the remote risk of being "primed" by subsequent creditors; but no lender would lend against unregistered copyrights if they couldn't perfect their security interest. As we read the law, unregistered copyrights have value as collateral, discounted by the remote potential for priming. As *Aerocon* reads the law, they would have no value at all.

Aerocon's argument also ignores the special problem of copyrights as after-acquired collateral. To use just one example of the multi-industry need to use after-acquired (really after-created) intangible intellectual property as collateral, now that the high-tech boom of the 1990s has passed, and software companies don't attract equity financing like tulips in seventeenth century Holland, these companies will have to borrow more capital. After-acquired software is likely to serve as much of their collateral. Like liens in any other after-acquired collateral, liens in after-acquired software must attach immediately upon the creation of the software to satisfy creditors. Creditors would not tolerate a gap between the software's creation and the registration of the copyright. If software developers had to register copyrights in their software before using it as collateral, the last half hour of the day for a software company would be spent preparing and mailing utterly pointless forms to the Copyright Office to register and record security interests. Our reading of the law "promote[s] the Progress of Science and useful Arts" by preserving the collateral value of unregistered copyrights, which is to say, the vast majority of copyrights. *Aerocon*'s reading of the law—which would force producers engaged in the ongoing creation of copyrightable material to constantly register and update the registrations of their works before obtaining credit—does not.

CONCLUSION

Regarding perfection and priority of security interests in unregistered copyrights, the California U.C.C. has not stepped back in deference to federal law, and federal law has not preempted the U.C.C. Silicon Valley Bank has a perfected security interest in the debtors' unregistered copyrights, and *Aerocon*, standing in the bankruptcy trustees' shoes, cannot prevail against it.

IN RE EXIDE TECHNOLOGIES
607 F.3d 957 (3d Cir. 2010)

This case presents the question whether the parties' Agreement is an executory contract. EnerSys Delaware, Inc., appeals the judgment of the District Court, which affirmed the Bankruptcy Court's order that the Agreement was an executory contract, subject to rejection under 11 U.S.C. §365(a), and that Exide Technologies could reject it. We conclude, however, that EnerSys has substantially performed the Agreement. As a result, EnerSys does not have any unperformed material obligations that would excuse Exide from performance. We hold, therefore, that the Agreement is not an executory contract. We will vacate the District Court's order and remand this case to the District Court with instructions to remand it to the Bankruptcy Court for further proceedings consistent with this opinion.

I. BACKGROUND

A. Factual Background

On April 15, 2002, Exide filed a voluntary petition for bankruptcy protection under Chapter 11 of the Bankruptcy Code, 11 U.S.C. §1101, et seq. After filing for bankruptcy, Exide sought to reject various agreements that it had with EnerSys arising from their June 1991 transaction. In June 1991, Exide sold substantially all of its industrial battery business to EnerSys for about $135 million. The assets that Exide sold to EnerSys included physical manufacturing plants, equipment, inventory, and certain items of intellectual property. To formalize the sale, Exide and EnerSys entered into over twenty-three agreements. Four of these agreements constitute the crux of the dispute: (1) the Trademark and Trade Name License Agreement, (2) the Asset Purchase Agreement, (3) the Administrative Services Agreement, and (4) a letter agreement. The Bankruptcy Court held, in an order predating the order challenged here, that the four agreements constituted a single integrated Agreement (the Agreement). In re Exide Techs., 340 B.R. 222, 227 (Bankr. D. Del. 2006). Neither Exide nor EnerSys have challenged this determination. We therefore take the next step of determining whether the Agreement is an executory contract.

Under the Agreement, Exide licensed its "Exide" trademark to EnerSys for use in the industrial battery business. Exide wanted to continue to use the Exide mark outside of the industrial battery business. To accommodate the needs of both parties, Exide granted EnerSys a perpetual, exclusive, royalty-free license to use the Exide trademark in the industrial battery business. This division worked, and, for almost ten years, each party appeared satisfied with the results of the transaction.

In 2000, however, Exide expressed a desire to return to the North American industrial battery market. After the parties agreed to the early termination of a ten-year noncompetition Agreement (thus granting Exide permission to reenter the market), Exide made several attempts to regain the trademark from EnerSys, but EnerSys refused. Exide wanted to regain the mark as a part of its strategic goal to unify its corporate image. Exide hoped to use a single name and trademark on all the products that it produced; this single name and trademark were, naturally, "Exide."

Exide reentered the industrial battery business by purchasing GNB Industrial Battery Company. Exide, however, remained bound by the ongoing obligation to forbear from using the Exide trademark in that business for as long as the license continued in effect. Thus, from 2000 until Exide filed for bankruptcy protection in 2002, Exide was forced to compete directly against EnerSys, which was selling batteries under the name "Exide." Then, when Exide filed for bankruptcy under Chapter 11, Exide was presented the opportunity to try to regain the Exide trademark by rejecting the Agreement. Exide sought the Bankruptcy Court's approval to do so.

B. Bankruptcy and District Court Proceedings

On April 3, 2006, the Bankruptcy Court entered an order granting Exide's motion to reject the Agreement. The court held that the Agreement was an executory contract, subject to rejection under 11 U.S.C. §365(a), and that rejection terminated Exide's obligations under it. About three months later, on July 11, the Bankruptcy Court entered an order approving the transition plan and denying EnerSys's motion to stay. EnerSys appealed these two orders to the District Court. The District Court, on February 27, 2008, affirmed the Bankruptcy Court's orders.

EnerSys appeals the District Court's order, arguing two issues: (1) the District Court erred in holding that Agreement was an executory contract, and (2) it erred in holding that rejection terminates EnerSys's rights under the Agreement.

II. DISCUSSION

We exercise plenary review of an order from a district court sitting as an appellate court in review of a bankruptcy court. We will review both courts' legal conclusions de novo. Furthermore, we will set aside a bankruptcy court's factual findings only if clearly erroneous. For mixed questions of law and fact, we will engage in "a mixed standard" of review, "affording a clearly erroneous standard to integral facts, but exercising plenary review of the lower court's interpretation and application of those facts to legal precepts." *Id.*

A. Executory Contract

The policy behind Chapter 11 of the Bankruptcy Code is the "ultimate rehabilitation of the debtor." Nicholas v. United States, 384 U.S. 678, 687 (1966). The Code therefore allows debtors in possession, "subject to the court's approval, . . . [to] reject any executory contract or unexpired lease of the debtor." 11 U.S.C. §365(a). But the Bankruptcy Code does not define "executory contract." Relevant legislative history demonstrates that Congress intended the term to mean a contract "on which performance is due to some extent on both sides." H.R. Rep. No. 95-595, 347 (1977).

With congressional intent in mind, this Court has adopted the following definition: "'An executory contract is a contract under which the obligation of both the bankrupt and the other party to the contract are so far underperformed that the failure of either to complete performance would constitute a material breach excusing the performance of the other.'" In re Columbia Gas, 50 F.3d at 239. "Thus, unless both parties have unperformed obligations that would constitute a material breach if not performed, the contract is not executory under §365." In re Columbia Gas, 50 F.3d at 239. The party seeking to reject a contract bears the burden of demonstrating that it is executory. And "[t]he time for testing whether there are material unperformed obligations on both sides is when the bankruptcy petition is filed." *Id.* at 240. Finally, to conduct this determination, we "consider contract principles under relevant nonbankruptcy law." *Id.* at 240 n.10. New York, because it is the forum selected in the Agreement's choice-of-law provision, provides the relevant nonbankruptcy law.

Accordingly, our inquiry is to determine whether the Agreement, on April 15, 2002, contained at least one obligation for both Exide and EnerSys that would constitute a material breach under New York law if not performed. If not, then the Agreement is not an executory contract.

Under New York law, a material breach, which "justif[ies] the other party to suspend his own performance," is "a breach which is so substantial as to defeat the purpose of the entire transaction." Lipsky v. Commonwealth United Corp., 551 F.2d 887, 895 (2d Cir. 1976); see In re Lavigne, 114 F.3d 379, 387 (2d Cir. 1997):

[U]nder New York law, only a breach in a contract which substantially defeats the purpose of that contract can be grounds for rescission. The non-breaching party will be discharged from the further performance of its obligations under the contract when the breach goes to the root of the contract.

But when a breaching party "has substantially performed" before breaching, "the other party's performance is not excused." Hadden v. Consolidated Edison Co., 356 N.Y.S.2d 249 (1974); see Merrill Lynch & Co. Inc. v. Allegheny Energy, Inc., 500 F.3d 171, 186 (2d Cir. 2007). New York's high court has instructed how to determine when a party has rendered substantial performance:

> There is no simple test for determining whether substantial performance has been rendered and several factors must be considered, including the ratio of the performance already rendered to that unperformed, the quantitative character of the default, the degree to which the purpose behind the contract has been frustrated, the willfulness of the default, and the extent to which the aggrieved party has already received the substantial benefit of the promised performance.

Hadden, 356 N.Y.S.2d 249. "The issue of whether a party has substantially performed is usually a question of fact and should be decided as a matter of law only where the inferences are certain." *Merrill Lynch & Co. Inc.*, 500 F.3d at 186.

The Bankruptcy Court here failed to properly measure whether either party had substantially performed. Our inspection of the record, however, reveals that the inferences are clear that EnerSys has substantially performed. Applying *Hadden*'s balancing test, EnerSys's performance rendered outweighs its performance remaining and the extent to which the parties have benefitted is substantial. Specifically, EnerSys has substantially performed by paying the full $135 million purchase price and operating under the Agreement for over ten years. EnerSys has been producing industrial batteries since 1991, using all the assets transferred under the Agreement, including real estate, real-estate leases, inventory, equipment and the right to use the trademark "Exide." Moreover, EnerSys has provided Exide with the substantial benefit of assuming the latter's liabilities, including numerous contracts and accounts receivable, within the business EnerSys purchased.

Exide argues that EnerSys's ongoing, unperformed obligations outweigh its performance. It relies on the following four obligations of EnerSys: (1) an obligation to satisfy the Quality Standards Provision, and obligations to observe, (2) the Use Restriction, (3) the Indemnity Obligations, and (4) the Further Assurances Obligations. We reject Exide's argument; these four obligations do not outweigh the substantial performance rendered and benefits received by EnerSys.

First, EnerSys's obligation to observe the Use Restriction, i.e., not to use the Trademark outside the industrial battery business, is not a material obligation because it is a condition subsequent that requires EnerSys to use the mark in accordance with the terms of the Trademark Licence. A condition subsequent is not a material obligation. See In re Columbia Gas System, Inc., 50 F.3d 233, 241 (3d Cir. 1995) ("Non-occurrence of a condition is not a breach by a party unless he is under a duty that the condition occur." (quoting Restatement (Second) of Contracts §225(3) (1981))). Moreover, the Use Restriction does not relate to the purpose of the Agreement — which is that Exide would transfer its industrial battery business and the concomitant assets and liabilities to EnerSys and EnerSys in exchange would pay Exide about $135 million. Therefore, even if the obligation were not a condition subsequent, it nevertheless would not affect the substantial performance of the Agreement.

Second, EnerSys's obligation to observe the Quality Standards Provision is minor because it requires meeting the standards of the mark for each battery produced; it does not relate to the transfer of the industrial battery business. Furthermore, the record reveals that Exide never provided EnerSys with any quality standards. (J.A. 297.) The parties, in fact, do not ever seem to have discussed any such standards. (See *id.* at 321-22.) It is an untenable proposition to find an obligation to go to the very root of the parties' Agreement when the parties themselves act as if they did not know of its existence. Finally, the other two obligations that Exide argues are substantial, the Indemnity Obligation and the Further Assurances Obligation, do not outweigh the factors supporting substantial performance. In regard to the Indemnity Obligation, under the Asset Purchase Agreement, all representations and warranties arising from it expired in 1994, on the third anniversary of the closing and Exide did not present any evidence that any liability assumed by EnerSys was still pending. Similarly, under the Further Assurances Obligation, EnerSys agreed to cooperate to facilitate the 1991 transaction. Exide has identified no remaining required cooperation.

Exide argues, however, citing *Hadden*, that the substantial-performance doctrine is "irrelevant here" because it applies only in cases involving construction or employment contracts. See *Hadden*, 356 N.Y.S.2d 249. Our review of New York law reveals that no New York court has held (or even intimated, see *id.*) that the doctrine should be confined to the construction/ employment contract areas. Indeed, the Second Circuit Court of Appeals, applying New York law, recently applied *Hadden*'s substantial-performance doctrine in a $490 million asset-purchase contract that formalized the sale of an energy trading commodities business to a larger energy business. See *Merrill Lynch*, 500 F.3d at 186. That contract was neither a construction nor employment contract. We also now conclude that we will not confine the doctrine to construction and employment contract cases.

III. CONCLUSION

For the reasons stated above, we have determined that the Agreement is not an executory contract because it does not contain at least one ongoing material obligation for EnerSys. Because the Agreement is not an executory contract, Exide cannot reject it. We will vacate the District Court's order and remand this case to it for remand to the Bankruptcy Court for further proceedings consistent with this opinion.

IN RE TEMPNOLOGY LLC
559 B.R. 809 (1st Cir. 2016)

At issue before the bankruptcy court was what rights Mission Product Holdings, Inc. ("Mission") Mission, as a licensee of intellectual property, retained as a result of its election under Bankruptcy Code §365(n) when the Debtor rejected the executory contract that gave rise to the license. The bankruptcy court ruled that Mission retained its nonexclusive license to use the Debtor's intellectual property as set forth in the rejected contract, but not its exclusive product distribution rights or right to use the Debtor's trademark and logo also contained in the contract.

Prior to a sale of substantially all its assets in 2015, Tempnology LLC, n/k/a Old Cold, LLC (the "Debtor") was a Portsmouth, New Hampshire-based material innovation company that developed chemical-free cooling fabrics for use in consumer products under the brand name "Coolcore." Mission is in the business of marketing and distributing innovative sports technologies.

On November 21, 2012, the Debtor and Mission entered into a Co–Marketing and Distribution Agreement (the "Agreement"). In section 1 of the Agreement, entitled "Territory," the Debtor granted Mission exclusive distribution rights within the United States and "first rights of notice and of refusal in certain other countries" (collectively defined in the Agreement as the "Exclusive Territory") with respect to an array of the Debtor's products defined as "Cooling Accessories" and identified on Exhibit A of the Agreement. The Debtor also granted Mission the non-exclusive right to sell Cooling Accessories anywhere else in the world.

In section 5 of the Agreement, entitled "Product Exclusivity," the Debtor agreed that in the Exclusive Territory it would not license or sell certain specified Cooling Accessories, defined in the Agreement as "Exclusive Cooling Accessories," to anyone other than Mission during the term of the Agreement.

In section 6, entitled "Distribution Exclusivity and Collaboration," the Debtor agreed that in the Exclusive Territory it would not sell any Cooling Accessories and certain other products directly or indirectly to any sporting goods and sport specialty retailers.

Section 7 of the Agreement, entitled "Cooperation and Further Assurances," provided:

> [T]hat (i) [the Debtor] shall take no actions to directly or indirectly frustrate its exclusivity obligations hereunder; (ii) [the Debtor] shall fully cooperate with [Mission] to ensure that no third parties take any actions that frustrate the purposes of the exclusivity provisions herein, and (iii) [the Debtor] shall take such actions as are necessary to enforce [the Debtor]'s intellectual property rights and contractual rights against third parties.

In section 15 of the Agreement, entitled "Intellectual Property," the Debtor granted Mission the following non-exclusive license (the "IP License"):

> Excluding those elements of the CC Property consisting of Marks [and] Domain Names, [the Debtor] hereby grants [Mission] and its agents and contractors a non-exclusive, irrevocable, royalty-free, fully paid-up, perpetual, worldwide, fully-transferable license, with the right to sublicense (through multiple tiers), use, reproduce, modify, and create derivative work based on and otherwise freely exploit the CC Property in any manner for the benefit of [Mission], its licensees and other third parties.

The Agreement defined "CC Property" as:

> [A]ll products (including without limitation the Cooling Accessories), personal products, inventions, designs, discoveries, improvements, innovations, ideas, drawings, images, works of authorship, formulas, methods, techniques, concepts, configurations, compositions of matter, packaging, labeling, software applications, databases,

> computer programs as well as other creative content, methodologies and materials in existence prior to this Agreement (or created outside the scope of this Agreement) or developed or provided by [the Debtor] hereunder and all Intellectual Property Rights with respect to any of the foregoing, excluding any materials provided by [Mission].

With respect to the Debtor's trademark and logo which were excluded from the IP License, section 15(d) of the Agreement granted Mission a limited license to use the Debtor's Coolcore trademark and logo as follows:

> During the Term of the Agreement and the Wind–Down Period, [the Debtor] grants to [Mission] a non-exclusive, non-transferable, limited license, which shall expire upon the termination of this Agreement except as necessary to allow either party to exercise its rights during the Wind–Down Period, to use its Coolcore trademark and logo (as well as any other Marks licensed hereunder) for the limited purpose of performing its obligations hereunder, exercising its rights and promoting the purposes of this Agreement as contemplated herein. . . .

The upshot of the Agreement was that during the term of the Agreement Mission enjoyed the exclusive right to sell the Cooling Accessories to sporting goods retailers in the United States and potentially certain other countries, and the exclusive right to sell Exclusive Cooling Accessories to anyone in that same territory. Additionally, Mission received a non-exclusive but perpetual license to exploit the Debtor's intellectual property and a limited license during the term of the Agreement to exploit the Coolcore brand and logo.

The Agreement had an initial term of two years and was subject to automatic renewal for additional one-year periods. Either party could terminate the Agreement with or without cause by providing written notice. Any event of termination, however, would trigger a two-year wind-down period during which Mission would retain certain rights to purchase, distribute, and sell the Cooling Accessories in accordance with the Agreement.

On June 30, 2014, Mission exercised its rights to terminate the Agreement without cause, triggering the two-year wind-down period. On July 22, 2014, the Debtor issued a notice of termination for cause, asserting that Mission had breached the Agreement. The ensuing dispute resulted in a two-phase arbitration process. On June 10, 2015, the arbitrator rendered a decision in the first phase of the arbitration, determining that the Agreement remained "in full force and effect." The second phase of the arbitration — as to whether either party had breached the Agreement — did not get very far as the Debtor's bankruptcy, and accompanying stay, brought the arbitration to a halt.

On September 1, 2015, the Debtor filed a voluntary petition for reorganization under chapter 11 of the Bankruptcy Code. The next day, the Debtor filed a motion seeking authority to reject certain of its executory contacts, including the Agreement. The Debtor also filed a motion asking the bankruptcy court to approve the sale of substantially all of its assets free and clear of liens, claims, encumbrances, and other interests.

Mission filed an objection to the sale motion and the rejection motion, which included its notice of election pursuant to §365(n)(1)(B). In its objection, Mission argued that notwithstanding the Debtor's rejection of the Agreement, by making an election under §365(n) Mission retained its exclusive product distribution rights as well as its rights under the IP License and the limited trademark license and that it could continue to exercise and exploit all those rights without interference from the Debtor or the purchaser of the Debtor's assets. Mission maintained that any sale of the Debtor's assets would be subject to, not free and clear of, Mission's rights under the Agreement.

After a non-evidentiary hearing, the bankruptcy court entered the order being appealed (the "365(n) Order") granting the 365(n) Motion and ruling: (1) Mission's election pursuant to §365(n) protected Mission rights as a non-exclusive licensee only as to any patents, trade secrets, and copyrights as were granted to Mission in section 15(b) of the Agreement (the section identifying the property subject to the IP License); (2) Mission's election pursuant to §365(n) provided no protectable interest in the Debtor's trademarks or trade names; and (3) Mission's election pursuant to §365(n) provided no protectable interest in the Debtor's "Exclusive Products" and the "Exclusive Territory" as those terms were defined in the Agreement.

II. ISSUES ON APPEAL

In the present case, it is undisputed that, due to its §365(n) election, Mission retained its rights under the IP License granted to it in section 15 of the Agreement and could exercise those rights free from interference by the Debtor.

Mission argues, however, that the bankruptcy court committed reversible error: (1) by ruling that Mission's §365(n) election applied only to the IP License and not to the exclusive product distribution rights granted in the Agreement; (2) by ruling that notwithstanding its §365(n) election Mission did not retain any rights to use the Debtor's trademark and logo because those items are not included in the Bankruptcy Code's definition of "intellectual property"; and (3) by not requiring the Debtor to bring an adversary proceeding against Mission in order to obtain the relief sought in the 365(n) Motion.

A. Whether the Bankruptcy Court Erred in Ruling that Mission's Exclusive Product Distribution Rights Were Not Protected by its §365(n) Election.

Mission argues that its exclusive product distribution rights were preserved as a result of its §365(n) election because §365(n) permits a licensee of intellectual property to retain its rights under the contract, "including a right to enforce any exclusivity provision of such contract" and "including any embodiment of such intellectual property." 11 U.S.C. §365(n)(1)(B) (emphasis added). According to Mission, the Debtor's grant to Mission of exclusive rights to distribute Cooling Accessories in section 1 of the Agreement, and the Debtor's agreement in sections 5 and 6 not to license or sell Cooling Accessories to anyone else during the term of the Agreement, were "exclusivity provisions" and they related to the IP License because the Cooling Accessories were the "embodiment" of the Debtor's intellectual property. Thus, Mission contends, its §365(n) election protected not only its non-exclusive IP License but also its exclusive product distribution rights.

As the bankruptcy court correctly observed, and the parties do not seriously dispute, an executory contract which may be subject to a §365(n) election can contain terms and provisions unrelated to the licensing of intellectual property. Upon rejection of such a contract, the licensee's §365(n) election applies only to its rights to intellectual property and not to any other rights that it might have received under the executory contract. To conclude otherwise would allow the narrow exception of §365(n) to upend the very purpose of §365. Any executory contract could be made "rejection proof" by inserting in it an intellectual property license no matter how remote or untethered the license provision was from the other terms of the agreement.

The Agreement here deals with far more than the licensing of intellectual property. As reflected in its title, "Co-Marketing and Distribution Agreement," it confers on Mission the exclusive right to distribute the Debtor's products, namely its Cooling Accessories, in the United States and elsewhere around the world. Even a cursory reading of the Agreement makes it clear that the parties had two independent goals in entering into the Agreement: first, to grant Mission the right to distribute certain of the Debtor's products on an exclusive basis in a defined territory during a limited period; and second, to grant Mission a non-exclusive license to use some of the Debtor's intellectual property in perpetuity.

Mission also argues that the Debtor actually granted Mission two separate intellectual property licenses in the Agreement — the non-exclusive IP License provided in section 15 and an implied exclusive intellectual property license to defined products in a defined territory provided in sections 1, 5, 6, and 7 of the Agreement. According to Mission, the provisions by which the Debtor agreed that it would not interfere with Mission's product distribution rights in the Exclusive Territory and would refrain from selling or licensing the same products to third parties in that territory constituted the grant of an exclusive intellectual property license to Mission.

Mission's attempt to re-characterize its exclusive product distribution rights under the Agreement as an intellectual property license are unsupported by either the letter or the spirit of the Agreement. The product distribution provisions in sections 1, 5, 6, and 7 of the Agreement never use the terms license or intellectual property. They confer on Mission the exclusive right to sell certain of the Debtor's products in a defined territory and restrict the Debtor's ability to do the same, nothing more. These rights would have been viable and valuable even if the Agreement had not gone on to grant Mission the IP License.

Nor does the fact that the product distribution rights happen to be exclusive allow Mission's §365(n) election to extend to those rights. The parenthetical reference in §365(n)(1)(B) to "a right to enforce any exclusivity provision of such contract" refers "to such intellectual property." Thus, exclusivity provisions unrelated to an intellectual property license such as the exclusive product distribution rights in the Agreement are not protected by a §365(n) election.

We conclude that the bankruptcy court did not err in ruling that the exclusive product distribution rights granted to Mission in the Agreement were unprotected by its §365(n) election.

B. Whether the Bankruptcy Court Erred in Ruling that Mission's Rights in the Debtor's Coolcore Trademark and Logo Were Not Protected by its §365(n) Election and, Therefore, Mission Did Not Retain Any Rights to the Trademark and Logo Post-rejection.

While the purpose of §365(n) is to protect licensees of intellectual property, the section does not define the term "intellectual property." Section 101(35A) does. It provides:

The term "intellectual property" means —

(A) trade secret;

(B) invention, process, design, or plant protected under title 35 [relating to patents];

(C) patent application;

(D) plant variety;

(E) work of authorship protected under title 17 [relating to copyrights]; or

(F) mask work protected under chapter 9 of title 17 [relating to microchips];

to the extent protected by applicable nonbankruptcy law.

11 U.S.C. §101(35A). Conspicuously absent from the Code's definition are trademarks and trade names.

After Congress enacted §365(n), several courts directly addressed the issue of whether trademarks are protected under the statute. Some courts reasoned by negative inference that the omission of trademarks from §101(35A) means that trademark licenses are not afforded any protection under §365(n) and therefore electing licensees have no rights to use trademarks post-rejection. See, e.g., In re Old Carco LLC, 406 B.R. at 211 (holding that "[t]rademarks are not 'intellectual property' under the Bankruptcy Code" and, therefore, §365(n) did not entitle licensees to retain their rights with respect to trademarks or to continue using them post-rejection); In re HQ Global Holdings, Inc., 290 B.R. 507, 513 (Bankr. D. Del. 2003) ("[S]ince the Bankruptcy Code does not include trademarks in its protected class of intellectual property, *Lubrizol* controls and the Franchisees' right to use the trademarks stops on rejection."); Raima UK Ltd. v. Centura Software Corp. (In re Centura Software Corp.), 281 B.R. 660, 674-75 (Bankr. N.D. Cal. 2002) ("Because §365(n) plainly excludes trademarks, the court holds that [the licensee] is not entitled to retain any rights in [the licensed trademarks] under the rejected . . . [t]rademark [a]greement.").

Other courts have expressed the view that reasoning by negative inference is inappropriate in the context of the rejection of trademark licenses and the scope of the §365(n) election. *See, e.g.*, In re Exide Techs., 607 F.3d at 966 (Ambro, J., concurring) ("I believe such reasoning [by negative inference] is inapt for trademark license rejections."); In re Crumbs Bake Shop, Inc., 522 B.R. at 772. Courts applying this approach rely on the legislative history of §365(n), concluding that "Congress intended the bankruptcy courts to exercise their equitable powers to decide, on a case[-]by[-]case basis, whether trademark licensees may retain the rights listed under §365(n)." In re Crumbs Bake Shop, Inc., 522 B.R. at 772 (adopting rationale set forth by Judge Ambro in In re Exide Techs.). After considering the equities, the court in In re Crumbs Bake Shop, Inc. concluded that it would be inequitable to strip the trademark licensees of their rights under §365(n) in the event of a rejection, as those rights were bargained away by the debtors.

Courts may use §365 to free a bankrupt trademark licensor from burdensome duties that hinder its reorganization. They should not . . . use it to let a licensor take back trademark rights it bargained away. This makes bankruptcy more a sword than a shield, putting debtor-licensors in a catbird seat they often do not deserve.

In Sunbeam Products, Inc. v. Chicago American Manufacturing, LLC, 686 F.3d 372 (7th Cir. 2012), the U.S. Court of Appeals for the Seventh Circuit declined to follow either approach in its entirety. While the Seventh Circuit agreed that a §365(n) election does not protect licensee rights in trademarks due to the omission of trademarks from the definition of intellectual property, it rejected both the line of authority embracing *Lubrizol*'s holding that a trademark license is terminated upon rejection and the reasoning of Judge Ambro that equitable principles could preserve a licensee's rights in trademarks post-rejection. Instead, the Seventh Circuit held that the debtor's rejection of a trademark license, which was part of a supply agreement that related to the manufacturing and sale of electric fans by a third party, did not automatically extinguish the licensee's right to use the debtor's trademarks. In response to cases such as In re Old Carco, LLC, supra, the court stated that "an omission is just an omission. The limited definition in §101(35A) means that §365(n) does not affect trademarks one way or the other." *Id.* at 375. The court examined the legislative history of §365(n) and suggested that "the omission [of trademarks from the definition] was designed to allow more time for study, not to approve *Lubrizol*." *Id.* (citations omitted). It then rejected any equity-based attempt to circumvent the statutory omission, stating that "[r]ights depend . . . on what the Code provides rather than on notions of equity." *Id.* at 376.

The Seventh Circuit determined it was more appropriate to focus on §365(g), which sets forth the consequences of a rejection under §365(a). Under §365(g) "the rejection of an executory contract or unexpired lease of the debtor constitutes a breach of such contract or lease. . . ." 11 U.S.C. §365(g). By classifying rejection as a breach, §365(g) establishes that in bankruptcy, as outside of it, the non-rejecting party's rights remain in place. *Sunbeam*, 686 F.3d at 377. Thus, rejection does not terminate the contract. *Id.* at 377-78. "[R]ejection is not the functional equivalent of a rescission [as *Lubrizol* suggests], rendering void the contract and requiring that the parties be put back in the positions they occupied before the contract was formed. . . . It merely frees the estate from the obligation to perform and has absolutely no effect upon the contract's continued existence." *Id.* at 377.

We agree that §365(n) incorporates the definition of intellectual property set forth in §101(35A), and that the definition does not encompass trademarks and logos. But we decline Mission's invitation to rule that, despite the omission of trademarks from the Code's definition of intellectual property, Mission's licensee rights in the Debtor's trademark and logo should be preserved under §365(n) on equitable grounds as suggested in §365(n)'s legislative history. "[C]ourts must presume that a legislature says in a statute what it means and means in a statute what it says there." Conn. Nat'l Bank v. Germain, 503 U.S. 249, 253–54 (1992). Thus, if a statute is unambiguous, the court need not resort to legislative history to construe its meaning. Moreover, "[w]hat the Bankruptcy Code provides, a judge cannot override by declaring that enforcement would be 'inequitable.'" *Sunbeam*, 686 F.3d at 375. While it is true that the legislative history expresses the sentiment that bankruptcy courts develop the "equitable treatment" of trademarks under §365(n), we are not bound by Congress' aspirational asseverations.

We agree with the bankruptcy court that, based on a plain reading of the statute, Mission's rights in the Debtor's trademark and logo were not and could not be protected by its §365(n) election. We must part company with the bankruptcy court, however, on the effect the Debtor's rejection of the Agreement had on Mission's licensee rights in the Debtor's trademark and logo. The bankruptcy court ruled that, because the Debtor's trademark and logo were not protected by Mission's election under §365(n), Mission did "not retain rights to the Debtor's trademarks and logos post-rejection." This conclusion endorses *Lubrizol*'s approach to the rejection of executory contracts, namely that rejection terminates the contract. *Lubrizol*, however, is not binding precedent in this circuit and, like the many others who have criticized its reasoning, we do not believe it articulates correctly the consequences of rejection of an executory contract under §365(g). We adopt *Sunbeam*'s interpretation of the effect of rejection of an executory contract under §365 involving a trademark license.

> What §365(g) does by classifying rejection as breach is establish that in bankruptcy, as outside of it, the other party's rights remain in place. After rejecting a contract, a debtor is not subject to an order of specific performance. *See* NLRB v. Bildisco & Bildisco, 465 U.S. 513, 531 (1984). The debtor's unfulfilled obligations are converted to damages; when a debtor does not assume the contract before rejecting it, these damages are treated as a pre-petition obligation, which may be written down in common with other debts of the same class. But nothing about this process implies that any rights of the other contracting party have been vaporized. *Sunbeam*, 686 F.3d at 377.

Applying *Sunbeam*'s rationale, we conclude that, while the Debtor's trademark and logo were not encompassed in the categories of intellectual property entitled to special protections under §365(n), the Debtor's rejection of the Agreement did not vaporize Mission's trademark rights under the Agreement. Whatever post-rejection rights Mission retained in the Debtor's trademark and logo are governed by the terms of the Agreement and applicable non-bankruptcy law.

Thus, we conclude that the bankruptcy court did not err in ruling that Mission's §365(n) election failed to protect its rights under the Agreement as licensee of the Debtor's trademark and logo, but it erred in ruling that Mission's rights in the Debtor's trademark and logo as set forth in the Agreement terminated upon the Debtor's rejection of the Agreement.

IN RE SPANSION, INC.
507 Fed. Appx. 125, 2012 WL 6634899 (3d Cir. 2012)

SCIRICA, Circuit Judge.

In November 2008 Spansion filed a patent infringement complaint over its flash memory products against Samsung and Apple with the International Trade Commission (ITC). In a letter agreement dated February 10, 2009 between Spansion and Apple, Spansion agreed to dismiss the ITC action against Apple and promised to refrain from filing future actions related to those patents. In exchange, Apple agreed to not disbar Spansion as a supplier, and to consider Spansion for future products if certain conditions were met. On March 1, 2009, Spansion filed for Chapter 11 bankruptcy in the Bankruptcy Court for the District of Delaware. Under 11 U.S.C. §365(a), Spansion moved to reject the letter agreement as an executory contract. The Bankruptcy Court granted the motion, and on September 1, 2009 it issued an order stating that "the Agreement . . . is hereby rejected; and further ordered that . . . this Order upon Apple, Inc. shall constitute adequate written notice of termination thereof." Apple then filed under 11 U.S.C. §365(n) electing to retain its rights under the agreement, contending the agreement was a license.

Spansion moved to enforce the September Order arguing it terminated the agreement. Apple moved under FRCP 60(b) to clarify the Order, positing termination was never at issue and that Spansion did not request termination as relief. The September Order had adopted Spansion's sample order language virtually unchanged, and there was no discussion before the Bankruptcy Court on the question of termination. Accordingly, the Bankruptcy Court amended its order to "provide that such order is without prejudice on the issue of whether . . . [the] agreement has been or can be terminated by Spansion." The Bankruptcy Court denied Apple's §365(n) election, finding the agreement was not a license, so §365(n) did not apply.

Apple appealed the Bankruptcy Court's denial of its §365(n) notice and Spansion cross-appealed its grant of Apple's 60(b) motion. The District Court of Delaware held the agreement was a license because it was a promise not to sue, and held §365 permits Apple to retain its rights under the patent license. The District Court further found the Bankruptcy Court did not abuse its discretion in granting the Rule 60(b) motion. Spansion appeals from the District Court judgment, but contends we do not have jurisdiction over the appeal because the District Court remanded to the Bankruptcy Court.

I

A

"The courts of appeals shall have jurisdiction of appeals from all final decisions, judgments, orders, and decrees entered" by district courts with appellate jurisdiction over bankruptcy court decisions. 28 U.S.C. §158(d). Finality is often assessed differently in the bankruptcy context because the bankruptcy court continues to determine the disposition of the debtor's other assets, even when there is a final order involving one of those assets. We consider several pragmatic factors to determine whether we have jurisdiction, including: "the impact upon the assets of the bankrupt estate, the necessity for further fact-finding on remand, the preclusive effect of our decision on the merits on further litigation, and whether the interest of judicial economy would be furthered." In re Meyertech, 831 F.2d 410, 414 (3d Cir. 1987).

Determining whether the letter agreement is a license and whether there was a valid §365(n) election impacts Spansion's patent assets. No other fact-finding is necessary to resolve whether the agreement was a license or whether the §365(n) election was valid. Furthermore, our decision on the merits will have preclusive effect on further litigation, because the state law termination issue is predicated on a valid §365(n) election. Determination of the license issue also impacts the Bankruptcy Court's interpretation of state contract law, because the ability to terminate contracts at will can be limited by federal intellectual property law. See, e.g., Rano v. Sipa Press, Inc., 987 F.2d 580, 585-85 (9th Cir. 1993) (finding licensing agreements without a stated duration not terminable at will, because under federal law copyrights expire after 35 years, creating an end date to the licensing contract).

Judicial economy favors jurisdiction. The validity of the license and the amended order leaves open the question whether Apple may continue to use Spansion's patented products, and whether Apple could be subject to further patent litigation by Spansion. The interests of judicial economy would be served by resolving the status of the letter agreement.

B

"We exercise plenary review of an order issued by a district court sitting as an appellate court in review of the bankruptcy court." In re CellNet Data Sys., Inc., 327 F.3d 242, 244 (3d Cir. 2003). Legal conclusions are reviewed de novo and the bankruptcy court's findings of fact are reviewed for clear error. In re Exide Techs., 607 F.3d 957, 962 (3d Cir. 2010).

"We review a district court's denial of a Rule 60(b) motion for abuse of discretion." Reform Party of Allegheny Cnty. v. Allegheny Cnty. Dep't of Elections, 174 F.3d 305, 311 (3d Cir. 1999).

II

A

The District Court upheld the Bankruptcy Court's judgment to amend the September Order under Rule 60(b)(6). Rule 60(b)(6) provides relief from judgment for "any [ ] reason that justifies relief." Fed. R. Civ. P. 60(b)(6). The rule seeks "to strike a proper balance between the conflicting principles that litigation must be brought to an end and that justice must be done." Boughner v. Sec'y of Health, Educ. and Welfare, 572 F.2d 976, 977 (3d Cir. 1978). Accordingly, "Rule 60 is to be liberally construed in order that judgments will reflect the true merits of a case." 11 Charles Alan Wright & Arthur R. Miller, Federal Practice and Procedure §2852 (3d ed. 2012). A Rule 60(b)(6) motion is generally reserved for extraordinary circumstances where extreme and unexpected hardship will result absent relief. Budget Blinds, Inc. v. White, 536 F.3d 244, 255 (3d Cir. 2008).

The termination issue was not before the Bankruptcy Court, not considered by the Bankruptcy Court, and not adjudicated by the Bankruptcy Court. Spansion provided no evidence or argument in support of termination. Accordingly, the Bankruptcy Court amended its order to reflect the fact that it made no determination on the termination issue. Ordering relief the court did not intend to grant is an extraordinary circumstance. The Bankruptcy Court did not abuse its discretion in correcting this error by granting the Rule 60(b) motion.

B

"[A] license . . . [is] a mere waiver of the right to sue by the patentee." De Forest Radio Tel. & Tel. Co. v. United States, 273 U.S. 236, 242 (1927) (quotations omitted). A license need not be a formal grant, but is instead a "consent[ ] to [the] use of the patent in making or using it, or selling it . . . and a defense to an action for a tort." Id. at 241. The Court of Appeals for the Federal Circuit explained that the inquiry focuses on what the agreement authorizes, not whether the language is couched in terms of a license or a covenant not to sue; effectively the two are equivalent. TransCore, LP v. Elec. Transaction Consultants Corp., 563 F.3d 1271, 1275-76 (Fed. Cir. 2009).

In the letter agreement, Spansion promised "to dismiss the ITC action against Apple, and [to] not re-file the ITC action or another action related to one or more of the same patents against Apple." This was a promise not to sue Apple for its use of Spansion's patented products. Accordingly, as the District Court found, the letter agreement is a license. Since all the evidence before the Bankruptcy Court showed the agreement was a license, the District Court properly held the Bankruptcy Court finding was clear error.

C

After a debtor rejects a contract under §365(a), section 365(n) allows the holder of an intellectual property license to elect to retain its rights under the contract. 11 U.S.C. §365(n)(1)(B). The Bankruptcy Court denied Apple's §365(n) election because of the "cessation of business between Spansion and Apple" after Spansion moved to reject the agreement. But §365(n)(1)(B) allows a licensee "to retain its rights . . . as such rights existed immediately before the case commenced." 11 U.S.C. §365(n)(1)(B), see also 2 William L. Norton Jr., Norton Bankruptcy Law & Practice 3d §46:57 ("The rights which may be retained are those existing 'immediately before the case commenced.' "). Accordingly, cessation of business after Spansion filed for bankruptcy is irrelevant to the §365(n) analysis. Since the letter agreement was a license, Spansion's rejection of the license under §365(a) triggered Apple's right to elect to retain its licensing rights under §365(n).

For the foregoing reasons, we will affirm the judgment of the District Court.

JAFFE v. SAMSUNG ELECTRONICS CO., LTD.

737 F.3d 14, (4th Cir. 2013)

NIEMEYER, Circuit Judge:

This appeal presents the significant question under Chapter 15 of the U.S. Bankruptcy Code of how to mediate between the United States' interests in recognizing and cooperating with a foreign insolvency proceeding and its interests in protecting creditors of the foreign debtor with respect to U.S. assets, as provided in 11 U.S.C. §§1521 and 1522.

Qimonda AG, a German corporation that manufactured semiconductor devices and was, for a brief time, one of the world's largest manufacturers of dynamic random access memory ("DRAM"), filed for insolvency in Munich, Germany, in January 2009. The principal assets of Qimonda's estate consisted of some 10,000 patents, about 4,000 of which were U.S. patents. These patents were subject to cross-license agreements with Qimonda's competitors, as was common in the semiconductor industry to avoid infringement risks caused by the "patent thicket" resulting from the overlapping patent rights of some 420,000 patents in the semiconductor industry.

Ancillary to the German insolvency proceeding, Dr. Michael Jaffé, the insolvency administrator appointed by the Munich court, filed an application in the Bankruptcy Court for the Eastern District of Virginia under Chapter 15 of the U.S. Bankruptcy Code, petitioning the U.S. court to recognize the German insolvency proceeding as a "foreign main proceeding" in order to obtain an array of privileges available under Chapter 15. Among other relief, Jaffé specifically requested that the bankruptcy court entrust to him, pursuant to 11 U.S.C. §1521(a)(5), the administration of all of Qimonda's assets within the territorial jurisdiction of the United States, which largely consisted of the 4,000 U.S. patents.

Contemporaneously with the Chapter 15 proceeding, Jaffé sent letters to licensees of Qimonda's patents under its cross-license agreements, declaring that, under §103 of the German Insolvency Code, the licenses granted under Qimonda patents "are no longer enforceable," including the licenses under the company's 4,000 U.S. patents. As Jaffé later indicated to the bankruptcy court, he intended to re-license Qimonda's patents for the benefit of Qimonda's creditors, replacing licenses paid for in-kind with cross-licenses with licenses paid for with cash through royalties.

The bankruptcy court entered an order recognizing the German insolvency proceeding as a foreign main proceeding and a separate order granting Jaffé the discretionary relief he requested under §1521(a)(5). But, following a four-day evidentiary hearing, it conditioned the §1521 relief with the requirement that Jaffé afford the licensees of Qimonda's U.S. patents the treatment they would have received in the United States under 11 U.S.C. §365(n), which limits a trustee's ability to reject unilaterally licenses to the debtor's intellectual property by giving licensees the option to retain their rights under the licenses. After balancing the interests of Qimonda's estate with the interests of the licensees of its U.S. patents, the bankruptcy court concluded that the application of §365(n) was necessary to ensure, as required by §1522(a), that the licensees were "sufficiently protected," even though it would adversely affect Qimonda's estate. The bankruptcy court also concluded, pursuant to 11 U.S.C. §1506, that allowing Jaffé to cancel unilaterally Qimonda's licenses of U.S. patents "would be manifestly contrary to the public policy of the United States," recognizing "a fundamental U.S. public policy promoting technological innovation," which would be undermined if it failed to apply §365(n) to the licenses under Qimonda's U.S. patents.

In this direct appeal from the bankruptcy court, Jaffé challenges both of these conclusions, arguing that the court erred in its construction of Chapter 15 and abused its discretion in applying it.

We conclude that the bankruptcy court properly recognized that Jaffé's request for discretionary relief under §1521(a) required it to consider "the interests of the creditors and other interested entities, including the debtor" under §1522(a) and that it properly construed §1522(a) as requiring the application of a balancing test. Moreover, relying on the particular facts of this case and the extensive record developed during the four-day evidentiary hearing, we also conclude that the bankruptcy court reasonably exercised its discretion in balancing the interests of the licensees against the interests of the debtor and finding that application of §365(n) was necessary to ensure the licensees under Qimonda's U.S. patents were sufficiently protected. Accordingly, we affirm.

II

Congress enacted Chapter 15 of the Bankruptcy Code in 2005 as part of the Bankruptcy Abuse Prevention and Consumer Protection Act of 2005, Pub. L. No. 109-8, 119 Stat. 23, stating that its purpose was "to incorporate the Model Law on Cross-Border Insolvency," which had been developed in 1997 by the United Nations Commission on International Trade Law ("UNCITRAL"), "so as to provide effective mechanisms for dealing with cases of cross-border insolvency." 11 U.S.C. §1501(a). In this respect, Chapter 15 replaced former 11 U.S.C. §304, which authorized bankruptcy courts to award appropriate relief in a case ancillary to a foreign proceeding but which was largely discretionary. See 11 U.S.C. §304(c) (2000). Chapter 15 lists five specific objectives: (1) to encourage cooperation with "the courts and other competent authorities of foreign countries involved in cross-border cases"; (2) to increase "legal certainty for trade and investment"; (3) to promote the "fair and efficient administration of cross-border insolvencies" so as to "protect[ ] the interests of all creditors, and other interested entities, including the debtor"; (4) to protect and maximize "the value of the debtor's assets"; and (5) to facilitate "the rescue of financially troubled businesses." 11 U.S.C. §1501(a).

To further these stated objectives, Chapter 15 authorizes the representative of a foreign insolvency proceeding to commence a case in a U.S. bankruptcy court by filing a petition for recognition of the foreign proceeding. 11 U.S.C. §§1504, 1509(a), 1515. If the petition meets the requirements listed in §1517, the court must enter an order granting recognition of the foreign proceeding. And if that foreign proceeding "is pending in the country where the debtor has the center of its main interests," it is recognized as a "foreign main proceeding." 11 U.S.C. §1517(b)(1); see also *id.* §1502(4). With the entry of an order recognizing a foreign main proceeding, the foreign representative of the proceeding automatically receives relief as stated in §1520, including the automatic stay created by §362 with respect to the debtor and its property within the United States and the ability to operate the debtor's business within the United States under §363, as well as the right to sue and be sued and the right to "intervene in any proceedings in a State or Federal court in the United States in which the debtor is a party." *Id.* §§1520(a), 1509(b)(1), 1524. Moreover, the statute provides that following entry of a recognition order, "a court in the United States shall grant comity or cooperation to the foreign representative," thereby implementing a principal purpose of Chapter 15. *Id.* §1509(b)(3).

Even before entry of the order granting recognition, §1519 authorizes the bankruptcy court, on the foreign representative's request, to grant preliminary relief when "urgently needed to protect the assets of the debtor or the interests of the creditors." 11 U.S.C. §1519.

In addition to the automatic relief that comes with the entry of an order granting recognition of a foreign main proceeding, §1521 authorizes the bankruptcy court to grant discretionary relief. Specifically, §1521 provides that "where necessary to effectuate the purpose of this chapter and to protect the assets of the debtor or the interests of the creditors, the court may, at the request of the foreign representative, grant any appropriate relief." 11 U.S.C. §1521(a). This discretionary relief may include "entrusting the administration or realization of all or part of the debtor's assets within the territorial jurisdiction of the United States to the foreign representative," *id.* §1521(a)(5), as well as "entrust[ing] the distribution of all or part of the debtor's assets located in the United States to the foreign representative," *id.* §1521(b). The bankruptcy court, however, may only grant discretionary relief under §1521 if it determines that "the interests of the creditors and other interested entities, including the debtor, are sufficiently protected." *Id.* §1522(a). It may also subject the discretionary relief it grants under §1521 "to conditions it considers appropriate, including the giving of security or the filing of a bond." *Id.* §1522(b).

Finally, all of the actions authorized in Chapter 15 are subject to §1506, which provides that "[n]othing in this chapter prevents the court from refusing to take an action governed by this chapter if the action would be manifestly contrary to the public policy of the United States." 11 U.S.C. §1506.

Chapter 15 thus authorizes an "ancillary" proceeding in a United States bankruptcy court that is largely designed to complement and assist a foreign insolvency proceeding by, among other things, "bring[ing] people and property beyond the foreign main proceeding's jurisdiction into the foreign main proceeding through the exercise of the United States' jurisdiction." In re ABC Learning Centres Ltd., 728 F.3d 301, 307 (3d Cir. 2013); see also H.R. Rep. No. 109-31, pt. 1, at 106 ("Cases brought under Chapter 15 are intended to be ancillary to cases brought in a debtor's home country . . ."). This structure reflects "the United States policy in favor of a general rule that countries other than the home country of the debtor, where a main proceeding would be brought, should usually act through ancillary proceedings in aid of the main proceedings, in preference to a system of full bankruptcies (often called 'secondary' proceedings) in each state where assets are found." H.R. Rep. No. 109-31, pt. 1, at 108. Notwithstanding this general policy, Chapter 15 also expressly contemplates that "[a]fter recognition of a foreign main proceeding, a case under another chapter of [the Bankruptcy Code] may be commenced . . . if the debtor has assets in the United States." 11 U.S.C. §1528.

Thus, taken as a whole, Chapter 15—like the Model Law on which it was based—takes "several modest but significant" steps toward implementing "a modern, harmonized and fair framework to address more effectively instances of cross-border insolvency." UNCITRAL, Guide to Enactment of the UNCITRAL Model Law on Cross-Border Insolvency, in Legislative Guide on Insolvency Law 307, 307 (2005) (hereinafter, "Guide to Enactment").

III

Jaffé contends that the bankruptcy court erred by employing §1522(a)'s sufficient protection requirement to subject his "right to administer [Qimonda's] U.S. patents to the . . . constraints imposed by §365(n)," thus allowing the Licensees to elect to retain their license rights under Qimonda's U.S. patents, contrary to German law as he understands it. In re Qimonda AG, 462 B.R. at 183. The bankruptcy court limited the authority it conferred on Jaffé under §1521(a)(5) by balancing the interests of the Licensees with the interests of Qimonda's estate under §1522(a) and concluding that the Licensees should receive the protection of §365(n). Id. at 180-83. In support of his challenge, Jaffé makes essentially three arguments: (1) that the district court and the bankruptcy court erred in even considering §1522(a), because that section applies only to relief granted under §1521, that the relief granted under §1521 may be requested only by the foreign representative, and that he, as the foreign representative, never requested the inclusion of §365(n) as part of the §1521 relief; (2) that the bankruptcy court misunderstood the type of protection afforded by §1522(a) by applying a test that balanced the debtor's interests and the creditors' interests instead of a test that placed all creditors on an equal footing; and (3) that in balancing the competing interests, the bankruptcy court overstated the risks to the Licensees, especially in view of Jaffé's offer to re-license Qimonda's patents to them, and failed to treat all creditors' interests equally. We address these points in order.

A

First, Jaffé argues that both the bankruptcy court and the district court erred in even considering §1522's sufficient protection requirement because §1522(a) applies to relief that may be granted under §1521, and §1521(a), in turn, provides that "the court may, at the request of the foreign representative, grant any appropriate relief." He asserts that he "never asked the bankruptcy court to include §365 in its Supplemental Order or sought other relief relating to §365(n)" such that the Licensees would have the option to retain their licenses under Qimonda's U.S. patents. Thus, according to Jaffé, because application of §365 was not specifically requested by him, the bankruptcy court's sua sponte inclusion of

§365 was legal error, the correction of which must precede any consideration of §1522(a)'s sufficient protection requirement.

We believe that Jaffé's view of the relationship between §1521(a) and §1522(a) is too myopic. While it is true that Jaffé "never affirmatively requested rejection authority under §365," he did request several forms of discretionary relief under §1521, among which was the privilege, pursuant to §1521(a)(5), to have the bankruptcy court entrust him with "[t]he administration or realization of all or part of the assets of [Qimonda] within the territorial jurisdiction of the United States," specifically identifying the company's U.S. patents as among the U.S. assets he sought to control. And, as a prerequisite to awarding any §1521 relief, the court was required to ensure sufficient protection of the creditors and the debtor. Section 1522(a) states this explicitly, providing in relevant part, "The court may grant relief under section . . . 1521 . . . only if the interests of the creditors and other interested entities, including the debtor, are sufficiently protected." 11 U.S.C. §1522(a). Additionally, the court was authorized to "subject" any §1521 relief "to conditions it considers appropriate." *Id.* §1522(b); see also H.R. Rep. No. 109-31, pt. 1, at 116 (describing §1522 as "giv[ing] the bankruptcy court broad latitude to mold relief to meet specific circumstances, including appropriate responses if it is shown that the foreign proceeding is seriously and unjustifiably injuring United States creditors").

This is precisely what the bankruptcy court did here. It granted discretionary relief under §1521 and, as mandated, considered the question of sufficient protection under §1522(a). Upon such consideration, it conditioned its §1521 relief on application of §365(n), finding that such protection was appropriate in the circumstances presented.

To be sure, the bankruptcy court did not frame its initial inclusion of §365 in the Supplemental Order as a condition on the authority it was granting Jaffé under §1521. Indeed, when initially faced with Jaffé's motion to amend, the court described the inclusion of §365 as "improvident." But on the Licensees' appeal, the district court correctly recognized that it was incumbent on the bankruptcy court, on remand, to consider whether "the interests of the creditors and other interested entities, including the debtor, [would be] sufficiently protected" under §1522(a) were the court to modify its earlier order so as to grant Jaffé control over the administration of Qimonda's U.S. patents without providing for the application of §365(n) to the licenses on those patents. See In re Qimonda AG Bankr. Litig., 433 B.R. at 557-58.

The bankruptcy court's consideration of §1522(a) was thus undoubtedly appropriate when authorizing relief under §1521.

B

Jaffé next contends that even if the bankruptcy court was correct to consider §1522's sufficient protection requirement in granting §1521 relief, the court nonetheless employed the wrong test in applying §1522(a). He maintains that the bankruptcy court's "ruling fundamentally misunderst[ood] the 'interests' §1522(a) protects" by failing to recognize that §1522(a) is merely a procedural protection "designed to ensure that all creditors [could] participate in the bankruptcy distribution on an equal footing" and thus should not be used to protect parties from the substantive bankruptcy law that would otherwise apply in the foreign main proceeding. He asserts that "[d]isregarding foreign law based on an open-ended balancing test under §1522(a) is contrary to Chapter 15's basic design," which, according to Jaffé, requires U.S. courts to defer to foreign substantive law except only as allowed under §1506, which provides a narrow exception when the court's action would otherwise violate "the most fundamental policies of the United States." H.R. Rep. No. 109-31, pt. 1, at 109. In sum, he argues (1) that the bankruptcy court erred by interpreting §1522's sufficient protection requirement as incorporating a balancing test that could achieve a result that treated creditors differently and that would therefore be in tension with German law, and (2) that, to the extent §1522(a) was implicated at all, the bankruptcy court should have limited its analysis to ensuring that the doors of the German insolvency proceeding would be open to the Licensees on equal footing with Qimonda's other creditors.

Jaffé's theory of how the sufficient protection requirement of §1522(a) operates is not illogical. The text of the statute is broad and somewhat ambiguous regarding the test that courts should employ to determine "if the interests of the creditors and other interested entities, including the debtor, are sufficiently protected." 11 U.S.C. §1522(a). But we are not convinced that Jaffé's theory can fully be squared with the text or with Congress's intent in enacting the text.

Section 1522(a) requires the bankruptcy court to ensure the protection of both the creditors and the debtor. 11 U.S.C. §1522(a). The provision thus requires the court to ensure that the relief a foreign representative requests under §1521 does not impinge excessively on any one entity's interests, implying that each entity must receive at least some protection. And because the interests of the creditors and the interests of the debtor are often antagonistic, as they are here, providing protection to one side might well come at some expense to the other. The analysis required by §1522(a) is therefore logically best done by balancing the respective interests based on the relative harms and benefits in light of the circumstances presented, thus inherently calling for application of a balancing test.

We also find support for this interpretation in the Model Law on Cross-Border Insolvency, on which Chapter 15 was based. In enacting Chapter 15, Congress stated that it intended to codify the Model Law. See 11 U.S.C. §1501(a). And, in doing so, it also indicated strongly that the Model Law, and the accompanying Guide to Enactment issued by UNCITRAL in conjunction with its adoption of the Model Law, should inform our interpretation of Chapter 15's provisions. Indeed, Chapter 15 provides that "[i]n interpreting this chapter, the court shall consider its international origin, and the need to promote an application of this chapter that is consistent with the application of similar statutes adopted by foreign jurisdictions." *Id.* §1508; see also H.R. Rep. No. 109-31, pt. 1, at 109-10 ("Interpretation of this chapter on a uniform basis will be aided by reference to the Guide and the Reports cited therein, which explain the reasons for the terms used and often cite their origins as well. . . . To the extent that the United States courts rely on these sources, their decisions will more likely be regarded as persuasive elsewhere"). Thus, the Model Law and its Guide to Enactment also provide relevant guidance in determining the appropriate meaning of Chapter 15's provisions.

The Guide to Enactment contains a number of paragraphs that bear directly on the question of how a court should assess the interests of others and protect them prior to granting the discretionary relief sought by a foreign representative. For example, the Guide acknowledges that the representative of a foreign main proceeding will "normally seek[ ] to gain control over all assets of the insolvent debtor." Guide to Enactment ¶158, at 347. But it stresses that the Model Law makes "[t]he 'turnover' of assets to the foreign representative discretionary," adding that "the Model Law contains several safeguards designed to ensure the protection of local interests before assets are turned over to the foreign representative." *Id.* ¶157, at 347. Chief among those "safeguards" is Article 22 of the Model Law, which is largely codified as §1522. According to the Guide, "The idea underlying [A]rticle 22 is that there should be a balance between relief that may be granted to the foreign representative and the interests of the persons that may be affected by such relief. This balance is essential to achieve the objectives of cross-border insolvency legislation." *Id.* ¶161, at 348. The Guide to Enactment separately indicates that Article 22 is designed to "protect the interests of the creditors (in particular local creditors), the debtor and other affected persons." *Id.* ¶35, at 314. Finally, the Guide states, "[i]n addition to [Article 22's] specific provisions," Article 6 of the Model Law "in a general way provides that the court may refuse to take an action governed by the Model Law if the action would be manifestly contrary to the public policy of the enacting State." *Id.* ¶36, at 314 .

Informed by the Guide to Enactment's description of the relationship between Articles 22 and 6 of the Model Law (§§1522 and 1506 in the U.S. Bankruptcy Code), we do not share Jaffé's view that §1506's public policy exception forecloses use of a balancing analysis under §1522. Contrary to Jaffé's position, Chapter 15 does not require a U.S. bankruptcy court, in considering a foreign representative's request for discretionary relief under §1521, to blind itself to the costs that awarding such relief would impose on others under the rule provided by the substantive law of the State where the foreign insolvency proceeding is pending. Instead, Chapter 15, like the Model Law, anticipates the provision of particularized protection, as stated in §1522(a).

We therefore conclude, through interpretation of §1522(a)'s text and consideration of Chapter 15's international origin, that the district court correctly interpreted §1522(a)'s sufficient protection requirement as requiring a particularized balancing analysis that considers the "interests of the creditors and other interested entities, including the debtor," 11 U.S.C. §1522(a), and, in this case in particular, a weighing of the interests of the foreign representative (the debtor) in receiving the requested relief against the competing interests of those who would be adversely affected by the grant of such relief (here, the Licensees). And we also agree that §1506 is an additional, more general protection of U.S. interests that may be evaluated apart from the particularized analysis of §1522(a).

In reaching this conclusion, we join the Fifth Circuit, which interpreted §1522(a) similarly, based largely on the language in the Guide to Enactment. See In re Vitro S.A.B. de C.V., 701 F.3d 1031, 1060, 1067 n. 42 (5th Cir. 2012).

C

Finally, Jaffé contends that the bankruptcy court's balancing analysis, even if assumed appropriate, was flawed in implementation. He argues that the court dramatically overstated the risk to the Licensees' investments made in reliance on the cross-license agreements, especially in light of his offer to re-license Qimonda's U.S. patents to the Licensees at a RAND royalty rate. In this regard, he maintains that the court's balancing analysis failed to recognize that "§1522(a) requires courts to protect the interests of all 'creditors and other interested entities, including the debtor'—not just one set of contracting parties."

The Licensees respond, arguing that "the bankruptcy court properly recognized that Dr. Jaffé's offer to relicense did not change the balance of harms" and that the bankruptcy court correctly "concluded that, without §365(n) protection, the Licensees would face both the immediate harm of a hold-up and the future . . . destabilization of the licensing regime in the semiconductor industry." They maintain that in light of the bankruptcy court's detailed findings and careful reasoning, Jaffé simply "cannot meet his heavy burden to demonstrate that the bankruptcy court abused its discretion in its application of §1522."

It should be noted that after hearing four days of evidence, the bankruptcy court considered the outcome of its balancing analysis to be a close one. But in the end it concluded, reasonably we believe, "that the balancing of debtor and creditor interests required by §1522(a), Bankruptcy Code, weigh[ed] in favor of making §365(n) applicable to Dr. Jaffé's administration of Qimonda's U.S. patents." In re Qimonda AG, 462 B.R. at 182. The court recognized Jaffé's claim that the "application of §365(n) [would] result in less value being realized by the Qimonda estate." *Id.* But it noted that "Qimonda's patent portfolio [would] by no means be rendered worthless" because the "U.S. patents [could] still be licensed to parties that [did] not already have a license, and Dr. Jaffé, to the extent permitted by German law, [would] be able to fully monetize the non-U.S. patents." *Id.* Additionally, the bankruptcy court found it significant that "[a]pplication of §365(n) . . . [would impose] no affirmative burden on Dr. Jaffé," *id.*, but instead would merely limit his ability — and, importantly, the ability of the patents' subsequent owners — to bring infringement actions against the very entities that Qimonda had previously promised not to sue. See Imation Corp. v. Koninklijke Philips Elecs. N.V., 586 F.3d 980, 987 (Fed. Cir. 2009) (characterizing a patent cross-license agreement as essentially "a promise by the licensor not to sue the licensee" for infringement (citation omitted)).

In considering and weighing the Licensees' interests, the bankruptcy court largely credited their evidence indicating that entrusting Jaffé with the right to administer Qimonda's U.S. patents without making §365(n) applicable to the preexisting licenses under those patents would have broad-ranging ill effects. It explained that "the risk to the very substantial investment the [Licensees] — particularly IBM, Micron, Intel, and Samsung — [had] collectively made in research and manufacturing facilities in the United States in reliance on the design freedom provided by the cross-license agreements, though not easily quantifiable, [was] nevertheless very real." In re Qimonda AG, 462 B.R. at 182-83. While the bankruptcy court acknowledged that the Licensees had been unable "to identify specific Qimonda patents implicated by the products they manufacture[d] and s[old]," it noted that the lack of such evidence was "not at all surprising, since the whole point of portfolio cross-licenses [was] to eliminate the necessity (and in some cases impossibility) of individually analyzing each and every patent that might possibly apply to determine if a new design infringe[d] on it." *Id.* at 181. Thus, although the bankruptcy court could not, in the course of its balancing analysis, make "a finding that cancellation of the [Licensees'] right to use Qimonda's U.S. patents would have a specific dollar impact on them," it did find that it "create[d] a substantial risk of harm," adding that "the threat of infringement litigation can be as damaging as an actual finding of infringement." *Id.*

We find the bankruptcy court's thorough examination of the parties' competing interests to have been both comprehensive and eminently reasonable.

Jaffé relies heavily on the mitigation that would result from his commitment to re-license Qimonda's patents to the Licensees on RAND terms, arguing that it would provide sufficient protection for their interests. Of course, his proposal — first mentioned after the district court's remand — does weigh in his favor by decreasing the Licensees' holdup risks. But just because the RAND proposal would reduce the Licensees' risks does not mean that their interests would be sufficiently protected by Jaffé's promise to re-license. The bankruptcy court expressly recognized this, explaining that "the hold-up risk is lessened by Dr. Jaffé's offer to re-license the patents on RAND terms," but emphasizing that "even if the WIPO expert determination process were to arrive at the same figure that would have been agreed to in an 'ex ante' scenario, the [Licensees], because of their sunk costs, [would] not have the option of avoiding royalties altogether by designing around the patent." In re Qimonda AG, 462 B.R. at 181-82. We conclude that the bankruptcy court's findings in this regard are not unreasonable and that the bankruptcy court was justified in its skepticism of Jaffé's claim that the Licensees' interests would now be "sufficiently protected" by his commitment not to charge them an exorbitant rate during their re-licensing negotiations.

Moreover, the bankruptcy court also noted that it remained an "open question" whether any new license issued by Jaffé on RAND terms would itself be secure, expressing its concern that

> Dr. Jaffé could still sell the underlying patents to a purchaser — whether a practicing entity or a "troll" — that might itself file for insolvency under German law or transfer the patent to a special purpose entity for the purpose of having it file for insolvency under German law.

Id. at 181-82 n. 13. The court's recognition of this concern was also reasonable, as it is far from clear whether, having once facilitated the termination of license rights in a foreign insolvency proceeding, the genie could ever be put back into the bottle. Rather, as indicated by expert testimony that the bankruptcy court credited, it would seem all too likely that such a result would introduce a dangerous degree of uncertainty to a licensing system that plays a critically important role in the semiconductor industry, as well as other high-tech sectors of the global economy.

At bottom, we affirm the decision of the bankruptcy court, finding reasonable its exercise of discretion in conducting the balancing analysis under §1522(a) and concluding that attaching the protection of §365(n) was necessary when granting Jaffé the power to administer Qimonda's U.S. patents. See In re Vitro S.A.B. de C.V., 701 F.3d at 1069 (noting in the course of affirming a bankruptcy court's decision not to enforce the reorganization plan adopted in a foreign main proceeding that "[i]t is not our role to determine whether the above-summarized evidence would lead us to the same conclusion" and adding that "[o]ur only task is to determine whether the bankruptcy court's decision was reasonable").

IV

It is important, we think, to recognize, as Jaffé would have us do, the importance of Chapter 15 to a global economy, in which businesses needing bankruptcy protection increasingly have assets in various countries. In mimicking the U.N.'s Model Law on Cross-Border Insolvencies, Chapter 15 furthers a policy of the United States of cooperating with other countries in providing fair and efficient insolvency proceedings for such international businesses. Consistent with its stated purposes, Chapter 15 provides for the ready recognition of foreign insolvency proceedings, see 11 U.S.C. §1517, and grants automatic relief to protect U.S. assets upon entry of an order granting recognition, see *id.* §1520. It also provides for a broad range of discretionary relief under §1521. Thus, it represents a full commitment of the United States to cooperate with foreign insolvency proceedings, as called for by the U.N.'s Model Law on Cross-Border Insolvency. And at bottom, such cooperation will provide greater legal certainty for trade and business to the benefit of the global economy.

But the United States' commitment is not untempered, as is manifested in both Chapter 15 and the Model Law on which it was based. Thus, §1522(a) requires that a bankruptcy court, when granting the discretionary relief authorized by §1521, ensure sufficient protection of creditors, as well as the debtor. And at a more general level, §1506, which covers any action under Chapter 15, authorizes a bankruptcy court to refuse to take an action that would be manifestly contrary to U.S. public policy.

In this case, it is sufficient for us to affirm the bankruptcy court, based on its application of §1522(a). But in doing so, we understand that, by affirming the bankruptcy court's application of §365(n) following its balancing analysis under §1522(a), we also indirectly further the public policy that underlies §365(n). The Senate Report accompanying the bill that became §365(n) explicitly recognized that licensees have a strong interest in maintaining their right to use intellectual property following the licensor's bankruptcy and that to deny them that right would "impose[ ] a burden on American technological development that was never intended by Congress." S. Rep. No. 100-505, at 1. The Report added that "[t]he adoption of this bill will immediately remove that burden and its attendant threat to the development of American Technology." *Id.* at 2.

In this case, the bankruptcy court, in weighing the respective interests of the Licensees and the debtor under §1522(a), found that without the protection of 365(n), the risk of harm to the Licensees would be very real, impairing the "design freedom provided [them] by the cross-license agreements." In re Qimonda AG, 462 B.R. at 183. And as the bankruptcy court otherwise found, this potential harm to the Licensees would, in turn, threaten to "slow the pace of innovation" in the United States, to the detriment of the U.S. economy. *Id.* at 185. Thus, the court's findings, which were, to be sure, focused on the Licensees' interests, nonetheless necessarily furthered the public policy underlying §365(n).

We thus recognize that by affirming the bankruptcy court, even though on its §1522(a) analysis, we too necessarily further the public policy inherent in and manifested by §365(n).

The judgment of the bankruptcy court is accordingly AFFIRMED.

IN RE CFLC, INC.
89 F.3d 673 (9th Cir. 1996)

PREGERSON, Circuit Judge.

Everex Systems, Inc., a buyer of certain of the assets of CFLC, Inc. in a Chapter 11 bankruptcy, appeals the district court's affirmance of a bankruptcy court order denying CFLC's motion as debtor to assume and assign to Everex a patent license from Cadtrak Corporation to CFLC.

FACTUAL BACKGROUND AND PROCEDURAL HISTORY

In a 1986 agreement, as modified by a 1989 supplemental agreement, Cadtrak, in return for a one-time $290,000 payment, granted CFLC, a personal computer company, a royalty-free, worldwide, nonexclusive license to use certain computer graphics technology for which Cadtrak holds a patent (the "Cadtrak license"). The license agreement specified, among other things, that the license was non-transferrable, that it extended to any company more than 50% of which was owned by CFLC, that it conferred on CFLC no right to sublicense, that it could be terminated by Cadtrak upon CFLC's bankruptcy, and that it was to be construed according to California law.

On January 4, 1993, CFLC began a Chapter 11 proceeding, in the course of which it sold certain divisions, foreign subsidiaries, and assets for nearly $20 million. It then sought and received approval to sell "substantially all" of its remaining assets to Everex. The sale closed on November 12, 1993; Everex paid approximately $4 million. The sale agreement provided that the parties would seek the assumption and assignment by CFLC to Everex of certain designated executory contracts, and for the designation up to 30 days after the closing date of additional contracts to be assumed and assigned; Everex acknowledged that the bankruptcy court had the final decision on the assumption and assignment of the contracts. On December 8, 1993, Everex designated additional contracts, including the Cadtrak license. On January 4, 1994, CFLC moved to assume and assign executory contracts, including the Cadtrak license; Cadtrak objected to the assumption and assignment. Bankruptcy Judge Randall J. Newsome held a hearing on the motion on February 4 and orally denied the motion as to the Cadtrak license; a written order followed.

Everex and CFLC appealed to the District Court, where Judge Wilken heard oral argument in September 1994 and affirmed the bankruptcy court's denial.

ASSUMPTION & ASSIGNMENT OF EXECUTORY CONTRACTS IN BANKRUPTCY

Section 365 of the Bankruptcy Code "gives a trustee in bankruptcy the authority either to reject or to assume executory contracts and unexpired leases. Ordinarily, a trustee may take either of these actions without the consent of the other party to the contract or lease and notwithstanding a provision in the applicable agreement that purports to restrict assignment. See 11 U.S.C. §§365(a) & (f)(1)." Metropolitan Airports Commission v. Northwest Airlines, Inc. (In re Midway Airlines, Inc.), 6 F.3d 492, 494 (7th Cir. 1993). Once a contract has been assumed, the trustee can assign it.

IS THE LICENSE AN EXECUTORY CONTRACT?

Everex argues that no meaningful performance remains on either side of the contract. If it were right on this point, Everex would lose the appeal since §365 only allows the assumption and assignment of executory contracts. However, Everex is clearly wrong. This court has held that the meaning of that term in this context is "a contract on which performance is due to some extent on both sides" and in which "the obligations of both parties are so far unperformed that the failure of either party to complete performance would constitute a material breach and thus excuse the performance of the other." Griffel v. Murphy (In re Wegner), 839 F.2d 533, 536 (9th Cir. 1988). Cadtrak owes significant continued performance to the licensee: it must continue to refrain from suing it for infringement, since a nonexclusive patent license is, in essence "a mere waiver of the right to sue" the licensee for infringement. De Forest Radio Telephone Co. v. United States, 273 U.S. 236, 242 (1927). The licensee also owes performance: it must mark all products made under the license with proper statutory patent notice. Since failure to mark deprives the patent holder of damages in an infringement action before the infringer has actual notice of the infringement, 35 U.S.C. §287, the licensee's performance of this duty is material. Therefore, the license is an executory contract under §365.

DOES FEDERAL OR STATE LAW APPLY?

Whether 365(c) bars assumption and assignment of the Cadtrak license thus turns on whether or not "applicable" law excuses Cadtrak from accepting performance from, or rendering performance to, anyone other than CFLC. The bankruptcy and district courts held that the applicable law is federal law, and that federal common law makes patent licenses non-assignable. Everex argues that the applicable law is California law, and that the California Supreme Court's opinion in Farmland Irrigation Co. v. Dopplmaier, 48 Cal. 2d 208, 308 P.2d 732 (1957).

The statutes governing patents are basically silent on the issue of licenses. The construction of a patent license is generally a matter of state contract law, Lear, Inc. v. Adkins, 395 U.S. 653, 661-62 (1969) ("[T]he California Supreme Court's construction of the 1955 licensing agreement is solely a matter of state law."), except where state law "would be inconsistent with the aims of federal patent policy," *id.* at 673. *See also* McCoy v. Mitsuboshi Cutlery, Inc., 67 F.3d 917, 920 (Fed. Cir. 1995) ("Whether express or implied, a license is a contract governed by ordinary principles of state contract law."). Two circuits have found such an inconsistency and expressly held that "[q]uestions with respect to the assignability of a patent license are controlled by federal law." PPG Industries, Inc. v. Guardian Industries Corp., 597 F.2d 1090, 1093 (6th Cir.), *cert. denied*, 444 U.S. 930 (1979); Unarco Industries, Inc. v. Kelley Co., 465 F.2d 1303, 1306 (7th Cir. 1972) ("[T]he question of assignability of a patent license is a specific policy of federal patent law dealing with federal patent law. Therefore, we hold federal law applies to the question of the assignability of the patent license in question."), *cert. denied*, 410 U.S. 929 (1973). . . .

Federal patent policy, however, does justify the application of federal law here. The fundamental policy of the patent system is to "encourag[e] the creation and disclosure of new, useful, and non-obvious advances in technology and design" by granting the inventor the reward of "the exclusive right to practice the invention for a period of years." Bonito Boats, Inc. v. Thunder Craft Boats, Inc., 489 U.S. 141, 150-51, (1989). Allowing free assignability — or, more accurately, allowing states to allow free assignability — of nonexclusive patent licenses would undermine the reward that encourages invention because a party seeking to use the patented invention could either seek a license from the patent holder *or* seek an assignment of an existing patent license from a licensee. In essence, every licensee would become a potential competitor with the licensor-patent holder in the market for licenses under the patents. And while the patent holder could presumably control the absolute *number* of licenses in existence under a free-assignability regime, it would lose the very important ability to control the *identity* of its licensees. Thus, any license a patent holder granted — even to the smallest firm in the product market most remote from its own — would be fraught with the danger that the licensee would assign it to the patent holder's most serious competitor, a party whom the patent holder itself might be absolutely unwilling to license. As a practical matter, free assignability of patent licenses might spell the end to paid-up licenses such as the one involved in this case. Few patent holders would be willing to grant a license in return for a one-time lump-sum payment, rather than for per-use royalties, if the license could be assigned to a completely different company which might make far greater use of the patented invention than could the original licensee.

Thus, federal law governs the assignability of patent licenses because of the conflict between federal patent policy and state laws, such as California's, that would allow assignability.

DOES FEDERAL LAW BAR ASSIGNMENT OF NONEXCLUSIVE PATENT LICENSES?

Federal law holds a nonexclusive patent license to be personal and nonassignable and therefore would excuse Cadtrak from accepting performance from, or rendering it to, anyone other than CFLC. "It is well settled that a non-exclusive licensee of a patent has only a personal and not a property interest in the patent and that this personal right cannot be assigned unless the patent owner authorizes the assignment or the license itself permits assignment." Gilson v. Republic of Ireland, 787 F.2d 655, 658 (D.C. Cir. 1986) (Friedman, J.). *See also* Stenograph Corp. v. Fulkerson, 972 F.2d 726, 729 n.2 (7th Cir. 1992) ("Patent licenses are *not* assignable in the absence of express language."); *PPG Industries*, 597 F.2d at 1093 ("It has long been held by federal courts that agreements granting patent licenses are personal and not assignable unless expressly made so."); . . . E.I. du Pont de Nemours & Co. v. Shell Oil Co., 498 A.2d 1108, 1114 (Del. 1985) (rights conveyed by nonexclusive patent license are personal to licensee and not susceptible to sublicensing unless specific permission given). The only decision cited to the contrary is Justice Traynor's opinion in *Dopplmaier.* While that opinion raises not insignificant questions about the actual holdings, relevance, and continued vitality of the nineteenth-century Supreme Court decisions which are cited for the origins of the federal rule, those questions are not so significant as to compel departure from the uniform rule of modern federal decisions reading those precedents as defining nonexclusive patent licenses as personal and non-assignable. [Citations omitted.]

CONCLUSION

Because federal law governs the assignability of nonexclusive patent licenses, and because federal law makes such licenses personal and assignable only with the consent of the licensor, the Cadtrak license is not assumable and assignable in bankruptcy under 11 U.S.C. §365(c). The decision of the district court is therefore AFFIRMED.

IN RE TRUMP ENTERTAINMENT RESORTS, INC.
526 B.R. 116 (Bankr. D. Delaware 2015)

GROSS, Bankruptcy Judge.

The Court is deciding the motion of Trump AC Casino Marks, LLC ("Trump AC") which seeks relief from the automatic stay pursuant to Section 362(d)(1) of the Bankruptcy Code in order to proceed with an action in the Superior Court of New Jersey (the "State Court Action"). Trump AC is attempting to terminate the Trademark License Agreement (defined below) under which Trump Entertainment Resorts., Inc. and certain of its affiliates (collectively, the "Debtors") are licensees. Because, for the reasons set forth below, under Section 365(c)(1) of the Bankruptcy Code the Debtors may not assume or assign the Trademark License Agreement absent Trump AC's consent and Trump AC has withheld such consent, the Court finds that cause exists pursuant to Section 362(d)(1) to lift the automatic stay. Accordingly, the Court will grant Trump AC's motion and lift the automatic stay in order to allow it to proceed with the State Court Action.

BACKGROUND

Prior to the Petition Date (defined below), Donald and Ivanka Trump (the "Trumps") and the Debtors entered into the Second Amended and Restated Trademark License Agreement (the "Trademark License Agreement"), dated July 16, 2010. The Trumps subsequently assigned all of their rights and obligations thereunder to Trump AC. Under the terms of the Trademark License Agreement, the Trumps granted the Debtors a royalty-free license to use the Trumps' names, likenesses, and other enumerated marks (the "Trump Marks") in connection with the operation of three hotel casinos located in Atlantic City, New Jersey. The Trademark License Agreement provides for three categories of uses of the Trump Marks: (1) over 200 "current uses," for which the Debtors need no prior approval and which cover a wide range of products and activities associated with the operation of a hotel casino; (2) "similar uses," which are similar to the 200+ current uses and for which the Debtors need no prior approval but which are subject to Trump AC's 10-day right to object; and (3) "proposed uses," which are neither current nor similar uses and for which the Debtors must obtain prior approval.

The Trademark License Agreement is exclusive as to a defined, six-state territory and perpetual, subject to the parties' termination rights as defined therein. Under the terms of the Trademark License Agreement, the Debtors may terminate at any time on 30 days' notice. The process by which Trump AC may terminate the Trademark License Agreement is somewhat more complex. In simple terms, the Trademark License Agreement requires that the Debtors use the Trump Marks in a manner consistent with a certain standard of quality and provides a mechanism for Trump AC to exercise quality control over the Debtors' use of the Trump Marks. Under the terms of the Trademark License Agreement, upon Trump AC's request, the parties must cooperate to appoint a neutral third party to conduct a review of the quality of the Debtors' properties (a "Quality Assurance Review"). If a property fails a Quality Assurance Review and the Debtors fail to cure any deficiencies within the applicable cure period (or if the Debtors breach any other provision of the Trademark License Agreement), Trump AC has the right to initiate an action in the Superior Court of New Jersey which, setting aside certain complexities not relevant here, could ultimately result in the termination of the Trademark License Agreement.

Finally, the Trademark License Agreement provides with respect to "Assignments and Sublicenses" that "without the prior written consent of [Trump AC], in their sole and absolute discretion, none of the [Debtors] may assign, sublicense or pledge any of their rights or obligations under [the Trademark License Agreement]" subject to certain exceptions not applicable here.

On July 16, 2010, the same day the Trumps and the Debtors executed the Trademark License Agreement, the Trumps, the Debtors, and the Debtors' most significant secured creditor (the "First Lien Lender") entered into an agreement ancillary to the Trademark License Agreement styled "Consent and Agreement" (the "Consent Agreement"). As of the Petition Date, the Debtors owed the First Lien Lender approximately $292 million under the terms of a pre-petition credit facility (the "Pre–Petition Credit Agreement"). Amounts due under the Pre-Petition Credit Agreement are secured by a lien on substantially all of the Debtors' assets and make up the vast majority of the Debtors' pre-petition capital structure and total outstanding debt. As is relevant here, under the terms of the Consent Agreement, Trump AC consented to "transfers . . . from time to time of the rights of any one or more of the [Debtors] under the [Trademark License Agreement] upon and following the enforcement by the [First Lien Lender] of its rights under the [Pre–Petition Credit Agreement] (each, an "Enforcement Action "). . . ." (emphasis in original). Under the terms of the Consent Agreement, following an "Enforcement Action," Trump AC "shall recognize" the First Lien Lender as a licensee under the Trademark License Agreement in the place of the Debtor or Debtors which were the subject of the Enforcement Action.

On August 5, 2014, Trump AC initiated the State Court Action alleging that the Debtors had failed a Quality Assurance Review and failed to timely cure any deficiencies, as well as other breaches of the Trademark License Agreement. Ultimately, in the State Court Action Trump AC seeks to terminate the Trademark License Agreement in accordance with the procedure contemplated therein.

Stepping back, on September 9, 2014 (the "Petition Date"), the Debtors filed voluntary petitions for relief under chapter 11 of the Bankruptcy Code, thus staying the State Court Action. As of the Petition Date, the Debtors operated two of the three hotel casinos which were originally subject to the Trademark License Agreement: the Trump Plaza Hotel and Casino (the "Plaza") and the Trump Taj Mahal Casino Resort (the "Taj Mahal"). Shortly after the Petition Date, on September 16, 2014, the Debtors closed the Plaza. The Taj Mahal remains open for business and the Debtors have represented that they have no immediate plans for its closure. According to the Debtors, use of the Trump Marks is "ubiquitous" throughout the Taj Mahal and it would be costly and problematic to remove the Trump Marks. The Debtors' proposed but not yet confirmed chapter 11 plan of reorganization (the "Plan") does not contemplate any sort of significant asset transfer. Instead, the Plan contemplates cancellation of pre-existing equity, a nominal distribution to unsecured creditors, and a debt-for-equity swap of substantially all amounts owing under the Pre–Petition Credit Agreement. The Plan further contemplates assumption of the Trademark License Agreement.

On September 24, 2014, Trump AC filed its motion seeking relief from the automatic stay to proceed with the State Court Action (the "Stay Motion"). On October 16, 2014, the Debtors filed an objection the Stay Motion, to which the First Lien Lender filed a joinder. On December 11, 2014, the Court held a hearing on the Stay Motion (the "Stay Motion Hearing") and thereafter took the matter under advisement.

ANALYSIS

Trump AC argues that cause exists for the Court to lift the automatic stay under the decision of the United States Court of Appeals for the Third Circuit in *West Electronics*, 852 F.2d at 82-84, because the Trademark License Agreement is not assignable absent Trump AC's consent under applicable non-bankruptcy law and thus is not assumable or assignable by the Debtors under Section 365(c)(1) of the Bankruptcy Code. For the reasons that follow, the Court agrees.

Section 365(a) of the Bankruptcy Code provides that the Debtors, "subject to the court's approval, may assume or reject any executory contract or unexpired lease." While the term "executory contract" is not defined in the Bankruptcy Code, the Third Circuit has adopted the following definition: "[An executory contract is] a contract under which the obligation of both the bankrupt and the other party to the contract are so far unperformed that the failure of either to complete performance would constitute a material breach excusing performance of the other." Sharon Steel Corp. v. Nat'l Fuel Gas Distrib. Corp., 872 F.2d 36, 39 (3d Cir. 1989).

The Trademark License Agreement is an executory contract of the kind generally subject to assumption under Section 365(a), a point neither the Debtors nor Trump AC has disputed. Indeed, this Court has previously found patent and copyright licenses to be executory contracts within the meaning of Section 365. The reasoning in those decisions with respect to whether an intellectual property license is an executory contract applies with equal force in the context of a trademark license.

The Debtors' right to assume the Trademark License Agreement, however, is subject to the limitation set forth in Section 365(c)(1), which provides:

> (c) The trustee may not assume or assign any executory contract or unexpired lease of the debtor, whether or not such contract or lease prohibits or restricts assignment of rights or delegation of duties, if —
>
> > (1) (A) applicable law excuses a party, other than the debtor, to such contract or lease from accepting performance from or rendering performance to an entity other than the debtor or the debtor in possession, whether or not such contract or lease prohibits or *122 restricts assignment of rights or delegation of duties; and
> > (B) such party does not consent to such assumption or assignment. . . .

The Section 365(c)(1) limitation on the assumption of executory contracts applies whenever the contract is "subject to a legal prohibition against assignment" to a third party and the non-debtor party to the contact does not consent to assignment. *West Electronics*, 852 F.2d at 83. Ultimately, the Third Circuit concluded in *West Electronics* that where an executory contract is subject to the limitation on assumption set forth in Section 365(c)(1), the non-debtor party to the contract is entitled to relief from the automatic stay pursuant to Section 362(d)(1) in order to seek termination of the contract. *Id.* at 83–84.

It is important to note that Section 365(c)(1) limits a debtor in possession's ability to assume an executory contract based on its ability to assign that executory contract to a third party and makes no reference to whether a debtor or debtor in possession actually intends to assign the executory contract to a third party. *See* In re Catapult Entm't, Inc., 165 F.3d 747, 750

(9th Cir. 1999). Thus, the plain language of Section 365(c)(1) establishes what courts have come to refer to as the "Hypothetical Test." In other words, "a debtor in possession may not assume an executory contract over the nondebtor's objection if applicable law would bar assignment to a hypothetical third party, even where the debtor in possession has no intention of assigning the contract in question to any such third party." *Catapult*, 165 F.3d at 750. The Third Circuit has adopted the Hypothetical Test.

It is also important to read Section 365(c)(1) in conjunction with Section 365(f)(1), which provides:

> Except as provided in subsections (b) and (c) of this section, notwithstanding a provision in an executory contract or unexpired lease of the debtor, or in applicable law, that prohibits, restricts, or conditions the assignment of such contract or lease, the trustee may assign such contract or lease under paragraph (2) of this subsection.

Under Section 365(f)(1), a debtor may assign a contract notwithstanding any provision in the contract or applicable non-bankruptcy law which would prohibit such an assignment. Section 365(f)(1), though, is expressly subject to any alternative rule provided in Section 365(c). As set forth above, Section 365(c)(1) provides that a debtor may not assume or assign an executory contract if assignment is prohibited by applicable non-bankruptcy law, seemingly eviscerating the rule with respect to "applicable law" set forth in Section 365(f)(1).

The United States Court of Appeals for the Ninth Circuit recognized the internal inconsistency of Section 365 in its *Catapult* decision and persuasively reconciled the conflict as follows:

> The Sixth Circuit has credibly reconciled the warring provisions by noting that "each subsection recognizes an 'applicable law' of markedly different scope." Subsection (f)(1) states the broad rule — a law that, as a general matter, "prohibits, restricts, or conditions the assignment" of executory contracts is trumped by the provisions of subsection (f)(1). Subsection (c)(1), however, states a carefully crafted exception to the broad rule — where applicable law does not merely recite a general ban on assignment, but instead more specifically "excuses a party . . . from accepting performance from or rendering performance to an entity" different from the one with which the party originally contracted, the applicable law prevails over subsection (f)(1). In other words, in determining whether an "applicable law" stands or falls under §365(f)(1), a court must ask why the "applicable law" prohibits assignment.

In line with the Ninth Circuit's reasoning, the Court is persuaded that "for section 365(c)(1) to apply, the applicable law must specifically state that the contracting party is excused from accepting performance from a third party under circumstances where it is clear from the statute that the identity of the contracting party is crucial to the contract. . . ." ANC Rental, 277 B.R. at 236.

C. Application to Trademarks

In applying the forgoing principles, the Court must first determine what the "applicable law" is in this instance. "The term 'applicable law' means any law applicable to a contract, other than bankruptcy law. . . . " In re XMH Corp., 647 F.3d 690, 695 (7th Cir. 2011). Since the Trademark License Agreement is just that, a trademark license agreement, it is clear that the applicable law here is federal trademark law. Based on the Court's research and cases cited by Trump AC, it appears that the substantial weight of authority holds that under federal trademark law, trademark licenses are not assignable in the absence of some express authorization from the licensor, such as a clause in the license agreement itself.

However, as recognized in the Ninth Circuit's *Catapult* decision, it is not sufficient to simply recognize a general ban on contract assignment under the applicable non-bankruptcy law, the Court must understand why the applicable non-bankruptcy law bans assignment. As explained by the Seventh Circuit in XMH:

> Often the owner of a trademark will find that the most efficient way to exploit it is to license the production of the trademarked good to another company, which may have lower costs of production or other advantages over the trademark's owner. Normally the owner who does this will not want the licensee to be allowed to assign the license (that is, sublicense the trademark) without the owner's consent, because while the owner will have picked his licensee because of confidence that he will not degrade the quality of the trademarked product he can have no similar assurance with respect to some unknown future sublicensee.

9647 F.3d at 696. "The purpose of a trademark, after all, is to identify a good or service to the consumer, and identity implies consistency and a correlative duty to make sure that the good or service really is of consistent quality, i.e., really is the same good or service." *Id.* at 695. Accord 4 McCarthy on Trademarks §25:33 (4th ed. 2010) ("Since the licensor-trademark owner has the duty to control the quality of goods sold under its mark, it must have the right to pass upon the abilities of new potential licensees.").

In other words, federal trademark law generally bans assignment of trademark licenses absent the licensor's consent because, in order to ensure that all products bearing its trademark are of uniform quality, the identity of the licensee is crucially important to the licensor. But this is only a default rule, which the parties to a license agreement are free to contract around. See XMH, 647 F.3d at 696. Nothing in the Trademark License Agreement indicates that the parties intended to contract around the default rule. In fact, the terms of the Trademark License Agreement provide just the opposite. Subject to certain narrow exceptions not applicable here, the Trademark License Agreement expressly prohibits the Debtors from sublicensing or assigning their rights thereunder absent Trump AC's consent. While such a provision is unenforceable in bankruptcy pursuant to Section 365(f)(1), it certainly underscores that the parties did not intend, at least at the time the Trademark License Agreement was drafted, to alter the default rule of non-assignability.

The Debtors argue, however, that even if the default rule is that the Trademark License Agreement is not assignable absent Trump AC's consent, under the terms of the Consent Agreement, Trump AC has provided the necessary consent. In the Consent Agreement, Trump AC consented to transfer of the license agreement to the First Lien Lender "upon and following" the enforcement of its rights under the Pre–Petition Credit Agreement. The Consent Agreement applies to only a narrow class of potential assignees, and only after the First Lien Lender initiates an "Enforcement Action." It is clear to the Court that in this context "Enforcement Action" refers to the First Lien Lender's state law rights to pursue its collateral under the terms of the Pre-Petition Credit Agreement. The First Lien Lender has initiated no such action. Bankruptcy is a collective proceeding initiated by the Debtors and while the First Lien Lender has taken steps to preserve its rights with respect to the Pre-Petition Credit Agreement, those actions to not rise to the level of an Enforcement Action as contemplated by the Consent Agreement.

While it appears that Trump AC viewed the First Lien Lender as a suitable licensee in the event of, for example, a state-law foreclosure, that does not change the facts that (1) the First Lien Lender has commenced no such action and (2) under the Consent Agreement, consent is only effective upon the commencement of such an action. Consent with respect to an isolated assignee, which is effective only upon the occurrence of some future event which, under the terms of the Plan, is all but certain to never occur is simply not enough to override the default rule of non-assignability applicable to trademark licenses.

Accordingly, the Court finds that under applicable non-bankruptcy law the Trademark License Agreement is not assignable. The Court further finds that federal trademark law prohibits assignment of trademark licenses under circumstances where it is clear that the identity of the licensee is crucial to the agreement. Thus, the requirement of Section 365(c)(1)(A) is satisfied.

As for Section 365(c)(1)(B), Trump AC clearly does not consent to the assumption or assignment of the Trademark License Agreement, as is evident from its filing of the Stay Motion. The Debtors argue again that Trump AC has provided the necessary consent under the terms of the Consent Agreement. First, as set forth above, under the terms of the Consent Agreement, consent is not effective unless and until the First Lien Lender initiates an Enforcement Action, which it has not. Second, the Consent Agreement deals with consent to assignment in the context of a state law enforcement action and not with consent to assumption and assignment under Section 365, which is a technical process specific to bankruptcy. And finally, even if the consent set forth in the Consent Agreement was effective, it would merely operate to override the default rule with respect to the non-assignability of trademark licenses thus making the Trademark License Agreement assignable under applicable law and obviating the need to apply Section 365(c)(1) at all.

For these reasons, the Court finds that under the Section 365(c)(1) Hypothetical Test adopted by the Third Circuit, the Debtors are prohibited from assuming or assigning the Trademark License Agreement, despite the fact that the Debtors have no immediate plans to assign the agreement to a third party. Consequently, under the Third Circuit's *West Electronics* decision, Trump AC is entitled to relief from the automatic stay pursuant to Section 362(d)(1).

CONCLUSION

For the reasons set forth above, the Court finds that the Trademark License Agreement is not assignable under applicable non-bankruptcy law and is thus not assumable or assignable under Section 365(c)(1). Accordingly, under the Third Circuit's *West Electronics* decision, Trump AC is entitled to relief from the automatic stay pursuant to Section 362(d)(1) in order to proceed with the State Court Action.

IN RE ROOSTER, INC.
100 B.R. 228 (Bankr. E.D. Pa. 1989)

FOX, Bankruptcy Judge.

Pincus Bros., Inc. seeks relief from the automatic stay, which motion is opposed by the debtor and the official committee of unsecured creditors. In essence, at issue is the nature of a licensing agreement between the debtor and Pincus, a corporation that is the "sole and exclusive licensee of the right to use Bill Blass' name and trademark . . . in connection with the manufacture and sale" of men's apparel. Ex. P-1, at 1. In particular, the issue raised is whether the licensing agreement constitutes a personal services contract which cannot be assigned or sold by the debtor.

I.

This chapter 11 debtor-in-possession is in the business of manufacturing and selling men's neckwear. In February, 1987 the debtor entered into a licensing agreement with Pincus, which granted to the debtor an exclusive sublicense to use the Bill Blass trademark on its neckties. This agreement, prepared by attorneys for Bill Blass and for Pincus, is representative of agreements into which Pincus has entered with its fifteen sublicensees. In fact, a Pincus senior vice president, Lawrence A. Smith — the managing director of "Bill Blass Menswear" — testified that the agreement under scrutiny is virtually identical to the fifteen current licensing agreements Pincus has with the other sublicensees. These fifteen parties were all selected by Pincus, with the approval of Bill Blass, to produce various items of men's apparel; each sublicensee pays royalties to Pincus in the average amount of 7% of gross sales of licensed items up to specified amount in gross sales, and a lesser percentage of additional gross sales. (The licensing agreements also call for minimum royalty payments.)

The clothing produced by these fifteen sublicensees is coordinated by Pincus, which creates a "package" for the entire Bill Blass menswear line. Pincus apparently prepares this "clothing package" for presentation to the sublicensees, which presentation includes the tone and selection of colors for Bill Blass' new line of menswear. After the sublicensees view the clothing package at Pincus and pick up tone and color combinations, they also view the "accent colors and tone" of related sublicensees. The object of this is to ensure that the sublicensees present in the retail marketplace the same idea as created by Pincus for the line of Bill Blass menswear.

Upon receiving information about the look to be created, the sublicensees then must choose appropriate patterns for their clothing items. The debtor's job as a necktie manufacturer was to research the "phenomenal libraries of patterns past" that are maintained by silk producers in Italy. From these old files of patterns Rooster selected patterns for the newly-created line, reproducing these patterns with the colors and tone set by Pincus. The neckties do not go into production until Bill Blass has examined and approved the chosen patterns. Smith testified that Bill Blass acted as an overseer of the actual designs of the neckwear, and that he changed the neckties size, shape and color before the manufacturing process started. In practice, both Bill Blass and Pincus reviewed all proposed Bill Blass neckties and gave express approval to the acceptable merchandise.

Indeed, under the licensing agreement sub judice, Ex. P-1, the debtor is subject to a substantial amount of supervision and control by Bill Blass and Pincus, its licensee. For example, the agreement provides that the debtor shall not have the right to use the [Bill Blass] trademark with respect to any item the design and material of which has not been approved by both Bill Blass, Ltd. and [Pincus] in writing, or which has not been designed by Bill Blass, Ltd., nor shall [Rooster] have the right, except with the consent of Bill Blass, Ltd. and [Pincus] to modify or change the design or designated material of any Licensed Items theretofore so approved, or so designed. Minor changes required by manufacturing demands may be made upon oral approval by Bill Blass, Ltd., and [Pincus], provided, however, that such minor changes do not materially affect the overall appearance of the Licensed Item. Ex. P-1, ¶7(a). Further, under the agreement, the debtor is required, at Pincus' request, to submit to Bill Blass and Pincus samples of the neckties the debtor proposes to sell. Should these samples not meet "standards of the highest quality" as determined by those entities, the debtor can be required to discontinue their manufacture or withdraw them from sale.

The debtor is required under the agreement to submit for Bill Blass' written approval "any and all labels, press releases, display, printed matter (including but not limited to stationery, invoices and business cards), advertising and promotional material involving the Trademark. . . ." Ex. P-1, ¶8(a). This subparagraph also provides that the parties "expressly understood and agreed that the 'Bill Blass' label will not be used on any item without the written approval of Bill Blass, Ltd. of the specific items, both as to the design and quality of raw material. . . ." In addition to delimiting the development, manufacture, final product and advertisement by Rooster of Bill Blass neckwear, the agreement provides for the accounting to Pincus of the debtor's sales, and the payment of certain royalties thereon.

The agreement expressly grants to Rooster the exclusive sublicense to use the Bill Blass trademark in distribution and sales "in the United States, its territories and possessions." Ex. P-1, ¶4. The agreement is silent as to the retail markets into which the neckties are to be placed; testimony indicated that Pincus decided to grant the neckwear sublicense to the debtor in large part because of the debtor's perceived good judgment in choosing appropriate retailers, ability to sell to these retailers, and, in general, the business acumen of the debtor's management and principals.

Evidence was received to the effect that Jerry Meyers, former president of Rooster, approached Pincus and sought the grant of the sublicense. Before granting this sublicense, for which candidates in addition to Rooster were considered, Pincus conducted its customary "extensive investigation" of each candidate, looking at the candidate's financial status, physical plant, key personnel (to see whether they will be "compatible" with other sublicensees and Pincus), existing products, channels of distribution and marketing, and reputation in the industry. After selecting Rooster as sublicensee-elect, Pincus introduced the debtor to Bill Blass; Blass inspected Rooster's sample merchandise and was requested, by Pincus, to approve this candidate. Blass, of course, did so approve.

Pincus introduced other testimony regarding the qualifications of its sublicensees, offering Smith's testimony that it attempts to choose manufacturers which possess, inter alia, a "taste level" which is in harmony with the fashion sense of Bill Blass, Pincus and other sublicensees, and an industry persona which "complements and enhances the status and prestige of Bill Blass' name and trademarks in the marketplace."

No written notice of default under the agreement has been provided to the debtor, either before or after its February 24, 1989 bankruptcy filing. Before commencement of the case, however, Rooster apparently arranged a meeting between Pincus and another manufacturer—Parklane—to see if this company would be acceptable as a replacement sublicensee. No agreement was reached. Pincus apparently wants three or four companies to make presentations, and it wants the ability to choose the sublicensee from among these candidates. The debtor, on the other hand, is negotiating to sell its rights under the licensing agreement. Richard Aron, chair of the debtor's board of directors, is negotiating with another entity for an assignment of rights; the assignee would pay $25,000.00 annually for five years to the debtor, plus reimburse the debtor for merchandise already on order for the Bill Blass line (including prepayments made in the approximate amount of $44,000.00). With this money Rooster would cure any contract default and sell the agreement to that entity.

Therefore, implicit in the litigation over the sublicensing agreement (as with most litigation under 11 U.S.C. §365) is a contest for control and recovery of the economic value of the agreement. Pincus wants control over the identity of the sublicensee for a number of reasons—including control over the economic value.

II.

The parties agree that the licensing agreement is an executory contract within the meaning of 11 U.S.C. §365. See generally Sharon Steel Corp. v. National Fuel Gas Distribution Corp., 872 F.2d 36 (3d Cir. 1989). Normally, an executory contract may be assumed or rejected by the debtor (subject to application of the appropriate standard). If the contract is properly assumed, the debtor may assign its rights under the contract, contrary contractual language notwithstanding. 11 U.S.C. §365(f)(1), (2), (3). An exception to this power to assume and assign is found at 11 U.S.C. §365(c)(1)(A). This exception provides that:

> (c) The trustee may not assume or assign any executory contract or unexpired lease of the debtor, whether or not such contract or lease prohibits or restricts assignment of rights or delegation of duties, if—

> (1)(A) applicable law excuses a party, other than the debtor, to such contract or lease from accepting performance from or rendering performance to an entity other than the debtor or the debtor in possession, whether or not such contract or lease prohibits or restricts assignment of rights or delegation of duties. 11 U.S.C. §365(c)(1)(A).

The words "applicable law" in this subsection refer to "applicable non-bankruptcy law." See H.R. Rep. No. 95-595, 95th Cong., 1st Sess. 348 (1977); S. Rep. No. 95-989, 95th Cong., 2d Sess. 59 (1978). Evidently, the purpose of this provision is to prevent the debtor from assigning (over objection) contracts of the sort ordinarily made unassignable by law. Matter of West Electronics, Inc., 852 F.2d 79, 83 (3d Cir. 1988). Here the issue is narrowly framed by the parties: does the licensing agreement constitute a contract for personal services, which applicable Pennsylvania law holds as unassignable? If it is not a personal services contract, there would be no basis on the evidence presented to grant Pincus relief from the stay; rather,

Pincus may file a motion to compel the debtor to assume or reject the contract. By so doing, Pincus will force the debtor either to reject the agreement or cure any defaults. If it is a contract for personal services that cannot be sold or assigned by the debtor, I would grant relief from the stay as the debtor concedes that it can no longer fulfill its contractual requirements as sublessee.

III.

The nonassignability imprint of personal service contracts is found, albeit sparingly, in Pennsylvania law. In Saxe v. Feinstein, 366 Pa. 473, 476, 77 A.2d 419, 421 (1951), the Supreme Court stated the principle:

> While a party to a contract may assign his rights and benefits thereunder, he may not, unless the contract so provides, assign his liability under the contract to perform duties involving his personal ability, integrity, credit or responsibility.

This recognition of a universally accepted common law doctrine arose in the context of the assignment to a subcontractor of an obligation to demolish a boiler and the resultant damage that occurred when the job was performed negligently. Without much explanation, the Court concluded that this was not a personal service contract, one which drew upon "personal ability, integrity, credit or responsibility." Id.

A contract for "personal services" contemplates performance of contracted-for duties involving the exercise of special knowledge, judgment, taste, skill, or ability. These services are not assignable by the party under obligation to perform without the consent of the other contracting party. Matter of Sentry Data, Inc., 87 B.R. 943, 950 (Bankr. N.D. Ill. 1988); In re Compass Van & Storage Corp., 65 B.R. 1007 (Bankr. E.D.N.Y. 1986).

Whether a contract is for personal services depends upon the sui generis attributes of the intended performance. Matter of Noonan, 17 B.R. 793, 798 (Bankr. S.D.N.Y. 1982). Contracts to perform "artistically" are clearly of a personal service nature. See Foster v. Callaghan & Co., 248 F. 944 (S.D.N.Y. 1918) (contract between author and publisher); Matter of Noonan (contract for singer/songwriter to record); Western Show Co. v. Mix, 308 Pa. 215, 162 A. 667 (1932) (duty of Tom Mix to accompany a circus tour). Compare, e.g., Devlin v. Mayor, 63 N.Y. 8 (1875) (duty to clean streets involves mechanical skills which are tested by objective standards). Certain employment contracts of individuals also create a categorical "personal services" exception, see In re Miller, 101 F.2d 323, 324 (6th Cir. 1939). Corporations can also, however, enter into such contracts. Ford, Bacon & Davis, Inc. v. Holahan, 311 F.2d 901, 904 (5th Cir. 1962), cert. denied, 373 U.S. 913 (1963). Generally speaking, nondelegable duties have been determined to be of a personal nature whenever the performance depends upon a special relationship, special knowledge, or a unique skill, upon which the other party is entitled to rely. In re Alltech Plastics, Inc., 71 B.R. 686, 688 (Bankr. W.D. Tenn. 1987). See, e.g., In re Bronx-Westchester Mack Corp., 20 B.R. 139, 143 (Bankr. S.D.N.Y. 1982) (distributor agreement); In re Taylor Mfg., Inc., 6 B.R. 370, 372 (Bankr. N.D. Ga. 1980) (lease of real property); Sackman v. Stephenson, 11 N.Y.S.2d 69 (N.Y. Sup. Ct. 1939) (contract between student and correspondence school).

I cannot conclude that the debtor's performance under the licensing agreement draws upon any special personal relationship, knowledge, unique skill or talent. The only actual discretion retained by the debtor in the area of development or manufacture is the choice of patterns to put into production. This activity allows the debtor to travel to Italy to review the catalogues of patterns there maintained by silk manufacturers. Rooster then chooses patterns that fit the design, color, and quality (the "look") already chosen by Bill Blass and Pincus. Thus, Rooster is not involved in creating the actual design of the trademarked neckwear; its artistic input is limited to choosing from established patterns. Pincus' own testimony conceded that "there is nothing new in the clothing business — everybody keeps reinventing the wheel. . . ." Thus, Rooster is not involved in the creation of a new or unique product.

The patterns chosen (and combinations created) by Rooster were not automatically adopted by Pincus and Bill Blass as part of the trademarked line, as explained above. The contracted-for review and ability to alter Rooster's intended product, actually and fully exercised by Pincus and Bill Blass, does not bespeak of any "personal ability, integrity, credit or responsibility," Saxe v. Feinstein, 366 Pa. at 476, 77 A.2d 419, with regard to Rooster's performance. Instead, I find that this actual control over Rooster's performance removes Rooster's duties from the sphere of personal service and from the ambit of §365(c)(1)(A). That is, Pincus relied on the exercise of its rights to control the design of trademarked goods, rather than on the "taste level" of Rooster or any of its employees.

Other indicia of an agreement contemplating personal services by the debtor are lacking as well. There simply are no contractual terms requiring the personal performance of any identified employee for any particular duty. For example, the agreement is silent on the question of who, representing Rooster, was to travel to Italy and choose the patterns that would be put back into circulation. No one is named as the person responsible for selecting the raw fabric; no named individual is responsible for marketing the finished product. Nor does the contract identify the markets into which Blass trademark items may be introduced.

The instant case is distinguishable from In re Little & Ives Co., 262 F. Supp. 719 (S.D.N.Y. 1966), a case upon which Pincus relies heavily. There, a contract to revise, publish and sell an encyclopedia was held to be nontransferable by the debtor's trustee to a third party. The court noted that a personal service contract had been created where the contract provided, inter alia, that the debtor was required to "dismiss any sales personnel whose conduct marred [the licensor's] prestige and reputation," and where the relationship between those entities "was based on trust and confidence." The court found that the licensor "not only placed its trust and confidence but its reputation as well in the hands of Little & Ives." Id. at 723. Unlike the case sub judice, Little & Ives does not suggest that its licensor exercised real control over its sublicensee.

More importantly, in Little & Ives, which involved litigation under the former Bankruptcy Act, the contract allowed the licensor to terminate the agreement in the event of Little & Ives' bankruptcy or insolvency. The licensor did so terminate; this termination was upheld by the court:

> We find most compelling the sound reason which prompts upholding the validity of an expressed and unambiguous termination provision in a contractual relationship such as confronts us here . . . in these circumstances Oxford's interests warrant the protection that it sought to preserve.

Id. (footnote omitted). Of course, this decision predates the current Bankruptcy Code, specifically 11 U.S.C. §365(b)(2) and (e)(1), which nullifies this type of ipso facto clause. See, e.g., In re Rose, 21 B.R. 272 (Bankr. D.N.J. 1982).

Pincus vigorously argues that it relied on the personal involvement and discretion of Rooster president Jerry Meyers, and employees Bernstein and Smeikle. In particular, it asserted that the agreement contemplates that Meyers would make the above decisions. However, Pincus conceded that Meyers did not consistently do this work personally. Pincus did not consider this a breach. In fact, under the licensing agreement it is possible for the entire roster of Rooster employees to change, without creating an event of default.

I appreciate Pincus' concern that the finished product look "right." Certainly, in the realm of fashion, appearance is a primary concern. However, to the extent that the final product must be finished with workmanlike skill, this task must be considered more mechanical than not. And, because of the extent that Pincus and Bill Blass retain and exercise plenary control over the trademarked product, they do not rely on the personal performance of Rooster. Thus, if they are dissatisfied with the product, they may exert reasonable veto power and prevent the products' being marketed. It is likely, given such power, that any prospective assignee of the debtor would ensure its "compatibility" with the fashion ideas of Pincus and Bill Blass.

An appropriate order shall be entered.

ORDER

AND NOW, this 31 day of May, 1989, upon consideration of the motion of Pincus Brothers, Inc. for relief from the automatic stay, and for the reasons stated in the accompanying Memorandum Opinion, the motion is DENIED.

V. PROBLEMS

1. Creditors are considering a large loan to Biomeva, a small biotech company located in Seattle, Washington. Biomeva owns a handsome portfolio of patents, patent applications, know how, software, and trademarks. Creditors would like their loan to be secured by Biomeva's property. Creditors have heard tales about others' failure to perfect security interest in various types of intellectual property. Explain to Creditors how their loan will be secured and how their security interest in different types of intellectual property will be perfected and entitled to priority.

2. Should there be a federal filing scheme for perfection of security interests in patents, patent applications, registered copyrights, unregistered copyrights, registered trademarks, and unregistered trademarks? This would mean a central filing for all security interests in such types of intellectual property. What are the theoretical foundations to support or not support central filing?

3. George Jones and CBS executed a recording contract in which Jones agreed to make master recordings and CBS agreed to pay Jones royalties from the sale of records. Jones later filed for Chapter 7 protection. Are Jones's royalty rights going to

become property of the bankruptcy estate? *See* Waldsmid v. CBS, Inc., 14 B.R. 309, 312 (M.D. Tenn. 1981).

4. Assignor of the trademark "Cuzcatlan" assigned the trademark to Assignee. Assignee recorded the assignment with the Trademark Office. A few years later, Assignor filed for bankruptcy under Chapter 7. The bankruptcy trustee has argued that the prior assigned trademark belongs to the property of the estate. You have been retained by Assignee to handle the matter. Your paralegal has done some investigation, and she discovered that Assignor continued to use the trademark after the assignment. There was no written license agreement permitting Assignor to use the trademark after the assignment. Is the trustee's argument correct? *See* In re Impact Distributors, Inc., 260 B.R. 48 (Bankr. S.D. Fla. 2001).

5. Are all intellectual property license agreements executory contracts? Explain. Whether an intellectual property license agreement is an executory contract is an important question that must be determined in a bankruptcy case involving intellectual property licenses. Why so?

6. The Intellectual Property Licenses in Bankruptcy Act excludes trademarks from the definition for "intellectual property." Only licensees of the defined intellectual property have a statutory right to continue to use the license after the debtor licensor rejects the intellectual property license agreement(s). What are possible reasons for the exclusion of trademarks from the Act?

7. What are some potential impacts from the ruling rendered in Jaffé v. Samsung? Is it fair to the foreign creditors with respect to their interests in U.S. licensing assets? Should other nations adopt similar protection under Section 365(n) for their licensees? Will Jaffé v. Samsung deter insolvency forum shopping?

VI. DRAFTING EXERCISES

1. Licensing attorneys generally include an "ipso facto" provision that purports to terminate the license agreements upon the filing of bankruptcy or on the insolvency or financial condition of a contractual party. Bankruptcy courts have routinely held that the Bankruptcy Code nullifies "ipso facto" provisions. *See* In re Rooster, Inc., 100 B.R. 228 (E.D. Pa. 1989) (stating that the current Bankruptcy Code "nullifies . . . ipso facto clause") (*citing* In re Rose, 21 B.R. 272 (Bankr. D.N.J. 1982)); In re Sapolin Paints, Inc., 5 B.R. 412 (Bankr. E.D.N.Y. 1980). *See also* In re Footstar, Inc., 337 B.R. 785 (Bankr. S.D.N.Y. 2005). Why do licensing attorneys continue to include "ipso facto" provisions in license agreements? Can you think of any reasons for the inclusion of such provisions in the drafting of intellectual property license agreements? Draft and submit the "ipso facto" provision in an intellectual property license agreement.

2. IPCo owns various intellectual property assets. IPCo licenses some intellectual property and receives periodic royalty payments. IPCo has requested that you draft a security agreement that contains, among other provisions, the grant of security interest in the intellectual property assets, intellectual property licenses,

and royalties from various intellectual property assets. IPCo explains that it is the debtor in the secured transaction. Submit your draft.

3. Instead of having IPCo as your client, Creditor in the secured transaction is your new client. Creditor wants you to draft the grant of security interest provision. How would you draft the grant provision for Creditor? What are some of Creditor's concerns? Submit your draft of the grant provision.

· CHAPTER ·

15

INTELLECTUAL PROPERTY LICENSES AND TAXATION

I. OVERVIEW

Ben Franklin said long ago that death and taxes are two certainties in life; we cannot avoid them. It should come as no surprise that the income received from intellectual property transfers such as licensing is subject to taxation. Yet, ordinary people do not like to pay taxes, nor do businesses.

In different stages of business transactions involving intellectual property, from technology development, acquisitions, transfers, to disputes and settlements, taxation is central to decision making. Knowledge about tax law relating to intellectual property transfers assists the intellectual property transferor and transferee in their tax planning.

Imagine that Company X is thinking about acquiring a target corporation with valuable intellectual property assets, notably a valuable brand name. Company X is aware that there are several potential purchasers of the target corporation. A purchaser with an attractive offer will definitely have a much better chance to acquire the target corporation. If Company X acquires the brand name separately from the acquisition of the stock of the target corporation, it will be able to come up with a better offering price and hence stand a good chance to succeed in the acquisition. How? If Company X structures the "acquisition" of the brand name as a "license" under tax law, it will be able to deduct the contingent payments and periodic payments as expenses. The deduction will save Company X a significant amount of tax in the long run and therefore the Company would be able to factor that tax saving into its tendering of a higher and more attractive purchase price. *See* Nabisco Brands v. Commissioner, T.C. Memo 1995-127.

The tax treatment of intellectual property development, acquisitions, transfers,* litigation, and damages is complex and beyond the scope of this book. To maintain the

---

* *See* Maine and Nguyen, Intellectual Property Taxation (Carolina Academic Press, 2d, 2014).

· 851 ·

licensing focus, this chapter focuses primarily on tax treatment in the context of the licensing of various types of intellectual property from the licensor's perspective and from the licensee's perspective. The cases included in this chapter are from both federal and state sources.

II. TAXATION ISSUES IN INTELLECTUAL PROPERTY LICENSING

A. Taxation Issues in Patent Licensing

1. In General

Tax issues are often a puzzle because what one would consider a patent license may not be treated as a license under tax law. Depending on how tax law characterizes a particular transfer — either as a license or a sale — payments received by the transferor will be subject to different tax treatment. The transferor most likely prefers to have the transfer characterized as a sale of a capital asset so the transferor can enjoy the favorable tax rate for capital gains. The transferor does not want the transfer characterized as a license because the tax rate would be higher for ordinary income.

On the other hand, the transferee would like the transfer to be characterized as a license so the transferor can immediately deduct the cost in the year incurred as business expenses. The transferee does not want the transfer characterized as a sale because then the transferee will not be able to take an immediate deduction of the transfer cost from its taxable amount. The transferee must instead amortize the cost over a long period of time, such as 15 years. Depending on the goal of the transferor and the transferee with respect to the taxation of the transfer amount, the transferor and transferee can decide how to structure the transfer, specifically how to structure the payment plan, reservation of rights, and control so that the transfer may be characterized in accordance with the desire of the parties.

2. Characterization of a Patent Transfer: Sale or License

In 1954, Congress recognized the importance of patents to the welfare of the country and provided incentives to inventors for their contribution by enacting Section 1235 of the Internal Revenue Code (the "Code"), which allows inventors to qualify for capital gain treatment if their patents and inventions are capital assets that were transferred as a sale or exchange. Section 1235 thus provides certainty to inventors, as the treatment of patent royalties received by inventors are treated as capital gains, even though they might otherwise be treated as ordinary income. Not all transfers of patents are treated favorably, however; only transfers that satisfy all the requirements under Section 1235 have preferential treatment. If a transfer does not qualify for the preferential tax treatment under Section 1235, the transfer is more similar to a license and subject to ordinary income tax treatment.

Section 1235(a) provides that a transfer (other than by gift, inheritance, or devise) of property consisting of all substantial rights to a patent, or an undivided interest therein, which includes a part of all such rights, by any holder shall be considered the sale or exchange of a capital asset held for more than one year, regardless of whether payments in consideration of such transfer are (1) payable periodically over a period generally coterminous with the transferee's use of the patent, or (2) contingent on the productivity, use, or disposition of the property transferred. *See* Spireas v. Comm'r, TC Memo 2016-163 (U.S. Tax Ct 2016); Blake v. Comm'r, 615 F.2d 731 (6th Cir. 1980).

Many inventors today are employees of either small or large business entities. The employees often transfer the inventions to the employers. Are monetary rewards to inventor employees qualified for capital gain treatment under Section 1235? *See* Lehman v. CIR, 835 F.2d 431 (2d Cir. 1987), which can be found in the Materials section of this chapter.

B. Taxation Issues in Trade Secret Licensing

1. In General

Tax issues arising in trade secret licensing are similar to those in patent licensing. Nevertheless, different issues are encountered in trade secret licensing due to the fundamental difference between trade secrets and patents. Recall that a trade secret is any information, formula, pattern, compilation, program, device, method, technique, or process that derives independent economic value because it is not generally known to a trade and is maintained in secrecy by reasonable efforts. To put it another way, the essential element of a trade secret is secrecy. Thus, if the trade secret owner does not convey the right to prevent unauthorized disclosure of the trade secret, no complete disposition of trade secret occurs.

Patents, on the other hand, are novel and non-obvious inventions. Patents are fully disclosed to the public in exchange for a monopoly to exclude others from selling, making, or using the patents for a limited time of 20 years from the date of filing the patent application. The patentee has the right to exclude others from the manufacture, use, and sale of the patent during the life of the patent. Thus, no complete disposition of a patent occurs if the right to prevent infringement is not included.

2. The Impact of Characterization of Trade Secrets

There is no specific Code provision that covers the taxation of transfer of trade secrets. Unlike patent transfers, which are governed under Section 1235 and related regulations, transferors of trade secrets must look to a general Code provision for intangible property, Section 1222(3). Under Section 1222(3), a transfer of intangible property may be entitled to long term capital gains treatment if the transferor can establish (1) that the information in question constituted a capital asset; (2) that there has been a sale or exchange of such information; and (3) that the transferor held such information for more than one year prior to the sale or exchange.

To determine whether a transfer of trade secrets is a sale or license, some courts have looked to tax cases concerning patent transfers for guidance. Courts also closely examined the provisions in the transfer documents in their inquiry. *See* E.I. du Pont de Nemours & Co. v. United States, 288 F.2d 904 (Ct. Cl. 1961), which can be found in the Materials section of this chapter. If the transfer includes "all substantial rights" in the trade secret, the transfer is a sale. What are the "substantial rights" in trade secrets that if retained by the transferor would render the transfer a license? *See* Pickren v. United States, 378 F.2d 595 (5th Cir. 1967); Glen O'Brien Movable Partition Co. v. Commissioner, 70 T.C. 492 (1978).

C. Taxation Issues in Copyright Licensing

1. In General

A transfer of a copyright is entitled to capital gain treatment for the amount received if the copyright qualifies as a "capital asset."

The definition of "capital asset" excludes certain types of copyrights. Copyrights created by individual authors are not deemed a "capital asset." That means the author is not entitled to the capital gain treatment when the author sells the copyrights to others. Similarly, copyrights created under the works-made-for-hire doctrine are excluded from the definition of "capital asset," and entity authors who own such copyrights are not entitled to the capital gain treatment when they sell the copyrights to a third party. Individual and entity authors will pay ordinary income tax rates when they sell their copyrights. *See* 26 U.S.C. §1222(3); Stern v. United States, 164 F. Supp. 847 (D.C. La. 1958), which can be found in the Materials section of this chapter.

Based on the definition of "capital asset," only holders of copyrights that are neither self-created nor works-made-for-hire can obtain capital gain treatment for the transfers of the copyrights, as long as the transfers satisfy the requirements for sale or exchange of capital assets. *See* Martin v. Comm'r, 50 T.C. 341 (1969). Copyright owners, such as a Hollywood producer who purchased a copyright in a script and subsequently sold the copyright to a film company with resources to make a movie, are qualified to receive the capital gain treatment for the income received from the sale.

The tax treatment of copyright transfers is rather confusing, particularly compared to the tax treatment of patent transfers. An inventor enjoys favorable capital gain treatment if he or she sells the invention or the patent. As long as the inventor can show that the transfer is a sale and not a license, the inventor can receive the capital gain treatment for the amount received. Why did Congress provide favorable tax treatment to inventors but not authors?

Tracing the history of the tax treatment of self-created copyrightable works reveals a substantial change in 1950. Prior to 1950, the tax treatment of a transfer of a copyright depended on the professional status of the author. If the author was a writer by profession, then the sale of his or her copyright resulted in ordinary income. If the author was an amateur, then the sale of the copyright produced capital gain. Indeed, prior to 1950, the definition of "capital assets" permitted creative individuals to sell their literary or artistic works and pay tax on the profits at capital gain rates as long as they could demonstrate that their works were not property held primarily for sale in the ordinary course of business. Congress then changed the definition of "capital assets" by section 210 of the Revenue Act of 1950. The legislative history shows that Congress intended to provide uniform ordinary income treatment for the sale of copyrights created by personal efforts, regardless of the status of the author, professional or amateur. The new definition of "capital assets" excludes self-created copyrights, literary, musical, artistic compositions, or similar property. *See* Picchione v. Comm'r, 54 T.C. 1490, 1492-93 (1970) (discussing the historical changes relating to tax treatment of self-created copyrights).

This drastic change may be due to several factors, including the organized lobbying efforts of the inventors and patentees, little or no initiatives from the authors, and the recognition of the importance of patent to both industrial progress and national defense. The explanation below illuminates the reasons for different tax treatment between patents and copyrights:

> It appears that the difference in tax treatment between patents and copyrights is due largely to legislation based on ad hoc reactions to isolated political and economic events rather than attempts to establish a consistent tax structure. For example, the 1950 amendment, which excluded copyrights and copyrightable works from the definition of a capital asset, was at least partly attributable to congressional disapproval of certain publicized transactions involving property of this nature. Perhaps the best-known transaction was General Eisenhower's sale of *Crusade in Europe* for a reported $1,000,000, all of which was taxed as capital gain. Also, while the inventors forcefully presented their views at the congressional hearings preceding recent revisions of the revenue code, the authors showed little initiative. As passed by the House, the bill which later became the Revenue Act of 1950 prevented both authors and inventors from reporting profits from the sale of patents and copyrights as capital gain. After testimony by inventors and representatives of patent organizations, the Senate amended the bill to allow capital-gain treatment of the sale of a patent by an inventor. Again in 1954, the patent interests successfully lobbied for a favorable act, while the authors were largely inactive. Another reason for the discrimination in favor of patents is the congressional desire to foster invention by means of tax incentives. While the justification for this encouragement has not been elaborated, it is clear that inventions, especially when patented, are considered important for our industrial progress and national defense.

A Comparison of the Tax Treatment of Authors and Inventors, Note, 70 HARV. L. REV. 1419, 1423 (1957).

2. Sale or License of Copyrights "Capital Assets"

If the copyright is qualified as a "capital asset," the transfer of the copyright is entitled to capital gain treatment if the transfer is a sale, not a license. The transfer is a sale if the transferor does not retain substantial rights in the copyrights. *See* Rev. Rul. 60-226, 1960-1 C.B. 26 (ruling that the transfer is a sale of a copyright if the copyright owner transfers "the exclusive right to exploit the copyrighted work in a medium of publication throughout the life of the copyright"). Determining whether a transfer is a sale or a license of copyright capital asset, courts look to provisions in the contract between the transferor and transferee. For example, in finding the agreement is a license the Tax Court in Brown v. CIR, 56 T.C.M. (CCH) 638 (1988), stated:

> For tax purposes, a sale of a motion picture occurs when there is a transfer of all substantial rights of value in the motion picture copyright; thus, no sale has occurred if the transferor has retained substantial proprietary rights in the motion picture. Durkin v. Commissioner, 87 T.C. at 1369; Tolwinsky v. Commissioner, 86 T.C. at 1042-1043. We first look at the specific terms of the transactions as reflected in the written agreements. Steel LP retained certain of the rights to STEEL when it executed the Steel LP/Cincoa agreement. Specifically, Steel LP retained "any interest whatsoever" in any of the literary and dramatic material "contained in the Picture or upon which the Picture is based and the copyright and any renewals and extensions thereof," as well as certain television and other ancillary rights. Identical language also was contained in the Cincoa/Somerset agreement. The purchase agreements transferred to the respective purchasers only "the right to rent, lease, exhibit, distribute, and otherwise deal in and with respect to" STEEL. The transfer of such rights, when considered together with Steel LP's retention of other rights, indicates to us that the true form of Steel LP's transfer of STEEL is that of merely a license or lease, not a sale transaction.

D. Taxation Issues in Trademark Licensing

A transfer of a franchise, trademark, or trade name is a sale or exchange of a capital asset under Section 1221[1] if the transferor does not retain any significant power, right, or continuing interest with respect to the subject matter of the franchise trademark or

---

1. Under section 1221 the term "capital asset" means property held by the taxpayer (whether or not connected with his trade or business), but "does not include

(1) stock in trade of the taxpayer or other property of a kind which would properly be included in the inventory of the taxpayer if on hand at the close of the taxable year, or property held by the taxpayer primarily for sale to customers in the ordinary course of his trade or business;
(2) property, used in his trade or business, of a character which is subject to the allowance for depreciation provided in section 167, or real property used in his trade or business"; and
(3) self-created copyrights.

Section 1222(3) defines "Long-term Capital Gain": The term "long-term capital gain" means gain from the sale or exchange of a capital asset held for more than one year, if and to the extent such gain is taken into account in computing gross income.

trade name. The income received is entitled to capital gain treatment to the extent the gain is realized. A transfer where the transferor retains rights or interests that are deemed significant with respect to the franchise, trademark, or trade name is a license under Section 1253. The income received by the licensor is treated as ordinary income for tax purposes, and the payments made by the licensee are generally deductible. *See* Robinson Knife Manufacturing Company Inc. v. CIR, 600 F.3d 121 (2d Cir. 2010) (holding that "a producer's royalty payments (1) are calculated as a percentage of sales revenue from inventory and (2) are incurred only upon the sale of that inventory, they are immediately deductible as a matter of law because they are not 'properly allocable to property produced' within the meaning of 26 C.F.R. §1.263A-1(e)").

In distinguishing a sale from a license or franchise, trademark or trade name, the difficult issue is determining whether a right or interest is significant. From the transferee's perspective, if the trademark transfer is a sale or exchange of a capital asset, the transferee must amortize the cost over a period of time. If the transfer is not a sale or exchange of a capital asset, the transferee is entitled to immediate deduction. The transferee can deduct the cost from its taxes. *See* 26 U.S.C. §1253(d)(1)-(2). *See* Stokely USA, Inc. v. Comm'r, 100 T.C. 439, 450 (1993), and Nabisco Brands v. Commissioner, T.C. Memo 1995-127, the latter of which can be found in the Materials section of this chapter.

Prior to 1969, the treatment of trademark transfers under case law was in conflict and lacked a coherent standard for determining whether a transfer was a sale or a license for tax purposes; consequently, no standard existed for tax treatment of payments, lump-sum, and/or contingent payments for the transfer. The main reason for such disarray was the extent to which the transferor could retain such rights or interests in the transferred trademark that would still render the transfer a sale. Congress responded to the need for a uniform treatment of trademark transfers and enacted Section 1253 as part of the Tax Reform Act of 1969. Under Section 1253(a), a transfer is not a sale or exchange of a capital asset if the transferor retains any "significant power, right, or continuing interest" with respect to the trademark. Under Section 1253(b)(2), the term "significant power, right, or continuing interest" includes, but is not limited to, the following rights with respect to the trademark transferred:

(A) A right to disapprove any assignment of such interest, or any part thereof.
(B) A right to terminate at will.
(C) A right to prescribe the standards of quality of products used or sold, or of services furnished, and of the equipment and facilities used to promote such products or services.
(D) A right to require that the transferee sell or advertise only products or services of the transferor.
(E) A right to require that the transferee purchase substantially all of his supplies and equipment from the transferor.
(F) A right to payments contingent on the productivity, use, or disposition of the subject matter of the interest transferred, if such payments constitute a substantial element under the transfer agreement.

Since Section 1253 is only applicable to trademark transfers occurring after December 31, 1969, for any trademark transfers occurring before that date, the statute is of no assistance. *See* Consolidated Foods Corp. v. United States, 569 F.2d 436, 437-38 (7th Cir. 1978) (noting that it could not look to Section 1253 in analyzing the trademark transfer at issue that occurred prior to 1969, but "the confused and unsettled case law").

III. MATERIALS

The Materials include seven cases centering on the tax treatment of various intellectual property transfers. First, Spireas v. CIR, T.C. Memo 2016-163 (U.S. Tax Court 2016) illustrates how the Tax Court determines whether a transaction is a transfer or a license of patents subject to tax. In comparison, Lehman v. CIR, 835 F.2d 431 (2d Cir. 1987), illustrates the tax treatment of a patent incentive award from an employer. Third, E.I. du Pont de Nemours & Co. v. United States, 288 F.2d 904 (Ct. Cl. 1961), is a decision on the tax treatment of trade secret transfers. Fourth, Stern v. United States, 164 F. Supp. 847 (D.C. La. 1958), is about the tax treatment of copyright transfers.

Next, Robinson Knife Manufacturing Company Inc. v. CIR, 600 F.3d 121 (2d Cir. 2010), focuses on the tax treatment of royalty payments under a trademark license. Nabisco Brands, Inc. v. Commissioner, T.C. Memo. 1995-127, provides an interesting factual background on tax planning and its consequences regarding the sale and acquisition of trademarks and associated businesses.

Lastly, TGS-NOPEC Geophysical Co. v. Combs, 340 S.W.3d 432 (Tex. 2011), addresses whether receipts from the licensing of geophysical and seismic data to customers in Texas should be categorized as receipts from the use of a license or as receipts from the sale of an intangible asset for state franchise tax purposes.

SPIREAS v. COMMISSIONER
T.C. Memo. 2016-163 (U.S. Tax Court 2016)

LAUBER, Judge:

The Internal Revenue Service (IRS or respondent) determined, for 2007 and 2008 respectively, deficiencies in petitioners' Federal income tax of $4,083,264 and $1,745,701. The deficiencies arose from respondent's conclusion that the royalties Spiridon Spireas (petitioner) received under a license agreement are taxable as ordinary income rather than as capital gain. The question we must decide is whether petitioner transferred "all substantial rights" to the relevant technology, such that the royalties he received are eligible for capital gain treatment under section 1235.

FINDINGS OF FACT

Petitioners resided in Pennsylvania when they filed the petition. He obtained his Ph.D. degree from St. John's University in 1993. Dr. Sanford M. Bolton, now deceased, was chairman of the pharmaceutical sciences department at St. John's when petitioner was writing his doctoral thesis and served as his faculty adviser.

A. The Liquisolid Technology and Patents

Petitioner's dissertation addressed techniques designed to improve, in laboratory-scale studies, the solubility of drugs not easily dissolved in water. Petitioner subsequently became a renowned expert in the science of drug delivery, including "liquisolid" technologies, which involve novel methods of drug formulation. He is an inventor and has secured, jointly or individually, more than 80 U.S. and foreign patents and/or patent applications.

In 1997 petitioner and Dr. Bolton organized Hygrosol Pharmaceutical Corporation (Hygrosol) for the purpose of exploiting the liquisolid technologies they were developing. At all relevant times, petitioner and Dr. Bolton each owned 50% of Hygrosol. . . .

Petitioner and Dr. Bolton applied for, and . . . they were issued [four patents: '500 patent, '337 patent, '339 patent, and '834 patent]. . . . We will refer to the technology underlying each of the Patents as the liquisolid technology.

B. Negotiations Toward Licensing Agreement

At the relevant times, Mutual Pharmaceutical Company, Inc. (Mutual), was a company whose business focused on developing and marketing generic drugs. United Research Laboratories, Inc. (URL), was an affiliate of Mutual that distributed pharmaceutical products and some health and nutritional supplements. We will refer to these companies collectively as Mutual.

On December 23, 1997, Mutual sent petitioner and Dr. Bolton a larger scale proposal that included a draft license agreement. . . . After several months of additional negotiations the parties executed a license agreement based on this principle.

C. The License Agreement

On June 12, 1998, Hygrosol, Dr. Bolton, and petitioner (collectively, licensors) entered into a license agreement with Mutual (1998 license agreement or agreement). The agreement granted to Mutual the right to use the liquisolid technology, on a product-by-product basis, to develop, produce, and sell within the United States new and generic pharmaceutical drugs, as determined by the parties on the basis of unanimous consent. The agreement began with the following recitals:

> WHEREAS, the founders of Hygrosol, Spireas and Bolton, have obtained a notice of allowance of their patent claims in their application for United States Letters Patent entitled LIQUISOLID SYSTEMS AND METHODS OF PREPARING SAME * * * (the "Patent") * * *; and
>
> WHEREAS, Spireas and Bolton developed and are the inventors of all the technology which is the subject of the Patent (the "Technology"); and * * *
>
> WHEREAS, Hygrosol, Spireas and Bolton desire to grant to Mutual and United the exclusive right to utilize the Technology only for the development of new generic drug forms and new drug products (the "Products"), unanimously selected by Hygrosol, United and Mutual and, after so selected, to be developed, produced and sold in the United States.

Section 2 of the agreement, captioned "Grant of Exclusive Rights," provided that the licensors granted to Mutual "[t]he exclusive rights to utilize the Technology only to develop Products that Mutual, United, and Hygrosol, acting in good faith will unanimously select." Mutual was also granted the exclusive right, within the United States, "to produce, market, sell, promote and distribute * * * said Products containing the Technology." The "Technology" was defined as "the technology which is the subject of the Patent," which denoted the original 834 patent.

Section 7.4 of the agreement addressed after-acquired technology. It provided that "[i]f, during development of a Product, a new patent of specific application claims is secured based on the original Patent, the new patent shall be the property of Hygrosol, Spireas and Bolton." However, Mutual in that event would have the right, without paying additional compensation, "to utilize such patent as if described in the definition of 'Patent' set forth above." Thus, the "Technology" that Mutual received the right to use ultimately included not only the 834 patent but also the 550 patent, which was a "division of" the 834 patent, and the 337 and 339 patents, which were "continuations of" the 550 patent.

The term "Products" was defined to mean "new generic drug forms and new drug products" developed using the Technology. "Products" could also include nutritional supplements that were either combined with pharmaceutical drugs or required FDA approval to be marketed as drugs. The term "Products" thus excluded nutritional supplements unconnected to any FDA-approved drug and not requiring FDA approval. Section 5.5 further provided that "[t]he group of potential Products to be selected by the parties to this Agreement shall exclude, at all times during the life of this Agreement, products that Hygrosol, Spireas, and Bolton are developing or are in negotiations to develop for another party."

Mutual's rights to use the Technology with respect to a particular Product began once the parties agreed in writing to develop that Product and Mutual paid petitioner $10,000 to conduct a feasibility study. During the agreement's first year, the licensors pledged to make a good-faith effort to propose three Products for development. If Mutual determined, after petitioner presented the results of his study, to dispense with further feasibility studies and discontinue developing that Product, the licensors were then free "to offer the Product to any other entity."

If the parties agreed, following completion of feasibility studies, to develop a particular Product, formulation studies would begin under petitioner's supervision with a view to producing a clinical batch of the Product meeting Mutual's specifications for dissolution and stability. That stage would be followed by clinical studies and (if they were successful) development of a marketing strategy for the Product. If Mutual sold a Product, 20% of the gross profit (as defined) was to be paid to Hygrosol quarterly.

If Mutual did not actively develop, produce, or sell a particular Product, the licensors could terminate its exclusive rights with respect thereto. Mutual would also forfeit its exclusive rights with respect to a Product, and such rights would revert to the licensors, if Mutual notified them that it was discontinuing development or marketing of that Product. On the other hand, the agreement permitted Mutual to sublicense to a third party its rights with respect to a particular Product; in that event, the licensors were entitled to 50% of the "net proceeds" as defined.

Apart from royalties to be paid on ultimate sale of Products, petitioner was paid in other ways for work performed at various stages of the development process. The $10,000 up-front fee was based on an estimate that the feasibility study for a given Product would take approximately 15 days to complete. For additional time devoted to feasibility studies, petitioner would be paid as an independent contractor at a daily rate of $600. In March 1999 petitioner entered into an employment agreement to serve as vice president of research and development for Mutual. His duties as an employee included laboratory and research activities related to obtaining FDA approvals for the company's products.

The 1998 license agreement granted Mutual rights to use the Technology only in the pharmaceutical field. Petitioner retained rights to use his liquisolid technology to develop vitamins, nutritional supplements, and other health-related products not requiring FDA approval. In February 1998 petitioner engaged one or more professionals to market the liquisolid technology to various companies in the health and nutrition fields. As of June 1998 the right to exploit the liquisolid technology in the health and nutrition fields had substantial value.

The 1998 license agreement was not petitioner's only effort to commercialize the liquisolid technology within the pharmaceutical field. During 1997 and through the date of that agreement, petitioner worked with other drug companies to develop at least one pharmaceutical product using the Technology. The Technology had potential application to thousands of pharmaceutical products, and Mutual obtained rights to use that Technology only with respect to Products that the licensors presented to it for development. By withholding his assent as to a particular drug, petitioner could reserve to himself and his co-licensors the exclusive rights to develop new formulations of that drug using the liquisolid technology. The licensors could also reacquire rights to use the Technology with respect to Products that Mutual declined to pursue or abandoned after development had begun. The right to use the Technology to develop drugs that were not proposed by the licensors to, or selected for development by, Mutual had substantial value at the time the 1998 license agreement was signed.

D. Selection of Products for Development

As of the date the agreement was signed, petitioner had not yet developed a commercially viable drug or other product using the Technology. While the Technology included patented concepts for addressing the "low bioavailability" problem, the parties recognized that these concepts would need to be adapted to the peculiar properties of each specific chemical or molecule in order to create a new, commercially successful, formulation of that drug. When they executed the 1998 license agreement, the licensors had not identified any Products that would be presented to Mutual for development.

Starting in mid-1998, petitioner screened up to 100 drugs, through preliminary tests, to determine their suitability for development under the 1998 license agreement. Of these, the parties selected more than 20 Products for further development. The agreement specified that these selections had to be memorialized "in writing," and the parties did this by executing short engagement letters. Between June 24, 1998, and December 30, 2002, the parties executed engagement letters committing themselves to pursuing "highly to maximally bioavailable formulations" of various drugs, including Ibuprofen, Lovastatin, and Viagra; and to pursuing "bioequivalent formulations" of various drugs, including Lovastatin, Paxil, and Zoloft.

A typical engagement letter was two paragraphs long and was signed by a representative of Mutual and by petitioner as the representative of Hygrosol.

By early 2000 the U.S. molecule patent had expired for a drug called felodipine, which is used to treat high blood pressure. It was manufactured by a large, unrelated pharmaceutical company and marketed under the brand name Plendil. Any pharmaceutical company could purchase the felodipine molecule; however, there remained a nonexpired formulation patent on the Plendil product.

Because of its chemical structure, felodipine has low water solubility and degrades if it is exposed to elevated temperatures or light. Petitioner performed preliminary tests on felodipine in early 2000. After doing so, he was hopeful that the Technology could be used to develop a new formulation of felodipine that would overcome the challenges posed by this drug, and achieve bioequivalance with the Plendil product, without infringing on the existing formulation patent.

On March 7, 2000, Mutual sent petitioner an engagement letter addressing the development of three Products, including felodipine. This letter read in full as follows:

> This letter is the formal engagement of Hygrosol and Mutual for generic bioequivalent versions of Rythmol and Plendil Extended-Release, as well as maximally bioavailable formulations of Propafenone, in accordance with the License Agreement between Hygrosol and Mutual dated June 12, 1998.
>
> Attached with this letter is a check for Thirty Thousand Dollars ($30,000) for engagement of these three products, in accordance with the License Agreement. Please sign below if this is acceptable to Hygrosol Pharmaceutical Corp.

Petitioner countersigned this letter (March 2000 engagement letter) in his capacity as vice president of Hygrosol. Felodipine was the 11th drug that the parties had selected for possible development under the 1998 license agreement.

When he signed the March 2000 engagement letter, petitioner had completed roughly 30% of the work that ultimately resulted in a successful new formulation of felodipine. The principal challenges this molecule posed were its low solubility in water and its high sensitivity to heat and light. In solving these problems, petitioner employed the Technology and (in particular) the claims governing "granular liquisolid systems" covered by the '339 patent. But considerable work was required to adapt the Technology to felodipine's idiosyncrasies, regulating the release of the drug from the generic tablet and making the active ingredient stable in tablet form. Petitioner and Mutual refrained from seeking a patent on this formulation in order to prevent competitors from seeing the disclosures that a patent application would require. However, the felodipine formulation was novel, useful, and nonobvious, and it qualified as patentable.

Under the 1998 license agreement, Mutual obtained the exclusive right to produce and sell within the United States any "Product[ ] containing the Technology," which included the felodipine formulation. It obtained FDA approval for that formulation, and it has successfully marketed a new generic form of felodipine that resulted from petitioner's application of the Technology. Felodipine and propafenone were the only Products developed under the 1998 license agreement that resulted in commercial success.

IRS EXAMINATION

Petitioners timely filed joint Federal income tax returns for 2007 and 2008 on Forms 1040, U.S. Individual Income Tax Return, on which they reported royalties received under the 1998 license agreement as long-term capital gain. The IRS examined those returns and issued petitioners a timely a notice of deficiency. That notice determined that the royalties received were not subject to section 1235 and should have been reported as ordinary income.

OPINION

The Commissioner's determinations in a notice of deficiency are generally presumed correct, and the taxpayer bears the burden of proving those determinations erroneous.

A. Governing Statutory Framework

Royalty payments received under a license agreement are generally taxed as ordinary income. However, section 1235(a) provides that a transfer of property "consisting of all substantial rights to a patent * * * by any holder shall be considered the sale or exchange of a capital asset held for more than 1 year." This treatment applies regardless of whether the consideration received in exchange is payable periodically or is contingent on productivity or use of the property. Sec. 1235(a)(1) and (2).

For payments to qualify for capital gain treatment under section 1235, it is not necessary that the property transferred be patented or be subject to a patent application at the time of transfer. See sec. 1.1235-2(a), Income Tax Regs. It is sufficient that the taxpayer transfer all substantial rights to a patentable product that is held as a trade secret, whether or not a patent application is ultimately filed. As the Third Circuit explained in Magnus v. Commissioner, 259 F.2d 893, 898-899 (3d Cir. 1958): "[O]ur inquiry is aimed at ascertaining * * * whether rights amounting to full and complete control were relinquished. A transfer of something less constitutes a mere license with the royalties * * * received thereunder taxable as ordinary income."

In determining whether "all substantial rights" have been transferred, the "circumstances of the whole transaction, rather than the particular terminology used in the instrument of transfer, shall be considered." Sec. 1.1235-2(b)(1), Income Tax Regs. We consider the practical effect of the terms to which the parties have agreed, but we will not reform the parties' agreement to alter its terms absent unusual circumstances.

Capital gain treatment is not available where the instrument of transfer "grants rights to the grantee, in fields of use within trades or industries, which are less than all the rights covered by the patent, which exist and have value at the time of the grant." Sec. 1.1235-2(b)(1)(iii), Income Tax Regs. To ascertain whether a taxpayer has transferred "all substantial rights," we consider whether he has retained rights that, in the aggregate, have substantial value. See E.I. du Pont de Nemours & Co. v. United States, 432 F.2d 1052, 1055 (3d Cir. 1970).

The central dispute between the parties may be encapsulated in the question: "All substantial rights to what?" Respondent submits that the instrument of transfer is the 1998 license agreement and that the crucial question is whether petitioner thereby transferred all substantial rights to the Technology. Respondent contends that the answer to this question is "no," urging that petitioner retained valuable rights to use the Patents and liquisolid technology both outside the pharmaceutical field (e.g., in developing vitamins and nutritional supplements) and inside the pharmaceutical field (e.g., in developing drugs on which he was then collaborating with other companies or might in future decline to propose to Mutual for development). Petitioners submit that the key document is the March 2000 engagement letter; that this letter was in substance a license agreement; and that the central question is whether petitioner thereby transferred all substantial rights to the felodipine and profafenone formulations. Petitioner contends that the answer to this question is "yes," urging that felodipine and propafenone have no value outside the pharmaceutical field but are useful only as drugs. We conclude that respondent has the stronger side of this argument.

B. Nature of the Rights Transferred

1. The 1998 License Agreement

We discern little if any ambiguity in the 1998 license agreement. That agreement is the "instrument of transfer." Sec. 1.1235-2(b)(1), Income Tax Regs. Section 2 of the agreement, captioned "Grant of Exclusive Rights," provides that the licensors granted to Mutual "[t]he exclusive rights to utilize the Technology" to develop new formulations of selected Products. The rights transferred were thus the rights to use the liquisolid technology embodied in the Patents and to make and sell any "Products containing the Technology," that is, any Products successfully generated by exploitation of the Technology.

Conversely, the 1998 license agreement did not transfer rights to the formulation of any specific drug. It could not possibly have done so, because no such formulations existed in June 1998. Indeed, the parties at that time had not selected any drugs for development using the Technology, and they did not know what drugs would in the future be proposed or selected for development. Felodipine and propafenone in particular, the 11th and 12th drugs proposed by the licensors, were not selected for development until March 2000.

The recitals to the 1998 license agreement confirm the parties' intent. The fifth "whereas" clause states that "Hygrosol, Spireas and Bolton desire to grant to Mutual and United the exclusive right to utilize the Technology only for the development of new generic drug forms and new drug products * * * unanimously selected by" the parties. This sentence leaves little doubt that what the licensors intended to transfer to Mutual was a limited right to use the Technology, coupled with the right to make and sell any drug formulations successfully developed using the Technology.

Section 4 of the agreement, captioned "Compensation," supports respondent's view that Mutual was paying royalties for rights to use the Technology generally, not for the felodipine formulation specifically. Petitioners submit that Dr. Spireas was "the sole inventor" of the felodipine formulation and that he "invented the felodipine technology in his individual capacity as an inventor." Dr. Enscore similarly testified that petitioner invented the felodipine formulation sometime after May 2000 and that it was an adaptation of the "granular liquisolid" technology covered by the 339 patent. That patent, unlike the other Patents, was issued to petitioner individually, not to petitioner and Dr. Bolton jointly. Thus, if Mutual were paying only for the felodipine formulation, one would have expected that petitioner would receive most, if not all, of the resulting royalties.

But that is not what the 1998 license agreement provided. Section 4 provided that, if Mutual received FDA approval for and sold a Product, then 20% of the gross profit would "be paid to Hygrosol quarterly." Hygrosol was owned 50-50 by petitioner and Dr. Bolton, and Dr. Bolton would thus receive 50% of all royalties paid under the agreement. This division makes perfect sense if the royalties were paid for use of "the Technology," which at that time consisted of the 834 Patent, which was jointly owned by petitioner and Dr. Bolton. This division is hard to reconcile with petitioner's theory that the royalties were paid exclusively for a product of which he, in his individual capacity, was the sole inventor.

The conclusion that Mutual was paying royalties for use of "the Technology" is supported, not only by the terms of the 1998 license agreement, but also by the "circumstances of the whole transaction." Sec. 1.1235-2(b)(1), Income Tax Regs. During the negotiations toward the agreement petitioner clearly had, as a primary goal, maintaining control over the liquisolid technology. He testified that he was hesitant to license this technology to Mutual because he was already collaborating with other companies to develop drug formulations using it. He was also interested in exploring use of the Technology in the field of nutritional supplements, such as CoQ10.

When Mutual in December 1997 proposed that it receive an exclusive license to use the Technology for all purposes, petitioner firmly rejected that idea. Under the agreement ultimately signed, Mutual was granted rights to use the Technology only with respect to Products "unanimously selected" by the parties. Mutual was explicitly denied the right to use the Technology with respect to "products that Hygrosol, Spireas, and Bolton are developing or are in negotiations to develop for another party." Rights to use the Technology would also revert to the licensors as to a given Product if Mutual did not follow through on its commitments. In short, the negotiating history confirms the parties' understanding that what was being licensed was a right to use the Technology, albeit a carefully circumscribed right to do so.

In asserting that petitioner "transferred his felodipine technology to URL [and] Mutual," petitioners ignore the dispositive provisions of the 1998 license agreement. In section 7.2, Mutual explicitly agreed "that all formulations relating to the Products containing the Technology and developed in Mutual's * * * facilities belong to Hygrosol, Spireas and Bolton," subject to Mutual's rights under the Agreement. Section 7.4 similarly provided: "If during development of a Product, a new patent of specific application claims is secured based on the original patent, the new patent shall be the property of Hygrosol, Spireas, and Bolton." Mutual was not entitled to outright ownership of subsequently developed technology, but only "the right to utilize such patent as if described in the definition of 'Patent' " set forth in the 1998 license agreement. This makes it clear that all rights Mutual obtained were governed by, and limited by, the 1998 license agreement.

2. The March 2000 Engagement Letter

In contending that petitioner transferred all substantial rights to the felodipine formulation, petitioners largely ignore the 1998 license agreement, which Mr. Gould opined was in substance an R&D agreement setting forth "a framework" for product development. Instead they rely on the March 2000 engagement letter, which Mr. Gould opined was in substance a license agreement. Mr. Gould's testimony on these points was unpersuasive because it ignored the terms, purpose, and effect of both documents.

The March 2000 engagement letter was just that—an engagement letter. It stated rather plainly that the parties had selected three drugs for development and transmitted a $30,000 check "for engagement of these three products." It was substantially similar to 20 other engagement letters the parties signed to memorialize their selection of certain drugs for further investigation. These engagement letters grant no rights and have no royalty payment terms. Far from constituting freestanding license agreements, they simply rendered the 1998 license agreement operative with respect to the Products that they identified.

The 1998 license agreement specified that Mutual was granted rights "to utilize the Technology only to develop Products that Mutual, United and Hygrosol * * * unanimously select." Section 2.2 of the agreement provided that the period during which Mutual shall have exclusive rights with respect to a Product "commences as soon as * * * said Product is identified by either party and agreed upon in writing by Hygrosol, Mutual, and United." The March 2000 engagement letter simply memorialized that felodipine and propafenone had been "identified * * * and agreed upon in writing" by the parties. The execution of this letter did no more than fulfill a condition stated in the 1998 license agreement: It served to trigger, with respect to those two Products, the "exclusive rights to utilize the Technology" granted to Mutual by section 2.1 of the agreement.

The 1998 license agreement is clearly the relevant "instrument of transfer," *see* sec. 1.1235-2(b)(1), Income Tax Regs., because it is the agreement that granted the rights for which Mutual paid. Indeed, in asserting that Mutual received "all substantial rights" to the felodipine formulation, petitioners necessarily rely on provisions of the 1998 license agreement stating that Mutual received rights throughout the United States for a perpetual term. Petitioners cannot logically contend that the March 2000 engagement letter served to license the felodipine formulation, while relying on the 1998 license agreement to establish that Mutual's rights in that formulation were unlimited temporally and exclusive geographically.

Petitioners assert that their view of the situation is supported by what they call the statute's "'in consideration of' requirement." Section 1235 provides that a transfer of property consisting of all substantial rights to a patent shall be treated as the sale of a capital asset "regardless of whether or not payments in consideration of such transfer" are payable periodically or contingent on productivity or use. Petitioners note that, among the 20-plus products the parties selected for development, felodipine and propafenone were the only two that resulted in commercial success. It therefore makes sense, they urge, to regard the royalties as having been paid "in consideration of" those two Products.

In advancing this argument, petitioners seek to redraft the 1998 license agreement, using hindsight, to achieve a more advantageous tax result. The liquisolid technology had potential application to thousands of drugs; in June 1998 the parties had no idea to which drugs it might usefully be applied. As a result, they necessarily crafted that agreement as a license to use the Technology to figure out which drugs might be developed successfully.

To employ an analogy from a different industry, an oil company that licenses drilling technology inevitably uses that technology no less in drilling dry holes than in drilling successful wells. The same was true here. Mutual necessarily "utilize[d] the Technology" every time petitioner performed feasibility studies on a Product in its laboratories. Petitioner performed feasibility studies for Mutual's benefit on more than 20 Products over four years; this amounted to a significant "utilization" of the Technology by Mutual.

When entering into the 1998 license agreement, Mutual could logically expect to derive value from all such uses of the Technology. Even if feasibility studies on a particular drug did not predict a home run, those studies might yield valuable know-how that would assist development of similar (or redirect development toward dissimilar) Products. Mutual might also derive value by using the Technology to cross unpromising drugs, or unpromising types of drugs, off of its list. As is true in many licensing arrangements, Mutual contracted to pay royalties not on the basis of actual usage of the Technology, but on the basis of sales of Products containing the Technology. The payment structure chosen by the parties does not alter the fact that Mutual paid royalties to "utilize the Technology." Those royalties were paid "in consideration of" its use of that Technology both when its use of the Technology was successful and when it was not.

In sum, the rights transferred to Mutual are those granted to it by the 1998 license agreement and only those rights. While resisting the conclusion that this agreement was the relevant "instrument of transfer," petitioners have not identified any other document that could have granted to Mutual, and defined, the specific rights that Mutual in fact possessed. We conclude that the terms of the 1998 license agreement and the extrinsic circumstances both support what we believe to be its clear meaning. The rights granted to Mutual under the agreement were the limited rights "to utilize the Technology * * * to develop Products" and to make and sell "Products containing the Technology." This resolves the first part of our inquiry, which required us to identify the nature of the rights transferred.

C. Substantiality of the Rights Retained

The remaining question is whether petitioner in the 1998 license agreement transferred "all substantial rights" to the Technology. We conclude that he did not. The rights granted to Mutual were less than all the rights in the Technology because the license was limited to the pharmaceutical industry and was restricted to specific Products selected by the parties. We find that the licensors' retained rights had substantial value.

A taxpayer does not transfer "all substantial rights" to a patent if the instrument of transfer "grants rights to the grantee, in fields of use within trades or industries, which are less than all the rights covered by the patent, which exist and have value at the time of the grant." Sec. 1.1235-2(b)(iii), Income Tax Regs. In determining whether a taxpayer has transferred "all substantial rights," the Third Circuit has evaluated whether the taxpayer has retained rights that, in the aggregate, have substantial value. See E.I. duPont de Nemours & Co., 432 F.2d at 1055.

In at least two respects, the 1998 license agreement did not transfer all substantial rights to the Technology. First, the agreement did not transfer to Mutual all rights to use the Technology within the pharmaceutical field. Section 5.5 of the agreement explicitly denied Mutual any rights with respect to drug products petitioner was already investigating. It provided: "The group of potential Products to be selected by the parties to this Agreement shall exclude, at all times during the life of this Agreement, products that Hygrosol, Spireas, and Bolton are developing or are in negotiations to develop for another party."

The agreement also gave petitioner and his co-licensors effective veto power over the drugs as to which Mutual could exercise its rights in the future. The Technology had potential application to thousands of drugs, but section 2.1 granted Mutual rights to use the Technology "only to develop Products that Mutual, United, and Hygrosol * * * will unanimously select." The agreement required the licensors to act "in good faith" when proposing (or declining to propose) Products for development. But situations can easily be imagined in which the licensors might have concluded, acting in good faith, that Company X would be a more logical development partner for a particular Product than Mutual.

The parties understood that additional work would be required to adapt the liquisolid technology to the variables of individual drugs. But this does not diminish the value of the Technology generally or of petitioner's retained rights to use it. Petitioner negotiated assiduously to maintain control over his patented liquisolid techniques; this strongly implies a belief that the rights he retained had value. Although felodipine and propafenone turned out to be the only drugs successfully developed between 1998 and 2004, when petitioner left Mutual's employ, this outcome was not foreseeable when the parties negotiated the agreement. We accordingly find and hold that the licensors' retained rights to use the Technology within the pharmaceutical industry, as of June 1998, had substantial value.

Second, petitioner retained under the 1998 license agreement all rights to use the Technology outside the pharmaceutical field, e.g., in developing nutritional supplements, vitamins, and other products not requiring FDA approval. The restriction of a license to one field of use, where a reserved field of use has value at the time of the grant, fails to convey "all substantial rights." *See* Mros v. Commissioner, 493 F.2d 813, 817 (9th Cir. 1974); sec. 1.1235-2(b)(1)(iii), Income Tax Regs.

When he executed the 1998 license agreement, petitioner was extremely interested in exploring use of the Technology to develop "super-bioavailable" or other new formulations of nutritional supplements like CoQ10. Indeed, in February 1998 he engaged one or more professionals to market the liquisolid technology to various companies in the health and nutrition fields. At trial, petitioner suggested that these retained rights had little commercial value because (for example) consumers might refuse to pay extra for a supplement containing a smaller dose of the active ingredient. But his testimony on this point was anecdotal and conclusory, and it was at odds with other portions of his testimony.

Once again, it is implausible that petitioner would have negotiated so insistently to retain rights to use the Technology in the nutrition field if he was convinced that these rights had no value. We accordingly find and hold that the rights petitioner and his co-licensors retained to use the Technology, both within the pharmaceutical field and in other fields, in the aggregate had substantial value.

D. Conclusion

Petitioner in June 1998 negotiated a deal to license use of the Technology to Mutual on a limited, product-by-product, basis. It is possible that he might have struck a different deal: He might initially have proposed an R&D arrangement, then waited several years to see what developed. The record does not establish what motivated his decision. Time may have been of the essence, or the "bird in hand" mantra may have carried the day.

"While a taxpayer is free to organize his affairs as he chooses, nevertheless, once having done so, he must accept the tax consequences of his choice * * * and may not enjoy the benefit of some other route he might have chosen to follow but did not." Commissioner v. Nat'l Alfalfa Dehydrating & Milling Co., 417 U.S. 134, 149 (1974). Petitioner wishes to revise the agreement he negotiated in 1998, which by its terms granted a limited right to use "the Technology," and replace it with a different arrangement that, in hindsight, might appear to generate a more desirable tax outcome. Petitioner is not at liberty to undo the deal he made or the documents he signed. *See* Commissioner v. Danielson, 378 F.2d at 775. Because petitioner in the 1998 license agreement did not transfer "property consisting of all substantial rights to a patent," section 1235(a) does not apply. We thus sustain respondent's determination that the royalties petitioners received are taxable as ordinary income.

LEHMAN v. CIR

835 F.2d 431 (2d Cir. 1987)

LUMBARD, Circuit Judge.

Herbert and Arlene Lehman appeal from a judgment of the United States Tax Court following a trial before Special Trial Judge James M. Gussis determining a deficiency of $8,320 in their federal income tax for 1981. They claim that the tax court misapplied §1235 of the Code, which accords capital gains treatment to amounts received by an inventor as consideration for the transfer of a patent, by finding that an incentive award received from International Business Machines Corporation (IBM) in 1981 by Herbert Lehman (employed by IBM since 1960 as a chemist) in recognition of a patent he transferred to IBM in 1965 did not qualify for capital gains treatment under §1235. The Commissioner maintains that the tax court properly characterized the corporate incentive award at issue as taxable as ordinary income under §61 of the Code, rather than as capital gain under §1235, because the award was not received in exchange for Lehman's assignment of his patent rights to IBM. We affirm the decision of the tax court.

I.

Herbert Lehman was a chemist employed by IBM in Poughkeepsie, New York throughout 1981. He was first employed as a chemist by IBM in 1960. The parties agree that he was not employed as an inventor. At the time he commenced his employment, he agreed to assign his rights in all future inventions to IBM. In accordance with this agreement, on June 30, 1965, he assigned to IBM his entire right, title and interest in his invention called "Method for Controlling the Electrical Characteristics of a Semiconductor Surface." The assignment also assigned to IBM Lehman's entire right, title and interest in a pending patent for that invention; that patent was subsequently granted to Lehman and was assigned Patent Number 3402081.

In May 1981, Lehman received from IBM an award of $30,000 based on Patent Number 3402081. This award was granted under an incentive award plan maintained by IBM, the basic purpose of which, according to literature distributed by IBM to its employees, is to "recognize employee achievements of significant or outstanding value, especially those that are beyond the levels of expected performance in the assigned jobs." The award was treated as part of the $96,733.40 of "wages, tips, and other compensation" on the W-2 Form issued by IBM to Herbert Lehman for the 1981 tax year. A letter from IBM to Herbert Lehman dated March 19, 1982 stated in part that "the award was granted to you above and beyond your normal compensation."

On Schedule D of their joint income tax return for 1981, appellants characterized the award as being in respect to the transfer of an invention or patent right and accordingly treated it as a capital gain under §1235 of the Code. The Internal Revenue Service determined that the

$30,000 award was ordinary income, not a capital gain under §1235, and issued a statutory notice of deficiency of $8,320 in federal income taxes on January 30, 1985.

Agreeing with the IRS's characterization of the payment, Judge Gussis concluded that the corporate award was ordinary compensation for services rendered by Lehman to IBM within the meaning of §61(a)(1) of the Code because it did not constitute consideration for the transfer of an invention or patent right under §1235. In reaching its decision, the court relied on the following facts: (1) that as a condition to his employment, Mr. Lehman had agreed to transfer all rights to any products or processes he might invent during his employment without any consideration in addition to any compensation that he might receive from IBM during the course of his employment, (2) that he received no payment at the time he transferred the rights to IBM in 1965, and (3) that the award was not made until 16 years after the transfer.

II.

On the undisputed facts, we agree with the tax court that this case presents the question of whether the $30,000 payment made in 1981 by IBM under its incentive award program to Herbert Lehman was (1) compensation which is to be treated as ordinary income under §61 of the Internal Revenue Code of 1954, or (2) a payment made in exchange for Lehman's assignment of his patent rights which would be treated as capital gain under §1235.

Section 1235 of the Internal Revenue Code provides in relevant part:

> **(a)** A transfer (other than by gift, inheritance, or devise) of property consisting of all substantial rights to a patent, or an undivided interest therein which includes a part of all such rights, by any holder shall be considered the sale or exchange of a capital asset . . . regardless of whether or not payments in consideration of such transfer are —
>> **(1)** payable periodically over a period generally coterminous with the transferee's use of the patent, or
>> **(2)** contingent on the productivity, use, or disposition of property transferred. . . .

The purpose of this section is to allow inventors to treat patent royalties as capital gains, even though they might otherwise be treated as ordinary income. The primary requirement to obtain this favorable treatment is that the payment be in exchange for the transfer of property consisting of "all substantial rights to a patent." Where, as here, there is an employment relationship between the transferor and transferee the question arises whether payments made by an employer to an employee who has agreed to assign his patent rights to his employer are payments made in consideration for the transfer under §1235 or simply additional ordinary income to the employee.

The question of whether payments by an employer to an employee are within the scope of §1235 is to be answered by consideration of the facts and circumstances under which the employer makes payments to the employee. This is the approach taken in several tax court cases that have considered §1235. See Beausoleil v. Commissioner, 66 T.C. 244 (1976); Downs v. Commissioner, 49 T.C. 533 (1968); McClain v. Commissioner, 40 T.C. 841 (1963); Chilton v. Commissioner, 40 T.C. 552 (1963). It was the approach followed by the tax court in this case, and, for the most part, we adopt that approach.

Payments received by an employee as compensation for services rendered as an employee under an employment contract requiring the employee to transfer to the employer the rights to any invention by such employee are not attributable to a transfer to which section 1235 applies. However, whether payments received by an employee from his employer (under an employment contract or otherwise) are attributable to the transfer by the employee of all substantial rights to a patent (or an undivided interest therein) or are compensation for services rendered the employer by the employee is a question of fact. In determining which is the case, consideration shall be given not only to all facts and circumstances of the employment relationship but also to whether the amount of such payments depends upon the production, sale, or use by, or the value to, the employer of the patent rights transferred by the employee. If it is determined that payments are attributable to the transfer of patent rights, and all other requirements under section 1235 are met, such payments shall be treated as proceeds derived from the sale of a patent.

Unlike the tax court, however, we believe that neither the fact that Herbert Lehman did not receive compensation at the time he assigned the rights to his patent, nor the fact that he did not receive the award until sixteen years after the transfer, militates against finding that the payment was within §1235. In fact, it seems to us that §1235 was designed to grant capital gains treatment to such delayed payments when the payments satisfy the basic requirement of §1235 that the payments in question were made in consideration of the transfer of patent rights.

Nevertheless, we agree with the holding of the tax court that Lehman's receipt of the 1981 incentive award from IBM does not qualify for capital gains treatment because it was not made in consideration of the transfer of his patent rights in 1965. We reach this conclusion on two independent grounds.

First, we interpret Herbert Lehman's employment agreement with IBM as not requiring IBM to provide any consideration for Lehman's transfer of patent rights in addition to his continuing employment and the ordinary compensation that follows from that relationship which includes the agreement to assign any patent rights that he might obtain during the course of his employment by IBM. We interpret this language to mean that the payment made by IBM to Herbert Lehman is to be characterized as ordinary income in the form of compensation for his employment, not as consideration for the transfer of the patent that he assigned to IBM in 1965.

Second, we believe that the tax court decisions in *Beausoleil*, *McClain*, and *Chilton*, *supra*, provide a principled distinction between (1) royalty-type payments made by an employer directly in consideration of the assignment of a patent by an employee which qualify under §1235 and (2) payments that recognize in a more general manner the contributions of an employee who has assigned certain patent rights to his employer but which do not qualify under §1235 because they were not made in consideration of the transfer of patent rights.

In *McClain*, the taxpayer, in consideration of his employment, had agreed to assign to his employer all inventions relating to his employer's business that he might make during his employment. McClain developed two patentable inventions during the course of his employment by Lockheed and executed assignments of the relevant patents to Lockheed. At some time after the transfer, during McClain's period of employment, Lockheed announced through a series of publications to its employees that it was implementing a program for paying employees specified percentages of income received by Lockheed as the result of its sale or licensing of employee inventions to third parties.

The plan in *McClain*, though terminable by Lockheed at its discretion, had several important provisions that distinguish it from the IBM plan at issue here. First, even if it was terminated by Lockheed, awards would be given to employees for patents assigned prior to the change or discontinuance of the plan. Second, an employee who had assigned patent rights either before the plan was created or while the plan existed was to share in revenue or royalties at a specified rate. Unlike the IBM plan at issue in this case, therefore, whether the employee received awards and the amount of those awards were unrelated to any subjective judgments by his employer about his continuing performance. Third, an employee whose assignment of patent rights was covered by the plan would continue to share whether or not he remained with Lockheed. Fourth, if an employee covered by the plan were to die prior to the expiration of the assigned patent, his designated heirs were to receive the continuing awards. The tax court found that, as the program was operated, the awards in question should be treated as consideration for the transfer of patent rights under §1235, and consequently accorded the payments capital gains treatment.

In *Chilton*, the taxpayer also had an agreement with his employer to assign to his employer all patent rights for inventions he might produce during the course of his employment; the taxpayer was to receive a 2 1/2% royalty on the sales of articles manufactured and sold by the employer that were covered by the assigned patents. Like the taxpayer in *McClain*, Chilton's receipt of these amounts was not conditioned on his continued employment because the royalties were to continue for the life of the patents. The tax court found that these amounts were made in respect of the transfer of patents he had produced and therefore constituted capital gains under §1235.

Like the case currently before us, the *Beausoleil* case also involved an IBM incentive program. Under the program at issue in *Beausoleil*, IBM employees received a specified number of points for each patentable invention that they produced and assigned to IBM under an employment agreement similar to the agreement at issue in this case. Over time, employees accumulated points; IBM would then make a cash distribution once they had accumulated a specified number of points. The taxpayer in *Beausoleil* received one of these awards and sought to characterize it as a capital gain under §1235. The IRS maintained that the amounts were ordinary income. The tax court agreed with the IRS's assessment of a deficiency because its examination of the facts indicated that the award to the taxpayer was not made in consideration of the transfer to IBM of the rights to his invention as required by §1235.

The *Beausoleil* court distinguished the *McClain* and *Chilton* decisions by stating "the payments [made in *McClain* and *Chilton*] were royalties geared to the use by, and profitability of the invention for, the employer. Moreover, the employees in those cases were to receive royalty payments for the life of the patent despite termination of their employment by the corporation. . . ." 66 T.C. at 250. We believe that the approach taken by the tax court in *Beausoleil*, *supra*, both in its construction of §1235 and treatment of the *McClain* and *Chilton* decisions, was sound because it recognized the important distinction between payments received from an employer which if made to an outsider would constitute royalty payments and payments made to an employee that could represent additional ordinary income.

The distinction made by these decisions parallels our belief that the exception from §61 created by §1235 for periodic payments made in consideration for the transfer of patent rights should not be extended to payments that include an element of ordinary compensation for services. It is true that some of the bonus received by Herbert Lehman in 1981 was in recognition of the value of the patent he transferred to IBM—if he had never transferred the patent to IBM, he would not have received the $30,000 award under the incentive program. We also believe, however, that the bonus represented ordinary income in the form of compensation for Herbert Lehman's continuing contributions to IBM—if he was no longer employed by IBM or if his job performance had become substandard, under the terms of the program as set forth in the explanatory materials distributed by IBM to its employees, it seems quite unlikely that IBM would have given him the $30,000 award in 1981. Neither his employment agreement nor the terms of IBM's incentive program give us a basis either for determining that the award was given solely in recognition of the patent assignment, or for designating part of the bonus as compensation for continuing service and part as consideration for the patent. Since we cannot identify that portion of the award that is in recognition of the assignment, and because we do not believe that Congress intended that the entire award, including the part which is merely compensation for services, be treated as capital gains, we must agree with the tax court that the entire award constitutes ordinary income under §61 rather than a capital gain under §1235.

The decision of the tax court is affirmed.

E.I. DU PONT DE NEMOURS & CO. v. UNITED STATES
288 F.2d 904 (Ct. Cl. 1961)

JONES, Chief Judge.

Whether a taxpayer receives capital gain or ordinary income when he makes a nonexclusive transfer of certain rights in a secret process.

[T]he transfer of a trade secret may be a transaction equivalent to a sale, in the same manner that a patent assignment is considered a sale. In each case the transferee or assignee gets more than mere information. Of greater importance, he obtains what he believes to be a competitive advantage, a means for commercial exploitation and reward.

Without question, there are important differences between patents and trade secrets. Under the Constitution a patent secures to the inventor the exclusive rights to his discovery. A form of monopoly is given in exchange for the full disclosure and public dedication of a new and useful invention. United States v. Dubilier Condenser Corp., 1933, 289 U.S. 178. Information contained in a patent is public, widely distributed, and generally known by those interested in a particular art. Inevitably the patented idea becomes common knowledge, yet the patentee retains the right to prevent the manufacture, use and sale of the invention during the life of the patent. 35 U.S.C. §154. The patent owner may affirmatively act to prevent anyone else from using the patented invention; even to prevent such use by a second inventor who discovers the same idea entirely on his own. It follows that no disposition of a patent is complete without some transfer of this right to prevent infringement.

A trade secret is any information not generally known in a trade. It may be an unpatented invention, a formula, pattern, machine, process, customer list, customer credit list, or even news. The information is frequently in the public domain. Anyone is at liberty to discover a particular trade secret by any fair means, as by experimentation or by examination and analysis of a particular product. Moreover, upon discovery the idea may be used with impunity. A plurality of individual discoverers may have protectible, wholly separate rights in the same trade secret. However, the owner of a trade secret has no protectible rights in the idea itself any more than a lawyer has in his estate plan or a doctor in his diagnosis. Unlike an estate plan or a diagnosis, a trade secret, as a tool for commercial competition, derives much of its value from the fact of its secrecy. It is truly valuable only so long as it is a secret, for only so long does it provide an advantage over competitors. It follows that the essential element of a trade secret which permits of ownership and which distinguishes it from other forms of ideas is the right in the discoverer to prevent unauthorized disclosure of the secret. No disposition of a trade secret is complete without some transfer of this right to prevent unauthorized disclosure.

However different these concepts of trade secrets and patents may appear to be, there is an important similarity; they are both means to competitive advantage. The value in both lies in the rights they give to their owners for monopolistic exploitation. The owner of a patent can make something which no one else can make because no one else is permitted. But circumstances are frequently such that the owner of a trade secret can make something which no one else can make because no one else knows how. The patent owner has a monopoly created by law; the trade secret owner has a monopoly in fact. In both cases there exists the possibility of either limited or complete transfers of the right to the exclusive use of an idea.

A person may pay the owner of a patent for the privilege of operating under the patent without liability for infringement. This is the simple license situation. De Forest Radio T. & T. Co. v. United States, 1927, 273 U.S. 236, and is not considered a "sale" under the tax law. Parke, Davis & Co. v. Commissioner, 1934, 31 B.T.A. 427. Again, a person may pay the owner of a patent for the privilege of operating under the patent without liability for infringement, and in addition may pay for the residual right possessed by the patent owner, that being the right to prevent all others from operating under the patent. This is an assignment, Waterman v. Mackenzie, 1891, 138 U.S. 252, and is treated as a "sale" under the tax law. Commissioner of Internal Revenue v. Hopkinson, 2 Cir., 1942, 126 F.2d 406. In both cases there has been a sacrifice of an exclusive market and the establishment of a potential competitor where formerly the law guaranteed there would be none. Yet unquestionably the money received from the license is ordinary income to the owner of the patent, while the money received from the assignment may be treated as capital gain.

Compare the situation which obtains with trade secrets. A person may pay the discoverer of a trade secret for its disclosure, but in fact the disclosure which is purchased carries with it the right to use the trade secret without liability to the owner. This is the instant case. Again, a person may pay the discoverer of a trade secret for disclosure (i.e., the privilege of using the trade secret) and in addition pay for the residual right possessed by the discoverer — the right to prevent unauthorized disclosure. And this right to prevent unauthorized disclosure is effectively as stated above, the right to prevent anyone else from using the secret process.

Just as the grant of the naked right to operate under a patent in exchange for money results in ordinary income to the owner of the patent, so the simple disclosure and grant of the privilege of using a trade secret in exchange for money must also result in ordinary income to the discoverer of the trade secret. In both instances there has been no disposition of interest sufficient to meet the "sale" requirement of the Code. . . . When a patent owner gives not only the right to operate under the patent but in addition conveys all or a part of his remaining rights in the patent (particularly the right to exclude others from using the idea) in exchange for money, the disposition is complete. The transaction satisfies the "sale" requirement of the Code, and any gain on the transaction may be entitled to capital treatment. Similarly, when the owner of a trade secret gives the right to use the secret and in addition conveys his most important remaining right, the right to prevent unauthorized disclosure (and effectively the right to prevent further use of the trade secret by others) there is a complete disposition of the trade secret. This transaction meets the "sale" requirement of the Code and any gain would be entitled to preferential capital treatment.

In the case before us the plaintiff did not transfer to Associated the right to prevent further disclosure of the secret process. In fact, Associated could do nothing to prevent the subsequent disclosure of the secret by plaintiff to Ethyl of Delaware. Because of this, we find that the disposition of the trade secret did not meet the requirements of a "sale." Accordingly, the gain realized on the transaction must be taxed as ordinary income. Any other rule would encourage tax avoidance by providing a broad avenue for the conversion of ordinary royalty income into capital gain.

STERN v. UNITED STATES
164 F. Supp. 847 (D.C. La. 1958)

WRIGHT, District Judge.

This case concerns "Francis," the talking mule. Francis is a product of World War II. It was created by a lonely second lieutenant in the Pacific theater of operations who sometimes wondered whether there was anything in the Army lower than a second lieutenant. Francis convinced him there was. Now, seven motion pictures later, that second lieutenant, the taxpayer here, is claiming that the income from "Francis" is entitled to capital gains treatment under the Internal Revenue laws.

In 1933, after attending Harvard University, David Stern, III, was employed as a dramatic critic for the Philadelphia Record, a newspaper owned by his father. . . . In 1938 he became publisher of the Courier-Post newspapers in Camden, New Jersey. . . . In the spring of 1943, Stern enlisted as a private in the United States Army. He was later commissioned as a second lieutenant. While in the Pacific, Stern wrote some imaginary dialogue between a second lieutenant and an old Army mule, some of which he sold to Esquire for approximately $200. . . .

After his release from the Army in 1946, Stern returned to Camden as publisher of the Courier-Post newspapers. . . . While so doing and at the suggestion of a book publisher, he rewrote in book form all of the episodes about the talking mule, Francis. During this period he also wrote a sequel to "Francis," called "Francis Goes to Washington." It, too, was published by Farrar-Strauss, publisher of "Francis." In July 1949 Stern completed negotiations for the purchase of The New Orleans Item and took over the controlling interest and active management of the newspaper as its publisher. Since that date, he has devoted virtually his full time to the newspaper business as publisher.

On June 2, 1950 Stern sold to Universal Pictures Co., Inc., all of his "right, title and interest . . . in and to . . . that certain character known as 'Francis' conceived and created by" him, together with all of his rights to the two novels mentioned above and all of his rights to any contracts with respect to the properties conveyed. In consideration of this transfer, Universal agreed to pay him $50,000 plus 5% of the net profits from photoplays based on the character Francis, and 75% of all sums received by Universal under contracts for the use of licensing of the property. Payment of the $50,000 entitled Universal to a "commitment period" of two years within which to make a motion picture. Thereafter, and following release of each picture, Universal was entitled to additional commitment periods by paying a similar fixed consideration of $50,000 as to each picture or period. The contract further provided that "if purchaser shall elect not to pay fixed consideration with respect to any next succeeding commitment period . . . the property shall revert to the seller," all rights in motion pictures produced to remain in Universal. Under this agreement, Universal produced six additional motion pictures in which the character Francis was used. Stern prepared the screen play for the first of these pictures but has had no connection whatever with the writing or production of subsequent pictures except occasionally and incidentally as a consultant.

Plaintiffs have reported . . . those amounts received from Universal for the character Francis . . . as capital gains, accrued during the years received. For the year 1950, the Internal Revenue Service originally accepted plaintiffs' treatment of this income as capital gains from the sale of the character Francis. In considering subsequent years, the Appellate Division of the Internal Revenue reopened the return for the year 1950 and ruled that income from the character Francis was not subject to capital gains treatment for the reason that the contract with Universal was not a sale of the character Francis, that if it were, Francis was property held by the taxpayer primarily for sale to customers in the ordinary course of his business and, further, under the provision of Section 210(a) of the Revenue Act of 1950, amending the provisions of Section 117(a)(1) of the Internal Revenue Code of 1939, 26 U.S.C.A. §117(a)(1), the character Francis was similar to a copyright, a literary or artistic composition and, therefore, not a capital asset. . . .

The question as to whether the taxpayer's contract with Universal Pictures is a sale will be considered first because if it is not a sale, it will be unnecessary to consider the other objections to capital gains treatment of the income made by the Government. It will be noted in the contract that Stern sold all of his interest in the books "Francis," and "Francis Goes to Washington," the character Francis, and all rights and pending contracts concerning them. The agreement makes reference to "the full and complete ownership in the property sold, transferred and granted to (Universal) hereunder." It declares that Stern "hereby sells, transfers and conveys . . . all right, title and interest" in the property to Universal and guarantees "the full benefit of (Universal's) full and complete ownership in the property."

Obviously, the draftsmen of this contract intended that it be a sale and called it such. Apparently they were familiar also with the one case, Cory v. Commissioner of Internal

Revenue, 2 Cir., 230 F.2d 941, which the Government cites as authority for its contention that this agreement is not a sale, because the language of the agreement leaves no doubt that Stern transferred his entire bundle of rights in all the Francis properties, together with rights of future exploitation, to Universal Pictures. Thus this agreement is different from the agreement under consideration in Cory v. Commissioner, *supra*, because there the agreement provided for "a transfer of a part of the cluster of rights" inhering in the taxpayer. Cory v. Commissioner, *supra*, at page 944. . . .

Finally, and unfortunately for the taxpayer, the Government's position on the 1950 amendment to the 1939 Code is well taken. That amendment excludes from capital gains treatment income from the sale of "a copyright; a literary, musical, or artistic composition; or similar property" held by "a taxpayer, whose personal efforts created such property." The purpose of this amendment is obvious. It is intended to deny capital gains treatment to income from the sale, by their creator, of literary, musical, or artistic compositions, or similar property. Prior to 1950, various rulings of the Internal Revenue Service had approved capital gains treatment of various literary, musical and artistic compositions, including books and radio programs. Congress determined to eliminate such treatment for such compositions. Hence the amendment.

The taxpayer contends that the character "Francis" is not covered by the amendment, that it is not subject to copyright, that it is not a literary, musical or artistic composition or similar property. He argues that he has paid his taxes at the regular rates on all his income from his writings. He states that the character "Francis" is an "intellectual conception" and that as such the income from the sale thereof is entitled to capital gains treatment.

The taxpayer cites several cases in support of his position that the character Francis is not subject to being copyrighted. And he spends much time in his brief arguing that the Internal Revenue Service itself has limited the words of the statute "or similar property" to property capable of being copyrighted. It is not necessary for this Court to appraise the taxpayer's citations, his argument on this point, or the counter citations and argument of the Government. It is this Court's view that the character Francis, irrespective of its susceptibility to copyright, is "a literary composition" and as such the income from the sale thereof is not entitled to capital gains treatment. The taxpayer concedes, as he must, that the novel, "Francis," in which the character Francis is the leading figure, is a literary composition, but he argues that Francis, the principal characterization in the book, is not. In this he is mistaken. The character Francis gets its definition and its delineation from the book. The literary description in the book composes the character. How can it be said that the book is a literary composition yet the main character delineated therein is not? A slice of the loaf is still bread. It would be absurd to attribute to Congress the intention, under the 1950 amendment, of covering whole literary compositions but not parts thereof, particularly in view of the catchall, "or similar property," which appears at the end of the amendment.

Without the literary description of Francis, his mannerisms and his manifestations, Francis would cease to exist. In any event, an amorphous Francis could hardly be called "property held by the taxpayer," the sale of which is entitled to capital gains treatment. Section 117(a)(1), I.R.C., 1939. If Francis is, as taxpayer suggests, an "intellectual conception," sans form and substance, existing in the mind alone, it is incapable of ownership and, therefore, of being "property held by the taxpayer." See Holmes v. Hurst, 174 U.S. 82, 86; Nichols v. Universal Pictures Corporation, 2 Cir., 45 F.2d 119, 121. If Francis has sufficient form and substance to be considered property capable of ownership, this is so because of its literary composition. Compare Warner Bros. Pictures v. Columbia Broadcasting System, 9 Cir., 216 F.2d 945.

The taxpayer is entitled to capital gains treatment on the income from the contract in suit for the year 1950 because the 1950 amendment to the Code does not apply to income received during that year. As to subsequent years, however, capital gains treatment of the income from the contract must be denied as proscribed by that amendment.

Judgment accordingly.

ROBINSON KNIFE MANUFACTURING COMPANY, INC. v. CIR
600 F.3d 121 (2d Cir. 2010)

CALABRESI, Circuit Judge.

Petitioner-Appellant Robinson Knife Manufacturing Company ("Robinson") sells kitchen tools labeled with trademarks licensed from third parties to whom Robinson pays royalties. In Robinson's income tax returns for its taxable years ending March 1, 2003, and February 28, 2004, Robinson deducted these royalty payments as ordinary and necessary business expenses under 26 U.S.C. §162. The Commissioner disagreed and issued a notice of deficiency stating that, under 26 U.S.C. §263A, the royalties are required to be capitalized and made part of Robinson's inventory costs. The Tax Court, T.C. Memo 2009-9, upheld the Commissioner. Robinson appeals. We hold that where, as here, a producer's royalty payments (1) are calculated as a percentage of sales revenue from inventory and (2) are incurred only upon the sale of that inventory, they are immediately deductible as a matter of law because they are not "properly allocable to property produced" within the meaning of 26 C.F.R. §1.263A-1(e). We therefore REVERSE the decision below.

During the taxable years at issue, Robinson used, inter alia, two well-known licensed trademarks: Pyrex, which is owned by Corning, Inc., and Oneida, which is owned by Oneida Ltd. The owners of these two trademarks have for many years conducted substantial and continuous advertising and marketing activities to develop trademark awareness and goodwill. As a result, it is much easier for Robinson to place a Pyrex or Oneida product at a major retailer than it is to place an otherwise identical house-brand product.

DISCUSSION

II. Legal Framework

A. Capitalization and Deduction

The income tax law distinguishes between business expenses and capital expenditures. Under 26 U.S.C. §162(a), taxpayers may deduct "all the ordinary and necessary expenses paid or incurred during the taxable year in carrying on any trade or business." By contrast, under 26 U.S.C. §263(a)(1), no immediate deduction is allowed for capital expenditures, which are "[a]ny amount paid out for new buildings or for permanent improvements or betterments made to increase the value of any property or estate." The immediate deduction of a cost is more favorable to the taxpayer than is capitalization. The primary effect of characterizing a payment as either a business expense or a capital expenditure concerns the timing of the taxpayer's cost recovery: while business expenses are currently deductible, a capital expenditure usually is amortized and depreciated over the life of the relevant asset, or, where no specific asset or useful life can be ascertained, is deducted upon dissolution of the enterprise. INDOPCO, Inc. v. Comm'r, 503 U.S. 79, 83-84 (1992).

The significance of the distinction is only slightly different where, as here, the expense would be capitalized to inventory. For inventory, especially inventory held for sale, the taxpayer usually does not have to rely on depreciation or wait for dissolution of the enterprise in order to obtain cost recovery. Instead, the taxpayer has to follow complex inventory accounting rules in order to get deductions over time. See 26 C.F.R. §1.263A-1(c)(4). These rules are designed to achieve a result that is as similar as possible to what would happen if it were administratively feasible to keep track of each individual inventory item, so that whenever an item were sold its cost basis would be known, and the taxpayer would pay income tax on the gain (or deduct the loss) from the sale of that inventory item. See INDOPCO, 503 U.S. at 84.

With ideal matching, a taxpayer would be permitted to deduct the costs of producing an inventory item no earlier, and no later, than the taxable year in which that particular inventory item is sold. Unfortunately, when a company has, say, 100,000 identical spatulas on hand at any given time and it is constantly creating and selling such spatulas (along with any number of other products), perfect matching may be difficult and the costs of producing an inventory item are sometimes recovered earlier or later than they ought to be. A distortion of income results.

[The Court rejected the capitalization of the royalty payments. "If the allocation methods in the regulations worked perfectly, this case would never have been litigated. Under a perfect allocation system, every cent Robinson paid in sales-based royalties would be allocated to exactly those inventory items whose sale triggered Robinson's obligation to pay. Because it is the sale of kitchen tools that triggers Robinson's obligation to pay royalties, all Robinson's royalties would be allocated to those inventory items that are sold, at the same time as, and therefore during the same taxable year as, the royalties are incurred. The result would be that Robinson would recover the cost of the royalties immediately — just as it would if, as Robinson claims, the royalties were deductible rather than subject to capitalization. In reality, the allocation methods do not work perfectly. And Robinson, presumably to save administrative costs, elected the least accurate of the permissible methods. A significant amount of money, therefore, rides on whether Robinson can deduct its royalty payments. If Robinson cannot deduct the payments immediately, then a substantial portion of them will be allocated to ending inventory, and Robinson will have to wait until a later taxable year to recover those costs."]

III. Deductibility of the Royalty Payments

Robinson presents three arguments that the royalty payments are not required to be capitalized under §263A: (1) that the royalty payments are deductible as "marketing, selling, advertising, [or] distribution costs," 26 C.F.R. §1.263A1(e)(3)(iii)(A); (2) that royalty payments which are not "incurred in securing the contractual right to use a trademark, corporate plan, manufacturing procedure, special recipe, or other similar right associated with property produced," id. §1.263A1(e)(3)(ii)(U), are always deductible; and (3) that the royalty payments were not "properly allocable to property produced," id. §1.263A-1(e)(3)(i).

We reject Robinson's first two arguments as addressing situations that go far beyond the case presented here, but we are persuaded that the third argument is correct. We conclude that royalty payments, which are (1) calculated as a percentage of sales revenue from certain inventory, and (2) incurred only upon sale of such inventory, are not required to be capitalized under the §263A regulations. . . .

C. Properly Allocable to Property Produced

Robinson's third argument is that the Tax Court's view that Robinson's royalties were "properly allocable to property produced" was based on an erroneous interpretation of 26 C.F.R. §1.263A1(e)(3)(i). We agree.

It would be contrary to the purpose of §263A and the regulations if commissions for sales of books that have already taken place were treated differently from similar royalties for sales of other types of goods. The position taken by the Tax Court and the Commissioner in this case would give rise to exactly the problem Congress crafted §263A to fix, for then "the treatment of indirect costs [would] vary depending on the type of property produced." S. Rep. No. 99-313, at 133. The preamble to the uniform capitalization regulations confirms that capitalization ought not to "depend[ ] on the nature of the underlying property and its intended use," as it did under the pre-§263A laws. T.D. 8482, 1993-2 C.B. at 78. And, the uniform capitalization rules would not be very uniform if they were to treat books and spatulas differently.

It would similarly be "inappropriate" for a kitchen-tool manufacturer to capitalize trademark royalties where such royalties are based only on those kitchen tools that have been sold by the manufacturer, and not on any kitchen tools that are still on hand.

Although the 1988 Notice does not explicitly state the reason why capitalization should not be required for "commissions for sales of books that have already taken place," the distinction drawn by the IRS is guided by the principles underlying inventory accounting. The purpose of inventory accounting is to reflect income clearly, by matching income with the costs of producing that income in the same taxable year. When a publisher incurs the obligation to pay a commission only for books that have already been sold, or when Robinson incurs the obligation to pay a royalty only for kitchen tools that have already been sold, it is necessarily true that the royalty costs and the income from sale of the inventory items are incurred simultaneously.

Had Robinson's licensing agreements provided for non-sales-based royalties, such as manufacturing-based or minimum royalties, then under the reasoning of Notice 88-86 capitalization would be required.

In the instant case, however, the record is clear that Robinson's royalties were sales-based. They were calculated as a percentage of net sales of kitchen tools, and they were incurred only upon the sale of those kitchen tools. They are therefore immediately deductible.

IV. Conclusion

For these reasons, we hold that taxpayers subject to 26 U.S.C. §263A may deduct royalty payments that are (1) calculated as a percentage of sales revenue from certain inventory, and (2) incurred only upon sale of such inventory. Accordingly, we REVERSE the judgment of the Tax Court and REMAND with instructions to enter judgment for Robinson.

NABISCO BRANDS, INC. v. COMMISSIONER

T.C. Memo. 1995-127 (United States Tax Court 1995)

COLVIN, Judge.

Respondent determined deficiencies in petitioner's Federal income tax of $2,016,773 for 1982 and $2,223,929 for 1983. Petitioner bought the Life Savers trademarks in 1981 as part of its purchase of the Life Savers business from Squibb, Inc. (Squibb). After concessions, the sole issue for decision is whether petitioner's payments to Squibb for the Life Savers trademarks are deductible under section 1253 in an amount greater than allowed by respondent. We hold that they are.

FINDINGS OF FACT

Some of the facts have been stipulated and are so found.

1. Petitioner

In 1982 and 1983, Nabisco Brands, Inc. (Nabisco), was the parent of the Nabisco group, an affiliated group of corporations (petitioner). Nabisco is a Delaware corporation. Its principal office was in Parsippany, New Jersey, when it filed the petition. The Nabisco group was formed on July 6, 1981. . . . On September 10, 1985, R.J. Reynolds Industries, Inc., bought the Nabisco group and changed its name to RJR Nabisco.

2. Selecting a Buyer for the Life Savers Group

In 1981, Squibb was a health care and consumer products company unrelated to the Nabisco group. Life Savers was one of Squibb's subsidiaries. Life Savers made and marketed several leading brands of hard candies such as Life Savers and Breath Savers, chewing gums such as Care*Free, Bubble Yum, Replay, and Beech-Nut, and other products.

During the 1970's, Squibb decided to concentrate on its health care business. Squibb decided in early 1981 to sell the Life Savers group. In April 1981, Squibb employed the investment banking firm of Brown Bros. Harriman & Co. (Brown Bros.) to help it sell the Life Savers group.

3. Petitioner's Consideration of Acquisition of the Life Savers Group . . .

4. Negotiations to Buy the Life Savers Trademarks

Petitioner believed the Life Savers trademarks were indispensable to Life Savers' business success. Petitioner would not have bought the Life Savers group if it could not also buy the Life Savers trademarks. Petitioner preferred to buy Life Savers' assets, primarily to avoid assuming Life Savers' liabilities. Squibb preferred to sell Life Savers' stock so it would transfer Life Savers' liabilities to petitioner.

Petitioner's principal negotiators were Powell, who handled the financial aspects of the negotiations, and Keith Thompson (Thompson), from Nabisco's legal department. J. Thomas Pearson (Pearson), Nabisco's vice president for taxation, also assisted petitioner. Squibb's principal negotiators were J. Elliston Murray, Squibb's controller, who handled the financial aspects of the negotiations for Squibb, and Daniel Cuoco, Squibb's assistant general counsel.

Pearson suggested to Powell and Thompson that petitioner buy the Life Savers trademarks in a way that would permit it to deduct the purchase price of the trademarks under section 1253. Pearson suggested a separate sale of the Life Savers trademarks. Powell proposed to Squibb that petitioner buy the Life Savers trademarks. Squibb did not accept that proposal when it was first raised.

. . . Squibb wanted to obtain the highest possible price for the Life Savers group and to sell it by the end of 1981. Squibb wanted substantial deferred payments rather than immediate cash for the Life Savers group. Petitioner and Squibb were initially unable to agree on the price for the Life Savers group.

Pearson concluded that a separate purchase of the Life Savers trademarks, if structured to comply with section 1253, would generate future tax deductions for petitioner with a 1981 present value of about $9 million; this would let petitioner raise its offering price and enhance its prospects of outbidding Rowntree. Petitioner raised the amount it was willing to pay for the Life Savers group by $18 million.

Squibb knew that petitioner intended to obtain a tax benefit under section 1253 from the trademark agreement. Both parties believed that if they structured the Life Savers' sale to comply with section 1253, Squibb would treat the payments as ordinary income rather than long-term capital gain.

5. The Purchase Agreement

Squibb chose petitioner to buy the Life Savers group. As a result of the negotiations, Squibb and petitioner agreed to structure the transaction as a sale of the shares of Life Savers and other members of the Life Savers group, and a separate sale of the Life Savers trademarks for an initial payment of $25 million and annual payments for 10 years. The parties designed the annual payments formula to reduce Squibb's risk by varying the payment rate based on the amount of sales, and by providing for higher annual payment rates in the first 5 years than in the second 5 years. . . .

Petitioner projected that its annual payments under the formula would be more than 50 percent of the amount that it would pay for the trademarks, and thus it would comply with section 1253(b)(2)(F), as interpreted by section 1.1253- 2(d)(6). Pearson believed that the annual payments would total more than $25,000,000, and thus the 50-percent requirement of the proposed regulation would be met, and that petitioner would pay little on sales above Life Savers' historical level (approximately $275 million) on the theory that future sales above that level would result from petitioner's efforts.

The parties expected that sales of the trademarked products would be at least as great through the term of the trademark agreement as they were in 1981 ($271.2 million) and that petitioner's 10 annual payments to Squibb would be at least $28,208,000. That amount is more than 50 percent of petitioner's total estimated payments for the trademarks.

The annual payments that Squibb was to receive under the trademark agreement would vary to some extent based on the levels of petitioner's future sales of the trademarked products. For example, if sales fell by $78,200,000 to $193 million, annual payments would fall by $346,600 for the first 5 years and $291,500 for the second 5 years.

The parties executed the purchase agreement on November 13, 1981. In December 1981, the boards of directors of the various companies approved petitioner's acquisition of the Life Savers group. On December 29, 1981, Life Savers assigned and distributed to Squibb the Life Savers trademarks and the stock of two foreign subsidiaries.

The Life Savers acquisition closed on December 31, 1981, and January 4, 1982. At the first closing, Squibb sold the stock of Life Savers to a Nabisco subsidiary and the Life Savers trademarks to petitioner. The second closing involved the sales of various foreign subsidiaries in the Life Savers group.

6. Terms of the Trademark Agreement

a. Best Efforts Clause

The trademark agreement required petitioner to use its reasonable best efforts to maintain or increase sales of Life Savers products (best efforts clause). The best efforts clause was important to Squibb, which was concerned about its financial risk. Petitioner believed that Squibb could sue under the best efforts clause if, for example, petitioner intentionally reduced sales of the trademarked products.

b. The 33-Percent Option

The trademark agreement included an elective remedy to encourage petitioner to maintain or increase sales of trademarked products. Squibb could elect the remedy if sales of any of the trademarked products fell below 33 percent of the 1981 sales level. If sales fell below 33 percent of the 1981 level, Squibb could: (i) Continue to accept annual payments from petitioner under the annual payments formula based on actual sales of the affected product, or (ii) require petitioner to make payments under the annual payments formula based on the 1981 sales of the affected product (the 33-percent option). If Squibb elected the 33-percent option, petitioner would pay Squibb for that year and for all remaining years of the trademark agreement based on 1981 sales.

The 33-percent option was intended to accommodate Squibb's desire to secure its expected future payments and petitioner's desire not to have Squibb interfere in its business operations.

Sales of Life Savers products subject to the trademark agreement totaled $271.2 million in 1981. If Squibb had elected the 33-percent option based on $271.2 million of sales, petitioner's annual payment to Squibb would have been $3,076,100 for the first 5 years of the agreement and $2,565,500 for the second 5 years. Squibb and petitioner did not know Life Savers' total 1981 sales when they agreed to the 33-percent option. However, they knew that sales were $279.4 million in 1980 and $279.9 million in 1979.

Petitioner and Squibb believed that, absent petitioner's neglect or mismanagement, circumstances would have to have been very different from what petitioner and Squibb forecast for sales to drop by more than two-thirds from the 1981 level. If such a drop had appeared imminent, the 33-percent option gave petitioner an incentive to stem the decline.

c. Transfer Option

Squibb had two options under the trademark agreement if petitioner proposed to transfer any of the Life Savers trademarks or business to a third party. Squibb could: (i) Continue to accept annual payments from the third party under the annual payments formula based on actual sales of the transferred product, or (ii) require petitioner to continue making annual payments based on 1981 sales of the transferred product (the transfer option). The transfer option also let Squibb receive payments based on 1981 sales if petitioner stopped selling any of the Life Savers products.

d. Points Relating to Both the 33-Percent Option and the Transfer Option

Petitioner and Squibb made no agreement about whether Squibb would elect under the 33-percent option or the transfer option if either became exercisable.

The trademark agreement required petitioner to certify sales of trademarked products and calculate its payments to Squibb each year. For the first 5 years (1982 through 1986), petitioner reported total sales of all trademarked products, not total sales of each trademarked product. In 1987, petitioner began to report total sales of each trademarked product. Squibb did not exercise the 33-percent option or the transfer option even though sales of several trademarked products fell below 33 percent of their 1981 levels during the term of the trademark agreement. . . .

Petitioner amortized the $25 million initial payment over 10 years and deducted the annual payments. Petitioner's total deduction under section 1253 was $5,562,189 ($2,500,000 + $3,062,189) for 1982 and $5,603,544 ($2,500,000 + $3,103,544) for 1983. Respondent disallowed petitioner's amortization of the initial payment and deduction of costs to acquire the Life Savers trademarks.

Squibb reported the $25 million initial payment and the annual payments as ordinary income for income tax purposes. Respondent has not challenged Squibb's reporting of any of the payments as ordinary income. Squibb was more concerned with guaranteeing payments under the trademark agreement than with the tax treatment of those payments.

In 1989, Squibb filed a claim for its 1981 taxable year seeking a refund of $10,325,167 in Federal income tax based on Squibb's reclassification of the $25 million initial payment for the Life Savers trademarks as a long-term capital gain. Respondent denied Squibb's claim. Squibb filed a protest with respondent's Appeals Office. To date respondent has not granted Squibb's protest.

OPINION

1. Introduction

This case involves the sale of Life Savers trademarks for an initial payment and 10 annual payments. The sole issue is whether for 1982 and 1983 petitioner may amortize the $25 million initial payment and deduct the annual payments it made to buy the Life Savers trademarks under section 1253.

Section 1253 provides that costs of acquiring a trademark may be deducted or amortized. Generally, whether a taxpayer may deduct or amortize trademark acquisition costs under section 1253 depends on the terms of the trademark purchase and the seller's degree of involvement in the buyer's business after the sale.

A taxpayer may deduct payments for acquiring a trademark that are contingent on the productivity, use, or disposition of the trademark. Sec. 1253(d)(1). A noncontingent single payment discharging a principal sum agreed upon in the transfer agreement may be amortized over a 10-year period if the transfer of the trademark is not treated as a sale or exchange of a capital asset under section 1253(a). Sec. 1253(d)(2)(A). A transfer of a trademark is not a sale or exchange of a capital asset if the transferor retains any significant power, right, or continuing interest with respect to the subject matter of the trademark. Sec. 1253(a). A right to receive payments contingent on the productivity, use, or disposition of the subject matter of the trademark transferred is significant for purposes of section 1253(a) if the payments are a substantial element under the transfer agreement. Sec. 1253(b)(2)(F).

The parties raise the following issues:

(a) Contingent Payments Issues: Whether, as respondent contends, $1,692,420 of each annual payment in 1982 and 1983 was not contingent on the productivity, use, or disposition of the Life Savers trademarks because either: (i) The 33-percent option effectively guaranteed that those amounts were minimum payments; or (ii) those amounts were not contingent on the productivity, use, or disposition of the Life Savers trademarks because of the annual payments formula and Life Savers' financial history and business operations; and

(b) Significant Powers Issues: Whether, as petitioner contends, Squibb retained a significant power, right, or continuing interest in the Life Savers trademarks under the trademark agreement for any of the following reasons (the significant powers issues): (i) The portions of petitioner's estimated annual payments for the Life Savers trademarks that respondent concedes were contingent were a substantial element of the agreement under section 1253(b)(2)(F); (ii) petitioner's obligations and Squibb's rights under the best efforts clause were a significant power not listed in section 1253(b)(2); (iii) the 33-percent option gave Squibb a significant power not listed in section 1253(b)(2); or (iv) the various powers, rights, and interests that Squibb retained with respect to the Life Savers trademarks collectively were a significant power not listed in section 1253(b)(2).

The parties agree that if petitioner prevails on either of the contingent payments issues or any of the four significant powers issues petitioner's annual payments for the Life Savers trademarks are fully deductible under section 1253(d)(1) and (d)(2), and the initial payment for the Life Savers trademarks may be amortized over 10 years under section 1253(d)(2). As discussed below, we conclude that petitioner prevails under the first of the significant powers issues. Thus, we need not consider any of the other issues.

2. Did Squibb Retain Any Significant Powers, Rights, or Continuing Interest in the Trademarks?

Petitioner contends that Squibb retained various significant powers, rights, or continuing interests (SPRI) with respect to the Life Savers trademarks under the trademark agreement.

Payments that are contingent on the productivity, use, or disposition of a trademark are an SPRI if the payments are a substantial element under the transfer agreement. Sec. 1253(b)(2)(F). Section 1253 does not define "substantial."

Respondent concedes that about 25 percent of the payments under the trademark agreement were contingent, on the theory that payments above those which respondent contends were guaranteed by the 33-percent option were contingent. Petitioner argues that 25 percent is a substantial element under the statute, and that the contingent payments were deductible because they were an SPRI under section 1253(b)(2)(F).

Petitioner maintains that contingent payments which are more than 20 percent of the consideration paid for trademarks are substantial. Petitioner points out that quantitative definitions of "substantial" abound in the tax field, and that 25 percent is toward the high end of the accepted range.

We agree that 25 percent is substantial in the present context. Whether contingent payments are a substantial element of the transfer agreement under section 1253(b)(2) is decided based on all of the facts and circumstances. See Stokely USA, Inc. v. Commissioner, 100 T.C. 439, 453 (1993). We apply the plain meaning of substantial. Zinniel v. Commissioner, 89 T.C. 357, 363-364 (1987); Huntsberry v. Commissioner, 83 T.C. 742, 747-748 (1984). Substantial means "of considerable value; valuable. . . . Something worthwhile as distinguished from something without value or merely nominal." BLACK'S LAW DICTIONARY 1428 (6th ed. 1990). It is difficult to view payments ranging from $1.4 to $1.6 million annually, constituting 25 percent of the total payments, as insubstantial. We hold that petitioner's payments were a substantial element under the transfer agreement within the meaning of section 1253(b)(2)(F).

Because we find for petitioner on this issue, we need not reach the other issues. We hold that petitioner's payments to Squibb are fully deductible under section 1253.

TGS-NOPEC GEOPHYSICAL CO. v. COMBS
340 S.W.3d 432 (Tex. 2011)

Justice **MEDINA** delivered the opinion of the Court.

This appeal arises from a franchise tax dispute involving the apportionment of receipts from the licensing of geophysical and seismic data to customers in Texas. The taxpayer complains that the Comptroller has mischaracterized these receipts as Texas business and thereby has erroneously increased its franchise tax burden. At issue is whether these receipts should be categorized as receipts from the use of a license or as receipts from the sale of an intangible asset. If the receipts are from the use of a license, then the Comptroller has correctly assessed the tax. If the receipts are from the sale of an intangible, then the Comptroller has erred in assessing additional taxes because receipts from the sales of intangibles are Texas receipts only if the legal domicile of the payor is Texas.

The lower courts concluded that the Comptroller had appropriately characterized the revenue as receipts from the use of a license in Texas and therefore correctly assessed the additional taxes. 268 S.W.3d 637 (Tex. App.-Austin 2008). We disagree and reverse and remand to the trial court for further proceedings.

I. BACKGROUND

The taxpayer is TGS-NOPEC Geophysical Company ("TGS"), a Delaware Corporation with its principal place of business in Houston, Texas. It gathers, interprets, and markets seismic and geophysical data regarding subsurface terrains worldwide with sophisticated seismic equipment and software technology. TGS collects and stores this data in a master library and licenses various parts of the library to customers who use the licensed data to evaluate oil and gas formations for drilling operations. TGS requires its customers to enter into a master license agreement, which governs the parties' rights and obligations. The master license agreement describes TGS's seismic data as proprietary information and as valuable and highly confidential trade secrets. The master license agreement also states that TGS retains title to the seismic data and that it only licenses the limited use of the information to its customers.

When a customer wants to access data for a particular location, TGS and the customer enter into a specific license agreement under the master license agreement. TGS generally charges its customers a flat fee to access data under these specific license agreements and does not receive any additional payments, such as royalties. TGS delivers the data to its customers in tangible media forms such as magnetic tapes, printed materials, or film. Each piece of data provided by TGS includes the following notice:

> These data are owned by and are trade secrets of [TGS]. The use of these data is restricted to companies holding a valid use license from [TGS] and is subject to the strict confidentiality requirements of that license. The data may not be disclosed or transferred except as expressly authorized by the license. Unauthorized disclosure, use, reproduction, reprocessing or transfer of this data by or to a third party is strictly prohibited.

The licensing agreements are nonexclusive, and TGS may license the same data to multiple customers. Its customers receive unlimited access to the data under the specific license purchased, but they cannot disseminate the information to third parties, nor is the license transferrable.

. . .

II. ANALYSIS

The question . . . is whether the act of licensing an intangible asset is the "use of a license" within the meaning of the franchise tax statute. To answer that question, we begin with the purpose and operation of the Texas franchise tax statute. See Tex. Tax Code ch. 171.

A. The Texas Franchise Tax

The franchise tax is a tax on the privilege of doing business in Texas. Bullock v. National Bancshares Corp., 584 S.W.2d 268, 270 (Tex. 1979), cert. denied, 444 U.S. 1016 (1980). It is imposed on each taxable entity that does business in this state or that is chartered or organized here. Tex. Tax Code §171.001(a). Before 2008, the franchise tax was imposed on an entity's capital or earned surplus. See 1997 Tex. Gen. Laws 4569, 4569-70. The tax code, however, presently imposes franchise tax on an entity's "taxable margin." Tex. Tax Code §§171.002. Because all of a company's capital, earned surplus, or taxable margin may not be attributable to business done in Texas, receipts must be apportioned between Texas and other jurisdictions. The tax code does this by multiplying an entity's capital, earned surplus, or taxable margin (depending on the applicable version of the code) by a fraction, the numerator of which consists of receipts from business done in Texas (Texas-sourced receipts), and the denominator of which consists of all receipts from business anywhere, including Texas. Tex. Tax Code §171.006.

In sourcing receipts to Texas, the tax code identifies business done in this state as the sum of the taxable entity's gross receipts from the following activities:

(1) each sale of tangible personal property if the property is delivered or shipped to a buyer in this state regardless of the FOB point or another condition of the sale;

(2) each service performed in this state, except that receipts derived from servicing loans secured by real property are in this state if the real property is located in this state;

(3) each rental of property situated in this state;

(4) the use of a patent, copyright, trademark, franchise, or license in this state;

(5) each sale of real property located in this state, including royalties from oil, gas, or other mineral interests; and

(6) other business done in this state.

Tex. Tax Code §171.103(a) (hereafter referred to as the "sourcing statute"). The issue here is whether the revenue TGS earns licensing its seismic data library is appropriately sourced under subsection (4) as receipts from the "use of a license in this state," *id.* §171.103(a)(4) or under subsection (6) as "other business done in this state," *id.* §171.103(a)(6). If subsection (4) applies, the Comptroller has appropriately sourced the receipts. But if subsection (6) applies, as TGS maintains, the receipts must be sourced to the state of the customers' domicile under the "location of the payor" rule, and the Comptroller's assessment must be revised. See 34 Tex. Admin. Code §3.549(e)(30)(B); *id.* §3.557(e)(25)(B).

. . .

C. Sourcing Receipts from Intangible Assets

The history of the franchise tax indicates that the Comptroller has been allocating receipts from intangibles to the state of the payor's domicile since 1917. This practice ended in 1959, in part, when the Legislature amended the sourcing statute to require use-based sourcing for two kinds of intangibles, patents and copyrights. See Act of August 6, 1959, 56th Leg., 3rd C.S., ch. 1, art. 12.02, 1959 Tex. Gen. Laws 187, 307 (sourcing "royalties from the use of patents or copyrights" to their place of use). Before this, the sourcing statute consisted of a single catch-all provision, for business done in the state, similar to subsection (6) of the current statute. And under the earlier statute, the Comptroller sourced all receipts from intangibles under the "location of the payor" rule.

After the 1959 amendment, receipts from intangible assets, other than patents and copyrights, continued to be taxed as other business under the "location of the payor" rule until 1988, at which time the Comptroller began sourcing revenue from three additional intangible assets based on location of use. The Comptroller made this change by promulgating a new rule. Rule 3.403(e)(11) provided that "[r]eceipts to the owner for the use of trademarks, franchises, and licenses are allocated according to the location where used." 12 Tex. Reg. 2971 (1988) (to be codified at 34 Tex. Admin. Code §3.549). After Rule 3.403(e)(11)'s adoption, the Comptroller began sourcing receipts from licensing trademarks, franchises, and licenses according to their place of use, like patents and copyrights. Receipts from licensing other types of intangible assets, however, continued to be sourced to the location of the payor under the catch-all provision pertaining to "other business."

Comptroller letter rulings from the period confirm this practice. Concerning the licensing of data, the Comptroller issued the following guidance in 1990:

... gross receipts from [licensing seismic data] are from a license to use the geophysical information. For franchise tax purposes, the gross receipts from the licensing of the use of the information would be considered receipts from the sale of an intangible and would be allocated to the legal domicile of the payor.

Comptroller Letter Ruling 9005L1019F09 (5/1/1990); see also Comptroller Letter Ruling 9103L1087B07 (3/1/1991) (issuing similar ruling to another licensor of seismic data). These rulings recognized that Rule 3.403(e)(11) did not apply to the receipts because the customers used seismic data rather than the license conveying the data.

The Legislature did not amend the sourcing statute to match the Comptroller's sourcing rule on trademarks, franchises, and licenses until 1997. After this amendment, subsection (4) of the sourcing statute provided that "gross receipts of a corporation from its business done in this state [includes] the corporation's receipts from . . . the use of a patent, copyright, trademark, franchise, or license in this state. . . ." Act of May 20, 1997, 75th. Leg., R. S., ch. 1185, §5, 1997 Tex. Gen. Laws 4569, 4570. The amendment equalized the tax treatment among similar intangible assets by adding licenses, trademarks, and franchises to the provision governing patents and copyrights. *Id.* Although other amendments to the franchise tax have followed, the sourcing statute has not materially changed since 1997. Gross receipts derived from a license continue to be sourced to Texas when the license is used in this state. Tex. Tax Code §171.103(a)(4).

D. Receipts from the Use of a License

The Comptroller argues that because TGS uses a license agreement to transfer seismic data to its Texas customers, the receipts are from the use of a license in Texas. She further argues that the phrase "use of a license" encompasses licensing because there is no qualifying language in subsection (4) or in any other part of the sourcing statute to suggest that the licensing of data does not constitute the use of a license. The Comptroller concedes that previously the licensing of seismic data was sourced as a general intangible under the "location of the payor" rule, but she maintains that the Legislature changed that practice in 1997 when it decided to tax licenses like patents and copyrights, according to their place of use.

TGS argues that the Comptroller and the court of appeals have confused "receipts from licensing" with "receipts from the use of a license." TGS submits that there is a critical distinction between receipts from licensing transactions (in which a license is merely the transfer mechanism) and receipts from the use of a license (in which the license itself is a valuable asset). Because TGS's customers do not use a license but instead use seismic data, TGS submits that the receipts at issue are not from the use of a license but are from its customers' acquisition and use of TGS's data. TGS contends that its receipts are therefore essentially a limited sale of an intangible asset, geophysical data. Because this data is not one of the intangible assets listed in subsection (4), TGS concludes that the receipts it derives from this data must instead be sourced as other business under the catchall provision, subsection (6), and allocated to the state of the payor's domicile. Tex. Tax Code §171.103(a)(4), (6).

As the arguments indicate, the term "license" has more than one meaning. It can be used as a verb to convey the act of giving permission or as a noun to represent the permission or right granted. See Webster's New International Dictionary 1425 (2d ed. 1960). As such, its use in the statute is ambiguous.

Instead of focusing on the word "license," as the Comptroller and court of appeals have done, the word must be read in the context of the whole statute and consideration given to what it means to "use a license." See *City of Sunset Valley*, 146 S.W.3d at 642; *Mega Child Care*, 145 S.W.3d at 176. Language cannot be interpreted apart from context. The meaning of a word that appears ambiguous when viewed in isolation may become clear when the word is analyzed in light of the terms that surround it. The word "use" poses some interpretational difficulties as well because of the different meanings attributable to it. "Use" and the "use of a license" therefore, draw their meanings from context, so we look not only to the words themselves but to the statute in its entirety to determine the Legislature's intent. It is a fundamental principle of statutory construction and indeed of language itself that words' meanings cannot be determined in isolation but must be drawn from the context in which they are used.

The statute sources to Texas "receipts from the use of a patent, copyright, trademark, franchise, or license" to the extent they are used in Texas. Tex. Tax Code §171.103(a)(4). The canon of statutory construction known as noscitur a sociis, or "it is known by its associates" directs that similar terms be interpreted in a similar manner. See Fiess v. State Farm Lloyds, 202 S.W.3d 744, 750 n. 29 (Tex. 2006). Thus, we interpret the similar terms license, patent, copyright, trademark, and franchise in a similar manner.

Considering how the statute applies to patents and copyrights is therefore instructive. When a business wishes to manufacture a patented item, it must purchase the patent or obtain permission to use the patent from the owner. Permission is usually granted in the form of a license. When the licensee thereafter produces the patented item, it uses the patent, and its payments to the patent's owner are "receipts from the use of a patent." See Tex. Tax Code §171.103(a)(4). The revenue or royalties that the patent owner receives is included in Texas receipts to the extent that the patent is used in production, fabrication, manufacturing, or other processing in Texas. 34 Tex. Admin. Code §3.549(e)(30)(A)(i). Even though a license is part of this transaction, the receipts are from the use of the underlying intellectual property, the patent, not from the use of a license.

Similarly, when a business wishes to publish copyrighted material, the owner of the copyright must grant permission through a license. When the licensee publishes the copyrighted material, it uses the copyright, and its payments to the owner are receipts from the use of a copyright. See Tex. Tax Code §171.103(a)(4). Revenue the copyright owner receives from the use of its copyright is included in Texas receipts to the extent the copyright is used in Texas. 34 Tex. Admin. Code §3.549(e)(30)(A)(ii). Even though a license is part of this transaction, the receipts are from the use of the underlying intellectual property, the copyright, not from the use of a license.

In these two situations, the owner of the intangible asset uses a license to convey limited rights to its intellectual property. But the revenue produced is not from the use of a license in Texas; it is from the use of the underlying intellectual property, the copyright or the patent. Similarly, the revenue TGS receives from conveying its geophysical data is not derived from the use of a license but from the use of the underlying intellectual property, the data. The term "license" in subsection (4) of the sourcing statute therefore refers to licenses that are themselves revenue-producing assets. It does not include the mechanism of licensing, which would subsume all intangible assets. Had that been the Legislature's intent, it would not have been necessary to name the intangible assets specifically as the Legislature has done in subsection (4). See In re M.N., 262 S.W.3d at 802 (presuming that the "Legislature included each word in the statute for a purpose . . . and that words not included were purposefully omitted").

E. The Comptroller's Rules

The Comptroller's own administrative interpretation of the sourcing statute further contradicts her argument here. The Comptroller's regulations provide: "revenue that the owner of a trademark, franchise, or license receives is included in Texas receipts to the extent the trademark, franchise, or license is used in Texas." 34 Tex. Admin Code §3.549(e)(30)(A)(iii) (former franchise tax); id. §3.591(e)(21)(A)(iii) (margin tax). Under this rule, the intangible asset that is "used" must be owned by the revenue recipient and used by someone else. The underlying asset in a licensing transaction meets this standard because it is owned by the licensor, who receives the revenue, not the licensee, who uses the intangible asset. In contrast, the license resulting from a licensing transaction does not meet this standard because the licensee owns the license.

TGS, the revenue recipient, owns seismic data, which is its intellectual property. TGS's customers want to access this valuable intellectual property, and TGS thus grants them a right to access the data through license agreements. TGS grants its customers a license, or a limited right, to use its seismic data. The customers, however, then use the seismic data and not the licenses that vest in them as a result of the licensing transaction. Because TGS is not the owner of the license but the owner of the data, its receipts from customers, who use its seismic data, should not be sourced under subsection (4), and the assessment here conflicts with the Comptroller's own administrative rule. See 34 Tex. Admin. Code §3.549(e)(30)(A)(iii); see also Rodriguez, 997 S.W.2d at 254-55.

Moreover, the Comptroller's construction of the statute conflicts with her rule regarding the licensing of software. By rule, the Comptroller allocates receipts from licensing software to the location of the payor under subsection (6) as sales of intangibles. See 34 Tex. Admin. Code §3.549(e)(30)(A)(iii), (e)(7); Tex. Tax Code §171.103(a)(6). Because a license is used to transfer the underlying intangible, however, the Comptroller's argument in this case would dictate allocation of the receipts under subsection (4). Tex. Tax Code §171.103(a)(4). The Comptroller accordingly is inconsistent when equating the licensing of an intangible asset with the use of a license in this state. See Tex. Tax Code §111.002 (providing that Comptroller's rules must not conflict with state or federal law).

III. CONCLUSION

The Legislature could have allocated receipts from the use of intangible assets in this state to subsection (4) of the sourcing statute, generally, but it did not. See, e.g., Tex. Tax Code §171.0004(d) (providing that an "entity conducts an active trade or business if assets, including royalties, patents, trademarks, and other intangible assets, held by the entity are used in the active trade or business of one or more related entities"). Some states do allocate revenues from intangible assets generally to the place of their use, but our

Legislature has chosen to specifically name the intangibles which qualify for such treatment. Because TGS's receipts from licensing its seismic data are not receipts from the use of a license in this state within subsection (4)'s meaning, the court of appeals erred in upholding the Comptroller's franchise tax assessment in this case. Receipts from this intangible asset are not allocated according to its place of use under subsection (4) but rather are included under subsection (6)'s catch-all provision as a limited sale of an intangible and allocated under the "location of the payor" rule. We therefore reverse the court of appeals' judgment and remand the case to the trial court for further proceedings consistent with this opinion.

IV. PROBLEMS

1. What are the differences between a sale and a license of patents? What are "substantial" rights in patents? Does a geographical limitation on a patent transfer render the transfer a sale or a license?

2. Researcher is a regular employee at University. Researcher assigned all of her inventions, know hows, and patents to University per the Employment Handbook. As the holder of numerous patents, University has recently licensed several patents, including a patent that Researcher is the inventor on, to Pharma. Researcher has just received $100,000 from University as an "award." Researcher believes that the award is for the patent with Researcher's name as the inventor. Researcher wants to report the award as "capital gains" to obtain a lower tax rate. Explain to Researcher the possible tax treatment for the award.

3. Does tax law treat transfer of trade secrets similar to transfer of patents? What are some reasons for such tax treatment?

4. What is the tax treatment for the transfer of self-created copyrights by individual authors? What is the tax treatment for the transfer of a copyright that is a work-made-for-hire? *See* TREAS. REG. §1.1221-1(c)(2), which provides:

> in the case of sales or other dispositions occurring after July 25, 1969, that a letter, a memorandum, or similar property is excluded from the term "capital asset" if held by (i) a taxpayer whose personal efforts created such property, (ii) a taxpayer for whom such property was prepared or produced, or (iii) a taxpayer in whose hands the basis of such property is determined, for purposes of determining gain from a sale or exchange, in whole or in part by reference to the basis of such property in the hands of a taxpayer described in subdivision (i) or (ii) above.

5. What is the tax treatment for a transfer of trademarks for the transferor? For the transferee? What are the differences and similarities to tax treatment of the other types of intellectual property transfers?

6. If TGS-NOPEC Geophysical Co. has received a patent related to its seismic data and subsequently licensed both the patent and the data to others, how will the receipts from the licenses be sourced under Texas law?

V. DRAFTING EXERCISES

1. Draft a grant provision that most likely will be deemed a sale of trademarks for tax purposes.
2. Consider the following provision and determine whether the transfer is a sale or a license for tax purposes.

> ... WHEREAS the Licensors are the beneficial owners of the Letters Patent short particulars whereof are set out in the first and second parts of the schedule hereunto annexed and are the registered proprietors of the Letters Patent short particulars whereof are set out in the first part of the said schedule AND WHEREAS one or other of the Trustees as appears from the said schedule is the registered proprietor of each of the Letters Patent short particulars whereof are set out in the second part of the said schedule but the Trustees as they do hereby acknowledge hold their interest in the said Letters Patent upon trust for the Licensors AND WHEREAS the Licensors have agreed with the Licensees for the grant to the Licensees of a sole and exclusive license under each and every one of the said Letters Patent upon the terms and conditions set out in a letter dated the Twenty-eighth day of November One thousand nine hundred and thirty two addressed to the Managing Director of the Licensees and signed by the President of the Licensors AND WHEREAS the Licensors have requested and directed the Trustees to joint in this Deed of License NOW THIS DEED WITNESSETH that in pursuance of the said agreement the Licensors as beneficial owners and the Trustees at the request and by the direction of the Licensors DO HEREBY grant unto the Licensees the sole and exclusive license under the said Letters Patent and each of them To HOLD the same unto the Licensees for their own benefit for the remainder of the term for which the said Letters Patent were respectively granted and any extension or renewal thereof upon and subject to the terms and conditions set out in the said letter dated the Twenty eighth day of November One thousand nine hundred and thirty two IN WITNESS WHEREOF the Licensors have caused this Deed to be executed under their Corporate Seal by their thereunto duly authorized officers the Trustees have hereunto set their respective hands and seals and the Licensees have caused their Common Seal to be hereunto affixed this day and year first before written.

See Cleveland Graphite Bronze Co. v. Commissioner, 10 T.C. 974, 981 (1948).

· TABLE OF CASES ·

Italics indicate principal cases.

·INDEX·